A Standing Commission of the European
Federation of Financial Analyst Societies
The European Bond Commission
in association with
International Securities Market Association

ISMA

THE EUROPEAN BOND MARKETS

An Overview and Analysis
for Money Managers and Traders

STUART K. McLEAN, EDITOR

Fifth Edition

PROBUS PUBLISHING COMPANY
Cambridge, England
Chicago, Illinois

Edited, designed and typeset by Nick Battley, London, England

ISBN 1-55738-286-7

Printed in the United States of America

BB

1 2 3 4 5 6 7 8 9 0

Contents

Preface

Jean Guy de Wael
President,
European Federation of Financial Analysts Societies

I am delighted to have this opportunity of introducing the fifth edition of *The European Bond Markets*, published by the Bond Commission of the European Federation of Financial Analysts Societies (EFFAS).

The Bond Commission of EFFAS began its activities in 1976. As a voluntary organization, it features not only unparalleled expertise covering the whole spectrum of bond-related activities, but also the motivation to share such expertise for the common good of the industry. One example of that motivation lies in this book.

Some sixteen member societies have contributed much thought, and much time, to providing a publication which brings together a wealth of expert knowledge on the European markets, in just one prestigious volume. It is precisely this sort of effort and co-operation which provides evidence of both the need, and the success, of EFFAS.

It is impossible to mention that success without paying tribute to the past chairmanship of Stuart McLean, Piet Versloot, William Zwager and Hasse Nilsson. Without their foresight and imagination, this book, and others published by the Bond Commission, would simply not have been possible. In particular, Stuart McLean's legendary expertise and effort demand special recognition.

Those involved in the contributions to this book are many and varied. Whether member companies, employees, or self-employed members, it is true to say that they have all donated much time, effort and knowledge to this project. A debt of gratitude is owed to each and every one of them.

Naturally, a few introductory remarks cannot do justice to a work of this quality and magnitude. The true value will again be demonstrated by those international bond market professionals throughout the world who have shown appreciation of previous EFFAS publications, and will undoubtedly do so again.

It is with pride and gratitude that I wish the EFFAS Bond Commission all the success they deserve with this, the fifth edition of *The European Bond Markets*.

Paris, 3 August 1992 — Jean Guy de Wael

Foreword

Hasse H. Nilsson
Chairman,
The European Bond Commission

Almost two decades have passed since the formation of the European Bond Commission. During the 1970s, the Commission gradually developed from being a study-group comprising a few 'bond scientists' to a formal group of 'bond enthusiasts' committed to the aims laid down in the Articles:

- to standardize the method of analysis of bonds across the markets,
- to provide information to market participants,
- to act as an exchange of information to encourage the promotion of international participation in the markets.

The abolition of exchange controls during the 1980s shifted attention from the eurobond market towards domestic bond markets, thereby providing further impetus to the work of the European Bond Commission. From a position of relative obscurity, the commission began to gain attention and appreciation from a growing number of market participants and market organizations, such as the International Securities Market Association (formerly AIBD). The 1980s also witnessed the expansion of the European Community and, with it, a broadening of national representation within the Commission. As a consequence of developments in eastern Europe, the present number of 16 countries is expected to increase further in the years to come. This fifth edition of *The European Bond Markets* represents the most detailed and comprehensive reference guide to the bond markets yet published. It makes a notable contribution to the list of authoritative works already published by the Commission, including the *European Futures and Options Markets* (1991), the *Glossary of Terms in the International Bond Markets* (in no less than six languages), and several working papers on bond techniques. Furthermore, preparations are in hand for publications on subjects such as bond indices and European institutional placing rules and restrictions.

In addition, the Commission aims to increase its involvement in education (preferably in co-operation with bodies like the ISMA) within a global framework, as the process of international capital market integration necessarily calls for international training and qualification programmes.

The European Bond Commission has been, and hopefully will continue to be, a 'people's institution'. Despite the pressures of increased competition and, indeed, the pressures of work in general, which everyone engaged in the securities industry has experienced in recent years, the members of the European Bond Commission have shown remarkable commitment and enthusiasm by voluntarily, and without remuneration, giving up their leisure hours for work on Commission projects. Though the list of names of those who have contributed to the success of the Commission is almost endless, some outstanding personalities deserve special mention. Stuart Millman, Commission chairman during the 1970s, was the driving force behind the Commission's transformation into a real 'European' institution. The chairmanship of Peter Versloot saw the first publications and fund-raising activities, events which were to set the pattern for the future. Stuart McLean, chairman until summer 1990, and currently vice-chairman, brought additional professionalism and quality to the Commission's publications. More than anyone, Stuart has shouldered the responsibility and therefore deserves both gratitude and respect for all his efforts in the co-ordination of the written contributions from 16 different countries - not to mention the gathering of the necessary sponsorships from all over Europe, without which our intentions would have vanished into the haze.

It is my sincere hope that, in the future, the European Bond Commission will attract those who, for reasons other than personal financial gain, will be prepared to meet challenges with total commitment and who seek the invaluable friendship which exists between members.

Happily, past evidence suggest that this hope will be fulfilled.

Copenhagen, 28 August 1992 — Hasse H. Nilsson

Contributing Authors

Christopher Anthony
UBS Phillips & Drew

Balazs Bathory
Creditanstalt Securities Ltd., Budapest

Dr. Werner Becker
Deutsche Bank Research

Françoise Beirens
Generale Bank

Steven Bell
Morgan Grenfell

Graham Bishop
Salomon Brothers International Limited

Malin Hedman Bjrkmo
Stockholm School of Economics & hman Fondkommission AB

Dr. Norbert Bräuer
DG Bank Deutsche Genossenschaftsbank, Frankfurt am Main

Bjarne Brynning
Vesta-group

Jacek Brzezinski
Creditanstalt-Bankverein, Vienna

Virginie Chapron du Jeu
CDC

Arnaud Clement-Grancourt
BNP

Stefan Clevhammar
Kommunernas Pensionsanstalt

Alexander Creutzberg
Postipankki Ltd

Miguel de Bragança
Citibank-Portugal S.A.

Jean Guy de Wael
European Federation of Financial Analysts Societies

John C. Diaz
Moody's Investor Services Limited

João Ermida
Citibank-Portugal S.A.

Ignacio Ezquiaga
Analistas Financieros Internacionales

Wolfgang Fast
Z-Länderbank Bank Austria AG

Peter Fertig
Dresdner Bank AG, Frankfurt am Main

Gilbert François
Belfox

Sonsoles Gallego
Analistas Financieros Internacionales

Enrique García
Ahorro Corporacion Financiera, Svb

Marie-Pierre Gontard
Cardif

Ernest Gnan
Oesterreichische Natinoalbank

Jean Granoux
CNCA

Gabor Grenczer
Europartners Kft., Budapest

Jan Gurander
Patricia Treasury AB

Mattias Hansmann
Commerzbank AG, Frankfurt am Main

Päivi Härkönen
Startel Inc.

Koos 't Hart
Pierson, Heldring & Pierson

Klaus Holschuh
Commerzbank AG, Frankfurt am Main

Gerald Holtham
Lehman Brothers International

José Ramón Jara
Analistas Financieros Internacionales

Sven Jarlöv
Skandinaviska Enskilda Banken

Lukas Julinek
LB-Capital Markets, Vienna

Dr. Klaus Kegler
Delbrck & Co. Privatbankiers, Kln

Steven Klop
Compagnie Parisienne de Réescompte

Richard Komarnicki
Consultant

Bert Korevaar
ABN AMRO Bank

Andrejs Landsmanis
Läns Kapital AB

Csaba Lantos
Creditanstalt Securities Ltd., Budapest

Alexandra Larsen
Translator

Philippe Laurendeau
CDC

Michael Lewis
Deutsche Bank Research

Arne Lidén
Arcona Fastighetsutveckling AB

Joanna Makris
Citibank NA - Athens

Dr. Patrick Mange
Deutsche Bank Research GmbH, Frankfurt

Eva-Maria Mann
Deutsche Bank Research GmbH, Frankfurt

Stanislaw Markowski
Bank Creditanstalt S.A., Warsaw

Eva Märzendorfer
LB-Capital Markets

Pat McArdle
NCB Stockbrokers Ltd

Stuart McLean
UNI Storebrand Investment Managers

Pilar Medina
Banco Hipotecario De España

Baste Nepstad
Vital Forsikring

Chris Nicodem
Stichting Unilever Pensioenfonds 'Progress'

Bernt Nilsson

Hasse H. Nilsson
The European Bond Commission
Sundberg & Co.

Agnès Peltier
La Mondiale

Jan Pollestad
Carl Kirulf & Co.

Gregor Pozniak
Creditanstalt-Bankverein

Giorgio Radaelli
Lehman Brothers International

Dr. Karl Eugen Reis
DG Bank Deutsche Genossenschaftsbank, Frankfurt am Main

Niels Retbøll
Sundberg & Co.

Dieter Ritter
DG Bank Deutsche Genossenschaftsbank, Frankfurt am Main

Leif Ola Rød
Pre Invest

Odd Sigmund Røste
Oslo Stock Exchange

Peter Schedling
Oesterreichische Kontrollbank AG

Roman Schremser
Girozentrale und Bank der Österreichischen Sparkassen AG

Oliver Seipt
Dresdner Bank AG, Frankfurt am Main

Erik Sjberg
Enskilda Kapitalförvaltning

Rodrigo Sousa
Banco Hipotecario De España

Morten Steinsland
Vestenfjeldske Bykreditt

Dr. Werner Stricker

Uwe Sundermeier
Dresdner Bank AG, Frankfurt am Main

Dick Taverne
PRIMA Europe Ltd.

Paul Temperton
Merrill Lynch, Pierce, Fenner & Smith Ltd

Halvard Tretvoll
Central Securities Depository (VPS)

Tiina Tuominen
Postipankki Ltd

Bob Tyley
Paribas Ltd

Chris van Aeken
Kredietbank

Peter van der Linde
Philips Pensioenfondsen

Jan van Roekel
Algemeen Burgerlijk Pensioenfonds

Wilma Vergi
Cariplo, Milan

Gert Verheij
Towers Perrin/Smit & Bunschoten

Yves Wagner
Banque Générale du Luxembourg

Philippe Willemetz
Consultant

Pehr Wissén
Svenska Handelsbanken

Edward M. Young
Moody's Investor Services Limited

Ernst Zbinden
Bank Leu

Peter Zelnik
Europartners Kft., Budapest

Chapter

1

Introduction

Stuart McLean
UNI Storebrand Investment Managers

At the time of publication of the last edition of the *European Bond Markets*, in 1988, little did we anticipate the massive interest in European bonds that was to manifest itself in the following years. This has been particularly noticeable in 1991 and 1992, as a result of the proposals for convergence which culminated in the Maastricht Treaty (though, it should noted that we go to press awaiting the result of the French referendum on the treaty, on 20 September 1992, and hence those contributors who have pondered the future of Europe are very much hostages to fortune). During this time, international investors came to believe that the move to European monetary union (Emu) would result in similar inflation rates, as well as similar levels of borrowing, among the different countries. As a consequence, it was therefore concluded that interest rate differentials would narrow, causing the yields of 'high-yielding' countries to fall rapidly. International investors began to investigate the (then) more peripheral countries of Belgium, Italy and Spain. These countries responded by making changes to their markets in order to encourage investment, and yield differentials subsequently fell. Later, the search for high-yielders turned to Finland, Sweden, Norway and Portugal. The former countries even linked their currencies to the Ecu as a precursor to possible membership of the EC. Only Sweden could really accommodate the flows of funds. Indeed, Portugal had to limit overseas investors in certain securities. However, starting with the run on the Finnish markka, 1992 was to see the reversal of the trend and growing fears of 'too much, too soon'. The Danish vote against the Maastricht Treaty exposed the economic fundamentals of some countries and yield margins over German Bunds widened, especially in Spain and Italy. The continuing financial difficulties in Scandinavia have caused a reversal in their fortunes and many international investors have been left with European bonds 'under water'. The French referendum will either put the positive trend back on course, albeit at a more cautious pace, or cause very serious disruption to many European bond markets. It is hoped that this book will help investors whichever direction the result points.

Almost immediately after the last edition was released, the Swedish and Norwegian bond markets were deregulated, thereby allowing international investors to participate. Many other countries have also seen major changes in the last four years. All of these reorganizations are in response to the growing volumes of international monies that are available for investment. By developing their domestic markets, governments were provided with the opportunity of raising finance cheaper domestically, rather than internationally. Some of the changes that have been made have concerned the taxation of securities, with moves such as the removal of withholding tax, the payment of interest gross to international investors, the extension of the maturity-date ranges of issues out to at least ten years (and in some cases even further) and the issuance of fixed-rate bullet bonds in preference to previous conventional structures. All of these changes are covered in this edition.

The European Bond Commission is proud of its role in advancing the evolution of the European bond markets. The demand for our last edition has been very strong and many participants cite this book as an essential source of reference, providing information which has been instrumental in their increased understanding and confidence - two essential ingredients for successful involvement in these markets. In addition to publications, the Commission holds regular meetings throughout Europe at which information on the various markets is exchanged; furthermore, the Commission as an entity works with its members to help promote interest in individual markets as appropriate. With the Commission comprising the heads of research of many major security firms and banks, much has been achieved in the area of information-flow to investors. In 1991, for example, the increased interest in Finland, Sweden and Portugal can be attributed to the efforts of the member network. In 1992, members of the Commission have been working with the authorities in Sweden and Ireland to promote these markets further, not just in Europe, but also in the USA. We eagerly await the opportunities that will arise in Eastern Europe, Greece, Turkey and Iceland, as new members join the group, thereby assisting the evolution of their markets and providing new avenues for successful investment.

Expanded edition

When we completed the last edition of the European Bond Markets in 1988, there was a sense of amazement at the sheer size and scope of the publication - at over 600 pages, it had exceeded anything we had previously produced. The main reasons for this growth lay not only in the dedication of the authors, but also to the gaining of access to more comprehensive data, thereby enabling deeper analysis to be undertaken. However, our amazement at the size of the last edition has certainly been surpassed by this 1600-page volume! (Indeed, because it is so large, we have decided to produce the non-European eurobond section separately at a later date.).

Part of the reason for this further increase in size is the addition of several new countries, (as well as the general availability of more detailed market data). As the European Bond Commission has grown so, too, has the number of markets that can be covered. The three most noteworthy newcomers are Finland, Greece and Portugal. Additionally, we are indebted to the Austrian Commission for their work and contacts which have allowed us to include, albeit in a rather basic way, Czechoslovakia, Hungary and Poland. Furthermore, the Belgian Commission has been able to furnish separate details of the Luxembourg market (which has a particularly close relationship with the Belgian market - indeed in many analyses, Belgium includes Luxembourg!). Finally, this edition also covers the European currency unit (Ecu) markets (see Chapter 6). This is a tricky area to analyse since Ecu bonds are issued both as domestic and eurobonds and it can be difficult to make the distinction. However, we are pleased to have, as members of the UK Commission, some of the leading practitioners in this market and we are grateful for their enlightening contribution.

In this edition, we are carrying leading articles on a wide range of subjects connected with the European bond markets, with some being particularly topical. These articles include:

- Aa analysis of **European monetary union** by Gerald Holtham of Lehman International (formerly head of the Economic Unit at the OECD in Paris),
- A political commentary on the **Impact of Maastricht** by Dick Taverne, one of the UK's first MEPs (Members of the European Parliament) and a celebrated political commentator,
- A discussion of **'Eculand' as a potential thirteenth member of the European Community** by Graham Bishop of Salomon Brothers, a major researcher in this market,
- Two articles by Deutsche Bank on the effects of **German unity** and **European convergence,**
- A proposal for the creation of a **European bond index**, including the possible weightings to be used, by Paul Temperton, chief European economist at Merrill Lynch International,
- An in-depth analysis of the **European currency unit**, by Paul Temperton, Bob Tyley of Paribas, and Giorgio Radaelli of Lehman Brothers International
- An article on **credit ratings in Europe** by Moody's Investor Services.

We hope that these articles will enlighten those investors who are new to Europe, as well as stimulating thought amongst experienced practitioners.

Finally, with increased familiarity with government bonds in most European countries, we have been asked to provide more details on other sectors of the market, such as bank, mortgage and corporate bonds. Hopefully, we have cast some light on these important sectors by identifying the major issuers and the opportunities for investment that their issues provide. Currently, these bonds tend to attract solely domestic investment but, with the search for greater returns and competition between fund managers, we anticipate growing international participation.

We have also included three new sections. As well as details on settlement, there are also sections on money markets and futures and options. These markets exercise an increasing influence on the cash markets and many investors need greater knowledge of the opportunities they present.

Size of Markets

One of the major problems with describing market size is actually obtaining good data. There are many systems which provide information on practically all recent issues; however, data on smaller, older, issues is extremely hard to find since they are usually illiquid and therefore few people keep records of them. Further difficulties are encountered in handling callable bonds, sinking funds, etc. where details of retired securities are hard to unearth. To date, one of the few really reliable sources for government bond information, in particular, has been the Salomon Brothers research team. Hopefully, we have been able to extend their work by including other sectors such as domestic bonds, medium-term notes as well as eurobonds. The members of the European Bond Commission have used the very best sources available to derive their numbers - in some cases, actually working from the individual bonds. We have been able to further refine these statistics using data from the ISMA database on eurobonds, and Webster Communications statistics on medium-term notes. The ISMA database includes details of private placements that have been notified to them.

From Figure 1.1, it can be seen that, in a number of countries, government bonds dominate, e.g. Belgium (96.29 per cent), Greece (85.91 per cent), Hungary (94.34 per cent), Ireland (97.34 per cent), Italy (82.80 per cent), Poland (100.00 per cent) and Portugal (80.33 per cent). For the developing countries this is understandable, because government debt has the highest credit-quality and therefore investments can be easily justified, as well as providing the greatest liquidity. However, it is interesting to note the size of the Belgian and Italian government bond sectors. Both governments have been major borrowers for some time and have therefore had to offer attractive rates in order to meet funding requirements. This practice usually squeezes out other borrowers, such as corporates, since the interest rates they would have to pay would be significantly higher. As a result, they turn to the banking sector or the international bond market or, even, issue equity.

The difference between eurobonds and international bonds (e.g. 'Bulldogs', 'Matadors', 'Navigators' and 'Yankees') is a fine one. The main difference cited is that eurobonds are intended for international investors whilst international bonds are for domestic investors. Another distinction is that the former are usually syndicated internationally and the latter, domestically. Switzerland, alone, has an international market, while the majority of countries have eurobond markets. Several countries have both, e.g. Austria, Belgium, Denmark, Ecu, France, Portugal and the United Kingdom. In many cases, those authorities who wished to retain control over the issuance of debt in their currency tended to discourage the growth of eurobonds by allowing international issues, as in the case of Portugal, Spain and the United Kingdom. Gradually, as the domestic markets evolved, such restrictions have been removed, allowing flourishing eurobond

	Government		Eurobonds[1]		International		Domestics		MTNs[3]		Total	
	Amount	%	Amount	%	Amount	%	Amount	%	Amount	%	Amount	%
Austria	401.60	39.53	71.5	7.03	19.9	1.96	523.0	51.48	0.0	0.00	1016.0	100.00
Belgium	4619.90	96.29	51.0	1.06	61.0	1.27	66.2	1.38	0.0	0.00	4798.1	100.00
Czechoslovakia	2.00	44.44	0.0	0.00	0.0	0.00	2.5	55.56	0.0	0.00	4.5	100.00
Denmark	410.00	34.33	26.0	2.18	5.0	0.42	752.0	62.97	1.1	0.09	1194.1	100.00
Ecu[2]	54.31	25.90	134.9	64.34	18.2	8.70	0.0	0.00	2.2	1.05	209.7	100.00
Finland	11.10	19.41	9.9	17.24	0.0	0.00	35.7	62.43	0.5	0.92	57.2	100.00
France	980.00	33.78	207.8	7.16	322.2	11.11	1390.0	47.91	1.0	0.03	2901.0	100.00
Germany	1204.80	43.13	295.9	10.59	0.0	0.00	1292.0	46.25	0.7	0.03	2793.5	100.00
Greece	3751.90	85.91	0.0	0.00	0.0	0.00	615.5	14.09	0.0	0.00	4367.4	100.00
Hungary	40.00	94.34	0.0	0.00	0.4	0.94	2.0	4.72	0.0	0.00	42.4	100.00
Ireland	13.73	97.34	0.1	0.35	0.0	0.00	0.3	2.13	0.0	0.18	14.1	100.00
Italy	1,027,049.00	82.80	26,672.0	2.15	0.0	0.00	183,807.0	14.82	2864.1	0.23	1,240,392.0	100.00
Luxembourg	0.00	0.00	561.4	100.00	0.0	0.00	0.0	0.00	0.0	0.00	561.4	100.00
Netherlands	225.85	69.71	28.3	8.72	0.0	0.00	69.9	21.56	0.0	0.01	324.0	100.00
Norway	87.04	33.35	2.6	1.01	0.0	0.00	171.3	65.64	0.0	0.00	261.0	100.00
Poland	7405.50	100.00	0.0	0.00	0.0	0.00	0.0	0.00	0.0	0.00	7405.5	100.00
Portugal	2292.85	80.33	152.5	5.34	409.0	14.33	0.0	0.00	0.0	0.00	2854.4	100.00
Spain	16,373.90	72.82	719.8	3.20	0.0	0.00	5392.3	23.98	0.0	0.00	22,486.0	100.00
Sweden	269.00	24.89	18.1	1.67	0.0	0.00	793.0	73.37	0.8	0.08	1080.9	100.00
Switzerland	12.30	3.64	0.0	0.00	189.9	56.25	135.4	40.11	0.0	0.00	337.6	100.00
UK	121.72	55.60	72.8	33.23	4.3	1.96	18.3	8.35	1.9	0.86	218.9	100.00

Figure 1.1 The European bond markets

Note: Amounts are in local currency (billions) as at 1 January 1992. Percentages shown for each sector relate to the total of the individual country

[1] *All eurobond data derived from ISMA database (includes notified private placements*

[2] *All Ecu data derived from BIS, using their definitions*

[3] *All MTN data from Webster Communications*

	Government		Eurobonds		International		Domestics		MTNs		Total	
	USD bn	%	USD bn	%	USD bn	%	USD bn	%	USD bn	%	USD bn	%
Austria	40.6	0.69	7.2	0.12	2.0	0.03	52.8	0.90	0.0	0.00	102.6	1.74
Belgium	159.7	2.71	1.8	0.03	2.1	0.04	2.3	0.04	0.0	0.00	165.9	2.81
Czechoslovakia	0.1	0.00	0.0	0.00	0.0	0.00	0.1	0.00	0.0	0.00	0.2	0.00
Denmark	75.7	1.28	4.8	0.08	0.9	0.02	138.9	2.36	0.2	0.00	220.6	3.74
Ecu	37.7	0.64	93.6	1.59	12.7	0.21	0.0	0.00	1.5	0.03	145.5	2.47
Finland	2.9	0.05	2.5	0.04	0.0	0.00	9.2	0.16	0.1	0.00	14.8	0.25
France	204.6	3.47	43.4	0.74	67.3	1.14	290.2	4.92	0.2	0.00	605.7	10.28
Germany	858.3	14.56	210.8	3.58	0.0	0.00	920.4	15.62	0.5	0.01	1990.1	33.77
Greece	21.4	0.36	0.0	0.00	0.0	0.00	3.5	0.06	0.0	0.00	25.0	0.42
Hungary	0.5	0.01	0.0	0.00	0.0	0.00	0.0	0.00	0.0	0.00	0.5	0.01
Ireland	7.3	0.12	0.0	0.00	0.0	0.00	0.2	0.00	0.0	0.00	7.5	0.13
Italy	957.2	16.24	24.9	0.42	0.0	0.00	171.3	2.91	2.7	0.05	1156.0	19.62
Luxembourg	0.0	0.00	21.8	0.37	0.0	0.00	0.0	0.00	0.0	0.00	21.8	0.37
Netherlands	142.8	2.42	17.9	0.30	0.0	0.00	44.2	0.75	0.0	0.00	204.8	3.48
Norway	15.7	0.27	0.5	0.01	0.0	0.00	30.8	0.52	0.0	0.00	47.0	0.80
Poland	0.6	0.01	0.0	0.00	0.0	0.00	0.0	0.00	0.0	0.00	0.6	0.01
Portugal	18.8	0.32	1.2	0.02	3.3	0.06	0.0	0.00	0.0	0.00	23.3	0.40
Spain	179.5	3.05	7.9	0.13	0.0	0.00	59.1	1.00	0.0	0.00	246.6	4.18
Sweden	52.5	0.89	3.5	0.06	0.0	0.00	154.6	2.62	0.2	0.00	210.8	3.58
Switzerland	9.8	0.17	0.0	0.00	151.3	2.57	107.9	1.83	0.0	0.00	269.0	4.56
UK	242.0	4.11	144.6	2.45	8.5	0.15	36.3	0.62	3.7	0.06	435.3	7.39
GRAND TOTAL	3027.5	51.37	586.47	9.95	248.17	4.21	2022.0	34.31	9.19	0.16	5893.3	100.00

Figure 1.2 The European bond markets

Note: Amounts are US dollar equivalents, based on currency rates as at 29 August 1992. Percentages shown for each sector relate to the total of all the markets described

sectors, albeit usually with some marginal controls. In this context, therefore, it is noticeable that France has a larger international bond market sector.

Usually, domestic bonds represent a major source of finance for bank, public authority and corporate borrowers. In the case of those countries which are dominated by a government market, it is no surprise to learn that these sectors are small. In most of the countries where large corporate sectors exist, these are usually found to be dominated by financial institutions, such as banks and mortgage institutions.

Finally, we have included medium-term notes. This sector, while still small, is growing very rapidly and such issues can be found in Denmark, Ecu, Finland, France, Germany, Ireland (only one small issue), Italy, Netherlands, Sweden and the United Kingdom. By offering investors any structure they desire, these notes are being used as a means to produce bonds that incorporate many of the financial engineering tools now available to meet investors requirements. By incorporating derivatives, they allow some investors with certain restrictions, to overcome these problems.

	Local value (billion)	**US dollar equiv.** (billion)	**Percentage**	**Government position**
Germany	2793.5	1990.1	33.78	(2)
Italy	1240.4[1]	1156.0	19.62	(1)
France	2901.0	605.7	10.28	(4)
UK	218.9	435.3	7.39	(3)
Switzerland	337.6	269.0	4.57	(15)
Spain	22,486.0	246.6	4.19	(5)
Denmark	1194.1	220.6	3.74	(8)
Sweden	1080.9	210.8	3.58	(9)
Netherlands	324.0	204.8	3.48	(7)
Belgium	4798.1	165.9	2.82	(10)
Ecu	209.7	145.5	2.47	(6)
Austria	1016.0	102.6	1.74	(11)
Rest	n/a	118.7	2.02	n/a

[1] *trillion*

The largest European bond markets are:

Eurobond markets

We are sorry that this book does not contain full details on the non-European eurobond markets; however, we will be publishing these later. In the mean time, we are able to provide a brief description of the relative sizes of the markets, based on the ISMA database as at 1 January 1992. If we look at the amounts outstanding (not issued) in US dollars then,

- The top 10 currencies are:-

	US dollars (million)	Percentage
US dollars	619,114	41.66
Deutschemarks	164,302	11.05
Japanese yen	159,395	10.72
UK sterling	122,546	8.25
Swiss francs[1]	122,263	8.23
Ecu	92,125	6.20
Canadian dollars	62,854	4.23
French francs	35,847	2.41
Australian dollars	27,750	1.87
Italian lire	21,172	1.42
Others		3.97
Total	1,486,276	100.0

[1]*these are classed as international bonds in Switzerland*

- The top 10 European currencies are:-

Deutschemark	164,302	11.05
UK sterling	122,546	8.25
Swiss franc	122,263	8.23
Ecu	92,125	6.20
French franc	35,847	2.41
Italian lira	21,172	1.42
Luxembourg franc	16,008	1.08
Netherlands guilder	14,465	0.97
Spanish peseta	6494	0.44
Austrian schilling	5914	0.44
Other	12,094	0.81

- The structure of the market by instruments is:-

Straights	1,163,628	78.29
Floating-rate notes	273,996	18.44
Convertibles	78,680	5.29

Features of each chapter

We have tried to standardize each chapter to enable the user quickly to find any desired information. However, with so many authors and with markets drawn from so many different countries, we have not been to do so in all cases. In the main, however, the following structure has been provided.

Introduction

This section provides a general overview of the markets in the individual country, as well as providing information of changes witnessed since 1988, and highlighting other important features.

Market composition

This section provides details of the size of the markets, including the various sectors such as government, public authority, corporate, bank, eurobond, medium-term note, asset- and mortgage-backed, convertible and international bonds. Each sector is described in detail and includes maturity structure and coupon structure - there is no doubt that these features can be important both to investors and to the structure of interest rates.

Types of security

Each bond market sector has details of the various types of security available and their extent. With many new structures available in the markets in general, individual securities can be of specific interest to both international and domestic investors.

Issuers

Details are provided of the types of issuer active in each sector, including examples and country of origin. The market structures in certain markets highlight the importance of particular issuers, the names of some of which may be unfamiliar to international investors. Some issuers may also be strong in one type of security, yet totally absent from another sector.

Investors

Details are provided of the investors in the markets, together with their preferences, and the influence of international investors.

Methods of issuance

Details of the issuance of a new bond - of great importance to both investors and issuers alike. The methods of issuance vary markedly from country to country.

New issue volumes

Details of new issuance volumes show the growth of particular sectors and the frequency of issuance ,which can be dramatic.

Methods of trading

This section gives details of how particular sectors are traded with the names of the major counterparties who are particularly strong in these sectors. (It should be noted that there are many counterparties who are not featured. This does not mean that the EBC has any opinion about individual companies/banks.)

Market practices

This section is a compilation of market features, failure to understand which, can often lead to errors and even losses.

Settlement (NEW!)

We have made settlement a specific section to reflect its importance. The settlement of securities can be a major factor in losses. This matter is very complicated and we recommend that investors should take advice ***before*** transacting, or else employ an experienced global custodian.

Yield calculation

An explanation of the most common method(s) of calculating the yield for particular markets. The most common standard in Europe is the ISMA (formerly AIDB) method. Details of this technique are available directly from:

- The International Securities Market Association
Seven Limeharbour
DOCKLANDS
London
E14 9NQ
United Kingdom

This is available in a separate publication for which a payment is required.

Taxation

A description of the different forms of taxation pertaining to the market; a crucial consideration for both the issuer and investor. With many countries, especially Belgium, Italy and Spain making major changes to the taxation of bonds for international investors, it is essential to be conversant with this sector.

Futures and options **(NEW!)**

One of the major events since the publication of our last edition has been the emergence of futures and options exchanges in most European countries. The market structures and contracts are continually being changed, with the result that publications can rapidly become out of date. The European Bond Commission published an extensive guide, *The European Futures and Option Exchanges* in 1991. With over 1100 pages, it covers all available contracts including both soft and hard commodities, interest rates, stock exchange indices and stock options. It is available from Probus Publishing.

Money markets **(NEW!)**

We have been asked by many investors to give details of the various money market instruments that are available, and are pleased to oblige.

Interest rate history

An explanation of economic factors affecting interest rates and a discussion of the development of yields in recent years.

Inter-market spreads

A presentation of the yield differentials between the various sectors, and their historical developments.

Sources of reference

This section gives details of the major references for each country. It includes details of the publications of central banks and similar authorities, together with other commercial sources, newspapers that provide coverage, and Reuters/Telerate pages. Two major sources of information are Bloomberg and Datastream International.

The authors

The authors are major practitioners in their markets. A real understanding of how domestic investors, as well as international investors, interact with the market and the factors which affect each group can only be legitimately commented upon by someone within that country. It is therefore hoped that this publication will provide a comprehensive guide of real value to investors, borrowers and counterparties alike.

Acknowledgements

In order to produce this publication a veritable army of participants have made their contributions. I wish to personally thank the following for their help, patience and vast amounts of work.

- The EFFAS Board
- The sponsors
- The authors and their assistants
- The translators
- Probus Publishing (especially Michael Jeffers)
- and, most importantly of all, Nick Battley

Nick Battley has been employed by the European Bond Commission, courtesy of the sponsors. By using an excellent professional editor, we believe that we have been able to produce an extremely high-quality product. Nick has been instrumental in determining the style of this book, and in creating the form that has been employed. It became apparent that, surprisingly, there was no agreed international convention for the abbreviations and common terms used in the European bond markets. This came to light after Nick had consulted many publishing houses, security firms and the international financial press. As a result, Nick has developed a convention, one which he hopes to make available in the future, for all financial writers and editors.

Nick not only controlled the format but also interacted directly with the authors, which enabled him to influence them in their writing. His ability to translate from many styles of 'European-English' to 'English-English' has been remarkable. We can not thank him enough.

The sponsors

The high quality publications that the European Bond Commission has been able to produce has been supported by the generosity of our sponsors who have provided funds to pay for all the essential facilities that are required for this book. Their support has been important to us, not only terms of the monies provided, but also for helping us by distributing the book to many participants. With the increasing complexity of European markets, we hope you remember their support when you come to act in their markets.

Our thanks go to our major sponsors:

• Barclays de Zoete Wedd	United Kingdom & International
• Caisse des Dépôts et Consignations	France
• Citibank Portugal	Portugal
• Caisse Nationale de Credit Agricole SA	International & France
• Credit Suisse First Boston	International & United Kingdom
• DnB Fonds as	Norway
• Deutsche Bank International	Germany & United Kingdom
• Dresdner Bank	Germany
• Goldman Sachs International	International & United Kingdom
• IBJ International	International
• ISMA	International
• JP Morgan	International & United Kingdom
• Kidder Peabody International	International
• Lehman Brothers International	International & United Kingdom
• Merrill Lynch International	International
• NCB Stockbrokers	Ireland
• Salomon Brothers International	International & United Kingdom
• Skandinaviska Enskilda Banken	Sweden
• Sveriges Föreningsbank	Sweden
• UBS Phillips & Drew	International & United Kingdom
• UNI Storebrand Fund Managers	International
• Unibørs Securities	Scandinavia & Denmark

Supported by our associate sponsors;

• Alicon	Denmark
• Amsterdam Stock Exchange	Netherlands
• Bank für Arbeit und Wirtschaft	Austria
• Bank Leu	Switzerland
• Banko Totta & Acores	Potugal
• Bloomberg	United Kingdom
• CARIPLO	Italy
• Christiania Fonds a.s.	Norway
• Copenhagen Stock Exchange	Denmark
• Creditansalt	Austria
• DnB Fonds A/S	Norway
• Elcon Securities a.s.	Norway

• European Options Exchange	Netherlands
• ESSAR Securities	Norway
• Fearnley Finans (Fonds)	Norway
• FG Inversiones Bursátiles S.A.	Spain
• FIMAGEST	France
• Financiële Termijnmarkt	Netherlands
• Finanshuset A/S	Norway
• First Austrian Bank	Austria
• Fokus Fonds	Norway
• Fondsfinans a.s.	Norway
• Grupo Ahorro Corporacion	Spain
• GZ Bank-Girozentrale Vienna	Austria
• Handelsbanken Fonds as	Norway
• Invest Securities as	Norway
• Kredietbank	Belgium
• Luthy Baillie, Dowsett, Pethick	United Kingdom
• Norske Finansanalytikeres Forening	Norway
• Norse Securities	Norway
• Oesterreichische Volksbanken AG	Austria
• Oslo Bors Informasjon	Norway
• Oslo Securities AS	Norway
• Oesterreichische Kontrollbank AG	Austria
• ÖVFA-Austrian Association of Financial Analysts	Austria
• Pre Fonds a.s.	Norway
• Raiffeisen Zentralbank Oesterreich	Austria
• Sundal Collier & Co. a.s.	Norway
• Z-Landerbank Bank Austria AG	Austria

Your Partner

Why UNI Storebrand?

As Norway's leading insurance company, we have an unmatched depth of understanding of the investment needs of our customers. The service we offer is a very personal and flexible one. We sit down with you to listen to your objectives and constraints. Together we build a working partnership.

You will not be asked by us to accept an off-the-shelf solution, and you will always be a top priority of our most senior managers.

Fixed Interest Performance

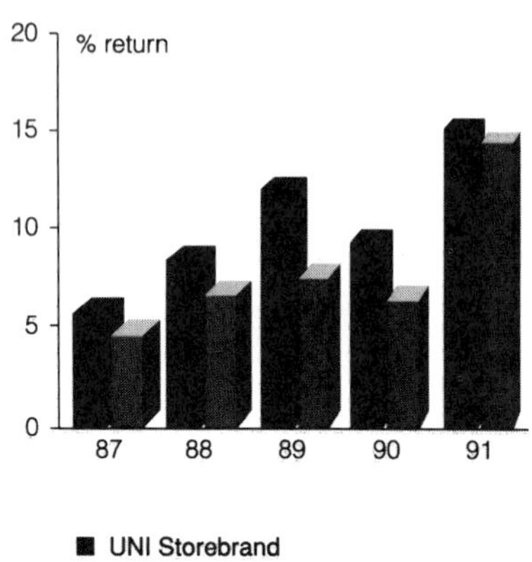

Source: UNI Storebrand annual reports

Equity Investment Performance

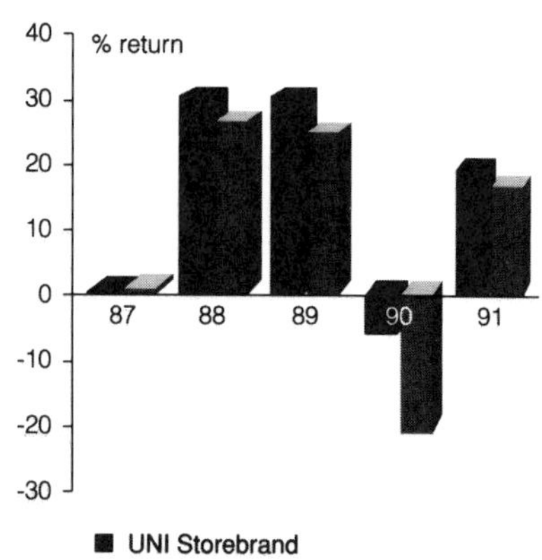

Source: UNI Storebrand annual reports

For over twenty years we have consistently outperformed accepted benchmarks in the international capital markets. Latterly, as the charts show, our international companies have outperformed both equity and bond markets in every year except 1987, in bad years as well as good.

in International Investment

Unit Trust

For funds up to around £5m (NKr 50m), we believe the Storebrand International Unit Trust (SIUT) is a suitable investment vehicle. This is a global balanced fund, split between bonds and equities. Its investment objective is growth with low risk. Performance since launch has been excellent relative to its London-based competition.

Portfolio Management

Alternatively, for clients who wish to invest larger sums internationally UNI Storebrand Portfolio Managers Ltd offers a personalised fund management service. Our expertise in devising and implementing investment strategy will allow you greater precision in matching your portfolio to your objectives.

As a first step, based on a detailed understanding of your requirements, we agree with you appropriate asset classes to satisfy your risk tolerance, investment horizon and liability structure. Our fund managers are then given clear guidelines and follow disciplined procedures in implementing the chosen strategy. We agree with you the appropriate benchmarks against which to measure our performance.

Of course, these guidelines and benchmarks are not cast in stone – we are always happy to discuss them with you in the light of experience and revise them as necessary. As a basic minimum we supply you with comprehensive quarterly reports and hold an annual investment seminar. Ours is a truly personal service, and we are happy to provide you with whatever information you need, when you need it.

Note:
- *The past is not necessarily a guide to future performance*
- *The value of investment units can fall as well as rise*

UNI STOREBRAND

Chapter

2

The future of

Credit ratings in Europe

Edward M. Young & John C. Diaz
Moody's Investor Services Limited

Overview

Although the emergence of credit ratings is a relatively new phenomenon in Europe, their use by European investors has nevertheless grown steadily since Moody's assigned its first eurobond rating in 1974. In 1991, Moody's rated roughly 82 per cent of the volume of eurobonds issued, bringing its rating coverage of all eurobonds to about 71 per cent of the volume outstanding. In the eurocommercial paper market the application of ratings has been more rapid, driven by a series of defaults which resulted in actual losses to investors. Within European domestic financial markets the use of ratings is also rising, guided to some extent by regulatory initiatives, but more importantly, by a growing recognition of the need for a mechanism that assesses credit risk and helps investors to price debt securities properly.

While ratings are not yet a universal requirement in the euromarkets there are several trends that, over the next decade, will further stimulate their use and expand their applications beyond their present role. These include:

Financial market integration

The removal of barriers between markets remains a priority for the European Community as it implements its plan for a single market. Removing barriers to capital movements and harmonizing standards should stimulate greater cross-border financial activity. If the European Community enlarges to incorporate the former members of the European Free Trade Association, as well as possible new members from the Eastern bloc countries, the number of potential debt issuers will expand dramatically.

The trend towards privatization

Continuing privatization of formerly state-owned entities coupled with their subsequent need to fund their capital requirements in the public markets instead of the national budget will add to the ranks of potential issuers. With greater capital market integration, these issuers will be able to diversify their funding sources well beyond their own domestic markets with relative ease.

Expanding funds for investment

The pool of investment funds is likely to expand because, as the European population ages, there should be a greater propensity to save rather than consume. The individual may be reluctant to be an active and direct participant in the market and may prefer to invest through a pension fund or a life insurance company. Since, in an integrated market, the investor will have a wider selection of investment opportunities from which to choose, there is reason to believe that over time more of the investment decision making process will pass to the professional institutional investor. The professional asset managers will thus play a more important role but, with an increasingly sophisticated clientele, will have to cope with more demanding performance standards. This will put a premium on identifying the best investment return commensurate with the risk appetite of the investor.

Growing complexity of credit analysis

The credit analyst of the 1990s faces a more complex and challenging task than ever before:

- The secular growth of information technology continues at an exponential rate making the creation of global communications networks and the completion of complex transactions easier and cheaper.
- There is a growing list of investment options available across thousands of possible issuers who operate in many different countries with differing cultures, languages, and business practices. At the same time, financial engineering continues to create new types of securities with complex and often risky features.
- Volatility in the debt markets is rising and there is an overall trend toward increased credit risk. The latter is partly spurred by the drive of many government bodies to foster competition and de-regulate markets. This is challenging long established practices and strategies of the major companies of the day. The trend toward privatization of state-owned and controlled companies is also creating long-term risks for investors.

The driving force for ratings will continue to be the investor. As investors respond to the aforementioned challenges, their reliance on a formal system of credit evaluation from an informed, independent, impartial and objective source will increase. Furthermore, as investors extend their investment choices to multiple industries and across national boundaries, a rating agency's breadth of coverage and its ability to provide ratings that are globally comparable will become critical.

As the use and importance of ratings increases, issuers will also benefit. Ratings provide broader access to new sources of capital at competitive costs. Provided that the ratings have credibility, are widely disseminated, and are understood by the market, they will expand an issuer's access to a greater range of investors. Ratings can also help stabilize access to the capital markets by helping issuers to manage investor perception of their credit risk. In times of stress, for example, investors are more likely to opt for rated securities where there is a greater degree of certainty about the level of risk.

The growth of debt securities markets

The dramatic changes in financial systems around the world over the last few decades have had a profound effect on the risks assumed by the providers of credit to the markets and on the nature of professional credit analysis. Evaluating a borrower's credit-worthiness has always been an integral part of lending money, but until recently that function rested almost exclusively with bank credit departments who had relatively small numbers of borrowers and the time and resources to examine the details of their clients' businesses. The credit analyst of the 1990s is more likely to work alongside an institutional portfolio manager, or perhaps on the sell-side of the market in a securities firm or universal bank. The transformation in the role of the credit analyst is part of a profound shift in the financial markets that has been driven by several factors:

Disintermediation

Historically, banks were the main intermediaries between savers and users of capital. They collected funds from savers in the form of deposits and then lent these funds to corporations, governments, or other producers in the economy. Over the past several decades that traditional role has been progressively replaced by a more cost-efficient process in the public securities markets.

Since its inception, outstandings in the eurobond market have risen dramatically, to an estimated $1.3 trillion by year-end 1990. That figure includes issues by corporates, sovereigns, and supranationals. More recently in Europe, users of capital in the industrial, public utility, and financial sectors have chosen to finance their short-term capital needs through commercial paper, having realized that short-term funding costs are generally lower in this market. The eurocommercial paper market has grown to around $70bn in outstandings, while domestic commercial paper markets in England, France, Spain, Sweden, and Germany account for approximately a further $90bn .

Several obvious advantages have helped promote this process of disintermediation. From the borrower's point of view, sidestepping the banking system, either through bond or commercial paper markets, usually means a substantial cost savings. The borrower does not have to pay a premium for the bank's credit department and lending staff, its equity base, and the costs of mobilizing the savings of thousands of individual depositors. Lending rates in the public debt markets are often more competitive, because credit-worthy borrowers can choose the most economical source of funds from a wide range of domestic and international alternatives, rather than from a few banks.

Technological developments

Paralleling the growth of public debt markets has been a steady increase in the willingness of corporations, financial institutions, and sovereign issuers to go beyond the confines of their own domestic markets to seek out the efficiencies and competitive benefits that are available in other larger financial markets. The most conspicuous example of this is the eurobond market. Advances in information technology have improved the efficiencies in the securities markets by lowering the expense of communication and calculation. More importantly, the exponential growth in information technology has enabled financial intermediaries to remove the barriers of geography, thus gaining opportunities in new markets.

Privatization and deregulation

A second underlying factor spurring the growth of debt securities is that governments and regulators are actively encouraging them. Around the world, governments are realizing that the task of national resource allocation is extremely difficult and that highly centralized authorities simply cannot process information fast enough to manage vast economies and their financial systems efficiently. Governments are taking steps to relax their control over public enterprise generally, and over their financial markets in particular. Government-owned enterprises are being transferred to private hands, while existing regulations are being adjusted to facilitate the development of the debt securities markets. From a public policy point of view, the open-market discipline inherent in a broad and competitive public market-place offers a more efficient means of channeling savings to national and local development. It also offers an economical and flexible source of funds for private companies that will help them meet the challenge of increasing foreign competition.

The move toward a single market within the European Community should spur the further development of debt securities markets. The financial integration of the European Community is seen as an important element of the move to a single market. Essentially all remaining restrictions on intra-market capital flows will be removed after 1992, with co-ordinated steps to liberalize securities trade and other capital flows as well as financial services. These reforms will help make the European community resemble a large national financial market.

The changing nature of credit decisions

Market liberalization and technological innovation have created an explosion of opportunities. Simply stated, the key advantage that broad-based debt markets offer to both investor and issuer is diversification. With a vast range of debt instruments from which to choose, investors are presented with new means of optimizing yields on the securities they buy while also picking securities with the currency, maturity structure, and other features to match particular portfolio requirements. The range of securities available also provides a means of diversifying risk. From the borrower's point of view, the growth in debt markets means a wider range of potential funding options, which may translate into an increased ability to finance in markets where interest rates are low or where particular funding needs in terms of currency or maturity can be more easily met.

Reaping the benefits of that diversification, however, hinges directly on being able to manage credit risk. Inadequate information flow creates uncertainty and uncertainty keeps investors away from new and unfamiliar markets. This in turn causes issuers to lose access to an important range of funding sources. The key from both perspectives is **credit information** or the ability to: (1) gather sufficient information to make correct credit evaluations on the new range of issuers, and (2) continuously update that information.

Credit analysis has always been central to the lending of capital. But in the more integrated markets of the 1990s, the nature of that analysis has altered considerably. This is true in several ways:

Complexity and innovation

Perhaps the most obvious development in fast-expanding markets is that credit decisions are becoming more complex. As investment horizons are expanded, investors are introduced to issuers in different cultures, who operate in different political and economic environments, who use different accounting systems and conventions in their financial reporting, and who operate with different standards of financial disclosure. In addition, more efficient technology is helping to spawn new and innovative types of debt securities with new and complex credit implications. To take full advantage of this diversity-- both to maximize returns and for portfolio diversification -- investors will increasingly be forced to commit more resources to credit analysis because appropriate, reliable means must be found to compare relative risks across the new range of debt instruments and cross-border debt issuers.

Volatility

Moreover, as the debt markets grow more complex, they are also becoming more volatile. And like most others in the financial services industry, investment managers are under mounting competitive pressure to meet stringent performance standards. The traditional emphasis in bond investments on buying and holding a security to term is changing. Increasingly, portfolio managers are concerned with optimizing the value of their portfolios on a total return basis, taking into account income from interest payments and reinvestment as well as the current market value of each bond in the portfolio. The value of each debt security must be continuously evaluated according to current market value and quickly adjusted for any changes in credit quality that may have a direct and immediate impact on secondary market prices. The role of the credit analyst is thus becoming increasingly time sensitive - the objective being not only to weigh the relative risk of default over the life of each debt instrument, but also to monitor and to forecast changes in credit risk over time.

Secular rise in credit risk

While the growth of the securities markets is affecting the nature of the credit analyst's task, the same forces that are driving market growth are having a fundamental effect on the underlying credit quality of issuers. Improvements in information technology and the world-wide trend towards open-market economies are having serious consequences for the competitive business prospects and risks -- thus the credit quality -- of a broad range of issuers. Continuous improvements in technology and technology transfer have enabled new entrants to put new production technologies to work to compete directly with major established companies. Japanese automobile manufacturers, for example, have adopted and developed state-of-the-art technology to produce high-quality, reasonably priced cars that compete with long established companies in their home markets. Not only are major corporations in Europe and North America having to respond to new and intense competitive pressures in order to preserve their markets, they may also face new sources of competition following the establishment of more market oriented economies in Eastern Europe.

Technology is also driving competition by shortening the traditional product development cycle. What used to take a decade now takes a few years. This puts a premium on making investments in research and development, and on understanding how a developing technology can meet real customer needs in widely dispersed markets. At the same time, faster technological development opens many opportunities for smaller, more nimble competitors who can challenge important business lines of major corporations. Not only is the cost of research is increasing, but the cost of making a strategic error is rising exponentially as well.

In addition to added risks for well-established issuers, the trend toward privatization of government-owned enterprises throws up new challenges for the credit analyst. During the 1980s, some 220 government-run enterprises around the world were privatized. The current accent on open-market efficiency, particularly in Eastern Europe, will likely produce more privatization programs in the 1990s. Like other private companies, these new entities typically choose to fund a significant portion of their operations through the issuance of debt. Following privatization there is a major shift from government funding to investor funding; this process is now occurring in the electric and water utilities in the

United Kingdom for example. One aspect of privatization is that the credit risks of an enterprise inevitably rise when it moves from government control to private ownership and management. Usually, fully-privatized companies relinquish formal government guarantees of their debt. Managers must also adjust to the realities of competition and to new, often unpredictable environments. In the event of a crisis, government support and intervention to support the company can no longer be automatically assumed.

In a globalizing and increasingly competitive free-market-oriented economy, the credit strength of issuers is becoming less certain and more volatile. All things considered, the risks of making uniformed credit decisions will rise in the 1990s. **The most profound implication of the shift in financial intermediation from governments and the banking system to the individual debt investor is that it is the investor, not the banking system, who is absorbing all of the credit risk.** It is the investor, not the credit department of a bank, who is responsible for the analysis of credit risk. In an environment of change and economic volatility, the task of forecasting credit risk is becoming more central to investment decisions while at the same time becoming more complex. If investors are to be able to take advantage of new opportunities to maximize yields and diversify investment risk, they must have access to timely and adequate information regarding the true nature of the credit risk to which they are exposed. Equally important, there is an essential need for a framework of credit risk evaluation that enables reliable comparisons across the new diversity of issues and issuers.

The role of ratings in the financial markets

The role of credit ratings in the financial markets is straightforward: to provide the investor with a relative ranking of the risk of default for a given fixed-income investment in comparison with all other rated instruments. The rating represents the quickest, most convenient means of communicating the rating agency's credit risk analysis to the market-place. By providing a simple, objective and consistently applicable indicator of relative default risks, ratings can be used to determine whether that security meets an investor's risk guidelines. In this way, the rating has the effect of reducing uncertainty about the investment risks of a much wider range of securities than the credit staff of any particular institution could follow on their own. Ratings provide a supplement to the institution's own credit assessment, and can open the institution's investment horizons to a broader spectrum of investment opportunities. This, in turn, helps the institution manage the risks in its fixed income portfolio through appropriate diversification. The wider range of choice will also help the institution to maximize returns on debt purchases while selecting the risk-adjusted currencies, maturity structures, and other features that will better conform to its particular investment needs.

Pricing

Ratings play a key role in the pricing of debt securities. The rating provides an essential indicator of how much added return, or risk premium, the investor should demand on progressively lower-rated securities to compensate for their relatively higher probability of default. Typically, this pricing is calculated against a proxy for a 'risk-free' investment (normally government debt securities of the country in whose currency the security is denominated). Figure 2.1 shows a ten-year history of spreads between various rating categories of corporate bonds and the ten-year US Treasury rate.

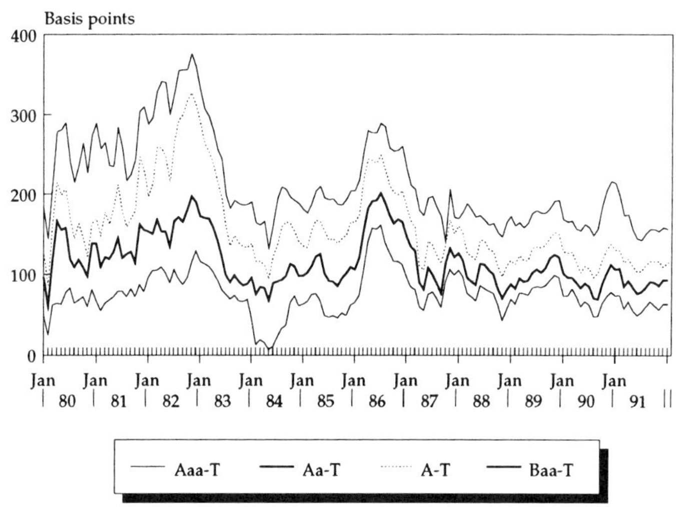

Figure 2.1 Corporate bond yield spreads vs. Treasury, June 1981 - October 1991

In markets where an independent rating system has not been fully established, investors have often relied upon the issuer's name or reputation, or a measure such as market capitalization, as a rough indicator of credit risk. Though this has often been accepted as market practice, it has the obvious disadvantage that many so-called 'name' companies have defaulted in the past. More importantly, a 'name' does not provide the relative ranking of the risk that sophisticated investors need to make risk-adjusted yield comparisons.

Investors in progressively-lower-rated bonds typically demand a proportionately higher margin of return above the risk-free rate, reflecting the higher risk of default. Higher-rated bonds will not require as high a yield because of the inherently lower credit risk. It is important to note that the price spread between different securities in each rating category is not a pure reflection of relative rating levels. There are other factors involved in determining the pricing of a specific bond. Differences in the liquidity of the bond issue or the risk of redemption can influence the yield over the risk-free rate. Investor perception of the overall risk in the credit markets can also lead to increased risk premiums. During periods of economic recession, when the probability of default by weaker or more highly geared companies increases, investors will demand proportionately higher yields.

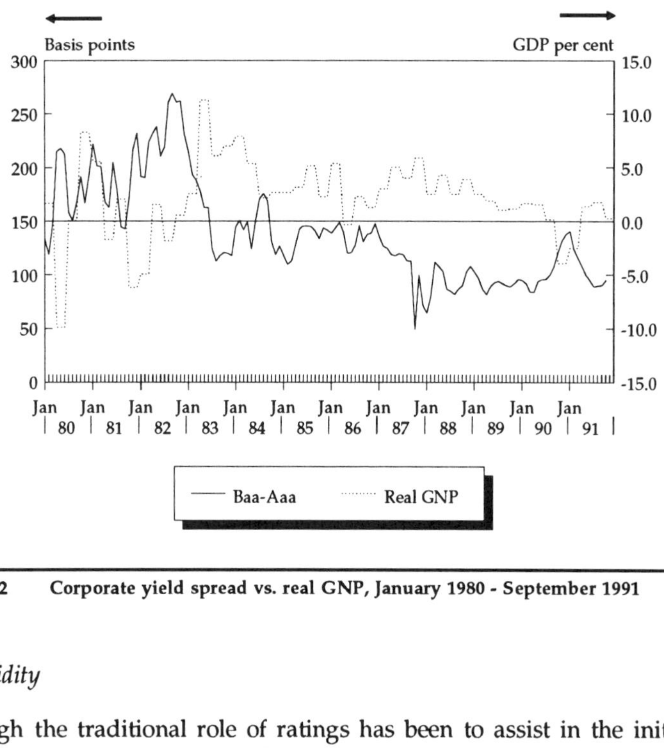

Figure 2.2 Corporate yield spread vs. real GNP, January 1980 - September 1991

Liquidity

Although the traditional role of ratings has been to assist in the initial investment decision, investors have found other uses for ratings as well. With the development of liquid secondary markets, ratings may provide investors with an indication of how readily the security may be sold in the secondary markets in times of market stress. As a general rule, the more highly rated a security, the more likelihood there will be of being able to sell the security in an illiquid market.

Portfolio management

As portfolio management techniques have become increasingly sophisticated, ratings have come to be used for assessing the current market value of the securities held in portfolio as well as a tool for managing investment criteria in regards to acceptable levels of credit risk. Some institutions choose to create a portfolio of bonds with approximately the same level of credit risk (that is, rated within a specified band), using ratings as their guide not only to establish the investment criteria but also to monitor the portfolio by following rating agency announcements as an early warning sign that the portfolio may require adjustment.

Rating agency credibility

There are several important ingredients that contribute to a rating agency's credibility:

- (1) *Independence and objectivity:* A rating agency's opinions must, first of all, be recognized as objective and impartial. The rating agency must be independent and free from the influence, or even the perceived influence, of interested market forces such as financial intermediaries, governments, or issuers themselves.

- (2) *Professionalism and experience:* To provide objective and relevant opinions on credit quality, a rating agency's analysts must be thoroughly professional and must have relevant experience.

- (3) *Global coverage:* Investors want to make risk/reward decision on the broadest range of securities available to them. The rating agency must be in a position to provide comparative opinions on credit quality and default risk. Greater coverage contributes to an important comparative perspective in the analysis. When investors extend their investment choices to multiple industries and across national boundaries, a rating agency's ability to provide rating opinions that are globally comparable becomes critical.

Moody's default rate studies

It is important to note that the ultimate accuracy of all ratings is difficult to evaluate in advance. Since ratings are intended to be a prediction of the future, the accuracy of the prediction can only be determined after the rated security has performed to maturity. However, the incidence of default by rating category can be calculated over a given period and this can provide an indication of a rating agency's track record.

Since 1989, Moody's has been has been publishing the results of an on-going study of corporate bond defaults and default rates by rating category. Data is now available for measuring actual default experience between 1970 and 1991. The purpose of the study has been to provide investors in the bond markets with some guidelines on historical default experience. The study grew out of the need to assess the level of credit support needed for structured securities backed by pools of corporate bonds. The study determined that average default rates across investment horizons spanning one to twenty years clearly show that default rates for lower-rated issuers exceed those of high grade issuers.

Moody's uses a strict test for default. A default is defined as any missed or delayed disbursement of interest and/or principal, including distressed exchanges. Using its own proprietary database, Moody's reviewed the rating histories of over 4000 US and non-US issuers of long-term bonds. This universe covered industrial companies, utilities, financial institutions, sovereigns, and structured finance entities. Over the study period (1970-1991), 425 rated issuers defaulted on their debt. The rating history of each of these defaulted issuers was traced to determine the original rating place on the bond. This was then converted to provide the cumulative default rate by rating category over various fixed points in time, i.e. five, ten, fifteen, and twenty years.

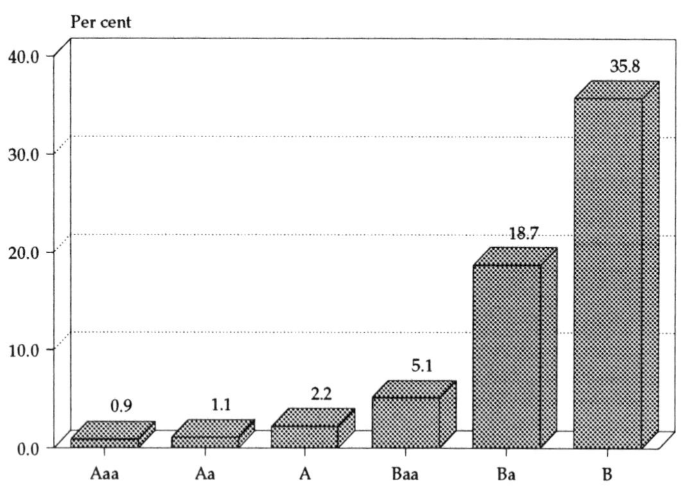

Figure 2.3 Average 10-year default rates

Figure 2.3 shows the average default rate, by rating category, over a ten-year period. The default rate for lower rated issuers is evident. As the chart shows, there is a sharp distinction between companies in the investment grade category (ratings of Baa and above) and companies in the speculative grade categories (ratings of Ba and B). Moreover, as Figure 2.4 shows, the volatility of default rates is also significantly higher at the lower end of the rating scale. In the speculative grade category, default rates are more volatile and less predictable in any given year.

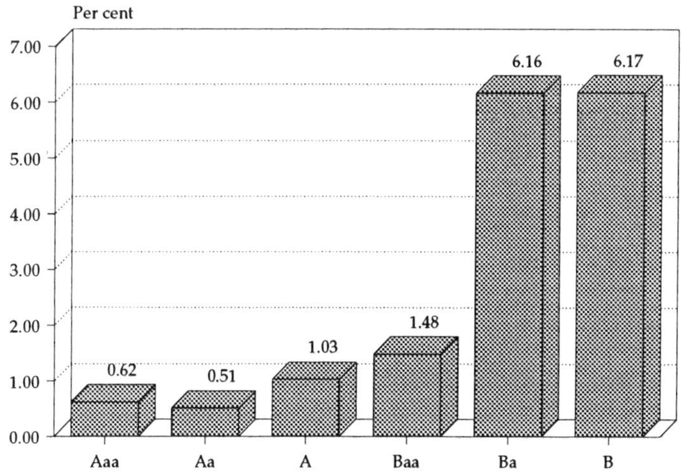

Figure 2.4 Standard deviation of 10-year default rates

While studies of historical default rates are a useful guide to a rating agency's track record, the immediate value of ratings to investors as a measure of future default experience must be judged by proxy, based on such indicators as the quality and foresight of the rating agency's analysts, its reputation for integrity and professionalism, and its responsiveness to the research needs of the market and the major investors it serves.

Conclusion

The expected growth in the number and diversity of participants in the fixed income markets will lead to escalating complexity and volatility. As the various markets merge and expand, there will be a growing need for transparency in order to maximize efficiency and minimize risk. Transparency will demand better and clearer information which will be expedited through technological advances. Among the information needs will be an efficient and comprehensive system to analyze credit risk. Ratings fill this need because they represent a fast and convenient method of communicating an independent credit risk evaluation to the market. By providing a simple, objective and consistently applicable indicator of relative default risks, ratings can be used to determine whether a security meets an investor's risk guidelines. However, it must be emphasized that ratings are only one of several important factors that affect the investor's purchase decision. Liquidity of a debt issue, foreign currency exposure and redemption risk are but a few of those ingredients. Furthermore, ratings are only opinions and do not represent assurances about the future performance of a particular security. Ultimately, it is up to both issuer and investor to become familiar with the rating system in order to use ratings effectively.

Appendix

The eurocommercial paper market: an example of rating development

The broadest and most active use of credit ratings in Europe today is in the eurocommercial paper (ECP) market. The development of this market over the past six years provides a good example of how the use of credit ratings has grown in a truly cross-border market. The ECP market began in the mid 1980s as an outgrowth of the note issuance facility and revolving underwriting facility market. Over the latter part of the decade, many NIF and RUF facilities were replaced by ECP programmes. The market began as, and remains, a cosmopolitan one, containing issuers and investors from a broad range of countries. At the end of 1986 there was approximately $14bn in outstandings. Commercial banks were active players in the market, especially as investors. Credit ratings were new to Europe and their use was not widespread. Some issuers who were active in the United States commercial paper market set up ECP programs and transferred their US ratings, while some of the larger European issuers sought ratings to help expand their programs. In a 1987 report by the Federal Reserve Bank of New York, it was noted that in the ECP market ratings were "common, but not required". The report estimated that only about 45 per cent of active ECP issuers were rated, but commented that practice in the ECP market would likely converge with the US market practice and require ratings.

By the end of 1991, the situation regarding ratings had changed markedly. In terms of total outstandings, the ECP market had grown to almost $80bn. Significantly, over 80 per cent of the active cross-border issuers were rated, representing 85 per cent to 90 per cent of the total volume of the market. The unrated sector had been sharply reduced and many ECP dealers reported difficulty in selling unrated commercial paper to investors in any quantity.

Two key factors contributed to the adoption of ratings by the ECP market:

1. Shift in the investor base

At its inception, commercial banks were the major investors in ECP. The banks did their own credit analysis and in many cases were buying the paper of their long-standing customers. To broaden and deepen the market (thereby making it more attractive and more available to a larger number of issuers) the major ECP dealers sought out new investors among sovereign governments, large corporates, pension funds and insurance companies who needed outlets for their short-term liquidity. At the same time earnings and capital adequacy pressures relating to BIS capital standards had led many commercial banks to sharply decrease their investment in ECP.

There was, however, one important distinction between these new investors and the commercial banks; few of them maintained large credit departments that could perform the required credit analysis. More importantly, these new investors wanted no risk to their principal. As the ECP market expanded in terms of the number and diversity of issuers, the task of selecting suitable investments from a list of hundreds of names became increasingly complex. This was a difficult task without a large supporting credit staff and so investors began turning to credit ratings for guidance.

2. *Defaults*

The second factor that contributed to the spread of credit ratings was a series of defaults in the ECP market that took place during 1989-1990. This proved dramatically (and painfully to some investors), that credit risk was a real issue that had to be constantly addressed and monitored. The defaults began in June 1989 when Integrated Resources, a US company, defaulted on approximately $63m worth of ECP. In quick succession, two other companies defaulted on $113m of eurocommercial paper, but the event that particularly shook the market was the default of DFC New Zealand Ltd. A year later, Polly Peck International plc defaulted on £90m of sterling commercial paper.

These defaults spurred not only a flight to quality in the ECP market, but also stimulated a concern for credit risk. While rated issuers continued to issue commercial paper and even increase their outstandings, the unrated sector of the market shrank as investors pulled back from companies that had no formal indication of relative risk. Investors took credit ratings more seriously than they had in the past, particularly when investing across borders. Name alone was no longer sufficient. More investors subscribed to rating agency research and followed announcements of rating changes. Many established ratings as a basic criteria for investment: unless an issuer had two ratings of Prime quality the investor simply would not invest in that issuer's commercial paper.

Chapter

3

Eculand

- The thirteenth member of the EC

Graham Bishop
Salomon Brothers International Limited

Eculand - the thirteenth member of the EC

In April, 1991 Salomon Brothers published a research report entitled *Eculand - The Thirteenth Member of the EC?*. Today, the question mark is unnecessary. The Treaty of Maastricht has been signed and it specifies the Ecu as the single currency of the EC. Because any political change which removed the will to achieve Emu would be seen as a dramatic turn in Europe's post-war history, market participants can now focus on the implications of the growth of the thirteenth member of the Community.

The question mark is also unnecessary because the Ecu has continued to display the swings in interest rates which are characteristic of an independent currency, albeit one which is tightly pegged. This peg creates a major investment opportunity, but one which hinges on the Ecu's independence - an intrinsic part of the Ecu banking system.

The nature of Ecu

Figure 3.1 shows the development of Eculand's banking system and illustrates some of the changes captured by the data up to September 1991. In the initial phase of the Ecu's growth, the demand for Ecu loans (the assets of the banking system) outstripped the available Ecu resources (the deposit liabilities of the banks). Therefore, the banking system closed the gap with baskets - a collection of financial liabilities, ultimately, of the various central banks of the EC. By the end of 1987, 18 per cent of Ecu credits were funded in this manner.

In effect, the basket-makers were functioning as a 'currency board' - standing ready to exchange Ecu and baskets at par (except for transaction costs). The banking system thought it ran very little risk, because the Ecu and baskets were

	1985	1986	1987	1988	1989	1990	Jun 1991
Assets	63.6	69.8	80.2	101.5	128.2	147.1	173.2
Liabilities	57.8	60.0	66.1	89.1	116.9	146.4	179.3
Net assets	**5.8**	**9.8**	**14.1**	**12.4**	**11.3**	**0.7**	**-6.1**
of which *vis-à-vis*							
External monetary institutions	-0.7	-0.6	-1.6	-3.5	-5.8	-8.5	-8.8
Non-banks	6.8	9.9	14.0	17.5	12.2	11.5	15.8
Interbank	-0.3	0.5	1.7	-1.5	4.8	-2.3	-13.1

Figure 3.1 Development of Eculand's banking system, 1985-Jun 91 (Ecu billion)
Note: Figures may not sum due to rounding
Source: Bank for International Settlements (BIS)

regarded as identical and interchangeable. Thus, an obligation to pay one could be settled by delivering the other through the banks' clearing system. The mechanisms of this process are documented in a working paper issued by the Ecu Banking Association.

Basket-making is a business that any good-sized international bank can enter. However, there are two particular hurdles to overcome to be successful: first, setting up the technical facilities to arrange instant loans and deposits throughout all the financial markets of the Ecu's constituents; and second, committing the necessary volume of available credit lines. Both factors require a major commitment to achieve a high volume, otherwise the fixed costs of the facilities can become a significant transaction cost per unit of basket.

In the early days, either Ecu or baskets could be delivered to the Ecu clearing banks in settlement of Ecu obligations. Many of the clearing banks did not particularly wish to acquire a position in baskets so, in late 1988, the clearing banks suspended interchangeability of baskets with Ecu, cutting the linkage with the EC's central banks. Thereafter, baskets of the component currencies were no longer accepted in settlement of Ecu liabilities. In October 1989, the remaining basket-maker, Kredietbank, began to charge for the risks involved in interchanging baskets and Ecus by quoting a two-way price. The involuntary holders of baskets rapidly left the market, so this date appears to mark the start of the Ecu's deviations from the basket.

Basket-making was virtually eliminated in 1990, as the banks' net asset positions fell close to zero. The process of shrinkage began, with a rise in the banks' Ecu liabilities relative to their assets - Ecu deposits by governments virtually doubled between 1988 and 1990. The banks therefore needed to lend baskets. As with any decision to lend, there is a question of credit lines to counterparties. A perfect basket requires adequate credit lines for banks operating in each currency, which can be a problem for those banks unwilling to make a major commitment to the Ecu/basket market.

The inability of Eculand's banks to lend all their Ecu liabilities resulted in a sharp rise in the interbank markets' net liabilities. Presumably, this rise was absorbed by the remaining Ecu/basket arbitrageurs, who would naturally reduce the interest rate they were prepared to pay. Unfortunately, the rise in the Ecu's exchange rate versus the basket imposed a serious book loss - especially relative to capital - even if an actual loss was avoided when the loans and deposits were unwound. The severity of this problem will depend on both the internal accounting and prudential supervision regimes.

The new international capital requirements pose additional problems. Interbank loans, under the Solvency Ratio Directive that came into force throughout the EC from January 1991, require capital equal to 20 per cent of the 8 per cent minimum capital/assets ratio. By early 1991, the Ecu was at a premium of 0.8 per cent versus the basket. The disappearance of this premium would represent a loss of 50 per cent of capital employed (8 per cent minimum capital x 20 per cent risk weighting for interbank assets = 1.6 per cent capital requirement).

This analysis demonstrates that the Ecu as a monetary unit is merely a set of liabilities of the commercial banks. There is no lender of last resort standing ready to exchange those bank liabilities, at par, for the liabilities of a central bank - whose solvency is underwritten by the tax powers of a national government. The limit on Ecu money creation of the commercial banks is not a monetary target set by a committee of central bankers, but rather the prudential limits set by the capital adequacy requirements of the EC Solvency Ratio Directive. The creation of Eculand's money will therefore substitute partially for the creation of existing national currency - but how much is substitution and how much is incremental?

Understanding the independent nature of Ecu money is critical to assessing the opportunities - and risks - offered by Ecu bond markets in the run-up to Emu. Figure 3.2 shows the fluctuations of the Ecu versus the basket.

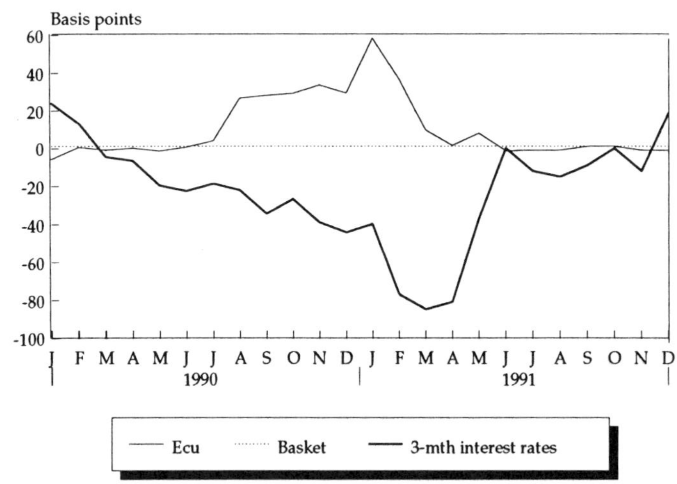

Figure 3.2 **Divergence in Ecu foreign exchange and interest rates from the basket**

The remarkable feature of the graph above is that, once the Ecu's independence as a foreign currency became recognized, it ceased to fluctuate in practice. However, the interest rate is not, and cannot be, pegged to that of the basket. Accordingly, Eculand is now set for a rapid expansion.

The expansion of Eculand

During the latter part of 1991, the Ecu exchange rate stayed remarkably close to its basket, despite large swings in the relative interest rate and major debate on the very definition of the Ecu.

...will be driven by a wide spread

That debate is now settled and the Ecu is frozen, so investors can confidently analyse the prospective returns from the Ecu and the basket. Surprisingly, Ecu bond yields continue to be 40-50 basis points below basket yields from three to ten years' maturity.

Accordingly, a rational arbitrageur should issue Ecu bonds, sell the Ecu proceeds and invest them in the basket - locking in a handsome profit. This would push down the Ecu foreign exchange rate versus the basket unless there is an offsetting flow, perhaps due to central bank transactions, which may amount to intervention to support the Ecu. Sharp falls in the Ecu would not enhance the image of the Community's future stable currency.

However, the result of such a wide spread at a time when national interest rates are converging is that Ecu bonds now represent one of the cheapest forms of funding in the EC. If this spread is sustained and the Ecu remains stable, it is reasonable to expect a significant substitution of Ecu funding for national currency funding. The attractions will rise as Emu comes closer and is more certain. This process probably has negligible impact at present, but may well accelerate and pose substantial problems to monetary policy-makers. Ecu funding will represent a relaxation of effective monetary policy relative to that expressed in national currencies.

...but will the spread remain so wide?

The answer is bound up with investor expectations about the certainty and timing of Emu. The Treaty has now specified that the European central bank will have the same objectives as the Bundesbank - price stability - but have even greater independence. These provisions are intended to ensure that the Ecu is at least as good as the Deutschemark so the Ecu is likely to assume the Deutschemark's 'hard-currency' mantle. Thus, after Emu, Ecu bonds should trade at the same yields as Deutschemark bonds - for a given credit. Cashflows occurring after Emu should therefore be valued with current Deutschemark rates. The yield curve can be decomposed into a series of segments by calculating the forward three-month rate. For example, the difference in yield between a bond maturing in five years and one maturing in five years and three months must represent the expected rate on three-month money in five years' time.

This analytical technique can be used to track the changes in investor expectations which are implicit in the shape of the yield curve. Figure 3.3 chronicles these changes by charting the expected spread between Ecu and Deutschemark three-month interest rates. In the extreme case, if they were identical then investors implicitly regard Ecu and Deutschemarks as perfect substitutes at that time.

At the end of October 1991, in contemplation of the Maastricht summit, investors apparently were relaxed and believed that some more convergence was possible, but were slightly sceptical that it would last. During the summit, there appeared to be serious misgivings that there could be short-run dislocations - a realignment within the ERM, for example - but this would be overcome for a period in the mid-1990s. After Maastricht and the full resumption of trading in the New Year, investor expectations have undergone a dramatic change: chances of a dislocation seem less and, crucially, investors expect a drastic narrowing of interest rate differentials by 1995, with no change thereafter. This expressed a powerful, though not total conviction, that the Ecu and Deutschemark will become virtual substitutes from 1995 onwards.

The implication is key: if investors retain this conviction, Ecu bonds will continue to trade at wide yield spreads below the basket yields; will offer cheap finance in the EC; and will provide a major incentive for the Ecu to substitute for many national currencies in the next few years.

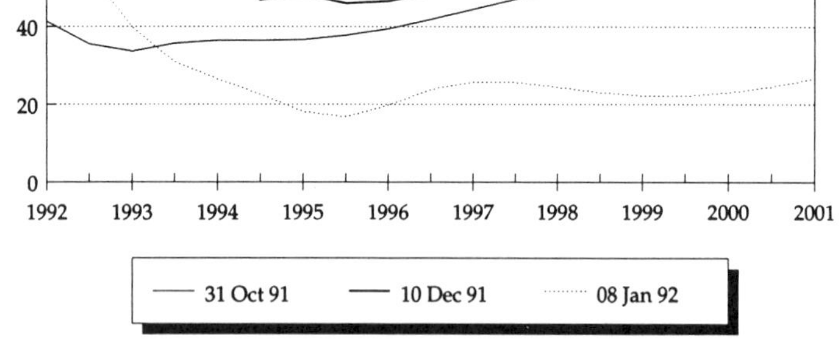

Figure 3.3 Three-month Ecu forward rates: spread vs. Deutschemark (basis points)

So far in 1992, investors have subscribed for Ecu 9 billion of bonds - an annual rate nearly three times greater than the hectic pace of 1991. Though the volume of issuance pushed yields back up to 50 basis points over forward Deutschemark rates, the curve remains flat. This suggests that investors have retained their new-found conviction that Emu will occur, leaving longer-dated Ecu bonds as very attractive assets. This mechanism will substitute private enterprise money - the Ecu - for money issued by EC central banks, unless the date of Emu is relatively early. How soon will the private money 'tail' wag the public money 'dog'? As this theoretical risk becomes a practical question driven by growing Ecu usage, there will be a corresponding pressure to advance the date of Emu as Eculand expands further.

The Ecu bond market

The attractions of longer-term Ecu bonds are clear enough - but where will the supply come from? Some of the governments of the EC have already set out to provide an answer.

The procedure for starting Emu begins with a report from the European Commission and the European Monetary Institute. These reports shall "take account of the development of the Ecu." For bond markets, the "store of value" function of Ecu money is more relevant.

That store of value function of the Ecu developed dramatically during 1991. The opening weeks of 1992 have witnessed a surge in new issuance, even before several EC Governments have implemented their issuing plans.

Once parliaments have ratified the Treaty, committing their countries to participating in an eventual single currency, debt managers will have to recognize that the longer term bonds they issue now will probably be repaid in Ecu. So the question they have to answer is: why should they issue longer bonds in anything other than Ecu? In fact, most EC countries are moving towards increased Ecu issuance - the French government has a formal target of 15 per cent of its annual debt issuance, the UK government has commenced an Ecu Treasury note programme, and the Italian government has issued a large volume of Ecu debt.

By the mid-1990s it is conceivable that 20 per cent of the debts of all EC governments (apart from Germany) could be denominated in Ecu. (Germany is unlikely to pay a premium interest rate in order to participate in the Ecu market.) The result is startling. The Ecu-denominated bond market of the EC governments would be the largest in Europe and twice the size of today's major long-term bond markets. At Ecu 450 billion outstanding, that would be ten times the volume of today's corresponding Ecu bond market. The magnitude of this development would represent an 'Emu boom' for the Ecu markets. So a natural and progressive development of Ecu capital markets will make them the largest financial market in Europe, even during the course of a prolonged Stage Two of the Emu process.

If the Ecu bond market has emerged as the single largest bond market in Europe by the mid-1990s, then it would be easy to conclude that the Ecu was accepted as a store of value by the citizens of Europe - setting the scene for a rapid move to Emu.

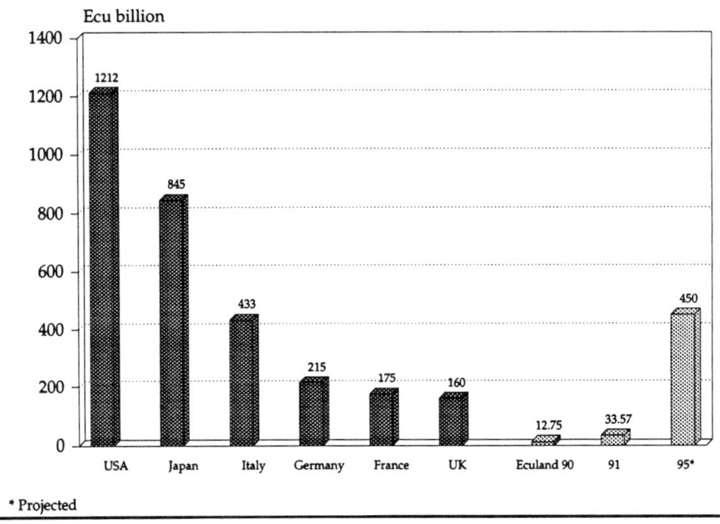

Figure 3.4 **Government bond markets at end-1990 vs. Eculand in 1990, 1991 and 1995. Large public sector issues only**

Expansion of the European Community

Today, the European Community dominates Western Europe while the European Free Trade Association (Efta) is on the periphery. The EC/Efta Accord, agreed in November makes the direction quite clear: most of the Efta states will join the EC in the foreseeable future, whether that Accord ever becomes effective or not. In fact, at Maastricht, the EC effectively invited Efta States to apply for EC membership before the end of 1992. Finland has now applied and Norway will probably joining the list of applicants later this year; even Switzerland is contemplating joining a list which which already includes Austria and Sweden. They will all be accepted and become members of the EC - perhaps even in January 1995 - forming EC17.

Tomorrow, Europe 2000 will be even more dominated by the EC 17. Leaving aside the associates to the East, the population of the EC 17 will be as big as the US and Japan combined. Rearranging current GNP figures, the GNP of that group is already a quarter bigger than that of the United States. This enlargement process will certainly stretch the EC's institutional structure to its limit and it is clear that another inter-governmental conference (IGC) will be necessary in the mid-1990s to consider how to cope with any subsequent expansion. 1996 has already been pencilled in.

The day after tomorrow, Europe 2010 could see the Community expand from the EC 17 to 30 - or even more, depending on whether some countries split up. Though such numbers seem large, we know that the Eastern associates, as well as many other countries such as Iceland and Malta, already are knocking at the EC's door.

What would be the international position of the economic group which could result from EC 30? The population will be significantly more than twice that of the US, but what about GNP? A rough assumption is that the new countries from Eastern and Central Europe will have closed the wealth gap with Western Europe, to the extent that they match the average GNP per capita of the EC today. This seems plausible over a twenty year time-frame. The result is that the

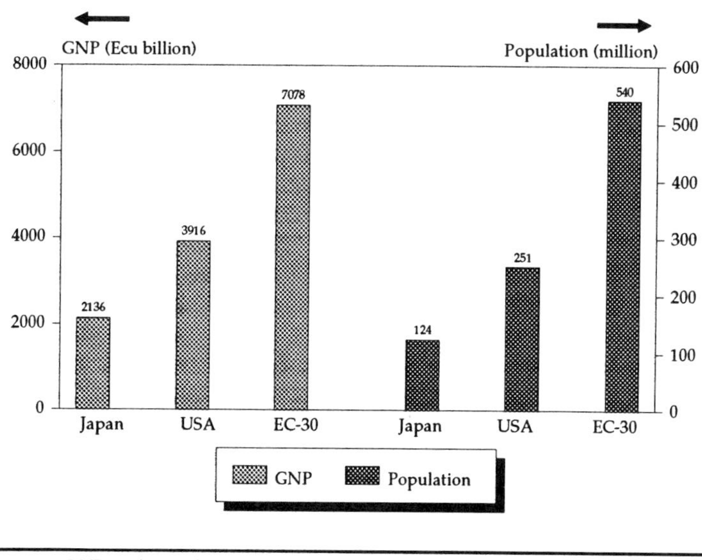

Figure 3.5 GNP and population of EC30
Note: Future pattern is based on 1990 data

GNP of EC 30 would be about 80 per cent bigger than that of the United States today, or three times that of Japan.

This would be an economic colossus and it could crystallize if the EC does little more than continue along the current path, following the signposts created in the Treaty of Maastricht. This grouping will have one currency - the Ecu. If this vision turns out to have any truth at all, then the Ecu will rival the dollar *tomorrow* and surpass it *the day after tomorrow*. That single currency will be the monetary 'canvas' for weaving the political tapestry which will result from the present revolution.

What does *tomorrow* - let alone *the day after tomorrow* - mean for the Ecu bond market, when the EC17 has the Ecu as its single currency? The chart simply rearranges today's data into the new group.

Tomorrow, the Ecu denominated government bond market of the EC17 would match that of the United States. *Today's* infant Ecu market, having passed adolescence in the mid-90s, will have reached maturity.

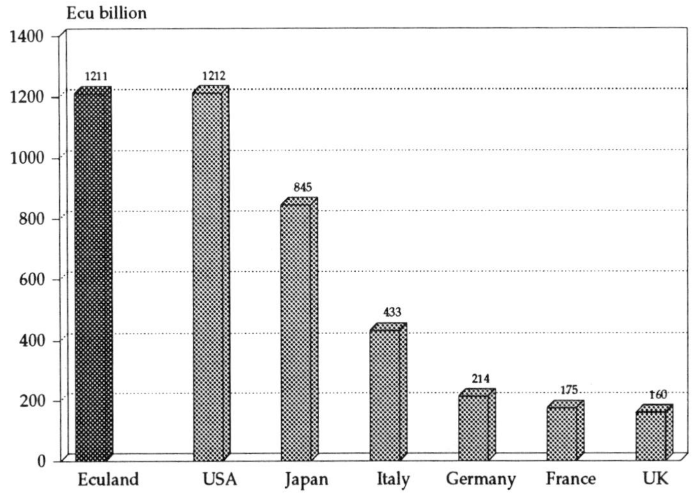

Figure 3.6 Government bond market, 2000

Chapter

4

Towards a

European bond index

Paul Temperton
Merrill Lynch, Pierce, Fenner & Smith Ltd

Introduction

The recent growth of interest in the investment opportunities available in European money and bond markets and the prospect of continued further substantial international diversification of bond portfolios, has raised the important issue of how best to structure a bond portfolio dedicated to the European markets.

A global investor has several available indices against which he might be assessed (for example, the Merrill Lynch, J. P. Morgan or Salomon Brothers indices), and the characteristics of each of the indices (in terms of the allocation to particular currency blocs, maturity distribution, duration etc.) are clearly defined. Given the benchmark against which the fund manager is assessed, his neutral portfolio allocation is also clearly defined.

An informal survey which Merrill Lynch have carried out amongst mangers of European bond funds shows a wide variety of benchmarks being used including: Deutschemark cash, Ecu cash, the European segment of one of the global bond indices, etc. Given this, there are no generally accepted guidelines for structuring a European portfolio.

This chapter discusses the alternative frameworks for asset allocation which might be used and develops an allocation system for the European markets which, although highly eclectic in nature, fulfils the requirement of setting a reasonable benchmark for European asset allocation. It can also readily be used as a basis for measuring portfolio performance.

Approaches to determining portfolio weightings

Typically, neutral portfolio weightings for a global bond fund are determined by relative bond market capitalizations. This is the basis, for example, of the strategy table in the Merrill Lynch bi-weekly *'Currency and Bond Market Trends'* publication. For the European markets, these market capitalizations are set out in the first set of columns in Figure 4.1. Included are both Salomon Brothers estimates for the end of 1990 and Merrill Lynch's estimates for mid-1991. But for investors in the European markets there are sound reasons for questioning whether this is an appropriate approach.

First, there are significant differences between markets in terms of liquidity. For example, although the Italian government bond market is very large it is relatively difficult to trade in that market. Thus, although market capitalization weights suggest a high allocation to Italian bonds - the market is the second largest after the Deutschemark market - the fund manager might find himself seriously constrained in terms of trading opportunities by allocating such a large proportion to the Italian market.

Second, persistent and excessive national budget deficits, by raising the outstanding stock of debt, would raise the portfolio allocation to that country. But

	Size of bond market			GDP				Total trade		Average of econ. factors	Ecu weights	Overall
	Salomon	Merrill Lynch		Current prices & exchange rates		Current prices & PPP rates		Current prices & exchange rates				
	($bn) 1990	($bn) 1991	(%)	$bn	%	$bn	%	$bn	%	%		
EC markets												
Bel/Lux	271	139	3.5	145	3.0	117	2.8	166	7.4	4.4	8.1	6.9
Denmark	213	182	4.5	101	2.1	68	1.6	51	2.3	2.0	2.5	2.2
France	575	451	11.3	880	17.9	712	16.9	301	13.5	16.1	19.3	16.5
Germany	1124	1032	25.8	1118	22.8	815	19.3	521	23.4	21.8	30.2	25.8
Greece	0	18	0.4	47	1.0	64	1.5	20	0.9	1.1	0.7	0.6
Ireland	0	21	0.5	29	0.6	27	0.6	30	1.3	0.9	1.1	0.9
Italy	755	1020	25.5	758	15.4	703	16.6	241	10.8	14.3	9.8	8.4
Netherlands	186	178	4.4	213	4.3	180	4.3	184	8.2	5.6	9.4	8.0
Portugal	0	7	0.2	37	0.7	61	1.5	22	1.0	1.1	0.8	0.7
Spain	90	100	2.5	289	5.9	337	8.0	83	3.7	5.9	5.3	4.5
UK	361	321	8.0	670	13.6	703	16.6	284	12.8	14.3	12.8	10.9
Total EC			86.6		87.3		89.6		85.4	87.4	100.0	85.4
Efta markets												
Austria	0	17	0.4	117	2.4	88	2.1	60	2.7	2.4		2.3
Finland	0	29	0.7	90	1.8	63	1.5	38	1.7	1.7		1.6
Iceland	0	0	0.0	5	0.1	4	0.1	3	0.1	0.1		0.1
Norway	47	12	0.3	83	1.7	65	1.5	44	2.0	1.7		1.7
Sweden	209	198	4.9	159	3.2	116	2.7	85	3.8	3.3		3.2
Switzerland	190	187	4.7	171	3.5	105	2.5	96	4.3	3.4		3.3
Ecu market	80	95	2.4									2.4
			100.0		100.0		100.0		100.0	100.0	100.0	100.0

Figure 4.1 Factors taken into account in determining European bond market weights

the attendant relatively poor inflation performance would argue against such a strategy. Conversely, a small and underdeveloped bond market - for example Spain - might offer some of the more attractive investment opportunities as its inflation performance converges on the European average. Finland, Sweden and Norway, countries which have generally run budget surpluses and consequently have low outstanding stocks of government debt, would have a low weight.

Third, European bond markets are often not particularly well traded along the yield curve. Long maturity bonds simply do not exist in some markets; and the concentration of trading in the latest (typically ten-year maturity) issued bonds in other markets might make the intermediate maturities relatively illiquid.

Given these difficulties, the relative sizes of the different European economies might provide a more appropriate framework for setting portfolio guidelines. The relative sizes of GDPs, set out in the second set of columns in Figure 4.1 could be used. But estimates of GDP based on current prices and exchange rates may give a distorted picture of relative size. An alternative approach, used by the OECD, is to use Purchasing Power Parity exchange rates to convert national GDPs into a common currency and estimates on this basis are also shown (of course, there are many different estimates of PPP, the OECD use their own estimates).

Another approach is to assess how important that country is within European trade. This can be measured by the ratio of the country's total trade (exports plus imports) as a proportion of total European trade, also shown in Figure 4.1.

Relative GDP and trade shares form the basis of the weights used in the Ecu and point to a straightforward solution to the problem under consideration: that is, use Ecu weights themselves. As can be seen from the column showing the average weight according to the three economic factors and the column showing the weight in the Ecu, there are still some substantial differences reflecting other (largely political) factors. But two other factors lend favour to the use of the Ecu.

First, the Ecu, if not already, will come to be regarded as the currency of Europe as the EC moves through Stage Two of Emu and eventually to the adoption of a single currency at the end of the century. It will represent one of the three main currency blocs: Yen, Ecu and dollar. In this context, portfolios may come to be structured in relation to, and measured against, the performance of the Ecu. Second, and in a similar vein, the Ecu bond market is already well on the way to becoming one of the world's leading bond markets. The Ecu was the fourth largest sector of the bond market in terms of new issuance in 1990; and the largest in the first quarter of 1991. Although new issuance receded after that, we think that the clarification of the role of the Ecu in the move to

European Monetary Union made at the Maastricht summit will help to secure the Ecu's role as one of the world's leading currencies.

Moreover, with several European finance ministries and central banks now actively promoting the use of the Ecu a growing importance for the market in the early to mid 1990s seems ensured. Reflecting these considerations, it seems likely that a growing number of European funds will have their performance assessed in relation to an Ecu benchmark.

There are, however, a number of drawbacks with using Ecu weights as the appropriate benchmark. First, not all European currencies are components of the Ecu. The Ecu weighting system would ascribe a neutral portfolio weight of zero to these markets. Second, the weights in the Ecu have been subject to five yearly revisions in the past - creating major discontinuities in the weights. Although this will not happen any longer under the Maastricht agreement to freeze the composition of the Ecu until the start of Stage Three, the weights of the currencies in the Ecu do vary day-to-day depending on exchange rate fluctuations against the Ecu. The weights shown in Figure 4.1 are the weights as calculated using central rates against the Ecu.

Third, such an approach would, itself, have no explicit role for an allocation to Ecu bonds. This could be dealt with by decomposing Ecu bondholdings into the national currencies according to their weights in the Ecu, but this approach itself has two drawbacks. First, it would still be necessary to identify in the asset allocation how much of the allocation to each currency was an actual rather than a 'decomposed Ecu' holding. Second, it would allow no specific role for expressing whether there were attractive opportunities between actual Ecu yields and yields in component markets.

Fourth, the Ecu weights make no allowance for relative bond market capitalizations, although as discussed above there are good grounds for questioning the validity of market capitalization weights.

These considerations indicate that a compromise approach is needed. Based on the above discussion we think that the following benchmark allocation is reasonable.

An eclectic approach to currency exposure

In the EC markets, weights are based on Ecu weights. But an explicit allowance is made for a neutral allocation to the Ecu (based on its market capitalization, the other factors being irrelevant) and the EFTA markets (based on the three economic factors). This means that only 85.4 per cent of the portfolio is allocated to the EC markets, with the rest split between the Ecu market (2.4%) and the EFTA markets (12.2 per cent).

The overall benchmark portfolio allocations are as set out in the final column of Figure 4.1

Maturity considerations

Consideration of the benchmark allocation along the yield curve poses slightly less of a problem. The approach we have used is to weight the different maturity sectors according the nominal value of bonds outstanding in that maturity category. In doing this we have used the Datastream/EFFAS indices. These are constructed for all of the European markets under consideration with the exceptions of Greece, Portugal, Finland, Iceland and the Ecu. Thus 96 per cent of the portfolio allocation is covered. The maturity breakdown of the indices is shown in Figure 4.2.

	1-3	3-5	5-7	7-10	Long
Austria	9	25	10	42	14
Belgium	21	39	30	10	0
Denmark	17	20	15	42	6
France	7	28	15	30	20
Ireland	24	12	15	18	31
Italy	5	52	43	0	0
Netherlands	17	28	11	43	0
Norway	28	0	0	15	58
Spain	71	14	11	2	2
Sweden	31	22	25	16	6
Switzerland	16	20	27	29	7
UK	16	13	18	22	32
Germany	17	28	18	37	1

Figure 4.2 Maturity breakdown of Datastream/EFFAS European indices

Although this approach is analogous to that used in the global indices, it sits, to some extent uncomfortably, with the eclectic method in which the currency weights were chosen. In particular, it might be appropriate to have an explicit neutral weighting for cash. And it could be that, bearing in mind the difficulties about trading bond markets along the yield curve mentioned above, that we should restrict the allocation to just the actively traded long benchmark bonds. Another alternative would be to have the same target duration in all markets, achieved by using an appropriate mixture of cash and bonds (although the shortness of some of the markets would prevent uniform use of such a technique).

	1-3	3-5	5-7	7-10	Long
EC markets					
Belgium/Luxembourg	1	3	2	1	0
Denmark	0	0	0	2	0
France	1	5	3	5	3
Germany	4	7	5	9	1
Greece	1	0	0	0	0
Ireland	0	0	0	1	0
Italy	0	4	4	0	0
Netherlands	1	2	1	4	0
Portugal	1	0	0	0	0
Spain	3	1	1	0	0
UK	2	1	2	3	3
Total EC	14	23	18	25	7
Efta markets					
Austria	0	1	0	1	0
Finland	2	0	0	0	0
Iceland	0	0	0	0	0
Norway	1	0	0	0	1
Sweden	1	1	1	0	0
Switzerland	0	1	1	1	0
Total Efta	4	3	2	2	1
Ecu market	0	1	0	1	0
Total	18	27	20	28	8

Figure 4.3 Neutral portfolio weightings

Given these difficulties, weighting by market structure along the yield curve does seem appropriate, even though the currency allocations are not based on bond market capitalizations.

Conclusions

With these problems that Merrill Lynch have identified in establishing guidelines for European bond portfolio allocation, the neutral portfolio weightings which are arrived at, and which are presented in Figure 4.3, should be treated essentially as a frame of reference rather than a hard-and-fast schema. Merrill Lynch use the approach as the basis for a table showing our recommended portfolio strategy which uses the allocation as the neutral basis of the portfolio, making their recommended allocations around that. A recent example is shown in Figure 4.4.

How to read Figure 4.4 (overleaf):
Asset mix recommendations are highlighted in **bold**. *The neutral weights, based on the Ecu (see 'The European Economy' Second Quarter 1991) are shown in italic. The extent to which the asset mix recommendations deviate from market capitalization weights represents Merrill Lynch's recommended overweighting and underweighting of the respective markets. The* **gross currency position** *indicates Merrill Lynch's recommended percentage allocation to each of the major income markets prior to currency hedging. The* **net currency position** *indicates Merrill Lynch's recommended exposure to each of the major currencies after adjusting the gross currency position for* **forward currency purchases(+)** *or* **sales(-)**. *Details on how the recommended portion of funds committed to bonds should be allocated is provided under* **bond selection decision**. **Currency risk** *is defined as the ratio of Merrill Lynch's recommended net currency position to the market capitalization weight.* **Interest rate risk** *is defined as the ratio of Merrill Lynch's recommended portfolio duration to the market's average duration multiplied by the ratio of the recommended gross currency position to the market capitalization weight. A reading above 1.00 for these risk measures would indicate greater recommended portfolio exposure to currency and/or interest rate risk than an Ecu weighted basket of European bonds would be exposed to and vice versa.*

	Currency decision:		Market decision:			Bond selection decision:					Portfolio risk			
						Maturity structure								
	Net currency position	Currency hedge	Gross currency position	Cash	Bonds	1-3	3-5	5-7	7-10	Long	Portfolio duration	Currency risk	Duration risk	Interest rate risk
DEM	**13**	**0**	**13**	**0**	**13**	**0**	**7**	**0**	**6**	**0**	**4.3**	**0.50**	**0.93**	**0.47**
	26	*0*	*26*			*4*	*7*	*5*	*9*	*1*	*4.6*			
FRF	**25**	**0**	**25**	**0**	**25**	**0**	**0**	**0**	**20**	**5**	**7.3**	**1.47**	**1.35**	**1.98**
	17	*0*	*17*			*1*	*5*	*3*	*5*	*3*	*5.4*			
NLG	**5**	**0**	**5**	**0**	**5**	**0**	**3**	**0**	**2**	**0**	**4.1**	**0.63**	**0.97**	**0.60**
	8	*0*	*8*			*1*	*2*	*1*	*4*	*0*	*4.2*			
BEF	**7**	**0**	**7**	**0**	**7**	**0**	**3**	**0**	**4**	**0**	**4.7**	**1.00**	**1.28**	**1.28**
	7	*0*	*7*			*1*	*3*	*2*	*1*	*0*	*3.7*			
ECU	**0**	**0**	**0**	**0**	**0**	**0**	**0**	**0**	**0**	**0**	**0.0**	**0.00**	**0.00**	**0.00**
	2	*0*	*2*			*0*	*1*	*0*	*1*	*0*	*5.0*			
DKK	**11**	**0**	**11**	**0**	**11**	**0**	**0**	**0**	**11**	**0**	**6.4**	**5.50**	**1.56**	**8.59**
	2	*0*	*2*			*0*	*0*	*0*	*2*	*0*	*4.1*			
IEP	**2**	**0**	**2**	**0**	**2**	**0**	**0**	**0**	**2**	**0**	**6.4**	**2.00**	**1.19**	**2.37**
	1	*0*	*1*			*0*	*0*	*0*	*1*	*0*	*5.4*			
GBP	**8**	**0**	**8**	**0**	**8**	**0**	**0**	**0**	**8**	**0**	**6.4**	**0.73**	**1.19**	**0.86**
	11	*0*	*11*			*2*	*1*	*2*	*3*	*3*	*5.4*			
ITL	**10**	**0**	**10**	**4**	**6**	**0**	**0**	**4**	**2**	**0**	**2.6**	**1.25**	**0.69**	**0.86**
	8	*0*	*8*			*0*	*4*	*4*	*0*	*0*	*3.7*			
ESP	**7**	**0**	**7**	**2**	**5**	**0**	**2**	**0**	**0**	**3**	**5.5**	**1.40**	**2.02**	**2.83**
	5	*0*	*5*			*3*	*1*	*1*	*0*	*0*	*2.7*			
SEK	**3**	**0**	**3**	**0**	**3**	**3**	**0**	**0**	**0**	**0**	**1.0**	**1.00**	**0.20**	**0.20**
	3	*0*	*3*			*1*	*1*	*1*	*0*	*0*	*5.0*			
NOK	**4**	**0**	**4**	**0**	**4**	**4**	**0**	**0**	**0**	**0**	**1.0**	**2.00**	**0.20**	**0.40**
	2	*0*	*2*			*1*	*0*	*0*	*0*	*1*	*5.0*			
FIM	**0**	**0**	**0**	**0**	**0**	**0**	**0**	**0**	**0**	**0**	**0.0**	**0.00**	**0.00**	**0.00**
	2	*0*	*2*			*2*	*0*	*0*	*0*	*0*	*5.0*			
CHF	**0**	**0**	**0**	**0**	**0**	**0**	**0**	**0**	**0**	**0**	**0.0**	**0.00**	**0.00**	**0.00**
	3	*0*	*3*			*0*	*1*	*1*	*1*	*0*	*3.7*			
Other	**5**	**0**	**5**	**5**	**0**	**0**	**0**	**0**	**0**	**0**	**0.1**	**1.67**	**0.03**	**0.05**
	3	*0*	*3*			*2*	*1*	*0*	*0*	*0*	*4.6*			
Total	**100**	**0**	**100**	**11**	**89**	**7**	**15**	**4**	**55**	**8**	**5.0**	**1.00**	**1.09**	**1.09**
	100	*0*	*100*			*18*	*27*	*20*	*27*	*8*	*4.6*			

Figure 4.4 **A recent example of a Merrill Lynch portfolio strategy**

1992 Second Quarter
Merrill Lynch
The European Economy
Prospects for currencies, money and bond markets
Merrill Lynch & Co.
Global Securities Research & Economics Group
International Fixed Income Research

Chapter

5

Economic convergence

in the European Community

Michael Lewis
Deutsche Bank Research

Introduction

Economic convergence is the process of approximation of economic performance ultimately leading to internal (price and cost) and external (exchange rate) stability, and is a necessary condition for European countries to meet in order to participate fully in the second and third stages of economic and monetary union (Emu).

The decision behind the creation of the exchange rate mechanism in 1978 can be traced back to the failure of floating exchange rates during the 1970s and the divergent monetary and fiscal policies adopted within Europe after the first oil price shock in 1973. Uncoordinated policy responses by European governments weakened the performance of economies which had, in any case, already begun to show signs of divergence at the end of the 1960s. Germany and the Netherlands maintained their fight against inflation by a tightening of monetary policy which was reinforced by a strong appreciation in their currencies so moderating imported inflation. However, the loosening in the authorities' fiscal grip in light of declining growth and rising unemployment led to a notable deterioration in these countries' budgetary positions.

Policy responses - particularly in the UK and Italy - were, however, directed at insulating their domestic economies from both the direct and indirect effects of the hike in oil prices. An accommodating monetary policy was adopted in these countries (with real rates of interest actually turning negative in Italy during 1974), so as to maintain a strong rate of growth. However, this policy turned out merely to delay the income effects of the shock. In both countries, nominal unit labour costs accelerated sharply and the large depreciation in the effective exchange rate, amounting to approximately 15 per cent (for both countries) over the 1972-74 period, also led to a significant rise in inflation rates, which exceeded 20 per cent in Italy and the UK in 1974 and 1975, respectively.

Just one year after the 1973 oil price shock, a notable deterioration was seen in the differences of economic performance with respect to inflation and current accounts. For example, as far as inflation was concerned, the gap between the best- and worst-performing countries had widened from approximately 6 percentage points, to around 15 percentage points by 1974. The rapid acceleration in unit labour cost in the accommodating countries (Italy and the UK) also led to a worsening in their current account positions. On the other hand, the hard-currency group, Germany and the Netherlands, having contained the acceleration in inflation experienced a noticeable improvement in their external positions with Germany's current account surplus of 0.4 per cent of GDP in 1972 rising to 3.1 per cent of GDP by 1974. These divergent current account trends exacerbated an already volatile foreign exchange market.

ERM and the oil shock of 1979/80

While the 1979/80 oil price shock did occur at the peak of the business cycle, the main reason why it proved less disruptive was helped by the co-ordinated policy action taken. If one lesson had been learned from the first oil price shock it was that any effort to achieve higher growth was doomed to failure beyond the very short run. However, at the beginning of the 1980s, the economic position of respective European member states remained highly divergent. Inflation ranged from approximately 15 per cent in Italy and Ireland to just over 6 per cent in the Netherlands and Germany. Meanwhile, current accounts had mushroomed by 1980, to around 4 per cent of GDP in France and Belgium.

At first, the strict anti-inflationary stance of the hard-currency group (Germany and the Netherlands) was skirted by the soft-currency group (France, Belgium, Denmark and Ireland) as they attempted to regain competitiveness and boost growth by large and frequent devaluations. While the size of the devaluations never fully offset inflation differentials, hence maintaining some pressure to bear on inflation, the devaluations did obstruct progress towards economic convergence and, in particular, convergence in the rate of increase in prices towards the best-performing country in the ERM, traditionally Germany (see Figure 5.1). Fiscal prudence, the tight monetary policy adopted by Germany and the strong appreciation in the Deutschemark, together brought the rate of consumer price inflation down to some 3 per cent in the Federal Republic by 1984. Despite the negative impact on the current account deficit from an appreciation in the effective exchange rate, this was offset by a collapse in real wages growth which turned negative in both Germany and the Netherlands during the 1980-85 period.

The success in containing wages growth, through the discipline of the exchange rate mechanism, was central in the role to bring down inflation across Europe during the first half of the 1980s. A number of factors brought about this positive development. Firstly, there was an increasingly interventionist style shown by governments in the setting of public sector wage levels - indeed, in all the soft currency countries, at one time or another, a wages plan has operated. Secondly, there was a growing recognition by the industrial partners that lower real unit labour costs would, by increasing the profitability of investment, provide an environment for lower inflation and sustainable growth and hence improve long-term employment prospects. This became increasingly important in France where inflation forecasts, rather than actual past rates, were used to set the level of wage increases in the important public sector. Perhaps most importantly of all, however, was the acceptance by trade unions across Europe and the electorate alike to high, and rising, levels of unemployment.

The hard-currency option

The varying speeds of convergence within the group of ERM countries has, by and large, been dictated by how early, and to what degree, governments have pursued the financial discipline set by the anti-inflationary Deutsche Bundesbank, and the commitment to the fixed-exchange rate parity. The fruits of

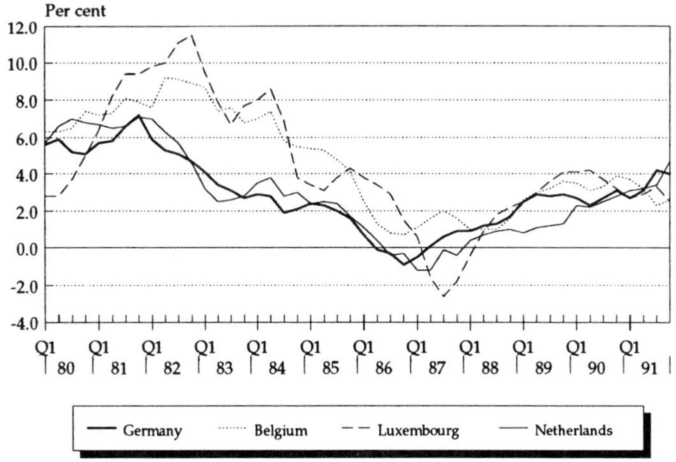

Figure 5.1 Fall in inflation rates (consumer prices, year-on-year)

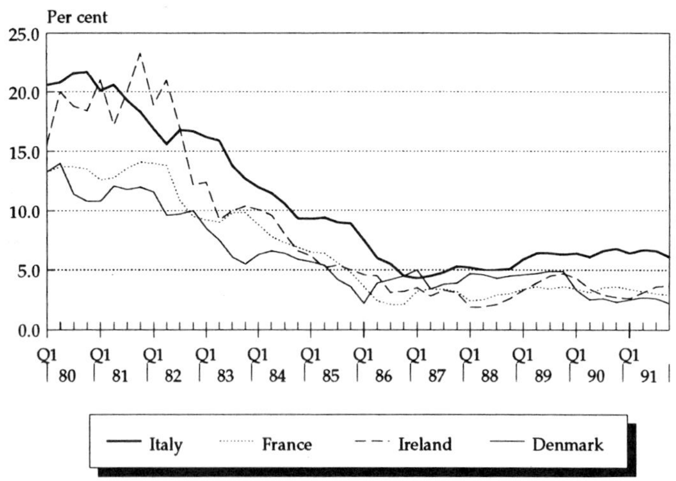

Figure 5.2 Fall in inflation rates (consumer prices, year-on-year)

adopting the 'hard-currency option' were seen first in Belgium, Denmark and Ireland. Indeed, Ireland, which started the 1980s with one of the highest rates of inflation and largest current account deficits in the Community, imposed a substantial fiscal contraction to curtail imports and eradicate domestic inflationary pressures. With the commitment to a stable exchange rate, and with deflationary forces taking hold, inflation fell steadily from 20 per cent in 1981 to around 4 per cent, five years later. The current account deficit also improved (partly due to a strong pick-up in export growth), falling from 14.3 per cent of GDP in 1981, to a small surplus by 1987 (see Figure 5.4). However, the economic cost paid was a drastic shake-out in the labour market which, while raising productivity and bringing pressure to bear on the rate of growth of nominal wages, had the effect of forcing the rate of unemployment to rise sharply, from 6 per cent to a level of over 15 per cent (at the time of writing).

In Belgium and Denmark, where trade links with Germany and the Netherlands were even stronger, currency devaluations and government involvement in wage-setting procedures helped improve competitiveness. For Belgium, this involved a once-and-for-all realignment, in 1982, of 8.5 per cent (the largest devaluation in the ERM's history), while Denmark saw two devaluations in 1979 - although a somewhat haphazard improvement in the performance of wages held up progress in its trade position.

A lack of firm commitment by the French authorities to its exchange rate parity in the first couple of years after the ERM's founding, meant a slight delay in its economic convergence. France's fragile trade position was behind her authorities' policy move towards a gradual depreciation in the French franc in the early 1980s. However, by the end of 1982, dissatisfied with the country's poor economic performance, they adopted the so-called 'Franc-fort' policy. This involved the freezing of wages and prices for a couple of months at the end of 1982, and the commitment to the French franc's parity position within the ERM from March 1983 onwards. Fiscal austerity, as well as monetary discipline, followed as the authorities tackled high unit labour costs, which had eroded French competitiveness *vis-à-vis* her major trading partners. By 1984, inflation had declined to under four per cent and her current account deficit dwindled to one per cent of GDP (see Figure 5.4). While this period of convergence was relatively fast, to sustain these gains, France had to go through several years of below-trend growth. Again, unemployment suffered.

The emergence of the narrow-band group (Germany, the Netherlands, Belgium, Denmark, France and Ireland) in the second half of the 1980s - a core of hard-Deutschemark currencies whose permitted band of fluctuation was 2.25 per cent - and who had swallowed the tough medicine imposed implicitly through its ERM commitment led to an impressive convergence in inflation and the external accounts though with mixed success over controlling the size of their respective public debts. The collapse in oil prices in 1986, accentuated by a steep decline in the US dollar provided a powerful boost to the convergence

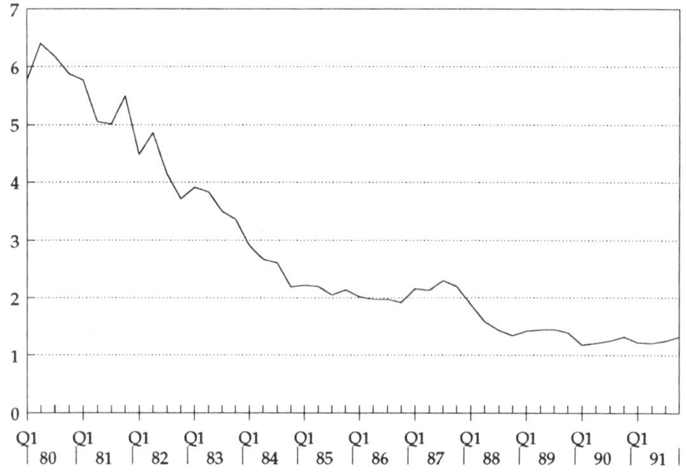

Figure 5.3 **Convergence of inflation rates (standard deviation of inflation in 8 ERM countries)**

process. Indeed, among this hard-currency group, the gap between the best and worst inflation performer ranged between 3-4 per cent after 1987.

Exchange-rate stability gained increasing credibility as foreign exchange participants considered realignments within the ERM a thing of the past (the last general realignment occurred in January 1987). This allowed interest rate differentials *vis-à-vis* Germany to fall steadily with, in some cases today, short-term money market rates a matter of only a few basis points above those in Frankfurt. This was in complete contrast to the early days of the system which was characterized by numerous devaluations and sharp fluctuations in ERM countries' interest rates.

A new wave of ERM members

The liberalization of capital markets which occurred across Europe during the 1980s also brought its advantages to the convergence process. International portfolio flows, led to large funds exploiting interest differentials that existed between the traditional hard currencies, the Deutschemark and the Dutch guilder, and the weaker currencies. This provided substantial support to the 'weaker country' currencies, aiding the anti-inflationary commitment. More recently, however, the danger has been that those countries facing the toughest

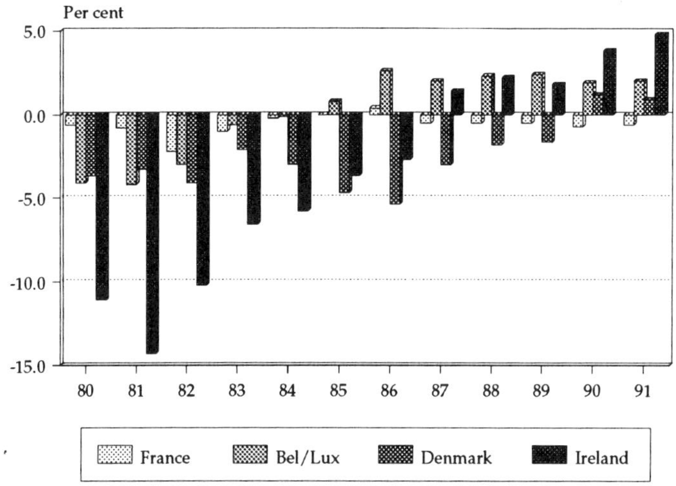

Figure 5.4 **Improvement in trade positions (current account, percentage of GNP)**

adjustment (currently Spain and Portugal) have seen their currencies rise to the upper limit of its permitted fluctuation band within the ERM thus threatening to trigger a premature reduction in interest rates. Despite this, the second wave of countries which are following the footsteps of the original narrow-band currencies are making some progress. The move by Spain and the United Kingdom into the ERM under the discipline of the 6 per cent fluctuation band, and the Italian decision to adopt the 2.25 per cent discipline in January 1990, has seen an improvement in these countries' economic performance, notably illustrated by inflation which, in the case of the UK, has fallen to within 2 per cent of the best-performing country (Denmark). However, further progress towards a sustainable trade position (i.e. under one per cent of GDP) in all three countries, will require several years of sub-trend growth to both rein-in import growth and quell domestic inflationary pressures.

The process of convergence in member countries' public debt positions, however, remains unsatisfactory and threatens to obstruct the convergence in long-term interest rates. Indeed there seems to be only a tenuous link between membership of the ERM and a sound fiscal position. For example, Spain and the UK, who are relative newcomers to the system, operate with a debt/GDP ratio under 60 per cent of GDP, whilst Italy, Belgium and Ireland, who belong to the original members of the ERM, face worryingly high debt levels. Ireland has scored some success in battling its debt overhang with public debt as a percentage of GDP having fallen, in 1991, to approximately 110 per cent - from over 130 per cent back in 1987. Buoyant economic growth in the second half of the 1980s has largely been attributable to this improvement but, with the economic slowdown now in place across Europe and so straining every government's fiscal purse, further progress in all three countries is likely to be slow. Indeed the sudden demand shock arising from German unification has led its inflation performance to become one of the worst in the ERM. While this has not led to a deterioration in other member states price performance, it has forced a significant hike in European interest rates to occur, so exacerbating the servicing of national debts.

Conclusion

The tough medicine taken by the governments of the traditional 'weaker' currencies in the early days of the ERM (French and Belgian Franc, Danish krone and the Irish punt) has paid off. Devaluations and sharp fluctuations in European currencies and interest rates in the first half of the decade have been replaced by a group of hard-Deutschemark currencies whose commitment to a stable exchange rate policy has brought considerable convergence in interest rates and trade positions across Europe. While progress has been restrained over the past two years by both the Iraqi invasion of Kuwait and the subsequent hike in oil prices, as well as by German unification, this setback is seen as only temporary. However, progress towards improving debt positions remains an important and more longer-term issue facing several European countries.

Chapter

6

The

European currency unit

Paul Temperton
Merrill Lynch, Pierce Fenner & Smith Ltd.

Giorgio Radaelli
Lehman Brothers International

Bob Tyley
Paribas Ltd

6.1 What is the Ecu?

Introduction

Twelve years after its creation, the Ecu has gained such prominence as to rank the third reserve currency and the second most-favoured currency of denomination for newly-issued bonds. This augurs well for the chances of economic and monetary union (Emu) in the not too distant future. Emu would no doubt make the Ecu the most widely-used currency. However, while Emu needs the Ecu the latter has, by now, got a life of its own. The role of the Ecu in international finance looks set to remain substantial no matter how fast we approach Emu.

Historical review

The idea of a European currency is logically and historically interrelated with the initiative, at political level, to promote closer links amongst European states. The path leading to today's Ecu debate started no less than forty years ago with the formation, thanks to the efforts of the then French foreign minister Schuman, of the European Coal and Steel Community (ECSC). This comprised France, Germany, Italy and the Benelux countries. European ties were extended with the Treaty of Rome, ratified by those six countries in March 1957. The Treaty established the European Economic Community and the European Atomic Energy Community. These, together with the ECSC, formed the European Community (EC). Stated objectives of the EC were the creation of a customs union with free movement of goods, services and capital, through common policies concerning agriculture, transport, and social aspects. (However, foreign policy was understood to remain under the control of member states.)

The idea of European economic and monetary union had to wait another twelve years. At the Hague summit of December 1969, the EC leaders agreed to the eventual establishment of a single European currency. Though all could agree to the eventual Emu goal sometime in the distant future, none could agree a timetable. The 1970 Werner Report, which aimed to establish an economic and monetary union by the early date of 1980, foundered. The Report set out the following targets: (1) a single Community currency, (2) a complete liberalization of capital movements within the Community, (3) a common central-banking system à la Federal Reserve, (4) a centralized economic policy-making body politically responsible to the European parliament. (Points 1 to 3 would be later incorporated in the Delors' report.)

However, well-known events (in particular the first 'oil-shock'), slowed down considerably the timetable of the Werner Report. At the same time, both high and diverse rates of inflation in the mid-1970's were not conducive to nurturing a system of fixed-exchange rates. Governments preferred to retain the safety valve of exchange rate devaluations in tackling adverse terms of trade shocks coupled with rigid real wages. Thus, the move towards Emu lost momentum. The Bretton Woods system of fixed exchange rates and the EC's first attempt, known as the 'Snake', also failed. However, the creation of the European Monetary Co-operation Fund (EMCF) in 1974 proved to be durable, indeed, it still exists today.

The following year saw the establishment of the 'European unit of account' (EUA), an embryonic Ecu. The EUA was adopted as unit of account for the ECSC in 1976 and, in 1978, made its first appearance in EC budgets.

That year saw the second, much more successful, attempt at exchange rate management. The European monetary system (EMS), the European exchange rate mechanism (ERM) and the European currency unit (Ecu), were established by a Resolution of the European Council on 5 December 1978, following summits in in Copenhagen, Bremen and Brussels between April and December of that year. The objective was to create a 'zone of increasing monetary stability within Europe'. The EMS came into operation on 13 March in the following year. The original hope was that the EMS would develop within two years to a final stage which would see the establishment of a European central bank, to be known as the European Monetary Fund (EMF). That hope, of course, was not realized. However, the EMS has been successful in achieving its first objective - greater exchange rate stability among member countries.

In Luxembourg, on 2-3 December 1985, the EC leaders reaffirmed their commitment to the 'progressive realization of Emu' with the Single European Act. This represented the first significant revision of the Treaty of Rome. At the centre of the Act was the desire to fulfil the original vision of a common European market with free movement of goods, services, capital and people. A target deadline was set for 31 December 1992. Detailed measures for the removal of internal barriers were set out in a European Commission White Paper, entitled *Completing the Internal Market*, produced under the direction of Lord Cockfield, Britain's senior commissioner in Brussels.

The Single European Act amended the original Treaty of Rome in a number of areas and recognized the EMS and the Ecu. However, it stated that further institutional changes in the monetary field would again require a change in the Treaty. Meanwhile, Article 236 of the Treaty still rules that "institutional changes can only be made by a conference of representatives of the governments of the member states, and that such a conference can only amend the Treaty by common accord" - generally thought to mean: by unanimity. In practice, therefore, the creation of a European central bank can be vetoed by any member. The Single Act was converted into law by each member country during the course of 1987.

On 27-28 June 1988, at the European Council Summit in Hanover, the EC members agreed to establish a committee chaired by the, then, president of the European Commission, Jacques Delors, to study and propose concrete stages leading towards the progressive realization of Emu, as reaffirmed in the Single European Act. Some member states wanted the communique to include an investigation into the possibility of a European central bank. However, there were strong objections to this, notably from the British. The so-called *'Delors Report'* was published in April 1989.

The Delors report recommended a three-stage approach to Emu. At the Madrid summit of June 1989, it was agreed that Stage One would start on 1 July 1990 with the following objectives: Firstly, completion of the internal market and strengthened competition policy. Secondly, reform of the structural funds and enhanced co-ordination (i.e., all members should join the ERM and have attained the narrow exchange rate fluctuation band) and surveillance. Finally, budgetary adjustments in high debt/deficit countries.

Stage Two, due to start in January 1994, will seek two objectives: evaluation and adaptation of Stage One policies and review of national macroeconomic adjustments. Moreover, Stage Two would see the Committee of Central Bank Governors being transformed into the European System of Central Banks, or Eurofed, a transformation that would necessitate amending the Treaty of Rome. Stage three, on schedule not earlier than 1997, would complete the budgetary co-ordination of the system while strengthening, if needed, structural and regional policies. At the beginning of this final stage, member countries should move to irrevocably-locked exchange rates and the national currencies would eventually be replaced by a single European currency.

The Ecu and the ERM

The Ecu is fundamental to the operation of the ERM as it is used to determine when a central bank must intervene in the foreign exchange market to either support or cap the rise of its domestic currency. One Ecu is equal to the sum of fixed amounts of the twelve EC currencies. To be specific:

1 Ecu = 0.624 Deutschemarks + 1.33 French francs + 0.0878 British pounds + 152 Italian lira + 0.22 Dutch guilders + 3.30 Belgian francs + 6.89 Spanish pesetas + 0.20 Danish kroner + 0.085 Irish punts + 0.31 Luxembourg francs + 1.44 Greek drachma + 1.39 Portuguese escudos

These amounts were adjusted in September 1989 following the inclusion of the Spanish peseta and the Portuguese escudo into the Ecu. Before this, they were adjusted only once, in 1984. The amounts reflect the relative importance of each currency's economy as measured by GNP, intra-EC trade and short-term financial flows. By statute, the amounts must be reviewed every five years or earlier if a new member country joins the EC.

Each currency in the basket has a central exchange rate against the Ecu, the degree of fluctuation from which, will indicate whether a country has to take 'corrective actions' to affect the external value of its currency. The central rates have been adjusted on a number of occasions, known as an EMS realignments. There have been twelve of such realignments since the ERM came into operation in 1989. Most of them occurred in the period to January 1987. The only realignment that has occurred since was a 'technical' one; a 3.75 per cent devaluation of the Italian lira in order to facilitate its adoption of the narrow fluctuation band.

Even though the fixed-amounts of each currency in the Ecu normally change only every five years, the importance or weight of each currency in the basket changes daily since its value depends on the spot Ecu exchange rate. For example, if there are 0.624 Deutschemarks in the Ecu and 1 Ecu is worth Dm 2.05586, then the German unit has a weight of (0.624 x 100)/2.05586 = 30.36 per cent. At today's central Ecu rates, the Deutschemark has the largest weight followed by the French franc and sterling. On a day-to-day basis, the weights will fluctuate as currencies deviate from their central Ecu rates. Dividing one central Ecu rate by another yields the target cross rate between each pair of currencies. These are known as cross-parity rates. For example, the Deutschemark/sterling central cross-parity rate is currently:

(Dm/Ecu = 2.05586)/(£/Ecu = 0.69690) = (Dm/£ = 2.950)

The ERM is the mechanism for keeping exchange rates close to their central rates. There are two types of constraint on currency movements: parity limits and divergence thresholds.

The parity limits define the maximum amount by which a currency can move within the ERM. They are derived from the cross-parity rates. For sterling and the Spanish peseta, the upper and lower parity limits are 6 per cent from the central cross-parities. For all other currencies, except the Portuguese escudo and the Greek drachma, the upper and lower rates are 2.25 per cent from the central rates. The escudo and the drachma are members only of the EMS, not the ERM so, for these currencies, a 'notional' 6 per cent band is adopted. If an exchange rate reaches its parity limit then the central banks of the two currencies involved are obliged to trade unlimited amounts of the currencies involved at those limits with any commercial bank.

Unlike the cross-parity limits which are defined between pairs of currencies, divergence thresholds are defined in terms of the exchange rate between a currency and the Ecu. Divergence thresholds are meant to give an indication as to the overall strength or weakness of a particular currency within the ERM. The thresholds are 75 per cent of the deviation that would put a currency at its limits against every currency in the Ecu. However, divergence thresholds are not simply equal to the Ecu central rates plus or minus 2.25 per cent times three-quarters. Instead, they are narrower than this, because movements in in each currency affects the Ecu itself. The divergence threshold for any currency *j* is computed as follows: 0.75 x 2.25 x (1-*j*), where *j* is the weight of currency *j* in the Ecu. The divergence threshold is generally, though not always, crossed before a parity limit is reached. If a currency reaches its divergence threshold, the central bank of the currency in question is expected, but not obliged, to intervene or to take action.

'Action' typically involves foreign exchange intervention and/or changing short-term interest rates. Intervention is of two types. At the cross-parity limits it is compulsory for both central banks to intervene under the EMS rules. However, so-called intra-marginal intervention, that is intervention within the parity limits, has become increasingly common. Intra-marginal intervention is expected (yet not obligatory) when a currency reaches its divergence threshold. Under the Nyborg-Basle Agreement of 1987 it was officially agreed that countries should take measures to prevent pressures developing within the system rather than reacting once the parity limits had been reached. (To this end, the EC central bank governors agreed extending the scope of the Very Short-Term Financing Facility to financing intra-marginal intervention.) Radaelli (1990) provides empirical evidence that intra-marginal intervention has been important in fostering EMS stability. Indeed, the author takes the view that the EMS stability to date owes more to increased co-ordination of monetary and intervention policies than to the operation of capital controls.

European integration

Economic integration is a rather wide concept, encompassing both goods and capital markets. Integration goes hand in hand with convergence (of economic performances). In fact, the higher the economic convergence, the easier it is to maintain free goods and capital markets. the road to Emu will see goods market integration with the implementation of the 'single market'. Capital market liberalization will take somewhat longer. While the majority of EC states are required to dismantle all their capital controls by the start of Stage Three, Greece, Spain and Portugal have been granted a later deadline (1995).

Many commentators have been (and some still are) worried at the prospect of an ERM deprived of the helping hand provided by capital controls. These typically serve one, or both, of the following purposes:

- 1) to boost the level of national savings, hence capital accumulation;
- 2) to limit the volatility of domestic interest rates in the face of exchange rate constraints and/or a high level of public debt.

Within the EC, (1) would apply to countries like Greece, with a tendency to significant current account deficits (to the tune of 3.6 per cent of GDP in the second half of the 1980s) hence high external debt. However, freedom of capital movement coupled with the single market for goods and services should make countries with relatively cheap labour, like Greece (and Portugal), a favoured destination for foreign direct investment. This favourable element should largely offset the tendency for 'hot money' to leave those countries once the net of capital controls is removed.

(2) applies to countries like Italy and Greece, whose stocks of public debt equal 103 per cent and 91 per cent of GDP, respectively. However, in this case as well, the phasing out of capital controls need not cause havoc, as suggested by the Italian experience. (Italy scrapped its capital controls in May 1990. That was followed by healthier capital inflows). This was due to three elements. First, the removal of administrative controls probably reduced political risk as perceived by non-resident investors. Secondly, by the time of liberalization, Italy's commitment to exchange rate fixity was seen as 'credible' by the markets. Thirdly, as shown by Gros (1987) and Radaelli (1990, *bis*) the effectiveness of capital controls tends to fade in the long run.

On the subject of convergence, the ERM-induced link with the Deutschemark has greatly helped those countries with relatively high rates of inflation in gearing their economic policies to the objective of price stability. As Figures 6.2-6.5 show, a great degree of convergence has already been achieved in the areas of both inflation and interest rates. The key mechanism in the disinflationary process in the ERM has been the tendency for high-inflation countries to lose export price-competitiveness. This has come about through an appreciation of their real exchange rates, i.e. their nominal exchange rates multiplied by relative price levels. Figure 6.1 shows that, during the first half of the 1980s, successive devaluations of high inflation currencies more than offset their inflation differentials with Germany (i.e., their real exchange rates against the Deutschemark were depreciating). However, in more recent years such devaluations have less than offset inflation differentials, causing a rise in their real exchange rates against the Deutschemark.

Though this disinflationary process has delivered inflation cum interest rate convergence, it has done so at the cost of higher unemployment (see Figures 6.6 & 6.7). Not only that, unemployment divergence amongst EC regions seems to have increased between 1979 and today. However, one should not be too pessimistic. In fact, Giavazzi and Giovannini (1988) provided evidence suggesting that the EMS inception had a favourable impact on inflation expectations in countries like France and Italy, thereby lowering the output cost associated with anti-inflation programmes.

In Europe, under the Treaty of Rome, there is *de jure* labour mobility and the 1992 single market legislation seeks to promote this by harmonization of some professional qualifications. But for many workers, particularly at the blue-collar

	B/Lux franc	Danish krone	French franc	Irish punt	Italian Lire	Dutch guilder	Narrow band	ERM
1979-83								
No. of realignments	5	7	4	4	5	2	22	27
Average size (%)	4.9	4.4	7.1	5.2	6.3	2	5.1	5.3
Average cumulative price differential	1.65	3.1	6.7	12.0	9.8	1.0	5.0	5.9
Degree of offsetting (%)	296.6	139.8	105.4	43.5	64.4	203.2	101.2	89.7
1984-87								
No. of realignments	2	2	2	3	3	-	9	12
Average size (%)	1.5	2.5	4.5	4.7	4.7	-	3.5	3.8
Average cumulative price differential	5.3	6.8	8.3	6.1	9.3	-	6.6	7.3
Degree of offsetting (%)	28.5	36.5	54.5	77.2	50.7	-	52.7	52.1

Figure 6.1 Realignments in the EMS (*vis à vis* the Deutschemark), 1979-87
Source: European Commission Services

Notes: All data refers to bilateral Deutschemark exchange rates. Cumulative price differentials (CPI, monthly data) are measured between two realignments. The offsetting of inflation differentials is measured by the ratio of central rate variation to the price differential by the time of realignment.

level, language and cultural differences remain huge barriers; it is hard to see European workers becoming as mobile as, say, Americans in the next few years. Indeed, Eichengreen (1990) concluded that regional unemployment differences in the EC are up to twice the level found in the USA. In the end, it will probably be up to fiscal transfers rather than wage flexibility to ensure that the process towards Emu does not see further widening of unemployment differences among EC regions.

Widening unemployment differentials may reflect not only differences in wage flexibility but also differences in production structures. The higher the latter the less homogeneous (or symmetric) the countries in question. Although the European Commission (1990) claimed that economic integration will make the occurrence of country-specific shocks less likely, there is some evidence against that thesis. Shearson Lehman Brothers (1990) looked at the issue of EC homogenization (or symmetry) by comparing the degree of country specialization at different points in time. This was done by measuring the degree of statistical similarity between the sectorial composition of GDP in different countries in 1979 and compare this with the same measure for 1986 (the most recent year

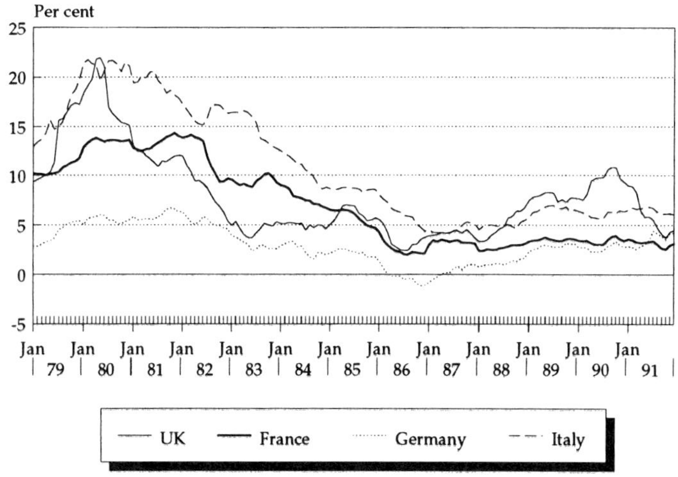

Figure 6.2 European inflation - UK, France, Italy and Germany

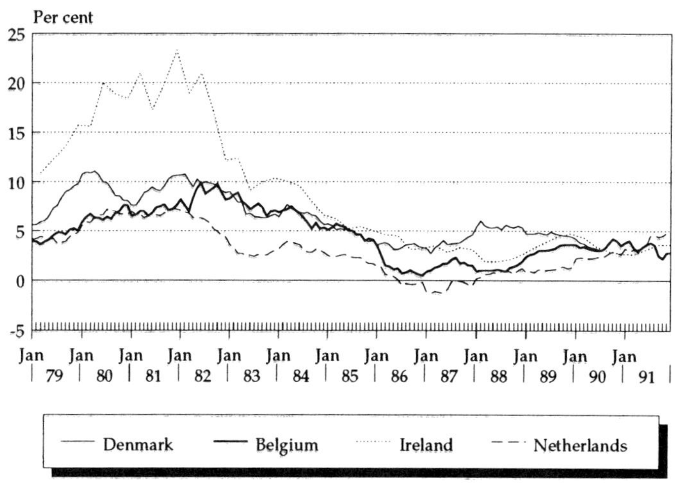

Figure 6.3 European inflation - Denmark, Belgium, Ireland and the Netherlands

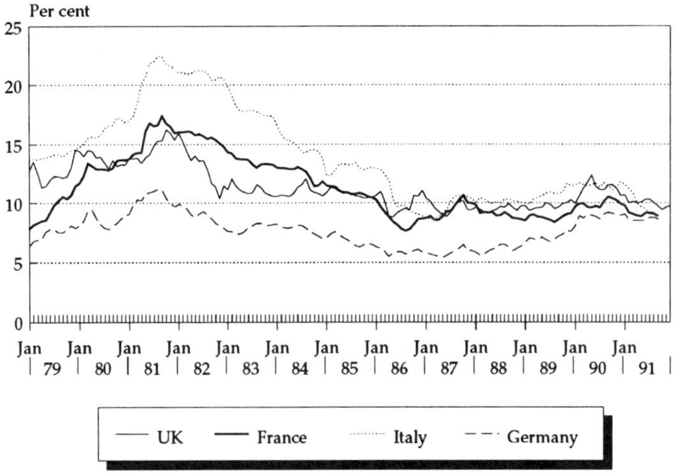

Figure 6.4 **European bond yields - UK, France, Italy and Germany**

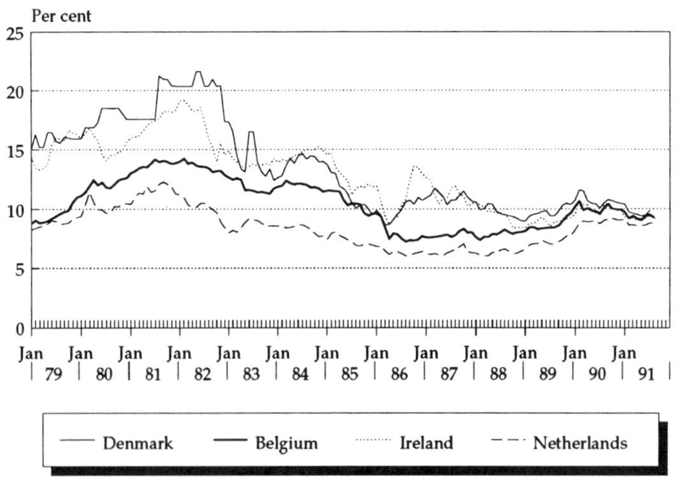

Figure 6.5 **European bond yields - Denmark, Belgium, Ireland and the Netherlands**

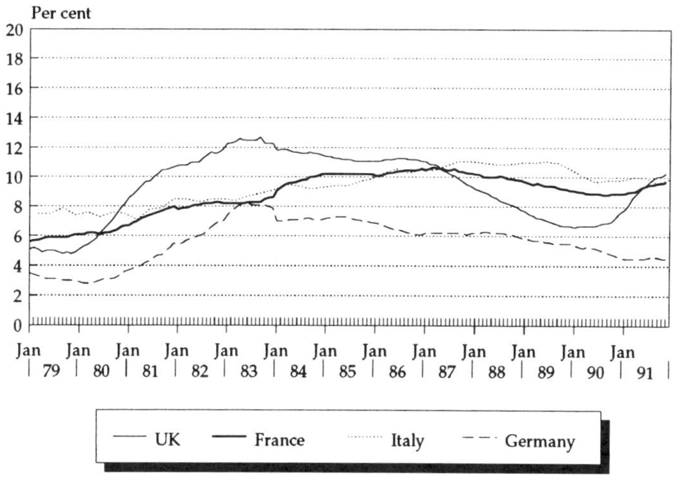

Figure 6.6 European unemployment - UK, France, Italy and Germany

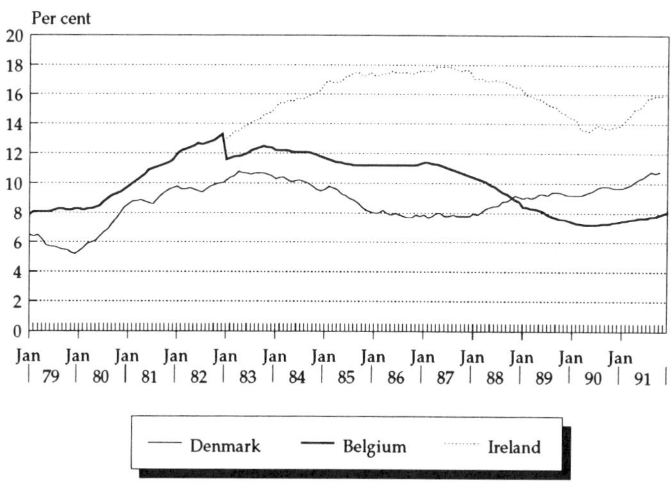

Figure 6.7 European unemployment - Denmark, Belgium, Ireland and the Netherlands

for which consistent data was available). It was found that, for the original ERM members, the production similarity index fell from 91 per cent in 1979 to 88 per cent in 1986. A similar result held for the EC as a whole.

Therefore, although intra-industry specialization may have been taking place (as claimed by the Commission), sectorial specialization has been significant tending to make economies less symmetric. This result reinforces the fear that progression towards Emu will have to battle against soaring unemployment differences.

Figure 6.8 provides a snapshot of the current degree of EC convergence on labour costs and public finances. Italy, Belgium, Portugal and Greece are the

	Unit labour costs (% growth)	**Budget deficit** (% of GDP)	**Public debt** (% of GDP)
Belgium	3.4	6.5	*128.1*
Denmark	1.4	1.3	62.3
Germany	5.4	4.6	45.4
Greece	*14.2*	*15.3*	86.0
Spain	5.7	2.7	44.5
France	3.3	1.6	37.3
Ireland	4.9	3.8	97.4
Italy	6.9	*10.1*	*103.3*
Luxembourg	2.8	-1.6	4.7
Netherlands	3.4	4.8	78.8
Portugal	*14.6*	5.5	63.8
UK	8.2	2.2	44.5
EC	5.9	4.6	60.0

Figure 6.8 **EC convergence as at May 1991**
Note: Figures in italic are the most divergent

countries currently showing the highest degree of divergence from the EC norm. Fiscal divergence looks like the most worrying aspect, particularly if it is true that the tendency for unemployment rates to diverge will be fought with EC-designed fiscal transfers rather than measures aiming at higher wage flexibility.

Finding the optimal trade-off between fiscal discipline and national autonomy is likely to prove a thorny issue on the road to Emu. The need for some degree of fiscal autonomy arises from the loss of exchange rate changes as a way to affect one country's relative price level in dealing with adverse price shocks (e.g., a surge in energy prices). In the absence of labour mobility and/or sufficient wage flexibility, budgetary transfers that redistribute income to areas facing falling demand and soaring unemployment would have the same stabilizing effect of a devaluation under flexible exchange rates. Indeed, many argue that fixed exchange rates would not survive adverse supply shocks (especially if asymmetric) without an adequate system of fiscal transfers.[1]

On the other hand, it is also generally acknowledged that Emu requires long-term consistency between the common monetary policy and members' fiscal policies. In fact, unsustainable individual budgetary trends would ultimately lead to debt monetization or default, threatening EC monetary policy. A first-best solution to this threat would be to endow the future EC central bank with sufficient pre-commitment not to renege on its promise of price stability. However, bail-out clauses would inevitably be disguised as fiscal transfer mechanisms. All the more so since political and economic integration would strengthen interdependence and solidarity among members. Another factor which would make it hard ruling out bail-out clauses is financial openness increasing the amounts of, say, the Republic of Italy being held by other EC citizens. therefore, the costs of one region's fiscal indiscipline would most likely spill over to other regions through higher taxation and/or higher risk premiums on their public debt.

A common sense answer to these problems seems to be that although Emu's survival would not require binding short-term fiscal rules, medium-term guidelines would undoubtedly help. This is often intended as requiring that fiscal policies be sustainable, that is, consistent with a stable debt-to-GDP ratio over the medium-term.

On this definition, fiscal sustainability requires maintaining a primary surplus (i.e., revenues in excess of spending net of interest payments) over the medium-term. Note that the higher the starting debt-to-GDP ratio, the higher the needed primary surplus. The European Commission (1990, pp109) estimates that no less than six out of the twelve member states need to improve their primary budget balance to achieve sustainability. (The countries in question are: Belgium, Greece, Spain, Italy, Holland and Portugal). However, generating high primary surpluses in a well-integrated Europe would be difficult since sharply increasing tax rates in region *A* would probably contract its tax base as production factors 'emigrate' to regions with more favourable tax regimes. This is one

[1] *In the US, this is replaced by a structure in which regional tax rates are a function of regional income trends. If, for instance, there an external shock such as a drop in the oil price enriches Nebraska at the expense of Nebraska, tax rates would be increased in the former while cut in the latter. It looks unlikely that the EC will adopt this type of solution to the problem of regional imbalances.*

reason behind the view that a country should not be allowed in Emu before it has achieved a sustainable debt-to-GDP ratio. The other reason, which is of even more concern to the debt markets, is that allowing a country with a very large outstanding stock of government debt to join Emu would risk it having too great an importance in determining the overall valuation of the common currency debt of the EC. (For example, if all of the twelve EC countries' outstanding government debt was converted into Ecu, Italy would account for around 50 per cent of the Ecu-denominated debt).

Ecu and Emu

Even if agreement can be reached on the need for a centralized independent European monetary policy, there is still debate over the necessity for a single currency. The Delors Report left open the possibility of permanently-fixed exchange rates rather than a common currency. The objective of a single currency has greater symbolic value and would provide a more credible anchor for influencing inflation expectations. Introducing a new currency is typically used as a means for taming inflation and/or devaluation psychology, particularly in the aftermath of hyperinflation.

There is a strong case to be made for moving to a single currency once it has been decided that exchange rates are to be permanently fixed. In fact, locked-exchange rates cum different currencies does not does not grant more monetary policy independence - at a national level - than a single 'federal' currency would. However, in that case the mere existence of differing currencies leaves open the possibility - however small - of future devaluations. Therefore, while maintaining differing currencies does not offer any advantage, it is a situation prone to instability.

Against that logic, in September 1989, Nigel Lawson, then chancellor of the Exchequer, presented a UK alternative to Stage Two of the Delors Plan. The idea was that of allowing EC currencies to 'compete', with the soundest, that is, the lowest inflation one, eventually emerging as the dominant (single?) European currency. This process would be facilitated, the UK Treasury argued, by a removal of unnecessary restrictions on the use of EC currencies, particularly impediments to the cross-border provision of financial services and to use the cheap and convenient means of payments. However, the proposal failed to convince Britain's EC partners of its ability to deliver a single European currency at the end of the process.[2]

[2] *The lack of plans for reforming legal tender laws was seen as a drawback of the UK proposal. Moreover, the other EC partners were unsure that one dominant currency would emerge at the end of a process - Emu's Stage One - featuring convergence of interest rates.*

The muted EC reaction induced the UK Treasury to modify its proposal by introducing a thirteenth 'competing' currency. This could well be the Ecu, whose banknotes would be issued and made legal tender in all the EC countries. This would require the creation of a European Monetary Fund (EMF) which would only provide Ecu in return for national currencies, thus ensuring no net addition to the EC money supply. This initiative got also known as the soft Ecu proposal. The idea was to get people familiar with transacting in a common currency. Moreover, it was thought that competition among monetary authorities would lead to a convergence of EC inflation on the best performance, and that the system could eventually evolve into one of fixed-exchange rates.

The soft Ecu approach was later superseded by another British proposal: the hard Ecu. Unlike the soft Ecu, which is a composite currency reflecting only the average performance of its constituents, the hard Ecu could not have its parity devalued against any other member currency. It would, in effect, always shadow the strongest currency. The exchange value of the hard Ecu in terms of national currencies would be guaranteed by the EMF which would have sole responsibility for issuing it. The EMF would acquire assets in the form of deposits denominated in national currencies and would issue interest-bearing liabilities in hard Ecu. As the private hard Ecu market developed, interest rates would be set, following current practice, by creating money market shortages and then relieving them at the chosen interest rate. To avoid any inflationary bias, all central banks would be obliged to repurchase any excess of their own currencies held by the EMF. Over time, as the hard Ecu's reputation was consolidated, it was proposed that it could develop into the dominant common currency or even a single currency.

As of today, it is clear that the hard Ecu plan has not won support among the Community. The majority of EC leaders showed little sympathy for the idea of an additional currency. Nearly as lukewarm was the reception to the proposals, later put forward by the Bundesbank and the Spanish government, for 'hardening' the Ecu via basket redefinitions (or ERM realignments) so as to avoid Ecu depreciation against any EC currency. The German/Spanish proposals are for a concept of 'hardening' which does not require a surrogate central bank like the EMF to be established[3].

If the EMF will be as politically independent and inflation-proof as the Bundesbank, there is no reason why, many would say, it should not be associated

[3] *At the time of writing, it seems that the only Ecu-hardening acceptable to the majority of the EC states is 'freezing' the basket ahead of Emu. This would involve a once-and-for-all redefinition of the amounts of each EC currency entering the basket. Consequently, if there were realignments of ERM currencies, the increase in weight of the appreciating currencies is permanent, not to be reversed by subsequent redefinitions. Freezing the Ecu basket, therefore, represents a modest hardening of the Ecu compared to the earlier UK and Spanish/German proposals.*

with a single currency *ab origine*. In all, what the UK proposals have achieved is to weaken somewhat a pre-existing concensus amongst EC leaders that Emu should proceed as fast as originally envisaged, It is increasingly clear that further thinking is required on what a future European central bank should look like. The EC concensus seems to be converging on a politically-independent central bank to replace (not complement as the hard Ecu proposal would have it) today's Bundesbank, Bank of Italy, etc. The national central banks could be transformed into regional arms of the future central bank which would thus be modelled on today's Bundesbank. As this scenario is independent from the establishment of a federal Europe, there seems to be no reason for ruling out a 'Eurofed' if, and when, Emu takes place.

The private Ecu and its future

The official Ecu, used for transactions among EMS central banks and EC institutions and as a unit of account by the latter, is defined, as we have seen, as a basket of currencies. However, the same cannot be said (anymore) for the private Ecu.

When Kredietbank Luxembourgoise (KBL) first started the private Ecu market, by accepting an Ecu 100,000 term deposit from the EC Commission, it had in mind the same basket as the official Ecu. In the early days, the Ecu money market was only a deposit market. When an investor bought an'Ecu' from KBL, he put up enough money for KBL to be able to buy the basket; and KBL then invested appropriate amounts in the respective money markets. When borrowers also started to use the Ecu , KBL and other banks shifted from investment in the national money markets towards investment in Ecu loans or commercial paper. Simultaneously, it became legally possible in most countries to sell Ecus among private agents. This saved transaction costs. Consider investor *A* who steps out of Ecus while *B* wants to buy Ecus; whereas in the old days *A* would have had to sell the basket and *B* to buy the basket, the cost and hassle of unbundling and re-bundling can now be avoided.

One problem with the private Ecu stems from the periodical redefinition of the official Ecu. Ignorance over the future weights often causes the spot Ecu to 'rationally' deviate from its official value. Another potential problem could arise if Ecu interest rates are not set correctly; then, in an efficient market, equilibrium would be upset, again leading the private Ecu value to deviate from its official counterpart.

Although the Ecu is a linear combination of component currencies, Ecu interest rates should not equal a linear-weighted average of the components' rates of interest. Sercu (1990) reminds us that the risk-free rate of return on the basket is a weighted harmonic mean of the components' risk-free rate of returns. Since a harmonic mean is lower than a standard mean, Ecu risk-free interest rates should always be below the weighted-average risk-free rate.[4]

In short, while the private Ecu is still 'defined' as a basket, there is no obvious force keeping its value within transaction-costs bounds around the basket itself. (Risk-premiums due to ignorance over future redefinitions of the basket are responsible for this and for the divergence of Ecu interest rates from their theoretical, risk-free, values.) Far from being a problem, this makes the private Ecu more akin to a normal currency.

The (private) Ecu has been gaining prominence in international finance. Adding together private deposits and official Ecus, the Ecu is already the third-biggest reserve currency, behind the dollar and the Deutschemark. Ecus are also proving popular in international bond markets. In the first half of 1991, 13 per cent of all international issues were denominated in Ecus, second only to the dollar. The future replacement of all existing EC currencies by the Ecu would automatically boost its share to near 50 per cent of all international bonds and near 40 per cent of all foreign exchange reserves.

[4]*Here is an example which shows that, for any basket such as the Ecu, the equilibrium (arbitrage-free) interest rate is lower than the weighted average. for simplicity, assume a basket containing just Dm 3 (=n1) and £1 (=n2). Use the Belgian franc as the reference currency together with the following data:*

	*Spot rate** S_j	n_jS_j	*Interest rates (1 year)*
Deutschemarks	*20*	*60*	*6.5%*
Sterling	*60*	*60*	*15%*
		Se = 120	*Avg = 10.75%*

** spot rates in units of Belgian francs*

If a banker accepts a one-year basket deposit, he cannot just buy and invest that basket if all risk is to be avoided. Indeed, investing Dm 3 and £1 at the ruling interest rates would generate a portfolio containing Dm 3.195 (=3 × 1.065) and £1.15 (= 1 × 1.15). Clearly, the future Dm/£ ratio is no longer 3:1; or, conversely, the portfolio does not contain a predictable number of basket units. Our banker will have too many pounds and too few Deutschemarks. The appropriate strategy in this case would be for the banker to buy:

Dm 3/1.065 = 2.817 at a cost of 2.817 × 20 = 56.338
£1/1.15 = 0.8696 at a cost 0.8696 × 60 = 52.174

at a total cost of 56.338 + 52.174 = BFr 108.512. By construction, this portfolio will contain Dm 3 and £1 (that is, one basket) one year from now. The immediate outlay is BFr 108.152, corresponding to 108.512/120 = 0.9043 basket units. Therefore, the one-year interest rate is 1/0.9043 - 1 = 10.587%, which is less than the weighted average, (0.5 × 15 + 0.5 × 6.5 = 10.75%). The example can be summarized into the following formula

$$1{+}i \text{ basket} = \frac{1}{\dfrac{0.5}{(1{+}i\ Dm)} + \dfrac{0.5}{(+i\ \pounds)}} = 1.10587$$

In words: unity plus the risk-free rate of return for the basket is a weighted harmonic mean of unity plus the component risk-free rates of return . As the example shows, the harmonic mean is lower than a standard mean.

However, these figures probably underestimate the future role for the Ecu. After Emu, the Ecu would be the currency of the world's largest trading bloc. Assuming that raw materials continue to be priced in dollars, the EC Commission (1990) reckons that some 10 per cent of EC trade could shift from dollar to Ecu invoicing, implying an extra demand for Ecus of $60bn. Moreover, Emu would make much of the foreign exchange reserves within the EC redundant. Assuming that the EC reduces its reserves by the same proportion as the share of intra-EC transaction costs in its total foreign exchange transactions, then the EC Commission (1990) estimates that more than $200bn of reserves could be converted into Ecus.

Finally, an additional boost to Ecu balances could come from its demand as a store of wealth, especially if the anti-inflation credentials of the future European central bank will be no less than that of the Bundesbank. In such case, its anti-inflationary credibility would exceed that of the US Fed. If one also considers that the EC is a net foreign creditor, in contrast to the USA, the attraction of the Ecu as a store of value increases further.

References

Eichengreen, Barry, *One Money for Europe? Lessons from the US Currency Union*, Economic Policy, n.8, 1990.

European Commission, *One Market, One Money*, European Economy, n.44, October, 1990,

Giavazzi, Francesco and Alberto Giovannini, *The Role of the Exchange Rate Regime in a Disinflation: Empirical Evidence from the European Monetary System*, in Giavazzi, Micossi and Miller (eds.), *The European Monetary System*, Cambridge University Press, 1988.

Radaelli, Giorgio, *EMS Stability, Capital Controls, and Foreign Exchange Market Intervention*, in Courakis and Taylor (eds.), *Private Behaviour and Government Policy in Interdependent Economies*, Clarendon Press - Oxford, 1990.

Sercu, Piet, *Ecu Spot Rates, Interest Rates and Yields: Are There Arbitrage Possibilities?*, EIASM Working Paper, January 1990.

Shearson Lehman Brothers, *European Monetary Union. Marriage - but a Long Engagement*, December 1990.

6.2 The international Ecu bond market

Primary market

Issuance

The first Ecu bond was issued in April 1981, for SFTE (Société Financière pour les Télécommunications et l'Electronique). Since then, the Ecu has grown to be one of the most popular currencies for new issuance in the international bond market. In the first quarter of 1991, for example, there was a greater amount of straight international issuance in Ecu (US$17bn equivalent) than in any other currency including the US dollar (US$ 13.6bn).

There are three types of Ecu bond issuance. They are traditional eurobonds; domestic issues designed to appeal to the international investor; and straightforward domestic issues. The first two categories comprise what is known as the international bond market, the focus of this section.

Eurobonds represent the largest portion of the international bond market. They include the myriad of traditional issues by corporates and supranational agencies. Along with these are sovereign issues such as those for the Republic of Italy, the UK, and the Kingdom of Denmark.

The international domestic market is represented primarily by the four French Ecu OATs (*Obligation Assimilable du Trésor*) and the two Kingdom of Spain issues. They qualify as international by being designed to appeal to international investors: they have gross coupon payments, are clearable through the international clearing systems, and so on. This may well be true for normal domestic issues anyway, and hence their 'international' status is solely a recognition of this appeal. This is the case with the French OATs. Alternatively, the usual domestic rules may need modifying to achieve international appeal. In the case of Spain, for instance, a special exemption was accorded to exempt non-residents from domestic withholding tax.

Pure domestic issues exist, for example, in the Italian and Greek markets. These are subject to all domestic rules and regulations, and therefore may not be homogeneous with the international issues. That is not to say that they are not important, as they can be quite sizeable. The amount of domestic Italian Ecu bonds, known as CTEs (*Certificati del Tresoro in Ecu*), that is currently outstanding is over Ecu 25bn. This is more than four times larger than their stock of Italian Ecu eurobonds outstanding. Although in theory CTEs are designed for domestic investors, non-residents hold over 60 per cent of the outstanding amount, primarily as a result of asset-swapping activity.

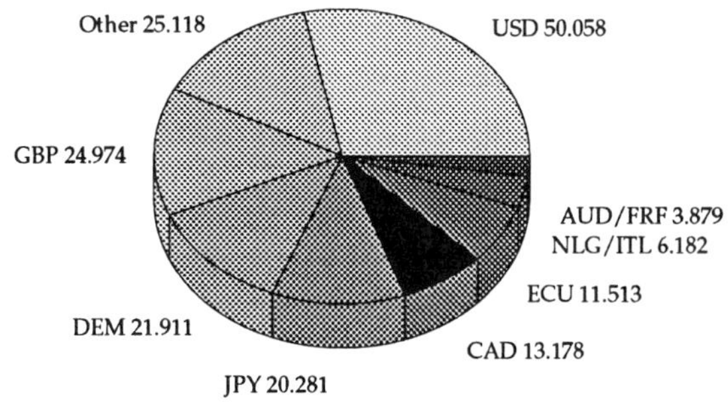

Figure 6.9 Eurobond new issue volumes (in US$ billion) by currency, 1988

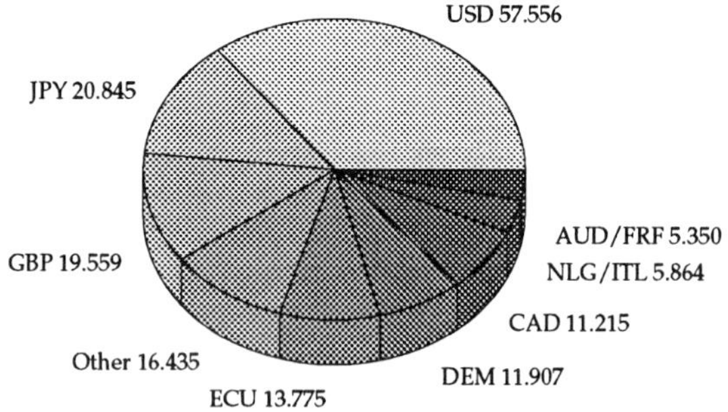

Figure 6.10 Eurobond new issue volumes (in US$ billion) by currency, 1989

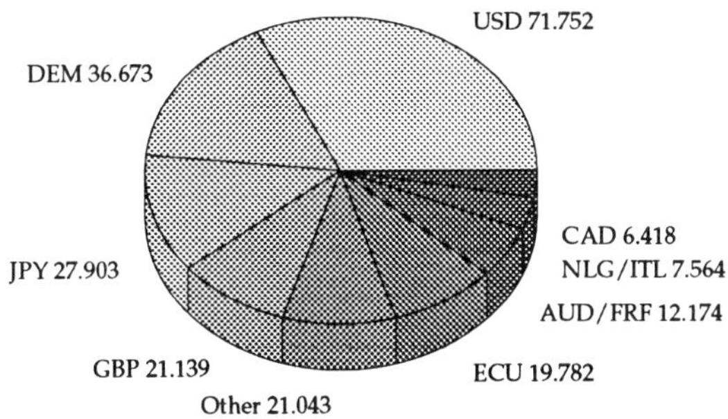

Figure 6.11 **Eurobond new issue volumes (in US$ billion) by currency, 1990**

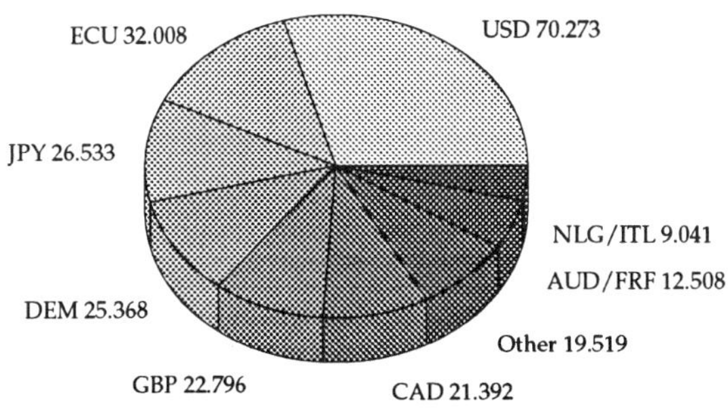

Figure 6.12 **Eurobond new issue volumes (in US$ billion) by currency, 1991 (to third quarter)**

Currently, there are no significant pricing differences between eurobonds and international issues, but pure domestic issues are valued differently. Some countries issue in several market categories. Already noted are the Italian issues in both the eurobond and domestic markets. Their recent issuance in the eurobond market was designed to increase the maturity profile of the Italian public debt. This was more easily achieved by targeting an international investor base, particularly as Italian investors have traditionally preferred shorter maturity investments. The UK has issued a super-jumbo eurobond, but its new 3-year note programme is designed as an international domestic. Similarly, Belgium is intending to issue international domestic issues in 1992, having issued in the euromarket previously. It is this current interchangeability between eurobonds and international domestic issues that allow us to regard the international bond market as a generic sector.

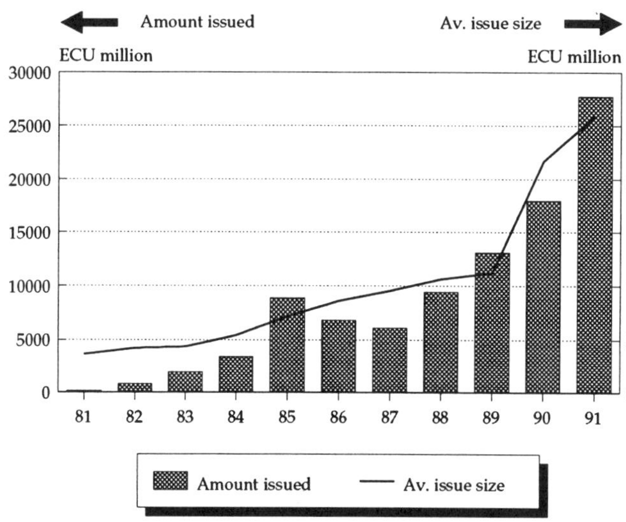

Figure 6.13 Growth of the Ecu bond market (first three-quarters of 1991, annualized)

Traditionally, the majority of issuance in Ecu has been of straight bonds. However, there are issues of significant size in FRNs (floating-rate notes) and zero-coupons, such as the Ecu 1bn issues for Italy and Crédit Local, respectively. Also, other issue types such as convertibles are appearing more regularly. Issuance has been increasing dramatically in recent years. Unlike the relative surge of issuance in 1985, which was caused by a bond market rally, the current increases have been driven by something more fundamental. The reasons for issuance have naturally varied from issuer to issuer, but the single biggest factor encouraging such activity has been the movement towards European economic and monetary union (Emu). In order to appeal to institutional investors, the average size of issuance has increased, too.

Issuance in the Ecu market follows normal euromarket procedures. Issues can be sold on a fixed re-offer basis, sold at a discount to reflect fees, or sold as a private placement. Sovereign issues can follow normal eurobond practice as the Italian issues have done, or a more normal domestic issue technique. Some issues, such as the French Ecu OATs, have been launched using both methods. There have also been conversions and exchange offers. The conversion from the 1997 OAT into a new 2002 OAT, for example, increased both the maturity of the French debt and future deliverable supply for the Matif Ecu future. The second was an exchange of seven small issues by EDF into a single 10-year issue of over Ecu 500m, providing the market with the liquidity it desired.

Within the eurobond market itself, the number of market-makers is increasing continually although, some houses, given their depth of coverage, have maintained their league table rankings.

	Rank of Paribas	Amount (Ecu million)	Market share (%)
1991 (Jan-Sep)	1st	6993	29.98
1990	1st	3209	23.19
1989	1st	2409	21.21
1988	1st	1876	19.86
1987	1st	1497	24.55
1986	1st	1990	31.32
1985	1st	1574	17.66

Figure 6.14 League table rankings of bookrunners in Ecu eurobond issues

Issuers

The Ecu bond market is made up of a wide range of borrowers where supranationals, sovereigns, private companies and public enterprises each provide a large share of new issues.

European supranational borrowers like the EC, the European Investment Bank (EIB), the European Atomic Energy Community (Euratom), and the European Coal and Steel Community (ECSC), contribute a significant proportion to

	1988		1989		1990		1991 Q3	
	% of total	No. of issues	% of total	No. of issues	% of total	No. of issues	% of total	No. of issues
Supranationals	25.0	19	17.4	20	13.1	10	19.2	15
Sovereigns	6.9	5	15.9	9	37.6	8	39.4	7
Public companies	21.3	24	21.1	32	27.1	33	15.4	23
Private companies	46.8	42	45.6	55	22.2	31	26.0	56
	100	90	100	116	100	82	100	101
Total value ($m)	11,513.46		13,774.74		19,782.48		32,008.03	

Figure 6.15 **Ecu issues by type of borrower (US$ equivalent, percentage of total volume and number of issues)**

new issuance. First, the statements of accounts and all financial operations conducted by these entities are denominated in Ecu, thus they issue Ecu eurobonds and, in some instances, Ecu domestic issues (targeted to one country), matching assets and liabilities from a currency standpoint. Secondly, European supranational entities want to encourage the development of the Ecu and its use as a financial instrument for purposes of investment and financing. It has therefore always made sense for them to borrow in Ecu and, most of the time, without the need to swap the funds into other currencies. This issuance will continue: for instance, the first financing for the new European Bank for Reconstruction and Development (EBRD) was in Ecu, and the EIB is increasing its Ecu funding requirements.

Sovereign issuers have contributed to the drastic increase in issuance. Sovereign issuers are not necessarily natural users of Ecu but they have become large borrowers, nonetheless. France and Italy, in particular, use the market considerably, but other countries such as the UK, Belgium and Spain are also active. In part, this involvement can be attributed to a political decision to promote the Ecu in the run-up to Emu; France, for instance, committed itself to raise 15 per cent of its borrowing requirement for 1991 in Ecu. Economic considerations do drive a country to issue, however; Italy, which has a large borrowing requirement, is attracted by the cheap funding compared to Italian yields, and the market acceptance of longer maturities as well as the pro-European aspect. This issuance obviously will continue.

Apart from the sovereign and European supranational issuance, there has been the usual swapped issuance by corporates, supranationals and sovereigns.

These issuers, who may have no natural need for Ecu will fund if the swap market opportunities are available. In this way the Ecu market is no different from any other euromarket. Fortunately, in the past, the domestic Italian CTE issuance has helped create swap opportunities for issuers. Although this factor has declined, other emerging ones have enabled the swap market to continue its growth. The most recent of these is the link to the Ecu by the higher-yielding Nordic currencies, which has provided a new source of paying-interest in Ecu.

The combination of these factors has led to most of the liquid issues in the Ecu market being of high credit quality. In general, sovereign and supranational issuers are at least AA, if not AAA, and because most corporate issuance is swapped, the issuers have to be of sufficient creditworthiness to obtain swaps. Even those that are unrated tend to have government guarantees.

Secondary market

Outstandings

For a market that only started in 1981, it is staggering that the straight sector is already the fifth largest international bond market in the world. A list of liquid issues is shown in the Appendix.

Benchmark issues

A major development of the Ecu market in the last two years has been the creation of liquid jumbo issues. These are high-quality sovereign or supranational names and are large in size.

The jumbo issues constitute those of Ecu 1bn, or more. They were either issued in one amount, such as the Italian bonds, or in several fungible tranches of the same issue, as in the case of some French Ecu OATs. These issues are now providing a quality yield curve for the Ecu market. However, given the short time-scale over which they have been issued, it is not surprising that this process is not yet complete, as the short end, in particular, not yet well covered. This is changing, however. The UK, for example, has announced the setting up of a regular auction schedule of three-year notes. It is particularly satisfying that the rationale for this was not a funding requirement, but to satisfy a market development need. Thus the Ecu bond market now has a liquid maturity span of up to 20 years. This is matched by only two other European bond markets: those of France and the UK. These issues have not only brought attention to themselves, but to the Ecu market as a whole, by their visibility and liquidity.

Size, of course, is not necessarily a good indicator of liquidity, but turnover volume is higher in these issues. Using the Cedel and Euroclear turnover figures for August 1991, all seven of the most actively traded Ecu bonds have issue sizes of Ecu 1bn or more. Note also that six of the 14 most actively traded bonds

Maturity	Amount (Ecu m)	Issuer	Coupon (%)	Date
3-month	1000	Italy	FRN	Oct 2005
5-year	1250	Belgium	9.125	Mar 1996
	1000	Spain	9.00	May 1996
	1000	Norway	9.00	July 1996
6-year	1104	EIB	10.0	Feb 1997
	1000	Italy	10.375	July 1997
10-year	1000	Italy	10.75	Apr 2000
	3370	France OAT	9.5	Apr 2000
	1150	EIB	10.0	Jan 2001
	1500	France OAT	10.0	Feb 2001
	2750	UK	9.125	Feb 2001
	1446	France OAT	8.5	Mar 2002
20-year	2500	Italy	9.25	Mar 2011

Figure 6.16 Ecu jumbo issues

through Cedel and Euroclear were Ecu bonds. Indeed, over the last year, Ecu bonds have consistently seen some of the highest turnover through the international clearing systems. The three super jumbo benchmarks, those of Ecu 2.5bn or larger, are always near the top of the most-traded list, with one of them quite often at the very top.

Rank	Currency	Name	Coupon	Maturity	Turnover vol. (US$ bn)
1	DEM	Bund	8.75	2001	11.2
2	DEM	Bund	8.375	2001	10.6
3	ECU	UK	9.125	2001	10.3
4	ECU	Italy	10.75	2011	8.4
5	ECU	OAT	9.5	2000	7.1

Figure 6.17 The most-traded fixed-rate bonds in August 1991 (Euroclear & Cedel turnover figures)

Ecu indices

There are two main types of Ecu index: the actual yield index and the theoretical yield index.

Actual yields

The concept of an actual yield is not as simple as it sounds. Although most Ecu issues are highly-rated, whether they be corporate, supranational, or sovereign, there are still significant yield differentials between them due to factors such as liquidity, tax-free status to Italian investors, and so forth. There are two alternatives for dealing with this.

The traditional approach is by using the yield on benchmark bonds. This is an easy approach, but unfortunately, there are still significant gaps in the range of issues and maturities. This was particularly the case over a year ago, prior to the recent benchmark issuance, but it is still a problem, particularly as different issuers have focused on different parts of the yield curve. Hence the various benchmarks along the curve will be inconsistent in terms of pricing, and with potentially significant maturity differences. Also, the changing of benchmark status, for instance, from the Ecu OAT 9.5% 2000 to the Ecu OAT 8.5% 2002, will create further inconsistencies.

As an alternative, one can attempt to average the bonds in each maturity band to reduce the effect of different pricing of individual bonds. By determining the yield of a portfolio of all liquid bonds at each maturity, one can reduce substantially the effect of differential pricing and hence provide a good estimate of true market yield for each maturity. This is the technique used at Paribas for their actual bond indices since January 1990. Known as the Paribas Liquid Bond Indices, these provide an actual yield level for each sector of the market, so that fair comparisons can be made with the theoretical yield.

As well as a yield index for the three-, five-, seven-, and ten-year market sectors, there are both price and total return figures available for each index, as well as for the total market including the Italy 9.25% 2011.

Theoretical yields

The theoretical yield is the yield which would exist if one were able to construct a synthetic Ecu bond from the underlying constituent markets. The actual yield is the yield existing on actual Ecu bonds trading in the market.

There are three principal types of theoretical yield model with their own pros and cons. the simplest model is that based on a reduced basket, that is, a selection, not all, of the underlying markets. third, there is the true or par theoretical yield based on all the underlying markets and calculated in a correct mathematical fashion.

The reduced basket model uses only the major component markets. typically, these are the four markets of Germany, the Netherlands, France and the UK. The intention is to replicate the Ecu with a major proportion of the underlying markets; currently these comprise 72 per cent of the Ecu's composition. This is the basis of the model known as SBC4 (developed by the Swiss Bank Corporation). These markets are chosen as being those with the greatest liquidity and the highest underlying turnover, although the Italian market is excluded. The inherent advantage in this technique is that it is simple to calculate and requires no assumptions with regard to yields in some of the minor markets. The disadvantage is that this is not a true model as it excludes eight of the twelve constituent markets. In total, the reduced basket is more of a trading tool than a theoretical yield. Indeed, this is recognized in some of the more modern reduced basket models, such as that recommended by CDC, based on the markets with Liffe- or Matif-based futures contracts.

A simple weighted theoretical yield utilizes all the underlying markets and weights them according to the current weighting of each currency in the Ecu. It is therefore relatively simple to calculate but, unfortunately, there are significant errors. These include the estimation error which is discussed with regard to the true theoretical yield, but also mathematical errors in the weighting of the components. Whereas, prior to the widespread use of computers, such a yield may have been of use, there is nothing these days to favour such a technique over a true theoretical.

A true theoretical utilizes all the underlying markets but weights them in a mathematically-correct manner. By doing so, it provides the true yield that would exist on a synthetic Ecu bond which was constructed of its individual components. The major disadvantage is that as some underlying markets are incomplete, estimates have to made with regard to some of the underlying yields. However, the true theoretical is a fundamental analytic tool.

Below is the formula for constructing the true theoretical yield, and is that calculated by Paribas since the mid-1980s. The Paribas theoretical yield is widely used in the Ecu market and has become widely regarded as an 'industry standard'. It is defined as:

$$C = \frac{1 - \sum_{k=1}^{K} \frac{W_k}{(1 + i_k)^N}}{\sum_{k=1}^{K} \sum_{j=1}^{N} \frac{W_k}{(1 + i_k)^j}}$$

C	Ecu theoretical yield
K	number of currencies in the Ecu
N	maturity (number of years)
W_k	weight of currency k in the Ecu
i_k	yield for currency k and maturity N
k, j	increments

It is not as complex as it looks; it is just the mathematical expression for discounting each individual cashflow of a par bond in each underlying market in the right proportion. One can in fact go beyond this theoretical yield, which is based on the current composition of the Ecu, by attempting to allow for future revisions of the Ecu's composition. This is the approach that is taken by CSFB, for example. Whereas this has some inherent attractions, there are problems. By requiring another set of estimates, it reduces the credibility of the yield as a market standard, particularly as revisions are based not only on economic criteria, but also on a political component which is difficult to model accurately. The technique is useful immediately before a revision to the weights of currencies in the Ecu, but given that there may well be no more such revisions, its usefulness is further reduced.

Interpretation of the theoretical yield

Interpretation of the theoretical yield is difficult. The simplistic view is to assume that the theoretical Ecu yield shows where the absolute level of the actual market should be trading. For this interpretation to be valid, it would have to be possible to arbitrage the difference between the actual and the theoretical yield. Given the obstacles in many of the component bond markets - from withholding tax in Italy to availability of bonds in Greece - this condition does not hold. Besides, there are additional problems, such as the deviations that occur in the value between the market and basket Ecu currency. These compound the difficulties in valuing this so-called arbitrage.

A weaker condition would be if we were to say that one was a substitute for the other. If this was the case, an investor who could choose between a basket (i.e., the theoretical) and the Ecu market would choose the one that gave him the highest yield. Again we would argue that the investor would have to settle for a basket different to that required and, in addition, suffer the inconvenience of reinvesting thirteen coupons each year instead of one. Even in its weakest form then, this idea that the theoretical shows the level at which the actual market should be trading is fundamentally flawed.

This brings us to the second interpretation of the theoretical yield: that the theoretical is a benchmark from which we can draw some guidelines about the behaviour of the actual Ecu market.

The two interpretations - absolute level versus guidelines - are different. The problem comes in that the Paribas index - now the market benchmark - was designed as one thing, and is being interpreted as another. The result is that there has recently been a certain amount of uninformed comment to the effect that the market will converge to its theoretical level. Since actual yields are well below the theoretical this implies a major fall in the level of bond prices.

Finally, these comparisons were being made between actual Ecu bond yields and the original Paribas Theoretical Ecu Yield. This doesn't allow for the difference in credit quality between the different underlying markets. Also, a much more important factor is that it doesn't allow for the move to Emu, with the Ecu eventually losing its basket status to become the single currency. The construction of the New Paribas Theoretical Ecu Yield now allows for these two factors.

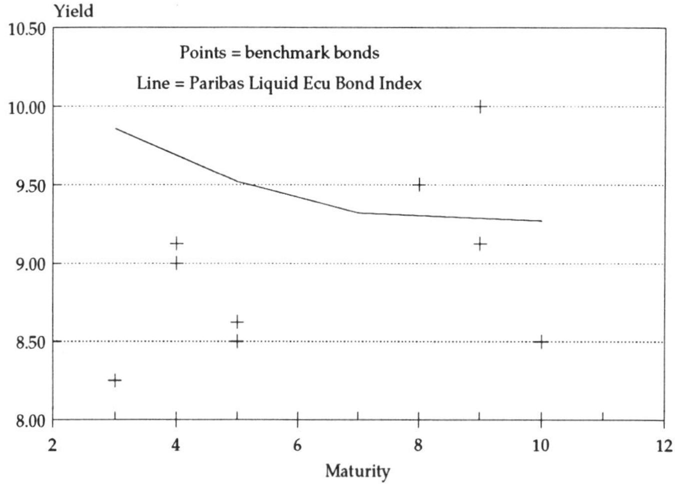

Figure 6.18 Paribas liquid Ecu yield

Valuation of Ecu bonds with reference to expected currency performance

As the most important factor that effects yield levels for an international investor is the expected currency performance, it is necessary to have a good idea of the likely future performance of the Ecu currency. How can this be determined?

In an efficient market, one would expect that the future value of an exchange rate would be equal to the forward rate, based on the yield differential between the two markets over the relevant time horizon. But, as many studies have shown (Fama 1983, Paribas 1990), the forward rate is a poorer predictor of future rates than the current spot rate. This is true even when there does not exist an exchange rate regime dedicated to exchange rate stability. Within such a regime, of which the ERM is a prime example, such a result is intuitively obvious. This provides us with the high yielding argument, that investments in higher yielding bond markets traditionally outperform low-yielding alternatives, as the currency depreciation is less than implied by the forward rate. Also complicating the use of the forward rate for the Ecu market is the discrepancy that occurs between theoretical and actual rates. As different rates give different forwards, which should be used to calculate the anticipated forward rate?

Fortunately for us, the Ecu is based on an official definition as a basket of 12 EMS currencies. We can therefore determine the future performance of the Ecu if we can do two things. First, we need to pin down the expected performance of the 12 component currencies. Second, we need to decide what deviations may occur between the market Ecu and its official definition.

We will start with the easier problem, being the second one. Before Stage 3 of Emu there is no official mechanism for holding the two in line. Until then, therefore, the only mechanism to hold them in line is that provided by market arbitrage. Fortunately, at the beginning of Stage 3 the Ecu will be fixed against the other inner group currencies. This will almost certainly occur at the official rate then. In other words, the deviation will be zero from the beginning of Stage 3 onward. This is due to occur in 1997, and as our interest is in long-dated bonds, the deviation at our time horizon will therefore be zero. The relevance of the deviation for currency expectations is therefore limited to possible volatility for short-term expectations.

Our main problem, therefore, is to decide on the expected performance of the various component currencies of the Ecu against the Deutschemark. Fortunately, we can utilize the working of the ERM and the expected behaviour of the various currencies in the lead up to Emu. With a freezing of the composition of the Ecu, we can then calculate the expected movement of the Ecu against the Deutschemark ahead of Stage 3. After then, of course, the Ecu loses its basket status and is fixed against the inner group currencies, and therefore the Deutschemark. There is therefore no movement in the Ecu/Deutschemark exchange rate after that date.

To start with, it is useful to get a feel of the level of currency risk that exists within the ERM itself. Consider, as a starting point, all the ERM currencies in a neutral position, i.e. at their bilateral central rates against the Deutschemark. Now let them depreciate against the Deutschemark to settle at their lower limits. The lower limits we shall use are the ERM band limits for most of the currencies but with the following exceptions. The Dutch guilder and Belgian franc

Currency	ECU weight	Central Rate #1	Central Divergence vs. DEM	Adjusted low Rate #2	Adjusted low Divergence vs. DEM	Change vs. DEM
DEM	30.36	1	0.00	1	0.00	0.00
NLG	9.49	1.12673	0.00	1.132377	-0.50	-0.50
BEF/LUF	8.09	20.6255	0.00	20.72888	-0.50	-0.50
FRF	19.32	3.35386	0.00	3.4305	-2.23	-2.23
DKK	2.52	3.81443	0.00	3.9016	-2.23	-2.23
IEP	1.11	2.67894	0.00	2.619	-2.24	-2.24
ITL	9.87	748.217	0.00	765.4	-2.24	-2.24
ESP	5.15	65	0.00	69.017	-5.82	-5.82
GBP	12.60	2.95	0.00	2.778	-5.83	-5.83
PTE	0.78	86.9393	0.00	98.03793	-11.32	-11.32
GRD	0.70	99.8662	0.00	112.6150	-11.32	-11.32
ECU		2.05586		2.01424		-2.02

Figure 6.19 Ecu Performance Currencies move from central rates to adjusted ERM lows

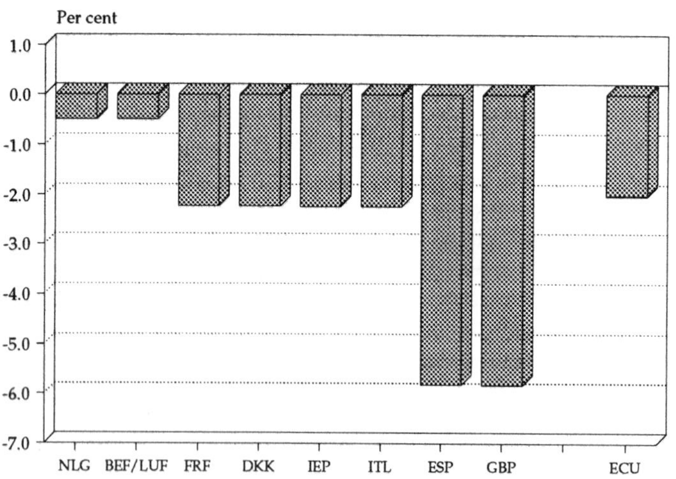

Figure 6.20 Percentage move of currency vs. Deutschemark (currency from central to ERM lows)

Currency	ECU weight	Central Rate #1	Central Divergence vs. DEM	1997 scenario Rate #2	1997 scenario Divergence vs. DEM	Change vs. DEM
DEM	30.50	1	0.00	1	0.00	0.00
NLG	9.53	1.1269	-0.02	1.12673	0.00	0.02
BEF/LUF	8.14	20.588	0.18	20.6255	0.00	-0.18
FRF	19.04	3.4135	-1.75	3.4305	-2.23	-0.50
DKK	2.49	3.8752	-1.57	3.9016	-2.23	-0.68
IEP	1.12	2.674	-0.18	2.619	-2.24	-2.06
ITL	9.92	747.783	0.06	775	-3.46	-3.51
ESP	5.34	62.95	3.26	69.017	-5.82	-8.79
GBP	12.48	2.9077	-1.43	2.778	-5.83	-4.46
PTE	0.79	85.96	1.14	94.556	-8.06	-9.09
GRD	0.63	112.1	-10.91	134.52	-25.76	-16.67
ECU		2.04680		2.01203		

Figure 6.21 **Ecu Performance Currencies move from central rates to anticipated 1997 scenario**

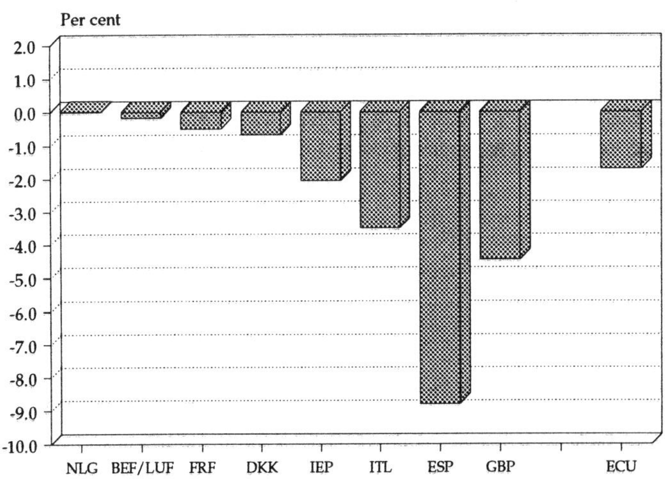

Figure 6.22 **Percentage move of currency vs. Deutschemark (currency from central to 1992 scenario)**

maintain their quasi-Deutschemark status and behave as if in 0.5 per cent bands, whilst the non-ERM currencies of the Greek drachma and Portuguese escudo behave as if in 12 per cent limits. From this we can derive the amount of depreciation suffered by the Ecu.

We can see clearly that the Ecu performs in line with, if not even a little better than, the other 2.25 per cent band currencies. This immediately provides an explanation for the intuitive feeling that the Ecu is similar to the French franc and the Danish krone in terms of risk.

Such a comparison was particulary useful in the pre-Maastricht days. Now, with the goal of Emu, we can attempt to be more quantitative. We have a likely time horizon, and expected currency behaviour for the various currencies on the route to Emu. We can therefore provide a realistic, viable scenario for the levels at which the various currencies will trade at the beginning of stage 3. The quasi-Deutschemark currencies fix at their current central rate against the Deutschemark. Excluding the ITL, the 2.25 per cent band currencies fix at their current lower limits against the Deutschemark. The Italian lire is the one 2.25 per cent band currency that may be devalued, but this would only be a small effect. We have assumed it trades almost 3.5 per cent below its current central rate. Both 6 per cent band currencies fall to their bottom limits against the Deutschemark, whilst the Portuguese escudo and Greek drachma fall by progressively larger amounts.

We are happy with a no-devaluation assumption for the other 2.25 per cent band currencies, as any slight economic advantage would be more than outweighed by the loss of exchange rate credibility. It is the scale of some of the economic problems facing Italy that may tempt a devaluation for that currency. The size of the 6 per cent band means a fall to the lower limits already enables a significant devaluation for those currencies. We can now look at the movement of each currency against the Deutschemark, and the implied movement in the Ecu.

So, though we allow for some significant falls against the Deutschemark, the Ecu still performs reasonably. This is the advantage that the functioning of the ERM provides for the Ecu. We can now take these implied currency movements and look at the yield premiums required to offset the currency losses sustained. We can do this for 5-year and 10-year bonds. This is where the second feature of the move to Emu comes into play. There are no currency losses for the Ecu against the Deutschemark and the other inner group currencies after stage 3 of Emu in 1997. Therefore the total currency loss for the Ecu is the same over both periods. With twice as long to obtain the required gains, the yield premium for a 10-year bond is just half that of a 5-year bond.

The above scenario requires 10-year Ecu bonds to yield just over 10bp more than French bonds. At 5-year maturities this reaches 25bp. For 5-year bonds, therefore, this confirms the conventional wisdom that they are expensive compared to other European bonds.

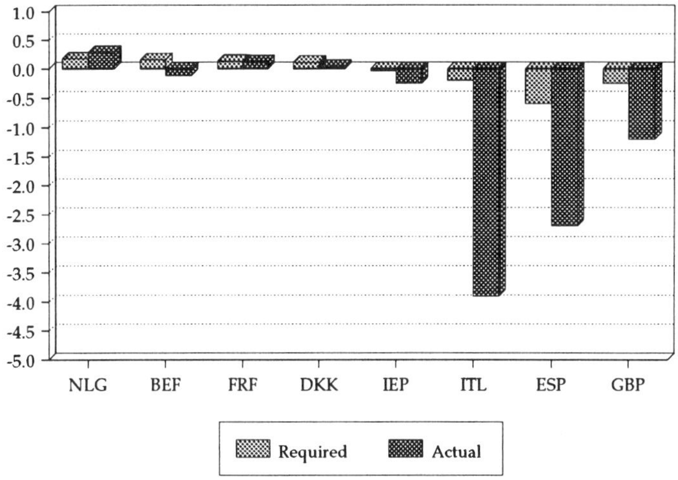

Figure 6.23 10-year bond spreads - 1

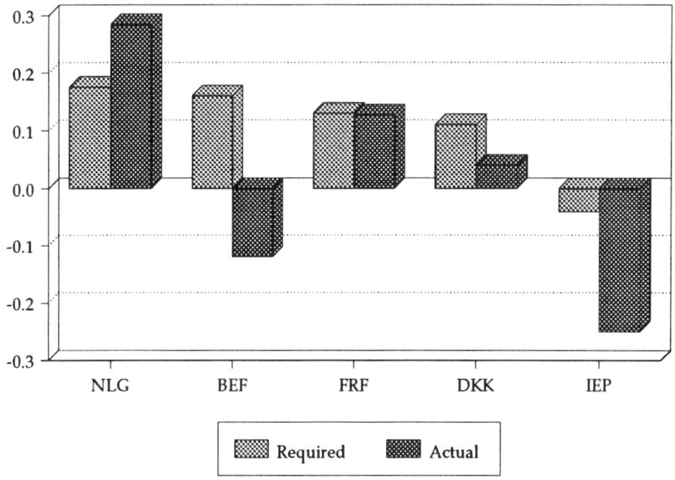

Figure 6.24 10-year bond spreads - 2

For 10-year bonds, the story is different. We can compare the required yield pick-up to cover the expected currency losses with the yield pick-up currently available in the market-place for switching into Ecu.

If the actual yield pick-up is lower than that required, it means that Ecu bonds will underperform that other countries bonds. We immediately note that the Italian, Spanish and UK markets are all expected to outperform Ecu significantly. But this calculation assumes that the three currencies fix to the Ecu in 1997. But this is not guaranteed. All three currencies are a higher risk. We can best sum up the result by saying that should any of the three countries show sufficient convergence so as to join Stage 3 of Emu, then these markets will outperform Ecu, but it is a higher risk.

If we just focus on the low risk currencies then the differences between them become a lot clearer. The outstanding feature is that the current differential between French and Ecu bonds is exactly that needed to offset the expected currency losses. Compared to the Belgian and Danish markets, the Ecu looks expensive, but both these have lower credit quality for instance.

Meanwhile, the required differential over France is near its high. Because the French franc is currently fairly low against the Deutschemark it doesn't have much further to fall. If it was at its central rate, for example, Ecu could just trade through French yield levels.

The above charts do not show Ecu bonds against German bunds. Based on the expected currency performance, 10-year Ecu bonds should be yielding less than 20bp over German bunds, and French franc OATs less than 5bp over bunds. (If we were to compare these markets against the Deutschemark* base that we discussed earlier, we might even see these markets through bunds.) Possibly the actual spread represents scepticism on the part of the market in believing the Emu convergence scenario. Therefore as the scenario becomes accepted, the yield differential will narrow. As we demonstrated earlier, the Ecu currency has a similar risk to the French franc. Thus even if scepticism grew over convergence in general, we would expect Ecu bonds to yield close to French bonds.

Credit concerns

Domestic and international investors perceive credit quality differently. Domestic investors usually regard the credit of the domestic government highly. This is a reasonable assumption in Europe. Of the EC countries, only Greece and Portugal have low implied ratings, yet even they are regarded satisfactorily by their domestic investors. International investors, though, have a wide selection of assets to choose amongst. They can therefore be a lot choosier over their investments. This is emphasized by the regular use of credit ratings to select allowable investments.

We can see the effect of this by looking at the trading levels of differently rated debt in the euromarkets. For a fuller analysis of this factor, refer to Paribas' publication *Arbitraging The Ecu*, December 1991. To summarize the results, the average credit quality of the theoretical yield requires a yield pick-up of around 8 bps compared to an AAA theoretical.

The actual Ecu bond market is composed of variously-rated issues. Given the international nature of the Ecu market, the AAA rated issues should therefore trade at a premium to the theoretical, and lesser credits weaker. There are a couple of factors that mitigate against this.

The first is Emu, which requires economic convergence. To become part of the single currency area countries have to achieve a high degree of economic convergence. To facilitate this, each country submits its economic proposals to the EC for surveillance and recommendations. As convergence in Europe is designed to be convergence on the best, the average rating over the life of a bond should be higher than the current evaluations. Credit ratings are static evaluations dependent on the current economic condition of the various countries. So for European sovereign debt, the credit rating should be a less important factor than would appear at first sight.

The second factor is due to the influence of domestic investors. Investors in non-AAA countries, such as Denmark and Belgium, will regard Ecu debt issued by their home government as creditworthy as their domestic currency government debt.

The one caveat to this is that due to the 'no bail-out' rule. To restrain countries from taking advantage of the single currency by issuing an unsatisfactorily high amount of debt, the EC will not guarantee the debt of any member. This allows the possibility of a sovereign default. Having a single currency removes the ability to devalue the debt and therefore increases the likelihood of default. This will not be a major problem though, since economic convergence remains a requirement prior to joining the single currency.

Therefore the following relationships should exist due to credit quality. European names should not be valued as rigorously as expected under a more traditional analysis. The EC names where a little more caution is deserved are those that may fail to achieve the necessary convergence, but still are allowed to enter Emu. Non EC names of less than AAA quality should not be rated so highly as equivalent EC credits.

Liquidity

International investors regard liquidity highly. They like to be able to react quickly to new opportunities and changing perceptions. This means that they need to be able to trade easily and cheaply. Therefore liquidity is important.

Indeed, what they require is specific liquidity. In other words they require liquidity in the instruments that they trade, not necessarily in the market as a whole. This is fortunate for the Ecu market, as there is substantial liquidity in the benchmarks, that does not exist in the market as a whole. Although this feature makes activities such as immunization difficult to envisage, it enables international investment.

There are jumbo issues (Ecu 1 billion or greater) of 5-year maturity, and in 1992 the UK and possibly the French will be issuing at shorter maturities. So there is some specific liquidity for the intermediate maturities. The greatest liquidity exists, though, at 10- and 20-year maturities. These represent the area of greatest interest for the international investor.

Not only is the 10-year sector the favoured for jumbo issuance, but we have two issuers who have specifically provided liquidity. The UK has issued one Ecu bond, designed as a highly liquid flagship issue. The UK 9.125 per cent 2001 has Ecu 2.75bn outstanding, of which Ecu 250m was kept by the Bank of England to aid the repo market in that bond, and therefore improve liquidity. France has issued 3 bonds with maturities 2000/2001/2002. The intention by the French authorities is for their issues to follow four essential characteristics. These are transparency, market need, regularity and consistency. Therefore they tap (issue further fungible amounts) their issues to build up liquidity. The French OAT 9.5 per cent 2000 is the largest outstanding issue in the Ecu market, with a size of Ecu 3.37 billion. These issues compare reasonably in size to the 10-year benchmarks in other European bond markets (see Figure 6.25)

We see the same sort of comparison if we look at the 20-year sector. The Italy 9.25 per cent 2011 is Ecu 2.5 billion in size. The exceptional feature here is that

Market	Size of 10-year benchmark (Ecu bn)
Germany	6.9
Netherlands	5.8
Belgium	3.0
France	7.6
Denmark	5.9
Ireland	0.9
Italy	6.8
Spain	3.0
UK	5.8
Ecu	2.75/3.37

Figure 6.25 Comparison of European bond benchmarks: 10-year

there is only two other European bond markets with bonds of such maturity. These are the UK and French markets:

Market	Size of 20-year benchmark (Ecu bn)
UK	4.4
France	5.2
Ecu	2.5

Figure 6.26 Comparison of European bond benchmarks: 20-year

That size is a meaningful comparison is shown by looking at the turnover figures. We can look at the two international clearing systems Euroclear and Cedel. The 3 Ecu issues that we have just considered are regularly in the top 5 of traded issues through the clearing systems. In many months, one or other of the Ecu issues is in top position. Although this ignores turnover through domestic clearing systems, it still shows significant liquidity in the Ecu issues.

Turnover in the Ecu bond futures contracts is still insignificant compared to other European bond market futures. Their existence, at least, will enable liquidity to increase on demand.

The conclusion is that the requirement for specific liquidity by international investors will continue to provide benchmark issues with a liquidity premium. This will exist particularly at maturities where the Ecu benchmarks compare favourably with the benchmarks in the underlying markets.

Other opportunities

It is not that domestic and international investors vary significantly in looking at other opportunities but the alternatives are different. The first comparisons for a domestic investor are short interest rates and equities. An international investor will look for a bond market with a better risk/reward ratio.

For an Ecu investor the other opportunities are the other European bond markets. Of course, if the theoretical yield were arbitrageable then it would be another opportunity, but it cannot and so is not. Paribas' analysis of currency performance shows that the Ecu currency has a similar risk as the safe inner band currencies, the French franc and the Danish krone. These are currently the similar risk alternatives. We would require a strong justification for the expected returns to differ significantly on these markets from the Ecu market.

The differences in yield between the German market and the Ecu market represents a differing level of risk. If Emu collapses, the Ecu market would be expected to underperform. Similarly, the countries with wide band currencies may not move to Emu in 1997, and therefore represent yet a higher level of risk. Either alternative may be a preferable market to invest in, but it requires the evaluation of a different level of risk.

Paribas' current evaluation of the European bond markets suggests that these risks are valued too highly, in other words, convergence of bond yields is likely to continue. However, it is the inner group of markets that represent the most obvious alternatives.

Tax considerations

The taxation of government bond markets is dictated by the domestic government involved. They can apply and change taxation of bonds, and apply withholding tax on interest payments.

Currently, of the major markets only Italy and the UK impose withholding tax. There are UK gilts that are tax-free to non-residents (the FOTRA gilts) but in Italy it is only through double taxation agreements that tax is reclaimable. Whereas in the past a rule of thumb was to regard the expected period for the reclaim of Italian tax as 5 years, tax repayments have started to arrive promptly in some cases.

Meanwhile, of the Ecu bonds that we consider in the international bond market, many are eurobond issues. In general these contain language in their prospectuses that provide for grossing up the coupon if a withholding tax is applied, for non-residents of the country of issuer. In other words, they will effectively remain tax-free to non-residents. The notable exception to this is provided by the Republic of Italy bonds in the euromarket. The language in the prospectuses of these issues appears to indicate that any tax imposed would be an act of default. Whereas this is always a possible outcome, it would appear to suggest that the issues would remain tax-free during their life. New issues could always have other language that would remove this possibility.

Other issues, such as the French Ecu OATs are international domestic issues. There seems to be no reason stopping the imposition of withholding tax. Although such taxation is not expected, there is always the possibility in the future that an EC wide withholding tax may be introduced. Over the life of some of the longer dated bonds this could be a possibility.

There are also some supranational issuers whose bonds are tax-free to Italian investors. These issuers are the EIB, the World Bank, Euratom and the ECSC. This exemption causes short-dated issues by such issuers to trade expensively. A change in the agreement providing this exemption would allow the issues to trade on a more normal valuation basis. Such a change could leave the outstanding issues tax-free and this grandfather status would cause them to trade more expensively.

Tax considerations are always complicated and fraught with legal difficulties. It would appear, however, that eurobonds are safer investments from a tax perspective than the international domestic issues. Of the eurobonds, the Republic of Italy issues appear best in this regard.

Sentiment

Sentiment is a catch-all phrase that covers movements due to chartism, fashion and so on. These are factors which cannot be defined by a conventional economic analysis, but can be significant in themselves. It is also the factor through which expectations of future developments are built in, i.e. fear of supply and inflation following German reunification.

For the Ecu bond market there are probably two significant sentiment factors. First is the deviation between actual Ecu bond yields and the theoretical. As we mentioned in an earlier section, this has been given much more credibility than is deserved, particularly as investors have been focusing on the old Paribas Theoretical Yield and not the new. This also highlights the fact that sentiment may even be based on incorrect analysis, but it is still an important factor.

The second sentiment factor for the Ecu market is one of ever increasing importance. Many international investors cannot cover all the global bond markets. It is important for them to focus on a number of key markets. Ecu is on its way to become the single currency of Europe. With only a small interim currency risk the Ecu bond market is an easy, relatively safe channel for international investment. We have already seen this factor operate in the past, with Ecu bonds being chosen as an easy way of gaining general European exposure. The move to a single currency reinforces this argument.

Volatility

The fact that Ecu bonds are more volatile than the theoretical yield is not a problem. Their volatility is similar to that of bond markets such as the French, and this is a more relevant comparison. The importance is that the volatility occurs in a rational way. Investors are more worried about sharp unexplained movements rather than normal day to day volatility.

Unfortunately for the Ecu bond market, it has suffered some sharp movements in the lead up to Maastricht. Fortunately, these were driven by two declining factors. The first was uncertainty as to the future development of the Ecu, the second the incorrect use of the theoretical yield.

In the future, we would expect volatility in the market to be similar to that in comparable markets, as such it should not be a particularly important factor.

Short interest rates

This is probably the area in which the Ecu markets differ from other government bond markets. There is no setting of short-term rates by any official authority. This will not change prior to the inauguration of the new European Central Bank in 1997. The European Monetary Institute that will exist in Stage 2 from 1994 to 1997 will not set official rates.

The theoretical short interest rate is similarly of little use. Deviations between actual and theoretical short rates have exceeded 100bp, greater than that seen at longer maturities. This is covered in some detail in the *Arbitraging the Ecu* document.

Therefore, the only driving force for short rates is supply and demand. We can estimate how certain events, such as government bond issuance, may impact on short rates, but in general they remain unpredictable.

This situation is likely to continue for some time. The depth of the money markets in Ecu will deepen, though, particularly as corporate users become more involved in the Ecu.

Fortunately, short interest rates are more important for domestic investors rather than international investors. There could be more effect on shorter dated bonds, once such maturities become more liquid.

Inflation

The Ecu bond market pays no attention to an Ecu inflation rate based on the component countries. Although this will change as we get near to 1997, inflation will not be a major factor directly for the Ecu bond markets. Whatever effect that occurs will be due to a knock on reaction to events in other government bond markets.

Supply

Supply is a somewhat neutral factor unless it is either particularly extreme, or changing dramatically. A limited supply can depress yields as much as an excess can push up yields. The UK gilt market was a notable example of this effect in the late-1980s. Due to the move by the UK into a budget surplus (including privatization proceeds) in 1987/1988, gross official sales of gilts became negative in the third quarter of 1988. This lack of supply held log gilt yields down , even as short rates were rising sharply to fight growing inflation fears. It comes as no surprise that the increase in yields in 1990 coincides with a diminution of this effect, with gross official sales again becoming positive in the second quarter of that year.

At the other extreme, we have countries such as Italy, where the amount of supply requires a sufficient yield premium to maintain domestic investment. As

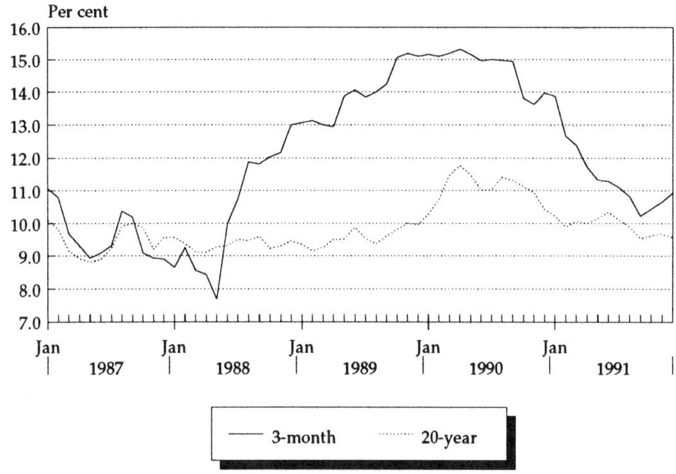

Figure 6.27 UK interest rates

it is the domestic investor who has most concern over supply, it is those markets that are dominated by domestic investors, such as Italy, that will be more affected by changing supply than those dominated by the international investor.

Supply is not a problem for the Ecu market. This is because, although it is the fifth-largest eurobond market, it is still a small market as far as global markets go (including domestic public and private sector bonds).

The successful agreement at Maastricht to move to a single currency, the Ecu, will ensure that domestic investment in Ecu will increase. Although there can obviously be periods of over-supply, as we saw in March 1991, supply is actually a positive for the Ecu market in providing the liquidity demanded by institutional investors. Indeed, if the domestic investor base in Ecu increases dramatically, the the Ecu market could even suffer from lack of supply. This could explain the expensive levels seen in shorter maturities. New issuance next year by the UK may demonstrate whether this is indeed the case.

Conclusion

The movement to Emu with the Ecu as the single currency of Europe has profound implications for the valuation of Ecu bonds. The New Paribas Theoretical

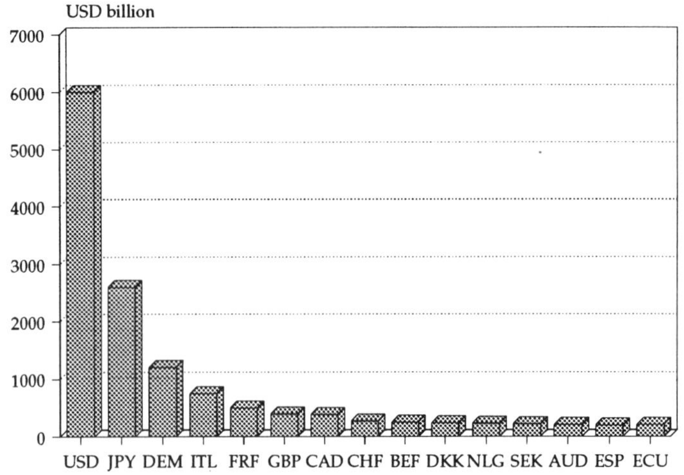

Figure 6.28 Size of global bond markets

Yield updates the theory of the theoretical yield for this move. However, it still does not provide us with a way of valuing Ecu bonds.

We have determined that the way to value Ecu bonds is driven by a comparison with other similar assets, and an understanding of the investor base. An analysis of all the relevant factors provides a number of guidelines for valuing Ecu bonds which can be summarized as follows.

Short-dated bonds are expensive. Most currency risks for the Ecu exist in the next five years. Reasons for the expensive levels seen include a lack of supply, which will change in 1992.

Ten-year maturities are cheap compared to German yields, but fairly valued compared to the French bond market. Ecu bonds should remain more highly correlated with French bonds than with German bonds. The high yielding markets of Italy, Spain and the UK look very cheap to Ecu, but only if they are expected to join Emu without significant currency losses. They remain a much higher risk alternative.

Twenty-year maturities in Ecu and France should be even closer to German levels given that there will be no further currency losses after 1997. Our analysis is based on Emu in 1997. Extending this to 1999 would not severely affect our valuation.

Convergence for Emu also implies some convergence of credit quality. Thus lesser rated credits will trade better of EC names than equivalent non-EC names. This is particularly the case for longer maturities.

The benchmark issues of Ecu 2.5 billion or more compete reasonably with other European benchmarks in terms of size. Liquidity, as indicated by turnover through the international clearing systems is also good.

Tax considerations would favour eurobonds over domestic issues. The Republic of Italy issues appear particularly attractive from this standpoint.

Supply is a positive for the Ecu market. Large liquid issues will remain sought after. Such issuance in the short end, though, could be responsible for pushing yields higher to fairer levels. Indeed, many expensive aspects of the Ecu market can be put down to lack of sufficient supply to satisfy current domestic type investors in the Ecu bond market.

Why investors consider J.P. Morgan the market source for ECUs.

J.P. Morgan provides the only continuously updated bond pricing for the twenty most actively-traded ECU issues on Reuters page XECU. As an active market-maker in ECUs and a primary dealer in all major European government bond markets, J.P. Morgan is uniquely positioned to offer authoritative pricing on ECUs and their derivatives. For more information please call

Trading: (44-71) 779 3152
Sales: (44-71) 779 3000
or Telex: (44-71) 895 4804.

JP MORGAN - LONDON					ECU BENCHMARKS	JP MORGAN - PARIS			XECU
TEL 071-779 3152		DAVID OVENDEN/L.FINDLAY				TEL 42 60 00 12			
U.K.	8.250	95	97.48-55	9.34	U.K.	9.125	01	101.21-28	8.89
BELGIU	9.125	96	100.24-34	8.98	OAT	10.000	01	105.51-61	9.02
SPAIN	9.000	96	99.54-64	9.10	FINLD	8.750	01	97.27-42	9.16
LOCAL	8.500	97	97.26-46	9.18	C O E	9.000	01	99.27-42	9.08
OAT	8.500	97	98.86-01	8.75	OAT	8.500	02	97.44-54	8.88
ITALY	10.750	97	104.09-19	9.28	DENMK	8.500	02	96.69-79	9.00
EEC	9.250	98	101.69-84	8.81	FONC	8.375	04	94.78-93	9.09
EIB	9.000	99	100.15-65	8.85	EUROF	8.500	07	95.50-65	9.04
ITALY	10.750	00	107.87-97	9.25	ITALY	9.250	11	98.88-03	9.35
OAT	9.500	00	102.26-36	9.05	OAT	8.250	22	92.58-73	8.95

With the addition of 10 more bonds to Reuters page XECU, all principal ECU market activity is now shown on a single screen. Pages XECV-Z carry the J.P. Morgan ECU index and the less active ECU issues.

JPMorgan

Chapter

7

European monetary union

Gerald Holtham
Lehman Brothers International

With help from colleagues
Peter Spencer & Jane Edwards

Introduction

The political process leading to European monetary union (Emu) is still under way, although signs of hesitation have recently emerged. Ten European states signed the Maastricht Treaty that endorsed the Delors Plan for three-stage progress to Emu. Two countries, UK and Denmark, however, insisted on opt-out clauses so that their commitment was not unconditional. Moreover, in Germany, for long a prime mover of the drive for monetary and political union, debate is only just getting under way on the costs and benefits of Emu. At the time of writing this seems likely to cause the German Parliament to insist on its own review or opt-out clause, before ratifying the treaty.

For whatever reason, the markets are clearly not yet convinced that Emu is inevitable. The structure, as well as the size, of yield spreads in European bond markets indicates that. The reasons for the markets' scepticism probably lies in the very protracted path to Emu set out in the Maastricht Treaty. On German insistence, Stage Two of the process, due to begin in 1994, will not look very different from the current situation. The Bundesbank in particular was unwilling to accept any gradual hand-over to new institutions, fearing a possible division of responsibility and consequent loss of monetary control. On the other hand, the Germans insisted on a long Stage Two because they wanted much more economic convergence among countries, in terms of inflation and government borrowing and debt, before union occurred in Stage Three. Meanwhile, countries like Italy and Spain fiercely resisted the idea of two or more speeds to Emu. Backed by the European Commission, they insisted that, as far as possible, everyone should enter Emu at the same time.

Those conditions together mean that nothing much is due to happen for a long time. Countries more eager for Emu, notably France and Italy, sought to counteract Emu's long incubation period by ensuring that the commitment to it was made final and binding now. That way, the train might move slowly but the passengers would be unable to get off. So they were bound to arrive at the destination eventually.

The quest for certainty via commitment was why the British and Danish opt-out clauses were so strongly resisted. Now, however, political developments in Germany could well mean that the Parliament refuses to ratify the Maastricht Treaty without reserving the right to reconsider the position in 1996. Should that happen, there will be no unconditional commitment. In effect, the decision on whether to have an Emu or not will simply have been pushed out four years or so, in spite of the efforts at Maastricht.

At this stage, the probability remains that Emu will take place eventually, though it is far from certain. If Germany insists on the literal application of the criteria for membership set down at Maastricht, that will ensure a two- or multi-speed system because it seems very unlikely that all current EMS countries will be able to meet the criteria this decade. Such insistence would also lead to a blazing political row because the government debt and borrowing provisions would certainly exclude Belgium and Italy, two countries most strongly supporting Emu. Germany, alone, will decide whether the criteria are applied literally because there is no Emu without her and the Germans, being happy with the Deutschemark, will not give it up unless they believe in the stability of whatever succeeds it. If Germany is uncompromising, France, which already meets all criteria for Emu, will then have to decide whether to go ahead with Germany, leaving out old allies. If those two countries hold together, Emu will happen, whoever else is in or out.

Although Emu is concerned with the co-ordination and eventual merging of monetary policies, many of the analytical issues come back to the role of fiscal policy, that is, the government's control over its tax and spending decisions. The optimal institutional arrangements for fiscal policy clearly depend on the monetary framework, but there is controversy on how far countries can, or should, retain complete fiscal autonomy after Emu.

While, in theory, it is possible to have a monetary union with fiscal autonomy, in practice, Emu will set up considerable pressures for a Euro-federal tax system. Any commitment to Emu should be in full awareness that, like the ERM itself, it will come to be seen and presented as a half-way house *en route* to a more satisfactory and stable end-point, namely a fully European economic policy. Indeed, the Germans, who are prepared to accept Emu only as part of a broader political union, no longer bother to disguise that point.

In the UK, a European political union has aroused fears of a rather bureaucratic, even 'socialistic', state - in terms of tax rates, welfare levels and degree of industrial regulation. Yet these fears are perhaps false or, at least, certainly exaggerated. If the United States and Sweden are regarded as the liberal and social democratic poles for fiscal and social policy in modern capitalism, it is arguable that a federal Europe will be driven inexorably towards the liberal, US, position compared with the current position of individual European countries. The sense of community will not be strong enough to support high taxes for cross-border transfers and the national elements of the tax and transfer system may be driven in a liberal direction by a continuing auction among tax regimes competing for mobile factors of production - capital or skilled labour. The more open the Union is to trade, immigration, or new members, the stronger those tendencies will be. Certainly, the 'social chapter' of the Maastricht Treaty is an attempt to resist 'regime competition' among countries with its liberalizing bias, but it is not very likely to succeed.

The road to Emu

Stretches back a long way...

The idea of a European economic and monetary union first came about 12 years after the Treaty of Rome was signed on 25 March 1957, founding the European

Economic Community (EEC). In December 1969, the EEC agreed to the eventual establishment of an economic and monetary union in Europe, but it could not agree a timetable. The Werner Report of 1970, which aimed to establish an economic and monetary union by 1980, foundered. The three conditions for Emu stated in the Werner Report were later reproduced in the Delors Report (1989). These are: the total and irreversible convertibility of currencies, the complete liberalization of capital transactions and full integration of banking and financial markets, and the elimination of margins of fluctuation and irrevocable locking of exchange rate parities.

The creation of the European Monetary Co-operation Fund (EMCF) came in 1974. It was created as a common-currency reserve to be used by the member central banks for foreign exchange market intervention at times of currency instability. The European monetary system (EMS), European exchange rate mechanism (ERM) and the European currency unit (Ecu), were established by a Resolution of the European Council in December 1978, and came into operation in March 1979. The original hope was that the EMS would develop rapidly within two years to see the creation of a European central bank, to be known as the European Monetary Fund (EMF). That hope, of course, was not realized. However, the exchange rate mechanism (ERM) of EMS has been successful in achieving its objective of greater exchange rate stability.

ERM: A half-way house and partial success

The external exchange rate link has greatly helped those countries with relatively high rates of inflation in gearing their fiscal and monetary policies to the objective of price stability. A high degree of convergence in inflation and nominal interest rates has already been achieved among EMS countries. The key mechanism in the disinflationary process in the ERM has been the tendency for the high inflation countries to undergo a rise in their real exchange rates, i.e. their exchange rates adjusted for movements in relative price levels. During the first half of the 1980s, successive devaluations of high inflation currencies more than offset their relative inflation differentials with Germany. However, in recent years, such devaluations have not fully offset inflation differentials. Though this disinflationary process has yielded inflation and nominal interest rate convergence, it has done so at the cost of higher unemployment. Now that Europe is in recession, with the inflationary consequences of German reunification keeping interest rates high, the system is coming in for increasing political criticism in some countries. The EMS has also served as the focal point for increased monetary policy co-ordination and has developed means by which member countries can monitor the relative stance of their monetary policy.

The new drive to Emu began in 1985 when the EC leaders reaffirmed their commitment to 'the progressive realization of Emu' in the Single European Act. The Single European Act represented the first significant revision of the Treaty of Rome. At the centre of the Act was the desire to fulfil the original EC vision of a common European market with free movement of goods, services, capital and people. A target deadline was set for 31 December 1992. Detailed measures for the removal of internal barriers were set out in a European Commission White Paper, *Completing the Internal Market*.

The three stages of Emu

The Report of the Committee for the Study of Economic and Monetary Union (the 'Delors Report') was published on 17 April 1989. The Delors report recommended a three-stage approach to Emu - and this remains at the core of the Maastricht Treaty.

During Stage One, all candidates for Emu should join the ERM and adopt the narrow 2.25 per cent currency band. The existing powers of the Committee of Central Bank Governors (CCBG) and the Council of Economic and Finance Ministers would be increased. Their present functions of co-ordinating economic and monetary policy would be enhanced to include greater policy surveillance of individual member countries. Though the CCBG would be free to express majority opinions, they could not impose them. During this period, all internal trade barriers would be dismantled, i.e. the '1992' reforms would be effected.

Stage Two was seen as a transitional one, during which the gradual change from co-ordinated national monetary policies to the implementation of a common monetary policy would be made. New institutions would be established. The CCBG would be transformed into the European System of Central Banks (ESCB). The existing 2.25 per cent bands in the ERM would be further narrowed and realignments only take place under exceptional circumstances

At the beginning of Stage Three, member countries would move to irrevocably-locked exchange rates and the national currencies would eventually be replaced by a single European currency. This would require the transition to a single European monetary policy under the control of the ESCB. All national foreign exchange reserves would be pooled, and the new ESCB would determine foreign exchange market intervention under the guidance of the Council of Finance Ministers (ECOFIN).

In 1989, Stage One of the Delors Report was agreed, with July 1990 set as its start date. Countries began a series of steps towards convergence.

Post-Delors momentum builds up

In January 1990, the Italian lira moved to the narrow 2.25 per cent band within the ERM, leaving only the Spanish peseta, which had joined the ERM in June 1989, on the wider 6 per cent band. Later, in May, Italy abolished its remaining exchange controls (ahead of the 1 July deadline), leaving only Spain, Portugal and Greece to remove theirs by 1992. That deadline may be extended until 1995.

In May 1990, Belgium announced that it was going to voluntarily maintain the Belgium franc within a narrower band against its central Deutschemark parity than the 2.25 per cent officially required by the ERM. The move followed the Dutch who, for some years, have maintained a voluntary 0.3 per cent band around their central Deutschemark parity.

In June 1990, Germany, the Netherlands, Belgium and France signed the Schengen Treaty which established a zone within which people could move without border controls. The Treaty, was important in demonstrating that some countries could meet the '1992' deadlines in advance, while others could not and thus it increased the prospect of a possible 'two-speed' Emu. Two of Schengen group, Netherlands and Belgium, are already essentially operating a fixed-exchange rate link with the Deutschemark.

In July 1990, Stage One of Delors began. Meanwhile, in September, the Bundesbank stated its views on Emu. As the current anchor of European monetary policy. the Bundesbank's views were influential. In essence, the Bundesbank wanted the new central bank to be modelled on itself. In the final stage of Emu, it was indispensable that the ECBS be obliged to pursue monetary stability and be independent at the institutional, functional and personal levels, from both national and EC influences. The ECSB must have sole control of external monetary policy, including exchange market intervention, and must not be obliged to extend credit to any public authority. The ECSB should have a council and an executive board; council members must be guaranteed their independence and a sufficiently long-term of office (without any possibility of dismissal).

The move to the final stage of Emu must be made only when inflation and price differences had been very largely eliminated, budget deficits had been reduced to tolerable levels, capital markets rates virtually harmonized, each member had been operating within the ERM for a sufficiently long period without capital controls, similar monetary policy instruments existed in all countries, and all the '1992' reforms had been realized in full. Most of these conditions were, indeed, incorporated into the Maastricht Treaty in some form.

On 8 October 1990, the UK became a full member of the ERM, joining the peseta on a 6 per cent band.

Also in October 1990, the Summit of Heads of State in Rome agreed to a 1 January 1994 start-date for Stage Two of the Delors plan for Emu, despite British opposition.

The Maastricht Treaty provisions

Further progress was made in the Maastricht Treaty agreed at the Summit in December 1991 - signed in March 1992, and currently awaiting ratification by member states. This must be completed by January 1993. The main provisions of the Treaty grew out of the Delors Report, influenced by the views of the Bundesbank. The key provisions are as follows:

An independent central bank à la Bundesbank

The ESCB will be set up, consisting of a European Central Bank (ECB) plus existing national central banks, each of which is to be independent of its government. The ECB will have an executive board and a governing council made up of the board plus national central bank governors. The board will have a president, vice president and four members elected for eight years, all independent of government. National governors must be appointed for at least five years and take instructions from the ECB, not member governments. The mandate of the ECB is price stability.

That all follows Bundesbank stipulations. However, the Treaty says that the Council of Finance Ministers can formulate "general exchange rate policy" after consulting the ECB. The ECB has day-to-day operation of the exchange rate policy and follows the general policy "without prejudice to price stability". That introduces an element of ECOFIN influence which the Bundesbank does not like.

Centralized controls on fiscal policy

The ECB is not to finance government deficits. States are to avoid 'excessive' deficits and these are to be monitored by the EC Commission and penalized by sanctions. Fines can be levied if a 2/3 weighted vote of the EC Council agrees (the vote excluding the country concerned). 'Excessive' relates planned and actual general government deficits and their direction of change to certain benchmarks. The benchmarks are deficits of 3 per cent of GDP and general government debt of 60 per cent of GDP. The treaty thus re-introduces binding constraints on national fiscal policy.

Start-date for Stage Two is confirmed as January 1994. The definition of the Ecu is frozen then and fixed for Stage Three. A European Monetary Institute (EMI) will be set up, taking over from the EMCF. It can hold reserves for member central banks, but will have no influence over policy until it is superseded by the ECB, at the start of Stage Three. The location of the EMI, and by implication the ECB, will be decided by the end of 1992. Amsterdam, Copenhagen and Madrid have all been proposed. The British are trying to insist on London, but the Germans may well hold out for Frankfurt.

Countries must meet convergence criteria

To qualify for Stage Three, a country must meet the convergence criteria. Those will be monitored by the EC Commission and the EMI. The criteria are:

- price inflation not more than 1 1/2 per cent above the average of the three lowest-inflation countries

- long-term interest rates not more than 2 per cent above the average of the three lowest for at least one year
- exchange rate in ERM narrow bands with no realignments for at least two years
- government financial position not 'excessive' as defined by the EC Council (see above).

All before the end of the century

The EC Council is to decide, by qualified majority, who is eligible by December 1996, and whether to go ahead with Emu. If no date is set by the end of 1997, Emu begins, in any case, in January 1999 and the Council decides by July 1999 who is in, and who needs a derogation. If even two countries wish to go ahead, they cannot be blocked by the others at that point.

Political problems on the road from Maastricht

As noted in the introduction, the idea behind this final stipulation was to make Emu a certainty, even if long-delayed. There is no doubt, either, that countries interpreted the convergence criteria broadly. Countries like Italy and Belgium took comfort in the fact that the Maastricht Treaty referred to the "direction of change" as well as the level of deficits and debt. Comments by German and other politicians encouraged them to believe the requirement need not be taken literally so long as they were moving in the right direction. With debt above 100 per cent of GDP, neither Belgium nor Italy could meet the criteria and Ireland would also be in acute difficulties.

Political discussion in Germany, however, has taken a pronounced turn since the Treaty signing. The public has woken up with apprehension to the idea of losing their 'lovely Deutschemark'. Germany stands to gain relatively little from Emu and it was always seen as a quid pro quo for political union. Germany wishes to exercise a political weight in the world commensurate with its economic power. But it wishes to do so without re-awakening fears, inside and outside the country, of resurgent nationalism. A European Union is seen as the means. Putting it crudely, Germany will give away seats on the Bundesbank council, thereby internationalizing its monetary policy, in return for France and the UK internationalizing their seats on the UN Security Council by merging their foreign policy in a European Union. (The French are ready to accept that; the British do not think they are).

German opinion now is that Chancellor Kohl did not get enough in negotiations on political union to make monetary union worthwhile unless it is entirely on German terms. Yet the snag is that, if the Parliament ratifies Maastricht as the Treaty stands, it loses control of the process. There are convergence criteria, but they are to be administered by the EC and EMI. And the Germans do not trust those bodies to apply sufficient rigour. It is feared that admitting countries with loose fiscal regimes could put excessive pressure on even an independent ECB, and accelerate inflation.

Hence the Social Democrats, who control the German Upper House, are insisting on the right to review the situation in 1996 - in effect another opt-out clause. They will probably get their way. Meanwhile, other voices, in the Bundesbank and elsewhere, are insisting on the literal application of the convergence criteria. All this clearly undermines the certainty which Maastricht tried to cement into the Emu process and leaves it needing another boost to its momentum. Events also threaten a spectacular political row in the future, with countries like Belgium and Italy resisting strict application of debt and deficit criteria, and consequent volatility in interest rate spreads as the political discussion fluctuates.

There are economic problems, too...

While the political problems are paramount, there are also economic difficulties. These stem from the use of over-valued exchange rates to depress activity and lower inflation. Unless inflation in any country following that path can be driven down below the rate ruling in Germany, thus allowing the country to slowly regain competitiveness, it will pay for its low inflation with high unemployment. The European countries have shown themselves ready to pay that price but the problems are being exacerbated by German unification which will keep interest rates high for some years, despite slow growth elsewhere in Europe.

Moreover, in some countries, the trade and current account deficits - lasting even during stagnation or recession - suggest the exchange rate is seriously over-valued. They may wish to realign before locking into Emu and, in any case, the market will suspect them of wanting to. The Maastricht Treaty, by specifying no realignments for two years before Emu, in effect puts a devaluation deadline at the end of 1994. Countries like Italy, Spain and UK (unless their circumstances change considerably in the interim) are likely to face massive speculative pressure on their currencies as the deadline approaches.

What do all these problems amount to? The odds remain that Emu will take place, though it is not certain. It depends on the French and Germans hanging together, with the French ready to pay the political price for monetary unification on German terms. It is too early to say exactly what convergence criteria will be imposed. France and Germany will certainly qualify, with Denmark and the UK doing so if they choose (though the political will in both countries is not consistently firm). The Netherlands will almost surely make it, with continued budget stringency as, too, will Spain, with a continued restrictive monetary policy in order to throttle inflation (again assuming political will holds out through more years of rigour). Belgium, Ireland and Italy are special cases in that the political will is not in doubt and they each qualify according to most criteria, while failing by miles on at least one. They represent the political 'hard cases'. (Luxembourg qualifies, but is in a currency union with Belgium). Austria and the outside Scandinavian countries can get into EC and qualify, though it is doubtful if they would be allowed to 'leap-frog' existing members like Belgium. The other existing EC members, Greece and Portugal, do not look likely to make the first wave, though the Portuguese could surprise.

It is unlikely that there will be an Emu without a 'final' quite large realignment, involving three or four countries, which could occur during 1993.

What will Emu look like?

Emu will set up pressures for a federal European state, both because that is its logic and because the Germans are likely to insist on it. Two questions dominate discussion of this outcome: First, how much freedom of fiscal policy action will individual states have within the union; will they have autonomy or will there be over-arching federal fiscal policy? Second, what will be the nature of this union; will it be closed, bureaucratic and social democratic, or will it be more open, liberal and free market?

A federal structure

Movement towards monetary union implies a progressive loss of national control over monetary policy. If the union is credible, and there are no barriers to trade in financial instruments, this will lead to interest rate equalization between the different financial centres. Ultimately, neither interest nor exchange rates are available as policy instruments. This means that adjustments to economic shocks, which might otherwise have been made relatively quickly and easily through the exchange rate, have to be made through changes in wages and other prices, which tend to be slow and painful.

In the long run, there is little that fiscal (or, for that matter, monetary) policy-makers can do to avoid adjustments to permanent real shocks, such as the decline of whole industries under the impact of technical change. One way or another, relative prices must change, the economy must adapt and that is that. The most the tax authorities can ever do is to smooth the effects out over time, preventing them from becoming too painful. In addition, policy can, in principle (though the practice is very difficult), smooth out the impact of temporary shocks, reducing the amplitude of the business cycle. But if monetary policy is dictated by a European central bank with a wider responsibility, this leaves fiscal policy as the only way for a national government to manage economic disturbances in its own country. That is the basic proposition which lies at the heart of the debate over the role of fiscal policy in the new Europe.

Puts the spotlight on fiscal policy...

There are various possibilities for the organization of fiscal policy in a monetary union. At one extreme, national fiscal authorities would have full constitutional autonomy but with the potential for international co-operation. At the other extreme, there would be a federal fiscal authority with minimal national autonomy and with automatic fiscal transfers through a unified tax structure, as in the United States. The Maastricht Treaty proposes a half-way house with national authorities doing most taxing and spending, subject to the harmonization of some tax rates, and with a relatively small amount of expenditure earmarked for, and spent at, the federal level; however there would be guidelines or constraints on national authorities set by a central authority.

The relative advantages of different systems depend on four considerations:

- *Symmetry*: how similar are the European economies in terms of production and consumption and so how susceptible are they to differentiated cycles or shocks; and are they converging?
- *Product market integration*: will the growth of intra-community trade dilute the effect of national policies ?
- *Labour mobility*: how far can it acceptably harmonize unemployment rates within the community?
- *Capital mobility*: how will interest rate equalization affect fiscal policy and finance?

Symmetry - a receding ideal

Symmetric disturbances, those which affect all countries in the system equally, can be adequately addressed by a common monetary or fiscal policy. Indeed, if the system were entirely symmetric, with all European economies being similar and sharing a general agreement about the relative costs of inflation and unemployment, all policy-makers would always agree on the appropriate policy stance and there would be no need for independent national fiscal policies. By the same token, asymmetry of one form or another is necessary to sustain arguments for autonomous national fiscal policy or federal transfers. Generalizing this argument, the greater the differences among countries, the greater the need for such policies.

The European Commission has argued that increasing economic linkages among the European countries will render them more and more alike. Symmetry will increase, and the need for differentiated fiscal policy will thereby diminish. Empirical work by Peter Spencer at Lehman Brothers, however, casts grave doubt on the Commission's proposition.

Traditional trade theory states that, when trade barriers between countries are removed, goods arbitrage tends to harmonize relative prices. Countries then tend to specialize in production according to their resource base and comparative advantage and production patterns in individual countries tend to diverge. Specialization destroys symmetry. However, much of the growth in trade has been intra-industry, the trade of similar manufactures between developed countries, which has expanded as barriers have come down. As a result, modern trade theories tend to emphasize the scope for specialization within sectors like manufacturing, which is due to the potential for economies of scale in production and the demand for variety in consumption, and to play down specialization across sectors.

The European Commission has naturally made great play of this point and the gains from trade in manufacturing which it implies. This is essentially the basis of the Ceccini Report on the benefits of the 1992 process. It is also the basis of the Commission's recent assertion (in Chapter 6 of its recent report, *One Market One Money*) that "economic integration will make the occurrence of country-specific shocks less likely since product differentiation tends to dominate product specialization".

The evidence does not support that assertion. The Commission's own empirical research is quite inconclusive while Spencer's work points in the other direction. He measured the degree of statistical similarity between the sectoral composition of GDP in different countries in 1979 (as the ERM started life) and compared this with the same measure for 1986 (the most recent date for which consistent data is available).

For the original ERM members, the ones which were most highly-developed and most likely to experience intra-industry specialization, he found that the production similarity index fell: from 91 (per cent) in 1979, to 88 in 1986. For the community as a whole, the index fell from 82 to 79. In other words, although intra-industry specialization may have taken place, sectoral specialization has also been significant, tending to make economies less similar.

A second set of tests measured the degree of similarity among relative price structures in different countries, at any point in time, using the detailed data used by the OECD to construct their purchasing power parity (PPP) measures. This raw data yields a series of different PPP exchange rates for different commodity groups. Comparisons of these structures between different European countries (using US prices as the benchmark) then gives a similarity index showing the degree of price harmonization. The data is available for 1980 and 1985 and shows a clear trend toward relative price harmonization in the community, with the highest degree of convergence in the core countries. The degree of convergence was much higher within Europe than between Europe, the US and Japan, and there was a high degree of harmonization in the service sector (excluding housing and telecommunications).

Product market integration favours fiscal federation

Where are these tendencies taking Europe? Imagine a fully-integrated European market, in which trade equalizes post-tax single-currency prices of most products throughout the region. It then follows from a basic theorem of international trade theory that, under competitive market conditions, this will also tend to harmonize the prices of immobile resources such as land and labour, and hence prices of non-traded goods and services such as housing. The idea behind this theory is that countries with exceptional endowments of land or other immobile factors of production will tend to export these resources indirectly through land-intensive items such as agricultural products.

In this hypothetical situation of complete integration, national output is determined on the supply side of the economy and changes in fiscal policy and other demand-side influences spill over into trade with other countries and are just reflected in the national current account. Similarly, capital market integration means that debt finance is reflected one-for-one in the capital account of the balance of payments. Unemployment could still occur if wages were slow to adjust but, with output impervious to fiscal policy, there would be little the national authorities could do about the situation. This makes a powerful argument for a centralized federal fiscal policy.

The tendency towards product market integration with sectoral specialization on the supply-side means there is no reason to think Europe is about to become an 'optimal currency area'. Differentiated shocks will remain possible. Differentiated fiscal policy will therefore remain necessary, despite Commission statements to the contrary.

Yet measures to influence demand within the region whose production has been affected by a shock, will be increasingly ineffective as integration proceeds. That implies that the differentiated fiscal response should be via balancing fiscal flows and regional policy within a more thorough-going federal system rather than via a national authority. Such a conclusion is probably correct on balance, but note that the fully-integrated situation is not yet with us and remains an extreme model for the future. In particular, closed-economy Keynesian characteristics are likely to remain in sectors which are impervious to trade, leaving some role for a national public expenditure policy which is targeted at the products of such sectors.

Cultural factors limit labour mobility

A degree of labour force immobility is also necessary to sustain arguments for both national and federal approaches. Otherwise, adverse economic shocks in any one sector or region will be reflected in outward migration, rather than structural unemployment, without any need for a regional stimulus. Even where this is physically possible, however, it may well be culturally or socially unacceptable. The preservation of regional communities and cultures is a legitimate aim of policy, particularly in the cultural and linguistic patchwork of Europe.

Capital mobility favours fiscal policy

Monetary union and capital mobility have other, more direct, implications for fiscal policy. The equalization of interest rates means that national fiscal authorities will find it possible to borrow much larger sums of money than they could in their national currencies, without pushing interest rates up unduly. In the absence of complete product market integration, this gives national authorities greater leverage over output and employment because it means that deficit spending no longer crowds out private spending through rising interest rates. Indeed, a regime of fixed-exchange and interest rates is the one in which national fiscal policy is most powerful, since the standard multiplier effects on demand can then work unhindered by the side-effects of high exchange and interest rates which occur in floating-exchange rate systems.

The authors of the Delors report regarded the attenuation of the interest rate effect as a bad thing, encouraging laxity in fiscal policy at the national level, which they argued would mean an excessively high interest rates at the European level. They suggested that there should be constraints on national deficits to prevent this happening. This recommendation has been opposed by politicians and academics, but has resulted in the fiscal pre-conditions for Emu set out in the Maastricht Treaty.

The argument for controls has several strands. The first is that financial markets mis-price risk. Their risk assessment of sovereign borrowers tends to be inadequate and there are periods of over-lending followed, eventually, by periods of credit contraction in which borrowers cannot obtain finance at any price. The markets thus cannot be relied upon smoothly to keep a check on government borrowing by steeply increasing the risk premiums on the Ecu debt of a heavily-indebted country. This is true even though the European central bank is to be truly independent and therefore not supposed to bail-out an indebted government by money creation.

Moreover, some analysts worry that a 'no bail-out' clause in the ECB's constitution would never be entirely credible because no monetary authority could stand by while a member government defaulted, endangering the European financial system. Those particular concerns seem over-blown, but the conclusion remains that the markets alone would not restrain excessive government borrowing until too late.

The second strand in the argument is that expansionary fiscal policies put up the cost of borrowing for other countries, by raising Ecu interest rates generally and that these financial spill-over effects must be taken into account by a central authority if the best combination of national policies is to be attained. Governments acting individually would reason as follows: 'Country *X* is borrowing heavily, pushing up interest rates and the cost of finance, whatever we do; fiscal rectitude earns us no reward in the form of lower interest rates, so we may as well spend more ourselves to counteract the effect on our economy of high interest rates; our own interest rates will not rise much in consequence'. There are already signs of such an effect as countries like UK and France begin to borrow and spend more in ERM in the face of high interest rates in Germany, where fiscal policy is expansionary.

The arguments for international co-ordination of fiscal policy, backed up by possible sanctions, are therefore persuasive in principle, though it is not clear how empirically important adverse fiscal spill-overs would be. It seems unlikely that any European country would go on a rakes' progress to insolvency and then blackmail the ECB to bail it out by threatening to default and bring down the banking system. Given the degree of integration in world capital markets, it is also doubtful if Ecu-borrowing by one country would raise Ecu interest rates of other governments' debt all that much. (German reunification makes for an exception because it affects the largest country in the system and has driven it to a fiscal policy that is enormously more expansionary than it would ever have contemplated otherwise.) Moreover, countries can already borrow in overseas currencies at the world interest rate, and some small community countries like Belgium and Ireland have made extensive use of this facility. So a move to a single currency does not change their situation very much. They can avoid the exchange risk associated with foreign currency borrowing at present (though, in principle, that risk is less for a government which can, after all, control its own monetary policy and therefore its exchange rate), but monetary union actually removes a domestic currency financing option. So there is little reason to think they would borrow more than they have in the past.

One should conclude that capital-market integration makes a strong case in principle for co-ordination of national fiscal policies backed up by the possibility of sanctions from the centre - just as national governments generally keep the power to restrain the access of local or regional authorities to the capital market. Emu would almost certainly be workable in the absence of such central sanctions or control, but could well be associated with too-high levels of public borrowing in that case.

Federation versus national autonomy

The balance of argument, given that capital market integration is a reality and increasing product market integration is in prospect, seems to favour a federal fiscal system. Federal systems having a larger, more diverse, tax base can more readily transfer resources from one region to another, depending on variations in relative income. National systems do make inter-regional transfers but, if all regions are in the same condition, they must attempt to transfer resources from one generation to another through variations in tax rates and public debt over time, which is much more difficult.

The difference between these two systems can be shown in terms of a specific case. Suppose that there is a surge in demand for capital goods in the Community, due to investment in Eastern Europe for example. This would naturally fall most heavily upon German producers, although investment goods industries in other countries such as France would also tend to benefit. A uniform tightening of monetary policy, designed to head off the inflationary demand pressure, would tend to leave Germany with an overheating problem and France with unemployment.

A federal tax and benefit system would automatically cushion these effects - raising extra tax revenue in Germany and paying it out, in the form of higher social security benefits, in France. Barry Eichengreen, the US economic historian who has studied the effects of monetary union in the US, estimates that the US federal system, despite its relatively low profile, automatically offsets about 40 per cent of swings in regional income and output.

Now suppose that separate national tax systems are in place, with similar tax rates for simplicity. Tax revenues increase in Germany, as before, but then are used to redeem German bond issues rather than being handed over to the French authorities. If the German population is unaware of these debt repayments, and the fall in future interest payments and taxes that they imply, then the macroeconomic effects will resemble those under the federal system. But, if the Germans realize that future taxes will be lower and lifetime disposable incomes higher than they would in a federal system, then they will tend to spend more and save less than in such a system. *Per contra*, lifetime disposal incomes and spending will tend to be lower in France than in a federal system. So, depending upon the degree of foresight in the system, national systems will tend to be less effective at offsetting regional swings.

Moreover, differential tax and benefit rates are likely to have adverse supply side effects if capital and labour are mobile. It is generally recognized that adverse supply side effects can lead to fiscal instability in a decentralized system with a high degree of factor mobility. This occurs when high relative tax rates reduce the tax base and cause tax rates to spiral upwards. The situation in which New York found itself during the 1970s gives an excellent example of such a spiral, and suggests that it is extremely difficult to arrest this kind of process without some sort of federal bail-out. This point is naturally stressed by the opponents of national fiscal policy.

A major drawback of the federal system concerns local democracy and accountability. Local taxation brings the costs of local spending home to voters, whereas federal taxation systems encourage pork-barrel politics. Local systems also allow for local discretion, whereas federal systems tend to work through automatic stabilizers. Political resistance to fiscal federalism thus remains strong, particularly among the more-favoured countries which expect to be providing, rather than receiving, most of the transfers. Nonetheless, one can reasonably believe that, if Emu takes place, the logic of the situation will dictate in favour of an increasing federal element in public finance and fiscal policy. That fact will, however, feed back on, and influence, the nature of the federation.

The drive to Emu has political motivation

If monetary union implies federal taxes and transfers, it implies, or ought to imply at least, a step in the direction of federal government - towards a 'United States of Europe'. That, of course, is precisely the intention of many who support Emu. They view it not as a technical notion, aimed simply at improving the material living standards of the majority of people living in the current EC; they see it as part of a political programme, with political objectives. If the economic arguments are inconclusive or finely balanced, that will be viewed by the federalists as a reason to go ahead, not as a reason to hesitate.

That attitude is certainly held by the French government. The French are preoccupied with the shape of a Europe in which a reunified Germany is economically dominant, while Soviet power is in eclipse. In a rather Gallic way, the complete opposite of English empiricism or muddling through, the French have thought intensively about their response to this situation and have come up with a grand strategy: They wish to cement their own ties with Germany, and bind that country into a European political structure. Thereby, they hope to abolish the possibility of resurgent German nationalism and renewed conflict.

The strategy may be rationally derived, but it is reinforced by the historical memories of over a century of conflict with a German state growing relatively more powerful all the time. The *entente cordiale* with the United Kingdom proved an inadequate counterweight. The French commitment to closer European integration is therefore great. At present, this finds its echo in important elements of the German government. Franco-German discussions before German unification led to a deal being struck. President Mitterand withdraw all his reservations about German unity and adopted a positive position in the Four Power Talks. The quid pro quo was that a unified Germany would accept, indeed promote, steps to European unity.

The German government feels itself bound by this agreement but, in any case, it coincides with the preferences of a number of leading personalities, notably Hans Dietrich Genscher, the former foreign minister. Many Germans note, with bemusement, the concern that some of their neighbours clearly feel about resurgent German power - but they are generally keen to allay the concerns. However, the fiscal burdens of unification are leading to disgruntlement among the German population and a reduced willingness to foot the bill for Europe. This feeling will inhibit the growth of the EC budget, as the Germans are indeed the principal paymasters and it could yet obstruct the path to Emu.

Beyond the perceived need to lock-in the new Germany, there is some support for European federalism on chauvinistic grounds. No European country, it is held, can be an economic great power like the United States, or even Japan.

But the EC, viewed as a whole, would be second to none. It would have a central role in determining the world financial arrangements. Obviously, that is an argument that appeals mainly to politicians, but then, the negotiations over Emu *are* among politicians and will remain so, unless popular discontent grows enough to break in. Support for the extreme Right in Europe, notable J-M Le Pen's party in France, provides a barometer for this risk.

Why UK attitudes are untypical

In the United Kingdom, there is a less lively concern about anchoring the Germans into Western Europe. Moreover, there has been more concern about the sacrifice of political sovereignty implicit in Emu. This is not because of any innate chauvinism on the part of the British, nor is it simple insularity; it is a consequence of the British electoral system. In Europe, all senior politicians are used to living with coalitions, to horse-trading over programmes and taking part in governments in which they never get all their own way. These things are facts of life in electoral systems characterized by some form of proportional representation and a multiplicity of parties. Little cultural change is implied when the politicians do exactly the same things at a supranational level.

In the UK, on the other hand, the first-past-the-post electoral system leads to single-party governments that sometimes have the aim, and ability, to make sweeping legislative changes without much negotiation. The restraints on national power implied by Emu are therefore more keenly felt.

The British system implies pendulum swings between parties that often adopt more ideological or extreme positions than their continental analogues. Any ideologist or 'conviction' politician who sees a realistic prospect of being able to implement his or her entire programme is naturally concerned about being forced towards some sort of European average. Concern about 'sovereignty' among British politicians is therefore positively associated with (1) their extremism and (2) their prospects of electoral success. It is therefore understandable that the Liberal Democrats, who are both centrist and have no realistic chance of office, should be Emu-enthusiasts. Equally, it is unsurprising that Mrs Thatcher, who was on the right wing of the Conservative party, and who was very successful electorally, should have been most concerned about 'sovereignty'.

The fading electoral popularity of the Conservatives between 1988 and 1992 led them to edge towards a more centrist political position under a new leader. Their concern about sovereignty diminished accordingly. The opposition Labour Party similarly moved towards a more pro- European stance as it became more centrist in pursuit of votes. Labour's enthusiasm for Europe increased as the Thatcher revolution unfolded in the UK. Mrs Thatcher's government moved UK social policy towards the United States model and away from the previous welfarism consensus. Compared to what was happening in the UK, social policy in most European countries and in the Community began to look quite 'social democratic'. Examples are the 'social chapter' of the Maastricht Treaty (rejected by the Conservatives), and the German practice of having obligatory workers' representatives on company boards. Despairing of 'socialism in one country', Labour began to see the Community as the most likely political framework in which to achieve a more social-democratic social policy.

Political characteristics of a European federal system

In fact, consideration of what a future United States of Europe might look like, suggests that Labour may be mistaken in this. It is quite possible that the development of the European Community in becoming a common-currency area, together with its widening to include other states, will lead to a breakdown of the social democratic consensus and a move towards economic and social liberalism (in the European sense of the word). If Europe comes to resemble the United States a little more in terms of having federal political arrangements and a common currency, it will probably come to resemble it more in terms of social policy and attitudes. Ironically, the 'Thatcherites' may have less to fear from a united Europe in the longer run than the 'social democrats'.

The essence of a social democratic or welfare-state policy is that relatively high levels of progressive taxation are levied to provide income support or a safety net for the least-fortunate, and to provide a high level of public services. These taxes and transfers have been found most tolerable and sustainable in relatively homogeneous, societies where the degree of identification with fellow citizens is high. (The origins of the welfare state, in Bismarck's Germany was in the nation-building process at the time of the first German unification). The most comprehensive social democracies have been in small countries like Sweden and, formerly, the Netherlands.

Such a system never became established in the United States, not only because the country is large and diverse, but also because its population has always been fed by immigration. It is hard to get the prosperous to agree to underwrite the living standards of the poor if the commitment is open-ended, due to mass migration.

Europe will not long remain social democratic, therefore, if its borders remain open and a liberal immigration policy is in force. The Schengen group of countries, who have agreed to unify their border controls, implicitly accepted that point by initially excluding Italy on the grounds that its control of immigrants from outside the EC was not tight enough.

There may, nonetheless, be problems if the EC is truly open to new member states, as many are urging. It is one thing to ask German burghers to make transfer payments to Portuguese small holders, but to ask them to extend the same to unemployed Poles, Czechs or whoever else may apply for membership, is surely to ask too much. The bigger and more open the Community becomes, therefore, the more politically difficult it is likely to be to maintain high levels of social provision.

Yet liberalizing forces will be at work even with a closed EC, with restricted membership, though they would be weaker than in the open-arms case. The integration of Europe will put together, in the same system, people whose sense of kinship and mutual responsibility is weaker than in the old nation states. The political difficulty is evident to Jacques Delors at least. He has decided that lobbying for larger cross-border transfer flows to compensate for the loss of the exchange rate instrument is politically ill-advised. Clearly, he does not believe the political will exists for cross-border transfers on anything like the scale of existing inter-regional transfers within nation states. Accordingly, he has tried to reduce the expectations of the Southern European countries in this regard. The Spaniards held out for more 'solidarity' funds at Maastricht. Other countries, such as Germany and Belgium, signed the post-dated cheque readily enough, but are now complaining about Mr Delors' most recent budget plan that seeks to give effect to what was promised at Maastricht.

But if social democracy cannot go supra-national, cannot it persist at the national level within the EC and currency union? Probably it can, but even there, liberalizing tendencies will exist. The free movement of labour and capital will tend to undermine the welfare state in any member country that has higher taxes and more comprehensive income support systems than average. There will be some tendency for equalization of provision.

The Commission's strategy in this area so far has been to try and 'level up' rather than accept levelling down, by requiring all countries to meet certain standards in terms of minimum wages, welfare provisions and conditions of work. That is the point of the social chapter. In that way, they hope to avoid 'social competition'. However, the lower-income countries with high unemployment will be uneasy about not being able to attract capital to take advantage of lower labour costs. Some competition is absolutely necessary for economic efficiency. Moreover, EC governments, if they collude to maintain the level of tax and welfare provision, will be in the same position as any cartel - vulnerable to anyone breaking ranks and bidding to increase market share by charging lower prices - or, in this case, attracting footloose capital with a lower tax-subsidy system. It will be difficult for countries to avoid, in the long run, having their tax rates bid down to the level of the most liberal countries in the system - a sort of competitive solution.

That will be true for taxes on any footloose factor, so it will be true of capital taxation. But labour, especially skilled labour, is mobile to an increasing extent and it is also a complement to capital anyway. So there is likely to be downward pressure at least on the the higher marginal income tax rates applying to the more skilled and generally mobile workers.

If socialism in one country is no longer on anyone's agenda, it is quite unlikely that a large open European Community will provide a very secure basis for a form of social democracy. Only a 'fortress Europe' which excludes new members would have any chance of doing so. The British Conservatives and others on the political right who insist that the EC and monetary union must be open to all European states in due course, are therefore being shrewd in the pursuit of their social preferences.

Chapter

8

The economic effects of

German unification

- two years on

Dr. Werner Becker
Deutsche Bank Research

Note: In general text, the abbreviation 'Dm' is used to denote the Deutschemark. Elsewhere, the international mnemonic 'DEM' is used.

The challenge of GEMU

German Monetary and Economic Union (GEMU) in mid-1990, was a milestone on the road towards the political unification of Germany, a process which was completed on 3 October 1990 with the accession of the five new Federal states - the former GDR - to the Federal Republic of Germany. Unification was not an isolated national event, but took place in the context of the profound political and economic change in the former eastern bloc countries in the late 80s. It was also firmly embedded in the framework of the EC.

Key elements of the monetary union were the introduction of the Deutschemark as sole legal tender in east Germany (replacing the inconvertible Ostmark), the transfer of full responsibility for monetary policy from the Staatsbank to the Deutsche Bundesbank, as well as the fixing of the conversion rate between the Deutschemark and the Ostmark. In parallel, an economic union was established, i.e. east Germany also adopted the fully-fledged (legal) framework of the smoothly-functioning social market economy of west Germany.

Basically, the rapid introduction of GEMU contrasts with traditional economic wisdom and theory. For example, the GEMU approach runs counter to the theory of optimum-currency areas. The tremendous divergence in terms of economic systems and structures, as well as of productivity and living standards, would have suggested employing a gradual approach towards convertibility of the Ostmark through phased plans, with German monetary union as the crowning achievement of the process. Such a procedure would have provided the exchange rate as a valve to alleviate adjustment pressures. It was, however, based on the assumption of the persistence of two German states - ignoring the historical opportunity to achieve unification.

In the mean time, it is widely acknowledged that the rapid implementation of GEMU was the right decision at that time for political and economic reasons. There was no genuine political alternative, because the residents of the former GDR expressed their deep-rooted distrust in the viability of a 'home-made' transition from the socialist system to a market economy, by massive migration to west Germany. Another clear signal was the famous slogan of the Leipzig demonstrations in early 1990: "If the Deutschemark does not come to us, we will go to the Deutschemark!" The continued lack of a substantially-improved outlook in East Germany could easily have led to unabated migration to the west, and increasing economic and social tensions in both parts of Germany.

GEMU also proved to be useful in economic terms, by avoiding the inherent risks of a time-consuming transition process within the framework of the former GDR. Given the fact that the state of the east German economy was much more desolate than initially expected, a gradual approach would not have worked without the creation of new protective economic walls between east and west Germany, including strict border controls. East German companies would not have been competitive on international markets at any exchange rate, and not even at very low prices, because of their outmoded and unattractive range of products (e.g. Trabant cars). On the other hand, the rapid introduction of GEMU had the advantage of giving east German companies and households immediate access to a fully-convertible currency, thus supporting confidence in a better future and providing full availability of western-style goods and services. Furthermore, a reliable legal framework for the establishment of the market economy laid the groundwork for entrepreneurial initiative in East Germany and the inflow of private capital urgently needed to restructure the desolate economy.

For the east German economy, the challenge of unification resulted in a fundamental, and painful, adjustment process. The transition to a market economy was initially - in 1990/91 - associated with a deep slump in industrial production; unemployment increased substantially, but there has also been - through massive public transfers from the west - a rising standard of living in east Germany. On the other hand, and in contrast to initial expectations, GEMU is also having a strong impact on the west German economy. The western 'big brother' has not only had to shoulder the burden of massive public transfer payments, but has also benefited substantially from the strong economic impulses of unification.

Despite the creation of GEMU, there are still two different economic areas in Germany, with different degrees of dynamism and a substantially higher level of productivity and standard of living being enjoyed in the west. However, the process of growing-together economically and the approximation of wages and income to west German levels is well under way, two years after the start of GEMU.

Against this background, several questions need to be addressed:

- What are the monetary and economic implications of unification, two years after the fact?
- To what extent are they influencing the prospects of German growth, interest rates and the Deutschemark exchange rate?
- Is Germany able to manage the historical challenge of unification in a manner that will preserve market confidence?
- What is the international impact of GEMU, especially in Europe?

Monetary implications of GEMU

Monetary policy in an enlarged Deutschemark area

The extension of the currency area of the Deutschemark to east Germany was managed, by the Deutsche Bundesbank, without any serious disruptions in the money, capital and foreign exchange markets. It involved a variety of technical and practical problems in the implementation of monetary policy in an enlarged

Deutschemark area. One important issue was the fixing of the conversion rate between the Deutschemark and the Ostmark (M). In this context, neither the inadequate statistical data of the former GDR, nor the various official exchange rates and the strongly-fluctuating free market rates of the Ostmark, provided economically-reliable clues. In the end, multiple conversion rates were set by a political decision (e.g. recurring payments like wages, rents etc. at a rate of 1:1; also savings accounts, depending on the account holder's age, to maximum amounts of M 2000, M 4000 and M 6000; all other assets and liabilities at a rate of M 2:Dm 1; the average conversion rate was M 1.8:Dm 1).

Another issue was that of the technicalities involved in the introduction of the Deutschemark in east Germany. Before the start of GEMU on 1 July 1990, the Bundesbank set up a 'provisional administrative office' in Berlin, with 15 branches in the former GDR, to take care of the technical aspects of monetary union. The conversion of Ostmarks into Deutschemarks was carried out only via bank accounts - around 24 million bank accounts were converted at the beginning of July. In order to supply the 16 million east German residents with an initial stock of currency, the Bundesbank provided Dm 28bn, in coinage and notes.

Currency conversion in east Germany resulted in a one-off increase in Deutschemark money supply, M3[1], of Dm 180bn, or 15 per cent. This exceeded the relationship between the former GDR production-potential and that of west Germany at the time (approximately 10 per cent). Initially, this has not resulted in inflationary problems, because a portfolio adjustment has been under way in east Germany and monetary wealth-formation has increased disproportionately, i.e. bank clients' assets - mostly in the form of savings deposits (which are included in M3) - have been replaced by the purchase of securities or other forms of long-term saving, which are not included in M3. In mid-1991, for the first time since the announcement of official money supply targets had been introduced in 1974, the Bundesbank revised its money supply target (from 4-6 per cent to 3-5 per cent) during the course of a year. This was attributable to the fact that the monetary adjustment process in east Germany was taking place more quickly than had originally been expected. Another factor in this context was the fact that the production-potential of east Germany - and therefore the basis for assessing an adequate money supply target - had initially been overestimated.

The conduct of monetary policy in East Germany was, in principle, based on the same instruments and techniques as in the West. However, during the initial phase of GEMU the rudimentary character of the East German banking system

[1] *M3 comprises currency in circulation, domestic banks' sight deposits, time deposits with less than 4-years' maturity and savings deposits at statutory notice*

had to be taken into account. For instance, trade bills eligible for re-discount, or marketable securities that might serve as a basis for repurchase agreements of Lombard loans, were not initially available at east German banks. Therefore, the Bundesbank granted them so-called refinancing quotas which - in contrast to traditional re-discount credit - could be utilized not only on the basis of trade bills, but also on the basis of bank promissory notes. Banks in east Germany were also allowed to submit bank promissory notes as collateral for Lombard credit. These special refinancing facilities had been gradually abolished by mid-1992. The central bank's funding of banks in east Germany is, therefore, now on the same footing as for banks in the west.

The implementation of monetary policy has been going hand-in-hand with the development of an efficient two-tier banking system in the east. Since the beginning of GEMU, the integration of east German banks has made rapid progress. West German banks, including their associations, undertook an immense effort in terms of investment, retraining and advisory services, in order to establish a universal banking system in east Germany, similar to that of the west, encompassing private banks, co-operative and savings banks, as well as a wide range of special banks. At the end of 1991, about 500 banks were operating in the east, with around 6000 branches (in comparison to west Germany, where there were 4000 banks with 43,400 branches). However, the number of branches per capita is substantially lower than in the over-banked west German market. Nevertheless, the quality of bank services in east Germany has been substantially improved since the beginning of GEMU and is already matching western standards. All in all, the Bundesbank successfully managed the transitional problems of monetary policy in the enlarged currency area.

Monetary policy and inflation performance

There had been strong sentiment, above-all abroad, that the introduction of GEMU would be inflationary because of the expansionary effects of the very high budget deficits caused by the tremendous public transfers to the east and the related spending spree of east German consumers. Given the fact that more than 90 per cent (1991) of the all-German productive potential is located in the west, monetary policy is focusing on the west German inflation rate (the special case of the east German inflation rate is referred to later in this chapter). In the initial phase of GEMU, from July 1990 to May 1991, the west German inflation rate moved between 2.3 per cent and 3.0 per cent (see Figure 8.1). This positive performance was partly due to the fact that the spending boom of east German consumers was concentrated on a few goods (like cars, consumer durables etc.) which could easily be satisfied by increasing imports. The risk of growing unemployment partly dampened the propensity to consume. Furthermore, the Bundesbank continued with its restrictive monetary policy. Nevertheless, in spring 1991, the price climate in west Germany deteriorated considerably because of two interrelated factors:

- Firstly, it became more and more obvious that the substantially higher demands on German fiscal policy, caused not only by unification, but also by additional financial contributions to eastern Europe and to the Gulf War effort, could only be met by higher taxes. In this context, some indirect taxes (on petroleum and insurance premiums) were raised in the middle of 1991, resulting in a one percentage point leap in the inflation rate in July 1991, to over 4 per cent.
- Secondly, the continuation of the unification-supported boom in west Germany, and the tax-induced higher inflation rates, triggered high wage settlements in 1991. As a consequence, the unit labour costs increased by 5 1/2 per cent - a clear deviation from the path of the stability-orientated wage policies of the 80s. The hike in unit labour costs in 1992 will be somewhat less.

Against that background, the inflation outlook will improve only gradually. The inflation rate peaked in March 1992, at 4.8 per cent (year-on-year). Due to the basis effect of higher excise taxes in July 1991, the inflation rate should be in the 3 per cent range in the second half of 1992 (June 1992 showed a level of 4.3 per cent). A temporary increase in the inflation rate - to some 4 per cent - is expected as of January 1993, because the one percentage point increase in VAT will result in an increase in the price index, of 0.5 to 0.6 percentage points. Therefore, the average inflation rate in 1993, of 3.6 per cent, will be only slightly lower than the average for 1992, which is estimated to be 3.8 per cent. A sustained reduction in inflation rates to less than 3 per cent is probably not on the cards before 1994. Although a turnaround in wage policy was not achieved in 1992, there is some hope that the 1993 wage round will be more moderate. The settlement in the metal industry, for 1993, gave a signal in this direction.

A special feature is the development of the east German inflation rate. In the initial phase of GEMU, east German prices were rapidly adjusted to market conditions (with a few exceptions, e.g. rents, energy and transportation). While prices of basic goods like food rose sharply, those of consumer durables and semi-luxuries (e.g. coffee) decreased substantially. On balance, the east German price level in the second half was around 3 percentage points below the average of 1989. East Germans also benefited from a substantial increase in both the quality and availability of goods and services - which cannot be covered by a year-on-year comparison of price statistics. The favourable price situation deteriorated substantially in the course of 1991, when the east German inflation rate surged to a peak of 22 1/2 per cent in November 1991 (year-on-year). However, this price trend is not primarily due to an inflationary process, but rather to the gradual introduction of market prices and the reduction of subsidies in the

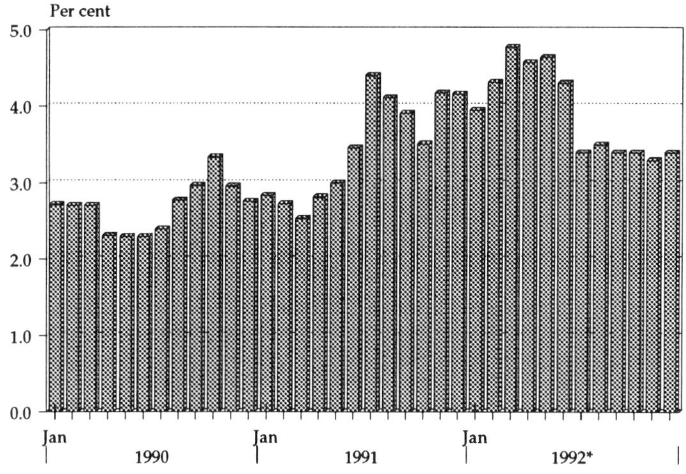

*) *July-December figures estimated*

Figure 8.1 West German inflation, 1990-1992

fields of rents, energy and transportation. On the other hand, the steep increase in east German labour costs since the beginning of GEMU, also contributed to higher inflation rates, especially as far as prices of services are concerned. The average rate of inflation, which came down to 17.5 per cent in the second half of 1991, is expected to fall to 12 per cent in 1992, and below 10 per cent in 1993.

All-German monetary target

In order to contain the inflationary effects of GEMU, the Bundesbank set (for the first time) an all-German monetary growth target for 1991 (see Figure 8.2). This target, which was lowered at mid-year from a 4-6 per cent range to a 3-5 per cent range was, by and large, met by the monetary growth rate of 5.2 per cent (Q4/Q4). In 1992, however, the monthly rates of monetary expansion in the first five months have been close on 9 per cent, and therefore well above the annual target range of 3.5-5.5 per cent. One reason for this is the continuing strong growth in bank credits to non-banks, in the wake of slower economic activity in the west, and the increasing economic activity and privatization in the east. Of course, as far as the latter is concerned, there is a special factor at work - credit expansion to east German firms is not susceptible to high interest rates since credits to east German firms are being subsidized to spur the eco-

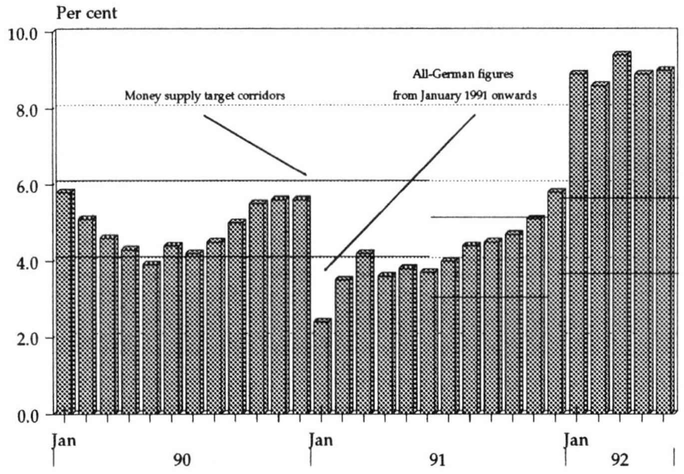

Figure 8.2 German M3 growth (annualized)

nomic recovery there. Another important element in monetary expansion is the inverted yield curve - individual and institutional investors are preferring to park liquidity in high-yielding short-term instruments, like time deposits (which are included in M3), rather than invest in longer-term, securitized, instruments (which are not included in M3). Usually, this situation tends to normalize as inflationary expectations diminish, and if higher bond prices are in the offing. Furthermore, the Bundesbank has to take into account the rising use of Deutschemark coinage and notes abroad, especially in eastern Europe.

Against this background, a temporary overshoot of the monetary expansion target seems to be tolerable. On the other hand, strong monetary growth, in an environment of relatively high inflation rates and budget deficits, leaves hardly any scope for lowering central bank interest rates in 1992. Therefore, in the foreseeable future, the Bundesbank will probably continue its current restrictive course in order to contain inflationary expectations.

Monetary policy, budget deficits and interest rates

The announcement of GEMU by Chancellor Kohl, in early February 1990, caused a precipitous rise in German capital market rates of around 1.5 percentage points to more than 9 per cent (for the 10-year maturity range). This rise reflected the market's early scepticism and uncertainty concerning both the inflationary and budgetary implications of GEMU. In the first two years of GEMU, capital market rates moved within the range of 8-9 per cent (10-year). Paradoxically, in contrast to the widespread apprehension felt both in Germany and abroad, the hikes in Bundesbank rates, in August and December 1991, were associated with lower capital market rates. As a result of the Bundesbank's monetary policy, capital market rates are somewhat above 8 per cent (10-year), at the time of writing. Given an inflation rate of over 4 per cent, this implies a real interest rate of about 4 per cent, which is at the upper end of the long-term fluctuation band (2-4 per cent). By contrast, real interest rates were excessively high in the first 12 months of GEMU, amounting to 5-6 per cent by June 1991.

Although market confidence in the policy of the Bundesbank has obviously remained unscathed, the continued highly-expansive fiscal policy is burdening the stabilization task of monetary policy. There is no doubt that massive state financial transfers are needed to support the restructuring of the east German economy. The public tasks that need to be financed are enormous, ranging from investment in infrastructure (transport, telecommunication etc.) via the establishment of efficient public administration facilities, to the fostering of private investment.

High public transfer requirements

The flow of public transfers from west to east totalled Dm 60bn in 1990, and Dm 140bn in 1991. The latter figure corresponds to roughly two-thirds of the east German national product. This means that the gap between production and demand is being filled by massive state financial support. The transfer will further increase to Dm 170bn in 1992, or 6 per cent of GNP. Given the fact that the state of the east German economy has been much worse than had initially been supposed, substantial public transfers, in the order of well over Dm 100bn (net) per annum, are highly probable in the years to come.

The deterioration in public sector finances in the wake of German unification is highlighted by the development of key financial ratios. The general government budget deficit rose to Dm 120bn in 1991, or 4.3 per cent of pan-German gross national product (GNP), and is expected to come to roughly the same amount (or 3.9 per cent of GNP), in 1992. By comparison, in 1989, the West German budgets had been more or less in equilibrium. The ratio of government spending to GNP was in excess of 53 per cent in 1991 for the united Germany. This is roughly 6 percentage points higher than in the pre-unification year of 1989. Two questions arise in this context:

- Will the German capital market be able to cope with the high public borrowing requirement?

- What are the consequences of sustained high transfer requirements for the stance of fiscal policy?

The financing of public deficits has so far been handled without any disruption to the Deutschemark capital market. The German Federal authorities have been, and will remain, top-rated in international financial markets. Additionally, the Deutschemark capital market is liquid enough to absorb large amounts of new issuance. The savings of private households, for instance, amounted to Dm 235bn in 1991, and are expected to increase to about Dm 250bn in 1992; the savings ratio will continue to be in the order of 14 per cent.

Although there is no financing problem in a technical sense, a certain risk premium has to be paid for tapping the Deutschemark capital market in such large amounts. It is, however, difficult to quantify the risk premium. Such a premium could be lowered if there is the prospect of a credible consolidation course in fiscal policy. It was gratifying to note that the Federal government presented a tight budget for 1993, curbing spending growth to 2 1/2 per cent. The same rate is targeted for the years 1994-1996, according to the medium-term fiscal plan.

Unfortunately, until mid-1992, most of the budgetary cuts behind the small increase in expenditure remained undisclosed - with the exception of the Federal Labour Office which, as of 1993, is no longer eligible for government grants, and which will cut expenditure by Dm 6bn, in 1993. No doubt, a further increase in taxes would prove counter-productive, given the high level of taxation and the disincentives involved.

It remains to be seen when, and if, substantial cuts will be decided upon. On the other hand, there are several budgetary risks, including the integration of the unification-induced off-budget items (such as Treuhandanstalt, for example) into regular budgets. Therefore, Federal spending is likely to increase more strongly than envisaged in the medium-term fiscal plan.

An important element of fiscal policy management is that the Federal states (Länder) and local authorities should also be integrated in the consolidation strategy, because they account for approximately two-thirds of total public expenditure (see Figure 8.3). According to the finance minister and the Fiscal Planning Council, west German Länder government and local authority spending should increase by only 3 per cent p.a. in the period 1993-1995. Experience shows, however, that this recommendation is likely to be exceeded. In fact, the Länder governments and local authorities have built an average annual growth of 4 1/2 per cent into their draft budgets for 1992-1995. Because of the relatively-high wage settlement in the public sector in 1992 - which will hit the Länder governments and local authorities harder than the Federal government, because they employ more public sector personnel - it is feared that the west German Länder governments and local authorities will again fail to substan-

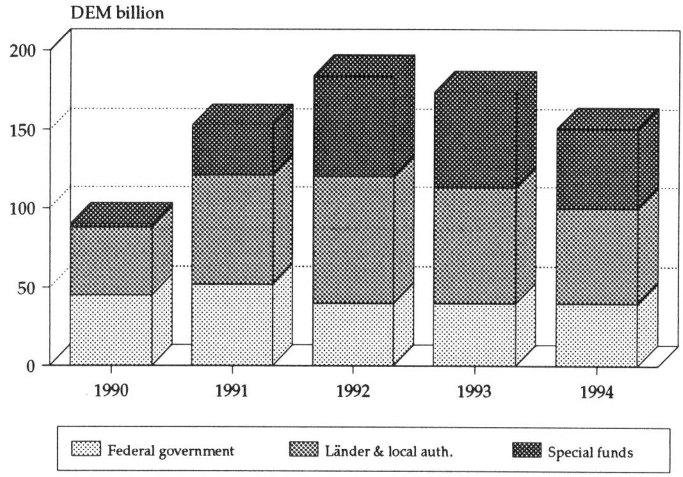

Figure 8.3 German public sector deficit, 1990-1994

tially contribute to fiscal consolidation, as they failed to do so in 1990/91, when they increased spending by an average of 6.8 per cent p.a.

On the other hand, a lack of consolidation will lead to a substantial increase in the interest rate ratio in German budgets, thus leaving no room for fiscal manoeuvre in the years to come. For instance, in the Federal budget, interest outlays per annum will reach 10 per cent of total expenditure in 1992 and are expected to increase to 13.5 per cent in 1995, under the medium-term fiscal plan. All in all, a less expansive fiscal policy is urgently needed in order not only to curtail the increase in the interest service burden, but also to create scope for lower Deutschemark interest rates and thereby to foster growth and alleviate the stabilization task of the Bundesbank.

Impact on the real economy

Since the introduction of GEMU, Germany has been a 'split economy', not only with respect to divergent productivity and living standards, but also as far as economic dynamics are concerned.

There have been two phases, the **first** of which was the period 1990/91: While business activity continued to boom in west Germany, with substantial gains in terms of output, employment and profits, the east German economy embarked on a process of fundamental restructuring, with shrinking production and increasing unemployment. West German GNP increased by around 4 1/2 per cent in 1990, and by a good 3 per cent in 1991. Strong domestic demand was a source of dynamism, and more than outweighed the dampening effects of the weakening world economy. A steeply-rising new order intake in the capital goods sector, and a double-digit increase in retail sales in the first year of GEMU, clearly showed that the west German economy benefited strongly from east Germans' pent-up demand and their focus on western products.

In contrast, the introduction of GEMU immediately highlighted east German companies' lack of international competitiveness. On the one hand, east German firms suffered from a steep decline in domestic demand because western products were clearly preferred by the east German population - there was no lack of demand, but rather a shift in that demand. On the other hand, east German exports to the traditional Comecon markets collapsed in the wake of the slump connected with the economic reforms in those countries. As a consequence, east German companies have had undergo shock therapy in their adjustment to market conditions. They have been compelled to reduce production to actual demand, to improve quality and styling of products, and to attach particular attention to cost-orientated pricing. In the process, industrial output declined by more than one third between the third quarter of 1990 and December 1991.

Changing pattern of business activity

In the **second** period, which emerged in the second half of 1991, the economic dynamism in west Germany slowed in the aftermath of the increase in indirect taxes, and the one-year income tax surcharge (solidarity levy) in July 1991. However, west German GNP is expected to grow by a good 1 per cent in 1992, and by 2 1/2 per cent in 1993.

There is also a changing pattern of economic activity in east Germany. The downward movement came to an end in the course of the second half of 1991. While an upswing is gaining momentum in the construction and the service sectors, the loss in manufacturing output is continuing well into 1992. Besides the financial transfer from the west, the improvement in east Germany is partly due to government measures in support of exports, and also partly to the fact that east German residents have returned to their own, more competitive, products. Despite the turnaround, however, it is too early to characterize the increasing economic activities in east Germany as evidence of a self-sustaining upswing.

As far as medium-term growth prospects are concerned, real average growth of approximately 2 1/2 per cent p.a. is expected for west Germany. In east Germany average growth rates in the order of 10 per cent p.a. seem to be possible; the process of recovery there is, of course, starting from a very low level. In 1991, per capita GNP in east Germany reached some 30 per cent of the west German level. However, differences in income and prosperity are much smaller because income and demand in the new Länder are twice as high as GNP. The gap between income and demand on the one side, and output on the other, is presently artificially narrowed through financial transfers from the west, but has to gradually be compensated for by increased local output in east Germany.

Support for sustained growth in Germany is expected to come not only from domestic sources, but also from exports in the wake of a recovering world economy - which, traditionally, was the driving force for west German business activity. On the domestic side, wage settlements are a decisive factor in both west and east Germany alike. In the west, the unification boom triggered a price/wage spiral, prodded by inflationary tax hikes in mid-1991. The high wage settlements resulted in an increase in unit labour costs of 5 1/2 per cent in 1991 though, to date, 1992 has seen a reduced figure. This trend has to be reversed in 1993, if rising pressures on company profits and their propensity to invest are to be avoided.

In east Germany, the attempt to reach the stated objective of increasing wages as rapidly as possible (by the mid-90s) to the higher west German levels, resulted in excessive double-digit wage hikes, which were often unmatched by increases in productivity. As a consequence, the nominal east German wage level in mid-1992 amounted to 60-70 per cent or more, of the west German level (compared to approximately 36 per cent in the second half of 1990), depending upon the type of industry. However, there are two sides to every coin and, as far as this wage policy is concerned, productivity must improve in line with investment, with little time-lag. If not, the consequences will be even more cuts in employment or higher public transfer requirements.

While most prices for goods and services are converging in the enlarged German single market, the integration of the two labour markets is proving more difficult. The final outcome, of course, will be a rough approximation of wage levels. A small step towards such integration is the increasing number of east-west commuters (estimated at more than 500,000). However, despite redundant east German labour, no significant pressure on west German real wages is visible - a phenomenon which should have occurred by now, at least according to single-market textbooks.

The key to revitalization of the east German economy is private investment. The fact that it increased from Dm 26bn in 1991, to around Dm 44bn in 1992, shows that many investors are using this window of opportunity. Private investment is strongly fostered by the government programme entitled 'Upswing East'. Treuhandanstalt is supporting private investment and business activities through the rapid privatization of the state-owned firms of the former GDR. Between its establishment in mid-1990 and the end of May 1992, Treuhandanstalt has privatized around 7600 firms, or about two-thirds of all state-owned firms, thereby securing 1.2m jobs and the commitment of more than Dm 130bn in private investment in the years to come. Privatization has advanced further in the food and the construction industry. It remains to be seen whether

Treuhandanstalt will succeed in achieving its objective by finalizing its active operations by the end of 1993. Privatization seems the more efficient and preferred method by comparison to the restructuring of firms under the aegis of Treuhandanstalt.

One remaining impediment to investment is the property rights issue. Under the German constitution, property which was expropriated under GDR law has to be restored to the former owners. Logistically, however, there have been problems and there is a large backlog of unsettled applications. A new law intending to improve the process of the property restitution, and thus the conditions for private investment, was passed by Parliament in June 1992.

International implications of GEMU

The GEMU-induced stimulus is not only propping up German GNP, but also supporting growth in the partner-countries via increased German imports. In the early 90s, Germany has been playing a locomotive role in a slackening world economy.

The interplay of relatively weak German export development and the unification-induced import boom of 1990/91, led to a remarkable turnaround in Germany's external position: The huge current account surplus of Dm 108bn in 1989 was replaced by a deficit, in 1991, of around Dm 35bn; meanwhile the trade balance still showed a surplus (of Dm 22bn, after Dm 135bn in 1989 - See Figure 8.4). In the wake of the anticipated recovery of the world economy, the current account deficit will disappear by the middle of the decade. On the other hand, the tremendous fiscal expansion in Germany is criticized for leading to relatively-high interest rates abroad, with consequent detrimental effects on business activity. In a global context, this argument is not particularly convincing, because the slackening of business activity in the big industrial countries has given scope for the easing of interest rates, as the example of the US has demonstrated. On balance, it is probably the stimulating effect of GEMU which has prevailed internationally - as the Reagan policy mix stimulated the world economy in the first half of the 80s.

The EMS dilemma

In an economically highly-integrated Europe, an interest rate dilemma has arisen for several EMS countries who have an interest in maintaining stable EMS parities and who are therefore unable to lower their rates, in spite of domestic needs, while the Deutschemark - the anchor-currency - enjoys a high rate. In this context, Germany has been been under pressure to change its policy mix, i.e. to create room for monetary relaxation, by pursuing a less expansive fiscal policy. However, under the constraints of unification, consolidation of fiscal policy has proved no easy task. Usually, the leading role of the anchor-currency is a key element in every workable fixed-exchange rate regime. There are,

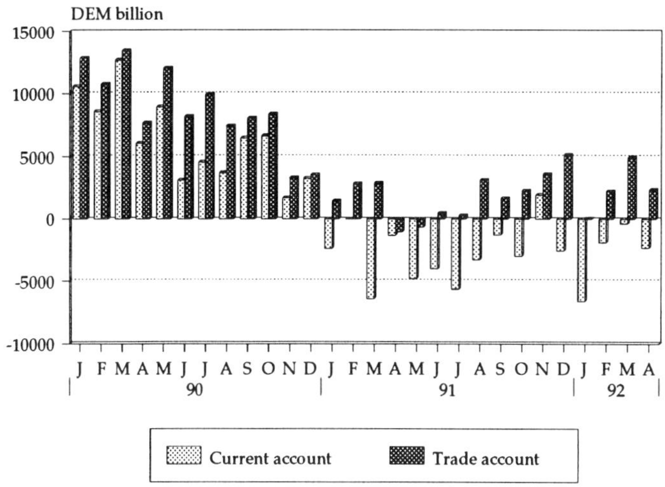

Figure 8.4 **German balance of payments, 1990-1992**

however, concerns, in some quarters, as to whether the Deutschemark can remain the anchor in the EMS in the light of the relatively high German inflation rate (4 1/2 per cent in May 1992, a figure which was above the level of the 7 other EMS countries). However, for the time being, there seems to be no alternative currency which could similarly reflect a policy of continuous stability, pursued by an independent central bank, and a broad and liquid financial market, as is the case of the Deutschemark. Moreover, the markets obviously have confidence in the Bundesbank's policy, since Deutschemark bond yields are still the lowest in Europe, and the spreads are even increasing following the negative Danish referendum on the Maastricht Treaty. This implies, of course, that Germany has a major responsibility in improving its stability performance in the foreseeable future.

As far as the exchange rate of the Deutschemark is concerned, fears of a GEMU-induced weakening have not materialized. The effective exchange rate of the Deutschemark as at mid-1992 is the same as at the outset of GEMU, two years ago.

Conclusion

The management of the unification problems was certainly helped by the fact that the west German economy was in favourable shape at the beginning of the unification process, in 1989: the inflation rate was low (2.8 per cent, annual average), economic growth was satisfactory (3.8 per cent, in real terms), the general government budget was roughly balanced after the strict consolidation course of the 80s, and there was a huge surplus on both the current account and trade balance.

Not surprisingly, these fundamental indicators have deteriorated in the wake of GEMU. The process of growing together is well under way but will need time, probably more time than initially assumed. What is also needed, is patience and a continuation of the strong efforts of all concerned. There is hope that both fiscal policy and wage policy will return to a more stability-orientated path, thereby facilitating the stabilization task of the Bundesbank, and creating scope for lower interest rates in the years to come. The transition to a fully-fledged market economy in east Germany is in full swing. Privatization is making rapid headway. There are reasons to be optimistic that the cost of unification will turn out to be a beneficial investment for the future. Provided that economic, fiscal and wage policy hold a realistic course, east Germany could become a highly-modern production location and service centre, perhaps a 'mini-Japan'.

Chapter

9

The

Impact of Maastricht

Dick Taverne
PRIMA Europe Ltd.

The impact of Maastricht

In the next few years, one of the major influences on bond markets will be progress towards a single currency. The Treaty of Maastricht is likely to prove the most important development in Western Europe since the European Community was founded, and the agreement on economic and monetary union (Emu) is likely to prove the most important part of the Treaty.

Three main conclusions can be drawn from Maastricht: that there will probably be a single currency; that there will be economic convergence among a number of key states; and that we can expect a decade of persistently low inflation. First, the probability must be that the Ecu will be established as a single currency.

In the face of mounting scepticism after the Danish referendum, and with the French referendum still to come, at the time of writing, this may seem a rash prediction. The need to reverse the Danish vote is only part of the problem. There are the misgivings of the Bundesbank, supported by a growing popular concern in Germany at the prospective loss of the Deutschemark. Quite apart from the chance that the French may vote 'No' simply to embarrass President Mitterand, there is clearly a strong streak of hostility to the loss of further sovereignty among the right-wing parties in France, which are likely to win the next elections and may well capture the Presidency before the beginning of Stage Three. There seems to be a continued lack of popular enthusiasm in Britain for granting further powers to Brussels, reinforced by concern that even the limited step of ERM membership has stopped Britain lowering interest rates to mitigate a severe recession.

In forecasting that a single currency will be established, it is also worth remembering that most forecasts come unstuck. Professional seers are best at telling us tomorrow why what they predicted yesterday did not come true today. No doubt there will be unexpected upheavals in the economies of a number of EC states before the end of the century. What, however, makes the emergence of a single currency likely, is the underlying trend which brought about the Treaty of Maastricht and which is also likely to carry its provisions into effect. This trend takes two forms: the drive towards political unity, which has been the power behind all major new developments of the EC ever since it was founded, and the internationalization of economics.

In the case of Germany, it is the political drive which is the most compelling. Germany is still scared of its own past and feels more secure inside a close-knit European Community. German politicians are also aware that their neighbours are deeply apprehensive of the threat that an unrestrained Germany might dominate the heart of Europe. It is extremely unlikely that Germany's consistent support for closer political union will suddenly collapse. It would have a devastating effect on her relations with her neighbours if she rejected Emu, which would be seen as a turning away from the European Community. Indeed, it is precisely the lack of clear commitments to closer political union in the terms of the treaty which lies at the heart of most of the German criticism of Maastricht.

Furthermore, the misgivings of the Bundesbank were to be expected. Its own role, of which it is rightly proud, will be greatly diminished once the European Central Bank is set up. The members of its Council who are also heads of the central banks of the German Länder will lose their influence. There is, however, no reason to suppose that Bundesbank reservations will stop Germany accepting the Ecu as a single currency, any more than the Bundesbank's opposition stopped the establishment of the EMS or the reunification of Germany. As for the French, their principal concern has been to see Germany tied into Emu. That is why they insisted on writing the inevitability of a single currency into the Maastricht Treaty. This concern is not likely to vanish even if the right wing is in power.

Moreover, political reasons are reinforced by economic trends, which will affect Britain as well as France. Every day sees a lessening of national control. National central banks and national Treasury ministers have only minimal, or largely illusory, control over money supply or the fixing of interest rates since exchange controls were abandoned; yet the re-imposition of exchange controls is out of the question. Fiscal policy is now the only effective weapon left to national exchequers; and there are clearly limits to how far fiscal and monetary policies can diverge. In addition, there is also a constant erosion of the geographical borders between the financial markets of the world. Continental markets are becoming more open because they are being prized open by the internationalization of economics. The traditional role of continental banks in lending to companies is being undermined by the international trend towards securitization. Some politicians may not like the results, but it is a trend they cannot resist. A single currency is the logical outcome of the trend in financial markets, just as a 'single market' for industry must logically lead to a single-currency zone.

In Britain, it is still conceivable that a tactical alliance between Conservative anti-Europeans - who have been given a new lease of life - and Labour champions of the 'social chapter', may defeat the treaty, or may force a referendum which, in the present confused mood, would lead to a vote against Maastricht. But, with the prestige of John Major and the government firmly on the line, the odds must be in favour of ratification by Britain. As for public opinion, it is significant that, both in the 1975 referendum and in the elections of 1983 and 1987, when Labour took an anti-EC stand, popular opinion endorsed EC membership. Whatever the views people expressed to opinion pollsters when the issue is reduced to the simple question: 'Should we be *in* or *out*?', the popular answer, realistically and sensibly, is always: '*In*'. Finally, even if the Danes do not reverse their 'No' vote, it is inconceivable that the other eleven, once they have all endorsed the treaty, will allow the Danish veto to stand in their way. There are ways - both technical and legal - round it. Bullying the Danes would not be an acceptable answer. But, if they vote 'No' again, after genuine attempts to meet their concerns (by strengthening the principle of subsidiarity, for example), the eleven will go on without the Danes. For all these reasons, it would be a prudent assumption that Stage Three of Emu will, in fact, begin before the decade is out.

The second main conclusion to be drawn from Maastricht is that the convergence criteria are likely to feature ever more prominently and cannot be ignored.

There are good reasons for questioning some of the Maastricht criteria in themselves, particularly the 3 per cent limit on budget deficits and the 60 per cent limit on the ratio of national debt to GDP. To start with, the limits are arbitrary. The only reason why the figure of 60 per cent was chosen was because that was the EC average at the time. Next, the criteria are ill-defined and easy to circumvent. The PSBR is differently defined in different EC countries. In so far as capital investment is excluded from the prescribed limit, there is ample scope for fudging the differences between capital and current expenditure. Indeed, it has not been unknown in the most reputable circles to find a temptation to cook the national books for political purposes. Thirdly, in some circumstances, formal limits on budget deficits may be undesirable. Some countries may be badly hit by an external shock and may suffer from renewed recession. To exceed the 3 per cent limit might then be not only acceptable, but wise. It is true that the small print of the Maastricht Treaty shows the convergence criteria to be flexible and subject to discretion. But in that case what they will actually be worth? Would they ever be enforced in practice?

However, the reality is that the criteria do matter to Germany. And in the case of monetary union, what Germany wants, it gets. Emu is inconceivable without Germany. Germany is also the one state which may lose economically more than it gains. It loses the Deutschemark and the control of monetary policy by the Bundesbank, both of which have a record of unparalleled success - hence the present malaise about Emu among the German public. The only way of laying to rest German fears that their financial rectitude will be replaced by laxity, that their currency may be partially controlled by nations like Italy and Britain with a history of greater profligacy and financial instability, is to ensure that only those who have proved themselves to be as disciplined as the Germans will be allowed into the inner circle. That is what the convergence criteria are for. That is why Germany will insist that they are not treated as meaningless. It follows that, whatever the small print and loopholes, no nation will be able to join Stage Three unless it has shown that it can manage a stable currency, that it has firm control of its budget deficit and that it has a manageable level of public debt.

This will mean some tough action in a number of member states. Whether Italy will sufficiently reduce its debt and deficit seems questionable. Britain will need to restore firm control over its public finances after the end of its recession. Germany itself is likely to exceed the 3 per cent deficit limit for some years. But certainly for Germany, and very probably for Britain and several other member states keen not to be left behind, the need to be eligible for membership of the first inner group will be an overriding priority of economic policy. In practice, there will be a two-speed Europe. That could have considerable political, as well as economic, advantages. It would help with the widening of Europe. The central European states, for example, could not hope to join in a single currency for very many years. But a two-speed Europe makes membership possible on a more workable basis. There would be an ante-chamber for those who could be full members of a single market and who accepted the political conditions of the EC, but who were not yet ready for Emu.

The third and final conclusion emerging from Maastricht is that the next decade is likely to be a decade of low inflation.

Again the sceptics may be able to point to past predictions, especially by politicians, which have proved hopelessly over-optimistic. And has not even Germany, the paragon of low inflation, shown in the last year that she is not immune from the inflationary disease? The prediction of low inflation is, however, based on the likelihood that three main causes of inflation in the past - devaluation, over-large budget deficits and political manipulation of the money supply - will no longer be operative.

Italy, Britain and, in the more distant past, France, have all suffered from relatively high inflation, which could at least partly be attributed to periodic devaluations. Since France ruled out the option of devaluation, its inflation rate has dropped dramatically. If Britain and other would-be Emu members made the same commitment, there is every prospect that they would see the same results. The contribution of high budget deficits to inflation is perhaps more disputable. As already mentioned, higher than normal temporary borrowing may sometimes be justified. But it would be a triumph of hope over experience to argue that persistently high deficits were compatible with sustainable low inflation or, conversely, that low deficits did not make low inflation easier to attain. And, as has already been argued, there will be almost overwhelming pressures in several countries to achieve lower deficits by the middle of the decade.

The third reason for expecting low inflation is that Maastricht requires an early move by would-be Emu members towards establishing the independence of their central banks. In the past there has been a significant correlation between success in achieving low inflation and the insulation of the money supply from political influence. British peacetime inflation began to grow after the nationalization of the Bank of England. The United States' relative inflation performance improved after the establishment of an independent Federal Reserve Bank. Germany has been a happy illustration of low inflation and an independent central bank. Other examples can be cited to suggest that the connection is more than a coincidence. In effect the Germans, supported by the Dutch, have won the battle of the independence of the European Central Bank. The next decade will almost certainly see a growing removal of political influence over decisions about interest rates and the money supply. As exchange rates become increasingly set and, as inflation policies gradually converge, there is every reason to expect that the virtues of the Deutschemark and the Bundesbank will be inherited by the Ecu and the ECB.

Chapter

10

The bond markets of

Austria

Wolfgang Fast
Z-Länderbank Bank Austria AG

Ernest Gnan
Oesterreichische Nationalbank

Eva Märzendorfer
LB-Capital Markets

Gregor Pozniak
Creditanstalt-Bankverein

Peter Schedling
Oesterreichische Kontrollbank AG

Roman Schremser
Girozentrale und Bank der Österreichischen Sparkassen AG

Note: In general text, the abbreviation 'Sch' is used to denote the Austrian schilling. Elsewhere, the international mnemonic 'ATS' is used.

10.1 Introduction

The Austrian capital market has undergone major changes since the mid-1980s. Traditionally the Austrian financial system was characterized by universal banking and a high degree of bank intermediation. Direct bank credits constituted the major source of corporate finance while the capital market played only a minor role.

Equity market deregulation

From the mid-80s, economic policy shifted its focus towards deregulation, structural reform and other supply-orientated measures. The development of a functioning capital market was considered important, with special emphasis being placed on the promotion of equity finance and the stock market. The most significant measures in this field were:

- The establishment, in 1982, of participation funds (*Beteiligungsfonds*). By issuing profit-sharing certificates (*Genußscheine*), these newly established institutions - mostly subsidiaries of banks - raised some Sch 13bn of risk capital between 1982 and 1989, which was invested in Austrian enterprises. The initial success of this instrument largely rested on the substantial tax allowances granted to private investors who bought profit-sharing certificates.

- Tax incentives for private share buyers. In 1986 a scheme of tax allowances for private investors' purchases of new share issues, was introduced. Simultaneously, the income tax rate on distributed profits was significantly reduced.

- Reform of corporate tax and net worth tax. The 1989 tax reform reduced corporate tax to a 30 per cent flat rate. Net worth tax levied on corporations was reduced indirectly by making it tax-deductible for the calculation of corporate tax.

- The 1989 Stock Exchange Act. In force as of 1 December 1989, the Stock Exchange Act led to major improvements in the fields of disclosure requirements (detailed prospectus etc.), information transparency, investor protection and access to stock market listings for potential issuers. It also led to the establishment of EC standards on the Austrian stock market.

All in all, these measures resulted in a noticeable upswing of the Austrian stock market in terms of prices, turnover, number of companies and issues listed, and a broader range of investors.

Bond market deregulation

The development of the bond market has been much more hesitant. The market is dominated by government (*Bundesanleihen*) and bank issues - there are only a few private sector non-bank issues. The reasons for this are not only the relatively small number of big companies in Austria and the high proportion of state-owned companies, but also the fact that bond issues simply cannot compete with cheap, customer-tailored bank credit (especially if subsidized) and cash advances.

However, major reform steps to promote the bond market have either been taken in recent years or are under way:

- Both the government authorities and the Austrian National Bank recognize the importance of a developed capital market for the financial system, for the conduct of monetary policy, and for overall economic development - their economic policy measures are therefore geared to this end.

- The Ministry of Finance, for example, completely re-shaped the issuing procedure for government bonds by replacing the traditional fixed-quotas with a competitive yield tender system. The secondary market in government bonds (*Bundesanleihen*) gained considerable liquidity through the introduction of a market-maker system.

- As of 1 January 1992, a new Capital Market Act took effect. This abolished the authorization requirements for bond issues (by the Ministry of Finance) while considerably increasing both disclosure requirements and investor protection.

- As of 4 November 1991, the Austrian National Bank established full liberalization of cross-border foreign exchange and capital transactions. There are no more restrictions or authorization requirements for foreign issues on the Austrian capital market (though, in practice, authorization had been very liberal from 1989 and had not, therefore, represented any real impediment).

- In recent years, a domestic institutional investor base has been developing. In particular, life insurance companies, investment funds and the newly-created pension funds, have all shown a strong demand for Austrian bonds.

- The step-by-step privatization course taken by the coalition government since 1987, in connection with the federal budget deficit consolidation programme, leaves room for future issues (like the Going Public bond by Austrian Industries).

- Domestic banks are putting more emphasis on their securities and investment banking activities such as the development of issuing, swap, derivative product and other securities-related departments, and, in some cases, special investment banking subsidiaries.

- On 4 October 1991, the Austrian Futures and Options Exchange (ÖTOB), which is financed and organized on a private sector basis, started operations.

The first signs of success are materializing: turnover figures have increased sharply in recent years, indicating a developing and maturing market. In 1990 alone, turnover almost doubled and a further increase - though not at quite the same pace - was seen in 1991. A variety of new instruments (Bull & Bear bonds, FRNs, reverse-floaters, various kinds of index-linked bonds, convertibles, bonds with warrants and related products), have been introduced to the market.

Both foreign investors and issuers are beginning to appreciate the Austrian schilling as an alternative to other hard currencies. Consequently, an increasing number of foreign issuers are showing up on the Austrian bond market whilst, at the same time, foreign investors are slowly discovering that the Austrian bond market can be an option to diversify their portfolios.

10.2 Economics

Exchange rates

The Austrian schilling is one of the most stable currencies in Europe. The Austrian National Bank - the country's monetary authority - has pursued a strategy of pegging the Austrian schilling to the Deutschemark since the mid-1970s. In recent years, the margin of fluctuation between the schilling and the Deutschemark has been extremely narrow (1990: 0.16 per cent; 1991: 0.079 per cent). In

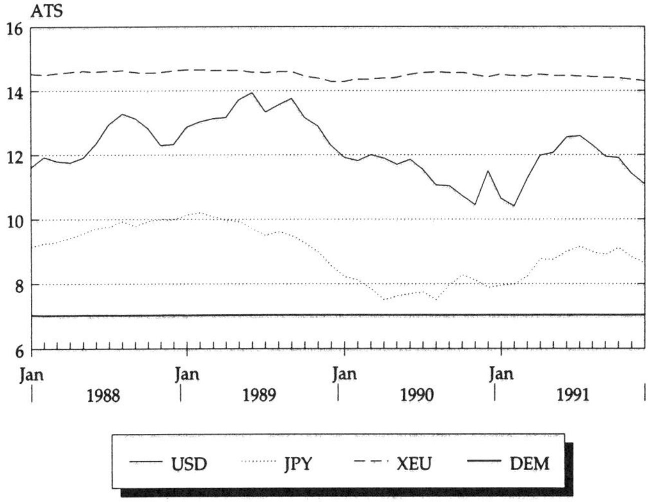

Figure 10.1 **Exchange rate of the Austrian schilling (ATS vs. DEM, USD, 100 JPY, XEU), monthly averages**

terms of exchange rate risk/opportunity for both issuers and investors, this makes the schilling equivalent to the Deutschemark.

Interest rates

Similar considerations apply with respect to interest rate developments (see Figure 10.2). Given the firm commitment to the 'hard currency' policy and an environment of liberalized capital flows, Austrian interest rates cannot differ significantly from those in Germany on risk-equivalent assets. In the last few years, the Austrian National Bank therefore closely followed German moves in official interest rates. Secondary market yields on the bond market were traditionally slightly above the corresponding German rates (1/2 to 1 percentage

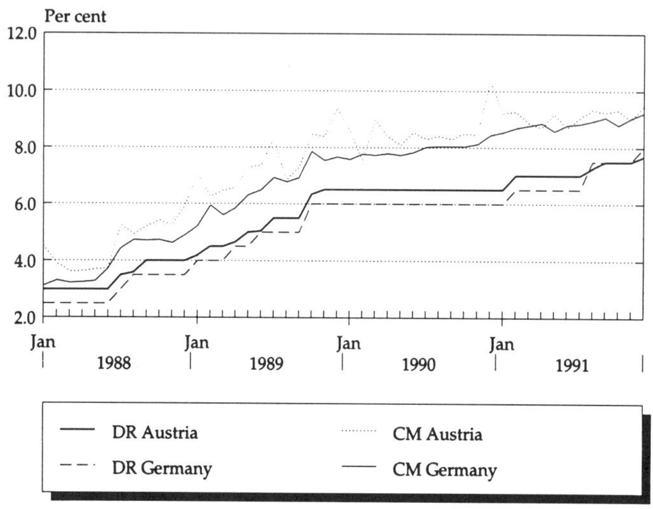

Figure 10.2 Discount rate and call money: Austria vs. Germany

point); however, from 1988, yield spreads continuously narrowed and, since 1989, have more or less disappeared. Money market rate differentials between Austria and Germany still show stronger fluctuations, possibly due to market imperfections and technical reasons; however, over the longer-term, they have been narrowing as well.

The Austrian hard currency strategy is based on the principle of the optimum currency zone, the chief aim of which is to ensure a maximum degree of overall economic stability for a small, open, economy. Moreover, this approach leads to an attitude of restraint in price and wage policy, which has a direct impact on the Austrian economy's price competitiveness. The so-called 'social partnership' between representative bodies of employers and employees continues to play an essential role in this context: The hard currency policy is based on a broad consensus between the Austrian National Bank and other economic decision-makers such as the federal government and the social partners, thereby ensuring extraordinary performance in terms of price stability, employment, economic growth and competitiveness.

It is worth mentioning that, in recent years, more and more European countries have come to regard the Deutschemark as their anchor, and have adjusted their monetary and economic policies accordingly.

Gross domestic product

The hard currency policy has been underpinned by the real sector development of the economy. Austria's macroeconomic fundamentals have, on average in recent years, developed more favourably than those in EC countries. Real GDP

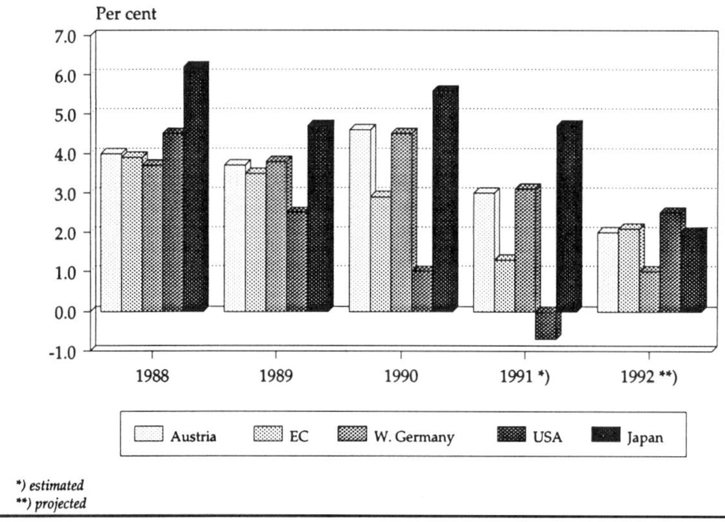

Figure 10.3 GDP growth rates Austria/EC/selected countries (Germany & USA)

progressed by 4.6 per cent in 1990 (see Figure 10.3), compared with 2.79 per cent within the EC. For 1991 and 1992 a slowdown to 3.0 and 2.0 per cent is expected. However, this is likely to be above the EC forecasts for 1991 and 1992.

Inflation

At 3.3 per cent, inflation (measured in terms of the consumer price index) in Austria was substantially below the EC average (5.7 per cent) in 1990. For 1991

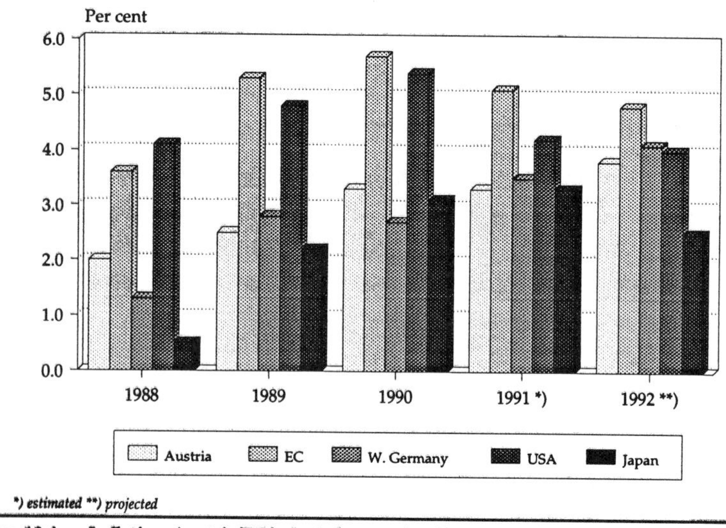

Figure 10.4 **Inflation Austria/EC/selected countries (Germany, US, Japan)**

and 1992, the inflation forecasts are 3.3 and 3.8 per cent, respectively, which would be well under the EC average (1991 and 1992 forecasts: 5.1 and 4.2 per cent), and even lower than German figures (1991: 3.5, 1992: 4.0 per cent).

Unemployment and unit labour costs

Unemployment stood at 5.4 (EC: 8.4) per cent in 1990 (see Figure 10.5), with a projected 5.8 and 6.0 (EC: 8.9 and 9.3) per cent in 1991 and 1992.

Special attention must be drawn to the favourable development of unit labour costs in Austria. While rising by 6.1 per cent in EC countries in 1990, they increased by a mere 2.9 per cent in Austria. For 1991, a 3.0 per cent improvement of relative labour costs, *vis-à-vis* the average of Austria's trading partners, has been forecast. According to available information, a further improvement is expected for 1992. Amongst other factors, this is due to the considerable influx of cheap labour from Eastern Europe.

Balance of payments

The external position of the Austrian economy has been roughly in balance during the last decade, with only minor fluctuations over time (see Figure 10.6).

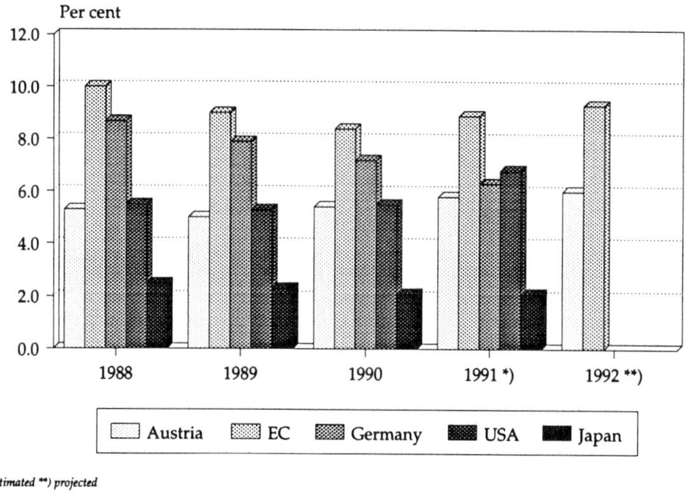

Figure 10.5 Unemployment in Austria/EC/selected countries (Germany, USA, Japan)

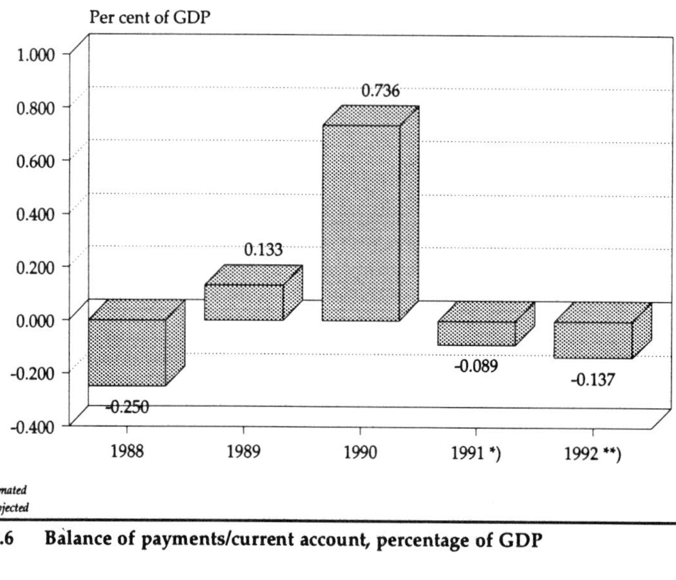

Figure 10.6 Balance of payments/current account, percentage of GDP

The 1990 current account surplus of Sch 13.2bn can be traced primarily to the boom in Germany, Austria's main trading partner, and to the shift in foreign tourists' preferences in favour of Austria. With around one hundred million overnight stays by foreign visitors in 1990, Austria is the most tourist-intensive country in the world.

The traditionally high Austrian savings ratio peaked in 1990 at 13.2 per cent of disposable income, the forecasts for 1991 and 1992 being similar at levels of 13.3 and 12.5 per cent, respectively.

Politics

Since 1987, Austria has had a coalition government formed by the Social Democratic Party (SPÖ) and the conservative People's Party (ÖVP). After the federal elections held on 7 October 1990, this coalition was maintained. The government is determined to continue its medium-term programme of fiscal consolidation, structural reform and EC integration. The main elements of this programme are:

- supply-side measures and structural reforms
- cuts in the net federal budget deficit
- participation in the European integration process, resulting in EC membership as soon as possible
- adherence to the successful hard currency policy strategy.

The reforms encompassed the re-structuring of the nationalized industries. In 1990, this programme remained on track with employment being reduced considerably and political influence on management being curtailed. These measures helped both to raise productivity and reduce unit labour costs which, in conjunction with improved market conditions, brought about a recovery in the financial position of nationalized industries.

The 1989 fiscal reform simplified the tax system by reducing the number of income tax brackets and abolishing several tax exemptions. The top marginal income tax rate was cut from 62 to 50 per cent, while the corporate tax rate was fixed at 30 per cent - internationally, a very favourable figure. As a result, the ratio of wage, income and profit taxes to GDP was reduced considerably.

Public sector deficit

The increase in federal debt, measured in terms of the net federal budget deficit, has been reduced in recent years in line with the Austrian medium-term budget consolidation strategy which was introduced in 1987 with the aim of reducing the net federal budget deficit to 2.5 per cent of nominal GDP by 1994. So far, considerable cuts in the net federal deficit have been achieved - despite the major reductions in tax revenues arising from the 1989 tax reform. In 1990, the deficit amounted to 3.5 per cent of nominal GDP (1991 preliminary figure: 3.3 per cent). The consolidation process has benefited much from both the buoyant economic development and additional revenue from privatization. However, in order to press ahead with consolidation, structural changes - in particular with respect to expenditure - will undoubtedly be necessary.

Changes in the Austrian banking system

In the financial services sector, major restructuring activities are under way. Banks and insurance companies are among those sectors of the economy affected most by Austria's integration into a common Europe. For this sector, participation in the European Economic Area is practically equivalent to EC membership. Together with the full liberalization of cross-border capital movements (as of 04 November 1991), participation in the European Economic Area and EC membership will lead to an unprecedented opening-up of the Austrian financial markets. In fact, restructuring in the Austrian financial services industry has already begun on a large scale as shown, for example, by the merger of Österreichische Länderbank and Zentralsparkasse in autumn 1991. It has been agreed that state influence in the Austrian banking sector is going to be further reduced by privatization steps. A new Banking Act is being prepared, which will ensure EC compatibility in banking.

In other countries there is a wide variety of specialist banks, such as investment banks, savings banks, and so on. In Austria, however, the existing banks can be viewed as general financial institutions, since they embrace all financial services. In the light of intended EC compatibility, the future of this Allfinanz characteristic will certainly be one of the leading financial topics of the decade.

EC membership

In 1989, Austria formally applied for EC membership. Being an Efta country, Austria is part of the European Economic Area, and therefore has already implemented a majority of the necessary economic and legal adjustments to meet EC standards.

Following a review of both economic and political issues, the EC Commission's official opinion (as required by the Treaty of Rome) recommended that the EC's political bodies consider Austria's application in a positive light. Given the new political and economic order in Europe, Austria's neutrality should not prove an obstacle to membership and it is therefore expected that it could be obtained by the mid-90s.

Eastern Europe

Last, but not least, the opening-up of Eastern Europe will certainly be of central importance in Austria's further economic development. Many Austrian companies have already established business relations in Hungary, the CSFR, the states of former Soviet Union and Poland. Austrian enterprises are among the most active in entering into joint ventures in Eastern Europe. In Hungary, for example, 25 per cent of all joint ventures have Austrian partners. Trade with Eastern Europe accounts for around 10 per cent of Austria's total foreign trade, a considerably higher level than for most other Western European countries.

The immediate effects of the breathtaking changes in Eastern Europe are being felt especially in the eastern parts of Austria. Having suffered for a long time from the negative effects of the Iron Curtain, economic activity in these regions has already been significantly stimulated by the opening-up of the CSFR and Hungary. Vienna, as the traditional centre of East-West trade, is also expected to benefit from this trend.

10.3 *Market composition*

Overview

Government bond market

The government bond market (see Figures 10.7 & 10.8) is the most mature and liquid sector of the Austrian capital market. In recent years, issue volume has increased while the issuing procedure has been improved substantially.

In 1989, motivated by the intention to establish a liquid and attractive market for public debt, the Ministry of Finance decided to shift its funding requirements, which had been covered by both government bonds and federal obligations (*Bundesobligationen*), primarily to government bonds. Prior to that time, federal obligations contributed up to 45 per cent of the Republic of Austria's fund-raising.

These measures were accompanied by the introduction of a tender system for government bonds. In favour of a higher market conformity, the original price tender system was replaced by a yield tender system in 1990. To achieve better market transparency and a noticeable improvement with respect to the principle of 'true interest rates', further modifications were introduced - starting with the second issue in 1991.

According to this new agreement between the Ministry of Finance and the 13 banks acting as market-makers, government bonds must be structured with maturities of 5 or 10 years.

The Republic of Austria is the most important borrower on the domestic market in terms of issue volume. Government bonds serve as schilling benchmark issues.

Local authority bond market

In addition to central government, public authorities such as federal provinces or municipalities also raise funds via the capital market but, as borrowers, their market share has declined. Indeed they have been absent from the market since 1988, presumably as a result of the generally high level of interest rates in recent years, which did not suit their tendency to raise capital on a long-term basis. Additionally, in most cases, these entities were able to receive funds from the central government at fairly attractive levels with any remainder being covered by loans.

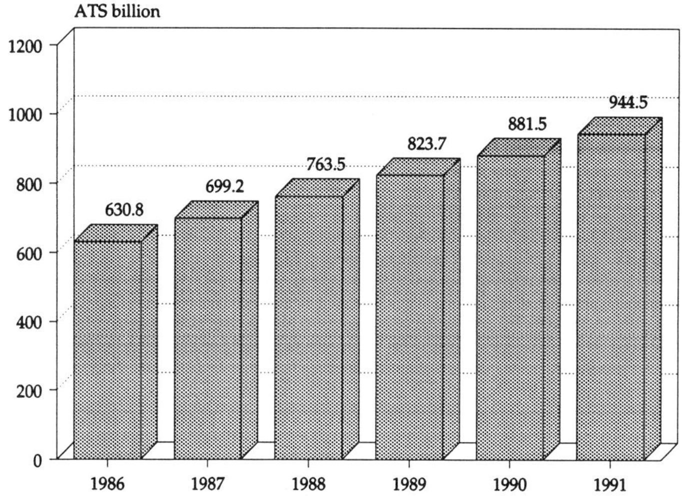

Figure 10.7 ATS bond market - total outstanding volume since 1986 (incl. *Daueremissionen*)

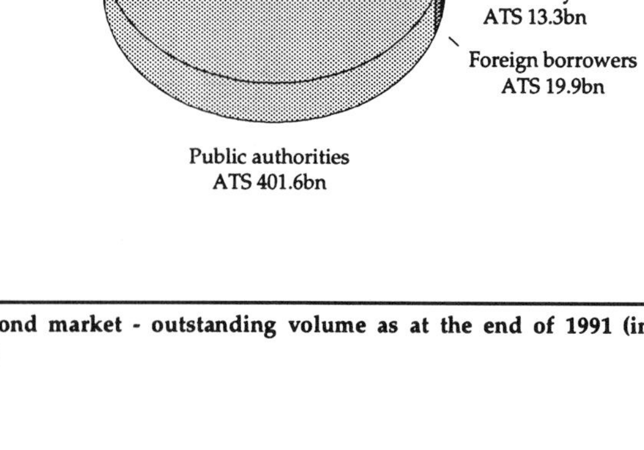

Figure 10.8 ATS bond market - outstanding volume as at the end of 1991 (incl. *Daueremissionen*)

Special financing agencies bond market

There are a limited number of special financing agencies in existence which - due to their ownership structure - can be subsumed under the public authority category. These agencies, owned or mainly-owned by the Republic of Austria or federal provinces, raise funds via the capital market to finance special infrastructure projects or other projects of common interest. The volumes raised are of marginal importance.

Within the last two years ASFINAG (Autobahnen- und Schnellstrassen Finanzierungs-AG) has been the sole user of the fixed-income sector.

Electricity utilities bond market

Until 1989 several electricity utilities occasionally tapped the Austrian market. Issuers included Verbundgesellschaft (the centralized part of the Austrian electricity industry comprising production and the supra-regional high-voltage grid system), and some regional producers and suppliers.

Floating-rate market

In 1986, the Republic of Austria launched the first floating-rate (Treasury) note (*Bundesschatzschein*). This issue served as a benchmark for further FRNs issued by the government, itself, and by financial institutions.

The positive yield spread in the three-month money market rates between the schilling and Deutschemark (50 to 70 basis points) made this instrument an attractive investment for both domestic as well as foreign institutional investors. The strong demand led to an extraordinary growth of this market sector: within just four years the outstanding volume reached a remarkable Sch 60bn. It also helped to establish a swap market, albeit on a rather small scale.

Bank bond market

To refinance part of their long-term loans, the banks not only float *Einmalemissionen* in the form of fixed- or variable-rate notes but, as the only market participants, they are also allowed to issue *Daueremissionen* (*Kassenobligationen*, mortgage-backed bonds and municipal credit-backed bonds). *Einmalemissionen* are issues offered during a certain subscription period having only one payment date, whereas *Daueremissionen* are issues offered on a continuous basis during an unspecified period having several payment dates. The combined outstanding volume of these two main types of issues - with an approximate ratio of 40:60 - far exceeds outstanding government bonds. Also, in terms of new issue volume prior to 1990, the banks launched a higher volume than the government. However, in 1991, Austrian financial institutions have slipped to become the second largest group of borrowers on the domestic market. This unprecedented development is due to a combination of the extraordinary increase of issues by the Republic of Austria - based on the shift from alternative sources of raising capital to bonds, as a consequence of the new issuing procedure - , on the one hand, and the strongly decreasing volume of bank issues on the other.

Daueremissionen market

This market sector can be regarded as a subdivision of the bank bond market, because, so far, only financial institutions have floated *Daueremissionen*. The main characteristic of these types of security is that they are not brought to the market during a certain subscription period, but are rather issued on a permanent basis until the individual issue is closed.

The most important of these instruments, in terms of issue volume, are the *Kassenobligationen*, with a volume, per year, which corresponds approximately to that of the banks' straight bonds.

Mortgage-backed securities and municipal credit-backed bonds complete the group of *Daueremissionen*. All three account for up to 60 per cent of the banks' complete issue volume and are, therefore, of real significance.

In some bond market statistics, *Daueremissionen* are not included.

Corporate bond market

Even though several liberalization measures have already been undertaken to encourage corporates to increase their use of the domestic capital markets, the market share of industry borrowers remains rather small.

One of the major obstacles is that corporates are still able to obtain government subsidized loans. In recent years several companies issued equity-linked bonds. The booming stock market of 1989 and 1990 favoured equity financing.

Foreign bond market

Due to limitations concerning foreign borrowers this sector of the Austrian bond market has been rather small, with only two or three issues per year until 1988. Supranational agencies such as development banks and institutions such as Eurofima have been the main borrowers, with the World Bank being the largest issuer. In line with the liberalization steps taken by the Capital Market Committee during early 1989, all foreign borrowers have been allowed to issue on the domestic market. Since then, a remarkable number of foreign bonds have come to the Austrian market. Due to the swap-driven character of such transactions, the volume has decreased to Sch 5bn in 1991, after the extraordinary increase of 54 per cent in 1990.

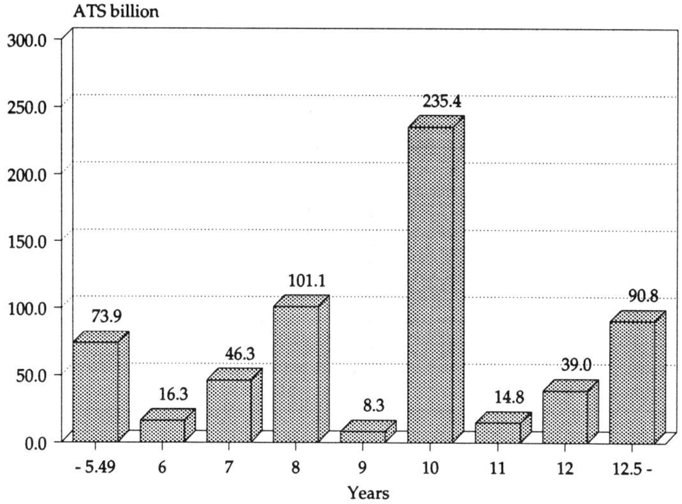

Figure 10.9 **Composition of market for *Einmalemissionen* by initial maturity**

Composition of market by initial maturity

As Figure 10.9 shows, 8- and 10-year maturities have been the most favoured. Together, they comprise around one half of the outstanding total volume of *Einmalemissionen*. In recent years, however, there has been a pronounced trend towards shorter maturities. While maturities of up to 10 years increased their share in the total volume of outstanding *Einmalemissionen* in 1990, those over 10 years stagnated or declined, both in terms of absolute outstanding volume, and in terms of market share. Issues with maturities of up to six years extended their share to 8.9 (1989: 3.4) per cent in 1990. In 1991, a trend towards bonds with shorter lives could be observed, resulting in an average initial lifetime figure of 7.08 years.

Composition of market by remaining life

More than 50 per cent of outstanding *Einmalemissionen* (as of 31 December 1991) had a remaining life of between 5 and 9 years, while 39 per cent had between 2 and 5 years, and 11 per cent had over 9 years (see Figure 10.10). *Einmalemissionen* with a remaining life of up to two years held only a 14 per cent share. While public sector and bank issues show relatively similar patterns in their distri-

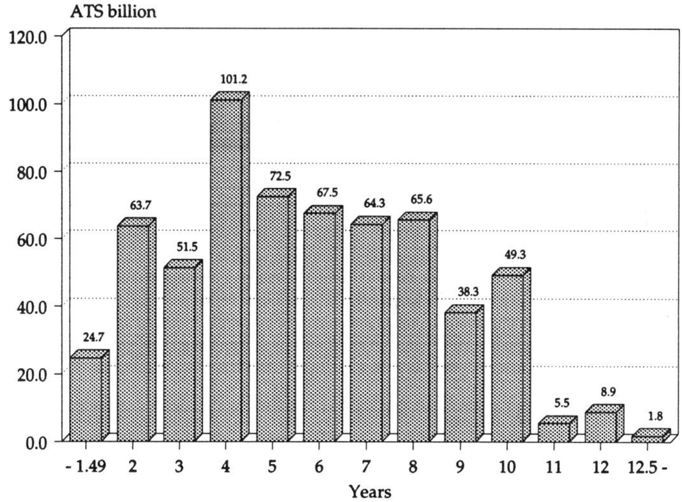

Figure 10.10 Composition of the market for *Einmalemissionen* by remaining life

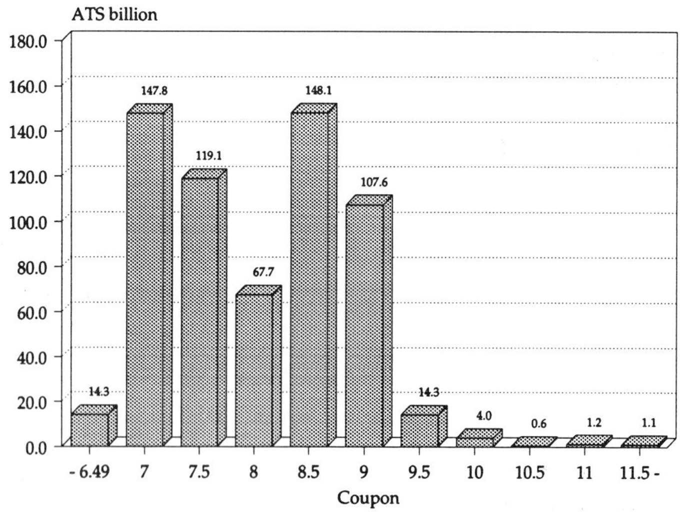

Figure 10.11 Composition of the market for *Einmalemission*en by coupon

bution over various ranges of remaining lives, issues by domestic and foreign non-bank private issuers are concentrated in the 5- to 9-year range, while there are very few issues with remaining lives of over 9 years.

Composition of the market for *Einmalemissionen* by coupon

Considering the bond market as a whole, more than 94 per cent of outstanding issues bear coupons of between 6 and 9 per cent. After a long period of slow decline (from over 8 per cent in 1983, to roughly 6 1/2 per cent in 1988), the second half of 1989 saw secondary market yields, and consequently coupons on new issues begin to rise sharply to stand at slightly under 9 per cent in the second half of 1990. Throughout 1991, they remained between 8 1/2 and 9 per cent, which explains the strong increase in the 8-9 per cent coupon range - by the end of 1991, these issues held a share of over 50 per cent of total outstanding volume against less than 25 per cent, two years earlier. Floating-rate securities, which were first issued in Austria in 1986 expanded significantly until 1990.

10.4 *Types of security*

Government bond market

According to the new agreement between the Ministry of Finance and the 13 banks acting as market-makers, the government is only allowed to issue bullet bonds. However, prior to the agreement being enacted in early 1991, the majority of issues had already been structured as bullet bonds.

Only a few government bonds are callable and redeemed at the option of the borrower. The last callable government bond was launched in September 1990.

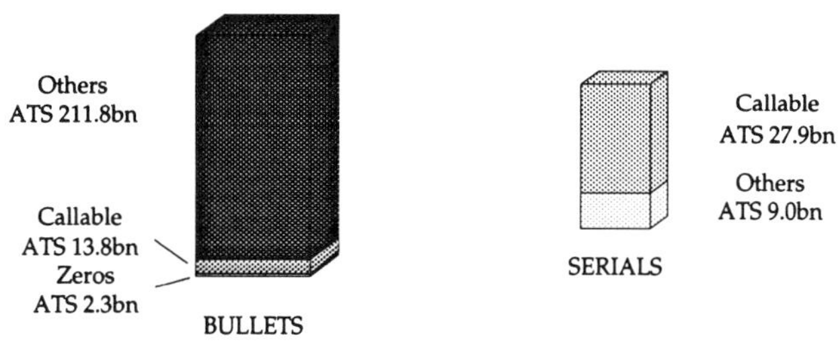

Figure 10.12 Government bond market - outstandings as at the end of 1991 (bullets, callables, zeros, serials)

However, the Republic of Austria has, on several occasions, pointed out that it does not intend to exercise this right.

The government bonds structured as zero-coupon or serial issues can be regarded as relics of the early 80s and, in terms of volume, are of decreasing importance.

Traditionally, the bonds of the AAA-rated Republic of Austria are the most liquid instruments on the domestic market. This situation results from a rather small denomination size (currently Sch 10,000, and previously, even smaller) which attracts not only institutional, but also private, investors and thus guarantees a high level of trading activity. With the introduction of the tender system and its continued improvement, liquidity has increased further, a situation helped by the merger of government bonds carrying the same coupon.

Austrian government bonds, which are recognized by both Euroclear and CEDEL, are targeted at domestic, as well as foreign, investors.

Federal obligations market (*Bundesobligationen*)

Federal obligations were of particularly great importance prior to the late 80s although, even at the end of 1991, the outstanding volume of this instrument still amounts to Sch 106.0bn (see Figure 10.13).

While government bonds have been mainly designed to satisfy retail demand, federal obligations have been targeted exclusively at institutions. As a result, their denomination size is usually very high (Sch 100,000). Most of these bonds are placed directly with a small number of final investors. Since the end of 1986, there have been several specific tranches issued and directly placed

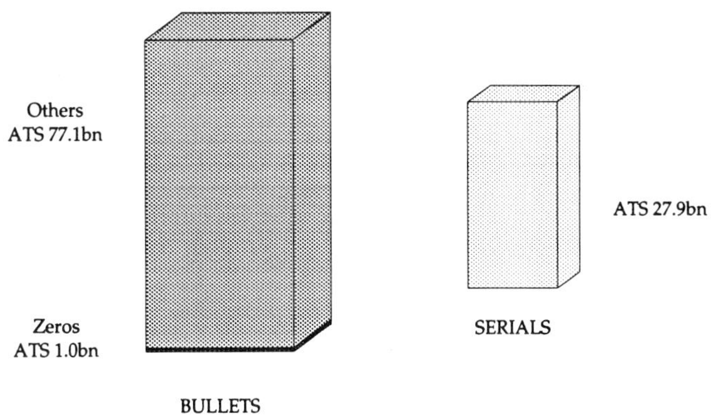

Figure 10.13 Federal obligations market - outstandings as at the end of 1991 (bullets, zeros, serials)

with foreign investors. The majority of federal obligations have been structured as straight bonds, while some have been structured as serials, zeros or floaters. The issue size has normally ranged from Sch 500m to Sch 1800m. Restrictions, which have excluded sales to non-banks or have required the owner to hold the paper until maturity, have usually been part of the bond agreement and have affected a considerable amount of the outstanding volume. Federal obligations have been gradually substituted by government bonds and, in 1991, constituted only a very small part of the total issuance (Sch 1.7bn).

Floating-rate note market

The FRN market was opened by the Republic of Austria in the fourth quarter of 1986 with a Sch 2bn issue. Due to the strong demand by domestic as well as by foreign institutions, this market sector grew extremely rapidly thereafter.

The FRN market is dominated by issues of the government, in the form of floating-rate Treasury notes (FRTN). Since 1989, these FRTNs have been placed not only by a domestic syndicate, but by an international one as well.

To avoid the stock exchange turnover tax, these FRTNs have a guaranteed maturity of just three years and will be renewed 2 or 3 times - depending on the 'final' maturity - for another three years, as long as the FRTNs are not called by the government; they are therefore known as renewable FRTNs.

These securities usually have a denomination size of Sch 100,000 to Sch 1,000,000 and are therefore mainly targeted at institutional investors. To broaden the investor base, the most recent FRTN, issued in February 1992, had a denomination size of Sch 10,000.

The interest rates of the FRTNs, payable quarterly, are linked to the three-month Vienna interbank offered rate (VIBOR) - the rates being fixed every three months for the following quarter. The three-month VIBOR constitutes a consensus rate of three-month market rates from a group of large Austrian banks (see Reuters page: VIBO).

The first FRTNs were brought to the market with a coupon of VIBOR plus 1/8 per cent. Since September 1989, FRTNs have carried a coupon of three-month VIBOR minus 1/8 per cent. Therefore, some of the early-issued FRTNs which provided interest rates above VIBOR have already been redeemed. However, in the current environment of inverted yield curves, and thus extremely high money market rates, this instrument still offers a very attractive return to the investor. Additionally, due to their reasonable issue volumes, FRTNs are very liquid instruments.

From 1989, when banks received permission to fund themselves via variable-debt issues, the FRN market has witnessed the involvement of financial institutions. Essentially, bank FRNs bear characteristics similar to the government FRNs in that the coupon is determined in connection with the VIBOR. However, there is a real difference because bank FRNs are structured as bullet securities and their denomination, as well as their issue size, is generally smaller than found in FRTNs. Their maturities have varied between 6 and 10 years.

A money market floater issued in 1990, with a volume of Sch 1.5bn, was the first to be offered by an international placement group. The willingness shown by the international market, in absorbing more than 40 per cent of the volume, illustrates that this bond was well received.

With the expectation of falling interest rates, three reverse-floaters have so far been issued by financial institutions. This instrument is basically equipped with a high fixed-interest rate from which a variable money market rate (usually three- or six-month VIBOR) is subtracted.

Bank bond market

The Austrian bank bond market can be divided into the following groups:

- according to their issuance method into *Einmalemissionen* and *Daueremissionen* (*Einmalemissionen* are issues offered during a certain subscription period having only one payment date, whereas *Daueremissionen* are issues offered on a continuous basis during an unspecified period having several payment dates)

and,

- according to their collateral into secured, non-secured, non-secured state-guaranteed and subordinated bank bonds.

Secured bank bonds

According to the Act on Secured Bank Bonds (*Gesetz über fundierte Bankschuldverschreibungen*, RGBl. no. 213 of 27 December 1905) Austrian banks are obliged to hold collaterals, which must always correspond, in their amount, to the sum of all outstanding secured bank bonds of the issuer. The assets are separated from all other assets of the bank and are continuously supervised by a government commissioner. These collaterals consist of borrower claims against the Republic of Austria, claims of the borrower against domestic or foreign enterprises (as far as they are guaranteed by the Republic of Austria), securities secured by mortgage, and cash. Therefore, the secured bank bonds can - as far as the standing of the borrower is concerned - be compared with issues of the Republic of Austria. This also explains the relatively small yield pick-up between these funded securities and the government issues.

With the enactment of the new Capital Market Act in 1992, the obligation for banks to fund their bonds has been abolished. Before this date, only a few types of bank issues were exempted.

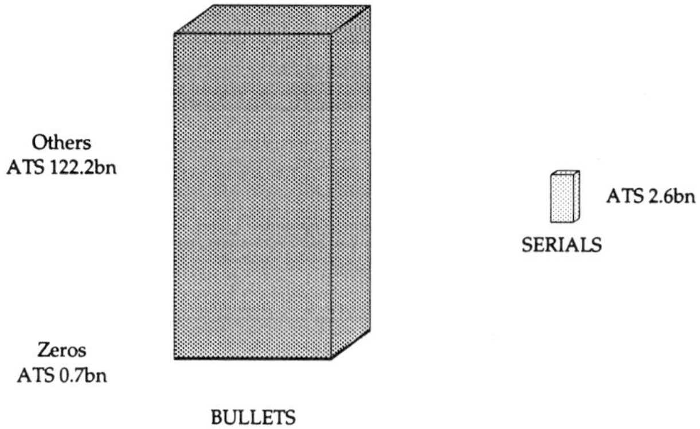

Figure 10.14 Bank bond market - outstandings as at the end of 1991 (bullets, zeros, serials)

Although the liquidity of these secured bank bonds is not as high as that of the government bonds (due to their smaller issue sizes), banks are prepared to support their own issues thereby providing the market with liquidity.

Because the banks' issues (except *Kassenobligationen*) are generally targeted at both private, and institutional, investors the typical denomination size is Sch 10,000.

■ Fixed-interest rate bank issues

In general, straight bank issues exhibit the same bond features as government bonds.

■ Variable interest-rate bank issues

- Money market floater: The FRNs and the reverse-floaters have already been discussed above.

- Capital market floater: The capital market floater is an instrument of the Austrian banks aimed primarily at domestic private investors. Specifically, the interest rate floats in line with the overall secondary market yield, or the secondary market yield for bank bonds, and is not linked to a money market indicator. Moreover, the adjustment of the coupon usually is done on an annual basis.

Some of these capital market floaters are equipped with a collar; the cap is often set quite close to the market level at issuance, so there is no substantial upward potential for the investor. Some capital market floaters even carry coupons of up to one percentage point below the secondary market yield.

■ Others

Banks have occasionally launched securities in which the redemption (and thus the yield) has been linked to other parameters such as stock exchange indices (Frankfurt's DAX and Vienna's ATX), or the price of oil.

Non-secured bank bonds

To a much lesser extent, Austrian banks have also issued non-secured bank bonds. The most active issuer in this sector is Österreichische Investitionskredit AG, which provides long-term financing for the domestic industry. To raise funds for financial institutions which are too small to tap the capital markets themselves, certain entities (*Finanzierungsgesellschaften*) were founded in the late seventies. These agencies mainly issue straight bonds and distribute the proceeds to smaller financial institutions in their respective banking sectors. Their bonds are not secured. Due to the fact that they are well-established names on the domestic market, no real yield difference to secured bank bonds can be observed.

At the end of March 1991 a new product was brought to the domestic market. The 'cash or share' certificate is a short-term instrument, with a maturity of one to two years, which offers a coupon far above the market and which will be redeemed, at the choice of the borrower, either at par or by delivery of shares at a fixed price (or payment of the equivalent schilling amount).

The first launch of this type of instrument was heavily oversubscribed and was followed by a couple of similar issues. However, due to the limited number of very attractive stocks in what has generally been sluggish equity markets, the number of 'cash or share' certificates has also been limited.

In view of the hedging requirements, issues sizes have not usually been above Sch 200m.

Kassenobligationen

See *Daueremissionen* market, later in this section.

State-guaranteed non-secured bank bonds

The bonds of the Oesterreichische Kontrollbank (OeKB), which are issued in order to raise funds for refinancing export credit insured by the government, are guaranteed by the Republic of Austria.

Subordinated bank bonds

According to 12 of the Austrian Banking Act 1979 (KWG), supplementary capital together with equity and participation capital constitutes the total equity of a financial institution.

To raise such supplementary capital, bonds can be issued. These supplementary capital bonds are a special kind of subordinated security which also has certain equity features.

The debt characteristics are:

- that the subscriber of the security does not become an owner of the financial institution,
- that the 'paid-in' capital will be redeemed at maturity.

The equity characteristics are:

- that the capital has to be given to the bank for a minimum of eight years,
- that the interest rate payments have to be covered by the net profits of the bank,
- that the investor also participates pro rata in the losses of the institution (meaning that the investors bear the risk of redemption of less than 100 per cent of the capital). Additionally, in the case of liquidation, these securities must not be redeemed before the satisfaction of all other claims (which do not have the quality of equity or participation capital) against the bank. On the Austrian market this higher degree of the investor risk is not always expressed in an adequate yield spread over government bonds.

Daueremissionen market

Overview

The main characteristic of this type of security is that it is not brought to the market during a certain subscription period, but is rather issued on a continuous basis all year long.

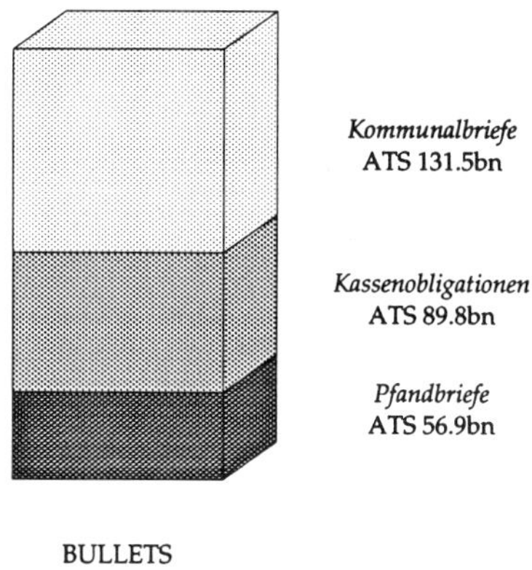

Figure 10.15 ***Daueremissionen*** **market - outstandings as at the end of 1991**

Daueremissionen seem to be a speciality of the Austrian capital market but, in view of their volume (see Figure 10.15), they are nevertheless quite important.

Kassenobligationen

The most frequently used *Daueremissionen* are the *Kassenobligationen*, which are issued by financial institutions to cover short- to medium-term capital needs. Accordingly, their maturities range from 1 to 5 years.

The yield is based on a coupon (between 3 and 7 per cent) and a bonus dependent on: the internal interest rate guidelines of the borrower, the maturity and the amount of the invested capital. The investor receives the interest and bonus annually on the coupon payment date.

As *Daueremissionen*, *Kassenobligationen* are not floated during a certain subscription period but can, instead, be bought during the course of a calendar year as a primary security. The security does not exist in physical, printed, form. The minimum denomination size is Sch 1m.

Although *Kassenobligationen* are one of the few types of non-secured schilling bank securities, they are nevertheless highly appreciated by investors. The main reason is that they are not subject to notable price changes because both issue, as well as redemption price, are usually close to par.

The subscribers of these securities are mainly institutionals and mutual funds. Due to their investment guidelines, mutual funds are primarily interested in those *Kassenobligationen* which are listed on the stock exchange, although the vast majority (90 per cent) of them are not listed.

Mortgage-backed and municipal credit-backed bonds

Another type of *Daueremissionen* are the mortgage-backed and municipal credit-backed bonds (*Pfandbriefe* and *Kommunalbriefe*). Because of their highly-qualified collateral mortgages and loans to domestic public entities, these types of security have a high level of financial credibility.

It should be noted that, currently, only a certain number of Austrian banks have the legal permission to issue such securities .

Due to their gilt-edged character, the guidelines concerning collateral are very rigorous. The banks are, for example, not allowed to float more mortgage bonds than are covered by mortgages; also, collateral cannot include more than 50 per cent of the estimated value of any real estate. If this collateral is insufficient, bonds issued by the government or provinces can be used as a short-term substitute. All regular and substitute collaterals have to be registered in a special register.

Mortgage-backed and municipal credit-backed bonds are commonly issued in the form of straight bonds or capital market floaters.

Corporate bond market

Corporates are not among the most frequent borrowers on the Austrian fixed-income market. Since most of the larger institutions have access to subsidized loans, which usually generate funds at a level well below the capital market rate, practically no straight bonds by this type of borrowers can be found on the domestic capital market.

Industry borrowers usually tap the market only with types of hybrid, all of which carry equity-linked features.

With the emergence of the booming Vienna Stock Exchange in 1989 and, thus, a relatively active warrant market, various bonds with warrants have been issued. In 1989 alone, six such bonds with a total volume of Sch 1.585bn appeared on the market. This relatively high number of issues demonstrated the positive acceptance of this instrument by investors.

Although issue volumes have been fairly small (see Figure 10.16), this development has been considered a real step towards realizing the ambitions of raising the market share of corporates as borrowers on the domestic capital market.

The same is true for the 'Bull & Bear' bonds, the first of which was launched for Unilever (Austria) in 1989 and soon followed by another one for Rank Xerox (Austria).

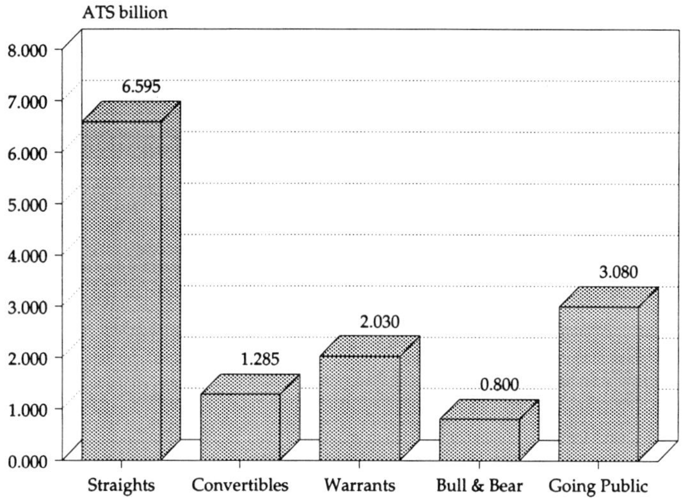

Figure 10.16 Corporate bond market - outstandings as at the end of 1991

These securities were floated in two tranches, the redemption prices (and thus the yields) of which are linked to the index of the Vienna Stock Exchange. In case of an increasing index, the redemption price of the Bull-tranche also increases whereas the redemption price of the Bear-tranche decreases, and vice versa.

Convertible bonds

In autumn 1990, the market for convertible bonds was re-opened by an issue of one of the largest Austrian construction enterprises (Allgemeine Bau Porr AG). This issue was followed by several other convertible bonds during the course of 1991.

Going Public bonds of Austrian Industries AG and Kärntner Landes-Hypothekenbank

The most remarkable corporate bond on the Austrian bond market in terms of the issue size was the 'Going Public' bond of Austrian Industries AG. During the second quarter of 1990, Austrian Industries AG (the holding company of Austria's nationalized industry) came to the domestic market with an Sch 3bn issue. This new financing instrument is intended as a method of floating equity during the maturity of the bond. The option coupons, which were issued together with the bond, provide the holder with the choice of either purchasing newly-issued shares at a discount or of redeeming the bond at slightly higher-than-par value. For the opportunity of purchasing shares at a discount, the investor pays an option premium, which is reflected in a reduced coupon. In the event that the company does not actually 'go public', the bond will be redeemed at a price far above par, which will compensate for the reduced yield during the time to maturity.

A similar construction has been chosen for a Sch 80m issue of the Kärntner Landes-Hypothekenbank.

Foreign bond market

Securities floated by foreign borrowers on the domestic market (see Figure - 10.17) are still limited to just a few different types. This fact can be explained primarily by the relatively low degree of diversification by issuers, who usually prefer to remain with the same instruments.

The vast majority of foreign issues are structured as straight bonds with maturities mainly between 5 and 10 years. In fact, it was a foreign borrower, the Swedish corporate, AB Electrolux, which issued the first straight bond on the

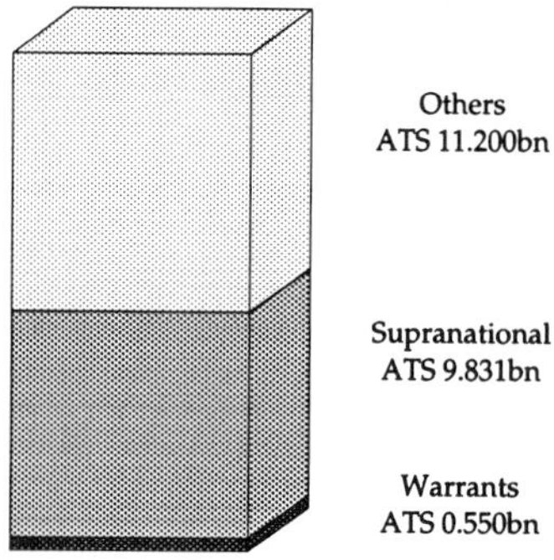

Figure 10.17 Foreign bond market - outstandings as at the end of 1991

Austrian capital market with a maturity below 5 years. This bond was brought to the market in April 1990 with an initial maturity of approximately 3.5 years. In July 1991, a Sch 1bn issue, with a life-time of just two years, was launched for the supranational organization, 'The Council of Europe Resettlement Fund for Refugees and Over-Population in Europe'.

An innovative idea was recently introduced to the domestic fixed-income sector by Asian Development Bank which, in September 1991, launched an issue which was structured as a bond with warrants. This supranational issue, of Sch 1bn, carries a coupon of 8.25 per cent and will mature in 2001 (but is callable at the option of the borrower, at par, in 1996). Together with the bond, warrants were floated as well. These warrants entitle the holder, in 1996, to receive a non-callable Asian Development Bank bond 1996-2001 with the same terms and conditions as the original bond, at the price of 100.25 per cent.

10.5 Issuers

The issuers on the Austrian capital market (see Figures 10.18 - 10.21) can basically be divided into four groups of which two, the public authorities and the financial institutions, dominate the market by far. The remaining two market groups are foreign borrowers and corporates. However, together these two account for no more than 10 to 15 per cent of the entire fixed-income sector.

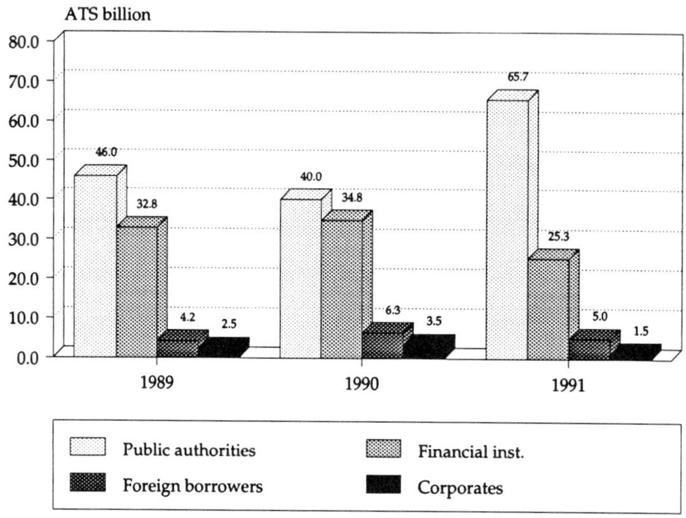

Figure 10.18 Issuers on the Austrian bond markets since 1989 (excl. *Daueremissionen*)

Corporate issuing activity showed a revival during 1989, as its market share rose from 0.3 per cent to 3.0 per cent. This increase was for two reasons: firstly, conditions on the fixed-income market compared favourably to traditional credit finance and, secondly, there was much interest in new hybrid products, such as bonds with warrants.

In 1990, the issue volume of public authorities (46 per cent) and financial institutions (41.2 per cent) played, by far, the dominant role on the domestic market. Foreign borrowers reached the encouraging amount of 7.4 per cent, which represents an extraordinary increase of 54.1 per cent. Industry borrowers have also been able to expand their issue volume to 4.2 per cent.

With nearly 70 per cent of new issue volume, excluding *Daueremissionen*, the Austrian government dominated the primary market during 1991. In fact, the Republic of Austria was the only issuer to enlarge its market share. This development can be explained by both the huge issue volume brought to the market by the Republic of Austria and the restrained attitude of the other borrowers.

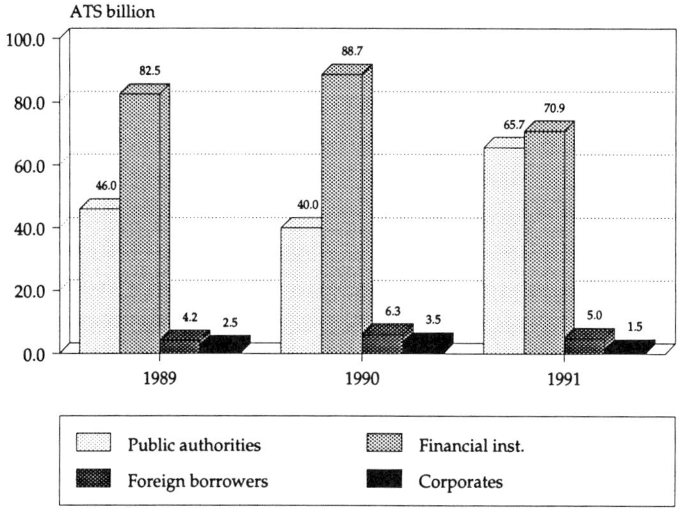

Figure 10.19 Issuers on the Austrian bond markets since 1989 (incl. *Daueremissionen*))

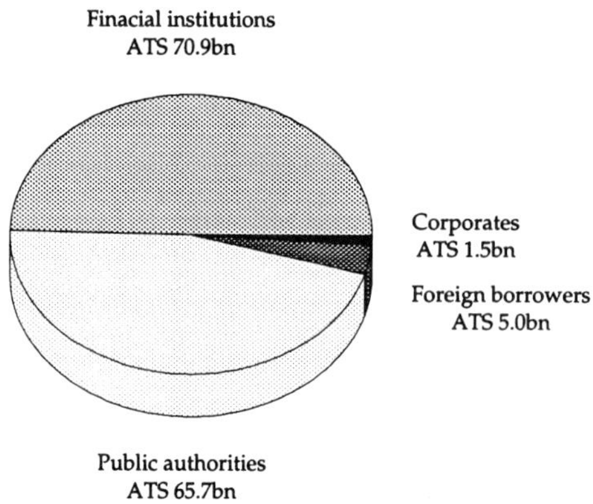

Figure 10.20 Issuers on the Austrian bond markets in 1991 (incl. *Daueremissionen*)

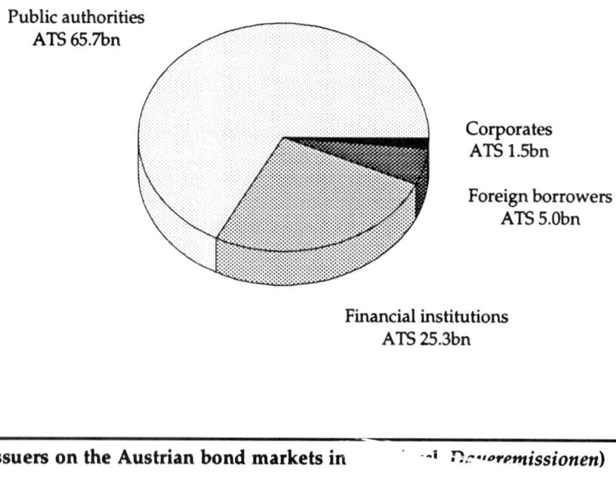

Figure 10.21 Issuers on the Austrian bond markets in [illegible] *Daueremissionen*)

10.6 *Investors*

Primary purchases

With a market share of around 50 per cent, banks are traditionally the most important buyers of bonds (see Figures 10.22 & 10.23). This situation is primarily attributable to two factors: Firstly, as underwriters of government bond issues, banks have to hold any issue not placed. Secondly, prior to the end of 1991, banks were only allowed to float secured securities. These secured bank bonds are, to a large extent, backed by claims against the Republic of Austria, therefore a portion of the collateral is in the form of government bonds.

The traditional pattern was turned round in 1990 when, due to an attractive level of interest rates, a strong growth in the buying interest of domestic non-institutional investors could be observed. The subscription portion of this investor group nearly doubled, to a noteworthy 31.8 per cent, or Sch 26.8bn. However, in 1991, that portion declined to little more than 20 per cent. The strong demand for schilling bonds from this investor class caused yields to drop below those of Germany and, because demand exceeded supply, it also led to the purchase of foreign currency bonds. According to reports of the Austrian National Bank, no corresponding fund inflows from the sale of schilling bonds to foreigners counterbalanced this development.

The importance of domestic institutional investors has decreased slightly, to 20.6 per cent. Within this group, insurance companies have played the dominant role. Mutual funds have had few funds available to invest because non-institutional buyers have preferred to purchase directly, rather than via the trusts.

As in previous years, the share of foreign investors continued to rise in 1990, to 5.4 per cent of the gross issue volume (although, at 4.0 per cent, the 1991 figure showed a slight reduction). This increased foreign interest was especially registered in the Going Public bond of Austrian Industries AG for which a syndicate of foreign banks underwrote (for the first time) a certain quota of the issue.

The market share of domestic banks was 54.1 per cent in 1991 and, hence, financial institutions remained the most important buyers of fixed-income products.

With the bond rally at the beginning of 1991, institutional investors largely changed their strategy by moving substantial amounts of cash into longer-term government bonds - in spite of the high money market rates. With the knock-on effect of stimulating the market further, this action thereby became both part-cause and part-effect of the rally.

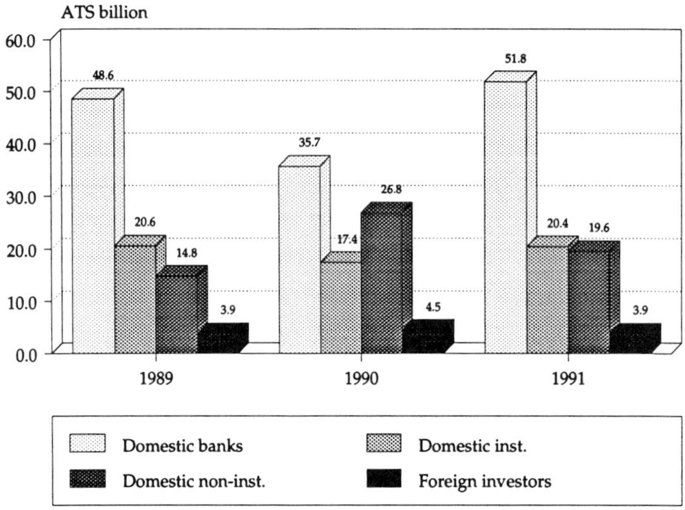

Figure 10.22 Primary purchases on the Austrian bond markets since 1989 (excl. *Daueremissionen*)

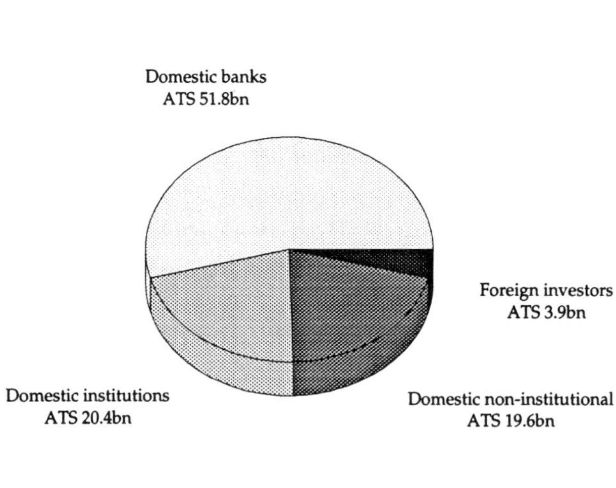

Figure 10.23 Primary purchases on the Austrian bond markets in 1991

After private investors had satisfied most of their demand during the second half of 1990, and after institutions had taken a significant stake in bonds during the first quarter of 1991, a considerable proportion of new issues remained in the banks' portfolios. This development meant that 1991 saw the return of the traditional investor structure, with the institutional buyers as second largest group (21 per cent) in the Austrian fixed-income market.

Unfortunately, foreign investment proved unable to continue the growth of previous years and dropped back slightly to 4.0 per cent of the gross issue volume.

Security holdings

By the end of 1990, around 60 per cent (Sch 531bn) of the total amount of outstanding bonds (see Figure 10.24) was in the portfolios of Austrian banks and non-corporate institutional investors (primarily insurance companies and mutual funds). Since the Austrian banks used mainly government bonds as collateral for their issues, they held roughly 40 per cent (Sch 355bn), whilst insurance companies and mutual funds held slightly over 9 per cent (Sch 82bn) each. The rest, i.e. around 40 per cent (Sch 351bn) of the total outstanding volume, was held by domestic private households, domestic corporate enterprises and for-

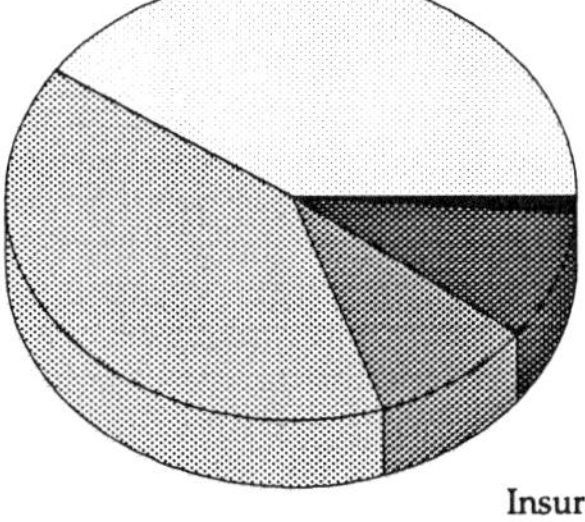

Figure 10.24 Security holdings in the Austrian bond markets, December 1990

eign investors (for statistical reasons these investors cannot be identified by volume).

Major long-term shifts in the importance of different groups of investors in recent years were:

- a reduction of the share of domestic banks (1983: 47.9 per cent, 1990: 40.3 per cent).

- a steady rise in the importance of insurance companies (1983: 7.9 per cent, 1990: 9.3 per cent).

- an explosive growth of mutual funds as a major group between 1984 (1.5 per cent) and 1989 (10.0 per cent). Note, however, that in 1990, mutual funds left their bondholdings virtually unchanged. Confronted with rising interest rates, domestic mutual funds were faced with more or less stagnating assets in that year. In the first nine months of 1991, their expansion regained some impetus, although they then invested almost exclusively in foreign currency assets.

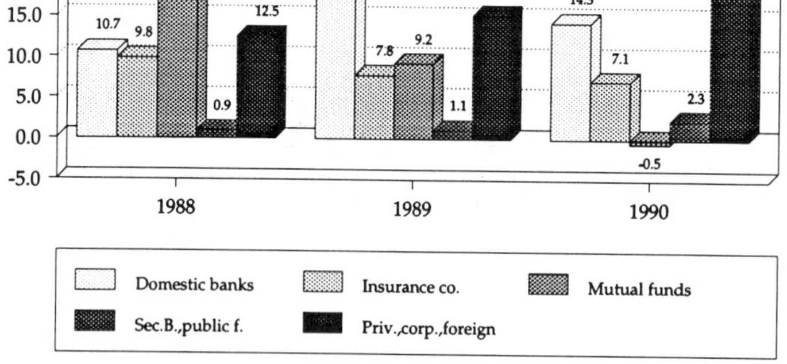

Figure 10.25 Net purchases of Austrian schilling bonds (1988-1990)

- a fluctuation in the holdings of domestic households, domestic corporate enterprises and foreign investors which, together, showed a slightly rising trend from 1983 (42 per cent) to 1986 (43.5 per cent), followed by a major decline until 1989 (38.4 per cent). Only in 1990 they did regain importance, due to strong interest in schilling bonds by domestic private households.

Net purchases (i.e. changes in portfolio holdings) of schilling bonds by different groups of investors accordingly showed major fluctuations in 1988 to 1990, as shown in Figure 10.25.

10.7 *Methods of issuance*

Statutory framework

Capital Market Act

At the beginning of 1992 a new Capital Market Act (*Kapitalmarktgesetz*) replaced the obsolete 1979 New Issues Act (*Wertpapieremissionsgesetz*). The new law represents a step towards those EC regulations relating to publicity requirements for new issues. Approval of the Ministry of Finance is no longer necessary, but investors are protected by the extended information requirements imposed on both issuers and sellers (lead-managers) of new, publicly-offered issues. The Act refers to three main topics:

■ 1. Production of offering circular
An offering circular, containing figures similar to the formats for prospectuses in the Stock Exchange Act 1989, has to be provided at the beginning of the offering period. The circular has to contain detailed information about the issuer, and the terms and conditions of the offering. Once the circular has been adequately prepared, it affords the opportunity to tap the market whenever placing conditions are favourable. There is a certain group of issuers and types of issues which are exempted from the obligation to deliver an offering circular, e.g. sovereigns, supranationals, eurobonds, private placements, etc.

All offering circulars have to be filed with Oesterreichische Kontrollbank AG, to which every intended new issue also has to be notified.

■ 2. Examination of circular
The offering circular has to be examined either by a bank with a certain amount of liable capital and/or by an auditor, for completeness and correctness.

■ 3. Liability
The issuer and the persons who have examined the offering circular, the offering banks and the auditor, if involved, all undertake responsibility for the correct figures in the offering circular and may be held liable for any false representation of the borrower's credit quality.

The Austrian banks entered into a 'gentleman's agreement' not to bring issuers of high credit risk to the market. In the event of failure of this agreement, the Austrian Ministry of Finance is entitled either to re-introduce the application procedure for new issues, or to introduce an obligatory rating for new bond issues.

Austrian National Bank

In the course of the deregulation and internationalization of the Austrian capital market, the requirement for approval from the Austrian National Bank for foreign borrowers wishing to tap the Austrian bond market was abolished in November 1991.

Standard issue procedures

Note that this subsection does not apply to government bonds and bank bonds.

Fee structure

Management fee:	0.25%
Underwriting fee:	Depends on the maturity of the bond; 0.25%-1.00%, or more
Selling fee:	1.00%
Introduction to the Vienna Stock Exchange:	0.10%
Paying agency fee:	
Coupon:	0.25% p.a. of the coupon
Redemption:	0.125%
Admission fee, Council of the Vienna Stock Exchange:	0.01% (up to 5 years); 0.04% (more than 5 years)
Contribution to Stock Exchange Fund:	0.01% p.a. max. ATS 50,000
Other expenses (advertising, printing etc.):	ATS 500,000 up to ATS 1,000,000

Figure 10.26 Fee structure in the Austrian bond market (excl. government and bank bonds)

Documentation

In addition to the obligatory offering circular, an information memorandum (a widely-distributed, 4- to 6-page brochure with a short description of the issuer and terms and conditions of the offering) plus advertising material (e.g. posters), have to be prepared.

Agreements required between the issuer and the bank(s) are: an underwriting agreement (containing: global note, terms and conditions, and list of documents to be provided) and a paying agency agreement. It must be mentioned that the usual clauses used in euromarket documentation (e.g. negative pledge, cross default, force majeure, etc.), are incorporated.

For the introduction to the Vienna Stock Exchange, which takes place after the offering period, a listing prospectus according to the provisions of the Stock Exchange Act has to be submitted to the Executive Committee of the Council of the Vienna Stock Exchange.

Draft timetable

Days	Action
x-	Working mandate to the lead manager; preparation of the offering circular; information memorandum; advertising; agreements
x-10	Invitation to the syndicate banks; meeting of the syndicate members
x-5	Dispatch of information memorandum and advertising material
x-2	Pricing of the bonds; launch date
x-1	Signing of the documents
x	Start of the subscription period
x+7	Payment date
x+8	Transfer of net proceeds to the issuer
x+14	Application for listing of the bonds on the Vienna Stock Exchange (listing prospectus)
x+35	Meeting of the Executive Committee of the Council of the Vienna Stock Exchange
x+40	First listing of the bonds

Figure 10.27 Draft timetable for new Austrian issues

Syndication

There are fixed syndicates of Austrian banks (Syndicate 'A') for certain public issues (Verbundgesellschaft, Oesterreichische Kontrollbank AG, Österreichische Investkredit AG). They are always led by Oesterreichische Kontrollbank AG, and totally underwritten by approximately 30 banks with fixed quotas. Partly-fixed syndicates (Syndicate 'B') for issues pertaining to regional electricity utilities, provinces, communities, special financing agencies, etc., are lead-managed by a bank from of a management group consisting of 4 - 6 banks, on a rotation system. Members of the underwriting group have fixed-quotas. Corporate bonds and bonds of foreign borrowers are freely syndicated. So far, Austrian banks have been reluctant to invite foreign banks to participate in schilling bond issues, although exceptions have been made for equity-linked issues.

Volumes

Suitable sizes for public bond issues range from Sch 500 to Sch 1500m (except domestic government and bank issues).

Tender system for government bonds

Government bonds are issued by tender (see Figures 10.28 & 10.29). The development of the Austrian tender system began in 1987. Prior to this date, government bonds were placed within a fixed syndicate of Austrian banks. After part-volume tenders and then price tenders, the final version of a yield tender was introduced in 1991.

There is an annually fixed number of banks which are allowed (indeed, obliged) to participate in a tender. The Republic of Austria usually taps the market once a month (except in July and August). At least one week before tender date, at the latest, the issuer indicates the maturity of the planned issue and the approximate volume (stating a maximum and a minimum volume within a range of Sch 2bn).

Every bank has to make competitive bids indicating the yield at which it is willing to buy the bonds. The minimum volume each bank has to bid for is the result of the upper-indicated new issue volume, divided by the number of bidding banks. The maximum volume each bank is allowed to bid for is limited to 30 per cent of the upper-indicated new issue volume. With an indicated volume of Sch 5 to Sch 7bn and 13 participating banks, therefore, the minimum volume to bid for is Sch 500m, while the maximum is Sch 2100m. The minimum size of a single bid is Sch 1m. There is no limit on the number of bids per bank.

Oesterreichische Kontrollbank AG (OeKB), as traditional lead-manager of the government bond issues, collects the bids and calculates their average weighted yield which provides the basis for the official issue features such as coupon and issue price. Issue prices, including fees, are close to par.

Dependent upon the volume allotted to a bank, the issuer pays a commission of between zero basis points (for an allocation of less than Sch 200m) and 30 basis points (for an allocation of more than 20 per cent of the total issue volume). Banks which receive less than Sch 200m have the opportunity to increase their stake to Sch 200m with additional allocations at the average yield ('non-competitive' bids).

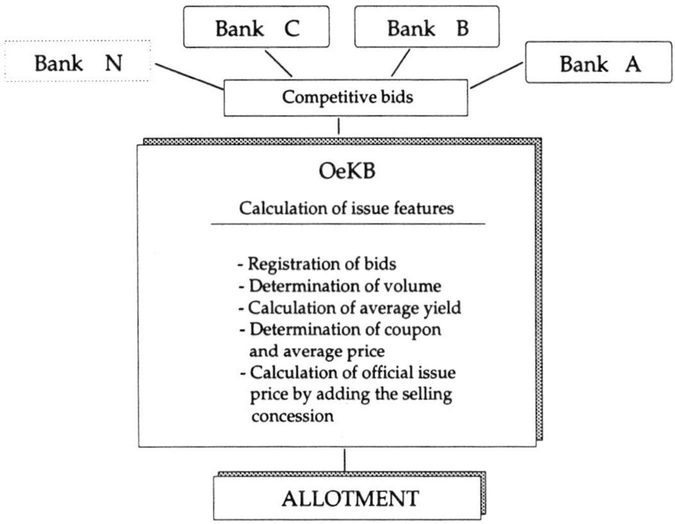

Figure 10.28 Tender procedure for a government bond (i)

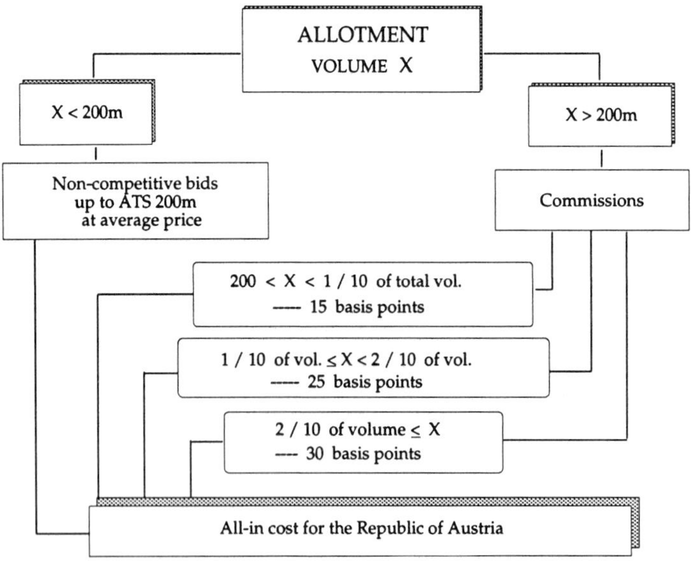

Figure 10.29 Tender procedure for a government bond (ii)

In order to create bigger and more liquid issues in the market the Republic of Austria has the opportunity to merge a new issue with a bond already traded subject to the coupon of the traded bond still reflecting market conditions and the issue price of the new bond being within a range of 99 per cent to 101 per cent.

This new system has proved to be a very successful innovation providing, as it does, liquid benchmark issues.

Unsyndicated bank bonds

Austrian commercial banks, as well as mortgage institutions and savings banks, issue bonds without the intermediation of external syndicates. This has several advantages including lower costs and less documentation.

For *Daueremissionen*, the volume of each issue (*Reihe*) is fixed in advance and the selling price can be adjusted at any time to meet both the requirements of the offering bank and the prevailing market situation. As soon as a *Reihe* is sold off, or the coupon no longer reflects the market, a new one can be floated.

Floating-rate Treasury notes (renewable)

This special capital market instrument, with a VIBOR-based coupon issued by the Republic of Austria (for more details, see Section 10.4), is mainly targeted at international investors. Lead-managed by an Austrian bank and completely underwritten by an Austrian syndicate, about 50 per cent of the issue or more (the 'international tranche') is placed abroad by an international co-ordinator via a syndicate of foreign banks (the 'international selling group').

10.8 New issue volumes

Overview

After a period of continual slight decline in issue volumes (excluding *Daueremissionen*, see Figure 10.31) from 1987 to 1990, a substantial increase was seen in 1991 (to Sch 97.5bn, from Sch 84.5bn, in 1990).

The combined gross issue volume of *Einmalemissionen* and *Daueremissionen* in 1991 reached an amount of Sch 143.1bn, which was 3.3 per cent above the level of 1990.

Other figures are: Sch 5.5bn, or 3.8 per cent of the issue volume, excluding *Daueremissionen*, which was issued as floating-rate securities (the volume of capital and money market floaters was in balance).

The issue volume of floating-rate Treasury notes (strictly-speaking, not bonds - but characteristically, very similar), peaked at Sch 26bn in 1990.

After three years of slightly decreasing issue volumes of *Einmalemissionen*, this trend reversed itself in 1991 with a new issue volume record (Sch 97.5bn). This result was mainly caused, as already noted, by the extraordinary rise in the Republic of Austria's issuing activity.

Only Sch 5.5bn, or 5.6 per cent, was issued as variable interest rate securities (most of this volume was launched in the form of capital market floaters). Due to the rather modest performance of the stock exchange, equity-linked products such as bonds with warrants or convertible bonds played only a minor role in 1991.

Floating-rate Treasury notes showed a sharp decline in 1991, with volume down 70 per cent.

The combined gross issue volume of *Einmalemissionen* and *Daueremissionen* reached Sch 143.1bn (+3.3 per cent) in 1991 - which, with the exception of 1988, was the largest annual amount raised via the fixed-income market.

Government bonds

Until 1988, the issuing activity of the Republic of Austria was split into government bonds and federal obligations (*Bundesobligationen*). Roughly 60 per cent of the borrowing needs were raised through government bonds, the remaining 40 per cent being covered by federal obligations. In 1987, federal obligations amounted to as much as 56 per cent of the Republic of Austria's issuing requirements.

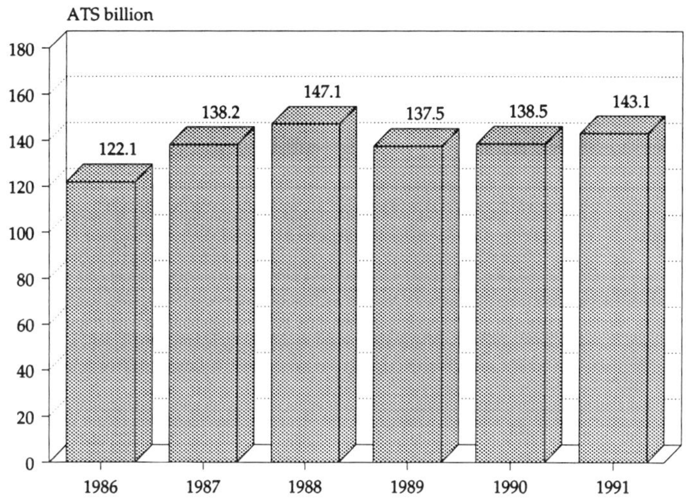

Figure 10.30 New issue volume since 1986 (incl. *Daueremissionen*)

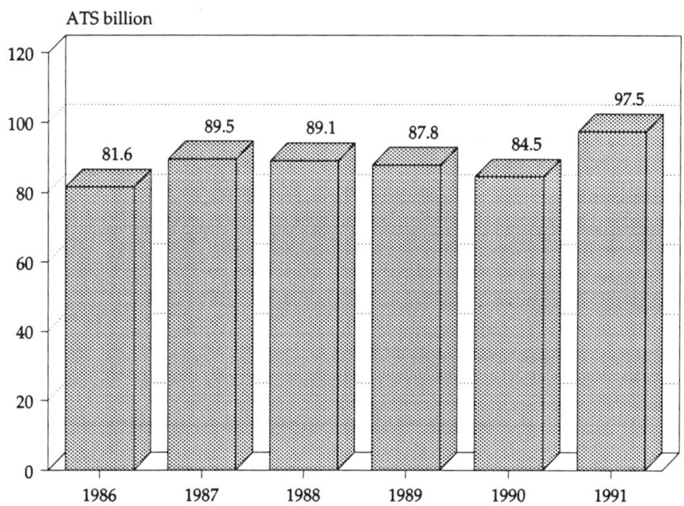

Figure 10.31 New issue volume since 1986 (excl. *Daueremissionen*)

Since 1989, only government bonds - with two or three exceptions - were brought to the market by the Republic of Austria. This explains the significant growth in government bonds, to Sch 43.5bn. in 1989 (see Figure 10.32).

After a year of rather moderate borrowing activity in government bonds during 1990, the issue volume for the first three-quarters of 1991 exceeded the corresponding figure of the previous year by a remarkable 20 per cent. By the end of 1991, the Republic of Austria had floated a total of Sch 65.2bn - a record amount.

At first glance, this surprising development may be thought to be simply due to a growth in the borrowing needs of the Republic of Austria but, in fact, the cause really lies in the lack of an active floating-rate Treasury note market. Due to the general expectations of falling money market rates, and consequently a

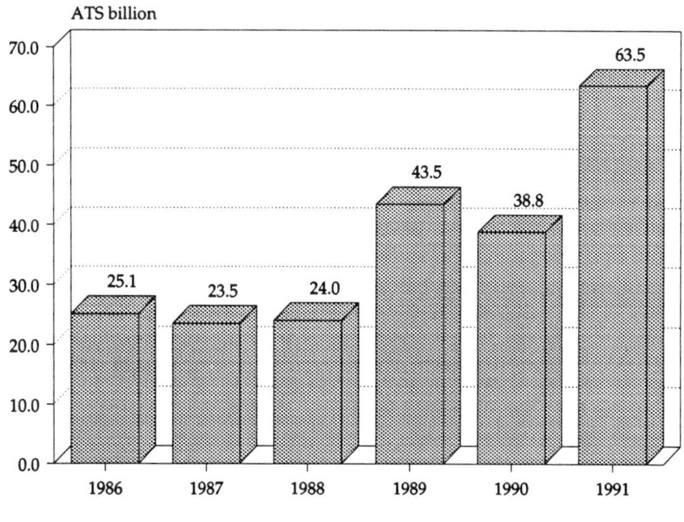

Figure 10.32 New issue volume of government bonds since 1986 (excl. federal obligations)

reluctance on the part of investors to buy money market-linked instruments, the Republic of Austria had to shift most of its funding requirement into government bonds. This caused, from time to time, a certain oversupply of government bonds, which contributed to a narrowing of the negative yield differential over Germany in the five-year maturity range, and to a widening of the positive spread in the longer maturities. In October 1991, to avoid such oversupply, the Ministry of Finance (in accordance with the banks acting as market-makers) launched a bond with a seven-year maturity. This was despite the fact that it was in apparent contradiction of the original intention of the market-maker agreement, which catered only for the issue of five- or ten-year government bonds.

Local authority and special financing agency bonds

The local authorities (provinces and communities) are steadily declining in importance. In the early eighties, these entities had tapped the market from time to time. In 1982, the year with the all-time highest issue volume (Sch 4.3bn), their market share was around 10 per cent of the *Einmalemissionen*. Since then, though, issue volume has continuously decreased. This is partly because they

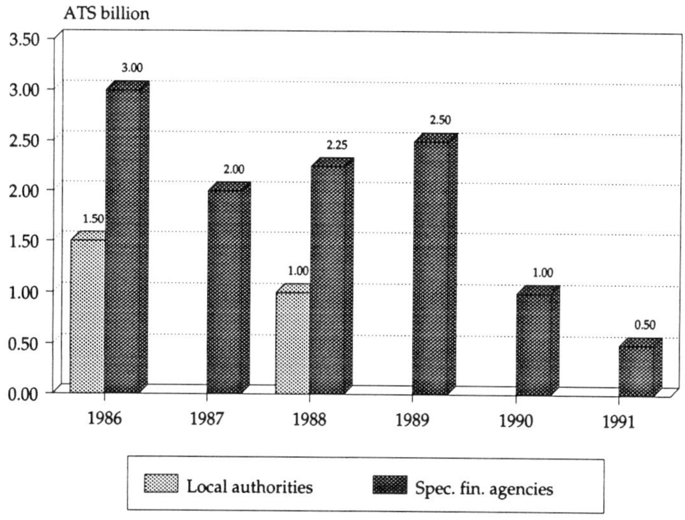

Figure 10.33 New issue volume of local authorities and special financing agencies (since 1986)

have preferred financing via loans, and partly because they have been able to receive funds from central government at levels more attractive than available on the capital market. The most recent issue of this group was a 7 per cent bond with 12-year maturity, floated by the Province of Styria in 1988.

More or less the same is true for the special financing agencies of the Republic of Austria. Since the mid-eighties, their rather modest market share, of approximately 6 to 7 per cent, has also been in decline. Nowadays, their

Einmalemissionen account for no more than roughly 1 per cent of the gross issue volume.

During recent years, ASFINAG has established itself as the special financing agency of the Republic of Austria. Of the small group of special financing agencies, ASFINAG has been the only one to have periodically tapped the domestic market. Due to the excellent creditworthiness of this borrower (triple A-rated), ASFINAG is not only able to issue remarkable volumes, but can also use the small sector of private placements - and tap foreign capital markets.

Floating-rate notes

The FRN market was opened by the Republic of Austria in late 1986 and, right from its inception, impressive growth has been recorded. Within only a few years (1986 to 1990), the per annum issue volume of floating-rate Treasury notes

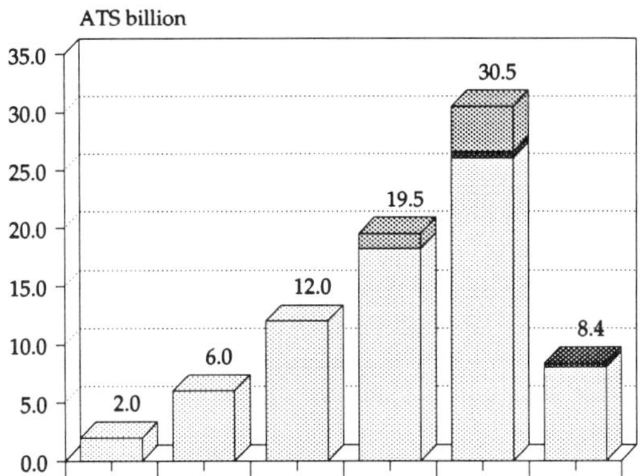

	1986	1987	1988	1989	1990	1991
FRNs				1.3	3.9	
Reverse-floaters					0.6	0.4
FRTNs	2.0	6.0	12.0	18.2	26.0	8.0

Figure 10.34 New issue volume of FRNs since 1986 (incl. FRTNs & reverse-floaters)

(FRTNs) increased from Sch 2bn, to a noteworthy Sch 26bn. The largest issue had a volume of Sch 8bn.

In 1989, when banks were allowed to fund themselves via variable-debt issues, this trend was supported as they took advantage of the widespread acceptance of FRNs.

The Austrian hard currency policy, and the positive yield spread to three-month money (50 to 70 basis points), both helped to cause this significant rise in FRN issue volume. Surprisingly, though, just as rapidly as the issue volumes had increased until 1990, so they decreased in 1991. This sharp decline, of around 70 per cent, can be attributed to the demand side, reflecting investors' expectations of an easing of monetary policy and, consequently, falling interest rates. The 'shortage' of FRTNs as a source of financing for the Republic of Austria was, to a major extent, compensated by a larger issue volume of government bonds.

The volume brought to the market in the form of reverse-floaters is only of marginal importance.

Bank bonds

Traditionally, the banks have been responsible for the largest per annum issue volume. The remarkable amount of *Daueremissionen* floated by financial institutions put them, as borrowers, ahead of the Republic of Austria. In terms of *Einmalemissionen*, the banks usually are the second-largest market users in Austria.

Until 1988, besides *Daueremissionen*, the banks issued mostly straights or capital market floaters. In 1989, the banks discovered FRNs and issues of up to Sch 1.5bn

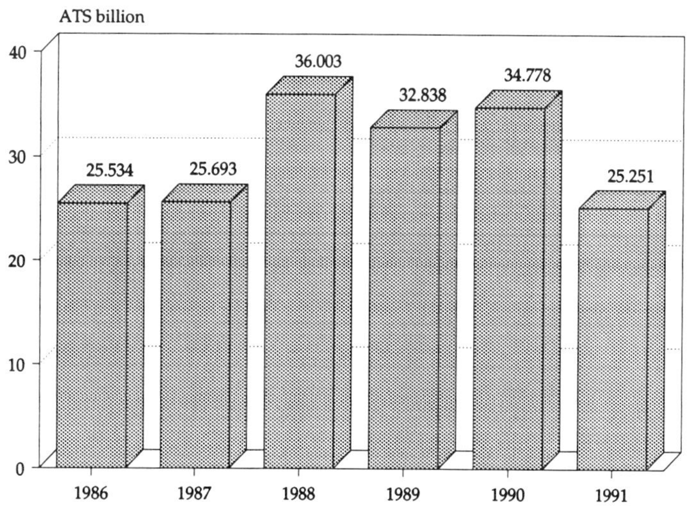

Figure 10.35 New issue volume of bank bonds since 1986 (includes straights, capital market floaters & FRNs)

were brought to the market. In 1990, the widespread acceptance of FRNs made possible the placement of a certain quota of the issues with international syndicates.

In the same year, some 11 per cent of the new issue volume (excluding FRTNs) was issued in the form of floating-rate securities (this volume being launched only by banks). The volume of capital market floaters and money market floaters (FRNs), was in balance.

In 1991, just Sch 5.5bn (or 5.6 per cent) was issued in variable-interest rate securities, the vast majority of the volume being launched in the form of capital market floaters.

Although innovative products, such as reverse-floaters and 'cash or share' certificates, have been appreciated for their structure, their low issue volumes mean that they remain of only marginal importance.

Daueremissionen

Historically, *Daueremissionen* have been the largest market sector of bank issues. In the early eighties this type of security made up a notable 80 per cent of the banks' issue volume. During recent years this percentage was reduced to roughly 60 per cent (see Figure 10.36). This trend of relatively decreasing issue

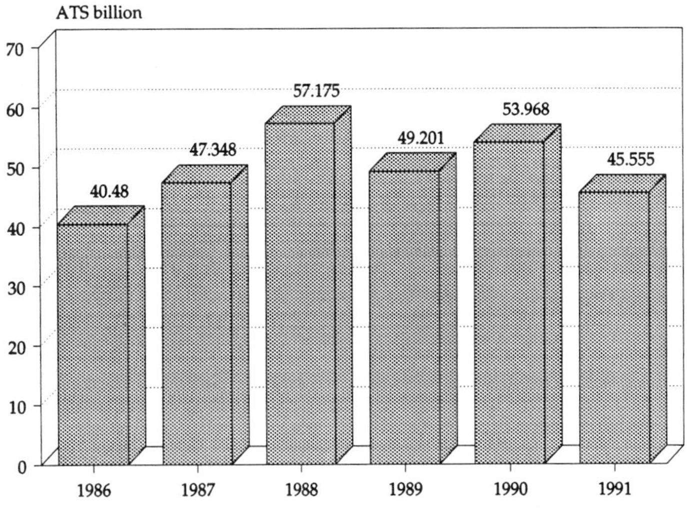

Figure 10.36 New issue volume of *Daueremissionen* since 1986 (includes *Kassenobligationen*, mortgage-backed bonds & municipal credit-backed bonds)

volumes is likely to continue throughout the coming years, in favour of an increased issue volume of other bank instruments.

Of the *Daueremissionen* which account for a total new issue volume of approximately Sch 50bn, the *Kassenobligationen* are by far the most important measured by issue volumes. *Kassenobligationen* have been floated at least twice as often as the other instruments. During recent years, some Sch 30bn has been annually issued.

The rest of the *Daueremissionen* volume is covered by mortgage-backed and municipal credit-backed bonds. Of these two products, the municipal credit-backed bonds are of relatively higher importance than the mortgage-backed bonds. The lower market share of these two types of bond can be explained by the fact that only a few Austrian financial institutions have the legal permission to issue them.

Corporate bonds

Although the new issue volume of corporates has seen an impressive growth during recent years (see Figure 10.37), their real market share is still quite modest. The issue volume increased from a rather low level in 1987 (Sch 305m), to a

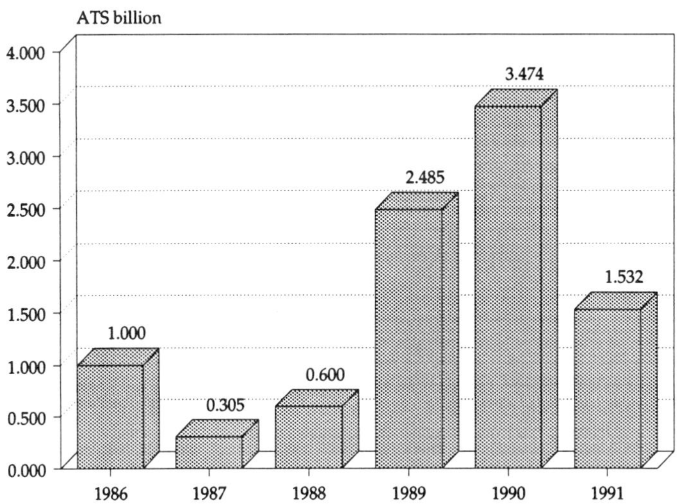

Figure 10.37 New issue volume of corporate bond issues since 1986 (includes straights, warrants, convertibles & 'Going Public' bond)

respectable Sch 3.5bn in 1990. In 1991, however, the new issue volume decreased to Sch 1.5bn.

The major obstacle to bringing more corporates to the capital market is probably the fact that most of the companies have quite good access to subsidized loans. Currently, there are more than 200 different types of government subsidized loan facility. This primarily affects the private placement market, because many Austrian corporates have neither the resources or, simply perhaps, the need to raise a volume of at least Sch 500m, which is regarded as the minimum size required to create a liquid bond issue in a public offering (although, in reality, common issue sizes are usually at, or below, this level).

Additionally, the vast majority of corporates which have used the capital market for fund raising during recent times have taken advantage of the prosperous equity market (especially in 1989), and financed themselves via equity.

In view of the intention to join the EC, plus the emergence of new markets in Eastern Europe, it is Austria's declared policy to erase the old system of subsidized loans while, at the same time, taking measures to attract corporates to the fixed-income sector. In the future, Austrian corporations will have to increase their use of the capital market for the purposes of both international investment and joint ventures.

Foreign bonds

Due to the limitations placed on foreign borrowers in the past, this part of the Austrian bond market has historically been fairly small (see Figure 10.38). However, during the course of 1989, the list of potential borrowers was extended by the allowance of all foreign issuers into the market.

Prior to this move, foreign issues had been limited to supranational agencies. Until 1988, there had been only two or three issues per year. Development banks and institutions like Eurofima were the main borrowers, with the World Bank being the largest single issuer.

Since 1989, several foreign borrowers (other than supranationals) have tapped the Austrian market:

- Bank of Foreign Economic Affairs of the USSR
- National Bank of Hungary (three times)
- Bayerische Hypotheken- und Wechselbank
- Commerzbank Overseas Finance N.V.
- AB Electrolux
- Omni Capital Markets Ltd.
- Petroleos Mexicanos (twice)
- AMAG Nederland B.V.
- JECC (Japan Electronic Computer Company)

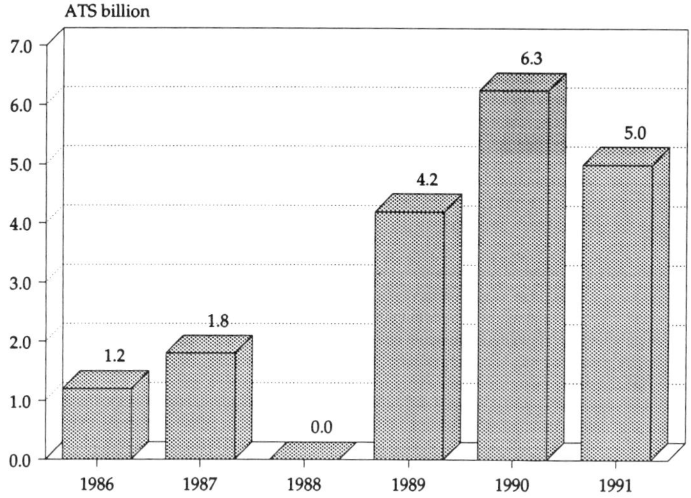

Figure 10.38 New issue volume of foreign bonds since 1986 (includes straights, warrants, supranationals)

In 1990, foreign borrowers' issuing activity increased by an extraordinary 54 per cent. In 1991, the issues of foreign borrowers developed in line with most other market participants. Their market share decreased in favour of Austrian government bonds and amounted to around 5 per cent.

In the third quarter of 1991, though, foreign issues reached an incredible market share of nearly 25 per cent. This unprecedented situation which, for this period alone, put the group in second place in terms of floated volume, had two major causes: Firstly, July and August are traditionally quiet months with only very moderate market activity - in 1991, practically no bank bonds were floated - and it wasn't until mid-September that the only government bond issue of the quarter, appeared. Secondly, most of the foreign bond issues are swap-driven and during the summer months of '91, the swap rates offered extremely attractive funding opportunities, especially among the shorter maturities. It was precisely this appealing market climate which drew three supranational institutions to tap the Austrian capital market, with Sch 1bn each. Besides the well-established Eurofima, a new issuer, 'The Council of Europe Resettlement Fund for Refugees and Over-Population in Europe', came to the domestic fixed-income sector. This bond was remarkable, insofar as it had an initial maturity of just two years (the same borrower again tapped the market with an identical maturity structure in early 1992). The short lifetime enabled the borrower to take full advantage of the almost flat yield curve in Austria, in relation to the strongly inverse yield structure in Germany, and to end up at an attractive all-in cost-level. In December 1991, the same advantage was realized by another new name on the domestic bond market, as the supranational, Nordic Investment Bank, launched Sch 1bn with a lifetime of three years.

After more than eight years of absence from the Austrian capital market, the Asian Development Bank re-entered this market in September 1991 (*see* Foreign borrowers, in Section 10.4).

Because of the tax advantage of supranational bonds (interest is paid out gross), these issues are exclusively targeted at the retail investor. As all of these bonds had different initial maturities, there were no difficulties in placement.

In general, bonds of foreign borrowers tend to have issue sizes of Sch 500m and above.

The easing of the issuing regulations have given (and will continue to give) a strong impetus to the foreign bond market, with the result that further growth and diversification can be expected.

10.9 *Methods of trading*

Overview

There are a number of trading methods practiced in Austria:

- on the Vienna Stock Exchange
  a) official trading (*Amtlicher Handel*)
  b) unofficial regulated trading (*Geregelter Freiverkehr*)
  c) OTC (*Sonstiger Wertpapierhandel*)

- Telephone trading (*Telefonhandel*)

The greater volume is traded off-exchange, as illustrated in Figure 10.39, below:

1991	**Turnover on the Vienna Stock Exchange**	**Total turnover**
January	2721	55,303
February	5025	81,230
March	2885	43,472
April	2267	28,643
May	1441	34,441
June	1903	37,161
July	2121	38,943
August	1986	16,543
September	2622	16,848
October	3078	30,070
November	1923	38,902
December	1759	77,684
1991 Total	29,732	499,240
1990 Total	23,049	435,517

Figure 10.39 Comparison of exchange and off-exchange bond turnover

Stock exchange trading

One function of trading on the stock exchange is the fixing of price, which is important for the other trading sectors. Bond prices are expressed as a percentage of par value.

On the Vienna Stock Exchange, the *Sensale,* official floor brokers, execute orders during the trading hours of 10.30 - 13.30. There are a certain number of *Freie Makler,* brokers who act as intermediaries between authorized credit institutions and private clients, in addition to dealing on their own account.

Telephone trading

Aside from trading on the official market, bonds are also traded on the OTC market. Bonds are traded before, during and after, official trading hours and are not required to go through the stock exchange.

OTC telephone trading takes place primarily in the interbank market and with institutional investors. Two-way prices (bid/ask) are quoted on Reuters, Bloomberg and Telerate by the largest banks. Deals vary in volume from Sch 1m to Sch 100m.

Orders

Orders with no limit at market (called *bestens,* meaning at the best market price available) are possible as, too, are orders with a specified limit, and stop orders.

Verbal orders (by telephone) are valid for one day and expire if they can not be executed. Written orders which do not specify a time limit remain valid until the end of the month.

As a result of the Stock Exchange Act of 1989, a third category of trading was established on the Vienna Stock Exchange called *Sonstiger Handel* or 'other trading', for which the listing requirements are not as strict as for the first two categories.

Market-makers

The names of the market-makers under the government bond tender scheme, together with their Reuters page codes, can be found in Figure 10.45 (in Section 10.18, Sources of reference).

10.10 *Market practices*

Coupon payment

By far the most common form of interest payment on the Austrian bond market is annual payment. At present, all straight *Einmalemissionen* on the market have a full-year coupon.

In the mortgage-backed and municipal credit-backed bonds markets some issues, particularly older ones, bear half-year coupons. For these issues, yields are commonly calculated including compound interest on the half-year payment. Similarly, some FRNs, whose interest rate is adjusted twice a year, bear half-year coupons. A few more recent FRNs (particularly money-market orientated ones, and reverse-floaters) have their interest rates adjusted (or will have them adjusted after an initial period of constant interest), quarterly. In these cases interest is also (or, will also be) paid out four times a year.

The coupons for FRTNs are fixed every quarter with the number of days of the next interest period being published together with the interest rate for this period (usually 88 - 93 days, depending on the months' length and weekends).

First coupon

On rare occasions, bonds have been issued with 'unusual' first coupons (longer or shorter than a normal coupon period). In these cases, interest is calculated on a 30/360 day basis.

In the past few years, the Republic of Austria has occasionally issued bonds with a shorter first coupon. These were identical in terms with previous issues and were consequently merged with them in order to obtain bigger and more liquid units.

Partly-paid

As yet, there have been no partly-paid bond issues in the Austrian market.

Interest payment and ex-coupon dates

Payment is made through the custodian bank free-of-charge, if the bank acts as paying agent for the issuer. Interest payments are usually made on an annual basis, 360 days a year, 30 days a month. The ex-coupon date is the first Monday of the month if the coupon date is between the 10th and 24th of that month; in any other case, it is the first Monday after the 14th day of the month. Bonds are traded ex-coupon on, and after, that Monday.

The pay and value dates may differ by one or two days, dependent on whether the bank is acting as paying agent.

Redemptions

Virtually all schilling bond issues redeem at par. Exceptions are a few callable issues which have to be redeemed at a premium if they called early (redemption at prices between 100.25 and 101.00), and the specific Austrian form of zero-coupon bonds, *Prämienanleihen*. These bonds were issued at a price of 100 and will be redeemed in a gross sum, including all accrued interest.

Call and put clauses

Although, until 1985, many government bonds were issued with a call option, this clause has since become less common. Since 1986, only four callable government bonds have been issued. The Republic of Austria has, however, repeatedly indicated that she does not intend to exercise this right. There are also few callable issues in the corporate and bank bond sectors .

In the mortgage-backed and municipal credit-backed market sectors, however, a call option is a common feature. Issuers have, in the past, frequently exercised their right to call an issue, combined with an offer to refrain from the call if the bond holder accepts a new (usually, lower) coupon rate.

Singular bank issues bear a put option, commonly (but not exclusively) in combination with a call option.

Serial bonds

Until around 1985, serial bonds (with predefined redemption schemes) were a common feature in most market segments, although they were rare in the *Daueremissionen* market. On some of these bonds redemption started just one year after issue whilst, in other cases, there were several years without capital repayment.

Serial bonds have become increasingly less important over the past few years - the last government issue was in 1985, with later single issues only until 1989.

Denomination

Government straight bonds usually have minimum denomination of Sch 1000 or Sch 10,000; a few issues also have Sch 5000 denominations. Federal obligations (with the exception of a very few, retail-targeted issues) have been issued in denominations of Sch 100,000 or Sch 1m, as have been FRTNs.

For corporate and bank bonds, the situation is similar, with usual minimum units being Sch 1000 to Sch 10,000. Being targeted primarily to small investors, mortgage-backed and municipal credit-backed *Daueremissionen* used to be issued in denominations of only Sch 1000; only recently have some of these bonds been issued in units up to Sch 10,000.

Form

Austrian schilling bonds are bearer bonds. However, for the bonds to be actually printed is rather the exception, than the rule; usually, the bond holder owns a share of one global note (*Sammelurkunde*) which is held in custody by Oesterreichische Kontrollbank.

Fees

Towards the end of 1991 the structure of fees on the secondary market came under extensive scrutiny, a process which is expected to last well into 1992. As a result, information can be given only about 1991 fee levels. Note that the figures given are for general indication only, since they may vary from bank to bank and according to order sizes or other determinants.

Buying and selling commissions

If bond transactions are not done on a net price basis, usually commissions of 0.75 per cent of transaction value are charged. These commissions include the stock exchange turnover tax and (if the transaction is carried out on the stock exchange) all stock exchange and broker fees. In the case of a net price transaction, the quoted price includes all commission elements, as well as the stock exchange turnover tax.

Custody fees

Usually Austrian banks charge approximately 0.0375 per cent custody fees for collective custody, and double this amount, for individual custody. The banks, however, normally reduce the custody fee by 50 per cent for their own issues.

Collection of fees

Since usually issuers pay respective fees to paying agents for their activities, the payment of interest and the repayment of capital of bonds are free of commission for the investor.

10.11 Settlement

For transactions on the Vienna Stock Exchange, the value date (settlement date) is normally the second Monday after the trading date. For business done between banks, the value date can be fixed individually but, in the absence of such an agreement, it will be seven calendar days after the trading date.

The settlement office, *Arrangementbureau*, which is operated by Oesterreichische Kontrollbank, assists the Vienna Stock Exchange in processing transactions. Together with the Central Depository (Wertpapiersammelbank), which is also a part of Oesterreichische Kontrollbank, this office minimizes physical delivery of stock exchange transactions. For cross-border transactions, Oesterreichische Kontrollbank provides a service through foreign clearing organizations (e.g. Deutscher Kassenverein, Deutscher Auslands Kassenverein, Euroclear).

10.12 *Yield calculation*

Overview

The yields of all Austrian bonds quoted on the Vienna Stock Exchange are calculated daily by Oesterreichische Kontrollbank and published once a week, together with the basic primary and secondary market data of each individual bond, in the brochure *Anleiheninformationen*.

These calculations form the basis for the calculation of average yields of issuer groups, as well as for the calculation of the Austrian Bond Performance Index (API). The results - group yields and bond performance indices - are published daily on Reuters screens OKBA-D.

The issuers for which group yields are calculated, are:

- government
- public funds
- special public agencies
- provinces and municipalities
- central electricity utility (Verbundgesellschaft)
- other electricity utilities
- corporates and other domestic issuers
- foreign issuers
- banks
- federal obligations (*Bundesobligationen*)

The group figures are computed by weighting the individual bond yield (average yield-to-maturity) by the amount outstanding at the moment of calculation. Omitted are bonds with a remaining life of less than a year as, too, are bonds with warrants, convertibles, index-linked bonds and money market floaters. In addition to the publication of the group figures daily on the Reuters network, and weekly in the *Anleiheninformationen*, the monthly arithmetic mean is published in the *Statistisches Monatsheft der Oesterreichischen Nationalbank*, the monthly statistical publication of the Austrian Central Bank.

The above-mentioned grouped and weighted figures play an important role in the Austrian banking sector, since they are commonly used as a basis for the charging of interest rates on many loans, as well as for capital market floaters.

Calculation method

The yield formula used to calculate yields in Austria corresponds to the ISMA formula:

$$P + a = \sum_{i=1}^{n} c_i \times r^{-\frac{i}{360}}$$

whereas the yield y is derived from r according to the following formula:

$$y = 100 \times (r - 1)$$

where,

P clean price
a accrued interest
n number of days between value date applicable to the calculation and the last payment of principal. The number of days is calculated on the basis of 30 days a month and of 360 days a year. Amounts falling due on the 31st of a month are regarded as falling due on the 30th of the respective month.
c_i cashflow due on the ith day according to the terms and conditions of the bond. This amount may comprise interest, principal, premium and - in the case of calculating effective costs - fees, commissions, taxes, etc.

Yields calculated by Oesterreichische Kontrollbank are based on the stock exchange value date. Prices are the clean prices quoted on the Vienna Stock Exchange. Accrued interest is normally a positive amount, calculated on a 30/360 basis. From the ex-coupon date onwards, they have negative values. Partial redemptions of principal in the case of serial bonds are not taken into account after the date of drawing, since there is usually no trade in those bonds already drawn. The drawing takes place between some four months and one month before due date, according to the conditions of the bond.

The average life published in the *Anleiheninformationen* is calculated as the mean of the life to next redemption and the life to last redemption. The duration, which nowadays is used by most analysts, is also calculated.

Contrary to other European FRN markets, the coupon of most Austrian floaters is not dependent on money market rates, but rather on capital market rates. These bonds are regarded as capital market instruments rather than short-term instruments and, therefore, prices tend not to be near par at the date of coupon fixing. For these reasons, the calculation of effective margins does not make sense. Oesterreichische Kontrollbank publishes yields computed under the assumption that all future coupons will be fixed under present market conditions. Since this form of yield calculation has been criticized on the basis that extreme high or low market rates certainly do not prevail during the whole life, the intention is to change the method described above, to one which uses long-term average rates.

The yields of money market floaters are already calculated by Oesterreichische Kontrollbank, on the basis of the respective VIBOR (Vienna interbank offered rate) for three or six months, and will be published in the near future.

Indices

At the moment two bond indices exist in Austria: a price index by Creditanstalt-Bankverein and a performance index by Oesterreichische Kontrollbank (API).

The price index of the Creditanstalt 'CA-Rentenindex' is based on an index-portfolio consisting of 60 Austrian bonds which reflect the structure of the traded bond market in terms of remaining life, coupon and type of issuer. Bonds exempt from withholding tax (issued before 1984) are not represented in this portfolio. The index is computed by weighting the quoted price of each bond with the amount outstanding. The index series started with the trade-date of 2 January 1985.

Name of index	Contents	Basis date (= 100)
API 1	Government bonds	02 January 1985
API 2	Bank bonds - fixed-coupon	02 January 1985
API 3	Bank bonds - capital market floaters	25 August 1986
API 4	Bank bonds - total	25 August 1986
API 5	Total market - *Einmalemission* (incl. capital market floaters)	25 August 1986
API 6	Total market - *Einmalemission* - fixed-coupon	02 January 1985

Figure 10.40 Austrian bond indices (API Indices)

The index portfolio of the Austrian Performance Index (API) is composed of all bonds quoted on the Vienna Stock Exchange. The essential idea of the index is that, at any given moment, the index portfolio comprises the same percentage of any bond quoted. Thus, cashflow from any bond (principal, interest, premium) is reinvested in the whole market, thereby increasing the percentage of all the bonds represented in the portfolio. In the case of a new issue, an amount of the old portfolio is 'sold' such that the receipts are sufficient to 'buy' the new bond in the necessary percentage of volume.

10.13 Taxation

Taxation of interest income

Under Austrian law, a tax on capital income (*Kapitalertragsteuer*) is levied on dividends, interest income from bonds (including money market instruments) and interest income from bank deposits. In the case of interest-bearing securities and bank deposits, the paying agent is required to withhold the tax.

The tax rate is 10 per cent of the interest paid on bonds, money market instruments and bank deposits.

As far as bonds are concerned, there are several exemptions from the tax on capital income. Tax-exempt is the interest on:

- Austrian schilling bonds issued before 01 January 1984;
- foreign currency bonds issued before 01 January 1989;
- bonds issued by supranational financial institutions (e.g. World Bank, EBRD, Eurofima, etc.).

Furthermore, the tax is not withheld if the securities are held as assets of a business - provided that this circumstance is made known to the paying agent and that the securities are deposited with a bank. Additionally, foreign private investors can claim tax-free payment of their interest on bonds and securitized money market instruments upon proof of their foreign, and non-resident, status.

In other cases (e.g. tax on the interest on a foreigner's cash account) investors from some 50 countries can gain full, or partial, tax relief on the basis of double taxation agreements.

Since the tax on capital income is a form of income tax, it is accounted as part of personal income tax liability.

Taxation of capital gains

Under Austrian tax law, the net profit from the sale of any kind of assets is generally taxable for business concerns while generally not taxable for private individuals. Profits from speculation, on the other hand, are taxable for individuals. For holders of securities, such speculative profits occur when the securities are held for up to twelve months and sold at a net profit.

For private investors, capital gains on bonds issued by Austrian domestic institutions are not regarded as speculative profits under Austrian tax laws. However, this exemption does not apply to convertible bonds and the bonds of foreign issuers.

There is a further exception which, in certain cases, re-introduces a taxation of capital gains on bonds issued by domestic institutions. Capital gains on bonds are subject to tax on capital income (to be withheld by the paying agent) if the official issue price of the bond was more than 2 per cent of face value lower than the redemption price. In such a case, it is assumed that any difference between the purchase price and the redemption (or sale) price contains an element of interest computed on the basis of the issue yield of the bond. This fictitious interest is calculated by employing a linear (non-compound) method, on a monthly basis.

In the case of a warrant bond, a theoretical value of the warrant is calculated which is then deducted from the historic issue price. If the coupon of the warrant bond is more than one percentage point lower than the average market yield at the time of issuance, this separation calculation is made immediately.

As indicated, this 'quasi-interest' element of capital gains on (warrant, discount and zero-coupon) bonds is regarded as taxable capital income (accounted at a 10 per cent tax rate).

Securities tax (*Wertpapiersteuer*)

The initial acquisition, in Austria, of bonds issued by a foreign issuer is subject to securities tax when these bonds are physically kept in Austria. The applicable rate is 1 per cent of the nominal value. In practice, this tax is of virtually no relevance.

Stock exchange turnover tax (*Börsenumsatzsteuer*)

Except for new issues, all sales and purchases of securities in Austria are subject to the stock exchange turnover tax whether or not the transaction takes place through the stock exchange.

For bonds the tax rate is between 0.04 and 0.1 per cent of the transaction price, dependent on the status of the issuer. It is halved when the transaction is done between securities traders. When the transaction takes place outside Austria, and if only one of the participants is an Austrian resident, the tax rate is also reduced by 50 per cent.

In practice, the stock exchange turnover tax is included in trading commissions, or in the net prices quoted by the banks. As in many other countries there have been discussions about the abolition of this tax, although no final decision has yet been made.

10.14 Futures & options

In 1989, the leading Austrian banks started preparations for the establishment of a futures and options exchange. They founded ÖTOB (Österreichische Termin- und Optionenbörse) as a joint-stock company which was to start and carry through the project, and which is today the organization which operates the futures and options market.

Presently, in 1992, ÖTOB has 42 shareholders - all the leading banks in Austria and one stockbroking company. The ÖTOB banks account for more than 95 per cent of all equity trading in Austria.

Organization of the market

ÖTOB is responsible for the fully-electronic trading and clearing of all derivative products. Commissioned by the Vienna Stock Exchange, the company safeguards the use and operation of the computer system, and ensures that transactions are done fairly, safely and quickly. It is the contract partner for both parties in all transactions and, as a clearing house, guarantees the fulfilment of all contracts. It uses the settlement system of OeKB to settle all related securities transactions. Furthermore, ÖTOB offers information and education services.

Contracts traded

Currently, stock options are traded on six of the most liquid equities on the Vienna Stock Exchange (Creditanstalt pref., EVN, Lenzing, ÖMV, Verbund, and Wienerberger). For each of the underlying securities, there are between four and eight market-makers, who continually feed quotes for the options into the trading system. This provides the transparency and liquidity essential for a derivatives market. The introduction of options on further underlying equities is planned for the future.

Contract specifications

On ÖTOB, both calls and puts (American-style) are traded. Trading hours are 10.30 to 14.00 local time. Expiration dates are the third Friday of each month (or the previous working day). For each underlying security, options with a maturity of one, two and three months are traded, as well as an option extending until the last month of the following quarter.

Further details concerning strike prices, tick sizes, fees, settlement, payment & delivery, etc. can be obtained from any market-maker (the large Austrian banks), or directly from ÖTOB, A-1014 Vienna (Tel: (43 1) 531 65).

Equity index products (to be launched in 1992)

ÖTOB intends to launch options on the ATX Equity Index during the first half of 1992. Futures on the ATX are also to be introduced soon, possibly on the same date. The ATX is a relatively new index for Austrian stocks, and has been developed by ÖTOB in co-operation with the University of Graz. It comprises (currently) 18 stocks in the consecutive trading segment of the Vienna Stock Exchange and is the first real-time index in the market. The ATX was introduced in 1991, and has gained a healthy reputation among both domestic and international investors.

Interest rate futures (to be launched in 1992/1993)

In addition to the above, there is the intention to introduce interest rate futures on a notional government bond (most likely one with a 10-year maturity) either in late 1992, or in 1993. The product specification can be expected to be similar to that of the DTB German Bund futures contract.

It is envisaged that a short-term interest rate futures contract will be introduced at a later stage.

10.15 Money markets

Overview

There is a schilling money market in Austria, but it is not securitized to any significant extent - only the 3-month VIBOR-linked FRTNs (see Section 10.4) are of relevance to foreign investors. Nevertheless, there are also listed Treasury notes to be found. These notes, which are exclusively held by Austrian banks, are described below.

Issuer

On several occasions during the past, the Republic of Austria has issued Treasury notes which have been allotted to certain Austrian banks, in fixed quotas.

Maturity

All Treasury notes are one-year instruments. However, upon original issue, the government and the buying banks have agreed on yearly extensions of the notes until certain, predefined, maturities. At present, final maturities range from 1994 to 1999.

Interest

The interest period always starts at the 25th of each month, even if such a day is a holiday. The Ministry of Finance informs the banks of the relevant interest rate for the following coupon period - the rate being dependent on the market yield for bonds, with a certain discount which, for the time being, may vary from bank to bank. Interest is paid annually on a 30/360 days basis, although this rule virtually never applies since the notes are, in practice, rarely traded.

Buyers

All Treasury notes are held by domestic banks. They may serve as collateral for open-market transactions with the Austrian National Bank and for interbank lending.

Calls

In principle, the original maturity agreements between the government and the banks are valid until maturity although, theoretically, the partners could agree on the cancellation of such a contract. One-sided calls or puts are not possible.

Prices

In theory, the Treasury notes are listed on the Vienna Stock Exchange. In practice, just one fixing (at 100) is made a few days after any renewal, followed by one before year-end, in order to provide an official level for the purposes of valuation in the banks' balance sheets.

10.16 *Interest rate history*

Due to the fact that the exchange rate between the Deutschemark and the Austrian schilling has not really changed since August 1981 (illustrated by a ten-year Sch/Dm high/low of 7.0555 and 7.003), capital and money market rates have not differed substantially from the corresponding German rates. However, the real rate of return (yield minus inflation rate) fluctuates more in Austria.

Since the early fifties, the average coupon of Austrian issues has been about 7.75 per cent, with a high/low of 11 per cent and 6.5 per cent (foreign issuers, warrant bonds, zero-coupons, excluded).

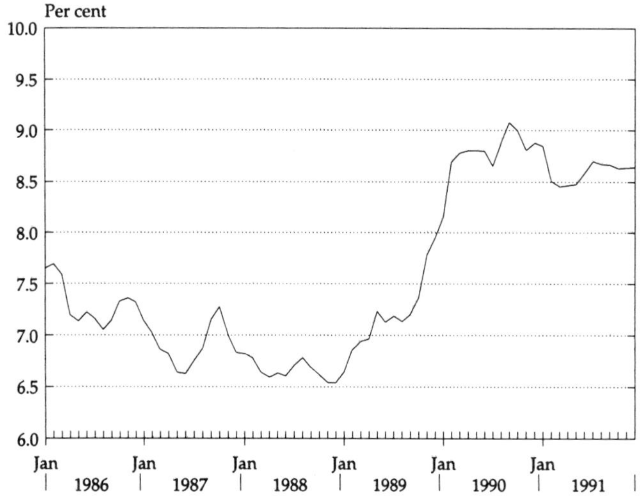

Figure 10.41 Secondary market yields of government bonds

Since the beginning of 1986 the volume-weighted average yield of government bonds has shown a steady decrease from 7.6 per cent to 6.5 per cent at the end of 1988. During 1989, and in the first quarter of 1990, yields increased again to just under 9 per cent, remaining at that level until the end of 1990. After somewhat lower yields in spring of 1991, the yield level reached 8.5 to 8.75 per cent at the end of the year. The yield decreased further, to 8.3 per cent at the end of February 1992, with the general expectation for mid-1992 being 8.0 per cent.

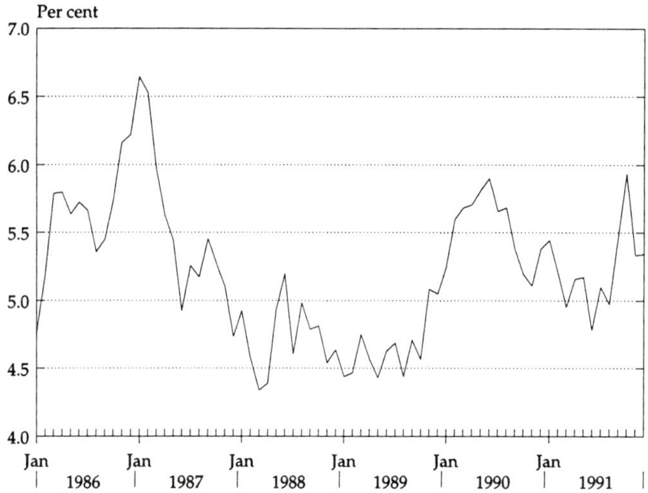

Figure 10.42 Real rate of return

The real rate of return (see Figure 10.42) was rather high between 1981 and 1991 with an approximate average of 4.5 per cent. The maximum rate of 6.8 per cent was recorded in January 1987, while June 1984 saw the minimum of 1.7 per cent.

10.17 *Inter-market spreads*

Domestic inter-market spreads

In the past - with few exceptions - the average secondary market yield of bank bonds (see Figure 10.43) was lower than the average government bond yield by up to 25 basis points. This can be explained, firstly, by the fact that bond-issuing Austrian banks have a very good financial standing (moreover, since most bank issues are collateralized, or state-guaranteed, there are no repayment risks) and,

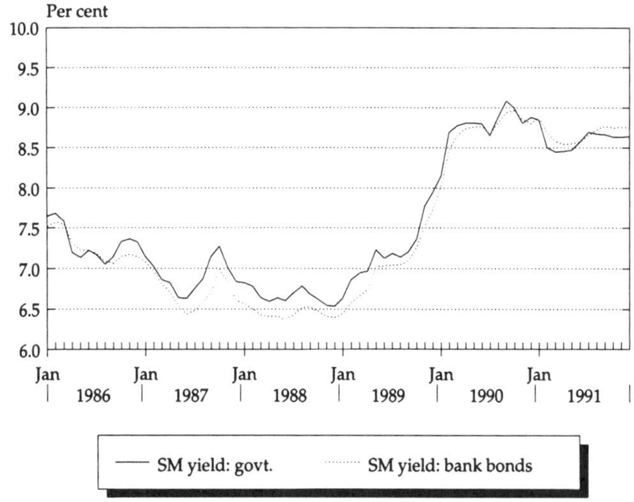

Figure 10.43 Secondary market yields of government and fixed-income bank bonds

secondly, by the fact that banks provide a very liquid market in their own issues.

In 1991, government bonds showed (for the first time) a lower return than bank bonds, reflecting the increase in liquidity caused by the introduction of the market-maker system. On average, the difference amounted to 10 basis points.

With the appearance of the first foreign issuers (other than supranationals) on the Austrian bond market, substantially higher secondary market yields emerged. Yield differentials between the foreign issues sector and the government sector amounted, in 1991, to 110 to 210 basis points.

The yield curve in Austria has always been characterized by a very rare pattern of two peaks. The reason is that there are two market segments: one with average lives to maturity up to 4 years, and dominated by bonds issued before 1984 (tax exempt and mostly serial bonds), the other with average lives of over 4 years (not tax exempt). Due to a lack of trade, the shorter market sector shows little reaction to interest rate changes.

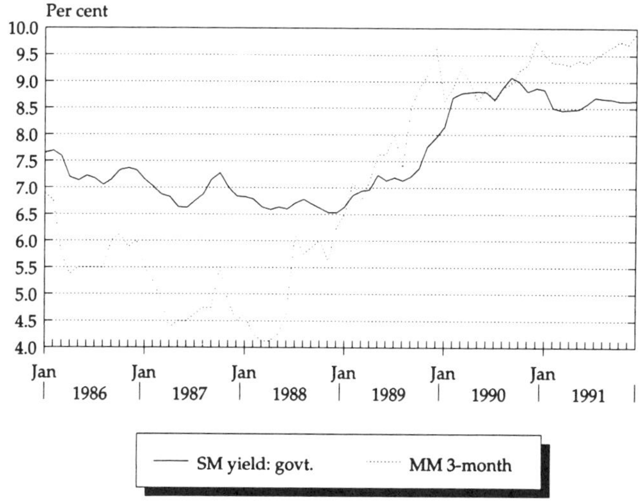

Figure 10.44 Secondary market yields of government and 3-month money rates

The differential between government bond yields and money market rates ranged between +50 and +200 basis points (see Figure 10.44). In 1988, it turned negative and vanished entirely from February to September 1990. Since October 1990, the yield curve has been inverse, with a maximum negative differential of 112 basis points seen in October 1991.

Spreads between Austria and Germany

As pointed out already (see Section 10.2, Economics), there has been a substantial change in the yield differential structure between Austrian and German government bonds. The spread between Austrian and German government bond yields was +150 to +50 basis points in the years 1986 to 1988, was balanced in 1989 and turned negative, by approximately -20 basis points, in 1990 and 1991.

10.18 Sources of reference

Financial publications

- *Statistisches Monatsheft der Oesterreichischen Nationalbank* (monthly): General economic data and statistics on Austria and detailed data on banking activities, including capital market statistics, published by the Austrian central bank

- *Berichte und Studien der Oesterreichischen Nationalbank* (Reports and Summaries of the Austrian National Bank) (quarterly)
More detailed papers and statistics on monetary policy, banking, financial markets and general economic developments, published by the Austrian central bank

- *Anleiheninformationen der Oesterreichischen Kontrollbank* (weekly): Detailed information on each bond listed at the Vienna Stock Exchange - basic primary and secondary market data including yields (to maturity, to next call, minimum and maximum yields in case of serial bonds), average lives, duration etc., as well as on issuers' groups

- *Kapitalmarktservice der Oesterreichischen Kontrollbank* (weekly): Information on planned and recent issues, yield curves, new instruments, issue procedures and adjusted coupons of FRNs; Austrian Bond Performance Indices (API)

- *Banking in Austria*
Girozentrale und Bank der österreichischen Sparkassen AG

- *Finanzmarktprognose*
Girozentrale und Bank der österreichischen Sparkassen AG

- *Investment Focus* (monthly, in German)
Bank Austria

- *CA Quarterly*
Facts and figures on Austria's economy (in German and English)

- *CA Bond Report*
Monthly, in German (English edition in preparation)

- *Girozentrale-Schilling Trends* (monthly)
  Girozentrale und Bank der österreichischen Sparkassen AG

- *Austrian capital market*
  Girozentrale und Bank der österreichischen Sparkassen AG

Quote vendors and news agencies

- Reuters provide screen information as shown in Figure 10.45

- Telerate provide screen information as follows:

17249, 51-52, 56	Girozentrale

- Bloomberg provide screen information as follows:

BAVI	Bank Austria AG

Page No.	Contributor	Subject
General bond and capital market screens		
BAUA-C	Bank Austria AG	Bond market information
CADZ-EE	Creditanstalt-Bankverein	Bond market information
ECOH	Oesterreichischen Nationalbank	Group yields (monthly averages)
GIRW-Z	Girozentrale und Bank der öesterreichischen Sparkassen AG	Bond market information
OKBA-C	Oesterreichischen Kontrollbank	Group yields & prices
OKBD	Oesterreichischen Kontrollbank	Austrian Bond Performance Indices (API)
OKBE-G	Oesterreichischen Kontrollbank	Issue calendar - explanation
OKBH-J	Oesterreichischen Kontrollbank	Issue calendar - single issues
OKBK-M	Oesterreichischen Kontrollbank	Issue calendar - permanent issues
OKBT	Oesterreichischen Kontrollbank	Government bond tender information
QQHH-I	Multi-contributor	Money market information
VIBO		Vienna Interbank Offered Rate
Market-maker screens for certain government bonds		
BAUA	Bank Austria AG	
BAVX	Bank für Arbeit und Wirtschaft AG	
BSVA	Schoeller & Co. Bankaktiengesellschaft	
CAEC	Creditanstalt-Bankverein	
DMLM	Deutsche Bank (Austria) AG	
FABG	DIE ERSTE österreichische Spar-Casse - Bank	
GIRX	Girozentrale und Bank der österreichischen Sparkassen AG	
OBKA	Bank für Oberösterreich und Salzburg	
OCCC	Österreichisches Credit-Institut, AG (will be merged with Girozentrale)	
OVAI	Österreichische Volksbanken-AG	
PFST	Pfandbriefstelle der österreichischen Landes-Hypothekenbanken	
PSKA	Österreichische Postsparkasse	
RZBA	Raiffeisen Zentralbank Österreich AG	
VPVH	Vindobona Privat-Bank AG	

Figure 10.45 Reuters pages

Chapter

11

The bond markets of

Belgium

Françoise Beirens
Generale Bank

Gilbert François
Belfox

Chris van Aeken
Kredietbank

Addendum on Luxembourg by

Yves Wagner
Banque Générale du Luxembourg

Note: In general text, the abbreviation 'BFr' is used to denote the Belgian franc. Elsewhere, the international mnemonic 'BEF' is used.

11.1 Introduction

Overview

At the level of 12.9 per cent seen between 1982 and 1990, Belgian government bonds have had the best annualized return (expressed in US$) when compared to the government bonds of the US (9.9 per cent), Germany (9.2 per cent), Japan (8.8 per cent), the Netherlands (8.4 per cent), France (10 per cent), the United Kingdom (11.5 per cent), Switzerland (4.7 per cent), and those Ecu issues for sovereign names (7.8 per cent).

This impressive performance can be attributed to the fundamental change in the Belgian approach to economic problems. This origins of this change, initiated in 1982, can be traced to the major increases in the price of oil seen in the 1970s which had resulted in a period of slow (even negative) economic growth and double digit inflation. These recessionary forces had, in turn, led to an increase in both current account imbalance and public sector borrowing requirement.

The turning point in economic policy was an 8.5 per cent devaluation of the Belgian franc against the Ecu, in February of 1982, followed by the introduction of strict austerity measures.

The results of this policy were: a fall in the rate of inflation to an absolute minimum of 1.2 per cent in 1988 (year-on-year), a growth in the surplus of the current account balance (towards 2 per cent of GNP), and a reduced public sector net financing requirement (down from 13.4 per cent of GNP in 1981, to 5.6 per cent in 1990).

Deregulation and reform

However, despite these successes, there is still a major macroeconomic problem to be resolved - that of the size and servicing of the public sector debt, which is one of the highest in Europe and well above the EC average.

To tackle this problem, a series of measures have been taken over recent years (see Figure 11.1). The reforms have already had an enormous impact on the government bond market. An indication of its success can be seen in the lowering of the borrowing costs for the Treasury as well as the growing participation of foreign investors in the market.

In addition to the benefits of reform and economic policy success, the Belgian money and capital markets have also benefited from a programme of modernization. So, although the Belgian debt burden is still high, at least the instruments required to manage it have been brought up to international standards.

The latest event in the overall process is the opening of the Belgian Futures and Options Exchange (Belfox) which traded its first bond futures contract on 6 December 1991.

Mar 1989	Weekly credit tenders on government issues and repos of commercial paper
May 1989	First linear bond issue
Mar 1990	Lowering of the withholding tax from 25 per cent to 10 per cent
	Abolition of the two-tier foreign exchange market
May 1990	Decision to peg the Belgian franc to the Deutschemark within the EMS
Oct 1990	Designation of primary dealers
Jan 1991	Abolition of the 'fixing' of foreign currencies by the National Bank of Belgium (NBB)
	Abolition of stamp duties on commercial paper
	Enlarged power for the Banking and Finance Commission
	Lowering of stock exchange duties
	New market for Treasury certificates (primary and secondary)
	New clearing system at the NBB for Treasury certificates and linear bonds
	New monetary policy by the NBB coming into force

Figure 11.1 History of Belgian bond market deregulation & reform

The reforms mentioned above were all aimed at the modernization of the Belgian money and capital markets. Moreover, the new-style money market put an end to the monetary financing of the Treasury and resulted in a more independent central bank - one of the conditions for later Emu membership.

11.2 Economics

Introduction

With exports of goods and services representing 41 per cent of total resources (GNP plus imports), the Belgian economy is one of the most open and internationalized in the world. Developments are therefore largely influenced by the international environment and, consequently, the key to Belgian economic health lies in having a competitive international stance.

While the adverse effects of weakened competitiveness in the late seventies took their toll, with symptoms such as a bulging current account deficit, rapidly contracting economic growth and a record public sector borrowing level, the successful remedial measures taken in the early eighties have put the Belgian economy back on the right track.

Currently, Belgian economic policy is aimed at the realization of three interrelated objectives: a strong currency policy, budgetary discipline and a stable, and competitive, corporate infrastructure.

The sustained performance of the Belgian economy has enabled Belgium to gradually strengthen the Belgian franc within the EMS during the last years. In June 1990, following recommendations by the IMF, the Belgian authorities announced the pegging of the Belgian franc to the German mark - a policy which has since been maintained rigorously. The introduction of this hard currency policy, which is designed to reduce imported inflation, was warmly received by the markets and has led to the short-term interest rate differential with Germany and the Netherlands (which was close to 2 per cent at the beginning of 1990), being substantially minimized (to around nil at the end of 1991).

A policy of budgetary discipline is aimed at the stabilization of the level of the public debt relative to GNP (around 110 per cent, end 1991) and to the reversal of the vicious circle of a self-feeding debt due to the interest burden (the so-called 'snowball effect'). To reduce the budget deficit, a dual constraint has been self-imposed by the central government: public expenditure growth, excluding interest payment, is not allowed to exceed the growth rate of inflation, while the central borrowing requirement cannot exceed that of the preceding year, in nominal terms (i.e. BFr 405bn, the target level for 1989).

The Belgian government is determined to defend economic competitiveness *vis-à-vis* the country's main trading partners. Keeping production costs under control is one of the top priorities. A law concerning corporate competitiveness, enacted in January 1989, allows the government to intervene in wage negotiations whenever the Belgian wage costs rise considerably above the average of the country's main competitors; however, it is unlikely that such drastic measures will be needed.

The Belgian economy has made such significant progress since 1982 that it is now ready, in every respect but one, to participate in EC economic and monetary union (Emu). The remaining problem is the substantial public sector deficit. While short-term objectives of stabilizing the debt/GNP ratio (at 125-130 per cent) have been achieved, a further reduction of the ratio in the medium- and long-term will prove hard to obtain, due to substantial overshoots in some government sectors, such as social security, and the probable deceleration in economic growth. The high ratio, therefore, is the main cause behind the relentless effort to reduce public borrowing - one of the three priorities of the current economic policy. However, already, the combination of renewed corporate investment, sustained surpluses in the current account, growth in GNP (above EC averages), a low rate of inflation and a strong currency, have all contributed to the return of the Belgian economy as one of the strongest in Europe.

Politics

Political environment

The Belgian state, covering an area of 30,518 square km and with just under 10m inhabitants, is a constitutional parliamentary monarchy. The Constitution (in force since 1831) defines the separation of powers: the legislative power rests with the King and Parliament collectively, executive power is exercised by the King and his Ministers, and judicial power belongs to the Courts of Justice.

Parliament consists of two assemblies - the Chamber of Representatives (212 seats) and the senate (184 seats) - both of which have the power to propose legislation and vote on it. Legislative proposals and draft laws have to be approved by both assemblies.

By way of constitutional reform in 1970, 1980 and 1988, the central state was regionalized and extensive powers were given to:

- Three territorially-defined Regions (Flanders, Wallonia and Brussels) having *regional powers (public works, economic policy, etc.), and*
- *Three Communities (the Dutch- , French- and German-speaking), whose* powers are restricted to matters relating to education, culture etc..

Despite the granting of substantial financial autonomy (27 per cent of total public expenditure), the fiscal autonomy of the Regions and Communities remains rather limited, as the financing of expenditure takes place mainly via the re-allocation of taxes collected by the federal government.

International relations

Since 1921, Belgium has formed an economic and monetary union with Luxembourg (BLEU or Belgo-Luxembourg Economic Union). The Belgian and Luxembourg francs are at par and based on the combined foreign reserves of both countries. The National Bank of Belgium is responsible for the monetary policy.

The customs union of Belgium, the Netherlands and Luxembourg (BENELUX), established in 1948, was transformed into an economic union in 1960.

Belgium is a founding member of the European Community (EC) established by the 1951 and 1957 Treaties of Rome.

Government

Following the collapse of Mr Martens' eighth coalition on 4 October 1991, a general election was held on 24 November 1991.

The following table shows the general election results for the major parties (per number of seats in the Chamber, of a total of 212):

	1987	1991
Flemish Christian Democrats (CVP)	43	39
French-speaking Christian Democrats (PSC)	19	18
Flemish Socialists (SP)	32	28
French-speaking Socialists (PS)	40	35
Flemish Liberals (PVV)	25	26
French-speaking Liberals (PRL)	23	20
Flemish Federalist Party (VU)	16	10
Flemish Nationalists (Vlaams Blok)	2	12
Flemish Ecologists (Agalev)	6	7
French Ecologists (Ecolo)	3	10
All other	3	7
	212	*212*

Figure 11.2 Belgian general election results 1987/1991 [per seats in Chamber]

Gross national product

During 1988 and 1989, economic activity in Belgium accelerated. The GNP, in real terms, reached BFr 5634bn. Growth averaged 4.3 per cent in 1988 and 4.0 per cent in 1989, compared to 2.0 per cent in 1986-87 (see Figure 11.3). This improved economic performance, which was due to a robust revival in corporate investment and a high growth in exports, pushed GNP figures above the EC average and turned the Belgian economy into one of the most buoyant in the industrialized world. Although the revival of 1988-89 was carried over into 1990, leading to a GNP of BFr 6520bn, economic activity decelerated modestly

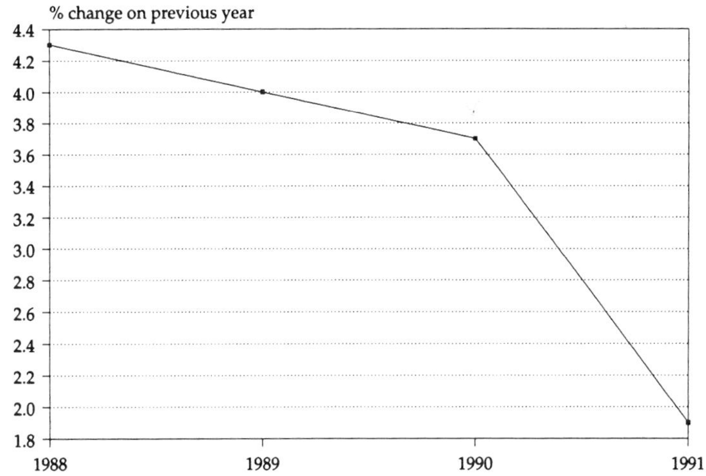

Figure 11.3 Belgian gross national product 1988-1991 (year-on-year percentage change)

during the year, to 3.7 per cent. In 1991 Belgium weathered a further, and more severe, slowdown in the improvement of economic performance (1.9 per cent).

Balance of payments

Belgium's improved competitive stance, along with the country's very open economy (exports of goods and services amount to 70 per cent of GNP), have together enabled it to take full advantage of strong growth in intra-EC trade. As a result, the volume of exports increased by an average of 8 per cent in 1988-

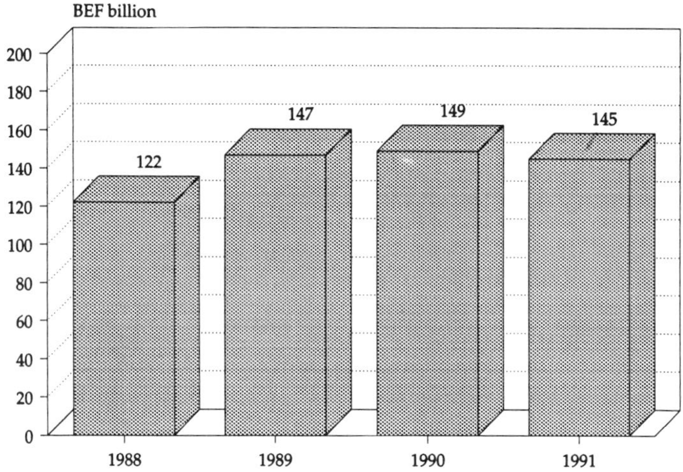

Figure 11.4 Belgian current account 1988-1991 (average of past 12 months, in BEF billion)

1989. Despite an acceleration in the real growth of domestic demand, to 5 per cent, the rise in imports remained in check. This strong trade performance, boosted particularly by exceptional demand from Germany, combined with the (automatic) indexation of wages and the deceleration of inflation, created a substantial surplus on the BLEU balance of payments current account - consistently amounting to some 2-3 per cent of GNP.

Another important evolutionary factor is the growing surplus in long-term capital transactions, especially in the balance of securities trading, due to the capital and money market reforms and the regained confidence in the Belgian franc. This resulted in a net capital inflow of BFr 128bn for the first six months of 1991, compared with just BFr 9bn for the same period in 1990.

Inflation

Inflation edged up, from 1.2 per cent in the second half of 1988 to 3.1 per cent in 1989 (see Figure 11.5), as a result of higher excise duties and food prices. The resultant increase in unit labour costs (of, roughly, 4 per cent) was even stronger in Belgium than in other EC countries, because of the system of automatic wage indexation which tends to reflect changes in the consumer price index very quickly (showing a lag of only around four months).

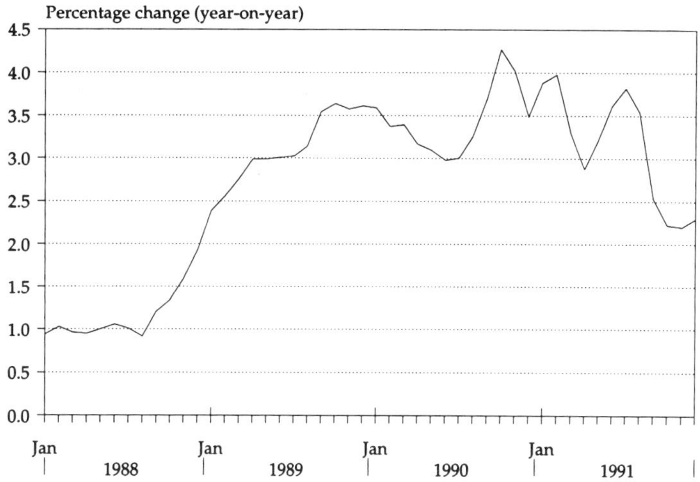

Figure 11.5 **Belgian inflation 1988-1991 (change per month, in per cent, compared with corresponding month of previous year)**

In 1990 inflation accelerated further, to an average of 3.4 per cent. To some extent this was due to the (short-lived) rise in oil prices; until the end of 1990, energy products had a high weighting in the Belgian CPI. The inflation differential *vis-à-vis* Germany remained limited (+120bp), as the Belgian franc was pegged to the Deutschemark in June 1990.

The second half of 1991 saw a cooling in the rate of inflation with CPI data showing a decline in the year-on-year rate of increase from 3.8 per cent (in July 1991), to 2.2 per cent (in October 1991). The inflation differential with Germany has been progressively reduced and, at the end of 1991, was maintained in Belgium's favour at -130bp (compared to +100bp in January 1991). The improvement in the inflation figure at the end of 1991 was chiefly due to the fact that Belgium benefited from a reverse 'oil effect' (relative to the autumn of 1990). Although this may be an exceptional factor, Belgium nevertheless currently enjoys one of the lowest rates of inflation in the EC.

Unemployment

The economic recovery registered since the mid-eighties has been accompanied by a commensurate decrease in the rate of unemployment (see Figure 11.6), which has fallen close to the average for the European Community. From a level

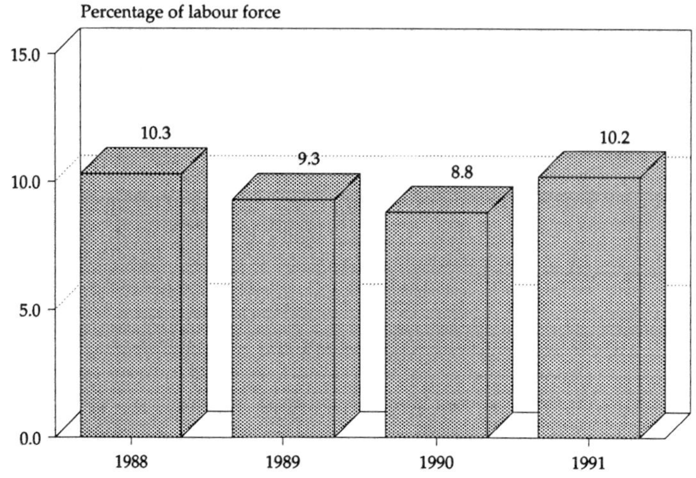

Figure 11.6 Belgian unemployment 1988-1991 (percentage of labour force, EC definition)

of 11.8 per cent in 1987, it fell to 8.8 per cent in 1990. However, recent developments are rather complex. By the end of 1991, the unemployed active population (391,000) was more than 10 per cent higher than in 1990. In particular, male and youth (under 25) unemployment have risen, suggesting a cyclical business cause.

Public sector deficit

The public sector net borrowing requirement reached record heights at the beginning of the 80s. Since then, budgetary policy has been aimed at reducing the deficit through austerity measures. As a result, the deficit declined, in terms of GNP, from 14 per cent in 1981 to 6.6 per cent in 1988. Despite this, the public debt/GNP ratio still rose from 83 per cent in 1981 to 122 per cent in 1988. In May 1988, the government set an objective of eliminating the self-fuelling nature of public debt (the so-called 'snowball effect') which is caused by the need to borrow to finance interest charges. To counter this vicious circle, two constraints were imposed on the central government budget: firstly, the rate of expenditure growth was not to exceed the rate of inflation and, secondly, a ceiling of BFr 405bn was placed on the deficit total

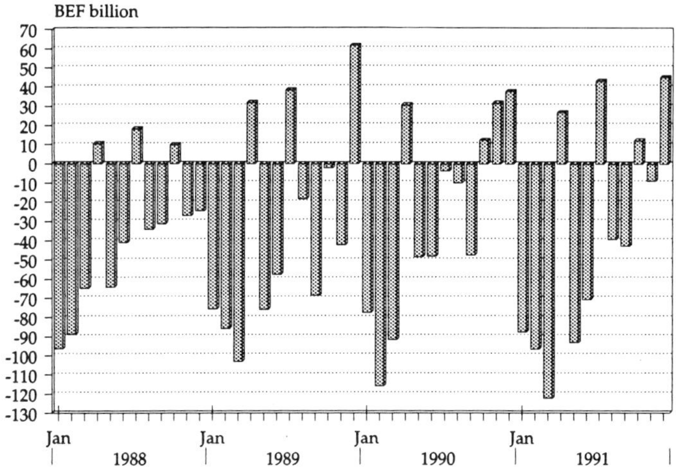

Figure 11.7 Belgian public sector deficit, 1988-1991

Because of high economic growth, in the 1988 - 1990 period, the budget deficit fell as a percentage of GNP to 5.6 per cent and the debt/GNP ratio was stabilized at 119 per cent. The improvement would have been more substantial, had it not been for the rising burden of interest payments.

However, a further deterioration of the budget deficit occurred in 1991 - in October 1991, the net financing requirement of the central government exceeded 1990's level by BFr 61bn. A combination of slow GNP growth and high interest rates has effectively stalled any further improvement in public finance. Nevertheless, in order to comply with the requirements of EC economic and monetary union, a further reduction in the public sector deficit (to 3 per cent of GNP by 1995) along with a significant improvement of the debt/GNP ratio, must be achieved.

Exchange rate

The participation of the Belgian franc in a narrow band within the EMS exchange rate mechanism means that fluctuations against the Ecu have remained relatively small by comparison to currencies outside the EMS such as the US dollar (see Figures 2.8, 2.9 & 2.11). The strength of the BFr led to the abolition, in March 1990, of the financial rate of the currency - more than two years ahead of schedule (a separate exchange rate for financial, as opposed to commercial, transactions had acted as a substitute for formal exchange control regulations).

It was the strength of the BFr, together with Belgium's excellent economic performance, that induced the Belgian authorities to link the BFr to the Dm in June 1990. This move ensured, firstly, that the BFr would be revalued in line with the Dm in any future EMS re-alignment and, secondly, that a limited informal fluctuation range of the BFr/Dm market exchange rate would be observed. The appreciation of the BFr against most EMS currencies, including the Dm and the Dfl, is telling proof of the favourable reaction of the market to the achievement of exchange rate stability. Throughout 1991, despite the November political crisis, the BFr remained steady against the Deutschemark (see Figure 11.10).

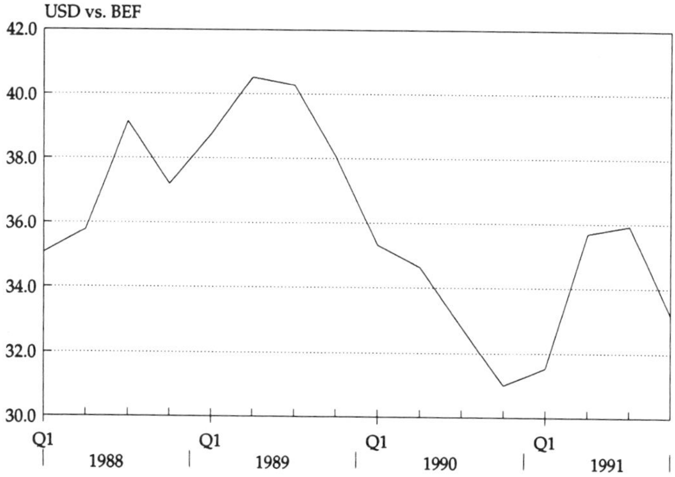

Figure 11.8 Exchange rate - USD vs. BEF (1988-1991, monthly)

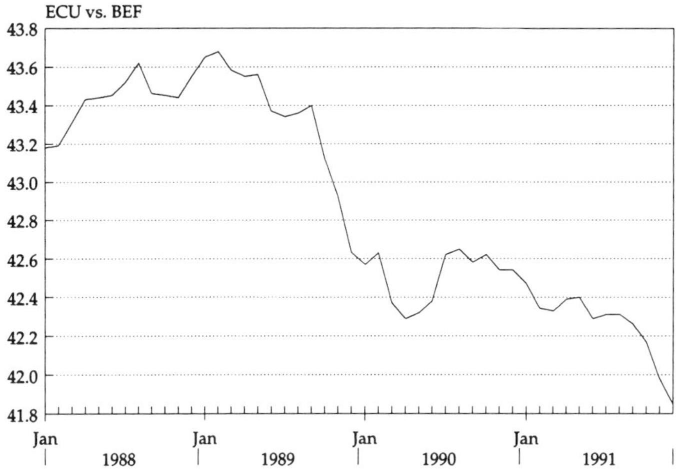

Figure 11.9 **Exchange rate - ECU vs. BEF (1988-1991, monthly)**

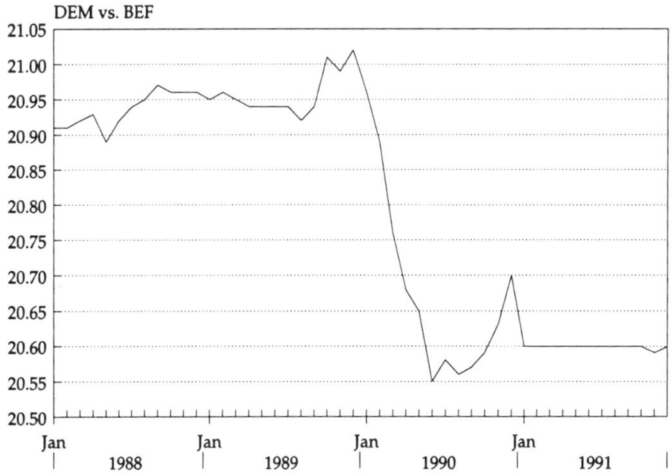

Figure 11.10 **Exchange rate - DEM vs. BEF (1988-1991, monthly)**

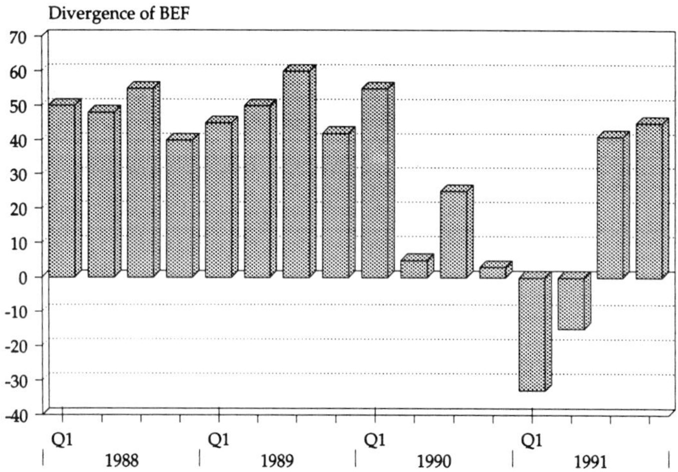

Figure 11.11 EMS bands 1988-1991, indicating divergence of the Belgian franc

11.3 Market composition

Overview

Government bond market

The government sector can be divided in three subsections: direct debt, indirect debt and state-guaranteed debt.

■ Direct debt
Direct debt, which is the debt issued by the Treasury of the Kingdom of Belgium, features three types of issue:

- 1) Classical bonds: straight bonds which were traditionally issued with calls.
- 2) 'Philippe' bonds: bullet bonds issued since March 1990, without underwriting by the banks.

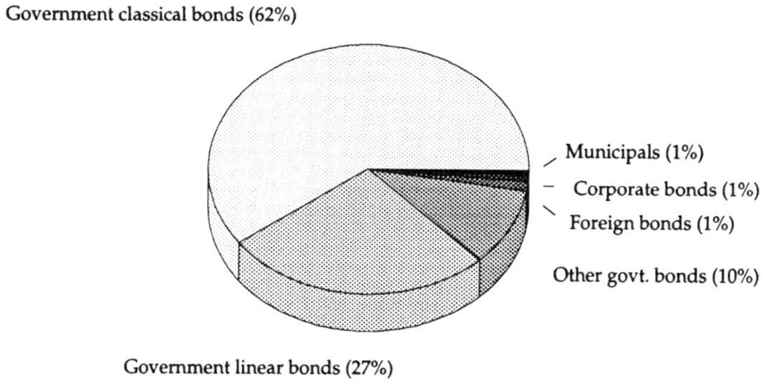

Figure 11.12 Composition of the Belgian bond market as at 31 December 1991

Classical bonds, which were underwritten by a consortium of banks, are no longer issued. Since the lowering of withholding tax, from 25 per cent to 10 per cent, they have been replaced by Philippe bonds and the Minister of Finance is now issuing 3 to 4 such bonds per year. Philippe bonds are mainly sold to the retail sector and liquidity is limited. Institutional and international investors concentrate their investments in linear bonds.

- 3) Linear bonds: issued since May 1989 as part of the modernization of the market.

These new securities, called *obligation linéaire - lineaire obligatie* (OLO), are straight non-callable bonds issued at monthly auction.

Eligible for both Euroclear and Cedel, these bonds have been created in order to enhance the liquidity of the secondary market (see Types of security).

■ Indirect debt

Indirect debt is issued by the Road Fund, which finances the building and modernization of roads. It has the full guarantee of the State and is part of the National Debt. These bonds have the same terms as direct state loans. However, it is expected that the Road Fund will not return to the market since it has been regionalized and can no longer benefit from state guarantee.

■ State-guaranteed debt

Examples of issuers in this subsection are: Telegraph and Telephone (RTT) and the Municipal Reform Fund, which have their interest and capital repayments guaranteed by the State. Issue sizes are modest and yields are above direct government bond yields.

Municipal bond market

Municipals no longer issue in their own name because the issuers have experienced financial difficulties in the past with the result that their credit standing has suffered.

A special Fund called 'Municipal Finance Reform Fund' has been set up to provide funds to the municipalities and is integrated in the state-guaranteed debt.

Corporate bond market

This sector of the market remains very narrow. Since the lowering of the withholding tax rate on coupons from 25 per cent to 10 per cent in March 1990, two issuers have come to the market: Generale Bank launched - and was lead manager

	March 1988	% Total	Dec 1991	% Total
GOVERNMENT (straight bonds)				
Direct debt				
Classical & Philippe bonds	2360.5	72.6	2851.8	60.1
Linear	-	-	1289.8	27.2
Indirect debt	478.5	14.7	340.6	7.2
State-guaranteed	261.8	8.1	137.7	2.9
Total	3100.8	95.4	4619.9	97.4
MUNICIPAL				
Municipal bonds	78.6	2.4	20.3	0.4
CORPORATE				
Straight	2.0	0.1	20.6	0.4
Convertible & cum warrants	17.9	0.5	25.3	0.5
Total	19.8	0.6	45.9	0.9
FOREIGN				
Foreign bonds	52.0	1.6	61.0	1.3
GRAND TOTAL	3251.3	100.0	4747.1	100.0

Figure 11.13 Composition of the Belgian bond market (BEF billion nominal)

for - a BFr 5bn public bullet issue in March 1991 with a life of 1991 - 1999, a coupon of 9.25 per cent and a coupon date of 02 April.

Petrofina tapped the market in November 1991 with an issue of BFr 5bn, featuring a life of 1991 - 2000, a coupon of 9 per cent and a coupon date of 01 February (the first payable being in 1993). The lead manager for this issue was Kredietbank.

Foreign bond market

Only supranational institutions of which Belgium is a member come regularly to the market.

Bank bond market

Bank savings certificates are tap issues made by semi-public financial institutions, savings banks or commercial banks, to obtain short- and medium-term financial resources. Banks regularly issue one- to five-year fixed-rate bonds with yearly coupons or capitalized interest. The conditions (especially the coupon rate) are usually fixed below the yield of the latest government bond.

Composition of market by maturity

Direct debt: classical bonds and Philippe bonds

The average life of the sector (see Figure 11.14) is relatively short by comparison with international standards. The classical bonds are 8-year maturity bonds usually with calls after 4 years, at decreasing call prices.

From March 1990 onwards, the classical bonds have been replaced by Philippe bonds (named after Philippe Maystadt, the Belgian Minister of Finance since 1988). They are issued by the Ministry of Finance directly into the market. Once withholding tax was reduced, the role of the consortium of banks became no longer relevant and the Minister of Finance now uses them only to sell the bonds over their counters. The continuing success of these issues is attributable to the very favourable reaction of domestic private investors. The advantage to the government is that the Minister of Finance has saved on fees, as well as issuing at a lower cost price.

Direct debt: linear bonds

Linear bonds were issued for the first time in 1989 as part of the process of modernization of the domestic financial markets. These bonds, which are auctioned monthly via a competitive tender system, are the most liquid instrument in the Belgian bond market.

New lines of OLOs are opened in order to offer a complete range of maturities. At present, the eight existing lines cover eight different maturities from 1994 to 2003 (see Figure 11.15)

Direct debt dominates the Belgian bond market, making up 87.5 per cent of the total outstanding volume.

Indirect debt

See Figure 11.16

State-guaranteed debt

Given the lack of new issues, the average life of the bonds in this segment is short and concentrated on the 1994 maturity (see Figure 11.17).

Municipal bonds

Since there have been no new issues in this segment since 1984 (see Figure - 11.18), it is likely to disappear altogether after 2007, when the last bonds will be redeemed.

Corporate bonds

■ Straight corporate bonds
See Figure 11.19

■ Convertible and warrant corporate bonds
See Figure 11.20

The low issuing activity by the corporate sector can be explained by the complicated regulatory framework as well as competition from Luxembourg issues. This is about to change, however, as a more market-orientated framework comes into force in 1992.

Foreign bonds

This sector of the market is very narrow (see Figure 11.21), there being only 11 issues outstanding - all of them supranationals (European Investment Bank, World Bank, Euratom).

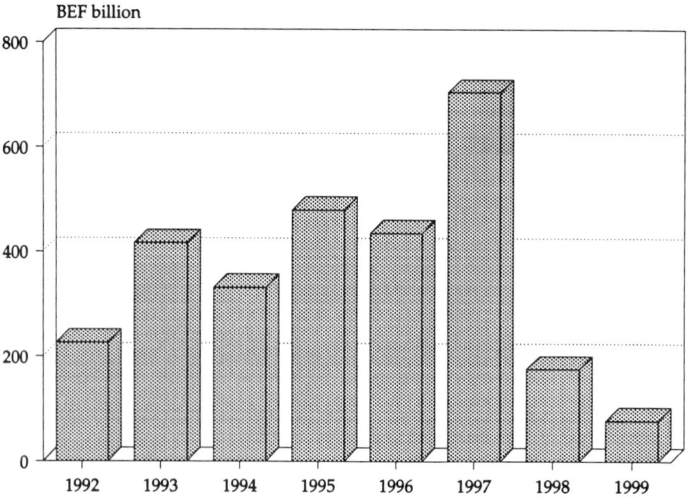

Figure 11.14 Maturity structure of classical and Philippe bonds

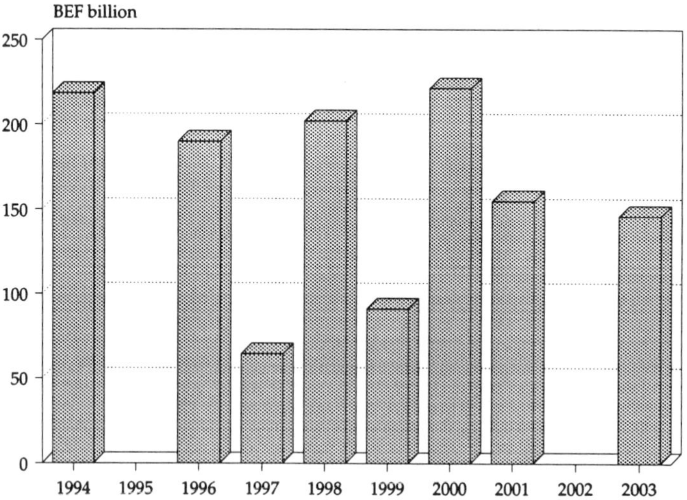

Figure 11.15 Maturity structure of linear bonds

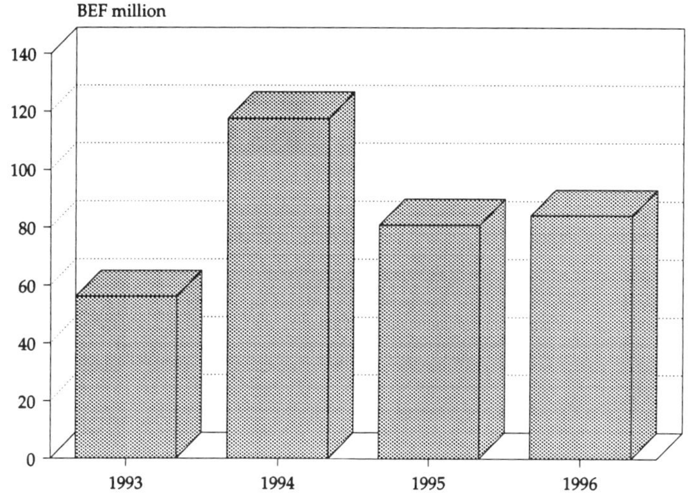

Figure 11.16 Maturity structure of indirect debt bonds

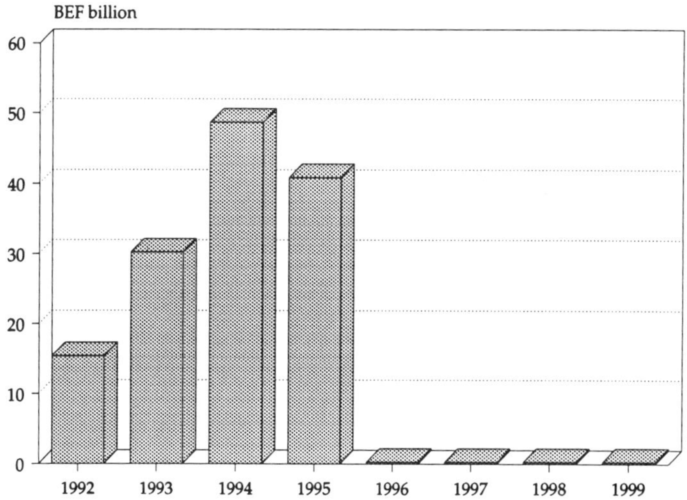

Figure 11.17 Maturity structure of state-guaranteed debt bonds

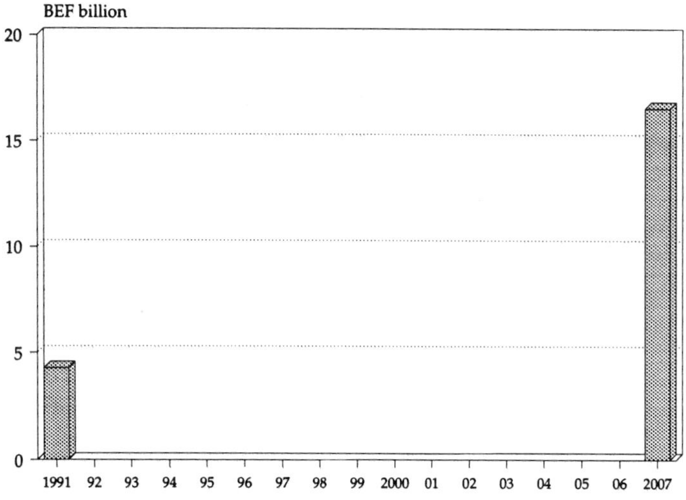

Figure 11.18 Maturity structure of municipal bonds

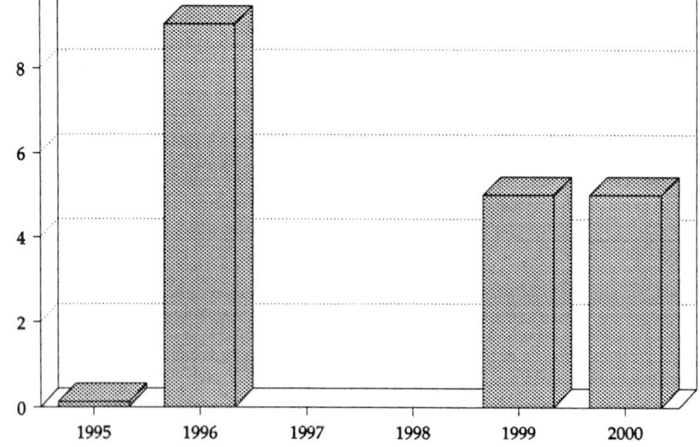

Figure 11.19 Maturity structure of straight corporate bonds

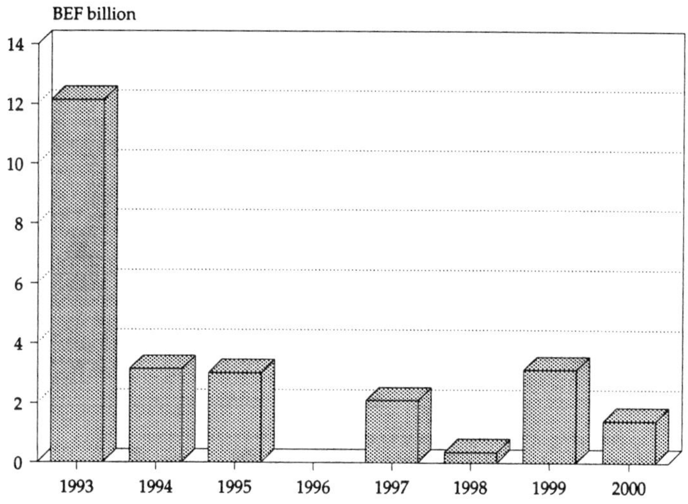

Figure 11.20 Maturity structure of convertible and warrant corporate bonds

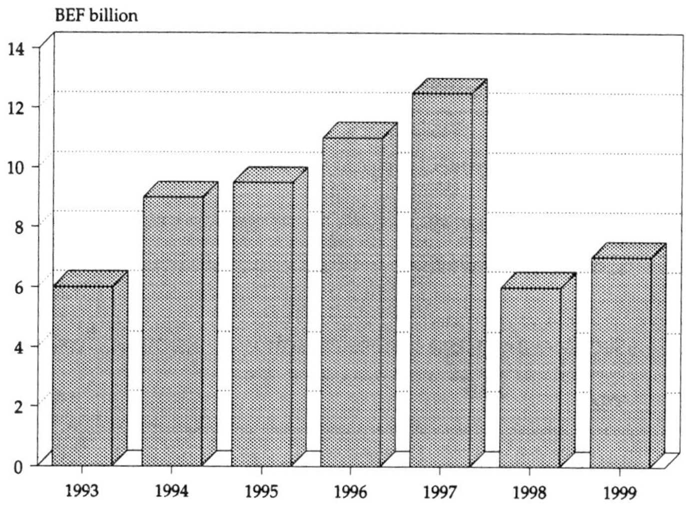

Figure 11.21 Maturity structure of foreign bonds

Composition of market by coupon structure

Direct debt: classical and Philippe bonds

The large variety of coupons (see Figure 11.22) reflects the past fluctuation of interest rates. The highest coupon rates, of 13 to 14 per cent, have been redeemed in 1990 and 1991. Bonds with 11 to 12 per cent coupon rates are short-dated, maturing in 1992, 1993 and 1994, and reflect the high interest rates of the first part of the eighties. The lowest coupon rate, of 7.60 per cent, is attached to a bond issued in February 1986 and maturing in 1994. The coupon rate of the most recent (fifth) Philippe bond is a 9 per cent bullet (1991-1999, 9 per cent with long first coupon from 12 December 1991 until 12 January 1993).

Direct debt: linear bonds

The narrow range of coupon rates (see Figure 11.23) reflects the recent emergence of this segment of the Belgian bond market.

Indirect debt

See Figure 11.24

State-guaranteed debt

See Figure 11.25

Municipal bonds

The absence of new issues and the low outstanding volumes in this sector of the market together account for the very irregular pattern of the coupon structure (see Figure 11.26).

Corporate bonds

■ Straight corporate bonds
See Figure 11.27

■ Convertible and warrant corporate bonds
See Figure 11.28

Foreign bonds

See Figure 11.29

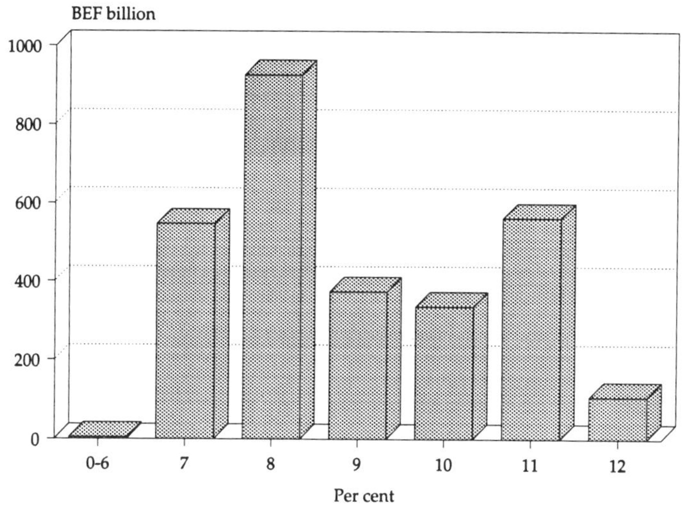

Figure 11.22 Coupon structure of classical and Philippe bonds

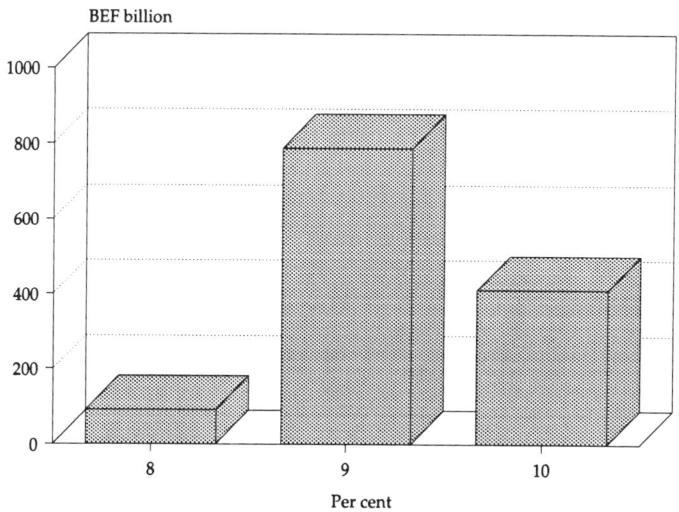

Figure 11.23 Coupon structure of linear bonds

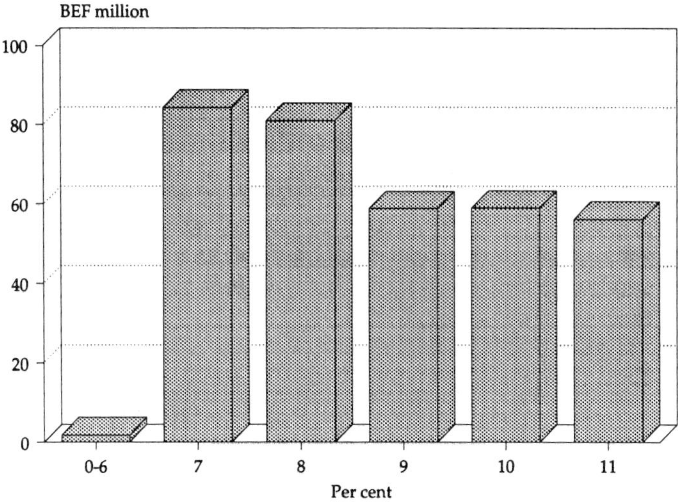

Figure 11.24 Coupon structure of indirect debt bonds

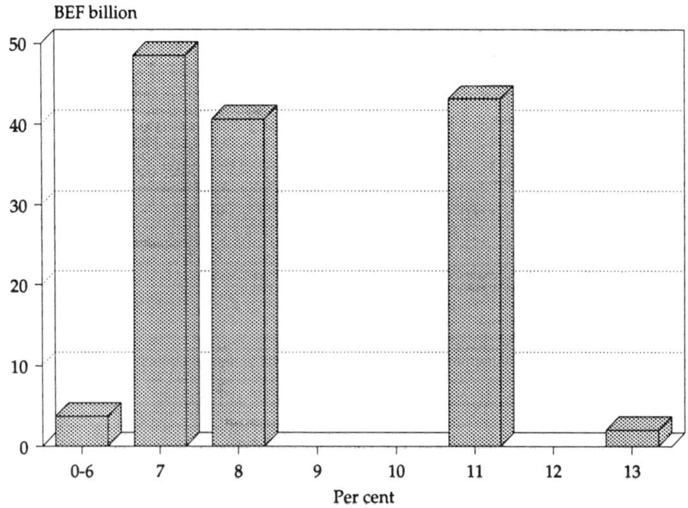

Figure 11.25 Coupon structure of state-guaranteed debt bonds

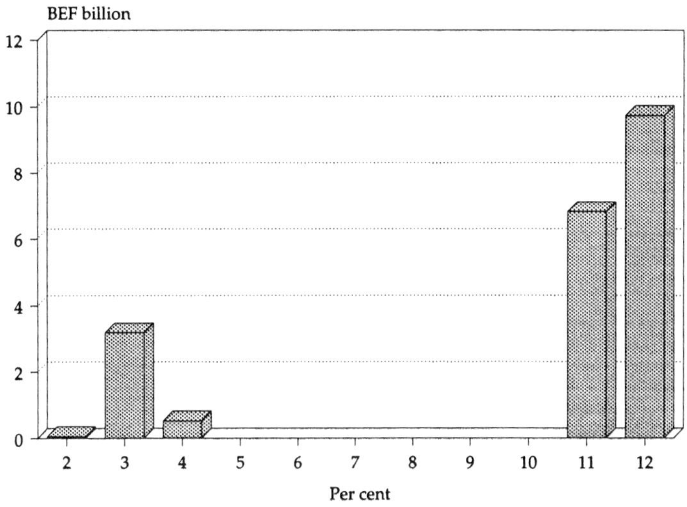

Figure 11.26 Coupon structure of municipal bonds

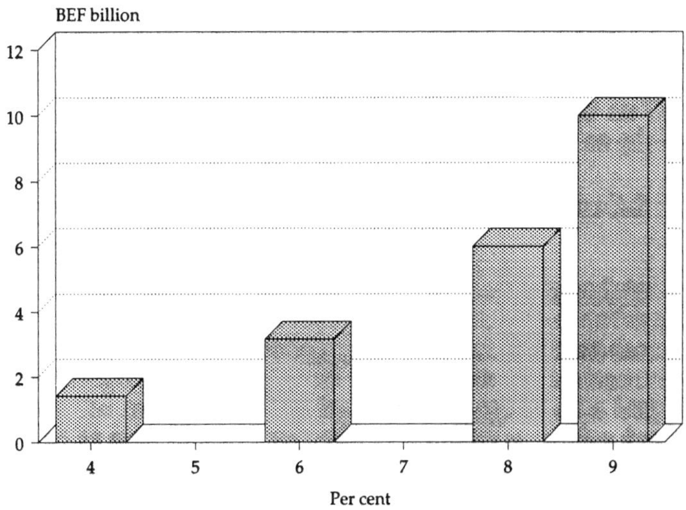

Figure 11.27 Coupon structure of straight corporate bonds

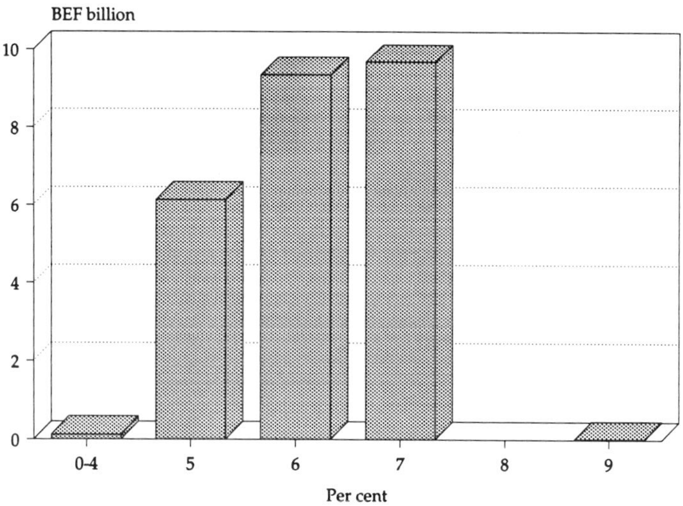

Figure 11.28 Coupon structure of convertible and warrant corporate bonds

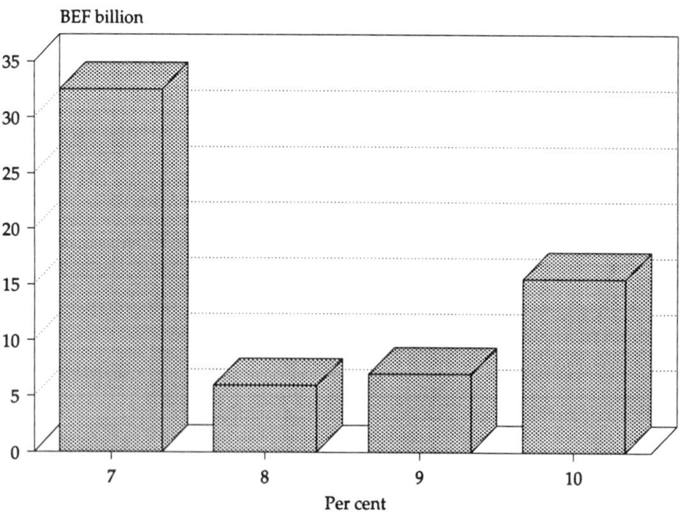

Figure 11.29 Coupon structure of foreign bonds

11.4 Types of security

Straight bonds

The straight bond is by far the most popular bond type in the Belgian market. The government bond market, making up 97 per cent of the whole bond market is dominated by the issuance of the classical and Philippe bonds, and the issuance, since 1989, of linear bonds (OLOs).

Classical and Philippe bonds

The classical bonds have more or less the same conditions, in each case the term being either 7 or 8 years, though with the possibility of anticipated redemption at pre-determined prices. Institutional and professional investors are generally not very pleased with this call option, owing to the (limited) insecurity it engenders for portfolio management.

Since 1989, they have been replaced by straight bullet Philippe bonds, which are issued mainly for the retail investor. The liquidity in the secondary market is limited.

Linear bonds (OLOs)

OLOs are a new type of security introduced in 1989 as part of the reform of the domestic financial markets.

The aim was to improve the liquidity of the secondary market. OLOs are non-callable bonds, with a fixed-coupon, issued in monthly auctions and entirely fungible.

Holdings are in book-entry form and exempted from the 10 per cent withholding tax for non-resident and most domestic investors. OLOs can be settled in Euroclear and Cedel.

The existing lines, as of 31 December 1991, are shown in Figure 11.30. Some other types of security can be found among existing government bonds or in the corporate bond sector.

Puttable bonds

Puttable bonds are not common, the only example being :

- Belgium 1987/1993/1997, 7.75 per cent, 05 January. Puttable and callable at 100 per cent from 05 January 1993 until 05 February 1993.

Denomination	Coupon (%)	Final maturity date	Issue size (BEF million)
OLO1	8.25	01 June 1999	91,420
OLO2	10.00	05 April 1996	190,000
OLO3	10.00	02 August 2000	221,295
OLO4	9.25	02 January 1998	202,406
OLO5	9.50	28 February 1994	218,720
OLO6	9.00	28 March 2003	146,195
OLO7	9.00	27 June 2001	154,985
OLO8	9.25	29 August 1997	64,755
		Total:	1,289,776

Figure 11.30 Belgian OLOs as at 31 December 1991

Convertible bonds

Bonds convertible into equity have returned to the domestic market in the 80's, largely as a result of the good performance of the equity market. The most innovative construction was issued by Barco Industries 1986/1998 with a coupon of:

- 2 per cent for 1987/89
- 4 per cent for 1990/93
- 5 per cent for 1994/98

and convertible into the issuer's stock until 1996.

Bonds with warrants

Bonds with warrants were the success story of the market during 1986 and 1987. There are 4 issues still outstanding:

- GBL 1987/93 6.00 per cent 01 August
- GIB 1986/94 5.75 per cent 01 December
- IMMOBEL 1987/94 5.25 per cent 30 June
- PCB 1989/97 7.00 per cent 31 July

Variable-interest bonds

There is only one public sector bond with a variable interest rate :

- Belgium 1984/1999 24 April:

  First rate: 12.125 per cent (11.50 per cent + 0.625 per cent)
  Current rate: 8.375 per cent since 24 April 1989
  Reference rate: savings bonds, with 5-year maturity, of 5 reference banks + 0.625 per cent
  Adjustment date : 24 April 1994

11.5 Issuers

Belgian government

The main feature of the Belgian bond market remains the predominance of the public sector borrowing, accounting for 97 per cent of the total bond market in 1991, with a total volume of BFr 4620bn.

The government (Kingdom of Belgium) bond market has become a two-speed market with:

- Classical and Philippe bonds
  issued through the counters of the traditional syndicate (consortium of banks and savings banks) directly into the market.

From March 1990, these bonds have been targeted on private investors.

- Linear bonds (OLOs)
  new-style government bonds targeted on institutional and foreign investors.

Corporates

The corporate bond market is very small. This is the result of low new issue activity, caused indirectly by the huge capital requirements of the government and the existence of attractive alternatives (private placements, commercial loans, Luxembourg franc issues). For a number of corporates, the burden of administrative regulation is also an obstacle to the issuance of a public bond.

Supranationals

The foreign sector of the Belgian bond market is also very narrow. Borrowers are supranational institutions of which Belgium is a member. The issue size is limited to BFr 3-6bn.

11.6 *Investors*

Banks and other financial institutions

For several years now, financial institutions have been the major investors in the Belgian bond market. In the recent past, government bonds were the only interesting asset because private sector credit demand was rather low after the successful re-capitalization operations in the early 1980s and the higher profit capability during the last economic expansion period. According to the latest available figures (see Figure 11.31), Belgian financial institutions hold around 58 per cent of the long-term public sector debt.

Private sector

Private individuals have invested less in the domestic market over the years for fiscal reasons (withholding tax) and because of a lack of confidence in the domestic

	31 December 1990		30 October 1991	
	BEF million	%	BEF million	%
Belgian financial institutions	**2,865,725**	**60.96**	**2,998,190**	**58.43**
Commercial banks	1,140,391	24.26	1,246,472	24.29
Public sector banks	1,010,970	21.51	1,029,796	20.07
Savings banks	59,6171	12.68	641,303	12.50
NBB	63,772	1.36	45,238	0.88
Miscellaneous	54,421	1.16	35,381	0.69
Other Belgian investors	**1,586,433**	**33.75**	**1,725,167**	**33.62**
Social security	139,433	2.97	144,100	2.81
Private sector companies & individuals	1,443,396	30.70	1,575,067	30.69
Other public sector	3600	0.08	6000	0.12
Foreign investors	**248,814**	**5.29**	**408,137**	**7.95**
Luxembourg	115,364	2.45	152,474	2.97
Rest of the world	133,450	2.84	255,663	4.98
Total	**4,700,968**	**100.0**	**5,131,494**	**100.0**

Figure 11.31 Holders of long-term public sector debt
Source: Belgostat, NBB

currency. They only returned to the market in March 1990, after the reduction of the withholding tax from 25 per cent to 10 per cent. Private companies are more interested in the short end of the market, as an alternative to bank deposits, for the investment of excess cash reserves.

The private sector, composed of companies and private individuals, accounted for nearly 50 per cent of the holding of the long-term public sector debt a decade ago, but now represents 31 per cent.

Institutional investors

The institutional holders of Belgian government bonds can be split into two main categories: financial institutions and insurance companies. Available data shows that almost 60 per cent of all long-term government bonds (having a

	Treasury certificates								OLO		Total	
	3-month		6-month		> 6-month		Total TC		Total		OLO + TC	
	BEF	%	BEF	%	BEF	%	BEF	%	BEF	%	BEF	%
Belgian banks (1)	616.7	49.7	204.7	60.7	125.1	58.4	946.5	52.8	544.4	50.0	149.1	51.8
Luxembourg banks (2)	383.6	30.9	78.3	23.2	71.1	33.2	533.0	29.7	113.8	10.5	646.7	22.5
Other Belgian fin. inst. (3)	66.1	5.3	2.2	0.7	1.7	0.8	70.0	3.9	96.2	8.8	166.2	5.8
Other Lux. fin. inst. (4)	73.5	5.9	25.7	7.6	9.3	4.3	108.5	6.1	49.3	4.5	157.7	5.9
Belgian public sector (5)	1.2	0.1	1.0	0.3	0.2	0.1	2.3	0.1	1.4	0.1	3.8	0.1
Other Belgian holders (6)	36.0	2.9	8.9	2.6	4.4	2.0	49.3	2.3	69.7	6.4	119.0	4.1
Other Lux. holders (7)	9.0	0.7	0.4	0.1	0.2	0.1	9.7	0.5	13.7	1.3	23.4	0.8
Holders outside BLEU (8)	54.3	4.4	16.0	4.8	2.3	1.1	72.6	4.1	199.9	18.4	272.5	9.5
Total	1240.3	100.0	337.2	100.0	214.2	100.0	1791.8	100.0	1088.5	100.0	2880.3	100.0
Geographical distribution												
Belgium (1+3+5+6)	719.9	58.0	216.9	64.3	131.4	61.3	1068.1	59.6	711.8	65.4	1779.9	61.8
Luxembourg (2+4+7)	466.1	37.6	104.4	31.0	80.6	37.6	651.1	36.3	176.8	16.2	827.9	28.7
Rest of the world (8)	54.3	4.4	16.0	4.8	2.3	1.1	72.6	4.1	199.9	18.4	272.5	9.5
Total	1240.3	100.0	337.2	100.0	214.2	100.0	1791.8	100.0	1088.5	100.0	2880.3	100.0

Figure 11.32 Holders of public sector debt (nominee inscriptions as of 31 December 1991)
Note: amounts are in BEF billion. Figures may not sum exactly due to rounding.

maturity over 1 year), are held by private commercial banks, savings banks, insurance companies and public sector credit institutions.

Amongst the insurance companies (holding 7-8 per cent of the outstanding public sector debt), life insurers are the major investors in the bond market, as they have to invest a substantial part of their mathematical reserves into BFr-denominated bonds for reasons of congruency.

Pension funds are less important in the Belgian market, by comparison to some other countries, because of the tax-funded social security system. Only the major private sector companies have extra pension schemes which are capitalized and, hence, they are natural long-term investors.

Non-residents

Until recently, foreign investors were not very active on the Belgian capital market for a number of reasons (e.g. low liquidity, long recovery period for withholding taxes, no long maturities, etc.).

Since the market reforms of January 1991, non-residents have become active players in the Belgian market, both in both the short- and long-term.

As shown in Figure 11.32, Belgian holders account for 59.6 per cent of Treasury certificates and 65.4 per cent of OLOs. Luxembourg investors, meanwhile, hold 36.3 per cent of Treasury certificates and 16.2 per cent of OLOs. Only 4.1 per cent of Treasury certificates are placed outside the BLEU, against a figure of 18.4 per cent for OLOs.

11.7 *Methods of issuance*

Classical and Philippe bonds

Until mid-1989, the method of issuance for all public sector debt was the banking consortium, which underwrote and placed all newly-issued government bonds, for a fixed commission.

The main borrowing instrument of the Kingdom of Belgium in the 80s was the classical bond, usually callable after four years at a premium.

Since March 1990, they were replaced by Philippe bonds, which are straight bullet bonds. The banks' counters are now used 3 to 4 times a year for the placement of these retail-targeted issues.

The lowering of the withholding tax from 25 per cent to 10 per cent in March 1990 encouraged private resident investors to come back to their domestic market and, as a result, these issues were a huge success.

Linear bonds

1989 saw the introduction of the *Obligation Linéaire - Lineaire Obligatie* (OLO) as a new borrowing instrument.

The main characteristics of OLOs are as follows:

- They are all bullet bonds.
- They are sold at a monthly auction and are open to all Belgian financial institutions, Luxembourg banks, Belgian stock brokers and Belgium-based institutional investors.
- Tendering and trading occurs in multiples of BFr 5m, with a minimum of BFr 50m per tender price.
- All tranches of the same bond are fungible.
- The bonds are held on a book-entry system at the National Bank of Belgium (NBB).
- Settlement occurs only via the clearing system of the NBB on a payment-against-delivery basis.
- Non-residents can open accounts in the clearing system of the NBB via Cedel or Euroclear.
- Coupons and accrued interests are free of withholding tax if held in the clearing system of the NBB.
- No stamp duty is due on secondary market transactions.

As from 29 January 1991, the Treasury has appointed 15 primary dealers and 1 candidate primary dealer whose role is to promote the placing of Treasury certificates and OLOs to improve their liquidity on the secondary market.

At the same time, access to the market for Treasury certificates has been extended to include all resident companies, both financial and non-financial, as well as non-resident companies.

Primary dealers are expected to:

- 1) regularly participate in the tendering for Treasury certificates (TCs) and linear bonds (OLOs) on the primary market;
- 2) actively participate as market-makers on the secondary market by setting realistic prices and undertaking to trade at fixed bid and offer interest rates (for TCs), or prices (for OLOs);
- 3) participate in the promotion of TCs and OLOs, in order to secure their placement both in Belgium and abroad.

Pursuant to this, the primary dealer is required to:

- a) acquire a minimum market share,

  on the primary market, of - on an annual basis - 0.5 per cent of the amounts allotted in the tendering for both TCs and OLOs, or at least 1 per cent of the combined (TC and OLO) amounts allotted;

  on the secondary market, of - on an annual basis - 2 per cent of the Treasury certificates and 1.5 per cent of linear bonds transacted, or at least 3 per cent of the combined (TC and OLO) total transacted;

- b) take concrete steps in respect of placement and
- c) provide monthly reports on primary and secondary market transactions to the Treasury and the National Bank of Belgium.

In return for these commitments, the primary dealers are entitled to:

- i) the sole right of non-competitive subscription, depending on the tendering allotment, that is in the amount of:

  * maximum 30 per cent of the average acquired in the
  a) 10 preceding auctions of 3-month certificates
  b) 4 preceding auctions of 6-month and 12-month certificates,
  and this against the weighted average interest rate for the allotment;

- * maximum 100 per cent of the average successful bids at the 4 preceding auctions, against the weighted average issue price of the OLO allotment; however, the Treasury reserves itself the right to reduce this non-competitive subscription to 30 per cent of the amount asked.

- ii) the sole right of access to an inter-primary dealer-broker, if such function were to be introduced (at the time of writing, no such Broker was active in the market);
- iii) attend regular meetings with the Ministry of Finance to discuss the trend of the markets and the issue policy to be followed;
- iv) evaluate, regularly, how the various primary dealers are functioning, set spreads, size, terms, etc. and settle payment and delivery transactions via the clearing system at the National Bank;
- v) act as principal intermediary for government intervention on the secondary market.

The function of primary dealer may be terminated only on one month's notice. Their operating terms and conditions are shown in Figure 11.33.

	Treasury certificates	**Linear bonds**
Maturity:	3, 6 and 12 months	The 'active' lines
Minimum amount:	BEF 25m + multiples of BEF 5m	BEF 50m + multiples of BEF 5m
Interest rate:	Money market yield	Fixed annual coupon
Price setting:	Per basis point	Per 5 basis points
Auctions:	Weekly for 3-month paper (Tuesday, every two weeks alternately for 6-month and 2-month paper (Tuesday)	Third (or fourth) Thursday of the month. Three OLOs are auctioned every month: one medium-term, one long-term, and one very long-term.
Settlement date:	Auction day + 2	Auction day + 7
Deadline for competitive bids:	10.45	10.45
Results available:	13.30	14.00
Tender system:	Multiple yield	Multiple price
Form of securities:	Dematerialized	Dematerialized
Settlement:	Via the book-entry system at the NBB (to be made via the local clearing system [CIK], as well as via Cedel or Euroclear)	Via the book-entry system at the NBB (to be made via the local clearing system [CIK], as well as via Cedel or Euroclear)
Non-competitive bids:	Auction day + 1	Auction day + 1

Figure 11.33 Operating terms and conditions for primary dealers

11.8 *New issue volumes*

Government bond market

Until 1989, the classical bond was the main borrowing instrument. Issuing these bonds via a consortium of banks, which underwrote a new issue and then placed it on the market, served the Treasury objectives of avoiding a monetary financing of the government deficit. A shift in the priorities, towards a reduction in the cost of the public debt and a greater appeal to foreign investors, led to the introduction of the linear bond in 1989. From March 1990, the classical bonds were replaced by the Philippe bonds.

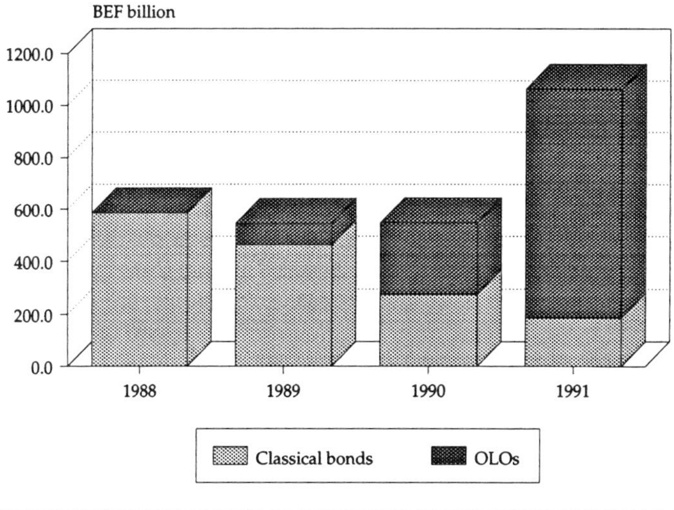

Figure 11.34 New issue volume of Belgian government bonds 1988-1991

After a rather slow start in 1989, OLOs made a substantial contribution to the net Treasury funding in 1990. The share of OLOs in the total government funding of 1990 amounted to 50 per cent, up from around 20 per cent in 1989.

In 1991, the growing importance of the OLO market was confirmed, achieving a relative share of the total issue volume of 80 per cent. At the same time, the share of outstanding OLOs in the Belgian public debt (BFr 355bn, or 5 per cent, at the end of 1990; BFr 1290bn, or 27 per cent, at the end of 1991) is also growing. This increase is partly due to the Treasury policy of encouraging institutional investors to exchange classical bonds, and other long-term BFr debt, for OLOs. During 1991, BFr 175bn of OLOs were created in exchange auctions or by surrender of so-called regularization bonds. However, the best measure of the growing interest in OLOs is that the total amount bid at the monthly OLO auctions approached around BFr 100bn in early 1991, from an average monthly amount of BFr 25bn in 1989, and BFr 31bn in 1990.

11.9 Methods of trading

Since the creation of OLOs, the Belgian bond market has become a two-tier market, one segment being the illiquid classical and Philippe bonds, and the other the OLOs. The classical bonds are both traded via the Brussels Stock Exchange and over-the-counter (for amounts above BFr 25m).

Secondary market activity on the stock exchange

Orders for small amounts of classical bonds are centralized by the brokers and traded at a price fixed on the stock exchange.

The market of the stock exchange is regulated by the Securities Regulation Fund (Rentenfonds/Fonds des Rentes) which stabilizes the market in direct government and government-guaranteed debt via its own portfolio.

In May 1990, an attempt was made to bring more business in the classical bonds to the Brussels Stock Exchange (BSE) by the creation of the CATS-BOND system, using the same hardware as for equity trading.

The CATS (Computerized Automated Trading System) technology has been under development since 1977 by the Toronto Stock Exchange since 1977 and is now in use in Paris, Madrid, Tokyo and Brussels. The CATS technology makes it possible for the exchange members to trade through a personal computer located in their office connected with the exchange's CATS mainframe. This results in an extended trading period during the day (see Figure 11.35), as well as in an increase in the volume traded through the exchange coming from over-the-counter business.

CATS-BOND membership is open to all members of the Brussels Stock Exchange. Information is provided on a continuous basis to investors by the BSE's BDB[1] information service and on quote vendors' pages (e.g. Reuters, Telerate).

CATS-BOND makes a distinction between:

- the *fixing market* where the Securities Regulation Fund (SRF) determines a unique daily price for all public sector bonds listed on the BSE;
- the *continuous market* with several prices during the day for a selection of more actively traded public sector bonds.

The fixing market

The SRF controls and organizes this market. There is no minimum amount required. The aim of this market segment is to offer small investors a fair price at which to trade. In OLOs, there is no fixing market - only a continuous one.

[1] *BDB: Bourse Data Beurs*

The continuous market

Most of the bonds issued by the Kingdom of Belgium and the Road Fund are traded in two sub-markets:

- the board lots where the minimum nominal value per transaction is BFr 5,000,000.
- the block sub-market where the minimum nominal value per transaction is BFr 25,000,000.

All bonds traded on the continuous market are also traded on the fixing market.

09.00	First connection between the admitted members of the BSE and the CATS mainframe.
09.15	Pre-opening for all bonds (continuous market and fixing market) during which the CATS-BOND members may introduce, cancel or modify their orders without dealing.
	The CATS mainframe calculates and displays the theoretical opening price.
09.30	The theoretical opening price is displayed without intervention of the SRF.
	The continuous market goes on till 12.30
	The Securities Regulation Fund may intervene in the continuous market, like any other CATS-BOND member.
12.30	Fixing by the Securities Regulation Fund, first for the bonds already traded in the continuous market and afterwards, for all the other bonds.
	The role of the Securities Regulation Fund is to balance the market and to stabilize the prices, except for OLOs.
12.30	As soon as the fixing has taken place, the continuous market resumes its activity the same way as between 09.30 and 12.30
16.00	Closing of the continuous market

Figure 11.35 Daily time schedule of CATS-BOND

Types of transaction in CATS-BOND

Figures 2.36 & 2.37 show the types of transactions in the continuous market and the fixing market

The CATS-BOND system was designed to allow for continuous trading in all direct government bonds, but failed to attract significant business activity - the market for sizeable blocs remaining over-the-counter. In 1990 and 1991, turnover in bonds on the BSE amounted to BFr 312bn and BFr 129bn respectively, representing only 10 per cent of the turnover on the OTC market.

Minimum volume:	BEF 5m
Maximum volume:	BEF 2bn
Volume display:	M = thousand
	M2 = million, e.g. 5M2 means 5,000,000
	M3 =billion
Price display:	With two decimals - e.g.: 100.14
Minimum price variation:	0.02 per cent (or 2 basis points)
Securities code number:	The securities code number followed by the letter C - e.g. Belgium 1989/99 8.25 per cent 01/06 (Code 239) would be displayed in the continuous market as 239C
Types of order:	
OPG:	At-market opening order
FOK:	Fill-or-kill order
AON:	All-or-none order
GTC:	Good-till-cancelled order
GTD:	Good-till-specified date
MON:	Minimum fill or nothing
Cross order:	Offsetting buy and sell order
On-stop order:	Triggered when the bid/ask price is higher or lower than the on-stop price.

Figure 11.36 Types of transaction in CATS-BOND - continuous market

Minimum volume:	The smallest denomination of the bond
Maximum volume:	BEF 2bn
Volume display:	The full amount has to be filled in
Price display:	Same as in the continuous market
Minimum price variation:	Same as in the continuous market
Securities code number:	The securities code number followed by the letter F - e.g. Belgium 1989/97 8.25 per cent 23/06 (Code 240) would be displayed in the fixing market as 240F
Type of orders:	At the opening limit orders

Figure 11.37 Types of transaction in CATS-BOND - fixing market

Secondary market activity by primary dealers

As may be seen by the obligations for the primary dealers, trading in OLOs is well organized and accounts for more than 90 per cent of the secondary market activity. The reforms have been followed by a substantial improvement in secondary marketability. In terms of individual linear bonds there are, of course, wide variations in market activity; during the second half of 1991, the OLOs maturing in 2000 and 2003 were the most liquid.

The operating terms and conditions for the primary dealers in the secondary market are shown in Figure 11.38

Secondary market activity in OLOs and Treasury certificates is increasing rapidly, with an average daily turnover in excess of BFr 20bn in OLOs, and around BFr 37bn for TCs. A relatively high turnover ratio of 5.00 - i.e. the stock of OLOs is turned over 5 times in a full year - has been reached in 1991. This is a substantial improvement compared to the 0.80 turnover ratio for Belgian bonds before the introduction of the primary dealers.

Bid/offer spreads are generally less than the 20 basis points quoted on the screen and the average deal size is around BFr 85m. Tradeable quotations for higher amounts (BFr 500-1000m) can easily be obtained.

	Treasury certificates	**Linear bonds**
Pricing	Bid and ask yields	Bid and ask prices
Menu	1,2,3,6,9,12 months	All outstanding OLOs
Size	BEF 50m-100m	BEF 25m-50m
Maximum spread	15 basis points	25 basis points
Opening hours	09.00-12.30[1]	09.30-12.301
	14.00-16.00	14.00-17.00
Value-date	Trade-date + 2	Trade-date + 7
Settlement	NBB	NBB

Figure 11.38 Operating terms and conditions for primary dealers[2] in the secondary market

[1] *Only until 11.00 on auction days*

[2] *A complete list of primary and candidate primary dealers is given in Section 11.18, Sources of reference*

11.10 Market practices

Coupon payment

All Belgian bonds pay annually in arrears.

First coupons

The first payment of coupons for broken periods is usually pro-rated in relation to the number of days between the date of issue and the date of payment (generally six months, sometimes more than one year), after which the annual interval continues.

Ex-coupon

Belgian bonds are traded cum-coupon up to, and including, the day before the next interest payment.

Redemption

Most of the listed Belgian public sector bonds (such as linear bonds or OLOs) are straight bonds with annual coupons.

All government and semi-government bonds issued before September 1986 are reimbursed at final maturity in a bullet payment. As a consequence, the average life of these issues for the bondholder is always equal to the life until maturity.

The issuer, on the other hand, has to purchase his bonds (except OLOs) in the open market (stock exchange) at a rate of generally 5 per cent of the nominal value issue size every year. The amount purchased every day may be variable. If the price of the bonds is above par, the Minister of Finance has to grant a special authorization to the issuer to enable him to re-purchase the bonds in the stock exchange.

Since September 1986, the listed bonds issued, or guaranteed, by the Kingdom of Belgium generally carry annual call options after four years for the issuer (with the exception of OLOs). There are also call provisions in listed bonds issued by international organizations, and in most listed private sector bonds. Most typically, an 8-year bond is callable after 4 years at 102.75 per cent, after 5 years at 102.00 per cent, after 6 years at 101.25 per cent and after 7 years at 100.50 per cent.

It is generally accepted that these call options are over-priced by comparison to bullet issues, i.e. the yield premium over-compensates for the slight risk of the bonds being called.

Denominations

All government bonds until March 1987 were issued in denominations of BFr 10,000, BFr 25,000, BFr 50,000, BFr 100,000 and BFr 500,000. Since then, government bonds have been issued in denominations of BFr 20,000 and BFr 50,000,

BFr 100,000 and BFr 500,000 supranational issues have only BFr 50,000 denominations.

Linear bonds are issued in denominations of BFr 5,000,000, but the bidding of the primary subscribers is not allowed for amounts smaller than BFr 50,000,000.

Form

All Belgian bonds (except the OLOs) are available in bearer form. Government bonds can be held in registered form, with the Ministry of Finance.

Linear bonds (OLOs) are dematerialized; they are represented either by book-entries with authorized subscribers or clearing houses (i.e. Cedel and Euroclear) directly or indirectly affiliated to the CIK, the Belgian domestic clearing organization, or by book-entries at the Treasury. Apart from two notes sent to the Belgian authorities (CIK and the SFR), no paper is delivered and trading takes place on a book-entry system managed by the clearing centre of the National Bank of Belgium (NBB) (which permits banking accounts to be used). The clearing centre guarantees the security of the transactions by means of a system based on payment against delivery.

Dealing quotations

Bond quotations are made in percentages of the nominal value. The price of all listed bonds is calculated without the accrued interest. The accrued interest is calculated on a 30/360-day basis and should be added to the price.

For OLOs, since January 1991, 15 primary dealers and 1 candidate primary dealer actively participate as market-makers on the secondary market by setting prices and undertaking to trade at fixed bid/offer prices. The normal trading size is BFr 50m - 100m. The minimum amount accepted is BFr 25m and a maximum spread of 25 basis points is observed. Actual quotation spreads are lower than required. The market is open on weekdays from 09.30 to 12.30 and from 14.00 to 17.00.

For bonds traded over-the-counter, there have been (since 01 October 1987) several market-makers providing firm or indicative bid and ask prices on Reuters and Telerate. The round lot size amounts to BFr 50m, although it is usual to trade larger blocks. The market-maker system has fallen into disuse since the inception of primary dealership.

The price of most public sector bonds is fixed by the Securities Regulation Fund every day between 12.30 and 14.30 (Brussels time) on CATS-BONDS, the computerized market for Belgian bonds (available since May 1990).

The role of the SRF is to stabilize the price and to balance the market (except in the case of OLOs). A selection of bonds issued by the Kingdom of Belgium and the Road Fund are also traded on the order-driven continuous market within CATS-BONDS. This market is open from 09.30 until 16.00, after a pre-opening of 15 minutes. Prices are quoted to two decimal places (e.g. 89.10) and have a minimum price variation of 0.02 per cent. In the case of OLOs, there is no fixing - only a continuous market.

In the secondary market for Treasury certificates, operated by the officially appointed primary dealers, the price setting is based on the money market yield. The quotations are made in bid/ask yields for a dealing size of BFr 50m-100m with a maximum spread of 15 basis points (in yield). These rules apply between 09.00-12.30 and 14.00-16.00.

Withholding tax

Income from Belgian bonds issued after 01 March 1990 is subject to a withholding tax set at 10 per cent. Coupons on classical bonds issued up to that date are paid net of a withholding tax of 25 per cent. In most cases the tax can be reclaimed by non-resident investors.

Coupons on OLOs are free of all withholding tax for non-residents. Accrued interest is paid gross.

Fees commissions and duties

Prices of OLOs are quoted on a net price basis. No stamp duty is levied for linear bonds.

A stamp duty is due on all other bond transactions by investors who are not Belgian banks or brokers. The stamp duty is 0.07 per cent on domestic bonds issued by the Kingdom of Belgium and the Road Fund and 0.14 per cent on other bonds. The maximum stamp duty per transaction has been limited to BFr 10,000. Generally speaking, the net prices quoted in the over-the-counter market for all classical bonds include stamp duty.

Bond transactions amounting to less than BFr 25m have to be executed through the Brussels Stock Exchange and are therefore be subject to the exchange fee (0.01 per cent - 0.025 per cent) and the commissions due to the stock broker, as determined by law.

11.11 Settlement

Settlement and value-date

Settlement for Treasury certificates is ordinarily two bank working days after trade-date.

The value-date for OLOs is seven calendar days (or, in case of a bank holiday, the next bank working day) after the transaction date. The same principle applies to other Belgian bonds in the over-the-counter market. However, other settlement periods are easily negotiable.

In the stock exchange, all bond transactions are settled three working days following the day of the transaction.

The central clearing system

The National Bank of Belgium has introduced a new central system for the efficient and reliable clearing of transactions of government book-entry securities (OLOs and Treasury certificates) on the primary and secondary markets. It is based on the principles of 'delivery against payment' and the matching of all transactions through the double notification of both buyer and seller to the clearing system. At the same time, it provides its participants with the possibility of (automatic) bond lending.

Belgian and Luxembourg financial institutions and brokerage houses may join this system directly or in a sub-participant capacity. The Securities Deposit and Clearing Office of the financial sector (CIK - Caisse interprofessionnelle de Dépôts et de Virement de Titres/Interprofessionele Effectendeposito- en Girokas) and the clearing houses of Cedel and Euroclear, have all joined the system. The participants are allowed to open and manage securities accounts in the clearing system, as are the international clearing houses (for non-residents only).

Settlement of classical bonds

It is possible for Belgian bond transactions to be settled through Euroclear and Cedel. Most of the trades are settled through CIK or through the National Bank. A similar settlement procedure to that used for OLOs is now available for classical bonds, under condition that the bonds are held with CIK or in book-entry form with the National Bank of Belgium. The delivery of securities in bearer form is not allowed. All procedures related to the withholding tax remain unchanged.

11.12 *Yield calculation*

Belgian bonds

The standard ISMA formula is used for determining yields since 01 September 1991, as laid down in the Royal Decree of 12 August 1991.

The calculation of the annual redemption yield is carried out as a present value calculation (on the value-date) implying that the redemption yield equals the interest rate at which all future proceeds such as coupon (on a gross basis) and redemption payments, are discounted. This present value expressed as a percentage of par (100 per cent) equals the clean price of the bond concerned, plus the interest accrued on the value-date. Note that Belgian bond prices are quoted on a clean price basis.

For full details of the yield calculation, see the ISMA publication *Formulae for Yield and Other Calculations* and the section dealing with yield calculation in the United Kingdom chapter.

Treasury certificates

The money market yield on Treasury certificates (3-, 6- and 12-month) is quoted on the basis of simple, instead of compound, yields. It indicates the annualized yield for the purchaser or seller of the certificates during the number of days from the value-date (included) to the redemption-date (not included), based on actual days, divided by 365.

11.13 Taxation

Domestic investors

Income and withholding tax

Pursuant to Belgian law, income from Belgian securities is subject to a withholding tax. The tax rate is 25 per cent on all debt instruments issued before 01 March 1991. Since then, it is set at 10 per cent.

It is very important to note that non-residents are exempt from this withholding tax.

For Belgian corporations, the withholding tax is considered as a down-payment on corporate income tax. Once paid, it becomes a tax credit for corporate income tax assessment.

For Belgian individual investors, the withholding tax means that there is no more income tax due on interest received, except in a case where the total interest income, net of withholding tax, exceeds an amount of BFr 505,000 per tax-paying entity. This amount is adapted every year when the tax laws are reviewed.

On some Belgian public sector bonds issued before 01 March 1991, the withholding tax has been reduced to 20 per cent, 12.50 per cent, 10.50 per cent or, in certain instances, even nil.

The withholding tax is not due on fixed-income securities held by financial institutions (private commercial and savings banks, public sector banks), by social security institutions and by insurance companies. Belgian pension funds are not exempt from withholding tax and are, therefore, unable to reclaim it.

A beneficiary of interest must provide to the debtor, or to the paying agent, a certificate stating the category of the exempted institution to which he or she belongs, and also stating ownership of the securities (see below). The securities must be held during the whole interest period (generally one year) in order to receive the full coupon. This rule does not apply to OLOs or to bonds issued by supranational organizations, on which the accrued interest is calculated without deduction of the withholding tax.

Proof of holding is provided by the nominative registration in the books of the issuer.

If an exempted institution holds a bond for a period which is less than the whole interest period, the investor will pay, when buying the bond, the accrued interest net of withholding tax and will receive the full interest net of withholding tax at the next coupon-date. The investor may then apply the withholding tax during the actual holding period against the corporate income tax due. The latter is due in quarterly provisional payments, so the withholding tax can be recovered within three months maximum, provided that the exempted institution has a taxable income. When selling the bond, the investor will receive the accrued interest on the value-date and will be able to apply the withholding tax for the actual holding period, from the last coupon-date, until the day before the value-date.

For all but exempted institutions, the withholding tax is also due on redemption premiums and on original issue discounts, if the yield-to-maturity calculated on the basis of the issue price is 0.75 per cent higher than the nominal coupon rate.

Capital gains tax

The actual Belgian corporate income tax is 39 per cent of the operating income, realized capital gains included. Capital gains non-realized are never taxable, unless they correspond to capital losses previously recorded on the same securities. Realized capital losses are always deductible as expenses during the year of their realization.

There is no capital gains tax for private investors.

Non-resident investors

Withholding tax

■ Linear bonds (OLOs)

Linear bonds held by non-resident investors are now governed by the significantly simplified tax regulations laid down in the Royal Decree of 25 January 1991, by virtue of which any income from dematerialized public debt securities, from transactions on these securities (e.g. from OLOs) or from related revenues (e.g. bond lending), is fully exempted from withholding tax. Therefore, coupons on OLOs are free of all withholding tax. Accrued interest is calculated on a gross basis.

A certificate of non-residence has to be completed through a Belgian financial intermediary (i.e. bank or broker), Cedel or Euroclear.

Three possible cases can be examined:

- Payment of interest at coupon-date: the holder receives the coupon at 100 per cent
- Sale on the secondary market: the seller immediately receives 100 per cent of accrued interest
- Purchase in the secondary market, or subscription at the monthly auction: the buyer has to pay 100 per cent of accrued interest.

■ Other Belgian bonds (except foreign bonds)
Interest on classical bonds is paid net of withholding tax of 25 per cent or 10 per cent (for issues since 01 March 1991). In most cases this tax can be reclaimed by foreign investors.

Non-residents are exempted from withholding tax provided that,

- the bonds are issued by Belgian government, public authorities, state-guaranteed public institutions, commercial and savings banks, finance companies and most public credit institutions;
- the holder signs a declaration of non-residency;
- the investor has taken a nominative registration in the register of the Belgian Ministry of Finance.

In the case of exempted investors, the coupon is paid gross for bonds purchased at issue or held for more than a year. For bonds purchased in the secondary market, the non-resident buyer pays 75 per cent (or 90 per cent for issues since 01 March 1991) of the accrued interest and, at coupon-date, receives 100 per cent of the coupon for the period during which the bond has been held and 75 per cent (or 90 per cent) of the coupon for the period prior to purchase. For bonds sold on the secondary market, the non-resident receives 75 per cent (or 90 per cent) of the accrued interest at sale and a fast reclaim procedure ensures Treasury repayment of the remainder within two weeks.

Applications for exemptions and the necessary administrative procedures for refunds may be handled by the investor's financial intermediary.

■ Foreign bonds (supranational issuers)
These bonds are payable free of withholding taxes if they are being paid to foreign investors outside Belgium.

Double taxation relief agreements

Non-residents of Belgium residing in a country with which Belgium has concluded a double taxation convention can also claim the exemptions and reductions foreseen in the agreements, besides the above-mentioned exemptions granted by Belgian legislation. Belgium has concluded agreements with the following countries:

All European Community countries, and Australia, Austria, Brazil, Canada, China, Czechoslovakia, Finland, Hungary, India, Indonesia, Israel, Ivory Coast, Japan, Malaysia, Malta, Morocco, New Zealand, Norway, Pakistan, Philippines, Poland, Rumania, Singapore, South Korea, Sweden, Switzerland, Thailand, Tunisia, USA, Yugoslavia.

These agreements reduce the rate of withholding tax to usually 10 or 15 per cent, and sometimes to nil. The rules differ from country to country as regards rates and conditions to be observed. Repayment or reduction occurs in principle according to the procedure of reimbursement. The simplified procedure of immediate reduction at source may be applied if the income is in respect of registered securities.

The formalities to be followed have been made uniform. The form 276 must always be used for application of exemption or reduction. It can be obtained from a financial intermediary or directly from the Belgian tax authorities. The application must be submitted within three years of the first day of the month of January following the due date of the coupon payment.

11.14 Futures & options

Introduction

Belfox s.c., the company responsible for setting up the Belgian Futures and Options Exchange, was founded on 23 January 1990 with a start-up capital of some BFr 500m. The London-based International Commodities Clearing House (ICCH) was appointed project manager. The Royal Decree of 10 April 1991 on the establishment and organization of the Belgian Futures and Options Exchange recognizes Belfox s.c. as the market authority and clearing institution with specific regulatory powers over its members.

The Belfox market is characterized by its fully automated and integrated trading/clearing system, which guarantees the reliable and efficient execution and settlement of all transactions.

Products

In its initial phase, Belfox will launch the following products:

- Futures on Belgian government bonds
- Options on six individual Belgian shares
- Futures and options on the BEL-20, the Brussels Stock Exchange price index.

Membership of Belfox

A professional intermediary who is legally allowed to act on Belfox, can do this under one of the capacities outlined below.

Public order members (POM)

Public order members are allowed to have orders executed by a broker through the Belfox trading system either in their own name and for their own account, or in their own name but for the account of clients.

Brokers

Brokers have the right to execute orders through the Belfox trading system, either in their own name and for their own account, or in the name of, and for the account of, a POM.

Market-makers

Market-makers have only the right to execute orders for their own account through the Belfox trading system. In addition, they are obliged to make a market in the option classes and/or futures contracts in which they has been accepted as a market-makers. During the sessions, the market-makers must at any time provide bid and offer prices for a minimum number of contracts as determined by the Board of Belfox for those option classes and/or futures contracts in which they have been accepted as market-makers.

Note: In addition to the technical requirements and the requirements regarding professional reliability, experience and the minimum number of trained personnel, all recognized professional intermediaries must comply with specific financial requirements, depending on the category in which they wish to act on Belfox.

Regulation

The Minister of Finance

The Minister of Finance has the following powers:

- Approval of the market regulations and any modification to them;
- Appointment of a government commissioner at Belfox;
- In the case of irregularities, the suspension of certain activities of Belfox and/or adjustment of the market regulations;
- Approval of the admission and deletion of any futures and/or option contract related to public debt.

The Banking and Finance Commission

The Commission has a direct prudential control over Belfox. If it suspects a breach of the law or other regulations, it can first set a period for rectification and eventually inform the Minister of Finance.

Belfox guarantee

The role of Belfox as a clearing house is essential for its members: Belfox is the counterparty for each contract registered in the name of one of its members. The Belfox guarantee takes effect as soon as the trading system matches an order between buyer and seller.

As Belfox is the counterparty to all transactions, it is legally required to guarantee the successful completion of each transaction which was registered correctly on

Belfox up to and including the possible delivery of the underlying assets. If one of the contracting members were to default, this guarantee will assure the security and stability of the market.

To cover this risk, the market regulations determine cover and margin obligations regarding transactions concluded on Belfox.

Financial cover

The credit risk Belfox runs as a counterparty for each registered contract in the name of its members has already been explained. It must also be pointed out that each client is allocated an anonymous account number so that a client position can be monitored without disclosure of identity. If a problem arises, Belfox will contact the appropriate intermediary.

The cover consists of a margin deposited at Belfox, which the exchange can use to meet its possible losses in case of a member's default. The margins are re-calculated every day.

These margin obligations are calculated at account level: the margin for the house accounts and the client accounts of a member are calculated separately. In this way a strict segregation is guaranteed between the activities for the member's own account, and those for the account of the member's clients.

Any netting of positions between client and house accounts or between client accounts of a POM is prohibited.

At the end of each trading day, the POM calculates the margin obligations for each of his clients. The client is obliged to deposit the total margin obligations for his open positions, at the request of the POM, and before the opening of the next session.

A POM is obliged to ask each of his clients separately for at least the minimum margin requirements as imposed by Belfox on its members under the market regulations.

The Belfox Board determines which financial assets are acceptable (in addition to cash) for its members to use in meeting margin requirements.

At the time of writing, acceptable collateral may comprise: BFr Treasury certificates, all listed bonds issued by the Kingdom of Belgium and the 20 stocks comprised in the BEL20 index of the BSE.

The daily cash flows between Belfox and its members are centralized through a specific payment system (the Protected Payment System), an automated debit and credit mechanism which is managed by the 5 founding member banks.

Contract specification

See Figure 11.39.

Contract size:	BEF 2,500,000 nominal value notional Belgian government bond with a 9 per cent coupon
Delivery months:	Three from the March, June, September and December cycle.
Expiry day:	Last business day of the expiry month
Last trading day:	Seven calendar days immediately prior to the expiry date, at 11.00
Quotation:	Percentage of par
Minimum price movement (tick size) and value:	0.01 per cent [BEF 250]
Trading hours:	09.15 - 17.00. Pre-opening commences at 09.00
Price limit:	The daily price variation is 200 basis points from the previous day's closing price, the Belfox Board may require that trading be halted for a certain time and/or an intra-day margin call be collected
Contract standard:	Only OLOs issued by the Kingdom of Belgium with minimum 7 years and maximum 10 years to maturity

Figure 11.39 Belfox bond futures - contract specification

Notes:

i) A new expiry month is introduced on the first business day of the nearest expiry month.

ii) Futures trading might be suspended whenever the Brussels' Stock Exchange stops trading in the deliverable bonds.

iii) The quote of a market-makers must always be for a minimum volume of 40 futures contracts in the nearest expiry month and 20 contracts in the second expiry month. Market-makers are requested to observe a maximum bid/offer spread of 10 and 15 basis points, respectively.

iv) At the close of each day's trading, a settlement price is fixed by the BELFOX Trading Department for each contract. This price is used by the Clearing House for the daily settlement to market of the open positions.

11.15 *Money markets*

An important reform within the management of the Belgian public debt was the modernization of the money markets and the implementation of a new monetary policy. The reorganization, which began in January 1991, was focused on the Treasury certificate market. These measures aimed at providing domestic and international investors with more attractive opportunities.

Background

From 1986 to 1988, a substantial part of the government's financing needs was met by short-term borrowing. This usually took the form of Treasury certificates with 1-, 2- and 3-month maturities, sold by the National Bank of Belgium on a tap basis to Belgian and Luxembourg financial institutions only. The rate, generally being slightly above interbank rates, was agreed by the National Bank and the Treasury. Non-banking financial intermediaries, corporations, and non-residents were all prohibited from purchasing these certificates. As a result, therefore, the secondary market was not developed at all.

Reform

In the first instance, the purpose of the reform was to reduce the cost of short-term borrowing for the Belgian government. At the same time, however, the government also wanted to separate the execution of monetary policy from the financing of the government borrowing requirements - in keeping with the parameters of EC Economic and Monetary Union.

Several steps have been made to open the market and to make it more secure, efficient and competitive. Treasury certificates are now accessible to all domestic and non-resident institutional investors.

Since 29 January 1991, Treasury certificates have been issued in fully Dematerialized form only, i.e. by book-entry form in a securities account with a financial intermediary approved by the Minister of Finance and participating in the National Bank of Belgium's (NBB) clearing system. Members of the clearing system include Euroclear and Cedel. The NBB clearing system guarantees that securities will be paid on delivery (in the primary and secondary market).

The Treasury issues three-month (91 days), six-month (182 days) and twelve-month (364 days) certificates at regularly scheduled auctions via a competitive tender system. This system guarantees that the primary market for Treasury certificates is transparent. The issues take place weekly (Tuesday) for the three-month certificates and monthly (Tuesday, every two weeks alternatively) for others. The announcement and results of the auctions are published on various information networks (see Section 11.18, Sources of reference).

All interested investors can submit bids to the Treasury (by 10.45 on auction day), in multiples of BFr 5m with a minimum of BFr 25m, at the auctions, indicating the quantities they are willing to take at different yields. A multiple-rate system is then applied, whereby successful bids are allocated at the rate bid proposed by the bidder. The Treasury may decide to scale down the bids at the stop-out rate. The results are made public by 11.30.

By the end of December 1991, the amount of outstanding new-style Treasury certificates amounted to BFr 1792bn, around BFr 1240bn of which was certificates of up to three months in maturity.

15 selected primary dealers and 1 candidate primary dealer were vested with the role of regularly participating in the auctions, subscribing sizeable amounts and promoting the market. They also ensure permanent bid and ask quotations. Each primary dealer quotes at least 6 certificate maturity months on screen, i.e. 1,2,3,6 and 12 months, with a size of BFr 50m-100m and a maximum spread of 15 basis points. In practice, the average amounts that can be traded are substantially higher (+/- BFr 510m per transaction) and the spreads at market level are generally tight (2-5bp).

Commercial paper and certificates of deposit

A legal structure permitting the issue of CPs and CDs in book-entry form, with the same legal and tax arrangements applied to the Treasury certificates, was set up on 22 July 1991.

The first commercial paper programme in BFr by a non-resident (within the new legal framework) was issued in November 1991 by the Dutch LEASE PLAN for an amount of BFr 3bn.

11.16 *Interest rate history*

1988

As in previous years, the Belgian interest rate trend closely shadowed that found abroad, specifically in Germany. The favourable trend in international rates, eased by the fall in oil prices and the contraction of inflation, provided a

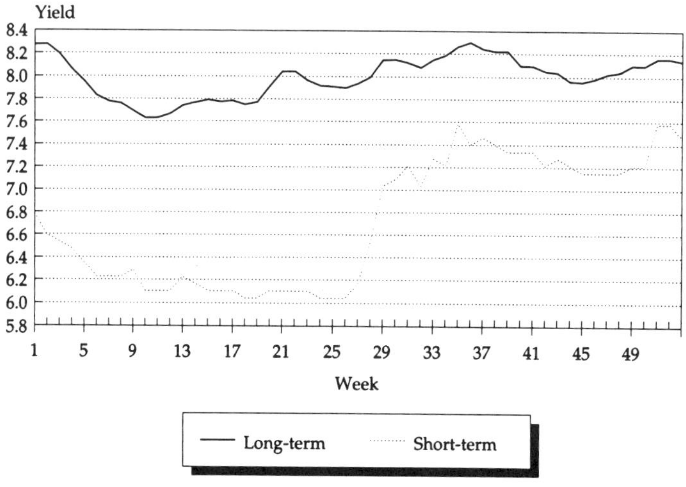

Figure 11.40 Belgian interest rates in 1988

background against which long-term (and short-term) Belgian interest rates were able to decline from 8.30 per cent (6.75 per cent) in January to 7.70 per cent (6.10 per cent) in May. By the late spring, however, interest rates moved up higher again to 8.30 per cent (7.50 per cent). The steady upturn in short-term rates gave a first warning of the inverted yield curve to come.

In 1988, the Belgian bond market was able to count on growing interest from specialized Luxembourg mutual funds. Liquidity on the secondary bond market remained limited, although it benefited from the appearance of OTC market-makers. Other innovations, in particular the introduction of an over-the-counter futures contract by Kredietbank, contributed to a modernization of the fledgling market. In May 1988, prompted by these innovations and a costly public debt, Minister of Finance Philippe Maystadt set up a commission to study the reform of the money and capital markets.

During the year, issuance of Belgian government bonds totalled BFr 657bn. The number of issues by private borrowers during the year remained limited to three, of which two were convertible bonds with warrants. On the international front, there was a single issue by the EIB for BFr 6bn. Various factors go to explain the fact that, compared to 1987, circa BFr 45bn more in savings found their way to the bond market in 1988. Among them is the probable after-shock from the stock market crash of October 1987, with investors switching to the bond market in their search for a safer investment.

It should be noted, too, that during the first half of the year, most news from the Belgian front was overshadowed by the animated battle for take-over of the Sociéte Générale de Belgique.

1989

In contrast with previous years, the mood on the Belgian bond and money market was rather restrained in 1989. The sharp upturn in short-term rates continued through 1989; from 7.50 per cent in January, they jumped to just above 8.30 per cent in March, and yields fluctuated at around this level for the first half of the year. Tensions in the forex market remained in evidence, while large interventions by central banks, the NBB included, could not stop the rise of the US dollar. As a result of the persisting economic uncertainty, German interest rates were hiked and Belgium followed suit. During the summer, the yield curve became flat at 8.40 per cent. However, the Belgian capital market did not prove immune to the spectacular autumn leap in German interest rates. During the last quarter of the year, an inverted yield curve came into place, with three-month rates in the area of 9.20 - 9.70 per cent and bonds 50 - 70 basis points lower.

The interest rate climate put a damper on the issue activity of the Belgian government. A total of BFr 545bn worth of bonds was floated on the market. In net terms, the amount of money raised shrank to BFr 192bn (from BFr 423bn in 1988). This development clearly ran counter to the government's intention to reduce the share of the short-term debt.

Just as the stock market was marked by capital increases in 1989, the bond market also underwent a face-lift. In co-operation with the banks, the Treasury implemented a number of reforms (quotas, commissions) in the working of the permanent issue syndicate (consortium of banks), with a view to make the issue of bonds less expensive. By far the most remarkable innovation in 1989, however, was the linear bond (OLO), issued via a tender system in consecutive

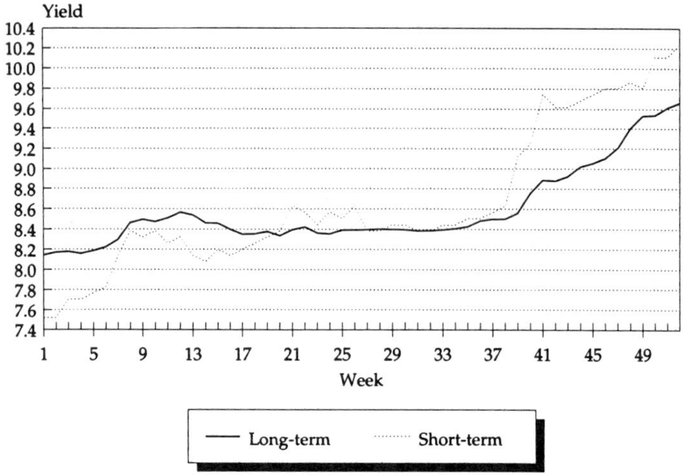

Figure 11.41 Belgian interest rates in 1989

tranches, each with an identical coupon and maturity, and with an advantageous fiscal treatment.

1990

With the fear of inflation hovering in the background, fuelled by the March announcement of German monetary unification and the outbreak of the Gulf crisis, the Belgian market was able to look to anything but a favourable investment climate. In all the tumult, the Belgian bonds held up relatively well. On balance, long-term yields barely rose in 1990 (the 9.80 - 10.30 per cent area), whereas money market rates plunged from 10.50 per cent (January) to 10.00 per cent (May) and, further, to 9.00 per cent (November).

The shrinking of the interest-rate differential between Belgium and Germany was given extra impetus by two measures which enhanced the attractiveness of Belgian franc investments: the pegging, on 16 June 1990, of the BFr to the Dm, and the lowering of withholding tax on bonds issued after 01 March 1990, from 25 per cent to 10 per cent. Furthermore, the repatriation of capital strengthened the position of the BFr within the EMS. All of this had a pronounced effect on the money market. Given the inauspicious mood on the bond market, liquidities

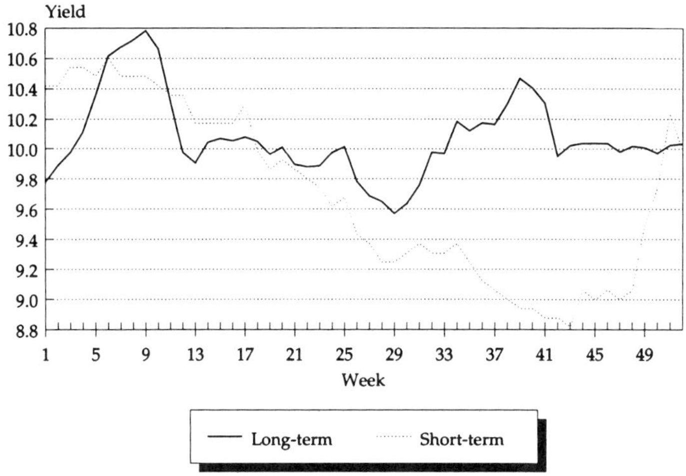

Figure 11.42 Belgian interest rates in 1990

were invested in principally short-term time deposits and savings certificates, with consequent pressures on the money market rates.

A total of BFr 548bn in government bonds was issued in 1990. A marked feature was the paucity of any issuers other than the Treasury. More than half of the total issue volume was placed via the issue of OLOs, actively transacted by institutional and professional investors, in line with the Treasury's intention to employ the OLO as their principal instrument of financing and of enhancing the international status of the Belgian bond market.

A first on the primary market was the launching in March of a government bond (the Philippe bond) aimed directly at the private investor, without the intermediary of the banking consortium.

1991

After the uncertainty in interest rates at the beginning of the year (brought about by the military operations in the Gulf), with bond yields slightly over 10 per cent and money market rates slightly under 10 per cent, the interest rate curve dropped and remained pretty flat during the first six months of the year (9.00 - 9.30 per cent). The advent of Red Monday only marginally increased bond yields (9.45 per cent), and rates for money market deposits remained virtually unchanged (9.20 per cent). Even the political deadlock at the end of 1991

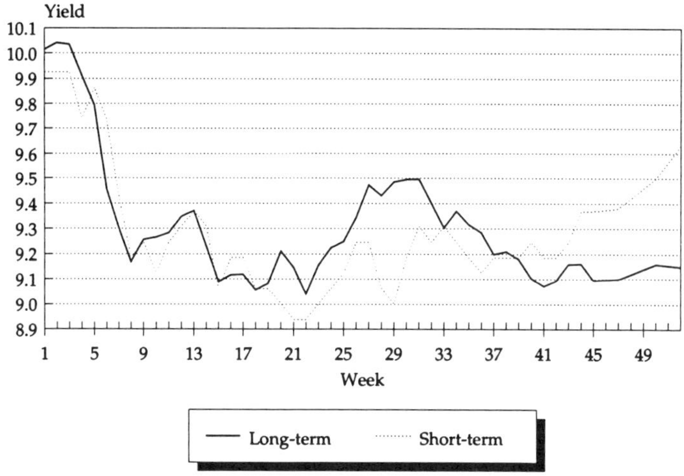

Figure 11.43 Belgian interest rates in 1991

hardly influenced the fixed-interest and money market rates, due to the persistently strong position of the BFr. As from October, the interest rate curve became inverted again (9.10 per cent vs. 9.50 per cent).

On 29 January 1991, an active secondary market in linear bonds and Treasury certificates was set up by an official corps of primary dealers. This introduction has taken the bond market by storm. Besides liquidity, a greater transparency in bond trading has been achieved. Furthermore, the December opening of the Belgian Futures and Options Exchange, will contribute to the efficiency of the underlying market. To enhance the attractiveness of the market, new OLO lines with new maturities were opened in 1991 and some classical bonds could be converted to OLOs. The total 1991 issue volume in government bonds amounted to BFr 969bn.

Even within the renewed framework, interest rate policy remains at the core of economic policy, which aims at reducing the budget deficit and maintaining the exchange rate stability with the Deutschemark to manage inflation. This policy is fostered particularly by the persistent surplus of Belgian cross-border securities trading - net purchases of government paper by non-residents totalling BFr 230bn - which makes the BFr perform exceptionally well. It has moved up to its central rate against Dm within EMS, and stayed there with the interest rate differential *vis-à-vis* Germany steadily narrowing.

11.17 *Inter-market spreads*

Overview

During recent years, spread trading has become one of the most important activities in the bond and money markets for professional and institutional investors. As such, it is now rightly judged to be of value despite requiring a good knowledge of different markets, products and techniques - be it in the bond, certificates or futures market.

Within the Belgian market, rather a limited number of spreads are available to investors, all of which, however, incur several problems.

OLOs versus OLOs

As the current OLOs entail an array of different maturity dates, and are all considered benchmarks for their respective term, the possibilities are limited. The introduction of Belfox, however, will probably create temporary (cash and carry) arbitrage opportunities.

OLOs versus classical bonds:

The lack of substantial liquidity in classical bonds makes it very hard to spread them. The absence of a developed bond-lending system in classical bonds also runs counter to efficient spread trading. As a final problem, the call features of these bonds are hard to price.

OLOs versus Luxembourg franc bonds:

In the absence of BFr-denominated Eurobonds, the LFr market is often considered as the unofficial euro-market of the BFr for private investors. However, the small issue sizes, the low liquidity and the mainly corporate issuers all make it very hard to use the market for spread trading.

Inter-government market spreads

An important factor in the determination of short-term interest rates are exchange rates and, in particular, their anticipated evolution. Generally, to compensate for the depreciation risk, an exchange risk premium is paid.

During the eighties, the lack of confidence in the Belgian franc was so great that even very high short-term interest rates appeared insufficient to entice capital

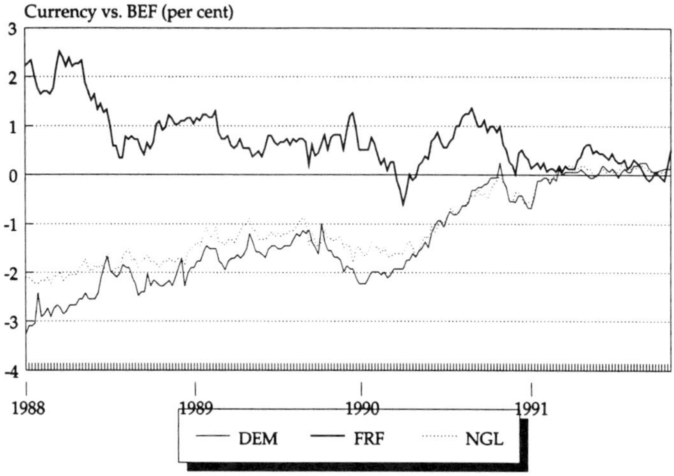

Figure 11.44 Short-term interest rate differentials 1988-1991 (BEF vs DEM/NGL/FRF)

from abroad. Consequently, there was substantial over-supply of BFr. To prevent the Belgian franc from being too much weakened, the NBB syphoned off the over-supply. The necessary foreign currency was drawn from its reserves, but at the same time the large-scale borrowing by the Treasury worsened the situation.

1984 saw the beginning of a gradual improvement in a more competitive Belgian economy. Greater confidence in the BFr and continuously wide interest rate differentials *vis-à-vis* Germany and the Netherlands served to make the expected yield on short-term BFr investments relatively attractive.

Since the pegging of the BFr to the Deutschemark, the yield differential has progressively disappeared as investors' confidence in the reformed monetary policy increased. Indeed, the official pegging involves a commitment to revalue the BFr in line with the Dm at any future EMS realignment. Yield differentials are, therefore, not really justified on account of an expected depreciation of BFr. The spreads BFr/Dm and BFr/Dfl, which were around 200 at the beginning of 1990, consequently fell to 40 basis points by the end of spring 1990. During the summer of 1990, the rise of German money market rates was followed by most EMS countries, except for France and the United Kingdom, and consequently, short-term interest rate differentials remained fairly stable. However, the disadvantage of pursuing such a tight exchange rate policy is that, when German interest rates rise, Belgium has little choice but to follow (e.g. at the end of 1990). The widening of the differential in the beginning of 1991 restored confidence in the BFr, which was strengthened and moved again above its central rate. Since then the BFr has achieved an exchange rate stability against the Dm and progress has been made in the field of monetary policy, which is clearly shown in the narrowing of the spread. It even became negative and was situated around 5-10bp at the end of 1991.

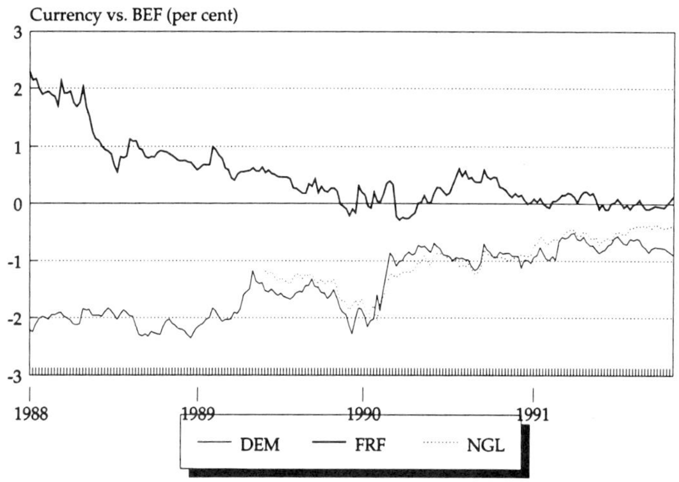

Figure 11.45 Long-term interest rate differentials 1988-1991 (BEF vs. DEM/NGL/FRF)

Because of Belgium's open economy and therefore its dependence on other countries, foreign investors do not look so much at the absolute level of Belgian interest rates, but rather at the interest rate differentials with other countries and especially those with Germany, France, Denmark and the Netherlands.

Yield differentials between government bonds are a function of the market's implicit expectation of currency depreciation of the higher-yielding currency, and of perceived differences in credit quality.

It is, in particular, compared to the German and Dutch bond market which have both systematically lagged behind, that the Belgian OLO market offers better yield prospects, especially as the spread amounts to more than 50 basis points.

On balance, in 1990, it proved possible for Belgian long-term rates to narrow to only 1 per cent, as against about 2 per cent, at the end of 1988 and 1989. The broadening of the interest rate differential immediately after the Gulf crisis was short-lived and was mostly due to a fear about the relatively substantial vulnerability of the Belgian economy. The positive trend can also be explained by the downward pressure on the Dm, resulting from the uncertainty of German monetary unification. This restored stability in the EMS and gave countries like Belgium and France scope for a narrowing of their interest rate differential with Germany. The impetus given by the pegging of the BFr to the Dm and the substantial capital inflow resulting from the lowering of the withholding tax, accelerated the shrinking of the spread.

The foundations for the current BFr parity *vis-à-vis* the Dm appears to be sound. Moreover, the reforms of 1990-1991 have corrected the traditional shortcomings of the Belgian bond market to such an extent, that less compensation needs to be offered for investing in Belgium.

Though this narrowing (115 to 66bp) was spread across the entire range of maturities, the long-term spread remained appreciably higher than the short-term. The main justification for the long-term yield spread with Germany (at 75bp at the end of 1991), the Netherlands (45bp) and France (14bp) remains the fact that the Belgian bond market is dominated by a single borrower with a huge public debt.

11.18 Sources of reference

Financial data

Banking and Finance Commission

- *Annual Report*

Brussels Stock Exchange

- *Official Stock Exchange List.* Daily quotations

Ministry of Finance (Treasury)

- *The National Debt.* Annual report

National Bank of Belgium

- *Monthly Bulletin*

Securities Regulation Fund (Rentenfonds/Fons des Rentes)

- *Annual Report*

Financial press

As from 01 December 1991 the daily official price list of the BSE appears in the following financial papers:

- *Echo de la Bourse* (in French)
- *Financieel Ekonomische Tijd* (in Dutch)

Quote vendors and news agencies

- Bloomberg
  Consult 'offerings' page (prices and analysis of all OLOs and the most liquid classical bonds are available in real-time)
- Reuters - see Figure 11.46
- Telerate - see Figure 11.47

Further reading

- Belfox: *Futures on Belgian Government Bonds*, October 1990
- Kredietbank: *The Belgian Economy and the Belgian Fixed-Income Markets. Growing International Status*, September 1991
- Kredietbank: *The Hard Belgian Franc Makes a Comeback*, September 1991
- Ministry of Finance and National Bank of Belgium: *Brussels - at the leading edge of finance*, May 1991
- Nomura Research Institute: *The Belgian Bond Market*, June 1991
- Petercam: *Belgian Economy*, November 1991
- Remy Freres: *The Belgian Bond Market 1990-1991*, December 1990

	Contributor	Treasury Certificates	OLOs
Prices			
Primary & candidate primary dealers			
	Multi-contributor	BTCX	BGBA-C
	Multi-contributor	BGBE-F (yields)	
	ABN	ABBR	ABKN
	Bacob	BACB	BACC
	Bank Paribas	PBXC	PBXT
	Banque Generale Lux	BGLP	BGLO
	Banque Indosuez	BISE	BISB
	B.B.L.	TBBL	BCEL
	Bcee Lux	CEE	BCEL
	B.I.L.	BILE	BILD
	Cera	CER	OCER
	CGER-ASLK	ASLB	ASLK
	Credit Communal	COMT	COMR
	Credit Lyonnais	CLPD	MANA
	Generale Bank	SGBA	GBBP
	J.P. Morgan	MORI	MORH
	Kredietbank	KRBQ	KBBP
	Dewaay	DEWK	DEWJ
Brokers			
	Petercam		PVCA
	Remy Freres		REMO-Z

Other useful pages

MFBA-C	Announcement and results of certificate auctions
BELA-F	Results of OLO auctions
NBVA-D	National Bank of Belgium money market intervention
NBBU-V	NBB daily turnover in certificates/OLOs
NBVE-F	Daily turnover in certificates/OLOs
KRBI	Kredietbank's bond market comments
KRBQ	Fair value Belfox futures prices
GBBO	Generale Bank's bond market comments
BQCB	Brussels Stock Exchange - cash bonds
BELU-W	Belgian financial report
BRNB	Belfox futures prices

Figure 11.46 Reuters pages

Page no.	Subject
Bond prices & information	
Primary & candidate primary dealers	
3272	General index
3718-19	Linear bonds composite page
3269	Kredietbank market commentary
Brokers	
3271	De Posson
8502	Finacor
Money markets	
3253	NBB indicative rates
3288	Long-term prime rates
3291	Brussels money market composite page
3705	Treasury certificates composite page
36350-53	Kingdom of Belgium Treasury
36360-74	National Bank of Belgium
36375-78	Volume on the secondary market (NBB)
Other useful pages	
36380	Belgian government securities
39519-34	Brussels Stock Exchange - cash market in bonds
25960	Belfox futures prices

Figure 11.47 Telerate pages

11.19 The Luxembourg market

Note: In general text, the abbreviation 'LFr' is used in general text to denote the Luxembourg franc. Elsewhere, the international mnemonic 'LUF' is used.

Introduction

The Luxembourg franc capital market is very different to other European capital markets. In terms of volume, the market is very successful and yet it features few of the characteristics normally considered pre-requisite for such success. It is, in effect, a tight market with little transparency and almost no liquidity. Additionally, the secondary market is almost non-existent and quotation spreads are substantial.

It seems a paradox, therefore, that an explosion in LFr-issue volume has occurred (with placement being made without difficulty).

Clearly, the market's apparent inefficiency has not deterred investors - a fact which, on the surface, appears hard to explain. It might be that the ultimate investors and the economic experts hold divergent views on the theoretical concept, and strategic importance, of market efficiency. One point beyond doubt, though, is that the category of investors to which the Luxembourg market is aimed, attaches importance to factors other than liquidity.

Development of the market

Until the sixties, the Luxembourg capital market was an exclusively domestic market, being essentially reserved for the state, the communities and other public institutions. The financial needs of a rather limited number of large-scale companies were insufficient to encourage a stronger development of the bond market. The market therefore remained somewhat parochial and insignificant.

At the beginning of the 1960s, the emergence of the euro-market had considerable impact on the Luxembourg financial industry, as both international and supranational issuers entered it's capital market. In 1962, the first international LFr-denominated public issue came from the European Coal and Steel Community (ECSC, LFr 300m, 4.75%, 1962 - 1977) followed, in 1965, by an issue from the Italian energy company, Ente Nazionale d'Energia Electrica (ENEL, LFr 30m, 6%, 1965 - 1970).

In 1967, the authorities defined the concept of private placement. In 1971, three placements were launched - for the European Investment Bank, the European Coal and Steel Community, and for Eurofima (the association which was established in 1956 in order to promote the modernization of the railway network in Europe).

Despite these first issues in the 1960s, the market still lacked authenticity. The number of the both public and private issues remained small, while the issues were not placed - remaining, instead, on the books of the banks. The market was totally illiquid and the ultimate investor non-existent. Outside interest in the market came mainly from the supranationals.

At the beginning of the 1970s, the official listing of the Luxembourg Stock Exchange (No. 9063, 01 July 1970) included, essentially, the different tranches of the grand ducal loan, loans granted by the state, loans for the cities and the communities, as well as the debenture bonds of some rare Luxembourg companies (Cofhylux, Hadir, Maria Rheinsheim, Rodange). The foreign companies listed on the Exchange remained ENEL and the ECSC.

Further development of the market in the 1970s was restricted by the introduction of new regulations: for public offers (1972) and public placements (1978). The first regulation introduced the calendar system, by which the number of issues per quarter was limited to two, with priority given to those issuers whose investments were either of interest for the Luxembourg economy, or which promoted inter-governmental relations within the EEC.

However, a certain amount of international issuing activity for private placements was seen in the so-called Luxembourg eurofranc sector. These were actually the first international LFr-loans. During this period, 14 loans (totalling LFr 9.8bn) were issued, compared with a modest private placement total of LFr 2.9bn.

The second regulation, in 1978, took effect at a time when private placement activity had just taken off again. The regulation limited the issue size to LFr 250m and requested denominations of, at least, LFr 1m. Furthermore, it stressed the private character of the transaction since neither advertising nor listing were admitted.

Between 1972 and 1980, the number of the private and public issues remained rather limited (see Figure 11.48). Private placements fluctuated between LFr 200m and LFr 2.57bn, while public issues ranged between LFr 1.1bn (1974) and LFr 7.1bn (1978). Foreign issuers had been active exclusively in the private sector, while the public sector was reserved for local issuers, as well as for the international institutions of which Luxembourg was a member.

The official listing of 1980 (No. 11651, 30 December 1980), consequently shows a number of foreign issuers scarcely higher than the listing of 1970. The LFr-securities listed essentially go back to the Luxembourg state (29 listed securities for the Grand Duchy), the issues guaranteed by the state (5 officially-listed securities for the Luxembourg railway society, the port of Mertert, the Electricity Society of the Our and the National Society for Investment Credits), the cities and the communities (3 securities), as well as Luxembourg companies (27 listed securities, especially from Arbed, Banque Générale du Luxembourg, the Banque International à Luxembourg, Cegedel, Kredietbank Luxembourg, Luxair, Philips, Rodange, Cofhylux, etc), and 3 convertibles. The category of the LFr-

	Public issues	Private placements	Euro-issues	Total
1972	2.600	1.100	6.100	9.800
1973	3.075	1,800	3.700	8.575
1974	1.100	0.200	-	1.300
1975	4.800	0.400	-	5.200
1976	3.770	0.325	-	4.095
1977	5.350	2.300	-	7.650
1978	7.100	2.570	-	9.670
1979	6.150	1.150	-	7.300
1980	5.850	3.210	-	9.060

Figure 11.48 The Luxembourg capital market during the 1970s (LUF billions)

denominated foreign loans contains 20 listed securities which were launched by the following: Akzo, Copenhagen Telephone, Eurofima, Mortgage Bank of Denmark, Norges Kommunalbank, Oslo, Renault Acceptance, Solvay Finance, Sveriges Investeringsbank, Volvo and Bergen Bank. For these debtors, a total volume of LFr 9.8bn was issued by the end of 1980. The category of the international LFr-loans comprised 29 officially-listed securities for the Asian Development Bank, the EIB, the ECSC, the Council of Europe and Euratom. These are essentially supranational issuers with an issue volume of LFr 14.4bn (by the end of 1980), four issues amounting to LFr 800m.

During the eighties, and especially during the second half of the decade, the LFr-capital market gained ground due to intense activity in the field of private placements.

Between 1980 and 1984, total issue volume increased from LFr 9.06bn to LFr 15.45bn , a 70 per cent improvement (see Figure 11.49). Over the same period, the volume of public issues increased by 87 per cent, from LFr 5.85bn to LFr 10.95bn, while private placements increased by 40 per cent, from LFr 3.21bn to LFr 4.5bn. The debtors were mainly supranational issuers and Luxembourg credit institutions. Between 1980 and 1984, the Luxembourg state also had recourse to enter the capital market, reflecting the increased financial needs of the state, particularly between 1981 and 1983. Since that period, the state's needs steadily decreased; indeed, now, the state budget generally shows surpluses.

In 1985, the lowering of interest rates and the introduction of newly-defined regulations by the Luxembourg Monetary Institute, both helped the market to

	Public issues	Private placements	Total	Private/Total (%)
1980	5.850	3.210	9.060	35
1981	7.964	1.900	9.864	19
1982	9.100	3.500	12.600	27
1983	10.650	3.700	14.350	25
1984	10.950	4.500	15.450	29
1985	15.900	11.275	27.175	41
1986	20.275	24.200	44.475	54
1987	14.600	41.937	56.537	74
1988	16.100	58.175	74.275	78
1989	17.700	49.350	67.050	73
1990	46.750	118.615	165.365	71

Figure 11.49 The Luxembourg capital market during the 1980s (LUF billions)

expand strongly. The regulations provided for greater flexibility in the issue calendar and an increase the maximum amount of private placements. As a result of these factors, total issue volume increased by 187 per cent within two years, from a 1984 figure of LFr 15.450, to LFr 44.475bn in 1986. Both public and private placement sectors saw improvement: Public issues registered an increase of 85 per cent, while private placements rose by more than 40 per cent, reaching a 1986 figure of LFr 24.2bn, or 54 per cent of the total issue volume. Some 75 per cent of private placements are issued by foreign borrowers, with the remaining 25 per cent being spread among the Luxembourg banks.

Deregulation

In common with other European and international markets, the Luxembourg market has seen recent deregulation. The general regulations concerning the issue of LFr-denominated securities were abolished with effect from 01 July 1990.

These measures have stimulated the market significantly. Total issue volume increased by almost 350 per cent, from LFr 67.050bn in 1989 to 165.365bn, in 1990. This surge continued in 1991 when, by the end of the third quarter, 1990 volumes had already been outstripped.

Along with the increase in volume, the Luxembourg market has seen strong diversification - attracting not only internationally-recognized issuers, but many less well-known ones, too. This broadening of the market has placed considerable responsibility on lead-managers, the quality of whom is of paramount importance for successful placement.

Types of issue

Over the last five years, instruments issued on the Luxembourg market have been almost exclusively fixed-interest securities. The three exceptions to this shown in Figure 11.50, below.

Type	Issue date	Issuer	Issue volume (LUF billion)
Floating-rate notes	13 December 1989	United Paper Mills	0.300
Convertible	06 June 1989	Pargesa	3.000
Equity-linked	27 March 1991	Bacob	1.000

Figure 11.50 Non-traditional Luxembourg franc issues for foreign debtors

Issuers

The breakdown of issuers by business activity illustrates that numerous financial institutions are having recourse to the LFr-capital market. These debtors often use subordinated issues which allow them to comply with the new Cooke regulations required by the Bank for International Settlements. It would appear that LFr investors accept somewhat lower risk premiums than are expected on other markets with the result that re-financing results look rather favourable.

During the formative years of the LFr-capital market, foreign issuers were practically non-existent (or, at least, of very little importance), the main market participants being supranational issuers. Developments over the past five years have, however, have dramatically created a broad geographical diversification whilst, at the same time, the share of domestic issuers has dropped steadily (to a figure of just 10 per cent, in 1990).

In 1986, at a time when the market had already shown some development with a total issue volume of LFr 45bn , Scandinavian issuers entered into competition with other European debtors and accounted for 35 per cent of the issues in the first semester and 41 per cent in the second. With such a considerable share of issuance, these Scandinavian - particularly Swedish - issuers promptly confirmed the significant role they were about to assume.

At that time, the Asian countries and the United States were scarcely present at all. The (then) seven countries of the EC were represented, in decreasing importance, as follows: Belgium, Luxembourg, France, the Netherlands, Germany, Italy and Great Britain. The supranational issuers (mainly the EIB, Eurofima and Euratom) had a market share of about 11 per cent.

Since 1986, in addition to a general geographic diversification, there has been a redistribution of market share in favour of France, Germany, Italy, the Netherlands and other new countries (albeit with rather insignificant amounts). This redistribution is at the expense of the Scandinavian countries (mainly Finland, Norway and Sweden,) as well as the supranational issuers.

In 1990, 21 countries had recourse to use the Luxembourg capital market, compared to a figure of 14, in 1986. The new issuers come from Australia (2 issues), Canada (3), Austria (2), Ireland (1), Spain (1) and Switzerland (2 issues). Although the market shares of these new issuers may be considered marginal, they nevertheless contribute to a significant expansion of the Luxembourg capital market. Figure 11.51 shows the market share by origin in 1991. The most important share is held by Belgium with 37.3 per cent (against 21.1 per cent in 1986). France follows with 19.4 per cent (against 11.1 per cent in 1986), Germany with 5.6 per cent (against 1.6 per cent), Sweden with 5.3 per cent (12.8 per cent) and Denmark with 2.6 per cent (4.8 per cent).

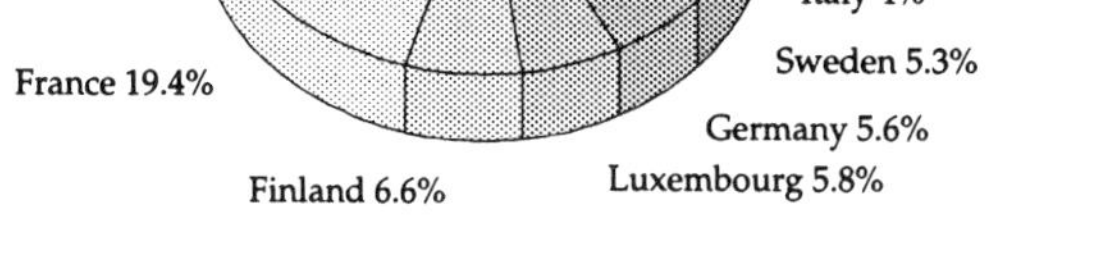

Others are: Supranationals 2.1%, Japan 1.5%, UK 1.5%, Norway 1.2%, Australia 0.8%, Ireland 0.3%, Switzerland 0.3%

Figure 11.51 Issuers on the Luxembourg market by origin (1991)

Type of issue by origin

There are essentially two loan categories to be considered: the public issue and the private placement. Officially-listed private placements have only been introduced since liberalization. It should be noted that, for the purposes of examining the link between origin and type of issue, the relative significance of the particular instruments and issues is discounted.

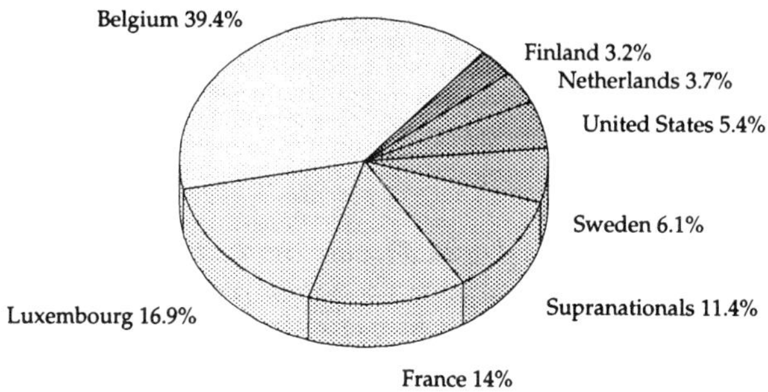

Figure 11.52 Private placements on the Luxembourg market by origin (1990)

In 1986, the Scandinavian countries accounted for 46 per cent of the total private placement issue volume, whereas western European countries accounted for only 31 per cent. Within the Scandinavian group, Sweden was at the forefront with more than 18 per cent of the total market. Among the other European countries, France was, by far, the principal foreign debtor ahead of Belgium, Germany and Italy. In 1990 (see Figures 11.52 & 11.53), the Scandinavian countries, led this time by Denmark, held a market share of only 21 per cent, in contrast to the other European countries which held the lion's share of 71 per cent. The current European order of rank is: Belgium, France, Luxembourg, Germany, the Netherlands, Italy, Great Britain, Spain, Switzerland and Austria.

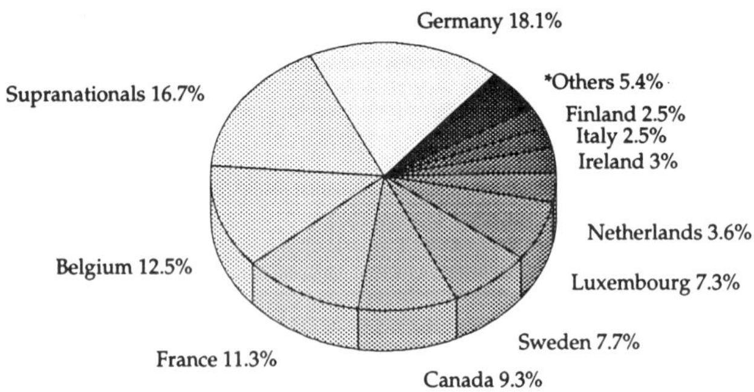

**Others are: UK 2.4%, USA 1.6%, Denmark 1.4%*

Figure 11.53 Public issuance on the Luxembourg market by origin (1990)

As far as public loans are concerned, the most apparent difference concerns the supranational issuers who, in 1990, occupied second place (behind German debtors), whereas their market share for private placements is below 1 per cent. As may be seen from the figure, the public market is clearly less geographically diversified than the private placement market.

The borrowers having recourse to the Luxembourg capital market are mostly excellent addresses with a good rating. However, their issues are generally not officially rated. Efforts to alter this situation have recently been made, albeit with only limited success.

Issue currency

Clearly, there are particular reasons for issuers to use the Luxembourg market. In general, an issuer looks to minimize the costs of his funding programme. To this end, consideration is often given to issuance in a foreign currency and such a move may be worthwhile for two reasons. Firstly, the foreign-currency yield may be lower than that found on the domestic market. Secondly, the issuer may be of the opinion that the issue currency risks depreciation against the domestic currency, thereby reducing the redemption amount denominated in the national currency. Such a strategy may well prove attractive if the anticipated exchange-rate losses are larger than the risk premium the issuer needs to offer to the market for the exchange rate risk.

The LFr has always belonged to the high-yielding currency group. Due to the close economic links between Belgium and Luxembourg, as well as the exchange parity between the Luxembourg franc and the Belgian franc, the yields of the two currencies develop mostly parallel to each other. Despite the relatively high yields of the Luxembourg franc against other traditional hard currencies, the currencies with a positive yield differential against the Luxembourg market were principally the Scandinavian currencies, the Italian lira and the French franc. A Danish krona debtor, for example, would have paid an average yield premium, between 1986 and 1991, of 140 basis points. For the Norwegian krona and Swedish krona, the premiums amounted to 333 basis points and 272 basis points, respectively.

Among the high-yielding EMS currencies, positive premiums could be found, for example, in the Italian lira (235 basis points) and the French franc (25 basis points). However, negative premiums could be seen in the Deutschemark (-211 basis points), the Swiss franc (-339 basis points), as well as the Japanese yen (-341 basis points).

These yield differentials can explain the strong presence of Scandinavian issuers in the LFr market. Indeed, it seems that the yield benefits largely compensated for possible losses caused by an appreciation of the LFr against the Scandinavian currencies.

If one considers, however, the evolution of the exchange rates of the respective currencies, one can see that both the Norwegian and Swedish currencies have depreciated against the LFr over the last five years by about 25 per cent and 17 per cent, respectively. Apart from coupon cashing, the debtors had to redeem their loans with 125 per cent and 117 per cent, respectively, of the issue value. Furthermore, the LFr has appreciated against the lire and the French franc by +10.2 per cent and +11.6 per cent, respectively. Against the US dollar, the LFr appreciated by an even more dramatic +46.4 per cent.

Among the payment flows connected with a security, the final redemption is, in general, crucial. Even a slight depreciation of the domestic currency at the moment of redemption, may effectively nullify the prior economies realized by a lower coupon level.

Since the majority of the currencies under review have drastically depreciated against the LFr, the issuers have had to accept higher financing costs than those prevailing in their domestic markets.

The secondary market

As noted earlier there is no real secondary market in Luxembourg. That the primary market can flourish in the absence of a secondary market seems to be attributable to the ultimate investor who seems to be an individual (there are, of course, no statistics for the secondary market) who subscribes via specialized dealers in the primary market, and who has an investment horizon corresponding to the maturity of the security. The liquidity and the existence of a well-structured secondary market seem to be, therefore, of little importance in the decision-making.

However, despite the foregoing, there is consensus that a good secondary market can only be of benefit for the Luxembourg market as a whole, particularly as it would encourage the participation of institutional investors. A first step in this direction would be for lead-managers to make a market for the issues they have launched. There are signs that the more innovative among them are already working to that end.

Chapter

12

The bond markets of

Czechoslovakia

Lukas Julinek
LB-Capital Markets, Vienna

This chapter has been supplied by the Austrian Bond Commission

Note: In general text, the abbreviation 'Kcs' is used to denote Czechoslovak korunas. Elsewhere, the international mnemonic 'CSK' is used.

12.1 General synopsis

Legal framework

The Bond Act, 1990

On 1 February 1991, the Federal Bond Act became effective. It governs the new issue procedure for all types of securities representing obligatory rights in written form. Bonds can either be issued in domestic or foreign currency in accordance with the ruling foreign exchange regulations. Application for the issuance of bonds has to be made to the Ministry of Finance, either the Federal Ministry or the Ministry of the Czech or Slovak Republic. The permit is granted with the approval of the Czechoslovak State Bank.

Stock Exchange Bill

The foundation of stock exchanges seems to be a matter of national pride in the CSFR. Until now, the three parliaments (Federal, Czech and Slovak) could not agree on a federal law governing stock exchanges. Only the Slovak government has passed a Stock Exchange Law - which led to the foundation of the Bratislava Stock Exchange. Prague has not yet decided on the organizational structure of its stock exchange, but has founded a so-called 'provisional secondary market for securities', which is organized and hosted by the State Bank. This market comprises ten domestic commercial banks, which meet weekly to trade securities that comply with the current listing requirements. Membership to the Prague Stock Exchange is also be open to foreign banks, but applicants need to obtain a banking licence in the CSFR.

In addition, the concept of a central depository has not yet found enough supporters to become real; Investicni Banka in Prague has been authorized to allocate ISIN (International Securities Identification Number) codes on Czechoslovak securities. By the end of August 1991, 125 ISIN codes were allocated in the CSFR.

Economic framework

Investors

Private investors prefer to keep their savings either in savings accounts or in the form of goods suitable for barter trading. Lack of confidence in the efficiency of the evolving domestic financial market and an unpredictable rate of inflation keep the private investor away from the market. Furthermore, a substantial decrease in real wages has forced people to reduce savings rather than acquire investments.

Institutional investors of a western type do not yet exist in the CSFR. Reorganization of social and other types of insurance, based on western models, will eventually create a stable demand for financial investments. Currently, only the obligatory 'reserve fund', which must be maintained by Czechoslovak companies, creates any real demand. Tight monetary policy by the State Bank leads to liquidity squeezes rather than to demand for investment opportunities.

Issuers

Until now, budget income has been mainly fuelled by taxation. Politically, the federal government tries to keep the state debt at minimum levels, except, that is, for the growing trade deficit which needs to be financed in foreign currency rather than korunas. From the corporate side there could, in the future, be a bottomless demand for funds, but more of a venture capital type than of a 'bond type'. Restructuring the Czechoslovak economy is a task for risk capital that is willing to wait for a dividend rather than expecting a constant cashflow.

Officially-traded bonds

See Figure 12.1, below. Trade volume amounts currently to Kcs 4m per session.

Issuer	**Kommercni Banka**	**Vseobecna uverova Banka**	**TOS Kurim**	**Federal Ministry of Finance**
Volume (CSK)	1bn	1bn	50m	2bn
Maturity	1995	1995	1996	2000
Coupon	23%	21%	18%+[1]	5%+[2]
Issue date	01 July 1990	01 November 1990	01 January 1991	30 October 1990

Figure 12.1 Officially-traded bonds (as at September 1991)

[1] *coupon 18% plus a variable coupon (max. +6%)*

[2] *plus redemption of 10% of principal*

Chapter

13

The bond markets of

Denmark

Hasse H. Nilsson & Niels Retbøll
Sundberg & Co.

Note: In general text, the abbreviation 'DKr' is used to denote the Danish krone. Elsewhere, the international mnemonic 'DKK' is used.

13.1 *Introduction*

Overview

In Denmark, a number of major changes have occurred since the previous edition of this guide. The *Little Big Bang* of summer 1988 (a nickname for the Danish Stock Exchange Reform) abolished the exchange-trading monopoly previously enjoyed by the 27 authorized broker firms, while simultaneously substituting the trading floor with a decentralized computer trading system. Participation in the system is now free to anybody complying with the rules and regulations appertaining to 'Stock Exchange Broker Companies'. Both prior to, and following, the reform, a large number of broker firms were acquired by banks and insurance groups, while competition forced others out of the market - some leaving voluntarily whilst others simply went bankrupt. As of today, only a handful of independent, privately-held, broker companies are left, while both the large mergers of Danish banks in 1990 and international deregulation, have made the broker companies owned by the two-largest Danish banking groups the major players in the Danish bond markets. Accounting for roughly two-thirds of total bond volume, the two banks act as quasi-stock exchanges in their own right, even though they are official members of The Copenhagen Stock Exchange.

Similar to the experience of other major bond markets, Danish margins and commissions have come under severe pressure since 1988, particularly as the substitution of mortgage benchmark issues by government benchmark issues attracted increased attention from foreign investors. Government bullet bonds, issued on a tap basis with maturities of up to 10 years, took the lead in terms of both issuing and trading volume, while the role of mortgage bonds faded. A contributory factor in the falling attraction of mortgage-backed issues was the crisis faced by mortgage institutions between 1988 and 1991. As the Danish economy suffered from a self-imposed cyclical downturn, property prices fell by up to 40 per cent and intrinsic mortgage values were accordingly eroded leading mortgage institutions to incur heavy losses and make substantial debt-provisions. Though the crisis has passed without any mortgage institution filing for bankruptcy, the yield premium on mortgage bonds over government bonds remains relatively high. While part of the premium may be explained by the fact that issuing volume has been reduced markedly in the mortgage bond sector (following the economic downturn and associated stagnation in the construction industry), the premium still contains an element of perceived risk.

A tax reform introduced in 1987, only reduced personal marginal income tax rates by a few percentage points, leaving Denmark to continue with the highest marginal tax rates in the OECD area (68 per cent on personal income). The tax value of provisions, i.e. interest payments etc., however, were reduced substantially. At the same time, corporate income tax and tax on capital income were also both reduced. These measures not only realized the desired aim of stimulating savings, but also produced a number of other macroeconomic benefits. Inflation decreased to a level of 2 to 2 1/2 per cent, the balance of payment swung into surplus, and the fiscal deficit stabilized at a lower and more acceptable level. However, growth remained modest and unemployment stayed high. The period 1988-1991 saw the introduction of new derivative instruments to the Danish bond markets. In particular, the arrival of futures and options (on mortgage and government benchmarks) has proved to be more than just a novel innovation; as liquidity has risen, these contracts have proved to be invaluable tools for market participants. The successive deregulation of neighbouring economies has stimulated issuers resident in Sweden, Norway and Finland, to launch, at the Copenhagen Stock Exchange, a number of issues denominated in their respective currencies. Whether this development should be regarded as setting a trend for the future or, (since all three are Efta countries) a first step towards EC integration remains, however, to be seen. Whatever the cause, though, the Copenhagen Stock Exchange has now become the main official exchange among the Nordic countries.

Market composition

At year-end 1991, the total market value of Danish bonds was standing at approximately DKr 1400bn, or roughly 150 per cent of Danish GNP. The bulk of new issues during the 1980s arose from the government sector, reflecting continued fiscal deficits. As mortgage-backed issues were hit by a considerable contraction in the construction industry, their relative market share was reduced markedly; ten years ago, mortgage-backed issues accounted for more than two thirds of all outstanding bonds - now the figure is fifty per cent. Domestic corporate bond activity is still negligible in Denmark, as most short- and medium-funding for private industry is handled by the banks, while long-term financing of real assets is provided through mortgage credit associations and 'Finance for Danish Industry'. The Danish Ship Credit Fund is a constant issuer, providing long-term financing for vessels build on Danish shipyards (which experienced a strong revival following the turnaround in world-wide shipping since 1986). Though municipalities do issue bonds, most financing is obtained in the form of direct loans from the government. Eurobonds denominated in Danish kroner never gained widespread popularity, in part due to the fact that the first issue was not launched until 1985, when domestic, and highly-liquid, issues were already available to non-Danish residents. Accordingly, the relative market share of eurobonds has dwindled. DKr-denominated issues launched by foreign entities emerged in 1988 but, as at the end of 1991 only DKr 3.6bn (or less than a

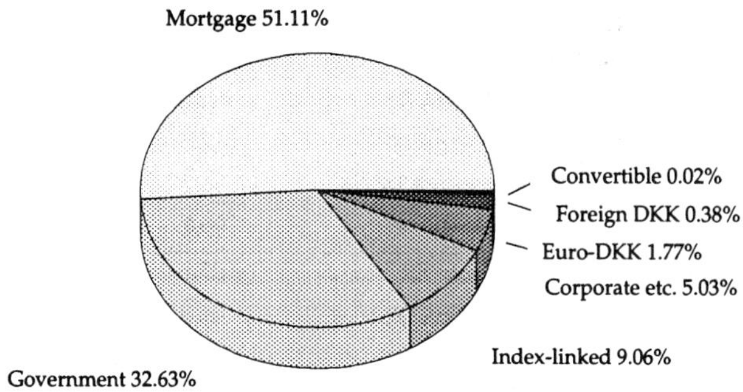

Figure 13.1 Composition of the Danish bond market

half per cent of the market value of all bonds outstanding) was issued by foreign, primarily supranational, issuers.

13.2 Economics

Macroeconomic factors

Gross national product

The past decade of Danish growth may be characterized by three distinct phases:

- a second oil crisis
- national euphoria and overspending
- self-imposed economic discipline

These phases are reflected in Figure 13.2. The aftermath of the second oil-shock was marked internationally by monetary tightening and fiscal abundance. In addition, Denmark changed government during 1982, when a Conservative-Liberal coalition replaced the Social Democrats and immediately stopped wage

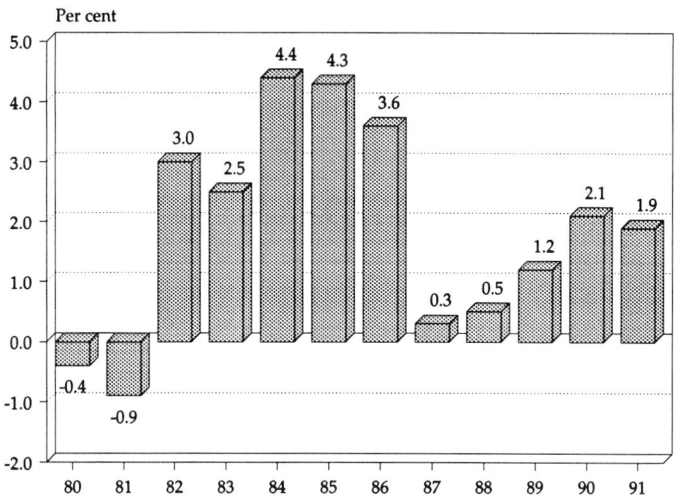

Figure 13.2 Danish gross national product

inflation by abolishing automatic wage indexation. Interest rates peaked in September 1982 at levels around 22 per cent for long-term bonds; by spring 1986, they could be dealt at yields just below 9 per cent. The substantial wealth-effect arising from this unprecedented fall in nominal yields triggered an enormous rise in private spending, with devastating impacts on the balance of trade. The brakes were applied in late 1986 with the simultaneous introduction of a tax reform reducing the tax value of interest expenditure, a penalty tax on consumer loans, and a doubling of real estate taxes. The savings ratio then started slowly but surely to increase during the following years and, by 1991, it stood at four times the level of 1986. Meanwhile, growth has stagnated, remaining below 2 per cent for the last 5 years, although both the balance of trade and inflation have improved markedly. Despite fiscal spending exceeding fiscal income, efforts have been successfully focused on cost reduction and productivity, making it possible to avoid an explosion of the fiscal deficit following the surge in unemployment from 1987.

Trade balance

Roughly 50 per cent of Danish trade is with EC countries, with Germany as the most-important single trading partner, accounting for approximately 40 per cent of total EC trading. Bearing in mind German reunification, it is not surprising

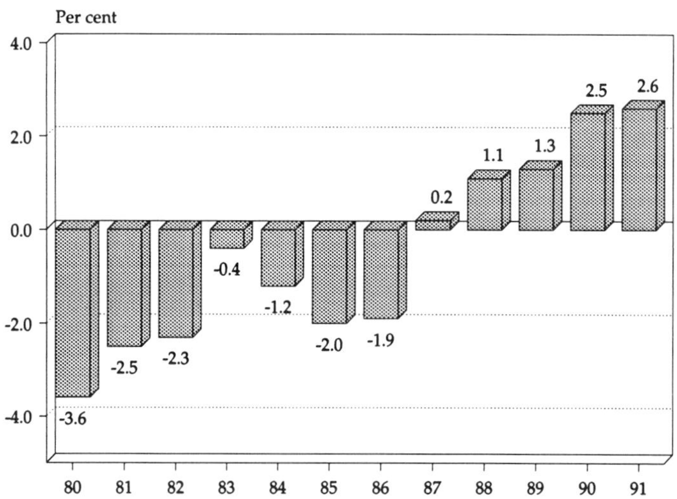

Figure 13.3 Danish trade balance

that Danish trading ties with Germany have been a major factor in the recent improvement in the trade balance (see Figure 13.3). Other important influences have been low Danish wage inflation, and high productivity gains.

Historic ties with former communist countries in the Baltic area, such as Poland and the Baltic Republics, as well as with the rest of Scandinavia, provides potential for further improvement in the Danish trade balance in the years to come. Following the successful turnaround of the balance of trade, the balance of payments has recorded a surplus in both 1990 and 1991, with the outlook for further improvement in the future. Until 1990, Denmark had 27 consecutive years of balance of payment deficits, accumulating foreign debt of up to 60 per cent of GNP at the 1989 peak.

Budget deficit

Government budget deficits rose to record levels in the beginning of the 1980s. This was mainly as a consequence of the second oil shock's impact on the business cycle (see Figure 13.4), but was also fuelled by expensive Parliamentary legislation which provided for an increase in unemployment benefits and social welfare bills, as well as a general expansion of public services and staffing. This unfortunate trend was brought to a halt, by the new Conservative-Liberal government coalition in 1983, primarily by the introduction of new special taxes

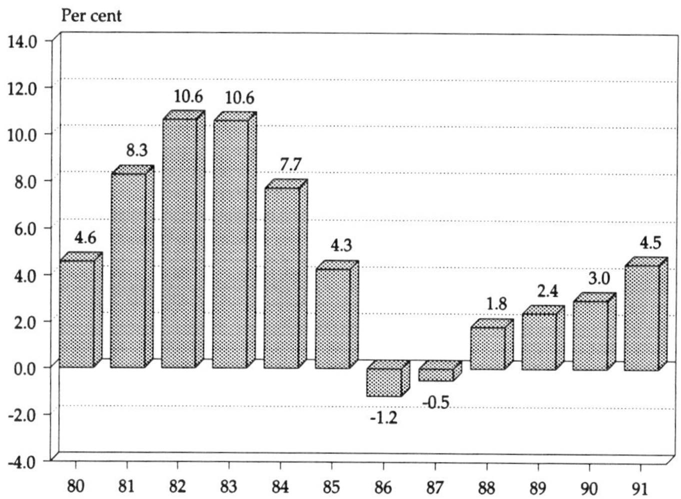

Figure 13.4 Danish budget deficit

such as the 'real rate tax' on pension schemes but also by commencing a modernization of the public sector and, also, by preparing for a general tax reform, which was finally implemented from January 1987. Though Denmark still upholds one of best welfare systems in the world, the government budget figures have stayed within acceptable limits since 1986. Total public employment is being steadily being reduced while total public debt is now below the Emu requirement of 60 per cent of GDP.

Unemployment and inflation

Unemployment has been hovering around 8 to 10 per cent during the last decade (see Figure 13.5), and is not expected to fall markedly during the next few years, as structural adaptations within both private industry and public services will only trigger demand for highly-skilled labour. The wave of mergers over the last few years in preparation for EC's 1992 single market has produced a number of redundancies - and this is likely to continue beyond the short-term. The extremely high Danish level of unemployment support, by comparison to other EC members, and rigid union conditions are also additional factors in the high level of unemployment; however, there is a growing recognition of the problem and labour market reforms may well be expected within the foreseeable future.

The abolition of automatic wage indexation in 1983, followed by a tight monetary policy and growing recognition by the unions that privileges must be paid for by reduced demand for wage increases, together promoted modest (but constant) real wage increases, whilst inflation (see Figure 13.6) has fallen almost throughout the whole decade, paving the way for a surge in exports and a stable exchange rate. The strong political consensus on exchange rate stability and commitment to market economics within an EC context, is probably the best guarantee that future inflation will be kept at a reasonable level.

Monetary policy

Since the origin of Danish commitment to the European exchange rate mechanism (ERM) in the beginning of the 1980s, the Danish central bank has strongly followed the footsteps of Germany's Bundesbank in its method of conducting monetary policy, although it should be noted that, with the development of the domestic economy, it had considerable scope for manoeuvre. Focusing on the monitoring of liquidity and short-term interest rates, new instruments facilitating the implementation of this strategy were introduced. Certificates of deposit (CDs), issued by the Bank exclusively for the banking system, were launched while, for the public, Treasury bills were issued. International co-operation and co-ordination between ERM central banks was developed to a level of sophistication. Growth in money supply was reduced from annually 10-12 per cent during the first part of the 1980s to the annual rate of approximately 5 per cent witnessed

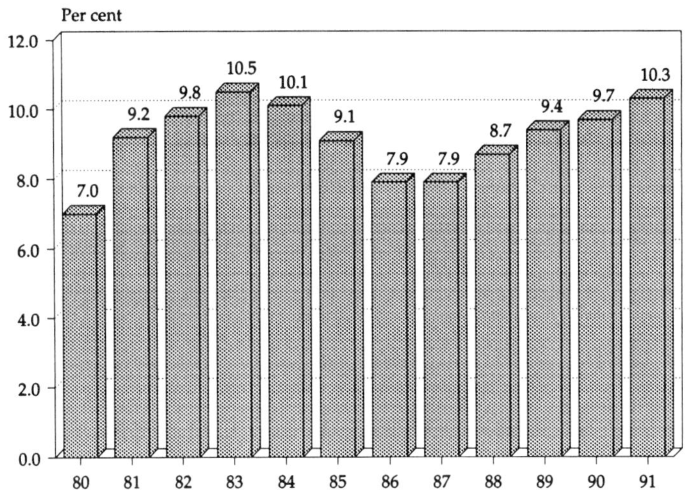

Figure 13.5 Danish unemployment

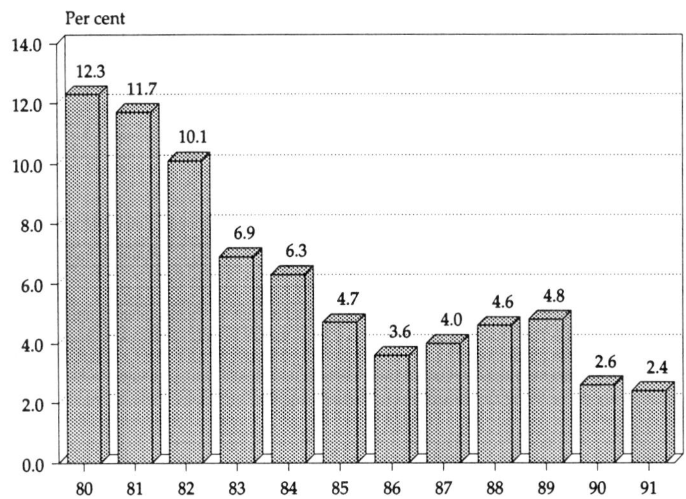

Figure 13.6 Danish inflation

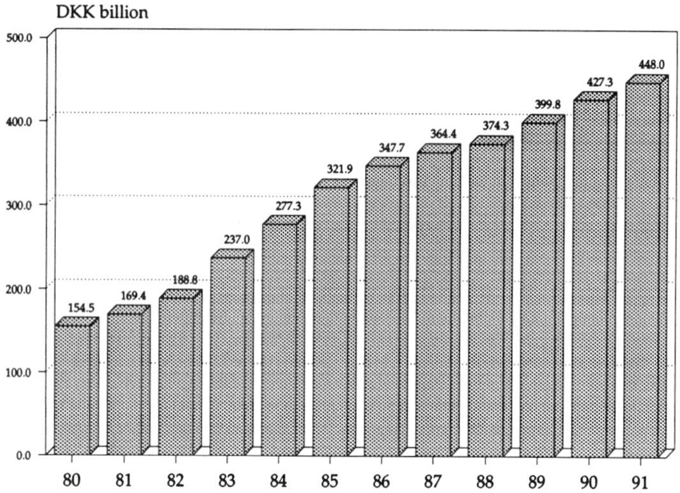

Figure 13.7 Danish money supply growth

during the last 6 years (see Figure 13.7). Apart from temporary fluctuations due to elections and external disturbances in the ERM, the Danish exchange rate has remained stable against the Deutschemark while the krone has joined the club of super-strong currencies within the ERM.

Exchange rates of the krone against the Ecu, the Deutschemark, the US dollar and the Japanese yen are shown in Figures 13.8 - 13.11.

Capital market structure

Deregulation, both external and internal, has characterized the development of the Danish capital market during the past decade. Exchange controls were completely abolished in 1989, though tax laws and regulations for the pension sector still represent minor impediments to the free flow of capital across borders. Domestically, deregulation has stimulated competition between financial institutions by abandoning privileges. Banks, saving banks, brokers, insurance companies, mortgage credit associations etc. are almost entirely free to compete with each other's product lines, while mergers and acquisitions (M&As) are now acceptable - indeed, many have already taken place. This is especially true of the banking sector which, with more than 200 banks and 3500 branches 'overbanking' a population of only 5 million, welcomed M&As. In 1990, the two largest banks merged under the name Den Danske Bank, and three larger banks merged under a new name - Unibank. Larger insurance groups such as Hafnia and Baltica have entered the banking and broking sector, and mortgage associations are being converted into corporate entities. The Stock Exchange Reform Act of June 1986 abolished the broker club system and created a new framework for future participants to deal under a decentralized computer system with direct links to a fully-automated settlement system - the Danish Securities Centre (previously established in 1983). Securities broking may now be carried out by any entity, if incorporated as *Børsmæglerselskab* and complying with rules and regulations laid down by the fiscal authorities and the Copenhagen Stock Exchange. Through mergers, acquisitions, insolvencies and voluntary terminations, 27 formerly-independent stockbroking firms have been reduced to just over a handful, while the stockbroking arms of banks and insurance groups have taken over the bulk of securities trading. Foreign participation has hitherto been confined to three Scandinavian-based houses and the Dutch concern, ABN-AMRO. The total number of authorized stockbroking companies, mainly bank subsidiaries, was 31 at year-end 1991. A complete list of current Danish authorized broker companies is provided in the Appendix to this chapter.

The substantial share of bonds in the total credit-flow illustrates the high degree of securitization of the Danish capital market. Considering the negotiability of private mortgages, and the bond element of foreign lending by the Kingdom of Denmark, securitization represents more than two-thirds of the flow of credit (see Figure 13.12).

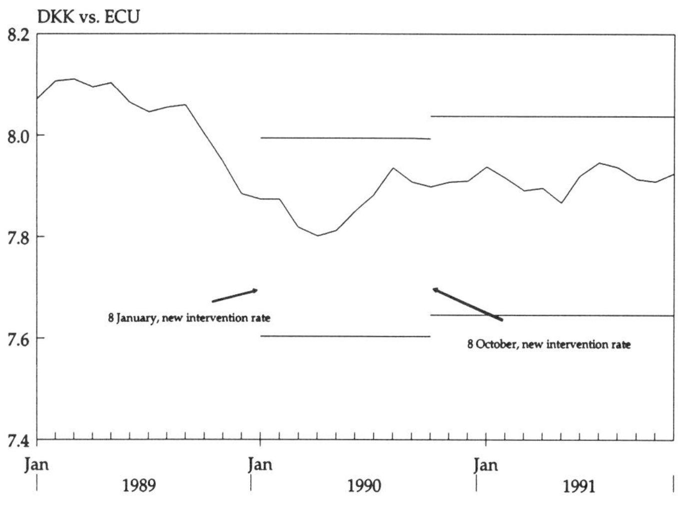

Figure 13.8 The performance of the Danish krone - DKK vs. ECU

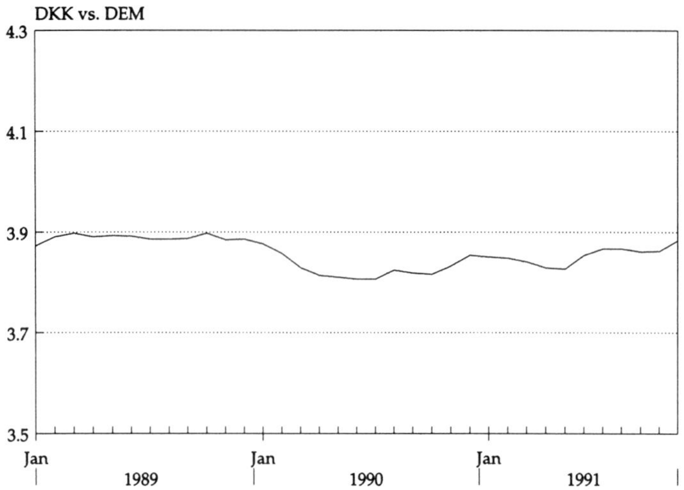

Figure 13.9 The performance of the Danish krone - DKK vs. DEM

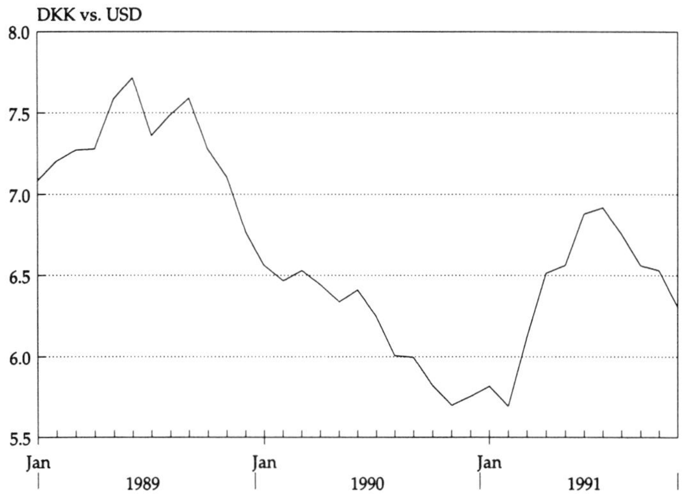

Figure 13.10 The performance of the Danish krone - DKK vs. USD

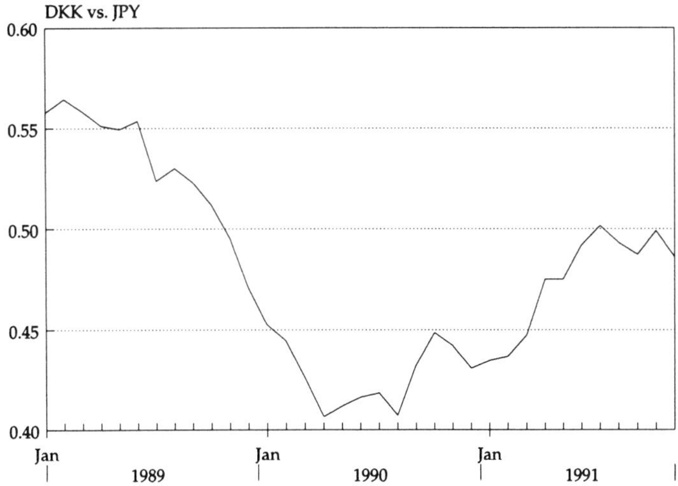

Figure 13.11 The performance of the Danish krone - DKK vs. JPY

	1980	1990
Bonds, incl. mortgage-backed	48	53
Direct lending	24	15
Private mortgages	10	7
Direct lending by government	5	3
Foreign lending incl. public bonds	13	22
Total	100	100

Figure 13.12 Distribution of credit by source

Banks & savings banks	202
Mortgage credit associations	7
Other bond-issuing intermediaries	3
Life insurance companies	23
Pension funds	183
Public pension & agency funds	25
Unit trust entities	22

Figure 13.13 Number of Danish financial intermediaries, 1991

Politics

Constitutional democracy was introduced in Denmark in 1849, although parliamentariansm (defined as the sole discretion of Parliament to actually form a government among its members), was established in 1901.

The present Constitutional Act dates back to 1953, when a general referendum substituted the former bicameral system with one single forum - Folketinget - but retained a constitutional monarchy and the tripartition of power. A total of 179 seats are allocated among the parties in the Parliament, of which four seats are occupied by the so-called North Atlantic members - Greenland and the Faroe Islands - whilst 175 seats correspond to mandates from the Kingdom of Denmark. Parliament members are elected for a four-year term though, in practice, early elections are predominant as it is in the power of any prime minister to turn a political issue into a cabinet question, and thus resigning if a parliamentary majority opposes the issue. The election system is proportional, thereby securing parliamentary representation in proportion to the total number of votes cast for each particular party. Any party obtaining more than two per cent of the total number of votes cast in a general election is represented in Parliament by at least four seats. This relatively-low 'entrance limit' facilitates the creation and existence of small parties which, at first glance, may seem inconsistent with political stability and decision-making, but if viewed in a wider perspective, it can be seen to necessitate a high level of co-operation and compromise; indeed, this has been borne out in practice to the point of almost becoming a Danish tradition. In retrospect, although general elections have been quite frequent in Denmark over the last two decades, only two different prime ministers have headed minority governments in 18 years. Furthermore, on most major issues, such as macroeconomic policy, EC and Nato, between 70 and 80 per cent of Parliament reaches consensus quite easily (this fact also reflects the lack of extremist parties in Denmark). Although the Social Democrats are still the largest single party in Parliament, the government leadership over the past decade has been in the hands of prime minister Poul Schlüter, leader of the Conservatives who, together with the Liberals, have formed the pillars of government over this period of deregulation and European integration, where Denmark is today one of the strongest economies within the Community.

13.3 Market composition

Overview

Government bonds

Over the past few years, government bullet bonds have replaced mortgage annuity bonds as benchmarks. The deliberate action of the Danish central bank in substituting serial issues by bullets served several purposes: Firstly, international demand for Danish issues continued to increase with a logical preference for sovereign credit, liquidity and bullet structures. Secondly, convergence of interest rates between Germany and Denmark - spreads were reduced from 600 to 100 basis points from 1986 to 1990 - and comfortable currency reserves, precipitated a conversion of foreign borrowings to the issuance and export of Danish kroner bonds. Thirdly, the credit crisis of Danish mortgage associations contributed to the flight to quality. Finally, public borrowing requirements continued to surge, forcing the central bank to meet investor preferences. In the future, no serial bonds are expected to be issued, while the policy-mix of bullets, short-term notes and Treasury bills seems set to continue to satisfy market participants.

Mortgage bonds

Though bonds issued by Danish mortgage associations still represent a majority in the total Danish bond market, their predominant role has been relatively reduced. Apart from the substantial increase in government issues, a number of events contributed further to a reduction in mortgage bond issuance. Economic slowdown, tax reform, and contractions on mortgage associations lending limits and lending profiles, together triggered falling prices on the family home market, as well as on business property. New construction has become negligible, and mortgage associations have been under financial pressure throughout the last five years. Accordingly, fewer (and smaller) issues were launched in this market segment, while credit premiums were raised relative to sovereign debt instruments. Though the crisis is over, the building sector is not anticipating a major turnaround within the next few years, while mortgage associations have not finalized restructuring and consolidation plans. Competition from within the mortgage sector, as well as competition from the rest of the Danish financial sector, may provoke mortgage credit associations to attempt new types of issue and methods of issuance in the coming years; these may include international fund raising.

	End-1991	% Total
GOVERNMENT		
Bullet	190	16.0
Serial	61	5.1
Floating-rate notes	85	7.1
Short-term notes	74	6.2
Total	410	38.6
MORTGAGE-BACKED		
Annuity	420	35.3
Serial	39	3.3
Floating-rate notes	3	0.3
Index-linked	56	4.7
Total incl. 2 mort.	647	54.4
SHIP CREDIT FUND		
Bullet	16	1.3
Index-linked	11	0.9
Total	27	2.3
MUNICIPALS		
Annuity	3	0.3
Serial	4	0.3
Index-linked	2	0.2
Total	9	0.9
BANKS		
Bullet & serial	8	0.7
FINANCE FOR DANISH INDUSTRY		
Bullet	2	0.2
FOREIGN BONDS		
Bullet	5	0.4

(cont.)

		End-1991	% Total
EUROBONDS			
	Bullet	21	1.8
	Zero-coupon	1	0.1
	GRAND TOTAL	1189	100.0

Figure 13.14 Composition of the Danish market (DKK billion nominal)

Ship Credit Fund

Inflation index-linked bullet bonds were introduced as a new financing instrument for vessels built on Danish shipyards from 1986. Similar to existing fixed-income bullet issues, Ship Credit Fund issues contain a large element of subsidy to the borrowers and security for investors, for the Fund carries a government guarantee.

After a decline in issue volume during the first half of the 1980s, the general improvement in international shipping and new financing techniques filled the order books of Danish shipyards, prompting new issues of Ship Credit Fund bonds, primarily for index-linked issues. During the period 1986 to 1991, the outstanding amount of Ship Credit Fund issues grew by 50 per cent.

Municipal bonds

Borrowing by Danish municipalities has been almost unchanged during the past five years, this being attributable to tighter central control, and co-ordination between central and local fiscal budgeting. Municipalities must obtain central permission to borrow; any loan subsequently being effected through the Danish Municipalities Mortgage Credit Association, through which individual municipalities are both jointly and severally liable for repayments of debt.

Bank bonds

Borrowings by banks remain an ingredient of the Danish bond markets, but they are of little overall importance; nevertheless, some innovations such as zero-coupon bonds, have emanated from this sector. Single issues tend to be relatively small, with maturities ranging between 5 and 10 years.

Finance For Danish Industry

This institution was established in 1985 by Danish banks, insurance companies and the central bank. Issues are typically medium-term bullets or serial bonds, though zero-coupon issues have recently been launched.

Foreign bonds

Bonds issued in Danish kroner on the domestic market by non-Danish entities were accepted by the central bank in 1986. However, only a few supranationals, e.g. World Bank, European Investment Bank and Nordic Investment Bank, coupled with a few Scandinavian borrowers, have tapped the market.

Eurokroner bonds

Since the first issue in early 1985, approximately 50 issuers have tapped the eurokroner market, with most persistent borrowers being of Danish origin (such as Finance for Danish Industry and the Kingdom of Denmark). Among foreign borrowers, Scandinavian and supranational names continue to dominate. Over the past three years, the eurokroner market has experienced little if any expansion, this being partly due to investor preferences and partly due to the opening of the domestic market to foreign borrowers. The total number of issues, at 80, is unchanged compared to 1988. Total outstanding volume is similarly unchanged at a level of approximately DKr 22bn.

Medium-term notes

Quite recently (during summer 1991), the first MTN programme in Danish kroner was launched by Australian Coles Myer Finance; this issue being followed shortly after by one from Goldman Sachs. It remains to be seen, however, whether MTNs achieve widespread popularity, or if these issues remain rare examples.

Composition of market by maturity

Government bonds

The total number of government bullet bonds, serial bonds and FRNs are respectively 11, 8 and 8. Figures 13.15-13.17 show the exact life against the actual outstanding nominal amounts.

As stated earlier, bullet bonds have become the dominating vehicle for long-term government borrowing requirements. Over time, maturities have lengthened as the rate gap versus German rates has narrowed and demand from

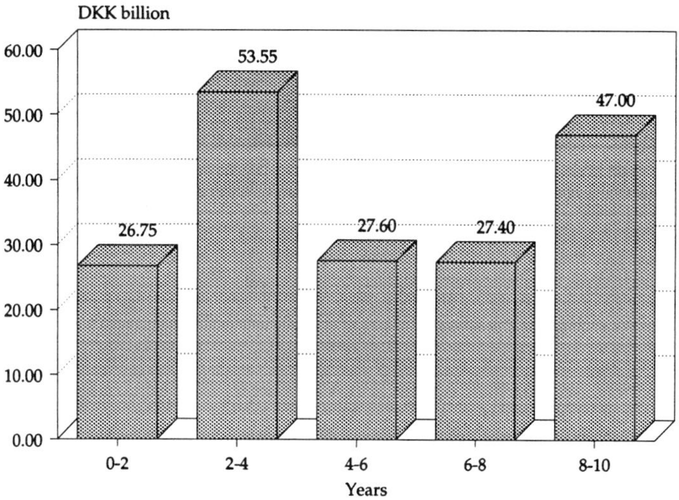

Figure 13.15 Maturity structure of the government bullet bond market

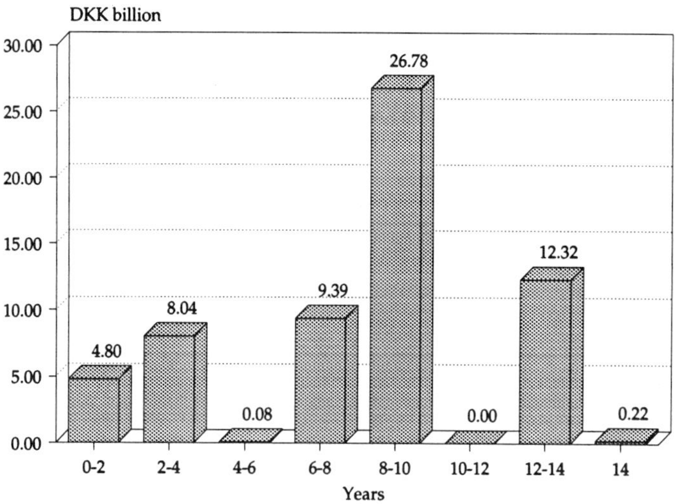

Figure 13.16 Maturity structure of the government serial bond market

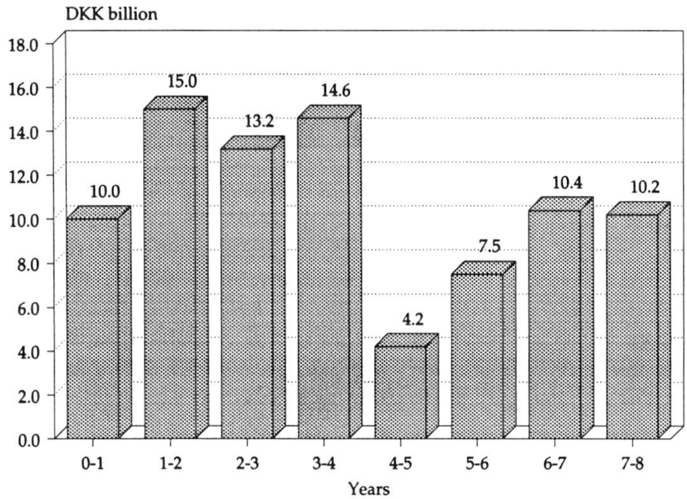

Figure 13.17 Maturity structure of the government FRN market

international investors for longer-dated issues has grown. Serial bonds, which are redeemed by equal annual redemptions, are disappearing gradually as the Danish central bank signals its intention to concentrate on long-term fund-raising by issuing bullet bonds. The average maturity of this segment is accordingly diminishing over time, and will almost disappear when the large issue, DKr 27bn (approx.) 12% 2001, is redeemed. FRNs are distributed almost equally over the time-scale, but their nature precludes meaningful analysis within the context of maturity profiles. Short-term government notes, which are not illustrated, are generally distributed equally at 3-month intervals ranging from 3 months up to 2 years. A new issue is being launched on a tap basis every third month. There has been no change in this structure over the past eight years.

Mortgage bonds

Though the issue volume of mortgage bonds has fallen substantially since 1986 due to the aforementioned lack of growth in the overall Danish economy, maturities have only shortened marginally in relative terms and the characteristic long-term nature of mortgage bonds is retained (see Figure 13.18). An additional factor in maintaining long maturities was the introduction of 30-year loans to new family homes in 1990 (formerly, the longest loans were for 20 years).

Ship Credit Fund bonds

Bullet bonds are issued on tap basis with maximum maturity of 10 years, while index-linked issues have a maximum maturity of 15 years (see Figure 13.19).

Municipal bonds

See Figure 13.20

Bank bonds

See Figure 13.21

Foreign bonds

See Figure 13.22

Eurokroner bonds

See Figure 13.23

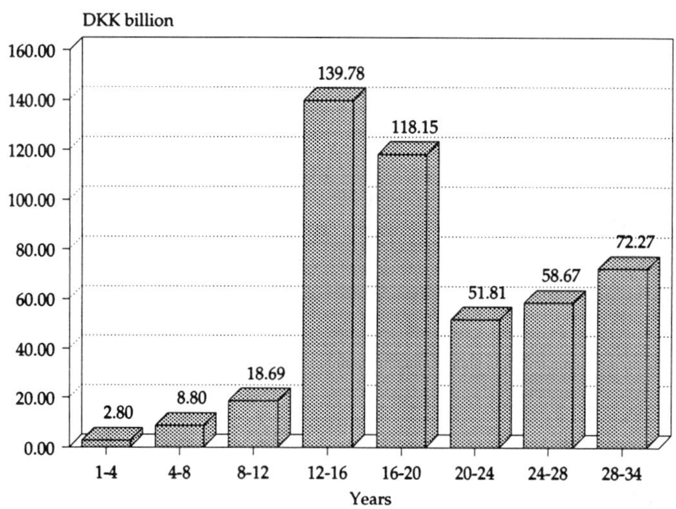

Figure 13.18 Maturity structure of the mortgage bond market

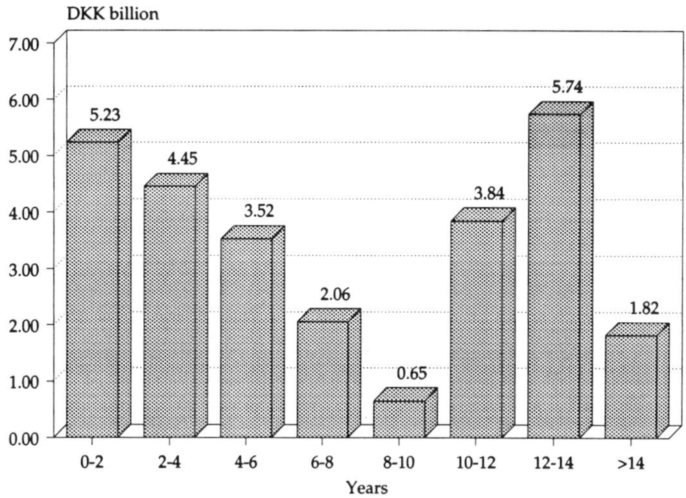

Figure 13.19 Maturity structure of the Ship Credit Fund bond market

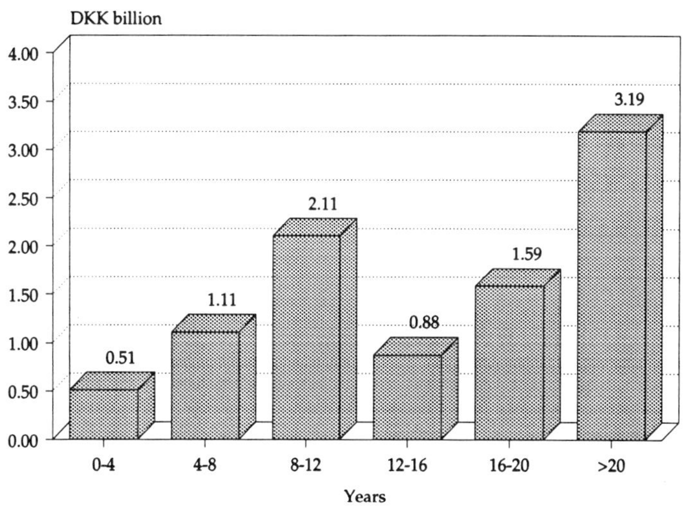

Figure 13.20 Maturity structure of the municipal bond market

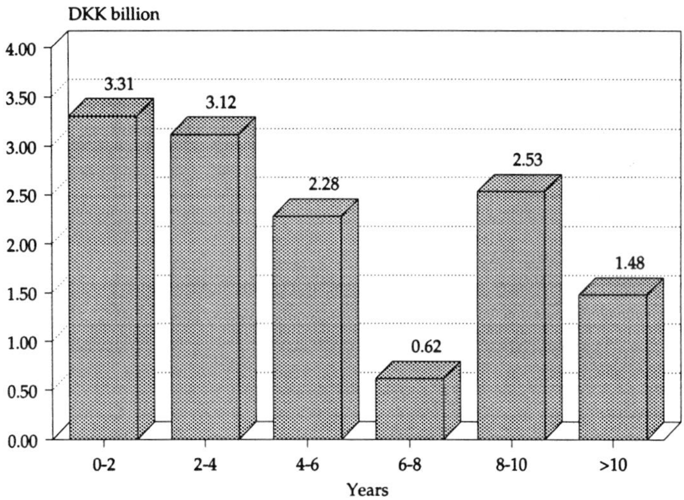

Figure 13.21 Maturity structure of the bank bond market

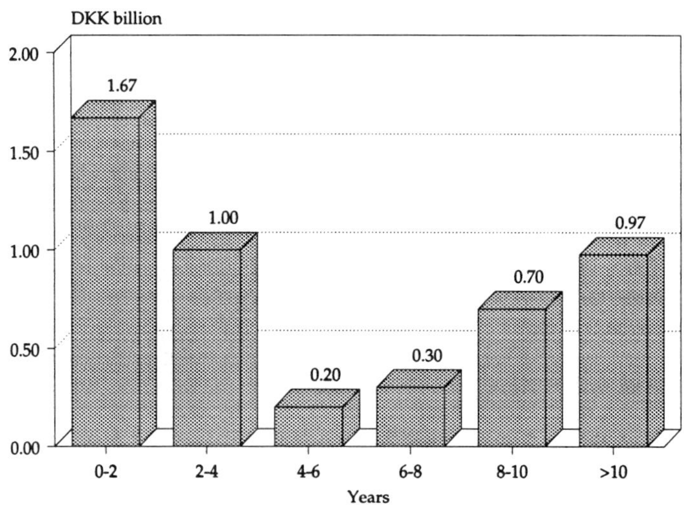

Figure 13.22 Maturity structure of the foreign bond market

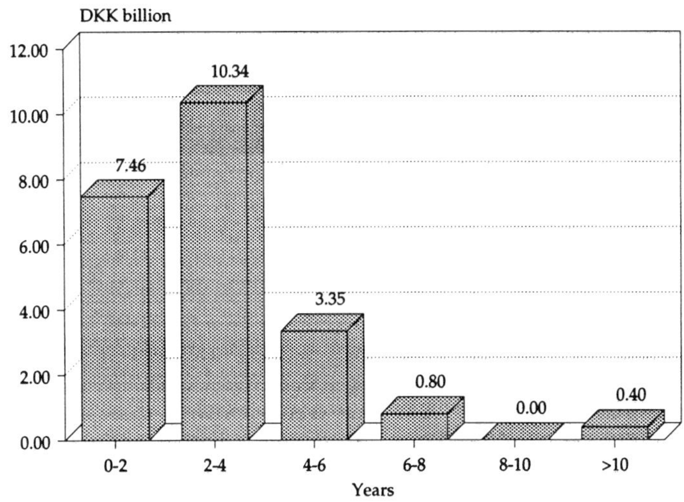

Figure 13.23 Maturity structure of the eurokroner bond market

Composition of market by coupon structure

Figures 13.24-13.30 suggest a high degree of stability of coupons ranging from 7 to 11 per cent accounting, as they do for around 90 per cent of all bonds outstanding. This however detracts from the fact that, until 1986, Danish bonds were issued at substantially-fluctuating discounts. Coupon settings between 8 and 10 per cent have been the convention, despite market rates of interest of more than 20 per cent during the high-inflation period of 1979-1982; the reason lies in the tax-free capital gains on bonds for private and corporate investors up until 1986. The tax reform implemented from January 1987, however, required coupon settings on new issues consistent with market rates of interest, in order to retain tax-freedom on capital gains for private individual holders of bonds. The minimum coupon in order for a new issue to achieve a so-called 'blue stamp', is 7/8 of the 20-business day average of market rates of interest preceding 15 June and 15 December respectively - rounded off to the nearest integer percentage. Between these two periods, adjustments may only be made if significant changes occur in market rates of interest, i.e. more than one percentage point change over a period of 10 consecutive business days. A blue stamp follows a bond issue for the rest of its life, irrespective of future changes in market rates. The law was not retrospective in the sense that holders of bonds with coupons below 'the minimum rate' continued to enjoy a tax-free regime.

Government bullet and serial bonds

Practically all fixed-rate government issues have coupons of 9 and 10 per cent (see Figure 13.24). Only 12% Serial 2001 has a coupon higher than 10 per cent. A new 10-year benchmark is to be launched in January 1992, with a coupon of 8 per cent.

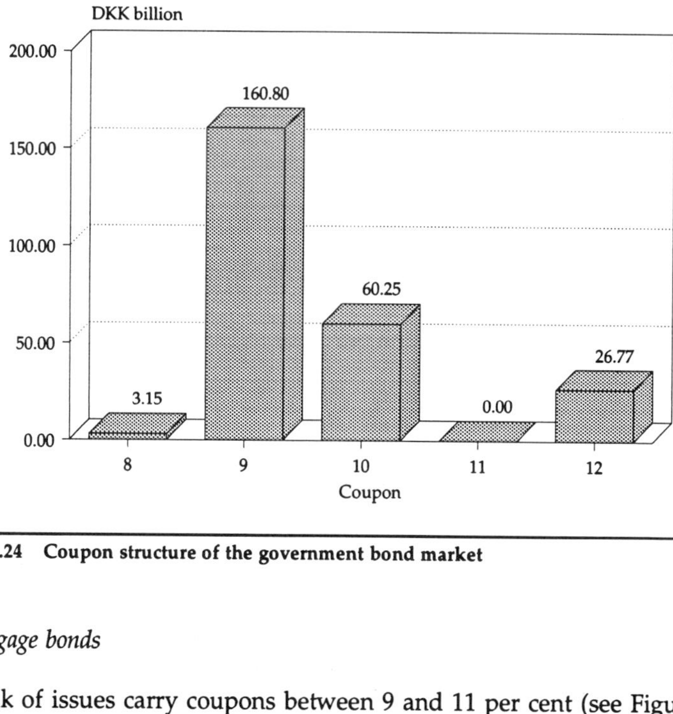

Figure 13.24 Coupon structure of the government bond market

Mortgage bonds

The bulk of issues carry coupons between 9 and 11 per cent (see Figure 13.25), while 'the top' appearing in the 2 1/2 per cent bracket reflects the mandatory coupon setting of index-linked issues. The general fall in interest rates over the past decade is naturally reflected in lower coupons.

Ship Credit Fund bonds

As most new issues of Ship Credit Fund Bonds have been index-linked since 1986, the coupon structure is clearly divided between 'old' and 'new' issues, the old issues varying between 7 1/2 and 10 1/2 per cent (see Figure 13.26).

Municipal bonds

The coupon structure of Municipal bonds (see Figure 13.27) also reflects the implementation of index-linked bonds with coupons of 2 1/2 per cent.

Bank bonds and Finance For Danish Industry bonds

Generally bonds carrying coupons below 9 per cent (see Figure 13.28) are older issues, while the zero-coupon segment reveals recent tap issues, launched by Den Danske Bank, Unibank and Finance for Danish Industry, specifically aiming at foreign investors (who not liable to capital gains taxation).

Foreign bonds

See Figure 13.29

Eurokroner bonds

Most of the Danish eurokroner issues were launched in the period 1985 to 1988. Accordingly the coupon distribution (see Figure 13.30) reflects market rates of interest during the same period, typically between 9 and 11 per cent. Only five zero-coupon issues have been floated: Kingdom of Denmark 92, Commerzbank Overseas Finance NV 93, Finance for Danish Industry 92, and two issues for Nordic Investment Bank (maturing in 92 and 93, respectively).

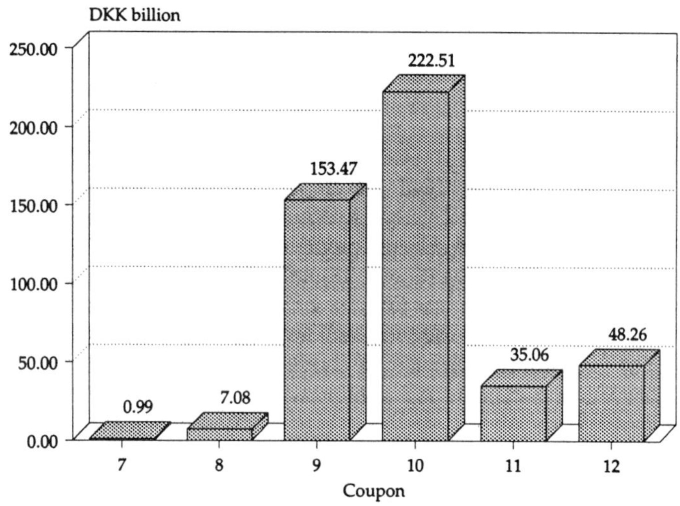

Figure 13.25 Coupon structure of the mortgage bond market

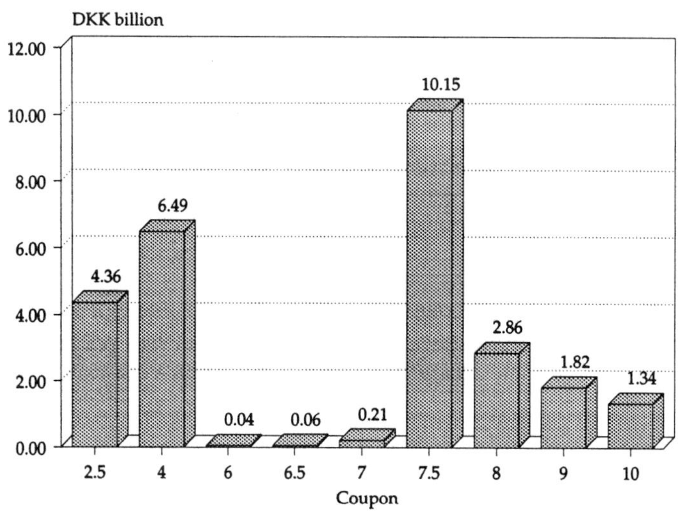

Figure 13.26 Coupon structure of the Ship Credit Fund bond market

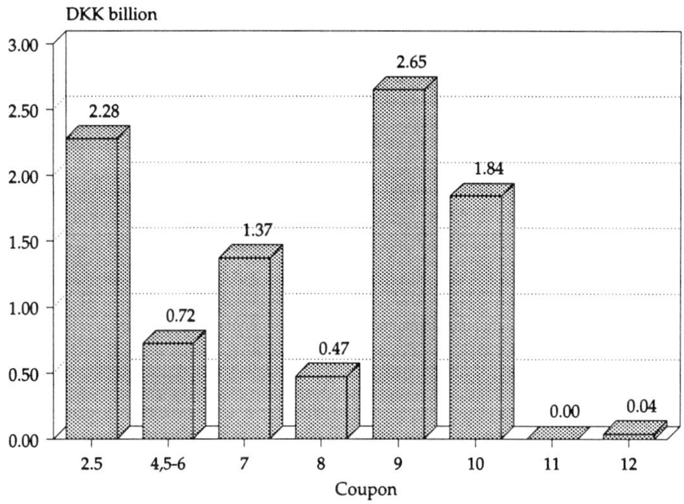

Figure 13.27 Coupon structure of the municipal bond market

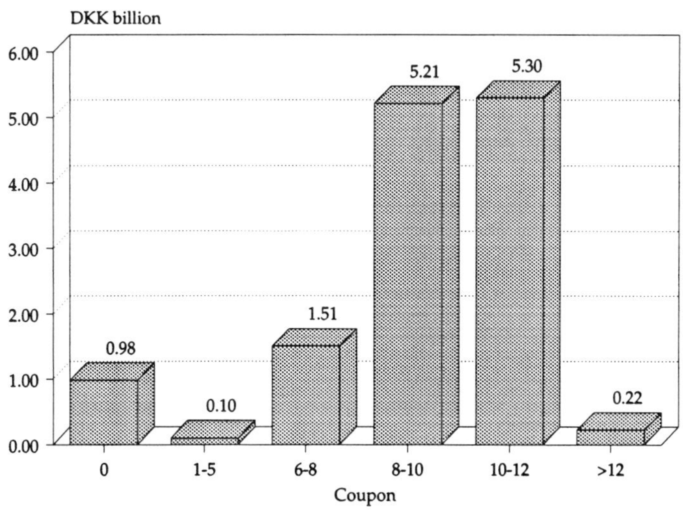

Figure 13.28 Coupon structure of the bank bond and Finance for Danish Industry bond markets

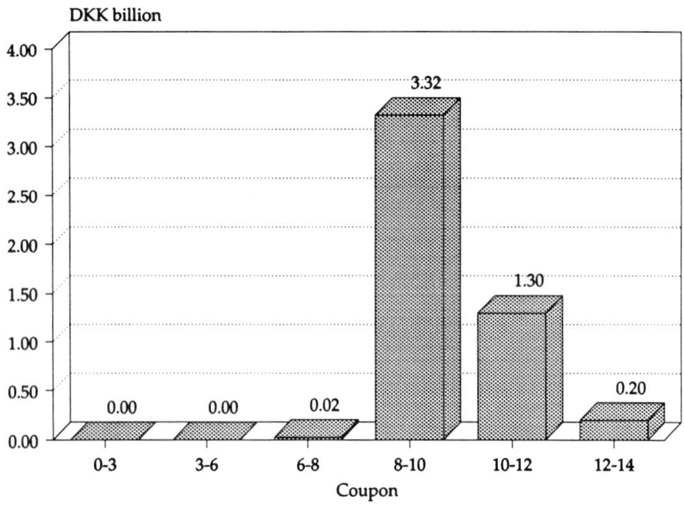

Figure 13.29 Coupon structure of the foreign bond market

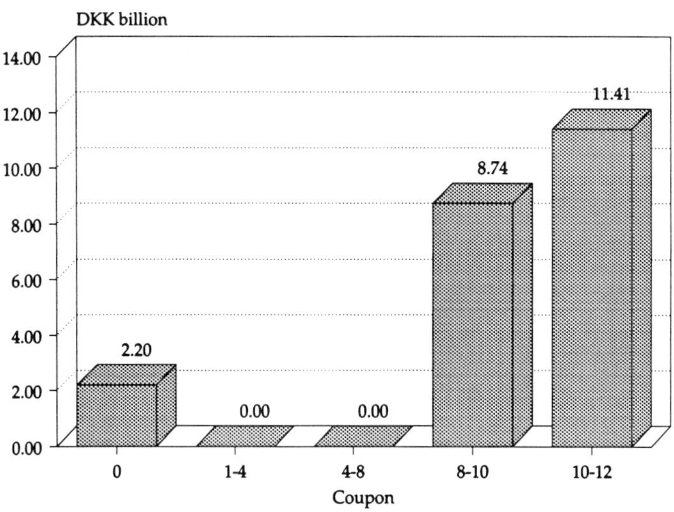

Figure 13.30 Coupon structure of the eurokroner bond market

13.4 Types of security

Government bonds

Bullet bonds

The vast majority of government bonds (see Figure 13.31) are bullet issues, i.e. with a single fixed-maturity date. Bullet issues are non-callable and pay coupon annually.

Serial bonds

The (diminishing) serial bonds are similarly non-callable, but are being successively redeemed by equal annual instalments on dates identical to the annual coupon.

Floating-rate notes

FRNs were introduced in November 1984 with 5- and 10-year maturities, on a non-callable bullet basis. At present, eight issues are outstanding with quarterly

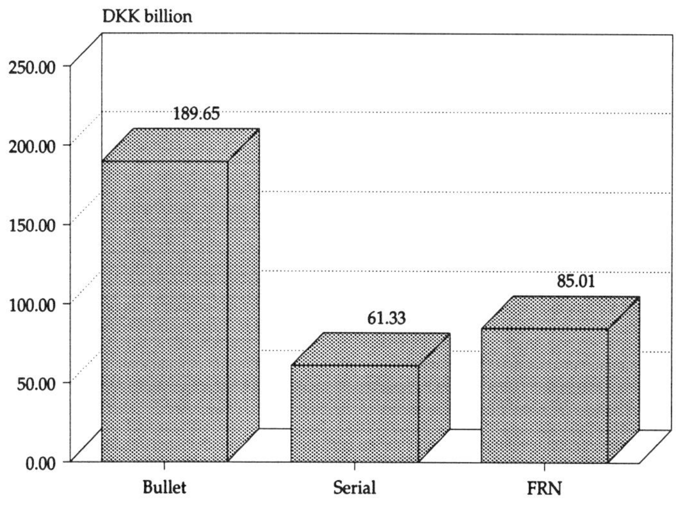

Figure 13.31 Types of issue in the government bond market

coupon dates: For 5-year issues, coupon dates are 20 February, May, August and November, while 10-year issues pay coupons on 15 January, April, July and October. The coupon is variable and, in principle, re-fixed every coupon-date. The basis is the daily official Copenhagen Stock Exchange average of effective yields on government bonds with less than 3 years to maturity. This average is defined as 'the reference rate of interest', and is observed for a period from 100 to 10 days preceding the upcoming coupon-date, and the average of the reference rate is fixed as the annualized coupon for the following 3-month period. The actual coupon paid on a given coupon-date to investor is accordingly based on a historical market rate development 190 to 100 days earlier. This lagged coupon fixing has procured a relatively stable price development, but also makes Danish government FRNs difficult to compare with, for example, euro-FRNs.

Premium bonds (zeros)

In Denmark, premium bonds are deemed as the 11 issues of 'gambling' paper with a total outstanding amount of DKr 1.2bn. Carrying no coupon and with long maturities, the bonds are numbered; semi-annual drawings by lot are made, corresponding to the intrinsic amount of interest the bonds should have carried, if having a coupon. Minimum face value is as low as DKr 50, allowing everyone to participate in the speculative hunt for profit.

Perpetuals

Four beautifully-decorated issues launched during the 'Golden Age' (more precisely, in 1886, 1894, 1901 and 1909) and representing a total nominal value of DKr 175m, are still circulating as irredeemable Danish government bonds. They pay an unprofitable, but stable, annual coupon. The debtor may, however, call the bonds at par on 3 months' notice, but it is difficult to find a reason for doing so. Firstly, many bonds have disappeared, as the issues originally were denominated not only in Danish kroner, but also in 'Reichmark', 'Franc d'Or' and 'Pound Sterling', and distributed across the old European continent before the Great Wars. Secondly, it is cheap funding!

Mortgage bonds

Annuity bonds

The most common type of mortgage bond is amortized according to the annuity principle, and issued with 10-35 years to maturity. Annuity bonds pay coupons semi-annually or quarterly in arrears together with instalments.

Serial bonds

Apart from having equal semi-annual or quarterly instalments, serial bonds are similar, in respect of coupon-fixing and maturity, to annuity bonds.

Variable-rate bonds

Variable-rate bonds have been issued since 1976 with the intention of giving borrowers access to adjustment of interest every 5 years, as opposed to the normal fixed-rate of interest through the entire borrowing period, which normally ranges from 10 to 35 years. The bonds are issued on a tap basis with final maturities from 1 to 5 years, mixed for the individual borrower to secure an amortization equal to a normal fixed-rate annuity bond.

Floating-rate notes

This type of instrument is issued with maturities ranging from 5 to 20 years. They are typically bullet issues with an adjustment mechanism for the coupon similar to government FRNs, i.e. quarterly. As can be seen in Figure 13.32, outstanding amounts are relatively small.

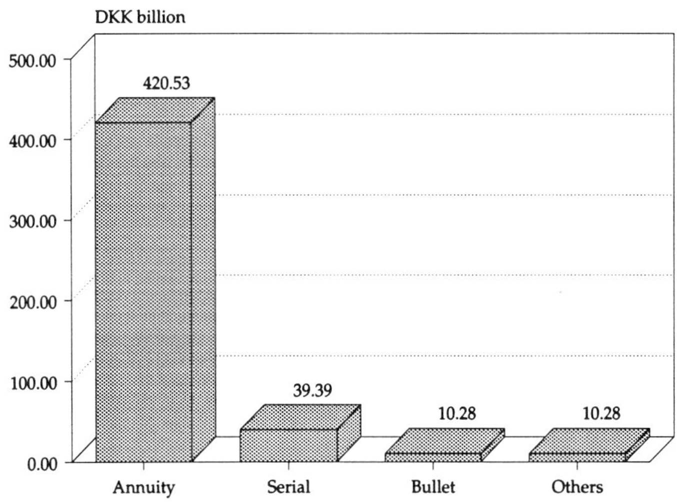

Figure 13.32 Types of issue in the mortgage bond market

Index-linked bonds

Index bonds are issued with a fixed 'real' coupon of 2.5 per cent, with maturities ranging from 20 to 35 years. The coupon is paid semi-annually, just as repayments, which are made according to either the serial (equal instalments), or the annuity, principle. Coupon, repayment and residual value is always multiplied by the index factor which is based on the development in the official net price index, which is identical to the CPI, excluding indirect taxes and subsidies.

Ship Credit Fund bonds

Bullet bonds

Fixed-rate bullet issuance is the traditional method of funding owners of new vessels contracted with Danish or foreign shipyards. Tap issues with a maximum of 10 years' maturity, are opened every year.

Index-linked bonds

Since 1986, index-linked bonds with 2.5 and 4 per cent coupons have been issued, on a tap basis, with maximum maturities of 15 years. The issues reflect

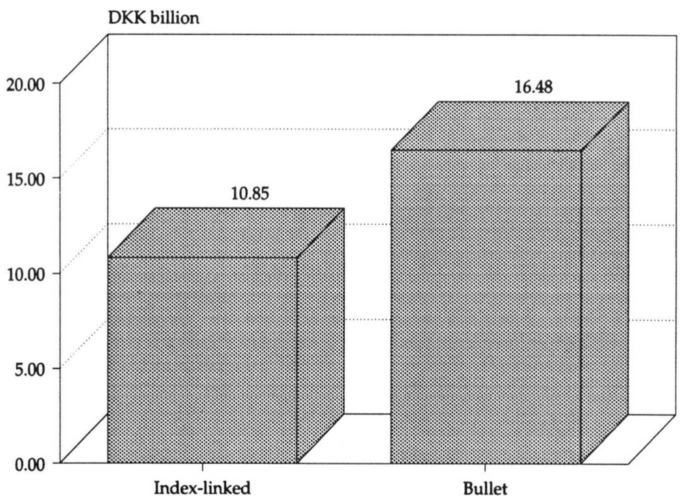

Figure 13.33 Types of issue in the Ship Credit Fund bond market

funding of vessels built on Danish shipyards (presently, up to 30 per cent of the contract value). The borrower is guaranteed a maximum index element of 3 per cent annually on 2.5 per cent coupons, and an index element of 1.5 per cent annually on 4 per cent coupons, while the investor always secures a full inflationary compensation. The difference is paid by the central bank as subsidies. Amortization is 9-year bullet, plus 6 years' equal instalments.

Municipal bonds

See Figure 13.34

Bank bonds and Finance for Danish Industry bonds

See Figure 13.35

Eurobonds and foreign bonds

See Figure 13.36

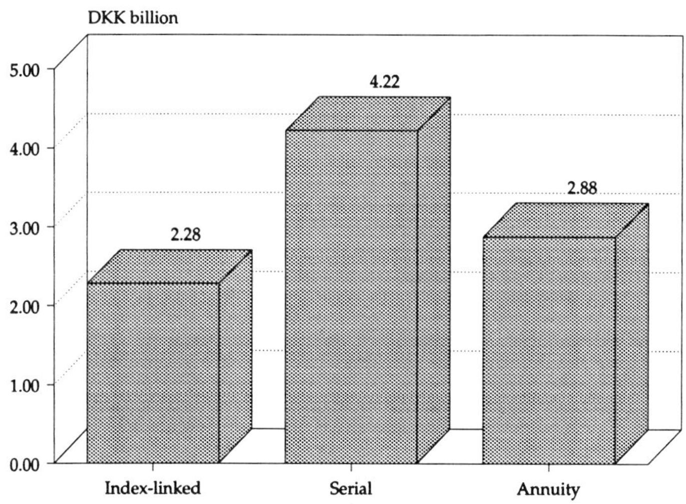

Figure 13.34 Types of issue in the municipal bond market

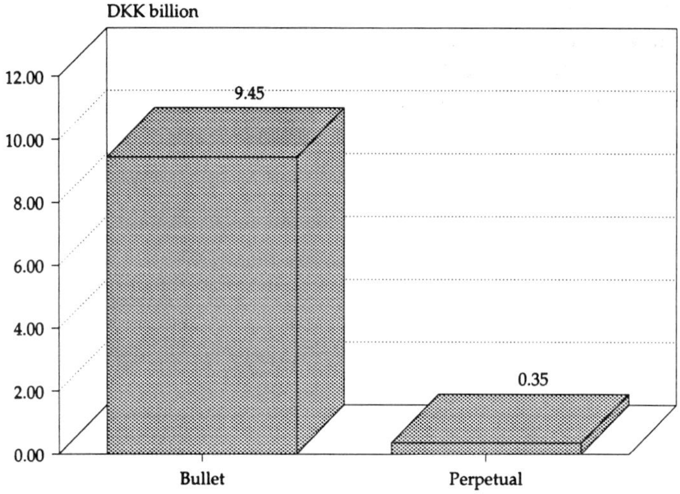

Figure 13.35 Types of issue in the bank bond and Finance for Danish Industry bond markets

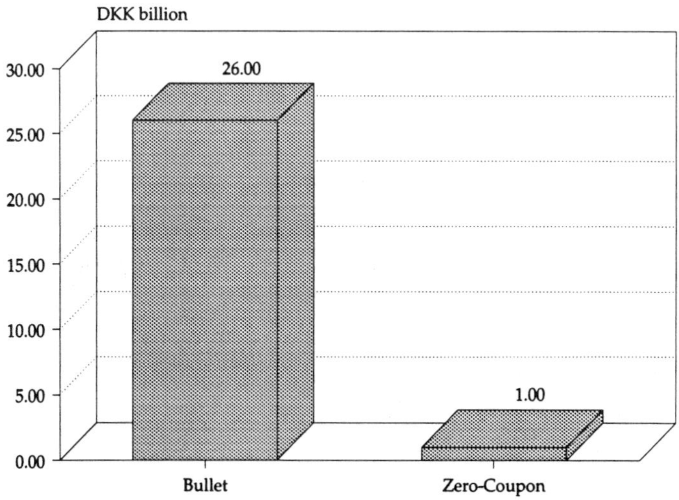

Figure 13.36 Types of issue in the eurobond and foreign bond markets

13.5 *Issuers*

Mortgage bonds

One may easily argue that Ship Credit Fund issues and Finance for Danish Industry issues should be included under this segment, as the actual collateral is a mortgage. However, as these specific issuers have already been dealt with thoroughly, this chapter only discusses the mortgage credit associations which cover a wide variety of property financing, i.e. private, public and business property. Mortgage bonds backed by secured credits are deeply-rooted in the Danish financial system - the first mortgage credit association was founded in the middle of the last century. By the 1880s, the associations were becoming dominant players in the provision of long-term financing for the Danish property sector, based on the principle of balanced lending. Any extension of credit creates its own financing at a cost decided by prevailing conditions in the bond market, because the credit is obtained by selling into the market the exact amount of bonds needed to cover the credit. The procedure is simply as follows: A loan is secured by the borrower through issuing a mortgage deed on his property to the mortgage credit association. The limit of mortgage association borrowing varies according to the type of property, subject to prevailing government rules, from 50 per cent up to 80 per cent of the assessed market value of the property in question. The mortgage deed is subsequently registered the Danish Official Register of Mortgages, with the order of priority of mortgages in a single property also being registered. In the event of default, the title and preferential position of the mortgage credit association are secured.

Owned by borrowers, who are jointly and severally liable for interest payments and instalments of bonds issued by the associations, mortgage credit associations are subject to relatively stringent statutory rules imposed by Parliament with the objective of securing both sound and stable operations. Before the Secured Credits Act of 1970, more than 20 associations were operating in a highly-regionalized market. The Act stimulated economies of scale by giving permission for more comprehensive associations, the result being massive mergers and acquisitions. As of today, only three large associations (plus one recent newcomer) are offering traditional mortgage services to borrowers:

- Kreditforeningen Danmark
- Nykredit
- BRF-Kredit
- Totalkredit

Mandatory provisions existing over many decades created huge reserves within mortgage credit associations - to the extent that market perception ranked mortgage bonds equal to sovereign risk, by not demanding a higher yield on mortgage bonds. The tax reform introduced in 1987 triggered a severe fall in prices across the whole property market and mortgage credit associations were forced to incur substantial losses, reducing reserves below legal limits. Subsequent restructuring and further deregulation of the Danish capital market will most likely change the structure of Danish mortgage credit associations in the years to come. Conversion into publicly-listed limited financial companies is in the pipeline, as well as possible mergers with other financial institutions, such as insurance groups and banks. Furthermore, deregulation (both domestic and international) will almost certainly lead to both more straightforward types of issue such as bullets, and more sophisticated placings in the international securities market.

Eurokroner bonds

For types of issue and country of origin of issuers, see Figures 13.37 & 13.38

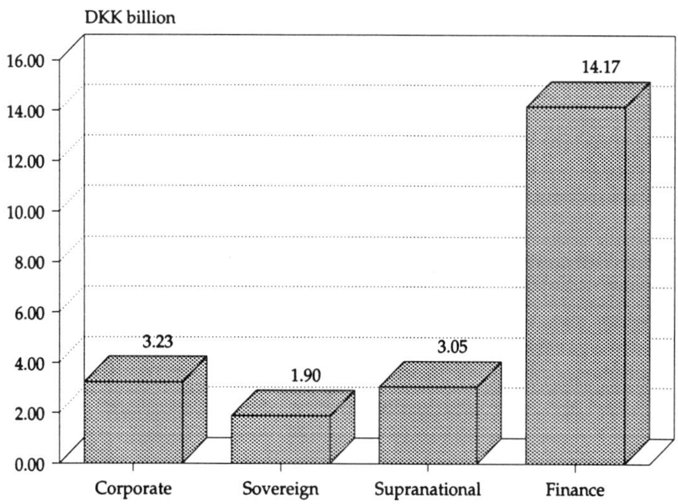

Figure 13.37 Types of issuer in the eurokroner bond market

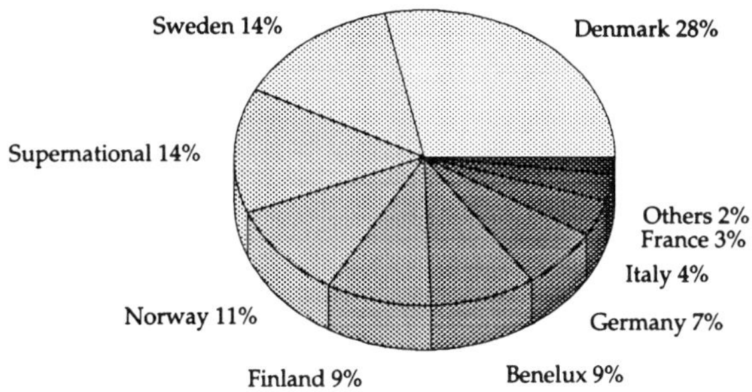

Figure 13.38 Country of origin of issuers in the eurokroner bond market

13.6 *Investors*

There is little statistical information available concerning the holding of bonds by different investor groups and, therefore, only a general overview can be presented here. It should be noted that, in this section, investment generally means the holding of domestic bonds in general (i.e. both mortgage bonds and government bonds).

The distribution of Danish bonds to end-investors is marked by the involvement of just two mainstay participants: The central bank, which is traditionally rather inactive on the portfolio side, and institutions (public and private), which traditionally pick up the vast majority of total net supply. Though placing rules for Danish institutions have been successively lifted during the latter part of the 1980s, more than 75 per cent of reinvestments and new money is annually channelled into the Danish bond market.

Less-consistent investment has been provided by the Danish banking sector and foreign investors. In fact, these two groups have acted in opposite ways over the past few years, with Danish banks converting bond holdings into money market instruments while foreigners have added substantially to their Danish portfolio holdings (a move primarily triggered by the convergence of

	Central bank	Banks & savings banks	Public pension funds	Insurance pension funds & private	Foreign investors	Total
1981	0.4	4.9	9.3	27.7	-0.2	42.1
1982	1.7	11.3	12.5	34.2	-0.6	59.2
1983	1.4	39.0	13.6	30.1	2.9	86.9
1984	-1.5	17.3	15.1	44.6	9.3	84.7
1985	-0.3	20.7	12.4	37.1	17.4	87.2
1986	12.1	-7.4	16.7	32.8	0.6	54.4
1987	-0.1	-33.6	12.7	50.5	17.3	46.7
1988	-0.1	15.7	12.3	19.3	12.6	59.9
1989	-0.3	10.5	11.5	18.3	-9.0	31.1
1990	2.0	-25.4	10.2	28.8	28.6	44.3
1991	12.0	-0.8	9.1	17.3	39.5	77.1

Figure 13.39 Net demand for domestic bonds, 1981-1991 (DKK billion)

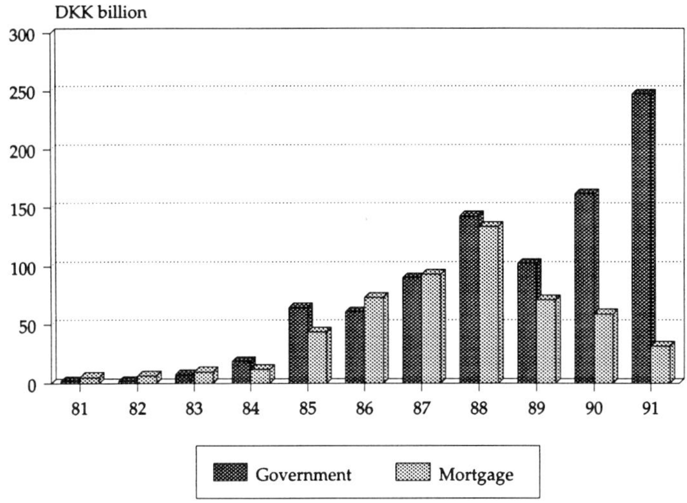

*) to third qtr.

Figure 13.40 **Turnover of domestic bonds by foreigners, 1981-1991**

	Benelux	Switzerland	UK	Germany	USA	Others
1985	44	12	7	19	-1	19
1986	-48	-2	16	32	2	100
1987	14	2	6	49	8	21
1988	-2	9	8	91	-7	1
1989	21	27	-22	69	7	-2
1990	6	1	26	43	11	13
1991	42	5	36	-4	3	18

Figure 13.41 **Net purchases of domestic bonds by foreigners, 1989-1991 [Relative distribution by country of origin, DKK billion]**

Danish and German interest rates). The popularity of Danish government bullet issues among foreign participants is clearly shown in Figure 13.41. An overview of the country of origin of international interest is provided in Figure 13.42, although, clearly, it does not account for the significant secondary trading of Danish kroner bonds between foreigners outside Denmark. The UK, Germany and Benelux have been the major players in the Danish market since 1989. Of particular interest is the UK demand, as it may well reflect underlying interest from (amongst others) the USA and Japan, since overseas investors often place their orders through large London-based broking houses and fund management entities (including London subsidiaries of Danish houses).

13.7 *Methods of issuance*

Overview

The two dominant market segments, government and mortgage bonds, are still issuing paper on a tap basis, thereby securing large outstanding amounts for the each individual issue. Furthermore, it is interesting to notice the total absence of primary dealers in the government bond sector, in which the Danish central bank is an equal participant amongst authorized stock exchange broker companies and a frequent user of market-makers - without being one itself.

Government bullet bonds

The issuance of government bullet bonds is carried out by the Danish central bank, which may stop the sale of bonds in the open market, temporarily or permanently, at its discretion at any time during the entire life of the bond. Conventionally, however, single bond issues are closed after a tap period of approximately 3 years.

Government FRN bonds

Issuance is normally on tap for a one-year period.

Mortgage bonds

All mortgage bonds, whether serial, annuity, variable-rate, FRNs or index-linked, are opened for tap up to 3 years from initial launch, depending on final maturity length and the type of bond.

Ship Credit Fund bullet bonds

Ship Credit Fund bonds are also tap issues. They may stay open throughout their entire life and, indeed, normally do so.

Bank bonds

Normally being bullet issues, bank bonds are frequently launched as tap issues with a cap on the total amount to be issued.

Eurokroner bonds

Eurokroner bonds follow the traditional pattern for euro issues. They are typically bullet issues which are placed through a suitable syndicate of international banks, lead- or co-managed by a Danish bank.

13.8 *New issue volumes*

As new issue volumes have been negligible in sectors such as the eurokroner market, the bank bond market, the municipal bond market and the foreign bond market, statistics are confined to the following sectors:

Government bond market

See Figure 13.42

Mortgage bond market

See Figure 13.43

Ship Credit Fund bond market

See Figure 13.44

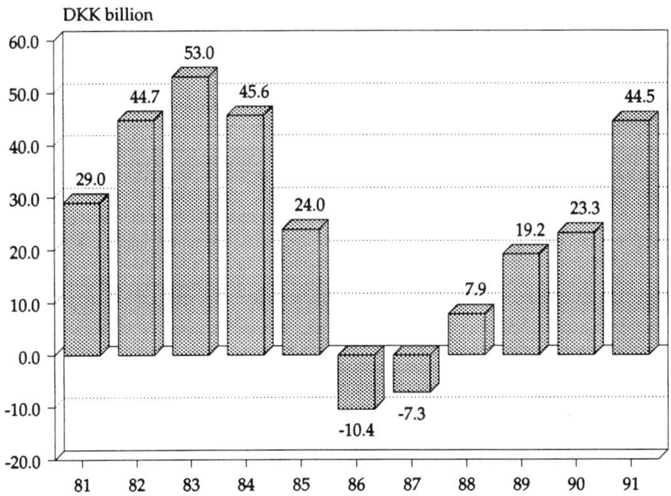

*) to third qtr.

Figure 13.42 New issuance volumes in the government bond market, 1981-1991

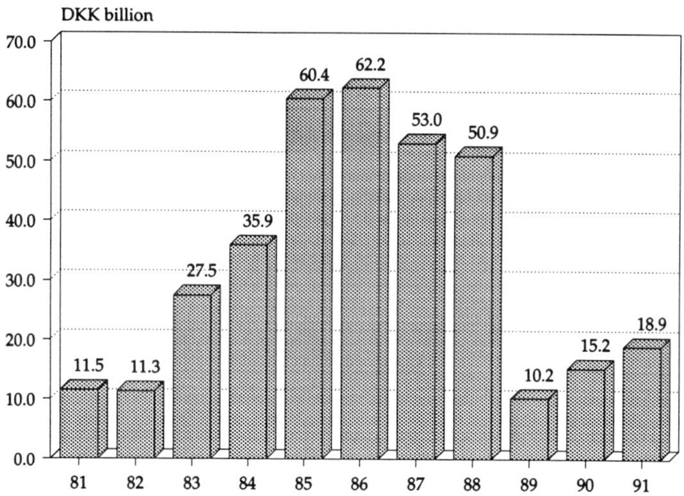

Figure 13.43 New issuance volumes in the mortgage bond market, 1981-1991

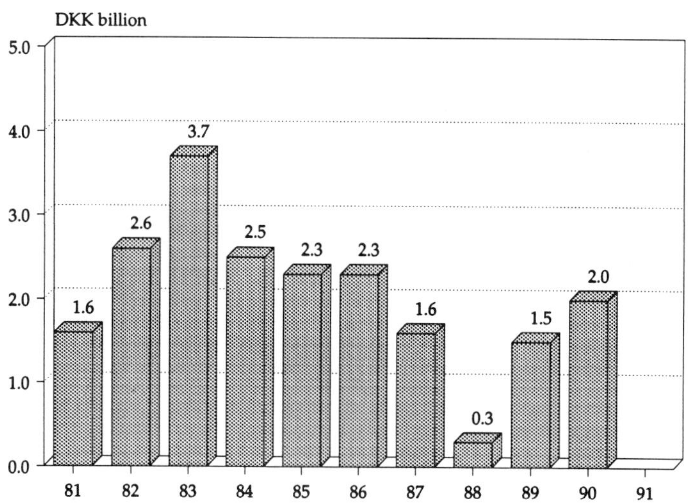

Figure 13.44 New issuance volumes in the Ship Credit Fund bond market, 1981-1991

13.9 Methods of trading

Overview

Apart from eurokroner bonds, the trading of all Danish kroner bond issues is domestically handled through a decentralized computer trading system under surveillance of the Copenhagen Stock Exchange Authorities. Prior to the *Little Big Bang* in 1988, trading was handled physically under an auction system at the stock exchange.

Though the system does not yet allow foreign entities to participate in the electronic trading system, broker houses in London and Frankfurt are major players in the benchmark sector, using Euroclear or Cedel for settlement purposes. At present, the domestic dealing system comprises 32 authorized broker companies, of which only a handful represent privately-held companies (former stockbroker firms), while the majority represents banks, insurance groups and other financial groupings.

Only a few foreigners have entered the market, three with Scandinavian coverage and origin, and one owned by the Dutch ABN-AMRO Bank. More than two-thirds of the total Danish market volume is handled by the two largest Danish banking groups, Den Danske Bank and Unibank. Recent mergers have allowed these two to take a clearly dominant position in general Danish banking and, in practice, compete as alternatives to the official Stock Exchange. In addition, the market has also been affected by the Stock Exchange Reform Act of 1987 (implemented during 1988) which had severe consequence for the less-active issues, making them almost impossible to trade in fair amounts.

Opening hours for the authorized trading system are 09.00 to 15.30 with, so far at least, no obligation for participants to act as market-makers. However, consideration is being given to the establishment of compulsory market-maker arrangements which will include a separation of stockbroker member companies into market-maker, and non-market-maker, participants in order to increase volume. The dominant participants, such as the big Danish banks are, in reality, market-makers *vis-à-vis* each other and large institutions on the parallel OTC market, with trading being handled via quote vendors such as Reuters, Telerate and Bloomberg, as well as by individual computer information systems which are distributed to large clients.

There is no 'primary dealer' system in Denmark, as the bulk of new issues are tap issues fronted by the central bank (government bonds) and the mortgage associations through the banking system (mortgage bonds). The Danish central bank deserves special attention in this context, as the bank is also a member of the group of authorized stock exchange broker companies. In its

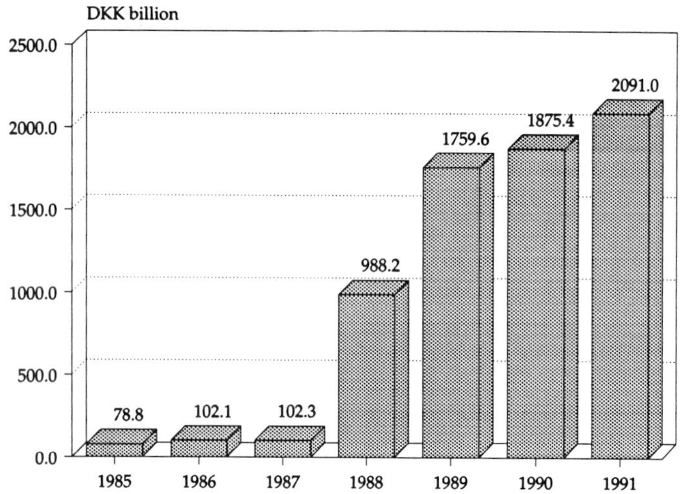

Figure 13.45 Turnover of domestic bonds, 1985-1991, as registered by the Copenhagen Stock Exchange

issuing capacity, the bank has sole discretion to issue government paper by selling in the open market - including sales to supranational institutions such as the World Bank, European Investment Bank and Nordic Investment Bank. On the buying side, the central bank acts as the exclusive broker for The Social Pension Fund, by far the largest public agency fund with assets well over DKr 100bn invested in Danish bonds. Finally, the central bank retains a high degree of independence in its conduct of monetary policy and, accordingly, one could justifiably question whether the bank qualifies for membership of, and direct participation in, the authorized trading system.

Price spreads among large participants for liquid issues such as government bullet bonds is normally 5 basis points, increasing to 10-15 basis points for mortgage bonds and Ship Credit Fund bonds. Smaller issues may easily show price spreads from 25-100 basis points.

Eurokroner bonds

Most issues are listed on Luxembourg Stock Exchange, but as with many other eurobonds, the majority of issues are traded OTC internationally between the large trading houses, among which large Danish banks are dominant.

Other bonds

Bonds issued by banks, Finance for Danish Industry, foreign entities (including the three existing medium-term note issues), are all traded OTC by members of the original syndicate, whether purely domestic or international.

13.10 *Market practices*

Coupon payment

Government straight bonds pay coupons annually in arrears, while FRNs pay coupon semi-annually. Mortgage bonds pay coupons semi-annually or quarterly. Ship Credit Fund bonds and municipal bonds pay coupons semi-annually. Most eurokroner bonds, foreign bonds and bank bonds pay coupons annually.

Ex-dividend

Apart from eurokroner bonds, which follow ISMA rules, Danish bonds trade ex-dividend when the value-date falls within 30 calendar days before the due date of interest. Negative accrued interest until the coupon-date is calculated accordingly. The official *Daily Quotation List,* published by the Copenhagen Stock Exchange, contains detailed information on this matter for all listed bonds.

Redemption

All domestic bonds are redeemed at par; this also includes the vast majority of mortgage bonds with call features by the issuer.

Denomination

Computerized book-entries of all listed Danish bonds have made set denominations almost obsolete; multiples of DKr 1000 are common for calculation purposes only.

Form

All bonds are in bearer form.

Dealing quotations

See Section 13.9, Methods of trading.

Commissions

There are no legal rules governing either the structure or size of commissions, which set entirely by competition. Large institutions normally deal with market-makers on a net basis, just reflecting professional price spreads, e.g. down to 5 basis points for benchmark government issues. 'Normal' round lots *vis-à-vis* clients usually are DKr 5m nominally, with a commission of 5 basis points on the price for liquid issues in the government and the mortgage bond sector of the market. Trade in odd lots, or illiquid paper, may be charged commissions of between 15 and 50 basis points on the price - there is a wide variation between stockbroker companies. Unfortunately, the authorized broker system under Copenhagen Stock Exchange gives only a poor indication of the accuracy of price information on less-liquid issues, which makes it difficult for clients to make judgements on the fairness of their broker's net price. Good personal relationships are still valid!

13.11 Settlement

All listed Danish bonds are settled three business days after the date of transaction, with accrued interest being calculated on a 30/360 days basis from, and including, the due date of the last paid coupon up to, but excluding, the value-date of the transaction. Since 1983, the settlement and safe-keeping of all listed Danish bonds has been in the hands of the Danish Securities Centre, the Danish abbreviation being VP, (VærdiPapircentralen). Governed and backed by Act of Law, VP has replaced all listed bond certificates, and share certificates for that matter, by computerized registration. Clearing of transactions, transfer of coupon payments, transfer and distribution of redemptions etc., are automatically handled at VP, at extremely low costs. VP is linked with Euroclear and Cedel, making it possible to settle transactions in liquid government and mortgage bonds through these systems, albeit only on a 7-calendar day basis similar to eurobonds. In contrast to Euroclear and Cedel, there is no borrowing facility in VP.

13.12 Yield calculation

Overview

The redemption yield, or just plain 'yield', is conventionally used as an evaluation criterion in the Danish bond market. This measure is, however, not exhaustive but, supplemented by the concept of 'duration', it does support portfolio decisions. Basically, the redemption yield is found as the internal rate of return of the cashflow of the bond including the price paid, along with accrued interest - assuming all future payments are reinvested at a rate of return equal to the internal rate of return. In order to proceed, it is necessary to know the exact cashflow and some definitions:

- 1 month = 30 days, 1 year = 360 days
- Accrued interest is calculated on a daily basis using 30/360 days system. Calculation includes the due date of the last paid coupon up to, but excluding the value-date of the transaction. 30 days before the due date of the next coupon, bonds are traded ex-coupon and negative accrued interest applies.
- Settlement is due three business days following transaction date.

The standard redemption yield is derived from the following formula:

$$p + a = \sum_{i=1}^{N} CFi\,(1+y)^{\frac{-Di}{Dy}}$$

where,

p	clean price paid on value-date
a	accrued interest
N	number of due dates
i	index, $i = 1,...,N$
CFi	cashflow to ith partial payment
Di	number of days to ith partial payment
Dy	number of days per year (=360)
Y	redemption yield

From the above formula, the standard yield is arrived at when using, interactively, the Newton-Rapson procedure, defining Y as the positive number that fulfils the formula.

Government bullet bonds

Government bullet bonds are characterized by a flow of equal coupons and one final redemption payment, arriving at the following calculation of cashflows:

Let,

N	number of due dates
Ny	number of due dates per year
i	index, $i = 1,\ldots,N$
CFi	cashflow to ith due date
Ci	coupon payment to ith due date
Ri	redemption to ith due date
C	annual coupon
P	principal

Then,

$$CFi = Ci + Ri \quad \text{, where,}$$

$$Ri = 0 \ , \quad i = 1,\ldots\ldots,N-1$$

$$RN = P$$

$$Ci = \frac{C}{Ny} \times P \ , \quad i = 1,\ldots\ldots,N$$

Government serial bonds

Government serial bonds are characterized by equal annual instalments and coupons until maturity, arriving at the following cashflow calculation formula:

Let,

N	number of due dates
Ny	number of due dates per year
i	index, $i = 1,\ldots,N$
CFi	cashflow to ith due date

Ci coupon payment to *i*th due date
Ri redemption to *i*th due date
C annual coupon
P principal

Then,

$$CFi = Ci + Ri\,,\quad i = 1,\ldots\ldots,N\,,\ \text{where}$$

$$Ri = \frac{P}{N}\,,\quad i = 1\,,\ldots\ldots,N$$

$$Ci = \frac{C}{Ny} \times \left(P - \sum_{j=1}^{i-1} Rj \right)$$

$$= \frac{C}{Ny} \times \left(P - (i-1) \times \frac{P}{N}\right)\,,\quad i = 1,\ldots\ldots,N$$

Mortgage bonds

Mortgage bonds are more complicated as far as cashflow projections are concerned, due to issuing procedures, call features and drawing procedures. Mortgage bonds are issued on tap over a period of 1 to 3 years, depending on the exact maturity. All mortgage loans based on a single issue are either annuity or serial loans with identical maturity, e.g. 10/15/20/30 years. Consequently, the cashflow does not provide us with a 'clean' annuity or serial bond, but is rather subject to detailed information given by the issuers via Copenhagen Stock Exchange and the Danish Securities Centre during the issuing period. Though non-callable issues have been issued over the past 7 years, the bulk of mortgage bond issues are callable at par by the borrower at six months' notice prior to the next regular coupon-date. However, call features are normally disregarded when calculating cashflows, though calls have been executed frequently during the last few years' general downtrend in market rates of interest, as borrowers recognized the advantageous conversions of their loan portfolios. Successive redemptions of mortgage bonds follows a drawing by lot procedure *vis-à-vis* bond holders. Consequently, holders of small positions are not certain to receive redemptions proportional to their positions. Again, conventional cashflow projections disregard the impact of disproportionate redemptions on small bondholdings.

Mortgage annuity bonds

As already mentioned, exact cashflows are calculated and published by the issuer. During the issuing period, a synthetic cashflow is projected on the anticipated final amount of the issue. An annuity loan is repaid by equal payments every due date, tantamount to a constant cashflow during the life of the bond whereby, over time, the coupon element decreases and redemptions increase. The following cashflow calculation applies:

Let,

N number of due dates
Ny number of due dates per year
i index, $i = 1,\ldots,N$
CFi cashflow to ith due date
Ci coupon payment to ith due date
Ri redemption to ith due date
C annual coupon
P principal

then,

$$CFi = (P \times \frac{C}{Ny}) \times (1 - (1 + \frac{C}{Ny})^{-N})^{-1} \quad , i = 1,\ldots,N$$

The cashflow CFi may then be divided into coupon payments, Ci and redemption payments, Ri:

$$CFi = Ci + Ri \quad , i = 1,\ldots,N \ ,$$

where,

$$C1 = \frac{C}{Ny} \times P$$

$$Ci = \frac{C}{Ny} \times (P - \sum_{j=1}^{i-1} Rj) \quad , i = 1,\ldots,N$$

$$Ri = CFi - Ci \quad , i = 1,\ldots,N$$

The example above illustrates the case of the former mortgage benchmark issue, 9 per cent 2006.

Mortgage serial bonds

Serial bond cashflow projections are exposed to the same set of problems arising with annuity bonds but, theoretically, cashflow calculations follow the procedure mentioned under government serial bonds.

Floating-rate notes

Whether issued by the government or by the mortgage institutions, the coupon rate is computed from the average yield on government fixed-rate notes and bonds with a remaining life of more than 3 months, and less than 3 years. The average yield is calculated from a period running from 6 months and 10 days before the coupon-date to 3 months and 10 days before the coupon-date. Since all fixed-rate government issues pay coupon annually, the coupon rate C on FRNs is adjusted using the following formula:

$$C = ((1 + r)^{.25} - 1) \times 100$$

Index-linked bonds

Calculations disregard the inflation-index element, and just follow the abovementioned procedures for 'normal' bonds, resulting in real-interest yields.

Eurokroner bonds and medium-term notes

Both are conventionally calculated on an ISMA (formerly, AIBD) basis.

Zero-coupon Treasury bills

The official conversion from price to yield is in accordance with Danish money market practice. The yield per day is calculated by dividing the capital gain until maturity by the actual number of days until maturity. On an annual basis, the yield is calculated by multiplying the yield per day by 360.

$$\text{Yield} = \frac{\text{1 million} - \text{price}}{\text{price}} \times \frac{360}{\text{actual number of days}}$$

In accordance with bond market practice, the yield per day is calculated on the basis of 'bond interest days': the period from a particular date in a certain month to the same date in the succeeding month counts as 30 days, to which number of days the additional actual number is added. A compound interest calculation applies:

$$\text{Yield} = \left(1 + \frac{\text{1 million} - \text{price}}{\text{price}}\right)^{\frac{360}{\text{bond days}}} - 1$$

As a consequence, the yield arising from 'bond market practice' overshoots the yield arising from 'money market practice'.

13.13 *Taxation*

Non-Danish investors

There is no withholding tax, turnover tax, or any other tax, on Danish kroner bonds purchased by foreign investors.

Danish private investors

Private individuals, who are not considered professionals (as stockbrokers etc. would be), are liable to capital income tax on current income from bond holdings at a rate varying between 50 and 56 per cent related to the size of total income. At the same time, capital gains on so-called 'blue stamped' bonds (which account for 99 per cent of all Danish bond issues - see Section 13.3), are free of tax.

Danish corporate investors

Corporations are liable to income tax on current income from bonds at the corporate tax rate of 34 per cent. Capital gains are taxed when realized, also at the corporate tax rate of 34 per cent.

Danish institutional investors

Defined as entities administering life and pension schemes, i.e. life insurance companies, public and private pension funds, and banks, these institutional investors are liable to a special tax, which is not found in other EC-member countries and is therefore frequently alleged to be tax-discriminatory. In January 1992, however, the EC Court of Justice ruled on the subject and allowed Denmark to continue collecting this special tax (called the 'Real Rate of Income Tax'). The tax is liable only on the total return stemming from fixed-income bonds, whether denominated in Danish kroner or foreign currency. Inflation index-linked Danish kroner bonds, as described elsewhere in this chapter, are exempt from the special tax.

Introduced in 1983, the tax has varied between 40 and 57 per cent (annually) of total return from institutional fixed-income bond holdings, accounting for approximately 10 per cent of total public revenue. Politically, the argument for introducing the tax was the relatively high real yields obtainable in the Danish fixed-income markets during the last decade which, over time, had the consequence of increasing consumption potential beyond production potential! As the original argument has been easily defeated both by numerous intellectuals as well as the events of international deregulation, the argument has turned rather more fiscal than political!

The structure and calculation of the tax is rather complex, but follows the following basic principles:

- A benchmark yield, based on historic cost and a complex formula known as 'the mathematical appreciation method', is derived from a sample of major life and pension funds.
- A benchmark inflation measure is calculated based on actual annual average inflation in the preceding 3 years.
- Taxable yield is derived by subtracting the benchmark inflation rate and a fixed 3.5 per cent adjustment factor (= the maximum real return permitted under the special tax system) from the benchmark yield.
- The gross tax rate is calculated by dividing the taxable yield by the benchmark yield.
- The tax-free ratio specific to the individual institution or fund in question, is calculated by dividing the value of the fund at the end of 1982 by the current value of the fund. Over time, pension contributions and financial income increase the vale of the fund and the tax-free ratio declines.
- The net rate is calculated by multiplying the gross tax rate by the tax-free ratio
- The net tax rate is applied to the actual yields (as reflected in the benchmark yield) achieved by individual life and pension funds to calculate the actual tax payable.

	1984	1985	1986	1987	1988	1989	1990	1991	1992[1]	1993[1]	1994[1]
Gross tax rate	40.5	40.6	44.1	56.9	56.0	56.0	44.0	40.5	44.9	50.0	49.0
Gross bond yield	14.0	9.9	11.6	11.7	9.9	10.8	11.0	9.9	9.5	9.0	9.0
Net bond yield	12.3	8.5	9.6	8.7	7.1	7.5	8.1	7.3	6.5	5.6	5.4

Figure 13.46 Calculation of historic and future net yields
[1] *estimated*

13.14 Futures & options

Futures and options first appeared on the decentralized electronic trading system administered by the Copenhagen Stock Exchange, when the so-called FUTOP market, consisting of both futures and options on the now former mortgage benchmark bond (9% 2006), was launched in September 1988. This move reflected the obvious advantage of simultaneous trading in FUTOPS and underlying assets on the same dealing system, providing as it does, for optimal pricing.

Following the replacement of mortgage bonds by government bullet bonds as benchmark paper during the course of 1990, FUTOPS on the latter were promptly launched, and soon they became the dominant contracts. Though FUTOPS still exist for the 9% 2006 issue, liquidity is low and attention is almost entirely devoted to the government bullet contracts. Turnover on FUTOPS has increased steadily since its inauguration in 1988 and, in 1991, a new annual record was posted with a total turnover of approximately 480,000 contracts, representing an underlying value of approximately DKr 480bn.

FUTOP business is cleared through the Danish Securities Centre, in a manner similar to that applying to the underlying assets. However, all participants, must be officially-registered broker companies and also members of the Guarantee Fund for Danish Options and Futures, which was established in 1987 as a non-profit making organization. The Fund guarantees the performance of obligations arising from trading in derivatives - a guarantee which extends to the clients of respective members. Originally initiated by the Danish central bank, banking organizations and the Association of Danish Stock Broker Companies, the Fund had 32 clearing members as at year-end 1991. All members must comply with rules, laid down by the Fund, covering the issuing, trading and settlement of transactions between members and the Fund, as well as between members and their clients. The Fund, furthermore, procures information concerning the risk on derivatives, as well as facilitating clearing and settlement.

Government bullet bond futures

The dominant futures contract is based on the government bullet benchmark, 9% 2000 (see Figure 13.48). Introduced in March 1991, the contract substituted an earlier version based on a basket of three government bullet issues, which was originally launched in September 1989. The success has been outstanding (see Figures 13.48 & 13.49), primarily due to international interest in the underlying Danish government bullet bond market following the marked increase in issuing volumes, as well as the general attraction of Danish bond yields during 1991. During January 1992, a futures contract on the 9% 1995 bullet issue, will be launched.

Contract size:	DKK 1,000,000 notional bond with 9% coupon
Delivery months:	March, June, September, December
Expiry:	Third business day of the delivery month
Last trading day:	Business day preceding expiry
Quotation:	Per cent of par
Minimum price movement (tick size) and value:	0.05 per cent = DKK 500
Trading hours:	09.30 - 15.30
Initial margin:	4 per cent
Price limit:	300 basis points
Contract standard:	Cash settlement
Settlement	Against Exchange delivery settlement price which is the Copenhagen Stock Exchange trading price at 11.00 on expiry date
Guarantee Fund fee:	1) DKK 50 per transaction; 2) DKK 50 per contract
Reuters pages:	DKOA

Figure 13.47 Government bullet bond futures - contract specification

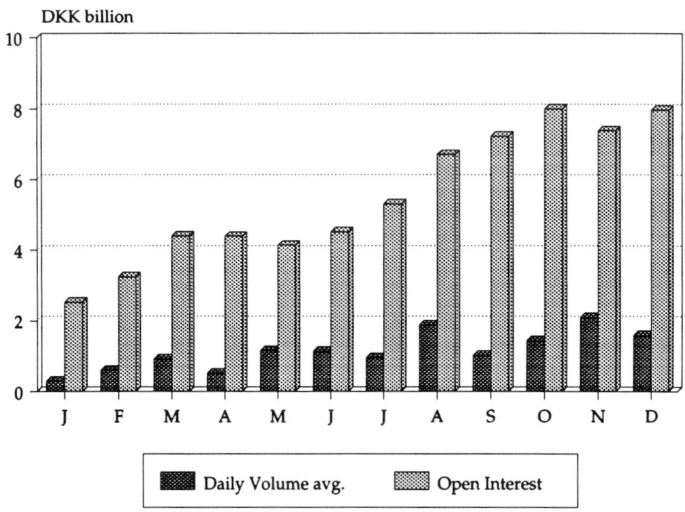

Figure 13.48 Government bullet bond futures - daily volume & open interest, 1991

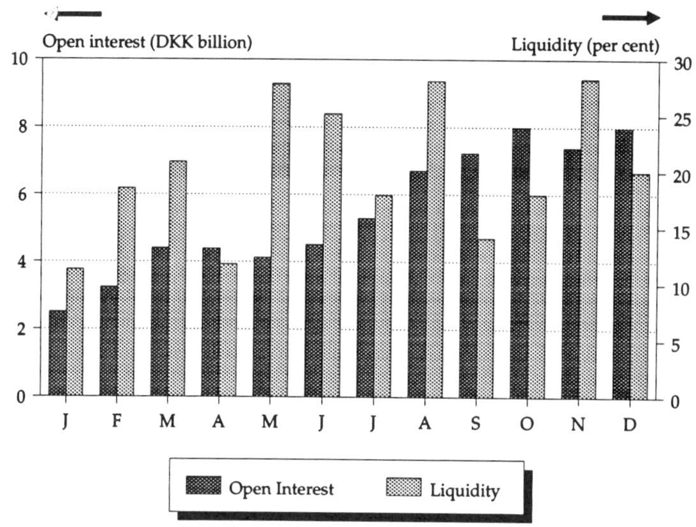

Figure 13.49 Government bullet bond futures - volume/open interest & open interest, 1991

Government bullet bond options

Introduced along with the futures contract in March 1991, calls and puts on the 9% 15 November 2000 bullet issue are, at present, the most popular derivatives in Denmark. Belonging to the European type, all options are settled in cash at expiry with a positive intrinsic value.

The option contract specification and turnover/open interest statistics are shown in Figures 13.50 - 13.52 incl.

Option type:	European
Contract size:	DKK 1,000,000
Delivery months:	March, June, September, December
Expiry:	Third business day of the delivery month
Last trading day:	Business day preceding expiry
Quotation:	Per cent of par
Minimum price movement (tick size) and value:	0.05 per cent = DKK 500
Trading hours:	09.30 - 15.30
Initial margin:	0-4% for seller only. Maintenance margin is the maximum of the settlement premium and the intrinsic value of the option
Price limit:	300 basis points
Contract standard:	Cash settlement
Exercise (strike) price:	One per cent intervals with a minimum of 3 prices above and below the current price. New series are added if price of underlying asset moves out of existing range
Guarantee Fund fee:	1) DKK 50 per transaction; 2) DKK 50 per contract
Reuters pages:	DKOA

Figure 13.50 Government bullet bond options - contract specification

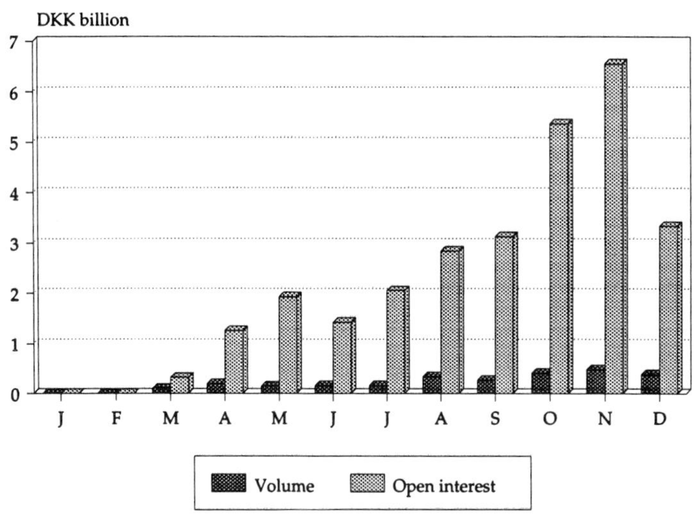

Figure 13.51 Government bullet bond options - daily volume & open interest, 1991

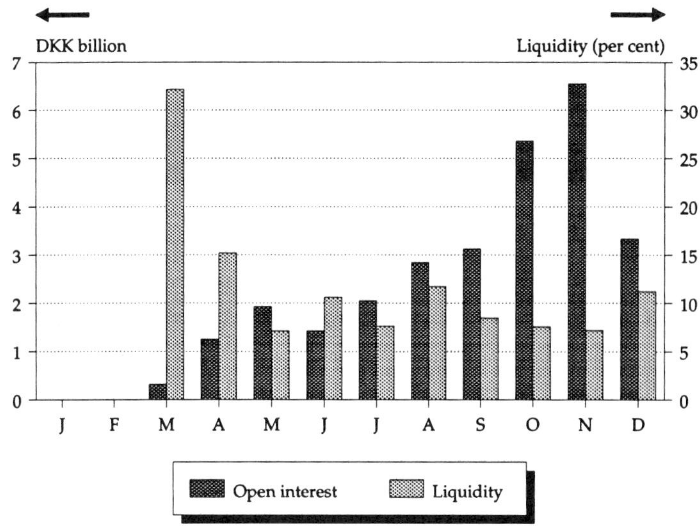

Figure 13.52 Government bullet bond options - volume/open interest & open interest, 1991

13.15 *Money markets*

Though Denmark is renowned for its history, variety and volume of bonds, the Danish money market has lagged significantly behind those of other countries and has only become relatively sophisticated during the past decade. Nevertheless, an almost total absence of interest rate futures within the organized market, means Denmark is compared unfavourably in this area *vis-à-vis* Sweden, for example. Short-term Treasury notes (*Statsgældsbeviser*) were introduced only a decade ago, while Treasury bills were launched as late as March 1990. CDs offered by the Danish central bank are available only within a closed system of banks and savings banks. As FRNs have already been dealt with in the context of the Danish bond market, earlier in this chapter, this section focuses exclusively on Treasury notes and bills.

Short-term Treasury notes (*Statsgældsbeviser*)

Officially, these instruments are categorized as government bonds, since they are issued as bullet issues with fixed-coupons. New issues are being launched quarterly with a final maturity of 2 years 1 month and 20 days, and they stay open for tap for the following 3 quarters.

Name	Maturity	Outstanding amount (DKK million)
8% STGB. III/93[1]	20 August 1993	5300
8% STGB. IV/93[1]	20 November 1993	1350
9% STGB. I/92	20 February 1992	10,750
9% STGB. II/92	20 May 1992	9350
9% STGB. III/92	20 August 1992	9700
9% STGB. IV/92	20 November 1993	10,100
9% STGB. I/93[1]	20 February 1993	14,050
9% STGB. II/93[1]	20 May 1993	13,000

Figure 13.53 Short-term Treasury notes outstanding as at end-1991
[1] *open for tap*

Zero-coupon Treasury bills (*Skatkammerbeviser*)

On 28 March 1990, the first auction for 3- and 6-month Treasury bills was held by Danmarks Nationalbank, the Danish central bank. The background was partly to strengthen the money market, but also enhance the central bank's monitoring of short-term interest rates. Though auctions are held at the end of every quarter, the central bank reserves the right to cancel, or postpone, the auction as well as the right to sell bills in the open market on a tap basis. Maturities, however, are kept firm at the first business day in the quarters of January, April, July and October. Issued in denominations of DKr 1m, the bills carry no coupon and are accordingly traded on a discount basis - being redeemed at par. The auction principle is Dutch: All bids submitted by Danish banks and brokers to the central bank before noon on auction day, form the basis for yield-fixing. All bids at, or above, the fixing are accepted, but allotments may be reduced at the central bank's discretion. The first couple of auctions were rather dissatisfactory, as the yield-fixings tended to be out of line with deposit rates, i.e. the bills were sold at a yield premium. However, as market participants, including foreigners, became more familiar with the new instrument, spreads disappeared and, in terms of volume, the security has, to an extent, replaced government FRNs. During 1991, 9-month bills were introduced.

Name	Maturity	Outstanding amount (DKK million)
SKBV 92/I	02 January 1992	15,500
SKBV 92/II	01 April 1992	16,700
SKBV 92/III	01 July 1992	16,550

Figure 13.54 Zero-coupon Treasury bills outstanding as at end-1991

13.16 Interest rate history

Over the period 1987-1991, Danish interest rate development has been increasingly based on international market trends, rather than by domestic determinants.

The increased international recognition of the Danish commitment to the ERM, reflected in rational macroeconomic policies, was the driving force behind the substantial reduction in the overall level of Danish interest rates from 1987-1988. The drop in long-bond rates, from approximately 12 per cent to below 9 per cent, stemmed primarily from a narrowing of yields *vis-à-vis* Germany, from 600 to 250 basis points (see Figure 13.55).

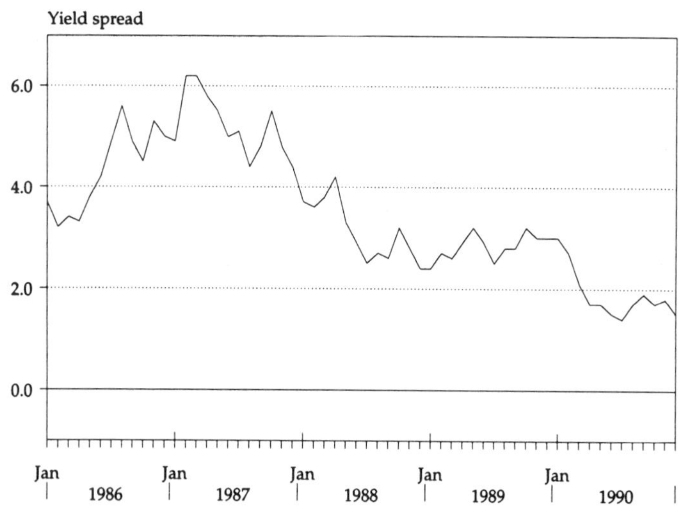

Figure 13.55 DKK/DEM yield spreads [10-yr government bullet bonds, 1986-1991]

Though macroeconomics have paved the way for this development since 1983, it was not confirmed by any real substantial foreign investments in the Danish bond market until 1987. Then, the marked evolution of government bullet bonds, which contributed further to the narrowing of yield gaps, was especially appreciated by foreign institutions. Last, but not least, domestic investors also jumped on the bandwagon in order not to miss the 'train of convergence'.

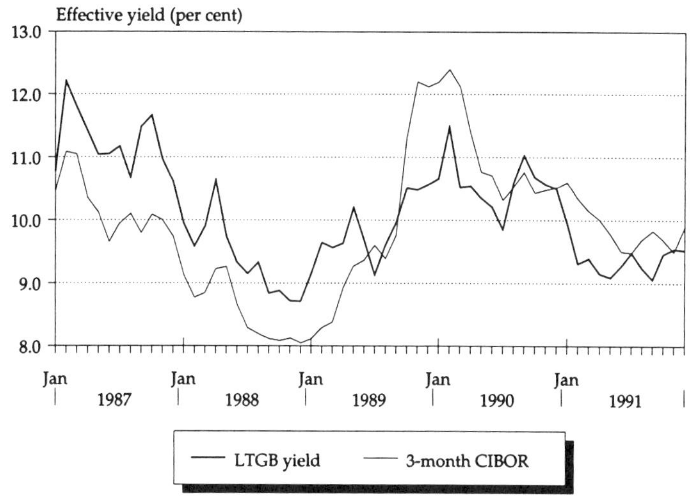

Figure 13.56 Long-term government bond yields & 3-month interest rates

Having re-established the old truth that "fundamental economic factors dominate long-term bond market performance", Danish rates have, since 1989, moved mostly in line with the European benchmark bond, the German Bund, although German reunification triggered further reductions in the yield gap, despite the overall increase in European bond rates at the announcement of the inter-German currency settlement in January 1990. At present (January 1992), Danish government bullet bonds are yielding 60 basis points more than German Bunds, representing the lowest spread so far seen. On a real rate basis, Denmark is on top among the hard-currency group within the ERM, and only conventions may justify the yield gap (see also Section 13.17, Inter-market spreads). Over the entire period, 1987-1991, short and long rates have moved parallel, (disregarding the shift to an inverse yield curve during mid-1989), along with most other European markets (see Figure 13.56).

13.17 *Inter-market spreads*

Spreads against German Bunds have already been discussed in the Section - 13.16, therefore this section is devoted to consideration of domestic spreads.

The spread between the two largest segments of the Danish bond market, government and mortgage bonds, have been rather volatile during the last five-year period for a variety of different factors. During the summer 1987, Danish long-term rates were represented by the mortgage bond benchmark, 9% 2006, trading at a slightly-negative yield spread against comparable government bonds, then represented by serial issues. With the emergence of longer-dated government bullet bonds (which are preferred by foreign investors), and the downturn of the Danish property market raising doubts on the solidity of Danish mortgage associations, a substantial increase in yield spreads was witnessed (see Figure 13.57).

From a peak of approximately 125 basis points in favour of government issues, Danish institutions made large conversions back into mortgage bonds during the second half of 1988, bringing spreads down towards zero in the beginning of 1989. Later that year, foreigners became net sellers of Danish

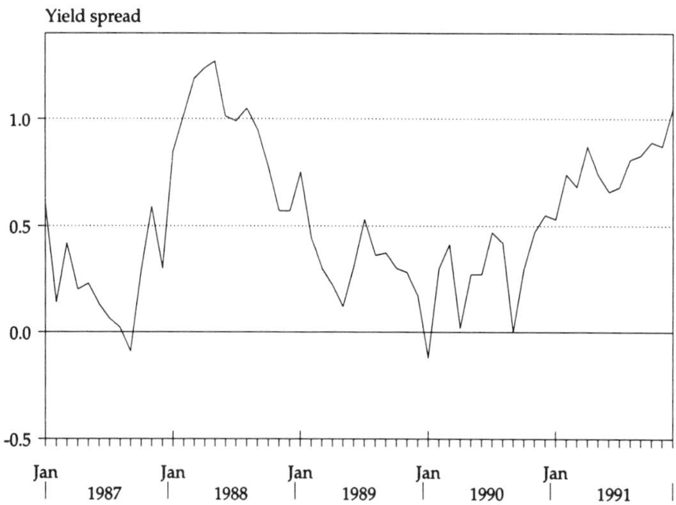

Figure 13.57 Yield spread between Danish mortgage bonds & government benchmark bonds

government bonds, re-establishing a small negative yield spread. As the interest rate turmoil caused by German reunification settled during the second quarter 1990, and interest rate levels started to resume a negative trend, foreign interest in Danish bonds accelerated. This interest was stimulated further by the launch of the first 10-year government bullet issue. Through 1991, government bonds have superseded mortgage bonds as benchmark issues, trading approximately 100 basis points lower in yield against comparable mortgage bonds as at year-end 1991.

13.18 *Sources of reference*

Financial data

The Copenhagen Stock Exchange

Several publications are issued by the Copenhagen Stock Exchange and are listed in the following:

- *Daily Official Price List* with headings translated into English
- *Weekly Official Price List* (Mondays), exhaustive
- *Monthly Official Price List,* covering price developments during the specific month
- *Quarterly Official Price List,* covering price developments during the specific quarter
- *Monthly Report,* comprehensive commenting, including turnover and price developments
- *Annual Report* and *Semi-Annual Reports,* also available in English
- A number of technical reports on yield calculations etc. are also available

Since the list of publications is expanding, interested readers are recommended to contact the Exchange directly.

Address:
The Copenhagen Stock Exchange
Nikolaj Plads 2
DK - 1067 Copenhagen K

Tel: +45 33 93 33 66

Danmarks Nationalbank (The Danish central bank)

The central bank publishes a number of comprehensive commented statistics covering the total Danish capital market including bond market statistics and developments as well as cross-border capital flow statistics.

- *Monthly Financial Statistics,* a short overview of interest rates, foreign exchange rates and cross-border capital flows
- *Quarterly Review,* published in English during February, May, August and November. Quite comprehensive
- *Annual Report,* published in English and very comprehensive

Address:
Danmarks Nationalbank
Havnegade 5
DK - 1093 Copenhagen K

Tel: +45 33 14 14 11

The Guarantee Fund for Danish Options and Futures

Apart from a prospectus on each futures and options contract launched on the Copenhagen Stock Exchange, a variety of information may be obtained from the Guarantee Fund, e.g. annual, semi-annual and quarterly reports on volume, open interest etc.

Address:
The Guarantee Fund for Danish Options and Futures
Kompagnistræde 15
DK - 1012 Copenhagen K

Tel: +45 33 93 33 11

Financial press

The leading daily newspaper, with extensive securities market information including a large, but not exhaustive, selection of bond prices is:

- *Dagbladet Børsen*

Address:
Møntergade 19
DK - 1014 Copenhagen K

Tel: +45 33 15 72 50

Quote vendors and news agencies

Page codes for Reuters, Telerate and Bloomberg are shown in the Appendix together with the names of the authorized brokers.

Appendix

Authorized Danish stockbroker companies

At the end of 1991, a total of 31 companies were authorized members of the electronic dealing system at the Copenhagen Stock Exchange, and also members of the Association of Danish Stock Broker Companies. A variety of information and research is produced and distributed by the broker companies including information which is fed through global quote vendor systems such as Reuters, Telerate and Bloomberg. The following table gives brokers' names in alphabetical order and, where applicable, (R)euter, (T)elerate and (B)loomberg access codes. As a vast majority of broker companies are affiliated, or associated, with other financial groups, primarily banks, the parent company is shown. Also note that all authorized broker companies must use the Danish expression for broker company, *Børsmæglerselskab,* in their name.

	Parent	Access codes
Aktiv Børs Børsmæglerselskab A/S	Aktivbanken A/S (owned by Top Danmark, insurance)	R: AKTI , T: n/s , B: n/a
AL Børsmæglerselskab A/S	Aktieselskabet Arbejdernes Landsbank	R: n/a T: n/a , B: n/a
Alfred Berg Børsmæglerselskab A/S	AB Volvo	R: ABDE++ , T: n/a , B: n/a
Alicon Børsmæglerselskab A/S	ABN-AMRO BANK NV	R: ACOM++ , T: 8601 , B: n/a
Alm. Brand Børsmægleraktieselskab	Controlled by Alm. Brand (insurance group)	R: n/a , T: n/a , B: n/a
Baltica Børsmæglerselskab A/S	Baltica Holding A/S (insurance group)	R: BABG++ , T: n/a , B: n/a
Benzon & Benzon Børsmæglerselskab A/S	Private	R: BENZ++ , T: 9342 , B: KORB - 0 (yellow)
Bikuben Børs A/S Børsmæglerselskab	Sparekassen Bikuben (savings bank)	R: BIKI , T: n/a , B: n/a
BMS Broker Børsmæglerselskab A/S	Private	R: n/a , T: n/a , B: n/a
A/S Bjørnskov & Co. Børsmæglerselskab	Former partners, pension funds and smaller banks	R: BJOR , T: n/a , B: n/a
DanskeBørs Børsmæglerselskab A/S	Den Danske Bank A/S	R: DANY++ , T: n/a , B: n/a

(cont.)

	Parent	Access codes
Fyns Børsmæglerselskab, Børs Fyn, Aktieselskab	Amtssparekassen for Fyns Amt (regional savings bank)	R: n/a , T: n/a , B: n/a
Gudme Raaschou Børsmæglerselskab A/S	Gudme Raaschou Holding A/S	R: n/a , T: n/a , B: n/a
Gyllenhammar & Partners Børsmæglerselskab A/S	Mercurius Gruppen AB	R: n/a , T: n/a , B: n/a
A/S Hafnia Børs, Børsmæglerselskab	Hafnia Holding A/S (insurance group)	R: HASE , T: n/a , B: n/a
H.C. Møller Brsmægleraktieselskab	Unibank A/S	R: MOLL , T: n/a , B: n/a
Interbørs A/S Børsmæglerselskab	Interbank af 1985 A/S	R: n/a , T: n/a , B: n/a
Jysk Børsmæglerselskab A/S	Jyske Bank A/S	R: JYSK , T: n/a , B: n/a
Carnegie-Jensen & Co. Børsmæglerselskab A/S	Nordbanken AB	R: CAJF++ , T: n/a , B: n/a
Lannung & Co. A/S Børsmæglerselskab	Akkumulator Invest A/S	R: n/a , T: 8228 , B: n/a
A/S Midtbørs, Børsmæglerselskab	Aktieselskabet Midtbank (regional bank)	R: n/a , T: n/a , B: n/a
Nordjyllands Børsmæglerselskab A/S	Spar Nord Holding A/S (regional bank)	R: n/a , T: n/a , B: n/a
P-H Børsmæglerselskab A/S	Private	R: AAPH , T: n/a , B: n/a
PS Børs Børsmæglerselskab A/S	Købjenhavnske Bank A/S	R: n/a , T: n/a , B: n/a
Rued Jørgensen Børsmæglerselskab A/S	Sankt Annæ Holding A/S (private)	R: BRUE+ , T: n/a , B: n/a
Samson Børsmæglerselskab A/S	Samson Holding A/S (private)	R: SAMS , T: n/a , B: n/a
Scanbroker Børsmæglerselskab A/S	Private	R: n/a , T: n/a , B: n/a
Sundberg & Co. Børsmæglerselskab A/S	Sundberg & Co. Holdingselskab ApS (private)	R: SUNA , T: n/a , B: n/a
Børsmæglerselskabet Børs Syd A/S	Sydbank Sønderjylland A/S (regional bank)	R: BSYD , T: n/a , B: n/a
Unibørs Børsmæglerselskab A/S	Unibank A/S	R: UDKG+ , T: n/a , B: n/a
Vestbørsen Børsmæglerselskab A/S	Aktieselskabet Varde Bank (regional bank)	R: VABA , T: n/a , B: n/a

Chapter

14

The bond markets of

Finland

Päivi Härkönen
Startel Inc.

Alexander Creutzberg
Tiina Tuominen
Postipankki Ltd

Note: In general text, the abbreviation 'FM' is used to denote the Finnish markka. Elsewhere, the international mnemonic 'FIM' is used.

14.1 Introduction

The Finnish financial markets experience a rapid evolution during the 1980s. The size of the markets grew from FM 100bn in 1980, to FM 600bn in 1990. During the same period, the relative proportion of bonds grew from FM 17bn to FM 108bn. Money market instruments, meanwhile, have increased to FM 150bn. It is important to note that the stock of money market instruments is now bigger than that of bond securities.

The liberalization of the financial markets, during the 1980s, contributed to a marked expansion of the economy - a fact which was reflected in the GDP growth rate of 4-5 per cent, recorded during the latter part of the decade. At that time, the Finnish economy was one of the fastest-growing in the world.

With growth, however, came inflation. In the late 80s, annual inflation - which was fuelled by rising real estate prices - grew by an average of 6 per cent. This level of inflation then caused interest rates to rise.

The start of the 1990s was marked by a rapid slowdown in the Finnish economy. Indeed, such was the magnitude of the slowdown, that growth rates actually turned negative in late-1990, and stayed that way throughout the following year. However, GDP is forecast to show some improvement during 1992, with a return to positive rates coming in 1993. In contrast, though, there is little optimism for an early fall in the unemployment figures, which have been swollen by the recession, and the current rate of around 10 per cent is expected to remain unchanged during the early 1990s.

The general economic climate worsened considerably during the autumn of 1991 with corporate bankruptcies growing in number and exacerbating the problem of unemployment. As a direct response to the situation, the central bank, the Bank of Finland, devalued the Finnish markka. It was the bank's belief that the currency had faced such uncertainty that such a move was unavoidable. The new range for the markka (which had been pegged to the Ecu in June 1991) was fixed at Ecu 5.39166 - 5.72516.

With a volume of FM 46.7bn, the Finnish bond markets meanwhile witnessed a 64 per cent growth in new issuance in 1991. This figure included FM 11bn from central government, FM 27.1bn from financial institutions and FM 7.3bn from corporates. During the same year, new issuance denominated in other currencies amounted to FM 33.1bn.

New issuance is expected to increase considerably in 1992, as the net financial requirement of Finland is expected to exceed FM 50bn. This figure means that net foreign debt/GDP will be more than 30 per cent.

14.2 Economics

Introduction

During the latter years of the 1980s, the money and capital markets in Finland experienced a period of very rapid liberalization which coincided with an unprecedented rate of growth in the domestic economy. However, in the 1990s, the Finns are now facing the stark contrast of a deep recession.

The downturn in the Finnish economy was abrupt. In 1989, the gross domestic product grew by 5 per cent but, in 1991, it fell by 5 per cent. As far as the future is concerned, it is assumed that 1992 will see zero growth while prospects for 1993-95 are modest and dependent, to a large extent, upon global economic growth.

At the moment, the two basic problems in the Finnish economy are the current account deficit and the high rate of unemployment. While the recession has eased inflationary pressures, it has increased unemployment (which is forecast to be at around 10 per cent for, at least, the early part of the 1990s). By comparison to GDP, the current account deficit is not expected to widen further, but will nevertheless remain large in the near future.

The performance of the Finnish economy, then, was very favourable in the 1980's, with total output and productivity growing faster than in other industrial countries. Strong domestic demand boosted the economy but the demand exceeded available resources, thereby creating both inflation and high interest rates. Additionally, public sector growth outstripped that of the private sector.

The present economic policy of the government is to reduce the current account deficit whilst improving the efficiency of the public sector in order to achieve the primary goal of a reduction in overall public expenditure. The government is also aiming to reduce unemployment while keeping the inflation rate as low as possible.

Finland will increase its borrowing from both international and domestic capital markets. Indeed, net foreign debt will reach about 30 per cent of GDP. The government's net financing requirement will be over FM 30bn in 1992, and will remain quite large during the rest of the early 1990's.

The recession has also created an unhealthy environment for corporations, with falling productivity and weak domestic demand, and this is reflected on the Helsinki Stock Exchange where share prices have fallen by approximately 15 per cent during the first nine months of 1991. Dividends, too, have fallen sharply. Fundamental factors are gloomy and are likely to remain so in the near future.

Exchange rate

Finland pegged the Finnish markka to the Ecu in June 1991. Prior to the linkage, the external value of markka was determined by a foreign trade-weighted exchange rate index, with the proportion of EMS currencies accounted for about 80 per cent of the basket. Following the linkage, the mid-point of the currency variation band stayed the same and the fluctuation range remained at 6 per cent.

After the Ecu-pegging decision, the yield difference between 3-month HELIBOR (Helsinki interbank offered rate) and 3-month Ecu was about 1.5 to 2 per cent. During the autumn of 1991 the differential widened to about 3 to 4 per cent, due to increased uncertainty about the economic situation and speculation on the external value of the markka.

On 14 November 1991, the Bank of Finland announced that the central bank had decided to withdraw, temporarily, its support for the markka. The currency was then allowed to float in order to find its own market level.

The next day, the central bank and the government announced that the markka would be devalued by 14 per cent. The new fluctuation range would keep the markka between 5.39166 and 5.72516 per Ecu, with a new mid-point of 5.55841. According to the Bank of Finland pressure against the markka had grown considerably. Interest rates had moved up sharply as the markets showed uncertainty about the level of domestic wage settlements as well as the general state of the economy. However, despite the high interest rates, currency out-flow had continued.

Since devaluation, interest rates have come down slightly but continued uncertainty over wage agreements and inflation have meant that the overall level is still high. It is expected, however, that the first few months of 1992 will show a marked fall in rates.

Gross domestic product

The Finnish economy expanded during the 1980s with a substantial increase in gross domestic product; indeed, the growth of the Finnish economy was one of the fastest in the world. Towards the end of the decade, GDP increased by 4 to 5 per cent annually for three consecutive years - in 1988 growth actually reached 5.4 per cent (see Figure 14.1).

The economy could not survive such a high growth rate without problems. Accordingly, the current account deficit deepened, inflation accelerated and interest rates rose. The economic downturn took place at the beginning of 1990 as industrial production started to fall and domestic demand was dampened by high interest rates.

In 1991, industrial production grew by less than one per cent and during the first quarter of that year, gross domestic product actually fell by 5.2 per cent. A

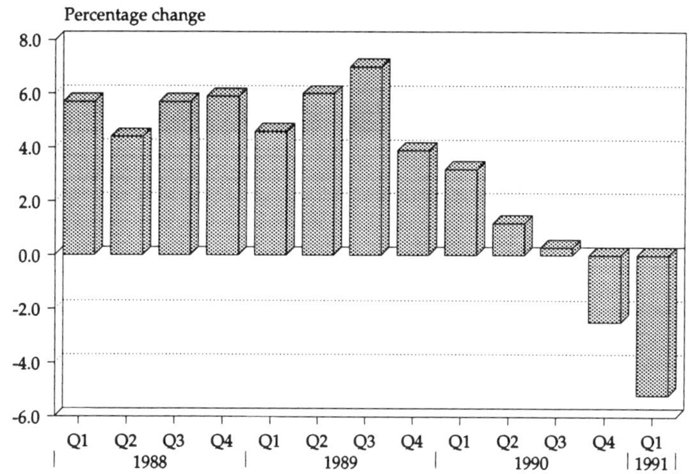

Figure 14.1 Finnish gross domestic product - percentage change per quarter (1988-1991)

zero-growth in GDP is forecast for 1992, after which a slow upward trend should be seen.

Trade balance

Due to rapid growth in domestic demand, imports exceeded exports in the late 1980s, while direct investment in Finnish industry grew tenfold during the period 1981-1989.

The trade balance began to move into deficit (see Figure 14.2). In 1989, the balance was in the red by some FM 6.1bn. The start of the 1990s saw a reduction in Finnish exports to what used to be the Soviet Union. The bilateral clearing trade between the Soviet Union and Finland ended as from 1991 and now trade with the new CIS republics is conducted in convertible currencies. Exports to the Soviet Union were about 5 per cent of the total export of goods in 1991. In contrast to the foregoing, it is expected that exports to the West will develop more favourably.

Engineering and forest products account for about 80 per cent of exports, with all other sectors accounting for just 20 per cent. In 1989, exports of goods and services amounted to FM 117bn compared to a 1992 budget forecast figure of FM 120bn.

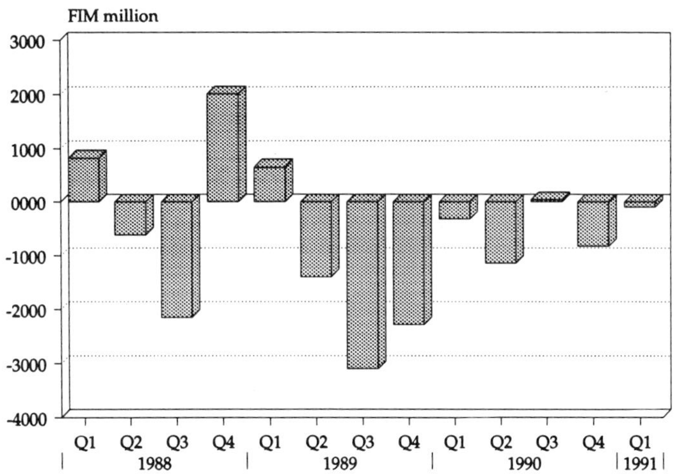

Figure 14.2 Trade balance in FM millions (per quarter, 1988-1991)

The widening of the current account deficit in the late 1980s is considered to be one of the major economic problems in Finland. Whilst interest rates have remained high in order to attract foreign investors (thereby countering the deficit), they have also had the effect of minimizing investment by Finnish industry and households.

The 1991 current account deficit was FM 25bn. It is forecast that, over the next few years, the deficit will diminish. A level of FM 18bn, or -3.4 per cent of GDP, is predicted for 1992.

Unemployment

During the years of growth, unemployment fell by approximately 3.5 per cent . In 1989, the number out of work was just 89, 000 and many sectors experienced a shortage of labour. By 1991, however, the effects of the recession were being felt with the rate of unemployment approaching 10 per cent - around 300,000 people (see Figure 14.3).

The construction and manufacturing industries were the first to implement lay-offs and redundancies. Soon after, the service sector began to be similarly affected.

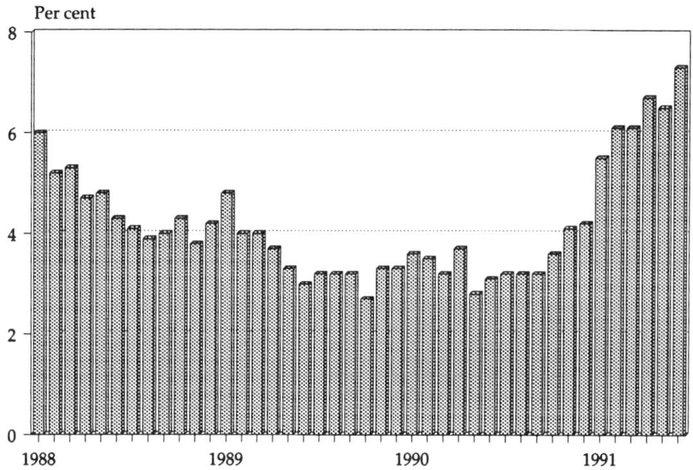

Figure 14.3 **Monthly Finnish unemployment (per cent, 1988-1991)**

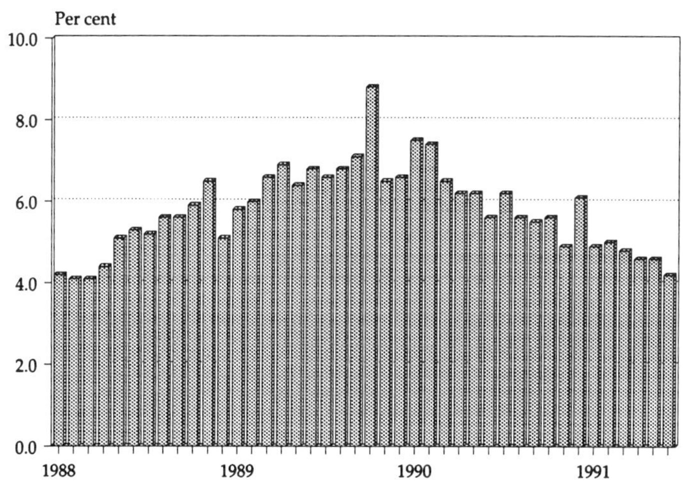

Figure 14.4 **Monthly inflation in Finland (per cent, 1988-1991)**

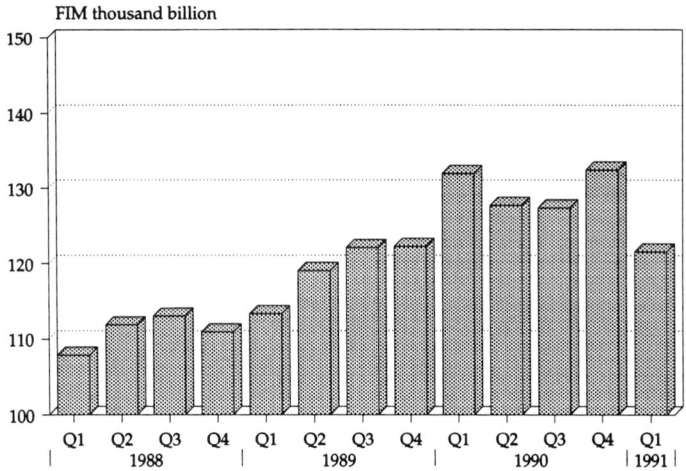

Figure 14.5 M1 money supply (per quarter, 1988-1991)

With the national budget forecast for 1992 seeing the rate remaining at around 10 per cent, a significant reduction in Finnish unemployment in the short-term is not anticipated.

Inflation

In the late 1980s, annual inflation in Finland grew by an average of approximately 6 per cent a year (see Figure 14.4). Rising real estate prices, in particular, helped push up the consumer price index. As noted earlier, interest rates rose so steeply that they started to affect domestic demand whilst, at the same time, investment by Finnish industry began to decline.

In 1991 the inflation rate is expected to be about 4 per cent although, as a result of devaluation, it is forecast to rise to 6 per cent in 1992.

The growth in M1 money supply, a key factor in inflation, is shown in Figure 14.5.

Politics

As an Efta member, Finland is moving closer to the European Community, the first step in the process being the establishment of the European Economic Area, which will create integrated markets in Europe.

After a long period as an observer, Finland became a full member of the Council of Europe in May 1989.

In March 1991, Finland had parliamentary elections at which the Centre Party won the highest proportion (25.2 per cent) of the 200 seats in the parliament . Behind them, the Conservatives took 19.2 per cent, the Social Democrats 22.1 per cent and the Greens 6.7 per cent. The new coalition government consists of the Centre Party, the Conservatives, the Swedish Peoples' Party and the Christian League and, with the absence of the Social Democrats, is therefore clearly to right of the political spectrum.

14.3 Market composition

The Finnish financial market saw rapid evolution during the 1980s. The size of the market grew from FM 100bn in 1980, to FM 636bn in 1991 (see Figures 14.7 & 14.8). At the same time, the structure of the market has seen marked changes. Money market instruments, bonds and equities have become eminent, while the proportion of traditional bank deposits has diminished.

Although the Finnish bond market is still small by international standards, it has nevertheless witnessed considerable growth. The recent liberalization of the Finnish money and capital markets has given added momentum to this development. At the end of 1991, the outstanding amount of Finnish bonds was FM 146bn which, as a percentage of gross domestic product, represents almost 28.5 per cent.

The markka bond market is usually categorized by issuer (see Figure 14.6) and is seldom divided into separate domestic and euromarket sectors. The FM-eurobond market developed between 1986 and 1990, during which period 11 such bonds were issued, with 5 of them coming from the World Bank (see

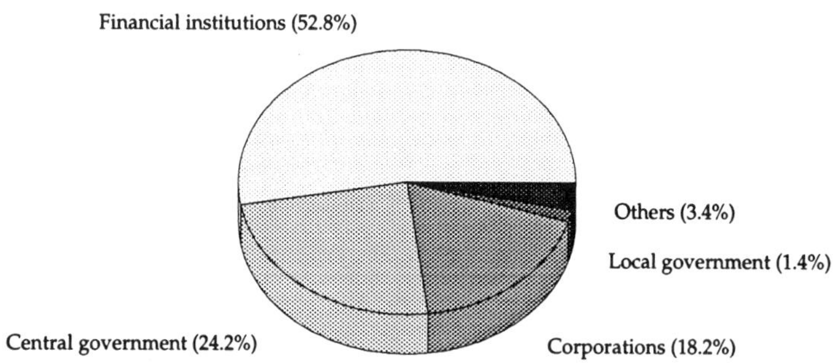

Figure 14.6 Composition of the Finnish bond market (June 1991)

	Coupon (%)	Maturity	Issue amount (FIM million)
NIB	9 5/8	1986-91	250
Postipankki	10 1/4	1987-92	150
Outokumpu Oy	10 1/4	1987-92	200
World Bank I	10	1987-94	300
World Bank II	9 7/8	1987-92	300
NIB	9 1/2	198-93	300
World Bank III	9 5/8	1988-96	300
IFC	9 5/8	1988-95	250
World Bank IV	9 5/8	1988-95	300
NIB	9 5/8	1989-94	400
World Bank V	9 3/4	1989-94	300
Total			3050

Figure 14.7 Foreign-targeted FIM-bonds issued prior to 1 January 1990

Figure 14.7). Since the re-opening of the market, in 1990, all the eurobond issues can be traded as domestic bonds.

Composition by coupon

The majority of Finnish bonds are fixed-rate. In taxable issues, the coupon ranges from 9 per cent to 14 per cent, with the average coupon being 13.4 per cent.

The interest rate of floating-rate markka bonds is either linked to the Bank of Finland's base rate, or to HELIBOR (Helsinki interbank offered rate), which is based upon the trading of certificates of deposit (CDs). HELIBOR rates represent the average bid-rate quoted by the five largest Finnish banks, i.e. Kansallis-Osake-Pankki, Okobank, Postipankki, Skopbank and Union Bank of Finland, each day at 13.00 (Finnish time).

Composition by maturity

The typical maturities of Finnish bonds are 1.5, 2, 2.5, 3, 4 and 5 years, with the 3- to 5-year maturities being the most common. The 5-year government bond is considered to be the benchmark in the Finnish bond market. All government housing fund bonds have maturities of 10 years.

So far, there are no bonds with maturities over 10 years although, once the market has fully developed, such bonds are very likely to be introduced.

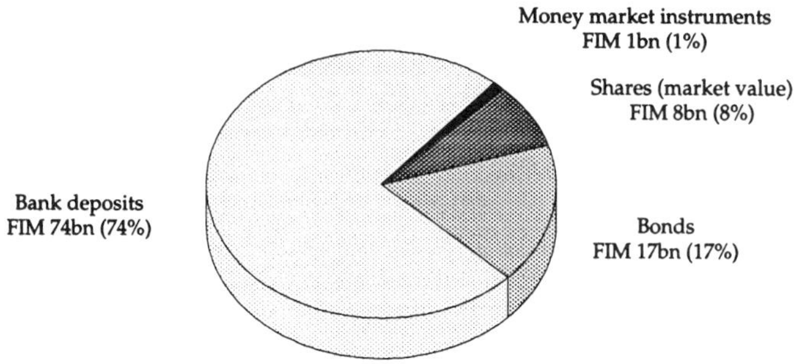

Figure 14.8 Composition of the Finnish financial markets in 1980

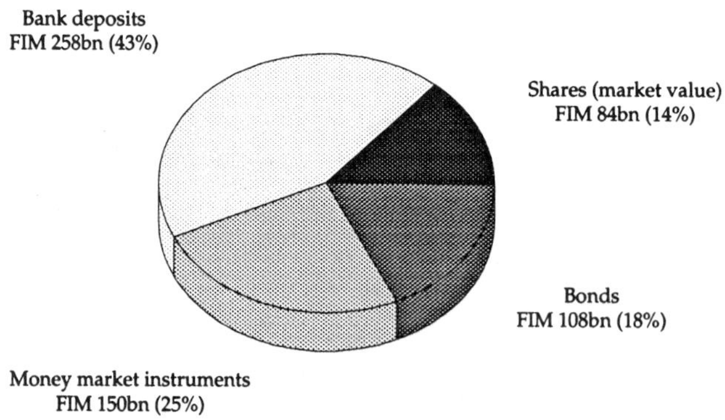

Figure 14.9 Composition of the Finnish financial markets in 1991

14.4 Types of security

Overview

Bullet bonds

With their proportion having increased significantly in recent years, bullet bonds now represent the majority of Finnish issues.

Convertible and warrant-linked bonds

Convertible bonds are scarce in the Finnish bond market. While some have historically been issued by corporates and financial institutions, the prolonged downturn in share prices since the second quarter in 1989 have made them less attractive, with the result that have not consolidated their position in the overall bond market.

The continuous fall in share prices has affected warrant-linked bonds as well. These warrant bonds had been particularly popular in 1987, reflecting the prosperous outlook of the equity market at that time. However, since 1988, there has been no new issuance; meanwhile, those bonds which have yet to be redeemed are scarcely seen in the secondary market.

Sinking funds

The old tax-exempt government bonds (see below) are all sinking funds which are redeemed in equal instalments during the life of the bond. Sinking funds have not been particularly attractive to investors and so their relative proportion in the market has declined.

Government and local authority bonds

Traditionally, government bonds are divided into taxable and tax-exempt categories. Since the beginning of 1991 the government has issued only taxable bonds. Although the old tax-exempt bonds still represent over 30 per cent of the outstanding government bond stock, their significance diminishes as they are redeemed.

Since the beginning of 1989 the Finnish government has issued four types of taxable bonds, each targeted at specific investor group.

Retail bonds

Retail bonds have maturities from 3 to 5 years and are targeted to private investors. These bonds have denominations of FM 5000, 10,000 and 50,000.

Serial bonds

Serial bonds are offered to institutional investors. These are normally tap issues and public bullet bonds with denominations of 1m and 5m. To date, the maturity of serial bonds has shown a variation of between 4 and 5 years.

Government Housing Fund bonds

The Government Housing Fund bonds are public bullet bonds, offered to institutional investors, with a maturity of 10 years and denominations of FM 5m and FM 10m. The first tranche was issued in 1990. By 15 September 1991, the amount of Housing Fund bonds outstanding was FM 3.6bn.

Special bonds

Special bonds are also offered to institutional investors. They have maturities of between six and ten years and denominations of FM 1m and 5m. These infrequent issues are private placements.

Corporate bonds

The corporate bond sector consists mainly of fixed-rate bullet bonds, convertible bonds and warrants. Traditionally, corporate bonds have had either a bank guarantee or other collateral, or they have been subject to private placement arrangements. However, the amount of non-guaranteed bonds is likely to increase, since guaranteed issues which show on the balance sheet strain the solvency requirements of the banks. Non-guaranteed corporate bond issues, to date, are: Repola 11.75% 1994, Metra 12.3% 1995, Novera 11.75% 1994 and Valio 12.1% 1995.

14.5 Issuers

In June 1985, the Bank of Finland banned the sales of markka bonds abroad. The ban was temporary and the rationale behind the move was that the strong demand for FM bonds induced capital in-flows which, at the time, were considered excessive. In 1986, the Bank of Finland reverted to allowing the sale of FM bonds abroad, albeit on a case-by-case permission basis. Between 1986 and February 1990, eleven foreign-targeted bonds, all listed in Helsinki, were issued. From the beginning of February 1989, Finnish entities were allowed to issue FM-denominated bonds abroad, while foreign entities were able to issue FM bonds in the Finnish market. Also, from that date, the sale abroad of convertible bonds and equity-warranted issues has been permitted. The last restriction, that concerning the sale of domestic bonds abroad, was lifted in January 1991.

Central and local government

Central and local government account for roughly one quarter of total bond issuance (see Figure 14.10). As noted earlier, the old tax-exempt bonds proved unattractive to investors. It is hoped that the new taxable bonds, which are targeted at specific groups, will promote investment and liquidity in this sector.

Liquidity will also benefit from an expected increase in new issuance caused by the continued severe recession and the government's increased net borrowing requirements.

Financial institutions

Financial institutions include finance companies, banks and mortgage banks. Due to the long-term nature of their liabilities, mortgage banks have been particularly active issuers and much of their funding is derived from the bond market. Another important issuer has been Finnish Export Credit, a special finance institution. Banks have issued mainly subordinated debentures.

Corporates

The corporate sector has not been particularly active in bond issuance. Although the proportion of corporate bonds in the market has increased by almost 60 per cent since the beginning of 1986, most of these issues have been private placements which are not traded in the secondary market.

That corporations have not issued many bonds may be attributable to the present Finnish pension fund system which allows corporations to borrow money from their pension funds. This sort of borrowing is very attractive to

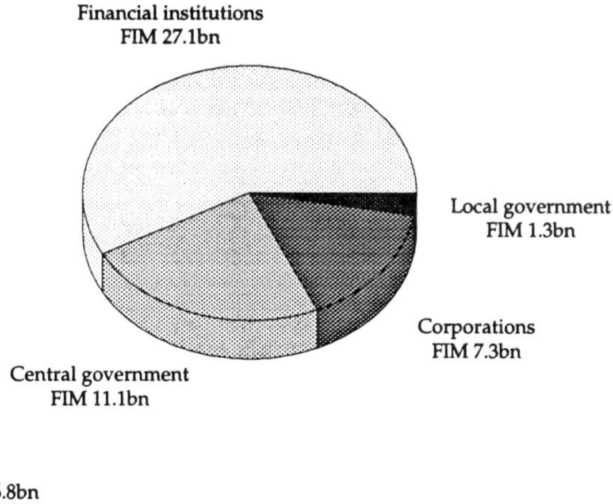

Figure 14.10 Issuers in the markka bond market, 1991

corporations in the short-term, since the interest rate on such loans is low by comparison to open-market rates.

Due to the new BIS risk-adjusted capital adequacy requirements for the banks, more corporate bond issues (rather than traditional bank loans), may be expected. Traditionally, all corporate bonds have had a bank guarantee or other collateral but, in 1991 the first non-guaranteed corporate bonds were issued.

Foreign borrowers

The most active international issuers have been supranationals such as the World Bank and IFC with other foreign borrowers like the Nordic Investment Bank, together with several Finnish and foreign banks. The largest single international markka-denominated bond issued thus far is the FM 500m Export Development Company 13.25% 1993.

14.6 Investors

Insurance companies

Insurance companies play a major role in the credit market. This is partly due to the fact that a considerable portion of their pension premium income is subsequently lent back to the companies which paid the premiums. About half of the credits granted by insurance companies consist of premiums lent back under the compulsory labour market pension scheme. In addition to this type of lending, insurance companies invest in both the capital and real estate markets.

Due to the long-term liabilities of these companies, most of their funds is invested in bonds with long maturities, i.e. from 5 to 10 years. As there are no FM bonds with maturities longer than 10 years, the insurance companies are forced to cover their liabilities with bonds of these maturities. Given the nature of their liabilities, it is most unlikely for insurance companies to hold short-term bonds.

Pension funds

The investment policy of the pension funds closely follows that of the pension insurance companies. Nearly 75 per cent of premium income is lent back to the parent company, with remaining assets normally being invested in bonds, equities, etc. As a result, although some bond investment is made by the funds, their overall level of activity is restricted by the scale of their lending.

Corporations

Corporations normally tend to hold bonds, as part of their investment portfolio, in order to diversify risk. However, the high short-term interest rates recently experienced have prompted them to reduce their exposure to bonds, in favour of the better returns provided by shorter investments. When the Finnish economy recovers, though, it is very likely that corporations will re-establish, and increase, their bond holdings.

Banks

Banks tend to hold investments in the one- to ten-year area, with the average maturity being two years. The application of BIS rules has made the less risky government and bank bonds more attractive than corporate bonds.

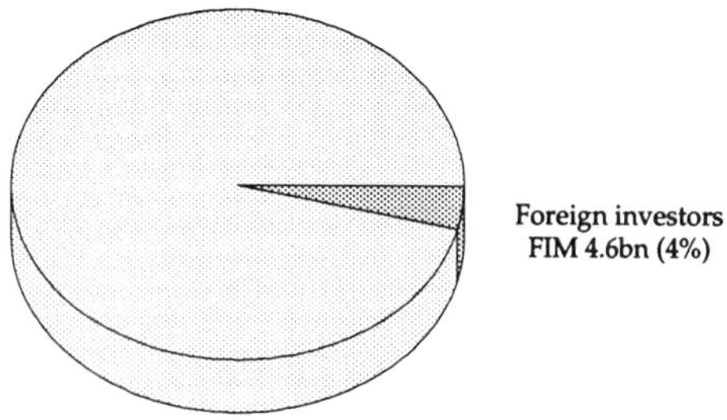

TOTAL STOCK: FIM 116bn

Figure 14.11 Foreign investment in markka bonds, 1990

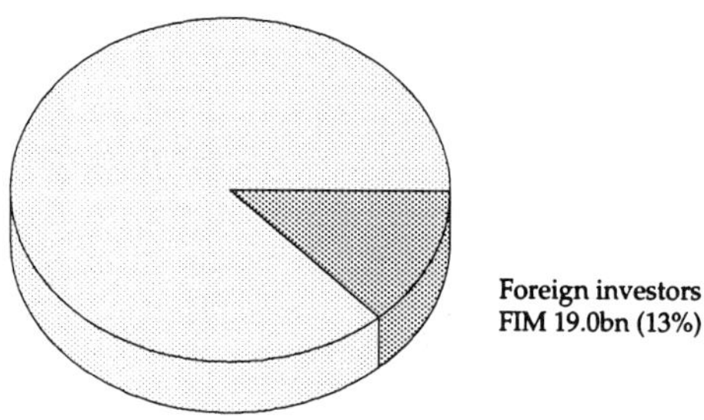

TOTAL STOCK: FIM 145bn

Figure 14.12 Foreign investment in markka bonds, 1991

Individuals

The government used to target tax-exempt low-coupon bonds at private investors but recent fiscal reform has meant that, since 1991, such bonds are no longer issued. However, the government has launched a new type of bond, the retail bond, which is especially aimed at private investors. The change from tax-exempt to taxable bonds (as well as other fiscal alterations) has, to some extent, confused private investors with the result that they have not been particularly active in the bond market since 1989.

Overseas investors

With high interest rates and relatively low risk, the Finnish market has attracted growing interest from overseas (see Figures 14.11 & 14.12) - mainly from European and Japanese investment funds. Generally, they tend to invest in the more liquid bonds such as international and government issues, as well as in bank bonds.

14.7 *Methods of issuance*

Auction

At present, all markka-denominated government serial bonds are issued through auctions. The Government Housing Fund, municipalities and certain corporations also use this method. Auction dates and amounts vary from issue to issue. Only the HELIBOR banks (Kansallis-Osake-Pankki, Okobank, Postipankki, Skopbank and Union Bank of Finland), banking firms and brokers, are allowed to bid in auctions (with investors bidding through them). Government serial bonds are issued on a non-competitive basis (Dutch auction), whereas Government Housing Fund bonds are issued on a competitive basis (American-style auction).

Other methods

Normally, Finnish domestic and international bonds are issued using a method by which the borrower calls for offers from the banks, or the banks offer to arrange an issue for the borrower. They can be either non-syndicated or syndicated issues and are underwritten by the lead-manager, with the terms fixed and agreed.

If a new issue is brought to the market as a syndicated issue, the lead-manager selects the co-managers who both underwrite, and agree to distribute, the issue. Rules for lead-management are stated in the recommendations of the International Primary Market Association, IPMA. The three major Finnish banks are members of this association.

14.8 *New issue volumes*

At the end of 1990, new issuance volume was almost FM 28bn. The amount of both foreign-targeted bonds, as well as domestic bonds, is on the increase. As a consequence of the unexpectedly sharp downturn in economic growth, the 1991 budget shows a deficit for the first time in three years and, for 1992, a larger deficit is forecast. With public net borrowing increasing, the majority of new issues are likely to come from the government sector. The expected increase in new issuance volume will boost liquidity in the market.

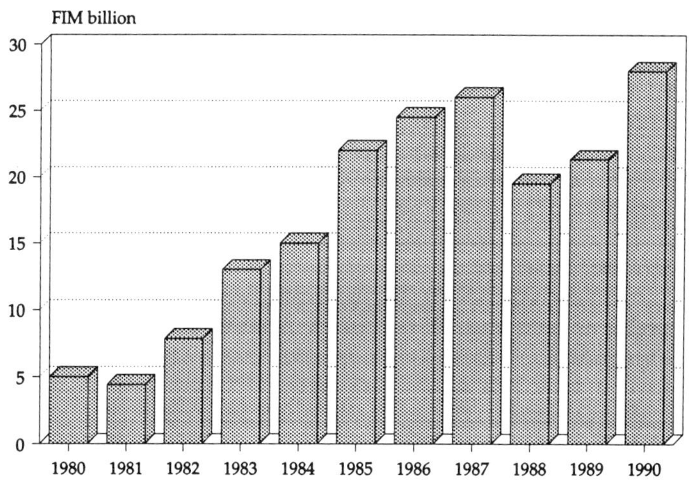

Figure 14.13 New issue volume of Finnish bonds (1980-1990)

14.9 *Market practices*

Trading practices

The majority of retail bond trading is conducted over the telephone and through banks. The role of the Helsinki Stock Exchange in bond trading is marginal. The most significant counterparties in both market-making and trading are the HELIBOR banks:

- Kansallis-Osake-Pankki
- Okobank
- Postipankki
- Skopbank
- Union Bank of Finland

Form

All domestic and euromarkka bonds are in bearer form.

Coupon payment

Generally, all markka bond coupons are paid annually. Some government retail bonds and international FM-denominated bonds are paid semi-annually, one example being the World Bank 10% -94 issue.

Redemption

Markka bonds redeem at par upon maturity. Redemptions on the old tax-exempt government bonds, and certain corporate issues, are made in equal instalments during the life of the bond. There are no put or call options in the Finnish bond market.

Denomination

Government serial bonds can be found in denominations of FM 1m and FM 5m, whilst housing bonds are in FM 10m denominations and retail bonds in FM 5000, 10,000 and 50,000 denominations. Other bonds are mostly in denominations of FM 10,000, FM 100,000 and FM 1m.

Dealing quotations

Dealing quotations are on a yield-per-annum basis. Government bonds are quoted on the interbank market with bid/offer spreads of 10 basis points (in yield). All other bonds are quoted between 10 and 50 basis points. Quotations are made either for bonds issued, or guaranteed by, one of the five HELIBOR banks, or for bonds which are issued, or guaranteed by, local government. Quotations are usually for amounts of FM 10m at a time.

Legislation

The legal regulations concerning issuance of bonds have been defined in the *Act of Bonds, Debentures and other Note Issues*. The *Securities Market Act* that came into force in August 1989, applies to the public issuance, marketing and exchange of securities.

The supervisory authority in Finland is the Banking Supervision Office which is responsible to the Ministry of Finance.

14.10 Settlement

It should be noted that all Finnish government bonds can be settled either domestically, or through Euroclear. The domestic settlement requires a custodian account in one of the Finnish banks. Following a transaction, bonds are transferred either between accounts within a custodian bank, or between banks if buyer and seller have accounts with different custodians.

The Finnish system for handling securities transactions is still based on physical certificates which, following transactions, are transferred from seller to buyer. To rationalize the processing of securities, a book-entry system is being gradually introduced over 1991/2 with the aim of replacing physical securities with computerized entries in securities accounts.

Euromarkka bonds are cleared by Euroclear or Cedel. For trades with foreign counterparties, the settlement period is normally five banking days. Trading with Finnish counterparties, however, requires two banking days.

14.11 *Yield calculation*

ISMA rules are followed in yield calculations. All counterparties use the ISMA general redemption formula:

$$P = \sum_{i=1}^{n} CFi \times vLi$$

where,

P	gross price (i.e. clean price plus accrued interest)
n	number of future cashflows
CFi	ith cashflow
Li	time in years to the ith cashflow
v	annualized discounting factor i.e. if the annualized yield is y then $v=1/(1+y)$ (y=0.08 for a yield 8%)

The coupon is paid annually and accrued interest is calculated on a 30/360 basis from, and including, the date on which the last interest coupon is paid up to, but excluding the settlement date of the transaction.

14.12 *Taxation*

Domestic investors

Income and withholding tax

Finnish residents are liable to income or withholding tax on capital gains and interest receipts. From the beginning of 1992, the prevailing rate of withholding tax on interest from deposits and bonds is, for individuals, 15 per cent.

Corporations are taxed at their normal rate of income tax. In Finland, bonds are not subject to stamp duty.

Capital gains tax

In Finland, the amount of capital gains tax is dependent upon the period of ownership of a security. If the security has been held for less than 5 years, the capital gain is taxed at the marginal rate whilst, if the period exceeds five years, the securities are tax-exempt.

Overseas investors

Withholding tax

Foreign investors are exempt from withholding tax on any interest income received from holding Finnish bonds. Also, they are not subject to any Finnish income or wealth tax related to coupon payments or capital gains incurred through the sale of markka bonds. The same applies to Finnish stamp duty, turnover tax and any other similar tax payable in connection with transactions in markka bonds.

14.13 Money markets

The development and liberalization of the financial markets has led to a rapid emergence of short-term financing which, in turn, has led to an equally rapid development of the money market. In 1980, money market instruments covered only 1 per cent of the total turnover in the financial markets but, by 1990, their share had grown to 25 per cent.

Markka certificates of deposit (CD), commercial paper (CP) and Treasury bills are all non-interest-bearing, negotiable, promissory notes which are issued at a discount to their face value. Their issue price is calculated as follows:

$$P = \frac{N}{1 + \frac{r}{100} \times \frac{t}{365}}$$

where,

P	present value
N	nominal amount
r	discount-to-yield rate (%)
t	actual days (365/365)

CDs, issued by commercial banks and the Bank of Finland, are the most liquid instruments in the Finnish money market. The CD market is also the basis of HELIBOR (Helsinki interbank offered rate).

Together with CDs, the CP market has expanded during the last couple of years and, at present, they provide a fairly liquid market for investors. Along with bonds, these instruments can also be traded on a repo basis. Following the expansion of these markets, trading in derivative instruments (e.g. interest rate options, caps and floors, forward rate agreements and swaps) has emerged.

The maturity of money market instruments varies from 1 month to 5 years. However, CDs, CPs and Treasury bills are seldom issued for periods longer than 12 months, while the average maturity for new issues is approximately 3 months.

CDs are issued in denominations of FM 1,000,000 - a figure which also represents the minimum investment amount.

14.14 *Interest rate history*

The most important money market interest rate in Finland is the 3-month market rate (HELIBOR). At the beginning of 1990, this rate stood at 16 per cent. During the first half of that year, though, a decline of 350 basis points was witnessed. This was mainly attributable to the improved liquidity of the money markets, but was also partly due to the background of the convertible foreign exchange reserves of Finland.

During the autumn of 1990, however, money rates started to rise again, and

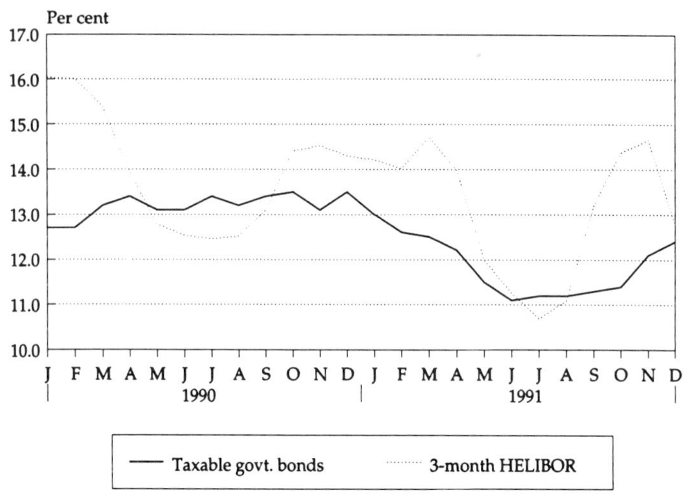

Figure 14.14 Three-month HELIBOR/taxable government bonds

the 3-month HELIBOR peaked at 16 per cent in the beginning of March 1991, at the time of the Parliamentary elections. Later, the rate started to drop gradually, reaching 11 per cent in June, as the markka became linked to the Ecu.

During the summer, the rate started to rise again, as speculation mounted against the markka. In November, during which month the markka was devalued, the rate again stood at 16 per cent. After devaluation, however, it again fell and closed the year at a level of 12.5 per cent.

In Finland, the yield on taxable 4- to 5-year government bonds is the most appropriate statistical indicator of long-term interest rates. The yield on taxable government bonds is quoted as of November 1987.

From 1988, until the beginning of 1991, the yield of taxable issues rose - in line with the development of other European bond markets. In the first quarter of 1991, long-term interest rates started to fall. This was partly due to the sharp downturn in economic growth and a substantial fall in the rate of inflation. However, it was also partly due to speculation over the linkage of the markka to the Ecu, an event which, as noted earlier, actually took place in June 1991.

14.15 Sources of reference

General financial publications

- *Finnish Bond Issues* by the Bank of Finland. A list of new markka bond issues. Published annually.
- *Bank of Finland Bulletin* (including the 1991 special issue, *Financial Markets in Finland*). 11 issues per year. The publication includes special articles on current issues, as well as statistics and charts. Special issues are published as required.
- *How to Trade in Finland,* by the Finnish Foundation for Share Promotion. An annual guide to the Finnish securities market.

Publications by the banks

Kansallis Banking Group

- *Economic Outlook.* A monthly guide to the Finnish money and bond markets.
- *Economic Review.* Published twice a year, it includes the economic outlook and future prospects for the Finnish economy.
- *FIM Interest Rates.* 1 to 2 issues per month
- *Finland's Money Market.* A general presentation on the money and bond markets

Postipankki

- *Bond Letter.* A fortnightly newsletter dealing with the current state of the Finnish bond market
- *Economic Outlook.* A quarterly publication intended to give a brief outlook on current economic trends and state of the market.

Union Bank of Finland

- *Finnish Markka Fixed Income Markets.* A general guide to the Finnish bond market, information on market conditions, instruments, market volumes, etc. Updated annually.

Säästöpankkien Keskusosuuspankki SKOP

- *SKOPBANK Focus.* Provides current information on Finnish equity and bond markets. 3-4 issues per year

- *The Finnish Economy and Financial Market.* A monthly publication which deals with the Finnish financial market.

Quote vendors & news agencies

Information on the Finnish markets is provided by:

- Datastream
- Startel Inc.
- Reuters
- Telerate

Appendix

Finnish markka-denominated bullet bonds issued by the Republic of Finland

	Coupon (%)	Maturity	Issued amount (FIM million)
Finland 1 (1988)	9 3/4	16 February 1993	500
Finland 2 (1988)	10.10	20 April 1993	500
Tap issues			
Finland 1 (1989)	11 1/4	15 December 1993	1200
Finland 2 (1989)	11.40	15 September 1994	330
Finland 1 (1990)	13.00	15 March 1994	1173
Finland 2 (1990)	12 3/4	15 September 1994	847
Finland 1 (1991)	12 1/2	15 January 1996	1500
Finland 2 (1991)	11 3/4	15 March 1996	1800
Finland 3 (1991)	11.00	15 June 1995	2460 (3500)
Finland 1 (1992)	11.00	15 January 1999	1377 (4000)
Housing bonds			
Housing Bond 1 (1990)	12 1/2	15 September 2000	1250
Housing Bond 1 (1991	11.00	15 March 2001	1000
Housing Bond 2 (1991)	10 1/2	15 June 2001	1673 (2015)
Housing Bond 3 (1991)	10.80	16 September 1996	300
Retail issues			
Finland 1 (1990)	13.00	21 May 1993	200
Finland 2 (1990)	12.80	13 August 1993	270
Finland 3 (1990)	12.80	17 September 1993	150
Finland 4 (1990)	12.90	15 October 1993	215
Finland 5 (1990)	13.00	19 November 1993	165
Finland 6 (1990)	13.00	10 December 1993	500
Finland 1 (1991)	13.00	02 January 1994	500
Finland 2 (1991)	12.25	04 March 1994	500
Finland 3 (1991)	11.50	06 May 1994	475
Finland 4 (1991)	10.80	12 August 1994	560
Finland 5 (1991)	10.80	14 October 1994	205
Finland 6 (1991)	11.00	18 November 1994	100
Finland 1 (1992)	11.50	07 January 1995	270
Finland 2 (1992)	11.50	27 January 1995	195

Finnish Markka-denominated bullet bonds issued by the Republic of Finland in 1991 & 1992 (to time of writing)

1991		
	Tap issues	FIM 5,760,000,000
	Retail issues	FIM 2,340,000,000
	Housing bonds	FIM 2,973,000,000
	Total	FIM 11,073,000,000
1992		
	Tap issues	FIM 1,377,000,000
	Retail issues	FIM 465,000,000
	Housing bonds	
	Total	FIM 1,842,000,000
	Total outstanding amount	FIM 19,023,000,000

Chapter

15

The bond markets of

France

Philippe Willemetz & Richard Komarnicki
Consultants
(Co-ordinators)

Arnaud Clement-Grancourt
BNP

Marie-Pierre Gontard
Cardif

Agnès Peltier
La Mondiale

Virginie Chapron du Jeu & Philippe Laurendeau
CDC

Jean Granoux
CNCA

Note: In general text, the abbreviation 'FFr' is used to denote the French franc. Elsewhere, the international mnemonic 'FRF' is used.

15.1 Introduction

The French financial markets can be traced back to Napoleonic times when, as in other European markets, business was monopolized by broker-dealers (*officiers ministériels*) who were appointed by the Minister of Finance . However, the last ten years have seen many changes throughout Europe, and the French financial markets have undergone a significant transformation.

The modernization of the French markets was initiated by the government through its *Dautresme Report,* which paved the way for a radical shake-up of the financial sector.

Modernization of the markets

When taking an overview of the events of the last decade, three milestones can be identified: In 1982, the tax on bond transactions in the stock exchange was abolished. Four years later, in 1986, the French Treasury began a regular auction plan for Treasury bills and bonds, with the first Treasury swap auction being done in 1987. A futures market opened on 20 February 1986 and met with swift success - the significant volatility of 1986-87 helping to lift volumes to a level of 50-100 thousand contracts per day, a level which has been maintained since the fourth quarter of 1987.

Equity market

The equity market witnessed a number of changes during the 1980s. From January 1988, the stockbrokers' monopoly (*les Charges d'Agent de Change*) was gradually abolished, as banks and insurance companies were permitted to purchase capital in the stockbrokers' firms, now called *sociétés de bourse.*

The *sociétés de bourse* are subject to regulations set by the Conseil des Bourses de Valeurs (CBV) and, specifically for their activity on the futures and options market, by the Conseil du Marché à Terme (CMT). These regulations, and the general activities of the *société de bourse,* are controlled by La Société des Bourses Française (SBF). The SBF also participates with the CBV in the preparation of new legislation. The Association Française des Sociétés de Bourse (AFSB) is the association of the *sociétés de bourse* and the SBF, and functions to represent them collectively, to defend their common interests, and to resolve problems between *sociétés de bourse* and the SBF

The COB (Commission des Opérations de Bourse) is the watchdog of the market, with a set-up similar to that of the Securities and Exchange Commission (SEC) in the United States.

In addition to the organizational changes, the equity market, itself, witnessed several new developments:

- equity savings accounts (CEA[1]) replaced 'Monory' accounts (tax-saving investments);
- capital development increased and capital risk funds were introduced;
- equity warrants, participating stocks, preference shares without voting rights, and investment certificates were all created.

Money market

The French money market has been reorganized to interconnect with the bond market.

- the tax on term deposits was increased in 1982;
- certificates of deposit (CDs) were announced in 1984: French franc CDs, foreign currency CDs, and commercial paper (CP), all appeared on the market in 1985;
- a repo market was inaugurated with the *pension livrée,* in 1989;
- Matif[2] introduced futures, and options on futures, on PIBOR (Paris interbank offered rate).

French institutions were no longer admitted on the interbank money market, and so the markets for both CDs and CP were given a boost as, too, was the general demand for money market funds.

Stock exchange

Stock exchange trading has also undergone a major transformation. Broker-dealer firms have been allowed to enlarge their capital base, although they have lost their Napoleonic monopoly of *officier ministériel.*

Computerization has replaced the open-outcry market for bonds and equities, with a screen-based 'telematic' market. Meanwhile, the CAC[3] system for day-long continuous trading has replaced the traditional fixing of prices for bonds. Additionally, a primary-dealer network for government bonds has been created.

[1] *Compte d'Epargne en Actions*

[2] *Marché A Terme International de France*

[3] *CAC, here, means Cotation Assistée en Continu*

In 1988, futures and options on equities were launched with two index contracts, CAC[4] 40 and OMF[5] 50. The latter failed to survive, but CAC 40 futures volume is steadily increasing, from 40-90,000 contracts (per month) in 1989, to 150-240,000 contracts, in 1991.

Bond markets

Like other sectors, the French bond market has also experienced both change and innovation. In 1988, mortgage-backed securities, to be held by special pass-through funds specifically created for them, were introduced. Also that year, the Cooke Ratio (which sets an 8% capital account/asset ratio for banks) was adopted. In 1989, mutual funds were authorized to capitalize their coupons. Also in 1989, the maximum tax on bonds and money market instruments was reduced to 15 per cent.

In 1990, Matif introduced a long-term Ecu bond futures contract, as well as a euro-Dm three-month contract. Meanwhile, the Treasury issued both a 30-year French franc bond and an Ecu bond. In 1991, a 30-year Ecu bond issue was launched with great success.

On the regulatory side, compliance codes have been established (with ASSFI[6], COB, and Commission de Déontologie Financière, being the main bodies).

Although the modernization of the bond market is described separately here, it is, of course, necessary to view it in conjunction with the changes seen in both the money market and equities market, particularly with the emerging importance of funds with guaranteed returns and the mixing of bonds, swaps and equity market index options. As new products are continually being introduced (such as two-year options on the CAC 40, which have been quoted since the 4th quarter of 1991), the ever-present demand for low-risk financial instruments is leading to greater sophistication, particularly in the development of hybrids.

Modernization of clearing and settlement

On the administrative side, modern delivery-against-payment systems are now available in Paris for the bond market, the money market and the stock market.

Since 1988, the Saturne system - managed by Bank of France - has handled Treasury bills and all short-term instruments with the delivery-against-payment

[4] *CAC, here, means Compagnie des Agents de Change*

[5] *Organisation des Marchés Financiers*

[6] *Association des Sociétés Financières*

system. All such transactions, repos, loans and borrowed short-term instruments, are included in this system.

As of June 1989, French franc CDs have been included in the Saturne system, while CDs denominated in foreign currencies will be included in the near future. Several clearing sessions a day, allow for money market participants both to trade and clear until late on the same day. The system can manage 6000 operations for more than FFr 1bn, the sort of figure seen on Bank of France auctions days.

In June 1990, the RELIT[7] delivery system began operations on all stocks deposited at SICOVAM[8]. Since October 1990, inter-broker and inter-dealer operations, as well as the transactions of all primary dealers, jobbers and brokers, are managed by this system.

RELIT features guaranteed delivery against payment, which is done at T+5 working days. Delivery can be done on T+2 to T+5. This system, which handles transactions on the primary market, grey market and secondary market, as well as repos, currently manages an average of 110,000 transactions a day. As far as French domestic clearing is concerned, RELIT is now on an equal footing with Euroclear and Cedel.

DTC in New York, JSCC in Tokyo, CDS in Toronto and MSTC in Chicago all have a depository service activity on their domestic market. In Paris, RELIT is also a depository service which allows for the possible adjustment of global transaction and delivery preparation. For a long time, however, SICOVAM in Paris, has managed all depository positions, and this now includes the positions of RELIT participants (whose cash accounts, incidentally, are all managed by the Bank of France). SICOVAM was created by a Decree of 4 August 1949 and became, by a law of 3 November 1984, the compulsory depository of depositories. This central stock bank keeps account of stocks which can no longer be physically materialized in France. To circulate French stocks outside France, SICOVAM issues certificates.

[7] *Règlement-Livraison de Titres*

[8] *Société Interprofessionelle de Compensation de Valeurs Mobilières (clearing house and depository)*

15.2 Economics

GNP/GDP

Cyclical forces are currently in operation. The economies of most OECD countries slowed down in 1990. After a period of steady growth in 1988-9, the French economy also slowed (see Figures 15.2 & 15.3), partly as a result of the Gulf War. Foreign demand, which had been good in 1989, also showed signs of weakness the following year but, against the world-wide trend, it showed renewed strength in 1991, a fact which can be directly attributed to heavy demand from Germany. On the domestic front, however, the growth in demand for industrial products decelerated in 1990 and actually went down in 1991. This fact was reflected by the figure for the utilization of industrial capacity which decreased in 1990, although it stabilized at 83 per cent at the end of 1991. Further evidence of the cyclical downturn was provided by industrial forecast and order-book figures, which both peaked in 1989 and then declined, a factor which contributed to a reduction in corporate investment, particularly in the services

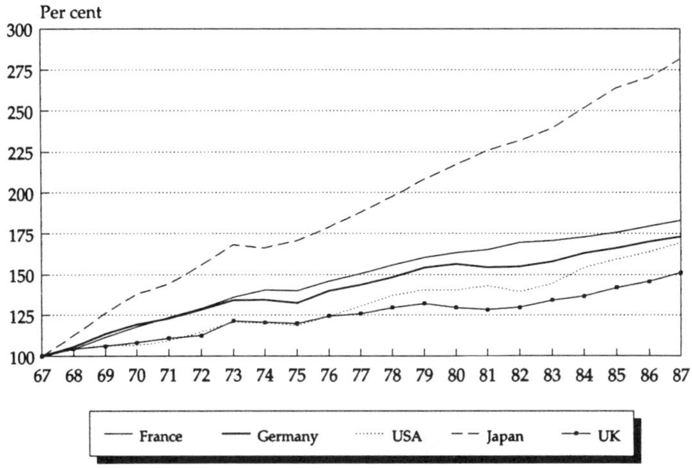

Figure 15.1 GNP at constant prices, 1967-1987
Sources: OECD, INSEE, Survey of Current Business, CSO, Statistiches Bandesamt

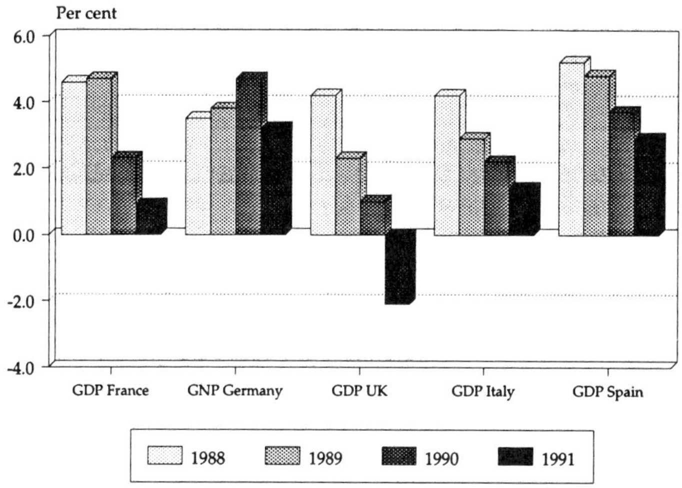

Figure 15.2 Growth in real GDP/GNP in selected European countries, 1988-1991
Source: Banque de France

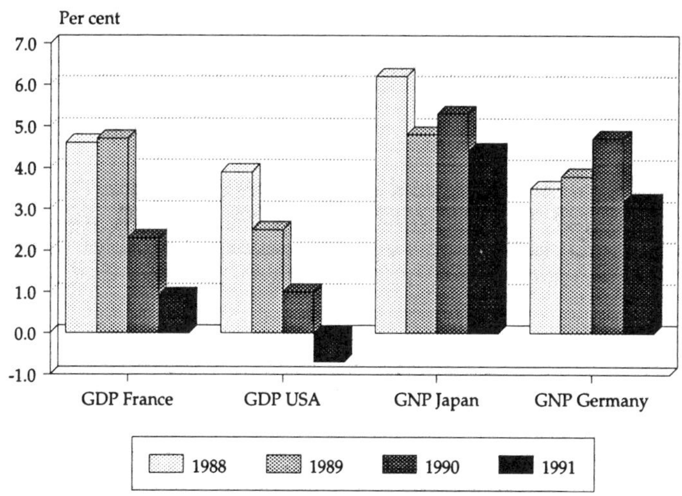

Figure 15.3 Growth in real GDP/GNP in France, USA, Japan & Germany, 1988-1991
Source: Banque de France

and building sectors. Public sector spending remained rather brisk despite the fact that the budget seemed under control. Currently, however, government investment is decelerating with the growth in spending being mainly attributable to an increase in both retirement and unemployment benefits. Nevertheless, despite the downturn, overall industrial investment remains rather healthy.

Trade balance

The French trade balance has generally shown deterioration since 1986, largely as a result of insufficient investment and competitiveness. However, an investment drive, coupled with a slowdown in domestic demand, have together turned this trend around in 1991 (see Figure 15.4); French industry managed to cut its trade deficit by half, although this performance was in contrast to the agricultural trade balance, which showed a reduction in surplus. Industrial exporters were able to improve their market share because the Italian lira was overvalued and the German market was still healthy, a fact reflected especially in its demand for automotive products. Meanwhile, French industrial imports have weakened in line with a weakening in domestic demand.

Being its biggest trading partner, France has benefited from Germany's health. There is a natural concern, therefore, that any future weakening of the German economy is likely to have a direct impact on France's trade balance.

Unemployment

For many countries (USA, Canada, UK, Australia etc.), unemployment bottomed at the end of 1990. Cyclical forces are certainly stronger in these countries, but France is not immune. Unemployment in France trended down during 1987-90 (see Figure 15.5). During this period, some 700,000 jobs were created but unemployment figures were only down by 300,000. Youth unemployment - which peaked at 25 per cent in 1984 - has been reduced, but has been replaced by a greater proportion of unemployed mature workers (40-50 years old) who have great difficulty in finding fresh employment. The number of long-term (over 1 year) unemployed has passed the 1m mark.

Industrial employment increased in 1989 and 1990 but, as forecasts became rapidly gloomier towards the end of the period, this trend was soon reversed. Overall unemployment surged in 1991 and, by the end of the annum, it reached its highest level for three years. By contrast, the cyclical move is late in Germany, where the high level of activity associated with unification has helped its economy.

The French economy needs an annual 2 per cent growth in GDP to achieve a downtrend in unemployment. The annual population growth of 0.5 per cent in France is much higher than that of Germany, which is minimal even with immigration now running at 0.5 per cent (the growth of the indigenous population is

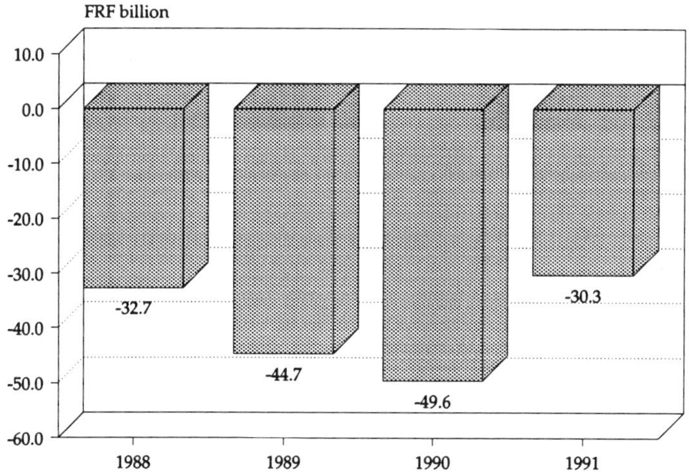

Figure 15.4 French trade balance, 1988-1991

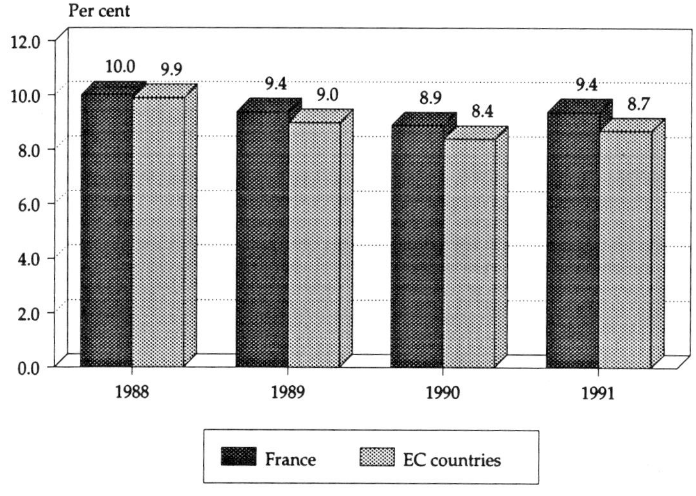

Figure 15.5 Unemployment, 1988-1991

actually decreasing). The current rate of unemployment in Germany is less than half that of France.

Inflation

The French consumer price index has been on a horizontal trend for more than four years (see Figures 15.6 & 15.7). In fact, excluding food and energy, the inflation rate was trending downward until early 1990. The implicit GDP deflator has been stable between 2.7 per cent and 3 per cent a year, for both 1990 and 1991 and OECD forecasts for 1992 and 1993 keep this range unchanged. During the first half of 1990 prices were held in check by European competition. However, the second half of that year saw the moderate impact of the rise in the price of oil following the Gulf War.

Since the German and French economies are linked by mutual trade, it is interesting to note that service sector prices are rising slower in France than in Germany. Prior to 1985, wage cost increases were lower in France than in Germany, but now the reverse is true, so that the inflation spread simply disappeared at the end of 1991. The inflation rates of 3.1 per cent in France and 4.1 per cent in Germany at the end of 1991 are partially due to effects of changes in German taxation.

The overall inflation picture for 1991-1992 (in the USA, UK and Japan) is one of decelerating inflation. Wage agreements in French civil service of 2.0 per cent (1991), 2.7 per cent (1992) and 1.8 per cent (1993) imply a 6.5 per cent increase for a two-year settlement. The German civil service union will no doubt see this as the lowest acceptable for one year.

In general, France's anti-inflation efforts will continue to be constrained by both German monetary policy and the European monetary system.

On the subject of inflation, it is particularly important to note the components of the CPI index, as well as their evolution, as shown in Figures 15.8 & 15.9.

Monetary policy

Recently, the policy of the French finance minister, Pierre Bérégovoy, is for a strong franc in order that France should follow a disinflationary path. The reward should be lower interest rates but, in the autumn of 1991, when short-term interest rates were pushed lower than German short-term interest rates, the French franc exchange rate became a problem, so that the spread to German rates had to be swiftly reversed.

The new Bank of France money supply benchmark, M3, had a slower growth in 1991 (see Figure 15.10), below the lower target limit of 5 per cent, based on 4th quarter of 1990. As funds were transferred by households from saving accounts to special retirement accounts (PEP[9]), they left M3.

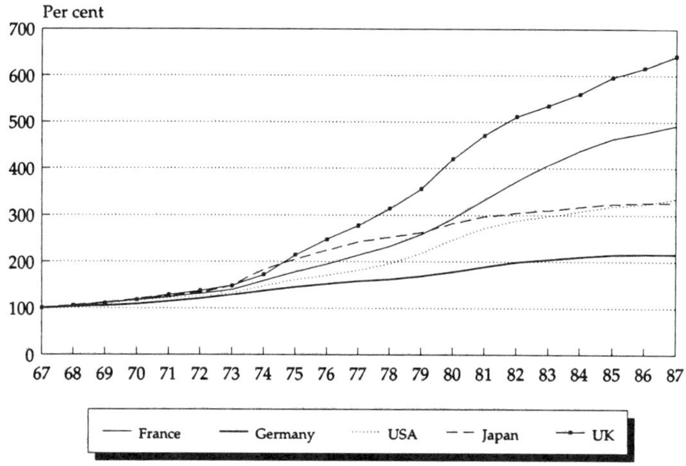

Figure 15.6 Increase in CPI, 1967-1987
Sources: OECD, INSEE, Survey of Current Business, CSO, Statistiches Bandesamt

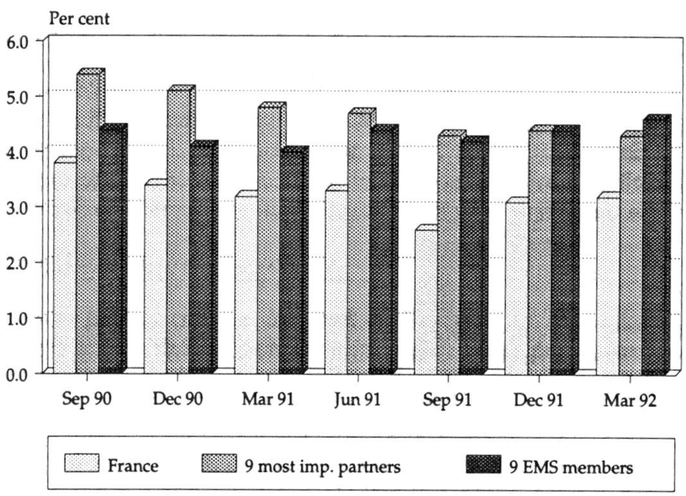

Figure 15.7 Quarterly CPI figures, Sep 1990 - Mar 1992 (per cent, year-on-year)
Source: Banque de France

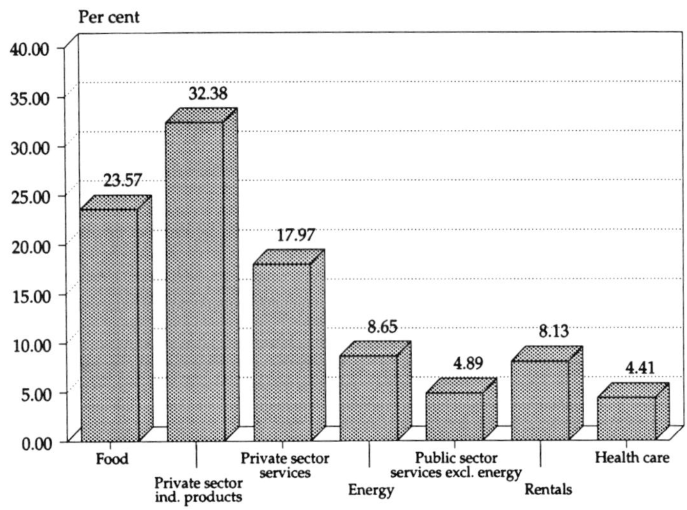

Figure 15.8 **Composition of the French CPI index (per cent, weighted)**
Source: INSEE

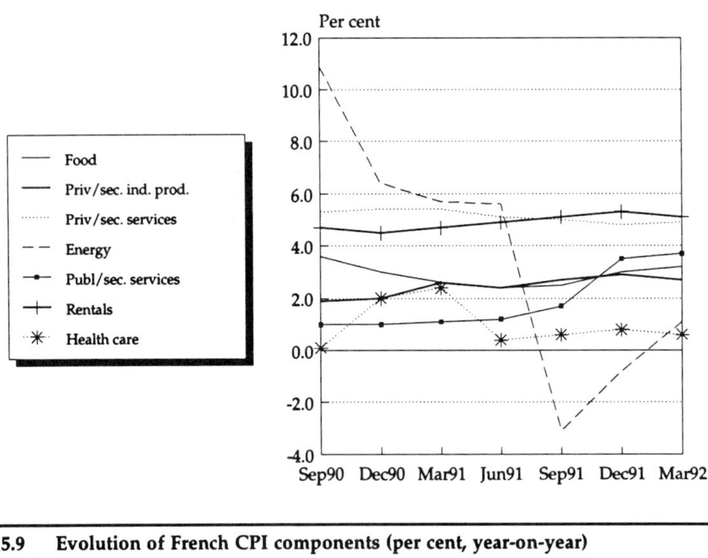

Figure 15.9 **Evolution of French CPI components (per cent, year-on-year)**
Source: INSEE

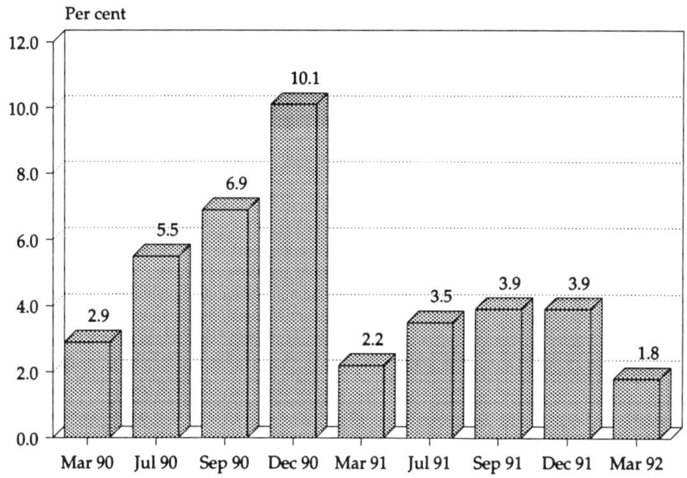

Figure 15.10 Growth of French M3 money supply (per cent, against end of previous year)
Source: Banque de France

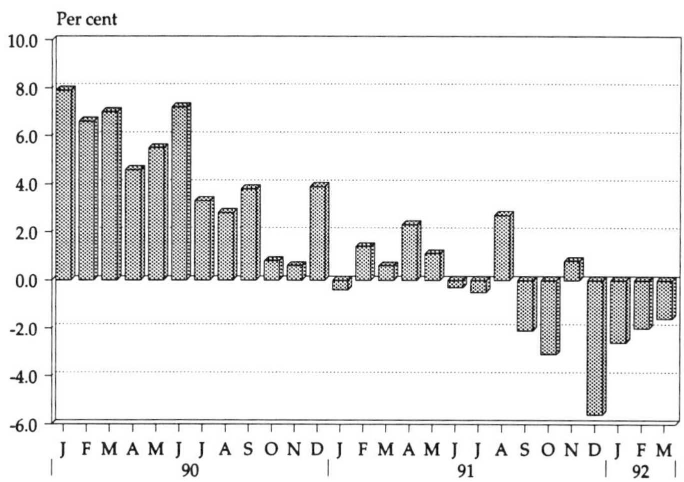

Figure 15.11 Evolution of French M1 money supply, Jan 1990 - Mar 1992 (per cent, year-on-year)
Source: Banque de France

The deceleration in growth of money market funds was also a factor in the deceleration in growth of M3. Bank credit for the economy is decelerating, too, due to the weakness of the domestic economy. As a result, M1 (see Figure 15.11) and M2 aggregates figures were both down in 1991.

Public sector deficit

The French public sector deficit was contained below the 1988 level, in both 1989 and 1990 (see Figure 15.12). In 1991, a weak economy meant a weakening of tax revenues. The government attempted to cut spending, but was politically hampered by regional elections. Social security provision continues to account for a major part of public expenditure, and there is little hope of a reduction in the near future.

Public debt increased from 15 per cent to 27 per cent of GNP during the eighties. High real interest rates have to be compared to GNP growth to foresee spiraling effect. When a primary public deficit surplus is needed, it means that a contra-cyclical policy is no longer possible.

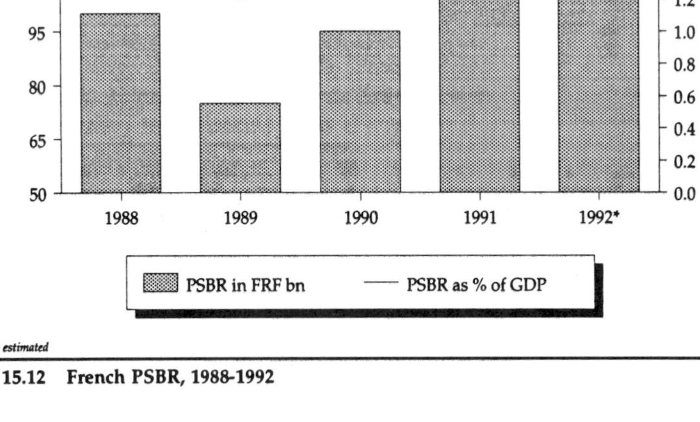

Figure 15.12 French PSBR, 1988-1992

Exchange rate history

The French franc was devalued by 3 per cent in 1981, by 5.75% in 1982 and by 2.5 per cent in 1983. This was followed, in 1985, by a revaluation of 2 per cent, although 1986 saw a further devaluation, of 3.0 per cent. For some time, the French franc has remained stable at the bottom end of the European monetary system, with the lowest possible short-term interest rates being used to maintain this position. A comparison of purchasing power between the franc and the Deutschemark shows that, with the exception of 1990, the Deutschemark has been over-valued.

The exchange rate to US dollar is largely dependent upon the EMS. Prior to February 1985, the dollar was particularly strong but, since then, it has declined. In 1990 the lowest rate seen was FFr 5.07 whilst, in 1991, the lowest point was FFr 5.40.

Politics

Between 1981 and 1983, the Mauroy government had to cope with disequilibrium problems with the result that, following the devaluation of 1983, a policy of austerity has been closely followed. Compulsory state borrowing and special tax increases both helped to limit the budget deficit to 3 per cent of GNP, while monetary aggregate growth goals were reduced from 10 per cent to 9 per cent. The subsequent Fabius, Rocard and Cresson administrations have all kept to tight monetary and budgetary aims, so that the disinflation process has necessarily led to a convergence to the German inflation rate. This has been reflected in the fact that the interest rate spread *vis-à-vis* Germany went down continuously for ten years.

As finance minister, Delors was able to erase wage indexation and, when Bérégovoy succeeded him, a strong franc policy was doggedly pursued, with the net result that foreign investors became confident in the belief that the previous vagaries of monetary policy would not return.

15.3 *Market composition*

Composition of market by maturity

Government bonds

The amount of long-term fixed-rate government bonds outstanding has almost doubled in the last four years. This increase is mainly seen in the 15- to 30-year range, while there has been little growth in the 8- to 12-year sector (see Figure 15.13). The cause of this difference has been the issuance of 15- and 30-year bonds from 1989 onwards - a policy which has increased the average maturity of French government debt to over 7 years.

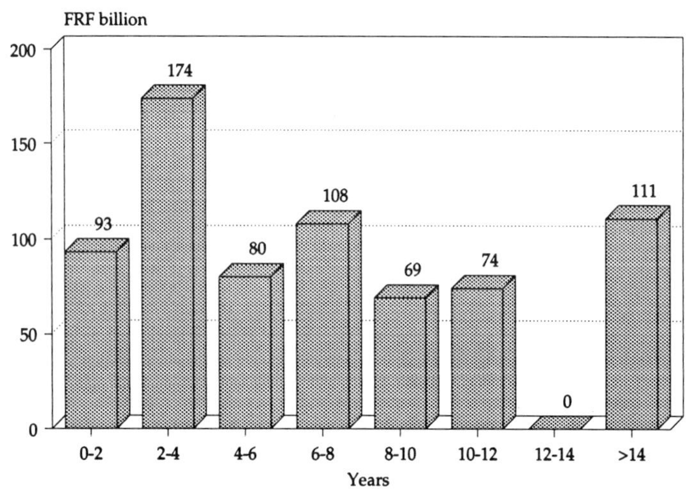

Figure 15.13 Maturity structure of the government bond market

Government-guaranteed bonds

The average remaining life of fixed-rate guaranteed bonds is shorter than for government bonds, with only FFr 20bn outstanding over ten years. Currently, the government only gives its guarantee to four public issuers, which are

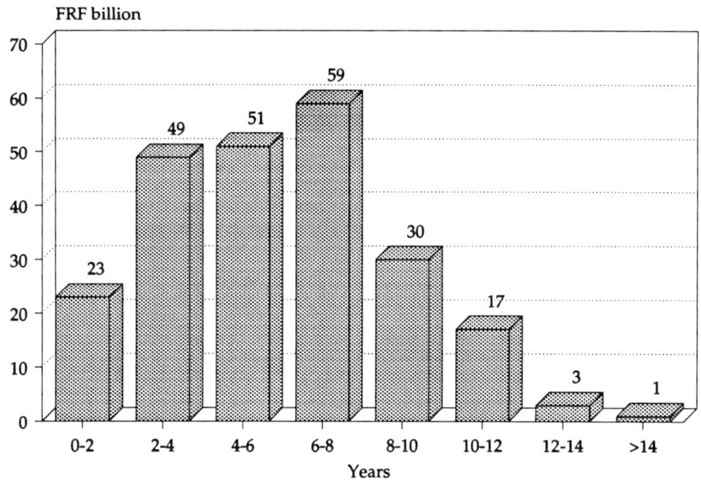

Figure 15.14 Maturity structure of the government-guaranteed bond market

owned by the state. The bulk of the issues outstanding in this category are medium-term fixed-rate (see Figure 15.14).

Public sector bonds

The outstanding amount of public sector bonds with remaining lives equal to, or longer than, ten years, has fallen by half compared to four years ago (see Figure 15.15).

Corporate bonds

The outstanding amount of fixed-rate corporate bonds with remaining lives greater than 8 years has, like that of the public bond sector, also been reduced (see Figure 15.16).

Composition of market by coupon

Government bonds

Most government bonds have coupons of between 8 per cent and 10 per cent (see Figure 15.17). This is very different from the pattern seen ten years ago, and

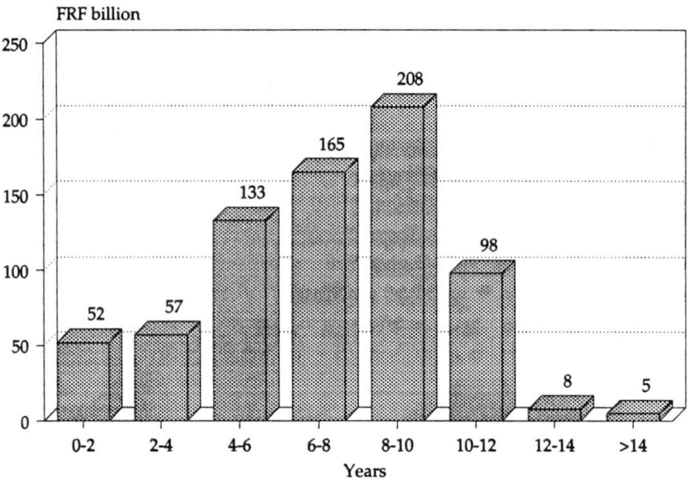

Figure 15.15 Maturity structure of the public bond market

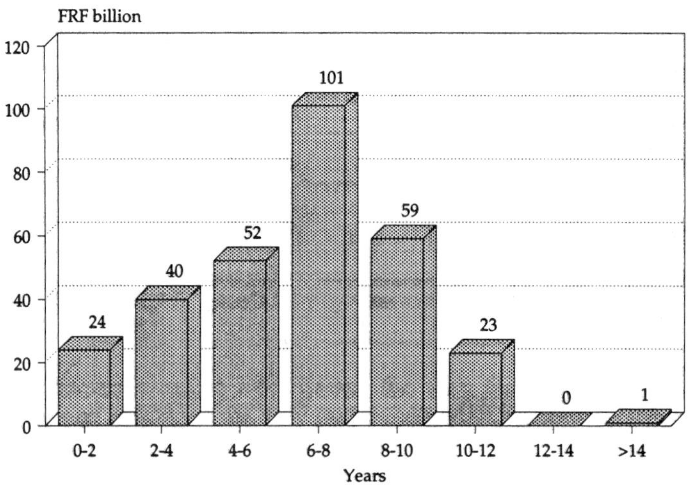

Figure 15.16 Maturity structure of the corporate bond market

reflects the fact that those *Emprunt d'Etat* state loan issues which preceded the large OAT bonds, are coming to the end of their lives; also, in recent years, interest rates (and therefore, coupons) have generally stayed in the 8-10 per cent range.

Guaranteed bonds

The volume of guaranteed fixed-rate bonds in the 10 to 14 per cent range reflects the rather large issues of the early 1980s. However, more than half the total outstanding amount in this sector have coupon rates between 8 and 10 per cent (see Figure 15.18).

Public sector bonds

Most of the outstanding amount is in the 8 to 10 per cent range. However, there is also a significant volume in the 10 to 12 per cent range (see Figure 15.19).

Corporate bonds

The coupon structure of the corporate sector is rather similar to that of the guaranteed bond sector, as indeed, it has been for some years (see Figure 15.20).

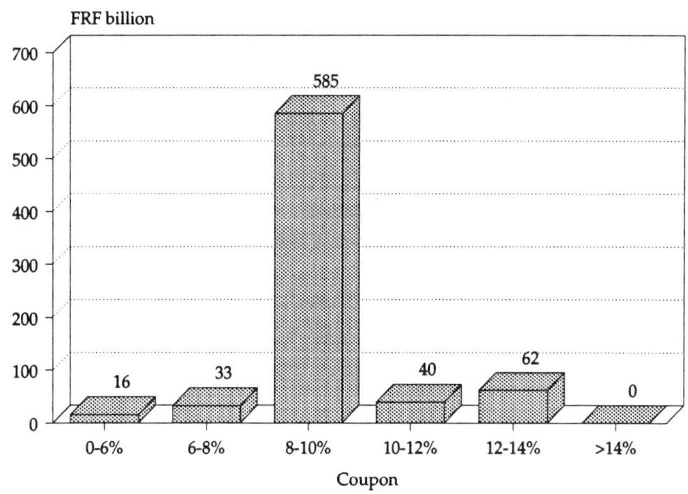

Figure 15.17 Coupon structure of the government bond market

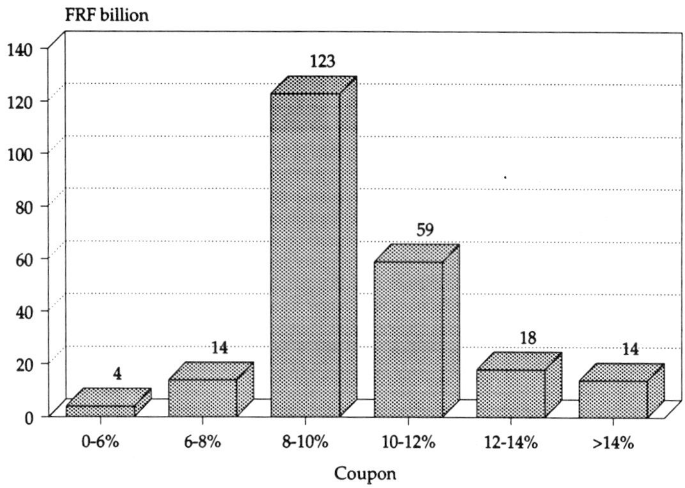

Figure 15.18 Coupon structure of the government-guaranteed bond market

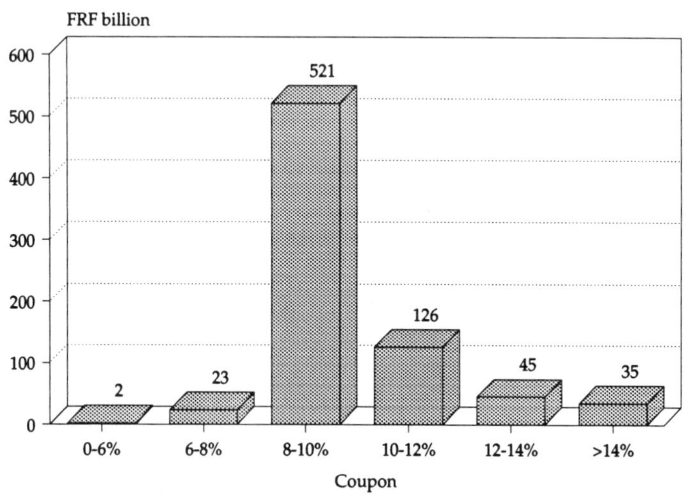

Figure 15.19 Coupon structure of the public sector bond market

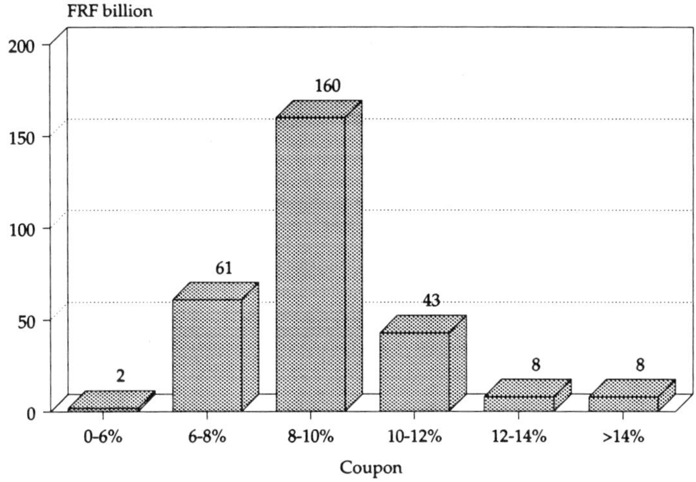

Figure 15.20 Coupon structure of the corporate bond market

15.4 Types of security

Government bond market

Before 1985, the principal long-term debt instrument of the French government was the syndicated state loan (*emprunt d'Etat*). Until that time, bond issues were irregular and handled by bank syndicates, a relatively uncompetitive method. Furthermore, the issues (see below) were numerous, small in size and highly dissimilar in their characteristics:

- Exchangeable bonds (*emprunts échangeables*) are fixed-rate bonds that can be exchanged for floating-rate bonds at a date set upon issue; there are eight bonds which are all bullet issues.

- Cum-warrant bonds (*emprunts à bons d'échange*) are fixed-rate bonds with detachable warrants that can be traded separately on the secondary market; the warrants are exercised for fixed- or floating-rate bonds. The warrants (11.5 million warrants are outstanding) entitle the holder to subscribe to a TRA December 1997, every year from December to February.

- Extendible bonds (*emprunts à fenêtre et prorogeables*) allow bearers to extend the maturity to a date of their choosing, under the conditions set at the time of issue. The extension 'window' is limited to two months per year.

- Renewable Treasury bonds (*obligations renouvelables du Trésor*, or ORTs) were issued in 1984 and 1985 with six-year maturities. These bonds can be exchanged for a comparable new issue with the coupon payable at maturity. There is only one issue outstanding.

- FELINS (*fonds d'Etat libres d'intérêt nominal*) are stripped fixed-rate bonds (and issued as such). Principal (*FELIN de capital*) and coupons (*FELIN d'intérêt*) are traded separately; FELINs have only been issued once and the amount outstanding is low.

- Index-linked bonds (*emprunts indexés*) are bonds with interest and/or capital that vary in accordance to a particular index. The last of its kind, the State bond 77/92 8.80 per cent, indexed to the Ecu, has just been repaid.

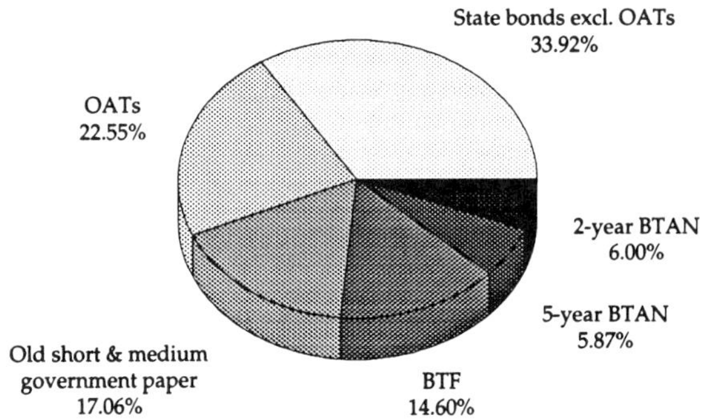

Figure 15.21 Breakdown of French government negotiable debt as at 31 December 1986

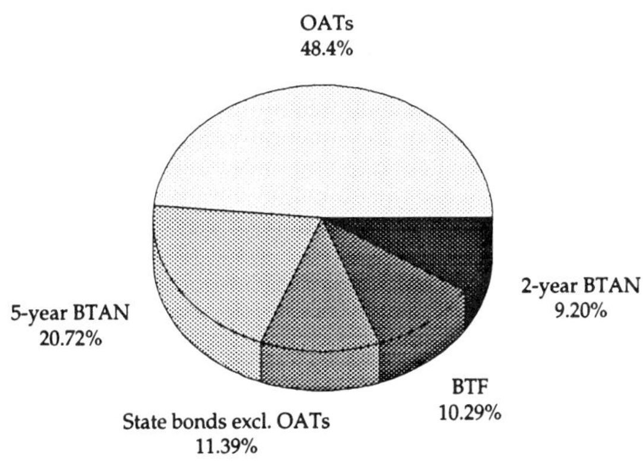

Figure 15.22 Breakdown of French government negotiable debt as at 31 December 1990

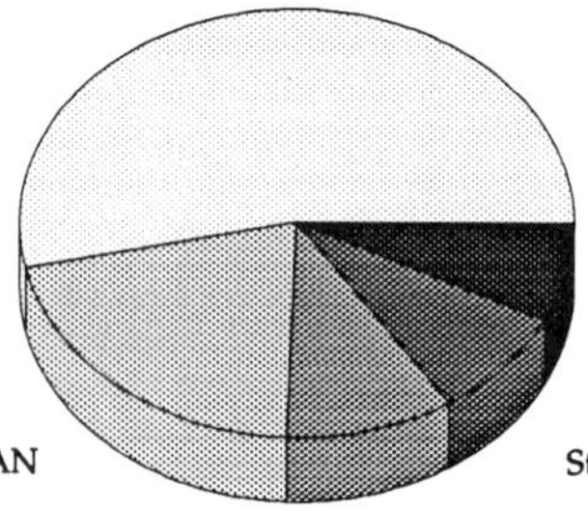

Figure 15.23 Breakdown of French government negotiable debt as at 31 December 1991

Fixed-rate OAT bonds (*obligations assimilables du Trésor*)

Fixed-rate OAT in French francs

Gradually, from 1985 onwards, the issuance policy of long-term bonds was concentrated on one new type of security, the OAT (*obligation assimilable du Trésor*), either in French francs or in Ecus (as of 1989). They are bullet issues and fungible, so the majority of OATs sold at auctions can be issued as tranches of existing issues. Their maturities range from 7 to 30 years and they represent the major portion of France's long-term debt. OATs are denominated in units of FFr 2000.

Fixed-rate OAT in Ecu

The French government was the first sovereign issuer to denominate a long-term issue in Ecus. In 1992, the Ministry of Finance again intends to issue 15 per cent of the government's borrowing requirement in Ecus (as it did in 1991).

Floating-rate OAT bonds

The Treasury also issues a small number of variable-rate bonds or bonds indexed to short-term references (TMB, TRB) and long-term references (TME, TRA):

■ TMB
TMB is based on the arithmetic mean of the average monthly yields on 13-week BTFs recorded during the year preceding payment of the coupon. This index is published by the Caisse des Dépôts et Consignations.

■ TRB
This reference is revised at each quarterly maturity according to the yield on the 13-week BTFs recorded during the auction preceding payment of the coupon.

■ TME
TME is the arithmetic mean of the average monthly yields on fixed-rate government bonds, with maturities of more than seven years, recorded during the year preceding payment of the coupon.

■ TRA
This is a reference rate that is revised in line with variations in the TME.

Stripped OATs

The French government was the first in Europe to approve the creation of a market in stripped bonds, patterned on the US market in Treasury strips. As at 31 December 1991, there was FFr 16.3bn nominal of OAT stripped from the OAT 8.5 per cent 10-2019.

BTANs

BTANs (*Bons du Trésor à taux annuel normalisé*) are fixed-rate Treasury notes with maturities of two and five years, at issue, and an annual coupon. The amount outstanding in BTANs totalled FFr 406bn at the end of 1990, and FFr 417.7bn in 1991. The number of lines has been gradually reduced to increase capitalization on the instruments. They are fungible.

BTFs

BTFs are also fungible, and some lines are in excess of FFr 10bn. Maturities are quarterly (13 weeks), half-yearly and annual. Occasionally, the Treasury issues 4- and 7-week bills, depending on its very short-term cash management requirements. Like BTANs, they are issued in units of FFr 1m nominal, but on a discount basis. Maturities are always set on a Thursday (or the following business day).

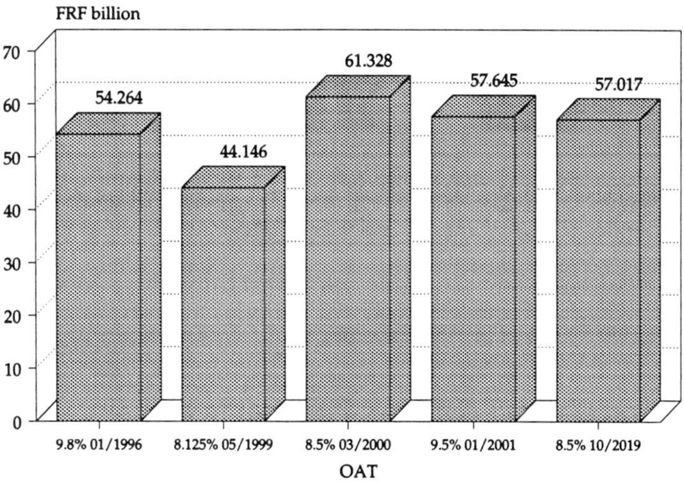

Figure 15.24 Selected fixed-rate OATs outstanding as at 31 December 1991

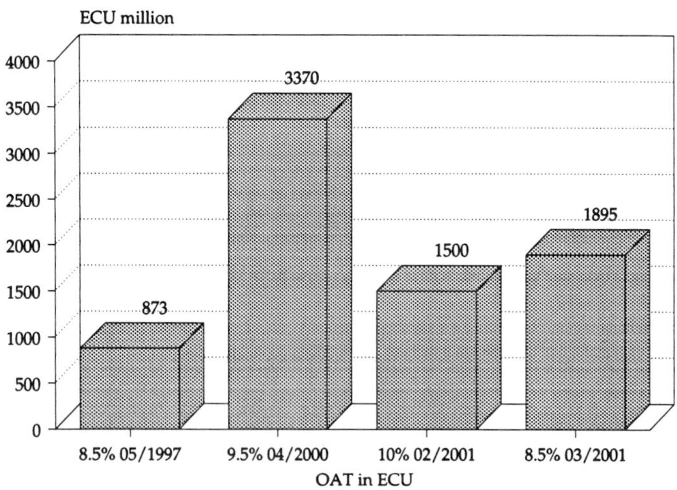

Figure 15.25 Selected fixed-rate OATs in Ecu outstanding as at 31 December 1991

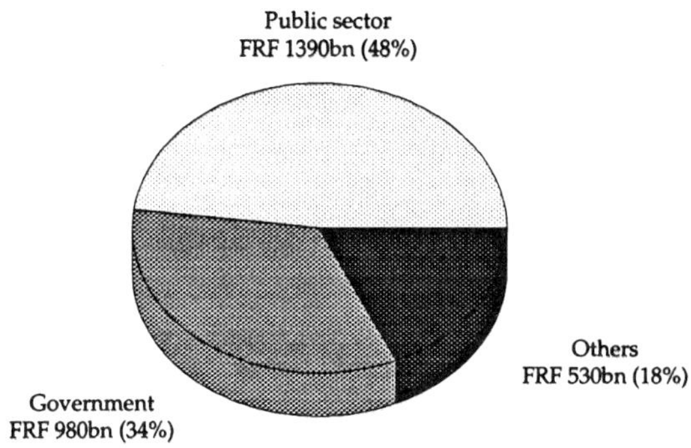

Figure 15.26 French bond market capitalization as at 31 December 1991

Domestic French franc bond issues

Apart from the Treasury, a large number of public and private companies regularly issue on the French bond market. The capitalization of the market in 1991 is shown in Figure 15.26, and described below.

Public issues

Some public sector issuers are backed by the government's guarantee. Examples include the Caisse Centrale de Cooperation Economique (CCCE), the Credit d'Equipement des Petites et Moyennes Entreprises (CEPME) and the issues of the Caisse de Refinancement Hypothécaire (CRH) which were issued before 1988. Some of the intermediaries maintain markets in these bonds as well as for issuers like SNCF, EDF, CFF and CLF. In some issues, blocks of up to FFr 100m can be exchanged. The healthy liquidity in these bonds is important. All the more so, as some fixed-rate issues are supplemented by new fungible stocks, thereby increasing the outstanding amount to levels of FFr 18bn, in some instances. Issuers now tend either to buy back the older, lower capitalized, issues, or propose exchanges for new fungible ones.

Bullet bonds

The most recent issues of public corporations are fixed-rate bullets.

Variable-rate

There are a number of different reference rates for these issues. Some of them (TMM, TMO) have been utilized since the early 1980s, but are less active now.

■ TMO
Indexed on the yield at which new issues are offered on the primary market.

■ TMM
Indexed on the monthly average of the overnight rate (linear, not capitalized).

■ TME
Indexed on the arithmetic mean of the average monthly yields of fixed-rate government bonds, with maturities of more than 7 years, recorded during the year preceding payment of the coupon.

■ TMB
Indexed on the arithmetic mean of the average monthly yields on 13-week BTFs recorded during the year preceding payment of the coupon. This index is published by the Caisse des Dépôts et Consignations.

■ TAM
Indexed on the annualized yield of the monthly averages of the overnight rate.

■ TRA
Emprunt à taux revisable annuel. Indexed on the current bond market, or the date of review, re-fixed annually.

■ TRO
Emprunt à taux révisable. Same as TRA, but re-fixed every three years.

■ P3M
Indexed on the average of 3-month PIBOR for the last three months.

■ P3R
Indexed on the spot 3-month PIBOR rate, as observed on the coupon re-fix date.

■ P1C
Indexed on the annualized yield of the monthly average, of the daily observations, of 1-month PIBOR.

Perpetual bonds

There are two types of perpetual bond:

■ TSDI (*Titres subordonnés à durée indéterminée*)
Subordinated perpetual bonds indexed on the TMO, or the TME.

■ TSIP (*Titres subordonnés à intérêt progressif*)
Subordinated perpetual bonds indexed on the TAM with a stepped-margin.

Both the above carry call features.

Zero-coupon securities

Some new zero-coupon issues were placed in 1991 (CEPME, Credit Lyonnais).

Subordinated bonds

Banks have issued many TSR (*Titres subordonnés remboursables*) bonds, which are all subordinated. In the event of a bank being wound up, they would be repaid after payments of deposits and unsubordinated bonds. They have a fixed maturity.

Puttable bonds

Only three issues have put features:

- EDF 9% Feb 1963-1964/1999
- EDF 7.75% (ex 16.7%) 65-71/01
- EDF 5.75% Feb 1966-76/06

They all have sinking funds.

Optional puttable and callable bonds (emprunts à fenêtres)

These bonds have both a call and put feature which can be exercised by the issuer and the bondholder on the 7th, 10th, and 14th year. This facility protects the holder against a rise in interest rates.

The BFCE 14 per cent Jan 1984 has such a feature - the call price is fixed, over par, while the holder can ask for redemption at par.

Callable bonds

There have been no call features on new public issues since 1987. The main callable issues are:

- BFCE 10% Feb 1986-99/01
- BFCE 7.90% July 1986-97/99
- EDF 10.10% Jan 1986-1998
- EDF 8% June 1986-01
- EDF 8.5% 87-99
- GDF 8% Dec 1986-1998
- SNCF 9.80% 86-01

Emprunts à BLK (Bons à lots kilométres - railway ticket vouchers)

Issued by the SNCF, these bonds bear a low nominal interest, but holders may 'win' (by lottery) railway ticket vouchers.

Titres participatifs (participating bonds)

These are close to 40 *titres participatifs* issued in the French bond market. Their characteristics are as follows:

- The coupon is equal to the sum of two variables:
  a) They are partly indexed on either a floating-rate reference, TMO or TAM, or a fixed-rate coupon. This part of the coupon resembles the minimum coupon on FRNs.
  b) The other part of the coupon is based on the year-on-year evolution of the issuer's financial results; it is either based, depending on the issue, on the evolution of net profits or turnover.
  The overall coupon is also capped against the TMO reference (120 to 130 per cent of TMO).

- They are perpetual bonds with call features. They will either be redeemed as the issue is refinanced or, in the case of a nationalized firm, if it goes public.

Corporate bonds

Bullet bonds

Most corporate bonds and ex-warrant bonds issued since 1987 are bullets.

Sinking funds

Nearly all ex-warrants bonds issued before 1987 have sinking funds (or purchase funds).

Bonds with call and put options (emprunts à fenêtre)

Three domestic corporate bonds have call and put features:

- Cie Bancaire 16.90% Aug 1982
- Michelin 10.80% 1975
- SICOFRAM 12.50% 1985

The issuers can call their issues at certain prices that are either fixed, or decrease with the remaining life to maturity, whilst holders can, at their option, ask for redemption at par.

Bonds with a reinvestment option for the coupon (obligations à réinvestissement optionnel du coupon, OROC)

If interest rates fall, the holders of the bonds can reinvest the coupon at the rate the OROC was issued and, in the event of a rate rise, they can reinvest the coupon at market rates.

Cum-warrant bonds

There are two types of warrants attached, they either give the right to subscribe to new bonds or to shares of the issuer, at a fixed price.

■ Warrants giving the right to new bonds
These warrants give the right to subscribe to new bonds which often have the same characteristics as the issue to which the warrant was attached, and are normally exercisable at all times. In some instances, however, the characteristics can be different, while the exercise period may be limited to certain months in the year.

■ Warrants giving right to new shares
There are over 110 warrants giving right to subscribe to French shares.

Perpetual bonds

Some commercial private banks have issued TSDIs. They are subordinated perpetual bonds indexed on the TAM and TME. Some TSIP are also issued by banks. They are subordinated perpetual bonds, indexed on the P1C, with a stepped-margin.

Subordinated bonds

Banks have issued a few TSR bonds, which are all subordinated. Should a bank be wound up, they would be repaid after payments of deposits and unsubordinated bonds.

Floating-rate notes

The two main references utilized in the corporate sector are the TME (long-term reference), and the P3R which is indexed on the spot 3-month PIBOR rate.

Medium-term notes

Medium-term notes, BMTNs[9], are new instruments created for corporations. They have a minimum maturity of 1 year and a minimum issue amount of FFr 1m. They can either be issued on a discount basis or with a floating-rate coupon.

Convertible bonds

As at the end of 1991, they were 68 convertible bond issues on the French market:

- 10 issues are ORA (*obligations remboursables en actions*) in which the issues are redeemed in stocks, rather than in cash like most convertibles;
- 1 issue is an ORCI (*obligations remboursables en certificats d'investissement*) in which the issue is redeemed in a certificate (a share without voting rights);
- 4 issues are OCBSA (*obligations convertibles avec bon de souscription d'actions*) which were issued with warrants attached, allowing subscription to new shares.

Eurofranc issues

Bullet bonds

Eurofranc issues are mostly fixed-rate bullets.

Zero-coupons

There are many zero-coupons with maturities from 1995 to 2002, mostly from French public and private sector issuers such as EDF, CLF, SNCF and Cie Bancaire.

[9] *Bons à moyen terme négociables*

Floating-rate notes

A few FRN issues have been issued recently. They are based on P3R and some of them have a call feature.

Bonds indexed on the performance of a specific stock or an index (CAC 40).

These bonds, which currently have a maturity range of 2 to 5 years, are zero-coupons. At worst, holders are guaranteed to receive their capital back. If the stock rises, holders participate in the performance of the stock at a greater degree by a ratio of 115 per cent to 130 per cent of the appreciation of the stock. For example, in the case of the Lafarge Coppée issue, the redemption formula in 1994 is the following:

$$\text{Nominal} \times 115\% \times \frac{LC - LCI}{LCI}$$

LCI Average of the stock price of Lafarge Coppée at 11h and 15h on the 17,18,19 June 1991 = FFr 392.13

LC Average of the stock price of Lafarge Coppée at 11h and 15h on the 14th, 13th, 12th, 11th and 10th business day prior to the 15 July 1994 while the amount repaid will not be inferior to the nominal, a ceiling of 160 per cent of the nominal is the maximum repayment possible.

Convertibles

There are two convertible issues, for Michelin and Lafarge Coppée.

Ex-warrant bonds

There are two such issues from Japanese issuers, both maturing in 1995.

Euro medium-term notes

There is one such issue for Credit Local de France, which is based on the formula: fixed-rate - PIBOR. This issue is similar to an issue brought by the Société Générale on the eurofranc market. The holder profits from a fall in short-term interest rates.

Subordinated issues

Only one issue on the market, for Société Générale, is a TSR - its index being P3R + margin.

Warrants on OAT

Many warrants have been issued by BNP, Banque Paribas, Crédit Lyonnais and Société Générale on OAT 8.5 per cent 2000, and OAT 8.5 per cent Oct 2019. Two warrants have been issued on OAT 8.5 per cent May 1997 in Ecu, by Crédit Lyonnais. These warrants can really be considered as negotiable securitized options.

15.5 Issuers

French domestic bond market

State and public agencies

The public sector (the state and public agencies) remains the principal issuer on the French primary market with about 50 per cent of the total issuance volume in 1991 (cf. 42 per cent in 1988). The rise in the public sector borrowing requirements has stemmed largely from the widening of the budget deficit.

The public services sector encompasses a wide range of corporations such as Eléctricité de France (EDF), Gaz de France (GDF), Société Nationale des Chemins de Fer (SNCF), Caisse Nationale des Autoroutes (CNA), Charbonnages de France and Caisse Nationale de l'Energie (CNE). EDF 9,30 per cent 2001(FFr 14bn) and SNCF 9 per cent 2003 (FFr 15bn) are the two issues with the largest outstandings. Since 1991, Eléctricité de France has been reducing its issue volume, while SNCF has increased its issue volume from FFr 7.4bn in 1990 to FFr 13.2bn in 1991.

Two new issuers appeared in 1991: La Poste and France Telecom (which replaces Caisse Nationale des Télécommunications (CNT)).

Financial institutions

Financial institutions represent the second largest group of borrowers after the state. The most significant issuers are the large financial institutions such as Crédit Foncier de France (CFF) and Caisse de Refinancement Hypothécaire (CRH). The biggest issues in this category are CFF 10 per cent 1998 (FFr 12bn) and CRH 8.50 per cent 1999 (FFr 18bn). Caisse de Refinancement Hypothécaire has recently been privatized. Other notable issuers are Auxiliaire du Crédit Foncier (a subsidiary of CFF), and Comptoir des Entrepreneurs.

Banks are among the largest issuers on the domestic market. Their refunding needs increased with the slowdown in deposits and the need to improve their risk ratios. Caisse Nationale de Crédit Agricole is the most important issuing-bank, with a total issuance volume, in 1991, of FFr 15bn.

Industrial and commercial sector

This group encompasses industrial and commercial corporates and specialized public financial institutions such as Crédit National, Crédit d'Equipement des Petites et Moyennes Entreprises (CEPME), Caisse Centrale de Coopération

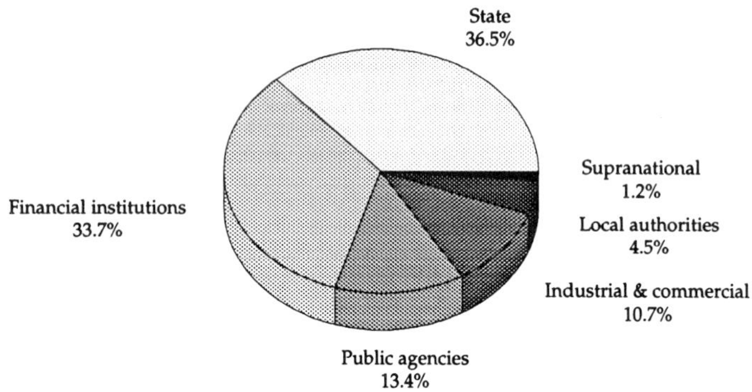

Figure 15.27 Types of issuer in the French domestic bond market (1991, per cent)

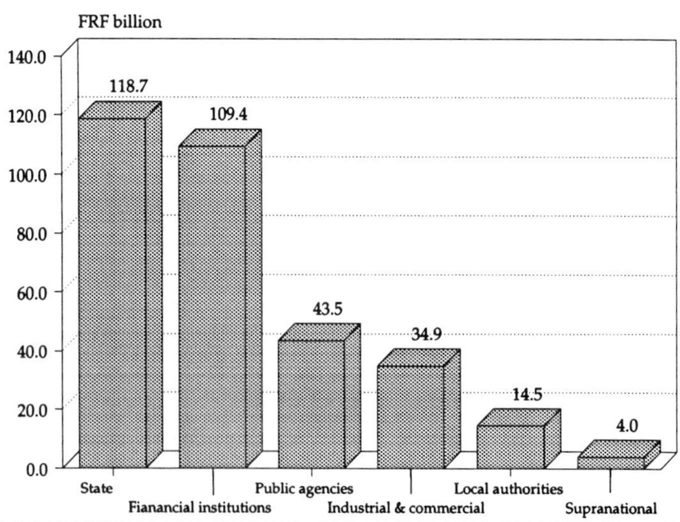

Figure 15.28 Types of issuer in the French domestic bond market (1991, FRF billion)

Economique (CCCE), Banque Française du Commerce Extérieur (BFCE), and Finansder. Finansder, CCCE, BFCE and CEPME are the last issuers to benefit from the French government guarantee on their new issues.

The issues of private sector corporates are essentially linked to asset operations, revenue-indexed bond issues, convertible bonds, bonds with equity warrants and, for the first time in 1988, redeemable subordinated bonds (*titres subordonnés remboursables* (TSR)).

Local authorities

Along with local authorities, Crédit Local de France (CLF) and its subsidiary Floral, Caisse Autonome de Refinancement (CAR) also belong to this group.

Crédit Local de France has almost disappeared from the domestic primary market in 1991, since it has found cheaper refunding on the international markets, using the opportunities to be found on the swap markets.

Supranationals

The European Investment Bank (EIB) is the main supranational issuer on the French domestic market, although there are also some issues by the World Bank.

	Issued amount (FRF bn)	Rank
Caisse Nationale de Crédit Agricole	15.3	1
Crédit Foncier de France	13.9	2
Société Nationale des Chemins de Fer	13.2	3
Caisse de Refinancement Hypothécaire	12.0	4
Société Générale	10.0	5
Crédit Lyonnais	9.8	6
Caisse Autonome de Refinancement	8.0	7
Finansder	6.5	8
Banque National de Paris	6.3	9
Crédit National	6.0	10
France Télecom	5.0	11
Caisse Nationale des Autoroutes	4.8	12
Caisse Epargne Ecureuil	4.8	13
Compagnie Bancaire	4.6	14
Floral	4.3	15
Banque Européenne d'Investissement	4.0	16
La Poste	4.0	16

Figure 15.29 Ranking of the largest issuers on the domestic market in 1991 (excl. state and public exchange offers)

The largest French issuers have focused on the internationalization of their debt, in an attempt to attract non-resident investors. To reach this objective, they have created very liquid fungible issues. Some of the largest issuers, such as Eléctricité de France and Société Nationale des Chemins de Fer, launched domestic issues with a syndicated international 'tranche', exclusively targeted towards non-resident investors. Additionally, major French issuers have increased their use of the eurofranc market in order to reach a wider investor base and achieve a more extensive placement.

Eurofranc bond market

Prior to 1989, the opportunities to be found in the eurofranc market were principally exploited by corporates, since the largest French public sector issuers concentrated on the domestic bond market. However, 1991 has seen the market open up and develop quite dramatically, with total new issuance volume double that of 1990.

French issuers

In 1989, French issuers accounted for less than 50 per cent of the total issuance on the eurofranc market. Corporates were the first French issuers to utilize the market as they readily appreciated the speed, flexibility and favourable costs available. In particular, corporates such as Rhône Poulenc, Pernod Ricard, Thomson, Michelin, BSN, and Elf Aquitaine, all came early to the market, principally with short and medium-term issues (1 to 5 years), and often taking advantages of the swap opportunities. Foreign corporates such as Olivetti followed the same policy.

In 1989, the French Treasury authorized French banks to borrow on the eurofranc market. The first bank issue was the one from Compagnie Bancaire - until 1989, the only French financial institutions to use the market had been Crédit Local de France and Interfinance Crédit National.

Prior to 1989, the largest public sector issuers had preferred to limit their French franc-denominated bond issues to the domestic market and their foreign currency-denominated issues to the international markets.

In 1991, French issuers accounted for up to 65 per cent of the eurofranc issue volume (see Figure 15.30). While traditional issuers such as Crédit National , Compagnie Bancaire and Crédit Local de France, increased their total eurofranc issue amounts, two public sector issuers, Caisse Nationale des Autoroutes and France Telecom, both launched their first issues on this market.

Recently, new bond structures have appeared: zero-coupon bonds (Société Nationale des Chemins de Fer, Eléctricité de France and Crédit Local de France), OROC (optional reinvestment of coupon bonds) and one-year bonds (Société Générale for FFr 6bn and Crédit Lyonnais for FFr 3bn).

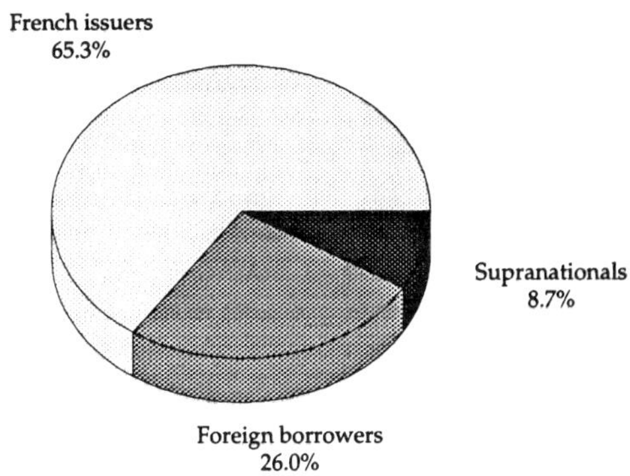

Figure 15.30 Issuers on the eurofranc market,1991

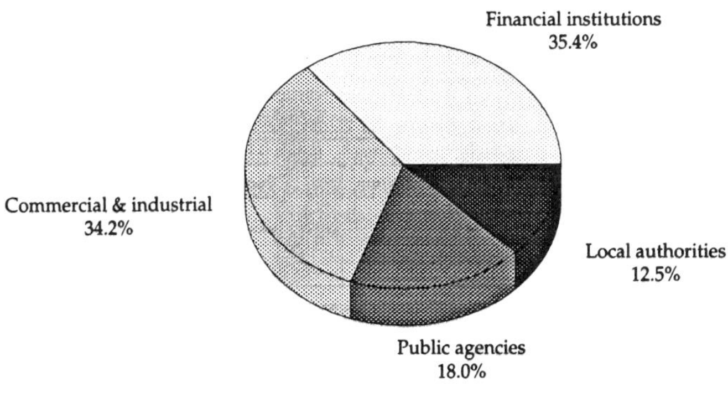

Figure 15.31 French issuers on the eurofranc market,1991

Foreign borrowers

In 1989, foreign borrowers were very scarce. The few that used the market were essentially Scandinavian public and private sector issuers (SAS, Norsk Hydro, Volvo, Kingdom of Denmark, Republic of Finland), and German banks.

In 1991, the jumbo issue of the Kingdom of Spain (9.25 per cent December 2004) of FFr 6bn was the highlight of a remarkable year, as new interest in the eurofranc market came from the sovereign issuers of the Province of Quebec and Republic of Finland, with issues of more than FFr 2bn. French banks strengthened their activity on the market, thereby allowing them to tap a wider range of investors. Société Générale and Crédit Lyonnais were particularly active on the market in 1991.

Supranationals

This category is dominated by the European Investment Bank and the World Bank.

	Issued amount (FRF bn)	Rank
Crédit National	9.7	1
Compagnie Bancaire	8.6	2
Société Générale	8.2	3
Crédit Local de France	7.0	4
Kingdom of Spain	6.0	5
Crédit Lyonnais	5.7	6
European Investment Bank	3.0	7
Republic of Finland	3.0	8
Banque Nationale de Paris	2.9	9
France Télecom Crédit Foncier de France	2.5	10
Eléctricité de France Province of Quebec Eurofima African Development Bank	2.0	12

Figure 15.32 Ranking if the largest issuers on the eurofranc market, 1991

Marketable loan securities

Commercial paper

The commercial paper market is highly concentrated (see Figures 15.33 & 15.34) - on 27 December 1991, the top thirty issuers represented 76.09 per cent of all commercial paper outstanding. In 1985, some 210 corporates had issued commercial paper. Today, there are about 100 with a total outstanding amount of FFr 160.2bn (as at 27 December 27 1991). The major issuers are the public agencies (Eléctricité de France, SNCF, Caisse Nationale des Télecommunications), and the big industrial corporates (Rhône Poulenc, Peugeot, Renault).

Certificates of deposit

The certificate of deposit market is also very concentrated (see Figures 15.35 & 15.36); on 27 December 1991, the top twenty issuers represented 62.48 per cent of the total amount outstanding. The prime issuers are the major banks, in addition to Compagnie Bancaire and Caisse des Dépôts et Consignations.

Bons des institutions et des sociétés financières (BISFs)

BISFs (see Figure 15.37) are issued by

- Specialized financial institutions such as Crédit d'Equipement des Petites et Moyennes Entreprises, Crédit National, Comptoir des Entrepreneurs, and SDR (Sociétés de Développement Régional) either directly, or through Finansder.
- Financial companies which act as mutual guarantee societies or real-estate companies, the major issuers being DIAC, Bail Equipement and Caisse Autonome de Refinancement.
- Crédit Local de France and Crédit Foncier de France, which have a medium-term note programme.

	Issuers	Outstandings
Outstandings of more than FRF 1.5bn	30	76.09%
Outstandings from FRF 500m to FRF 1.5bn	32	18.56%
Outstandings from FRF 100m to FRF 499m	27	4.79%
Outstandings up to FRF 100m	19	0.56%

Figure 15.33 Outstandings on the commercial paper market

	Outstandings (FRF million)	Market share (%)
Rhône Poulenc	11,145	7.08
Caisse Nationale des Télécommunications	7734	4.92
Renault (Cofirem)	7510	4.77
SNCF	7435	4.73
LVMH	7156	4.55
Fiat France	6740	4.28
Eléctricité de France	6646	4.22
Peugeot (Sofira)	5330	3.39
Usinor Sacilor	5075	3.23
Aérospatiale	4640	2.95
Gaz de France	4188	2.66
Cie Générale de Eaux	4038	2.57
Schneider SA	3665	2.33
Lafarge Coppée	3479	2.21
Thomson	2900	1.84

Figure 15.34 Outstandings of the top fifteen issuers on the commercial paper market (as at 27 December 1991)

	Outstandings (FRF million)	Market share (%)
Banque Nationale de Paris	98,187	9.44
Crédit Lyonnais	84,088	8.09
Société Générale	56,182	5.40
Caisse Nationale de Crédit Agricole	50,125	4.82
Compagnie Bancaire	46,298	4.45
Banque Paribas	40,656	3.91
Caisse de Dépôts et Consignations	34,885	3.35
Crédit Commercial de France	25,799	2.48
Banque Française du Commerce Extérieur	24,810	2.39

Figure 15.35 Outstandings of the top nine issuers on the certificates of deposit market (as at 27 December 1991)

	Issuers	Outstandings
Outstandings of more than FRF 10bn	20	62.48%
Outstandings from FRF 5bn to FRF 10bn	14	9.33%
Outstandings from FRF 1bn to FRF 5bn	82	19.79%
Outstandings from FRF 500m to FRF 1bn	71	4.88%
Outstandings from FRF 100m to FRF 500m	124	3.08%
Outstandings up to FRF 100m	148	0.44%

Figure 15.36 Outstandings on the certificates of deposit market

	Outstandings (FRF million)	Market share (%)
Crédit Foncier de France	23807	17059
Comptoir des Entrepreneurs	13486	9.96
DIAC	12957	9.57
Caisse Autonome de Refinancement	11146	8.24
Crédit National	10818	7.99
Crédit d'Equipment des Petites et Moyennes Entreprises	8688	6.42
Franfinance Crédit	4505	3.33
Bail Equipement	3676	2.72
Crédit Local de France	2926	2.16

Figure 15.37 Outstandings of the top nine issuers on the BISF market (as at 27 December 1991)

15.6 *Investors*

Overview

Since 1980, individuals and corporates have been reducing their exposure to bonds, mainly in favour of SICAV[10].

The investment portfolios of insurance companies, especially those in the life business, are still heavily biased towards bonds, with over 50 per cent being placed in such securities. At first sight it would appear that, since 1985, many of these institutions have been apparently reducing their exposure to bonds. In reality, however, bonds held by them through SICAV or FCP[11] have increased - from 5 per cent of total investment in 1985 to 7.5 per cent in 1990.

	Individuals	Institutional investors	Corporates	Foreign investors	Others	Total
1980	56.8	32.8	5.9	-	4.5	100.0
1981	55.3	31.3	9.2	-	4.2	100.0
1982	54.1	34.9	9.3	0.1	1.6	100.0
1983	44.9	45.6	5.1	2.2	2.2	100.0
1984	41.8	47.0	5.5	2.4	3.3	100.0
1985	36.0	54.9	4.1	3.5	1.5	100.0
1986	30.6	58.1	5.2	4.2	1.9	100.0
1987	31.6	56.4	5.7	4.7	1.6	100.0
1988	32.3	53.6	9.9	2.7	1.5	100.0
1989	33.9	51.2	10.8	2.9	1.2	100.0
1990	35.2	49.2	10.9	3.9	0.8	100.0
1991[1]	37.9	49.6	8.0	3.4	1.1	100.0

Figure 15.38 Distribution of French bondholding, by investor type (per cent, as at 31 December)
Source: BDF Quarterly Survey

[1] *end-March*

[10] *Société d'Investissement à Capital Variable (mutual funds & unit trusts)*
[11] *Fonds Commun de Placement (mutual funds)*

From 1983 to 1986, OPCVM[12] exposure to bonds increased to 66 per cent, but by 1990, this figure had decreased to 40 per cent. In the meantime (from 1986 to 1990), OPCVM investment in money market instruments has increased from 7 per cent to 44 per cent, the main reason being that, since 1986, only financial institutions have had direct access to the money market, with the result that others have had to invest in money market funds.

Insurance companies

Life insurance companies

The majority of their funds (around 52 per cent) is invested in bonds - this being mainly due to the nature of their liabilities, especially their with-profit policies which feature guaranteed high returns. The other reason is the former investment requirements of French insurance regulations - until 1990, life insurance companies were subject to a minimum bond investment requirement of 44 per cent.

Property-casualty companies

These companies invest less in bonds and more in stocks and real estate. Nevertheless, around 44.5 per cent of their investment is in bonds, of which 7.4 per cent is held through SICAV or FCP.

OPCVM

From 1982 to 1986, OPCVM (SICAV and FCP) have grown very rapidly (see Figure 15.39). OPCVM net investment in bonds has increased from FFr 269bn in 1984 to FFr 644.7bn in 1986. In 1987, this figure was slightly lower at FFr 629bn but, since that year it has been steady, at around FFr 750bn.

Institutional investors (incl. insurance companies, pension funds & OPCVM)

After a sudden rise in 1982 (see Figure 15.40), the percentage of bonds in institutional portfolios has remained rather stable. However, this apparent stability has actually resulted from a decrease in bondholdings by insurance companies and a corresponding increase in holdings by OPCVMs (although this must be viewed purely in relative terms, since part of insurance companies' portfolios is invested in OPCVMs). In addition, it is quite likely that new regulations and tax laws may induce insurance companies to make new portfolio allocations in the future.

[12] *Oragnismes de Placement Collectif en Valeurs Mobilières - designates all types of mutualized investments in securities, including SICAV and FCP*

	SICAV	FCP	Total	% change (year-on-year)
1979	47.2	10.9	58.1	+22.3
1980	62.6	17.0	79.6	+37.0
1981	72.3	27.3	99.6	+25.1
1982	104.2	54.2	158.4	+59.0
1983	190.9	105.4	296.3	+87.0
1984	298.7	162.4	461.1	+55.6
1985	449.6	229.1	678.7	+47.2
1986	701.8	320.0	1021.8	+50.5
1987	821.6	316.2	1137.8	+11.4
1988	1074.5	417.8	1492.3	+31.2
1989	1269.9	517.1	1787.0	+19.7
1990	1447.3	569.4	2016.7	+12.9

Figure 15.39 Total outstanding value of SICAV & FCP (FRF billion, as at 31 December)
Source: ASFFI

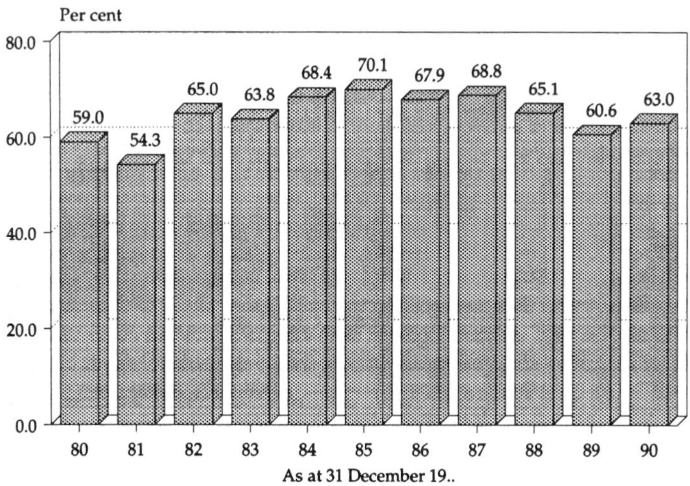

Figure 15.40 Distribution of bonds held by institutional investors as a percentage of their own portfolios *Source: BdF Quarterly Review*

Individuals

At the beginning of the 1980s, individuals were the prime investors in bonds - indeed, half of the bond stock was in their hands (see Figure 15.41). However, with bond market deregulation, it has become difficult for individuals to purchase bonds. As a consequence they have been more and more attracted by SICAV which additionally offers them tax advantages. Figures 15.42 - 15.45 analyse the patterns of bondholding by individuals.

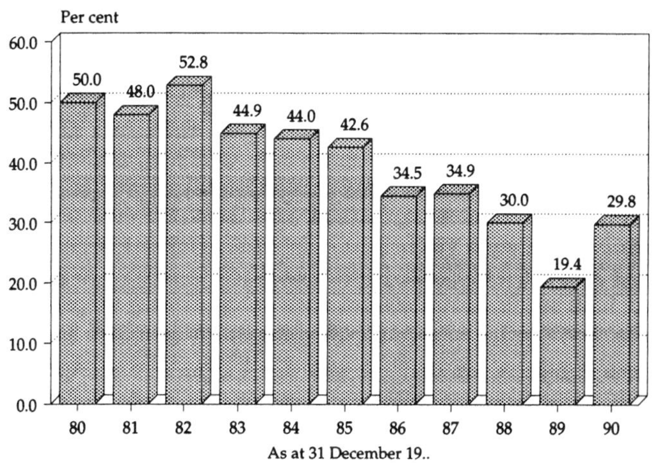

Figure 15.41 Distribution of bonds held by individuals as a percentage of their own portfolios
Source: BdF Quarterly Review

Corporates

Corporates, too, have been reducing their direct exposure to bonds in favour of SICAV (see Figure 15.46), but less so than individuals.

Overseas investors

An overwhelming 96 per cent of the international investors in the French bond market are of the institutional, rather than individual, type. Since 1986, overseas investors have increased their purchases of French bonds (see Figure 15.47), mainly in OATs. At the beginning of 1992, their market share stands at around 30 per cent. Net purchases of OATs were high in both 1989 and 1990, at FFr 100bn each year (together with BTANs and BTFs) but, at FFr 30-40bn, this figure was rather less in 1991.

	1979	1987	1991
Directly	1.7	2.2	4.0
Through SICAV	-	2.6	4.0

Figure 15.42 Individual holders of French bonds (in millions)
Source: COB Bulletin no. 250 (September 1991)

	Farmers	Skilled workers & tradesmen	Managers	Employees	Freelance	Non-workers[1]	Others
1987	5.6	8.8	13.3	4.0	7.0	55.6	5.7
1991	2.2	6.0	10.0	4.7	5.8	63.0	8.3

Figure 15.43 French bondholding by occupation group (per cent)
Source: COB Bulletin no. 250 (September 1991)

[1] *Non-working includes students, retired and unemployed persons*

	Under 25	25-34	35-44	45-54	Over 55	Total
1987	0.5	2.1	8.1	22.4	66.9	100.0
1991	0.5	7.4	8.4	15.6	68.1	100.0

Figure 15.44 French bondholding by age group (per cent)
Source: COB Bulletin no. 250 (September 1991)

	Bondholders	Population
Countryside	21.6	26.0
2000-20,000	13.1	16.4
20,000-100,000	13.8	13.2
>100,000	31.6	28.0
Paris	20.0	16.4

Figure 15.45 French bondholding by population density (per cent)
Source: COB Bulletin no. 250 (September 1991)

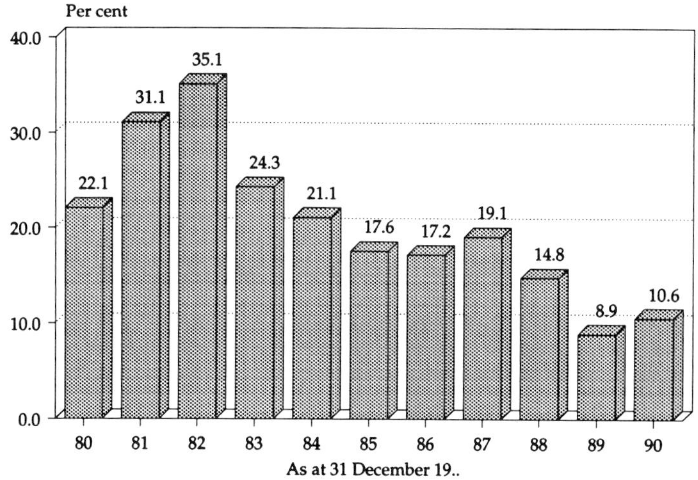

Figure 15.46 Distribution of bonds held by corporates as a percentage of their own portfolios
Source: BdF Quarterly Review

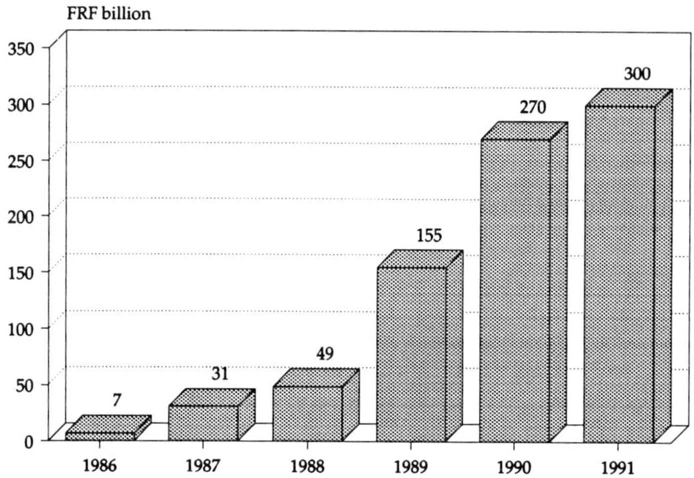

Figure 15.47 Distribution of bonds held by non-residents (FRF billion)
Figures supplied by Trésor

15.7 *Methods of issuance*

Long-term bonds

Within the French bond markets, there are different issuance methods with each one corresponding to the specific needs of the issuer.

	Domestic market	Eurofranc market	Total
Auctions	38.1	-	29.4
Syndicated placements	43.9	100.0	56.7
Other placements	18.0	-	13.9

Figure 15.48 Composition of 1991 issuance (per cent)

Auctions

Until 1990, the auction technique was essentially used by the largest issuers on the domestic market (besides the French Treasury), such as Crédit Local de France (CLF) and Caisse de Refinancement Hypothécaire (CRH) in order to place large issue volumes on the market. In 1990, however, these issuers abandoned the method due to the excessive refunding costs. Today, the Treasury is the sole user of auctions.

■ Treasury bond auctions

Prior to 1985, the principal long-term debt instrument of the French government was the syndicated state bond issue (*emprunt d'Etat*). Bond issues were irregular and handled by bank syndicates. As a consequence, the lines were numerous, small, and highly dissimilar in their characteristics.

As a result of the financial reform, initiated in 1984 by the minister of economy, finance and budget , the French government radically changed its issuance policy to encourage simpler products. By concentrating issues on heavily-capitalized pools of bonds, liquidity was also enhanced. Gradually, issuance policy concentrated on new securities, OATs (*obligations assimilables du Trésor*), fungible, denominated in French francs or Ecus (as of 1989), redeemable at maturity and bearing annual fixed-rate, or variable-rate, coupons.

These bonds are issued through the Dutch auction system (also called the 'bid price auction system'), and are open to all institutions having a cash account with the Banque de France and a securities account with the SICOVAM clearing house. Participants compete through a system of competitive bidding.

Two business days before the auction, the Treasury sets a range[13] for the issue volume and specifies the bonds to be issued. The minimum bids are FFr 50m for OATs denominated in French francs, and Ecu 5m for OATs denominated in Ecu. The Banque de France centralizes all the bid prices and amounts through a computerized bidding system. (Treasury officials do not have access to this information, thereby ensuring that bids remain anonymous). Bids are then classified in decreasing order of prices. Taking into account prices and volumes offered, the Treasury decides upon the amount it allocates for each issue. To obtain an issue amount as close as possible to the one announced before the auction, the Treasury has the right to reduce, proportionally, the bids given at the lowest accepted price. Each bid is settled according to the Dutch auction principle, that is to say, at the bidder's price. The results of the auction are announced immediately after the bids have been passed through the computerized system, and are displayed on screen by specialized agencies. An annual auction calendar is published specifying the dates and the lines that are likely to be issued, with minimum amounts set for each line. Auctions of French franc OATs are held on the first Thursday of each month. Successful bids are settled on the 25th of the month. OATs are issued in nominal amounts of FFr 2000, except for the OAT TRB 1993 (FFr 50,000).

French franc OATs are issued with maturities ranging from 7 to 30 years. Ten-year OATs are the French market's benchmarks. A new 10-year OAT is now issued each year, and the outstanding supply is increased through monthly auctions. The last two 10-year OATs, issued in 1989 and 1990, both have outstandings of more than FFr 50bn. Since 1987, issues with longer maturities have been created: a 25-year bond (OAT 8.50 per cent December 2012) and a 30-year bond (OAT 8.50 per cent 2019). In addition to fixed-rate bonds, the Treasury also issues a smaller number of variable-rate bonds, indexed on short-term (TMB, TRB), or long-term (TME, TRA) references. The authorities tend to give priority to fixed-rates, because it is determined to reduce the sensitivity of its debt yield to short-term rate fluctuations. However, the Treasury now makes increasing use of the swap market, so that its debt is actually less fixed-rate than it seems. Swaps are sometimes rapidly unwound as the management of the debt is quite active.

[13] *The minimum amount to be issued is always a multiple of FFr 1bn, and the maximum is always equal to the minimum plus FFr 2bn. Range is equal to FFr 2bn.*

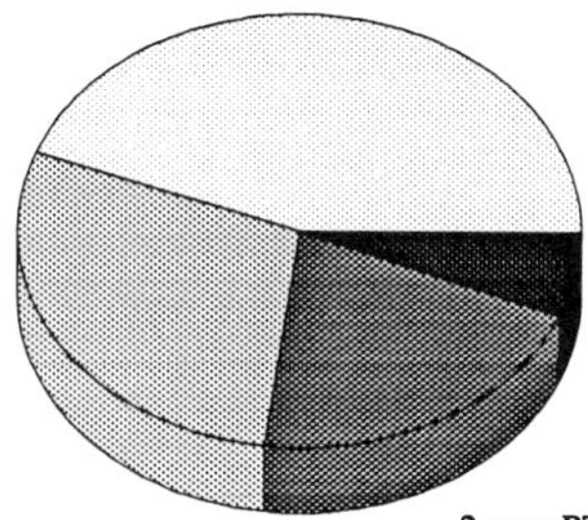

Figure 15.49 Composition of state issues in 1991

The first Ecu-denominated OAT was issued in April 1989. Today, the French government is the largest sovereign issuer on the long-term end of the Ecu market. In 1991, 13 per cent of the government's bond issues were denominated in Ecu. To allow for the same degree of transparency as enjoyed by the French franc OATs, the government specifies which bonds will be issued and sets a range for the total amount two business days before the auction, which is held quarterly. Ecu-denominated OATs are issued in nominal values of Ecu 500 and carry an annual fixed-rate coupon.

■ Treasury bill & note auctions

BTANs (*bons du Trésor à taux annuel normalisé*) are interest-bearing fixed-rate Treasury notes with maturities generally of two and five years at issue, and an annual coupon. BTANs are issued by auction according to a half-yearly issue calendar which gives the minimum amount to be issued by maturity. Two business days before the auction, which is held on the third Thursday of each month at 11.00 (or the following business day if such a Thursday is a public holiday), the Treasury announces the upper and lower limits of the amount it intends to auction. Bids are made in price terms, as a percentage of the nominal amount, and to two decimal places. Successful bids are settled on the 5th of each month for 2-year BTANs, and the 12th for 5-year paper.

BTFs (*bons du Trésor à taux fixe*) are short-term discount bills, issued by auction according to a quarterly calendar which specifies the maturities of the bills to be auctioned; 13-week long bills are issued every week, 26-week long bills are issued every two weeks, 1-year long bills (can be 51-54 weeks) are issued every four weeks.

In addition to the calendar issues, the Treasury also issues BTFs with maturities ranging from 4 to 7 weeks, depending on its cash management requirements. Two business days before the auction, which takes place on a Monday, the Treasury announces the exact amount which will be issued. Bids are submitted in discount rate terms, to two decimal places, on the basis of a 360-day year, and are settled on Thursdays. BTANs and BTFs are issued in units of FFr 1m nominal.

BTAN and BTF auctions are opened to all institutions having a securities account on the Saturne settlement system, in addition to a cash account with the Banque de France. Beside the differences of pricing and calendar, the auction procedures for BTANs and BTFs remain the same as those used for OATs.

■ Reverse auction

The so-called reverse auction is a conventional auction, but bids are made in terms of sale price rather than purchase price. The Treasury sets a maximum amount for the bonds it wishes to repurchase, within which the lowest-priced offers are accepted. The state then acquires the bonds at the sale prices given by the bidders.

As in the case of conventional auctions, the Treasury announces in advance the lines it intends to repurchase, and the volume of the operation in terms of upper and lower limits. The first reverse auction took place on 28 March 1991.

Syndicated issues

The Issues Committee (Comité des Emissions) is the controlling body which must authorize any new type of bond to be issued. The Committee can delay an issue either in the event of market saturation or poor market climate, but only if the issue size exceeds FFr 500m. This committee, which is under the authority of the Treasury, comprises eight banks (Banque Indosuez, Banque Nationale de Paris, Banque Paribas, Caisse des Dépôts et Consignations, Caisse Nationale de Crédit Agricole, Crédit Commercial de France, Crédit Lyonnais, Société Générale), and meets every two weeks.

If an issue amounts to more than FFr 1bn, a more formal procedure is necessary. The issuer has to register its issue on a calendar, at least three weeks before the planned issue day, with the Secretariat of the Issues Committee held by Crédit Lyonnais. As the calendar is very often crowded, it may be necessary to register earlier than 3 weeks before the issue, in fact the sooner the better! The Committee tries to keep to the calendar, even though it manages issuance according to market conditions. Of course, the State (which sometimes still uses the syndication system, especially for those issues designed particularly for the individual investor) always has priority over other issuers and does not need to register in advance.

The bank syndicate, *de prise ferme,* is the traditional method which involves the issuer choosing a bank, or a group of banks, to act as lead-manager(s) as a result of a process of competitive bidding. The lead-manager sets up an underwriting syndicate which has the responsibility to sell the whole issue, and to guarantee the successful outcome of the operation. To support the grey market, the underwriting group performs repurchases of the bonds when necessary. The lead-manager sets up a selling group and then allocates a share of the issue to each member of the group. The allocated commissions depend on the level of risk taken by each participant of the syndicate as lead-manager, co-lead-manager or manager.

Increasingly, issuers concentrate their issues on heavily-capitalized pools of bonds, creating fungible *souches* in order to improve their debt liquidity. The first to adopt this policy were public agencies (Crédit Local de France and Eléctricité de France). They have since been followed by private sector issuers (Compagnie Bancaire and Comptoir des Entrepreneurs). Issues are presently in bullet form with redemption *in fine.* Syndicated bonds are essentially issued on a fixed-rate basis (61 per cent of the total in 1988, substantially more in 1991). Prior to 1992, the minimum maturity for bonds issued on the primary market was 7 years. The French Treasury has recently decided to reduce this limit to 5 years, with a further reduction (to 3 years) to follow in 12 months' time.

■ Fixed price re-offer

Recently (since April 1991), as a result of the influence of the international market, the leading banks have introduced the fixed price re-offer system. This method requires the managers of the deal to agree not to offer bonds below a consensus price until the syndicate is broken. This was established in order to stop managers, with no placement capacity, from dumping the bonds on the market-place and thereby forcing the lead-manager to absorb them. The period of syndication can last from 24 hours to three days, dependent upon the success of placement. The fixed price re-offer system is now used for all the public syndicated issues on the domestic market, as well as on the eurofranc market.

Other methods

■ Private placements

The Tricot Commission Report compares private placements to the German *Schuldschein* and other formulae. Until now, some issues on the French bond market have been placed in the hands of a small number of institutions, which have agreed not to sell them, at a price held unchanged and set by the issue manager. For these issues, there is no grey market between the launch and quotation of the issue.

The development of these 'controlled issues' was linked to the rapid expansion of short-term mutual funds (short-term SICAV) which, until 1990, had to hold 40 per cent of their assets in bonds. With the whole issue, they could control the market quotation of the bond and avoid large fluctuations in pricing.

This technique has almost disappeared with the abolition of the above-mentioned regulation, and the new investment ratios for mutual funds.

■ Public exchange offers

A new technique of large-scale exchange offers, has been promoted on the French domestic bond market. This technique, known as *offres publiques d'echange* (OPE), is now common - many of the large public sector borrowers such as Crédit Local de France, Electricité de France and Société Nationale des Chemins de Fer have used OPEs to replace a number of old and illiquid issues with new liquid issues. In the two years 1990-1991, seven *offres publiques d'echange* were launched. This technique represents an ideal way of actively managing significant amounts of issuers' debts.

Medium-term

Marketable loan securities

Marketable loan securities are treasury management instruments which were developed following the monetary market reform of 1985. The aim of this reform was to break the frontiers between short-term and long-term rates, and between monetary agents and other investors. It gave every participant access to all products with monetary references. Besides BTFs and BTANs, there are four different types of instruments, with each one corresponding to a specific type of issuer.

Despite that, though, they do have common characteristics:

- maturities from 10 days to 7 years
- discounted coupon up to one-year maturity
- annual coupons on a fixed or variable basis after one year
- minimum amount of FFr 1m for each security
- equal fiscal treatment
- no official quotation

For marketable loan securities with initial maturities of less than two years, issuers must announce whether they have applied to an agency for a rating. When the initial maturity exceeds two years, a rating is required by regulation.

Credit institutions, securities houses, stockbrokers, and Caisse des Dépôts et Consignations, all place and trade these securities.

Certificates of deposit are issued by the banks on a continuous-offer basis and can be denominated in French francs or foreign currencies. The average maturity at issuance is around one year. The banks have created fungible issues.

Commercial paper has been a major innovation for corporates, since it enables them to refund themselves directly without bank intermediation. CP issues are concentrated in short-term maturities (from 20 days to 365 days).

The notes of the financial institutions and companies (BISFs - *bons des institutions et sociétés financières*) are generally issued on a continuous-offer basis. Certain financial institutions used to include BISF issues in their syndicated issue programmes, but they have now ceased this practice.

BMTN

A new instrument has recently been made available to the issuers of negotiable medium-term notes. Known as BMTN (*bon à moyen terme négociable*), it groups together:

- the certificates of deposit of banks
- the commercial paper of corporates
- the medium-term notes of financial institutions and companies (BISFs).

The nominal amount of a BMTN is at least FFr 1m (or its equivalent in foreign currency), whilst its minimum maturity is one year. A rating from one of the specialized rating agencies, such as Moody's, Standard and Poor's, Euronotation or IBCA, is required for each BMTN issue.

Until now, the medium-term note market only allowed issues with maturities of 2 days to 7 years and it has suffered from a lack of liquidity. As a result, issuers have had to face relatively expensive refunding costs. Because of this, the upper limit of the maturity date will be reduced and, as a consequence, the long-lived 'gap' between the short-term market and the long-term market will progressively disappear and there will soon be a global interest rate market with all maturities available, as exists in the United States, for example.

15.8 New issue volumes

French domestic bond market

New issue volumes grew continuously from 1981 to 1986. Although there was a decrease for the first time in 1987, volumes since 1988 have remained quite stable (see Figure 15.50). The percentage of state issuance, meanwhile oscillated from 35 per cent to 40 per cent between 1988 and 1991. Even though public sector borrowing requirements increased, the major issuers actually reduced their issuance on the domestic market - preferring, instead, to exploit the attractive opportunities to be found on the international market.

The programme announced by the French Treasury for 1992 amounts to FFr 135bn, 15 per cent of which is to be in Ecu.

As far as government and public sector issuance is concerned, and leaving aside the influence of market conditions, the most active periods are traditionally the first few months of each year, reflecting the fact that these issuers have pre-set annual borrowing programmes. August volumes are traditionally low (see Figures 15.51 & 15.52).

By contrast, the borrowing needs of corporates tend to be on a more immediate basis, with the result that there is no discernible pattern of new issuance.

Eurofranc bond market

The eurofranc market closed in 1981, but re-opened in 1985. Following the abolition of withholding tax on all new issues on the domestic market since 1 January 1987, demand for public sector bonds increased. The liquidity of some government bonds (OATs) was been greatly enhanced by the French Treasury's practice of issuing monthly taps on existing issues, rather than issuing new bonds. International clearing houses such as Cedel and Euroclear helped the distribution of these domestic securities. These factors together encouraged, for large holders, the switching out of eurofranc bonds into domestic bonds, and was one of the reasons for the slow pace of new eurofranc issues in 1987.

Nevertheless, since 1989, eurofranc volumes have been growing rapidly (see Figure 15.53), largely as a result of enhanced opportunities for issuers, improvement of the liquidity of the market and international demand for French franc.

Marketable loan securities

The prevalence of certificates of deposit (see Figure 15.54) reflects the good quality of banking names. However, even if certificates of deposit are good refunding instruments, banks have to take into account the impact of the contingency reserves on the cost of the product - a fact which, for them, reduces the attraction of certificates of deposit.

Commercial paper

See Figure 15.55. In 1991, the inverted yield curve made short- and medium-term refunding less attractive by comparison to bond issue refunding.

Certificates of deposit

Since 1986, the refunding needs of the banks have been continually increasing (see Figure 15.56).

BISFs

See Figure 15.57.

BTAN + BTF

See Figure 15.58.

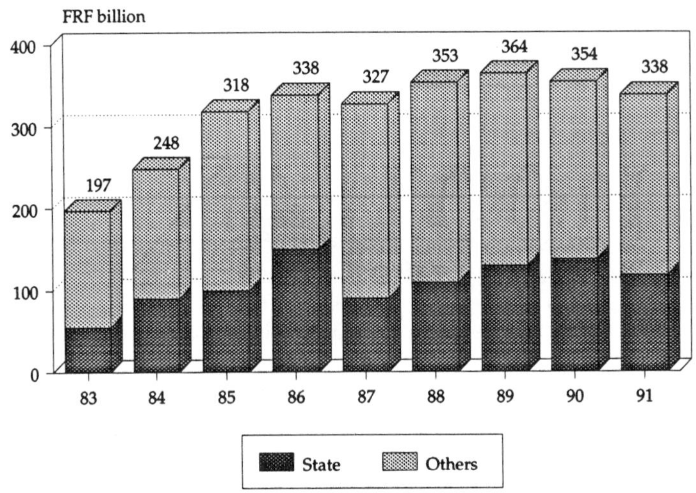

Figure 15.50 New issue volumes, 1983-1991

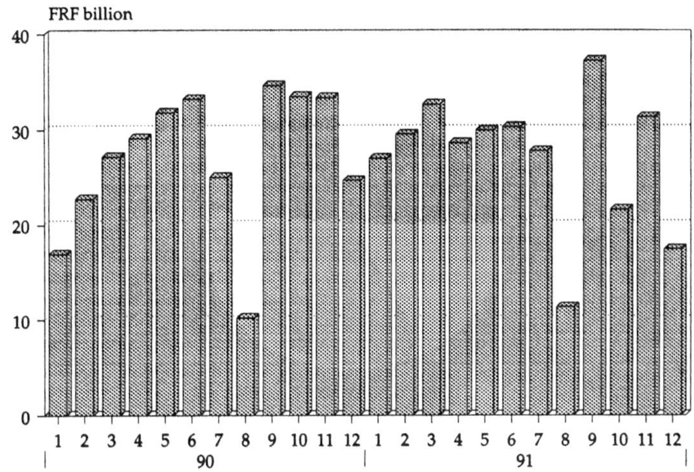

Figure 15.51 Monthly new issue volumes (excl. public exchange offers)

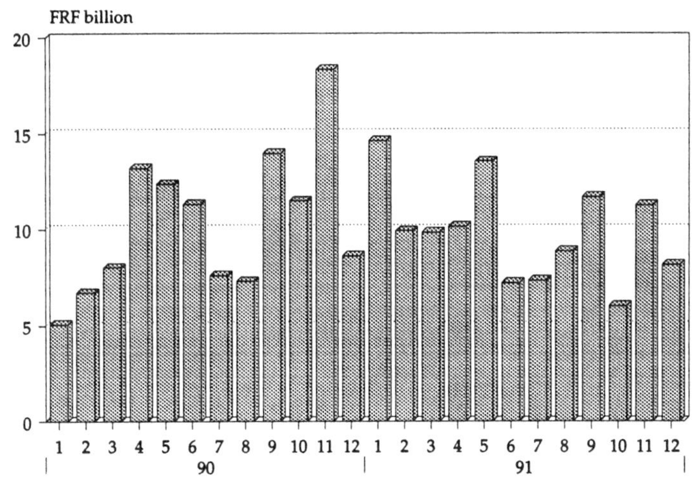

Figure 15.52 Monthly new issue volumes of the state sector (excl. public exchange offers)

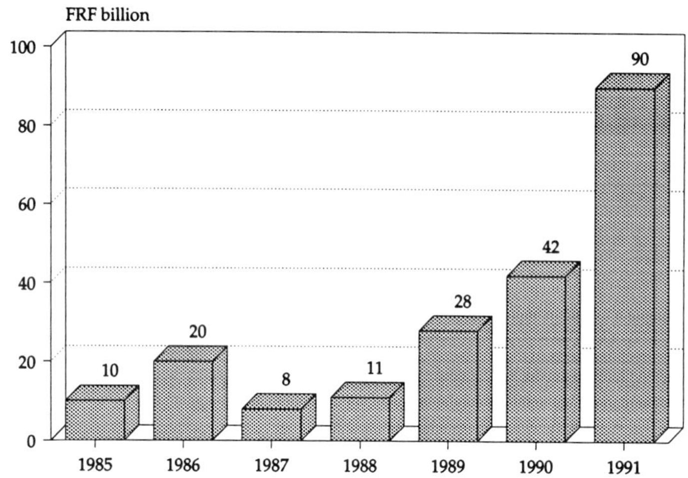

Figure 15.53 New issue volumes in the eurofranc market, 1985-1991

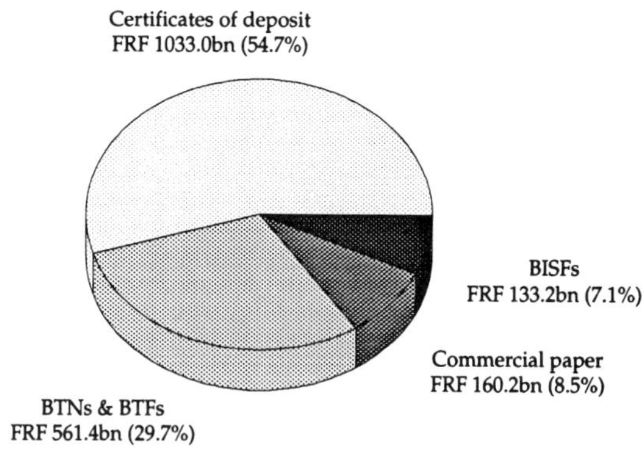

Figure 15.54 Short- and medium-term negotiable debt outstanding as at December 1991

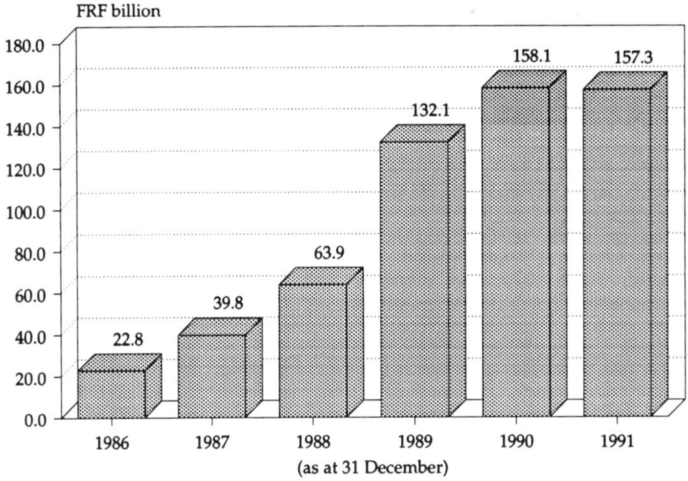

Figure 15.55 Commercial paper issued, outstanding at year-end (1986-1991)

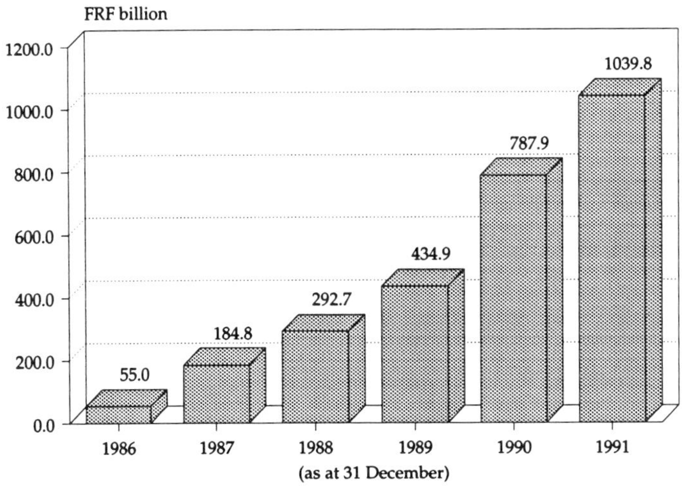

Figure 15.56 Certificates of deposit issued, outstanding at year-end (1986-1991)

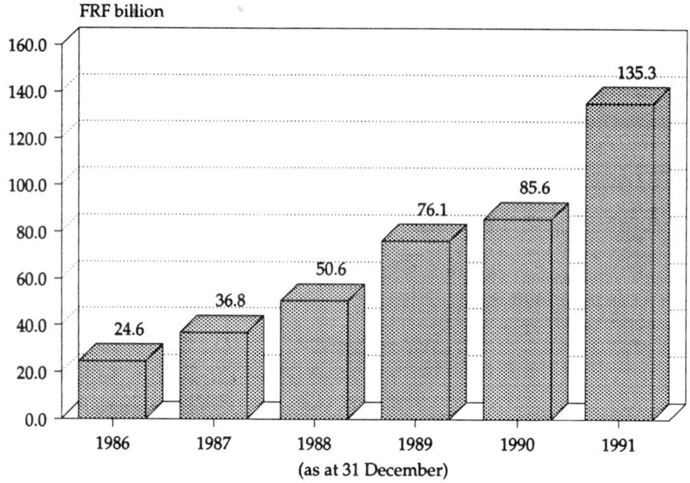

Figure 15.57 BISFs issued, outstanding at year-end (1986-1991)

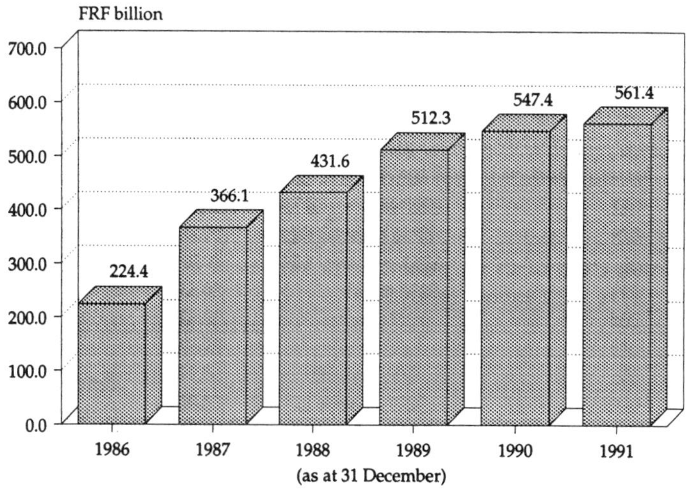

Figure 15.58 BTANs & BTFs issued, outstanding at year-end (1986-1991)

15.9 Methods of trading

Treasury bond specialists (SVTs) (15 in number)

To foster the placement of French government securities and to improve the liquidity and security of the market, the Treasury has selected a group of specialized intermediaries, similar to the primary dealers in the USA, who are authorized to buy and sell government securities in direct dealings with the Treasury. These practitioners are known as *Spécialistes en Valeurs du Trésor*, or SVTs. Two selections were made (in 1986 and 1990). Since 1 July 1990, the 15 institutions designated as SVTs are as follows:

- Banque d'Escompte
- Banque Indosuez
- Banque Nationale de Paris
- Banque Paribas
- Caisse Centrale des Banques Populaires
- Caisse des Dépôts et Consignations
- Caisse de Gestion Mobilière Intermédiation
- Caisse Nationale de Crédit Agricole
- Crédit Commercial de France
- Crédit Lyonnais
- J.P. Morgan
- Nomura France
- S.G. Warburg - Bacot-Allain SA
- Société Générale
- UBS France SA (succeeding Banque Finance Plus)

The choice of primary dealers reflects the diversity of the institutions that are active players in the government bond market, including leading high street banks and specialized financial institutions, both French and foreign. The composition of the group changes in line with developments in the markets, and the activities of the establishments themselves.

To qualify for selection as an SVT, an institution must have a minimum of FFr 150m in shareholders' equity. In addition, it must prove its capacity to act as a primary dealer (see Figure 15.59) with a one-year trial period as a reporting dealer or *Correspondant en Valeurs du Trésor*, CVT. There are 4 CVTs. They have the same function as SVTs, although not so strictly governed.

Primary dealers are required to:

Quote prices on request for negotiable government securities. SVTs are required at all times to quote bid and offer prices for principal government securities, together with the quantity of bonds for which those prices are firm.

Participate regularly and significantly in auctions (2 per cent of the annual volume issued in each category of security; the arithmetic mean of the three percentages must represent at least 3 per cent).

Play a significant part in trading in the primary and secondary markets for government securities, thereby contributing to liquidity (the annual minimum participation in these transactions is 3 per cent for each category of security). Figures are based on statistics prepared by the Banque de France using the Saturne System (BTFs and BTANs) and on data on volumes gathered by the Treasury (OATs).

Participate actively in placing government securities with final investors both inside and outside France.

Figure 15.59 Terms of reference for primary dealers

France's primary dealers play a key role in bolstering the government securities market:

- They play a significant part in auctions for government securities and all other active debt-management operations.
- They make markets in all government securities, giving bid and offer prices by telephone to interested parties. Furthermore, they undertake to quote firm prices, for set quantities, of the most actively traded OATs, BTFs and BTANs.
- They participate actively in placing government securities with final investors inside and outside France, and regularly organize or participate in promotional campaigns for French government securities abroad.
- They advise the Treasury on the elaboration and implementation of its issuance policy, as well as on matters concerning the efficient operation of the market.

In return for committing themselves to these obligations, primary dealers are permitted to submit non-competitive bids after auctions have taken place. The overall amount accepted in this manner is limited to a maximum of 20 per cent of the volume issued - any such amount being divided up among the SVTs in proportion to each dealer's participation in competitive bidding at the three previous auctions for the same type of paper.

To improve efficiency, the SVTs have set up Prominnofi, a broker specialized in government securities. Prominnofi gives primary dealers instant access to the best bid and offer prices quoted by other SVTs. Restricted to primary dealers, Prominnofi guarantees anonymity by acting as counterparty for all SVTs. In addition, it handles securities lending for the dealers' books.

SVTs can also take individual initiatives in offering customers new products derived from government securities, such as stripped bonds and OAT warrants. This ensures that investors will find, on the French market, the same broad range of instruments that are available in other international financial centres.

As a formal group, and with the authorization of the Treasury, SVTs offer investors the opportunity to acquire stripped bonds (See Section 15.4, Types of security).

During the 1980s, market liquidity improved tremendously. Recently, transaction volumes have levelled at around FFr 3000bn (1989: FFr 3180bn; 1990: FFr 3200bn; 1991: FFr 3000bn).

Government OATs are the driving force of this liquidity; in 1990, they represented 56 per cent of the annual turnover with just 27 issues. The turnover of public and corporate bonds meanwhile amounted to FFr 1298bn.

Continuous trading - CAC system

Overview

Continuous trading began in June 1986, with a selection of French stocks that were listed on the monthly settlement market by the end of 1987. As of February 1988, French bonds were added to the CAC system. This move has been gradual, beginning with bonds which were not actively traded, but CAC now includes the very actively traded bonds. The development of specialists has increased overall market liquidity. Using RELIT, the French market has automated routing of orders and automatic settlement and delivery procedures.

Technical operation

The CAC system is based on the CATS programme developed by the Toronto Stock Exchange. Each operation takes only five seconds. Orders receive equal treatment on a first-come first-served basis, with the system then matching bid and ask prices directly. It maintains a centralized market that is error-free, tamper-proof and totally confidential. Screen quotations are made from 10.00 to 17.00 for all bonds except government bonds, which are quoted by open outcry. The 10.00 price fixing is considered the most important compared to later quotations. All orders transmitted to any *société de bourse* appears on the screens of all the others as well. A specialized computer system provides print-outs of all the deals which have been automatically made. Specialists pledge to have an inventory of FFr 20,000 minimum of any bond to smoothly execute small orders.

Public bond specialists (SVPs[14]) (10 in number)

Just as the SVTs were established for French government securities, SVPs were instituted in December 1991 in order to develop the liquidity of the public bond issues of four institutions:

- Crédit Foncier de France
- Crédit Local de France
- EDF
- SNCF

As at December 1991, there were ten institutions designated as SVPs:

- Indosuez
- BNP
- Paribas
- CDC
- CNCA
- CCF
- Crédit Lyonnais
- Société Générale
- J.P. Morgan
- S.G. Warburg - Bacot-Allain SA

SVPs pledge to display bid and ask prices all day long on Reuters screens.

Teneurs de marché (market makers - 20 in number)

Like the SVPs, *teneurs de marché* pledge to display bid and ask prices.

Contrepartistes (75 in number)

As their name suggests, *contrepartistes* act as counterparties, making bids and offers for their own account.

[14] *Spécialistes en Valeurs du Secteur Public*

Buying and selling BTFs

BTFs are fixed-rate short-term discount Treasury bills with 3-, 6- and 12-month maturities at issue. The bills are issued by auction according to a quarterly calendar, which is published in advance and which specifies the maturities of the bills to be auctioned (BTFs with maturities of between 4 and 7 weeks can be issued outside the calendar period dependent upon cash-management requirements.) One 13-week BTF is issued each week and is augmented by a half-yearly, or yearly, line of BTFs.

Buying BTFs at auctions

The Treasury announces the exact amounts that will be issued two business days before the auction, which takes place on a Monday. Bids are submitted in discount rate terms to two decimal places, on the basis of a 360-day year. Bids at the marginal discount rate are reduced on a pro rata basis, rounded up to the nearest million (i.e. the minimum quantity).

■ Example:
Auction of the 3-week BTF (9 September 1991). Treasury borrowing requirement: FFr 6bn.

- Marginal discount rate: 8.91 per cent. Percentage accepted at marginal (accepted low price): 81.81818 per cent.
- An FFr 500m bid at the low price will be accepted for FFr 409.09m rounded up to FFr 410m, i.e. a real percentage of 82 per cent, owing to rounding-up.
- Total issued by the Treasury: FFr 6.004bn on 9 September.

Calculation of net amount due for a competitive bid of FFr10m at a discount rate of 8.90 per cent:

n number of days (91)
t discount rate (8.90%)
c capital subscribed (FFr 10m)
P net due

$$P = \frac{c \times [100 - (t \times \frac{n}{360})]}{100}$$

$$P = \frac{\text{FFr } 10\text{m} \times [100 - (8.90 \times \frac{91}{360})]}{100}$$

$$= \text{FFr } 9{,}775{,}027.28$$

The Banque de France, acting on behalf of the Treasury, debits the exact amount (centimes included) from the bidder's Saturne account without notification by the bidder, or matching of the trade.

Transactions

The procedures for buying BTFs in the markets (when-issued, secondary or forward) differ slightly from those described above. Trades are based on a money market ('in fine') yield to two decimal places, expressed as a percentage, on a 360-day year basis. Primary market transactions are based on the settlement date.

Using the following formula, where t is the discount rate and R the 'in fine' rate, we obtain:

$$R = \frac{t}{[1 - (\frac{t \times n}{36000})]}$$

and

$$t = \frac{R}{[1 + (\frac{R \times n}{36000})]}$$

after rounding-up:

$$R = 9.12 = \frac{8.91}{[1 - (8.91 \times \frac{91}{36000})]}$$

and

$$t = \frac{9.12}{[1 + (\frac{9.12 \times 91}{36000})]} = 8.91$$

- Method of calculating the amount due on a when-issued transaction

Buy FFr 10m of the BTF maturing 12 December 1991, quoted at 9.12 per cent

n no. of days (91)
R in fine rate (9.12 per cent)
C nominal amount (FFr 10m)
P net amount due

$$P = \frac{C}{[1 + (\frac{R \times n}{36000})]}$$

$$P = \frac{\text{FFr 10m}}{[1 + (\frac{9.12 \times 91}{36000})]} = \text{FFr } 9{,}774{,}661.47\text{, rounded up to } 9{,}774{,}661.00$$

Trades between domestic counterparties are generally settled on T+1, and on T+7 calendar days, when non-residents are involved. The method of calculation is identical, the only variable being the number of days.

Settlement and delivery

■ Transactions between residents

Note: The same rules apply to both BTFs and BTANs
Transactions of BTFs and BTANs are cleared by the Banque de France through its Saturne system, which is based on the principle of two-way notification.

Both counterparties (or their representatives at the Banque de France) notify the Banque de France of the conditions of the trade: buy or sell, value-date, counterparty, category of security (code, maturity, coupon), nominal amount, and the net amount to be settled in French francs.

These details are transmitted electronically (or, where unavoidable, by telex or hard copy). The Banque de France matches the instructions given by each counterparty and specifies the status of the operation, which is displayed on the Saturne members' terminals:

101 notification received
102 notification received from both parties and matched
103 transaction finally cleared - the Banque de France has processed the cash and securities)

In the event of a mismatch, the Banque de France informs the counterparties of the anomaly. Each is then responsible for taking corrective action to ensure the trade is cleared.

In the event of failure to deliver, which would be observed at the last clearing session of the day, the Saturne system automatically calculates a penalty. This is immediately debited from the cash account of the defaulting counterparty and credited to the other counterparty. Two rates of penalty are applicable depending on the remaining life of the securities: FFr 700 per FFr 1m nominal for securities with less than two years to maturity, and FFr 1500 for securities with 2 years or more. Saturne then halts the operation in question.

■ International transactions
Counterparties using Cedel or Euroclear as custodians must go through their respective sub-accounts with Saturne. Cedel and Euroclear members give details of the Saturne account of the custodian for the resident buyer or seller of the securities; the Saturne member specifies the Cedel or Euroclear sub-account of the non-resident buyer or seller.

Buying and selling BTANs

BTANs are fungible fixed-rate Treasury notes with maturities of two and five years, and an annual coupon. They are auctioned on the third Thursday of each month in accordance with a previously-published calendar. The Treasury issues one new 5-year and one new 2-year BTAN semi-annually, from which new issues are made every month. In certain cases, 2-year BTANs are now issued to be fungible with old 5-year issues maturing in 2 years' time..

Buying BTANs at auction

Two business days before the auction, which is held on the third Thursday of each month, the Treasury announces the upper and lower limits of the amount it intends to auction. Bids are made in price terms as a percentage of the nominal amount excluding accrued interest, to two decimal places. Successful bids are settled on the 5th of the following month for 2-year BTANs, and the 12th for 5-year BTANs.

BTANs are denominated in units of FFr 1m - they are therefore reserved for professional investors. Accrued interest is calculated on the basis of a 365-day (or 366-day) year. Maturities and coupon dates for BTANs are fixed on the 12th of the month.

Transactions

Trading is based on the yield-to-maturity, expressed as a percentage, on a 365-day (or 366-day) year basis.

■ Primary market

BTANs are traded in the primary market on a settlement-date basis. Accrued interest is calculated to the settlement date.

■ Secondary market

As an example, suppose a buyer purchases FFr 10m of the BTAN 8.50 per cent due 12 November 1996, quoted with a spread of 9.08 per cent (offer) - 9.12 per cent (bid) for settlement on 12 September 1991.

The following formulae can be used to evaluate the price as a function of the yield-to-maturity, as well as the corresponding amount to be paid in French francs:

$$P + CC = 100 / (1 + TA / 100)^{(A - n / 365)} + \sum_{i = 1,A} TN / (1 + TA / 100)^{(i - n / 365)}$$

$$CC = TN \times n / 365$$

$$M = N \times (P + CC) / 100$$

where,

Note: In this example there are 366, rather than 365, days in the year

P	price in per cent of nominal net of accrued interest	97.47873%
CC	accrued interest as a per cent of nominal	7.06010%
M	amount paid in francs	10,453,883
N	nominal in francs	10,000,000
TN	nominal interest in francs, for a capital of FFr 100	8.50%
TA	yield-to-maturity expressed as a percentage on an actual (366-day) year basis	9.08%
A	maturity of the BTAN (years)	6
n	no. of days between date from which interest begins to run and date of assimilation (0 for a new bond)	304

Note:

1) The calculation of accrued interest in the bond market includes one extra day.

2) The above formulae are based on 366 days in the event of a leap year.

The difference between the 1-day and the 7-day rates is that, when no value-date is specified, the yields quoted on screen are good for T+1. The same calculation would show that the 7-day and the T+1 yields are highly similar.

Settlement and delivery

Same conditions as for BTFs (see earlier).

Buying and selling French franc OATs

Since the financial reform initiated in 1984, OATs have become the French government's favoured means of selling its long-term debt. These fungible securities, with maturities of 7-30 years, are generally issued by auction according to a previously-published annual schedule.

Ten-year OATs, which form the bulk of the basket of bonds deliverable against the notional 7-10 year future traded on Matif, are the market benchmark. Each year, the outstanding supply of a ten-year OAT is increased through regular auctions.

Buying French franc OATs at auction

Two business days prior to the auction, the government announces details of the bonds concerned and defines the upper and lower limits of its borrowing requirement. Auctions of French franc OATs take place on the first Thursday of the month, with settlements being made on the 25th. OATs are issued with a nominal of FFr 2000 (except for the OAT TRB 1993, which has a nominal of FFr 50,000). Bids are submitted as a percentage of par, net of accrued interest.

■ Transactions
SVTs quote net prices on screen, valid for amounts of up to FFr 20m, with a price spread of only 10 basis points for the most liquid securities.

■ Primary market
Between 2 and 5 days prior to the monthly auction, and up until the auction settlement date (the 25th of the month of auction), OATs can be traded in the primary market. The value-date for primary market transactions is the auction settlement date, with accrued interest being calculated to that date.

■ Secondary market
Interest calculation depends on whether the settlement is domestic or international.

■ Domestic settlement
Accrued interest is calculated on the trade-date. The settlement date is three business days after the trade.

- Example of the calculation of amount due:

Bond:	9.5 per cent 25 January 2001
Price:	103.50
Trade date:	6 September 1991
Coupon value-date:	6 September 1991
Settlement date:	11 September
Last coupon-date:	25 January 1991
Days accrued:	224
Accrued interest:	9.5 x 224/365 = 5.83

Amount due: $10{,}000{,}000 \times [(103.5/100) + [(9.5/100) \times (224/365)]]$

$$= 10{,}000{,}000 \times \left[(103.5/100) + \frac{(9.5 \times 224)}{36500} \right]$$

= FFr 10,933,000

International settlement

Accrued interest is calculated on the settlement date, i.e. seven calendar days after the trade-date. The seven-day price is therefore calculated as follows:

7-day price = domestic price - 7 days' accrued interest + 2 or 4 days of funding.

- Example of calculation:

Bond:	9.5 per cent 25 January 2001
Domestic price:	103.5
Overnight rate (*Tjj*):	9.25
7 day price:	103,5 - (7 x 9.5) + 2 ((103.5 + 5.83) x 9.25) = 103.37
Trade date:	6 September 1991
Coupon value-date:	13 September 1991
Settlement date:	13 September
Last coupon-date:	25 January 1991
Days accrued:	231
Accrued interest:	9.5 x 231/365 = 6.012
Nominal:	FFr 10m
Amount due:	$10{,}000{,}000 \times [(103.37/100) + [(9.5/100) \times (231/365)]]$

= FFr10,938,232.88

Other possibilities can be negotiated by the two counterparties.

Settlement and delivery

There are three systems for clearing OAT trades:

- An inter-SVT system, reserved for primary dealers and managed by SICOVAM.
- A system for non-SVT French clients. Transactions are settled three days after the trade-date by a transfer of funds from a Banque de France account and a transfer of securities within SICOVAM. This system has recently been replaced by the RELIT payment-against-delivery system.
- Clearance through Cedel and Euroclear for international counterparties (transaction date + 7).

15.10 *Market practices*

Coupon payment

On French fixed-rate bonds, coupon payments are annual. On variable-rate instruments, coupons can be paid semi-annually or even quarterly.

First coupon

If the first coupon does not run for a whole year, it is usually calculated *pro rata temporis*. Some recent assimilable issues have first coupons which are reckoned in such a way that yield-to-maturity is adjusted on market rates at the date of issue though the issue can be assimilated, after the first coupon, to a previous issue.

Partly-paid issues

There have been no new partly-paid issues, as fund managers have used futures and options for leverage.

Ex-dividend

French securities do not go ex-dividend prior to coupon-date. There are plans to introduce the UK practice (where gilt-edged securities go ex-dividend 37 days before the next interest payment).

Redemption

At present, both the Treasury and many public sector borrowers issue bullet bonds, but corporate issuers still have some constant annuity issues outstanding. These issues can be constant annuity by series, yearly equal reimbursement, redemption by series, every *N* years redemption by equal series, or yearly unequal series. Nearly all new corporate bonds are bullet issues.

Denomination

Usual denominations are FFr 2000 (OATs) or FFr 5000 (other issues), but there are also a few FFr 10,000 and FFr 20,000. Some old issues, however, can be found with denominations of FFr 1000 nominal, or below.

Form

On the French bond market, both registered and bearer forms of bonds can be used. As of 3 November 1984, bearer securities are no longer represented by paper certificates in France, but are rather held as book entries. Management and transfer of ownership are done through current account with SICOVAM.

Dealing practices

Quotations are made on a clean price basis and a percentage of nominal value. The minimum fluctuation is 0.01 per cent, while the maximum change from one day to the next is 2 per cent - beyond this limit an indicative bid (or asked) price is published. Exceptions to this convention are convertible bonds, and some indexed or variable-rate bonds, which are quoted in French francs (to two decimal places); the quoted price includes accrued interest.

Withholding tax

See Section 15.13 (Taxation).

Settlement

See Section 15.11 (Settlement).

Sinking funds

Fewer and fewer issues feature sinking funds, of which there are two types:

Mandatory sinking funds

In the case of mandatory sinking funds, all bonds redeemed have to be drawn, the issuer having no right to buy bonds below par in the secondary market and deduct the amount bought back from the amount to be drawn. This is the form of sinking fund used in France.

Non-mandatory sinking funds

In the UK, the USA and the euromarket, sinking fund provisions allow the issuer to buy bonds in the secondary market (if the price is below par) and to 'surrender' them to the sinking fund. If the issuer has not been able to buy back part, or all, of what has to be sunk, then the necessary amount of bonds must be drawn. The American form of non-mandatory sinking fund is sometimes termed the 'mandatory purchase fund'.

In some cases in the USA, the issuer can accelerate the redemption process by drawing (and/or purchasing) twice the yearly amount normally drawn, provided an indenture has such a provision.

Neither of the two situations noted above apply to French sinking funds - everything must be drawn.

Semi-sinking / semi-purchase funds

In France, some indentures provide an opportunity to buy back bonds, up to half the amount of the drawing every year, when the yield-to-maturity is half the sum of the two following yields:

- yield-to-maturity computed disregarding the possibility of the issuer buying-back bonds
- yield computed by replacing the maturity with the next drawing date and replacing redemption price with the next drawing price

Exceptionally, some issues are more flexible: specifically, average-maturity, floating-rate issues can sometimes be bought at a bid price higher than the market price.

Yield-to-maturity calculations

When an indenture authorizes the buying-back of bonds by up to K per cent of the amount of the drawings, the yield-to-maturity is computed as the weighted average of yield N_1, with a weight of $1-K$, and a yield N_2, with a weight of K.

This method makes two assumptions:

- that the prevailing long-term rates are constant
- that the issuer buys back ex-coupon bonds

The assumptions are enough to justify approximation of the true yield-to-maturity for those who keep their bonds up to drawing. There is, however, a more refined method which gives the yield-to-maturity without the second assumption and which is called the 'Aspro[15] Method'.

Aspro is not a complicated method, as may be seen below. Averaging for the whole bond market, the difference in yield computed by these two methods is

[15] *Algorithme Simple Pour Rendements Obligataires (simple algorithm for computing bond yields)*

about 5 basis points. The Aspro Method is used by Data Finance in its weekly *Yield Book*. The method aims at determining a true yield-to-maturity for bondholders who wish to hold their bonds until drawing. It takes into account, for every drawing, a drawing probability for the bondholders.

$$Q_i = \frac{(1-K)\,M_i}{N_{i-1} - K.M_i}$$

Q_i		the probability for a bond to be drawn at the *i*th drawing
K		the proportion of the issue that the issuer can buy back as authorized by the indenture
M_i		number of bonds to be drawn at the *i*th drawing
$N_i{-}1$		number of bonds remaining before the drawing
p	$1\text{-}q$	probability of not being drawn
$p_0 ; p_1 ; p_{i-1}$		probabilities of not being drawn
q_i		probability of being drawn
Q_i	$p_0 \bullet p_1 \bullet p_{i-1} \bullet q_i$	probability of a bond being drawn at the q_i drawing
U_i	$p_0 \bullet p_1 \bullet p_{i-1} \bullet p_i$	probability of a bond not being drawn
E		bond price
C_i		coupon
R_i		repayment price

Fundamental equation: $E = E1 + E2$

or,

$$E = \sum_{i=1}^{i=n} \frac{Q_i \bullet R_i}{(1+t)^i} + \sum_{i=1}^{i=n} \frac{U_{i-1} \bullet C_i}{(1+t)^i}$$

E1 is the present value of the drawing, weighted by time probability for a bondholder to be reimbursed at time $i = Q_i$.

E2 is the present value of the coupon weighted by the probability for a bond to not be drawn at time $i = U_i$ ..

15.11 Settlement

French listed securities

All French listed securities, except OATs, primary market and *gris* (grey) market transactions are cleared through the RELIT payment-against-delivery system (see below).

The SLAB system is based on two-way notification of the conditions of transaction, whereas the ISB/SBI system is based on one-way notification.

ISB	SBI	SLAB
Between sociétés de bourse	Between sociétés de bourse and intermediaries	Deliver system through bilateral arrangements
All French securities		• Primary market
(bonds in RPTA, equities.. except primary and grey market, OAT)		• Grey market
		• OAT (introduced 16 March 1992)

Settlement is carried out by payment against delivery on T+5 business days, although for *comptant* equities this date was changed to T+3 from 9 March 1992. The clearing of OATs in Ecu is currently under review.

BTFs & BTANs (Saturne)

Settlement and delivery for BTFs and BTANs is based on the principle of delivery against payment and operates by means of the Saturne system implemented by the Banque de France.

The system is accessible to all institutions that hold cash and securities accounts with the Banque de France. Each Saturne member has sub-accounts to ensure the separation between BTFs and BTANs held for its own book and those held on behalf of the various categories of customers.

Relying on remote transmission, Saturne allows operations to be cleared on the trading day (spot clearing). The system is based on two-way notification of the conditions of transaction, i.e. by both counterparties. In the event of a mismatch, the Banque de France informs the counterparties of the anomaly. Each is then responsible for taking corrective action to ensure the trade is cleared. Counterparties using Cedel or Euroclear must go through their respective sub-accounts with Saturne.

Lending, borrowing and repurchase of securities

The development of lending and repurchase of securities in France has long been hampered by legal, fiscal and accounting restrictions.

The market has expanded recently under the impetus of a more detailed definition of the legal and regulatory framework (with particular reference to securities lending), the rapid growth of money market funds (SICAVs) and the forthcoming implementation of the highly-efficient RELIT system.

Temporary sales of securities are sales of stock against cash (or against other securities in the case of lending operations). The operation yields revenue similar to the money market rate (generally the average weighted rate, TMP, minus a margin), for a fixed period of time. These operations allow professional investors to hedge short positions by borrowing securities, and to finance long positions by selling securities on a temporary basis. They improve portfolio yield and enable institutions that do not have access to the money market to invest liquid assets at close to money-market rates. A temporary sale of securities involves a transfer of ownership from the seller to the buyer throughout the duration of the operation. In the case of the *remere* (see definitions below), the securities are removed from the seller's balance sheet. In the case of *prêt de titres* and *pension livrée,* they are reclassified and allocated to a different item on the balance sheet. If a coupon is detached during the operation, the market rules state that the buyer must give back the interest to the seller, with good value-date.

Under the French system, there are three types of repurchase agreement — the *remere*, the *pension livrée* and the straightforward repo - and a borrowing and lending facility (*prêt de titres*).

Prêt de titres

This operation allows holders of securities to increase the value of their portfolios through the yield from the temporary sales of those assets. Cash or collateral is sometimes delivered against the securities lent. The advantages of securities lending include highly-streamlined administrative procedures and a clearly defined legal and fiscal framework.

Securities lending operations between French residents are cleared through SICOVAM, in the case of OATs, and Saturne, in the case of BTFs and BTANs. Transactions involving non-residents can be dealt with by Cedel or Euroclear.

Pension livrée

A *pension livrée* is defined as an operation whereby the seller transfers the ownership of government or private instruments, transferable securities or negotiable debt securities, to the buyer. Under the agreement, which is irrevocable and binding on both parties, the buyer undertakes to return the securities to the seller for a set price and on a specified date; the seller undertakes to repurchase the instruments.

The specific features of the *pension livrée* are the irrevocable agreement between the two parties to unwind the transaction at a set date and the exchanges of funds at both ends of the operation. All these movements are recorded on the Saturne system.

Remere

A *remere* is a contract for the sale of securities that includes a repurchase option. The operation is unwound when the seller exercises that option. In view of the risk that the option will not be exercised, securities sold under this type of agreement often trade at a discount to the market. In a *remere,* ownership of the securities is transferred from the bond lender to the bond borrower.

Repo

Repos can be used in exactly the same way as in the USA and British markets. Typically, repos involve either the sale of securities with an undertaking to repurchase them at set dates and prices, or a loan of securities collateralized by other securities.

15.12 Yield calculation

The redemption yield on fixed-rate bullet bonds in France is more straightforward than in those countries which have semi-annual coupon bonds, because coupons are annual.

The formula is as follows:

$$P + cc = \sum_{k=1}^{n} \frac{C(1+y)^{-k} + 100(1+y)^{-n}}{(1+y)^{a}}$$

where,

y	yield-to-maturity
P	clean price, to two decimal places
C	annual coupon
n	number of whole years to maturity
a	fraction of year to the next coupon payment, equal to the number of actual days divided by 365 (366 in a leap year or, more specifically, when a 29 February falls between the last and next coupon)
cc	accrued interest, equal to C, multiplied by the number of days since last coupon payment, plus one, divided by 365 (or 366), to three decimal places

Eurofranc bonds

It is a market convention to use the ISMA formula in determining yields. The results are very close to those given by the domestic method.

Comité de Normalisation Obligatairs (CNO)

This official commission of bond experts, whose members are SVT primary dealers on the bond market, has created a number of indices capable of measuring the total return of various components of the French bond market. The work of this commission, in creating the indices, was designed not only to improve public knowledge of the performance of the markets, but also to be a reliable reference for index-linked fund management, as well as a tool for the measurement of the performance of mutual funds.

The main indices are as follows:

- Fixed-rate: government, public sector & private sector bond indices
- Floating-rate: three indices with a monthly, quarterly reset reference, plus a long-term reference

15.13 Taxation

Taxation of securities traded in the cash market

French residents

■ Bonds

• Individuals liable to income tax.
Interest (exempt from withholding tax) is subject to either a flat 18.1 per cent levy in discharge of all other taxes, or progressive taxation after an annual rebate of FFr 16,000 for a married couple and FFr 8000 for single persons (a single rebate on income from French equities and bonds). Capital gains on the sale of securities are taxed at 18.1 per cent, if the total proceeds exceed FFr 307,600 for 1990 income. The total should be raised to FFr 316,900 for 1991 income

Generally, redemption premiums are not taxable if an investor 'carries' the bonds until redemption, and if the premium does not exceed 5 per cent of the issue price. Exceptions to this rule include premiums on securities such as FELINs, where the revenue is calculated annually on the basis of the yield-to-maturity of the security at issue.

• Non-profit organizations.
Income from *emprunts d'Etat* bonds issued before January 1987 is tax-exempt. For bonds issued after that date, the rate of taxation is 10 per cent. Capital gains on the sale of securities are not taxed.

• Legal entities subject to corporate income tax.
Interest, redemption premiums and capital gains are taxed at the standard corporate income tax rate of 34 per cent. Interest paid on bonds is taxable when cashed.

■ BTANs and BTFs

• Individuals liable to income tax
Interest, redemption premiums and capital gains are subject either to a flat 18.1 per cent levy in discharge of all other taxes, or at the progressive rate of income tax.

• Non-profit organizations
Income is taxed at 10 per cent. Capital gains are exempt.

• Legal entities subject to corporate income tax
Interest, redemption premiums and capital gains are included in a company's profits and taxed at the standard corporate income tax rate of 34 per cent. Income from BTFs and BTANs is taxed on the basis of interest accrued to year-end closing.

Non-residents

Interest on bonds, BTFs, BTANs, and other short-term instruments, are exempt from the flat 18.1 per cent levy.

■ Non-residents located in countries bound by tax treaties with France
Non-residents establish their status by means of a sworn declaration, submitted each time they change fiscal domicile.

This simplified system, applicable to non-resident individuals and legal entities whose paying agent is domiciled in France, was implemented by ministerial decisions of 17 March 1988 (*emprunts d'Etat* bonds held by corporate investors) and 5 May 1988 (Treasury bills held by corporate entities and *emprunts d'Etat* and Treasury bills held by private investors). This regime is also valid for non-resident corporate members of Cedel and Euroclear.

■ Non-residents located in countries that have no tax treaty with France
Non-resident status must be proved for each interest payment.

Taxation of futures and options

All income received by private individuals is taxed at 18.1 per cent. Losses can only be charged against gains of a similar nature made during the same year, or the five following years. Income earned by legal entities is taxed at the standard rate of corporate income tax (34 per cent), except in specific cases of hedging operations that have been duly identified and can be used to offset gains on Matif and losses in the cash market (or vice versa). One exception to these rules involves the gains made by locals (NIPs - Négociateurs Individuel de Parquet or 'private floor negotiators') on Matif, which are subject to personal income tax.

Non-resident customers

Non-residents are exempt from taxation on Matif transactions on three conditions:

- they are not permitted to have a permanent establishment in France
- the country in which they reside must be bound to France by a tax treaty
- they must submit a simplified declaration of non-residence

15.14 *Futures & options*

Overview

Le Marché à Terme International de France (Matif), was created in 1986. Its operations are managed by the Chambre de Compensation Matif SA (clearing house), which is responsible for the organization, negotiation , compensation and guarantees the *bonne fin*, or contract performance, of all transactions.

A third of all members of the Matif are foreigners. With 32 members out of 95 in 1991 (cf. 3 in 1986), and with 30 to 50 per cent of the open position (varying by contract) held by foreign investors, these statistics confirm how international the Matif has become. With the Globex trading system becoming operational later this year (1992) Matif is remaining at the forefront of technology, and thereby enabling international investors to trade Matif contracts around the clock. With a 29.9 per cent rise in the number of contracts traded in 1991, Matif has become the fastest growing financial futures exchange in the world (see Figure 15.60).

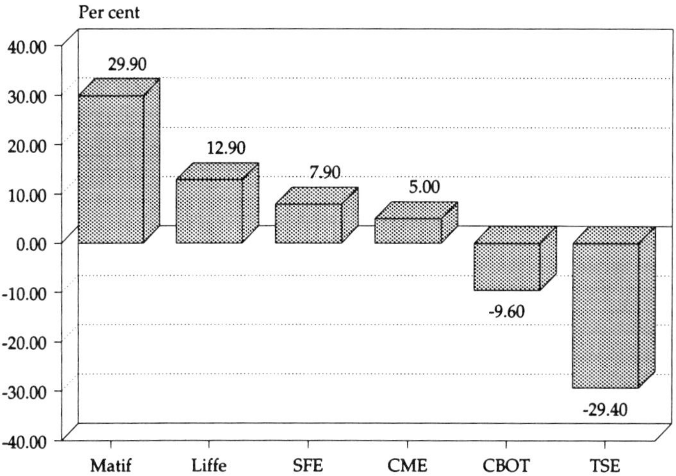

Figure 15.60 Change in activity on the world's six most important financial futures exchanges, 1991 vs. 1990
Source: Matif SA

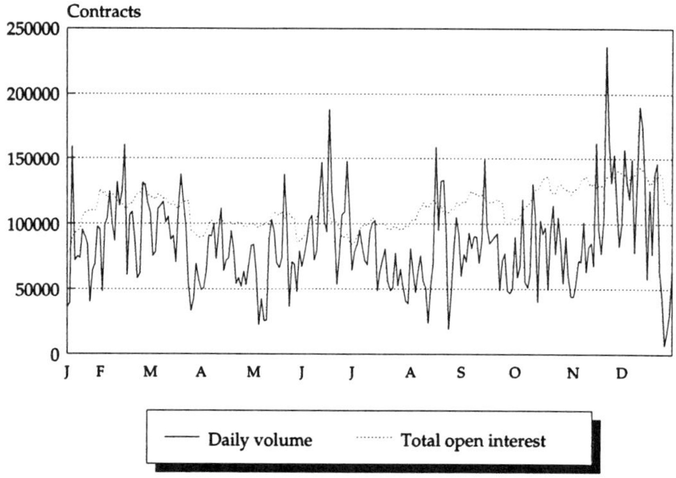

Figure 15.61 Matif's notional bond futures contract - daily volume & open interest, 1991
Source: Matif SA

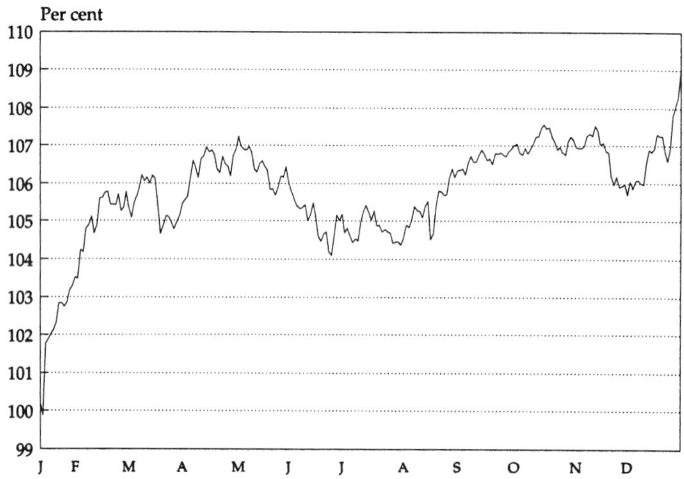

Figure 15.62 Matif's notional bond futures contract - price history, 1991 (2nd contract month)
Source: Matif SA

Notional bond futures contract

With over 21 million contracts cleared in 1991, the 7-10 year notional bond futures contract has become the second most-traded long-term interest rates futures product in the world.

Open interest in the contract has constantly remained at an average daily level of 80,000 contracts (see Figure 15.61). This figure could be wrongly attributed to a static situation in which players hedge portfolios and maintain positions for long periods. However, if one looks at the liquidity levels, the correct interpretation is quite different: The definition of liquidity is: volume ÷ open interest. A figure of 0.5, for instance, would indicate that the exchange turns over 50 per cent of the open interest in a single day - the higher the figure, the greater the liquidity. For the first half of 1990, liquidity on the notional bond contract averaged around 0.8 or 80 per cent, which is one of the highest figures in the world.

The price history of the futures contract (see Figure 15.62) has been staying very much in line with that of the cash market. As usual, when long-term yields are higher than short-term rates, then the more distant the contract month, the lower its price becomes compared to those nearby.

As France has experienced inverted, rather than flat, yield curves, it should be no surprise to learn that the prices of the different contract months have been crossing each other. The difference in price between the futures and a cash price enables the calculation of an implied repo rate, and the difference between the implied repo rate and the cash market rate signifies whether the futures contract is either cheaper, or more expensive, than it 'should' be.

The historical volatility of a futures contract (see Figure 15.63) is an interesting statistic, in the sense that it can explain at the same time sharp movements in:

- the volume of futures contracts traded
- the volume and the price of options on such a futures contract

Options on the notional bond futures contract

With over 8 millions contracts traded in 1991 (a rise of 13.5 per cent on 1990), this contract remains one of the most liquid options markets in the world, with the average open position being above 300,000 contracts (see Figures 15.64 & 15.65). The correlation between options volume and futures volume is very high, with options volume averaging about 40 per cent of the futures volume.

Option market-makers account for 45 per cent of the volume and contribute particularly to the liquidity of out-of-the-money and long options. By agreement

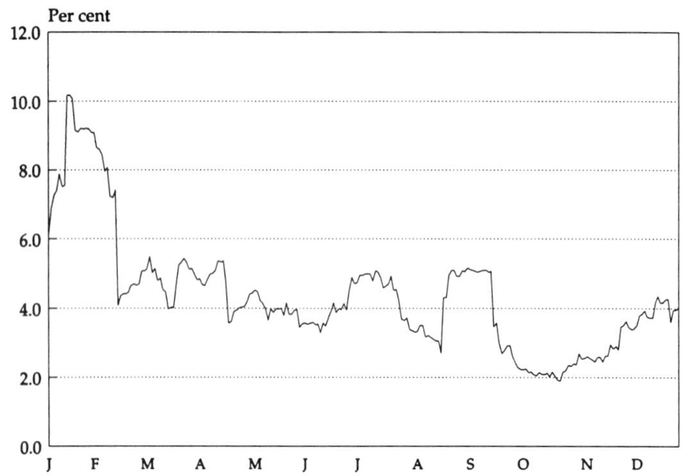

Figure 15.63 Matif's notional bond futures contract - historical volatility, 1991
Source: Matif SA

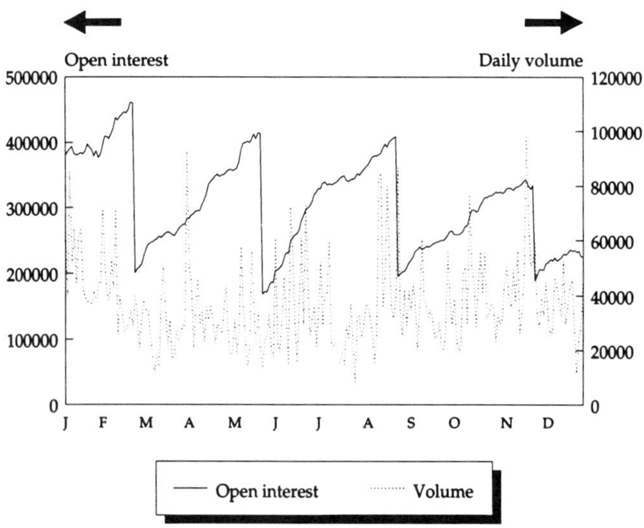

Figure 15.64 Matif's options on bond futures contract - daily volume & open interest, 1991
Source: Matif SA

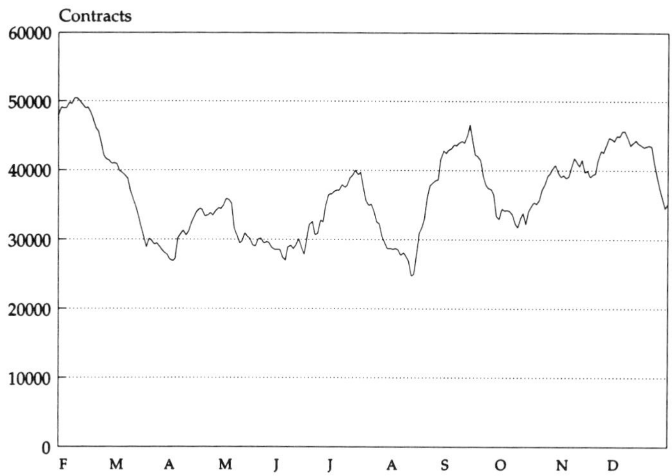

Figure 15.65 Matif's options on notional bond futures contract - 20-day moving average of volume, 1991
Source: Matif SA

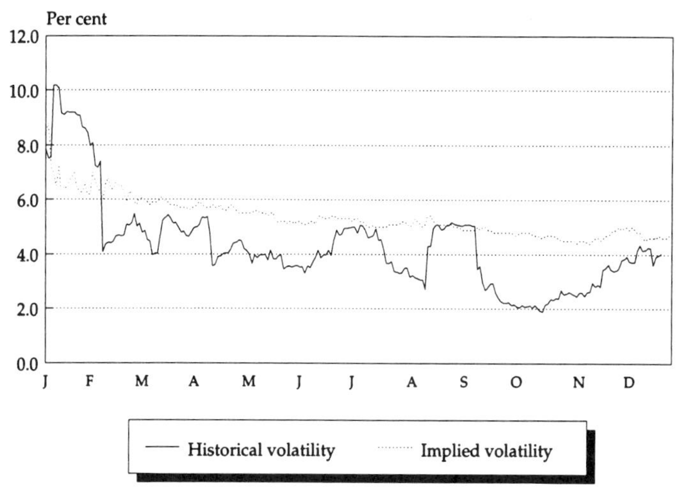

Figure 15.66 Historical volatility of futures contract & implied volatility of the options contract, 1991
Source: Matif SA

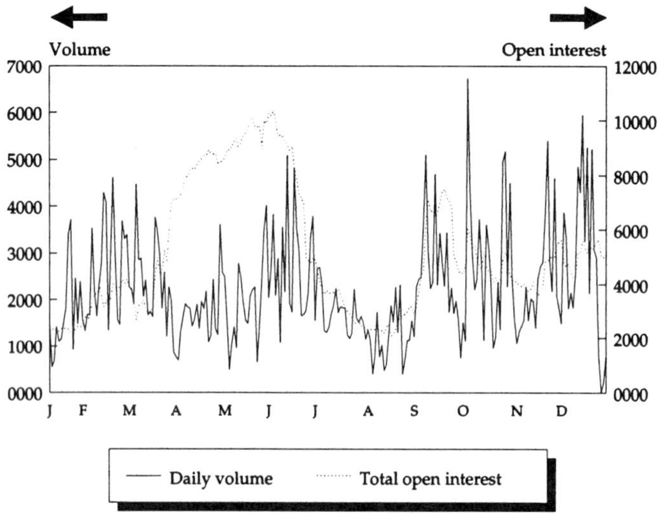

Figure 15.67 Matif's Ecu bond futures contract - daily volume & open interest, 1991
Source: Matif SA

Figure 15.68 Matif's Ecu bond futures contract - 1991 price history (2nd contract month)
Source: Matif SA

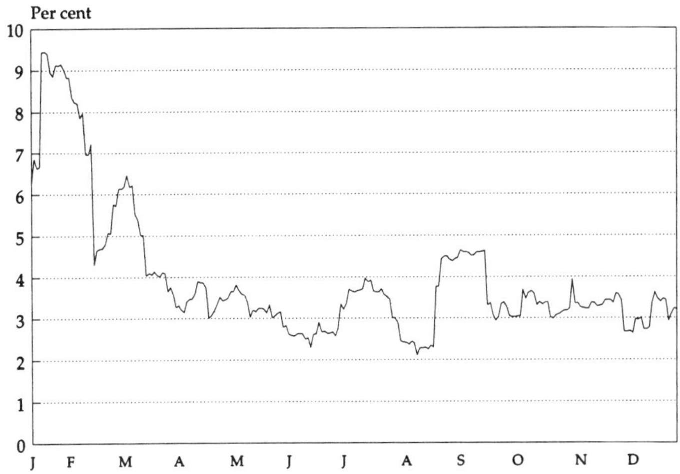

Figure 15.69 Matif's Ecu bond futures contract - historical volatility, 1991
Source: Matif SA

with Matif, market-makers maintain live prices in 9 options, with strike prices around the at-the-money option, and maximum spreads of 10 basis points.

Ecu bond futures contract

This contract (see Figures 15.67 - 15.69) was created in September 1990. With 55 per cent of the open position held by non-residents, the contract's international dimension is clear, a factor which contributes to making Matif a major source of reference in the Ecu financial markets.

Options on the Ecu bond futures contract

These options (see Figure 15.70), which have been quoted over-the-counter since March 1991, were listed on Matif from May 1992. The exchange has selected 5 market-makers which have the obligation to maintain markets in 9 options, with strike prices around the at-the-money level, and with a maximum spread of 10 basis points - the quoted premium price being good for up to 100 contracts.

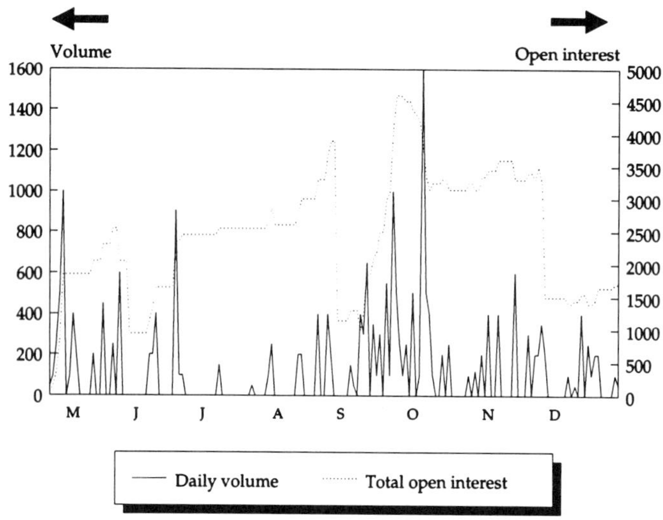

Figure 15.70 Matif's options on Ecu bond futures contract - daily volume & open interest, 1991
Source: Matif SA

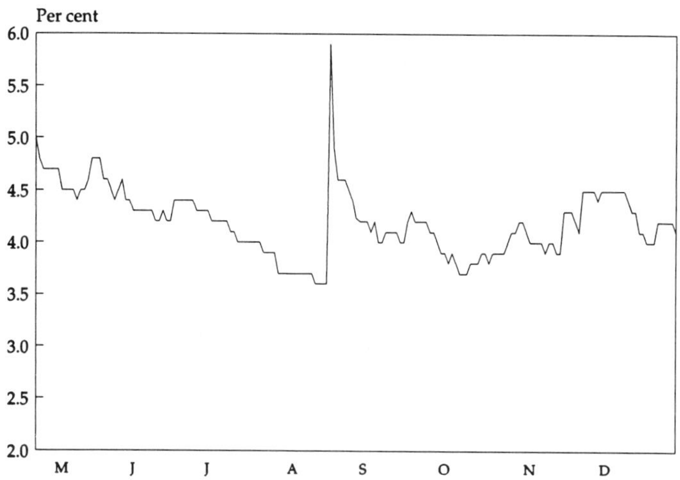

Figure 15.71 Ecu OTC options - implied volatility, Apr-Dec 1991
Source: Matif SA

15.15 Money markets

Overview

Negotiable money market instruments available to non-banks are called TCNs. (*titres de créance négociables*). They break down into categories according to maturity:

Short-term

Short-term instruments are issued for maturities shorter than a year. They include BTFs (*bons du Trésor à taux fixe*), BTs (*billets de Trésorerie*) issued by corporate entities, CDNs (*certificats de dépôt négociables*) issued by banks and BISFs (*bons des institutions et des sociétés financières*).

One year is the upper limit for mandatory reserve requirements with Banque de France.

Medium-term

Medium-term notes, BMTNs (*bons à moyen terme négociables*), are issued for maturities longer than one year; no upper limit has been formally set. They include BTANs (*bons du Trésor à taux annuel normalisé*), CDNs, BTs, BISFs. Rating of programmes is *de facto* compulsory. This category was introduced on 13 February 1992.

Hybrids

Some CDNs, and BISFs, retain a hybrid status; qualifying borrowers can issue CDNs, and BISFs for up to two years while freeing themselves from BMTN issuance regulations. These two-year CDs mostly address unrated subsidiaries of big institutions and are treated as short-term instruments.

Short-term instruments

Common features

Denomination:	FRF 1m
Coupon:	Fixed-rate, prepaid. These securities are issued at a discount.
Maturity:	More than 10 days and less than one year

(cont.)

Interest payment:	None. Redemption at par
Prices and interest calculation:	The yield rate 'in-fine' is used: n = actual number of days; R = yield in-fine; C = nominal amount; P = net amount due $P = \frac{C}{[1 + (R \bullet \frac{n}{36000})]}$

Specific features

■ BTF

Outstanding volume:	FRF 139bn
Maturity:	Generally 13, 26, 52 weeks
Issuance conditions:	Weekly auctions
Prices and interest calculation:	At the auction, discount rate is used for bids

n = number of days; t = discount rate; C = nominal amount; P = net amount due

$$P = C \bullet \frac{[100 - (t \bullet \frac{n}{360})]}{100}$$

On the market, either when-issued, or secondary (cash and/or forward), the yield rate 'in-fine' is used, instead of the discount rate.

n = number of days; R = yield in-fine; C = nominal amount; P = net amount due

$$P = \frac{C}{[1 + (\frac{R \bullet n}{36000})]}$$

t = discount rate and R = yield in fine, are related by the formula:

$$R = \frac{t}{[1 - (\frac{t \bullet n}{36000})]}$$

$$t = \frac{R}{[1 + (\frac{R \bullet n}{36000})]}$$

Issuer:	The French Treasury
Investors:	Financial institutions, central banks and money-market funds (OPCVM monétaires)

■ BTs (*billets de Trésorerie*)

Outstanding volume:	FRF 158bn
Issuers:	About 100 corporate entities
Investors:	Financial institutions (56 per cent) money-market funds (OPCVM) (31 per cent)

■ CDN (*certificats de dépôt négociables*)

Outstanding volume:	FRF 1044bn
Issuers:	Banks (art. 18 Law of 18/01/84) 21 of which account for 63 per cent of activity
Investors:	Financial institutions (33 per cent), corporate treasurers (29 per cent), money-market funds (OPCVM) (22 per cent), insurance companies (10 per cent)

■ BISF (*bons des institutions et des sociétés financières*)

Outstanding volume:	FRF 135bn
Issuers:	IFS (*institutions financières spécialisées*) which include Crédit Foncier (17 per cent), CAR (8 per cent), CEPME (8 per cent) Crédit National (7 per cent), and *sociétés financières* such as DIAC (10 per cent) CDE (10 per cent)
Investors:	Financial institutions (70 per cent), money-market funds (OPCVM) (22 per cent)

Medium-term instruments - BMTNs

Common features

Issuers:	French and foreign entities
Rating of programmes:	Compulsory
Currency:	Any. Banque de France may suspend issues in a specified currency for the purposes of monetary regulation
Denomination:	FRF 1m, or equivalent
Coupon:	Can be fixed-rate or floating-rate; in this case, re-fixed no more frequently than monthly

(cont.)

Maturity:	1 year and over (no upper limit)
Interest payment:	Fixed-rate: paid annually; floating-rate: depending on re-fix.
Prices and interest calculation:	Prices are quoted on a yield-to-maturity basis, to two decimal places. Coupon accrues on actual days over a 365/366 days basis
Investors:	No accurate information yet available on this new instrument

Specific features

■ BTANs

Issuer:	French Treasury
Currency:	FRF. Issues in Ecu are scheduled for 1992
Issuance conditions:	For each maturity, an auction of fungible BTANs is held monthly, until the issue is shorter than 2 (resp. 5) years, then a new tap is opened
Outstanding volume:	FRF 417bn
Maturity:	2 and 5 years (approximately)
Coupon:	Fixed
Investors:	Central banks, financial institutions, insurance companies, managed funds

■ BMTNs issued by banks, IFS and SF

The qualifying issuers (art 18.99, Law of 18 January 1984) can affix the name of CDNs, or BISFs, to the generic name of BMTNs. Investors are financial institutions, insurance companies and managed funds.

■ Hybrids - CDNs and BISFs which are not BMTNs

Qualifying issuers (mostly unrated subsidiaries) must choose between issuing BMTNs (in which rating is mandatory, while maturity is unlimited), or issuing CDs (in which rating is not necessary, but maturity is limited to up to 2 years only). Investors are financial institutions and managed funds

Sources for this section: Cahier des TCN (published monthly by Banque de France). No statistics for BMTNs are currently available.

15.16 *Interest rate history*

Prior to 1989

After the first presidential election of Mr Mitterand in 1981, French rates rose strongly. Short-term rates peaked at 20 per cent, while bond rates moved above 17 per cent. The real long-term rate went up from 2 per cent to 6 per cent, although it later fell back to 3 per cent in the 4th quarter of 1983; later it stabilized in the 5 to 7 per cent range. Following this period of strength, rates followed a downtrend which ended in mid-1986 with short-term rates at 7 per cent and long rates at 8 per cent. Bond turnover increased from FFr 150bn in 1982 to FFr 1675bn in 1986. This increase continued through 1988, when turnover reached FFr 3425bn, as long-term rates began trending up in Germany, Japan and the UK.

Short-term rates were rather stable in 1986 and 1987, despite the fact that short-term rates were beginning to rise in the US, because the French economy was sluggish. By the autumn of 1987, French long-term real rates peaked above 7 per cent.

From the end of 1986 to the 4th quarter of 1987, long-term rates trended up, at a time when the oil price was on a downturn.

The Matif long bond contract, which was launched in February 1986, peaked at 114 by mid-1986 but, by the time of the Crash in 1987, it had reached a low-point of 86. As a result of the Crash, however, the long-term trend in rates was instantly reversed. This one day reversal, which was seen in all bond markets, was followed by a quiet period in the market, which lasted for two years, until August 1989.

1990-1991

From August 1989 until September 1990, there was a mild bear market which came to an end during the Gulf crisis. Prior to the conflict, Matif's long bond contract was at 96. As the war unfolded, it rose to 108.50, with long-term rates accordingly falling from 10.50 to below 9 per cent

With the ending of the Gulf War, the long-term real rate went down by 1 per cent, to 6 per cent, a level which was maintained throughout 1991. Short-term rates fluctuated in a 9-10 per cent trading range. Long-term rates also showed some small fluctuations.

In summary, the downtrend of rates remained as long as inflation was on a downtrend. Inflation rates have followed a see-saw pattern since 1986, following the fluctuation in the price of oil and, naturally, long-term rates in France have been influenced by these factors.

French monetary policy, under Mr Bérégovoy (as minister of finance), is designed to ensure that the behaviour of the French franc in the European monetary system allows the spread against German rates to diminish steadily. The short-term spread with Germmany became negative for a few days after the reduction of official French rates in October but, with German rates being higher than those of France (which were aggravated by the effects of a weakening dollar), an equilibrium could not be achieved.

The convergence of French long-term rates can be compared to the situation in Denmark, where the long-term spread fluctuates within a stable range similar to that experienced in France (0.30 - 0.60). The Dutch long-term rate spread, meanwhile, has fluctuated in the range of 0 - 0.50, for years.

The narrow spread with German rates is now the principal feature of the French market (see French rates in Figures 15.72 & 15.77, in Section 15.17). This situation is similar to that which prevails between the Deutschemark and the long-term rates of those other countries which are pegged, either formally or informally, with the German currency (e.g. Denmark, Belgium and Holland).

15.17 *Inter-market spreads*

Three-month PIBOR vs. 10-year government bonds

The potential for a fall in short-term interest rates, which was side-tracked in 1990 by the uncertainty arising from the Gulf Crisis, was back in earnest in 1991.

With the global financial environment favouring a decrease in long-term rates, France, with its inflation well under control and with one of the highest levels of real interest rates world-wide, attracted investors to French franc bonds in the expectation that they would outperform others. At the beginning of the year, between mid-January and mid-March, an important fall in short-term interest rates took place, as the 3-month PIBOR moved from 11.29 per cent to 9.81 per cent on an actuarial (or 'bond equivalent') basis. Nevertheless, the magnitude of German economic growth caused by reunification, precluded all possibility of a further decline in French short-term rates. The change of government which took place at the end of the semester was very negative for the 3-month PIBOR, as subsequent attempts to disconnect the French monetary policy of the Banque de France from that of the Bundesbank brought the central bank's

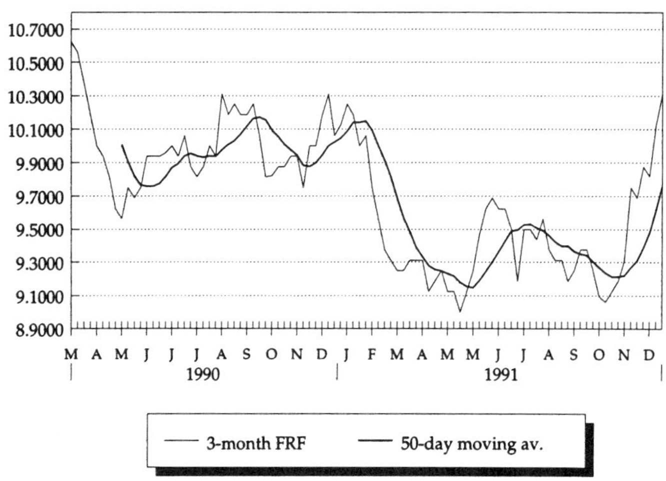

Figure 15.72 Three-month PIBOR

money deposit rate down to 8.75 per cent on the 17 October 1991. However, persistent difficulties of the French franc within the EMS forced the monetary authorities to take action and raise the same key rate to 9.60 per cent in December 1991 (cf. 9.25 per cent at the beginning of the year).

Thus, 1991 will be remembered as the year of inversion for the French yield curve with the 3-month PIBOR/10-year government bond spread moving from -0.5 per cent in the third quarter of 1990 to +1.5 per cent in December 1991 (see Figure 15.73).

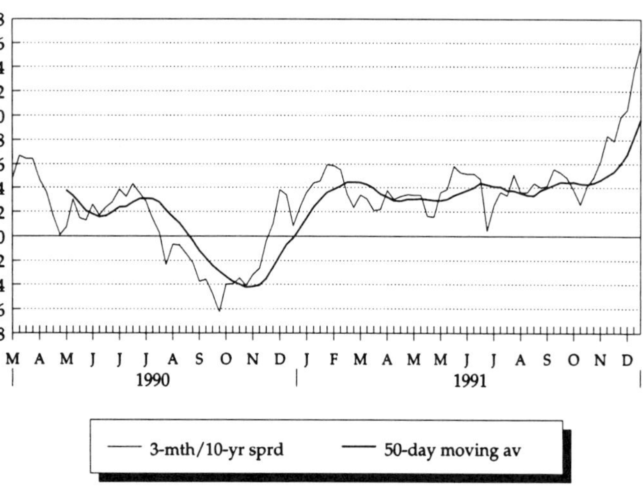

Figure 15.73 3-month/10-yr government bond spread

TME margin on FRN

The TME reference is indexed on average yield of state loans with 7 to 10 years' maturity. The actuarial margin of the FRNs moves in relation to the shape of the yield curve. It may be noticed in Figure 15.74 that there is an excellent correlation between the 3-month/10-year spread and the margin of FRNs indexed on the TME. As the yield curve steepens, the demand for FRNs on the TME reference, increases. To cover OATs indexed on the TME, arbitragers purchase the Matif bond contract and sell the Matif PIBOR contract. The inversion of the yield curve in 1991 explains the historically high level of actuarial margins of TME indexed bonds.

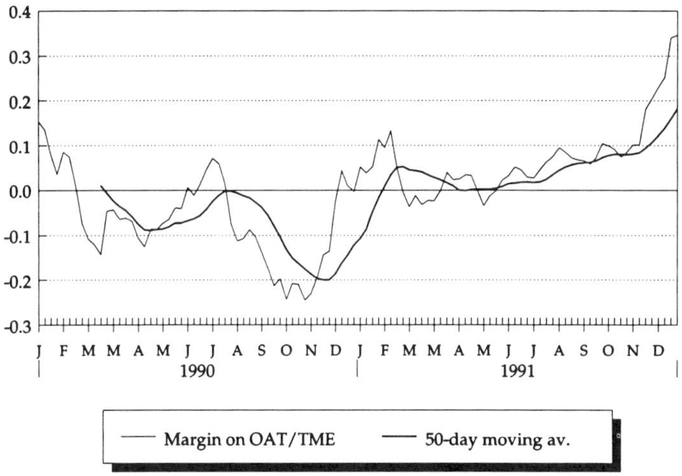

Figure 15.74 Margin on OAT bond indexed on TME

Public sector bonds vs. government bonds

During 1990 and 1991, investors have been less demanding in terms of yield pick-up on public sector bonds. From a level of 50 basis points prior to the Gulf War, the spreads increased due to a flight to quality at the end of 1990. But the fall in spreads (from 55 bp to 40 bp) in 1991, is important. This evolution has made it possible for the better-rated public issuers to issue new debt at an average of 80 bp lower than in 1990. The major reasons are as follows:

- The fact that new issues were fungible to older bonds has increased the size of the issues and therefore their liquidity.
- The restructuring of the debt of major public issuers by means of open market exchange (OPE). These operations have reduced the number of illiquid issues and created some benchmarks issues.
- The creation of specialist dealers in public bonds (SVP) to enhance the liquidity in the bonds of 4 major issuers (Crédit Foncier de France, Crédit Local de France, EDF and SNCF). Ten dealers, based in Paris, have entered an agreement to make markets with buy and sell quotes on the screens for these issues. This price guarantee has made non-residents more interested in these bonds.

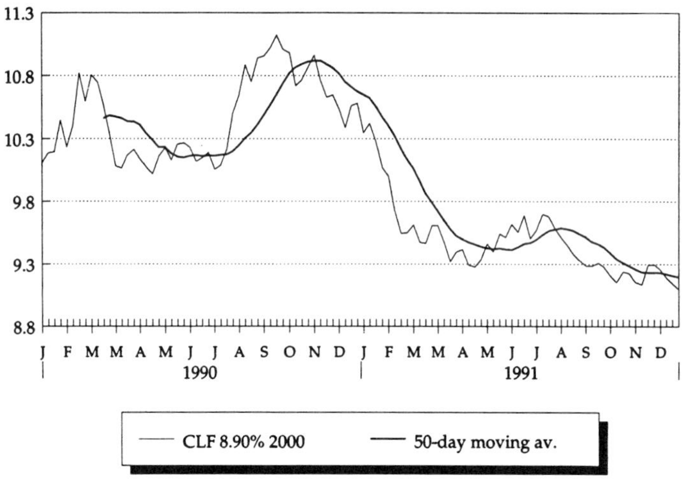

Figure 15.75 Public sector 10-yr bond: CLF 8.90% 2000
Source: Fininfo

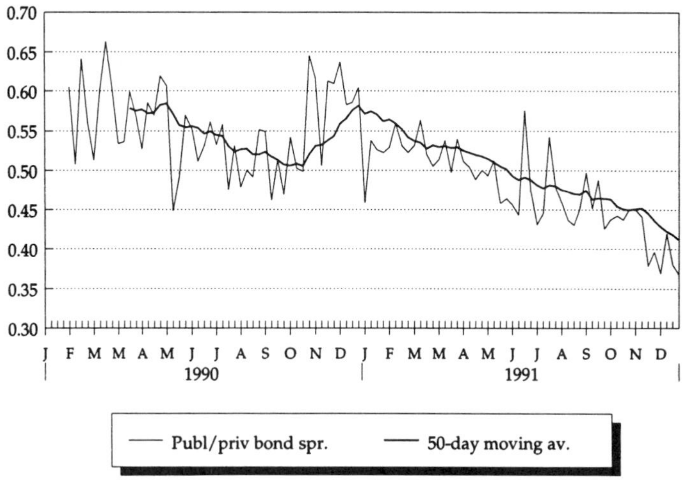

Figure 15.76 Public sector bond (CLF 8.9% 2000) vs. government bond (OAT 8.5% 2000)

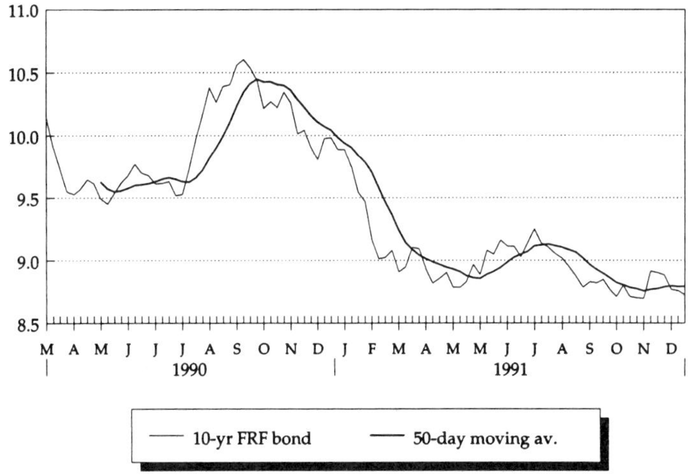

Figure 15.77 FRF OAT 8.5% 2000
Source: Fininfo

OAT vs. BTAN

Historically, OATs were dearer to BTANs by 25 bp. In the summer of 1991, OATs with less than 5 years to maturity lost their fiscal advantage. The attraction of the higher coupons of OATs is offset by the fact that they are less liquid than BTANS on the secondary market.

10-year bonds

During the second half of 1990, when the invasion of Kuwait took place, the yield on 10-year bonds in France surged from 9.5 per cent to 10.5 per cent (see Figure 15.77). The speedy outcome of the war created a bond rally during the first quarter of 1991. Investment demand, from both domestic sources and non-residents, brought the 10-year yield to nearly 9 per cent. Buoyed by optimism, international investors bought at the long end of the French market to hold bonds, rather than just trade them. The French bond market outperformed other bond markets with the yield spread with Germany reducing from 120 bp to 60 bp by the end of the year

The change of government that took place at the beginning of summer 1991, together with the hopes of a fall in short-term interest rates, brought the yield back up to 9.20 per cent in a bond market which, by that time, had been deserted by non-residents. With the confirmation of a recession in the US, French franc long-term rates fell during the last quarter and came close to the objective of 8.5 per cent which was expected by investors on the French market. With a volume of FFr 3000bn, two-thirds of which was transacted by non-residents, 1991 will be remembered as the international year of the French bond market.

10-year French/German spread

Since the end of 1989, the date of the reunification of Germany, the French/German spread (see Figure 15.78) has been continuously reduced from 180 bp to 35 bp (in Oct 1991). The evolution of the unified Germany has affected the economic performance of the ex-West German economy with regard to both infla-

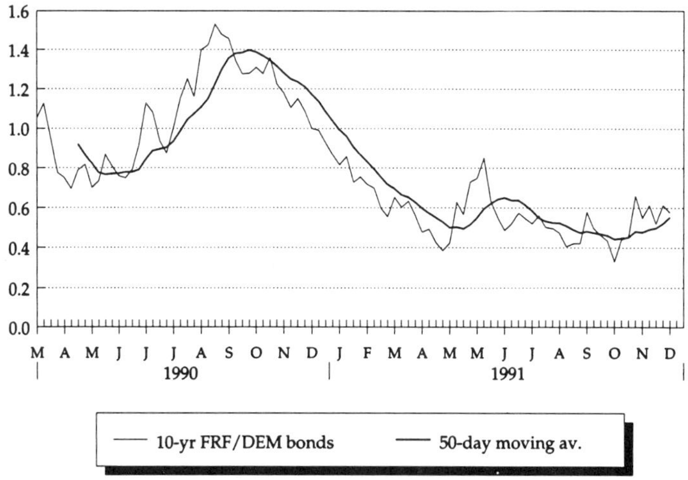

Figure 15.78 FRF OAT 8.5% 2000 vs. DEM 8.0% 2002
Source: CDC, Fininfo

tion and borrowing requirements. The Bundesbank's tightening of short rates, and the increase in new issuance of bonds, made the 10-year yield rise from 7.0 per cent in Oct 1989, to 9.2 per cent in Oct 1990.

Furthermore, the economic policies of Mr. P. Bérégovoy, which are based on a stable franc *vis-à-vis* the Deutschemark, has brought about a reduction in the inflation differential between Germany and France (from +2.5 per cent in 1989 to -1.5 per cent in 1991). However, this long-term evolution was halted by two problems:

- In August 1990, the impact of the war in the Gulf affected OATs more adversely than Bunds, reflecting the different types of investors in these two markets.
- In June 1991, the spread increased from 50 bp to 90 bp following the change of government in France, together with rumours of Mr. P. Bérégovoy's departure and the nomination of an unpopular prime minister, Mme Cresson.

Also, the failure of the last fall in the official rates, which took place in October 1991 in a weak dollar environment (creating friction within the EMS), has put a stop to any further narrowing of the spread. If the Maastricht Summit Agreement can stabilize them, then fundamentals which are still in favour of France, should work to its advantage.

10-year French franc vs. US dollar

Because of the lack of correlation of the French and US economies, the analyses of the 10-year spread requires a multitude of explanations, if it is to be understood completely. For the period under review, the political events in Europe and in the Gulf are of particular importance; the evolution can be broken down into three phases:

- From April 1990, there is a restrictive monetary policy in Europe, while the US economy slows down, the banking sector goes through a crisis and the level of inflation falls. The spread widens from 70 bp to 130 bp. With the Gulf War (August 1990 to January 1991), the lack of transparency on bond markets as a whole is relatively favourable to Treasury notes; OATs are sold and the spread reaches 190 bp at its widest.
- The end of the war, and the expectations of a growth in the US economy cancel the previous movement, and bring the spread down to 90 bp.
- The lack of economic growth, the major improvement in the level of US inflation (down from 6 per cent at the end of 1990 to 3 per cent at the end of 1991), the slack monetary policy of the Fed. (Fed. funds fell from 6 per cent to 4 per cent from May to December 1991) and a continued restrictive European monetary policy (headed by the Bundesbank), together make US bonds more attractive, and the spread increases to 180bp.

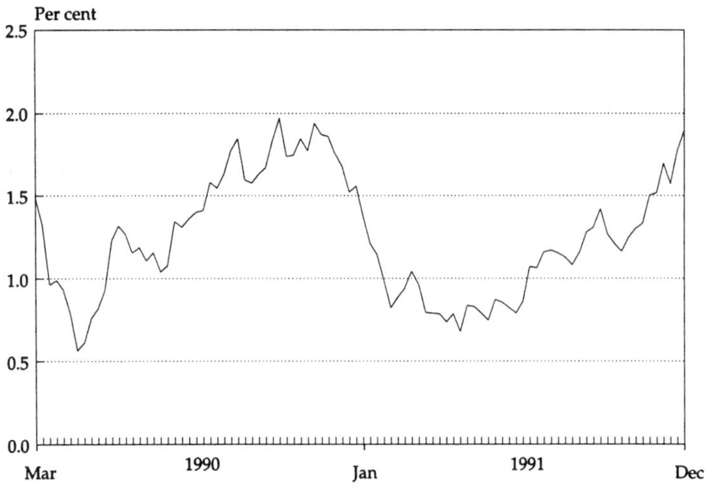

Figure 15.79 10-yr spread: French government bonds vs. US bonds

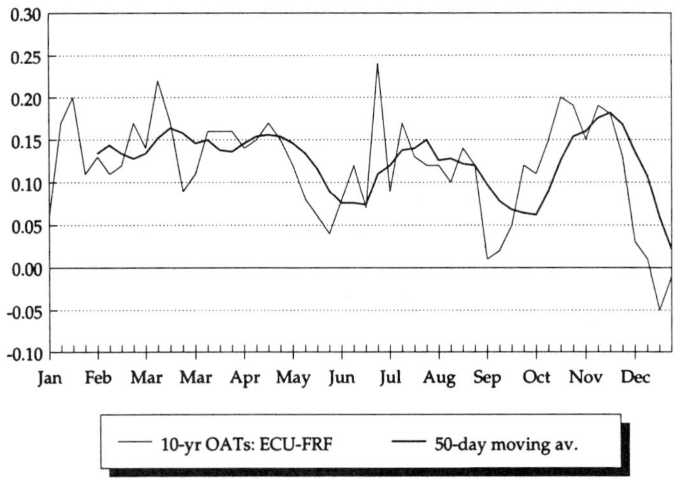

Figure 15.80 10-yr spread: OAT in ECUs vs. OAT in FRF

For 1992, with growth in the US economy now more probable and with growth in Europe under strain with a strong monetary policy (arising from German inflation and the effects of Maastricht) means that there will probably be a fourth phase which will signal a significant reduction in the spread.

Ecu vs. French franc

The 10-year Ecu/French franc bond spread evolved in 1991 in a narrow range (+ 30 bp-5 bp). In the period under review, the variations of the Ecu market, as against those of the major currencies of which it is composed (French franc, Deutschemark, British pound and Italian lira) are 70 per cent correlated to movements in the French franc bond market. Therefore, the differential between the Matif bond contract and Matif Ecu bond contract are being constantly watched by arbitragers as, too, are the spreads of these contracts against the cash market.

Two important periods may be identified:

- The spring of 1991, when a major fall in the French/German 10-year bond spread consequently made the French market dearer against the Ecu.
- From the 15th of September until the end of the year (the Maastricht Summit and the frozen Ecu discussions). At the beginning of the period, dealers disregarded the Ecu market - it would be left to fall back to its theoretical value. Later, when international dealers gathered that, after 1999, the Ecu was to be the currency of the strongest countries, they gave preference to the Ecu bond market over the French franc markets, and the spread duly went into negative territory.

This type of arbitrage, which features limited risks, is going to remain active for the foreseeable future.

15.18 Sources of reference

Newspapers and periodicals

- *La Tribune*
- *La Cote Defosses*
- *Les Echos*
- *La Synthese Financière*
- *L'Agefi*
- *Investir*
- *Journal des Finances*
- *Le Figaro* (pink pages of)
- *La Vie Française*
- *Option Finance*
- *Plus Values*
- *Haute Finance*
- *Dynasteurs*

Other financial publications

- *French Government Securities*
The Ministry of Finance and the Primary Dealers

- *En Direct des Marchés*
Fimagest (weekly)

- *La Lettre des Marchés des Taux*
Société Générale (weekly)

- *Fimat*
Société Générale (weekly)

- *Marché Financier*
CDC (monthly)

- *Financial Outlook*
CDC (monthly)

- *Accélérations*
Crédit Lyonnais (monthly)

- *Le Marché Obligataire Français*
Crédit Lyonnais (monthly)

- *Emprunts d'Etat*
Robert Lefèvre Vega Finance (monthly)

- *Marchés Obligataires et Monétaires*
Paribas (monthly)

- *Obligations Convertibles*
Didier Philippe (monthly)

- *La Semaine Obligataire*
Oddo (weekly)

Quote vendors and news agencies

- Reuters and Telerate provide information as shown in Figures 15.81 & 15.82

	Contributor	Subject				
TRES	Treasury	Menu				
SVTF-H	Banque de France	Reference rates for T-bonds				
Bond prices						
		BTF	*BTAN*	*OAT*	*OAT -ECU*	*Public sec.*
	Banque d'Escompte	BTFF	BEPG	BEPF		
	Banque Indosuez		ISVY	ISVT-V	ISVS-W	INDT-O
	BNP	TBNS	TBNQ	OBNP-Q	BNBB	OBNS-T
	Banque Paribas	PBAK	PBAA	PBAB-E	PBAG	PBAD-E
	CCF	MCCD-E	MCCE	OCCF-L	OCCI-X	OCCL-M
	CCBP	CBPX	CBPX	CBPX	CBPF-G	
	CDC	CDCJ	CDCK-L	CDCO-P-C	CDCE-F	CDCX-Y
	CGMI	CGMD	CGMD	CGMO-P-A		
	CNCA		CNCU	CNCV-W-U		
	Crédit Lyonnais		CLTB	CLYO	CLBJ	CLYO-R
	J.P. Morgan	CLTC	MGPB	MGPC-D	XECU-G-V	
	Nomura France	MGPB	NSVU	NSVT		
	Société Générale	NSVU	SGPF	SGOF		SGOG-I
	S.G. Warburg Bacot-Allain	SGPF	WFRC	WFRD-E	WSIQ	WSRF-G
	UBS France SA	WFRB	PLUT	PLUU		
	CPR	CPOB	CPOB	CPOA	CPOD	CPOC

Figure 15.81 Reuters pages

Page No.	Contributor	Subject			
20009-10	Treasury				
20018-19	Banque de France	Reference rates for T-bills			
Bond prices					
		BTF	*BTAN*	*OAT*	*OAT -ECU*
	Banque d'Escompte	2542	2542	2541	
	Banque Indosuez	2532	2532	2535-2533	
	BNP				
	Banque Paribas	20106		20105	
	CCF	20082	20081	20080	20080
	CCBP			8335	
	CDC				
	CGMI	8320	8320		
	CNCA		2545	2545	
	Crédit Lyonnais				
	J.P. Morgan	20101	20005-20101	20005	
	Nomura France				
	Société Générale				
	S.G. Warburg Bacot-Allain				
	UBS France SA		2527	2526	

Figure 15.82 Telerate pages

Number One retail bank in France

■ Key figures

FRF billion	**1991**
Capital funds	91.2
Consolidated net income	4.93
Customer loans	988.2
Customer deposits and bonds	1081.5
in number	
Customers	15,106,000
Employees	74,113
Automated teller machines	4,388

Number One retail bank in France

■ Market share

(percentage of total outstanding at year-end)

	1991	1990
Funds collected	19.5	18.6
Demand deposits	17.7	17.4
PEP savings plans	45.0	47.0
Home savings	30.5	30.4
Mutual funds (net assets)	14.7	15.2
Total loans	13.6	13.6
Loans to householders	25.2	24.9
Corporate loans	7.2	6.8

Number One retail bank in France

■ Total funds collected & managed

(in FRF million, as at 31 December)

	1991	1990
Demand deposit accounts	248,076	259,548
Home-savings accounts and plans	187,206	180,513
PEP savings plans	71,230	39,998
Savings certificates and time deposit accounts	197,682	220,355
Passbook accounts	100,099	98,989
Negotiable certificates of deposit	115,506	85,955
Total deposits	**919,799**	**885,358**
Long-term debt	161,740	148,831
Total funds collected (deposits & bonds)	**1,081,539**	**1,034,189**
Total funds managed (off-balance sheet)	368,635	316,493
Total funds	**1,450,174**	**1,350,682**
Mutual & investment funds (net assets)	*257,367*	*223,800*
(incl. money market funds)	*165,145*	*139,684*
Insurance products	*95,891*	*78,626*
SCPI real-estate investment companies	*10,377*	*9,367*

Chapter

16

The bond markets of

Germany

Klaus Holschuh & Mattias Hansmann
Commerzbank AG, Frankfurt am Main

Dr. Klaus Kegler
Delbrück & Co. Privatbankiers, Köln

Eva-Maria Mann & Dr. Patrick Mange
Deutsche Bank Research GmbH, Frankfurt

Dr. Karl Eugen Reis, Dr. Norbert Bräuer & Dieter Ritter
DG Bank Deutsche Genossenschaftsbank, Frankfurt am Main

Peter Fertig, Oliver Seipt & Uwe Sundermeier
Dresdner Bank AG, Frankfurt am Main

Note: In general text, the abbreviation 'Dm' is used to denote the Deutschemark. Elsewhere, the international mnemonic 'DEM' is used.

16.1 Introduction

Rising public sector deficit boosts liquidity

With an outstanding volume of more than Dm 2200bn, at the end of 1991, the German bond market is one of the world's largest. The government bond market, in particular, was given a strong boost following the economic and monetary union of the two German states, in July 1990, and the subsequent unification in October 1990. Since then, the move towards harmonizing the economies of the two German states has made it necessary to undertake the modernization of the infrastructure of the former GDR (in particular, its roads and telecommunications), to compensate for its geographical disadvantage. Additionally, high transfer payments for the unemployed, job creation measures, and the financing of investment incentives, have together necessitated a steep rise in public sector debt, with the result that the Federal Republic of Germany had to increase its borrowing requirements on the capital markets by a very substantial amount. Net public sector borrowing of the Federal Republic rose from Dm 27bn in 1989, to Dm 86bn in 1990 (from July 1990, this figure includes the bonds of the former Staatsbank of the old GDR), and to roughly Dm 88bn, in 1991.

This rise in government debt increased the outstanding volume of public sector bonds by a significant amount; it rose from Dm 470bn in 1989, to Dm 555bn in 1990, and reached Dm 643bn, at the end of 1991.

Bank bonds showed a similar development; the outstanding volume of this market segment rose from Dm 761bn (1989), to Dm 901bn in 1990, and reached Dm 1000bn at the end of 1991. This development is not only a strong reflection of the increased borrowing requirements of the Länder governments and local authorities, but also the demand for mortgage loans for modernization (particularly in the new Federal states).

The growth of the Deutschemark eurobond market, however, was less strong; its outstanding volume rose from Dm 210bn in 1989 to Dm 242bn by the end of 1991. This was mainly attributable to the high level of German interest rates - particularly by comparison to those of the USA - and therefore excessive financing costs for issuers. However, a change in this trend has become apparent since the 4th quarter of 1991.

New issuers and more flexible borrowing

In the wake of unification, new issuers came to the German capital market. These included Staatsbank, the German Unity Fund (which is guaranteed by the

Federal Republic of Germany and considered to be a government bond), Deutsche Reichsbahn and, finally, Treuhandanstalt.

Due to the large financing volumes involved, it became necessary for public sector borrowers to show flexibility in adjusting their financial requirements to meet those of their potential investors. As a consequence, public sector issuers have made use of the entire range of financing instruments available and, clearly, they have succeeded in meeting the wishes of buyers - for example, the sales of *Bundesobligationen* (special Federal bonds) have risen strongly, to reach an issuance figure of some Dm 10-12bn. Staatsbank, on the other hand, has issued FRNs (almost without exclusion), with the result that this sector has also shown strong growth.

To be able to meet the huge financing requirements of state and government entities, the Federal government decided to offer Federal Treasury notes (*Bundesschatzanweisungen* - four-year bonds) by tender on a recurrent two-month basis, so that the regular investment range for investors was broadened. But the new Federal states, such as the State of Brandenburg, have recently also issued *Landesschatzanweisungen*, the maturities of which can be as long as required.

Treuhandanstalt has so far mainly financed itself via loans against borrowers' notes (*Schuldscheindarlehen*), but has also launched a commercial paper programme. From mid-1992, Treuhandanstalt is likely to have the opportunity of refinancing itself through bond issuance since, by that time, the necessary Treuhandanstalt Act should have been passed by Parliament. The Act stipulates that Treuhandanstalt, like the German Unity Fund, is established as an ERP special fund and, therefore, that repayment is guaranteed by the Federal Republic of Germany. To what extent this borrower will find investors' acceptance will, amongst other things, depend on whether the bonds of Treuhandanstalt, like those of the German Unity Fund, will be deliverable into the DTB bond futures contract.

Increasing number of hedging instruments

Following the successful launch of the DTB bond futures contract, at the end of 1989, DTB decided (in October 1991) to introduce a futures contract on *Bundesobligationen*, with the aim of additionally providing investors with a hedging instrument for intermediate maturities. All *Bundesobligationen* and Federal Treasury notes (*Bundesschatzanweisungen*) with maturities of 3.5 to 5 years are deliverable into the contracts. The introduction of the futures contracts has therefore contributed to a steep increase in demand for both *Bundesobligationen* and *Bundesschatzanweisungen*, and this has been reflected in their issuance volumes.

The above-mentioned developments in the German bond market clearly demonstrate that, across the institutional spectrum, there is not only a willingness to adjust to changed financial situations with flexibility, but also to grasp the opportunities provided by new instruments and methods.

Creation of a commercial paper market

Since 1 January 1991, Germany has met the legal requirements for the issuance of commercial paper programmes. The statutory authorizations which governed the issue of such securities have been abolished. The Federal government also decided to abolish stock exchange turnover tax which, in particular, had made the issuance of short-term paper excessively expensive. The volume of CP programmes increased to close on Dm 17bn by the end of 1991, reflecting the broad acceptance that this segment of the money market has already found. This development should continue in the next few years, as the demand for short-term tradeable securities, from both institutional investors and corporations, has increased perceptibly.

With the establishment of a commercial paper market, the German money market is developing from being a purely interbank market, primarily concentrating on trading central bank money, into a market in which short-term securities are traded as well (this is already common practice in both the UK and the USA). As soon as the shape of the German yield curve has normalized again, and in view of the high borrowing requirements in the future, it is indeed possible that Treasury bills issued by the Federal Republic of Germany will also one day come to the market.

16.2 Economics

Introduction

Major events came thick and fast in 1990 and 1991. The 'peaceful revolution' in Eastern Europe - especially the former GDR - has developed a self-sustaining dynamism, the political and economic impact of which has changed the face of the world. Communism has failed miserably as a political and economic concept, and hopes are now being pinned on democracy and the market economy. The changeover is by no means completed yet - above all in the former USSR - and will require time and patience.

In political terms, the end of the Cold War has left a strategic power vacuum. Bloc thinking is passé, as too is the associated political/military disciplinary pressure; for Europe, the military threat has undoubtedly diminished. In contrast, however, the balance of political power has become less predictable. Social, demographic and ethnic problems are surfacing, harbouring the potential for major conflict, a potential which may not be easy to control. Movements towards national autonomy - for example in Yugoslavia and, much more importantly, in the Soviet Union - are gaining ground and promoting political destabilization, which saps strength. At this point in time, only America is in a position to maintain world order, but the USA cannot police the world alone. New security concepts are therefore imperative; but these must also be practicable. The UN has a special role to play here, since it would have to sanction such a unified front and the use of appropriate force - as happened in the Kuwait conflict. The necessary means would, however, have to be provided by others, primarily the USA, but also by Europe which, in future, will have to assume greater responsibility for ensuring peace.

In economic terms, the collapse of the centrally-planned economies of the East has left chaos in its wake. The prosperity gap with the West has widened, a fact which poses the danger of mass immigration from Eastern Europe. In social policy terms, Germany, like the other Western European countries, is not prepared for such an influx. However, since it will be scarcely possible to replace the fallen political boundaries with new social barriers, Europe (particularly Germany) is being confronted with the considerable cost of integrating these people. Greater economic and development aid could help encourage potential emigrants to stay put. However, this would require vast sums, which would make capital scarce for the foreseeable future and keep interest rates relatively high.

Politics

The outstanding event of the period under review was the unification of Germany and the incipient economic integration of the new Federal states. The introduction of the Deutschemark resulted in the almost total collapse of the east German economy. Consumers rushed to buy western goods, thus triggering a drastic slump in production in the eastern part of the country. This was compounded, on the export side, by the breakaway of major Comecon countries. Unemployment rose abruptly as a result, though the social effects are being cushioned by substantial transfer payments from west Germany. The process of structural adjustment in east Germany is now in full swing. Treuhandanstalt, which initially took over the firms in east Germany, has meanwhile had considerable success with re-privatizations and companies it has restructured itself. So although tensions remain, the drive to restore the east German economy should succeed.

The financial expense is enormous. For social reasons, the public sector has to bear the brunt, and budget deficits have risen appreciably. These deficits will tend to decline in the years 1992 to 1995, but will still remain high. This is tolerable if most of the funds are used for investment, as this is the only way to lay the foundations for a modern industrial structure, to create value added, and to fuel a steadily-widening income flow. The high level of capital spending in 1990 (+13.4 per cent) and 1991 (+9.3 per cent) points in the right direction. Capacities are being built up rapidly; some of the capital goods are destined for east Germany - since the necessary production facilities do not exist there yet, the initial capital equipment needed for the east currently still has to be produced in the west. The trough could be reached in the course of 1991. A recovery may even start in some sectors, widening in 1992 and bringing more rapid progress towards general growth.

The focus on revitalizing the new Federal states has released a substantial growth impetus in Germany, enabling neighbouring European countries to export more. This is crimping Germany's trade and current account surpluses appreciably but, at the same time, it cuts the volume of trade-related credit to other countries, which can then be re-channelled increasingly into 'internal financing'. Nevertheless, there is no denying that the German capital market faces a trying time, so interest rates could stay relatively high. This may not be welcome for the economies of the other EC countries, but they will be more than compensated by the spur to growth from German imports.

Gross national product

In the period from 1988 to 1991, Germany's real GNP has expanded by 16.0 per cent or 3.8 per cent p.a. (see Figure 16.1). In 1990, and especially in 1991, growth has been strongly affected by unification: west Germany experienced a full-scale

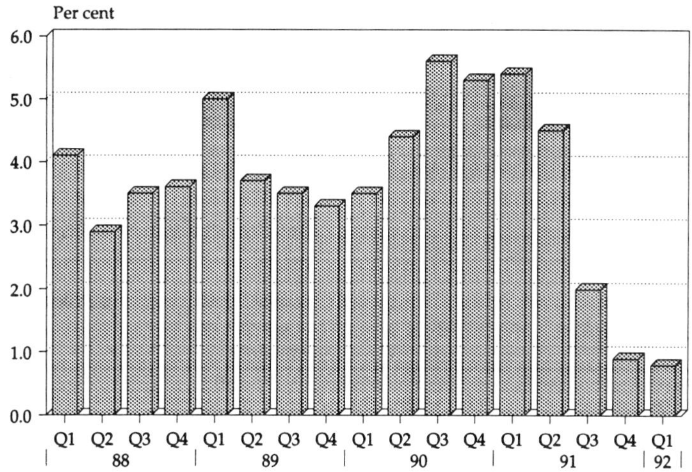

Figure 16.1 German GNP, 1988-1992 (year-on-year)

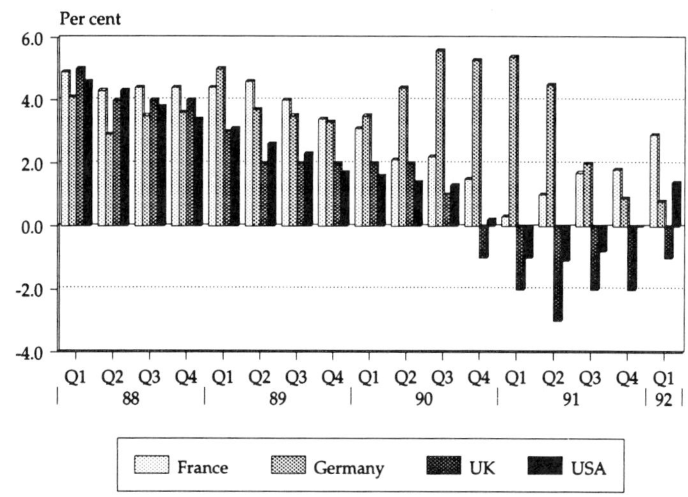

Figure 16.2 GNP/GDP of Germany and selected countries, 1988-1992 (year-on-year)

boom, while the economy of east Germany practically collapsed, as reflected in a slump in production and employment. But this shift did not amount to a pan-German zero-sum game. The huge financial transfers, especially by the state, created income and demand in east Germany which - being met in the west - acted as a large-scale economic support programme, and boosted real growth. Other European countries also profited through higher German imports, though this led to dramatically falling surpluses on Germany's external accounts.

From 1988 to 1990, real GNP rose by 12.5 per cent or roughly 4 per cent p.a. The first-half of 1991 brought a further increase, of 4.8 per cent in real terms, but this was not maintained during the remainder of the year, and 1992 is unlikely to see much improvement. The jump in public sector deficits required tax increases in 1991/92 which dampened growth in the second half of 1991, and will continue to do so in 1992. Private consumption has been particularly hard hit; the real rate of expansion has seen a decline and it is also curbed the momentum of capital spending (1988-1991: +45.2 per cent = +9.8 per cent p.a., real). However, the restructuring of east Germany is progressing, so that domestic production will gradually be able to replace imports and the GNP effect will then be countered by return to mounting trade surpluses. Real growth of 3.1 per cent was therefore realized in 1991, and 1992 should still bring roughly 2.0 per cent for the united Germany.

Trade balance

The strong surge in pan-German demand from unification had to be met through higher imports. From 1988 to 1991, imports jumped a whopping 57.2 per cent in nominal terms (=12.0 per cent p.a.), with the main thrust (roughly +14.5 per cent) coming in 1991. The main reasons were firstly the (at times) very firm Deutschemark (averaging 1.62 against the US dollar in 1990; 1991: 1.66), which made imports much cheaper and, secondly, the fact that German industrial capacities were working almost flat out. Imports were concentrated mainly on finished consumer goods, which went straight to east Germany. The bulk came from neighbouring EC countries; this not only prevented supply gaps but also reduced the danger of imported inflation.

Exports, on the other hand, increased by only 26.3 per cent between 1988 and 1991 (= 6.0 per cent p.a.), and almost stagnated in 1991. There are two reasons for this: tighter production capacities, used to supply east Germany, and the soft economies (above all in the UK and USA) which resulted in a drastic break in the investment cycle, thereby putting a tangible dampener on exports of German capital goods.

This widening gap between imports and exports triggered a steep decline in the German trade surplus (see Figure 16.3). This should not, however, be interpreted as a basic deterioration in the competitiveness of German products on

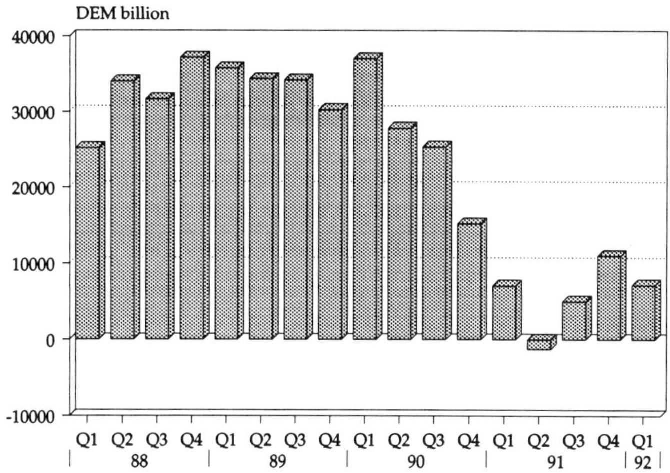

Figure 16.3 Germany's visible trade balance, 1988-1992

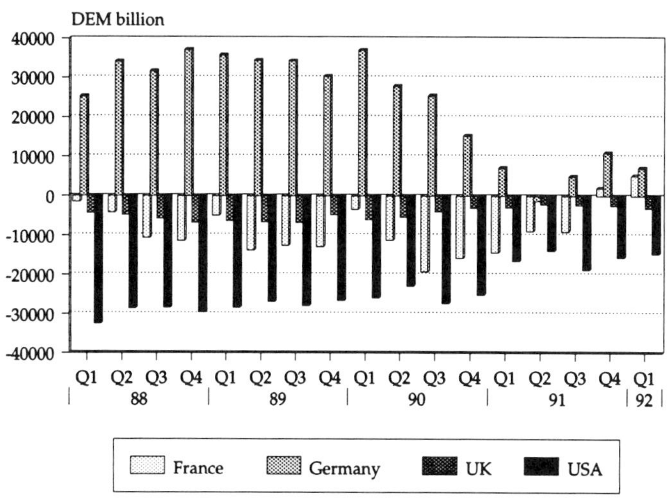

Figure 16.4 Visible trade balances of Germany and selected countries, 1988-1992

the world markets; it is rather due, in the main, to the special case of German unification. So although the German trade surplus fell to Dm 21.9bn in 1991 (1990 surplus: Dm 105.4bn), this is not a permanent feature. On the contrary, the import-pull will ease as production picks up in east Germany, whilst investment creates more production capacities in west Germany. Export efforts will be stepped up at the same time, so 1992 is already expected to produce a trade surplus of Dm 30bn. This will also spill over onto current account which, after a deficit of roughly Dm 32.9bn in 1991, will post only a small deficit of about Dm 10bn in 1992.

Unemployment

At the end of 1987, unemployment (employed wage and salary earners) in west Germany stood at 8.9 per cent, or 2.25 million jobless, while the labour force totalled 27.259 million. By December 1991, the labour force had risen to 28.913 million while the number out of work was 1.675 million, making the rate 6.2 per cent (see Figure 16.5). So, within 4, years the number of working persons increased by 1.654 million, while the number of jobless decreased by only 560,000. The gap was filled by a growing number of ethnic German settlers from eastern Europe and, before the Wall came down, from the GDR. After unification, about 400,000-600,000 commuters from east Germany also found work in the west, where the favourable economic situation offered better openings.

The situation in east Germany has been different. There, the collapse of the existing production structures led to large numbers of redundancies. In the last quarter of 1990, the aggregate number of jobless, and people on short-time work, came to 2.29 million; by April 1991 the figure had risen to 2.86 million (the majority of short-time workers are employed for less than 40 per cent of their usual working hours). However, from April 1991, career promotion programmes, re-training and job-creation schemes have all come into effect and are intended to improve the income situation of those taking part whilst also helping the labour force adjust to the working environment of the west - the way it is organized and the technology in use. As a result of these measures, the combined figure for unemployed and short-time workers decreased to 1.59 million by May 1992. The decline also reflects successful placement of growing numbers in new jobs, though the latter are increasing only slowly. The most favourable picture is in the east German construction industry, in small firms and in the services sector. In industry which is dependent on production technology, jobs are still very much at risk. Even when the east German economy gradually picks up (as is happening at the time of writing in some sectors - and this will accelerate and spread in 1992), unemployment in east Germany will no doubt remain a problem for quite a while, requiring correspondingly high state transfer payments.

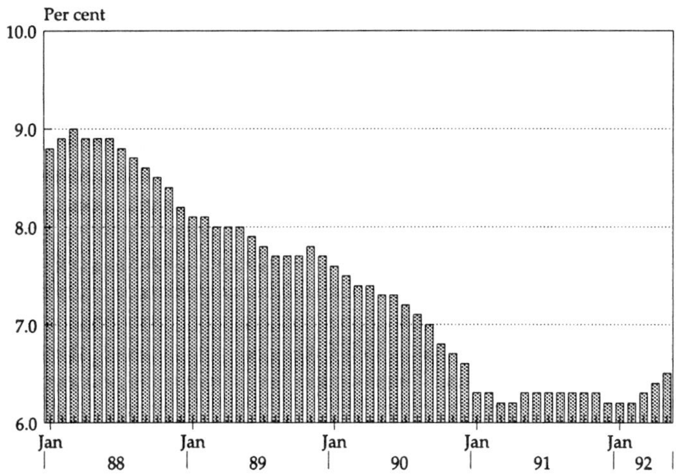

Figure 16.5 **German unemployment, 1988-1992**

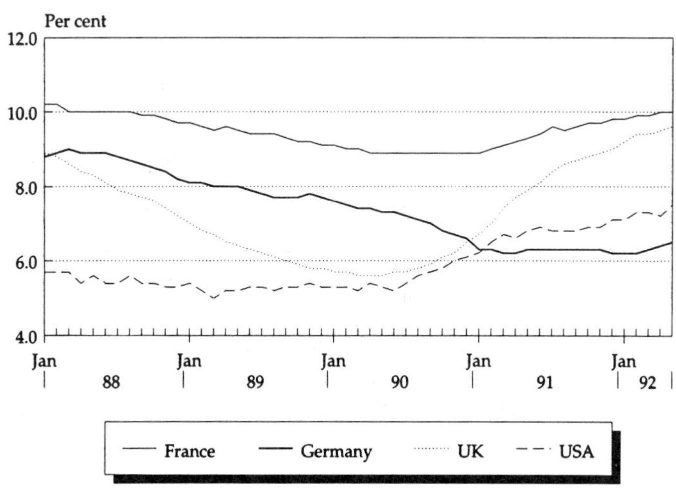

Figure 16.6 **Unemployment in Germany and selected countries, 1988-1992**

Inflation

Inflation was not a problem in the years from 1985 to 1987 - it stagnated, even moving slightly into the deflationary zone. From 1988, however, it began to move up again (see Figure 16.7), owing partly to administrative price increases, reaching a still moderate 2.7 per cent annual figure by the end of 1990 (despite a fairly strong price push towards the end of the year from the oil price hike due to the Gulf conflict). One reason for the relatively moderate pace of price increase during the period was the steady appreciation of the Deutschemark; domestic inflationary pressures were extensively neutralized by favourable import prices.

Since the beginning of 1991, however, a number of factors have impacted negatively. After the Gulf War, the dollar gained strongly and the Deutschemark weakened accordingly with the result that, especially in the dollar-dependent commodities sector, import prices climbed steeply thus driving up inflation. On the domestic side, there were substantial wage increases, which pushed up unit wage costs, causing companies to adjust their prices. But the final decisive factor was the tax increases implemented by the government in mid-1991: inflation jumped by 0.7 of a percentage point. In July it grew to 4.4 per cent, the highest since 1985. It has eased again slightly since then, to 4.1 per

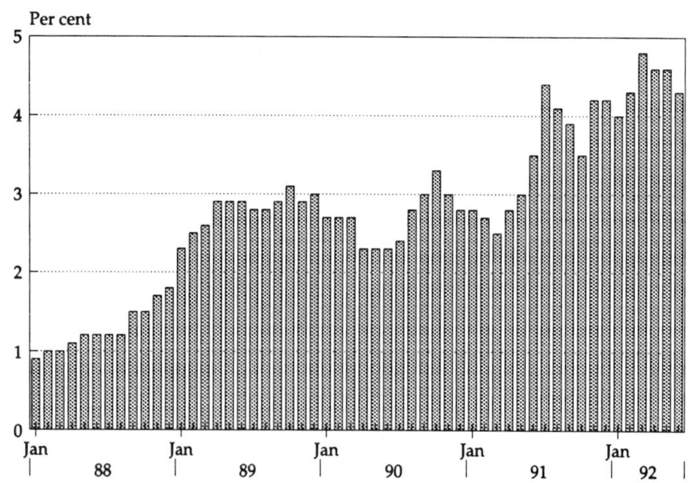

Figure 16.7 German inflation, 1988-1992 (year-on-year)

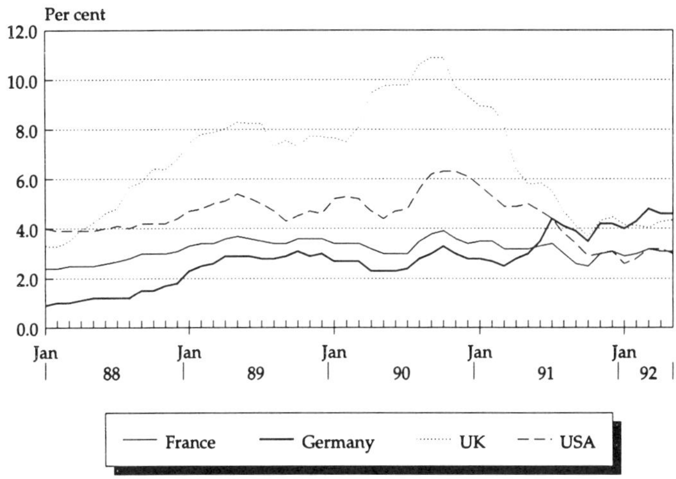

Figure 16.8 Inflation in Germany and selected countries, 1988-1992 (year-on-year)

cent in January 1992, although this is mainly due to the positive basis created by last year's oil price hike. This effect will fade more and more, so that inflation will hover around 4 per cent and remain there until mid-1992.

Monetary policy

The unification of Germany and the introduction of the Deutschemark in east Germany confronted the Bundesbank with a considerable challenge. The currency changeover went smoothly, but resulted in a large increase in money supply (M3 went up by about Dm 247bn - see Figure 16.9), which proved excessive in the face of shrinking east German production. One cause of the liquidity overhang was the political decision to exchange Ostmark into Deutschemark at 1 for 1, pushing up time deposits by roughly Dm 111bn, and sight deposits by about Dm 122bn This additional liquidity meant that east Germans were able to alter their consumption habits overnight and spend much more generously, even before the position regarding incomes, wages and pensions was finally clarified.

Since then, the level of wages in east Germany has risen appreciably. This has been accompanied by strong welfare support for the unemployed, short-time workers, pensioners etc., provided mainly by the public sector through

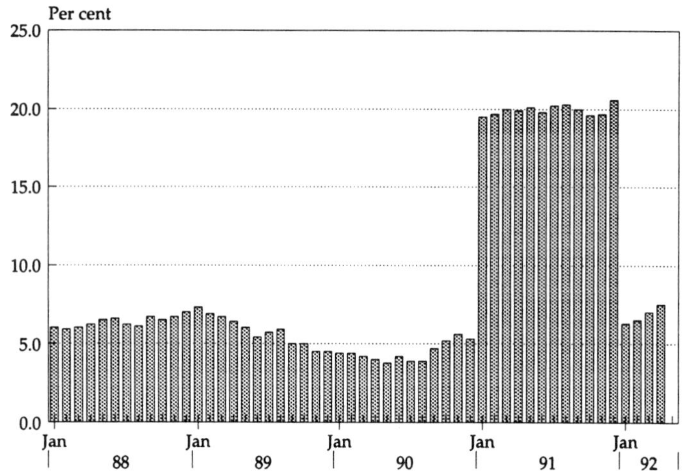

Figure 16.9 German M3 growth, 1988-1992 (year-on-year)

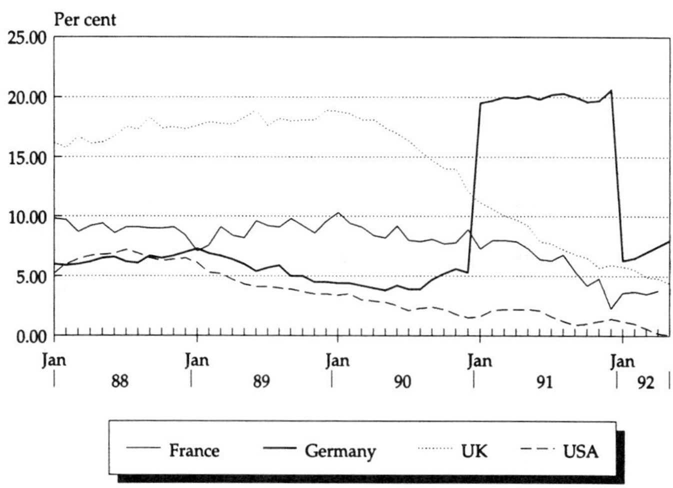

Figure 16.10 M3 growth in Germany and selected countries, 1988-1992 (year-on-year)

increased deficit spending. However, to prevent excesses in this field, the Bundesbank has followed a very restrictive course since the start of 1991. It hiked key interest rates, in four stages, to a level last seen in 1948. At the same time, it narrowed the target corridor for money supply growth. It is currently below the expected rate of nominal GNP expansion and will tend to hamper growth. But the Bundesbank has succeeded in making the public sector exercise deficit-discipline. Taxes are being increased and a start has at least been made to weeding out subsidies. However, from mid-1991, this has triggered a jump in inflation and a temporary weakness of the Deutschemark. Both these elements should, nevertheless, be blunted by the, now, relatively high international interest rate level, so that the Bundesbank can allow the ripples caused by interest rate cuts abroad - especially in America - to spread to Germany, leading to a slow reduction of rates, here, too.

Public sector deficit

Between the end of 1987 and March 1991, public sector debt (see Figure 16.11) expanded by Dm 248.1bn (or 29.0 per cent). Almost exactly half (Dm 123.3bn) is attributable to the Federal government, while the remainder is made up by the other central, regional and local authorities (approx. Dm 56.7bn) and the off-budget 'German Unity Fund' and 'Debt Liquidation Fund' (the latter has to settle the debt of east German companies taken over by Treuhandanstalt). Up to mid-1990, public sector debt had risen by Dm 95.8bn (11.3 per cent, or 3.1 per cent p.a.), giving a 'normal' level of incremental debt of Dm 27.4bn p.a. The ratio of new debt to nominal GNP actually declined: 1988 = 1.6 per cent; 1989 = 1.8 per cent; H1 1990 = 1.3 per cent.

But with unification and the kick-start financing needed for the east German economy, public borrowing has accelerated considerably. Just between mid-1990 and the end of September 1991, public sector debt jumped by Dm 183.9bn. The Federal government accounted for roughly Dm 69.2bn of this, while the off-budget funds, set up in mid-1990, borrowed Dm 82.7bn. The tax hikes in July 1991 allowed net new debt from budget items to be limited to Dm 116.8bn in 1991, though this still represents an increase to roughly 4.5 per cent of nominal GNP. A lower ratio should be feasible in 1992, even though the tax increases are due to expire at mid-year, for the east German economy seems to be bottoming out and some sectors are even starting to pick up, generating tax revenues in the eastern part of the country and reducing the volume of financial support. In addition, residential rents, transport fares and energy prices are being gradually liberalized, so that the subsidies granted in these areas in the past are decreasing. The forecast of a Federal government deficit in the region of Dm 48bn in 1992, after Dm 52.1bn in 1991, may therefore be quite realistic. This could, in turn, impact positively on the capital market and on interest rates.

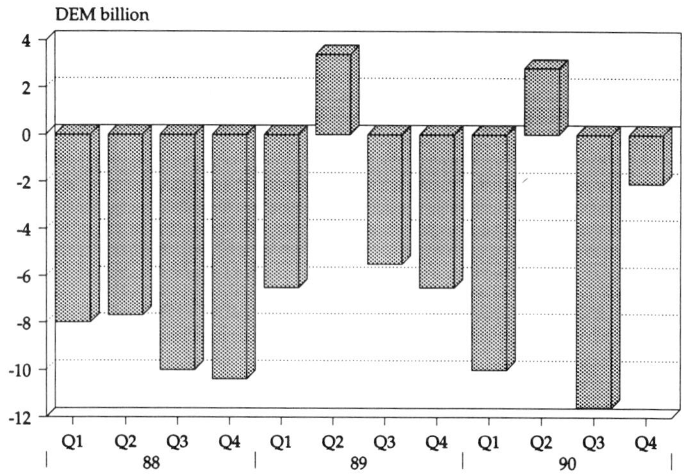

Figure 16.11 Germany's federal budget, 1988-1990

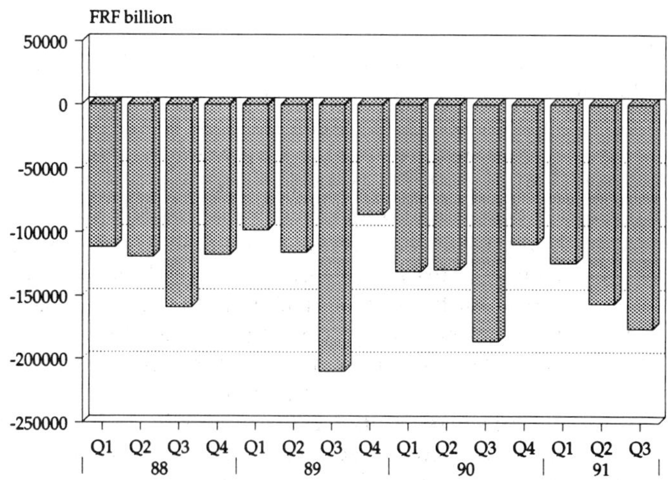

Figure 16.12 France's budget deficit, 1988-1991

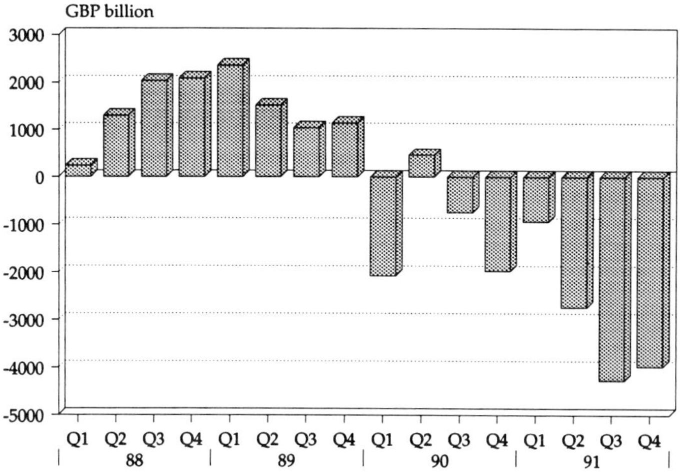

Figure 16.13 UK's budget deficit, 1988-1991

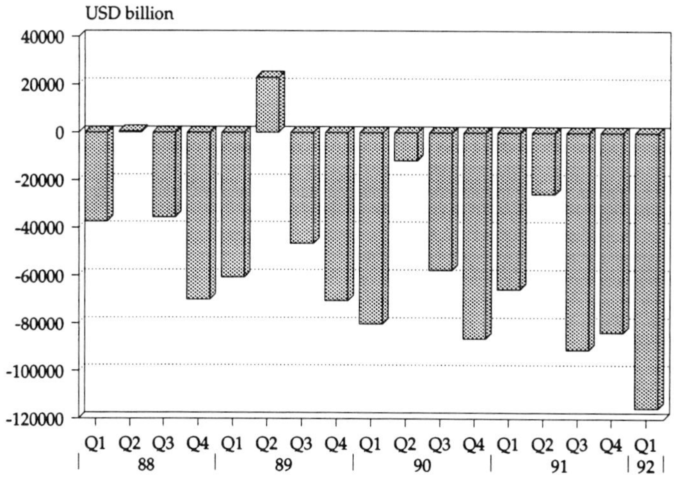

Figure 16.14 USA's federal budget deficit, 1988-1991

Currencies

Since 1988, the German currency has generally appreciated versus the most important free-floating currencies. From October 1988 to May 1992, it appreciated by an average of roughly 7.7 per cent against the GBP (member of the exchange rate mechanism of the EMS since October 1990) and roughly 14 per cent against the Japanese yen, and around 12.4 per cent versus the US dollar. This process was, however, by no means a one-way street and there were, at times, strong fluctuations. Major factors were economic growth, inflation and the impact of money supply on interest rates.

In 1988, GDP growth in Germany was slightly lower than in the other countries, which explains why these countries outperformed the Deutschemark in relative terms. In the following years, however, German economic growth was far above the growth rates of the other countries, with the exception of Japan. There was an additional boost from German unification, a factor which was an economic driving force all over Europe. As this process - at least until 1990 - was accompanied by high German foreign trade surpluses, there was an increasing capital allocation in favour of Germany, so that the Deutschemark gained strength.

This growth process was accompanied by declining unemployment which had a clearly stabilizing impact on inflation, especially as the Bundesbank pursued a cautious money supply policy. Due to the upward trend in interest rates, real differentials increased and found their preliminary peak after the opening of the east German border and the resultant surge in interest rates (February/March 1990). Market participants were right in their assessment that the German capital market would be confronted with considerable borrowing requirements for east Germany and the restructuring of that economy. Initially, however, this did not have any negative impact on the Deutschemark. Only when it was realized that the east German economy was in a worse-than-expected shape, and that west German financial aid would have to be long-term, did the climate for the Deutschemark change to its disadvantage. This was aggravated by the Gulf conflict, which required higher solidarity payments from Germany to the allied forces.

At the time of writing, the forex environment has calmed down somewhat. Yield spreads in favour of the Deutschemark, as well as the still-robust economic growth, are together having a stabilizing effect. This factor mix, however, can shift to the disadvantage of the Deutschemark if the economic recovery in the UK/USA, which is expected in 1992, is stronger than in Germany. Although this is doubtful, the Deutschemark could become more volatile.

16.3 Market composition

Overview

In terms of total volume of fixed-income securities outstanding, the German bond market ranks third in the world, smaller only than the US dollar and Japanese yen bond markets. The total of Deutschemark-denominated fixed-income securities outstanding at the end of 1991 amounted to more than Dm 2.7 trillion.

The market comprises a wide range of investment vehicles, with domestic bearer bonds playing the most important role. They have a total volume of Dm 1.7 trillion and therefore account for approximately 62 per cent of bonds outstanding. A particular financing pattern in Germany are the *Schuldscheindarlehen*. Public authorities, especially, rely heavily on this instrument and in fact, by the end of 1991, the *Schuldscheine* of public issuers reached a total volume of Dm 560bn. Registered bonds are of smaller, but increasing, significance in the domestic market. As an important financing instrument for banks, their volume reached about Dm 235bn at year-end 1991, accounting for 9 per cent of total issues. The market for Deutschemark bonds of foreign issuers (usually called eurobonds) which gained in importance in the introduction phase of the withholding tax in the first half of 1989, reached a total volume outstanding of Dm 242bn, accounting for 9 per cent of all Deutschemark bonds. The unification of the two German states caused a stronger growth of bearer bonds outstanding since mid-1990, while the other sectors did not show unusual growth rates during this period. The growing importance of bearer bonds is also due to the brisk issuing activity of east German issuers. In order to effect the necessary restructuring of the financial sector and their own balance sheets, east German special banks issued bonds with a total volume outstanding of around Dm 100bn.

Public authority bonds

The liberalization process since 1985 and in particular the abolition of the old 25 per cent coupon tax as from 1 August 1984, stimulated growing interest in German bonds on the part of foreign investors. The foreign demand concentrates mainly on the particularly liquid bonds of public authorities which, at the end of 1991, accounted for some 37 per cent per cent of all domestic bearer bonds outstanding. Despite the introduction of the 10 per cent withholding tax, which was in force in the first half of 1989, the growth of this sector did not show a recognizable break. The issues of public authorities (*Öffentliche Hand*) can be categorized in six major groups:

- Federal government
- Unity Fund
- Bundesbahn (Federal Railways)
- Bundespost (Federal Post Office)
- Länder (state) governments
- Local authorities

Within this group, the Federal government has a various number of investment vehicles.

In view of its more extensive capital raising activities, the Federal government is now much more flexible in its debt management. In this context, non-residents have been entitled to buy *Bundesobligationen* since October 1988. Since then, several steps to modify issuing practices - with increasing dominance of issuance by auction - have improved the marketability of this sector. Accordingly, renewal of the medium-term Federal Treasury notes in form of *Bundesschatzanweisungen* in May 1991 has enhanced the attraction of the public sector bond market. Meanwhile, Federal government bonds (Bunds), in particular, have shown good liquidity. Due to the high financing requirements for developing the east German economy, special government bonds have been created for refinancing the German Unity Fund. But these bonds, called Bundesrepublik Deutschland (*Fonds Deutsche Einheit*), are regarded as a similar instrument to Bunds and not really as a new instrument. The share of domestic public authority bonds in all domestic bearer bonds outstanding, increased from 35 per cent (at the end of 1987) to 38 per cent (at the end of 1991). Although, in principle, foreign investors are not subject to any restrictions regarding investments in the German bond market, it must be noted, that certain tap issues of the Federal government (*Bundesschatzbriefe* and *Finanzierungsschätze*) may not be purchased by non-residents. Considering the total volume of public authority bonds, there is no doubt that their market share is increasing, but in comparison with other countries, the proportion is still small. The reason is a remarkable feature of public sector borrowing, which is financing by a very large extent by means of *Schuldscheindarlehen.*

Schuldscheindarlehen

Due to the specific financing habits of public authorities in Germany, large amounts are borrowed in the form of so-called *Schuldscheindarlehen.* This instrument is unique to the German market, and not a security in the true sense, but a loan documented by negotiable promissory notes called *Schuldscheine.* These notes can be transferred by written assignment which gives them a marketability, so they are ascribed to the bond market. The *Schuldscheine* market is open to all types of domestic and foreign borrowers. As there are no reliable estimates for the volume outstanding of private borrowers - a rough estimate puts them

	March 1988	% Total	Dec 1991	% Total
DOMESTIC BEARER BONDS				
Public authority bonds	410.9	20.7	643.2	23.5
Federal government				
Bunds	157.1	7.9	278.7	10.0
Unity Fund	-	-	26.0	1.0
Federal bonds (Bobl)	87.7	4.4	137.7	5.1
Federal savings bonds	34.2	1.7	34.8	1.3
Federal Treasury notes	42.0	2.1	47.9	1.8
Federal Railways, Reichsbahn	24.7	1.2	31.2	1.1
Federal Post Office	28.8	1.4	43.9	1.6
States	36.3	1.8	47.6	1.7
Local authorities	0.2	-	0.2	0.0
Bank bonds				
Municipal bonds	367.7	18.5	392.2	14.3
Mortgage bonds	140.9	7.1	142.8	5.2
Specialized bank bonds	75.8	3.8	221.0	8.7
Other bank bonds	131.0	6.6	284.4	10.4
Corporate bonds				
	2.5	0.1	3.2	0.1
Total	1128.7	56.8	1686.8	61.6
DOMESTIC REGISTERED BONDS				
Municipal bonds	94.5	4.8	124.1	4.5
Mortgage bonds	78.7	4.0	95.9	3.5
Specialized bank bonds	7.7	0.4	10.0	0.4
Other bank bonds	0.8	0.0	2.1	0.1
Total	181.7	9.1	232.1	8.5

(cont.)

	March 1988	% Total	Dec 1991	% Total
PUBLIC AUTHORITY *SCHULDSHEINE*[1]				
Federal government	122.5	6.2	59.8	2.2
Unity Fund	-	-	24.8	1.0
States	244.9	12.3	298.1	10.9
Local authorities	116.4	5.9	136.4	5.0
Federal Railways	16.1	0.8	20.0	0.7
Federal Post Office	10.8	0.5	9.8	0.4
Credit Processing Fund	-	-	12.7	0.5
Others	5.7	0.3	16.3	0.6
Total	516.4	26.0	577.9	21.1
EUROBONDS[2]				
Sovereign issuers	n/a	n/a	25.3	0.9
Public authorities			5.5	0.2
Supranational issuers			49.5	1.8
Banks			66.5	2.4
Corporations			95.0	3.5
Total	160.2	8.1	241.8	8.8
GRAND TOTAL	1987.0	100.0	2738.6	100.00

Figure 16.15 Composition of the German market (DEM billion nominal)

[1] *Schuldscheine issued by private borrowers are estimated to amount to an additional DEM 150bn at the end of 1991*

[2] *Dresdner Bank estimates*

at some Dm 125 to Dm 150bn - , this section is necessarily restricted to describing the sector of public authorities' *Schuldscheindarlehen*. This group is the largest borrower of *Schuldscheindarlehen*, with a total amount of around Dm 578bn outstanding at the end of 1991.

The importance of *Schuldscheindarlehen* is indicated by the fact that they account for 90 per cent of the total volume of public authority bearer bonds (Dm 643bn outstanding). At the end of 1985, the volume of *Schuldscheindarlehen* was no less than twice that of public sector bonds - hence, this shows a changing trend in the structure of public sector financing. An increasing preference for negotiable bonds, in particular, has lead to a stagnation in the volume of *Schuldscheindarlehen* outstanding since 1984. A rise in foreign demand, particularly, has permitted public authorities to issue a higher volume of bonds and Treasury notes in the longer maturity range - at the expense of *Schuldscheine*. This has, meanwhile, increased the share of bonds in total public sector debt from just under 20 per cent in 1981, to some 45 per cent at the end of 1991. One reason was the restricted access to the *Schuldscheine* market for foreigners - they were not permitted to purchase those *Schuldscheine* which bear clauses prohibiting their sale to non-residents. Now, new issues of the public sector are no longer subject to this restriction clause (although the sale of those *Schuldscheine* of domestic banks with a maturity of up to four years is prohibited to non-residents). Extraordinarily high financing requirements in east Germany as a result of reunification have caused a revival of this market segment since mid-1990. In order to finance liquidity bottlenecks in particular, arising from the restructuring of east Germany's economic and financial system, special funds have been set up which are refinanced through the issuance of *Schuldscheindarlehen*.

Bank bonds

In contrast to the markets of many other countries, the German domestic bond market is dominated by bank bonds. The total volume of bank bonds outstanding at the end of November 1991 reached Dm 1272bn (including registered bank bonds), and accounted for 47 per cent of the whole German bond market (incl. *Schuldscheine*). The majority of bank bonds (82 per cent) are still issued as bearer bank bonds, amounting to 62 per cent of all domestic bearer bonds). However, over the years the proportion issued in registered form has been steadily increasing, to a total volume of Dm 232bn (or 9 per cent of all German bonds). Registered bonds are not officially listed, but are nevertheless actively traded in the over-the-counter market. Due to German accounting principles, institutional investors, particularly insurance companies and pension funds, invest large amounts in these bonds as they are not required to state write-offs in their balance sheets. Thus, a glance at the shares of bearer and registered bank bonds relative to all bank bonds outstanding during the last ten years, shows that there was a trend toward a preference for registered bank bonds when the level of interest rates in the German bond market was relatively low (reflecting a fear of losses in subsequent years). In fact, a decline in the share of these bonds has been seen since the beginning of 1990, when the yield level in Germany came near to 9 per cent - which is an historically high yield level.

The high level of direct borrowing by public authorities both via *Schuldscheine* and via bank loans explains why the German bond market is dominated by bank bonds. Mortgage banks and public sector credit institutions refinance their loans and their purchases of public authorities' *Schuldscheine* by issuing *Kommunalobligationen* (municipal bonds) which, as at year-end 1991, totalled Dm 516bn - representing 19 per cent of the German bond market, of which registered bonds accounted for 5 per cent. On the other hand, real estate credit institutions issue *Pfandbriefe* (mortgage bonds) to finance mortgage loans. At the same point in time, these mortgage bonds had a total volume outstanding of Dm 239bn, representing a market share of 9 per cent. In addition, specialized bank bond and 'other' bank bonds - totalling Dm 518bn, or 19 per cent of all German bonds - are issued by central savings banks (Girozentralen), commercial banks and specialized credit institutions such as the KfW (Reconstruction Loan Corporation). Within this group, the share of registered bonds is hardly 3 per cent. Particularly significant is the sector of special bank bonds, which have gained increasing importance since the unification of Germany with a growth of more than 170 per cent since the end of 1989, mainly due to the changed refinancing structure of commercial banks and the brisk issuing activity of the Staatsbank Berlin, a successor to east Germany's central bank.

Corporate bonds

Compared to other bond markets, German corporations as an issuing group play a negligible role in the domestic market. With a total volume outstanding of Dm 3bn at the end of 1991, their share is only 0.1 per cent of the whole bond market. The main reasons for this are the regulations which make issuance both a costly and lengthy process. Consequently, there has been a growing tendency to resort to foreign subsidiaries in the eurobond market for the issuance of corporate bonds. After abolition of government approval requirements and stock exchange turnover tax, the market for Deutschemark-denominated corporate securities has celebrated a revival, since the beginning of 1991, in the form of commercial paper (see Section 16.15 - Money markets).

Deutschemark eurobonds

During the past ten years, the German market for foreign Deutschemark bonds has grown considerably in size. Compared with 1985 - which was the year of abolition of the 25 per cent coupon tax and the final liberalization of the German capital market by the Bundesbank - the volume of Deutschemark-denominated eurobonds doubled to Dm 242bn outstanding, at the end of 1991. The announcement of a 10 per cent withholding tax on domestic issues in Germany also strengthened the growth of the market for Deutschemark eurobonds, which were not subject to this tax. Further stimulation was provided by the reduction of the minimum maturity for public bonds and private placements to 2 years, as well as the abolition (with effect from July 1989) of the compulsory period of notice to the Bundesbank for new issues - thereby allowing the issuers more flexibility in their financing arrangements. This has helped to increase the portion of this sector from 7 per cent in 1985, to 9 per cent in 1991. A view of the structure of Deutschemark eurobonds outstanding shows that issues of industrial borrowers are dominant, with a share of 40 per cent, followed by the borrowings of banks, with 27 per cent. For German corporates, both the length and cost of issuing in the domestic market, plus the introduction of the 10 per cent withholding tax, resulted in a trend towards resorting to foreign subsidiaries for cheaper funds. At the end of 1991, supranational borrowers accounted for 20 per cent of this sector, while sovereign borrowers held 10 per cent.

Deutschemark medium-term notes

In mid-1989, in line with the gradual liberalization of the market, the Bundesbank reduced the minimum life for foreign Deutschemark bonds to 2 years,

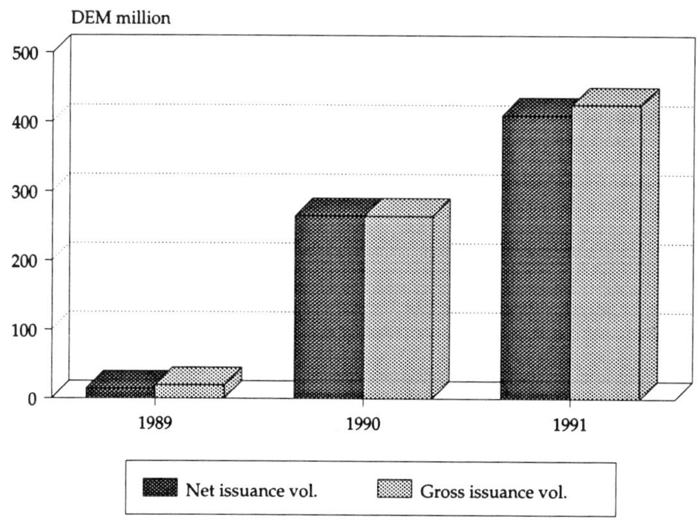

Figure 16.16 New issue volumes in the medium-term note market

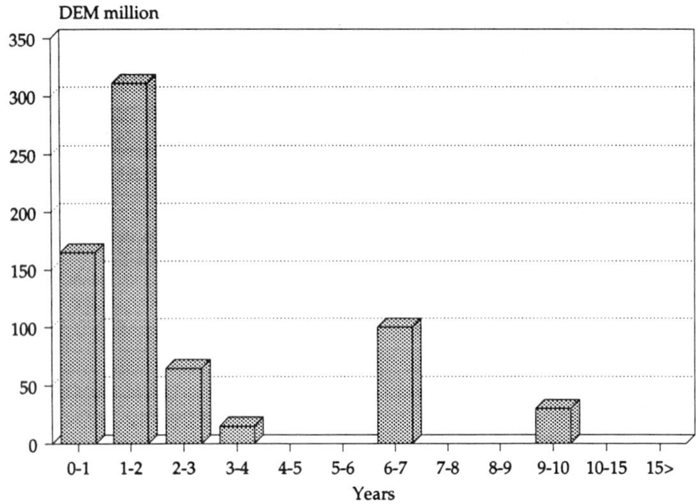

Figure 16.17 Maturity structure of the medium-term note market

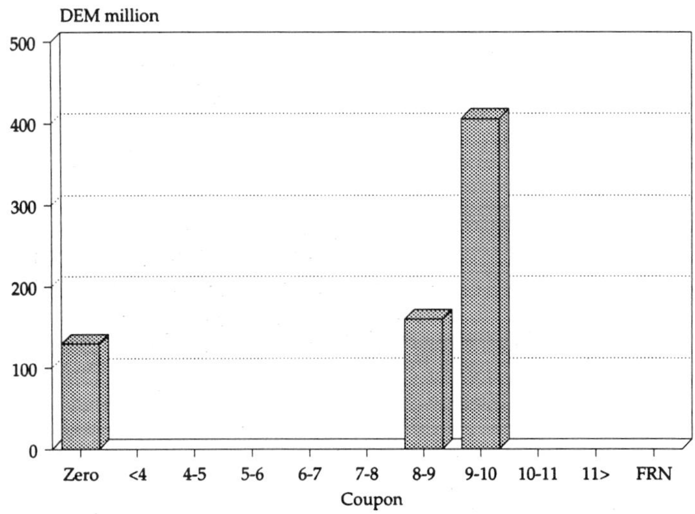

Figure 16.18 Coupon structure of the medium-term note market

thereby creating the pre-conditions for the issue of new capital market products with a Deutschemark component.

Since that time, Deutschemark-based medium-term notes have been issued in the Federal Republic as well. They have a high degree of flexibility in terms of utilization of the programmes (volume/maturity); however, at about Dm 0.7bn, the total amount outstanding is still very low.

The focus of current Deutschemark medium-term notes (Dm MTNs) is on the short-term maturity range. The reason is that these investment vehicles - in addition to the commercial paper programmes of industry - are mainly used for liquidity control. The respective maturities are shown in Figure 16.17.

The coupons of the Deutschemark MTNs (see Figure 16.18), issued since 1989, are in line with the interest rate level at that time, which was between 8 per cent and 9.5 per cent, whilst one tranche was issued in the form of a zero bond.

Composition of market by maturity structure

Public authority bonds

The following remarks on maturity structures relate to bearer bonds only, as there is insufficient statistical material available on the *Schuldscheindarlehen* and registered bank bond sectors.

A look at the maturity structure of the public authority bond market (see Figure 16.19) reveals that, in contrast to the discernible concentrations in the short or medium-term range that are to be found in other market segments, the redemption times of public authority bonds are comparatively evenly spread over the 1- to 10-year range. The reason for this continuity is the consistency of issuing policies, particularly on the part of the Federal government which permanently draws on the domestic bond market to finance its budget independently of cyclical market developments. This constancy factor is supported by the wide variety of financing instruments which almost completely cover the maturity spectrum. Even so, it is possible to detect a certain preponderance in the maturity ranges of 3 to 5 years as well as 9 to 10 years, reflecting a stronger tapping of the capital market by the Federal government through the issuing of *Bundesobligationen* (Federal government bonds) and *Bundesanleihen* (bunds) in the past two years in the wake of German reunification.

To date, public authority bonds with a maturity period of more than 10 years have only been issued in the single year of 1986. Then, the Federal government exploited the historically low level of interest rates to float two 30-year bonds, with a volume of Dm 1bn each, to secure favourable long-term refinancing rates of 5.625 per cent and 6 per cent, respectively. Besides these, the same issuer also floated two 12-year bonds, while the German Federal Post Office issued a 15-year bond. The introduction of the Federal Treasury note as a 4-year instrument

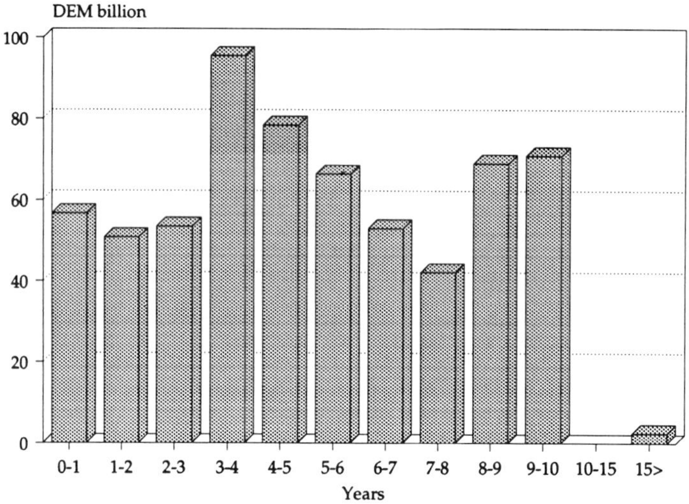

Figure 16.19 Maturity structure of the public authority bond market

in a new guise, as well as the increased attraction of the 5-year Federal bond through stocking up the outstanding volumes via market support quotas, give rise to expectations that the future will see the medium-term sector growing in importance.

Bank bonds

Municipal bonds (*Kommunalobligationen*) and mortgage bonds (*Pfandbriefe*) are usually issued with a maturities of 2-10 years (see Figures 16.20 & 16.21). Occasionally, maturities of 1- or 10-15 years are also seen in the market. Despite these exceptions, maturities of new issues tend to be concentrated in the medium-term range, which is accounted for by the fact that the mortgage loans and municipal loans behind these issues look for matching maturities in their refinancing. In phases of very high interest rates, such as at the beginning of 1981, it could be noted that new issues were temporarily only being offered in the short-term maturity range as the issuers were only prepared to lock in interest rates on a long-term basis at a depressed (interest rate) level. A number of bonds with lives, at issuance, of around 40 years are still in circulation. These were mainly issued in the period between 1950 and 1970 and served the needs of longer-term refinancing during the reconstruction phase in Germany.

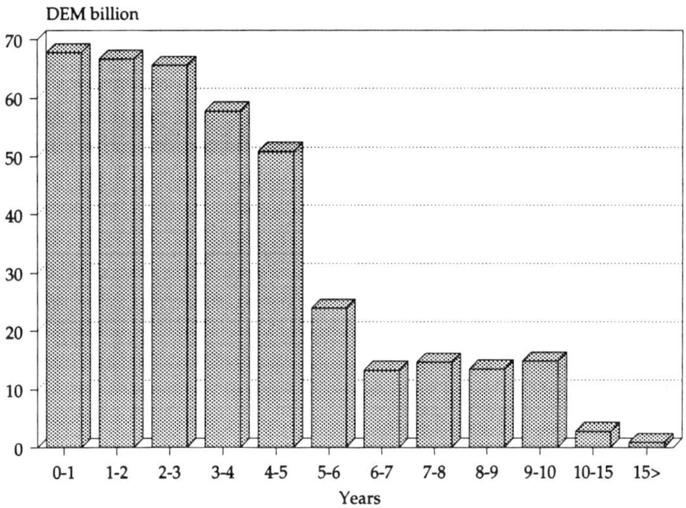

Figure 16.20 Maturity structure of the municipal bond market

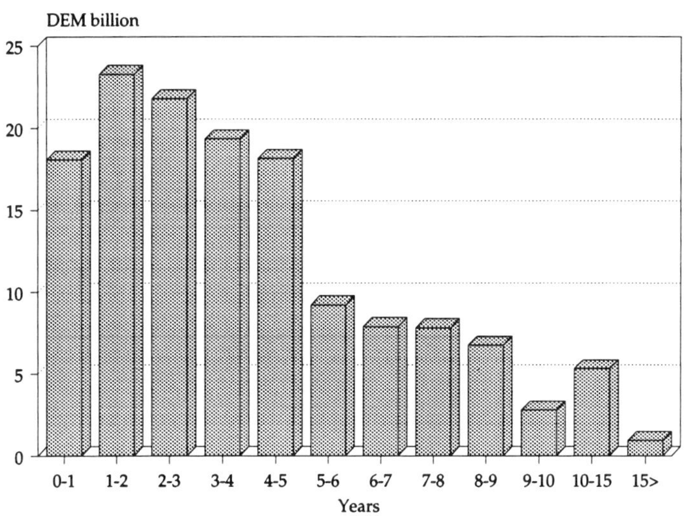

Figure 16.21 Maturity structure of the mortgage bond market

Whereas these bonds were once frequently offered with regular redemptions, for some years now only bullet bonds have been floated.

Specialized bank bonds

The bond issues of specialized banks cover the whole maturity spectrum from 1 to 10 years with the emphasis, however, on 2-5 years (see Figure 16.22). Infrequently, bonds with longer maturities may also be offered in the market. The

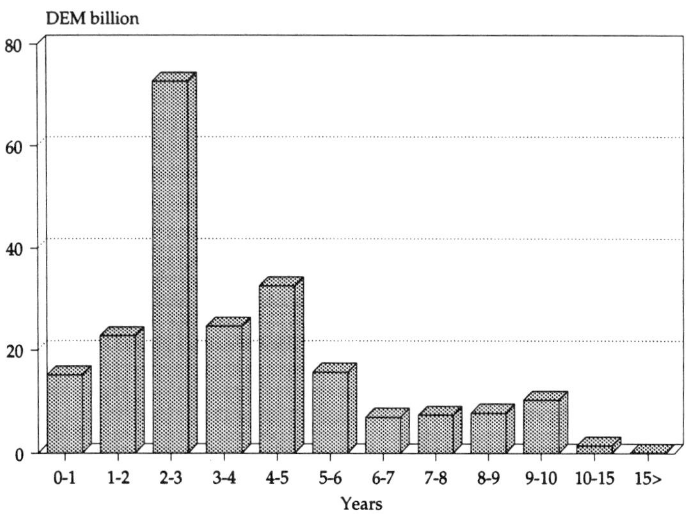

Figure 16.22 Maturity structure of the specialized bank bond market

special nature of many of these specialized banks, charged with the task of financing reconstruction in the post-war period, resulted, even as late as the 1960s, in a number of issues with very long maturities of 40 years or more.

Other bank bonds

Issues in the sector of 'other bank bonds' are mainly floated in the range from 1 to 10 years (see Figure 16.23), with the emphasis on the medium-term range up to 5 years. Bonds of less than two years are rarely issued, since the proceeds from the sale are always subject to minimum reserve requirements and therefore cause higher financing costs. Occasionally, issues with remaining lives of

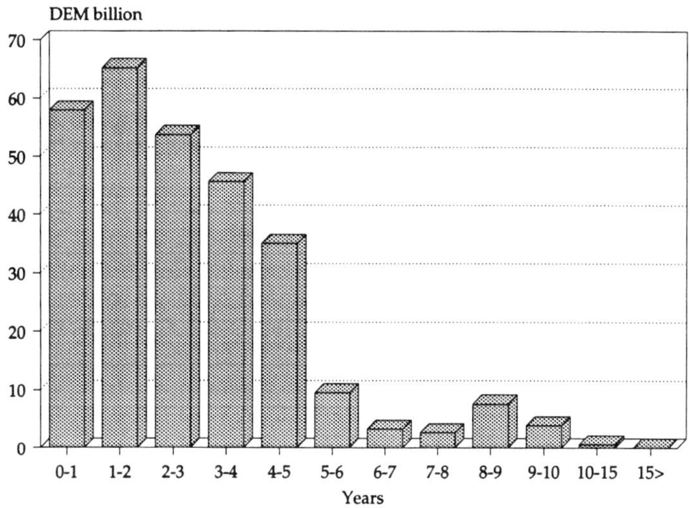

Figure 16.23 Maturity structure of the other bank bond market

less than 2 years may be offered to banks that are subject to reserve requirements and which add such bonds to their own portfolios. These issues are then exempted from the minimum reserve requirement. On the whole, longer-term issues with a maturity period of more than 6 years are of minor importance. The reason for this is the fact that the rules about matching the maturities of assets and liabilities are less strict here than in the case of mortgage banks, so that longer-term refinancing is not necessary. On the other hand, long-term, uncovered bank bonds would compete with public authority bonds and covered bank bonds, and are therefore of less interest to issuers.

Corporate bonds

Bonds from corporations in the non-financial sector were originally floated almost exclusively with maturities of 5, 10 or 15 years with a dominance of the 10-year issues (see Figure 16.24). Bonds with an original maturity period of less than five years are no longer to be found. The background to this unusual maturity structure consisted, on the one hand, of the complex issuing procedure for domestic corporations due to the requirement for official government approval that was valid up to the end of 1990 - this made costly short-term issues appear hardly a sensible proposition. On the other hand, these corporate bonds

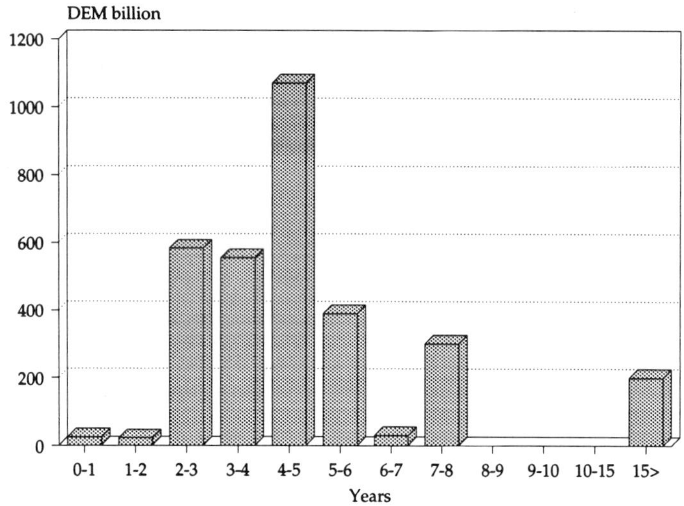

Figure 16.24 Maturity structure of the corporate bond market

were predominantly issued in the form of bonds cum warrants or convertible bonds, which required a longer maturity period because of the warrant. Correspondingly, the redemption periods concentrate on the medium remaining life range. Whereas in recent years there were only very few new issues in this market segment, or even none at all in 1990, since the beginning of 1991 the market has again seen the issuing of some bonds cum warrants with a 5-year maturity (e.g. 9.25 per cent Agima 1996), and with a 20-year maturity period (FRN Haniel 2011).

Deutschemark eurobonds

Up to the end of June 1989, restrictions imposed by the Bundesbank prevented the issuing of Deutschemark eurobonds with shorter maturities than 5 years, for public subscription, or shorter than 3 years, for private placements. It is only since July 1989 that the minimum maturity has been reduced to a uniform two years in both cases. A preferred maturity for new issues was 10 years. It was only in recent years that the medium-term maturity range up to seven years has managed to establish itself firmly in the market at a comparatively high interest rate level (see Figure 16.25). A closer scrutiny also reveals that supranational issuers are relatively frequent among the 10-year paper issuers, whereas the me-

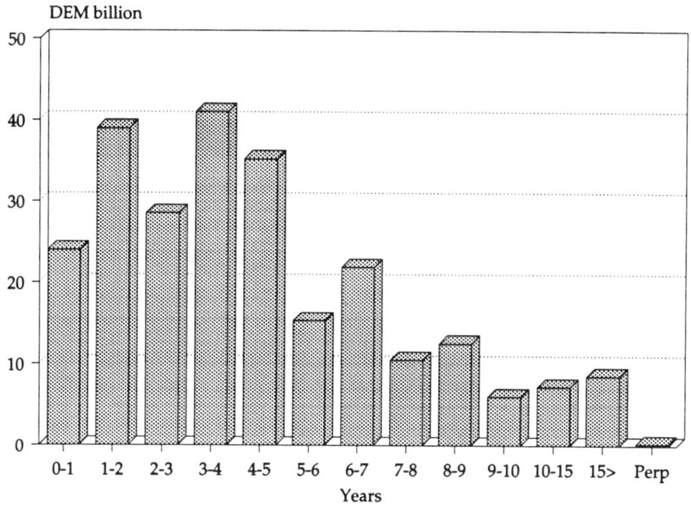

Figure 16.25 Maturity structure of the DEM eurobond market

dium-term maturity range is dominated by banks and corporations. Among the Deutschemark eurobonds with due dates longer than 10 years, maturities of 15 years are frequent. When the bond market was very bullish in 1986, a number of 30-years bonds were issued. The longest-dated bond is a zero bond from Euro-Deutschemark Securities Ltd., which falls due in 2026. The heterogeneity of the issuers with their very different refinancing requirements results in a comparatively even distribution of redemption dates over the whole remaining life spectrum.

Composition of market by coupon structure

Public authority bonds

The coupons of public authority bonds are concentrated in a range between 5 and 10 per cent (see Figure 16.26), corresponding to the yield level prevailing at the time of issue; coupons between 8 and 9 per cent account for the biggest share. This high share can be attributed to the comparatively large volume of issues resulting from the increased borrowing requirements since 1990 after the reunification of Germany, a period in which yields have risen accordingly. Only one bond with a coupon of less than 5 per cent is now in circulation, namely the

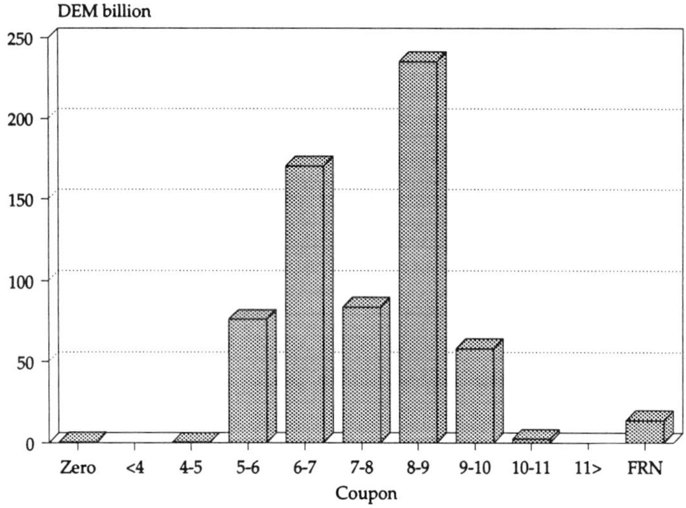

Figure 16.26 Coupon structure of the public authority bond market

4.25 per cent Hamburg *Kassenobligationen* 1992 (medium-term note), issued in 1988. Bonds with coupons of 10 per cent and more, date from 1981 and 1982. FRNs among public authority bonds have been seen in the market only since 1990 and, with a total outstanding volume of approximately Dm 13bn, they are still of small significance. Zero bonds in the form of Treasury notes have a total volume of only Dm 500m and are therefore also without significance in this sector.

Bank bonds

The coupon structures of municipal bonds and mortgage bonds (see Figures 16.27 & 16.28) also exhibit a normal distribution in the range between 5 and 10 per cent. In both sectors, however, the focus is on coupons of 6 to 7 per cent. The explanation lies partly in disciplined spending policies up to 1990, especially on the part of local governments, which resulted in reduced borrowing requirements and made it less necessary to raise refinancing capital via the issuance of municipal bonds during the phases of high yields that have prevailed in recent years. In the case of the mortgage bonds, the comparatively small share of high-rate coupons reflects an understandable reluctance to take up construction financing during phases of high interest rates. When credit demand slackens, so too do the refinancing requirements of the mortgage bonds that are

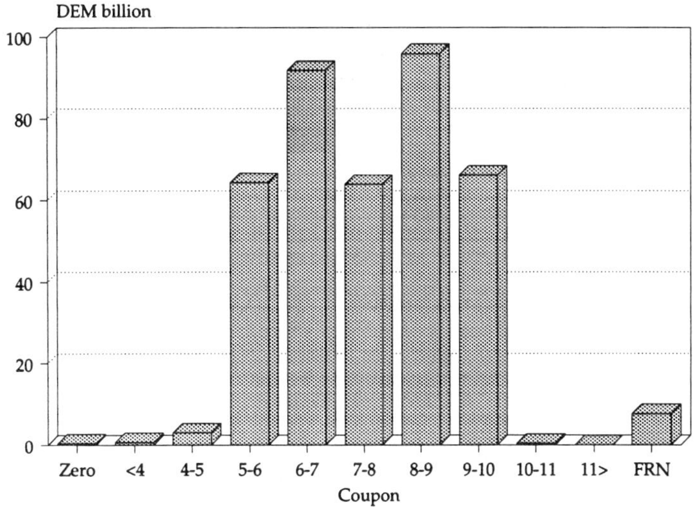

Figure 16.27 Coupon structure of the municipal bond market

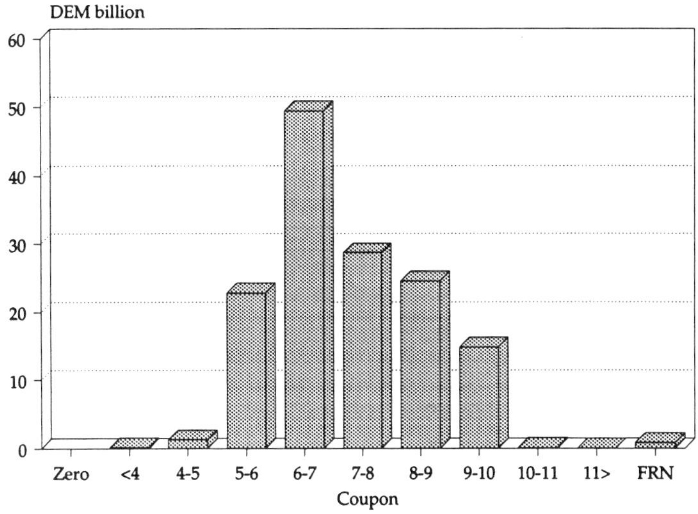

Figure 16.28 Coupon structure of the mortgage bond market

directly linked to the construction projects. Most of the coupons under 5 per cent date from the low yield phase in Germany from 1986-88. Zero bonds are of negligible importance with a total volume of approximately Dm 350m. Only among the municipal bonds do FRNs have an appreciable volume of around Dm 8bn. Besides these bonds with a yield subject to regular taxation, this segment of bank bonds hitherto included a number of tax-exempt issues from the period before 1955, with a total outstanding volume of approximately Dm 4bn. However, at the start of 1992 this tax-exemption was cancelled by law.

Specialized bank bonds

A striking feature of the coupon structure of issues of specialized banks (see Figure 16.29) is that the usual distribution of coupons in the range between 5 and 10 per cent is accompanied by an exceptionally large share of FRNs - and that even zero bonds carry some weight. On closer examination, this distorted picture in comparison with the other market segments is found to result from the special conditions in connection with the reconstruction of the financial sector in the east of Germany. The outstanding volume of zero bonds is accounted for almost exclusively by a single issue of Staatsbank Berlin in September 1990, with a nominal value of Dm 30bn, which was taken up mainly by West German banks. The FRNs are also represented by several borrowings of the same issuer

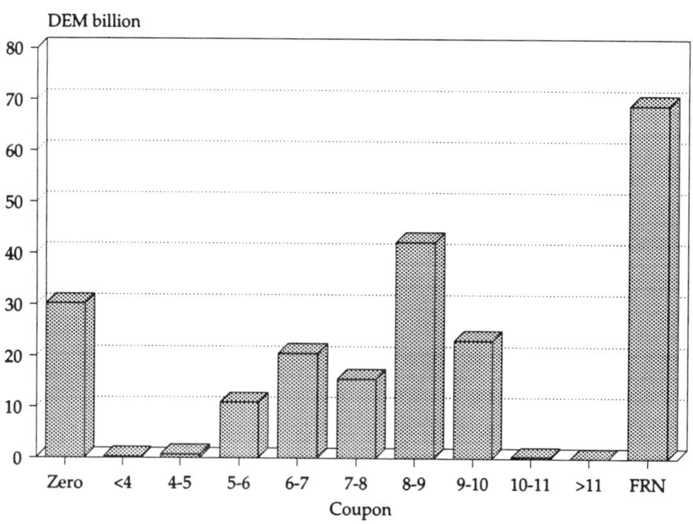

Figure 16.29 Coupon structure of the specialized bank bond market

totalling more than Dm 60bn. Nevertheless, other issuers are also to be found in the FRN segment, with loans totalling about Dm 7bn.

Other bank bonds

The coupons of other bank bonds (see Figure 16.30) show a distinct prominence of nominal yields in the 8-9 per cent range. This can be traced back to the explosive increase in new issues in the last three years, as a result of expanding credit demand in a booming economy, as well as to the fact that heavy demand for high-yielding investment alternatives coincided with large-scale re-allocations of funds from the sector of time and savings deposits. Besides these, there are also a number of tax-attractive bonds with coupons lower than 5 per cent, which were mainly issued in the period from 1986-1987. Although zero bonds are of

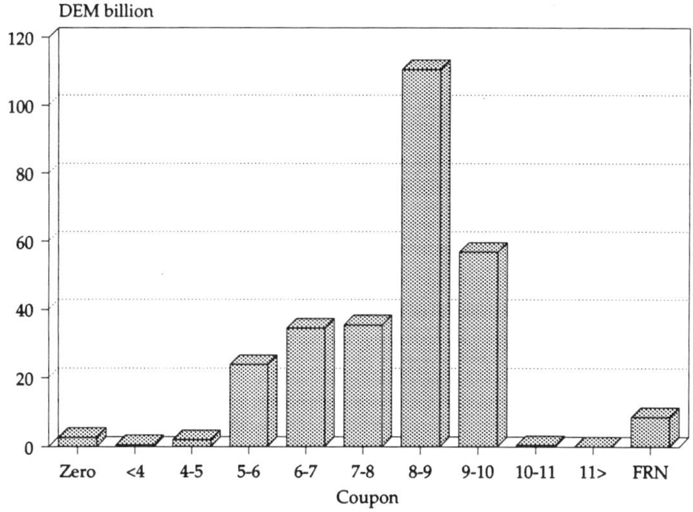

Figure 16.30 Coupon structure of the 'other' bank bond market

small importance in this sector with a volume of approximately Dm 3bn, they are currently experiencing a revival of interest with a number of issues in 1991.

Corporate bonds

In the market for corporate bonds, which has a total volume of only a little over Dm 3bn, about one half of all issues have a coupon of less than 4 per cent (see Figure 16.31). Without exception, these are bonds cum warrants dating from

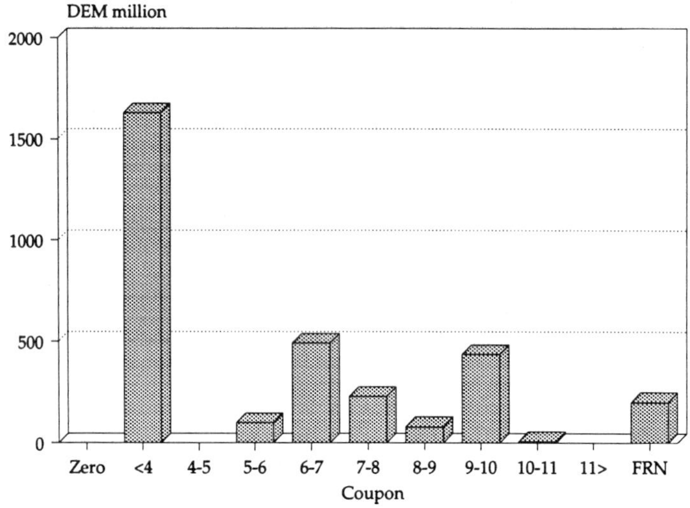

Figure 16.31 Coupon structure of the corporate bond market

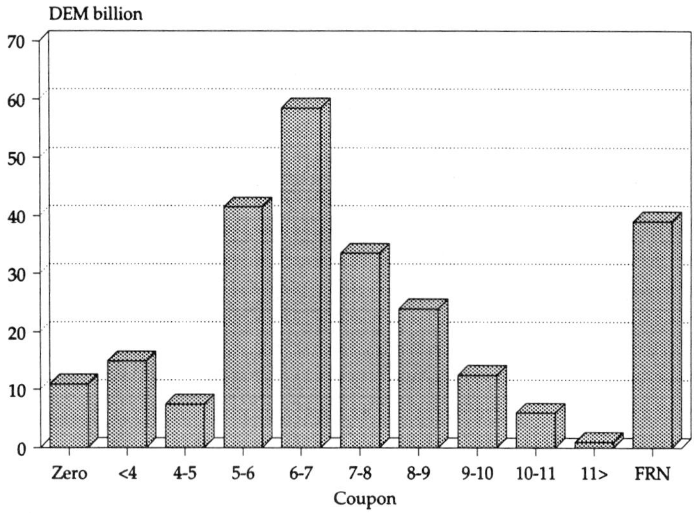

Figure 16.32 Coupon structure of the DEM eurobond market

1984 to 1986. Two high-coupon bonds, 8.875 per cent AGAB bond cum warrants 1996 and 9.25 VK Mühlen bond cum warrants 1996, were issued in 1991. Zero bonds are not represented in this segment, whilst one FRN from Haniel falling due in 2011 with a volume of Dm 200m is currently outstanding.

Deutschemark eurobonds

Of all market segments, Deutschemark eurobonds can point to the most varied coupon structure (see Figure 16.32). To begin with, here, too, there is a concentration in the standard coupon range of 5-10 per cent. Of special note is a comparatively large block of coupons of less than 4 per cent with a volume of approx. Dm 13bn, consisting exclusively of convertible bonds and bonds cum warrants. In the case of zero bonds, which have total redemptions of about Dm 10bn, it is that of the World Bank - maturing in 2015 - which features the greatest liquidity at Dm 2bn. High-interest yielding bonds, with coupons from 9 per cent, mostly date from 1990 and 1991 and correspond to general market yield levels. With a total volume of almost Dm 40bn, FRNs account for a large slice of this segment. Also noteworthy is the fact that, with the exception of the low-yielding bonds, a very varied spectrum of issuers can be found in all coupon ranges.

16.4 *Types of security*

Public bonds

Federal government bonds

The most popular instruments in the German bond market are the long-term government bonds, which have maturities of 8 to 30 years, with 10 years being the most common. They are issued by the Federal government (*Bundesanleihen*), the Federal Post Office (*Postanleihen*), the Federal Railway (*Bahnanleihen*) and by the Bundesländer (*Länderanleihen*). After German reunification a new debtor came into the market - the Unity Fund (*Fonds Deutsche Einheit*). This fund was created to finance the restructuring needs of East Germany. The target is to raise Dm 95bn by the end of 1994, guaranteed by the Federal government and by the West German states.

The local authorities usually do not issue bonds directly, but use *Kommunalobligationen* (see below). The only true communal long-term bond listed today is the Stuttgart 83/93, with a fixed annual coupon of 8 per cent.

Previously, the standard size of an issue of a *Bundesanleihe* was 4-5bn Dm (Post, Bahn and Länder were smaller). Since 1990, the Federal debt authorities have changed their behaviour in two ways: Firstly, the amount launched has been increased and, secondly, instead of placing new bonds, an issue is augmented several times. So the size of a *Bundesanleihe* has grown quite remarkably - to a record level of Dm 18bn in 1991's September placement. By the end of that year, total outstandings reached Dm 279bn, thereby giving the market considerable depth and liquidity. The turnover increased even more after the launching of Bund futures, on Liffe in August 1989, and on the German Options and Futures Exchange (Deutsche Terminbörse), in November 1990. The investor can count on a bid/offer spread which does not exceed 10 pfennigs under normal circumstances. *Bundesanleihen* usually yield lower than other straight domestic bonds.

Government bonds can be bought by retail clients free of charge within a three-day submission period (*Zeichnungsfrist*). After this deadline, they are listed on all eight German stock exchanges in the first section. The minimum denomination is Dm 100, the round lot for trading with varying notation, Dm 1m and, for off-floor trading, Dm 5m.

All *Bundesanleihen* are bearer bonds, but physical certificates do not exist anymore. Instead, proof is via debt book-entry (*Bundesschuldenbuch*). The interest is paid annually (up to March 1990, every issue had a fixed-coupon) and principal refunded in one amount at maturity. Neither lender nor borrower have a put or a call option.

In March 1990, the government came to the market with its first floating-rate note, which was endowed with a coupon of 3-month FIBOR (Frankfurt interbank offered rate) minus 20 basis points, quarterly adjustment and interest payment, and a maturity of 10 years. The actual coupon is 9.7 per cent.

Since then some other public entities started to raise their debt on floating-rate terms; examples are the Federal Railways (March 1990 to March 2000; 3-month-LIBOR minus 20 basis points) or the Federal Post Office (May 1990 to May 2000; 3-month-FIBOR minus 10 basis points).

The most active player in this field is the Staatsbank Berlin (former National Bank of the East German State) which, to date, has issued 21 floating-rate notes with maturities between 2 and 5 years and coupons between FIBOR minus 10, and FIBOR plus 5 basis points. The market has gained quite a remarkable acceptance among investors. It is very liquid, so that even large lots may be traded without difficulty.

Federal government medium-term notes

Federal government medium-term notes (*Bundesobligationen*) were launched in December 1979. However, real importance was not gained until 1989, when foreigners were allowed to buy them in the secondary market. The fact that the primary market is still off-limits is of no practical significance. The market now has quite a remarkable depth with total outstandings of Dm 134bn at the end of 1991.

Bundesobligationen have maturities of 5 years. Initial purchase is restricted to private persons and charitable organizations, which can buy them free of any charges from a bank acting as selling agent for the government; a service for which it, in return, receives a compensation fee.

The notes are issued on an ongoing basis (tap issue), parted into series with a fixed-coupon. The fine tuning of the yield is done by the variation of the price. When the planned volume of the tranche is reached, or when the market has moved away from the nominal interest rate, the series is closed (after prior announcement) and a new one introduced. After that, the then fully-placed note is listed in the first sections of the German stock exchanges. The minimum denomination is Dm 100, the round lot for the trading with varying notation is Dm 1m, and for off-floor trading is Dm 5m. Usually the bid/offer spread is about 10 pfennigs. The difference from the yield of the *Bundesanleihen* depends only on the slope of the yield curve.

Like the long-term Federal government bonds, the *Bundesobligationen* are bearer bonds with debt book-entry and therefore physical delivery is impossible. Interest is paid annually and principal is refunded in bullet form at maturity. Neither lender nor borrower has a put or call option.

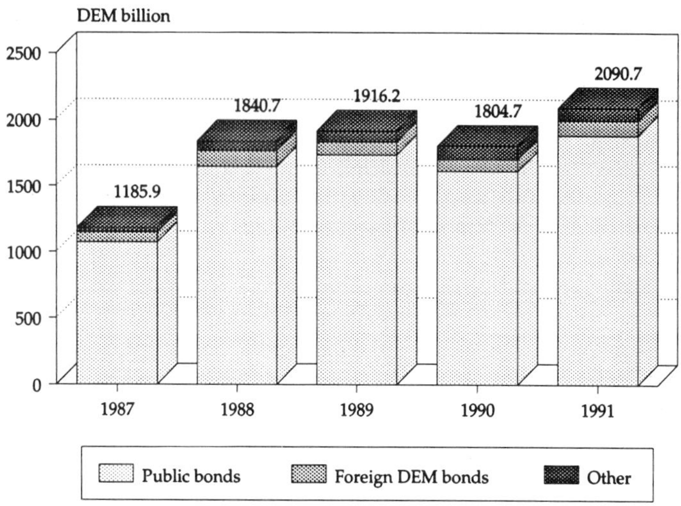

Figure 16.33 Annual development of turnover at the stock exchange

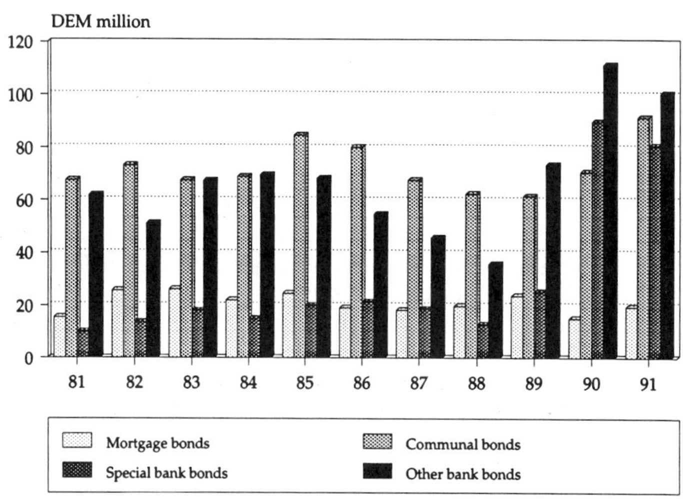

Figure 16.34 Bank bonds - annual development of gross sales

Before 1989, medium-term notes (*Kassenobligationen*) had been quite popular among international investors. But since the secondary market of the *Bundesobligationen* has been open to foreigners, their significance has waned. The Federal government does not use them any longer, and the total of its outstandings was Dm 34bn at the end of March 1991.

In May 1991, the Federal debt authorities revived the medium-term instrument for wholesale clients, central banks, supranational organizations, etc. - under the name of Federal Treasury notes (*Bundesschatzanweisungen*) - by implementing some important changes:

- The bonds are issued regularly (usually in a 2-month cycle) on the 25th, or the following business day, of the month in question. The listing is in the first section and the size of every issue should be large enough to guarantee a deep and liquid market.
- As regards the maturity, the authorities want it to be different from the well-known 5 or 10 years. The first tranche, in May 1991, was endowed with a 4-year life. The issuance procedure is by auction, in which all banks are authorized to make a tender offer. Private clients must place their orders through a bank. To secure a liquid market, the allotted amount is augmented by a quota for market intervention.

The new *Bundesschatzanweisungen* are designed mainly for institutional clients. Therefore, the minimum denomination is Dm 5000, the round lot for variable notation Dm 1m and, for off-floor trading, Dm 5m. Interest payment is annual and the principal is refunded in one amount at maturity. Neither a put nor a call option exists. Physical delivery is not possible, as the notes are entered into the debt book.

In 1991, the Federal Government launched 4 issues of the new instrument, with a size of Dm 6bn in May, July and September, and Dm 7bn in November. So, by the end of that year, the total outstandings (including the old *Kassenobligationen*) were Dm 48bn.

Another tool destined for wholesale investors are zero-coupon Treasury notes (*Unverzinsliche Schatzanweisungen - U-Schätze*) with a denomination of Dm 100,000, and more. As an unlisted money market instrument, with maturities up to 2 years, they are mentioned here for reasons of completeness only.

There are also some bonds tailored for private clients, the most popular being the two types of Federal Treasury letters (*Bundesschatzbriefe*). Type A has a maturity of 6 years while Type B has a maturity of 7 years. Minimum denominations are Dm 100 for Type A Dm 50 for Type B. Whereas Type B is a zero-coupon bond, Type A is endowed with fixed-rates. The characteristic of *Bundesschatzbriefe* is that their nominal interest rate rises every year, which gives investors a strong incentive to hold them until maturity although, they have the

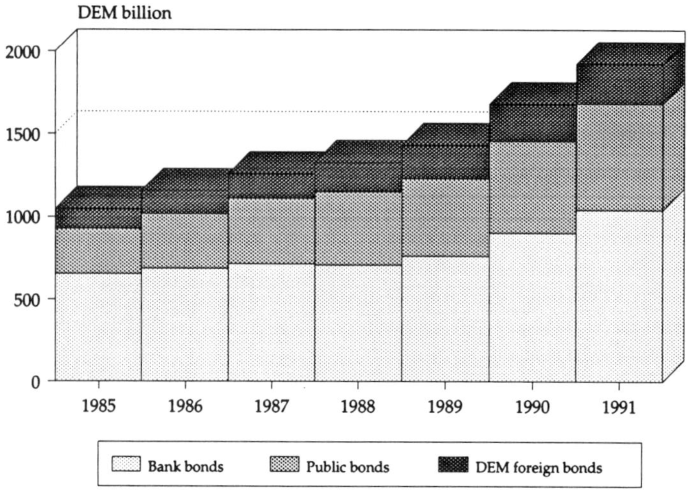

Figure 16.35 Annual development of total outstandings since 1985

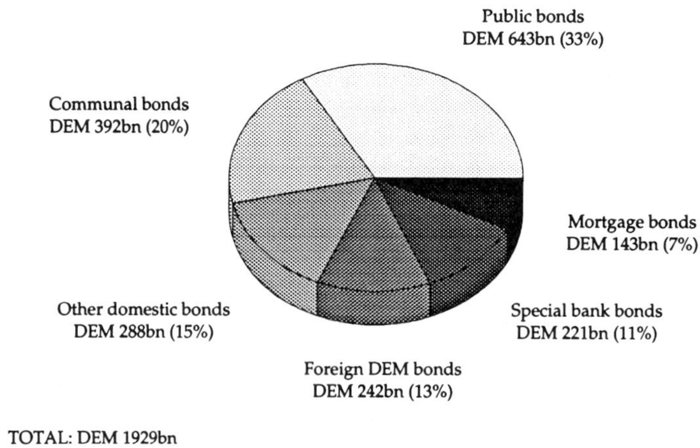

Figure 16.36 Total outstandings as at 31 December 1991

right, commencing one year after issuance, to demand redemption. Because of this there is no secondary market.

The last security to be mentioned here is *Finanzierungsschätze*, an unlisted money market instrument with zero-coupon, maturities of 1 or 2 years, and a minimum denomination of Dm 1000. As the purchase of *Bundesschatzbriefe* and *Finanzierungsschätze* is restricted to German residents, further analysis is superfluous.

Loans against borrowers' notes

Although loans against borrowers' notes (*Schuldscheine*) are not securities they should be mentioned here, briefly, because of their popularity among institutional investors. By the end of September 1991, the total outstanding public debt was Dm 1129bn, of which Dm 535bn were in *Schuldscheine* - nearly the same amount as in securities (Dm 578bn). The attraction of this arrangement lies, for the investor, in the better yield while the main disadvantage lies in the lower marketability. As it is not a bearer instrument, it is not quoted on any securities exchange. The initial sale, and all later sales, can only be realized by means of a separate written assignment; the purchases require the authorization of the borrower. As most *Schuldscheine* are unsecured, the bank which has arranged the initial transaction normally acts as trustee for the ultimate owner by keeping the original certificate in safe custody. There is always physical delivery.

Besides the public sector, there are important other institutions which use this instrument, namely banks, special credit institutions under public law, international organizations and, sometimes, industrial corporations. The maturities range from 5 to 10 years, in some cases even longer. Designed for wholesale investors, the minimum lot is Dm 1m. Accrued interest is not paid but divided on the coupon-date proportionally (on a 360 day/year basis) to whoever held the paper during the preceding period. Usually repayment is in bullet form, instalments over a fixed series of dates are an exception. In recent times, the Federal government endowed its *Schuldscheine* with a put option. Call options normally do not exist.

The main advantages for the issuer lie in the relatively low costs of borrowing, the uncomplicated way it can be arranged (as *Schuldscheine* are not subject to most of the restrictions governing securities), the flexibility and the discretion by comparison to the launching of a bond. For the lender, the fact that there is no necessity for depreciations (since there is no official trading) is sometimes important.

To summarize, the *Schuldschein* is an instrument, the conditions of which can be negotiated individually, with the possibility of trading it in a secondary OTC market.

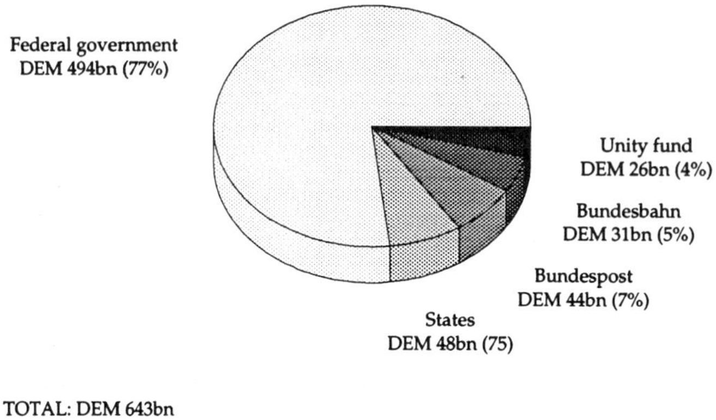

Figure 16.37 Public debt - total outstandings as at 31 December 1991

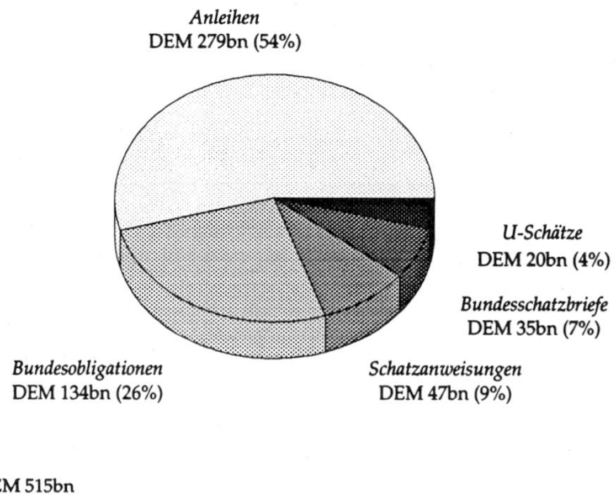

Figure 16.38 Federal government securities - total outstandings as at 31 December 1991

Bank bonds

Mortgage bonds (*Pfandbriefe*) are a special instrument created to fund housing (and shipbuilding) loans. As such, they are subject to the regulations of the Mortgage Bond Act, the Mortgage Bank Act and the Shipbuilding Mortgage Bank Act. These laws state that the bonds always have to be fully collateralized by first-ranking mortgages which must carry interest rates at least as high as the bonds themselves. Besides this, the issuing bank must guarantee coupon and repayment. Due to these provisions no *Pfandbrief* has ever gone into default.

The right to issue these bonds is reserved for 20 private and 8 public mortgage banks, 11 state banks (Landesbanken and Deutsche Girozentrale) and 2 special purpose semi-public banks (Depfa-Bank, DSL-Bank). These institutions place their *Pfandbriefe* on an ongoing basis. When the planned amount of a series has been raised, or if the market conditions have changed, a new tranche with a new coupon is launched. The fine-tuning of the yield is done by the variation of the price. Every new issue needs the approval of the minister of finance. A prospectus is only required, if the most recent one (of the bank in case), is more than 3 years old.

Mortgage bonds normally have a maturity of 3-10 years, and a minimum denomination of Dm 100. Usually, they are listed in the first section. Some issues tailored for wholesale clients are designed as registered bonds (*Namenspfandbriefe*) and are therefore not traded on a stock exchange. Though total outstandings by the end of 1991 were Dm 143bn, the market at the stock exchange is not very important, as most retail investors hold their *Pfandbriefe* until maturity.

Most of the dealing is done between banks, where round lots of Dm 5m are the usual size. Since issues are seldom larger than Dm 500m, two-way quotations for a particular series cannot be achieved in most cases. Due to the lower fungibility, the yield in normal times is a bit higher than that of public bonds, the spread varying due to the market conditions.

Nowadays, with only a few exceptions, interest is paid annually and the redemption in one amount. Some older issues are refunded prematurely via draws. By law, bonds with a maturity of more than 10 years must be callable by the borrower. Put options may not be given to investors and redemption above par is illegal.

Most of what has been said about the legal framework, design and market conditions for mortgage bonds also applies to communal bonds (*Kommunalobligationen*, in recent days also called *Öffentliche Pfandbriefe*). The main difference is the form of the collateral. The loans must be guaranteed by a German public sector entity (the EC and some of its agencies count as domestic public institutions). In addition, up to 10 per cent of the collateral may consist of loans to, or guaranteed by, an EC member state. With a total outstanding of Dm 392bn at the end of 1991, the *Kommunalobligationen* sector is one of the most important in the German bond market.

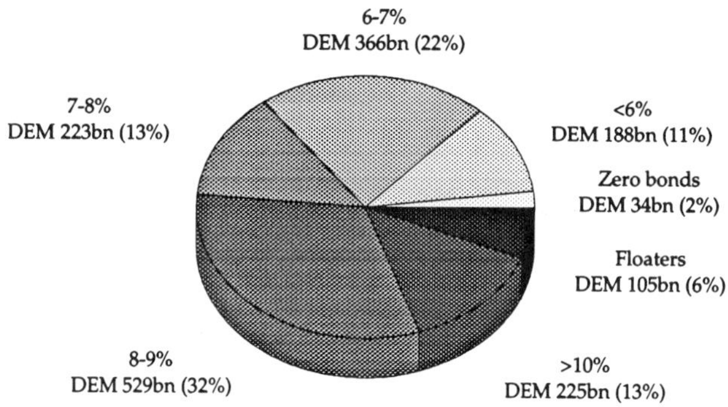

TOTAL: DEM 1682bn

Figure 16.39 Total outstandings by coupon as at December 1991

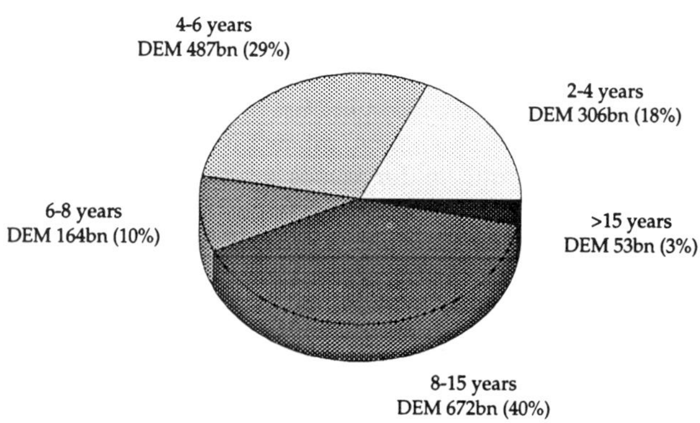

TOTAL: DEM 1682bn

Figure 16.40 Total outstandings by maturity as at 31 December 1991

Among the other bank bonds, a differentiation is made between those issued by special-purpose banks and those of private banks. The first group consists of such institutions as the Kreditanstalt für Wiederaufbau (Reconstruction Loan Corporation), Deutsche Pfandbriefanstalt (German Mortgage Bond Corporation), Deutsche Siedlungs- und Landrentenbank (German Housing and Agricultural Mortgage Bank), Deutsche Ausgleichsbank (German Equalization Bank), Landwirtschaftliche Rentenbank (Agricultural Mortgage Bank), Deutsche Industriekreditbank (Industrial Loan Bank), Staatsbank Berlin (former National Bank of East Germany) and the home loan banks (Bausparkassen), which all have special purposes and in the most cases a (semi-) public status. Also subsumed under this category is the DG Bank (the central institution of nearly 3500 co-operative banks), in spite of the fact that it is a globally-operating universal bank. These banks all issue bearer bonds (*Inhaberschuldverschreibungen*) with a higher credit standing because of their public backing. By the end of 1991 the total outstanding was Dm 221bn (cf. the Dm 284bn of the remaining bank bonds). All-in-all, the total of bank bonds outstanding amounted to an enormous Dm 1040bn.

Other domestic bonds

Among the other bonds, industrial bonds (*Industrieobligationen*) have almost no significance. Only 4 issues are listed in the first section of the stock exchange, with a total outstanding of Dm 3.2bn at the end of 1991:

- Harpener 4.5 per cent of 1959
- Schenker 7.375 per cent of 1985/95
- Thyssen 7.25 per cent of 1977/92
- VIAG 6.75 per cent of 1987/97.

This poor prominence can be principally blamed on tight legal restrictions. But, as the very cumbersome and time-consuming issuance authorization procedure (according to sections 795 and 808a of the German Civil Code) was repealed in 1991, there is a chance that this section of the market will be revived.

Formerly, the minimum maturity of a bond had to be 5 years. In 1984, however, the Bundesbank lowered this requirement to 2 years, thus paving the way for private medium-term note programmes. Such programmes are based on a general agreement between a capital-seeking institution and a bank acting as arranger, and give the institution the right to issue medium-term notes within a given volume, whenever it deems this appropriate. The notes may have fixed-floating- or zero-coupons, and maturities of between 2 and 30 years. Until now, this instrument has not been of great significance. Only about 15 programmes exist, with sizes between Dm 200m and Dm 2bn, the utilization being negligible.

Deutschemark foreign bonds (Dm-eurobonds)

Over the last few years, most of the borrowing needs of German corporations have been satisfied through the euro markets, normally by foreign outlets, founded especially for financing purposes. In fact, there is no marked difference between Deutschemark foreign bonds and Dm-eurobonds. The first are underwritten by a syndicate consisting of German institutions, the latter by an international one (under the leadership of a German institution, which could be a subsidiary of a foreign one).

Several times, the Bundesbank has declared (the most recent occasion was in June of 1989), that it wants the market for Deutschemark bonds anchored in Germany. To strengthen this market, it relaxed the existing restrictions further:

- The minimum maturity was reduced to 2 years and the requirement of prior notification of an issue waived. Foreigners were allowed to run continuously-offered programmes.
- Issuance permission of the public authorities is no longer needed. However, if the bonds should be listed officially, they have to fulfil the quality standards set by the rules of the stock exchange. A prospectus is obligatory.

By the end of 1991, total outstandings of all Deutschemark bonds of non-resident borrowers amounted to Dm 242bn (included in this figure are all issues where at least one German bank has been a member of the syndicate).

The market has developed such a variety that very little can be said about typical design. There are fixed-coupons (including zeros) as well as floating-rate notes (including capped ones); there are bonds with warrants, convertibles, dual-currency bonds, bonds with currency options, bonds linked to stock exchange indices, etc. Most of these issues are placed with the retail customer.

The following brief examples should serve to illustrate this wide spectrum:

- CPC International Inc. (USA) 86/01 is a 6.75 per cent fixed-rate straight bond with an annual coupon and redemption in one amount.
- Postipankki (Finland) 90/93 is also a fixed-rate (11 per cent) straight bond with yearly interest payment, but the refunding is linked to the notation of the German Equities Index (DAX) on 3 September 1993.
- Nord LB Finance (Curacao) 91/93 is endowed with an interest rate of 10.25 per cent, which is paid annually. The issuer may choose to redeem at 100 per cent, or in 14 common shares of Daimler Benz AG.
- Kingdom of Denmark 90/95 has an annual coupon of 13.125 per cent. The repayment is linked to the exchange rates of Dm/£ and Dm/Ecu.
- Series B Euro-Dm Securities (Island of Jersey) 86/06 is a zero bond secured by the German Federal Railways.

- BMW Finance B.V. (Netherlands) 87/08 is also a zero bond, but is repaid in equal amounts of Dm 969.32 each year, from 2008 to 2012, on 21 April.
- Export Development Corp. (Canada) 85/93 is a dual-currency bond. The 7.7 per cent interest is paid in Dm yearly, but refunded in US$.
- African Development Bank 87/97 is a floating-rate note based on 6-month LIBOR + 25 basis points. The interest is paid and adjusted twice a year.
- Sumitomo Bank (Japan) 89/94 is a convertible with a coupon of 2.625 per cent and may be converted between 13 February 1989 and 2 March 1994 into 36 shares of Sumitomo Bank, at a price of ¥3606.80, with a fixed exchange rate of 69.74 ¥/Dm.
- AGAB Finance B.V. (Netherlands) 90/93 is a straight 7.875 per cent bond with 3 warrants, each of which gives the holder the right to buy one AGAB share at a price of 328 Dm between 1 March 1990 and 15 December 1992.
- Nordiska Investeringsbanken (Norway) 87/92 bears a fixed-rate coupon of 4.875 per cent and has attached to it 20 warrants to buy US$50 at an exchange rate of Dm 1.673 in the period between 13 May 1988 and 7 May 1993.
- World Bank 89/94 is a 9 per cent straight bond with embedded currency options, which means that the issuer has the right to choose whether interest and redemption is paid in Dm or in US$.
- Ireland 89/99 is endowed with a fixed annual coupon of 7.25 per cent but, in this case, holders may choose, whether they want the payments in Dm or Irish punts.

Notes on Figure 16.41 (overleaf)

[1] *Bearer bonds. Debt book-entry - no physical delivery. Issued by the Federal Bond Syndicate (Bundesanleihekonsortium)*

[2] *Issued by an underwriting syndicate, usually led by the Landesbank of the particular state*

[3] *Bearer bonds. Debt book-entry - no physical delivery. Institutions and non-residents can only buy them in the secondary market*

[4] *Bearer bonds. Debt book-entry - no physical delivery. Issued by auction. Institutions and non-residents can only buy them in the secondary market. Significance waning*

[5] *Bearer bonds. Debt book-entry - no physical delivery*

[6] *Money market instrument. Mentioned for completeness only*

[7] *For resident retail clients. Sale to non-residents prohibited*

[8] *Not a bearer instrument. A loan, not a security*

[9] *Bearer bonds and registered bonds. Secured by first-ranking mortgages*

[10] *Bearer bonds and registered bonds. Secured by a guarantee of a German public sector entity (also partly by an EC member state)*

[11] *Without significance (only 4 issues listed in 1st section)*

[12] *No significant difference between DEM foreign bonds and DEM eurobonds*

Issuer	Maturity (years)	Typical issue size (DEM million)	Minimum denomination (DEM)	Listing
PUBLIC BONDS *(Öffentliche Anleihen)*				
Federal government bonds *(Bundesanleihen)*[1]				
Federal government Federal Railway *(Bundesbahn)* Federal Post Office *(Bundespost)* Unity Fund *(Fonds Deutsche Einheit)*	8-30 (usually 10)	4000-5000 (recently 10,000+)	100	1st section Variable notation (since Oct 1988)
State bonds *(Länderanleihen)*[2]				
States *(Bundesländer)*				
Federal government medium-term notes *(Bundesobligationen)*[3]				
Federal government	5	Permanent issue 5000-10,000	100	1st section Variable notation (since Oct 1988)
Medium-term notes *(Kassenobligationen)*[4]				
Federal government Federal Railway Federal Post Office States Special credit institutions	3-6 (usually 10)	100-2500 (recently, 10,000+)	5000	2nd section
Federal Treasury notes *(Bundesschatzanweisungen)*[5]				
Federal government	4-7	6000	5000	1st section
Federal government zero notes *(U-Schätze)*[6]				
Federal government Federal Railway Federal Post Office	1-2	Permanent issue (no predetermined amount)	100,000 or more	Not listed
Federal government savings bonds *(Bundesschatzbriefe)*[7]				
Federal government	Type A: 6 Type B: 7	Permanent issue (no predetermined amount)	Type A: 100 Type B: 50	Not listed

(cont.)

Federal government retail zero notes *(Finanzierungsschätze)*[7]				
Federal government	1-2	Permanent issue (no predetermined amount)	1000	Not listed
Loans against borrowers' notes *(Schuldscheine)*[8]				
Federal government Federal Railway Federal Post Office States Major banks Special credit institutions Foreign institutions	Typically 3-10	10-100	1,000,000	Not listed
				1st section
BANK BONDS				
Mortgage bonds *(Pfandbriefe)*[9]				
Mortgage banks (*Hypothekenbanken*) State banks (*Landesbanken)*	3-10	Permanent issue 20-100, up to 500	Normally 100 (can be 500 /1000/ 5000)	1st section
Communal bonds (*Kommunalobligationen / Öffentliche Pfandbriefe)*[10]				
Mortgage banks State banks	3-10	Permanent issue 20-100, up to 500	Normally 100 (can be 500 /1000/ 5000)	1st section
Other bank bonds *(Bankschuldverschreibungen)*				
Banks	1-10	Varies	Normally 100 (can be 500 /1000/5000)	Listed
OTHER BONDS				
Industrial bonds *(Industrieobligationen)*[11]				
Corporations	5-10	Varies	100	Listed
DEM foreign bonds *(DM-Auslandsanleihen)*, **DEM eurobonds**[12]				
Non-resident institutions (often outlets of domestic corporations for financing purposes only)	2-10, up to 30	200-500	1000 (straights) 10,000 (FRNs)	Listed

Figure 16.41 The German bond market - types of security

The market has gained quite remarkably in depth and liquidity. The main dealing takes place not at the stock exchange, but between the banks. The typical trading lot varies between Dm 1m and 5m, while the bid/ask-spread ranges from 10 pfennigs in liquid issues of high-quality borrowers, up to Dm 1 or more. The yield is equal to, or recently even a bit lower than, that of government bonds in the case of supranational organizations, rising to a difference of 250 basis points, as in the case of Mexico, or even more in lower-rated debts.

16.5 Issuers

Overview

Following the collapse of the Berlin Wall in November 1989, German Monetary Union (July 1990) and finally German unification in October 1990, new issuance activity in the German bond market has picked up significantly. In 1989, the net amount placed by all domestic issuers was nearly double that of the previous year (1988: Dm 40.1bn, 1989: Dm 80.6bn). By 1990, this amount had risen to record heights (1990: Dm 226.7bn); at the end of 1991, the net amount of new issues launched by domestic borrowers reached Dm 227.8bn.

During the same period the new net issuance activity of foreign borrowers contracted steadily (1988: Dm 45.2bn, 1989: Dm 39.1bn, 1990: Dm 36.8bn, 1991: Dm 38.0bn).

Public authorities

The most important issuing group in Germany is that of the public authorities. At the end of 1991, their market share was 38.6 per cent (net issue amount: Dm 87.9bn) of all domestic bearer bonds issued. Typical borrowers in this market sector are the Federal government, the Federal Railways (Bundesbahn), the Federal Post Office (Bundespost), the state governments and local authorities. Since German unification a new government-guaranteed issuer, the German Unity Fund (*Fonds Deutsche Einheit*), has tapped the market. The Reichsbahn, now under management of the Deutsche Bundesbahn, was the other issuer to make a first-time appearance.

Within this group, the Federal government is by far the most important issuer. In 1991, it issued a gross volume of Dm 148.3bn, followed by the German Unity Fund (1991: Dm 17.0bn gross). The state governments came third that year, with an issuing volume of Dm 9.5bn gross, while the German Post Office launched a volume of Dm 7.9bn gross, and the Federal Railways (including Reichsbahn), Dm 6.1bn.

Public authorities are not only active as issuers in the bearer bond market. From time to time they also issue medium-term notes, discount notes and - to a growing extent - certificates of indebtedness (*Schuldscheindarlehen*).

In the past, public authorities launched issues mostly with maturities of eight to ten years (the Federal government also tapped the four- and five-year sectors, in the form of *Bundesobligationen* and *Kassenobligationen* or *Bundesschatzanweisungen*). But with the high volume of previous issuance needing to be financed, the authorities have now adopted a more flexible approach. Every six weeks, the

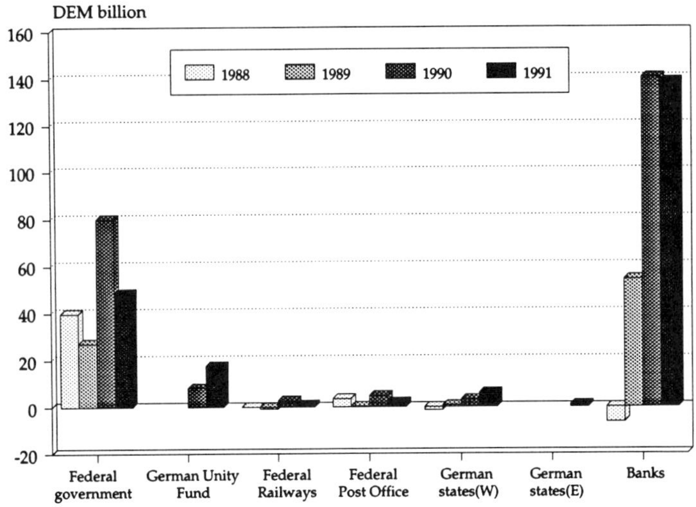

Figure 16.42 Issuers in the German bond market, by growth in vol. of bearer bonds outstanding
See below for data

Year-end:	1988	1989	1990	1991
Federal government	+39.6	+27.0	+80.0	+48.7
German Unity Fund	-	-	+8.2	+17.5
Federal Railways	+0.0	-0.8	+2.8	+0.9
Federal Post Office	+3.6	+0.2	+4.7	+2.0
German states (West)	-1.2	+0.7	+3.2	+6.1
German states (East)	-	-	-	+1.0
Banks, *of which*:	-6.4	+54.3	+140.5	+138.7
Regional giro institutions	-12.5	+11.1	+18.4	+16.4
Mortgage banks	-1.4	+3.5	+17.8	+29.9
Special credit institutions	-0.5	+9.0	+77.5	+62.9
Other banks	+8.0	+30.7	+26.8	+29.5

Figure 16.43 Issuers by growth in outstanding volume of bearer bonds (DEM billion)

Federal government currently offers its *Bundesschatzanweisungen* (four- and five-year bearer bonds), whilst it has increased the volume of its short-term discount notes (*Unverzinsliche Schatzanweisungen*). The same circumstances have arisen for other issuers in this sector.

As a result of increased issuance activity, bond volumes have also increased. In the past, issuance volumes for new bonds were normally Dm 4-5bn for Federal government bonds (*Bundesobligationen*: Dm 1-3bn), and Dm 1-2bn for all other issuers. Over the last five years, these volumes have increased sharply. For the German Unity Fund and the government itself, the normal issuance volumes are now Dm 8-10bn and, for *Bundesobligationen*, Dm 10-12bn. Amounts for the Federal Post Office and the Federal Railways, meanwhile, are Dm 5-6bn each.

Mortgage banks and other domestic banks

This subsection comprises the second most important group of borrowers in the German bond market. By the end of 1991, the total amount of their bonds issued (i.e. mortgage bonds, municipal bonds and the so-called 'other bank bonds'), accounted for 61.4 per cent, or Dm 1040.3bn. In 1991, this group issued bearer bonds with a total net volume of Dm 139.4bn (gross volume: Dm 292.1bn). The most important borrowers within this issuing group are mortgage banks, central savings banks and commercial banks.

Mortgage banks offer mortgage loans for housing, industrial and agricultural investments, as well as loans for both medium and small-sized municipalities. In order to refinance these loans, they issue either mortgage bonds or municipal bonds which, in turn, are also issued for refinancing purchases of *Schuldscheindarlehen* (for public authority entities). Most of these banks are majority-owned by big German commercial banks. The issuing amount for mortgage and municipal bonds is usually Dm 100-300m, with maturities ranging from two to ten years.

The other main issuers in this group of banks are the central savings banks (Girozentralen), which are jointly owned by the saving banks and the respective German states (e.g. Hessische Landesbank). Third place is taken by the commercial banks - an important element in German banking - and particularly the big three: Deutsche Bank, Dresdner Bank and Commerzbank, who are all frequent borrowers in the German bond market. Besides credit business and deposit taking, these banks work in the field of investment banking as well as handling the financial side of foreign trade. Their issues in the capital market serve predominantly as a means of refinancing loans and deposits.

The maturity spectrum of the bonds offered by these borrowers range from two to ten years. Maturities with a life of less than two (and one day) years are subject to minimum reserve requirements, and therefore not offered. The average issuing volume is approximately Dm 50-300 m.

Specialized credit institutions

Behind this group of issuers one can find names like the Kreditanstalt für Wiederaufbau. (Reconstruction Loan Corporation). Specialized credit institutions in Germany are normally public-owned banks with a particularly special function, such as refinancing capital investment in the east German states. Other specialized credit corporations are the Lastenausgleichsbank and the DSL Bank. In 1991, they issued a total volume of Dm 80.7bn, of which net new issuance accounted for Dm 66bn (1988: minus Dm 2.9bn; 1989: Dm 9.2bn; 1990: Dm 73.3bn). At issue, the maturities of these bonds range between five and ten years.

Corporates

In 1991, business enterprises launched just Dm 0.5bn net (Dm 0.7bn gross) in the German bond market. Traditionally, domestic enterprises have never raised large funds in the domestic bond market since they normally rely on traditional financing methods such as bank loans and *Schuldscheindarlehen*. The most likely reason for this is the relatively high cost of issuing small-sized bonds with long maturities. In recent years, however, this group of issuers has mainly issued bonds cum warrants and convertible bonds, with practically no issuance of straight bonds.

However, since the beginning of 1991, there have been some changes in the issuing behaviour of corporates. Parent companies of German enterprises now offer medium-term note programmes with maturities of between two and ten years. They are also allowed to offer Deutschemark commercial paper programmes with a life up to one year, in order to finance short-term borrowing requirements.

Foreign borrowers

Basically, all sovereign, public and private foreign borrowers can tap the Dm-euromarket (*Markt für DM-Auslandsanleihen*). Within this group of foreign borrowers, sovereigns and supranationals, the European Investment Bank and the World Bank are the most important single issuers. Other major issuers are borrowers whose issues are guaranteed by their respective home governments or public authorities. In addition, many corporate borrowers have tapped the market for Dm-foreign bonds.

However, since German unification, and in light of rising German yields, foreign issuers have significantly reduced their issuing activity. Whilst, in 1988, the borrowing activities of foreign borrowers reached a high of Dm 28.6bn net, this was reduced to Dm 18.6bn in 1991 (Dm 32.8bn gross), down from Dm 22.8bn in 1989 and Dm 21.7bn in 1990. Another reason for the lower issuance activity was the abolition of the 10 per cent withholding tax which had made Dm-foreign bonds (which were subject to this tax) less attractive.

Furthermore, the introduction of the new 30 per cent interest equalization tax on 1 January 1993 will probably impact on the Dm-eurobond market. In the past, there has been a constant demand for Dm-eurobonds from German residents who wanted to avoid part of their taxation on interest income from bonds. But, from the beginning of 1993, the tax rate for interest income from bonds which are not held in the portfolio of the owner will be taxed at 35 per cent. To attract German residents to buy Dm-eurobonds, it is therefore necessary to offer the investors a higher yield (compared to the domestic sector), implying an increase in borrowing costs. Only the future will tell whether this will further discourage the issuance activity of foreign borrowers.

16.6 *Investors*

Overview

Aggregate savings in the Federal Republic of Germany (excl. eastern Germany) have been growing steadily since the end of 1987 and, at the end of 1991, totalled Dm 267.4bn. As a percentage of net national product, and at market, prices this amounts to 11.7 per cent. At Dm 190.8bn, private households account for the lion's share. Owing to lively investment activity and the accompanying high credit demand, total savings in eastern Germany were negative in 1991 (minus Dm 12.2bn). Positive developments were registered for savings of private households, which - according to preliminary data - reached Dm 4.1bn in 1990 and Dm 12.5bn in 1991.

A look at the net sales figure for fixed-interest-bearing securities reveals that, since German reunification, net recourse to the capital market has soared and, at the end of 1991, was 2.8 times higher than at the end of 1989.

This change in the tapping of the capital market was also reflected in investor behaviour as interest rates rose after reunification due to the steep increase in financing volumes and, at the same time, a restrictive Bundesbank policy caused an inverse structure of the yield curve.

Higher yield levels induced not only domestic, but also foreign, investors to purchase bonds; meanwhile, the banks made a gradual retreat owing to rising refinancing costs.

Banks

Between 1987 and 1991, banks remained the most important group of investors in the German bond market (see Figures 16.44 & 16.45), even though their share in net purchases varied greatly due to several special factors (such as the introduction of an interest income tax at source, in 1988). At the end of 1991, the banks' share of net bond purchases amounted to a mere 18 per cent, compared with just under 48 per cent in 1987. A prime reason for banks tapping the bond market is an expectation of falling interest rates and resultant price gains. At the same time, banks' investment opportunities in fixed-income securities are basically dependent on their liquidity reserves, current credit demand and the level of refinancing costs. The process of restructuring in eastern Germany boosted credit demand noticeably, so that less funds could be made available to the capital market by the banks. The ever-more inverse yield structure also caused the banks' refinancing costs to soar, rendering investments in the bond market less attractive. Since the introduction of Bund futures at Liffe and the DTB (the

German futures exchange), the banks have made increasing use of these instruments, in order to achieve short-term trading profits. Lower costs (by comparison with the cash market), increased flexibility, and lower capital requirements, have all encouraged an increased shift of trading activities to this market.

Private investors

In 1987 and 1988, private investors were net sellers of German fixed-income securities. This was a result of both rising long-term interest rates and the announcement of the introduction of an interest income tax at source on fixed-interest securities. In the main, investors moved out of domestic bonds and into Deutschemark eurobonds (see Figures 16.46 & 16.47) and foreign currency bonds. Only after the abolition of interest income tax at source, and the unification-induced rise in interest rates, did private investors return to longer-term fixed-income securities. In 1991, their commitment in the bond market grew as it became clear that long-term interest rates had clearly passed their peak.

At the end of 1991, private households accounted for a good 26 per cent of net sales of fixed-interest-bearing securities, a figure twice as high as 1990. Private investor interest was primarily focused on 4- and 10-year maturities, but also included zero bonds and new financing instruments.

Corporates

The share of companies in net domestic sales of fixed-interest securities has remained relatively stable. Given the slowdown in economic activity, however, the amount of liquid funds invested in the bond market has been growing since 1989. Investments have centred on maturities of up to one year, but there has also been increasing demand for paper with maturities of up to 5 years. Investment in maturities of up to 12-months declined considerably after the introduction of commercial paper programmes (not included in sales figures for fixed-income securities since they are a classed as a money market instrument), which companies increasingly used to 'park' their short-term funds. This was attributable to the fact that commercial paper programmes with 3- and 6-month maturities closed the supply gap.

Investment funds

There are two groups of investment funds in Germany. The first is that of mutual funds (e.g. ADIG, DIT, DWS, Deka), which manage private savings. Mutual fund units can be purchased by any private individual. The second group comprises so-called Special fund companies, which manage funds from firms and insurance companies (i.e. pension funds). Shares in these Special funds can only be purchased by the unit holders (no more than ten). The share in net sales of

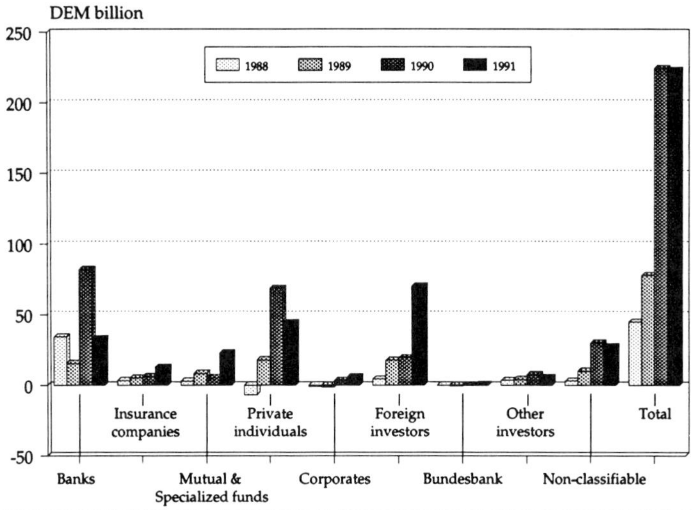

Figure 16.44 Purchases of domestic bonds
See below for data

	1988	1989	1990	1991
Banks	+34.3	+15.6	+82.3	+32.8
Insurance companies	+3.5	+5.3	+6.3	+12.8
Mutual funds and Specialized funds	+3.0	+8.5	+5.6	+22.8
Private individuals	-6.7	+18.1	+68.8	+44.2
Corporates	-0.8	-1.2	+3.6	+6.0
Foreign investors	+4.5	+18.0	+19.7	+70.2
Bundesbank	+0.1	-0.5	+0.2	+0.7
Other investors	+3.6	+4.2	+7.7	+5.6
Non-classifiable	+3.3	+10.1	+30.2	+27.7
Total	+44.8	+78.1	+224.4	+222.8

Figure 16.45 Purchases of domestic bonds[1]

[1] *Bearer bonds in DEM billion, nominal value (+ = net purchases, - = net sales)*

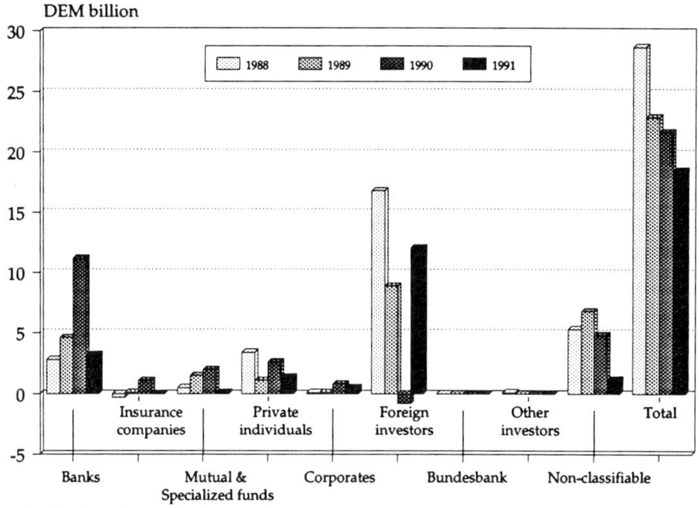

Figure 16.46 Purchases of Deutschemark eurobonds
See below for data

	1988	1989	1990	1991
Banks	+2.8	+4.6	+11.2	+3.2
Insurance companies	-0.3	+0.1	+1.1	-0.0
Mutual funds and Specialized funds	+0.5	+1.5	+2.0	+0.1
Private individuals	+3.4	+1.1	+2.6	+1.4
Corporates	+0.1	-0.1	+0.8	+0.5
Foreign investors	+16.8	+8.9	-0.8	+12.1
Bundesbank	-	-	-	-
Other investors	+0.1	-	-	-
Non-classifiable	+5.3	+6.8	+4.8	+1.2
Total	+28.7	+22.9	+21.7	+18.5

Figure 16.47 Purchases of Deutschemark eurobonds[1]

[1] *Bearer bonds in DEM billion, nominal value (+ = net purchases, - = net sales)*

fixed-interest-bearing securities accounted for by investment funds, varies greatly. Operating under the conditions laid down in the regulatory framework, such investment funds aim at producing profits, i.e. they are performance-orientated. Whether they are prepared to invest in the domestic bond market or not, therefore depends, above all, on the expected development of interest rates and the price gains to be achieved.

It is mainly in times of low interest rates that the mutual funds see an inflow of large amounts of money. This phenomenon is an example of the differences in investor behaviour seen in the various interest rate phases. Whilst private investors tend to invest directly in the bond market in periods of high interest rates, or in anticipation of falling rates, they show a preference for funds when interest rates are low. This results in relatively modest flows of liquidity to the funds in phases of high interest rates.

At the end of 1991, mutual funds accounted for only 3.7 per cent of the total net sales of fixed-interest securities, compared with more than 19 per cent at the end of 1989. The decline in the share of this investor group in net sales of domestic fixed-interest securities is, however, also attributable to another trend. The anticipated convergence of interest rates in the EMS countries led to the introduction of European bond fund products, inducing German investors to place their liquidity in such funds.

Foreign investors

Between 1987 and 1991, the share of foreign investors in the buying of domestic fixed-income securities varied considerably. Whilst, in 1987, it still amounted to 37.6 per cent, it fell to just under 5 per cent in 1988, after the announcement of interest income tax at source. In 1991, however, foreign investors once again showed a increased presence in the German bond market. At the end of that year, they accounted for more than 26 per cent of net sales, a fact which can be attributed, first and foremost, to expectations of an appreciation of the Deutschemark and declining interest rates. As had been the case in previous years, investors preferred government bonds because of their excellent liquidity and high degree of solvency. Another reason for the trend towards government bonds (including the German Unity Fund) and Treasury bonds, is the existence of hedging instruments, for such paper, in the form of futures. In 1991, non-resident investors accounted for more than 50 per cent of total net sales of government bonds. It should be clear, therefore, that the success of a bond issue depends, in no small measure, on this investor group.

16.7 Methods of issuance

The primary bond market comprises all activities relative to the distribution of new issues. In Germany the primary market is segmented in sectors for:

- government bonds
- municipal bonds and bonds of the *Länder*
- bank bonds and mortgage bonds
- bonds of domestic corporations
- international bonds

Statutory framework

There is no general law governing the German primary market like the Securities Act of 1933 in the USA. The main regulations regarding new issues are stated in the German Securities Prospectus Law, in the regulatory provisions by the Bundesbank based on its authority to provide for orderly capital market conditions, or are derived from the provisions of the German Stock Exchange Law.

Government bonds

By law, German government bonds and all bonds of Federal authorities (Railways, Post Office, German Unity Fund) are issued by the Bundesbank.

Since 1990, the Bundesbank applies a mixture of a syndication and tendering system to issue *Bundesanleihen* (Bunds). Every bond is issued in two tranches, one being issued by the consortium and one by open tender. The consortium tranche usually is issued on a Wednesday, amounting to about one third of the entire issue. One day later, the open auction takes place with another third of the volume. The remainder is kept by the central bank for market intervention purposes.

At present, over 110 banks are included in the consortium, roughly half of them being foreign banks based in Germany. Since October 1991, commitments are sized according to the effective amounts that the banks bid for in Bund auctions. Thus, their bidding will be taken as a measure of their placement abilities. For the syndicated tranche, there is a fixed-fee income ('reallowance') of 7/8 per cent. Usually, in the professional market, more than half of this amount is passed on by the banks to investors.

For open tender there are two ways of offering: Either a fixed price is set at which banks or investors are asked to bid for amounts only, or a minimum price is given which has to be matched, or exceeded, with the possibility of asking for different amounts at different prices. The highest offers are served first, followed by those with the next highest price.

Bond issues of the Federal authorities (e.g. Railways - Bundesbahn and Reichsbahn, Post Office - Bundespost, Unity Fund - *Fonds Deutsche Einheit*) are also lead-managed by the Bundesbank. They are issued through a traditional syndicate, through auctions or by the two systems operating simultaneously. The agencies normally opt for only one of them. Due to the smaller size of these new debt transactions, they usually are not traded abroad, are less liquid and pay a yield about 1/8 above Bunds.

Intermediate and short-term government bonds are sold either like the tap issues of bank bonds (five-year special Federal bonds - *Bundesobligationen*, Federal savings bonds - *Bundesschatzbriefe* and Treasury financing papers - *Finanzierungsschätze*) or by tendering procedures at fixed dates (medium-term notes - *Bundesschatzanweisungen*, Treasury discount papers - *Unverzinsliche Schatzanweisungen*).

Certificates of indebtedness (*Schuldscheine*) are issued in the form of private placements.

Bank bonds and mortgage bonds

Upon application, the issuers of mortgage bonds (*Pfandbriefe*) and the different kinds of German bank bonds (*Bankschuldverschreibungen* - bank bonds, *Sparbriefe* - savings bonds, *Kommunalobligationen* - communal bonds,) are assigned the special status of a *Daueremittent*, meaning 'frequent issuer' by a special provision of the German bank law. This status enables them to issue numerous bonds based on a general prospectus usually published every three years, and on a very short information prospectus only with every single bond.

Mortgage bonds and communal bonds are offered by the issuers (mortgage banks and savings banks) both to other banks - who either take them as assets or re-offer them to other investors - and to non-bank investors. The amounts are sold on request. Other domestic bank bonds are usually issued by banks within their retail chains and are not offered to other banks.

There is no fixed payment date for such an issue and it is on offer until the desired amount is reached, or until the coupon has to be changed because market rate variations can no longer be adjusted for by changing the issue price. In all cases, the only risk lies in the failure to place the required amount of bonds in the designated time-scale, and it is entirely born by the issuer.

Municipal bonds and bonds of the *Länder*

The bonds of the German Federal states (*Länder*) and municipalities are issued by the banks owned by these entities: *Sparkassen* (savings banks) and in particular

Landesbanken, which are the central banks of the *Sparkassen*. Syndicates are local and the issuance of the very few bonds of this sector is very similar to a private placement. However, these bonds are formally public bonds. By law, they do not have to go through an application procedure for such status.

German corporate bonds

The market segment for German corporate bonds is very small. The launching procedure is the same as that for international bonds (see below).

International bonds

The distinctions between domestic bonds, international bonds and eurobonds are derived from the borrower's country of registration, the consortium members and the investors.

A Deutschemark bond of a borrower registered in Germany is a domestic bond. If the issuer is registered in a foreign country, it is an international bond (*Auslandsanleihe*). A eurobond is a special type of international bond; according to the definition of the European prospectus, eurobonds are 'transferable securities which:

- are to be underwritten and distributed by a syndicate at least two of the members of which have their registered offices in different countries, and
- are offered on a significant scale in one or more countries other than of the issuer's registered office, and
- may be subscribed for or initially acquired only through a credit institution or other financial institution'.

Since, in Germany, there is no legal discrimination between domestic and foreign buyers of bonds - i.e. there is completely free capital import and export - today, nearly all foreign bonds are eurobonds.

For international Deutschemark bonds, the Bundesbank has set the following rules which are designed to maintain both control over all issuing activities and a distinct separation between the Deutschemark money markets and the Deutschemark bond market:

- The lead-manager of a Dm-denominated bond issue must be a bank which is incorporated in Germany, and the issue must also be launched in Germany. In a case where this bank is a subsidiary of a foreign house, it may lead-manage the bond only if the home country of this bank grants complete reciprocity for German banks. The existence of this rule is the main reason why there is no new issuance activity for

Deutschemark bonds outside Germany and the Deutschemark eurobond market is mainly located in Frankfurt. In addition:.

- German law and the use of the German clearing system are obligatory
- Deutschemark bonds must have a minimum tenure of two years. It is prohibited to issue shares of money market funds.
- Innovative issues must be reported to the Bundesbank in advance in order to allow for sufficient time to comment on it.
- Every lead-manager has to inform the Bundesbank of the issuer, amount, launch date, terms and placing method on the day of launch.
- Public bonds have to be listed on a German exchange. Private placements have to be introduced to the regulated market (*Geregelter Markt*) or to another system which assures availability of prices.

In the international bond sector, bidding procedures are the most common. The syndication and placing procedures are the same both for bonds which materialize through bidding, and those through an established relationship between borrower and issuing house.

Because of the large size of the funds raised through bond issues, banks often co-operate in underwriting and placing them with investors. For that purpose, they form a consortium or syndicate. The syndication process usually starts with the announcement of the bond to the primary market. The members of a consortium are classified by the responsibility they take over during the primary market period. Their obligations commence as soon as they agree to enter the syndicate.

The book-runner is the bank mandated to issue the bond. It is the main underwriter and always the lead-manager of the consortium. It is expected to take over at least a third of the bond volume. In case the bond should suffer from a very weak primary market, the lead-manager should try to manage the bond in a way avoiding disorderly market conditions (stabilization). The lead-manager is also responsible for continuously providing price quotations in the secondary market (market-making).

Sometimes, there is also a joint lead-manager who will also underwrite a major part of the bond and who might influence the pricing. Both lead- and joint lead-managers preserve the right to pre-place their commitments, that is, to place the bonds before opening the consortium.

Co-lead-managers and co-managers usually form the bulk of the members of a syndicate. They are selected according to their relationship with the book-runner, or the issuer, and according to their placing capacity with certain customers or in certain regions. They only differ in the amount of the bond they are willing to underwrite, or their commitment.

16.8 *New issue volumes*

Overview

The development of new issues of bearer bonds in the German bond market since 1988 has been characterized by two momentous events. The announcement of the introduction of a 10 per cent withholding tax for 1989 had already led, in 1988, to sizeable shifts in refinancing from domestic issues to bonds of foreign subsidiaries through the floating of Dm-eurobonds. Domestic net new issues plunged a dramatic 50 per cent to Dm 41bn, and the total volume of issues also dropped about 15 per cent from the previous year's figure to Dm 209bn (see Figure 16.48). The surprising repeal of the withholding tax, which was therefore only in force for the first half of 1989, together with a strong expansion of domestic loans business in a bullish economy, brought about a marked reversal of the 1988 relapse. Net new issues of domestic bonds doubled, to Dm 81bn in 1989, bolstered by brisk issuing activity, especially by

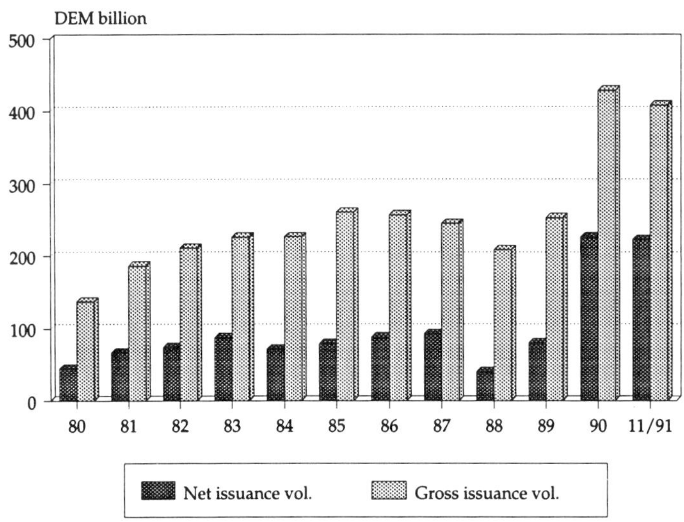

Figure 16.48 New issue volume in the German bond market

the commercial banks. This pushed gross new issues up 21 per cent to Dm 253bn

A further significant turning-point for structures in the German bond market was the reunification process in Germany. The huge funding requirements to finance the necessary economic and social adjustments in both west and east Germany, sparked off an explosive increase in the issuing of domestic bearer bonds. Net new issues reached a record level of Dm 227bn. As this coincided with an increase in the refinancing of expiring bonds, gross new issues shot up 69 per cent to reach, by far, the highest level of bond sales ever reached in Germany, at Dm 429bn. In 1991, the integration process in Germany still involved enormous borrowing requirements, so that net new issues stabilized at the very high level of around Dm 227bn overall, while the total volume of new issues only climbed by 3 per cent to a new record of Dm 442bn.

Public authority bonds

The sustained economic upswing since 1987, and the efforts of governments to consolidate their budgets, improved the financing situation of the public authorities to such an extent that gross new issues of public authority bonds declined appreciably in 1988 and 1989, by 17 per cent and 12 per cent respectively (see Figure 16.49). The smaller volume of public sector new borrowings correspondingly had an even greater impact on the figure for net new issues, which dropped 22 per cent and 56 per cent in these two years. In the wake of monetary union and reunification of the two German states, the situation in public sector budgets has changed completely in the last two years. The financing required to cover the greatly-enlarged deficits is reflected in a doubling of the gross new issue volume, totalling Dm 142bn in 1990 and about Dm 150bn in 1991. Net borrowings via bonds trebled in 1990, to more than Dm 86bn, and nearly reached the same amount in 1991.

Municipal bonds

The improved cash position of the local authorities was also reflected in the new issues of municipal bonds from 1988 to 1990 (see Figure 16.50). In each of the two years, 1988 and 1989, annual net new issues were only around Dm 1bn. In 1990, redemptions slightly outweighed the gross total new issue volume of Dm 71bn, so that total bonds outstanding marginally declined. However, on its own, this development gives a distorted picture of new borrowing by local authorities, since alternative forms of financing such as registered municipal bonds and *Schuldscheindarlehen* exhibited growth rates during the same period. The high borrowing requirements connected with the reunification of Germany had a delayed effect and did not show up in the budgets of local authorities until 1991. Net new issues of municipal bonds made out to bearer grew again for the first

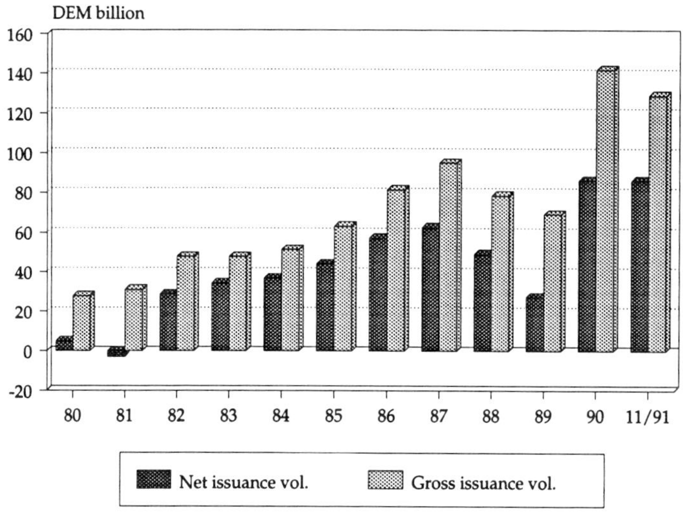

Figure 16.49 New issue volumes in the public authority bond market

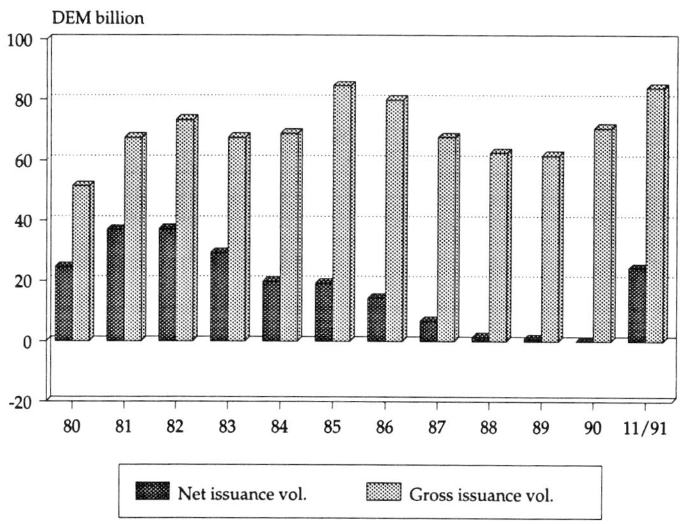

Figure 16.50 New issue volumes in the municipal bond market

time since 1982, to reach Dm 22bn at the end of the year. Gross new issues even chalked up a new record level at Dm 91bn.

Mortgage bonds

The market for mortgage bonds had already been benefiting from a favourable interest rate climate and a strong pick-up in construction activity, ever since 1986. This development is inadequately reflected in the new issue volume figures for mortgage bonds because net new issues of registered mortgage bonds, in particular, achieved strong growth rates. Thus, for example, although net new issues of bearer bonds in 1988 booked negative growth, the volume of out-

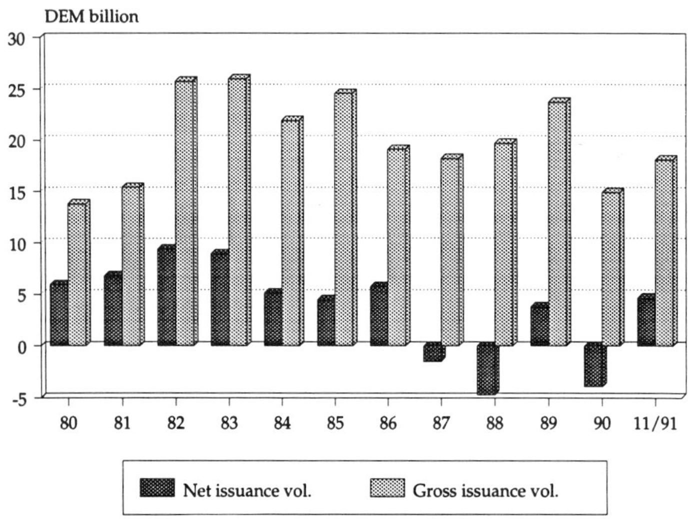

Figure 16.51 New issue volumes in the mortgage bond market

standing registered bonds managed to add Dm 9bn. It was not until 1990 that a weakening of overall construction activity was also reflected in a low net new issue volume of registered bonds, while mortgage bearer bonds outstanding continued to decline. In 1991, against a background of stabilizing interest rates, bonds issued in connection with public residential housing promotion schemes again induced a revival of this market segment, so that bearer net new issues improved to Dm 5bn and gross new issues to about Dm 18bn (see Figure 16.51).

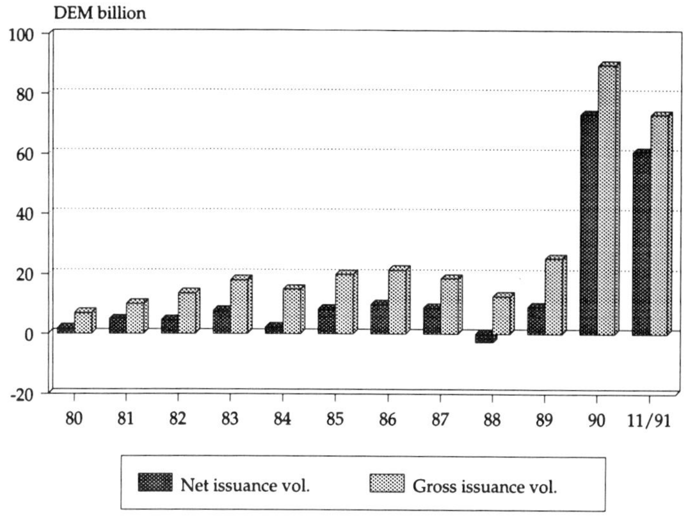

Figure 16.52 New issue volumes in the specialized bank bond market

Specialized bank bonds

Whereas the importance of the specialized banks entrusted with specific tasks had been tending to wane up to 1988 (see Figure 16.52), the reunification of Germany presented these banks with new tasks, and this led to an impressive trend reversal from mid-1989. The heavier demand for interest-subsidized loans from public promotion programmes favoured this development. Above all, however, it was the brisk issuing activity on the part of the successor of the East German central bank which drastically enhanced the importance of this market segment. The Staatsbank Berlin issued bonds with a nominal value of Dm 65bn in 1990 alone, thus receiving more than 70 per cent of the gross new issue volume of Dm 90bn. Dm 30bn of this figure is accounted for by a single so-called *Umwandlungsschuldverschreibung*, aimed at restructuring the liabilities of this banking institution. Net new issues had achieved a record volume of Dm 73bn in 1990 whilst, in 1991, they still managed to total Dm 66bn. Gross new issues declined from Dm 90bn (1990) to around Dm 80bn in 1991.

Other bank bonds

Over the period 1985-88 gross new issues of other bank bonds had recorded declining volumes (see Figure 16.53). Net new issues in 1988 were even negative,

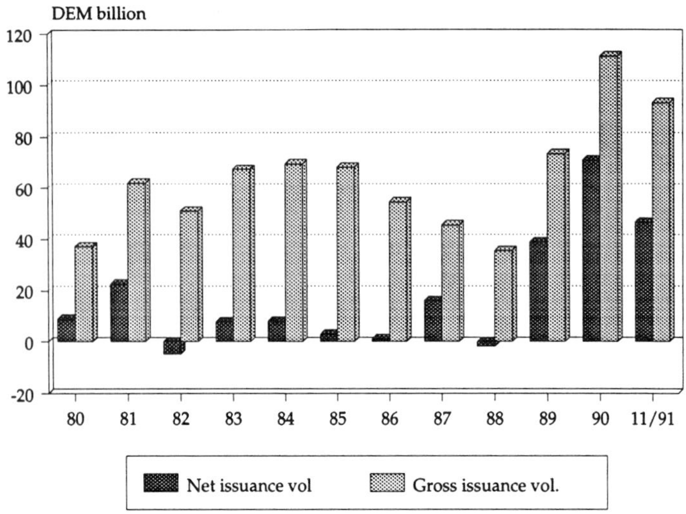

Figure 16.53 New issue volumes in the other bank bond market

as the introduction of the 10 per cent withholding tax induced domestic banks to increasingly channel their search for refinancing funds via their foreign subsidiaries. In 1989, expectations of rising refinancing rates prompted banks to increase their issuing activity. This development was fostered not only by higher credit demand from the industrial sector due to the quickening economy, but also by higher demand from private customers for fixed-income securities that yielded substantially more than savings deposits. Furthermore, after the 10 per cent withholding tax had been repealed, the practice of raising capital via foreign financing subsidiaries was resorted to very much less frequently by domestic banks in 1989, than in the preceding year. Net new issues of these bank bonds reached about Dm 39bn in 1989. In 1990, a strong expansion of the lending volume of the banks and savings banks generated additional brisk new issuing activity amounting to approximately Dm 111bn gross, while net new issues even soared to a historical high of Dm 71bn. Although this trend generally reversed in 1991, new issues of this borrowing group still reached Dm 100bn gross (only Dm 46bn net, however).

Corporate bonds

After the market for domestic corporate bonds practically came to a standstill in 1988-1990 (see Figure 16.54), the environment for this market segment was im-

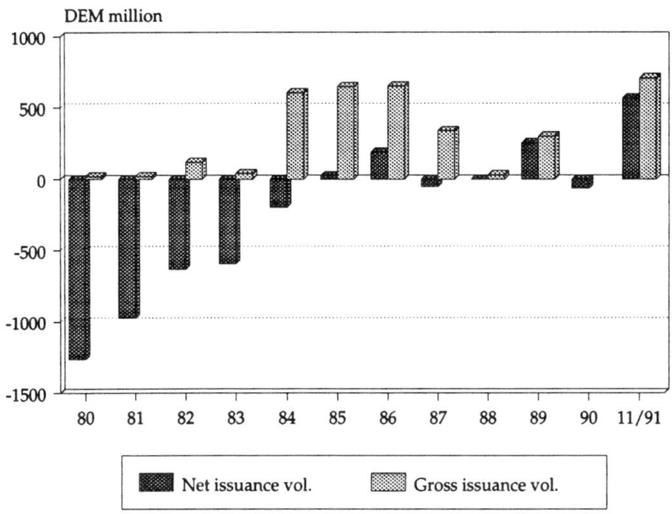

Figure 16.54 New issue volumes in the corporate bond market

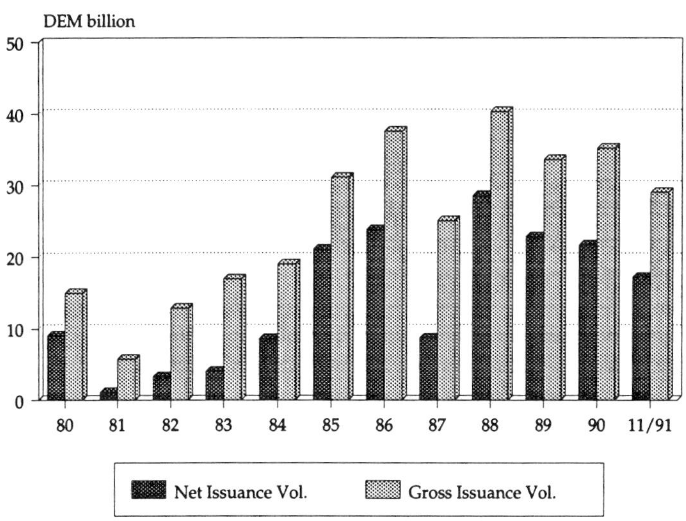

Figure 16.55 New issue volumes in the DEM eurobond market

proved in 1991 by the lifting of the requirement for government approval of bond issues, as well as by the abolition of stock exchange turnover tax. Although corporations continued to use their foreign subsidiaries as a platform for raising capital, 1991 nevertheless did see, once again, a few bonds cum warrants being issued by domestic enterprises, albeit with a total volume less than Dm 1bn.

Deutschemark eurobonds

With the 10 per cent withholding tax looming in the background, there was a sales boom in this market segment, with the large number of new issues occasionally leading to congestion. Gross new issues in 1988 reached a new record at Dm 40bn (highest bond sales hitherto were Dm 37.6bn in 1986), which meant that the previous year's figure was exceeded by no less than 60 per cent. Due to the lifting of the 10 per cent withholding tax, the strong demand for these instruments in 1988 and in the first quarter of 1989 gradually normalized again (see Figure 16.55). In spite of the fact that yields rose higher than at the domestic level, gross new issues of these bonds in 1989 dropped 17 per cent, against the record high of 1988, to almost Dm 34bn. These bonds benefited from foreign interest in the Deutschemark in the following two years. The volume of Dm 35bn in 1990 was slightly up from the previous year's figure although, in 1991, domestic investors, in particular, showed strong resistance and gross new issue volume therefore again fell, to Dm 33bn.

16.9 Methods of trading

Overview

Securities which are already in circulation are traded on the secondary market. In Germany, the secondary market consists of official bourse trading (*Amtlicher Börsenhandel*), the regulated market (*Geregelter Markt*), and unofficial transactions (*Freiverkehr*).

While official trading and the regulated market are limited to the stock exchange, unofficial dealings are carried on by telephone throughout the entire country, and also on a cross-border basis.

Official bourse trading

In the Federal Republic, official bourse trading takes place at the eight stock exchanges in Berlin, Bremen, Duesseldorf, Frankfurt, Hamburg, Hannover, Munich, and Stuttgart.

The German stock exchanges are legally-bound public institutions, which are subject to the 1896 Stock Exchange Act. The stock exchanges are supported by either the respective chambers of commerce and industry, or associations specially created for this purpose. The Stock Exchange Act stipulates that the setting-up of a stock exchange shall be dependent upon the Federal state government in question giving its approval, and this authority is also responsible for the supervision of the stock exchange.

Admission procedure

An admission procedure must, as a matter of principle, precede any official listing. The application, which has to be made by one of the banks admitted to the stock exchange, must contain the information required by the 1910 Announcement relating to the admission of securities to bourse trading.

Prospectus

For a bourse introduction, a listing prospectus has to be submitted to the Admission Committee (Section 39, Stock Exchange Act). The prospectus represents a wide-ranging collection of information in written form which permits an assessment of the securities from the legal and commercial standpoint that is as accurate as possible. Upon admission, the prospectus is published in the *Federal Gazette* and at least one authorized journal for the publication of such mandatory announcements.

A prospectus is not necessary for German public sector bonds, nor for mortgage and communal bonds if less than three years have elapsed since the publication of a similar prospectus.

The signatory of the prospectus is liable *vis-à-vis* the holder of the securities, as is the bank which makes the application and the issuer, if it was known that the information supplied was incorrect or incomplete or, in the absence of any serious misdoings, should have been known to the signatory (liability for false information, Sections 45, 88, Stock Exchange Act). The compensation claims arising from this liability are enforceable for no more than five years after admission.

Exemptions from admission procedure

Exempted from the admission procedure are German public sector bonds, which are automatically admitted to every German stock exchange. In order to secure an official listing for such issues, the Federal finance minister or the supreme authority at state level informs the board of directors of the stock exchange about the conditions for the securities that are to be issued. No bourse-listing prospectus is necessary for these bonds.

For fixed-income securities with interest payments and redemption which are guaranteed by the Federal government or one of the states, as well as for the fixed-income securities of a local government body and its bank and those of a state-supervised special mortgage bank, the Admission Committee can, upon request, waive the requirement that a prospectus be published. The approval of the Admission Committee is sufficient to secure an official listing of these issues.

Official brokers

From the legal standpoint, official brokers (*Kursmakler*) are individual businessmen. Consequently, their activities are covered by the provisions of the German Commercial Code (HGB). Given the significance of their functions, further stipulations relating to them are contained in the Stock Exchange Act.

Official brokers are appointed and sworn in by the relevant minister of the state in which the stock exchange in question is situated, the board of directors and the board of the Official Brokers' Chamber having indicated their agreement.

Official brokers may only arrange transactions in officially-quoted securities. For this, they receive a brokerage fee based on the nominal value in the case of fixed-income securities. The level of the brokerage fee is set by the state government in accordance with Section 30 of the Stock Exchange Act. The brokerage fee for bonds is inversely proportionate to the size of the transaction.

Official price fixing

At stock exchanges with a Chamber of Official Brokers, the fixing of official prices is performed by the official brokers under the supervision of the Chamber. If no such chamber exists, the board of directors is responsible for the fixing of prices. The price has to reflect the actual order position for the respective security, i.e. the buy and sell orders received.

In official trading, transactions can be effected at both spot and consecutive prices. Official trading covers the official hours, namely weekdays from 10.30 to 13.30.

Spot quotations

For most bonds, a daily price, the so-called 'single quotation', is established at which all transactions are settled. The single quotations are also referred to as 'spot quotations'.

At around 10.45, the official brokers start calling out the individual securities assigned to them. Up to this point, the official brokers collect the incoming buy and sell orders and enter them in their order books. Once the official brokers have stopped accepting fresh orders, they begin to compute the spot price which yields the highest turnover when buy and sell orders are compared. If no balance is possible between supply and demand, it is often created by the Bundesbank (in the case of Bunds), the issuer, the issuing banks or by self-dealing on the part of the brokers.

Continuous quotations

For some convertible bonds and bonds with warrants attached, continuous quotations are established, as they have been also for certain public sector paper with a transaction volume of Dm 1m and upwards, since 3 October 1988.

In continuous price trading, transactions may be effected at any time during bourse trading hours. The prices established in such cases are referred to as continuous prices. Continuous quotations come about in the following manner:

The first quotation, the opening price, and the last consecutive quotation, the closing price, are established in the same way as the single quotation. Between the two, transactions are effected for which an individual quotation is established. As certain minimum volumes are laid-down for variable-price trading, a single quotation is established alongside the continuous ones, and this is the price at which all trades that fall short of the minimum volume are settled. If the client so wishes, the transaction may be settled at the single quotation price, regardless of its volume.

Market quotation

The market quotation for fixed-income securities is usually graduated into units of 0.05 percentage points. Exceptions in this respect are the issues of the Federal government, the Federal Post Office and the Railways as well as floating-rate and zero-coupon paper. Here, quotations are based on gradations of 0.01 percentage points. The base unit is the percentage quotation.

The quotations are published in the official price lists of the German stock exchanges in the form of collective or individual prices or, if no turnover occurred, as bid and asked prices, i.e. reflecting the level of the buy or sell offers received or as estimated prices.

Significance of official trading

Fixed-income securities are only traded to a marginal extent on the stock exchange. A large part of trading is conducted off the exchange directly between the banks. One exception here are public sector bonds, which also feature prominently in official trading.

The regulated market

In May 1987, the regulated market (*Geregelter Markt*) was created, a new market segment taking its place between official trading and unofficial transactions. In order to channel bourse activities into only two market segments, securities from the so-called regulated free-trading (*Geregelter Freiverkehr*) tier of the stock exchange have, for the most part, been transferred to the regulated market, which has *de facto* replaced regulated free-trading as a result.

In the regulated market, trade in paper which is not officially-quoted takes place on the stock exchange floor. As a rule, these are low-turnover securities and are issued in small volumes, or they are paper which was not introduced into official trading for cost reasons.

The legal basis for the regulated market was established by the Stock Exchange Admission Act of 16 December 1986. This created the overall framework for the new market tier, leaving the details (e.g. fixing of prices, admission procedure) to be laid down by the individual exchanges in their regulations.

The following admission rules apply in the case of the regulated market:

Admission procedure

Admission to the regulated market depends on the decision of a committee, half of whose members are not by profession involved in stock exchange securities trading. The members of this committee are appointed by the board of directors for three years.

Admission must be refused if:

- the issue has already received an official listing
- there are formal shortcomings
- it is likely that the public is being deceived, or the public interest harmed
- orderly trading is not guaranteed

Minimum capital requirements

For a first-time admission of securities to the regulated market, the minimum nominal amount of capital that may be issued is Dm 500,000. Admission to the regulated market may, however, be restricted to part of the issue only.

Compulsory disclosure

The information required in order to gain a listing on the regulated market must be published in at least one authorized journal for stock exchange announcements. It is sufficient, however, for the issuer to announce that the relevant information is available free of charge from the official payment offices.

Players in the regulated market

Trading in the regulated market is handled by the 'free brokers' and the banks admitted to trading.

Like the official brokers, the so-called free brokers (*Freimakler*) are sole traders, subject to the provisions of the German Commercial Code.

After examination of their professional qualifications and the financial circumstances, free brokers are admitted to bourse trading by the board of directors. However, they do not have any official function, do not have to swear an oath and may not, for this reason, be involved in establishing official prices. Free brokers are also entitled to do business in their own name and for their own account.

In contrast to the official brokers, who may only do business in securities assigned to them, free brokers are able to trade in all securities that are not officially listed. For their services as intermediaries, they receive a brokerage fee equal to that charged by the official brokers.

Fixing of prices

The rules which apply for official trading determine the fixing of prices in the regulated market; nonetheless, these prices do not count as official quotations.

The prices are fixed by the official brokers who are appointed by the board of directors, under whose supervision they stand.

Unofficial trading (inter-office transactions)

Unofficial (and unregulated) trading is conducted between banks and free brokers. As business is usually handled by telephone, unofficial transactions of this type are often referred to by the term 'telephone trading' (*Telefonhandel*) in German.

Unofficial trading is not subject to the German Stock Exchange Act; instead, it is covered by the German Civil Code (BGB) and the German Commercial Code (HGB).

Inter-office transactions comprise the following elements:

- before-hours and after-hours dealings in listed securities
- trading in unlisted paper
- the placing of underwriting shares
- trading in new issues prior to the first bourse quotation

The paper traded unofficially includes securities which are not, or perhaps not yet, eligible for an official listing or for trading in the regulated market, and also securities already admitted to official trading, or to the regulated market segment of another stock exchange.

As a rule, customers' orders for listed securities are handled at the stock exchange during bourse trading hours.

Paper which may not be traded on the stock exchange includes registered bonds and private placements. At the same time, borrowers' notes, which are legally-speaking not securities, are traded in the unofficial market. No legal obligation to accept contracts exists with regard to trading in unlisted securities.

Fixing of prices

Prices are quoted as spreads, i.e. with bid and ask prices both being given.

Significance of inter-office dealings

Although most bonds are admitted to official trading, a large share of the trading in such paper is taken care of by inter-office transactions between banks.

IBIS

Since 1991, German banks use IBIS - the Inter-Bank Information System - to establish a computerized bourse based on the auction principle, which makes off-floor trading more transparent. Prices are determined by the size of turnover in given securities, which is in line with the current system of spot prices, and not by a market-maker principle. Bunds are traded continuously, from 09.00 to 17.00. The next phase of the reform is planned for 1995.

	DEM domestic bonds	DEM foreign bonds	Total
1980	81.1	19.5	100.6
1981	84.1	19.1	103.2
1982	146.4	28.5	174.9
1983	137.8	34.8	172.6
1984	220.8	44.9	265.7
1985	336.9	62.2	398.2
1986	475.2	74.5	549.7
1987	1113.0	72.8	1185.8
1988	1719.4	121.3	1840.7
1989	1814.3	101.9	1916.2
1990	1712.0	92.7	1804.7
1991	1979.7	111.1	2090.8

Figure 16.56 Stock exchange turnover in DEM billion
Note: Since 1987, the statistics are extended to include turnover before, and after, official trading

16.10 Market practices

Form

The German market has both bearer and registered bonds. However, most bonds and especially Federal government, Länder (State) and municipal bonds (public-sector bonds) as well as convertibles and bonds with warrants attached, are issued as bearer bonds (*Inhaberpapiere*). Occasionally, mortgage bonds (*Pfandbriefe*) and municipal bonds (*Kommunalanleihen*) are issued in registered form (*Namenspapiere*).

Public sector bonds are not delivered as physical documents but as bond certificates mostly in collateral form. *Schuldscheindarlehen* are registered loans which are usually transferable only three times when issued by the Federal Republic of Germany or public authorities.

Denomination

Domestic public sector bonds are issued in denominations of Dm 100 or a multiple thereof, with the exception of Type B Federal Savings bonds (*Bundesschatzbriefe*) which are available in denominations of Dm 50. The most common denominations of Dm eurobonds are Dm 1000 and Dm 5000. Domestic and international German bonds with warrants attached as well as convertibles are normally denominated in Dm 1000 and Dm 5000 or multiples thereof. *Schuldscheindarlehen* are denominated in Dm 100,000 or a multiple thereof.

Coupon

In general, coupons are paid annually on fixed dates, and sometimes semi-annually in arrears.

The first coupon of a Dm eurobond may be specially adjusted with regard to the interest period only. Both shorter and longer first interest periods are frequently encountered.

Ex-dividend

According to ruling of the security-clearing organization (Kassenverein), ex-dividend dates are determined as follows. If the next coupon-date is on a day between the 3rd and 16th of a month, then the ex-coupon-date falls on the first business day after the last day of the previous month. When the next coupon-date falls on a day between the 17th of the current month and the 2nd of the next month, then the first business day after the 15th of the current month is the ex-dividend date.

- Examples:
  A bond pays an annual coupon on June 15th; ex-coupon-date is the first business day after May 31st.
  A bond pays its annual coupon on February 20th; ex-coupon-date: first business day after February 15th.

Accrued interest is positive if the trade-date is before the ex-coupon-date, or if the trade-date is on the ex-coupon-date or later and the day before settlement date is in the new coupon period. Conversely, it is negative if the trade-date is the ex-coupon-date or later and the day before the settlement date falls in the current coupon period.

Accrued interest is calculated for all Dm-denominated bonds (international and domestic) on a 30-day month and 360-day year basis (30/360) with exception of FRNs (30/365).

Schuldscheine are normally bought net of accrued interest so that at coupon-date the issuer divides the interest proportionally among the holders on a 30/360 basis.

Redemption

As a rule, redemption takes place at pre-specified fixed dates. Sometimes, bonds are redeemed by annual drawings at lot at fixed dates (drawing schedule specified together with redemption price at issue).

Another redemption technique so far used only once for a Dm eurobond consists of repaying the principal in equal annuity amounts (so-called annuity bonds). For further information, please see chapter Types of Securities.

Sinking funds

Sinking Funds are unheard of for German domestic bonds. They are frequently used for repayment of Deutschemark eurobonds.

Dealing quotations

Most Deutschemark bonds are officially listed on one of the eight German stock exchanges. Dm eurobonds are mainly quoted in Frankfurt, some in Luxembourg and London. Official quotation is carried out according to the standard price (*Einheitskurs*) principle in steps of Dm 0.05 for domestic and Deutschemark eurobonds. For Government issues with an outstanding volume of more than Dm 2bn, consecutive trading takes place on the German stock exchange. Prices are dealt in steps of Dm 0.05. Bond prices are quoted exclusive of accrued interest.

Dealing spreads range from Dm -0.08 (public sector bonds, highly liquid Dm eurobonds) up to Dm 0.25. *Schuldscheine* are quoted on a yield spread basis normally with a spread of 2-5 basis points. Bank bonds are quoted on a yield spread basis as well, with a yield spread of 3-5 Bp.

Liquidity

Typical block trades range from Dm 5 million to Dm 10 million for public-sector bonds, to Dm 1 million to Dm 5 million for bank bonds to Dm 1 million for Deutschemark eurobonds. *Schuldscheindarlehen* (certificates of indebtedness) are usually traded in block of Dm 5 million to Dm 10 million.

However, public sector bond benefit from buying and selling activities of the Bundesbank (Federal Government and Federal Post Office bonds) or the corresponding state banks (Länder bonds) with the exception of Federal Railway bonds that are supported by Deutsche Verkehrskreditbank (DVKB). Mortgage bonds are usually supported by the issuer.

Transaction costs

Transaction costs comprise three different elements. Broker fees (*Maklercourtage*) range from 0.06 per cent for blocks over Dm 5 million to 0.75 per cent (block of Dm 50,000 or less).

Only banks can transmit order to brokers. Banks usually charge their private clients commission of around 0.50 per cent for both domestic and Deutschemark eurobond transactions.

Stock exchange turnover taxes are payable on the acquisition and sale of securities if the business was transacted in the Federal Republic of Germany or in a foreign country involving at least one German resident. In the later case the turnover tax is reduced to one half of the ordinary rate.

Settlement

Value-date for domestic bonds is usually two banking days after trade-date, seven calendar days after trade-date for Deutschemark eurobonds in over-the-counter trading. The settlement date is the same as the value-date. However, it is quite common for banks outside Germany to trade domestic bonds on the basis of value and settlement dates seven days after trade-date like in the euromarkets.

Clearing of domestic and Deutschemark eurobonds is carried out by seven regional Kassenvereine (security clearing associations). Transactions involving foreign customers are mainly settled through Euroclear, Brussels and Cedel, Luxembourg.

16.11 Settlement

Settlement of stock exchange trades

According to the stock exchange rules, the settlement of cash transactions normally requires that the payment and delivery of securities be effected on the second trading day following the trading day in question.

Trade data comparison system

Official brokers of the stock exchange enter the data of the trades into the stock exchange computer, which prints contract notes for both sides. In addition, the participants can get the data by computer link either in several tranches during the day or, on the same afternoon, in one file. This data is put into the bank's computer system and compared with its own records.

Settlement system

The selling party either releases trades directly into the stock exchange computer or, alternatively, marks those items which it cannot deliver on special lists, approves all others for release and returns them to the stock exchange. On the value-date, the stock exchange computer then starts the settlement procedure by debiting the seller's securities account and crediting his cash account at the Kassenverein (central securities depository), and vice versa for the buyer. The daily balances of the cash accounts of the banks are automatically settled by order of the Kassenverein at the local subsidiary of the German central bank.

A second file transfer for all securities debits and credits with the Kassenverein (from stock exchange and other transactions) is also produced by the stock exchange computer and delivered to the banks for approval to enable them to update their records with the Kassenverein.

There is also the possibility of settlement, along these lines, between two banks which are members of different German stock exchanges (settlement of cross-city trades).

Settlement of off-exchange trades

The value-date for the settlement of off-stock-exchange trades is negotiable. Almost all of the international dealers use the ISMA's 7th calendar day's practice, although Dm-denominated securities are not generally subject to the ISMA rules and recommendations. Here, international dealers must ensure that the value-date of a transaction does not coincide with a local bank holiday (this may be different from one region to the other).

Trade data comparison system

In the Kassenverein systems, a database is available wherein the market participants may enter their instructions (via their local custodians) for the settlement of off-stock exchange transactions in Deutschemark securities, prior to the settlement date.

The seller's instruction to deliver is compared with the buyer's instruction to receive, based on certain match criteria: DKV account number of the German counterpart or custodian, the amount of equities or bonds, the securities code (ISIN), the currency code (DEM) plus the counter-value and the settlement date. Within the matching of the counter-value, as a market rule, a difference of up to Dm 50.00 is accepted. The settlement will take place on the basis of the seller's amount.

(Same-day) settlement system

The standard settlement procedures within the DKV system remain unchanged, but a second (same-day) settlement cycle has recently been introduced. This means that the vast majority of the transactions should continue to be settled in the cycle during the night before the value-date, the results being available in the early morning of the value-date. It is then possible for the account holder to turnaround incoming receipts into a second settlement cycle for same-day value. This enables active market participants to have back-to-back trades settled on the same day in certain circumstances (i.e. those cases where the purchase side of the transaction is received out of the standard overnight settlement cycle and the sale side can be delivered in the same-day-settlement cycle). In these cases, the requirement to finance one day overdrafts will be eliminated. The situation, with an in-built one-day delay, will occur if the purchase side of a turnaround transaction is received out of the second settlement cycle for that day's value. At the beginning of 1993, the DKV plans to build an additional chaining facility into its systems, which will be designed to solve this problem.

The same-day-settlement facility will not be available for transactions in equities, or bonds, where the settlement day coincides with a cut-off date in the Kassenverein system with regard to dividend or interest payments or any other entitlement.

16.12 *Yield calculation*

The ISMA, Braess/Fangmeyer and the Moosmüller yield calculation methods apply to government securities (*Bundesanleihen, Bundesobligationen,* Länder bonds), local authorities (*Kommunalobligationen*) eurobonds, state agencies (Post and Railways), bank and savings bonds (*Kassenobligationen, Pfandbriefe*). Although the ISMA method is the most commonly used, for example by the Bundesbank, stock exchanges quote sheets, the Börsen-Datazentrale and institutional investors, it should be noted that some domestic institutional investors, as well as savings banks prefer the Braess/Fangmeyer and Moosmüller yields.

In contrast to the ISMA method, interest received after a fraction of a year is discounted according to the simple interest in the Braess/Fangmeyer and Moosmüller formulae.

In all methods the yield is calculated by solving, iteratively, the corresponding formulae (e.g. by using the Newton Raphson Method). The following formulae (proposed by the Securities Industry Association) can be used to estimate the start yield of the Newton-iteration:

$$\ddot{e} = 100 \bullet \left[\left[\frac{z \bullet J + 100 + A - K}{\left[100 \bullet J - J \bullet \frac{(100+A-K)}{2} - \frac{(100+A-K)}{4} \right] \bullet 100 \bullet p} + 1 \right] P - 1 \right]$$

1a. ISMA method

- Day count: 30/360

$$Pd = K + S = \frac{1}{q^{f}} \bullet \left[\frac{z}{p} \bullet k + \frac{\frac{z}{p} \bullet \frac{q^{n}-1}{q-1} + 100 + A}{q^{n}} \right]$$

$$q = 1 + \frac{\hat{e}}{100} \qquad e = [(1 + \frac{\hat{e}}{100})^{P} - 1] \bullet 100$$

$n = \text{INT}\,(T_m - T_{s)} \bullet P]$ integer coupon periods

$$f = \frac{T_1 - T_s}{B}$$ fraction of coupon period

$$S = \frac{T_s - T_{-1}}{B} \bullet \frac{z}{p}$$ accrued interest

1b. Braess Fangmeyer method

- Day count: 30/360

$$Pd = \frac{\left[z \bullet (1 + \frac{P-1}{P} \bullet \frac{e}{200}) \bullet \frac{q^j - 1}{q - 1} + 100 + A \right] \bullet \frac{1}{q^j} + \left[1 + r \bullet (1 + \frac{r+1}{p} \bullet \frac{e}{200}) \right] \bullet \frac{z}{p}}{1 + f \bullet \frac{e}{100}}$$

$L = (T_m - T_s)$ remaining life
$j = \text{INT}\,(T_m - T_s)$ integer years
$f = \text{FRAC}\,(T_m - T_s)$ fraction of year

$S = [1 - \text{FRAC}(L \bullet p)]\,\frac{z}{P}$ accrued interest

$r = \text{INT}\,(f \bullet P)$ number of coupon payments fractional year

Moosmüller method

- Day count: 30/360

$$Pd = \frac{1}{(1 + f \bullet \frac{\hat{e}}{100})} \bullet \left[\frac{z}{p} + \frac{\frac{z}{p} \bullet \frac{q^{n-1}}{q-1} + 100 + A}{q^n} \right]$$

$$q = 1 + \frac{\hat{e}}{100} \qquad e = [\,(1 + \frac{\hat{e}}{100})^P - 1] \bullet 100$$

$n = \text{INT}\,[\,(T_m - T_s)\,P\,]$ integer coupon periods

$$f = \frac{T_1 - T_s}{B}$$ fraction of coupon period

$$S = \frac{T_s - T_{-1}}{B} \bullet \frac{z}{P}$$ accrued interest

2. ISMA method applicable to non-interest-bearing securities (*Schuldscheine, Schuldscheindarlehen*)

- Day count: 30/360

$$K = \frac{1}{q^f} \bullet \left[\frac{z}{p} \bullet f + \frac{\frac{z}{p} \bullet \frac{q^n - 1}{q - 1} + 100 + A}{q^n} \right]$$

$q = 1 + \frac{\hat{e}}{100}$ $\qquad$ $e = [(1 + \frac{\hat{e}}{100})^P - 1] \bullet 100$

$n = \text{INT}[(T_m - T_s) \bullet P]$ integer coupon periods

$f = \frac{T_1 - T_s}{B}$ fraction of coupon period

3. ISMA method applicable to all types of security in which the maturity period is not an integer at issue date

3a. Short-ending coupon period (last coupon period is not an integer)

- Day count: 30/360

$$\text{a) } K + S = \frac{1}{q^1} \bullet \left[\frac{z}{P} + \frac{\frac{z}{P} \bullet \frac{q^n - 1}{q-1}}{q^n} + \frac{100 + A + \frac{z}{P} \bullet b}{q^{n+b}} \right]$$

b) with $q = 1 + \frac{\hat{e}}{100}$; $\quad e = [(1 + \frac{\hat{e}}{100})^P - 1] \bullet 100$

c) $n = \text{INT}[(T_1 - T_s) \bullet P]$ integer coupon periods

d) $f = \frac{T_1 - T_s}{B}$ fraction of coupon period

e) $b = \frac{T_m - T_1}{B}$ accrued interest

f) $S = \frac{T_s - T_{-1}}{B} \bullet \frac{z}{p}$ short-ending coupon period

3b. Short beginning coupon period (first coupon period is not an integer)

Day count: 30/360

$$Pd = \frac{1}{q^f} \bullet \left[\frac{z}{p} \bullet k + \frac{\frac{z}{p} \bullet \frac{q^n - 1}{q - 1} + 100 + A}{q^n} \right]$$

$q = 1 + \frac{\hat{e}}{100}$ $\qquad$ $e = [(1 + \frac{\hat{e}}{100})^P - 1] \bullet 100$

$n = \text{INT}[(T_m - T_s) \bullet P]$ integer coupon periods

$f = \frac{T_1 - T_s}{B}$ short beginning coupon period

$S = \frac{T_s - T_e}{B} \bullet \frac{z}{p}$ accrued interest

3c. Long beginning coupon period (first coupon is longer than one period)

- Day count: 30/360

$$Pd = \frac{1}{q^f} \bullet \left[\frac{z}{p} \bullet 1 + \frac{\frac{z}{p} \bullet \frac{q_n - 1}{q - 1} + 100 + A}{q^n} \right]$$

$q = 1 + \frac{\hat{e}}{100}$ $\qquad$ $e = [(1 + \frac{\hat{e}}{100})^P - 1] \bullet 100$

$n = \text{INT}[(T_m - T_1) \bullet P]$ integer period

$1 = \frac{T_{-1} - T_e}{T_{-1} - T_{-2}} + 1$ first coupon period

$f = \frac{T_1 - T_s}{B}$ fraction of coupon period for $T_s < T_{-1}$

$f = \frac{T_{-1} - T_s}{T_{-1} - T_{-2}} + 1$ fraction of coupon period for $T_s < T_{-1}$

$$S = \left(\frac{T_s - T_{-1}}{B} + \frac{T_{-1} - T_e}{T_{-1} - T_{-2}} \right) \bullet \frac{z}{p} \text{ accrued interest for } T_s < T_{-1}$$

$$S = \left(\frac{T_s - T_e}{T_{-1} - T_{-2}} \right) \bullet \frac{z}{p} \qquad \text{accrued interest for } T_s < T_{-1}$$

4. ISMA method applicable to all types of security in which coupon is stepped (case below: two coupons)

- Day count: 30/360

$$Pd = \frac{1}{q^f} \bullet \left[\frac{z_1}{p} + \frac{\frac{z_1}{p} \bullet \frac{q^{n1} - 1}{q - 1}}{q^{n1}} + \frac{\frac{z_2}{p} \bullet \frac{q^{n2} - 1}{q - 1} + 100 + A}{q^{n1+n2}} \right]$$

$$q = 1 + \frac{\hat{e}}{100} \qquad e = [\,(1 + \frac{\hat{e}}{100})^P - 1] \bullet 100$$

$$n_1 = \text{INT}\,[\,(T_c - T_s) \bullet P] \quad \text{period step 1}$$

$$n_2 = \text{INT}\,[\,(T_m - T_c) \bullet P] \quad \text{period step 2}$$

$$f = \frac{T_1 - T_s}{B} \qquad \text{fraction of coupon period}$$

$$S = \frac{T_s - T_{-1}}{B} \bullet \frac{z_1}{P} \qquad \text{accrued interest}$$

5. Calculation of zero bond yields

5a. Yield of zero bonds in the last 'quasi-period' (less than one year)

- Day count: 30/360

■ ISMA

$$\hat{e} = \left[\left(\frac{100 + A}{K}\right)^{\frac{1}{f}} - 1\right] \bullet 100$$

$f = \dfrac{T_m - T_s}{\frac{B}{P}}$ fraction of coupon period

■ Moosmüller

$$\hat{e} = \left(\frac{100 + A}{K} - 1\right) \bullet \frac{100}{f}$$

$$e = \left[\left(1 + \frac{\hat{e}}{100}\right)^{P} - 1\right] \bullet 100$$

$f = \dfrac{T_m - T_s}{\frac{B}{P}}$ fraction of coupon period

■ Braess/Fangmeyer

$$e = \left(\frac{100 + A}{K} - 1\right) \bullet \frac{360}{T_m - T_s} \bullet 100$$

5a. Yield of zero bonds with remaining life longer than one 'quasi-period'

- Day count: 30/360

■ ISMA

$$\left[\left(\frac{100 + A}{K}\right)^{\left(\frac{1}{n+f}\right)} - 1\right] \bullet 100$$

$$q = 1 + \frac{\hat{e}}{100} \qquad e = [(1 + \frac{\hat{e}}{100})^P - 1] \bullet 100$$

$$f = \frac{T_1 - T_s}{\frac{B}{P}} \qquad \text{fraction of coupon period}$$

■ Moosmüller

$$\frac{f \bullet \hat{e}}{100} = \left(\frac{100 + A}{K \bullet q^n}\right) - 1$$

$$q = 1 + \frac{\hat{e}}{100} \qquad e = [(1 + \frac{\hat{e}}{100})^P - 1] \bullet 100$$

$$f = \frac{T_1 - T_s}{\frac{B}{P}} \qquad \text{fraction of coupon period}$$

■ Braess/Fangmeyer

$$1 + \frac{e}{100} \bullet \frac{T_1 - T_s}{360} = \frac{100 + A}{K \bullet (1 + \frac{e}{100})^J}$$

6. Yield calculation for annuity bonds

- Day count: 30/360

■ ISMA

$$K = AN \bullet \frac{q^n - 1}{q - 1} \bullet \frac{1}{q^{n - 1 + c \bullet P}}$$

■ Moosmüller

$$K = AN \bullet \frac{q^n - 1}{q - 1} \bullet \frac{1}{q^{n-1+\text{INT}(c \bullet P)}} \bullet \frac{1}{1 + \text{FRAC}(c \bullet P) \bullet \frac{\hat{e}}{100}}$$

$$q = 1 + \frac{\hat{e}}{100} \qquad e = [(1 + \frac{\hat{e}}{100})^P - 1] \bullet 100$$

$$c = \frac{T_a - T_s}{360}$$

7. Yield calculation of pay-off bonds

- Day count: 30/360

■ ISMA

$$Pd = \frac{1}{q^f \bullet (q-1)} \bullet \left[\frac{z}{p} \bullet q + \frac{1}{h \bullet q^n} \bullet \left[100 \bullet (q^h - 1) - \frac{z}{p} \bullet \frac{q^h - 1}{q - 1} \right] \right]$$

■ Moosmüller

$$Pd = \frac{1}{(1 + f \bullet \frac{\hat{e}}{100} \bullet (q-1)} \bullet \left[\frac{z}{p} \bullet q + \frac{1}{h \bullet q^n} \bullet \left[100 \bullet (q^h - 1) - \frac{z}{p} \bullet \frac{q^h - 1}{q - 1} \right] \right]$$

$$q = 1 + \frac{\hat{e}}{100} \qquad e = [(1 + \frac{\hat{e}}{100})^P - 1] \bullet 100$$

$n = \text{INT}\,[(T_{1t} - T_{s}) \bullet P] + h + 1$ integer coupon periods

$f = \frac{T_{1z} - T_s}{B}$ fraction of coupon period

$S = \frac{T_s - T_{-1}}{B} \bullet \frac{z}{P}$ accrued interest

9. Calculation of yields of *Bundesschatzbriefe*

- Day count: 30/360

9a. Bundesschatzbriefe, Type A

$$100 = \sum_{j=1}^{J} \frac{zj}{q^j} + \frac{100}{q^j}$$

$$q = 1 + \frac{e}{100}$$

9b. Bundesschatzbriefe, Type B

$$e = \left[\left[\prod_{j=1}^{J} (1 + \frac{z_j}{100}) \right] \left(\frac{1}{J}\right) - 1 \right] \bullet 100$$

10. Calculation of money market yields

10a. Yield calculation for discount bills (payment upon maturity at par)

As for zero-bonds, effective interest calculation is based on simple interest (comparable to straight bonds in their last period). Examples are non interest-bearing commercial papers (*Handelswechsel*), Treasury bills, bankers acceptances.

Since 1 July 1990, the day count is actual/360 (was previously 30/360).

$$e = \frac{100 - K}{K \bullet f} \times 100$$

$$f = \frac{T_m - T_s}{B}$$ fraction of period

$$d = \frac{100 - K}{100 \bullet f} \times 100$$ discount rate

Note: Both above formulae also apply to savings bonds.

10b. Yield calculation for papers with interest paid at maturity (interest-bearing commercial papers)

As these papers do have a coupon, accrued interests are to be taken into account.

$$e = \frac{100 + A + L \bullet z - K - S}{f \bullet (K + S)} \bullet 100$$

$f = \dfrac{T_m - T_s}{B}$ fraction of period

$L = \dfrac{T_m - T_e}{B}$ life

$S = \dfrac{T_s - T_e}{B} \bullet z$ accrued interest

11. Floating-rate notes (EFFAS formulae)

$$(K + S) \bullet (1 + \frac{L* + DM}{100} \bullet \frac{d1}{360}) = C1 + \sum_{i=1}^{n} \frac{(La + QM) \bullet h}{[1 + (La + DM) \bullet \frac{h}{100}]^i}$$

$$+ \frac{100}{[1 + (La + DM) \bullet \frac{h}{100}]^n}$$

Abbreviations valid for all formulae above:

_	day-correction factor (_ = 365.25/360)/coupon payments per year)
A	call penalty (per cent)
AN	annuity (per cent
B	number of days in coupon period ($T_1 - T_{-1}$)
c	years without payments
d	discount rate
$d1$	number of days in the broken period
DM	discounted margin

e	annually compounded yield (per cent)
$\hat{e}$	yield compounded P times per annum (per cent)
$\ddot{e}$	estimated yield
h	number of pay-offs
FRAC	fraction
f	fraction of period
INT	integer
J	years
K	clean price (per cent)
L	remaining life
L^*	floating-rate at the time of bonds purchase
La	assumed floating-rate in the following periods
$C1$	first floating-rate coupon
P	number of coupon (annuity) payments (periods) per annum
QM	quoted margin
P_d	dirty price (per cent); $Pd = K + S$
q	effective interest rate
T_1	next coupon-date
T_{-1}	last coupon-date
T_{-2}	previous last coupon-date
T_{1z}	next coupon payment
T_{1T}	next pay-off rate payment
T_a	first annuity payment
T_c	conversion date
T_e	issue date
T_j	next coupon-date
T_1	last coupon
T_m	maturity date
T_s	settlement date
z	coupon (per cent annual)

16.13 Taxation

Taxation of residents' securities earnings

Investment income tax

Investment income tax is a special form of income or corporate income tax. The earnings from financial assets are immediately subject to investment income tax, just as wages and salaries are to normal income tax.

Convertible and income bonds

The interest earnings on securities offering not only a coupon, but also the right to exchange the paper for shares in the company (convertible bonds) or an extra interest payment, which is determined by the size of the profit distribution on the part of the borrower, are subject to a 25 per cent investment income tax.

The interest earnings from the above-mentioned securities have to be included in income tax statements, the capital yields tax which has already been levied being taken into account when the amount of income tax or corporate income tax is being calculated.

Taxation of non-residents' securities earnings

Foreign holders of securities

The External Trade Act defines non-residents as all natural persons who reside, or are usually resident, abroad, as well as legal persons and business partnerships with their legal seat or commercial headquarters abroad. As a result, actual nationality is irrelevant.

Levying of capital yields tax

The income generated by non-residents in Germany bears a limited tax liability. Only specific types of income, therefore, are subject to German taxes. In the case of fixed-income securities, this is the interest paid on the convertible bonds of German issuers and on both income bonds and profit-sharing certificates. Here, a 25 per cent withholding tax is levied on the gross interest distribution.

Double taxation agreements

Investors from countries which have signed a double taxation agreement with Germany are able, within the terms of such treaty, to demand a refund for part, or even the whole, of the amount deducted by means of the withholding tax. To this end, they have to present a refund application to the relevant German tax authorities. This application must be signed by the holder of the securities and certified by the relevant authority abroad. A refund is made once the application has been processed, which can take several months.

A few foreign central banks, which are specifically exempted from the investment income tax in double taxation agreements, need not pay this tax.

Capital gains

Germany does not impose a capital gains tax on non-residents.

Tax on interest income

The Federal government intends to levy a 30 per cent tax on interest income[1] from 1993 to comply with the ruling of the Federal Constitutional Court of 27 June 1991, according to which, the current practice for the taxation of interest income is unconstitutional. When the new tax is introduced, the tax allowance for savings is also to be increased from Dm 600 to 1200 (single persons/married couples) to Dm 6000 to 12,000. The tax on interest income is an advance payment imputable towards total income tax debt. As before, interest income must be stated in the wage and income tax declaration, and is taxable at the tax rate applicable to the individual taxpayer. The body which pays out the interest, e.g. a credit institution or building society, is responsible for withholding the tax. The tax saver's allowance is to be taken into account when the tax is deducted. The saver gives his bank an exemption order, in which he states his name, address and date of birth, and declares up to what amount (below the saver's allowance limit) interest is to be exempted from the tax deduction. Interest income below the allowance is thus to be tax-exempt right from the start. The exemption order can be spread over several accounts at various banks. It can be checked by the tax office in accordance with the provisions in Section 50b of the Income Tax Act. This is to prevent taxpayers from claiming tax allowances several times via different accounts. According to the Banking Order (Section 30a Tax Code), however, tax offices still have no access to accounts. Persons considered as non-residents for tax purposes - these are natural and juridical persons with residence, customary place of abode, registered office or business management abroad - are to be exempted from the tax. Furthermore, sight deposits at an interest rate of not more than 1 per cent and income from interbank business, are tax-exempt.

[1] *For anonymous over-the-counter transactions, 35 per cent*

Quite a few questions of detail, which are likely to come up when the planned legal provisions are put into practice, currently still seem unclear. these include the treatment of zero bonds or ex-warrant bonds.

Unlike the previous model - withholding tax - the planned new tax on interest income is not to be withheld by the issuer, but by the paying agency. This ensures that interest income from securities of foreign issuers is also subject to the new tax. In contrast to the former situation, advance tax payment will not be avoided by the buying of securities of foreign issuers. For this reason, the repercussions on the capital market should be much less pronounced than in 1989.

16.14 *Futures and options*

The world economic crisis of the thirties led to a legal ban on options trading in Germany. It was not until 40 years later, in 1970, that option trading on shares was resumed. On 1 April 1986, option trading on 14 bonds started. Following satisfactory trading volumes in the beginning, bond option business began to dry up and soon after, ceased to exist. This was attributable to a number of different reasons, most of them of a legal nature.

The German Speculating and Gambling Law (*Differenzeinwand*)

Until 1 August 1989, German banks were confronted with major difficulties when private customers dealt in options. Until then, a private investor's liability in connection with futures and options trading was treated as a gambling debt. Consequently, the law treated a private investor's liability as non-collectable by the banks, with the result that banks could rarely make claims against private customers having such liabilities. In order to insure themselves against this, the banks imposed harsh conditions on futures and options trading by private investors.

Short positions

In the past it was not possible to close a short position in the secondary market. If the option writers wanted to hedge themselves by buying the same options they had written, the law still required that the writers keep securities until they were exercised, or until their expiry date.

Capital investment and insurance companies

In the past, capital investment companies, as well as insurance companies, were been very restricted in their ability to use derivative instruments for hedging purposes. Since 1 March 1990, capital investment companies have been permitted to invest up to roughly 20 per cent of their fund assets in futures and options, as instruments for hedging purposes. Insurance companies can invest only a small part of their free capital. These restrictions keeps potential liquidity away from the markets. A revision of the Insurance Supervision Act (VAG) is planned and this will allow insurance companies to use futures and options for transactions not related to hedging.

Paradoxically, given the importance of the Deutschemark as an international investment and reserve currency, these legal obstacles meant that Dm-based interest futures were first introduced on foreign exchanges. On 29 September

1988, the London International Financial Futures Exchange (Liffe) started futures trading on German Federal government bonds and this contract soon became one of the most actively traded in Europe. In April 1989, options on Bund futures were also introduced. At the same time, futures on the 3-month interest rate for euro-Dm deposits were added to Liffe's product range. At practically the time, Matif started the trading of a similar contract; however, this was suspended in 1991 as a result of low volume. The range of instruments available for interest rate management on Liffe was expanded by the launch of options on euro-Dm futures in March 1990.

Deutsche Terminbörse DTB (German Futures and Options Exchange)

In order to allow trading of futures and options on the German Futures Exchange (DTB), a reform of the Stock Exchange Act was necessary. It was passed in June 1989, and took effect on 1 August 1989. The most important changes for DTB were:

- Prior to the reform, the physical presence of exchange players was mandatory during trading. In the reform, stock exchange trading was given a broader definition which paved the way to set up the DTB as a fully-computerized exchange. Dealing in futures and options need not be through an open outcry system and can, instead, be executed via electronic data transmission.
- Trading in futures and options was made accessible to private investors, provided they had been adequately informed of the risks involved. The responsibility lies with the investment consultant, such as a bank, to inform the private investor of these risks. For this purpose an 'information model' was created by the Federal Association of German Banks (Bundesverband Deutscher Banken). This information is supplied through:
    - a 'risk information' document, which must be signed by the client,
    - a standard product brochure, and
    - individual service.

Once clients have signed the form, they can trade futures and options, i.e. they can no longer avoid the responsibility of their actions by resorting to the speculation and gambling law.

For certain strategies with futures and options, short sales of the underlying securities are necessary. However, a cashflow can be generated only if the sale is settled. This can be accomplished either by entering into a repurchase/reverse repurchase agreement, or by borrowing securities.

Since securities lending was exempted from stock exchange turnover tax on 1 January 1990, this product has also been offered in Germany by the larger banks and the Deutscher Kassenverein. There is practically no repo market for Deutschemark issues in Germany.

DTB was registered as an Exchange in September, 1989. The DTB office is located in Frankfurt am Main and subject to legal supervision, i.e. stock exchange supervision, by the Federal State of Hesse. The legal body for the exchange is DTB GmbH, a private limited company with capital of Dm 10 million, which fulfils two distinct functions:

- it provides the facilities necessary for futures and options trading, at the DTB, and
- it guarantees, through an integrated clearing house, the proper settlement of transactions concluded at the DTB.

Reflecting these two functions of the DTB, are the two types of membership:

- exchange membership and/or
- clearing membership.

The conditions governing exchange membership are:

- a registered office in Germany,
- special qualifications in accordance with Section 14 of the Stock Exchange Act, and
- for a non-bank applicant, collateral of Dm 500,000.

Exchange members are entitled to execute futures and options transactions for their own account (principal account) and for the account of third parties (agent account). A market-maker is also necessarily an exchange member, but only qualifies after fulfilling the special qualification requirements laid down in section 17 of the Stock Exchange Act.

As a fully-computerized exchange, the DTB offers equal access to every potential exchange player, no matter where their location in Germany - with its electronic trading system, the result is the effective concentration of all trading on just one exchange.

All data and information relevant for trading in futures and options is shown on-line, and real-time, on the DTB trading screens. As a result, all players receive comprehensive information at the same time.

Clearing involves two key functions:

- the DTB is the contractual partner for each transaction. Business relations only arise between the clearing house and its members, who are responsible for the settlement of all transactions, and
- the DTB guarantees all obligations assumed on the exchange.

Clearing participants are:

- the clearing house
- the clearing members
- the Landeszentralbank (LZB) Frankfurt (as the cash-settlement agency)
- Deutscher Kassenverein (DKV) (as custodian)

There are two kinds of clearing membership:

- General clearing members (GCM) can settle their own transactions, customers transactions and the transactions of non-clearing members (NCM)
- Direct clearing members (DCM) can settle only their own transactions and those of their customers

NCMs must settle their transactions through a GCM.

Collateral system

The collateral system is of major importance for the security of trading and business settlement at the DTB. The collateral system ensures that the financial integrity of the clearing system is maintained. Factors making it possible for the clearing house to fulfil its obligations are:

- capital adequacy requirements for clearing members
- a clearing guarantee from a third-party bank
- the margin system

As collateral from its clearing-members, the DTB accepts either cash, a third-party bank guarantee, or securities eligible as collateral for Bundesbank advances. The margin limits are structured to maximize the clearing organization's ability to fulfil its commitments. On the other hand, margins required are kept as low as possible to avoid compromising cost efficiency. The clearing agency calculates the value of each position continuously throughout the day and, in the event of a cover shortfall, immediately demands further collateral from the members affected.

With the introduction of the German Stock Index and the Bund futures contracts, the DTB introduced a new risk-based margining system similar to the one used by OCC, Chicago. The system takes into account all DTB products in a given portfolio for margin calculation purposes.

On 19 January 1990, DTB started with the trading of stock options. On 23 November 1990, these were followed by futures on the DAX and on Federal government bonds. The latter contract is largely the same as that on Liffe - differences exist only in the trading hours (and the trading hours on the last trading day) and the settlement procedures. On 16 August 1991, just one trading day before the 'Red Monday', the DTB also introduced options on Bund futures. Only a few weeks later, on 4 October 1991, the DTB launched medium-term *Bobl* futures. Thus, the DTB is the only futures exchange which provides Dm-denominated interest rate futures in the maturity range of 3 1/2 - 5 years.

German government long bond (Bund) futures

Bund futures were first launched on Liffe in September 1988 (see Figure 16.57) and, by the end of 1989, it was the most active contract on the Exchange. The

Contract size:	Dm 250,000 nominal value notional German government bond (Bund) with 6 per cent coupon
Delivery months:	March, June, September, December
Delivery day:	Tenth calendar day of the delivery month. If such a day is not a working day in Frankfurt then the delivery day is the next following Frankfurt working day
Last trading day:	11.00 Frankfurt time three Frankfurt working days prior to delivery day
Quotation:	Per Dm 100 nominal value
Minimum price movement (tick size) and value:	0.01 per cent = Dm 25
Trading hours:	07.30 - 16.15 (floor trading hours) & 16.26 - 17.55 (APT trading hours), London times
Initial margin:	Dm 2000
Price limit:	No price limit
Contract standard:	Physical delivery may be made of any *Bundesanleihe* - including issues to the German Unity Fund (*Fonds Deutsche Einheit*) - with 8 1/2 - 10 years remaining maturity as at the tenth calendar day of the delivery month on a free-of-reallowance basis, as listed by Liffe. Delivery takes place through the Deutscher Kassenverein AG (Frankfurt). Delivery may be made via (i) a bank that has an account in its own name at a branch of Deutscher Kassenverein AG; (ii) Euroclear, or (iii) Cedel S.A. Delivery day in respect of Bund futures is the day on which Sellers' Bunds and Buyers' funds arrive at the Clearing House's delivery Agent in the Deutscher Kassenverein (Frankfurt).The invoicing amount is credited to Sellers' account on the same day. Buyers' Kassenverein account is credited with Bunds two Frankfurt working days later
Reuters pages:	LFJC (Monitor); FDB (Equities 2000)

Figure 16.57 Liffe Bund futures - contract specification

immediate success of the contract was mainly due to two factors. Firstly, the market for Deutschemark-denominated bonds is the world's third largest, after US Treasuries and Japanese government bonds. Furthermore, some other currencies are closely-linked to the Deutschemark (EMS, Austrian schillings) and thus, interest rates on these markets are dominated by the yields on Deutschemark bonds. Secondly, the contract represented the first efficient instrument to enable the taking of short positions in the market, a fact which was especially important in the environment of rising interest rates.

The German DTB launched an almost identical contract (see Figure 16.58) more than two years later, in November 1990. Both contracts were designed as deliverable contracts allowing the seller to select which Bund, with 8 1/2 - 10 years to maturity, to deliver. The invoice amount is adjusted by means of a price factor.

During 1991, the monthly trading volume at Liffe hovered mainly in the range between 600 thousand and one million contracts. This upper boundary was only exceeded during the rally in February, and again in August - as a consequence of 'Red Monday'. However, trading volume at DTB increased continuously in 1991; at the end of the year, the turnover reached more than 50 per cent of Liffe's trading volume and enabled DTB's market share of total volume

Contract size:	Dm 250,000 nominal value notional German government bond (Bund) with 6 per cent coupon
Delivery months:	March, June, September, December
Delivery day:	Tenth calendar day of the delivery month. If such a day is not a working day in Frankfurt then the delivery day is the next following Frankfurt working day
Last trading day:	11.00 Frankfurt time two Frankfurt working days prior to delivery day
Quotation:	Per Dm 100 nominal value
Minimum price movement (tick size) and value:	0.01 per cent = Dm 25
Trading hours:	08.00 - 17.00, Frankfurt time
Initial margin:	Dm 2500
Price limit:	No price limit
Contract standard:	Physical delivery may be made of any *Bundesanleihe*-including issues to the German Unity Fund (*Fonds Deutsche Einheit*) - with 8 1/2 - 10 years remaining maturity as at the tenth calendar day of the delivery month. Delivery takes place through the Deutscher Kassenverein AG (Frankfurt) with a two-day settlement. Notice day is two business days prior to the delivery day
Reuters pages:	DTSZ; BDL (Equities 2000)

Figure 16.58 DTB Bund futures - contract specification

to exceed one-third. As a result, Bund futures are the first contract traded successfully on two exchanges within the same time-zone. The ratio of trading volume to open interest, however, is significantly higher at the DTB than at Liffe - indicating that intra-day trading is more dominant at the DTB.

German government bond (Bund) option

Options on Bund futures were first launched on Liffe in April 1989 and grew quickly as the volume of the underlying futures contract increased. The DTB launched of Bund options on 16 August 1991. The combined DTB and Liffe trading volume of Bund options at the end of 1991 ranked third in the world. after options on US Treasury bonds (CBOT) and Matif's notional bond options. The ratio of options to underlying futures monthly volume, fluctuated at Liffe between one fifth and one third while, by the end of 1991, had already achieved a level of between 10 and 20 per cent at the DTB.

Bund options are options on the futures contract, and have the same face value and expiry cycle as that futures contract (see Figures 16.59 & 16.60). However, Bund options expire before trading ceases in the underlying futures contract. Bund options are American-style and may be exercised on any business

Option type:	American (exercise by 17.00 on any business day, extended to 18.30 on last trading day)
Unit of trading:	One Bund futures contract
Delivery months:	March, June, September, December
Assignment of futures:	On the first business day after the exercise day. Expiry at 18.30 on the last trading day
Last trading day:	6 business days prior to the first day of the delivery month
Quotation:	Multiples of Dm 0.01
Minimum price movement (tick size) and value:	0.01 per cent = Dm 25
Trading hours:	07.32 - 16.00, London time
Initial margin:	Liffe's option contracts are subject to London SPAN margining which reflects the price risk of the overall portfolio of options (or options and futures combinations)
Exercise (strike) prices:	Dm 0.50 intervals. 13 exercise prices are listed for new series. Additional prices are introduced on the business day after the Bund futures contract settlement price is within Dm 0.25 of the fourth highest or lowest existing price
Reuters pages:	LFJD - LFJK

Figure 16.59 Options on Bund futures (Liffe) - contract specification

Option type:	American (exercise on any business day to last trading day)
Unit of trading:	One Bund futures contract
Delivery months:	March, June, September, December
Assignment of futures:	On the first business day after the exercise day. Expiry at 18.30 on the business day following the last trading day
Last trading day:	6 business days prior to the first day of the delivery month
Quotation:	Multiples of Dm 0.01
Minimum price movement (tick size) and value:	0.01 per cent = Dm 25
Trading hours:	08.00 - 17.30, Frankfurt time
Initial margin:	DTB's option contracts are subject to the risk-based margining system
Exercise (strike) prices:	Dm 0.50 intervals. 9 exercise prices are listed for new series. Additional prices are introduced on the business day after the Bund future's nearby contract settlement price is above the average of the fourth and fifth highest or below the average of the fourth and fifth lowest strike price
Reuters pages:	BDLM-Y (Equities 2000)

Figure 16.60 Options on Bund futures (DTB) - contract specification

day prior to expiry, with exercise resulting in the assignment of the appropriate futures position.

German government medium note (Bobl) futures

Bobl (*Bundesobligationen*) futures, which were launched on the DTB on 4 October 1991 (see Figure 16.61), are the only futures contract for medium-term German government notes. During the first three trading months, the average trading volume was very satisfactory, at slightly above 4 thousand contracts. The ratio of volume to open interest was below one third, thus pointing to good market liquidity.

The deliverable contract allows the seller to choose for delivery *Bundesobligationen* or *Bundesschatzanweisung* with 3 1/2 - 5 years to maturity and an issue volume of at least Dm 4bn. The invoice amount is adjusted by means of a price factor.

Three-month euro-Deutschemark interest rate futures

Three-month euro-Deutschemark interest rate futures were launched in April 1989 on both Liffe and Matif. However, the low turnover led to a suspension of trading at the Matif whereas, on Liffe, the contract (see Figure 16.62) has grown

Contract size:	Dm 250,000 nominal value notional German government note (*Bundesobligationen* and *Schatzanweisungen*) with 6 per cent coupon
Delivery months:	March, June, September, December
Delivery day:	Tenth calendar day of the delivery month. If such a day is not a working day in Frankfurt then the delivery day is the next following Frankfurt working day
Last trading day:	12.30 Frankfurt time two Frankfurt working days prior to delivery day
Quotation:	Per Dm 100 nominal value
Minimum price movement (tick size) and value:	0.01 per cent = Dm 25
Trading hours:	08.00 - 17.00, Frankfurt time
Initial margin:	
Price limit:	No price limit
Contract standard:	Physical delivery may be made of any *Bundesobligationen* or *Bundesschatzanweisung* with 3 1/2 - 5 years remaining maturity as at the tenth calendar day of the delivery month and an issue volume of at least Dm 4bn Delivery takes place through the Deutscher Kassenverein AG (Frankfurt) with a two-day settlement. Notice day is two working days prior to the delivery day
Reuters pages:	BDM (Equities 2000)

Figure 16.61 DTB *Bundesobligationen* futures - contract specification

to be the second most-active contract on short-term interest rates, after the short sterling contract. The contract is cash-settled, with all positions being closed out against the Exchange Delivery Settlement Price.

Options on three-month euro-Deutschemark interest rate futures (see Figure 16.63) were launched in March 1990. However, the volume of the options in relation to the underlying futures has remained low. The option is American-styled. All options which are in-the-money on the last trading day are exercised automatically.

Note: prices, open interest etc. for the contracts mentioned above, are illustrated in Figures 16.64 - 16.75, at the end of this section.

Contract size:	Dm 1 million
Delivery months:	March, June, September, December
Delivery day:	First business day after the last trading day
Last trading day:	11.00 two business days prior to the third Wednesday of the delivery month
Quotation:	100.00 minus rate of interest
Minimum price movement (tick size) and value:	0.01 per cent = Dm 25
Trading hours:	08.00 - 16.10 (Floor trading hours) & 16.29 - 17.59 (APT trading hours), London times
Initial margin:	Dm 500
Price limit:	No price limit
Contract standard:	Cash settlement based on the Exchange Delivery Settlement Price which is based on the interest rates for three-month euro-Deutschemark deposits being offered to prime banking names between 09.30 and 11.00 on the last trading day, stated by a random sample of 16 from a list of designated banks. Having disregarded the three highest and three lowest quotes, the settlement price is 100.00 minus the average of the remaining 10 rates. From June 1992 onwards, the EDSP will be calculated using the FRABBA fixing in London on the last trading day
Reuters pages:	LFEA; FED (Equities 2000

Figure 16.62 Liffe three-month euromark futures - contract specification

Option type:	American (exercise by 17.00 on any business day)
Unit of trading:	One three-month euro-Deutschemark futures contract
Delivery months:	March, June, September, December
Assignment of futures:	On the first business day after the exercise day. Expiry at 17.00 on the last trading day. Fully-automatic exercise of in-the-money options on last trading day
Last trading day:	11.00 on the last trading day of the three-month euro-Deutschemark futures contract
Quotation:	Multiples of Dm 0.01 (i.e. 0.01 per cent)
Minimum price movement (tick size) and value:	0.01 per cent = Dm 25
Trading hours:	08.02 - 16.10, London time
Initial margin:	Liffe's option contracts are subject to London SPAN margining which reflects the price risk of the overall portfolio of options (or options and futures combinations)
Exercise (strike) prices:	Intervals are set of 25 basis points. 9 exercise prices are listed for new series. Additional prices are introduced on the business day after the three-month euro-Deutschemark futures contract settlement price is within 0.12 of the fourth highest or lowest existing price
Reuters pages:	LFEB - LFEG

Figure 16.63 Options on euromark futures (Liffe) - contract specification

Figure 16.64 Liffe Bund futures - 1991[1] price history
[1] *21 Jan - 31 Dec*

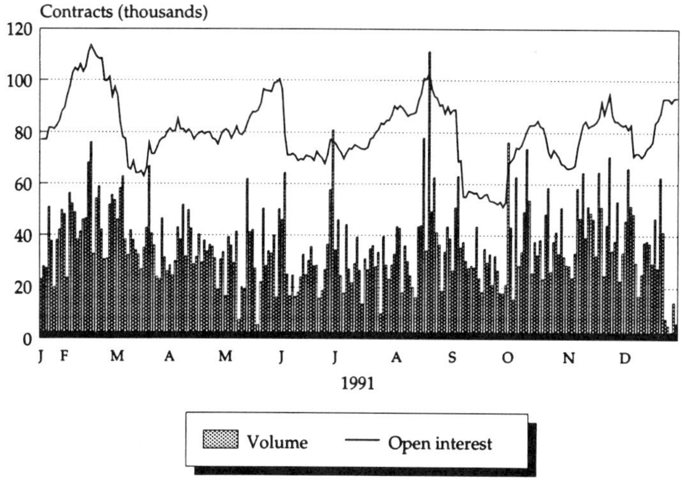

Figure 16.65 Liffe Bund futures - 1991[1] volume & open interest
[1] *21 Jan - 31 Dec*

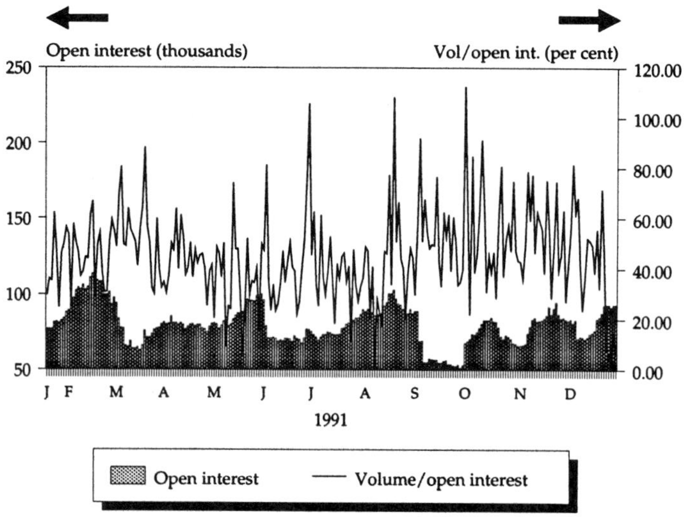

Figure 16.66 Liffe Bund futures - 1991[1] open interest & volume/open interest ratio
[1] *21 Jan - 31 Dec*

Figure 16.67 DTB Bund futures - 1991[1] price history
[1] *14 Jan - 31 Dec*

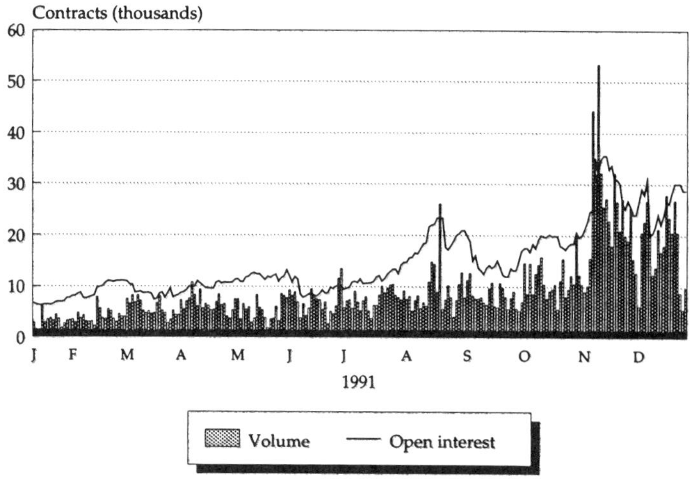

Figure 16.68 DTB Bund futures - 1991[1] volume and open interest
[1] *14 Jan - 31 Dec*

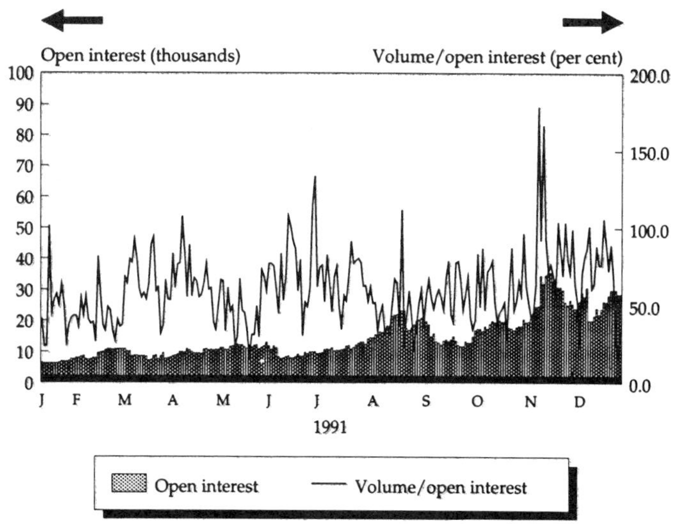

Figure 16.69 DTB futures - 1991[1] open interest & volume/open interest ratio
[1] *14 Jan - 31 Dec*

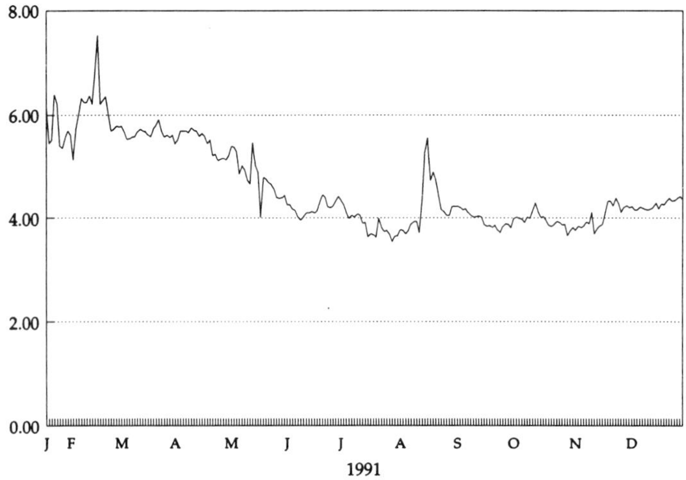

Figure 16.70 Options on Bund futures - implied volatility during 1991[1]

[1] *21 Jan - 31 Dec*

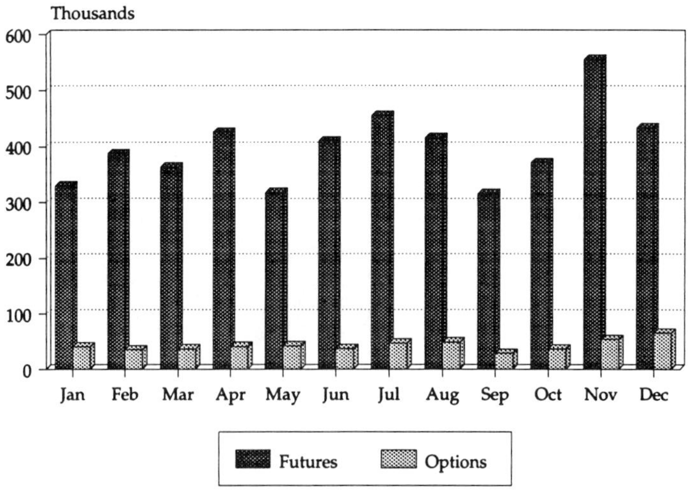

Figure 16.71 Liffe euromark futures - 1991[1] **monthly volume**

[1] *21 Jan - 31 Dec*

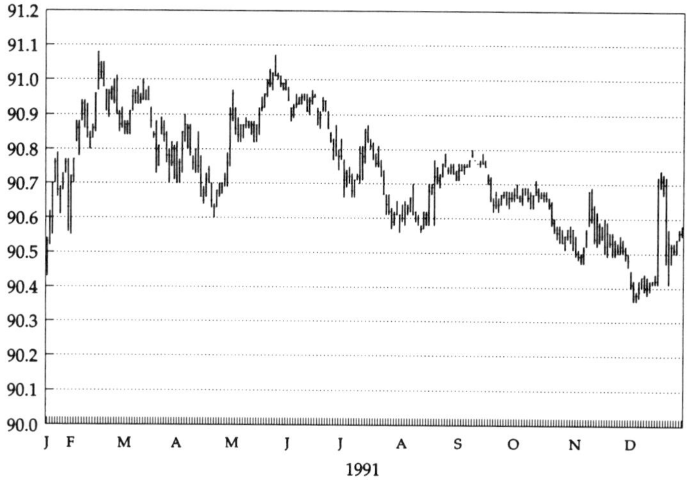

Figure 16.72 Liffe euromark futures - 1991[1] price history
[1] *21 Jan - 31 Dec*

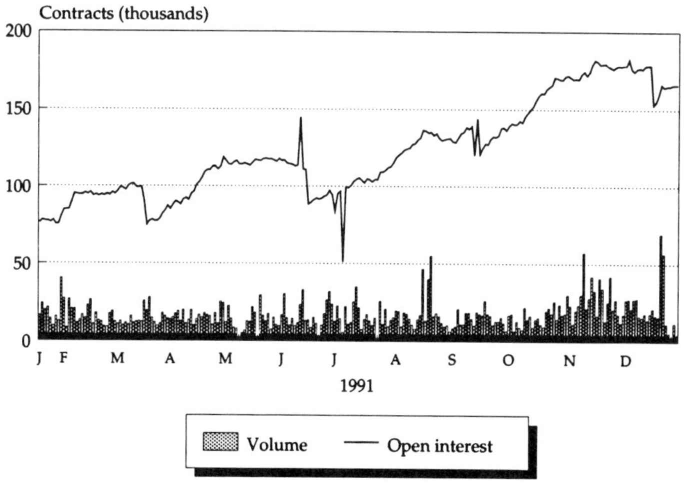

Figure 16.73 Liffe euromark futures - 1991[1] volume and open interest
[1] *21 Jan - 31 Dec*

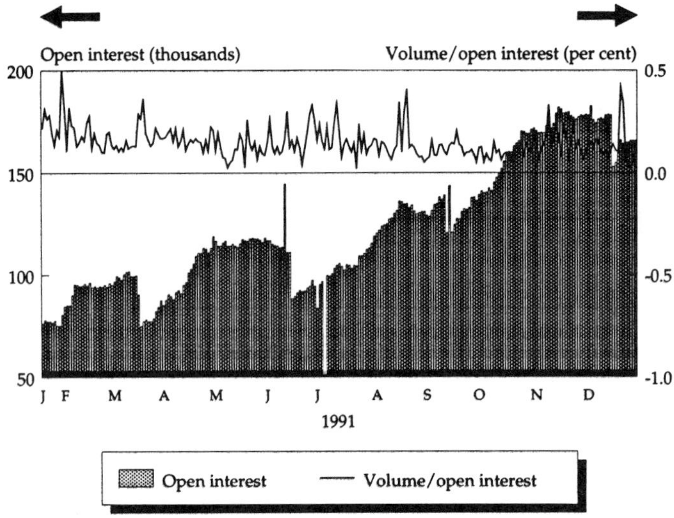

Figure 16.74 Liffe euromark futures - 1991[1] open interest & volume/open interest ratio
[1] *21 Jan - 31 Dec*

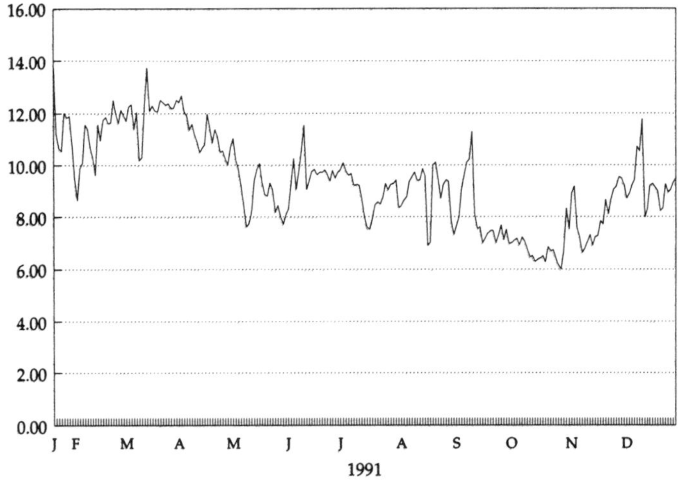

Figure 16.75 Options on euromark futures - implied volatility during 1991[1]
[1] *21 Jan - 31 Dec*

16.15 *Money markets*

Introduction

The German money market differs from other money markets in that interbank business predominates and that market behaviour depends, almost entirely, upon the policy of the Deutsche Bundesbank. Unlike other money markets, legal and other stipulations on the German market ensure that, in line with one of the basic principles of German banking (customer protection), deposits have to be soundly backed.

The principal differences between this market and the capital market can be found in an examination of:

- the most frequently-used instruments, with their economic and legal differences
- the maturities of the instruments, and associated accounting regulations
- the method of calculating interest
- the method of trading (over-the-counter or official stock exchange trading).

Instruments

Time deposits are the main instruments traded in the German money market. Legally, these are non-fungible claims. Turnover is highest in the 3- and 6-month maturities and there is brisk dealing in overnight money in order to square daily positions. Depending upon the state of the market, the traded volume of maturities of 6 to 12 months is generally lower, while maturities of 1 to 10 years are traded only sporadically.

Maturities

In the past, according to the breakdown for balance-sheet purposes, the money market was considered to cover maturities of up to 4 years, while maturities of over 4 years were treated as capital market transactions. Although the threshold for accounting purposes remains at 4 years, the money market is now considered to comprise maturities of up to 2 years, with the capital market covering those of 2 years and over. However, it is not possible to draw a clear dividing line, since the variety of instruments in use obviously leads to areas of overlap, while the need to place, or take up, funds on a tailor-made basis adds to the blurring of this boundary.

Calculation of interest

On the money market, unlike the capital market, interest is calculated on the basis of the actual number of days. This means that overnight money is paid back with interest, on the following day. By extrapolation, this gives a compound interest effect (× 364). For all longer-dated instruments, apart from time deposits, the prevalent method is discounting.

Method of trading

As a rule, deposits are traded, in interbank business or in customer operations, either direct or via a broker. This also applies to derivatives such as FRAs, options or swaps.

Only fungible claims (notes etc.) are traded on the stock exchange. Although the residual life may correspond with money market maturities, this paper is usually regarded as part of the capital market. The yield, however, tracks money market rates.

Money market rates/FIBOR

The money market, in a narrower sense, consists of trading in overnight money, time deposits and derivative products (e.g. FRAs). In the German money market, the maturities usually traded are from one day, up to 12 months. Trading is exclusively between domestic and foreign banks - the Bundesbank does not participate. Rates are usually fixed anew for each transaction. The quotation is given as a percentage, e.g. 8.45 per cent and the bid/offer spread is mostly 10bp.

At 11.00 Frankfurt time, the Deutschemark FIBOR is fixed. FIBOR is the equivalent of Deutschemark LIBOR in the euro-money market. Rates are fixed for 1 to 12 month maturities (and can be found on Reuters page, FIBO). The fixing is an average of the bid rates of 19 banks in Germany. The two highest and two lowest bids are omitted, and a simple arithmetical average is taken of the remaining 15. Since 1 July 1991, FIBOR has been calculated by the international method, i.e. on the basis of actual/360. In interbank trading, the settlement period is two days.

- Example: Bank *A* deposits Dm 100m with bank *B*, at 3-month FIBOR of 9.00 per cent, for the period from 2 March 1992 to 2 June 1992. Value-date 4 March; final amount Dm 102.25m.

FIBOR has gained importance as a reference rate for domestic floating-rate notes. Floating-rate notes, e.g. of the Bund and Staatsbank Berlin, are linked to 3-month or 6-month FIBOR. This may, however, refer either to old or new

FIBOR. The floating-rate note of the Federal Republic is linked to the old FIBOR, which is still calculated on a 30/360-day basis. A precise value-date is given. In the example shown above, the final amount, on the basis of the old FIBOR, is Dm 102.3m.

Interest rates for overnight money, or time deposits, are strongly influenced by Bundesbank measures. The different Bundesbank repo rates, the Lombard rate, and the Treasury bill rate, are especially important since its is via these rates that the Bundesbank steers the banks' refinancing. Bundesbank funds can be taken up against certain securities, which are determined by the Bundesbank. Repurchase transactions are offered by the Bundesbank for 1 month or 2 months at most; refinancing can be obtained at the Lombard rate, for a maximum of 3 months. As a result, these rates have a direct impact on money market rates for maturities of up to three months.

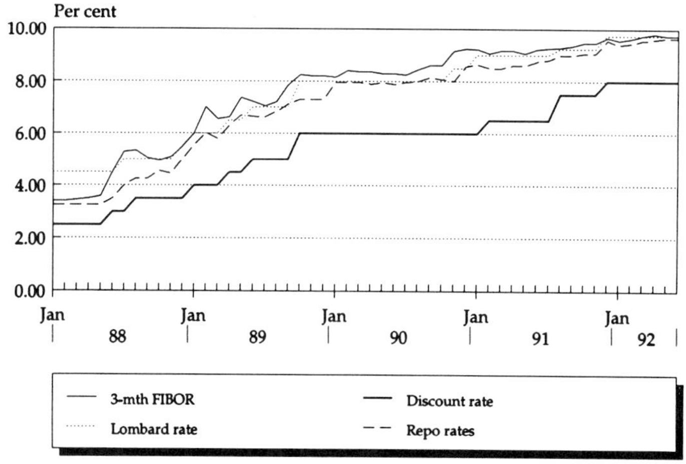

Figure 16.76 Money market rates, 1988 - 1992

The discount rate has lost significance as a guide to the level of money market rates ever since the Bundesbank began to steer the banks' liquidity entirely through securities repurchase transactions. Nevertheless, it is important for the banks' funding costs, as it is the cheapest rate at which they can obtain central bank money. The volume of funds which the banks can take up at the discount rate is limited by the size of the re-discount quotas (which are set by the

Bundesbank as an aggregate ceiling), and the volume of available bills of exchange; these are required as security for borrowing from the Bundesbank under the re-discount quotas. The level of the discount rate also determines the level of interest rates on loans which have conditions linked to the discount rate.

Money market instruments

Besides trading in overnight money and time deposits, the money market in a broader sense, includes trading in money market paper. The main issuer of money market paper in Germany is the public sector. The Federal Government, the Deutsche Bundespost (Federal Post Office) and the Deutsche Bundesbahn (Federal Railways), all issue paper on the money market to finance short-term capital requirements. These instruments are issued in agreement with the Bundesbank.

Mobilization paper

Money market instruments can also be issued by the Bundesbank, particularly to drain short-term liquidity surpluses. Pursuant to Section 42 of the Deutsche Bundesbank Act, the Bundesbank, which has equalization claims on the Bund (up to Dm 8bn), can ask the Bund to mobilize funds in the form of money market paper (mobilization paper). Furthermore, Section 42a of the Deutsche Bundesbank Act gives permission to mobilize a further Dm 8bn in money market paper (liquidity paper), if the original equalization claim of Dm 8bn has been exhausted. The Bundesbank mobilizes such paper, from time to time, to prevent an excessively strong decline in the overnight rate. Although the Bundesbank has these instruments at its disposal, it has not offered such paper for four years. The Bundesbank uses Treasury bills, which it offers to the banks, to drain off excess liquidity and stabilize the overnight rate.

Discount paper

Discount paper is created by public-sector borrowing. Two types are on offer: *U-Schätze* and *Finanzierungsschätze*. They differ in issuance procedure, and attract different buyers.

■ *U-Schätze*
U-Schätze, or *Unverzinsliche Schatzanweisungen*, are issued by the Federal Republic, the Debt-Processing Fund, the Federal Railways and the Federal Post Office. The most important issuers are the Federal government and the Debt-Processing Fund (responsible for financing the debt incurred through the changeover from the Ostmark to the Deutschemark within the framework of economic and

monetary union with the former GDR). *U-Schätze* are issued for account of the issuer. Maturities of *U-Schätze* range from half a year, to two years, with a difference of roughly half a year between maturities. *U-Schätze* are discounted (non-interest-bearing) paper.

U-Schätze are issued via tender. Bids at the tender have to be at least Dm 100,000 or a multiple thereof, and must be submitted to the Bundesbank (or one of its branches) no later than 11.00 on the last day of the bidding period. Foreign investors can place bids through a domestic bank. Bids are not made on the price, but on the yield - which must be indicated in steps of a full 0.01 percentage point. Bids 'at best' are also possible. They are allocated at the weighted average allocation rate. Those at the cut-off rate may only be partially allocated, but bids at lower yields will definitely be accepted.

Outstanding *U-Schätze* are eligible for collective custody and, at a maturity of one year or less, eligible as collateral for borrowing from the Bundesbank, and for securities repurchase agreements. *U-Schätze* are not listed on the stock exchange. The minimum denomination is Dm 100,000 or a multiple thereof; there are no maximum amounts. As *U-Schätze* are not listed, they cannot be returned (sold) before final maturity. The yield is calculated on the basis of 365/360 days. Only banks and institutional investors can buy *U-Schätze.*

■ *Finanzierungsschätze*

Finanzierungsschätze (Treasury financing notes) share similarities with *U-Schätze.* Like *U-Schätze,* they are discounted paper and are issued by the public sector and the Federal special funds (Debt-Processing Fund, Federal Railways, Federal Post Office).

At the time of issue, *Finanzierungsschätze* have a maturity of one or two years. Depending on the maturity, a distinction is made between type A (1-year maturity) and type B (2-year maturity). Type A is redeemed directly by the issuer at the nominal value at maturity. For type B, the holder's account is credited by the custodian bank.

Finanzierungsschätze are tap issues. They are issued once a month via the Bundesbank. The minimum denomination is Dm 1,000; the maximum that may be invested is Dm 500,000 per person, per business day. Like *U-Schätze,* they are issued on an interest-rate basis. The issuer fixes the rate for the sale in agreement with the Bundesbank. Interest is calculated on the basis of 365/360 days.

Finanzierungsschätze can be purchased by all domestic and foreign investors, with the exception of credit institutions. The banks receive a fee from the issuer, which is paid via the central bank and intended to cover the cost incurred in purchases and sales. Like *U-Schätze, Finanzierungsschätze* are not listed on the stock exchange - thus the paper must be held until maturity.

Finanzierungsschätze comply with the provisions of the German Civil Code, Section 1807, on trustee status, and Section 54 of the Investment Act on the investment of assets of insurance companies. For this reason, *Finanzierungsschätze* (along with securities) are especially appropriate for investment by insurance companies and pension funds.

At the end of 1991, the outstanding volume of *Finanzierungsschätze* and *U-Schätze* (public sector, Federal Railways and Federal Post Office) was Dm 34.7bn (cf. the end-1989 figure of Dm 12.154bn). The volume increased particularly strongly following German unification, a fact which reflects the diversification of issuance of public sector paper.

	1988	1989	1990	1991
Federal government	5.3	11.8	19.5	19.9
of which: *Finanzierungsschätze*	(1.7)	(1.5)	(7.8)	(18.2)
Federal states (West)	0.2	0.3	-	-
Debt-Processing Fund (*Kreditabwicklungsfonds*)	-	-	18.8	14.8
Federal Railways	0.1	0.7	0.1	-
Federal Post Office	-	-	-	-
Total	5.6	12.8	38.4	34.7

Figure 16.77 Outstanding volume of discounted paper , by issuers (DEM billion)

Commercial paper

Commercial paper (CP) consists of short-term financing instruments with maturities of between seven days and two years. A CP programme is a blanket agreement between an issuer and arranger (often a bank syndicate). The issuer, who generally has excellent standing, is entitled - but not obliged - to draw on the agreement at any time to obtain funds. CP is generally issued in relatively large denominations of at least Dm 500,000, and on a discounted basis. Since CPs tend to be designed for large investors, and programmes are generally not listed, they are more like a private placement.

CP issues, already an established feature in other money markets (such as in the USA and the euro-money market), have only been permitted on the German money market since 1 January 1991 when Sections 795 and 808a of the Federal German Civil Code, which had precluded CP issuance, were abolished. The other major obstacle to CP issuance was the stock exchange turnover tax, but this was also abolished at the same time. In the past, the purchase of securities forming part of an issue, was taxed at a rate of 6 per cent - regardless of the maturity. The tax therefore had a particularly negative impact on transactions in securities which had a maturity of less than one year.

Since its authorization, a rapidly-growing CP market has developed in the Federal Republic of Germany. At the end of 1991, the volume of arranged programmes amounted to Dm 16.9bn, or more than three times the figure for the first half of the year. This trend will probably continue as CP bridges the maturity gap between the Deutschemark money market and euro-Deutschemark medium-term note programmes. In addition, being bearer paper, CP facilitates the trading of money market maturities.

	Total volume of agreed CP programmes	Outstanding volume	Draw-down ratio (%)
1991			
1st half	5.6	-	-
2nd half	11.3	8.2	72.6

Figure 16.78 Deutschemark commercial paper of domestic issuers (DEM billion)

Conditions for Deutschemark commercial paper

Issuer:	Company of prime standing
Maturity:	Between 7 days and 2 years, less 1 day
Nominal interest rate:	None (discounted)
Yield basis:	365/360 days
Denomination:	Dm 500,000 min.
Size of series:	Dm 5m min.
Settlement:	2 banking days in Germany
Delivery:	Via Euroclear and Cedel
Listing:	Not listed
Callable by holder:	Only in exceptional cases
Trading:	On a yield basis

The formula for calculating the yield is:

$$P = F \times \left(1 - \frac{R}{100} \times \frac{Dsm}{360}\right)$$

where,

P price
F face value
R rate of discount per cent
Dsm number of days from settlement to maturity.

To compare the yield of commercial paper with other money market instruments (traded on a yield basis), the rate of discount can be converted using the following formula:

$$Y = \frac{100 \times R \times 360}{(100 \times 360 - R \times Dsm)}$$

where,

Y yield per cent
R rate of discount per cent
Dsm number of days from settlement to maturity

Issuers

Most of the issuers on the German commercial paper market are listed industrial companies. However, large companies from the public sector (e.g. Flughafen AG) and subsidiaries of foreign firms, also bring CP issues to the market.

Issuance procedure for commercial paper

The framework under which individual commercial paper is issued is provided by the programme and is based upon an agreement between the issuer and the banks which have been jointly-appointed as placing agent. Under the agreement, the issuer has the right to issue paper on the Deutschemark market at any time, but is not obliged to do so. The issue is closely co-ordinated with the banks, who contact appropriate investors. The banks do not underwrite the issue - they merely place it on a 'best-effort' basis. If it cannot be placed, the banks are under no obligation to take up paper already issued. As noted, the issuer is not obliged to issue commercial paper, and even if the placing agents have found interested investors, the issuer can refuse to make further issuance. The issuer should, therefore, have access to other funds - in sufficient quantity - to ensure his ability to redeem commercial paper already issued.

Deutschemark commercial paper programmes have a minimum volume of Dm 500m. The total amount of commercial paper outstanding may not exceed the current size of the programme. It is, however, possible to enlarge the programme at any time.

Since Deutschemark commercial paper programmes form part of the German money market, yields therefore follow the corresponding money market rates, i.e. Deutschemark LIBOR or FIBOR. However, they may well be higher, depending on the standing of the issuer.

Investors

Banks, investment institutions, life insurers and other companies, all invest in commercial paper.

16.16 *Interest rate history*

Overview

In Germany, bond market trends are only partly dependent on domestic factors. This is primarily attributable to the prominent position of the Deutschemark among the leading world currencies, the Deutschemark being the second most-important international investment and reserve currency, after the US dollar. There are basically three reasons for this: In view of the remarkable track record of the Federal Republic of Germany in respect of price stability - especially by comparison to other countries - the Deutschemark has become practically synonymous with currency strength. At the same time, the German capital market is distinguished as being highly liquid and freely accessible. Against this background, the share of public sector bonds owned by foreigners has increased by almost Dm 130bn since the end of 1985, to a recent level of Dm 175bn (cf.. all domestic bonds total of Dm 245bn), even though the Deutschemark, just like the Swiss franc and the Japanese yen, is regarded as a low-yielding currency. However, these shifts in foreign investor behaviour did not materialize as a continuous development over time, but rather in fits and starts. For example, expectations of a Deutschemark appreciation in May 1987, in particular, contributed to yields reaching their cyclical low.

Over and above this, domestic factors certainly do have significance. The general debate in connection with the introduction of a 10 per cent withholding tax as from 1 January 1989 generated predominantly negative stimuli to the bond market from October 1987. Additionally, domestic fundamentals showed signs of worsening - money supply expanded with fast growth rates, and the price climate gradually deteriorated. In consequence, the Bundesbank switched to a restrictive policy in the course of 1988. Since then, money rates have steadily climbed.

In an environment of already upward-moving yields, the announcement, in February 1990, of a pan-German currency along with economic and social union, came as a shock and drove yields up to a level not seen since summer 1982. The main worries in this respect focused on a sustained rise in PSBR, as well as the likely inflationary effects of an excessive money growth, plus an artificial lengthening of the economic cycle in Germany (resulting from a demand push from the new Federal states). Admittedly, however, the highest level that has so far been reached in the current interest rate cycle can be attributed to inflationary fears after the outbreak of the Gulf crisis. In summer 1991, the subject of tax on interest income again shifted into the foreground. The Federal Supreme Constitutional Court put the legislator under an obligation to make provision for a

	Start	End	High	Low
1987				
Bundesbank average yield[1]	5.87	5.88	6.93	5.24
3-month money[2]	4.85	3.55	4.90	3.55
10-year Bunds[2]	6.05	6.45	7.25	5.55
10-year bank bonds[2]	6.65	6.55	7.20	6.25
Yield spread[2 3]	1.90	2.70	2.75	1.90
1988				
Bundesbank average yield[1]	5.83	6.35	6.51	5.59
3-month money[2]	3.45	5.35	5.45	3.25
10-year Bunds[2]	6.55	6.55	6.85	6.15
10-year bank bonds[2]	6.60	6.70	6.95	6.30
Yield spread[2 3]	2.80	1.05	2.85	1.05
1989				
Bundesbank average yield[1]	6.38	7.60	7.73	6.38
3-month money[2]	5.45	8.20	8.35	5.45
10-year Bunds[2]	6.65	7.25	7.40	6.60
10-year bank bonds[2]	6.75	7.75	7.90	6.75
Yield spread[2 3]	0.90	-0.30	0.90	-0.55
1990				
Bundesbank average yield[1]	7.80	9.09	9.21	7.80
3-month money[2]	8.35	9.20	9.20	8.10
10-year Bunds[2]	7.45	9.00	9.10	7.45
10-year bank bonds[2]	7.95	8.95	9.05	7.95
Yield spread[2 3]	-0.40	-0.30	0.10	-0.50
1991				
Bundesbank average yield[1]	9.14	8.40	9.17	8.40
3-month money[2]	9.15	9.55	9.55	8.90
10-year Bunds[2]	8.95	8.05	8.95	8.05
10-year bank bonds[2]	9.00	8.30	9.00	8.30
Yield spread[2 3]	-0.30	-1.05	-0.30	-1.05

Figure 16.79 German bond yields (per cent) 1987-1991

[1] *daily data*

[2] *end-week data*

[3] *10-yr vs. 1-yr bank bonds (basis points)*

more effective method of ascertaining interest income for tax purposes, as from 1 January 1993.

In the course of the general rise in interest rates, the period covered by this review saw some considerable changes in the yield curve. As a consequence of the Bundesbank's switch towards a restrictive monetary policy in 1988, money market rates rose substantially faster then the yield of long-dated bonds. This resulted in an inversion of the yield curve. As the long rates had already passed their cyclical high, in late summer 1990, the Bundesbank continued to stick to its restrictive policy. As a result, there was no chance of a change in interest rates towards a 'normal' yield curve in 1991. On the contrary, the grade of inversion even widened at times, as long rates came down. Levels of price volatility fluctuated markedly and reached their high, for the period covered here, in February 1990, when the Federal chancellor submitted his proposal for economic, monetary and social union of the two German states.

1987

The strength of the Deutschemark had already been exercising a strong influence on the bond market since the end of 1986 - indeed, the German currency, in company with the Dutch guilder and the Belgian/Luxembourg franc, underwent an upward revaluation within the EMS, in January 1987. Not even the

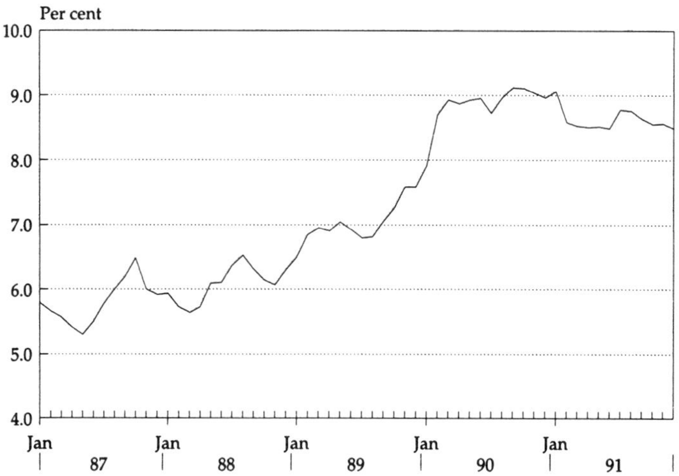

Figure 16.80 Bundesbank average yield

Louvre Accord, which was designed to support the US dollar, was able to shake confidence in the strength of the Deutschemark. In view of the expectations of an appreciating currency, there was a sharp rise in foreign buying in the German bond market. In May 1987, yields reached their lowest level since the 2nd quarter of 1978, with the Bundesbank average yield dropping to 5.24 per cent.

This was followed by the trend reversal in the interest rate cycle. In the initial phase, yields climbed up 1 to 1.5 percentage points by October. The change of sentiment had been brought about by foreign selling as well as by inflationary fears in the USA. After 9 October, the market was further burdened by the announcement of a 10 per cent withholding tax on interest income of domestic bonds and other interest-bearing instruments from 1989.

The stock market crash on Black Monday (19 October) then set off a temporary recovery in the bond market. The central banks freed liquidity in order to avert the danger of breakdowns in credit chains, with resultant upheavals in the world system of finance. In the course of this development, short-term interest rates initially fell faster than long-term ones.

1988

As a result of the ample supply of liquidity through the German Bundesbank, yields in Germany fell until the beginning of March. The Bundesbank average

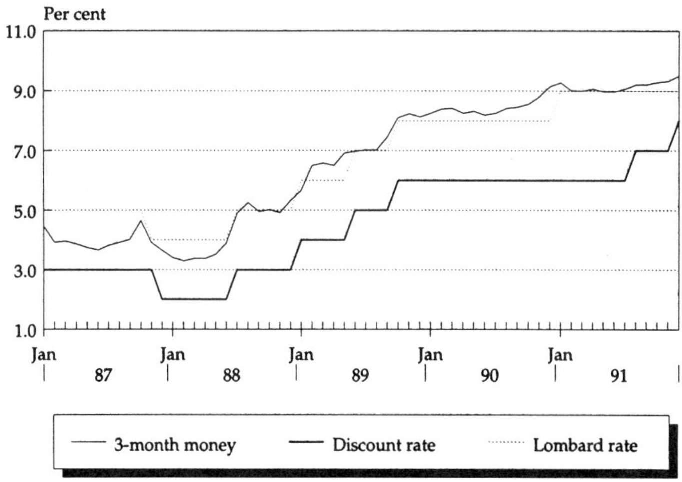

Figure 16.81 Bundesbank interest rates and money market

yield dropped to 5.59 per cent, 24 basis points below its level at the beginning of the year (see Figure 16.80).

A sharp upsurge in US interest rates, and waning expectations of a Deutschemark appreciation, then led to price losses in the German bond market. The upward movement of interest rates gained momentum when the Bundesbank switched to a restrictive policy in mid-year. With the increase of the discount rate from 2.5 to 3 per cent, the period of cheap money, which had begun in 1982, came to an end. At the same time, foreign investors were holding back on new investments, or were liquidating positions. With the Bundesbank average yield rising to 6.64 per cent in August, capital market rates reached their high for the year. In the following months the Bundesbank stressed its intention to keep the monetary aggregates under control by further increasing key interest rates.

As a result of the change in central bank policy, money market rates rose far faster than the yields at the long-end of the capital market. This led to a flattening of the, still upward-sloping, yield curve.

1989

The strongly restrictive central bank policy resulted in a further flattening of the yield curve. In spring, the yield curve became inverse - for the first time since August 1982.

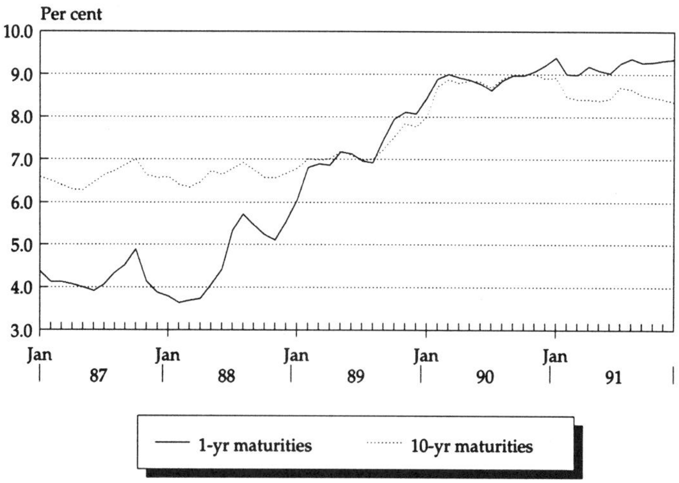

Figure 16.82 Yields on bank bonds

From March, a temporary switch from interest rate-linked tenders to volume-linked tenders in repurchase agreements, as well as comments from the Bundesbank that the, then rampant, inflationary fears were exaggerated, induced a recovery in the bond market. Also, the decision to abolish, from 1 July, the 10 per cent withholding tax that had been introduced at the beginning of the year, fostered a temporary fall in interest rates.

At the end of April, a further tightening of monetary policy, and a temporary firming of the US dollar to more than Dm 2, sent German bond prices tumbling. In May, the Bundesbank average yield reached its highest level in four years, at 7.16 per cent. The ongoing economic boom in West Germany, plus inflationary fears and the tight monetary policy, all strengthened the trend of rising yields. Furthermore, after the fall of the Berlin wall on 9 November, the spotlight then turned on political developments. At the end of that month, the Bundesbank average yield soared to 7.73 per cent, its highest level that year and about 130 basis points higher than when the year started.

1990

In that year, it was primarily the expected consequences of German economic and monetary union and of reunification, that determined the way interest rates developed. International interest rate trends and currency influences faded into

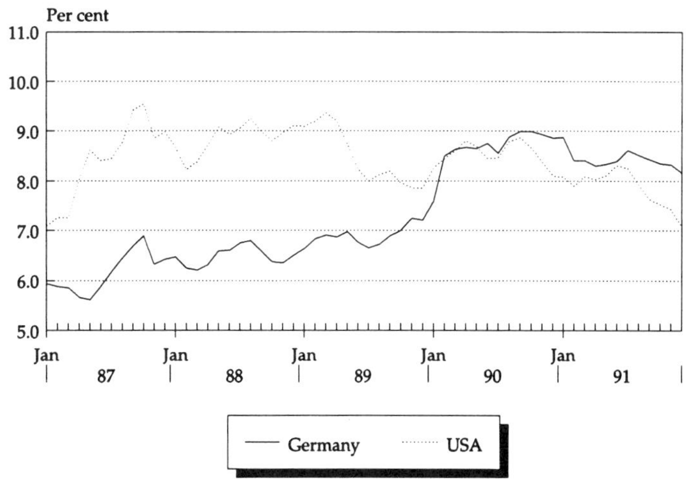

Figure 16.83 Yields on 10-yr government bonds in Germany and the USA

the background. The announcement, in February, of economic and monetary union with the former GDR (from 1 July 1990) was greeted by a substantial jump in yields; the Bundesbank average yield reached 9.15 per cent, its highest level since mid-August 1982. At the same time, the yield on 10-year government bonds was temporarily higher in Germany than in the USA, for the first time since the end of 1976. Market operators had fears about the government debt, which was in danger of getting out of hand, as well as about the inflationary pressures resulting from a consumer shopping spree in the former GDR.

Despite a temporary relaxation on the interest rate front, concern about monetary stability, and about the ability to finance German unity, persisted over the next few months. The oil price shock, in the wake of the Gulf crisis, drove interest rates up yet again from the beginning of August. The Bundesbank average yield reached its annual high at the end of September, at 9.21 per cent. This was then followed by a temporary recovery, with the bond market receiving support from a significant decline in interest rates in the USA. A new, and significant, fall in bond prices was seen from mid-December, triggered by heightened tension in the Gulf as well as the (unrelated) resignation of the Soviet foreign minister, Shevardnadze.

1991

In the first three weeks of the year, yields fluctuated in a narrow sideways trend. However, an increase in the key interest rates effective from 1 February then strengthened investor confidence that the Bundesbank would resolutely stick to a stability-oriented monetary policy. In addition, reports of the initial successes of the Allied troops after the outbreak of the Gulf War occasioned a fundamental improvement of sentiment in the international bond markets. Correspondingly, the Bundesbank average yield dropped to 8.40 per cent in mid-February, its lowest level for the year.

This was followed by a renewed sideways drift, which persisted until the end of June. During this period, the German bond market generally revealed itself to be exceptionally robust in the face of bad news. In large part, this is certainly due to astute debt management in the public sector. The Federal government held back with new issues of long-term Federal government bonds and, by means of regular floatings of comparatively liquid Federal bonds in the medium-maturity range, it has taken issuing pressure off the long-end of the market.

It was only after the decision of the Federal Supreme Constitutional Court, which necessitated new regulations on the taxing of interest income by the start of 1993, that yields started to rise again. The slack taxation rules concerning investment income, in force at the time, tempted many investors not to declare their taxable interest income to the fiscal authorities. The probability of being sued was small. As a result, the Federal Supreme Constitutional Court forced the government to establish more effective measures to collect taxes on interest

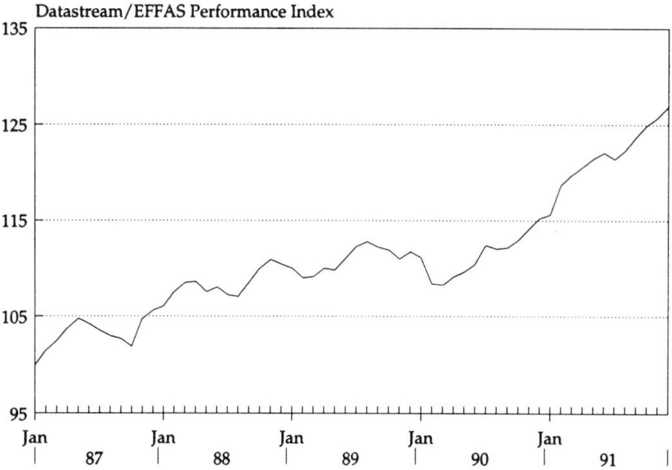

Figure 16.84 Performance of the German bond market since 1987

income. However, the corresponding government bill, presented in November and envisaging a 25 per cent deduction at the source of payment of investment income, made fears of a large-scale flight of capital appear unfounded. The tax-free status of foreign investors was particularly welcomed. Furthermore, under the bill in its present draft form, 80 per cent of domestic savers will in future not be liable to tax on investment income, since the tax-free amounts for the purpose of income taxation are to be set substantially higher.

Additional positive influences for the market over the last quarter of 1991 came from a renaissance of the Deutschemark, which recovered against all currencies, and triggered some tensions in the EMS for the first time in a year.

In December, the Bundesbank lifted key interest rates to record levels (discount rate 8 per cent, Lombard rate 9.75 per cent). Growing expectations that this was the last restrictive measure of the Bundesbank in the current cycle led to a rally, especially at the long-end of the market. At the end of 1991, the yield of long-term government bonds reached their lowest level for nearly two years.

16.17 Inter-market spreads

Government bond market/Dm-euromarket

The development of yield spreads between Bunds/*Bundesobligationen* and Dm-eurobonds (see Figures 16.85 & 16.86) is dominated, above all by the 'withholding tax story'.

The 'normal' spread should be positive, i.e. yields of Dm-eurobonds are usually higher than those of Bunds and *Bundesobligationen* (*Bobls*). The main reason for this, when looking at AAA-rated Dm-eurobonds (which is the case here), is liquidity. Whereas Bunds and *Bobls* (non-residents have only been allowed to purchase *Bobls* since mid-September 1988) have an issue volume of up to Dm 12bn, a Dm-eurobond is considered highly liquid when it has an issue volume of Dm 1bn.

Dm-eurobonds have also always exhibited a liquidity premium when there was no withholding tax, when there was no discussion about introducing such a tax, or when an existing withholding tax was abolished.

The higher demand for Dm-eurobonds when there was a tax on interest income was understandable, since the two withholding taxes which have so far existed affected only domestic paper. The coupon tax currently under discussion will, however, also affect Dm-eurobonds.

In July 1984, when the 25 per cent coupon tax on Deutschemark domestic bonds was abolished, yields of Dm-eurobonds, which until then had been 20-30bp lower than those of Bunds, then rose quickly to the 'normal' level of 25-35bp above Bunds (although highs of up to 60bp were observed at the long-end and of up to 40bp in the intermediate maturities).

It took another three years before there was renewed talk of introducing a tax on investment income. In October 1987, the government, in the person of the then finance minister Stoltenberg, announced (practically at the same time as the 1987 Crash) that the government was planning to re-introduce a 10 per cent withholding tax on domestic issues. This immediately turned the yield situation, on both the Dm-eurobond and Bund markets, upside down. The wave of selling orders for public sector bonds and the brisk demand for Dm-eurobonds, or the attractive investment opportunities in neighbouring European countries, saw Bund yields surge while Dm-eurobond yields headed south. The spreads between Dm-eurobonds and Bunds, which had still averaged roughly 30bp in October 1987, became negative again and hovered around minus 20bp until spring 1989.

The Tax Reform Amendment Act was passed on 8 July 1988 and the 10 per cent withholding tax was introduced on 1 January 1989. The capital flight which

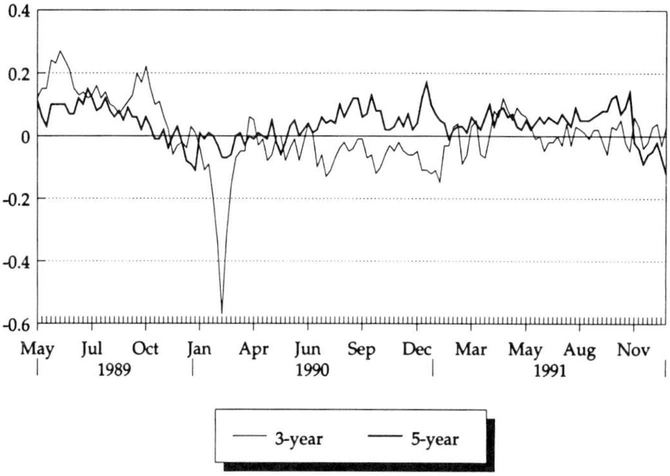

Figure 16.85 3-yr and 5-yr yield spreads: *Bundesanleihen* vs. *Bundesobligationen*

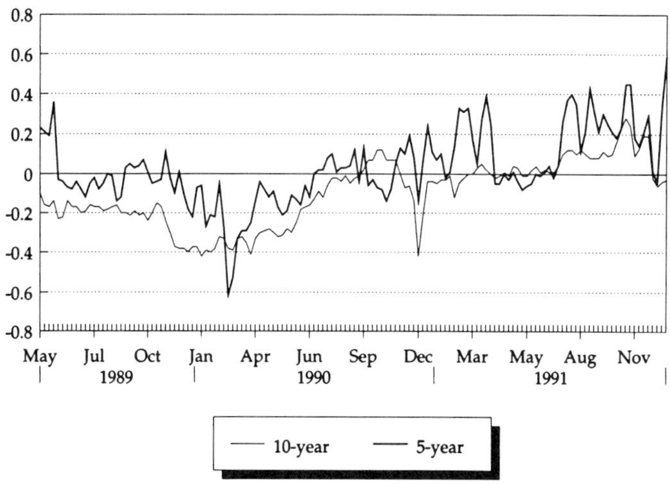

Figure 16.86 10-yr and 5-yr yield spreads: Bunds vs. DEM-eurobonds

had set-in shortly after the announcement, then assumed drastic proportions. It is estimated that Dm 45bn left the country in the initial weeks following introduction of the tax. This, together with other factors, triggered a renewed bout of Deutschemark weakness (the US$/Dm exchange rate rose from roughly Dm 1.70 at the start of the year, to over Dm 2 at mid-year) and put additional pressure, above all, on the more liquid Bunds.

The enormous capital flight, coupled with a drastic increase in administrative costs, quickly made the government realize that the 'Stoltenberg model' should remain an experiment. Not only did the hoped-for incremental tax revenues fail to materialize, but funding state spending also became more expensive. On 1 July 1989, the 10 per cent withholding tax was abolished again by the newly-appointed finance minister, Waigel. This followed talk of its possible abolition since May.

The yields of Dm-eurobonds also remained below those of Bunds after abolition of the withholding tax, even though they converged strongly. The main reasons for this were that only part of the paper transferred abroad was repatriated and, above all, that issuing activity in this already illiquid sector eased strongly.

Issuing activity on the Dm-euromarket picked up considerably at the beginning of 1990. But German unification also triggered a tighter monetary stance on the part of the Bundesbank, which caused a steady appreciation of the Deutschemark. Since this raised expectations of longer-term stability, longer-dated investments became more attractive which, overall, resulted in an inversion of the yield curve. The combination of these factors resulted in a renewed reversal in the development of yield spreads between Bunds (*Bobls*) and Dm-eurobonds, i.e. spreads soon turned positive again. At mid-year, issuing activity on the Dm-euromarket tended to flag, and yields in both sectors converged again.

At the same time, however, the spectre of inflation and public sector debt was looming on the horizon, and this prompted institutional investors to switch out of the Deutschemark. Parallel to that, the government - because of reunification and the concomitant higher-funding requirements - had greater recourse to the capital market. This hit the government bond sector more. Spreads between Dm-eurobonds and Bunds tended to widen and became negative again.

This situation was exacerbated in June/July 1991 when the first rumours of the introduction of a new coupon tax hit the market. Domestic investors began switching portfolios around again. Deliverable Dm-eurobonds were in demand, to the detriment of Bunds. The door was open for all sorts of speculation. For example, no one knew exactly to what extent foreign investors were going to be affected by the tax, or even how much the tax would be, or which form it would take. Above all, the 'shy' German investor (Federal Constitutional Court) was concerned about what would happen to Germany's cherished bank secrecy. The only certainty was that the tax - according to the Federal Constitutional Court ruling - had to be introduced by 1 January 1993, at the latest.

A little more light was shed on the tax debate at the start/middle of December 1991, when it became known that the tax was to be a 25 per cent coupon tax, affecting both domestic and foreign bonds and also OTC business. Many investors heaved a sigh of relief when it was officially announced that bank secrecy was to be retained, that non-residents were not to be affected by the tax, and that tax allowances were to be increased from Dm 600/1200 (singles/married couples) to Dm 6,000/12,000. Above all, the last point revealed that roughly 80 per cent of all savers would be exempt from the tax.

Spreads between Dm-eurobonds and Bunds/*Bobls* which, by that time, had fallen to a low of roughly minus 30bp in the 10-year segment and to approximately minus 70bp for 5-year bonds, contracted only moderately. Not only was the exact form of the tax not known (it is still under discussion at the time of writing), but issuing activity eased and tightened supply on the euromarket.

Government bond market/bank bonds and government/Post or Bahn

Bunds and *Bobls* have enjoyed advantages over bank bonds, mainly because of their higher liquidity, but also because of their better rating. The liquidity/rating premium on bank bonds, i.e. the spreads between the two types of bond was, however, determined above all by foreign interest in the German bond market. It should be noted that bank bonds are purchased mainly by domestic - usually private - investors and are usually held to final maturity.

As a result, all factors which make the German bond market less attractive, or cause speculation that the German market could become less attractive, have a greater impact on the much more volatile Bund and *Bobl* market. Nevertheless, the development of bank bond yields is closely-linked to that of the Bund sector, albeit with a certain time lag (one or two days).

One of the main factors negatively affecting German bank bonds is, of course, the withholding tax. Since small private investors play a much greater role in the bank bond market than in the Bund sector, any announcement of plans to introduce or abolish a tax on investment income naturally has a greater impact on the bank bond sector, with corresponding repercussions on spreads to Bund/*Bobls*.

Between 1988 and 1991, the highest spread to Bunds/*Bobls* was 60bp at the long-end and 33bp in the intermediate maturities. The lowest was minus 7bp and minus 16bp respectively.

In 1991, yield spreads averaged 10bp for 10-year bonds and 5bp for 5-year bonds. At the end of 1991, they widened again slightly. The main factor here was speculation about Bundesbank easing which would favour the more liquid Bunds/*Bobls*.

The foregoing also applies, in large part, to spreads between Bahn/Post bonds and Bunds/*Bobls* (see Figures 16.87 & 16.88) although, in this case, there

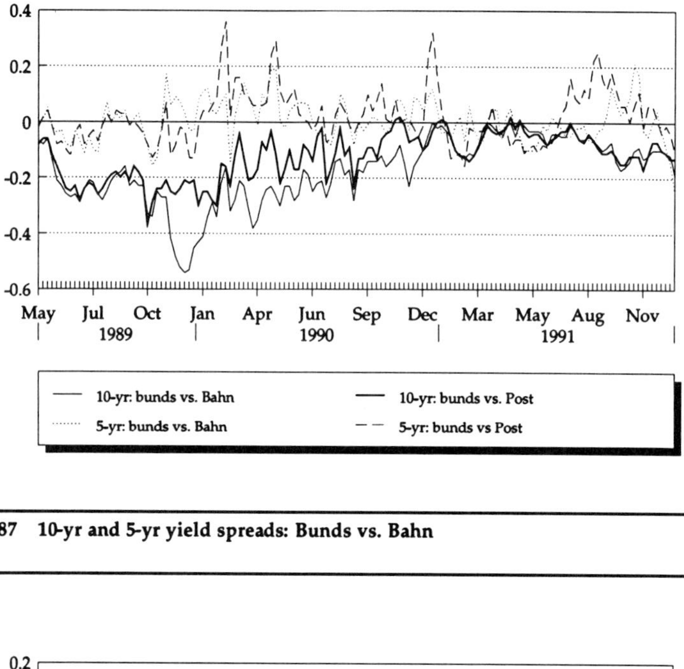

Figure 16.87 10-yr and 5-yr yield spreads: Bunds vs. Bahn

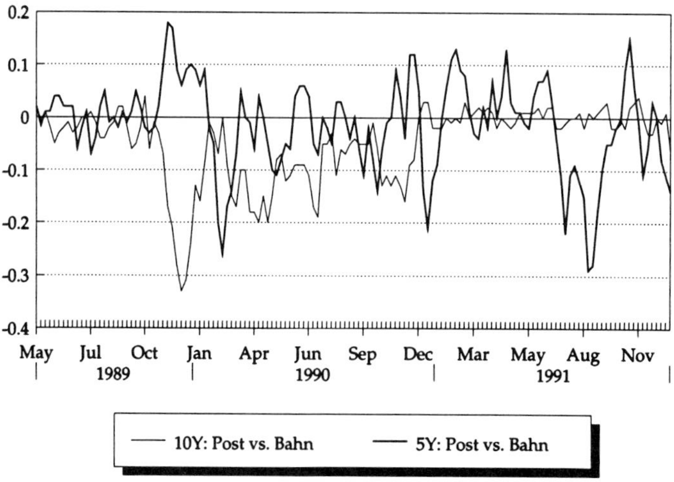

Figure 16.88 10-yr and 5-yr yield spreads: Post vs. Bahn

can be no talk of a solvency risk, since both the Federal Railways and the Federal Post Office are public sector entities.

Between 1988 and 1991, spreads between Bunds/*Bobl*s and Bahn/Post bonds hit a high of 55bp at the long-end and a low of roughly minus 2bp. For intermediate maturities, the yields of Bahn and Post bonds were a maximum of 30bp above, or below, the respective Bund/*Bobl* yields.

On average, the liquidity premium of Bahn and Post bonds over Bunds is between 10bp and 20bp.

16.18 Sources of reference

Financial data

German central bank - Bundesbank

- *Monthly Reports* of Deutsche Bundesbank
- *Statistical Supplements* to the *Monthly Reports* of Deutsche Bundesbank, especially *Series 2: Securities Statistics*

Other bank reports

- Commerzbank AG: *Rund um die Börse*, published yearly.
- DM Bonds - *Structure and Rules in Germany*, Dresdner Bank AG, Frankfurt, updated at irregular intervals.
- Special Report: *The German Bond Market*, DB-Research of Deutsche Bank Group, updated at irregular intervals.
- Commerzbank AG, Frankfurt: *Der deutsche Rentenmarkt*, Second Edition, Frankfurt 1990.

Financial press

Daily newspapers:

Boersen Zeitung
Handelsblatt
Frankfurter Allgemeine Zeitung

Publications/books

- Deutsche Bank: Deutschemark *Floating-rate Notes. Fixed Income Special Report*, October 15, 1987.
- Deutsche Bundesbank: *Its Monetary Policy Instruments and Functions*, Deutsche Bundesbank Special Series No. 7, 3rd Edition, Frankfurt 1989.
- Fage, Paul: *Yield Calculations* (CSFB Bond Manual), London 1986
- Herrmann, Armin: *Die Geldmarktgeschäfte*, Frankfurt 1980
- Köllner, Lutz: *Chronik der deutschen Währungspolitik: 1871-1991*, Frankfurt 1975
- Lipfert, Helmut: *Der Geldmarkt (mit Euro-Geldmarkt)*, Frankfurt 1975
- Lohmann, Karl: *Finanzmathematische Wertpapieranalyse*, Göttingen, 1979

- Lynch, John J.: *Standard Securities Calculation*
- Jan H. Mayle: *Securities Industry Association*, New York, 1986
- Mobbs, Stephen: *Bewertungsmethode für Euro-Dollar-Anleihen mit variabler Verzinsung*, 1987
- Wagner, Eckehard: *Effektivzins von Krediten und Wertpapieren*, Frankfurt am Main, 1988

Quote vendors and news agencies

- Reuters provide information on the German market as shown in Figure 16.89
- Telerate provide information on the German market on screen pages 1744, 3605, 3629 & 3630

Page No.		Subject
Bonds		
DBFA	Menu	Bond price quotations
DBFA	Menu	Bond price quotations
ABOG-M		*Bundesobligationen*
DRBC		Bank bond yields
BUND-G		Ministry of Finance, new issues
DGZF		Bank bond yields
ANLA	Menu	Stock exchange quotations
TUBA	Menu	Government bonds, DEM-eurobonds
DGDD		DEM-eurobonds
Futures		
Quote pages		
BDL		
BDM		
FDB		
Money market		
BIER		DEM-euro & domestic rates
FWDT		Domestic rates and DEM forwards
RMIG		German interbank rates
Bond indices		
Quote pages		
.GREX		REX Bond Index
.GREX1		REX Bond Index
.GREX5		REX Bond Index
.GREX10		REX Bond Index
Monitor page		
REX A,B		REX Bond Index

Figure 16.89 Reuters pages

IBJ

Chapter

17

The bond markets of

Greece

Joanna Makris
Citibank NA - Athens

Note: In general text, the abbreviation 'Dr' is used to denote the Greek drachma. Elsewhere, the international mnemonic 'GRD' is used.

17.1 Introduction

The Greek bond market has traditionally enjoyed the participation of local investors and has been dominated by government-issued securities. It is relatively small when compared to other European markets, but has grown rapidly over the last three years and this growth is expected to accelerate. Total bond outstandings have risen nearly threefold, from Dr 1480bn (US$ 8.2bn) in 1988, to the present level of Dr 3430bn (US$ 19.1 billion). Changes in the regulatory environment and plans for harmonization with the EC, which have led the Greek market to be characterized as 'emerging', are expected to contribute to growth.

The principal characteristics of the Greek bond markets are: short maturity ranges, limited liquidity and few types of issues.

As a result, despite the theoretical classification into four broad market types

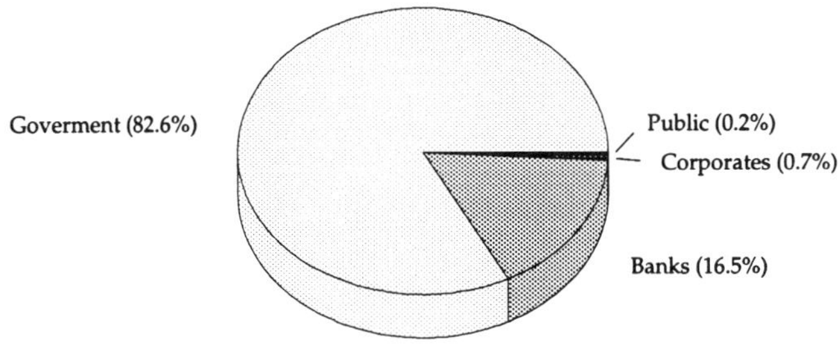

Figure 17.1 Composition of the Greek bond market

(see Section 17.3), only one of them, government, can be defined as a 'market'. The other three consist of issues which have been for special purposes and offered through private placements, as in the case of the majority of corporate bonds and public sector bonds (which are not available for active trading) and thus, most activity centres around Treasuries and government foreign currency-indexed (FCY) state bonds. However, it is expected that, as the primary market continues to grow with a greater variety of issues and extended maturities, the secondary market will gradually develop alongside, both as a result of the need to accommodate an increased number of participants and because of the adoption of European market practices.

During recent years, in spite of the considerable liberalization of the financial markets, obstacles associated with high PSBRs have restricted private sector forces. One element of deregulation, that of interest rates, drove government paper yields up to market rates, while government financing continued at preferential rates through other means, such as the obligation placed on commercial banks to invest in Treasury bills. This had the effect of pushing private sector lending rates to much higher levels, thereby limiting the competitive effects of deregulation. Furthermore, since January 1991, a 10 per cent tax has been applied on interest income earned on all bonds except government securities. By attracting investors' liquidity to finance the high PSBR, this has had a similarly restrictive effect.

Nevertheless, positive steps are being taken to strengthen competitive forces: In addition to the abolition of exchange controls on equity and fixed-income investments, the central bank, the Bank of Greece, has announced the phasing out of the obligatory investment ratio by mid-1993. It is also expected that the book-entry system will be introduced to allow for more flexible trading, higher turnover, and expansion of the secondary market.

On the broader economic front, a Medium-Term Adjustment Programme 1991-1993, was introduced in February 1991 with the aim of bringing PSBR, inflation and the current external deficit all to within manageable levels by 1993. For 1992, GDP growth is expected to reach 1.5 per cent, close to its trend rate in the 1980s, while productivity is projected to increase (reflecting restructuring), following the cyclical fall in 1991. Consumer price inflation is expected to fall from 17.8 per cent, at the end of 1991, to 15 per cent at the end of 1992, and to 12 per cent by the end of 1993. To achieve these targets the authorities intend to maintain tight credit conditions whilst, at the same time, hoping that a restoration of business confidence, a more favourable international environment and the prospective recovery in a large number of OECD countries, will together encourage a sharp rise in investment, both from expatriate Greeks as well as foreign institutions.

Greek bond market deregulation

Deregulation of the bond market (see Figure 17.2) began in late 1986, following increased interest from non-resident investors in securities listed on the Athens Stock Exchange. In order to encourage further investments, liberalization of currency exchange controls on the acquisition and liquidation of Greek securities was effected. Throughout 1987-1990, a number of new types of issues were introduced, some of which were modern reproductions of older ones issued during the 1940s and 1970s.

Initially, the government decided to borrow again in foreign currency; principally Ecu but, on two occasions, US dollars. This activity was followed by the public sector, in the form of the sole issuer, the Public Power Corporation (PPC), which borrowed in Deutschemarks. In mid-1990, a couple of corporates (already listed on the stock exchange) offered, through public subscription, the first bonds convertible into equity shares.

As of January 1991, all interest income became taxable, applying to all

1986	Exchange controls lifted for all investments in Athens Stock Exchange listed securities.
1986-7	First FCY-indexed bond, since 1940, issued by the government
1990	First FCY-indexed bond, since 1977, issued by the public sector
1991	First convertible (ex-warrant) corporate bonds issued by companies already listed on the Athens Stock Exchange
	Introduction of 10% tax on all interest earned income except for government bonds
	FCY-indexed bonds are traded at the Athens Stock Exchange on a net price basis
	Commissions on Stock Exchange traded bonds drops from a max. of 1 per cent to 0.25 per cent

Figure 17.2 History of Greek bond market deregulation

drachma deposits and fixed-income securities issued from that date onwards (with the exception of government bonds).

Most recently, a series of measures have been taken to rationalize trading practices through the stock exchange and develop a more efficient secondary market. Until 1989, bonds carrying accrued interest were traded on the floor on a gross price basis i.e., including accrued interest. This hindered the setting of realistic bond prices through natural supply and demand forces. In addition, brokerage commissions reached a high of 1 per cent, with a minimum of 0.5 per cent. The net result was that very few orders were directed from professional investors to the stock exchange brokers and this resulted in low volumes and limited secondary trading. Since, the introduction of the new measures, there have been signs of gradual improvement in floor trading and it is expected that the further modernization of existing practices will bring the market in line with other European standards.

17.2 *Economics*

Introduction

Over the past decade, expansionary fiscal policies and inappropriate government intervention in the markets have generated increased macroeconomic imbalances and microeconomic distortions which have, in turn, impeded the resumption of sustained non-inflationary growth. After the weak recovery in 1988-89, largely due to lagged effects of the 1986-87 Stabilization Programme, the growth of GDP fell to 0.1 per cent in 1990 (see Figure 17.3), compared with 2.6 per cent in the OECD area; by the end of 1991, though, it managed to reach 1.0 per cent. Consumer price inflation jumped from 14.8 per cent in 1989 to 22.8 per cent in 1990 (see Figure 17.4), while the external deficit grew to 54 per cent of GDP. It became generally recognized that the economic situation had, over two years, become untenable and that a change in policy course was urgently needed.

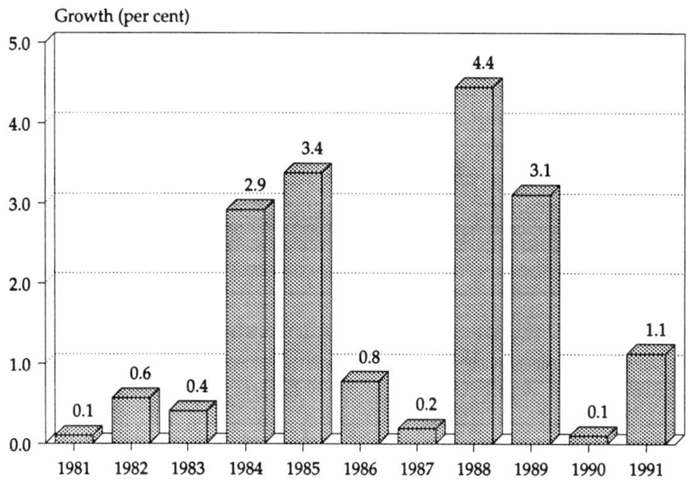

Figure 17.3 History of gross domestic product

In February 1991, a Medium-Term Adjustment Programme 1991-93, was presented by the government. It was designed to rectify the substantial internal and external imbalances in the Greek economy and to achieve greater convergence between the Greek economy and those of its European partners. It covers a wide-ranging programme of market-orientated structural reforms together with macroeconomic targets and policies. The principal objective of the Adjustment Programme was the reduction of the PSBR from 15.7 per cent of GDP in 1991, to just 3 per cent in 1993. Additionally, it targeted an inflation figure of 10 per cent by the end of 1993 (a rate not seen since 1973), down from the 18 per cent seen at the end of 1991. In the mean time, however, targets have been

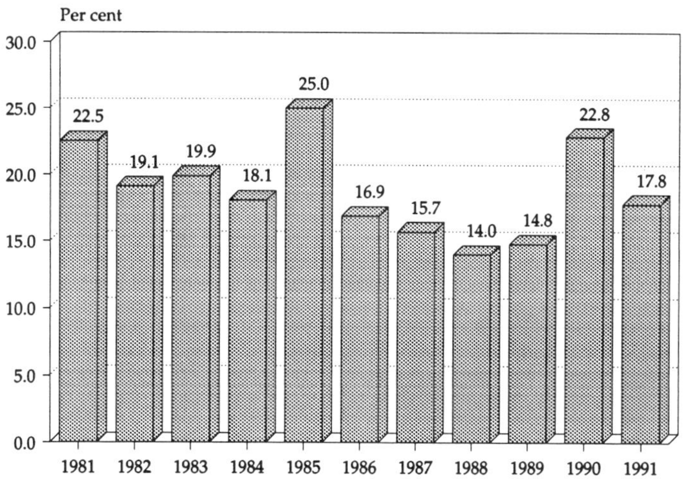

Figure 17.4 History of inflation

relaxed slightly. The 1992 budget proposal projects a PSBR of 9.1 per cent of GDP for 1992, and 7.1 per cent for the following year.

Over the period, government consumption is expected to gradually decrease, in contrast to public sector investment which is anticipated to show brisk growth due to multi-year programmes and other projects which are being prepared in collaboration with the private sector. During 1991, substantial progress has been made in both the financial area, and in the labour market.

The OECD short-term projections point to a marked improvement in underlying conditions helped by growing business confidence and a better social climate.

The positive benefits on output are not likely to take real effect until 1993, when growth potential should start to be boosted as both investment and exports gradually become the main elements of strength.

The full extent of the Adjustment Programme's dynamic effects, both short- and long-term, are difficult to predict and temporary adjustment costs may be high. However, it is widely considered essential for the Programme to be pursued vigorously, and in its entirety, to ensure that the Greek economy is put on a sustainable growth path.

Politics

Traditionally, macroeconomic policies in Greece are strongly influenced by the electoral cycle and this became even more pronounced in the 1980s. The 1986-87 Stabilization Programme, introduced after the general elections of 1985, paved the way for recovery by successfully producing a marked reduction in inflation, current external deficit and the PSBR, while at the same time stimulating a sharp rebound in profit rates.

Foreshadowing the 1989 general election, the policy stance was relaxed in 1988. Despite the steady reversal of the earlier stabilization gains, there was no change in policy until April 1990, this being due to a prolonged electoral period (three general elections between June 1989 and April 1990) and the return of weak coalition governments which were unable to pursue coherent anti-inflation programmes, the net effects being an undermining of confidence, increased pessimism of future inflation figures and the stockpiling of imported goods.

The political uncertainty ended after the general election of April 1990, as the New Democracy formed a single-party government. Since then, the macro-economic policy stance has shifted.

In the first months of 1990, there had been major concerns about the growing general crisis of confidence, the resurgence of destabilizing speculative forces and the need to boost government credibility by correcting public finances. In response to these concerns, the policy of the new administration was to tighten control over the economy. In parallel to this tightening, the new government started to introduce market-orientated institutional and structural reforms in order to reduce the microeconomic distortions which were impeding the resumption of self-sustained growth. International endorsement of these macro- and micro-economic policies came in February 1991 when the EC agreed a loan of Ecu 2.2bn, payable in two tranches - the second being subject to certain criteria set by the EC.

The performance of the Greek economy over the last decade is illustrated by Figures 17.5 to 17.12, on the following pages, which illustrate trends in foreign trade, unemployment, money supply, public sector deficit and exchange rates.

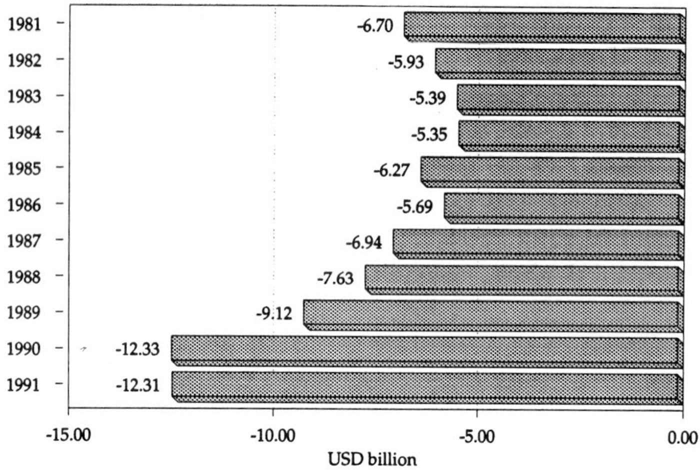

Figure 17.5 History of trade balance

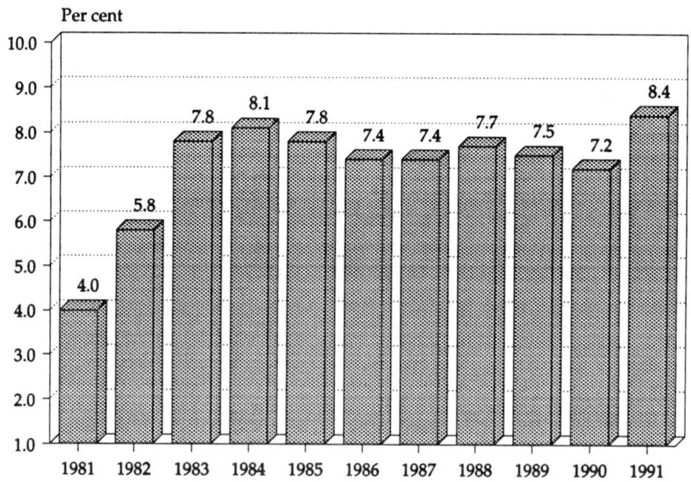

Figure 17.6 History of unemployment

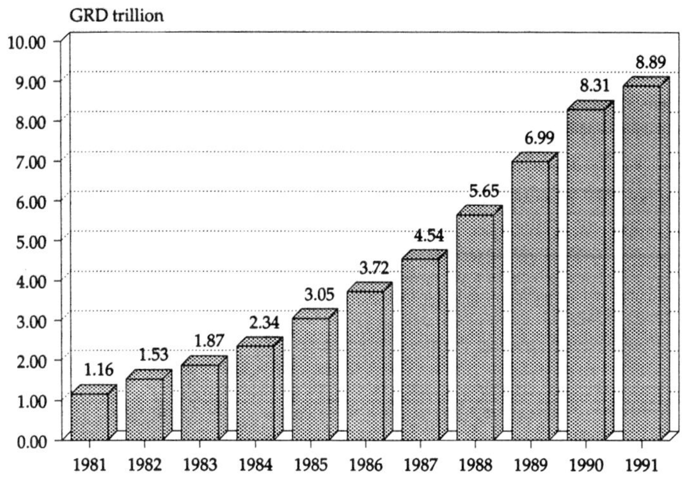

Figure 17.7 History of money supply (M3)

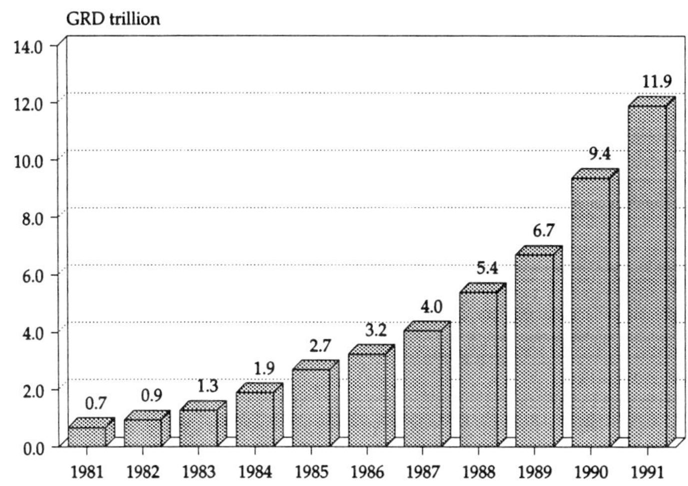

Figure 17.8 History of public sector deficit

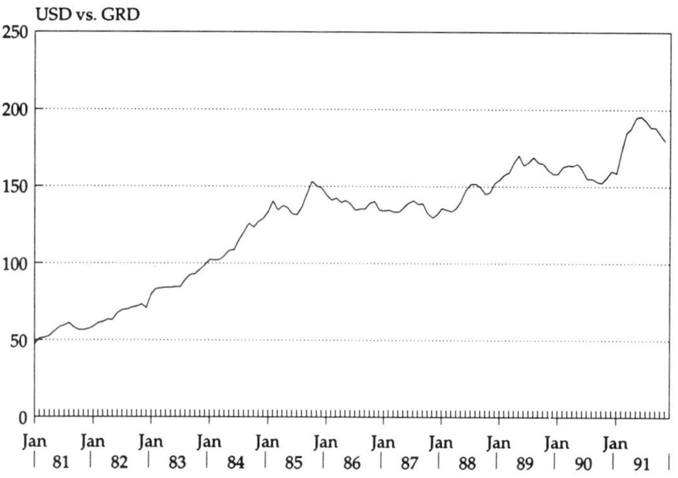

Figure 17.9 Exchange rate history: USD vs. GRD

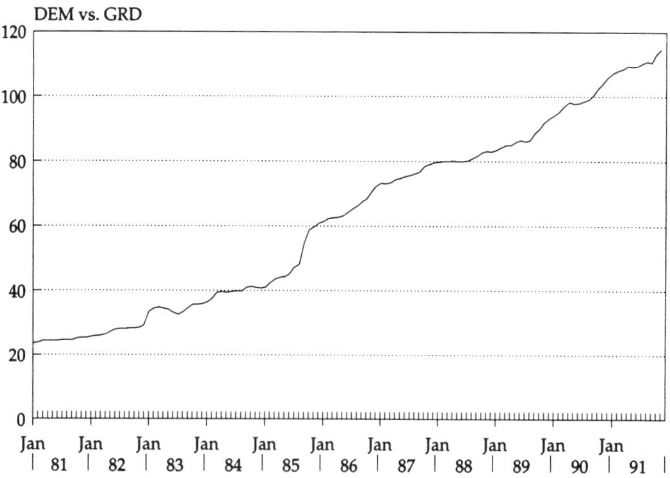

Figure 17.10 Exchange rate history: DEM vs. GRD

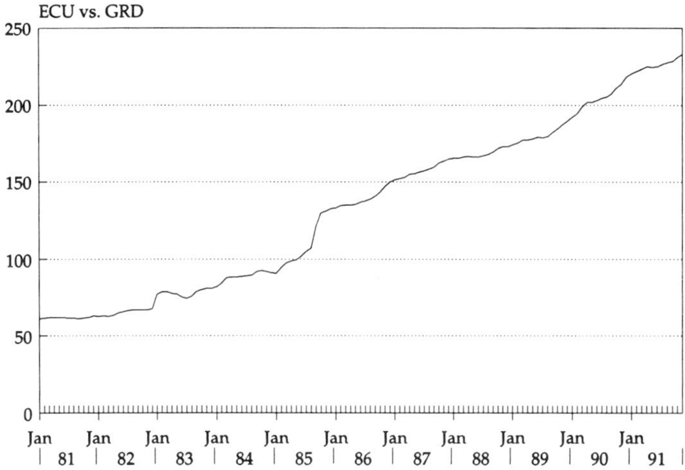

Figure 17.11 Exchange rate history: Ecu vs. GRD

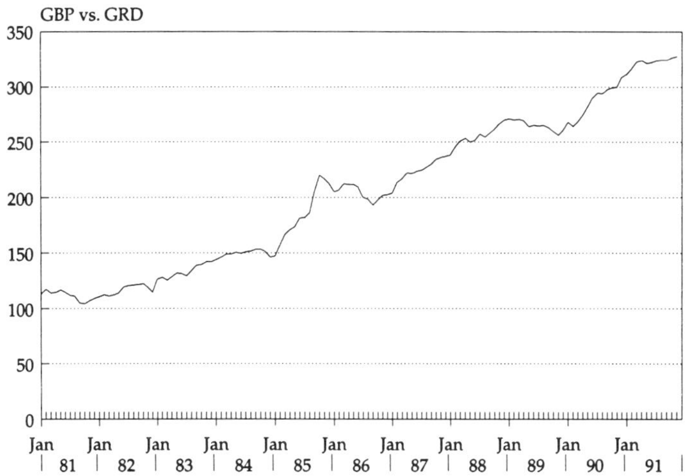

Figure 17.12 Exchange rate history: sterling vs. GRD

17.3 Market composition

Overview

The increasing borrowing needs of the Greek public sector have forced the government to enter the capital markets with aggression. As a result, in 1991, the government sector accounts for about Dr 3.7 trillion, or 86 per cent, of the total of Dr 4.3 trillion outstanding (see Figure 17.13). This contrasts with a figure in 1988 of Dr 0.9 trillion, or 63 per cent.

The remaining Dr 0.6 trillion is mainly dominated by the banking sector which represents about 13 per cent of outstanding issues. Higher interest rates, coupled with better terms on new issues, have led to a significant increase in demand for government paper by resident investors over the last three years. The corporate sector, in the mean time, managed to reach about a mere 1 per cent of total volume. This low proportion is due to two factors: firstly, issuers are still reluctant to borrow through capital markets and, secondly, corporate interest income is taxable (unlike government paper which is, at present, tax-free).

Pre-War II bond market

This part of the government sector has traditionally been illiquid, with very few transactions taking place each year - indeed, it hardly qualifies to be deemed a market. It comprises bonds which were offered in 1965, as a replacement to the originally-issued (prior to 1931) Pre-War II bonds, to which they owe their name. Initially, these bonds paid both capital and interest in a number of currencies. After their replacement, however, nearly all payments were due in sterling, with only three of them being due in US dollars. At the time of writing, outstandings are about Dr 10.4bn (nominal), accounting for a mere 0.3 per cent of the total government figure. It is expected that these bonds will be completely redeemed by the year 2000.

Post-War II bond market

The Post-War II bond market was created during the 1960s, when the Greek government re-entered the bond market, for the purposes of long-term financing, by issuing so-called 'Economic Development' bonds. Even though all government bonds subsequently issued are technically 'Post-War II', it has been commonly accepted that Treasuries and state bonds, in view of their size and importance, actually form two separate groups. Therefore, the Post-War II market

	1988	% Total	1991	% Total
GOVERNMENT				
Government bonds				
Pre-War II bonds				
Irredeemable/FCY-indexed	10.4	0.70	10.4	0.24
Post-War II bonds				
Lottery	0.9	0.06	0.8	0.02
Treasuries				
Renewable	626.0	42.31	2641.2	60.48
Bullet	237.0	16.02	311.3	7.13
State bonds				
FCY-indexed	57.0	3.85	788.2	18.05
Total	931.3	62.94	3751.9	85.91
PUBLIC SECTOR				
Public sector bonds				
Bullet	1.7	0.11	0.6	0.01
FCY-indexed bonds	6.3	0.43	5.3	0.12
Total	8.0	0.54	5.9	0.14
CORPORATE SECTOR				
Corporate bonds				
Floating	10.0	0.68	20.7	0.47
Convertible	-	-	3.0	0.07
Zero-coupon	0.4	0.03	1.9	0.04
Total	10.4	0.70	25.6	0.59
BANK SECTOR				
Bank bonds				
Renewable	530.0	35.82	436.0	9.98
Bullet	-	-	62.0	1.42
Zero-coupon	-	-	82.0	1.88
Total	530.0	35.82	580.0	13.28
MORTGAGE BONDS	-	-	4.0	0.09
GRAND TOTAL	1479.7	100.00	4367.4	100.00

Figure 17.13 Composition of the Greek market [GRD billion nominal]

effectively consists of both the 'Unified' and 'Economic Development' bonds. The Unified bond, bearing 2.5 per cent interest, was issued in tranches through the gradual replacement of all those drachma bonds issued prior to 1940. It became listed in the Athens Stock Exchange in 1962. The Economic Development bonds were issued between 1960 and 1970, with 20-year maturities. The majority of these bonds have been held in bank portfolios as a means of satisfying their reserve requirements.

Treasury bill/note market

Treasuries not only form the largest part of the whole bond market (86 per cent), but also dominate the government sector itself, accounting for some 80 per cent of its total. Over the last three years, the Treasury market has grown significantly, from Dr 863bn in 1988 to about Dr 3 trillion in 1991, thereby providing the government with a major source of funding. They are both issued and managed by the central bank (the Bank of Greece) on behalf of the government (Ministry of Finance) for the purposes of covering the expenses of productive public investments (under Law 3795/1957). Treasury bills were first introduced to the public in June 1985 - prior to that date they could only be purchased by banks for reserve-requirement purposes. They are issued at a discount regularly at each month-end and represent the very short end of the yield curve, with maturities of 3, 6, and 12 months. Treasury notes, on the other hand, have only recently entered the market, in July 1988. Issues prior to December 1990 carried limited maturities of between 2 and 3 years, while their coupons were fixed in the range from 20 per cent to 24.5 per cent. However, there was no issuance between that date and January 1992, when they reappeared - again with limited maturities, but this time as floaters (FRNs).

State bond market

Despite the fact that most government issues, such as Treasuries, are effectively state bonds, it has actually been common practice to restrict this term to one specific class, namely foreign currency-indexed (FCY) issues. These bonds, which were first offered in November 1986, linked to the Ecu, are issued and managed by the Bank of Greece under Law 3745/57, just as for Treasuries. The market has subsequently grown spectacularly - from Dr 57bn in 1988, to about Dr 788bn in 1991 (i.e. by a factor of 14). The majority of issues are indexed to the Ecu, with just two being tied to the US dollar (in June 1990 and July 1991). FCY-indexed bonds can be purchased both by domestic and foreign investors. Those domestic investors who have purchased them by paying in drachma have enjoyed full currency-protection, though not always at competitive yields when compared to other high-yielding drachma investments. Foreign investment, which is dependent on the spreads against the Ecu and US dollar in the euromarket, has been attracted by most issues. One issue which was particularly heavily-subscribed was the Ecu January 1990-91 12 per cent, which attained a figure of some Dr 180bn, of which about 65 per cent was purchased by foreign investors. FCY-indexed bonds are usually issued with maturities ranging from 1 to 4 years, and therefore represent the medium-term segment of the government market. They have been offered at irregular intervals, and have traditionally carried fixed-rate coupons. It is expected that most new issues in 1992 will be in the form of FRNs.

Public sector bond market

The public sector bond market is totally dominated by one issuer, the Public Power Corporation (PPC), which is the only electricity company in Greece. In the past, the PPC has issued bonds to fund various programmes, such as the full distribution of electricity to the whole of the country. PPC bonds have been issued since 1968 and reached total a total outstanding figure of Dr 8bn in 1988. However, between 1972 and 1986, the PPC placed no issues at all, but this hiatus was broken in 1987, when it offered a seven-year FCY-indexed bond, linked to the Deutschemark. Between 1988 and 1991, total outstandings declined by 25 per cent, this being due both to the lack of fresh issuance and the redemption of maturing issues.

Corporate market

The corporate bond market is a fairly new market. Historically, corporates have funded their needs for working capital through the banking system, at rates which have discouraged the growth of alternative sources. It is only recently that a small number of corporates have entered the capital markets by issuing corporate bonds.

The first bonds were structured during 1988 and accounted for Dr 10.4bn, a mere 1 per cent of total bond outstandings in Greece. The majority of corporate bonds are floaters (FRNs) with maturities ranging from 3 to 7 years. By comparison to other European markets, the Greek corporate sector has remained in a state of infancy. Furthermore, it is still an indirect substitute for bank loans, since most corporates have privately placed their bonds with banks.

Bank bond market

This market is the second largest within the Greek bond market, representing about 13 per cent of total outstandings. Its growth, however, has remained stagnant over the last two years. This can be attributed to the introduction of interest income tax which, since January 1991 when the tax became applicable, has discouraged continued investment in bank bonds. Indeed, in 1991, only Dr 150bn was offered, against a figure of Dr 388bn in 1990. Despite limited issuance activity, however, outstandings have not declined. This is due to the special characteristic of the majority of bank bonds, known as 'renewable' bonds, which carry the facility of being able to have their life extended for a series of years beyond their maturity date.

Those bank bonds issued to date have come from state-owned investment banks, after special approval from both the Monetary Committee and the Capital Markets Committee. Bank bonds are specifically issued to support industrial development and modernization, and aimed at the overall economic growth of the country (Law 3746/1957). They were initially offered in 1975, since when they have been regularly issued at the end of each month. They carry fixed-coupons and, generally, 1-year maturities (although there have been occasional issues with 2- and 3-year maturities).

In December 1990, the Hellenic Investment Development Bank (HIDB) offered the first zero-coupon bond; however, there have been no zeros issued since January 1991.

Mortgage bond market

This market is practically non-existent since, until very recently, it has comprised just one bond. In February 1989, the state-owned National Mortgage Bank (NMB) issued the first mortgage bond (Dr 4bn 14% NMB 1989-97). Under the terms and conditions of this bond, holders can present their bonds as collateral to NMB and claim a mortgage loan for up to three times their nominal value, at fixed-rate of 17.5 per cent.

Composition of market by maturity

Government bond market

Most of the maturities found in the government bond market lie in the range between three months (Treasury bills) and three years (Treasury notes and foreign currency-indexed bonds). About 80 per cent can be found in the one-year area. There is a significant lack of issuance in the medium- to long-term (see Figure 17.14), while attempts to issue paper for 20- to 50-year ranges have taken place only in the pre-war period, between 1880 and 1931.

Since 1985, the government has been borrowing for shorter dates by offering, on a monthly basis, 3-, 6-, and 12-month Treasury bills. Two-year and three-year Treasury notes were introduced in November 1987 but, since the end of 1990, there have been no further issues. In the mean time, despite foreign currency bond offerings with one- to four-year ranges, investor appetite favoured 1-year paper rather than the longer alternatives. In the case of local investors, this can be attributed to the relative attraction of high-yielding drachma bonds in a climate

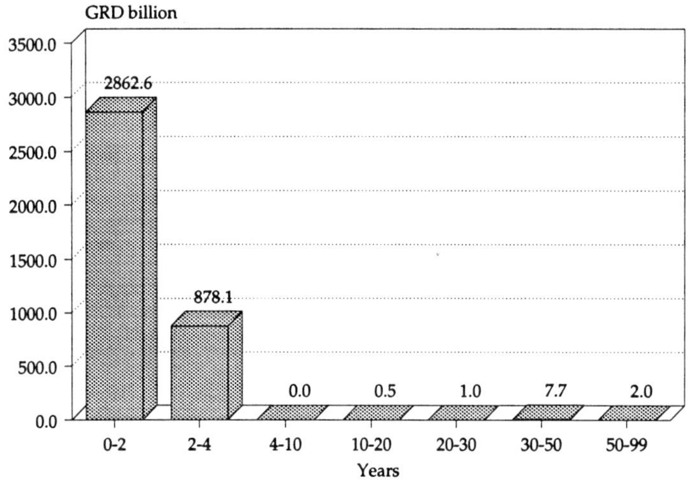

Figure 17.14 Maturity structure of the government bond market

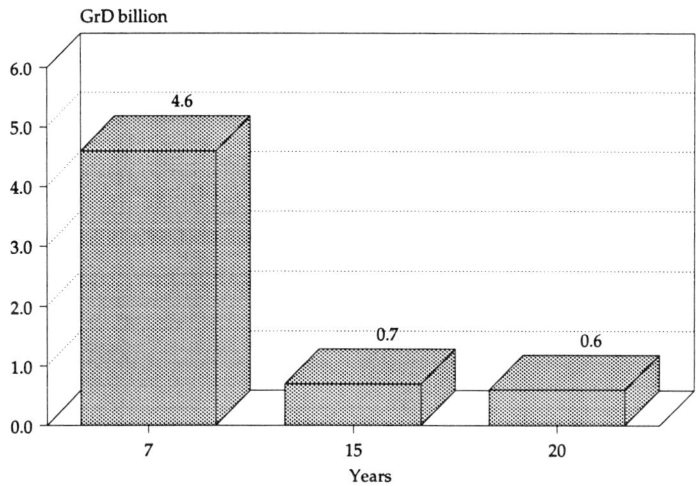

Figure 17.15 Maturity structure of the public sector bond market

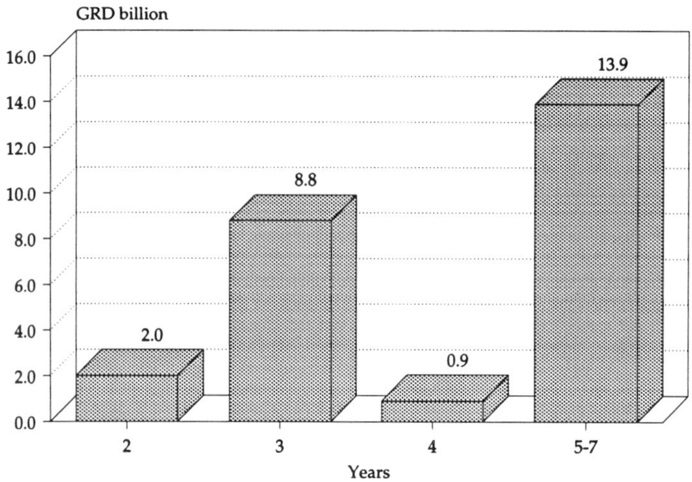

Figure 17.16 Maturity structure of the corporate bond market

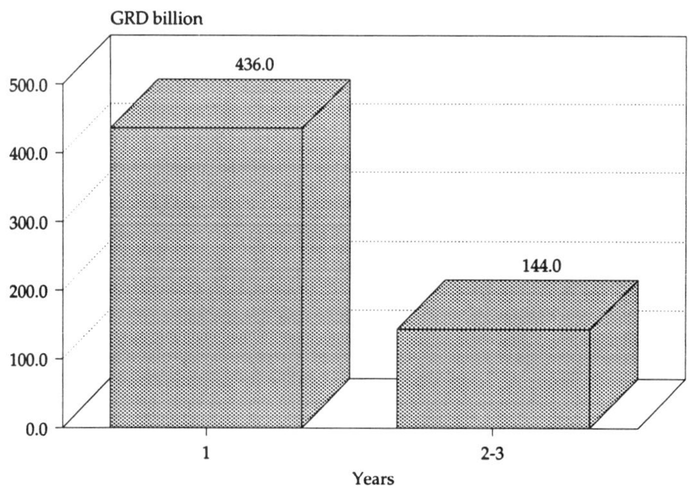

Figure 17.17 Maturity structure of the bank bond market

of uncertainty over the duration of the currency's weakness. Foreign investors, on the other hand, seemed reluctant to accept even medium-term Greek credit exposure during the fragile pre-election period between late-1989 and early-1990.

Public sector bond market

The public sector bond market is very small - containing just one issuer, the Public Power Corporation, which has been borrowing for medium-term periods ranging from 7 to 20 years. The shortest period, of seven years, represents a recent 1987 issue indexed to the Deutschemark. The 15- and 20-year ranges belong to 1970s issues (see Figure 17.15).

Corporate bond market

Corporate bonds are a relatively recent addition to the market. They are dominated by the debt-range of five to seven years, which accounts for approximately 55 per cent of the total sector outstandings (see Figure 17.16). The type of issue to be found in this area is mainly the FRN; these are primarily bought by commercial banks and represent a substitute for equivalent direct bank loans to the corporate sector. The remaining 35 per cent accounts for 3-year issues, mainly Citileasing FRNs, and 4-year issues which are mostly zero-coupon bonds. Finally, convertibles have usually been 4- to 6-year offerings.

Bank bond market

Since they are offered by state-owned banks, bank bond ranges (see Figure 17.17) usually follow the government bond maturity structure. Traditionally, bank bonds have been issued with one-year ranges although, until recently (1989), Hellenic Investment Development Bank (HIDB) offered 2- and 3-year paper.

Composition of market by coupon structure

Government bond market

The coupon structure of the government bond market (see Figure 17.18), can be divided into two distinct sections, one comprising low-coupon foreign currency-linked bonds and the other, high-coupon drachma bonds.

Only about 0.5 per cent of the total outstandings are to be found in the 2 to 6 per cent coupon area, and these are Pre-War II bonds (from 1880). The medium-coupon area of 9 to 11 per cent is closer to European standards and reflects Ecu coupons paid by the government for indexed bonds issued from 1986 onwards.

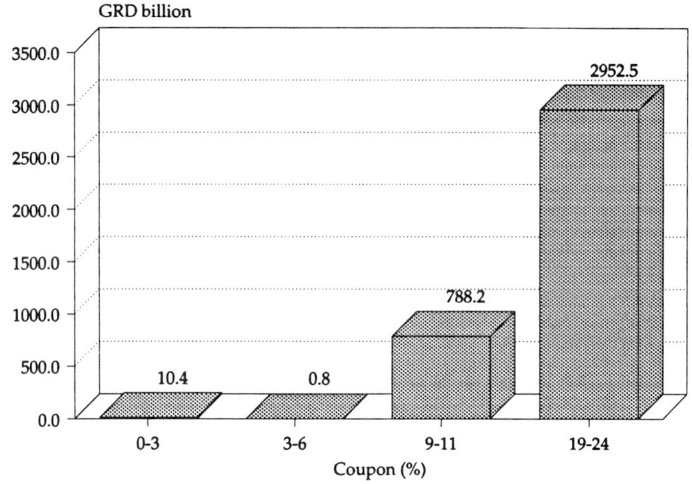

Figure 17.18 Coupon structure of the government bond market

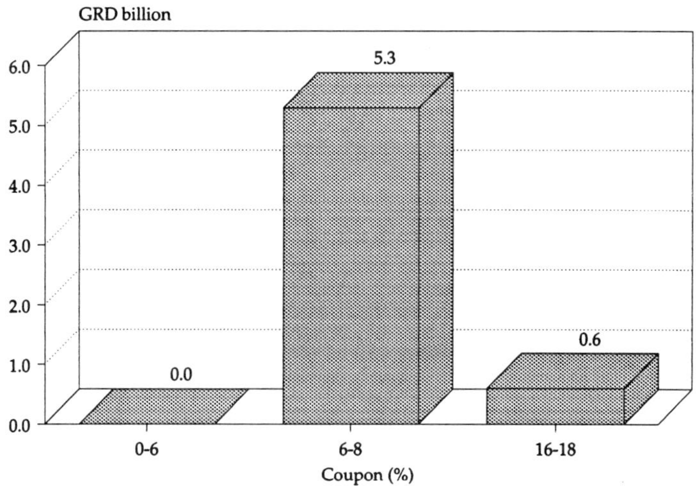

Figure 17.19 Coupon structure of the public sector bond market

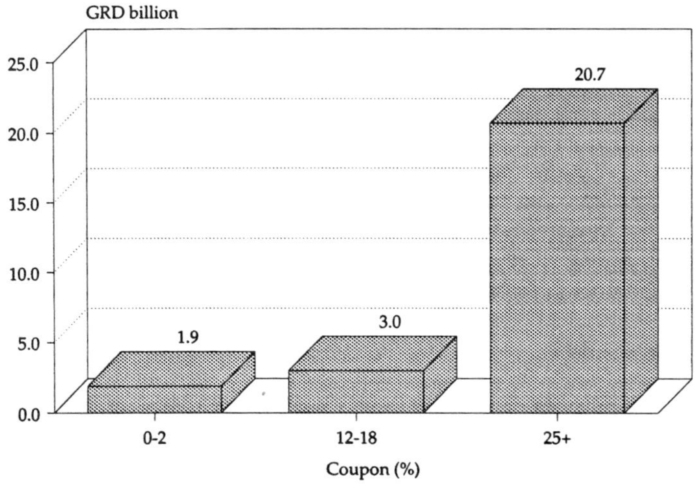

Figure 17.20 Coupon structure of the corporate bond market

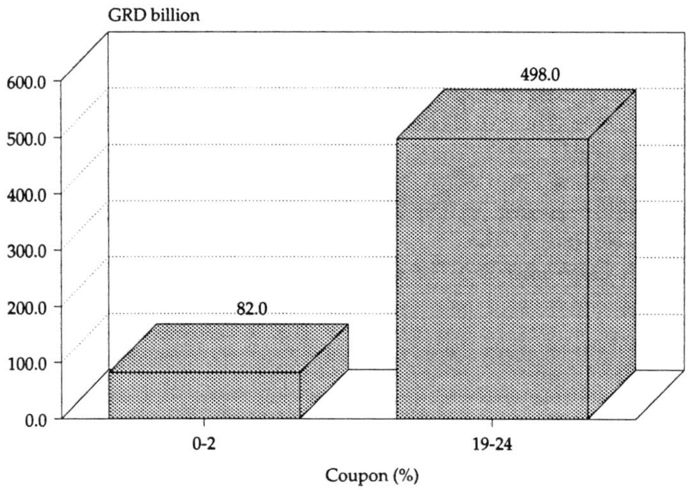

Figure 17.21 Coupon structure of the bank bond market

These account for 21 per cent of the government sector outstandings. The remaining 78.5 per cent belongs to drachma-denominated bonds (Treasury bills and notes) which have been issued since 1985. Fixed by the government, they reflect the yield trend towards market rates and, in recent years, have provided a major source of funding for the PSBR.

Public sector bond market

The public sector market (see Figure 17.19), again represented by the PPC, can also be divided into two coupon segments, namely foreign currency and drachma. In the former are 7 and 8 per cent coupons representing the 1977 and 1987 issues (indexed to the US dollar and Deutschemark, respectively) which account for 91.5 per cent of the total outstandings in the public sector.

Corporate bond market

About 81 per cent of the corporate sector total outstandings (see Figure 17.20) are floating-rate bonds, which have been issued since 1988 with coupons usually based on each bank's working capital loans base rate. To date, these coupons have ranged from 23 to 27 per cent dependent upon factors relating to both the individual corporate and its respective bank. Only 7.5 per cent are zero-coupon corporate bonds, while convertibles offer coupons from 12 to 18 per cent.

Bank bond market

The majority of bank bonds are fixed-coupon issues which are paid annually. Their coupon structure, like their maturity structure, closely follows that of the government bond market structure ranging, in recent years, from 19 to 24 per cent (see Figure 17.21).

Yields, however, do not align with the government pattern because bank bond returns differ, owing to the effect of the introduction of interest-earned income tax (see Section 17.12).

Zero-coupon bonds account for about 14 per cent of total bank bond outstandings.

17.4 Types of security

Government bond market

Irredeemable / FCY-indexed bonds

At present there are about Dr 10.4bn bonds outstanding and they fall into two categories:

- the so-called 'Unified bond'
- all the Pre-War II issues

The Unified bond was issued in 1962. It has no final maturity, but is annually redeemed through the stock exchange at a 3 per cent rate of the nominal value, an amount which is included in each year's government budget. It is expected that this bond will be fully redeemed by the year 2000 (43 years from issue). It carries a coupon of 2.5 per cent and also has the characteristics of a lottery bond.

All the Pre-War II bonds are expected to be redeemed by 2006. Redemption rates range from 0.5 to 3 per cent of their nominal value and they pay a semi-annual coupon. These are also lottery bonds and indexed to FCY.

The bonds mentioned above are not recommended for any type of investment, not even for the lottery, as returns have been very low (around 4 to 5 per cent for 1974-84), and are expected to remain at similar levels.

Lottery bonds

These bonds, very few of which are now outstanding, were issued during the 1960s and 1970s with 20-year ranges. Lottery bonds usually pay annual interest. Additionally, each bond automatically enters a yearly lottery. The winning bonds are redeemed at premium of 10 per cent, for the first ten years, and at 15 per cent for the remaining ten years of their nominal value. All Economic Development bonds are lottery bonds.

Renewable bonds

The majority of government bonds are renewable bonds, Treasury bills, which account for about 70 per cent of total government bond outstandings. They carry a special feature for the investor in that, upon maturity, the holder can roll-over the bond for a period equal to the initial range, for one more period at the prevailing coupon, without having to redeem the old bond and purchase a new issue.

Bullet bonds

About Dr 300bn represents bullet Treasuries (Treasury notes) which are issued with a fixed maturity date, a format unchanged since they were first launched. All FCY-indexed state bonds issued since 1986, are bullets.

FCY-indexed bonds

These bonds were issued in response to the need to hedge drachma holdings in the light of the weakness of the currency, and possible devaluation. To date, these bonds (which account for 21 per cent of government outstandings) have all been indexed to the Ecu, with the exception of two issues which have been indexed to the US dollar.

The characteristic of indexation to a foreign currency offers the advantage of receiving both interest payments and final redemption value in that foreign currency. This sector has been rather attractive to those drachma investors who have feared the decline of the drachma would outweigh the benefits which

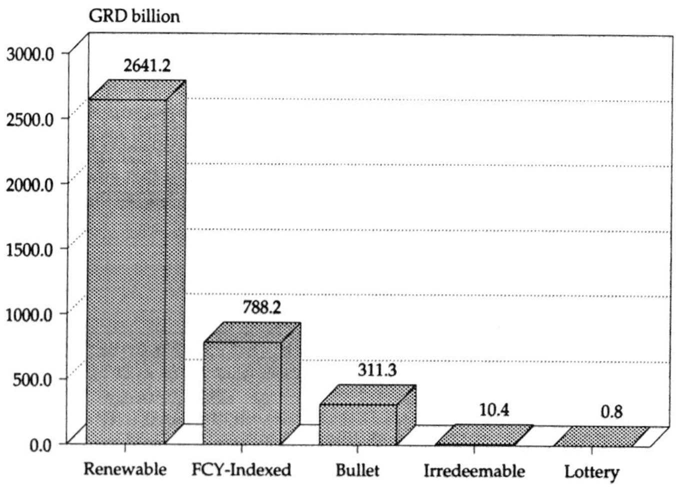

Figure 17.22 Types of issue in the government bond market

could be derived from alternative high-yielding drachma instruments. It has also been of great interest to foreign investors as these bonds can be treated wholly as Ecu eurobonds. Foreign currency investors pay in Ecu upon purchase and also receive all future payments in Ecu, thereby removing any exposure to the drachma throughout the life of the bond.

Public sector bonds

Public sector bonds are classified by two types, namely foreign currency-indexed (FCY) bonds, and bullet bonds (see Figure 17.23). Nevertheless, despite this difference in classification, all public sector bonds (except the PPC Deutschemark issue) share a common characteristic in that they are also lottery bonds, redeemed by lot at par.

FCY-indexed bonds

There are two such bonds, both issued by the PPC (Dr 3bn 8% 1977-92 and Dr 15bn 7% 1987-94), which are indexed to the US dollar and the Deutschemark, respectively. The latter is the only public sector bond which is not a lottery bond and pays at par upon maturity.

Bullet bonds

Only one bond is now outstanding as a bullet bond, the Dr 1.8bn PPC 7.5% 1972-92.

Corporate bond market

Floating-rate notes (FRNs)

The majority of corporate bonds are floating-rate notes (see Figure 17.24), based on a spread against working capital base rate (WCBR). A small number of corporate FRNs are priced on a spread against the 3-month Treasury bill. FRNs first appeared in 1988 reaching a total, that year, of Dr 10bn. Since then, they have almost doubled in volume and are becoming an interesting source of funding for well-known corporates. Interest payments are either annual or semi-annual, while some of them offer put options.

Convertible bonds

Only three corporate bond issues are convertible at present. Convertibility is into equity shares and the issuers are just two companies (Shelman and Petzetakis), and one bank (National Housing Bank) - all listed on the Athens

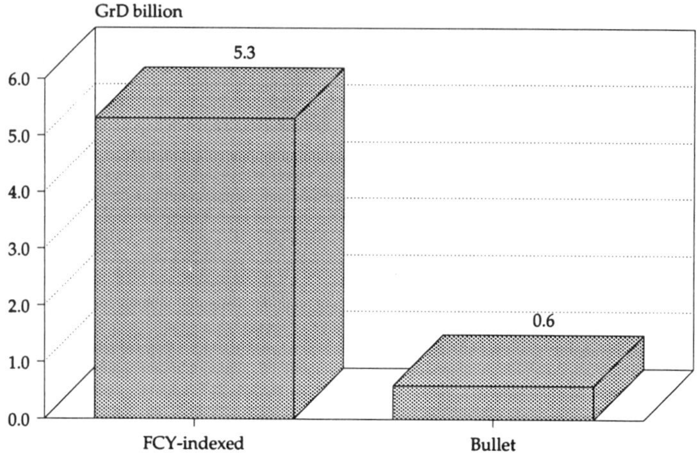

Figure 17.23 Types of issue in the public sector bond market

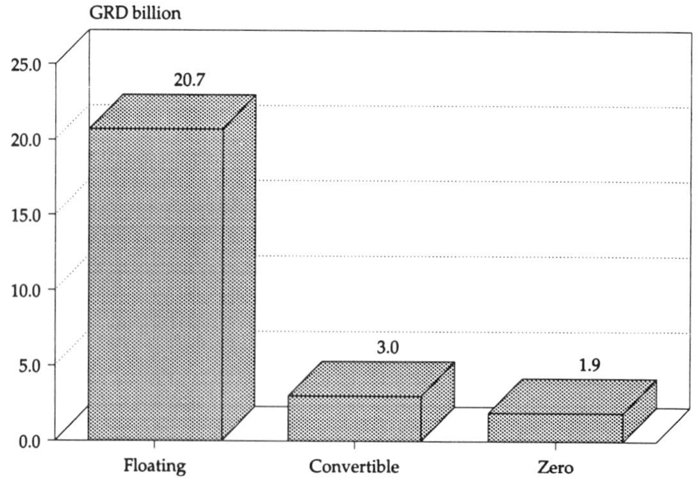

Figure 17.24 Types of issue in the corporate bond market

Stock Exchange. They have been only recently introduced to the market (since the second half of 1990) and carry maturity ranges of between 4 and 6 years (Dr 1bn Shelman 14% 1990-96, Dr 1.2bn Petzetakis 12% 1990-95 and Dr 0.8bn National Housing Bank 18.5% 1990-94).

Zero-coupon bonds

Zero-coupon bonds first appeared in 1988, as leasing company bonds offered by Citileasing, a Citibank subsidiary (Dr 0.4bn Citileasing 1988-91). Since then, they have only re-appeared (at the beginning of 1990) in the form of corporate bonds, directly placed with banks as lower cost funding alternatives.

Bank bond market

The bank bond market (see Figure 17.25) is dominated by state-owned investment banks. To date, no paper has been offered by private banks.

Annual renewable notes (ARNs)

ARNs are one-year notes, issued at the end of each month. They are renewable, upon maturity, for a period equal to their initial range, i.e. annually, for up to five years final maturity at the prevailing coupon.

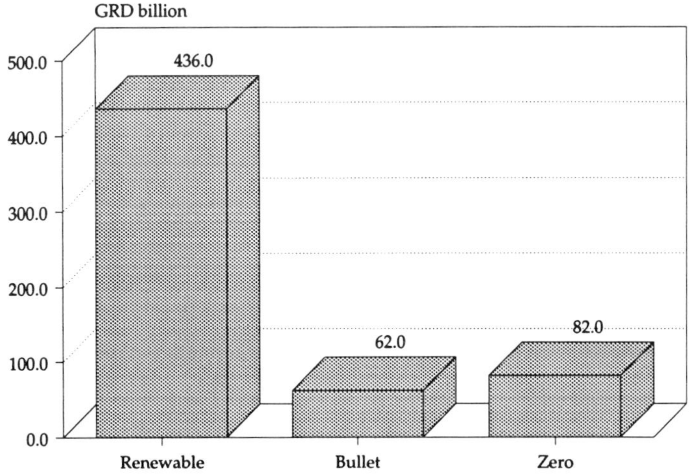

Figure 17.25 Types of issue in the bank bond market

Zero-coupon bonds

The first zero-coupon bonds were issued by the Hellenic Bank of Industrial Development (HBID) in December 1989 (Dr 8.4bn HBID 1989-92, also called the '1992' bond) followed, in March 1990, by Dr 5.9bn HBID 1990-1993. From March 1990, HBID offered 3-year zero-coupons on the 15th of each month, although the issuance of such bonds has ceased since January 1991.

Bullet bonds

These bonds, which have been offered monthly by HBID, bear fixed-coupons and lives of 2 and 3 years.

17.5 Issuers

Public sector bonds

The public sector bond market features only one corporation, the Public Power Corporation (PPC) which is a wholly state-owned electricity company.

Corporate bond market

Leasing companies

With about 40 per cent of the sector's outstandings, the corporate bond market (see Figures 17.26 & 17.27) is dominated by a single leasing company, namely Citileasing, a Citibank subsidiary. Citileasing has repeatedly entered the market since 1988, with different types of issues such as zero-coupons, straights, and FRNs.

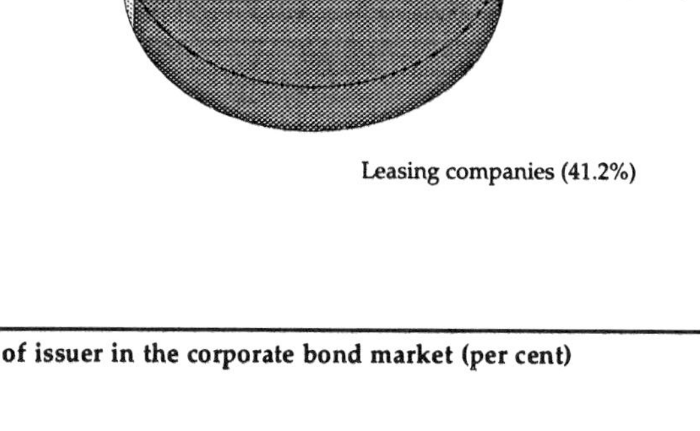

Figure 17.26 Types of issuer in the corporate bond market (per cent)

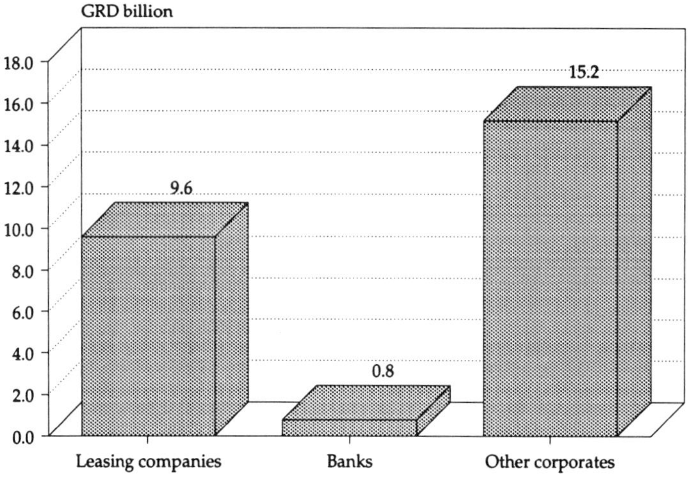

Figure 17.27 Types of issuer in the corporate bond market (volume)

Banks

At present, there is only one issue, that being the fixed-coupon National Housing Bank 1990/94. The bank is listed on the Athens Stock Exchange.

Other corporates

Other issuers in the corporate sector are varied. There are issues, for example, from oil companies (Mobil and Shell), chemical companies (Petzetakis 1990/1995) and wood companies (Shelman 1990/1996), as well as other renowned corporates such as Pirelli, Chalcor and Sidenor.

Bank bond market

Both types of issuer, investment banks and mortgage banks (see Figure 17.28), are state-controlled and they issue bonds in accordance with the decisions of the Capital Markets Committee and Monetary Committee. Issues are dependent on a bank's needs at the time, and are limited to amounts set by the Monetary Committee.

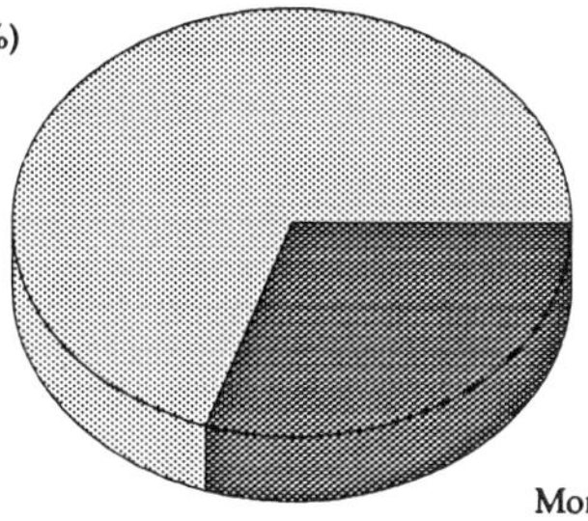

Figure 17.28 Types of issuer in the bank bond market

Investment banks

This group comprises the Hellenic Bank of Industrial Development (HBID), the National Investment Bank of Industrial Development (NIBID), and the Investment Bank.

Mortgage banks

This group comprises the National Mortgage Bank (NMB) and National Housing Bank (NHB). NMB has also issued mortgage bonds.

17.7 *Methods of issuance*

The Greek bond market features few different methods of issuance. As noted earlier, the majority of issues are in the government sector (which still controls a large number of activities in the financial markets) and the most common method is 'offer for sale by tender'. Other issuers offer their bonds through private placements.

Government bond market

Offer for sale by tender - public subscription

In Greece, unlike in other European countries, government securities are not offered in an auction system. Both Treasuries (bills/notes) and foreign currency-indexed bonds are issued through the offer for sale method, at a fixed-price. Treasury bills are regularly offered on the last calendar day of each month by the Bank of Greece, for the account of the Ministry of Economy. The price is fixed by the joint decision of the Ministry of Finance and the Bank of Greece and the offer is open to any amount. The subscription period lasts for five calendar days (issue-date inclusive), within which one can apply for subscription to the requested amount at the pre-determined price. The issue amount is announced after the subscription period, when all purchases have been completed. Purchases after the issue date, within the subscription period, are charged accrued interest.

Treasury bills are offered through commercial banks and brokers registered at the Athens Stock Exchange. Upon subscription, the investor receives a receipt confirming the purchase as valid proof of ownership. Physical delivery of the paper takes place within about one month although, in the past, it has taken more than three months for the issuer to deliver the bonds on very high volume issues, this being due to the physical nature of the Treasury bills. Treasury notes and foreign currency-indexed bonds are similarly issued, although not on the same regular basis as bills.

Corporate bond market

Corporate bonds issued to date have been offered through private placements. Dependent upon the type of bond, they have been placed either through rights offerings, or directly.

Private placement - rights offerings

This method has been used by all convertible bond issuers to date, i.e. Shelman, Petzetakis and the National Housing Bank. After determination of the terms and conditions of the loan in the prospectus and the granting of approval from the Capital Markets Committee, bonds are privately placed with shareholders during the subscription period, by the exercise of their rights. Such rights offer the shareholder the right to subscribe to the bond issue at a certain share/bond ratio. For example, Shelman shareholders could exercise their right to buy one bond for every 160 shares. In the case of Petzetakis, besides the private placement through rights offering, bonds have also been offered to the public during the same subscription period. Priority, however, is given to the existing shareholders, and only if the offering has not been fully subscribed by them, are bonds then allocated to the public. Rights are physically represented by a designated coupon attached to the body of the stock certificate and are tradeable through the stock exchange during the subscription period.

Direct private placement

The majority of corporate FRNs are usually privately placed. Corporate issuers usually employ a bank to structure the issue and, in most cases, they place the issue directly with the same bank. In effect, these bonds serve as a replacement for traditional working capital loans. In certain instances, banks may not wish to place bonds themselves, in which case they normally agree to structure and underwrite issues, before placing them with other banks.

Bank bond market

Offer for sale by tender - public subscription

Bank bonds (ARNs) are usually offered on the last calendar day of each month, with both price and issue amount being fixed. ARNs are offered through the issuing bank network, commercial banks, and Athens Stock Exchange brokers. Bank bonds are physically delivered immediately upon purchase.

17.8 *New issue volumes*

Government drachma bond market

During the subscription period, Treasuries are offered for any amount, i.e. the issues are 'open', and therefore the issuance figure is clearly determined by investor demand. A study of the overall drachma government bond market in recent years, shows that, with the exception of 1989, demand has been steadily growing (see Figure 17.29). During 1989, a large volume of new FCY-indexed government paper was issued and, in a period of repeated elections and fears for currency devaluation, these issues attracted most of the free liquidity.

During 1991, however, despite concerns about the weakness of the drachma, the government has managed to attract a near twofold increase in investor income over 1990, and threefold over 1989. Hopes of a lower inflation rate, and therefore a possible fall in interest rates, together with the tax-free interest income received, has attracted investors to one-year Treasury bills which have shown a record issuance of Dr 2809bn in 1991, against a figure of Dr 1441bn in 1990 (see Figure 17.30).

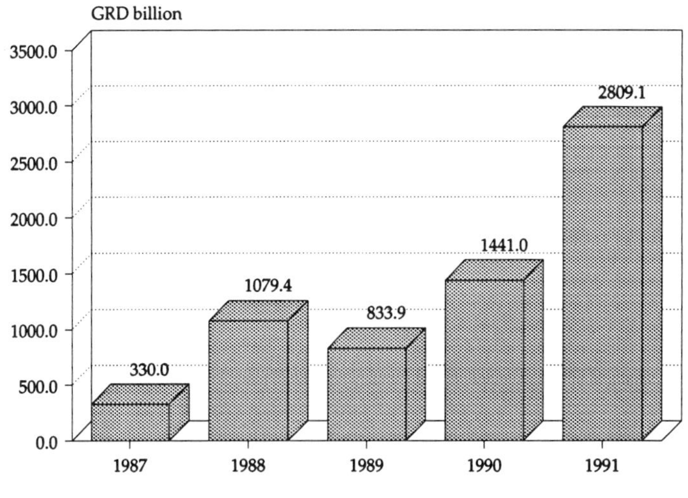

Figure 17.29 New issuance volume in the government drachma bond market, 1987-91

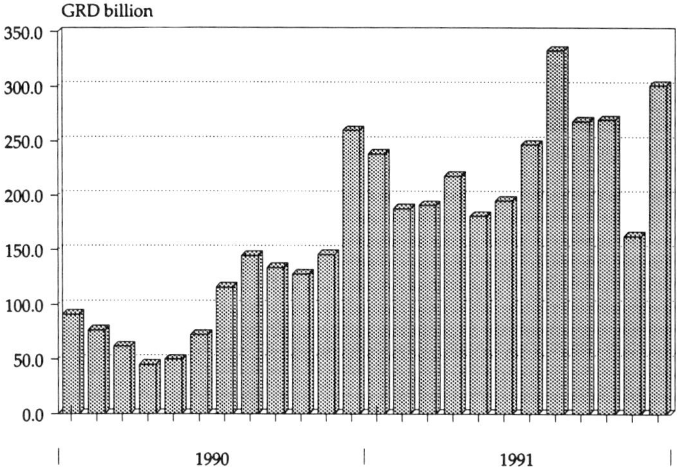

Figure 17.30 New issuance volume in the Treasury bill market, 1990-91

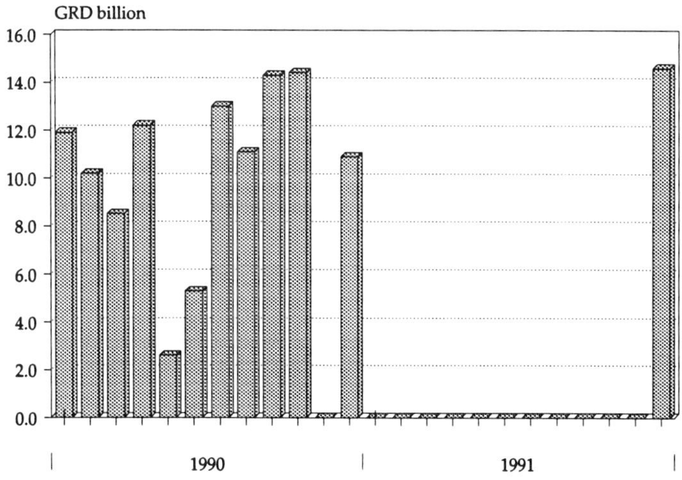

Figure 17.31 New issuance volume in the Treasury note market, 1990-91

Government FCY bond market

Foreign currency-indexed bonds (see Figures 17.32 & 17.33) were first issued in 1986. Since then, growing interest for these types of issues has attracted both resident and non-resident investors. As noted earlier, short-term issues during periods of domestic uncertainty have always attracted local interest and high volumes, while high-yield issues, which offer competitive spreads over similar eurobond issues, have attracted significant foreign investments.

One of the most successful issues was the 12% January 1990/1991, which reached a record Dr 182bn, about 40 per cent of the year's total new issuance amount. Since then, notable amounts have been issued reflecting the continuing requirement of domestic investors to hedge drachma holdings and the growing interest of foreign investors in the competitive yields to be found in emerging markets.

Public sector bond market

With only one issue, the 1987/1994 Dr 4.6bn Deutschemark-indexed bond brought by PPC, this sector has become stagnant over the last four years (see Figure 17.34).

Corporate bond market

In the corporate bond market, issuance activity first began in 1988 (see Figure 17.35), when the first cheaper sources for corporate funding appeared. Since then, the market has witnessed an important increase in activity in the area of medium-term bonds.

Bank bond market

As previously noted, bank bonds have always been issued subject to strict Monetary Committee conditions. It is important to note, however, that until recently, banks could not purchase such bonds for their own account. Furthermore, foreign investors can only purchase such bonds if they are individuals (Monetary Committee Decision No. 151/22.11.76). In the case of corporate investors, they are only allowed to purchase bonds with a minimum initial maturity of 2 years (Monetary Committee Decision No. 479/22.07.91).

Nevertheless, despite these restrictions, bank bond issuance grew steadily through 1990 (see Figure 17.36), reflecting the continued increase in the borrowing requirements of state-owned banks. However, a significant decline was witnessed during 1991, this being clearly attributable to the introduction of interest income tax, which was extended to cover bank bonds in January of that year. As a result, government paper bearing the same nominal coupon, at that time, as bank bonds, offered the competitive advantage of higher yields after tax.

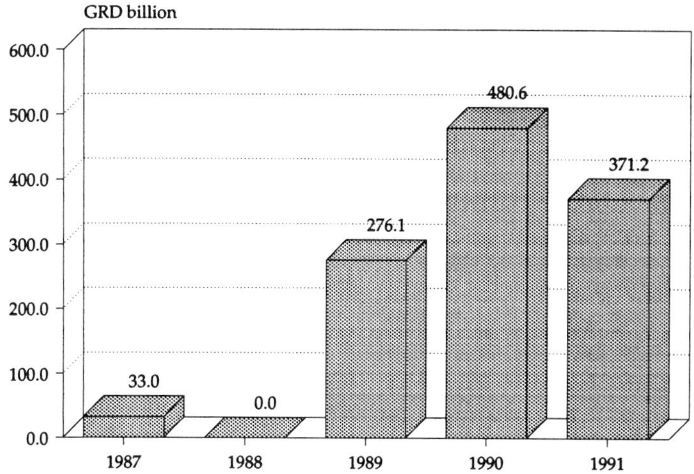

Figure 17.32 New issue volume in the government FCY bond market, 1987-91

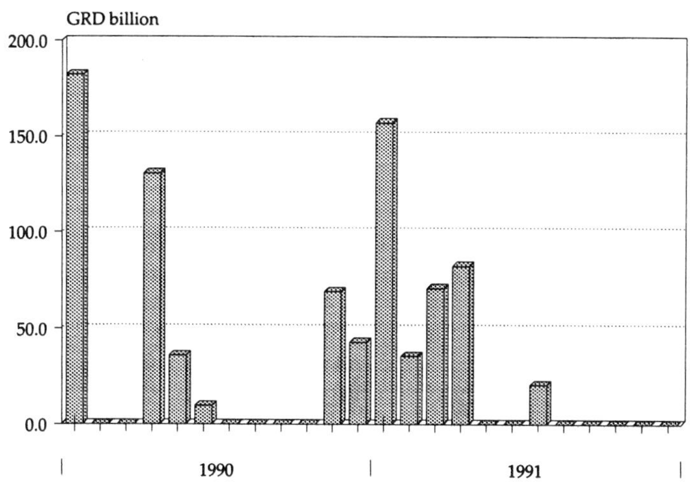

Figure 17.33 New issuance volume in the government FCY bond market, 1990-91

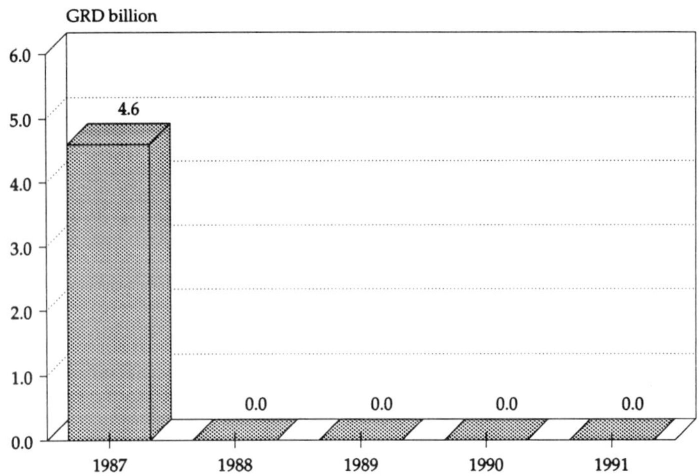

Figure 17.34 New issuance volume in the public sector bond market, 1987-91

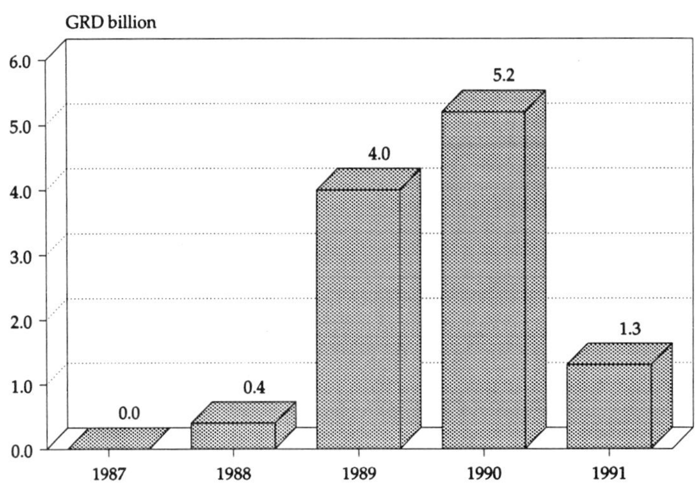

Figure 17.35 New issuance volume in the corporate bond market, 1990-91

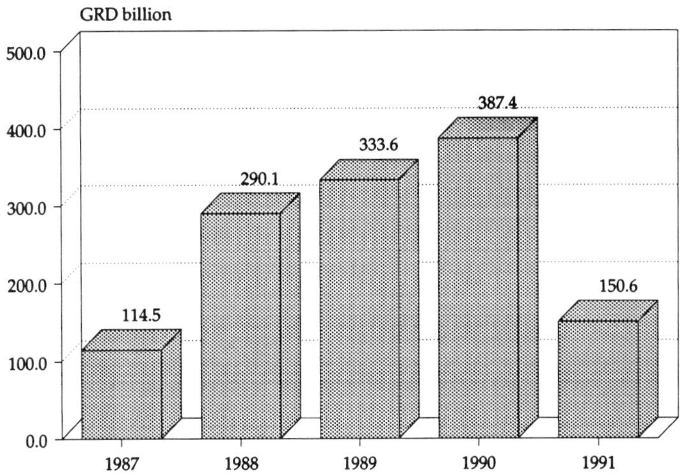

Figure 17.36 New issuance volume in the bank bond market [1987-91]

17.8 Methods of trading

Overview

While new issuance activity has rapidly increased over recent years, the secondary market has evolved only very slowly. As noted earlier, Greek bond trading is dominated by the government sector, while the other types of issues are very rarely traded. This means that bonds are usually held throughout their entire life. In cases where no secondary activity exists, the investor always has the alternative of discounting to the issuer, albeit with penalties.

Generally, bond trading is channelled either through brokers, members of the Athens Stock Exchange, or the over-the-counter market. Brokerage firms can act either as agents for investors, dependent on the size of their company capital, or as principals by buying/selling for their own account. However, very few are active in the bond market, the majority of them preferring to specialize in stocks. In contrast, a significant percentage of bond activity is handled by a

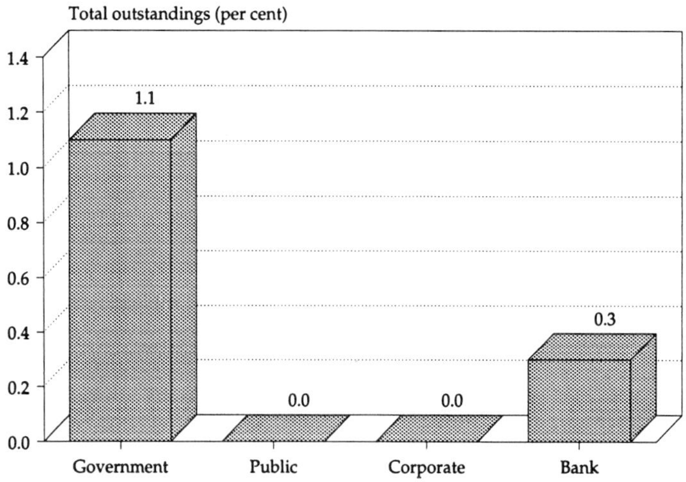

Figure 17.37 Athens Stock Exchange - bond trading volume

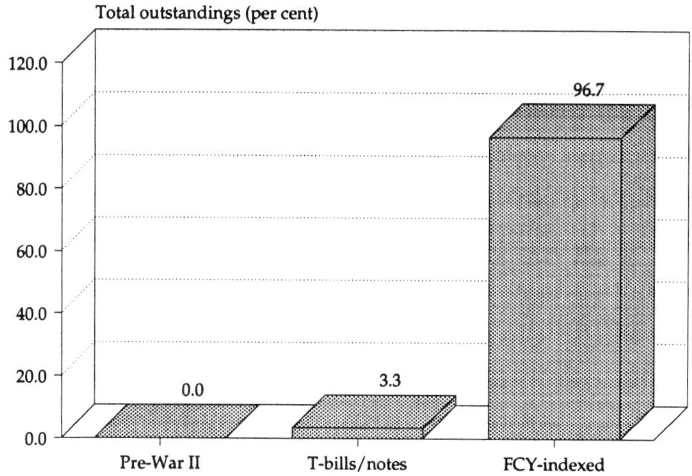

Figure 17.38 Athens Stock Exchange - government bond trading volume

small number of banks which are primarily market-makers for government bonds.

Not surprisingly, in view of the diminutive nature of the Greek market compared to other European countries, liquidity is limited, with the result that bid/offer spreads are rather wide, ranging from 1/2 to 1 per cent.

High-volume transactions have historically been traded over-the-counter, rather than on the stock exchange (this being due to the fact that over-the-counter participants are banks, mutual funds, investment, and insurance companies). Indeed, during 1991, bond transactions through the stock exchange amounted to only about 12.5 per cent of the total turnover (see Figure 17.37).

Government bond market

As noted above, most government paper trading takes place over-the-counter. Only about 1.3 per cent of total government outstanding volume is directed to the Athens Stock Exchange (see Figure 17.38), of which almost 97 per cent is attributable to trading in FCY-indexed bonds, the growth of which has been spectacular - from Dr 4bn in 1989, to Dr 48bn in 1991.

Treasury bill trading is limited, this being due to the frequent issuance and short range of the instrument - an investor can cover his purchase needs at the end of each month in the primary market and the maximum one-year holding period is considered sufficient, while not usually creating liquidations. Additionally, in the present circumstances, high spreads encourage straightforward investment rather than trading. However, it is expected that, in the near future, the effects of deregulation and harmonization with EC standards will encourage the development of a more efficient secondary market.

Other bonds

Public and corporate bonds are not frequently traded and, until recently, banks were not permitted to hold bank bonds in their portfolios. As a result, no market-making activity was possible except, that is, for monthly purchases in the primary market or at penalized discounts through the issuers.

Bank bond issuers can redeem bonds during their life, but only after six months from the issue-date, and at a price determined by accruals during the holding period, minus 3 months. For example, if the holding period is 8 months, the accruals received would only cover 5 months. HIBD, however, has been issuing 1-year bank bonds with no penalty upon discounting on the 6th and/or the 9th month - the so-called '6, 9, 12 bonds'.

There is, however, always the alternative of stock exchange trading at any time during the bond's life.

17.9 *Market practices*

Coupon payment

All government bonds pay annually. Most corporate bonds, and a few bank bonds, are zero-coupons. Corporate FRNs usually pay quarterly.

Denomination

For the most actively-traded bonds, denominations are as follows:

- Drachma government bonds (in Dr 000s): 100, 200, 500, 1000, 5000, 10,000
- Ecu government bonds (in Ecu 000s): 1, 2, 5, 10, 20, 50, 100
- Bank bonds (in Dr 000s): from 5 to 1000

Form

All bonds are presently in bearer-physical form and are therefore physically delivered upon settlement. It is expected that a book-entry system will be applied in the near future.

Dealing quotations

Bid/offer spreads are wide, ranging from 50 to 100 basis points for foreign currency (Ecu) government bonds, and from 100 to 200 basis points for drachma government bonds, which is the same spread currently applied to money market interbank trading.

Redemption

All issues are redeemed at par upon maturity, except lottery bonds which are gradually redeemed each year by lot for a specified number of bonds outstanding.

Withholding tax

There is no withholding tax for any government bonds. Corporate bonds, however, are subject to withholding tax, currently set at 25 per cent. Finally, for bank bonds, withholding tax of 10 per cent is applicable. International investors, though, may be treated in different ways, according to double taxation agreements (see Section 17.13, Taxation).

Puts

Only bank bonds (ARNs) are puttable in the sense that the holder can roll-over the investment upon maturity for another period, upon maturity. There are also ARNs offered by HBID with put options at the end of a 6- or 9-month period. Citileasing 1990/1995 has put options, at par, for years 3 and 4. There are also some corporate bonds with put options.

Commissions

Trading through the stock exchange incurs brokerage commissions of 0.25 per cent on the value of the transaction for each individual purchase/sale. Over-the-counter trading is free of commission.

17.10 Settlement

As all bonds are physically delivered, settlement is made in cash against delivery. There is no fixed settlement period for any bond type.

Settlement depends on the method traded rather than the type of issue. If traded through the Athens Stock Exchange, settlement is normally the next day (trade-date + 1). If traded over-the-counter, the settlement period is mutually agreed between the counterparties. Forward settlement can be arranged by the market-maker, provided either side can sustain credit and funding restrictions for more than the normal set period.

The only restriction applies in the case of transactions from foreign currency into drachma and vice versa - foreign exchange settlement periods are then used, usually for spot value, i.e. two business days (trade-date + 2).

17.11 Yield calculation

Government drachma bond market

Treasury bills

A simple yield calculation is used:

$$Y = \frac{100}{P} - 1 \times \frac{(365)}{(DTM)} \times 100$$

where,

Y yield (%)
P price (%)
DTM days from settlement to maturity

Treasury notes

The ISMA method of calculation is used, as applied for US Treasuries. For the calculation of the time period, actual days are used, counting from the settlement date to the maturity date of the bond. The general algorithm employed, and usually overcome by the use of an ISMA calculator, is:

$$P + g(1-f) = \frac{100R}{(1 + \frac{Y}{100})^{n+f}} + \frac{100g}{Y(1 + \frac{Y}{100})^{f-1}} \left[1 - \frac{1}{(1 + \frac{Y}{100})^{n+1}} \right]$$

where,

p price (%)
g coupon (%)
R redemption price (%)
Y yield (%)
$n+f$ life of the bond, where n = integer and $0 < f \leq 1$

Settings for the ISMA calculator would be:
365
ALT
ANN

For full details on ISMA calculator applications, see the *Bond Calculator Manual* by ISMA-Elgindata.

Government FCY bond market

FCY-indexed bonds, i.e. Ecu state bonds, can be treated as fully-paid fixed-coupon eurobonds, paying once a year, with an assumed single redemption date. Again, the ISMA formula and calculator can be used to avoid cumbersome calculations.

The time period is determined by actual/365 days, as for Treasury notes. It should be noted that the above calculations represent secondary market conventions and, as yet, are not determined by any regulatory body. Primary market calculations, however, differ from the above in the method used for counting the time period. Specifically, the Bank of Greece, the issuer for all government bonds, sells bonds on a actual/360 basis, whilst it discounts them during their life on a actual/365 basis!

17.12 Taxation

Domestic investors

Income and withholding tax

All government-issued bonds are free of income and withholding tax across all investor types and groups. Investments on corporate bonds, however, are subject to income tax. The rate of tax applied depends on the class of investor. In the case of corporates or financial institutions, interest is withheld at source and can be offset against their overall tax liability. If the investor is a mutual fund, then interest is taxable - not to the mutual fund, however, but to the ultimate recipient according to their specific tax status. Finally, since January 1991, as noted earlier, interest income on bank bonds is taxed at 10 per cent, withheld at source upon coupon payment. For individuals, this is treated as final settlement of tax on the relevant income, instead of advance payment of tax, and can be offset against overall liability. In the case of zero-coupon bank bonds, tax is withheld upon issuance.

Capital gains tax

In general terms, no capital gains tax is applied to any type of bond investment. Specifically, whilst individuals are tax-exempt from capital gains tax, corporations are liable to such tax, unless they present capital gains under their profit and loss (P & L) account, in a reserve account, in which case they are also tax-exempt.

Overseas investors

Of all the various bond types, only corporate and bank bonds are taxable - and therefore subject to withholding tax. As far as overseas investors are concerned, taxation depends upon the existence and nature of double taxation agreements with Greece (see below).

Double taxation relief agreements

A total of 17 countries have concluded agreements with Greece to avoid double taxation, i.e. both by Greece and by their own tax authorities, in respect of dividends, interest and royalties. Within this context, the tax rate applicable is the lowest of the rates in the specified agreement between the two countries (see

Figure 17.39). It is interesting to note that, in certain cases, such as the UK, interest income is totally tax-free.

In addition to the reliefs on taxable bonds arising from double taxation agreements, there are instances in which overseas investors may not only be tax-exempt from income tax on a non-taxable bond, but can actually claim tax credits from their tax-base country. Specifically, investors can claim tax credits provided the interest income earned is exempt from Greek tax for the promotion of economic development in Greece. Therefore, any investments in Greek bonds which are issued under Law 3745/57 granting economic development status, such as government bonds (Treasury bills, Treasury notes and FCY-indexed), are eligible for tax credits. For example, in Germany, any interest income will be fully taxable under its domestic laws. However, residents of Germany, to whom the income tax treaty between Germany and Greece applies, may be entitled to

Country	Tax
Austria	Tax free[1]
Belgium	15 per cent
France	10 per cent
Germany	10 per cent[2]
Denmark	8 per cent
Switzerland	10 per cent
USA	Tax free[3]
United Kingdom	Tax free
India	*
Italy	10 per cent
Spain	10 per cent
Cyprus	10 per cent
Holland	10 per cent[4]
Hungary	10 per cent
Czechoslovakia	10 per cent
Finland	10 per cent

Figure 17.39 Countries with double taxation agreements with Greece
* *local tax legislation applies*
[1] *tax-free, under certain conditions*
[2] *10 per cent with some exceptions*
[3] *tax-free up to 9 per cent interest rate*
[4] *except interest from banks, which is 8 per cent*

claim a credit against their German income tax, equal to the amount of Greek income tax that was not paid. Article XVII of the treaty provides for a credit, computed in accordance with German law, against the German tax payable on the interest, for 10 per cent of the amount of interest "if such interest is exempt from Greek tax due to special provisions of Greek law for the promotion of the economic development of Greece".

Withholding tax

In cases where no double taxation agreement exists, the interest income from taxable bonds is withheld at source at the relevant tax rate applied by the Greek authorities, as for domestic investors. Tax withheld, however, can be offset against the overall tax liability of overseas investors in their tax-base country.

17.12 *Interest rate history*

Introduction

Historically, the interest rate environment in Greece has been highly regulated. The central bank (the Bank of Greece), which applies monetary policy, has maintained tight control over the financial markets and their participants. Both the foreign exchange markets and the money markets have operated under restrictions which have not only created significant distortions, but have also limited competitive forces. As a result, the markets have only slowly (if at all) adapted to the rapidly-changing economic conditions - thereby further emphasizing rate imbalances.

However, with the onset of plans for European financial integration, the Bank of Greece has loosened its tight grip over interest rates during the last two years in preparation of an environment in which market forces can freely determine levels.

Before analysing the last four years in detail, however, it is important to note that those rates which have been, and continue to be, directly fixed by the central bank are:

- minimum savings account rates
- minimum working capital loan rates
- commercial bank overdraft rates to the Bank of Greece
- government bond rates

1987-1988

Throughout 1987, the interest rates applied to both bank deposits and loans were specified by central bank decisions. Within an ever-changing economic environment, this inevitably led to time-lags. Furthermore, interest rates remained at levels lower than inflation, a situation which had a negative impact on both currency stability and the balance of payments. During 1987, however, the first signs of a deregulation in interest rate policy appeared. This, coupled with lower inflation rates (from 16.9 per cent, in 1986, to 15.7 per cent in 1987, and 14 per cent in 1988), led to positive real interest rates at significantly-high levels - in contrast to the strongly-negative rates witnessed during the preceding fifteen years. Since 1987, the target of monetary policy has been to maintain high interest rates in order to control liquidity-growth and credit expansion, improve the balance of payments, and to support an anti-inflationary exchange policy.

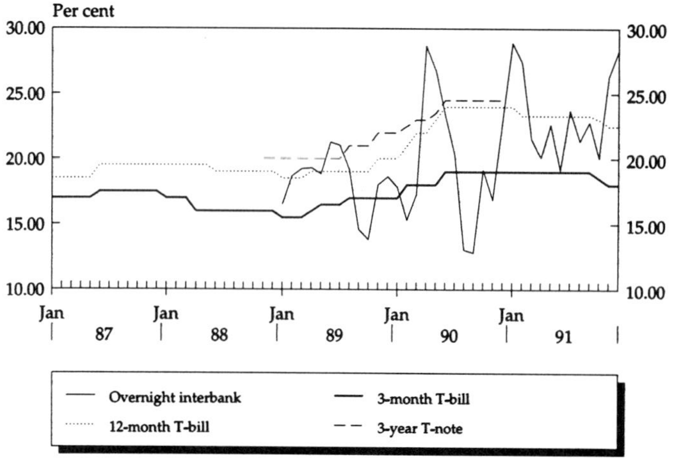

Figure 17.40 History of Greek interest rates, 1987 - 1991 (monthly)

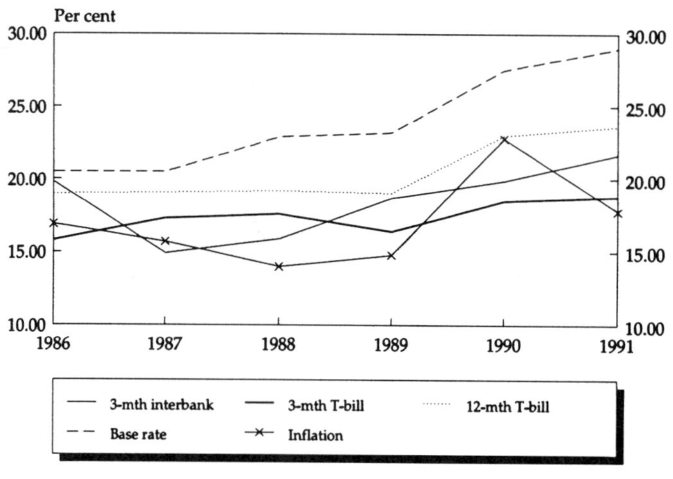

Figure 17.41 Greek interest rates, 1986 - 1991 (annual)

During 1988, nominal bank loan rates to the private sector stabilized at high levels. Base rates for working capital loans, for example, remained at about 22.9 per cent, with long-term loans at 18.5 per cent. At the same time, bank deposit rates did not show any change from their 15 per cent level.

Despite a degree of liberalization, the limited fluctuations in nominal interest rates again proved their close interaction with the rather stable government bond rates and savings account rates seen during the period - and demonstrated the need for further deregulation. It should be noted that bond rates and savings account rates are determined by the government and the Bank of Greece, respectively, while bank deposit and loan rates, which had been liberalized to a large extent, maintained a minimum fixed-level.

1989

During 1989, financial deregulation continued apace, with further relaxation of credit restrictions and interest rate controls. Banks were allowed to extend credit to any sector, subject to criteria of their own. Meanwhile, bank deposit rates were fully liberalized, the only exception being savings accounts, on which a minimum 16 per cent interest rate was applied. The reason for setting a minimum is given, by the Bank of Greece, as being the need to apply efficient monetary policy, since credit extension to the public sector is not freely-determined by market forces. Additionally, most bank loan rates were liberalized, albeit with the application of minimum lending rates (for the reasons mentioned above) of 17 per cent on long-term loans and 18 per cent on short-term working capital loans.

Finally, a new method of intervention was applied by the central bank to support high interest rates within its targets: Repurchase agreements (or, repos) enable liquidity to be drained by selling and buying Treasury bills to commercial banks for an agreed period, at an agreed rate. It is important to note that repo rates were determined, for the first time, through the auction system by free market forces. In cases of tight liquidity, the Bank of Greece engaged in reverse-repos.

1990

During 1986-1989, a substantial growth in liquidity and a significant overshoot in credit and monetary targets were largely due to both financial liberalization, and excessive public sector claims. In 1990, the first time in a number of years, a restrictive monetary policy, with credit targets, was closely followed and the trend of increased liquidity was halted. Despite this tightening by the Bank of Greece, however, credit to the private sector continued to grow rapidly in the first half of the year. In order to restore confidence, stop speculation against the drachma and drain liquidity once more, the Bank of Greece twice raised the minimum levels of savings account interest rates (at the end of March and in early July) and intervened in the interbank market through the auction of government bonds from its own portfolio. This resulted in the stabilization of short-term lending rates by commercial banks at around 29 per cent (which is an effective rate of 33 per cent for the borrower, who pays an additional tax on nominal lending rates for bank transactions). In addition to this, government bond rates followed the uptrend in interest rates - but at a higher rate. 1-year Treasury bill rates, of 24 per cent, proved serious competition for both time deposits, at 21 per cent, and savings deposits, at 18 per cent (which, together with a high inflation rate of 22.8 per cent, resulted in negative real rates). It is particularly important to note the 10 per cent spread between deposit and loan rates. This is partly attributable to the high cost of deposits which are, in turn, due to high reserve-requirements. It also reflects the oligarchic nature of the Greek banking structure.

1991

The principal characteristics of monetary and credit developments in 1991 were the marked slowdown in the rate of growth of money supply (M3) and aggregate domestic credit expansion which, coupled with the stability of high interest rates and a significant fall in inflation (from 22.8 per cent to 17.8 per cent), resulted in a significant rise in real interest rates. These developments reflect the substantial reduction in bank credit to the public sector due to the successful sales of government bonds to the non-banking public, together with the continuing deregulation of the banking system. One major factor which has affected the rate of growth of M3 is the decrease in private deposits, which resulted in the substantial rise of interbank rates - reaching the Bank of Greece overdraft levels of 26 - 32 per cent. Supply was, in fact, shifted from bank deposits to government bonds, due to the 10 per cent tax on all interest-earned income, except for government bonds. On average, overnight interbank rates reached 23.5 per cent, against 19.5 per cent in 1990.

During 1991, the Bank of Greece did not intervene through repos or reverse-repos, but selectively entered the overnight interbank market. Overall, during 1991 - the first year of the Medium-term Adjustment Programme - significant progress was achieved in reducing macroeconomic imbalances and distortions, by lower inflation rates, an improvement in the balance of payments, and lower real interest rates.

17.13 Inter-market spreads

Introduction

The analysis of spread relationships in bond markets which are rather young and small, like those of Greece, is not easy. The limited issuance in sectors other than that of the government (which accounts for about 86 per cent of total outstandings), creates obvious difficulties as far as inter-market spreads are concerned. As a result, the only such spread considered here is that which exists between the two most representative sectors, of government and bank bonds. In addition, though, it is useful to examining intra-market spreads within the government sector itself, between drachma bonds and FCY-indexed bonds. Finally, a performance comparison of two different types of market, for equities and bonds, could prove a useful tool in fund management decision-making.

Treasury bills vs. ARNs

In the past, Treasury bill yields have not varied greatly from renewable bank bond yields, indeed, they have followed almost the same pattern for a number of years. Since January 1991, however, spreads of about 150 to 200 basis points in favour of Treasury bills, have been observed. This, as noted earlier, is clearly due to the introduction of 10 per cent tax on interest income earned from all bonds with the exception of government issues.

Treasury notes vs. Ecu-indexed bonds

It is quite interesting to compare high-yielding drachma investments in Treasury notes with the alternative Ecu-indexed bonds which provide a hedge for drachma-based investors. Ecu bonds offer returns from both their coupon and the Ecu/drachma exchange relationship, while Treasury notes offer returns based only on their coupon. It is difficult, however, apply a full spread analysis for the past few years, as issues in the two markets have not been regular and do not follow the same maturity patterns. By comparing, though, two specific issues: drachma T-note 20% May 1989-92, and Ecu 9.75% May 1989-92, returns have been in favour of the Ecu bond, offering a negative spread of 7 per cent on Treasury note investments. However, in periods when drachma devaluation was limited, spreads have increased significantly and, in certain cases, have become positive. For example, the drachma T-note 24% January 1991-92 against the Ecu 12%, for the same period, reached a spread of about 4.5 per cent.

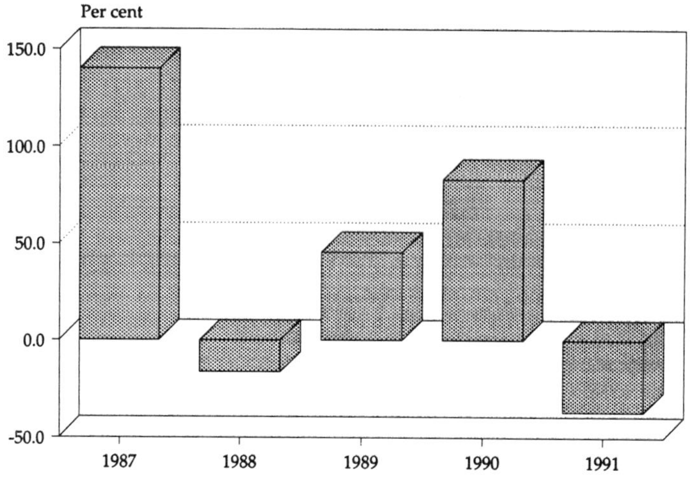

Figure 17.42 Yield spread: equities vs. Treasury bills, 1987-1991

Equity yields vs. Treasury bills

In Greece, equities have traditionally been characterized by their extreme volatility. The Athens Stock Exchange General Index, despite having shown significant overall gains for the equity sector during recent years, has also shown repeated corrections when observed closely, on a year-to-year basis. During the last five years, comparisons against the fixed-income market have displayed interesting results. In 1987, the best-performing year for equities, spreads against the January 1987-88 18.50% T-bill reached a high of about 140 per cent! In 1988, however, year-to-year returns on equities reached a mere 3 per cent, showing a negative spread of 16.5 per cent against the high-yielding January 1988-89 19.50% T-bill.

Spreads for the years of 1989 and 1990 remained positive, ranging from 40 to 80 per cent. In 1991, however, the equity market showed a negative yield of about 13 per cent, dropping the spread to -37 per cent against the 24% January 1991-92 T-bill (see Figure 17.42).

17.14 Sources of reference

Financial data

Bank of Greece

- *Long-Term Statistical Series of the Greek Economy* (annual, in Greek only)
  Provides data for at least the last 30 years. Figures for the two years prior to publication are based on estimates

- *Monthly Statistical Bulletin* (in Greek and English)
  Provides data for about the last 10 years

- *Annual Governors Report on the Bank of Greece Balance Sheet* (in Greek only)

National Statistical Service of Greece (NSSG)

- *Statistical Yearbook of Greece* (in Greek and English)
  Provides data for the last 5 to 10 years

- *Monthly Statistical Bulletin*

- *National Accounts*

Quote vendors & news agencies

- Reuters provide information as shown in Figure 17.43

- Telerate provide information as shown in Figure 17.44

Further reading

Athens Stock Exchange (ASE)

- *Yearbook of the Athens Stock Exchange* (in Greek only)
  Detailed description of all listed securities on the ASE, both equity and fixed-income

- *ASE Annual Statistical Bulletin* (in Greek and English)
- *ASE Monthly Statistical Bulletin* (in Greek and English)
- *ASE Daily Newspaper* (in Greek and English)

Page No.	Contributor	Subject
ATGI	Sigma Securities	Ecu bond prices
ATGJ-K	Athens Stock Exchange	Ecu bond prices
ATGL	Athens Stock Exchange	Corporate bonds
BBTA	Barclays	T-bill & Ecu bond prices
BVGT-U	Bayerische	T-bill & Ecu bond prices
CATH	Citibank	Ecu bond prices
CBGA	Commercial	T-bill prices
EMBA-B	Euromerchant	T-bill & Ecu bond prices
JPBD	Ionian	T-bill prices
MBGU-V-W	Midland	T-bill & Ecu bond prices
MTTD	Macedonia-Thrace	T-bill prices
NBGB	National	T-bill prices
TCBG	Traders Credit	T-bill prices
AMGR	American Express	Money market rates
AZGR	ANZ Grindlays	Money market rates
BAAG	Bank of America	Money market rates
BBAT/BBGD	Barclays	Money market rates
BQNP	BNP	Money market rates
BVGR	Bayerische	Money market rates
CATG	Citibank	Money market rates
CBGA	Commercial	Money market rates
CCAG	CCF	Money market rates
CNBA	Chase	Money market rates
CRBG	Credit	Money market rates
DRAA-B	Composite	Overnight rates
EMBA	Euromerchant	Money market rates
ETEB	Eteva	Money market rates
GHBG	General Hellenic	Money market rates
IPBA	Ionian	Money market rates
MBGR	Midland	Money market rates
MTTD	Macedonia-Thrace	Money market rates
NBGA-B	National	Money market rates

(Cont.)

Page No.	Contributor	Subject
(cont.)		
NWBA	NatWest	Money market rates
QGR1-3	Composite	Money market rates
SGAG	Société Général	Money market rates
TCBG	Traders Credit	Money market rates
AMGR	American Express	USD,DEM,JPY,GBP / GRD
ANZD	ANZ Grindlays	USD,DEM,AUD,ECU,GBP / GRD
BBXG	Barclays	All currencies / GRD
BGAN	Bank of Greece	Exchange fixings / GRD
BQNP	BNP	USD, DEM, FRF / GRD
CBOG	Commercial	USD, DEM, FRF, ECU, CHF / GRD, & fixings
CCAG	CCF	USD, DEM, FRF / GRD
CMBA	Chase	USD,DEM,FRF,ECU / GRD & fixings
CRBG	Credit	All currencies / GRD
GHBG	General	USD,DEM / GRD
GRDQ-S	Composite	Exchange: USD / GRD
GRDT-V	Composite	Exchange: USD / GRD
MTTD	Macedonia-Thrace	USD, DEM / GRD & fixings
NBGX	National	All currencies / GRD & fixings
NWAX	NatWest	All currencies / GRD
PARG	Paribas	USD, DEM, FRF / GRD
TCBG	Traders Credit	USD,DEM / GRD
ATGA	Alpha Trust	Stock exchange commentary
ATGD	N.D. Devletoglou	Stock exchange commentary
ATGG-II	Sigma Securities	Stock exchange commentary
BVGS-V-W	Bayerische	Money market & foreign exchange commentary
ETEC	Eteva	Money market commentary

Figure 17.43 Reuters pages

Page No.	Contributor	Subject
8692	Composite	T-bill prices
8695	Composite	Ecu bond prices
8693-4	Composite	Money market rates
8698	Composite	Overnight rates
8697	Telerate	Money market graph: overnight rates
20641-8	Telerate	FX graphs: All currencies / GRD
8689	Traders credit	FX technical analysis
8690	Bank of Greece	Exchange fixings / GRD
8691	Composite	Exchange / GRD
17890	Sigma Securities	Stock exchange commentary
17893	N.D. Devletoglou	Stock exchange commentary
17896	Alpha Trust	Stock exchange commentary

Figure 17.44 Telerate pages

Chapter

18

The bond markets of

Hungary

Csaba Lantos & Balazs Bathory
Creditanstalt Securities Ltd., Budapest

Peter Zelnik & Gabor Grenczer
Europartners Kft., Budapest

This chapter has been supplied by the Austrian Bond Commission

Note: In general text, the abbreviation 'Ft' is used to denote the Hungarian forint. Elsewhere, the international mnemonic 'HUF' is used.

18.1 General synopsis

Introduction

When studying the Hungarian market, one must be mindful of the restrictive conditions which have affected, and in some cases continue to affect, the development of a Western-style bond market:

- As yet, the national currency, the Hungarian forint is not a convertible currency. This means that Hungarian issuers may only launch bonds in a foreign currency, or targeted to foreign investors, with Hungarian National Bank (Magyar Nemzeti Bank, MNB) permission - as is the case with foreign issuers launching Ft-denominated bonds.

- In addition, foreigners cannot convert any income (interest) or repayment (principal) of bonds or notes, without MNB permission, into foreign (convertible) currency, even if they acquired the bonds by converting foreign currency into forints. In practice, therefore, foreigners do not buy Ft-denominated bonds at present (with the exception of the McDonald's and CSFB issues, which were launched in 1991 with MNB exemptions, and some municipal issues).

- In the past, capital from abroad could be channelled into the forint bond market only through companies founded in Hungary and 100 per cent-owned by foreigners. Recently, however, a new Investment Fund Law was enacted which allows foreigners to invest also through investment funds.

- Until 31 December 1987, the forint bond market was strictly divided into two segments: certain bonds could be purchased only by private individuals, others only by public institutions. On 1 January 1988, this separation of markets was abolished, although some of these restricted types of bond are still outstanding.

- Bonds for the private investor segment which were issued before 31 December 1987 had an automatic state guarantee, no matter who had issued the bond. As of 1988, this provision was also abolished.

- Until 31 December 1987, bonds offered to private persons were exempt from tax on both interest and capital gains.

- Until quite recently, the Hungarian government partly financed its budget directly through the banking system. Therefore, the Republic of Hungary has only occasionally appeared as issuer. In 1991 however, the Treasury started to launch issues, such as state bonds and Treasury bills, and plans to extend its market presence in the future. It can be expected that, in the forthcoming years, the Treasury will be, by far, the most important issuer of Ft-denominated bonds.

- Prior to 1990, there was no legislation governing the financial markets and the stock exchange. However, this was rectified that year when the State Securities Supervision (SSS) was legally established, as was also the Budapest Stock Exchange, which started activity on 21 June 1990.

Market history

The history of the Hungarian bond market can be divided into three clearly distinguishable chapters.

1981-1987 - the emergence of the bond market

In 1981-1982 some 'communal bonds' were issued. The issue sizes were small and the proceeds served for the development of the local infrastructure of rural settlements. However, the rules regulating the issue of government bonds, which were drafted in late 1982, took into consideration the experience made with these first experiments.

The main elements of the 1982 regulations were as follows:

- Bond issues targeted to companies or institutions did not need any authorization. The special permission of the Minister of Finance was required, however, for any bonds offered to private individuals (as mentioned above, these bonds were government-guaranteed).

- All income from bonds held by private individuals was exempt from taxes and fees, while the interest income of companies was subject to the general rules of taxation.

- The maximum life of these bonds was 15 years and the coupon could be fixed relatively freely. (Theoretically, the government had the right to set a ceiling for coupons. It was, however, never exercised.)

The first bond issue based on these new regulations was realized in March 1983, and was restricted to institutional investors. After this, the market quickly expanded; until 30 September 1986, some 140 bonds with a total volume of

Year	Number of issues	Total issue volume	Institutional purchases	Private sector
1983	23	819	595	224
1984	29	863	258	605
1985	50	2203	520	1683
1986	72	5028	1376	3652
1987	142	17,285	4594	12,692
Total	316	26,199	7343	18,856

Figure 18.1 HUF bond issues, 1983-1987

Ft 8.4 billion were issued. However, compared with the size of the economy, this figure was still rather small. The overall volume of the bond market amounted to only 1 per cent of GDP, and to 3 per cent of the total loan volume outstanding.

Active on the issuing side were trading companies (35 issues, 13 per cent of the volume), co-operatives (31 issues, 10 per cent), municipalities (22 issues, 8 per cent), the Post Office (for telephone network expansion; 6 issues, 19 per cent) and financial institutions (4 issues, 13 per cent). The share of manufacturing companies and agricultural enterprises in the bond market was relatively small by comparison to their importance within the national economy.

The average coupon of corporate bonds issued is between 12 and 13 per cent for bonds targeted to companies and institutions, and 9.5 per cent for bonds for private investors. This latter figure includes the 'telephone bonds' - without these the average coupon is approximately 10.4 per cent. The yields increased continuously, reflecting the slowly-increasing inflation and savings-book interest rates. Several bonds, amongst them those of the telephone companies, offered additional benefits to the investors and were therefore issued with lower coupons than the rest of the market. The telephone bonds, for example, entitled the holder to preferential treatment in the allocation of telephone lines, thus reducing the waiting period drastically - for non-investors this period was usually measured in years, if not in decades!

In the beginning, all bonds were issued with fixed-coupons. However, from 1985, bonds which - in addition to a minimum interest rate - paid 'bonuses' depending on the issuer's (the company's) results, were also issued. These bonuses were either paid out annually, together with the coupon, or as a premium at redemption. Floating-rate bonds, as known in the West, were absent until 1991. In 1986, a type of zero bond (issued at par, with all cumulative interest paid at maturity) was issued. The maturity of these bonds was usually five to seven years; some large issues, though, had maturities of ten to fifteen years.

The sale of bonds was always undertaken by the financial institution underwriting the issue. In 1981-1982, the experimental communal bonds were underwritten by the National Savings Bank. After the publication of the 1982 regulations, the State Development Bank took over the leading role and dominated the primary market with a market share of 80 to 90 per cent in 1983-1984. In 1985-1986, the Hungarian National Bank gained importance and underwrote some 40 per cent of issues. Indeed, the overall joint market share of the National Savings Bank, the Foreign Trade Bank, the Construction Innovation Bank and some 15 Savings Co-operatives, failed to reach 10 per cent.

As of 1 January 1987, following the reorganization of the banking system, the situation changed considerably. The 'Share Office' in the State Development Bank was transferred to Budapest Bank Ltd., while the functions of the 'Bond Office' of the Hungarian National Bank were transferred to two new banks, namely the Hungarian Credit Bank Ltd. and National Trading and Credit Bank Ltd. The competition between the banks was intended to promote both the bond and stock markets in the country.

In 1987, the opening-up of the market, together with the accelerating decline of Hungary's economic indicators (especially the inflation rate), resulted in a significant change in the balance between issuers and investors. Until then, bonds were seen both by private and by institutional investors as a very profitable and attractive form of savings (due to the relatively high yields compared to other forms of savings, as well as the possible capital gains on the secondary market). As these advantages were eroded, real interest rates turned negative, and the population gradually reduced its savings.

1988-1990 - a collapse in issuance

From 1 January 1988, the division of the market into two segments according to the status of the purchaser ceased to exist, as did the state guarantee for private investor-targeted issues.

A withholding tax was then introduced, and private investors had to pay 20 per cent tax on both interest and capital gains. At the same time, a totally new personal income tax system was introduced, while the inflation rate soared and the former upper limit on coupons was abolished.

These changes in market conditions led to a reduction of the new issues volume to less than 10 per cent of the preceding year's volume. Total forint bond issues in 1988 amounted to no more than Ft 1.6bn (compared to Ft 17.3bn in 1987).

At the same time, the secondary bond market - which was dominated by banks - also changed drastically. Previously, secondary market prices had been calculated by individual banks in isolation. This meant that investors could sell and buy bonds only in the branches of certain banks, and at the prices dictated by those banks.

As a consequence of both the high inflation rate and the opportunities offered by alternative forms of saving, the banks soon got into a difficult situation. The secondary market lost its balance - nobody wanted to buy bonds, whilst everybody wanted to sell. The banks' own bond books grew quickly during the first months of 1988 with the financial institutions buying back as much as 10 per cent of the outstanding volume per month.

The banks sought their way out of this dilemma in three ways: Firstly, they introduced repurchase agreements favourable for the investors. Secondly, in some cases they offered (and some continue to offer) voluntary bonuses on the yearly coupon of an issue. Thirdly, they established an organized secondary bond market between themselves in the form of a weekly auction mini-exchange meeting with the participants being the banks' traders. This first form of a preliminary exchange was called 'Securities Trading Agreement' (*Ertekpapir Kereskedelmi Megallapodas* - EKM), later to become Budapest Stock Exchange (BSE).

From 1988 onwards, the MNB has been organizing government Treasury bill auctions with maturities of 1 and 3 months. These securities are only available for institutional investors. Since 1991, the yields resulting from the auctions have served as the indicator for floating government bonds.

At the beginning of 1990, the bond market was totally moribund. There was practically no new issuance and the volumes on the secondary market diminished considerably. At that time the Securities and Stock Exchange Act governing the procedure of new issues and the obligation of information-disclosure by the issuers, was promulgated. The law prohibited banks, who had played the leading role before, from trading in securities. Banks with existing EKM membership were granted a seat in the new BSE, if they so desired, but were requested to set up their own securities firms (which they may wholly-own) by the end of 1992. As a direct consequence, many securities firms have been established - today, they exceed fifty in number - and they have taken over the leading role in both the primary and secondary markets.

On 21 June 1990, the Budapest Stock Exchange officially opened, taking over the responsibilities of the former EKM. Provisionally, all bonds which were traded within EKM were admitted to the BSE with the requirement that the issuer, together with a broker, had to file for final admission by the end of 1991 and had to fulfill all the necessary disclosure requirements (amongst others, this meant the issuance of a full prospectus). In the mean while, these bonds were also traded OTC at the sponsoring bank or broker. As it so happened, no application for listing was filed with the BSE by 31 December 1991 and, consequently, all bonds were de-listed.

On 21 June 1991, the first new issue for several months was launched by Postabank, with a coupon of 12 per cent + the yearly dividend of the bank (at that time, 20 per cent). This issue was duly introduced on the BSE and remained, for most of 1991, the only bond quoted on the exchange.

1991 and the future - a hopeful outlook

In 1991, inflation and interest rates hit an all-time high. Inflation reached 35-36 per cent, while time deposits for institutional investors could be fixed at up to 40 per cent for large institutional investors, and for maturities from 6 months upwards.

As the inflation expectations of some investors slowly declined, more interest concentrated on the OTC secondary market organized by the banks, where yields, especially for longer maturities, gradually fell. Issuers naturally concentrated on extremely short maturities, which could be successfully launched.

The following issues revived the debt security market:

- The government issued Treasury bills, to the general public, in two tranches (with a volume of Ft 25bn). Maturity is up to one year, interest varies from 28 per cent (one to three months) to 36 per cent (one year), with a redemption guarantee by the issuer at any time at par. This issue successfully competed with short-term bank deposits.

- The government additionally issued a floating-rate note with a 3-year maturity (with a volume of Ft 15bn). The interest rate is 2 percentage points above the Treasury bill auction rate (3-month), fixed semi-annually, paid annually. Although the issue was fully underwritten by the banks and the brokers, the appearance on the secondary market was not an unqualified success. In January 1992, it was trading at approximately 98 per cent, two points below the issue price.

- MATAV, the Hungarian telephone company ('Hungarian Telecom'), issued two bonds each with a fixed 35 per cent coupon, and maturities of 12 and 15 months, respectively. Coupon payment is quarterly and total volume amounts to Ft 2bn. Both issues were heavily in demand.

- McDonald's and CSFB launched (with MNB permission) the first Ft-denominated bonds targeted at foreign investors. Their maturities are 4 years, with coupons gradually reducing from 29 to 24.75 per cent. The issue volumes amounted to Ft 400 m each. The payments are freely convertible.

As expected, issue volumes of Treasury bills increased markedly in the first half of 1992, due both to the fall in inflation (to just above 20 per cent), and to high savings volumes. As at mid-1992, the total volume outstanding of Treasury bills placed with the general public amounted to Ft 24bn; meanwhile, the figure for Treasury bills sold by auction to institutional investors, was Ft 38bn. In addition, some Ft 115bn of liquidity bills (issued by the MNB) were sold into the domestic banking system. New investment funds, the first of which were launched in 1992, may also serve as a source of demand. Through these funds, foreigners will be able to participate in the Hungarian bond markets.

Until 1992, bonds traded both on the BSE and OTC included interest (dirty prices). From 1992 onwards, the BSE changed its rule to comply with international standards.

Chapter

19

The bond markets of

Ireland

Pat McArdle
NCB Stockbrokers Ltd

in association with:

John Corrigan
National Treasury Management Agency

Daniel McLaughlin
RIADA Stockbrokers Ltd

Note: In general text, the abbreviation 'Ir£' is used to denote the Irish pound. Elsewhere, the international mnemonic 'IEP' is used.

19.1 Introduction

The Irish bond market is almost totally dominated by Irish government issues. Currently, there are some 38 government issues outstanding, representing a market capitalization of Ir£14bn - equivalent to almost 60 per cent of GNP. There is a small number of corporate issues outstanding and more recently an active market in euro-Irish pound paper has begun to emerge.

The size of the government bond market is accounted for by a rapid expansion in the Exchequer's demand for funds from the mid-1970s. In the period to 1981, when the Exchequer borrowing requirement (EBR) peaked at almost 16 per cent of GNP, the central government's demand for funds grew rapidly both in absolute terms and relative to GNP. Since then, the EBR has been sharply reduced by successive governments and, in 1991, was 2.1 per cent of GNP.

A key development in the Irish market in recent years has been the increasing involvement of overseas investors in the market. Compared with 13 per cent of the market at the end of 1987, international institutional investors now hold about 30 per cent of outstanding domestic Irish pound issues. This reflects, among other things, the external investor's confidence in the domestic economic fundamentals - a low and stable rate of inflation, an expanding balance of payments surplus on current account and, as outlined above, a sharp reduction in the EBR. Critically, from the point of view of overseas investors, the Irish pound continues to be extremely stable within the European monetary system. Ireland confidently expects to satisfy the Emu convergence tests when that decision-making process gets under way.

It is not surprising, therefore, that there is a strong correlation between the yield on Irish government bonds and other narrow-band sovereign paper, notably that of Germany. In 1991, for example, Irish 10-year gilts traded in the range 93 to 157 basis points above the yield on 10-year Bunds. Irish interest rates are still higher than in any other hard-core EMS narrow-band country (with the exception of Denmark) and the range of foreign investment is continually broadening.

With the increasing participation by international investors in the market, the liquidity of Irish government securities continues to improve. Average daily turnover on the secondary market is Ir£160m. The recently established National Treasury Management Agency, which has responsibility for the funding of the EBR, is implementing a programme aimed at improving the liquidity and transparency of the market. Irish pound-denominated government debt has an AAA rating from both Standard and Poor's and Moody's rating agencies. Ireland has an AA long-term rating from the Japan Bond Research Institute, an AA3 rating from Moody's, and AA- from Standard and Poor's.

19.2 Economics

Introduction

Despite, or perhaps because of, its small size and geographical location at the western tip of Europe, Ireland has enthusiastically embraced initiatives for both trading and forging economic links with other nations. Over the past thirty years, industrial policy in Ireland has focused primarily on attracting foreign investment. More recently, the establishment of the International Financial Services Centre in Dublin, with substantial tax benefits, has attracted a wide range of banks, funds management institutions and other financial services companies to Ireland.

Ireland was a founder member of the OECD and a member of Efta until joining the EEC in 1973. The Irish government has supported various initiatives over the years for greater economic integration in Europe and the Irish pound became a full narrow-band member of the European monetary system (EMS) when it was established in 1979. Ireland was the first country to ratify the Maastricht Treaty, and did so by an overwhelming majority.

The Republic of Ireland is a parliamentary democracy with a long record of political stability. The two dominant political parties - who between them take about 75 per cent of the vote - are, in social and economic terms, centre/right parties. There is a broad political consensus on economic policy with the control of government spending and a commitment to exchange rate stability within the EMS central elements of policy. There is also a strong commitment to progress on Emu.

Gross national product

Facing into the 1980s, the Irish economy was beset by problems on a wide front. Inflation was running at over 20 per cent, the balance of payments was in serious deficit, reaching its nadir in 1981 with a current account deficit of almost 15 per cent of GNP, and government borrowing, of the same order of magnitude, was threatening to generate an explosive debt situation.

A sustained period of fiscal retrenchment during the 1980s (though it took time to significantly reduce government borrowing and stabilize the public debt), imposed a severe squeeze on domestic demand, resulting in minimal growth in overall national output. However, the associated rise in unemployment produced a sharp correction in domestic costs, substantially improving competitiveness and contributing to a sustained reduction in inflation. Moreover, the conjunction of depressed conditions at home and booming external demand brought a complete turnaround in the balance of payments' position.

The improvement in inflation and the balance of payments and a radically-reduced fiscal deficit strengthened the credibility of the Irish pound/Deutschemark link in the EMS and resulted in a fundamental re-rating of Irish financial markets, leading to a lowering of interest rates. These developments also produced a renewal of confidence among consumers and producers which saw a recovery in consumer spending and investment and revived growth in GNP from 1987 (see Figure 19.1).

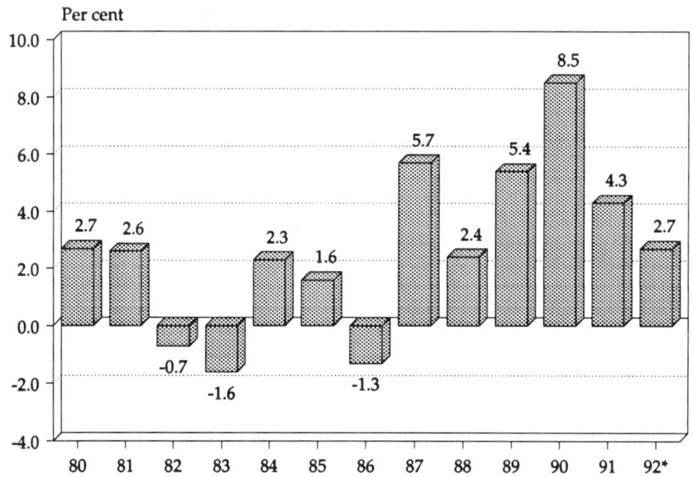

*) *forecast*

Figure 19.1 Irish GNP growth, 1980-1992

The period 1987-90 was one of high growth, rapidly falling budget deficits, a stable Irish pound within the EMS, low inflation, and sharply declining interest rates. Much of this emanated from a change in policy at the beginning of 1987, when a new government took strict action to curb government spending, committed itself to a firm exchange rate policy, and concluded a three-year wage agreement with employers and trade unions which provided for low wage increases. Unemployment, which had more than doubled in the first half of the eighties, began to decline, albeit from very high levels. More recently, the end of the domestic mini-boom and declining activity abroad have seen growth fall back sharply. The authorities are committed to a strict medium-term fiscal policy as part of their preparations for Emu. Inflation remains close to the bottom of the EC league and the balance of payments is in substantial surplus.

Balance of payments

Ireland is an extremely open economy with the combined value of exports and imports equivalent to over 110 per cent of GNP. As the world economy grew strongly during the 1980s, Irish exports boomed. At the same time, the domestic economy was depressed, constraining import growth. This combination saw the trade account move into surplus in 1985. Two years later, in 1987, the current account, too, moved into the black and growing surpluses have been recorded each year since then (see Figures 19.2 & 19.3).

The composition of Irish exports is now heavily-weighted towards manufactured goods, the share of which has increased, over time, to its current level of 70 per cent. Food and drink exports, on the other hand, have declined steadily to 22 per cent of the total. The geographical distribution of trade has also changed considerably (see Figures 19.4 & 19.5). While the UK remains the largest single source of imports and destination for exports, dependence on that market has fallen sharply. The share of other EC markets in Irish exports continues to grow and now exceeds that of the UK. Germany and France are, apart from the UK, Ireland's largest trading partners in the EC and Ireland has consistently recorded a bilateral trade surplus with Germany in recent years. EC countries account for about 70 per cent of Ireland's total imports and exports. While the US is Ireland's fourth most important single destination for exports, it is second largest as a source of imports, reflecting the presence of US-owned companies in Ireland who use it as a base for exporting into continental Europe.

The competitiveness of Irish industry has been improving in a sustained way over the past number of years. Productivity has been growing strongly, while

	1980	1985	1990	1991[1]	1992[2]
Trade balance	-1342	137	1814	2000	2600
EC transfers	480	901	1440	1750	1450
Profit repatriations	-258	-1321	-2452	-2050	-2200
Debt interest	-193	-795	-1009	-1050	-1150
Current balance	-1038	-650	556	1616	1750
External reserves	1346	2272	2892	3256	n/a

Figure 19.2 Analysis of Irish balance of payments, 1980-1992 (IEP million)
[1] *estimated*
[2] *forecast*

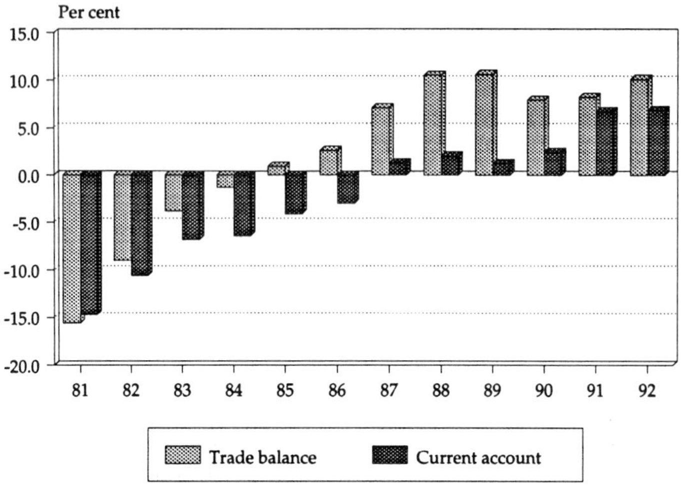

*) forecast

Figure 19.3 Irish balance of payments (as percentage of GNP), 1981-1992

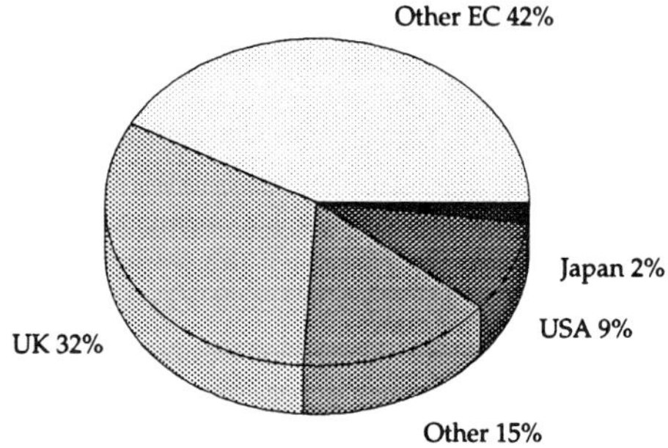

Figure 19.4 Distribution of Irish exports, 1991

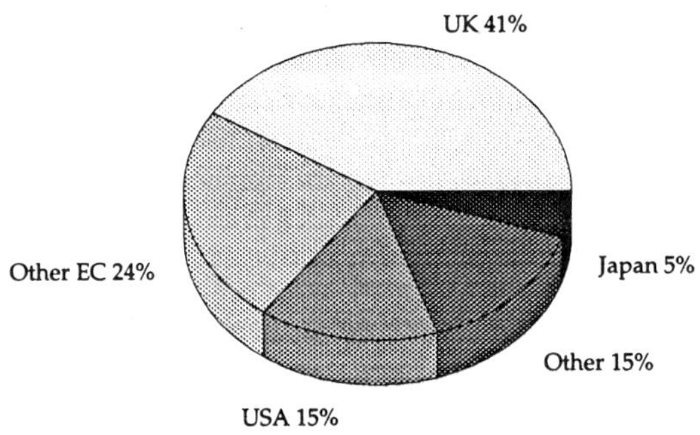

Figure 19.5 Origin of Irish imports, 1991

wages growth has been moderate. In the period since 1987, unit wage costs in Irish manufacturing industry have declined by close on 13 per cent. In relative terms, the decline has been over 20 per cent given rising unit costs in trading partner countries. It is notable in this context that, at a time of declining or slowing demand in those countries, Ireland's export growth has remained buoyant.

Unemployment

The unemployment rate in Ireland more than doubled between 1980 and 1987. In part, this reflected strong growth in labour supply, with the labour force growing, on average, by close to one per cent per year in the first half of the decade. More importantly, however, the rise in unemployment reflected a fairly steady decline in employment in the period. Total employment fell by 76,000 in the years 1980-1987. Continuing a long-term trend, employment in the agricultural sector fell by 45,000, a reduction of more than one-fifth, while industrial employment declined by 71,000, more than reversing the employment gains made over the previous decade. These reductions were partly offset by rising employment in the services sector, where numbers rose by 40,000. Declining industrial employment largely reflected falling numbers at work in the manufacturing sector, and this occurred despite growth in manufacturing output over the 1980-1987 period, of an average 6 per cent per year. This is partly explained by the fact that manufacturing output growth tended to be concentrated in the newer, more capital-intensive and export-orientated industries rather than in the more labour-intensive, domestically-orientated industries. It is also likely to have been due, in part, to relatively-high employment taxes and factors such as the impact of technological change on production techniques. The rise in unemployment would have been greater, but for the high rate of emigration which occurred. This has been a feature of Irish demography since the middle of the last century, the trend being reversed only briefly in the 1970s.

The economic boom in the latter part of the eighties saw employment grow by over 40,000, despite significant reductions in public sector employment. Net emigration continued to feature strongly and the unemployment rate fell from almost 18 per cent to under 14 per cent in 1990. More recently, unemployment has again started to rise strongly as employment has levelled off and net emigration has ceased, reflecting poor employment prospects in neighbouring economies. The unemployment rate in April 1991 was 15.6 per cent. This figure is based on the annual labour force survey. There is also a monthly indicator based on the number of persons claiming unemployment benefit. This latter measure is currently showing an unemployment rate of over 17 per cent.

The rise in unemployment and it relative level has not, however, resulted in any significant increase in social tensions. In part, this may reflect the source of the unemployment rise, i.e. cessation of emigration rather than falling employment, and the hope that it will prove temporary. It may also reflect a history of relatively high unemployment in Ireland and the realization that recent experience

	1980	1987	1988	1989	1990	1991
Total employment	1156	1080	1091	1090	1126	1125
of which:						
Agriculture	209	164	166	163	167	154
Industry	371	300	300	306	320	322
Services	576	616	626	621	639	649
Unemployment	91	232	219	202	179	208
(% of labour force)	(7.3)	(17.7)	(16.7)	(15.6)	(13.7)	(15.6)
Labour force	1247	1312	1310	1292	1305	1334
Net migration	-8	-27	-32	-46	-31	-1
Population	3401	3543	3538	3515	3503	3524

Figure 19.6 Population and labour force (mid-April estimates, thousands)

is not unique, with unemployment rising in most industrial countries. a further factor may be the recognition that past attempts to reduce unemployment by fiscal action - particularly in the 1970s - had little lasting impact, but were largely responsible for the sharp increase in the national debt in that period and the consequent rise in the burden of taxation during the 1980s.

Inflation

Ireland's inflation performance was radically transformed during the 1980s. At the beginning of the decade, the rate of increase in consumer prices was running above 20 per cent (see Figure 19.7), and close to twice the average rate in the EC as a whole. On the one hand, this reflected the high rate of inflation experienced internationally at the time and, on the other, a steady depreciation in the trade-weighted exchange rate of the Irish pound in the early years of the EMS, as severe economic imbalances and a delayed domestic policy response weighed on the currency. The inflation rate declined in the first half of the 1980s mainly in response to the general moderation in international inflation. For an economy as small and open as Ireland, the trend in the international price of traded goods, as transmitted through the exchange rate, tends to dominate the

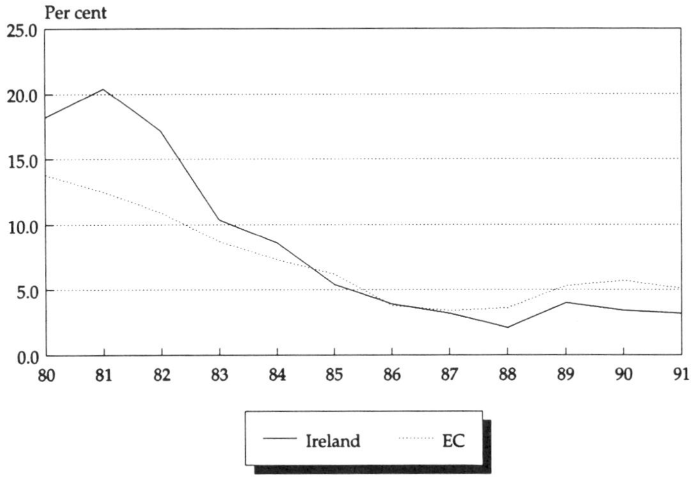

Figure 19.7 Irish inflation, 1980-1991 (annual percentage change)

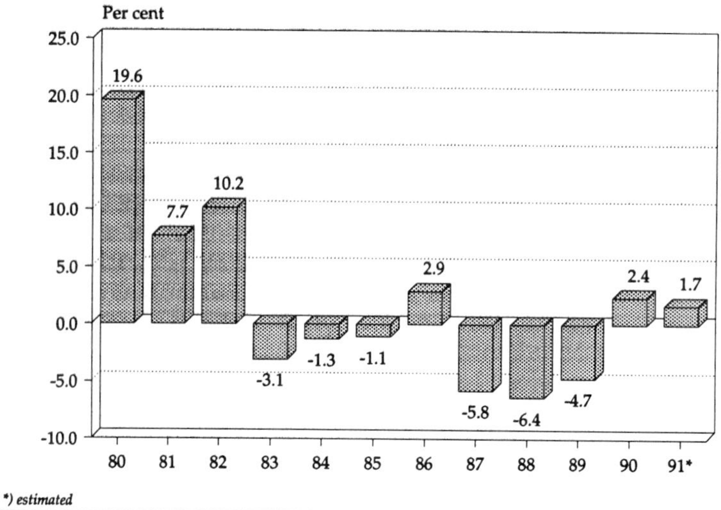

Figure 19.8 Unit wage costs in Ireland, 1980-1991 (annual percentage change)

inflationary experience. Thus, as currency stability was gradually established, Ireland's inflation rate began to converge on the EC average.

From the mid-1980s, however, the rate of increase in Irish consumer prices moved below that of the EC as a whole. Two factors were chiefly responsible. Firstly, commitment to exchange rate stability within the EMS was hardened and gathered increasing credibility. Secondly, the restrictive fiscal policy stance, pursued from about 1983 onward, along with the depressed condition of the domestic economy and higher unemployment, together brought about a significant adjustment in inflationary expectations. Average earnings increases, which had been consistently in double-digits through the first half of the 1980s, subsided. A watershed, in this respect, was the conclusion of a three-year national pay agreement in 1987 which limited wage increases to an annual 2.5 per cent. Contrary to earlier experience with pay bargains negotiated at national level, the 1987 agreement was closely adhered to and was followed in 1990 by a further three-year agreement under the Programme for Economic and Social Progress (PESP). The terms of this deal limit annual pay increases to an average of around 3.5 per cent over its life with the possibility of a further 1 per cent annual increase on the basis of local, productivity-related, bargaining.

Ireland's status as one of the low-inflation EC member states appears secure. The commitment to exchange rate stability remains firm. The benefit of low inflation in terms of the downward adjustment in Irish interest rate differentials is widely recognized. Ireland's strong commitment to full participation in Emu is broadly supported, and the required economic discipline this implies is understood.

Public finances

For much of the 1980s, the performance of the Irish economy was undermined by very large budget deficits. Attempts to reduce the level of borrowing focused on raising taxes and curbing capital spending. However, as current public spending was not tackled effectively, the Exchequer borrowing requirement (EBR) stayed high and the economy was left with tax rates at disincentive levels.

This situation changed dramatically in 1987, when a new government launched a programme of fiscal correction which yielded substantial results. Progress was made on both sides of the budget balance sheet. Government spending was cut back. The determined action helped get interest rates down and stimulated confidence in the economy which led to a buoyancy in tax revenue which went beyond expectations. As a result, the EBR fell from 13 per cent of GNP in 1986 to 2 per cent in 1990 (see Figure 19.10).

The impact of slower economic activity, both at home and abroad, caused the 1991 budget to overshoot and the deficit was 2.1 per cent of GNP, as compared to the original target of 1.7 per cent. Revenue was lower than expected, reflecting depressed consumer spending, and government spending rose because of higher unemployment. The overshoot would have been greater but for a Ir£100m package of measures introduced at mid-year to curtail the deficit. The

	1980	1985	1990	1991	1992[1]
Current deficit	547	1284	152	300	339
Capital deficit	670	731	310	201	253
Exchequer borrowing requirement	1217	2015	462	501	592
Public sector borrowing requirement	1559	2444	681	816	884
National debt					
Domestic	5689	10060	16255	16500	n/a
Foreign	2207	8441	8862	8900	n/a
Total	7896	18501	25117	25400	n/a

Figure 19.9 Analysis of Irish public sector deficit (IEP million)
[1] *forecast*

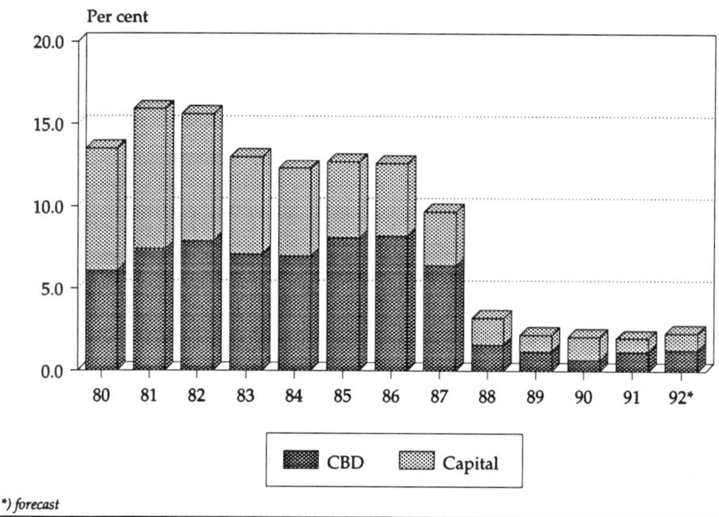

Figure 19.10 **Current budget deficit & EBR (percentage of GNP)**

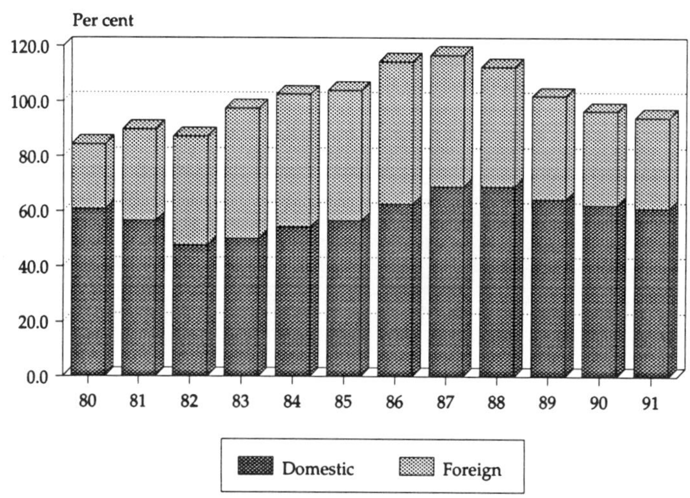

Figure 19.11 **Irish national debt (percentage of GDP)**

1992 target deficit is 2.3 per cent of GNP. The government are committed to lowering further the EBR, as a percentage of GNP, in 1993.

This is in line with the expectation that Ireland will satisfy the Emu convergence criteria. One of the conditions for transition to full Emu is a debt/GDP ratio which is steadily declining towards the EC average of 60 per cent. Ten years of high government borrowing saw Ireland's national debt (and therefore government bond market!) grow rapidly until the mid-eighties. The debt/GDP ratio was stabilized at 120 per cent of GDP by the initial tightening of fiscal policy in 1987 and has subsequently declined steadily to 95 per cent in 1991 (see Figure 19.11). The government has stated that they intend to continue to maintain the declining trend in the ratio, implying a tight medium-term fiscal stance.

The government are also committed to a programme of tax reform which involves lowering marginal tax rates and compensating by widening the tax base to remove exemptions and anomalies.

Exchange rate and monetary policy

For over a century prior to 1979, the Irish pound was linked to sterling on a one-to-one, no-margins basis. This ended when Ireland joined the EMS at its inception, on 13 March 1979. Since then, exchange rate policy centres on maintaining the value of the pound within the narrow, 2.25 per cent, band of the exchange rate mechanism (ERM) of the EMS. High government borrowing, relatively high inflation and balance of payments deficits resulted in the pound's central rate being devalued on two occasions: in March 1983, by 3.5 per cent and, in August 1986, by 8 per cent. The drawback of a depreciating currency in the context of a small open economy with a relatively centralized wage bargaining process (quick pass-through to inflation) are widely appreciated and, since 1987, the policy of a firm linkage of the exchange rate to the ERM is an important element of overall economic strategy. The Irish pound's deviation from its average Deutschemark rate has been less than half a per cent since 1988.

Given the extremely open nature of the Irish economy, the primary objective of monetary policy is to minimize imported inflation by maintaining the 'integrity of the currency'. To this end, it focuses on the external value of the Irish pound, seeking to keep it stable through the maintenance of adequate external reserves. The central bank focuses on interest rates and, in particular, on the differentials between Irish and foreign interest rates necessary to ensure adequacy of reserves. While the dominant influence on Irish interest rates is, thus, the trend in international rates, domestic factors are also important, as evidenced by the steady decline in the differential of Irish over, for example, German rates in recent years. Although the central bank does not attempt to resist fundamental interest rate trends, whether domestic or external in nature, it does pursue, in a purposeful way, the important function of smoothing short-run fluctuations and predictable seasonal patterns in liquidity.

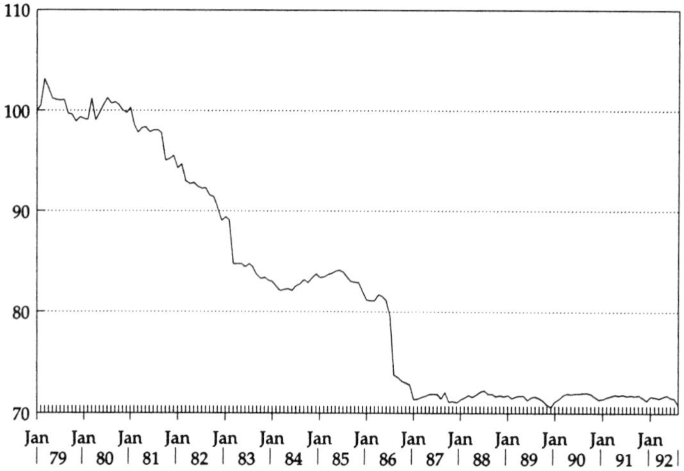

Figure 19.12 Exchange rate history: IEP vs. DEM, 1979-1992 (Jan 79 = 100)

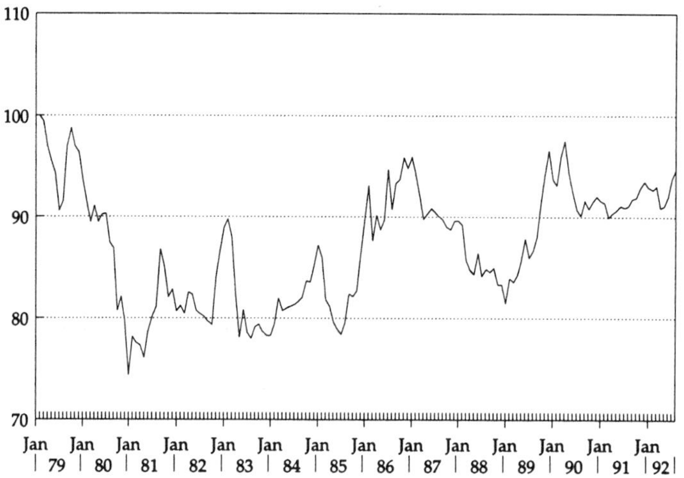

Figure 19.13 Exchange rate history: IEP vs. GBP, 1979-1992 (Jan 79 = 100)

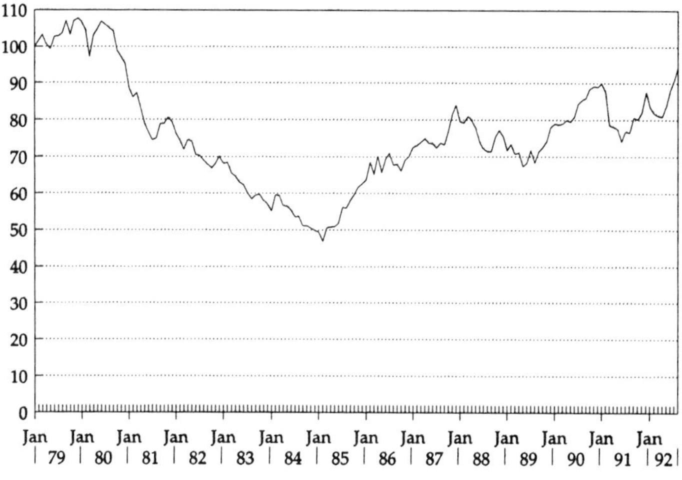

Figure 19.14 Exchange rate history: IEP vs. USD, 1979-1992 (Jan 79 = 100)

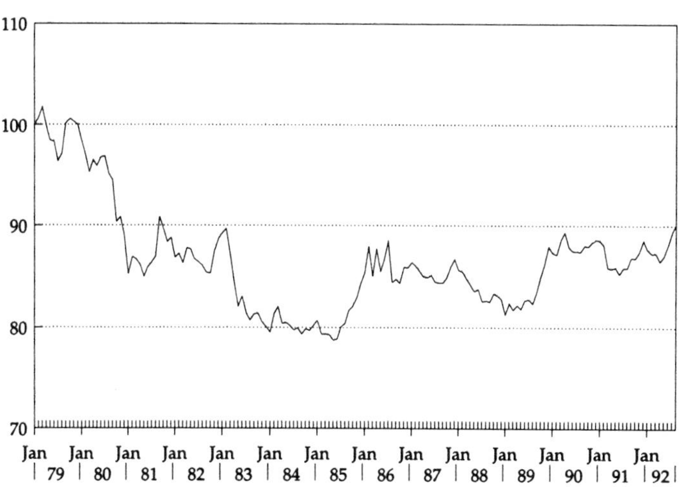

Figure 19.15 Exchange rate history: effective index of the Irish pound, 1979-1992 (Jan 79 = 100)

Emu

Ireland has adopted a very positive approach to Emu as reflected, for example, in the strenuous measures to curb the fiscal deficits in 1991 and 1992 so as to ensure that the debt/GDP ratio continues to decline. A recent study by Merrill Lynch concluded that Ireland, along with Belgium, Germany, the Netherlands and the UK, was highly likely to pass the Emu convergence tests. A separate study by Salomon Brothers confirms that Ireland currently meets the Emu convergence criteria on inflation, interest rates, exchange rates and the budget deficit. At present, Ireland's debt/GDP ratio is well above 60 per cent but this is unlikely to be a disqualifying factor as the EMS requirement is for steady downward pressure in the ratio towards 60 per cent and the Irish authorities are determined to satisfy this criterion.

Politics

The national parliament of Ireland, known as the Oireachtas, formally consists of a President and two Houses - the Dail, or Lower House, and the Seanad, Upper House. The Constitution confers legislative primacy on the Dail and the government is responsible to it alone. Presidential powers are limited and most can be exercised only on the advice of the government. Legislation may be initiated in the Seanad but its powers, too, are limited. It cannot initiate money bills and the Dail may pass a bill rejected by the Seanad, or may pass it without accepting amendments proposed by the Seanad.

Elections to Dail and Seanad occur at least once every five years. The Dail consists of 166 members, elected by adult suffrage under the proportional representation system. The Seanad has 60 members, 43 of whom are elected by 5 vocational panels, 6 by the universities and 11 members are nominated directly by the Taoiseach (Prime Minister). The Taoiseach is appointed by the President on the nomination of the Dail and government ministers are nominated by the Taoiseach for the approval of the Dail.

The current government has held office since July 1989. It is a coalition of the Fianna Fail and Progressive Democrat parties. The Fianna Fail Party holds 77 Dail seats and the Progressive Democrats 6. The coalition parties are centre-right in terms of the political spectrum as is the main opposition party, Fine Gael, which holds 55 seats. Together, these three parties account for over 83 per cent of Dail members. Left-wing party representation in the Dail is relatively small, accounting for 23, or 14 per cent, of seats. The Green Party holds one seat and the remaining four are independent, non-party members.

In the 23 governments since Ireland achieved independence in 1922, the Fianna Fail Party has been in power on 15 occasions, 14 of them as a single-party government. Most of the remaining eight governments have been coalitions of two or more parties with the Fine Gael Party as the major partner. Irish governments have rarely lasted the full term of five years permitted under the Constitution. The average duration in office since 1922 has been three years, with a median period of four years.

19.3 *Market composition*

Overview

Irish government issues account for 97 per cent of the total bond market. Some state-owned companies, most notably the Housing Finance Agency, the Electricity Supply Board, Telecom Eireann and the Agricultural Credit Corporation, whose issues carry a government guarantee, have a small number of bonds in issue. There are no private issues of significance traded in the Irish bond market. Recently, an active market in euro-Irish pound paper has begun to emerge.

There are at present 38 government bonds on issue, with a nominal value of Ir£14bn. This has grown from Ir£4.3bn, in 1981, and is considerably larger than the domestic equity market, which is valued at Ir£8.5bn. However, this rate of growth is not surprising given the scale of borrowing by the authorities in the first half of the 1980s. There was also significant recourse to foreign currency-denominated borrowing in this period. Since 1987, in contrast, the authorities

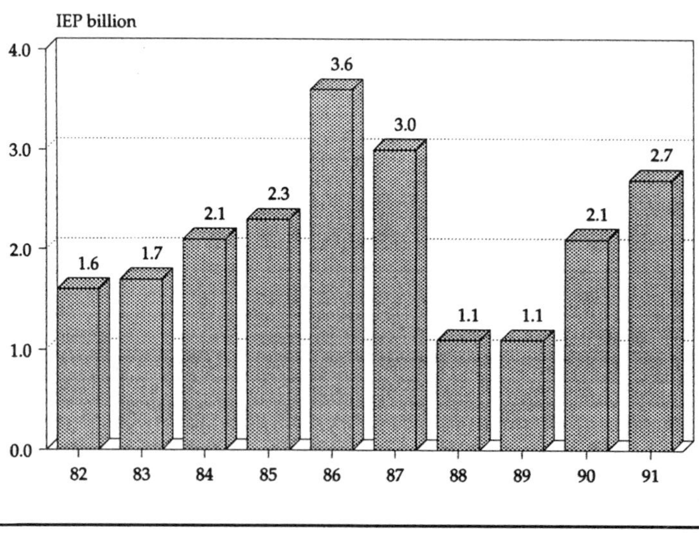

Figure 19.16 Gross issuance of Irish government bonds, 1982-1991

have become net repayers of foreign debt and the domestic bond market has again become the primary source of funding.

There is a variety of titles used for government stock including Capital Stock, Exchequer Loan, National Loan, etc. The title is of no significance as each stock ranks *pari passu* with every other government stock. However, the authorities issued a new 10-year benchmark in 1991 which they entitled 'Government Bond' to avoid any ambiguity for international investors. The date listed in the title of all government bonds is the date of final redemption of the stock. In some cases there are two dates specified in the title, such as the 9.25% National Loan, 1 July, 1989/94. In such cases, the stock may be redeemed at the option of the issuer, in whole or in part, at any time after the earlier date specified but, in any event, not later than the final date. Normally, three months' notice is required for any redemption prior to the latest redemption date. The authorities may, in the course of their day-to-day operations, repurchase stock from the market and such stock is usually cancelled without delay.

Composition of the market by maturity

The average maturity of government bonds (see Figure 19.17) has tended to shorten in recent years, following a marked reduction in the issuance of longer-dated stock. Consequently, the proportion of the market with a maturity of over

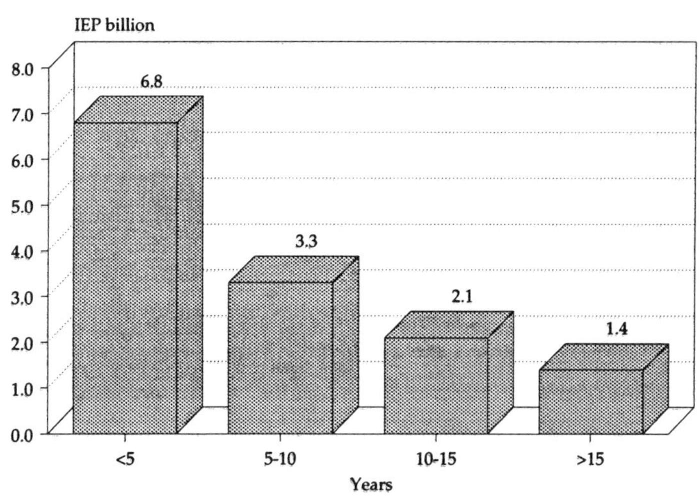

Figure 19.17 Composition of Irish market by maturity

10 years has fallen from over 36 per cent in 1986 to 25 per cent at end-1991. This change also reflects the growth in the importance of non-resident interest in the market, particularly from Europe, where the focus tends to be on maturities at the 5- to 10-year level. The shortening of the debt profile has also ensured a steady supply of issuance at a time when net borrowing has fallen to a range equivalent to 2-3 per cent of GNP, from over 12 per cent in the first half of the 1980s.

Composition of the market by coupon

Coupons on government stocks range from 6 per cent to 14 3/4 per cent, although the majority of stocks have coupons between 7 per cent and 10 per cent (see Figure 19.18). Given the relatively high level of Irish bond yields seen until recently, this has meant that most stocks were issued at a considerable discount to the market. Most recent issues have had coupons of 9.5 per cent or less.

There is a small number of variable-rate stocks (generally called 'floaters' elsewhere) on issue in the Irish government securities market. The dividend paid is a margin over the appropriate reference rate which, for all existing stocks, is the 3-month Dublin interbank offered rate. This paper is similar in nature to floating-rate notes in the eurobond market and holdings are concentrated in the hands of banking institutions.

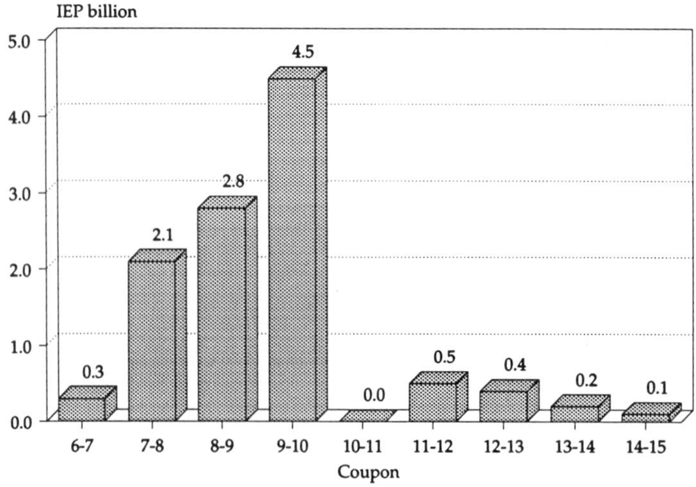

Figure 19.18 Composition of the Irish market by coupon

The Housing Finance Agency has issued three index-linked stocks. Two carry coupons of 2 per cent, and one of 4 per cent. The total amount on issue is only Ir£170m.

Benchmark issues

The National Treasury Management Agency has pursued a stated policy of building up large liquid issues which, relative to market size, compare with other EMS sovereign benchmark stocks. The Agency has recently designated the following stocks as benchmark stocks in the 5-, 10-, 15- and 20-year maturity ranges, with the broad objective of building up, where necessary, the amounts outstanding to around Ir£1bn in each case. Funding will be concentrated in these stocks:

- 8 3/4% Exchequer Bond 1997,
- 9% Government Bond 2001,
- 9% Capital Stock 2006,
- 8 3/4% Capital Stock 2012.

Apart from the stocks expressly designated as benchmark issues there are other large liquid stocks where the amounts outstanding are close to, or in excess of, Ir£1bn. These include the 7% Capital Stock 1994, 9% Capital Loan 1996, 9 3/4% Capital Stock 1998 and the 9 1/4% Capital Stock 2003.

19.4 Types of security

Bullet bonds

The majority of government securities (27 stocks out of the total of 38 on issue) have a single, fixed maturity date.

Callable bonds

The remaining 11 stocks have dual redemption dates (e.g. the 11% National Loan 1993-98) where the authorities have the option to redeem the stock at any time between the two dates shown in the title, provided they give three months' notice of their intention to do so. The circumstances in which the authorities would have an incentive to exercise their option in this regard depend on the relationship between current yield levels and the coupon. If the coupon exceeds current yield levels, the Exchequer's interest bill can be reduced by redeeming the stock at par and issuing a new stock at prevailing yield levels.

Dual redemption-date stocks priced over par trade on the basis that the option of early redemption will be exercised. The 11% National Loan 1993-98 is, thus, priced on the assumption that it will be redeemed in 1993.

Convertible bonds

There are no convertibles issued by the government on the Irish market although, in recent years, a number of private sector firms have issued convertible bonds. There are currently eight in issue.

Variable-rate stocks

There are four variable-rate stocks traded on the Irish market, with maturities in 1993, 1994, 1995 and end-1996. In general, dividends are calculated as the sum of the 'reference rate' and the 'margin' divided by the number of dividend dates in the year. The reference rate for the existing stocks on issue is the average of the three-month Dublin interbank offered rate (DIBOR) for the ten business days immediately preceding the second business day before the commencement of the relevant dividend period. The margin rates vary from zero to 0.1 per cent and the yield on the stocks is generally valued in the secondary market in relation to DIBOR.

The terms relating to each of these stocks are summarized in Figure 19.19.

	Variable 1993	Variable 1994	Variable 1995	Variable 1996
Redeemable at par	01 Feb 1993	01 June 1994	16 April 1995	30 Sep 1996
No. of dividends per annum	4	4	4	4
Reference rate[1]	Av. 3-mth DIBOR (10 days)	Av. 3-mth DIBOR (10 days)	Av. 3-mth DIBOR (10 days)	Av. 3-mth DIBOR (10 days)
Margin	0.10%	0.05%	0.00%	0.00%

Figure 19.19 Terms for variable-rate stocks
[1] *Further details given in text*

Index-linked stocks

There are three index-linked stocks trading on the Irish market, all issued by the Housing Finance Agency. These stocks will mature in 1993, 2008 and 2015 respectively. The amount due on redemption of these stocks and the interest payable is related to movement in the consumer price index (CPI). For example, interest is calculated as

$$\frac{\text{annual coupon}}{2} \times \frac{CPI_{t-6}}{CPI_{bm}}$$

where,

t month in which interest payment falls due
bm base month, CPI at date of issue of stock

19.5 Issuers

Government

The government dominates the Irish bond market although small quantities of stock have been issued by the Housing Finance Agency, the Electricity Supply Board, Telecom Eireann and the Agricultural Credit Corporation. The lack of any corporate issuance of note is partly due to tax considerations and partly to a crowding out effect as a result of the scale of government borrowing in the past. In terms of the former, the main factor relates to stamp duty and capital gains tax. Corporate bonds are liable for both, whereas government bonds are exempt.

Housing Finance Agency

The Housing Finance Agency (HFA) is a state-sponsored company incorporated in February 1982. The principal objects of the Agency are:

- to provide, by way of mortgage or charge loans, for the acquisition or construction of houses;
- to provide moneys to enable such loans to be made by housing authorities;
- to borrow or raise money for these purposes.

All of the issued share capital of the HFA is beneficially-owned by the Minister for Finance. The HFA initially involved itself in the business of providing finance directly for house purchase purposes to low-income individuals but it has now disengaged itself from such direct lending. Since July 1986, the Agency has operated only as funding agency for local authority mortgages. The Agency has four stocks on issue. Three of these (due in 1993, 2008 and 2015 respectively) are index-linked stock. The most recently issued HFA Stock, redeemable at par on 15 February 2018, is an 8 3/4 per cent fixed-interest stock. All HFA stocks are guaranteed by the Minister for Finance.

Electricity Supply Board

The Electricity Supply Board (ESB) is a state-owned utility engaged in the monopoly generation and transmission of electricity. It has an extensive investment programme to which the proceeds of its stock issues are applied.

Other state bodies

The Agricultural Credit Corporation (ACC) is a state-owned bank lending mainly to the agricultural sector. It has one stock on issue. Telecom Eireann, the state telecommunications company, also has one stock on issue.

Corporates

Other than state-owned corporations such as the ESB and the ACC there is no corporate bond issuance of significance.

Municipals

There are no municipal bonds of significance on issue in the Irish market. It is over 30 years since such a bond issue last took place.

19.6 *Investors*

Traditionally, the principal investors in Irish government stocks have been domestic banks for short-dated securities and other domestic institutions for longer-dated securities. The principal non-bank domestic purchasers of government bonds are insurance companies and pension funds who, in total, own one-third of the market (see Figure 19.20). Other financial institutions, such as building societies, are also significant purchasers of securities. Unlike a number of continental European markets, direct purchases of bonds by private investors are very small. The rapid growth in the market size and liquidity, together with Ireland's membership of the EMS since 1979, has led to a growing involvement by non-residents as active investors and traders in the Irish market in the last decade. This trend accelerated from the mid-1980s reflecting two major policy changes: Irish monetary policy became geared more firmly to maintaining the value of the currency within the ERM, and fiscal policy became much tighter. From 13 per cent of the market in 1987, the non-resident share increased to 30 per cent by 1991, with German institutions accounting for around two-thirds of the foreign total. However, the spectrum of foreign ownership has broadened of

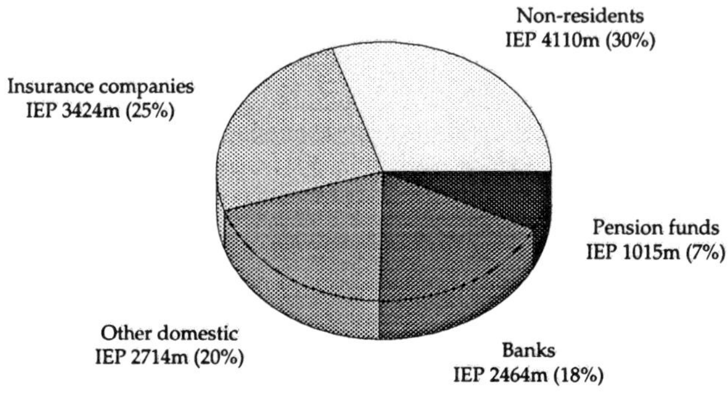

Figure 19.20 Holdings of Irish government bonds as at the end of 1991

late, with German investors becoming less important, and US, UK, other European and Japanese investors increasing their share of the non-resident uptake of securities.

International bond indices

Salomon Brothers' new Global Composite Index of government bonds, now includes Ireland, and arrangements have been finalized with Lehman Brothers and with Bloomberg to include Ireland in their respective government bond indices.

19.7 *Methods of issuance*

National Treasury Management Agency

In 1990, legislation was enacted to provide for the establishment of the National Treasury Management Agency to manage Ireland's national debt and borrowing programmes. The management of the national debt of Ir£25bn had become increasingly complex and the government decided that a separate public agency was required to manage the debt cost-effectively and to exploit fully the potential for savings. A key element identified as being essential to that task was the ability of the new Agency to recruit personnel skilled in modern debt management techniques.

The Agency came into being on 3 December, 1990. Under the National Treasury Management Act 1990, the borrowing and debt management functions of the Minister for Finance, and related operational responsibilities, were delegated to the Agency. The Agency operates under the general control of the Minister and is subject to whatever directions and guidelines he may give.

In the domestic debt management area, which accounts for approximately Ir£16 billion of the national debt, a key stated objective of the Agency is to improve the liquidity of the market. In January 1992, the Agency announced important changes in the gilt issuance procedures (outlined below) which will enhance the market's liquidity and transparency. Further significant changes in the market structure aimed at liquidity improvement are expected.

Primary market

The gilts funding programme of the government is met through sales by the National Treasury Management Agency via a form of tap, supplemented by occasional auctions. The tap operates as follows:

The market is advised of the target size of each tap. While a tap stock is open, the Agency does not offer for sale by tap, auction or otherwise, another stock within an announced maturity range of the open stock. The tap is closed when the funding target is reached, or earlier at the discretion of the Agency.

The Agency states the amount of a tap stock on offer at each posted price, which is firm. As market conditions change, the price and/or the specified amount on offer may be varied (without necessarily having sold the previously specified amount). In the event of simultaneous demand in excess of the specified amount of stock on offer at a posted price, the Agency, at its discretion, may supply up to the full amount demanded.

The opening of a tap is announced not later that 15 minutes before the next trading session commences on the stock exchange.

Announcements regarding the tap (including prices) are made on behalf of the Agency by the government broker on the stock exchange and, for information, by the Agency itself on Reuters (pages NTMB and NTMC).

Auctions

Auctions are held from time to time to supplement sales via the tap mechanism. In announcing an auction, the Agency indicates a restricted period during which it will not sell stocks within a specified maturity range of the auction stock.

If the amount of stock on offer in an auction is not fully taken up, the Agency is free to sell the residual amount by the tap mechanism, subject to not selling during the specified restricted period at a price below the average price accepted in the auction.

Two business days' notice of each auction is given, including detailed conditions governing the auction. The Agency is committed to selling the 20-year benchmark issue - 8 3/4% Capital Loan 2012 - by auction only during 1992.

19.8 New issue volumes

The tap system currently in use means that recourse to the market by the NTMA is spasmodic, and there is no regular calendar of supply. The NTMA has, however, announced that, subject to market conditions, there will be two auctions of the 8 3/4% Capital Stock 2012, one in September and one in the final quarter of 1992.

19.9 *Methods of trading*

Overview

Irish government bonds are listed and dealt on the the Irish Stock Exchange in Dublin. The exchange is a regional component of the International Stock Exchange in London. The stock exchanges merged in 1973, and all members of the Irish Stock Exchange are members of the London Stock Exchange, and are bound by its rules.

Turnover in gilts has increased considerably in recent years and the normal bargain size ranges between Ir£1m and Ir£3m.

Primary market

The bond market used to be managed by the Department of Finance, with the Central Bank of Ireland having responsibility for short-dated stock. However, in 1990, the government set up the National Treasury Management Agency (NTMA) to manage all aspects of government debt, domestic and foreign. The NTMA is responsible for issuing stock to the market and quotes bid prices for the benchmark stocks. The bid prices quoted often fall considerably behind market levels, so the NTMA's role is effectively that of buyer of last resort. The market officially opens at 10.00 and closes at 16.30.

Most of the dealing in government securities takes place without the involvement of the NTMA in what is termed the 'secondary market' and market prices are effectively established there.

Secondary market

As noted above, the bulk of trading takes place in the secondary market, as only four benchmark stocks are bid for by the NTMA, and the prices are usually well below market levels. Consequently, brokers match buyers and sellers of existing stock. A broker may also deal, on behalf of a client, with another broker. Over 85 per cent of market transactions are currently done in the secondary market. Prices available in the market are indicated on Reuters, Telerate and Bloomberg.

All transactions, whether client-matching or broker-to-broker, must be 'put through' the market. The prices at which such transactions take place are recorded and quoted by the stock exchange. The transaction will be permitted only where there are no superior bids or offers in equivalent size established within the market

Brokers as agents

Brokers are not permitted to deal as principals, and may act only as agents of their clients. This combination of the prohibition of principal trading and the 'put through' requirement ensures a high degree of investor protection. Brokers transmit guidelines as to current dealing levels through information agencies such as Reuters, Telerate and Bloomberg. These prices are shown on behalf of different clients and, in normal circumstances, can be taken as firm prices and dealt in at the size indicated.

19.10 *Market practices*

Coupon payment

All fixed-rate bonds have coupons paid semi-annually, although the NTMA has announced that, in future, new issues will carry an annual coupon. All the three variable-rate stocks (floaters) currently in issue pay dividends on a quarterly basis.

First coupon

As in the UK, it is sometimes the case that the first coupon-date may be more or less than one full coupon period after the date of issuance. As a result, this payment is usually pro-rata in relation to the number of days between the commencement of the dividend period and the date on which the stock is dealt.

Partly-paid

Irish government stock is not issued in partly-paid form.

Ex-dividend

Securities generally go ex-dividend on the Wednesday nearest to three weeks before the semi-annual coupon is paid.

Special ex-dividend

No Irish securities trade on a special ex-dividend basis.

Redemption

All Irish government securities are redeemed at par. The three index-linked stocks issued by the Housing Finance Agency have a redemption value linked to the CPI.

Puts

No gilt-edged issues confer the right of a put option on the holder.

Denomination

All stocks are transferable in any sums which are multiples of one penny.

Form

All Irish government bonds are in registered form.

Dealing quotation

Prices are quoted in decimal form rather than 32nds.

Liquidity

The most common dealing size is Ir£1m though it is not unusual for Ir£5 million to be transacted. The market turns over about three times per year, implying that weekly turnover is about Ir£800m. Prices in the 'runner' stocks are readily available but the agency broker system means that prices in the less-liquid stocks normally take longer to find. To help liquidity, the NTMA has begun to issue large amounts in a number of benchmark bullet stocks and has also, on occasion, offered switch terms out of dual-redemption date stocks into bullets.

Withholding tax

There is no withholding tax on Irish government bonds and the prospectus for each current issue states that the stock and interest payable thereon is exempt from all Irish taxation, present or future, if the beneficial ownership is held by a non-resident.

Commissions

Foreign investors generally deal on a net basis but Irish-pound liability clients pay commission on the basis of a predetermined scale of charges, set out below. There are no other charges.

Life of stock	Minimum commission
0 to 5 years	At discretion
5 to 10 years	.0161% on first IEP 1m (rates vary for smaller amounts) .0293% on next IEP 3m .013% on next IEP 6m .0065% on the excess
10 years plus	.0714% on first IEP 1m (rates vary for smaller amounts) .0585% on next IEP 3m .026% on next IEP 6m .013% on the excess

19.11 Settlement

Both primary market and secondary market gilt dealings are normally subject to settlement (payment) in full on the business day following but, in the case of overseas clients, brokers can arrange deferred settlement. Accrued interest will of course arise in this situation and will be calculated to the date of settlement. The National Treasury Management Agency, in its primary market operations, quotes terms for up to 7 days' delayed settlement.

About 80 per cent of all transactions in bonds are settled through the Gilt Settlement Office (GSO), which is operated by the Central Bank of Ireland. The GSO deals with transactions in government bonds in excess of Ir£100,000. The main objective of the GSO is to provide an efficient and risk-free system for the transfer of, and contemporaneous payment for, bonds between market participants by matching transfer of stock with simultaneous payment (guaranteed by approved settlement banks), thereby removing the risk of default. All holdings of government stock in the GSO are in book-entry form, i.e. the bank maintains an inscribed register, and, therefore, stock certificates are eliminated for deals carried out by GSO members. The authorities, the major domestic institutional players in the bond market, and most stockbrokers are members.

Non-resident investors in bonds can avail of the risk-free settlement procedure also by arranging for a member of the GSO to act on their behalf.

Payment for stocks not settled through the GSO is normally made against delivery of certificates accompanied by stock transfer forms (signed by the transferors) or certified transfer forms (certified by the Registrar, the Central Bank of Ireland, as constituting good delivery).

Irish bonds denominated in foreign currencies can be cleared through Cedel and Euroclear and discussions are well advanced with both these organizations on the question of including Irish pound-denominated government bonds in their settlement systems.

19.12 *Yield calculation*

The methodology and conventions adopted for the calculation of Irish bond redemption yields are similar to those employed in the UK gilt market. Yields are calculated on a semi-annual basis, reflecting the standard coupon period. The semi-annual yield calculations are based on standard discounting principles.

There is a slight variation in the case of index-linked stocks. Dividend and capital redemption payments are related to movements in the consumer price index (CPI). The relevant CPI figure for any payment is that pertaining six months prior to the month in which the benefit is received.

19.13 *Taxation*

Tax privileges

Interest on government stock is paid without deduction of income tax but is assessable to income tax in the hands of the recipient. Gains arising on the disposal of stock are exempt from capital gains tax. However, gains arising to private individuals within a minimum holding period of two years are subject to income tax and gains arising to financial institutions other than pension funds are subject to corporation tax.

The prospectus for all current issues of Irish government securities states that stocks and the interest payable thereon will be exempt from all Irish taxation, present or future, if the beneficial ownership of the stock is held by a person not ordinarily resident in the State.

Thus, payment of dividends is made without any deduction of tax and the absence of a withholding tax is guaranteed under the terms of the prospectus for all current issues of Irish government securities. It would be in breach of the prospectus terms, therefore, to introduce a withholding tax on dividends attaching to existing securities.

Exchange controls

The capacity of non-residents to invest or disinvest from the Irish government securities market is not restricted in any way by exchange control regulations.

19.14 Futures & options

IFOX

The Irish Futures and Options Exchange (IFOX) opened for trading on 29 May 1989, providing a new market in futures instruments covering Irish bonds and interest rates and the foreign exchange market.

IFOX was set up as a self-regulatory body, under the formal supervision of the Central Bank of Ireland. The task of supervising the risk management system is handled internally by the IFOX guarantee and compliance officer. He reports directly to the board of the exchange. The IFOX risk management system provides for an initial margin (e.g. 5 per cent of the nominal value of the bond contract), a variation margin, minimum capital requirements for membership, a limit on total open interest and position limits. Additionally, to provide security to the exchange clearing system, there is a guarantee system, which is underwritten by members.

There are 24 members in the exchange who have each subscribed Ir£60,000 for an exchange seat. The members are drawn from the leading Irish banks, stockbrokers, fund managers and treasury operations.

Trading on the exchange occurs via a computerized trading system. Dealers enter orders and match prices via screens linked to the central IFOX computer. There is no central exchange floor.

The main contracts traded on the IFOX are as follows:

IFOX short bond futures contract

The IFOX short bond contract is based on a Ir£100,000 notional 5-year Irish government stock with an 8 per cent coupon. This contract runs to delivery, i.e. outstanding contracts at maturity oblige the seller to deliver, and the purchaser to take delivery of, short-dated Irish government stocks. The seller chooses the cheapest to deliver in a range of bonds in the 3- to 6-year maturity area. In 1991 some 3100 lots were traded.

IFOX long bond futures contract

The IFOX long bond contract is based on a Ir£50,000 notional 20-year Irish government stock with an 8 per cent coupon. This contract also runs to delivery. The seller chooses the cheapest stock to deliver in a range of bonds in the 15- to 20-year maturity area. Long bond volumes at 9500 lots (underlying value Ir£475 million) in 1991 were 20 per cent up on the previous year with open interest also up proportionately.

The delivery requirement for the two bond contracts operates as follows: the exchange specifies a nominal amount of each deliverable stock which has a value of Ir£100,000 (short bond) and Ir£50,000 (long bond) when discounted at 8 per cent. The seller delivers a deliverable parcel of the stock. The settlement price is based on the final exchange price on the last trading day.

Some 90 per cent of contracts are in fact closed out prior to the dealing date. Delivery months are March, June, September and December. There is no stamp duty or turnover tax on the futures market, nor is there a withholding tax.

IFOX Three-month DIBOR contract

The IFOX DIBOR contract is based on a Ir£500,000 deposit at the three-month Dublin interbank offered rate. A cash settlement system operates, i.e. at maturity those holding outstanding contracts either pay or receive the difference between the final settlement amount specified by the exchange and the value as of the previous margin call. The exchange settlement price uses the same formula as that used to settle forward rate agreements (FRAs). In 1991 some 5500 contracts were traded. The DIBOR contract is expected to grow significantly with the recent introduction of three new market-makers on the contract - BNP, Citibank and Irish Intercontinental Bank (a subsidiary of Kredietbank) have agreed to join the existing market-makers, AIB and Bank of Ireland, by providing continuous liquidity to the contract.

The Reuters page IFOX is an index to the services.

19.15 Money markets

Introduction

In March 1979, the Irish pound joined the narrow-band ERM of the EMS, breaking the traditional one-for-one link with sterling. The focus for the daily determination of interest rates shifted from London to Dublin, and the Dublin interbank market developed rapidly over the following decade:

	1981	1986	1991
Volume (IEP billion)	23.5	55.2	60.5

From the outset, all the major Irish banks participated and some 26 banks are currently active. Rates are quoted throughout the day for terms ranging from overnight to one year, or sometimes longer. While the overnight rate can fluctuate from day to day, the key one-month and three-month rates, which account for two-thirds of the turnover, move more gradually and are the best indication of the general cost of funds in the market.

Irish pound deposits

About one quarter of the total turnover in Irish pound deposits is in certificates of deposit (CDs). There are twelve issuing banks and the market has grown rapidly since the relaxation of exchange controls in 1990. Interest on Irish deposits is paid without deduction of any taxes to non-residents.

Exchequer bills

This is the only government paper auctioned on a regular basis, with a tender taking place every Wednesday. Some Ir£25m to Ir£50m of debt is issued per week, with maturities of three and six months. Exchequer bills are issued at a discount and the nominal amount is repaid without deduction of any taxes. They normally trade between 20 and 30 basis points below the equivalent cash rate and there is an active secondary market. The volume of bills outstanding peaked at Ir£1bn in 1990. Since then, the outstanding amount has fallen steadily, to about Ir£550m at the end of 1991, and to about Ir£200m in September 1992. The decline has accelerated since the introduction of exchange notes (see below), which are more flexible instruments.

Exchequer notes

Exchequer notes, which are a flexible form of short-term government paper, were introduced in December 1991, with maturities ranging from 7 to 120 days. The National Treasury Management Agency quotes continuous two-way prices directly to banks, fund managers, insurance companies and stockbrokers. Unlike Exchequer bills, the notes are not bearer securities and a register of ownership is kept. By September 1992, some Ir£400m notes were outstanding.

Short gilts

- There are four variable-rate stocks available with a total issue size of about Ir£2bn. The coupon is related to over 3-month DIBOR, with the premium varying between 0 and 10 basis points, and the maturity ranging from 1993 to 1996.

- There are a number of fixed-interest, short-dated stocks available at any time to the international investor. However, because of the attractiveness of low-coupon stocks to domestic investors who are liable for income tax, it is only the higher-coupon stocks which tend to give a competitive gross yield in the very short maturities. The current runner stocks in the shorter maturities are the 8% Capital 1993, the 7% Capital 1994, the 9% Capital 1996 and the 8 3/4% Exchequer 1997.

The return on Irish government securities is paid without deduction of any taxes to non-residents.

Forward rate agreements and interest rate swaps

The FRA market has become very active in recent years with the central bank taking an active role in developing the market and with the advent of the 3-month contract on IFOX. Turnover in FRAs in 1991 was Ir10.9bn.

The interest rate swap market is developing rapidly and, at present, there are about 5 banks quoting prices. Prices are normally quoted with a 10 to 15 basis point spread and are about 40 - 60 basis points above the equivalent gilt yield.

Commercial paper

In recent years an active commercial paper market has developed and now totals about Ir£2bn. Unlike certificates of deposit, commercial paper is exempt from deposit interest retention tax (DIRT) in the hands of residents. Plans to reduce DIRT significantly have been announced, and this is likely to curtail the CP market.

Exchange controls

Exchange controls on transactions by Irish residents are being progressively abolished in the run-up to the end of the first stage of Emu in December 1992. There are no restrictions on foreign investment in Irish stocks. Restrictions on Irish investment in foreign securities were substantially removed in 1988 and 1989. From January 1992, all restrictions on foreign banks' Ir£ deposits with Irish banks were eliminated. Foreign banks may purchase Ir£ CDs and commercial paper but this paper may not be sold back to Irish residents until three months has elapsed. This remaining restriction will be removed by the end of 1992.

The role of the Central Bank of Ireland

Changes in the external reserves are the most important influence on liquidity and, therefore, on money-market interest rates. Net spending - positive or negative - by the government and its activities in selling or buying gilts is the other main influence on domestic liquidity. Both of these can give rise to large movements in liquidity which, if unchecked, would lead to considerable interest-rate volatility.

The Central Bank of Ireland endeavours to counter and smooth random fluctuations or distortions in rates, but not to resist the underlying economic trends. It does this by providing and absorbing liquidity on a day-to-day basis. To this end, the Bank estimates in advance what the overall liquidity requirements will be on a particular day. Unlike the Bank of England, however, the Central Bank of Ireland does not publish its estimated surplus/shortfall, rather it provides an early morning indication as to whether liquidity will be in surplus, shortfall or square, thereby influencing opening rates.

19.16 *Interest rate history*

The changed perception of the Irish currency resulted, in 1988, in a major shift in the relationship between Irish and overseas financial markets. Historically, Irish interest rates traded largely by reference to, and at a varying premium over, corresponding UK rates. This situation prevailed even after the Irish pound had joined the ERM of the EMS while sterling had remained outside the system. The relationship reflected the close historical links between the Irish and UK economies, particularly the importance of the UK in Irish trade, and the fact that Irish economic policy and performance, particularly on inflation had, for a time after the start of the EMS, remained more akin to the UK experience than to that of the strong-currency EMS countries.

The copper-fastening of the position of the Irish pound in the EMS from 1987 onwards and the continuing improvement in other economic fundamentals resulted in a decoupling of Irish financial market developments from those in the UK. The timing of this decoupling was, clearly, most fortuitous as it coincided with a period of sharply-rising interest rates in the United Kingdom.

As the credibility of the position of the Irish pound in the EMS was established, Irish financial markets were influenced increasingly by developments in other EMS countries; Germany replaced the UK as the dominant external influence on Irish interest rates. As the Dm/Ir£ exchange rate relationship has become more secure, the sustainable differential between Irish and German interest rates has narrowed considerably.

By the beginning of 1990, the differential of Irish over German money market rates had fallen to about 350 basis points. A year later, this had narrowed to about 200 basis points. The differential fell by a further 75 basis points in 1991, despite some scepticism at the beginning of the year that this would be possible. In the main, this move reflected the strong rise in the official external reserves that occurred and this, in turn, reflected the growing surplus on the balance of payments. Over the year to early-September 1992, the three-month differential over Germany has ranged from a high of 125 basis points to a low of 13 basis points. Belgian and Dutch short-term rates have fallen to German levels, while French rates are currently about 50 basis points above, pending the outcome of their referendum on Maastricht. Irish short-term rates thus remain high relative to those in other EMS countries.

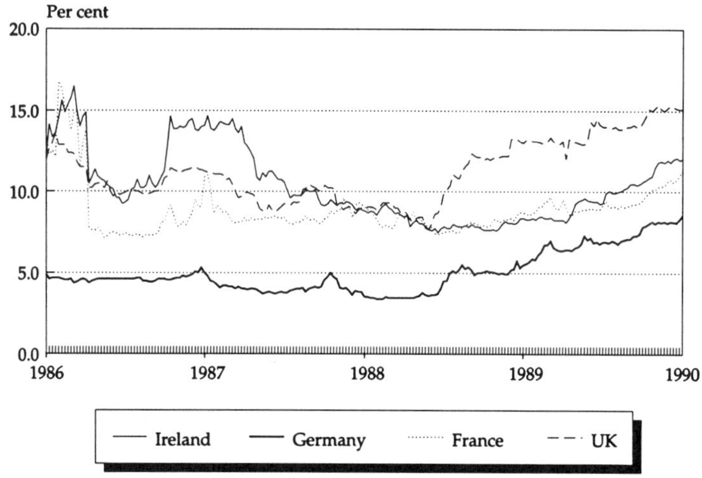

Figure 19.21 Interest rates in Ireland, France Germany and the UK, 1986-1990

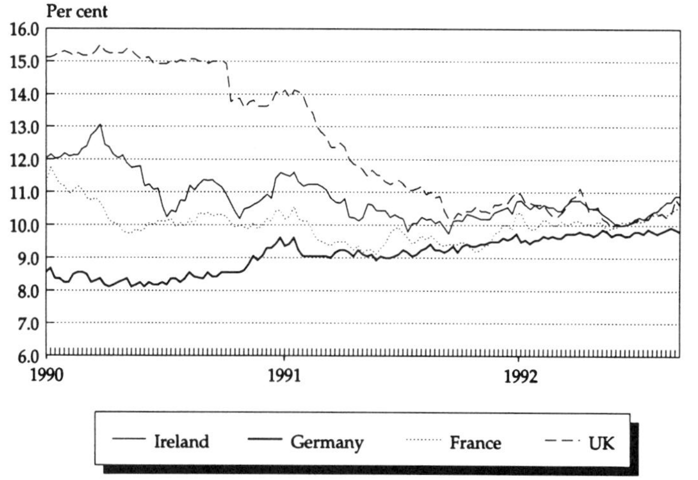

Figure 19.22 Interest rates in Ireland, France Germany and the UK, 1990-1992

19.17 *Inter-market spreads*

As the Irish pound came to be seen as a secure 'proxy Deutschemark', the high yields in Irish bonds began to attract substantial interest from international investors. Initially, international investment in the Irish market came primarily from Germany as investors in Frankfurt were quick to see the potential for falls in Irish yields as the Irish financial system reaped the benefits of a hard currency regime. The spread of international investment in the Irish bond market has widened considerably over the past few years. Funds management institutions and banks in the US, UK and, to a lesser extent, other continental European countries and Japan, have come to recognize the potential of the Irish market as an important part of core EMS bond holdings or as one side of yield spread plays within the EMS.

The upshot of this process was a narrowing of yield spreads over Bunds (see Figures 19.23 & 19.24), which paralleled that in the money market. By end-1990, the 10-year differential had fallen to 150bp. A year later, it was around 125bp. Over the year to August 1992, the differential has averaged 120bp, ranging from

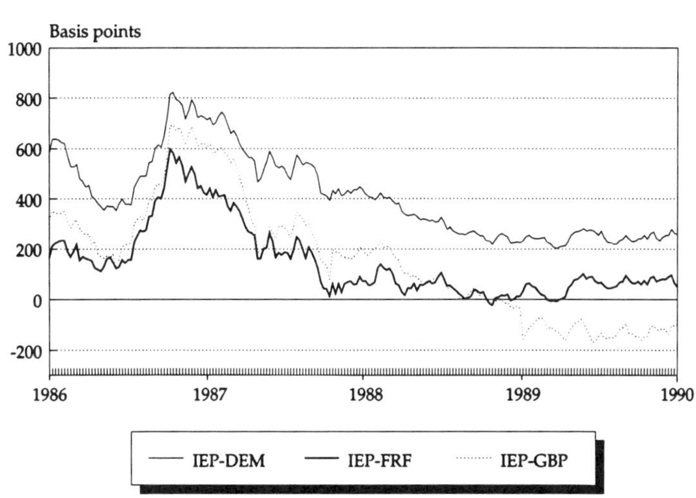

Figure 19.23 10-yr bond yield differentials, 1986-1990

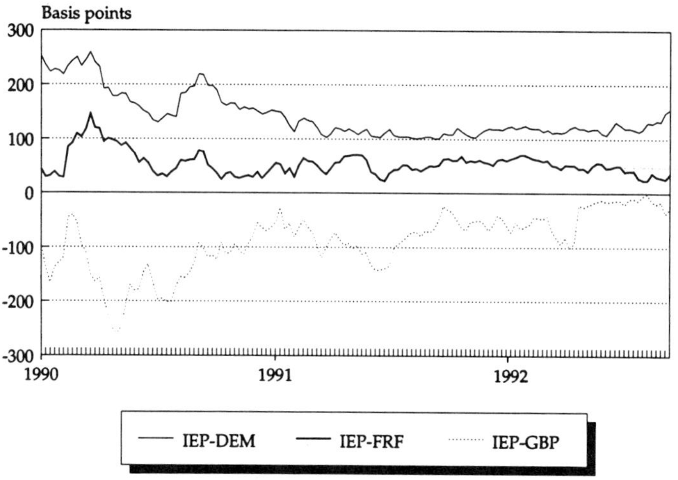

Figure 19.24 10-yr bond yield differentials, 1990-1992

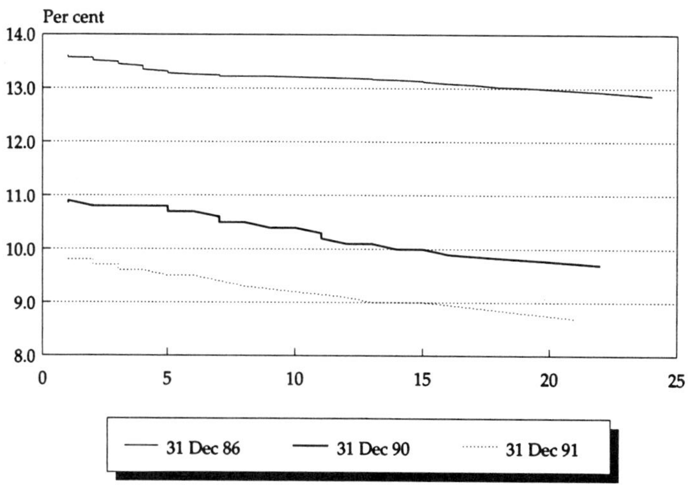

Figure 19.25 Irish yield curve

156 to 99bp. Ireland's strong economic fundamentals give rise to the prospect of further narrowing of differentials, if progress towards Emu continues.

The Irish yield curve (see Figure 19.25) has typically been inverted in recent years. In part, this reflected the falls in yields from very high levels in the mid-1980s and the virtually continuous expectation of further falls. For much of the period, the authorities refused to fund at the long end in the expectation of declining interest rates. More recently, the NTMA has again funded in the longs and the scarcity premium attaching to long-dated paper is no longer a factor. The yield curve inversion currently mirrors the position in other EMS member states and reflects the expectation that Ireland will participate fully in Emu at its inception.

19.18 Sources of reference

Financial data

National Treasury Management Agency (NTMA)

- Daily information on open stocks, tranching and switching (Reuters NTMB,C) and details of weekly Exchequer bill tender (Reuters NTMA).

Department of Finance

- *Annual Budget Statement*, Quarterly returns on Exchequer receipts and spending and monthly *Iris Oifigiuil* statement of receipts and issues.

Central Bank of Ireland

- *Monthly Statistical Supplement* on banking, external reserves and some government funding data. Quarterly Reports include macroeconomic forecasts, articles on monetary developments and detailed banking statistics (Reuters CBII,X).

Central Statistics Office

- Monthly, Quarterly and Annual macroeconomic data (Reuters CSOK,L).

Financial press

Daily:

- *Irish Times*
- *Irish Independent*
- *Irish Press*
- *Cork Examiner*

Weekends:

- *Sunday Business Post*
- *Sunday Tribune*

Quote vendors and news agencies

- Reuters provide information on screen pages NCSG-K, RIDA-C, DAVA-F, GDAA-D.

- Telerate provide information on screen pages 3911-4
- Datastream and Bloomberg also cover the Irish market (check with vendor for page codes)

Other publications

The following brokers provide daily, weekly, monthly and quarterly comment, analysis and forecasts:

- NCB Stockbrokers Ltd.
- Riada Stockbrokers Ltd.
- Davy Stockbrokers
- Goodbody Stockbrokers

Additionally,

- The Economic and Social Research Institute (ESRI) provides quarterly economic commentaries and occasional medium-term economic forecasts.

Chapter

20

The bond markets of

Italy

Wilma Vergi
Cariplo, Milan

Note: In general text, the abbreviation 'Lit' is used to denote the Italian lira. Elsewhere, the international mnemonic 'ITL' is used.

20.1 Introduction

With estimated total outstandings of Lit 1211 trillion (as at year-end, 1990), the Italian bond market is the third largest in the world, after the US and Japan. The market is clearly dominated by government issues (see Figure 20.1), which account for around 85 per cent of the total (Lit 1039 trillion in 1990, and an estimated Lit 1570 trillion in 1991 - see Figure 20.2).

The fact that such a level of public debt can be absorbed is largely due to the high savings ratio to be found in Italy - more than 95 per cent of government bonds are held by domestic investors.

Historically, foreign investors had been reluctant to invest in the Italian market, this being attributable not only to a lack of liquidity and transparency, but also to problems concerning clearing and settlement, as well as a complicated tax system. That Italian bonds now represent an increasing percentage in diversified international portfolios provides evidence that most of these problems have now been overcome. As far as administration is concerned, for example, settlement of government bond business can now be made through Euro-

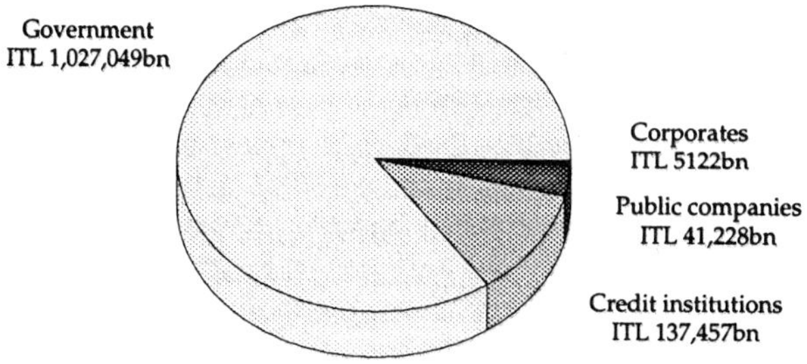

Figure 20.1 Composition of the Italian market

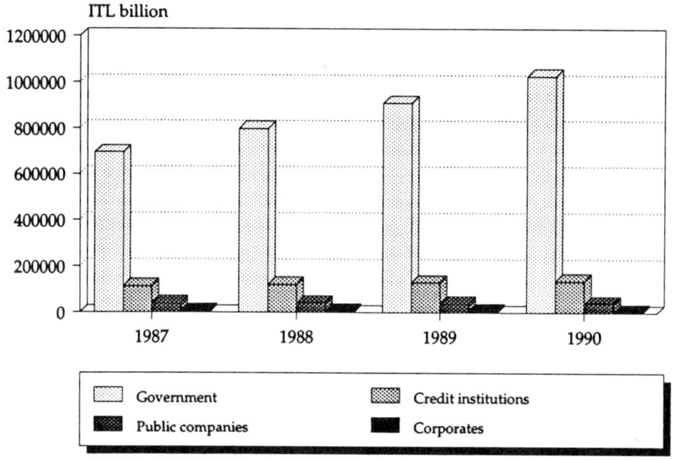

Figure 20.2 Total outstandings on the Italian market

clear/Cedel while fiscal improvements mean that withholding tax is now refunded in a few months.

The problems of liquidity have been addressed in a number of ways. For example, the introduction of an active screen-based market secondary market has improved trading efficiency.

The Italian bond market has undergone a period of dramatic change during the last ten years, but there are still areas requiring attention. Importantly, at the time of writing, there is no regulatory provision for a much-needed futures and options market (although it is hoped that such a market will appear in 1992).

Note: Unless stated otherwise, all figures given in this chapter refer to year-end 1991.

20.2 Economics

Introduction

Through the 1980s, Italy has made significant progress towards achieving economic stability. This steadiness, which has enabled the country to pursue a firm currency policy and budgetary discipline, has resulted in a major decline in the rate of inflation.

Nevertheless, the Italian economy is still characterized by a huge public debt, which is mostly composed of interest on government bonds. The financial structure of public debt is such that it is self-fed by its own interest charges. Attempts have been made, through budgetary discipline, to contain the growth in primary public debt and, as a result, this value has been successfully reduced since 1985. Meanwhile, the healthy performance of the Italian economy has enabled the government to apply a determined currency policy which has led to a strengthening of the lira within the EMS over the last ten years.

As mentioned above, Italian inflation has fallen steadily over the last ten years and the expectation is for a sharper rate of decline to be achieved before the end of 1992. One of the reasons for this, and for other encouraging prospects, is the discipline which has been brought about by Emu - European economic and monetary union - which obliges Italy to remain competitive with the other countries and to tackle the problems which have beset its economy.

Exchange rate

The Italian lira joined the European monetary system (EMS) in March 1979. At the beginning, it was allowed to fluctuate within a 6 per cent band but, since 8 January 1990, it has been restrained within a narrower margin. Between 1981 and July 1985, the currency was depreciated five times, but no further modifications to the parity have been made since then. When the lira joined the narrow band, new central levels were calculated relative to the existing lower limits.

1991 was characterized by an appreciation against the Deutschemark in the first months of the year (see Figure 20.3) but, after October, this trend was reversed and the German currency subsequently reached its highest level against lira. Meanwhile, the relative value of the US dollar grew during the first months of the year (see Figure 20.4) although, after August, the cross-rate declined.

Gross national product

Italy is the fifth-largest industrialized economy. Since 1983, economic activity has accelerated, reaching a growth rate of 4.1 per cent in 1988 (see Figure 20.6).

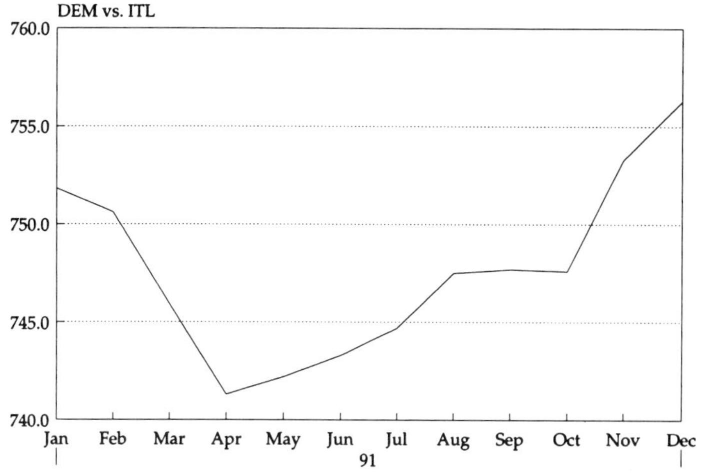

Figure 20.3 **The performance of the Italian lira against the Deutschemark in 1991**

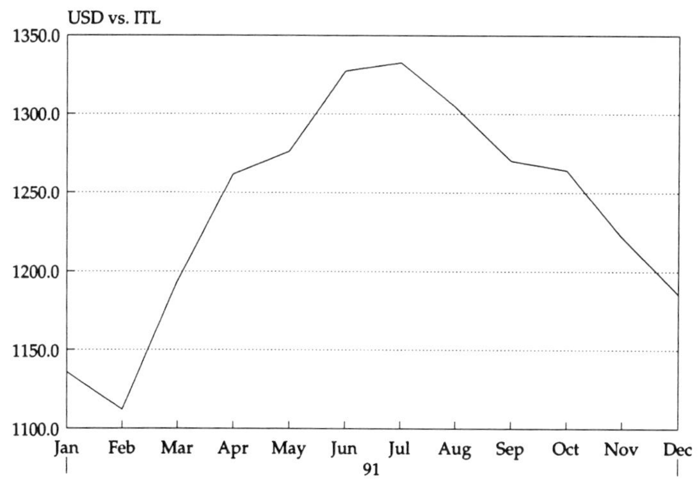

Figure 20.4 **The performance of the Italian lira against the US dollar in 1991**

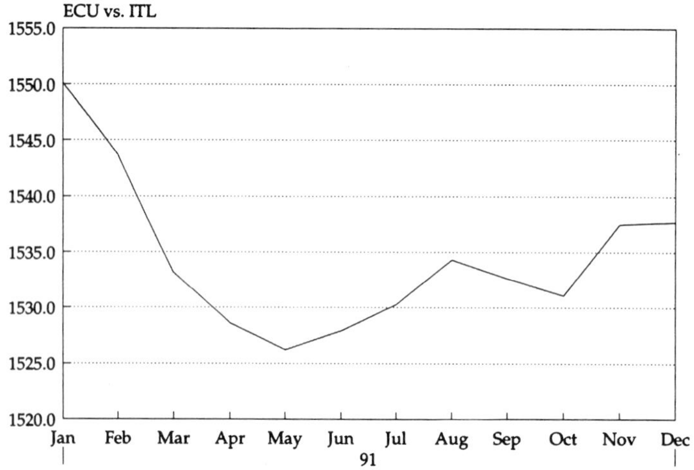

Figure 20.5 The performance of the Italian lira against the Ecu in 1991

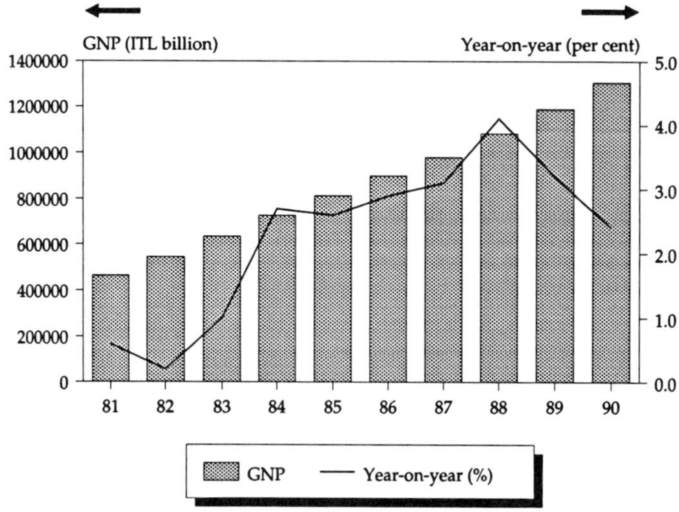

Figure 20.6 History of Italian GNP

In 1990, GNP reached Lit 1,306,833bn, an increase of 2.4 per cent on the previous year. The slowdown in economic activity during 1991 has, however, resulted in a reduction in this growth, to a level of around 0.8 per cent.

Inflation

During the 1970s, Italy had a rather liberal economic policy - which took little notice of inflation. As result, prices increased and inflation peaked at 21 per cent in 1980. Since 1981, however, the rate has been in decline, and it has been moving towards to the European average, although it needs to be reduced still further to achieve the target rate of 4.5 per cent before the end of 1992.

In 1991, however, annual inflation actually increased to 6.4 per cent, against a level of 6.1 per cent in 1990 (see Figure 20.7). Upon closer analysis, it can be seen that the rate peaked in June, at 6.9 per cent, before steadily declining to close the year at 6.0 per cent (see Figure 20.8). Producer prices, meanwhile, showed a fall from 4.2 per cent in January, to 2.3 per cent in November.

Balance of trade

During 1991, the balance of trade (see Figures 20.9 & 20.10) was adversely affected by a decrease in the competitiveness of Italian industry, and by the increase in the price of oil which resulted from the Gulf crisis.

Imports increased in volume by just 2.3 per cent (year-on-year) in the first six months of 1991 because, with a gap in production, there was a decrease in both the import of raw materials, and in machinery investment. In the same period, exports decreased in volume by 0.3 per cent (year-on-year), reflecting the slowdown in global demand. The spread in the growth of exports between other OECD countries is widening.

Balance of payments

Italy's current account closed 1991 with a deficit of Lit 8571bn (see Figure 20.11). In December, particularly, the deficit was Lit 7728bn, a figure which contributed substantially to the annual total. During that month, there were increased pressures on exchange rates, primarily against the Deutschemark. The Bank of Italy supported the Italian lira and modified the central repo rate, but these measures proved incapable of limiting the capital outflow. The previous deficit was recorded in 1985 (Lit -13,651bn).

Unemployment

During the last few years the unemployment rate has fluctuated from 11 to 12 per cent (see Figures 20.12 & 20.13).

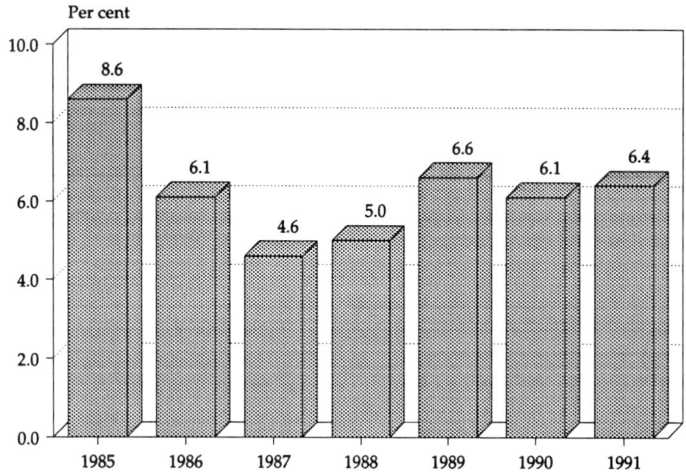

Figure 20.7 Italian inflation, 1985-1991

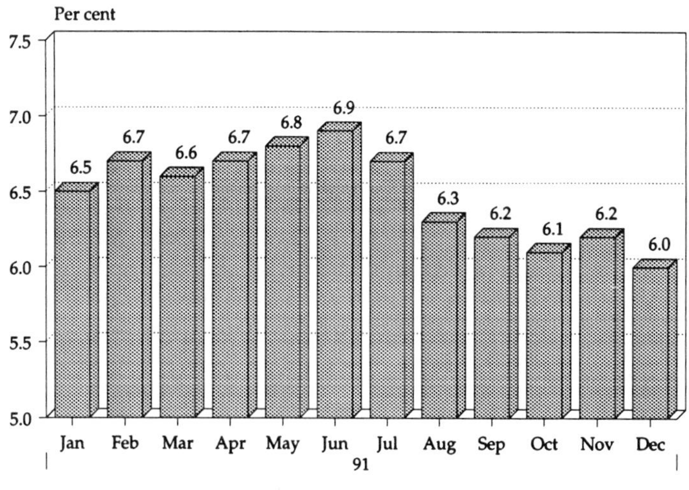

Figure 20.8 Italian inflation in 1991

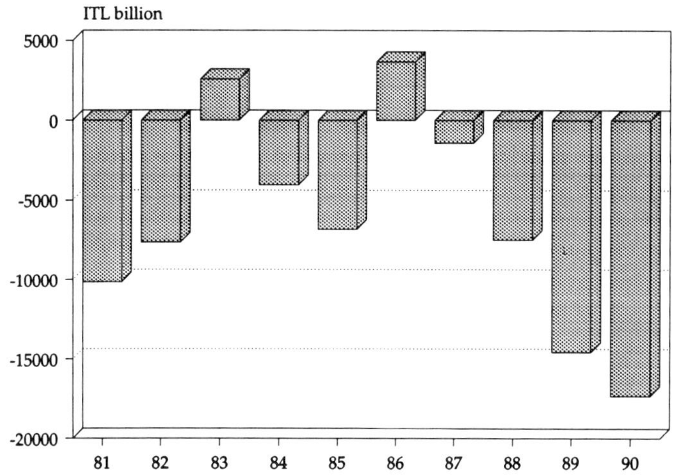

Figure 20.9 Italian balance of trade

	Imports (cif)		Exports (fob)		Trade balance	
	1990	*1991*	*1990*	*1991*	*1990*	*1991*
January	18,863	20,366	14,968	15,371	-3895	-4995
February	17,591	18,364	15,607	17,424	-1984	-940
March	19,819	17,597	16,570	17,065	-3249	-532
April	17,564	19,793	16,678	17,461	-886	-2332
May	19,814	20,407	17,322	17,205	-2492	-3202
June	18,098	19,005	19,348	19,409	1250	404
July	17,763	20,106	19,694	20,279	1931	173
August	11,272	11,173	11,509	11,494	237	321
September	18,383	19,888	16,509	16,861	-1874	-3027
October	20,649	21,341	19,177	19,952	-1472	-1389
November	20,534	19,486	16,898	17,084	-3636	-2402
December	17,355	18,239	19,333	20,132	1978	1893
Total	217,705	225,765	203,613	209,737	-14,092	-16,028

Figure 20.10 The structure of Italy's trade balance (ITL billion)

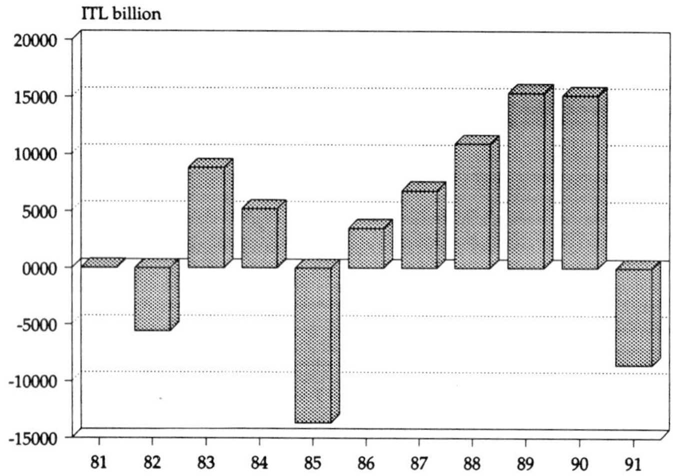

Figure 20.11 Italian balance of payments

		Number employed by sector (thousands)				Unemployed
		Agriculture	*Industry*	*Building*	*Others*	
1986		2242	4940	1883	11,795	2611
1987		2169	4867	1849	11,952	2832
1988		2053	4928	1823	12,181	2868
1989		1946	4953	1801	12,305	2866
1990		1896	4986	1859	12,564	2621
1990						
	1st qtr.	1944	5030	1861	12,454	2641
	2nd qtr.	1894	4970	1856	12,603	2602
	3rd qtr.	1846	4942	1857	12,675	2601
	4th qtr.	1830	4986	1881	12,726	2569
1991						
	1st qtr.	1817	5025	1928	12,815	2686
	2nd qtr.	1845	4974	1965	12,847	2640

Figure 20.12 Analysis of Italian employment

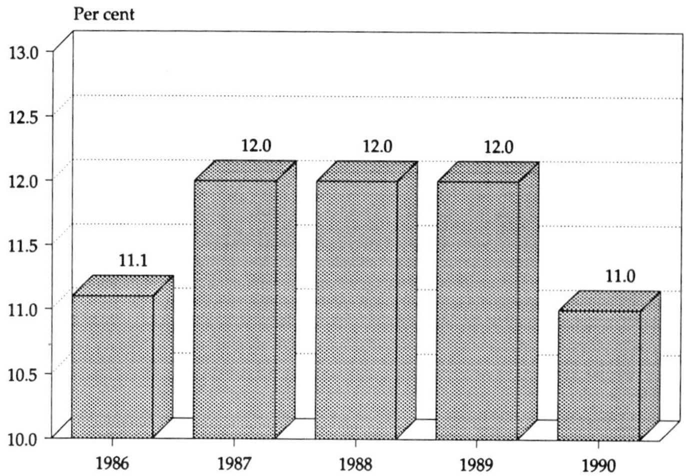

Figure 20.13 Italian unemployment

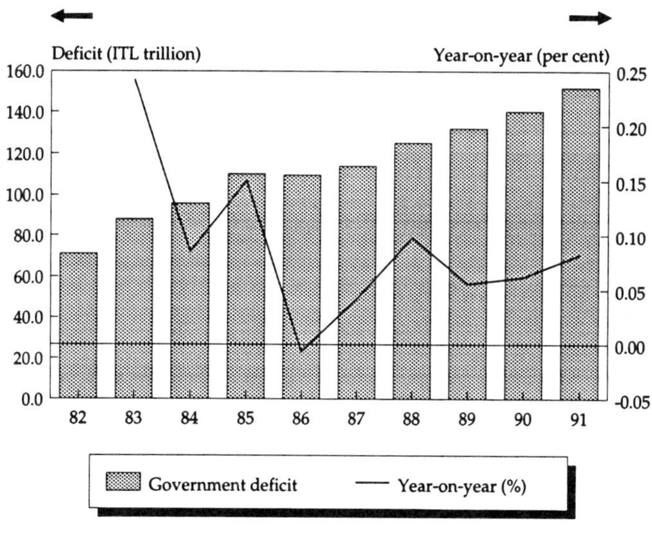

Figure 20.14 Central government deficit

	Fiscal revenue	Other revenue	Current spending	Other spending	Deficit
1985	177,645	43,945	279,238	54,562	112,210
1986	202,090	51,779	307,338	56,690	110,159
1987	224,676	56,867	333,987	61,384	113,829
1988	257,274	54,801	366,805	70,180	124,911
1989	293,462	60,531	394,547	92,846	133,400
1990	329,971	76,893	465,810	81,733	140,680

Figure 20.15 The structure of Italian government deficit, 1985 - 1990

Central government deficit

In 1991, central government deficit (see Figure 20.14) reached almost Lit 152.2 trillion, 20 trillion lira more than the amount estimated by the government in its yearly economic plan. Interest on government bonds represents more than Lit 150 trillion. The 1992 economic plan sets the central government deficit at Lit 127.8 trillion. Figure 20.15 shows the structure of central government deficit.

Money supply

The increase in money supply (M2) during 1991 remained within the target range of 5-8 per cent with a growth rate of 7.1 per cent being recorded in the first nine months of the year (see Figure 20.16). The reasons for this can be attributed to the high level of short-term interest rates, the decline in the level of economic activity, and the fall in inflation seen during the last half of the year.

	1990		1991
	January - September	*Year*	*January - September*
Bank reserves	8.5	10.4	7.5
Monetary basis	9.7	10.1	9.2
Bank deposits	8.7	9.2	5.9
M2	9.6	9.9	7.1

Figure 20.16 Italian money supply (M2/month, in per cent)

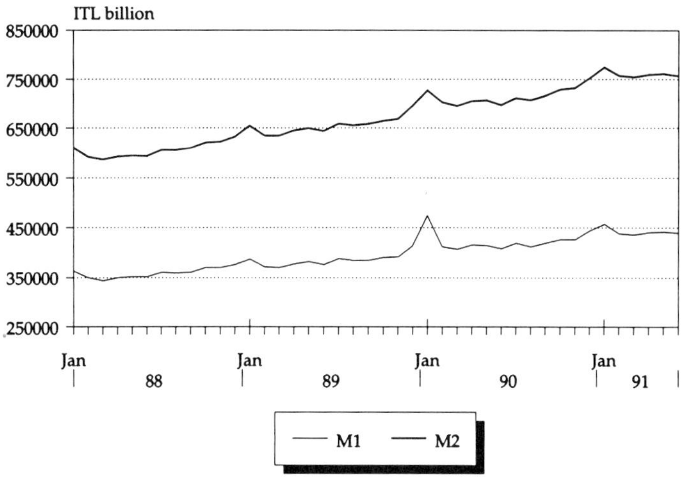

Figure 20.17 Italian money supply

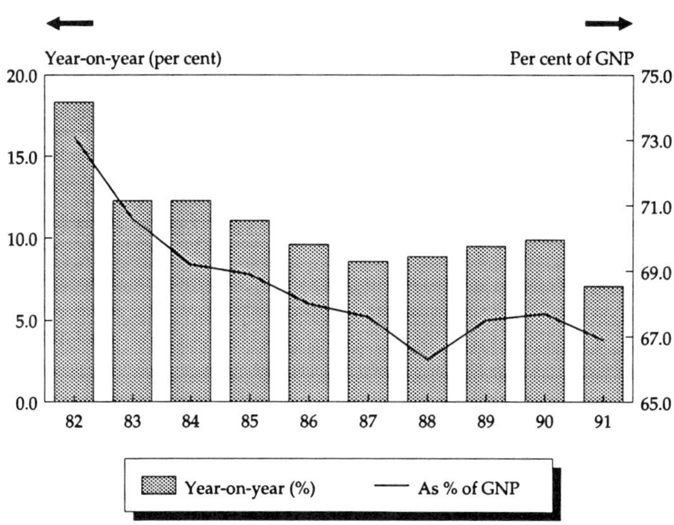

Figure 20.18 History of M2 money supply, 1982-1991

Politics

Since the end of WWII, the Italian political system has been characterized by the weakness of short-term government; successive administrations have rarely lasted more than two years. Despite this, the Christian Democrats held uninterrupted power from the 1940s to the early 1980s. Since then, however, governments have been formed by ministers from five different parties (Christian Democrats, Socialist, Republican, Social Democrats and Liberal).

Party	1976	1979	1983	1987	1992
Christian Democrats	38.7	38.3	32.9	34.2	29.7
Communists	34.4	30.4	29.9	27.8	21.7[1]
Socialists	9.6	9.8	11.4	14.3	13.6
Republicans	3.1	3.0	5.1	3.7	4.4
Social Democrats	3.4	3.8	4.1	2.9	2.7
MSI	6.1	5.3	6.8	5.6	5.4
Lega Nord	-	-	-	-	8.7

Figure 20.19 Percentage of vote for main parties in past Italian general elections
[1] *Partito democratico della sinistra (16.1) & Rifondazione Comunista (5.6)*

The Italian government is due to debate fundamental constitutional reform, including changes to the electoral system, the election of the president, and the differentiation of the roles of the two houses of Parliament.

20.3 *Market composition*

Overview

As noted earlier, the government sector comprises 84 per cent of the total Italian market. The growth of this sector has been particularly strong during the 1980s, this being due largely to two factors: Firstly, the government's tax treatment favoured its own bonds at the expense of other issues and, secondly, the high interest rates available on the state debt instruments ensured investor attraction.

The breakdown of distribution within the government sector reveals a number of changes over the last decade. Figures 20.20-20.22 show the dominance of Treasury notes over long-term bonds. The majority of government bonds still constitute Treasury certificates of credit (*Certificati di Credito del Tresoro* - CCT), although their percentage relative to the total is declining in favour of fixed-rate bonds (*Buoni del Tresoro Poliennali* - BTP, and *Certificati del Tresoro con Opzione* - CTO). The reduction in floating-rate notes reflects the Treasury policy of

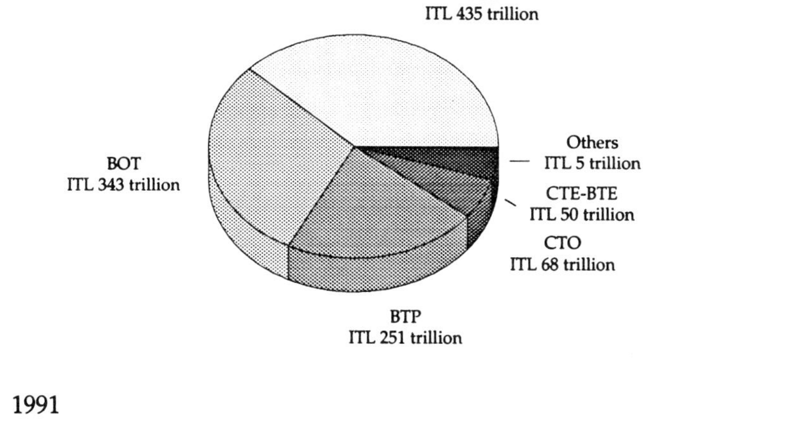

Figure 20.20 Distribution of instruments within the government sector (1991)

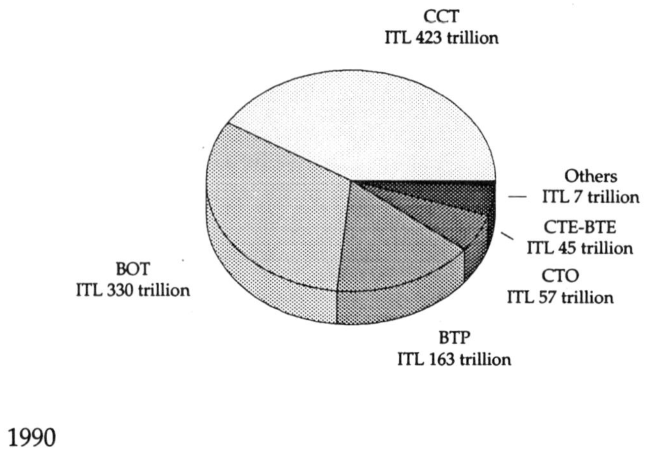

Figure 20.21 Distribution of instruments within the government sector (1990)

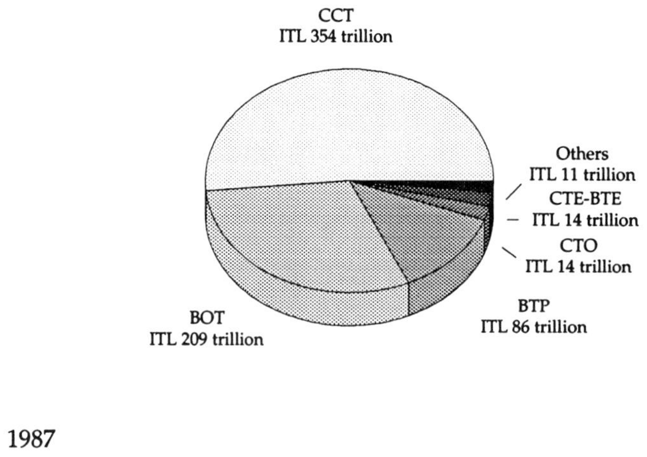

Figure 20.22 Distribution of instruments within the government sector (1987)

providing the Bank of Italy with more autonomy in the management of the monetary policy.

The others issuers are mostly represented by special credit institutions and public companies (FFSS, ENEL, IRI, ENI, etc.), but the issues are generally small and the market, therefore, quite limited.

Composition of market by maturity

The bond market can be divided into two distinct areas, namely the short-term and the medium/long-term.

Short-term market

■ Treasury bills
The short-term market is mostly composed of Treasury bills with ranges of 3-, 6- and 12-months (BOT). There are also short-term Treasury bills which are denominated in Ecu and issued with a maturity of one year (BTE). At the end of 1991, BOTs and BTEs accounted for Lit 343,000bn and Lit 2490bn, respectively. During that year, net issues of BOTs decreased markedly to Lit 13,865bn (from Lit 44,641bn, in 1990), as a result of which the average life in the government sector has begun to lengthen. In December 1990, the average was 2 years and five months, but is now around 3 years.

Medium/long-term market

■ Government bonds
Government bonds are generally medium-term bonds with ranges of 5-7 years but, in March 1991, the government issued its first ten-year fixed-rate bond (BTP 12.5% 01 March 2001). Floating-rate notes (CCTs) used to be issued with maturities of 2-10 years (the first CCT in 1977 carried a 2-year maturity), but are now commonly issued with 7-year maturities. Fixed-rate bonds (BTPs) used to be relatively short (some had just 2-year lives), but are now usually issued with 5-, 8-, or 10-year maturities (see Figure 20.17). Fixed-rate bonds with options (CTOs) are generally in the 6-year maturity range, although the first issue carried an 8-year maturity. Government Ecu-denominated bonds are generally in the range of 6-7 years.

■ Credit institution bonds
The longest maturities to be found in the Italian market, 20-30 years, are solely those of credit institutions' issues. However, such terms are not very common and the maturities in this sector are more generally between 10 and 15 years.

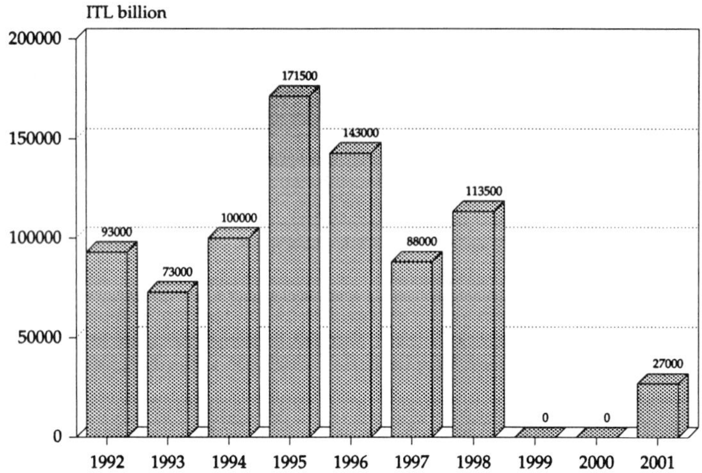

Figure 20.23 Maturity structure of the government bond market (excl. BOTs & BTEs)

■ Public company bonds

Public company bonds are medium-term bonds with ranges of 7-10 years. Until 1989, issues generally carried maturities no longer than 7-8 years (although a few 15-year issues appeared, exceptionally, in 1985 and 1986 - see below). Since then, a number of 10-year bonds have been issued (see Figure 20.18).

ABI code	Borrower	Amount issued (bn)	Maturity date	Year of issue	Type of security
13854	ANAS	500	01 May 2000	1985	FRN
13853	FFSS	1000	01 May 2000	1985	FRN
14223	ENEL	800	01 October 2000	1985	FRN
13870	ENEL	1000	16 May 2000	1985	FRN
14089	IRI	123	01 July 2000	1985	FRN
14614	ENEL	900	16 February 2001	1986	FRN

■ Corporate bonds and convertibles

Corporate bonds and convertible bonds have ranges of 5-7 years (see Figure 20.19).

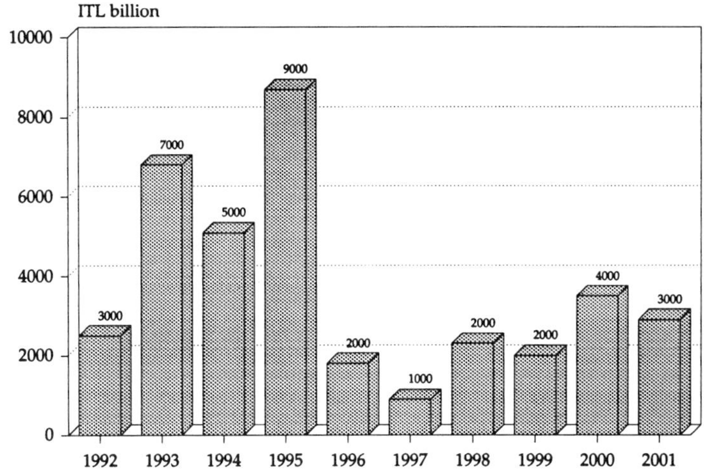

Figure 20.24 Maturity structure of the public company bond market[1]

[1] *listed bonds only*

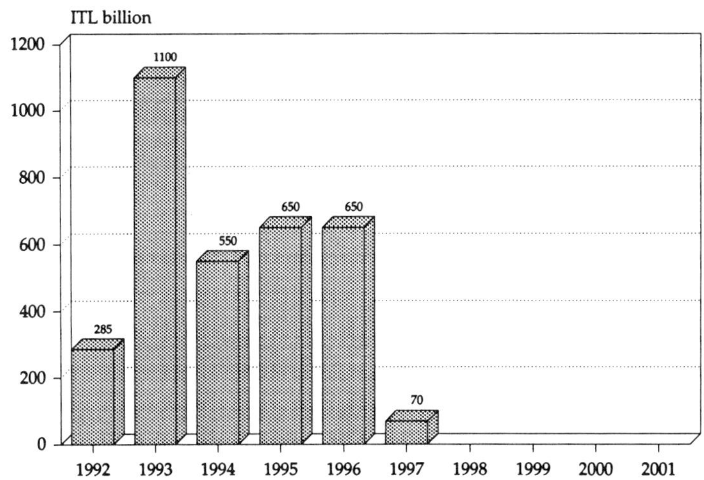

Figure 20.25 Maturity structure of the convertible bond market[1]

[1] *listed bonds only*

Composition of market by coupon structure

Government bond market

Government bonds (see Figures 20.20 & 20.21) generally have semi-annual coupons. However, CTRs and CTEs have annual coupons as, too, do those CCTs issued from January 1985 to September 1987. CCTs with annual coupons determine the following coupons on the yield of 12-month BOTs issued at the four auctions during the second and the third month preceding the coupon date.

- Example: ABI code 12885 CCT 01 MAY 1997
  The coupon that will be paid in May 1992 is calculated on the yield of 12-month BOTs issued in February and March 1991, plus a spread of 75 basis points.

CCTs with a semi-annual coupons were issued from 1977 to 1985, and from November 1987 onwards. During the first period, coupons were indexed to the yield of six-month BOTs relating to the second and the third months which precede the coupon date and carried a very high spread of between 75 and 100 basis points. Since November 1987, coupon have been indexed to the semi-annual

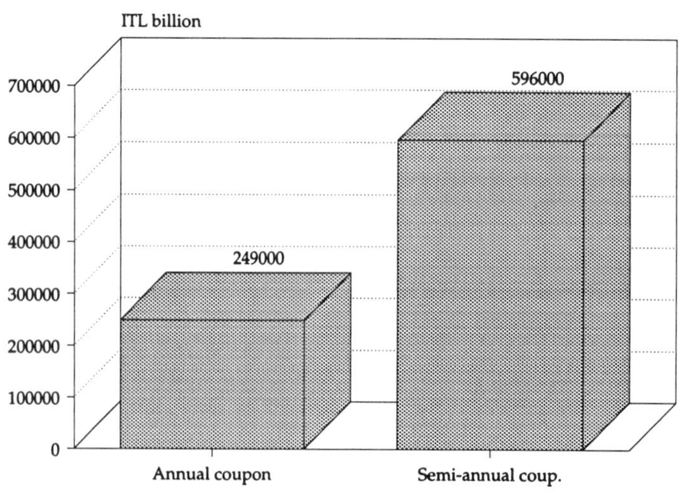

Figure 20.26 Coupon structure of Italian government bonds (annual & semi-annual)[1]

[1] *BTE/BOT not included*

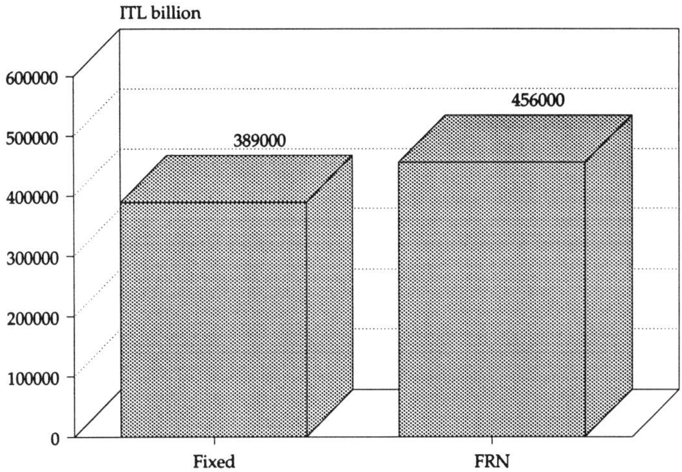

Figure 20.27 Coupon structure of Italian government bonds (fixed & FRNl)[1]
[1] *BTEs/BOTs not included*

yield equivalent of 12-month BOTs and carry a reduced spreads of 30 to 50 basis points.

- Example: ABI code 13096 CCT 01 March 1998
  The coupon that will be paid in March 1992 is calculated an a semi-annual yield equivalent of 12-month BOTs issued in June and July 1991, plus a spread of 50 basis points.

Credit institution bond market

Bonds issued by special credit institutions (see Figure 20.22 & 20.23) and banks generally have semi-annual coupons. Of the 908 bonds listed on the Milan Stock Exchange, 776 have semi-annual coupons, whilst only 132 have annual coupons. The more common coupon-dates more common are 1 January-1 July, or 1 April-1 October.

Floating-rate notes, which form the majority of issues in this sector, are generally indexed on financial or monetary ratios. One of the most common parameters used to calculate the coupons of floating-rate notes is an average of the yield of 12-month BOTs and the yield of bonds which have been issued since 1974 by credit institutions (RENDIOB).

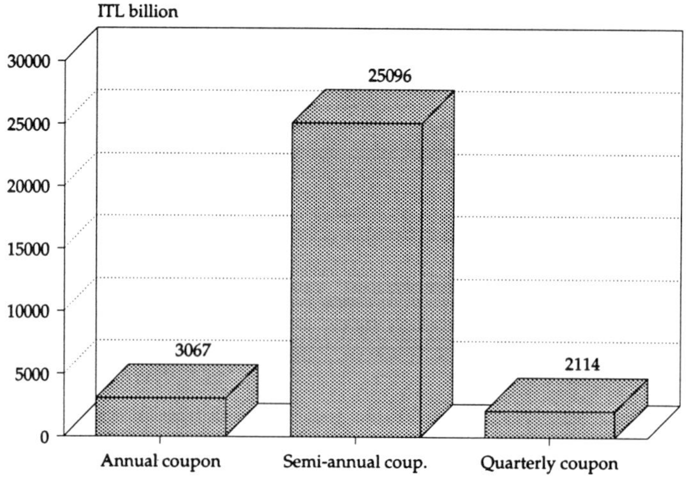

Figure 20.28 Coupon structure of credit institution bonds (annual & semi-annual)[1]
[1] *listed bonds only*

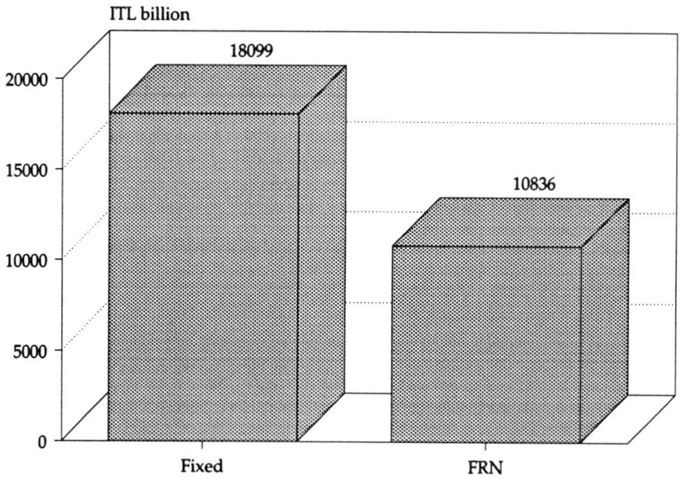

Figure 20.29 Coupon structure of credit institution bonds (fixed & FRN)[1]
[1] *listed bonds only*

RENDIOB is calculated by Bank of Italy each month and published in its bulletin, as well as in financial newspapers. Sometimes a monetary value, such a a 3-month interbank rate or an average of overnight interbank rates, is used.

Note that only a few issues are linked to an inflation index and that the first coupon of floating-rate notes is always determined on the issue date.

Public company bond market

Public company bonds generally pay semi-annual coupons. On 63 issues listed on the Milan Stock Exchange two issues are a zero-coupon bonds, six have annual coupons and the others pay semi-annual coupons. 16 issues are fixed-rate notes, 45 are floating-rate notes and 2 issues are fixed-rate revisable.

Bonds issued by ENEL (Ente Nazionale Energia Elettrica - National Board for Electric Power) are generally indexed on an average of the yield of 12-month BOTs and RENDIOB. Some issues have a minimum-guaranteed coupon.

- Example: ABI code 11611 ENEL 84/92 1′

Amount issued	Maturity	Coupon date	Minimum coupon
100bn	01 February 1992	01 February- 01 August	6.5%

Bonds issued by IRI (Istituto per la Ricostruzione Industriale - Industrial Reorganization Corporation are generally indexed on an average of the yield of 12 month BOTs and RENDIOB. Some issues have a minimum-guaranteed coupon.

- Example: ABI code 16010 IRI 87/94 2′

Amount issued	Maturity	Coupon date	Minimum coupon
500bn	01 June 1994	01 June- 01 December	3.75%

Bonds issued by FFSS (Ferrovie dello Stato - State Railways) are generally indexed on an average of the yield of 6-month BOTs and RENDIOB. Some issues have a minimum-guaranteed coupon.

- Example: ABI code 11627 FFSS 84/92

Amount issued	Maturity	Coupon date	Minimum coupon
800bn	01 Mar 1992	01 March- 01 September	6.5%

Bonds issued by ENI (Ente Nazionale Idrocarburi - National Hydrocarbon Corporation) are indexed on the average of the yield of 12-month BOTs and RENDIOB.

Corporate and convertible bond market

Corporate bonds and convertible are mostly fixed-rate bonds and coupons are paid annually. Of the 40 convertible bonds listed on the Milan Stock Exchange, 33 pay annual coupons whilst only 7 have semi-annual coupons. All the issues listed are fixed-rate bonds.

20.4 Types of security

Short-term bonds

Buoni Ordinari del Tesoro - BOT

BOTs are Treasury bills which are issued twice a month as short-term zero-coupon bonds. They are subject to a 12.5 per cent withholding tax which is calculated on the difference between issue price and face value. In the case of BOTs alone, tax must be paid in advance, with the result that they are quoted on a net price basis on the secondary market.

BOTs are not listed on the Milan Stock Exchange, but are nevertheless quoted on the Telematic market. Generally, the liquidity of BOTs decreases a few weeks following the date of issue. On occasions, brokers make a grey market by quoting new BOTs on their Reuters pages ahead of the actual auction.

BOTs are auctioned both at the middle and end of each month, with competitive bids. The dates of each issue are established by the Bank of Italy in an annual schedule issued at the beginning of each year, with the actual amounts decided only a few days prior to each auction (Reuters page ATIE). The tendency is for the issues at the end of the month to be larger, and therefore more important, than those issued at mid-month.

Each participant at the auction can submit a maximum of five competitive bids. These bids then filled, in order of price, until the issue is fully covered.

Until 1981, the Bank of Italy was under a Treasury obligation to take up any issue amount not placed on the market.

The most important issue in 1991 was a Lit 40,000bn face value issue which was placed in February of that year.

Buoni Ordinari del Tesoro in Ecu - BTE

First issued in October 1987, BTEs are short-term Ecu-denominated bonds which are issued, at par, by Dutch auction. The Bank of Italy defines the maximum coupon accepted, the amount offered and the maturity. The coupon is paid on maturity and subject to a 12.5 per cent withholding tax. BTEs are unlisted and treated on a simple net annual yield basis on the OTC secondary market, with accrued interest being calculated on an actual day formula.

Italian underwriters must pay for BTEs in lira at a fixed Lit/Ecu exchange rate which is determined, on the issue-date, by the Bank of Italy (non-residents, however, must pay in Ecu). Repayment may be made in either lira or Ecu, dependent upon detailed instructions which must be given to Bank of Italy at least one month before the maturity date. In the absence of such instructions, repayments must be made in lira. The Lit/Ecu exchange rate applied is the average of the Milan/Rome fixings of the two working days prior to maturity date.

Medium/long-term notes

Floating-rate notes: Certificati di Credito del Tesoro - CCT

CCTs, which were first issued in June 1977, are Treasury floating-rate notes indexed to BOT yields, plus a fixed spread. Although their volume has declined, CCTs still account for some 40 per cent of the government sector.

Generally, CCTs are initially offered on the first day of a month (although the re-opening of issues can take place at any time) and are auctioned in a fixed amount, at a minimum basis price (which is the same for each re-opening issue - the discount being used to calculate the withholding tax to be paid on maturity).

- Example: 13205 CCT 01 Sep 1998

Date	Amount issued	Base price	Price
01 Sep 91	Lit 7000bn	96.65	97.65
15 Sep 91	Lit 2500bn	96.65	98.60

CCTs exempt from withholding tax are indexed to BOT net yield while those subject to 12.5 per cent withholding tax are indexed to BOT gross yield. CCTs which are subject to 6.25 per cent withholding tax are indexed to BOT gross yield adjusted by a factor of 93.3333% ((1-12.5%)/(1-6.25%)). In this way, all the net coupons can be compared on a given date without the effect of withholding tax.

During 1991, the government issued CCTs on which the first coupon had a lower value than the corresponding hypothetical rate calculated on BOTs.

CCTs are listed on the Milan Stock Exchange, although new issues only appear on this market after the maturity of the first coupon.

Some 33 CCTs are quoted on the Telematic market by the primary dealers, with new CCTs generally being listed a few days after the auction. Liquidity is very good, reflected by the spreads which are generally only 1 or 2 basis points. It should be noted that, on occasions, prices may be obtained in the 'grey market' (when new bonds are announced but not yet auctioned).

CCTs can be classified by maturity, tax, spread and by annual or semi-annual coupon. The spread over BOT yield is fixed for each issue. Over the years, the value has shown a change in trend from a 0.75 or 1 point spread, to a more recent figure of 0.5.

The most important issue that year was the Lit 11,000bn face value CCT 01 October 1998 (ABI code 13207), while the highest issue price paid was at the second auction (on 15 May 1991) of CCT 01 May 1998 (ABI code 13099).

Indexed notes: Certificati di Credito del Tesoro - CTR

A CTR is a bond which is linked to an inflation index. The coupon is fixed at 2.5% and paid once a year on a revalued principal. There has only been one small CTR issue (Lit 1000bn), on 01 August 1983.

The lack of attraction of CTRs may be attributed to the use of an inflation index which was not widely-recognized and a yield which was less competitive than others to be found in the government sector.

Fixed-rate bonds: Buoni del Tesoro Poliennali - BTP

BTPs are fixed-rate bonds with semi-annual coupon and bullet repayment at maturity, which is generally from 5 to 10 years from issue (although, in the past, 2 to 5 years was more usual).

BTPs are issued by Dutch auction. They are often issued with an 'open series clause', enabling the amount issued to be more representative and thereby improving liquidity on the market. For each auction, the Bank of Italy defines the coupon, the maturity, the amount issued and the minimum price. In common with CCTs and CTOs, there is only one minimum basis price for BTPs, even if there are few auctions, because withholding tax (payable on maturity) is calculated on the difference between this price and par.

- Example: 12677 BTP 01 Mar 2001 12.5%

Date	Amount issued	Base price	Price
01 Mar 91	Lit 3000bn	92.20	95.75
01 Apr 91	Lit 3000bn	92.20	97.40
01 May 91	Lit 4000bn	92.20	98.00

BTPs pay interest semi-annually and are generally subject to 12.5 per cent withholding tax.

All BTPs are listed on the stock exchange after the payment of the first coupon. The most representative BTPs, plus new additions, are also listed on the screen-based market where spreads as narrow as one or two cents are common. Daily turnover on the Telematic market amounts to around Lit 3 trillion per day. A grey market in new issues is conducted by some dealers.

During 1991, total issuance of 5-year BTPs amounted to Lit 37,500bn, with the single most important issue being the Lit 11,000bn 01 March 1996 (ABI code

12676). Total 1991 issuance of BTPs with 10-year and 7-year maturities amounted to Lit 27,000bn and Lit 28,500bn respectively.

Fixed-rate bonds with option: Certificati del Tesoro con Opzione - CTO

CTOs are fixed-rate bonds which carry a put option and semi-annual coupon. The option gives the investor an opportunity of early redemption, at par, at the end of the third year. For the first issue only (December 1988), the option can be exercised at the end of the fourth year. Generally, options are exercisable, upon notice to the Bank of Italy during a specified period - normally one month before the exercise date.

With the exception of the first issue, which carried a maturity range of 8 years, most CTOs are in the 6-year range. CTOs are issued by Dutch auction with a minimum base price in amounts of Lit 2-3 trillion.

All CTOs, with the exception of the first issue, have mid-month coupon dates. Some CTOs are listed on the Milan Stock Exchange after the first coupon payment, but most are listed on the Telematic market. New issues are generally attract the most liquidity with spreads between 2 and 10 basis points. However, the limited size of each CTO issue means that liquidity on the secondary market compares unfavourably with that of BTPs.

Yields are often higher than on bonds with a similar maturity and, in such cases, the option is undervalued. A CTO grey market is usually available. The most notable CTO issue in 1991 was the Lit 7000bn 19 September 1997 (ABI code 13206).

Ecu-denominated bonds: Certificati del Tesoro in Ecu - CTE

CTEs are fixed-rate bonds with annual coupons, and were first issued in February 1982. They are issued at par with maturities of 5 or 6 years (although, in the past, CTEs have carried maturities of between 4 and 8 years).

Italian underwriters must pay for CTEs in lira at a fixed Lit/Ecu exchange rate, which is determined by Bank of Italy on the date of issue. Coupons and repayment are made in lira and the exchange rate used for these payments is the average of the Milan/Rome fixings of the two working days before the coupon or the maturity date. Foreign underwriters may pay in either Ecu or lira. If the payment is made in Ecu, the bonds are held in a special account at the Bank of Italy for coupons and repayment to be made also in Ecu. Non-resident underwriters may pay in lira and request that their payment, too, be put in a special account, after which both coupon and principal payments are made in Ecu. The facility to change account is very important as it enables investors to buy bonds from Italian dealers and then to convert them in an Ecu account.

CTEs are listed on the stock exchange but only one issue is quoted on the screen market. CTEs placed, or transferred, abroad are listed on the Luxembourg Stock Exchange.

Special credit institution bonds

These are bonds issued by credit institutions which specialize in the mortgage, agricultural and public works sectors.

After WWII, special credit institutions and banks started issuing bonds in order to refinance and maintain industries and companies. Until 1972, bonds which were issued by credit institutions were characterized by a fixed-rate and chance draw. The highest level of coupon rate was of 7 per cent and coupons were generally paid semi-annually. The first bond to pay an annual coupon was IMI S.S. 1964/1984, issued for Lit 468bn in 1964, but annual coupons only became commonplace after 1973. After that date, the first floating-rate note was placed, while issues generally showed an increase in the coupon rate and a shortening of the maturity range - in the 1960s the maturity range was over 17 years, but by the end of 1970s was nearer to 10 years.

In 1980s floating-rate notes, which are linked to financial ratios, represented more than 50 per cent of this market and coupons surpassed the 20 per cent level. Generally, these bonds have a predetermined repayment plan, semi-annual coupons and maturity ranges of 10 to 15 years. There are also few issues which pay interest quarterly.

- Example: ABI code 16401 IMI 87/92 5'

Amount issued	**Maturity**	**Coupon date**
500bn	01 October 1992	01 January - 01 April - 01 July - 01 October

Fixed-rate bonds have coupons which range from 10.5 per cent to 13.5 per cent. A group of these bonds is listed on the stock exchange, although they attract little trading volume. On rare occasions, some issuers quote their bonds via their Reuters pages. The minimum size of each deal on the Milan Sock Exchange is 1m lire but, on the OTC market, it is 1 or 2bn lire.

In 1990 the net issue of bonds by special credit institutions was Lit 5985bn against Lit 8205bn, placed in 1989.

Public company bonds

Before 1974, public company bonds had fixed-rate coupons. The first floating-rate note was issued by ENEL in 1974, but it remained the only issue of its kind until 1976, when ENEL placed a further issue.

During the 1980s, public companies mainly issued floating-rate notes in order to offer competitive instruments in a high interest market. Some bonds had also a minimum-guaranteed coupon.

Generally these bonds, which have maturities of 8-10 years, are issued as floating-rate notes linked to financial indices such as the Italian Banking Association's prime rate for bank account overdraft, average yield for interbank rates, Treasury bill yield, etc. Some of the bonds have an indexed redemption value.

In addition to floating-rate notes, there are also some fixed-rate notes and zero-coupon bonds.

Although public company bonds are listed on the Milan Stock Exchange, prices for most of them are usually obtained from dealers via their Reuters screens. Secondary market liquidity is poorer than that for government instruments, due mainly to the fact that the amounts issued do not equate with investment demand.

At the end of 1991, there were 71 public company issues outstanding, totalling Lit 41,000bn. Most of them are listed on the Milan Stock Exchange, although prices are normally obtained from dealers via their Reuters screens.

The most-recent issues, in 1991 were:

ABI code	Amount issued	Borrower	Issue date	Maturity date	Type	First coupon
26808	1500bn	FFSS	Dec 1990	01 Jan 2001	FRN	6.55%
28614	1000bn	ENEL	Nov 1991	12 Nov 2003	FRN	5.85%
28294	1500bn	IRI	Dec 1991	01 Dec 2001	FRN	6.30%

Corporate and convertible bonds

Corporate bonds are either ordinary or convertible. At the end of 1990, there was Lit 5122bn outstanding, with families and private corporations holding Lit 2039bn lire, and banks and mutual funds holding Lit 3083bn. The amount outstanding has decreased since 1988, when the total was Lit 6700bn.

Most of these bonds are listed on the Milan Stock Exchange, although the volume is rather limited and concentrated in the convertible issues (of which 40 are listed, with a total face value of Lit 350bn). The prices on convertible bonds are quoted either for settlement in cash (three days after the date of trade), or at full-term (as share settlement on the stock exchange).

Eurolira bonds

The eurolira market, which began in October 1985, initially lacked the potential for the sort of expansion and innovation seen in other comparable markets because the monetary authorities retained restrictions on foreign instruments, primarily in the hope that such a policy would maintain the stability of the lira. In July 1987, however, the Government partly deregulated the market by abolishing some of the restrictions. Since then, the eurolira market has seen an increase in both amounts issued and, consequently, amounts traded. In 1985, new issue volume totalled Lit 225bn - by 1991, it amounted to more than Lit 10,000bn. The most important issues during 1991 were:

Amount issued	Borrower	Maturity date	Coupon	Issue price
600bn	World Bank	23 April 1998	11.625%	101.45
1000bn	EIB	18 Jun 2001	11.10%	101.50
1000bn	Crediop	05 May 2001	11.20%	101.325

Eurolira bonds are issued outside Italy by supranationals, sovereigns, government agencies and societies.

They are issued through a syndicate of 30/35 banks or financial corporates, and investors can only buy bonds from the members of the syndicate. The Treasury and the Bank of Italy establish a queuing system with a lead-manager for each syndicate. Each of the syndicate members receives commissions to underwrite and place the bonds. At the end of 1991, the eurolira market comprised 136 issues, with a total outstanding amount of Lit 25,867bn. Most of these issues have annual, fixed-rate, coupons (indeed, fixed-rate bonds account for some 85 per cent of the market, with a total of Lit 22,192bn - see Figure 20.30)

There is only one zero-coupon bond, this being the Lit 150bn 27 August 1993 issue of Nordbanken, which was issued in August 1991 at an issue price of 80.55.

Floating-rate eurolira notes account for Lit 3675bn, with the most important issuers being supranationals and Italian public companies. These issues are generally indexed on financial and monetary ratios, such as the average of the yield of 12-month BOTs and the yield for interbank rates (usually a 3-month rate).

During 1991, there was no new issuance of floating-rate notes. The most important issues placed in 1990 were:

Amount issued	Borrower	Maturity date	Issue price	Issue date
500bn	FFSS	16 January 1998	100.00	January 1990
500bn	ENEL	28 April 2000	100.50	April 1990
500bn	FFSS	07 November 2000	101.00	November 1990

The liquidity of the market is influenced by the application of a specific taxation structure to these international bonds - all the issues are tax-exempt for non-resident investors while, for the Italian counterparties, only those bonds issued by supranationals and public companies are tax-exempt. There is a 30 per cent withholding tax on company bonds.

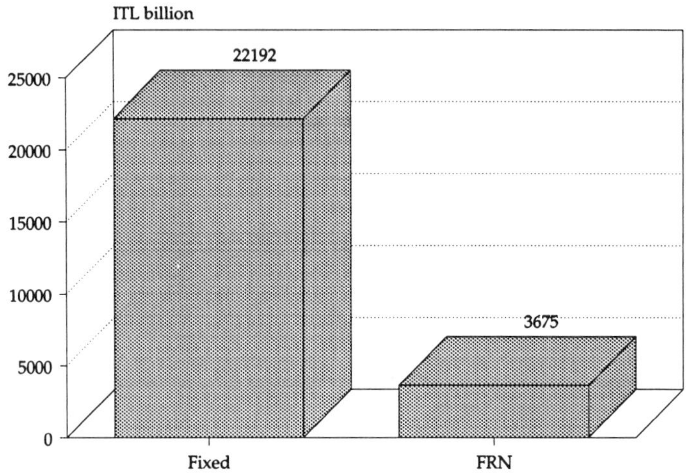

Figure 20.30 Composition of the eurolira bond market, 1991

Eurolira bonds are listed on the Luxembourg Stock Exchange, as well as the International Stock Exchange in London, although most of them are also quoted on Reuters pages by dealers. Spreads are generally around 50/60 basis points for supranationals, but wider for taxable issues. The minimum size of each trade is Lit 1bn for fixed-rate bonds and Lit 0.5bn for floating-rate notes.

All dealings done on the market are registered within 7 days on Euroclear/Cedel. Eurolira bonds are denominated in Lit 2/5m.

20.5 Issuers

The Italian government is the biggest issuer on the Italian bond market. Figure 20.31 shows the net issue amount on bonds over the last years, as well as the detail of issuance during 1991. Figure 20.32, meanwhile, shows net government issuance against GNP.

	Government	Special credit institutions	Public companies
1985	107,490	5178	2195
1986	97,740	6805	6071
1987	85,628	11,012	4038
1988	103,850	7966	709
1989	108,588	8205	35
1990	116,753	5985	-2592
Aug 90	7368	738	-103
Sep 90	7182	789	-24
Oct 90	15,965	682	-96
Nov 90	12,754	1025	-228
Dec 90	15,389	969	-584
Jan 91	3905	507	107
Feb 91	11,512	1482	2044
Mar 91	10,230	266	-15
Apr 91	12,521	2289	-296
May 91	13,758	643	-61
Jun 91	7624	1265	760
Jul 91	7805	247	-926
Aug 91	10,494	523	-260

Figure 20.31 Net issuance of bonds, by issuer

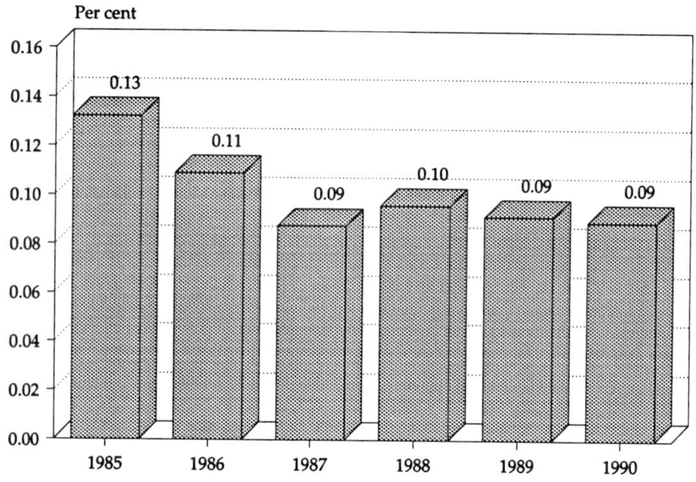

Figure 20.32 Net government issuance against GNP.

20.6 Investors

Investors on the Italian bond market can be divided into the following large groups, namely:

- families and corporates
- banks, mutual funds, insurance companies
- Bank of Italy
- non-resident investors

Families, banks and companies hold the highest proportion of securities (see Figure 20.33). Until 1981, the Bank of Italy was obliged by the Treasury to take

	Families & corporates	Mutual funds	Bank of Italy	Banks
1985	65,969	12,203	24,431	12,261
1986	60,994	27,866	10,139	11,618
1987	100,274	-2971	-2600	5975
1988	133,795	-9555	-798	-10,918
1989	125,089	-4170	4969	-9060
1990	127,542	3784	-2450	-8730
Aug 90	6450	-1108	-6649	9310
Sep 90	2875	235	-10,063	14,900
Oct 90	14,928	1164	930	-470
Nov 90	16,489	128	5284	-8350
Dec 90	-13,722	674	4493	24,330
Jan 91	36,535	-556	2050	-33,510
Feb 91	17,597	1007	6294	-9860
Mar 91	9801	2378	-5678	3940
Apr 91	17,071	1058	-6715	3100
May 91	12,796	867	-1073	1750
Jun 91	-1801	244	5166	6040
Jul 91	15,778	105	2323	-10,870

Figure 20.33 Net bondholdings of different investor groups

up any issue-balance not subscribed on the market. However, this rule was rescinded to allow the Bank to pursue an independent monetary policy.

Demand for Italian bonds by foreign investors has been increasing during the last five years due mainly to the high interest rates and attraction of a stable ERM currency. However, despite this increase, the contribution of foreign investment to the overall market remains marginal. During the recent years Bank of Italy reduced its importance as investor. Mutual funds, families and corporates increased their percentage.

20.7 *Methods of issuance*

Primary market

There are three principal methods of issuance which are used on the Italian bond market, namely:

- public auction
- syndicates
- private placement

Public auction may be either competitive or non-competitive (Dutch auction).

Competitive auction

This type of auction is generally used in the BOT Treasury bill market. Participants can make a maximum of five offers at different prices, with no limit on the amounts. They may also make an offer without indicating a price. Competitive bids are accepted from the highest price down. Non-competitive bids are accepted in full at an average price, plus a spread which is calculated by the Treasury. The minimum spread accepted between the different offers on 12-month BOTs is 5 basis points whilst, on 3- and 6-month BOTs, a 1 basis point spread is also permitted. All the offers must be sent to Bank of Italy by 12.00 on the day of auction.

Dutch auction (marginal auction)

This type of auction is mainly used by the Treasury to issue BTPs, CCTs, CTOs, CTEs and BTEs. For each bond, a minimum price (or maximum rate) is defined by the Treasury at, or below, which level bids are not accepted. Different issues of the same bond must have the same minimum price because the difference between that price level and par provides the basis for the calculation of withholding tax (which is paid on maturity). Participants must hand-deliver their offers to the Bank of Italy in Rome by 12.30 on the day of auction.

Underwriters can make a maximum of five bids. The minimum acceptable spread between the different offers is 5 basis points. All bids are filled at the marginal price which enables allocation of the global amount (see Figure 20.28)

Participants receive either 75 or 100 basis points placement commission and benefit from two to five 'bonus' days in respect of the value-date.

Amount offered: ITL 5000bn

Base price: 97.50

Participant	Bid price	Amount bid	Amount allocated	Price
A	97.75	1500	1500	97.55
B	97.70	1500	1500	97.55
C	97.65	500	500	97.55
D	97.60	1000	1000	97.55
E	97.55	1000	500	97.55

Figure 20.34 Example of a Dutch auction

	FFSS	ENEL	ENI	IRI	Convertibles	Corporates
1987	2000	2741	500	2350	1077	265
1988	1000	1693	118	1500	381	954
1989	1000	2660	100	100	563	474
1990	3200	1085	0	0	443	73
Sep 90	0	0	0	0	9	0
Oct 90	0	0	0	0	24	36
Nov 90	0	52	0	0	0	0
Dec 90	1500	0	0	0	52	7
Jan 91	0	150	0	0	0	431
Feb 91	0	1000	1403	0	0	0
Mar 91	0	0	0	0	0	0
Apr 91	0	0	0	0	0	0
May 91	0	50	0	0	0	70
Jun 91	0	0	0	1000	0	12
Jul 91	0	0	0	0	0	25
Aug 91	0	0	0	0	0	0

Figure 20.35 Net issuance of public sector bonds

Syndicates

Syndicates are used to place bonds issued by the public sector, such as ENEL, FFSS, IRI (see Figure 20.35). This method of issuance is also used in the eurolira market. Although there are no laid-down procedures, guidelines based on international practice are given to the participants by the Bank of Italy.

Syndicate members, who receive placement commission, are banks or financial companies. Although corporations often use this method of issuance, they sometimes also resort to private placement through banks. This method is widely-used by special credit institutions which issue their bonds through bank channels or through the issuer's shareholders.

20.8 *New issue volumes*

During 1990 new issuance totalled Lit 782,426bn (see Figure 20.36, below)

	1987	1988	1989	1990	1991[1]
BOT	316,110	409,411	198,553	559,196	602,421
BTE	2311	7289	11,313	6109	4000
CCT	55,480	27,350	21,300	75,538	99,000
BTP	19,020	75,383	41,100	74,460	93,000
CTO	-	594	15,620	27,161	23,000
CTE	2231	11,167	9025	8017	2400
Others	10,605	697	634	4582	n/a
Total government	405,757	531,891	597,545	755,063	823,821
Special credit institutions	25,100	21,789	21,368	22,364	n/a
Public companies	7591	4311	3860	4285	7103
Company	265	954	474	73	n/a
Convertible	1077	381	563	443	n/a
Others	450	550	300	200	n/a
Grand total	440,239	559,875	624,110	782.426	n/a

Figure 20.36 New issuance volumes, 1987-1991
[1]*Some of the 1991 figures are estimates*

It is important to analyse the composition of the net amount issued during the last few years in the government sector as shown in Figure 20.37.

	1987	1988	1989	1990	1991[1]
BOT	25,171	36,275	39,778	44,641	13,865
BTE	2311	5738	3264	-4072	-4750
CCT	35,267	-7848	20,916	54,214	12,000
BTP	13,538	59,781	27,006	-13,347	88,000
CTO	-	594	15,336	26,678	23,000
CTE	2231	11,167	7434	7262	1000
Others	6674	-1032	-2968	-114	n/a
Total government	85,192	104,645	110,766	115,262	113,115

Figure 20.37 Net issuance in the government sector, 1987-1991
[1]*Some of the 1991 figures are estimates*

20.9 Methods of trading

There are three markets which can trade Italian bonds: the Milan Stock Exchange, the over-the-counter market (OTC) and the Telematic market.

Stock exchange

Bonds on the stock exchange are listed 'on call', but the daily amount traded is mostly irrelevant.

OTC market

The OTC market was developed in order to improve liquidity on the secondary market, which had previously been confined to the official stock exchange market. The OTC market is principally a telephone market but quotations are posted on Reuters pages. Although rather illiquid (reflected in the typical spreads of 10/20 basis points) and with a thin daily turnover, the OTC market is nevertheless important because, historically, it paved the way for the introduction of a true screen-based secondary market on 16 May 1988.

Telematic market

This market, known as the 'Telematic' market was developed to counter the deficiencies of both the official stock exchange and the OTC market. On the Telematic market 25 primary dealers list prices on over than 75 government bonds during the periods 09.30-13.30 and 14.30-16.30 on each day that the stock exchange is open.

The minimum size of each deal is Lit 5bn and liquidity is good (although activity is concentrated among just a few primary dealers) with spreads generally in the region of 3/5 basis points, but often as narrow as just 1 cent.

Italian Treasury bills, or *Buoni Ordinari del Tesoro* (BOTs), have been quoted on the screen market since 26 October 1989. Dealings are concentrated in new issues and the market is mainly used to trade BOTs immediately after an auction.

Every day, the Bank of Italy provides a list of bonds with prices and amounts traded during the previous day (Reuters pages BITI-BITP) on this important market, which has seen steadily increasing volumes (see Figure 20.38) to a present-day level of more than 10,000bn per day .

The market is overseen by the *Comitato di gestione del Mercato Secondario* which is a committee composed of representatives of primary dealers.

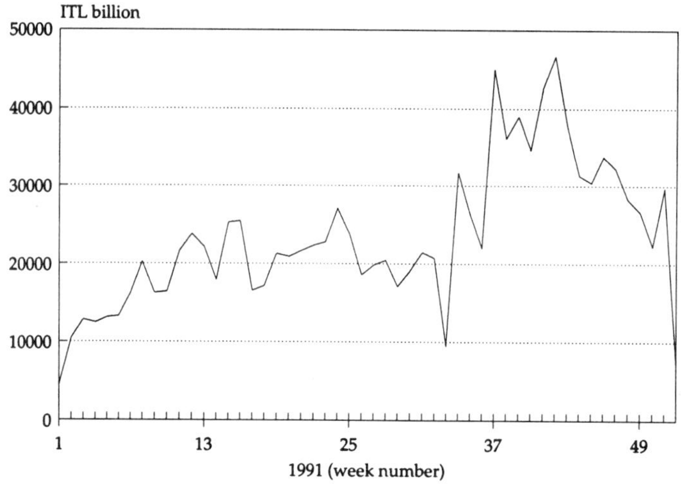

Figure 20.38 Weekly traded volume

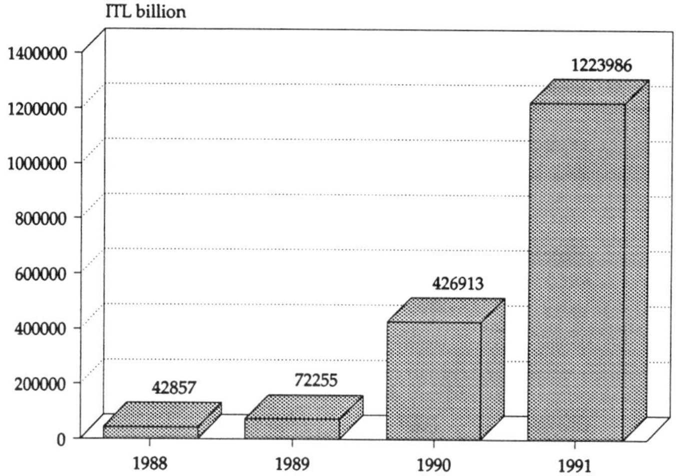

Figure 20.39 Traded volumes, 1988 - 1991

The Italian bond market has undergone a period of dramatic evolution during the last ten years, but there are still areas requiring attention. Importantly, at the time of writing, there is no regulatory provision for a much-needed futures and options market (although it is hoped that such a market will appear in 1992).

The primary dealers, and the major traders on the bond market are:

- Banca Commerciale Italiana
- Banca d'America e d'Italia
- Banca del Salento
- Banca Euromobiliare
- Banca Nazionale del Lavoro
- Banca Nazionale del l'Agricoltura
- Banca Popolare di Milano
- Banca Popolare di Novara
- Banco di Napoli
- Banco di Roma
- Banco di Santo Spirito
- Banco di Sardegna
- Banco di Sicilia
- Caboto
- Cariplo
- Cassa di Risparmio di Torino
- Cassa di Risparmio di Verona
- Credito Italiano
- Credito Romagnolo
- Eptaconsors
- Iccri
- Istituto Bancario San Paolo di Torino
- Monte Paschi di Siena
- Morgan G. Trust
- Sigeco

20.10 Market practices

Settlement

Bonds are normally settled on a three-day basis and, where either Cedel or Euroclear is used for the settlement, the value-date is the seventh day after the date of trade. No physical bonds are issued unless specifically requested by holders - most trading is handled by book-entry system through specified accounts held at Bank of Italy.

Non-resident holders may hold and dispose of the bonds through an Italian depository bank (agent bank) holding an account with the Bank of Italy. They may deal in bonds directly through Euroclear/Cedel. Underwriting transactions have to be handled by an Italian depository bank.

Upon request, foreign investors may withdraw bonds from the Bank of Italy for transfer abroad, in which case the bonds are stamped 'payable abroad'.

Redemption

Most of the domestic issues redeem at par (minus the withholding tax):

- Example: ABI code 12688 BTP 17 January 1999 12 per cent

Amount issued	Base price	Issue price	Redemption price
2000bn	94.95	99.60	99.369

The redemption price is calculated as:

100-94.95 = 5.05

(5.05 x 12.5)/100 = 0.63125

100 - 0.63125 = 99.369

A few of them, notably issues of ENEL, have a premium upon reimbursement which represents a cumulative percentage of the coupons:

- Example: ABI code 13086 ENEL 1985/1995 1'

Amount issued	Coupon date	Maturity date	Redemption value
900bn	01 Jan - 01 Sep	01 Sep 1994 01 Mar 1995	10 per cent of each coupon will be cumulated and will be paid as premium upon the principal

All government bonds redeem the principal in full upon maturity, but many securities have a predetermined repayment plan, often based on the plan used in France whereby principal repayments coincide with a coupon-date by reducing the bond's face value, or by chance draws. This method of redemption is mainly used by the older issues of special credit institutions. Drawing dates are established in the debt issue rules.

- Example: ABI code 4499 Cariplo Op. 1979/1999

Amount issued	Coupon date	Drawing date	Redemption date
25bn	01 May - 01 Nov	During the first fifteen days of August	01 May - 01 Nov

Redemptions are always made net of withholding tax.

Denomination

Most bonds have a minimum denomination of Lit 5m. Eurolira issues can be generally found in with denominations of Lit 2m (and multiples thereof), although differences do occur from issue to issue.

There are some old and rare bonds still in existence which have a minimum denomination of Lit 1m.

Coupon payment

Most domestic bonds pay coupons semi-annually. However old CCTs and CTEs pay annual coupons, while there are a few zero-coupon issues and bonds with quarterly coupons.

Eurolira fixed-rate bonds carry an annual coupon, but floating-rate notes generally have semi-annual coupons.

All coupon payments are made net of withholding tax, which is deducted at source by the Treasury and turned over to the Minister of Finance.

First coupon

The first coupon is always determined in the issue plan, even if the bond issued is a floating-rate note. It may be a pro-rata coupon, which is calculated on the number of days between the date of the issue and the date of payment.

Puts

CTOs give the holder the right to put bonds. Only a few eurolira issues have a put option.

Commissions

Commissions are given to brokers when they deal on the stock exchange. Broker commissions for bank trading are generally 0.1 basis points of the nominal value of bonds and 0.05 basis points for government securities.

Commissions for OTC dealings are regulated and agreed by the contracting parties; generally they apply a commission ranging from 1 to 5 basis points which is added to the price of the bond traded.

20.11 Settlement

Overview

All bonds are normally settled on a three day basis and, where Cedel or Euroclear is used for settlement, the value-date is the seventh day after the date of trade. Convertible bonds can be either settled in cash (three days after the date of trade), or at full term (as share settlement on the Milan Stock Exchange).

Book-entry system

No physical bonds are issued unless specifically requested by holders. Most trading is handled by book-entry system through specified accounts held at Bank of Italy.

Monte Titoli SpA

Monte Titoli SpA is a society which holds and manages physical bonds and shares. It was founded on 15 February 1978 by the Bank of Italy, with the principal purpose of reducing both the risks and the costs associated with bond trading. At the end of 1988, 168 banks joined Monte Titoli, a figure which represents a significant proportion of the Italian banking system. The society provides for the collection of coupons, redemption values and all other matters connected with bond management.

Non-resident holders may hold and dispose of the bonds through an Italian depository bank (agent bank) holding an account with the Bank of Italy, or with Monte Titoli; they may also deal in bonds directly through Euroclear/Cedel. Underwriting transactions must be handled by an Italian depository bank.

20.12 Yield calculation

Coupons on Italian bonds are calculated an the basis of a 30-day month and a 360-day year. They take into account the coupon payment date and the settlement date is therefore usually a day more than in other euromarkets.

Accrued interest on BTEs is calculated on actual days, on a 365-day year basis. Yields on BOTs are calculated using the same parameters, while Treasury bills are all quoted on a simple yield:

Simple yield = ((100/price) - 1) x (365/days to maturity)

- Example: 12029 BOT 15 Oct 1992

This bond was issued on 15 October 1991. There were 366 days to maturity and the gross issue price was 89.10.

Gross yield = ((100/89.10) - 1) x (365/366) = 12.20%

Withholding tax = (100 - 89.10) x 0.125 = 1.3625

Net price = 89.10 + 1.3625 = 90.4625

Net yield = ((100/90,4625) - 1) x (365/366) = 10.51%

The internal rate of return is used to calculate yield on all Italian bonds. It is the accepted market convention to use the appropriate international formula for such a return:

$$p + a = \sum_{j=1}^{n} C_j (1+r)^{-t_j}$$

where,

p	clean price
a	accrued interest
c_j	cash flow (coupons and redemption)
t_j	fraction of a period from the value-date to the first/next payment
r	internal rate of return

This formula has its limitations, however, because it does not allow for the fluctuation of interest rates on the market, which can alter the cashflow of the investment.

Yields on floating-rate notes are calculated by estimating future coupons on the basis of the latest reference index value. The IRR formula has been improved to optimize the value obtained. New formulae include the estimated inflation rate, the reinvestment rate, the probability of redemption, etc:

For full details on bond yield see the CSFB publication, *Yield Calculation* and ISMA publication, *Formulae for Yield and other Calculations.*

20.13 *Taxation*

Overview

In the past there has been a wide variety of Italian tax rates (see Figure 20.40) but, now, all bonds issued in Italy are subject to a 12.5 per cent withholding tax. Only supranational and government issues on the eurolira market remain tax-free (although corporate issues are subject to a 30 per cent withholding tax).

Treasury bonds & public administration (ENEL, FFSS)	Long-term bonds issued by banks	Bonds issued by IRI, ENI, EFIM, quoted societies	Convertibles
Issued before: 20 Sep 86 *No tax*	Issued before: 01 Jan 74 *No tax*	Issued before: 01 Jan 74 *No tax*	Issued before: 01 Jan 74 *No tax*
Issued between: 20 Sep 86 - 31 Aug 87 *6.25%*	Issued between: 01 Jan 74 - 02 Jul 80 *10.8%*	Issued between: 01 Jan 74 - 31 Dec 80 *21.6%*	Issued between: 01 Jan 74 - 31 Dec 80 *10.8%*
Issued after: 01 Sep 87 *12.5%*	Issued between: 03 Jul 80 - 30 Sep 82 *No tax*	Issued between: 31 Dec 80 - 30 Sep 82 *No tax*	Issued between: 31 Dec 80 - 30 Sep 82 *No tax*
	Issued between: 01 Oct 82 - 31 Dec 83 *10.8%*	Issued between: 01 Oct 82 - 31 Dec 83 *10.8%*	Issued between: 01 Oct 82 - 31 Dec 83 *10.8%*
	Issued after: 01 Jan 84 *12.5%*	Issued after: 01 Jan 84 *12.5%*	Issued after: 01 Jan 84 *12.5%*

Figure 20.40 Taxation of Italian bonds

Non-residents

Non-residents may apply to the Italian Ministry of Finance for refunds of withholding tax. Alternatively, they can claim a tax credit equal to, or a percentage of, the amount withheld at the source by the Italian government. On 11 April 1991, the Ministry of Finance defined a new method to claim these refunds:

Non-residents (assuming their country is linked with Italy by international agreement providing a special fiscal treatment for such interest) may ask a refund of withholding tax, but only that paid on government bonds or on public administration bonds. Non-residents have to fill in a form which consists of five parts and four copies. Once filled in, it has to be dated and signed by the recipient, then submitted to the depository bank (whether resident in Italy or in the effective beneficiary's country). The depository bank will file its own copy, after the appropriate checks, and after the signature of each enclosure and sheet of which it is composed, and the addition of the requested statement. The remaining copies have to be forwarded to the fiscal authority of the recipient's residence state which, after the appropriate checks, will keep one copy for its own files. Of the two remaining copies of the form, one will be kept by the non-resident, while the other will be sent by the same recipient to the Italian fiscal administration (Intendenza Di Finanza Di Roma, Via Del Clementino 91/A, 00186 Roma) within 10 years from the date on which the interest is available for collection.

The application for refund must relate to the interest on the bonds lodged in a single bank - in case of bonds lodged in different banks, a separate application for each has to be submitted. As for the period in respect of which the refund is claimed, the recipient can choose to fill in an application either referring to the coupon payment for each type of bond, as well as cumulatively, at the end of each assessment period; or for the total amount of coupons expiring in the duration if referring to different assessment periods. In a case where the bonds have been deposited (with a bank resident in Italy, or resident in the effective recipient's country), not directly on behalf of the beneficiary, but rather through a corporate which has made on indistinct deposit, jointly with other bonds held by different subjects, there is a part of form which should be filled in by the corporate depository. The depository must indicate the name of the bank with which the bonds have been deposited.

For bonds denominated in Ecu, figures have to be indicated, both in Ecu and in Italian lire, at the exchange rate pointed out and reported by the Ufficio Italiano Cambi and used for the coupon payment.

Italian corporates

This tax can be refunded to Italian corporate investors (such as banks and companies) who may then show the value on their balance sheets. Corporates must show all bond investments and trading income in their balances. Trading revenue is considered as a contribution to annual profits and is therefore taxed at a rate of 46.3 per cent.

There is also a tax on transactions amounting to some 0.9 per cent of the value traded. This tax is not applied to foreign investments or to the underwriting of government bonds.

There are minimum and maximum amounts, payable under this tax, of Lit 1000 and Lit 1,600,000 respectively.

20.14 *Futures and options*

There is no official futures and options market in Italy. However, there is an OTC market in derivatives and quotations may be obtained from dealers via Reuters pages. Nevertheless, although volumes have been increasing over the last few years, the numbers of contracts actually dealt on this market is still rather limited. It is expected that the Italian financial authorities will regulate the market by the end of 1992.

Investors wishing to trade Italian instruments should use the Marché à Terme International de France (Matif), or the London International Financial Futures Exchange (Liffe), both of which offer futures contracts on the fixed-rate bonds - *Buoni del Tesoro Poliennali* (BTPs). Matif's contract (see Figures 20.41 & 20.42 for specification and volume traded) began on 5 September 991, whilst Liffe's contract was launched shortly after, on 19 September 1991 (see Figures 20.43 & 20.44).

Since October 1991, it has been possible to trade options on BTP futures on both markets (see Figures 20.45 & 20.46 for specifications).

Contract size:	ITL 100m nominal value notional BTP with 10 per cent coupon
Delivery months:	March, June, September, December
Last trading day:	Fourth business day prior to the last business day of delivery month
Quotation:	Per ITL 100 nominal value
Minimum price movement (tick size) and value:	ITL 0.01; ITL 10.000
Trading hours:	09.00-16.30 (Paris time)
Contract standard:	Delivery may be made of any BTP with 6/10 years remaining maturity, provided that any such BTP has a minimum amount, in issue, of ITL 2000bn

Figure 20.41 Matif's BTP futures - contract specification

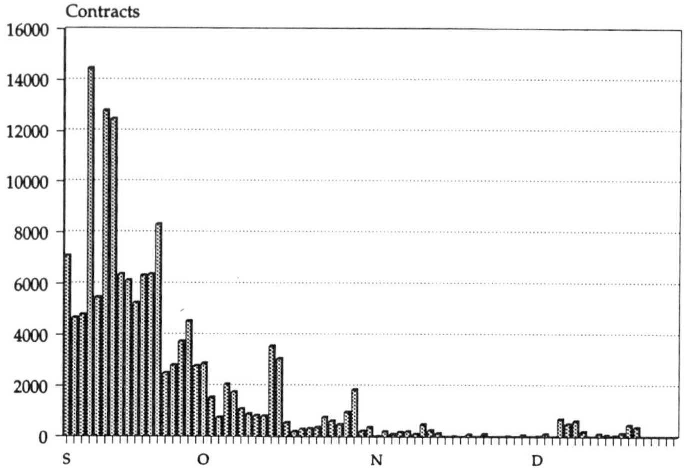

Figure 20.42 Matif's BTP futures - daily volume

Contract size:	ITL 200m nominal value notional BTP with 12 per cent coupon
Delivery months:	March, June, September, December
Deliver day:	Tenth calendar day of delivery month
Last trading day:	Fourth working day prior to the delivery day
Quotation:	Per ITL 100 nominal value
Minimum price movement (tick size) and value:	ITL 0.01; ITL 20,000
Trading hours:	08.10-16.05 (London time)
Contract standard:	Delivery may be made of any BTP with 8-10 1/2 years remaining maturity as at the tenth calendar day of the delivery month, provided that any such BTP has a minimum amount, in issue, of ITL 4000bn

Figure 20.43 Liffe's BTP futures - contract specification

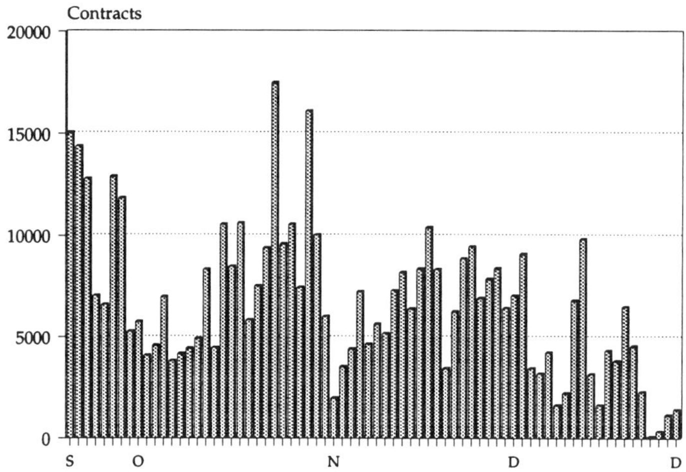

Figure 20.44 Liffe's BTP futures - daily volume

Option type:	American
Unit of trading:	BTP futures contract
Delivery months:	March, June, September, December
Assignment of futures:	Automatic exercise of in-the-money options on the last trading day
Last trading day:	Last working Thursday of the month preceding the Italian bond futures delivery month
Quotation:	Multiples of ITL 0.01
Minimum price movement (tick size) and value:	ITL 0.01; ITL 10,000
Trading hours:	09.05-16.30 (Paris time)

Figure 20.45 Matif's options on BTP futures - contract specification

Option type:	American. Exercise by 17.00 on any business day, extended to 18.30 on the last day of trading
Unit of trading:	BTP futures contract
Delivery months:	March, June, September, December
Assignment of futures:	On the first business day after the exercise day
Last trading day:	Seventh business day prior to first day of delivery month
Quotation:	Multiples of ITL 0.01
Minimum price movement (tick size) and value:	ITL 0.01; ITL 20,000
Trading hours:	08.10-16.10 (London time)
Strike prices:	At multiples of 50 basis points, with at least 9 bracketing the at-the-money price. Additional exercise prices are introduced on the business day after the BTP futures contract settlement price is within ITL 0.25 of the fourth highest or lowest existing exercise price

Figure 20.46 Liffe's options on BTP futures - contract specification

20.15 *Interest rate history*

Overview

Throughout a long period prior to 1987, Italy saw a steep reduction in interest rates (see Figure 20.47). This trend was halted by a temporary rise in 1987, since when it has been hard to identify a distinct pattern, as the rate has fluctuated in a narrow band.

Figure 20.47 Italian lira interest rate, 1987-1991

1991 in detail

In January, interest rates declined (see Figure 20.48), reflecting the new monetary policy of the Bank of Italy. At the beginning of February, this policy was modified, as a result of the rise in German interest rates but, later that same month, the Bank of Italy returned to its previous policy and the bond market reacted positively by reducing rates. February was also notable as a month in which cross-rates against the Deutschemark strengthened, a factor which, together with the successful conclusion of the Gulf War, supported a firm trend in government bond prices.

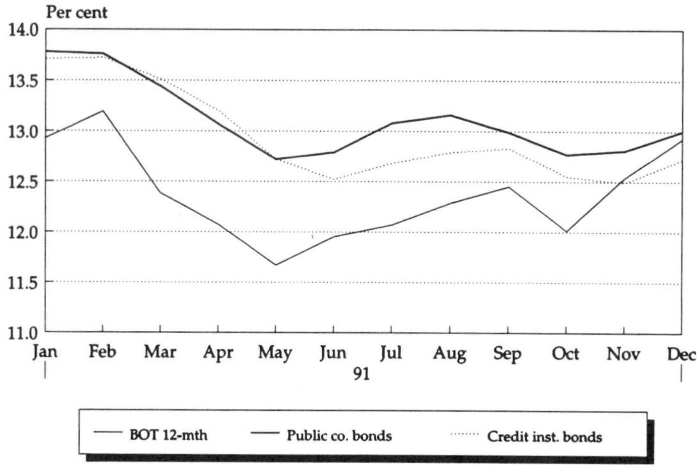

Figure 20.48 Italian lira interest rate, 1991

In March, the Treasury issued the first BTP with a ten-year maturity as it tried to modify the life of its debt. During this period, the yield curve became flat. The positive trend was underlined, in April, by the decision to admit government bonds into the Cedel/Euroclear system. Meanwhile, the finance minister modified the methodology of withholding tax reimbursement.

In May, the Bank of Italy reduced the prime rate to 11.5 per cent and, consequently, the Treasury reduced the face value of coupons on new issues.

The summer was marked by an inverse trend on the market, as prices declined under the pressure of sales by investors who preferred to monetarize their portfolios. During this period, the yield curve became convex (and was to remain so, until October).

The launch of new futures contracts based on BTPs (see Section 20.14, Futures & options) attracted widespread attention to the high rates available on Italian bonds, with the result that the rates subsequently declined under buying pressure; indeed, in October, rates reached their lowest level for the year.

An increase in inflation, however, led to the downward trend being reversed in November. After the Maastricht Treaty, the Bundesbank modified the main German rates and the Bank of Italy was forced to raise its prime rate to 12 per cent. Not surprisingly, this move prompted the bond markets to show a decline although, as the year closed, the fall in prices became less marked.

20.16 *Inter-market spreads*

Italian government bonds vs. UK government bonds

The spread between Italian government bonds and those of the UK, widened during the first part of the year (see Figure 20.49) but, in the period between April and July, it actually narrowed - the spread reaching a minimum value of just 34 basis points at the end of that period. Thereafter, the spread steadily began to widen again although this trend was halted as the year closed.

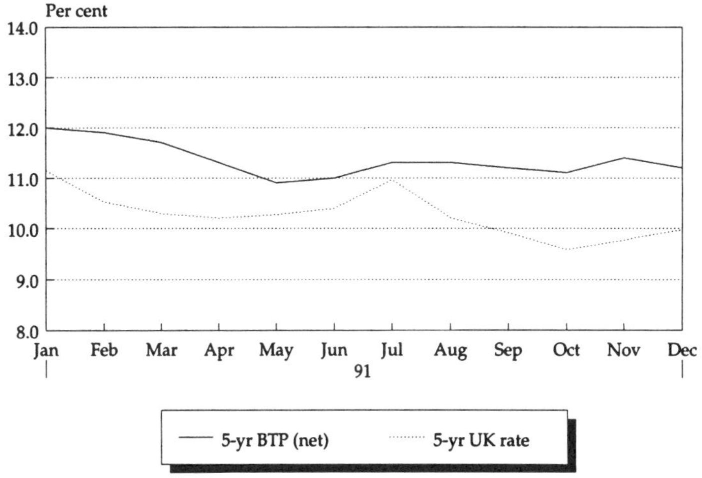

Figure 20.49 Inter-market spread - Italian government bonds vs. UK government bonds

Italian government bonds vs. German government bonds

The rates on German short-term bonds were reduced during the first two months of 1991, with the consequence that the spread became wider (see Figure 20.50). From March, however, this spread narrowed, with the minimum level, of 226 basis points, being recorded in May. The summer period saw a slightly higher level of around 235-240 basis points. In November, the spread showed signs of widening again, but a narrowing was recorded in December.

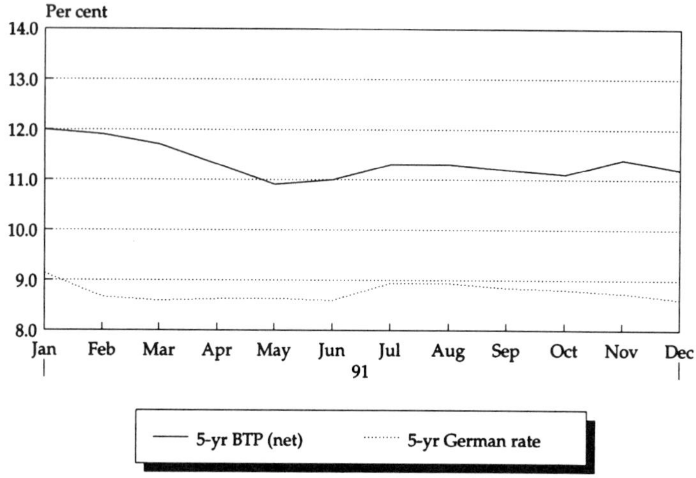

Figure 20.50 Inter-market spread - Italian government bonds vs. German government bonds

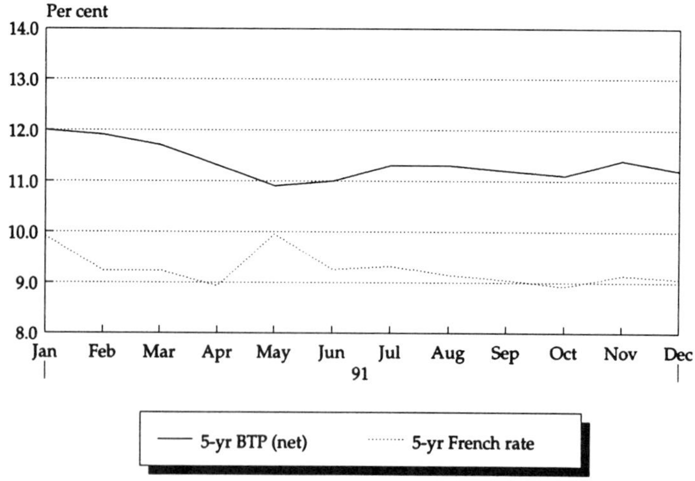

Figure 20.51 Inter-market spread - Italian government bonds vs. French government bonds

Italian government bonds vs. French government bonds

The spread between short-term Italian and French bonds (see Figure 20.51) showed a similar pattern to the others described in this section, albeit on a slightly smaller scale.

20.17 *Sources of reference*

Financial data/publications

Banca d'Italia

- *Bollettino*
- *Relazione Annuale*

Mediocredito Lombardo

- *Mercato Finanziario, Credito*
- *Speciale e Finanziamento degli Investimenti - Aavv 1984*

Borsa Valori Milano

- *Listino Ufficiale*

Credito Italiano

- *Guida del Risparmiatore 1985-1991*

Comitato di Gestione

- *Report Settimanale dei Mercati*

Mercato Secondario Titoli di Stato

- *Finanziari*

Ministero Delle Finanze

- *Circolare N. 12 Del 11-4-1991*

Further reading

- *Il Mercato Mobiliare Italiano,* by F. Cesarini
- *Struttura e Prospettive,* by F. Cesarini, 1973
- *Moneta e Politica Monetaria in Italia,* by P.Ranci, 1977
- *Il Sistema di Credito Speciale in Italia,* by V.Pontolillo, 1980
- *Il Nuovo Operatore di Borsa,* by S.Burattelli, 1989

Chapter

21

The bond markets of the

Netherlands

Peter van der Linde
Philips Pensioenfondsen

Bert Korevaar
ABN AMRO Bank

Koos 't Hart
Pierson, Heldring & Pierson

Chris Nicodem
Stichting Unilever Pensioenfonds 'Progress'

Steven Klop
Compagnie Parisienne de Réescompte

Jan van Roekel
Algemeen Burgerlijk Pensioenfonds

Gert Verheij
Towers Perrin/Smit & Bunschoten

with thanks to the
Economics Department
ABN AMRO Bank

Note: In general text, the abbreviation 'Dfl' is used to denote the Dutch guilder. Elsewhere, the international mnemonic 'NLG' is used.

21.1 Introduction

The Amsterdam Stock Exchange is the oldest continuously-traded stock market in the world. It has flourished ever since The Dutch East India Company, founded in 1602, made world history by inaugurating the public offering of shares and, unsurprisingly, the Exchange has become the model for many others around the globe.

Additionally, the Dutch bond market offers, relative to its size, some of the widest variety of liquid issues available in Europe. The size and liquidity of the market, which is dominated by government issues, have resulted from continuing, substantial, budget deficits.

This success, however, is relatively recent. Almost without exclusion, the Dutch government has historically issued state loans with mandatory pro rata sinking funds, making Dutch bonds both too unusual and parochial for most international investors. Recently, though, this position has changed dramatically. As of 1986, nearly all state loans have utilized bullet structures, thereby bringing the market into line with standard international practices and naturally improving the global attraction of the Dutch bond market. Only two issues (one in 1987 and one in 1989) had a sinking fund character.

The market has a few peculiarities of which the investor should be aware. In addition to the large number of sinking fund bonds, the short- and long-term bond market comprises a significant amount of private loans - very similar to the *Schuldscheine* market in Germany. These private loans are tailored to meet the specific requirements of both issuer and borrower, and include such advantages as the absence of an issue calendar, higher yields for investors and lower costs for borrowers (i.e. low commission and marketing costs). This sector is dominated by domestic issuers and institutional investors, - with foreign borrowers being admitted to this system only on a small scale.

However, as the government has stepped up its borrowing through the public capital market rather than through the private loan market, the preponderance of these bonds in Dutch institutional portfolios is changing. In 1980, the private loan market had a 67 per cent market share but, by 1991, it had dwindled to about 45 per cent. Additionally, the yield spreads between private loans and government bonds have recently narrowed to around 10-20 basis points in 1991, from a level of 15-30 basis points in 1990.

Market deregulation

A milestone in the history of the Dutch capital market (see Figure 21.1), was its liberalization on 1 January 1986. The aim of the liberalization was both to improve Amsterdam's position as an international financial centre and to do

1986	First issuance of bullet bonds
	Elimination of new issue calendar
	Underwriting and size restrictions on domestic and euroguilder bond issues lifted
	First floating-rate note issued
	Issue of CP and CDs permitted
	Start of Amsterdam Interprofessional Market (AIM)
1988	Zero-coupon bonds and discounted bonds permitted
	Medium-term notes permitted
1990	Abolition of stamp duty
	Introduction of open-order book
	Minimum commissions are lifted
	New rules for settlement
	First issue on tap of government bonds
	Issue of indexed loans permitted
1991	First issuance of government bullet bond with life of 15 years
	Issuance of government private bullet loans with lives of 20 to 40 years

Figure 21.1 History of Dutch bond market deregulation

everything possible to retain in the Netherlands, the trade (and, consequently, the price-setting thereof) in guilder-denominated paper.

The liberalization gave issuers more freedom in the choice of instrument. The Dutch central bank is now more flexible in its application of the issue calendar system, while a great many restrictions on the form of loans to be issued have been lifted. Restrictions concerning redemption schemes have disappeared (before liberalization, a bond had to be redeemed in at least four annual payments), while the legal minimum average life has been reduced from 5.5 years to 2 years. As a consequence of these measures, the distinction between the money market and capital market has faded somewhat. The results of liberalization can be defined as follows:

- It will become difficult for the Dutch central bank to regulate the money market in the traditional way, i.e. via swaps or special loans; on the other hand, the bank intends to intervene on the capital market with a Dfl 3bn bond portfolio.

- Large businesses can issue short-term paper. This means that they are able to cover their short-term financing needs directly on the market, instead of through bank overdrafts or cash loans.

Developments since deregulation

Developments since the beginning of 1986 have shown that the more flexible issue strategy of the Dutch central bank has made it possible for issuing institutions to respond with greater alertness to changes in market conditions. One consequence has been that issues are now less evenly spread throughout the year; rather they come by leaps and bounds, dependent on interest rate developments. By comparison to pre-1986, therefore, the success of issues now depends more strongly on the correct assessment of prevailing market conditions.

From its introduction in 1986, the bullet loan instrument has clearly satisfied a demand. Practically all recently-issued government loans fall into this category - in 1991, the Dutch government issued three 10-year bullet loans (as well as one with a 15-year maturity). The growth in issuance of bonds of less than 5.5 years maturity is slower than that of bullet loans, the modest use made of this facility being mainly attributable to the introduction of the medium-term note.

Since January 1986 the issue of both guilder commercial paper (CP, issued by companies and municipalities) and guilder certificates of deposit (CDs, issued by financial institutions), has been permitted. The minimum issue amount is Dfl 1m and terms can vary between 14 days and 2 years. At the end of 1991, the total value of announced CP programmes was Dfl 17.8bn, while CD programmes accounted for Dfl 17.2bn. The amount of CP and CDs actually outstanding on the market was Dfl 3.6bn and Dfl 4.5bn, respectively.

To date, the total number of floating-rate note issues is just two. The lack of appeal to borrowers is mainly due to the development of the interest rate swap market, while the very small difference between short-term and long-term interest rates has also played a role.

In January 1988, medium-term notes (MTNs) were introduced in the Netherlands. The minimum life for these notes is 2 years, while the minimum amount per coupon is Dfl 1m. As 14 programmes have already been issued on the domestic market, it seems that there is a good demand for this type of instrument. At the end of 1991, the total MTN value amounted to Dfl 21.1bn, with Dfl 14.4bn actually outstanding on the market.

Issue of zero-coupon bonds and deep-discount bonds has also been permitted since January 1988. However, the attraction of these instruments is limited because, for Dutch private investors, a yield which includes the capital gain to nominal value is used to calculate income tax liability.

Since 1986, the trading of blocks of shares (in excess of Dfl 1m) and bonds (in excess of Dfl 2.5m), without the intermediacy of specialist firms, has been made possible by the initiation of the Amsterdam Interprofessional Market (AIM). This effectively allows banks and stockbrokers to negotiate with clients and conduct transactions on a net basis (without the charging of commission, which is integrated in the negotiated price). AIM block trading transactions have steadily increased since 1986.

Issuance and trade in the government bond market

Recently, the Dutch government introduced an over-the-counter tap issue system. Under this system, the Agent of the Ministry of Finance can issue bonds which have already been introduced to the market by an issue under one of the two tender systems (Dutch or American), but where the subscription date has passed. The Agent fixes the price every day. This over-the-counter issue is limited to subscriptions over Dfl 2.5m. Thus far, the nominal value outstanding of these loans is relatively large and therefore fairly liquid.

It is estimated that over 50 per cent of secondary market trading of Dutch state loans takes place over-the-counter in London. To reclaim a larger share of trading volume, the Amsterdam Stock Exchange has taken steps to make its domestic secondary market more attractive. In an attempt to make the market more transparent, domestic market-makers have, since 16 July 1990, been inserting the bid/ask prices for 10 bonds into a public-access information system. At a later stage, it is envisaged that these prices will become transactional prices, although it is not clear how successful this effort will be. In addition, and for the first time, banks will be allowed to make markets in Dutch state loans in competition with *hoekman* firms, or jobbers, who will then have to choose between acting as either an agent or inter-dealer broker. Between 10 and 15 banks and brokers are expected to make markets.

Modernization

The Netherlands has not remained on the sidelines during the worldwide, and rapid, development of a more international and professional securities trading industry. The Amsterdam Stock Exchange has continuously taken measures to improve its position as an international financial centre. The last decade has seen the first wave of financial liberalization (1986) followed, in 1990, by the abolition of stamp duty, the scrapping of minimum commissions, the introduction of the open-order book and the enactment of new settlement rules. This continuing programme of reform and innovation ensures that the Dutch bond market is ready for the nineties.

21.2 *Economics*

Introduction

In ranking by population size and national product, the Netherlands is the sixth largest of the twelve European Community countries. The Dutch economy is essentially an export economy, with a high degree of international activity and its business structure is characterized by a few very large multinational companies and a relatively high number of medium-sized companies. The openness of the Dutch economy is reflected by the fact that exports of goods and services account for approximately 55 per cent of gross national product (GNP), which is substantially higher than in either Germany or the United Kingdom (both being around 30 per cent). This openness of the Dutch economy, and its dependence on international trade, help explain the Netherlands' involvement in the foundation of the European Community in 1958 and its commitment to the creation of a single European market.

The Netherlands' geographical location on the North Sea has enabled the country to become a major trading nation - it is often called 'the Gateway to Europe'. A considerable share of Dutch international trade consists of goods in transit to and from its EC partners. In particular, Rotterdam, the world's largest port, and Amsterdam International Airport at Schiphol, the fourth biggest cargo transport airport in western Europe, are important distribution centres for the EC.

Political relations in the Netherlands are not marked by any great conflict so that, in general, changes of government take place relatively smoothly. None of the political parties has ever had an overall majority in parliament, with the result that Dutch governments are always coalitions. Social attitudes in the Netherlands are characterized by a remarkable degree of harmony and willingness to co-operate. This is reflected, for example, in the low number of labour disputes and restrained nominal wage rises during the past decade.

Due to its political stability, economic performance and highly-developed financial markets, the Netherlands ranked third in the world (and first among the EC countries) in *Euromoney's* 1991 assessment of country creditworthiness.

Economic performance

In 1989 and 1990, the Dutch economy reached its highest level of growth since 1976, with GNP rising by 4.9 per cent and 3.8 per cent, respectively (see Figure 21.2). Although this strong economic growth slowed down in 1991 and is expected to be lower still in 1992, the Dutch economy remains healthy. The relatively strong economic position at the beginning of the 1990s is in stark contrast to the perilous position in which the Netherlands started the last decade. At the beginning of the 1980s, economic growth was stagnating, unemployment was climbing at an alarming rate, government finances were completely unbalanced and a large number of companies were facing financial problems. To counter this, a much-needed, and drastic, economic restructuring programme was initiated, which has since begun to bear fruit.

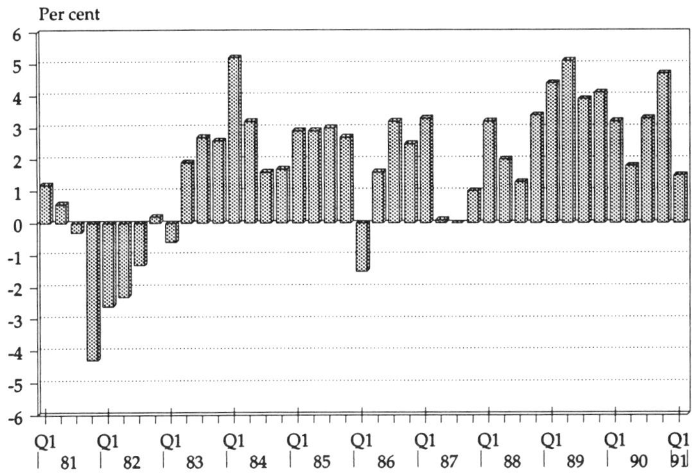

Figure 21.2 Dutch gross national product (year-on-year growth)

The Netherlands has a sizeable surplus on both its trade balance and current account (see Figures 21.3 & 21.4). In 1990, the latter amounted to almost 4 per cent of GNP. The surplus on the trade balance reflects the Netherlands' competitive strength in international trade, a position which has been brought about, in part, by the modest wage rises of the past decade. The important manufacturing sector accounts for the majority of exports. The Netherlands' involvement with the international trade of machinery, transport equipment, petrochemicals and food (Dutch agriculture is highly capital-intensive and technologically-advanced), ensures its worldwide importance.

By far the largest proportion of international trade is with the Netherlands' EC partners, particularly Germany, who absorb about three-quarters of Dutch exports. The sharp increase in demand for imports resulting from reunification,

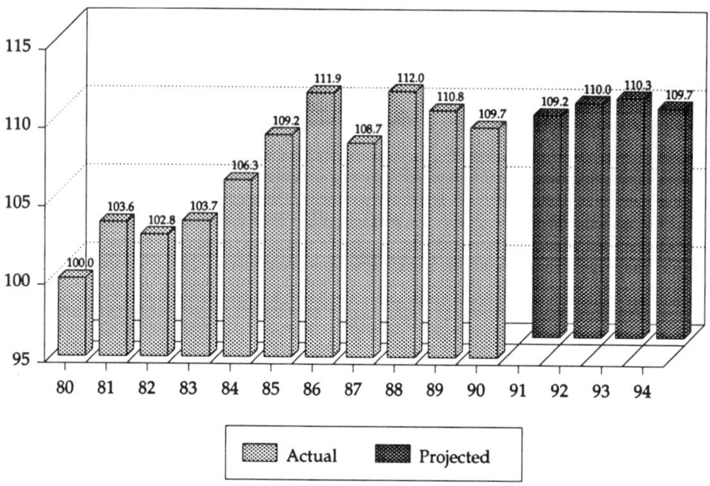

Figure 21.3 **Share of export markets, excluding energy, geographically weighted (1980 = 100)**

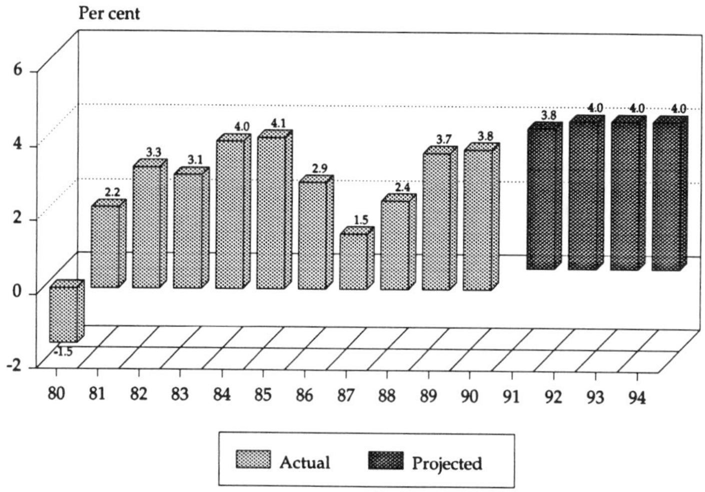

Figure 21.4 **Current account surplus (percentage GNP)**

boosted Dutch exports to Germany - in the period July 1990 - June 1991, they increased by 18 per cent year-on-year - in contrast to exports to other countries which stabilized over the same period. This trend has continued; the first half of 1991 saw Germany's share of Dutch exports rise by three percentage points to more than 30 per cent, although the expected slow-down in German economic growth may reduce this figure in the years to come.

Unemployment

As noted above, the beginning of the 1980s was marked by an alarming increase in the unemployment rate. However, mainly as a result of rapid economic growth and moderation in wage demands (and also a relative increase in the number of part-time jobs), the second half of the eighties saw a sharp rise in the number of people employed (see Figure 21.5) - particularly in the services sector. In the period 1985-1990 the number of people employed rose by an average 1.9 per cent per annum in the Netherlands, compared with an EC average of 1.2 per cent.

The fall in unemployment, though, was less spectacular than one might expect on the basis of these employment figures. The reason was a sharp rise in the numbers seeking work in the 1980s, particularly amongst women who had traditionally represented a low proportion of the labour market in the Netherlands.

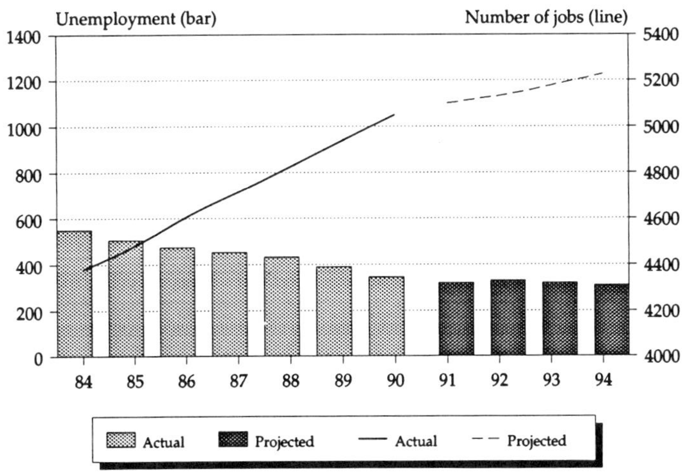

Figure 21.5 **Unemployment and number of jobs ('000 persons)**

Nevertheless, although the fall in the unemployment rate has been offset in this way, the larger working population offers a broader base for economic growth in the long-term.

Monetary policy, inflation and exchange rate history

In the early 1980's, the Dutch central bank (De Nederlandsche Bank, DNB) adopted the maintenance of a very close link between the guilder and the Deutschemark as its primary objective. Germany is the Netherlands' major trading partner and has an excellent reputation for combating inflation. The stable guilder-Deutschemark exchange rate is securely rooted in the wide-ranging convergence of the Dutch and (West) German economies.

Inflation in the two countries has been almost the same in the past decade, and among the lowest recorded in the OECD countries. Around mid-1991 however, Dutch inflation climbed to over 4 per cent (as it did also in Germany), mainly as a result of government fiscal policy. For the whole of 1991 an average inflation rate of slightly less than 4 per cent was reported, a figure which was a little higher than the German rate. Inflation rates in the member states of the European Community are expected to converge further in the years to come and the Dutch rate is not expected to exceed the European average.

Before German reunification, both countries consistently had large surpluses on the current accounts of their balances of payments. Since East Germany will continue to absorb much of West German production in the years to come, German surpluses will be (temporarily) relatively low by historical standards, whereas the Dutch current account is expected to maintain, at the least, its current surplus of about 4 per cent of GNP.

Tying the guilder to the Deutschemark has had a strong disciplinary effect on Dutch monetary policy. The guilder has become one of the firmest currencies in the European monetary system (EMS) and this strength can be attributed, in part, to the exchange rate policy pursued by DNB. Despite large fluctuations in the exchange rates of major currencies such as the US dollar and sterling, DNB has been able to keep the Deutschemark/guilder exchange rate within narrow margins (see Figure 21.7). In 1991, the guilder was in a position to shadow the Deutschemark for the eighth consecutive year, so it seems justified to speak of a 'Deutschemark/guilder bloc'. The differential between German/Dutch short-term interest rates is adjusted to maintain a stable exchange rate.

The fact that, in recent years, long-term interest rates in the Netherlands have only been fractionally higher than those in Germany (see Figure 21.6), indicates that investors consider the Dutch guilder to be virtually as sound as the Deutschemark.

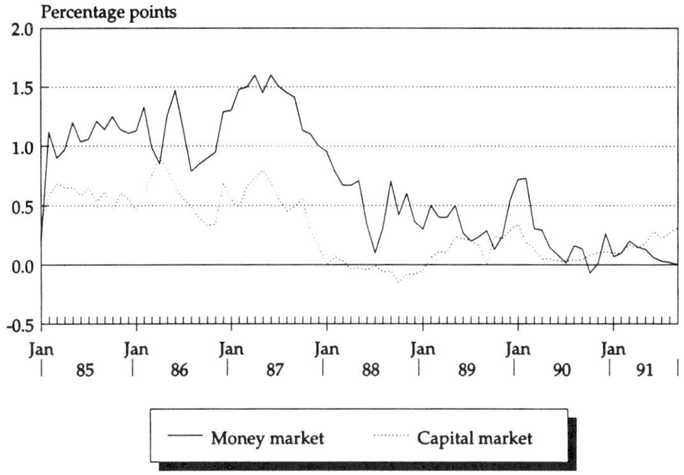

Figure 21.6 Dutch minus German interest rates

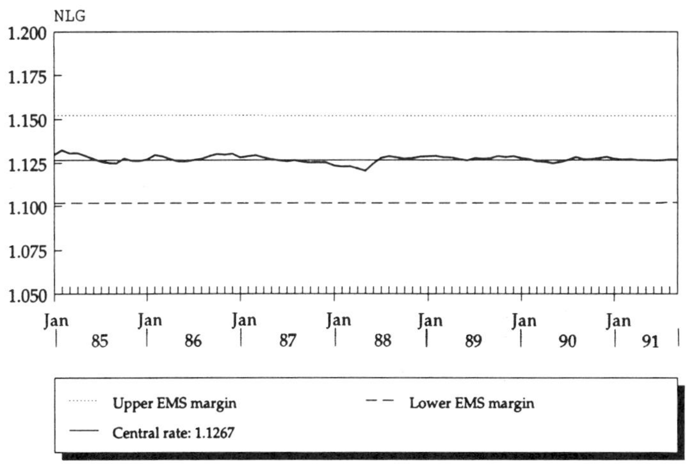

Figure 21.7 DEM/NLG exchange rate

Public sector

During the 1970s, public expenditure climbed steeply because of the expansion of income transfers, particularly in social security. Total public sector outlay reached a peak of 64 per cent of GNP in 1983, compared with 43 per cent in 1970. In spite of the rising tax burden and huge revenues from natural gas, the public sector budget deficit rose markedly until 1983. In 1983 the central government deficit amounted to 9 per cent of GNP, or nearly 22 per cent of public spending.

Since 1983, public finances have been dominated by the government's aim to reduce this deficit. Public expenditure was cut *inter alia* by reducing civil servants' wages and social benefits in 1984, and by freezing social security benefits in the period 1985-1989. As a result of this tight budgetary policy, public sector spending was reduced to 57 per cent of GNP in 1990.

A major setback in reducing the deficit was the decline in natural gas revenues of Dfl 14bn from 1985 to 1988, a figure representing more than 3.5 per cent of GNP. This decline was mainly caused by falling energy prices, although the depreciation of the US dollar was also significant since energy prices are set in dollars. Despite this setback, the government budget deficit was reduced further, to 4.8 per cent of GNP, in 1990.

The Dutch government has never had any problems in financing its debt, thanks to the high savings of Dutch households. Private sector savings have exceeded government expenditure for many years now and the Dutch economy, as a whole, is a net lender to foreign countries.

Thanks to its policy of curbing expenditure, the government did not need to increase the collective burden[1] in order to put public finances on a sounder footing. In fact, the tax burden was reduced from 49 per cent of GNP in 1983 to about 46.5 per cent in 1989, but gradually increased again, to almost 48 per cent of GNP in 1991. In recent years, several taxes have been revised.

In 1988, corporation tax was reduced to 35 per cent for profits higher than Dfl 250,000 and from January 1989, the standard rate of VAT was cut from 20 per cent to 18.5 per cent. The most significant change in taxation, though, was the introduction of a new income tax system in 1990. The *Oort* reform, as it is known, reduced the number of tax brackets from nine to three and lowered the top rate from 72 per cent to 60 per cent. This major streamlining of the tax structure was combined with a substantial tax relief, equivalent to around 1 per cent of GNP, which contributed significantly to economic growth.

[1] *The collective burden is defined as the ratio of tax and social security receipts plus non-tax revenues with the character of collected taxes (mainly associated with domestic gas sales), to national income.*

One of the most irksome problems with which the Dutch economy has had to cope is the very low number, by international standards, of individuals actually participating in the country's work-force. The chief cause of this is a high level of disability; for more than a decade, the percentage of personnel suffering from disabilities in the Netherlands has been twice as high as that in surrounding countries and between 1970 and 1980, sickness, disability, and public health payments almost doubled as a percentage of GNP. Although this percentage fell somewhat in the eighties, the Netherlands is still in a unique position. The Dutch government has taken some important decisions with regard to this problem and, in the summer of 1991, introduced an extensive package of measures:

- Duration of the disability payments will be shorter, and the level lower, depending on age and past employment history.
- The concept of 'appropriate labour' will be broadened.
- Employers will be fined if an employee becomes unfit for work, and receive a bonus if they employ an individual formerly in the 'unfit for work' category.

It is hoped that the new measures will reverse the trend with regard to disability.

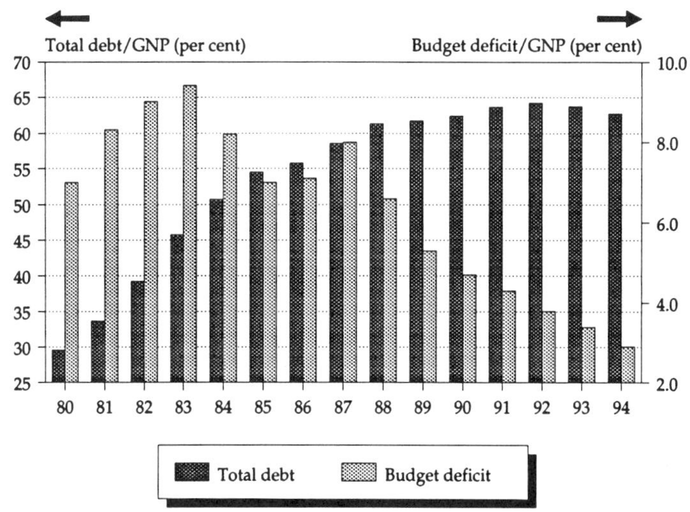

Figure 21.8 Total debt and budget deficit (as percentage of GNP)

The government's budget deficit will be reduced in steps of approximately 0.5 percentage point to 3 per cent of GNP in 1994 (see Figure 21.8), with the collective burden not exceeding the (still excessive) upper limit of 48 per cent of GNP. The debt/GNP - ratio is expected to peak in 1992, at a level of about 65 per cent, and will then start to decline.

21.3 Market composition

Composition by sector

Government market

Since 1986, the number of government bullet loans has soared and, in 1991, they accounted for more than 50 per cent of the market (see Figures 21.9 & 21.10). During 1989 and 1990, the Dutch government almost exclusively issued 10-year bullet loans. In 1991, the Dutch government issued four bullet loans with maturities of 10 (3) and 15 (1) years. The number of outstanding sinking funds has plummeted in recent years, the last one issued dating back to the beginning of 1989. Given the relatively large difference between the interest rates at the time of issue and those in 1985, 1986 and 1987, it became attractive for the Dutch government to redeem the callable bonds early. Since 1989, however, interest

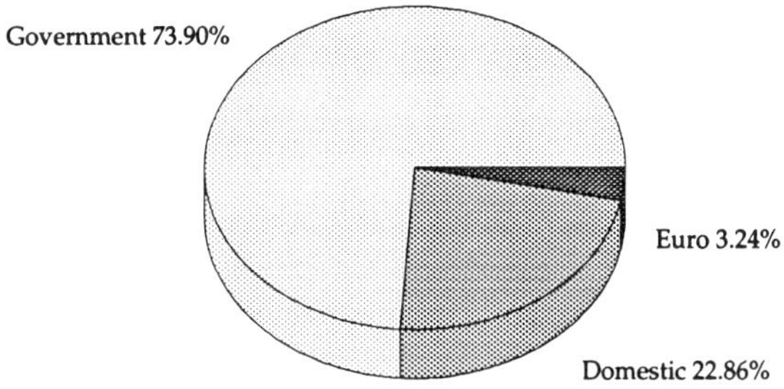

Figure 21.9 Composition of the Dutch market by sector (end-December 1991)

		End-December 1991	% Total
GOVERNMENT			
	Bullet	164.40	53.81
	Sinking funds	56.54	18.50
	Callable	4.86	1.59
	Total	225.85	73.90
EURO			
	Floating-rate notes	0.35	0.11
	Euroguilder	9.55	3.13
	Total	9.90	3.24
DOMESTIC			
Corporate			
	Bullet	4.40	1.44
	Sinking funds	2.16	0.71
	Total	6.56	2.15
Local authority			
	Bullet	3.05	1.00
	Sinking funds	0.40	0.13
	Callable	2.50	0.82
	Total	5.95	1.95
Financial institutions			
	Bullet	10.54	3.45
	Sinking funds	2.50	0.82
	Callable	3.26	1.07
	Total	16.30	5.34
Capital bonds			
	Bullet	1.37	0.45

(cont.)

Sinking funds	4.42	1.45
Callable	0.26	0.09
Total	6.05	1.99
Mortgage bonds		
Bullet	2.50	0.82
Sinking funds	2.41	0.79
Callable	0.02	0.01
Total	4.93	1.62
Bank certificates		
	12.12	3.97
Foreign bonds		
Bullet	7.77	2.54
Sinking funds	7.48	2.57
Callables	0.96	0.31
Total	16.57	5.42
Convertibles		
Bullet	0.12	0.04
Sinking funds	0.25	0.08
Callable	0.99	0.32
Total	1.38	0.44
Total domestic	69.86	22.86
GRAND TOTAL	305.56	100.00

Figure 21.10 Composition of the Dutch market (NLG billion nominal)

rates have been higher, making early redemption less frequent. In recent years no new early-redemption bonds have been issued on the public market.

Since the end of 1990 indexed bonds have been allowed (although none have been issued as yet).

Euroguilder market

The main difference between domestic guilder and euroguilder issues is that domestic issues require domestic documentation while euroguilders require euro-documentation. The principal advantage of euroguilder issues is the speed at which they can be launched, a facet which is essential to swap-related issues. A domestic issue requires the publication of a prospectus before the subscription date; in contrast, the prospectus of a euroguilder issue may be published after subscription. After a few relatively quiet years, the first half of 1991 saw the issue of Dfl 7.8bn worth of euroguilder bonds.

Originally, the main attraction of euroguilder bonds lay in the fact that they were bullet bonds. Since the 1986 liberalization of the Dutch capital market which lifted the ban on domestic bullet bonds, this advantage no longer exists. Another result of liberalization is that there is no longer a maximum amount per issue. Now, the main attraction of euroguilder bonds is the speed at which new issues can be launched, along with their relatively low issue costs. Nevertheless, despite these attractions, interest in euroguilder bonds has waned in recent years.

Since January 1986, the issue of floating-rate notes (FRNs) has been permitted in the Netherlands. One FRN was issued in 1986 and a reversed-floater was launched in 1990. Due to the development of the interest swap market, though, the market for floaters has never really got off the ground.

Domestic corporate market

■ Corporate bonds

Corporate bonds make up only a very limited part of the Dutch bond market and the number of new loans has fallen sharply over the past few years. The issued loans are mainly bullets. The share of sinkers in this sub-market continues to shrink every year.

■ Local authority market

In both 1990 and 1991, the BNG (Bank for Dutch Municipalities) issued a zero with a nominal value of Dfl 1.0bn. These bullet loans are the only noteworthy issues in the past two years. Only a handful of sinkers has been issued in recent years. The last callable issue dates from 1987.

BNG is the largest issuer of medium-term notes, accounting for 74 per cent of the total value of Dfl 21.1bn (as at the end of 1991). Some 80 per cent of these MTNs have been placed.

■ Financial institutions

After fairly buoyant years - in terms of issues - in 1988 and 1989, this market also suffered a contraction in 1990 and 1991. The majority of loans issued have been bullets. In 1990, only a single sinker was issued. No callables have been issued in this market in the past few years.

Capital bonds

1991 saw an extremely large issue of over Dfl 1bn, the biggest ever in this sector of the market. The number of callables has been declining for years - the last callable issued dates from 1980. In recent times only a few sinkers per year have been issued.

■ Supranationals

Supranational institutions regularly issue bond loans on the Dutch capital market and foreign governments are no strangers to the market either.

In the past two years, though, only a few issues have been made. The last sinker issue dates from 1988. The number of callables in this market has been falling sharply over the past few years.

■ Convertibles

This is the only sub-market where bullet bonds have so far failed to oust sinkers and callables. The majority of convertibles are callables. Following a fairly quiet 1990, the number of issues started to rise again in 1991.

Composition of market by maturity

Government market

Until the beginning of the 1970s, the maximum maturity of a government bond - usually a sinking fund - was 25 years. In the 1980s, there was a trend towards increasingly shorter terms but, since 1989, the Dutch government has almost exclusively issued 10-year bullet loans, causing the average duration of issued bonds to rise again. As a result of such issuance, a shortage has arisen in the 5- to 7-year sector (see Figure 21.11).

In 1991, the Agent of Finance surprised the market by issuing 15-year bullet loans. This is an indication that the government is generally looking to extend the maturity of its loans. In the next three years almost 75 per cent of the currently outstanding sinking funds will be redeemed.

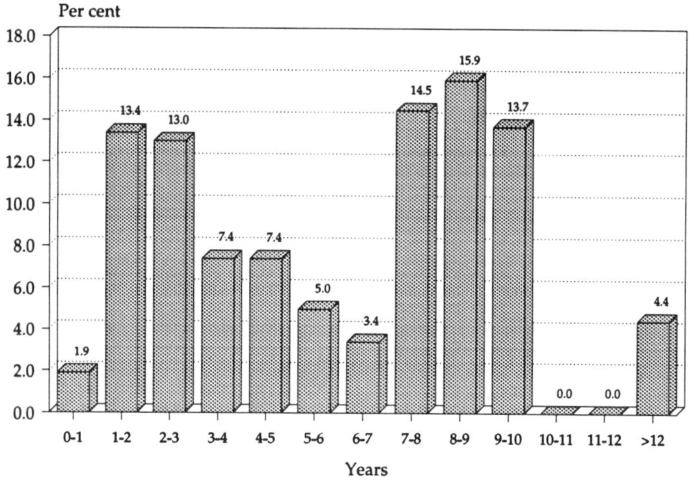

Figure 21.11 Maturity structure of the government bond market

The number of outstanding callables is steadily diminishing although, in the 4- to 5-year sector, there are still some callables with currently attractive coupons. The low coupons and short remaining lives of the other callables make early redemption unlikely.

Euroguilder market

Both short- (0- to 2-yr.) and long-term (7- to 10-yr.) euroguilder loans are issued in this market (see Figure 21.12). Medium-term loans are hard to come by, at present, because relatively few loans were issued in 1987 and 1988 and those that were issued had short terms.

Only two floating-rate notes are available in the euroguilder market: one issued by Security Pacific Corp. in 1986, with a maturity of ten years, and the other issued by AEGON in 1990. The latter is a reversed-floater with a maturity of 7 years.

Domestic corporate market

The striking features of this market are the relative lack of bonds with an average life of less than 2 years and, by contrast, the existence of 8- to 9-year and 10-

to 11-year maturities (see Figure 21.13). Two loans were issued in the 7- to 9-year sector, one by SHV and one by the PTT. The 10- to 11-year category is fully taken up by a callable issued in 1959 by Hendrick de Keyser, with a maximum life until 2022.

Local authority market

By far the largest issuer in this sector is the municipal bank, BNG. The other issuing institutions, such as local authorities, are increasingly retreating from this largely long-term bond market. The issue of two large zero issues by BNG has somewhat distorted the maturity spread (see Figure 21.14).

Financial institutions

The declining number of issues in this market has led to a sharp fall in the average maturity, a fall which has been accentuated by the fact that many of the bonds issued have been medium-term (see Figure 21.15).

Capital bonds

The duration spread in this market is good, mainly thanks to the sinking funds available - only bonds with lives of up to 2 years are scarce (see Figure 21.16). Bullets are rare, with one bond of the ING representing approximately 85 per cent of all bullet loans in this sector.

Mortgage bonds

Many old loans are still listed in this market. These loans are due to mature soon and the new loans being introduced have relatively short lives, with the result that there are virtually no long-term bonds left (see Figure 21.17).

Bank certificates

In the past few years a substantial number of loans have been issued in this market, mainly with lives between 1 and 5 years (see Figure 21.18). There is also a fair amount of loans with longer terms, but their nominal value is modest.

Foreign bonds

There is a fairly good maturity spread in this market (see Figure 21.19). Among those bonds with lives longer than 12 years are two loans of the World Bank, from 1986, which are due to mature in 2006. In the past few years it has been fairly quiet in this sector.

Convertibles

The lives of the issued loans tend to be relatively short (see Figure 21.20). Rolinco has the convertible with the longest maturity, dating from 1967 and maturing in 2007.

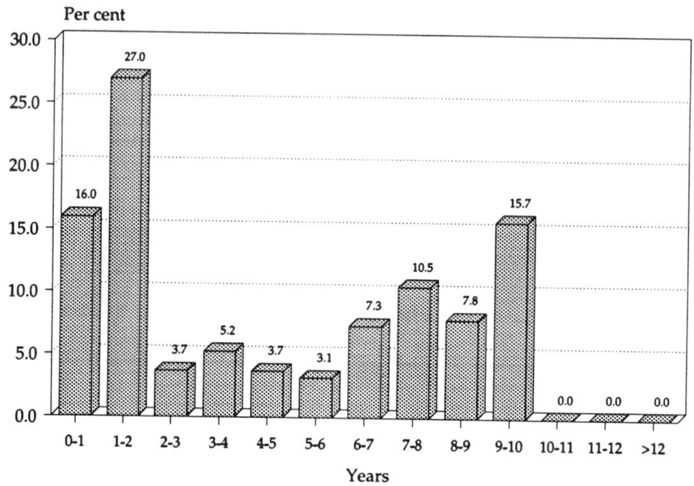

Figure 21.12 Maturity structure of the euroguilder bond market

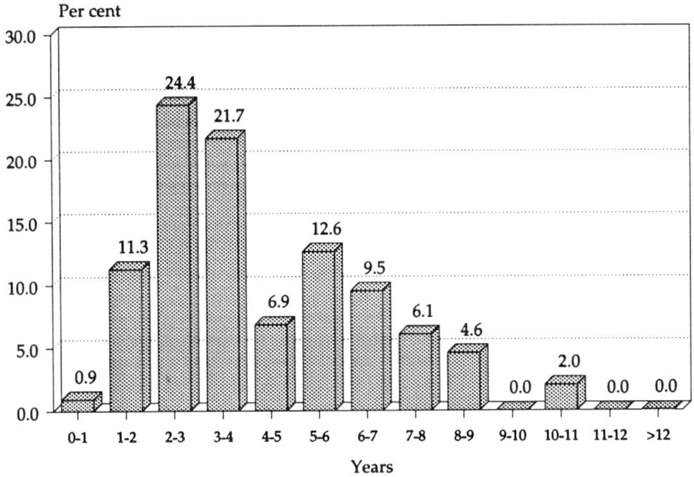

Figure 21.13 Maturity structure of the domestic corporate bond market

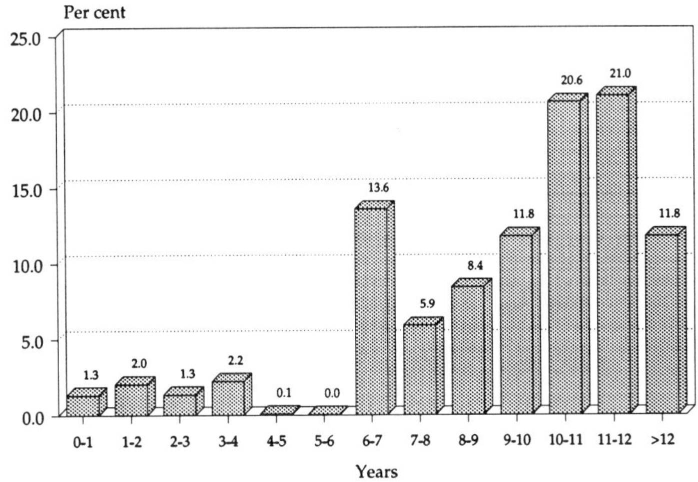

Figure 21.14 Maturity structure of the local authority bond market

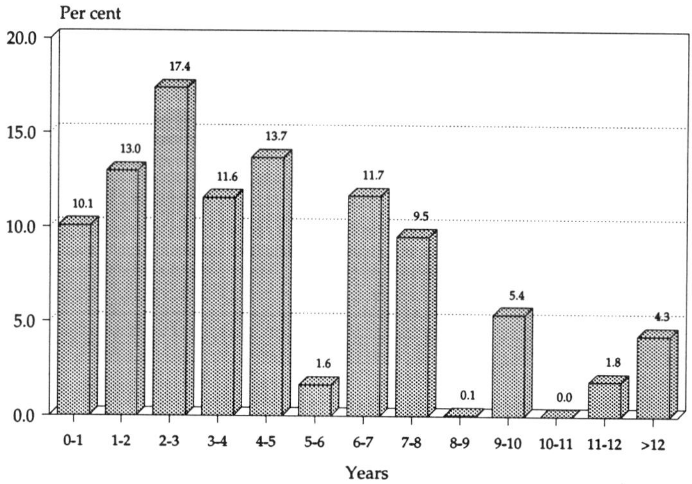

Figure 21.15 Maturity structure of the financial institution bond market

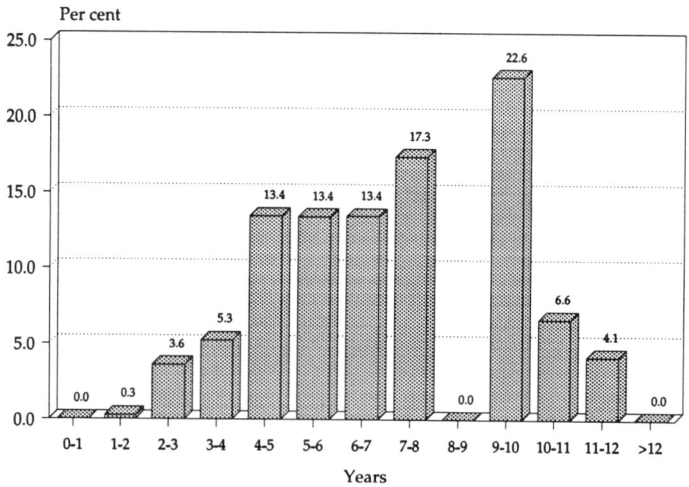

Figure 21.16 Maturity structure of the capital bond market

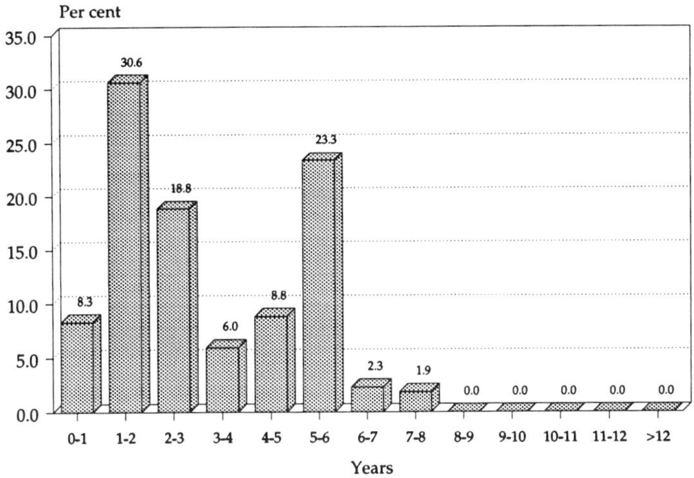

Figure 21.17 Maturity structure of the mortgage bond market

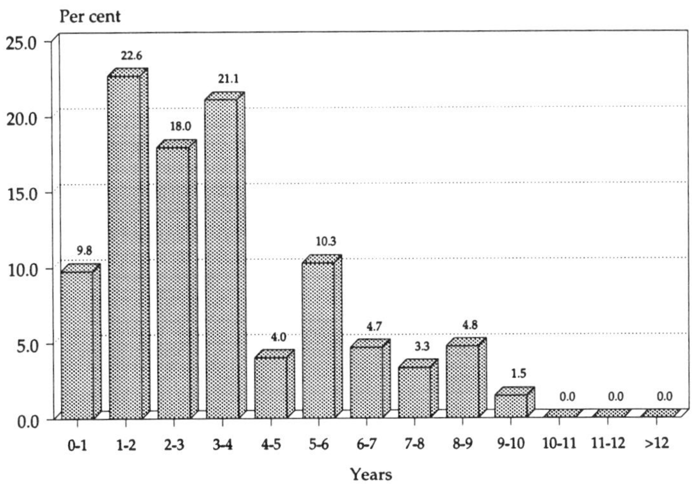

Figure 21.18 Maturity structure of the bank certificate bond market

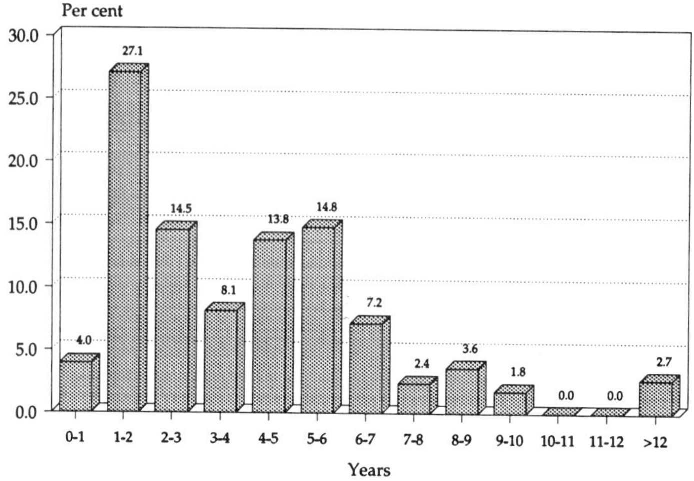

Figure 21.19 Maturity structure of the foreign bond market

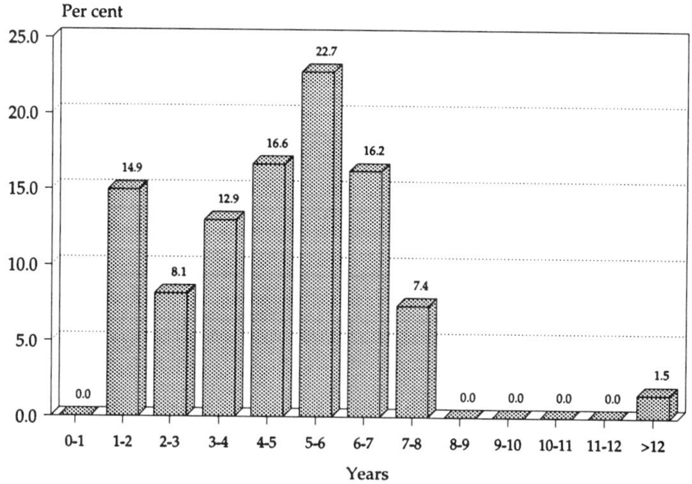

Figure 21.20 Maturity structure of the convertible bond market

Composition of market by coupon

Government market

The low rate of inflation from 1986 up to, and including, 1988, meant that virtually all loans issued in this period had a low coupon. Over the past few years inflation has started to rise again and this has led to higher interest rates and, consequently, a rise in coupons (see Figure 21.21). There are still a few loans, issued more than 25 years ago, with coupons below 5 per cent. The loans with coupons of more than 10 per cent generally date from the early 80s.

Euroguilder market

There are only a few loans with a very low coupon (smaller than 2 per cent) in this market (see Figure 21.22), these having been mainly issued between 1987 and 1989. Since 1989, virtually no low-coupon bonds have been issued largely due to Dutch taxation rules which make these bonds unattractive for many investors.

Domestic corporate market

Because most of the outstanding loans were issued in the period from 1986 up to, and including, 1988, the coupons are relatively low (see Figure 21.23). In the past few years, new issues have been limited, causing only a slight increase in the higher coupon sector. The loans with coupons of twelve per cent and upwards (two subordinated bonds from SHV) date from 1981.

Local authority market

The coupon spread in this market has left a wide gap between 1 per cent and 7 per cent (see Figure 21.24). The low-coupon sector marks the issue of two zeros by BNG, while the high coupons still date from loans issued in the early 80s.

Financial institutions

Most coupons in this market range from 6 to 8 per cent (see Figure 21.25), with levels largely being determined by the period in which the loans were issued. There are still two zeros listed, these being issued by Bank Mees & Hope in 1988 and 1989.

Capital bonds

This market is characterized by relatively high coupons (see Figure 21.26), mainly the result of the relatively large number of loans issued in the early

1980s. The high coupons will disappear in the coming period as the loans have residual lives of only 1 to 2 years.

Mortgage bonds

The mortgage bonds with coupons ranging from 3 to 4 per cent (see Figure 21.27) all date from before 1955 -there are even a few loans dating from before 1940. The market consists of a relatively large number of loans with small outstanding amounts.

Bank certificates

Most of the loans are in the 6 to 7 per cent coupon region (see Figure 21.28). In the past two years the majority of loans issued have coupons ranging between 8 and 10 per cent, resulting in a better spread in the market.

Foreign bonds

The 6 to 7 per cent coupon region also dominates this market (see Figure 21.29). The high coupons generally belong to bonds issued in the early 1980s.

Convertibles

Convertibles generally have lower coupons than the other kinds of bonds (see Figure 21.30). One exception, though, is the 11 per cent convertible which was issued by Bredero in 1981 - the level being attributable to the interest rates prevailing at the time (12.75 per cent for the Dutch government). No other convertibles dating from this high-interest period are currently listed.

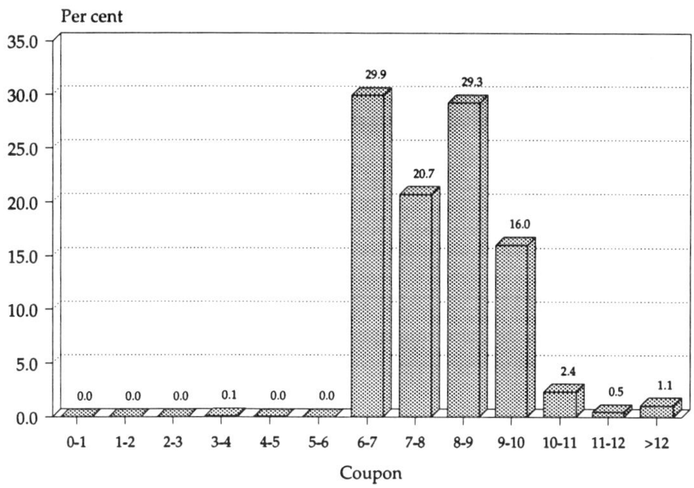

Figure 21.21 Coupon structure of the government bond market

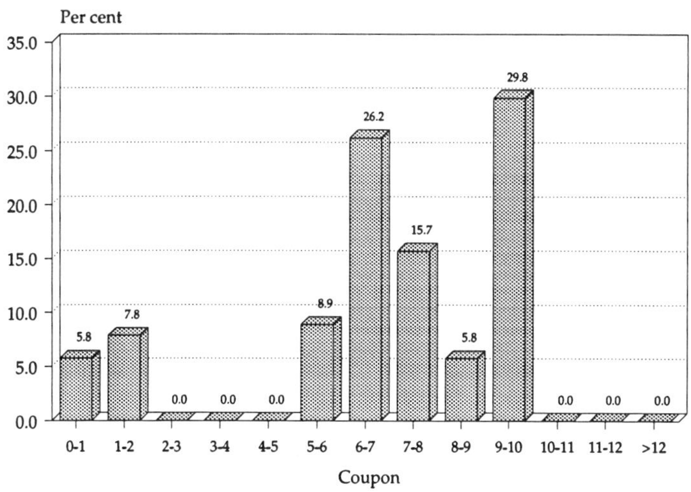

Figure 21.22 Coupon structure of the euroguilder bond market

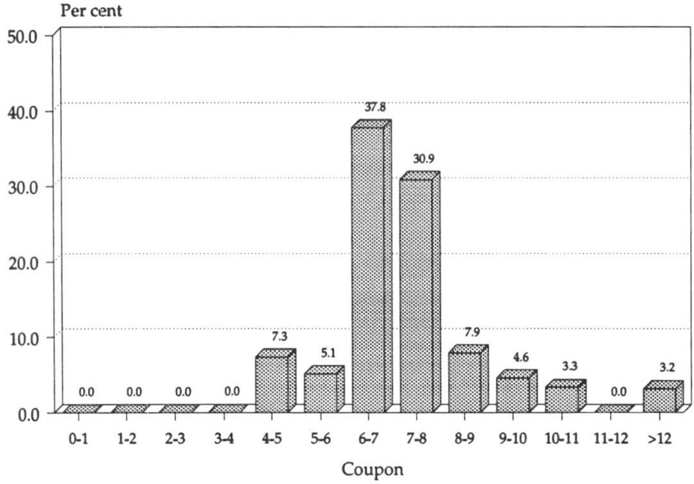

Figure 21.23 Coupon structure of the domestic corporate bond market

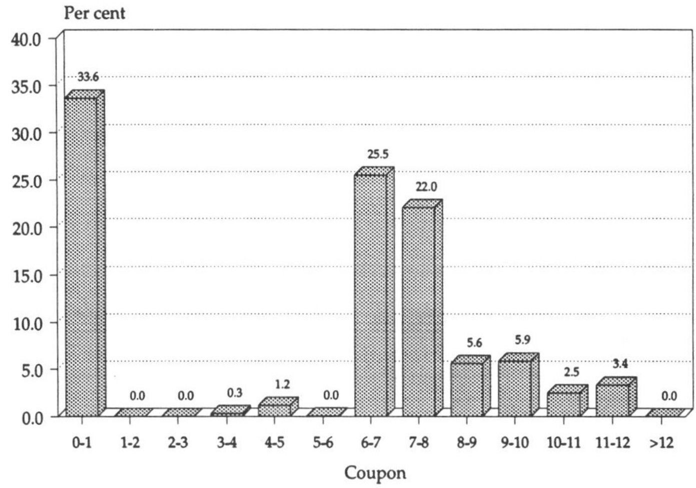

Figure 21.24 Coupon structure of the local authority bond market

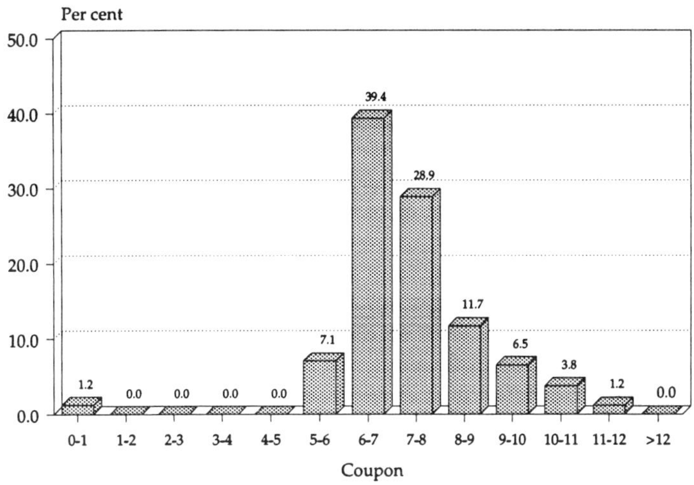

Figure 21.25 Coupon structure of the financial institution bond market

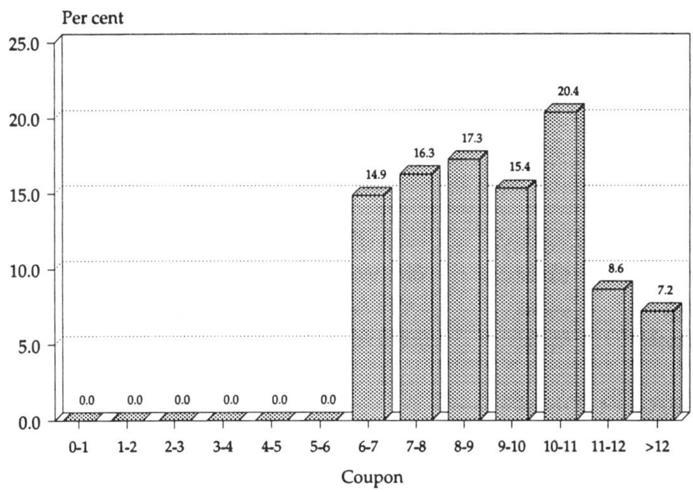

Figure 21.26 Coupon structure of the capital bond market

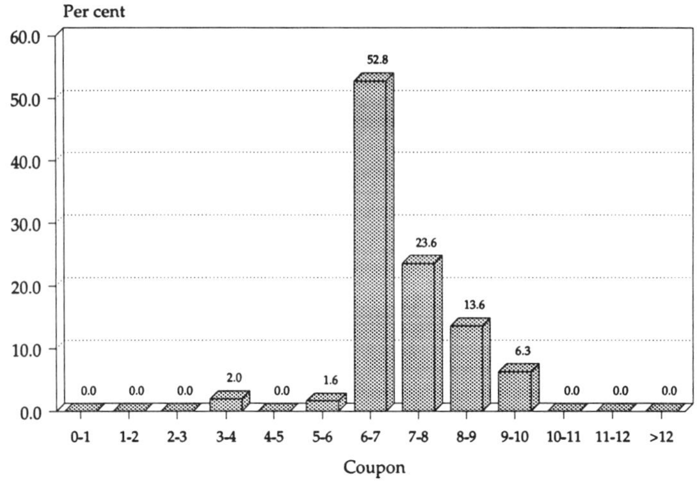

Figure 21.27 Coupon structure of the mortgage bond market

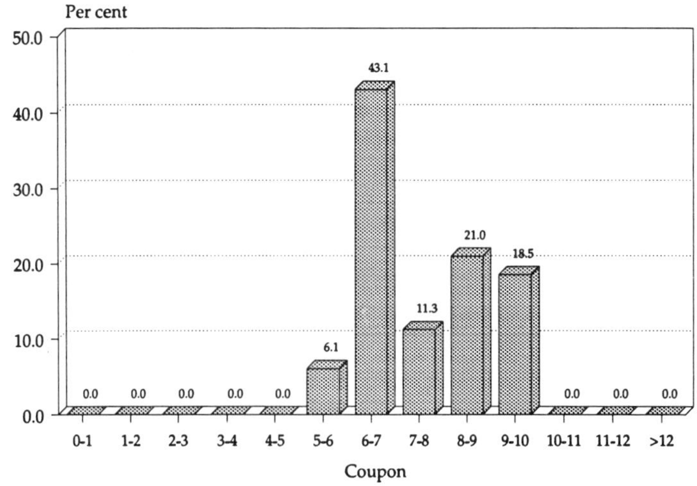

Figure 21.28 Coupon structure of the bank certificate bond market

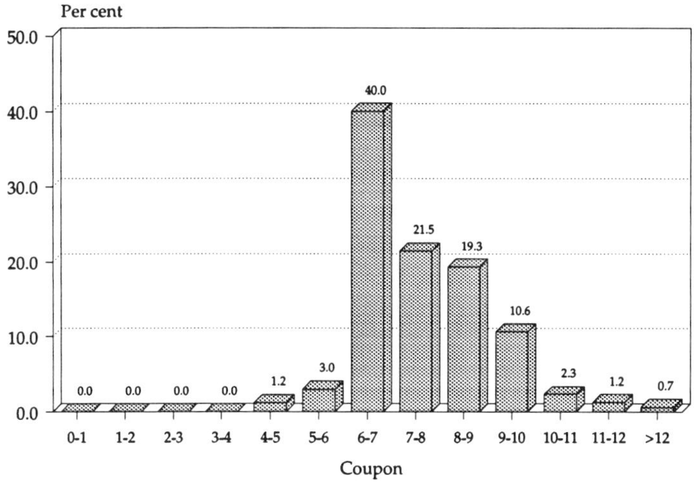

Figure 21.29 Coupon structure of the foreign bond market

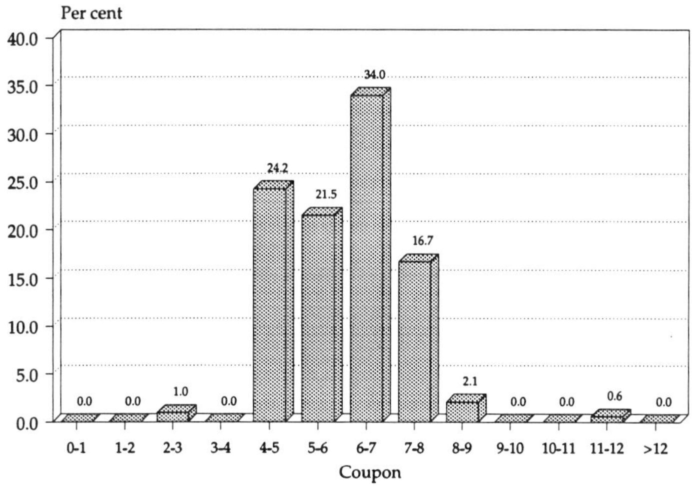

Figure 21.30 Coupon structure of the convertible bond market

21.4 Types of Security

Fixed or bullet

Bullet bonds were permitted after 1 January 1986. The table below shows that it now far more common for market participants to satisfy their financing needs by issuing bullet bonds (which redeem in a lump sum at maturity), rather than the so-called sinking funds (which redeem in several annual instalments).

	No. of bullet bonds issued	No. of non-bullet bonds issued
Central government	44	6
Other domestic institutions	74	18

Figure 21.31 Dutch bonds issued by domestic market participants since 1986
Source: Quarterly Bulletins/Dutch Central Bank
Note: These are ordinary bonds with fixed-coupons only

The popularity of bullet bonds among foreign investors has contributed to their increased issuance in the Netherlands. For reasons of maturity, and the preference of international investors, yields on bullet bonds tend to be somewhat lower than on comparable non-bullet bonds (see Figures 21.32 & 21.33).

Repayment by drawing

The issuer redeems parts of the issue on dates set out in advance in the terms of the issue. Until 1986, this was by far the most customary procedure in the Netherlands.

Serial repayment

It is possible to register certain bonds (Staat der Nederlanden, Bank voor Nederlandse Gemeenten, Nationale Investeringsbank, Nederlandse Ontwikkelingsbank and Nederlandse Waterschapsbank). Through this system the holder of the bond receives a proportional repayment.

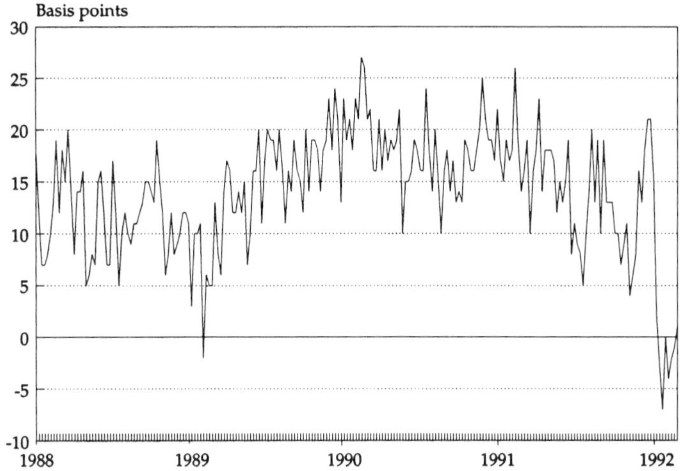

Figure 21.32 Yield on Dutch bullets and serial bonds (7% 1985/92-96 -/- 7% 1987-93)

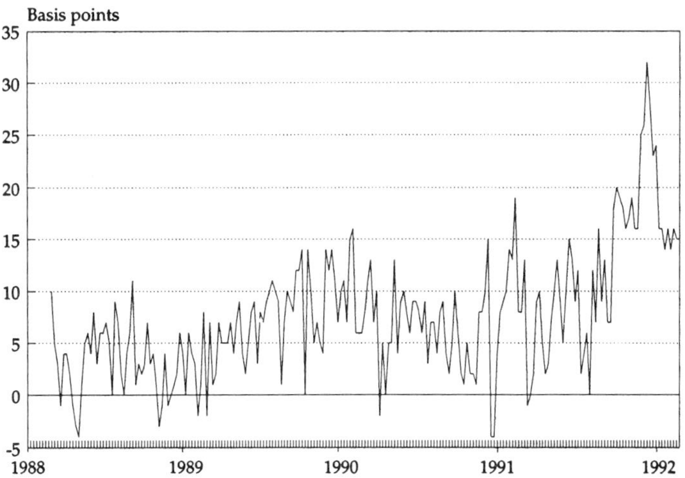

Figure 21.33 Yield on Dutch bullets and serial bonds (6.25% 1988/94-98 -/- 6.50% 1986-96)

Extendible

The holder of an extendible bond has the option, during a certain period of time, to convert the original bonds into bonds with a longer life, at the same rate.

At present, all extendibles that have been issued in the early eighties have largely been converted. Some of the issues have already been fully redeemed.

Callable

Long-term bonds (i.e. longer than ten years) often permit the borrower redemption before maturity against a given (descending) penalty expressed in a redemption price above par.

Fixed-coupon

The most common type of issue is with a coupon fixed throughout the life of the bond. However, a notable exception occurred in 1987, when the multinational, Hoogovens, issued a 12-year bond with a coupon rate that was allowed to vary between 6.75% and 10%.

Zero-coupon

Zero-coupon bonds were permitted after 1 January 1988. There are no coupon payments. Two types are available:

- priced at discount, ultimate value at par
- issued approximately at par, redeemable above par.

To date, two institutions have issued zeros: the Bank of Dutch Municipalities (BNG) and the general commercial bank, Mees and Hope.

Others

On a very limited scale, the Dutch bond market has witnessed a variety of securities such as coupon paid in equity, dual-currency, floating-rate notes, debt warrants, bond warrants, bull and bear, and partly-paid.

Discussions aimed at securing permission for the issuance of index-linked bonds have recently taken place, but the Ministry of Finance has yet to be convinced of their economic merit.

21.5 Issuers

Dutch government

The State of the Netherlands is by far the largest borrower in the Dutch market. At the end of 1991, the total nominal value of bonds listed on the Amsterdam Stock Exchange amounted to Dfl 326bn - of which 71 per cent was issued by the State.

The total bond turnover through the Stock Exchange was Dfl 212bn, of which Dfl 187bn (88 per cent) consisted of government bonds. The concentration of trading activity in government bonds is a result of continuing State deficits as well as its (the State's) growing preference for public issues. In 1991, the 25 most-traded bonds were all government issues, so it is clear that the liquidity of bonds by non-State borrowers is modest by comparison. Over the past few years the State merely issued bullet loans with an original life of 10 years. However, in April 1991, the State issued a bullet loan with an original life of 15 years, which did not carry an option for early repayment. This was seen as a sign that the State is willing, more than before, to accommodate the wishes of both domestic and foreign investors.

Local authorities

This category includes the Bank for Dutch Municipalities (BNG) and the Netherlands Polder Boards Bank (NWB). Both serve as paying institutes by transferring government payments, and granting loans to, the local authorities while attracting the necessary funds in the money and capital markets.
BNG has an aggregate outstanding amount of Dfl 4.2bn. The State owns 50 per cent of its shares, lower public authorities the other 50 per cent. Since January 1989, BNG has enjoyed the status of a money-creating, commercial bank and, for that reason, BNG is included also in the financial institution sector. In recent times, BNG has issued only 2 or 3 times a year on the public bond market, its main activity being in private placements (and in particular, the medium-term note sector).

Financial institutions

In 1990 the legal separation of the insurance and banking sectors was abolished. This allowed several mergers to take place in the Dutch financial community. Examples are the Internationale Nederlanden Groep N.V. (ING), Rabobank's acquisition of insurer Interpolis and its link-up with the Robeco investment fund

	1987	1988	1989	1990	1991
Central government	20,100	31,850	33,600	33,900	41,250
Local government					
Ordinary bonds	-	-	-	-	-
Eurobonds		150	150	-	-
Bank for Dutch Municipalities (BNG)					
Ordinary bonds	200	550	302	363	381
Eurobonds	-	-	202	-	-
Banks, trade, industry & miscellaneous					
Ordinary bonds	4355	4508	2168	780	336
Subordinated bonds	607	486	780	295	1600
Convertible bonds	10	320	315	45	365
Eurobonds	1720	4110	2604	2124	4449
Savings certificates	2905	4947	3672	4480	2770
Mortgage bonds	1477	1285	908	187	378
Public health	-	275	-	-	-
Foreign & supranational borrowers					
Ordinary bonds	1750	890	375	-	-
Eurobonds	133	3171	2173	1430	961
Bonds, parallel market					
(Bonds & miscellaneous)	25	-	-	-	-
TOTAL NEW LISTINGS	33,282	52,543	47,250	43,603	52,490

Figure 21.34 New listings on the Amsterdam Stock Exchange (NLG billion)
Source: Amsterdam Stock Exchange Facts & Figures. DNB, Annual Reports

group, and the acquisition by insurer AMEV N.V. of Verenigde Spaarbank (VSB), a Dutch savings bank. AMEV/VSB later merged with Belgium's leading insurance company, Groupe A.G.

The rapidly increasing international competition arising from the integration of EC financial services markets, led to the creation of ABN AMRO Holding. Financial institutions, and in the majority of cases they are still banks, regularly issue four types of bonds:

- Ordinary bonds
- (Subordinated) capital debentures
- Savings bonds; interest on which is not paid annually but in an aggregate amount on the final redemption date. These savings bonds are issued on tap.
- Bank bonds; issued on tap until a pre-fixed final date. Interest is paid annually, but the issue price can vary from day to day in accordance with the current market conditions. Their lifetime is limited to approximately eight years.

Mortgage banks also issue bonds. In spite of their name, these mortgage bonds are ordinary bonds that differ from those issued by other debtors only in their tap system of issue. All the mortgage banks have now been taken over by insurance companies or conventional banks, with the result that the market in mortgage bonds has declined sharply in recent years.

Since 1983, for statistical purposes, savings banks have been considered to be money-creating financial institutions.

Corporates in trade and industry

Several Dutch corporates, e.g. Ahold, KLM and Philips, have issued bonds with warrants attached. Because these bonds offered a lower coupon yield, they were attractive to private Dutch investors whose income from all types of bonds is subject to income tax. However, as a result of measures taken by the Ministry of Finance, this advantage no longer exists.

Corporates also issue convertibles. At the end of 1991, 33 convertible bonds of Dutch corporates were quoted on the Amsterdam Stock Exchange. Some convertible bonds were issued in the euroguilder market.

Foreign and supranational borrowers

Foreign governments and supranational institutions like the World Bank (IBRAD), the Inter-American Bank and the European Investment Bank (EIB) once regularly issued guilder loans on the Dutch bond market, but their interest in these instruments has fallen considerably over the past few years.

21.6 *Investors*

Banks

Dutch commercial banks hold bonds for four reasons, namely:

- as a liquidity reserve, and in connection with re-discounting and special loan transactions with the central bank. This applies in particular to government bonds and, to a lesser extent, BNG bonds.
- as underwriters to new issues.
- as dealers on the Stock Exchange for trading purposes (commercial banks are members of the Stock Exchange).
- as investment of their outstanding (savings) deposits.

Institutional investors: pension funds and insurance companies

Institutional investors hold bonds as part of their fixed-interest investments. For pension funds, fixed-interest values account for approximately 70 per cent of their portfolios, of which about 20 per cent represents negotiable bonds. For insurance companies, these figures are 55 per cent and 10 per cent respectively.

Insurance companies can reasonably ascertain their future cash inflows and outflows, but this is less so in the case of pension funds because their obligations are expressed in real terms and inflation erodes the nominal value of fixed-interest investments.

The Insurance Chamber, a semi-governmental institution, supervises all pension funds and insurance companies, including their investment policies. However, this supervision is very informal and the written rules are rather vague, which leaves a large degree of freedom.

Many institutional investors have their own restrictions regarding investments laid down in 'Articles of Association' and supervisory boards often apply their own rules. However, these rules sometimes stand in the way of a rational investment policy; indeed, many institutions are not allowed to acquire bonds (or fixed-interest assets) above par, or to make changes in their portfolios if a book loss results.

Investment funds

There are a few bond investment funds that operate (partly) on the Dutch bond market. Their investment in bonds amounts to about Dfl 13bn.

	Banks		Pension funds		Insurance companies	
	1989	1990	1989	1990	1989	1990
Bonds						
Domestic	50.6	52.7	53.4	60.2	10.6	14.8
Foreign	21.8	24.2	12.5	12.0	3.1	3.8
Private loans	224.7	232.9	198.5	197.4	65.9	68.1
Total assets	901.1	969.9	374.0	387.5	146.2	154.6

Figure 21.35 Assets of Dutch banks, pension funds and insurance companies (NLG bn)
Source: DBN, 1990 Annual Report

	Banks & institutional investors	Dutch private investors	Foreign investors
1988	52	12	36
1989	50	12	38
1990	36	18	46

Figure 21.36 Subscribers for Dutch public government bond issues (per cent)

Private resident individuals

Private resident individuals are subject to a progressive tax rate on interest income (including accrued-interest in the case of the sale of bonds), whereas both redemption profits and realized capital gains are tax-free. This often causes a preference for low-coupon bonds.

Foreign investors

Foreign ownership of Dutch government bonds is subject to fluctuation. Allocations to foreign investors of Dutch government issues amounted to 46 per cent in 1990. The percentage of all outstanding Dutch government bonds in foreign hands is estimated at 25 per cent.

21.7 *Methods of issuance*

Government bonds

Dutch auction

Government bonds are normally issued by tender, the principle of which is both simple and common to other primary markets.

The coupon and redemption schedule of an issue are both announced, on the Friday before tender, by the Agent of the Ministry of Finance (on behalf of the government) and investors submit bids, on the following Tuesday at 15.00, for a certain number of bonds at a specified price(s). These bids are made through authorized banks and brokers.

All bids at prices higher than the issue price are met in full; bids at the issue price receive a proportionate allotment; bids lower than the issue price receive nothing. This system is known as a Dutch Auction.

Tap issue

In March 1990, the Agent introduced the first tap issue, the methodology of which is as follows:

On the Friday before issue, the Agent announces the coupon and redemption of the issue. Before 08.30 Monday, the Agent determines the price at which he is willing to sell bonds. During the day he can change the price, but is not allowed to fix a price below the stock market quotation.

Investors can buy these bonds, from 08.30 to 15.00, through the authorized banks and brokers (plus fee). The minimum amount is Dfl 2.5m. In theory, the subscription period can last some weeks.

American tender

In 1990 there was also an American tender in the Dutch primary market.

Other bonds (excl. BNG)

All other bonds, except those of the BNG, are underwritten.

BNG

The bonds of the Bank voor Nederlandse Gemeenten, are sold through a group of major Dutch banks on a 'best-effort' basis.

Private placement

In the private placement market, lenders and borrowers negotiate, via a bank or a broker, details of amount, date of payment, redemption scheme, yield, price etc.

For the issuance of MTNs only, the maximum amount of a programme must to be determined in advance. MTNs are issued in denominations of Dfl 1m.

21.8 *New issue volumes*

Overview

New issues on the Dutch market are dominated by those of the central government and, in Figure 21.37 which shows new issuance from 1986-1990, the 'non-government' category represents the combined issuance of banks, insurance companies and industrial enterprises, a fact which further illustrates its dominance.

Government

The total value of Dutch government bonds issued in 1991, was Dfl 41bn (compared with Dfl 36bn in 1990). As at the end of 1991, about 71 per cent of the total value of bonds on the Dutch bond market were government bonds. Besides these issues on the public market, the government has also sought large sums on the private loan market (amounting to Dfl 8bn in 1991). Figure 21.38

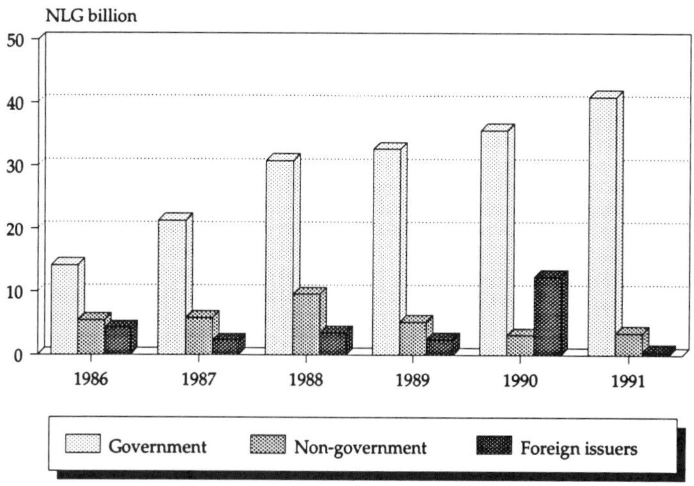

Figure 21.37 New issue volumes, 1986-1991
Source: De Nederlandsche Bank (Dutch Central Bank)

shows the breakdown of government issuance, on the public and private markets from, 1976 to 1991. Details of the government's 1990 and 1991 public issues can be found in Appendix 1.

	Public	Private	Private vs. public (%)
1976	2750	1156	29.6
1977	2590	2134	45.2
1978	3200	2973	48.2
1979	3950	3319	45.7
1980	7350	4824	39.6
1981	10,900	7772	41.6
1982	18,100	10,085	35.8
1983	22,850	9694	29.8
1984	25,050	6493	20.6
1985	20,350	14,456	41.5
1986	14,250	7790	35.3
1987	21,350	5892	21.6
1988	27,200	9628	26.1
1989	32,650	8681	21.0
1990	36,650	7855	17.7
1991	40,950	6923	14.5

Figure 21.38 Dutch government bonds on private and public markets (NLG million)

Non-government

Non-government issuance is relatively small. Details of the 1990/91 public issuance by financial institutions, trade & industry and foreign borrowers may be found in Appendix 1

Local authority

The main issuance activity of BNG and NWB is concentrated in the private placement market, particularly the medium-term note sector. A list of BNG's outstanding MTN volumes is shown in Appendix 2.

21.9 *Methods of trading*

Organization

In the Netherlands, there is one official body through which all securities are dealt, namely the Amsterdam Stock Exchange. However, deregulation of the market brought the arrival, on 5 May 1986, of AIM, the Amsterdam Interprofessional Market System. As a result, banks and stockbrokers are allowed to make direct deals with large investors for blocks of stocks and bonds with an effective value of Dfl 1m (shares) and Dfl 2.5m (bonds), trading on a net basis (i.e. fees are included in the price).

There are about 160 member firms in three categories, distinguished by their specific activities: banks, brokers and *hoekman* firms (jobbers who act as intermediaries between the banks and the brokers on the floor, and who are prohibited from any dealings with clients).

The control office of the Stock Exchange Association supervises the observance of the rules and the financial health of member firms. Furthermore, the Exchange has the statutory duty of protecting security holders and, to that end, it imposes strict rules governing both the issuance and subsequent information given by issuing bodies, through its mechanism for inclusion in the *Official Daily Quotation Record.*

By government decree, all domestic transactions, including subscriptions to new issues, must be executed through an intermediary who is a member of the Stock Exchange (the major commercial banks are members and play an important role). Holders, or potential purchasers, of stocks must therefore give their orders to either a bank or stockbroker, who will then act as buyer or seller on their clients' behalf and, in doing so, usually calls upon the services of the specialists - the jobbers, or *hoekman* firms.

Jobbers are both agents and own-account dealers, and will act as market-maker for a number of securities, although they are under no obligation in this respect and therefore make markets voluntarily according to their own trading requirements. For the majority of securities listed on the Stock Exchange, the jobbers collect the buying and selling orders from the brokers and endeavour to find a price at which they can execute the greatest number.

Besides this trading system, in which the specialist plays a major role and fixes the prices (with one or, sometimes, two quotations a day), there is a separate system for dealing in a number of actively-traded shares and bonds. For these securities, an opening price is fixed by the specialists and brokers conclude transactions with each other in open and continuous trading.

As of 1 April 1990, trading hours were extended and, for the most important Dutch shares and bonds, are now 10.00 to 16.30.

The official Stock Exchange hours remain at 11.30 to 13.15 and orders received without any specific indication are executed during this period.

Until recently, the less active shares and bonds were traded from 11.30 to 16.30. However, as from 2 January 1992, the times were changed as follows:

08.30 to 09.00	Unofficial trading hours for bonds (OOB securities - see below)
09.00 to 17.00	Official stock exchange hours (government bonds)
09.30 to 16.30	Official stock exchange hours (shares and non-government bonds)

The official list contains approximately 1900 securities, 70 per cent of which are domestic and foreign bonds, with the remaining 30 per cent being domestic and foreign shares.

In 1984, the Amsterdam Stock Exchange started a regular eurobond market for odd-lot trades, with daily price and volume publication. Trading takes place under ASAS (Amsterdam Security Account System) and the trading rules set by the ISMA are applicable.

Before liberalization in 1986, there was a difference in structure between euroguilder notes and bonds on the domestic market. The structure of repayment by drawing (obligatory on the domestic market), did not appeal to many foreign investors and issuers. As the eurobond market flourished elsewhere, the Dutch Central Bank decided, in 1969, to grant permission for a euroguilder market. Euroguilder notes could be in bullet form, were not listed (no prospectus required) and were placed on a 'best effort' basis without underwriting.

Whilst international borrowers and lenders were given the opportunity to be active in both the euroguilder and domestic guilder market, Dutch resident investors were not allowed to invest in the euroguilder market. At the moment, the 'destination' of the bonds, in terms of investor origin, is considered the most relevant factor in determining whether a bond is euro or domestic.

These days, eurobonds may be listed on the Amsterdam Stock Exchange, as well as underwritten.

OOB

Monday 16 July 1990 saw the inauguration of trading by Open-Order Book (OOB), a professional trading system for the most recent issues of government bonds. In the first phase, stockbroking firms were able to place limit orders in the system, with the minimum amount being Dfl 2.5 m. In the second phase, suitably qualified market-makers (stockbroking firms, Members of the Stock

Exchange Association) also get the opportunity to enter quotes (bid and offer prices) in the system, with the minimum amount being Dfl 5m. Through a *hoekman* acting as intermediary, the stockbroking firms can take up the orders and quotes entered in the OOB. Eleven government loans, including the most recent ones, were selected for the first phase.

The second phase will see the inclusion of five loans for which the OOB market-makers declare that they will be continuously in the market.

The OOB trading system is the result of two important steps mentioned in the action plan of the initiative group entitled 'Amsterdam as an International Financial Centre', which was formed in March 1989.

Initiative (14) contained in the action plan, urges intermediaries to establish themselves more positively as market-makers, both through the allocation of increased risk capital and by being more prepared to engage in large block transactions.

Initiative (15) initiated a special working group of Stock Exchange Members (the Committee for Bond Trading) which was to come up with further proposals to stimulate the function of trading in bonds in Amsterdam.

These initiatives were considered necessary because, for some years now, there has been evidence of an increase in the professional trading of Dutch government bonds in London.

In May 1989 the report of the Committee for Bond Trading appeared. One of its recommendations was the establishment up of an open-order book for the most recent government bonds.

Now that it has coupled the OOB trading system to its existing trading system, the Amsterdam Stock Exchange considers that is has established an efficient link between two market models, namely the auction market (which is order-driven and on which the current market system of the Amsterdam Stock Exchange - the Trade Support System ('HOS') - is based), and the dealers market (quote-driven and the system on which the OOB is based). In the case of the auction market, supply and demand are brought together and the price fixed at the level at which the greatest volume of transactions can be generated ('equilibrium price'). In contrast, the quote-driven market is formed by the market-makers, who elicit supply and demand.

The unique aspect of the combination of both systems is that the price-fixing which takes place within the auction market is, through the introduction of the function of the *hoekman*, coupled to the price-fixing as it occurs within the OOB. In this way, the pricing for non-professional investors, whose orders are handled in the normal way in the central market, is optimized by OOB pricing.

The establishment of the Open-Order Book system is a step on the way to creating the optimum conditions under which professional trading in government bonds can further develop in Amsterdam.

The abolition of the stock exchange tax, as from 1 July 1990, has removed an important cost factor from transactions made through the Amsterdam Stock Exchange.

The charges for the OOB are competitive with those of comparable trading systems in other countries, particular the London inter-dealer broker system. Furthermore, a start was made in February 1990 with the introduction of the seven calendar-day fixed settlement, in accordance with the recommendations of international umbrella organizations in this field (FIBV, Group of Thirty). The completion of both this process and that of the linkage to Cedel/Euroclear will finalize the modernization programme.

For the technical implementation of the OOB trading system use has been made, as in the case with the HOS system, of software developed by the Midwest Stock Exchange (MSE) of Chicago. This software has been adapted for local use in co-operation with the MSE and in close consultation with the users (members of the Stock Exchange Association). OOB processing takes place in a computer system which operates autonomously, although it is directly linked with the HOS computer. As is the case with HOS, there is a second identical OOB computer on full standby to take over processing in the case of a fault.

Transaction Costs

Average negotiable fees for non-AIM bond transactions (AIM transactions are not subject to buying or selling commission):

first NLG 5000:	1.75%
over NLG 20,000:	1.00%
over NLG 100,000:	0.40%
over NLG 500,000:	0.40%
over NLG 1,000,000:	0.25%
from NLG 1.0m to NLG 2.5m:	0.360% (on the total amount)
from NLG 2.5m to NLG 5.0m:	0.270% (on the total amount)
from NLG 5.0m to NLG 10.0m:	0.180% (on the total amount)
from NLG 10.0m to NLG 15.0m:	0.190% (on the total amount)

Minimum commission for a transaction: NLG 50

Size of trades

Normal transactions in government bonds can be as large as several tens of millions of guilders. The daily turnover in bonds at the Amsterdam Stock Exchange usually fluctuates between Dfl 350m and Dfl 1300m.

In 1991 average turnover totalled Dfl 845m, the highest being Dfl 2620m and the lowest Dfl 115m. Annual turnover for the years 1988-91 is shown in Figure 21.39.

Bond type	1988	1989	1990	1991
Government	159.6	144.4	166.9	186.5
BNG	1.7	0.6	0.5	0.5
Banks	26.9	18.7	15.7	18.7
Mortgage bonds	5.3	1.7	1.4	1.6
Savings bonds	3.6	1.6	1.4	0.9
Convertibles	1.2	2.2	1.5	1.2
Foreign bonds	8.2	3.9	2.0	3.0
Total	206.5	173.1	189.3	212.4

Figure 21.39 Effective turnover in Dutch bonds (NLG billion)
Source: Amsterdam Stock Exchange

In terms of debtor categories, the trading volume in Dutch government loans is by far the largest - about 90 per cent of the total bond turnover - mostly concentrated in recently-issued bonds. The government bonds most traded in 1991 are listed in Appendix 3.

21.10 *Market practices*

Coupon payment

For loans issued after 1960, interest is usually paid once a year (floating-rate notes excluded). Some older loans, issued before 1960 and carrying semi-annual coupons, are still outstanding. Most of the loans have a fixed-coupon during their whole lifetime.

Ex-dividend

After 1990, no guilder bonds trade ex-dividend.

Redemptions

Before 1986 the repayment of a loan in a lump sum on the final maturity date was not permitted; bonds had to be redeemed by the sinking fund method, with at least four annual payments of (nearly) equal size. Bonds to be repaid are selected by drawing three weeks before maturity date (in the case of government bonds), and sometimes up to three months before the maturity date (for others). Various drawing schemes can be used. Often the first repayment takes place either one or five years after the date of issue. Presently, however, the number of loans with a single instalment on the final maturity date is increasing. Redemption usually takes place at par, except for those bonds with calls, which are redeemed at a (descending) premium which is determined by the terms of the individual issue.

In the private market, a substantial number of redemption schemes are possible. An overview of the issue volumes relating to the different schemes may be found in Appendix 4.

Puts

Normally guilder bonds do not give the holder the right to put bonds. However, there are some bonds with special put features.

Denomination

Most bonds have a nominal value of Dfl 1,000 (CF pieces, K pieces: Dfl 5,000). Only very rarely are smaller denominations (of Dfl 100 and Dfl 500), or larger denominations (of Dfl 10,000 and Dfl 50,000), issued. In some cases, notably in the case of government bonds and the BNG, debt register entries are possible (the minimum amount for state loans is Dfl 100,000 and for BNG loans, Dfl 50,000). The advantage of a debt register is that redemptions are made proportionally and not by drawing.

Form

All quoted guilder bonds are in bearer form.

Dealing quotations

All guilder bonds are quoted in percentages, to two decimal places.

Withholding tax

In the Netherlands there is no withholding tax on interest payments.

Commissions

Minimum rates for transactions were abolished on 1 July 1990. Transaction costs of securities traded through the AIM system are negotiable.

21.11 Settlement

Physical delivery is a thing of the past in Amsterdam. Transactions taking place on the Amsterdam Stock Exchange result in a financial obligation to the Securities Clearing Corporation ('Effectenclearing'). All members of the Stock Exchange Association must be clearing members. The Effectenclearing balances out as many stock exchange transactions as possible and draws up overall statements - members then need only to settle their accounts. Settlement takes place on the 7th day after transaction.

In order to keep costs under control, the Centre for Securities Administration ('CF') has been set up. The CF registers the total shareholding, per security, which every bank and stockbroker holds in custody for clients. Once payable, dividend and interest payments are passed on to the custodians via the CF to enable the former to credit the accounts of those entitled to the securities in question.

The Netherlands Central Institute for Securities Clearing ('Negicef') acts as the central depository for all stock exchange members, so that physical movements of securities are rarely necessary. Approximately 90 per cent of all transactions are made through Negicef. The financial settlement system is channelled through the Kas-Associatie, which is a subsidiary company of the Stock Exchange Association. All securities movements are via a giro system, with physical delivery only being effected if specifically required by clients.

Every Dutch bond instrument can also be settled through Euroclear. The domestic clearing system links Euroclear with the Dutch banks. Euroguilder bonds and domestic foreign bonds can also be settled through Cedel.

21.12 Yield calculation

The calculation of the annual redemption yield is carried out as a 'present value' calculation, implying that the redemption yield equals the interest rate at which all future proceeds, such as coupon and redemption payments, are discounted. This present value, expressed as a percentage of the (remaining) loan amount, equals the price of the loan concerned plus the interest accrued on the date of calculation.

$$P + A = \sum_{t=1}^{n} \frac{CF_t}{(1+RY)^{t-s}}$$

P	clean price
A	accrued interest, based on 30/360
n	number of cash flows
CF	cash flow at time t: interest payment and/or redemption payment
s	time from last coupon payment date to the date of calculation, expressed as a fraction of a year
RY	redemption yield

21.13 Taxation

Capital gains and income tax

There is no capital gains tax in the Netherlands; equally, losses are not tax-deductible. However, income from all shares and bonds is subject to income tax. The absence of capital gains tax obviously encourages domestic private investors to concentrate on shares and on low-coupon bonds priced below par, as the redemption profit is free of income tax.

Withholding tax

Importantly, there is no withholding tax on interest payments in the Netherlands and there is certainly no intention of introducing such a tax in the near future. The dividend tax in the Netherlands is 25 per cent and is withheld at source, which means that dividends are paid less tax. Most non-residents, however, may claim a (partial) refund (see Figure 21.40).

Country of recipient (with tax treaty)	Withholding tax at source (%)	Possible claim or refund (%)
EC		
Belgium	25	10
Denmark	25	10
France	25	10
Germany	25	10
Greece	25	10
Ireland	25	10
Italy	25	25
Luxembourg	25	10
Spain	25	10
United Kingdom	25	10
Japan	25	10
United States	25	10

Figure 21.40 Withholding tax (dividends) for non-residents

Corporate tax

Domestic corporate investors pay the standard corporate tax rate on both interest and dividend revenues, and capital gains (including redemption profits). Corporate income tax amounts to 35 per cent.

Pension funds

Pension funds, and a number of other institutional investors, do not pay any tax at all. This is to avoid double taxation, since income tax is due on pension payments by these funds.

Investment funds

Investment funds that meet certain requirements can acquire the status of a 'Fiscal Investment Fund' (*Fiscale Beleggingsinstelling*). These funds have a corporate tax rate of 0 per cent. The most important requirement is that all investment income such as dividends, interest and rent (minus costs), must be paid out to the shareholders. The shareholders are liable to taxation on this income.

21.14 Futures & options

History

The Amsterdam Stock Exchange Association initiated the establishment of the European Options Exchange (EOE) which started trading call options, in the Merchants Exchange Building, on 04 April 1978.

In March 1979, put options were introduced, followed by gold options in April 1981. Bond options were introduced in November 1981 and, a year later, the trading of currency options was inaugurated.

As trade flourished, a modern Options Exchange Building was opened in April 1986, an event which was followed, in October 1986, by the start of trading in long-term options. In May 1987, EOE introduced stock index options.

The EOE widened its activities by establishing the FTA Financial Futures Exchange (Financiële Termijnmarkt) Amsterdam, which opened its doors on 19 June 1987. The FTA is housed in the Options Exchange Building.

In October 1988, the FTA presented EOE stock index futures (FTI). The FTA's futures programme was later extended with the introduction of guilder bond futures (FTO, June 1989) and futures on the Dutch TOP 5 Index, an index constructed from the five top Dutch multinationals listed on the Amsterdam Stock Exchange (FT5, March 1990) and dollar/guilder futures (FUS, August 1991).

Organization of the markets

The Vereniging European Options Exchange (EOE) was formed to regulate the trade in options. The EOE owns 100 per cent of the shares of Financiële Termijnmarkt Amsterdam N.V. (FTA).

Commercial activities are carried out by the wholly-owned Optiebeurs N.V. which owns 100 per cent of both the European Options Certificates B.V. (EOC) and the EOE-Services B.V. The latter renders various services such as the selling of information regarding option quotations and leasing of trading equipment. The EOC issues bearer certificates on options traded on the EOE.

The clearing activities are carried out by the holding company Holdingmaatschappij European Options Clearing Corporation B.V. (EOCC) through the 44.2 per cent-owned subsidiary International Options Clearing Corporation B.V. (IOCC), the 100 per cent-owned subsidiaries of European Stock Options Clearing Corporation B.V. (ESCC) and Associated Clearing House Amsterdam B.V. (ACHA), and the 70 per cent-owned European Futures Clearing Corporation B.V. (EFCC). The EFCC is 30 per cent owned by N.V. Nederlandse Liquidatiekas (NLKKAS) which, in turn, is 60 per cent-owned by EOCC.

The products of the FTA are traded by open outcry on the floor of the EOE. Trading is conducted under the supervision of market governors and the FTA ensures that transactions are open and fair, as well as being solely the result of supply and demand. An extensive network of rules and monitoring procedures prevent price manipulation and guarantee the integrity of the market. Margins and position limits are also governed by the regulations.

The clearing house for the FTA is the European Futures Clearing Corporation (EFCC). The responsibilities of the EFCC include the registering of all futures transactions and the daily calculation, and settlement, of profits/losses resulting from futures transactions. The main participants in the futures market are banks, pension funds, insurance companies, brokers and market-makers. The exact ratio in which the first three parties act as clients is not known. It is, however, clear that client orders account for roughly 40 per cent of total futures turnover.

With the permission of the Supervisory Committee, The European Options Exchange has raised the position limit, for certain institutional investors in the bond options classes, from 1 to 2 per cent of the nominal value of the underlying Dutch government bond. As a result, the position limit now equals the position limit for market-makers.

Institutional investors who wish to qualify for this dispensation must meet the following conditions and criteria:

- 1. The institutional investor must be recognized as such by the European Options Exchange.
- 2. The institutional investor must submit a written request which shows that the investor has, in his portfolio, fixed-interest securities valued at no less than Dfl 1bn.
- 3. For written positions, the margin requirements prescribed by the EOE apply. For written positions in bond call options, the limit cannot be exceeded unless the position is fully covered.

Contract specifications for bond options, options on bond futures and bond futures, are given in Figures 21.41-21.43.

Option type:	American; the holder of the option is entitled to exercise the option before the expiration date; positions may however be liquidated by means of a closing transaction before expiration
Contract size:	Dfl 10,000 nominal
Delivery months:	Initial lifetime: 3, 6 and 9 months; cycle: February, May, August and November
Last trading day:	Until 16.00, Amsterdam time, on the third Friday of the contract month, provided this is a business day
Quotation:	Dfl per Dfl 100 nominal
Minimum price movement (tick size) and value:	Dfl 0.05 = Dfl 5
Trading hours:	09.00 - 16.30, Amsterdam time
Initial margin:	Margin short call/put: (options price + % (2 × the price of the underlying value - exercise price)) × the unit of trading. For daily margin percentages, consult the *Daily Official List*
Price limit:	None
Exercise (strike) prices	Intervals of Dfl 2.50
Contract standard:	Physical (giro) delivery of one of the following bonds: 8 1/2% Nederland 1991 per 2006 (symbol: NLC) 8 1/4% Nederland 1992 per 2002 (symbol: NLT) 8 1/4% Nederland 1992 per 2007 (symbol: NLV) 9% Nederland 1990 I-II per 2000 (symbol: NLF) 6 3/4% Nederland 1988 per 1998 (symbol: NLW)
Position limits:	Applicable. Check with EOE for details

Figure 21.41 EOE Dutch bond options - contract specifications

Option type:	American; the holder of the option is entitled to exercise the option before the expiration date; positions may however be liquidated by means of a closing transaction before expiration
Contract size:	One FTO bond futures contract (Dfl 250,000 nominal)
Delivery months:	Initial lifetime: 3 and 6 months; cycle: February, May, August and November
Assignment of futures:	End of the last day of trading
Last trading day:	Until 16.00, Amsterdam time, on the third Friday of the contract month, provided this is a business day
Quotation:	Dfl per Dfl 100 nominal
Minimum price movement (tick size) and value:	Dfl 0.01 = Dfl 25
Trading hours:	09.00 - 17.00, Amsterdam time
Initial margin:	Margin short call/put: (options price + % (2 × the price of the underlying value - exercise price)) × the unit of trading. For daily margin percentages, consult the *Daily Official List*

Figure 21.42 EOE options on Dutch bond futures (OOF) - contract specifications

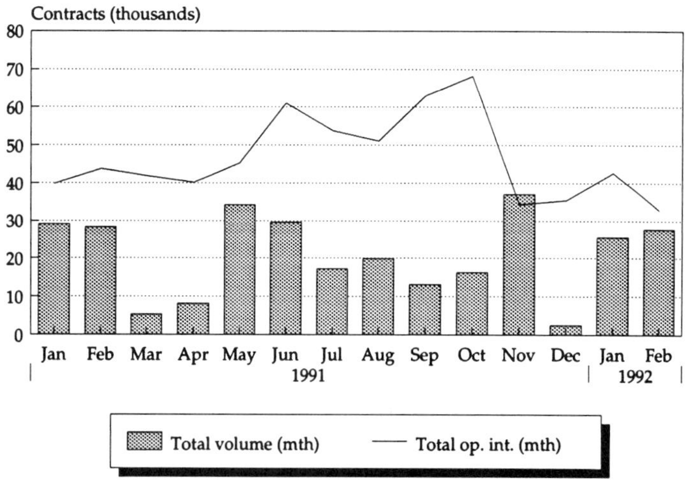

Figure 21.43 EOE options on bond futures - total mothly volumes and open interest.

Contract size:	A notional Dutch government bond with a nominal value of Dfl 250,000 and a 7% coupon
Delivery months:	March, June, September and December
Last trading day:	The 7th calendar day of the delivery month, provided this is a business day. Trading in the expiring contract will end after a special closing call starting at 16.00
Quotation:	Points per Dfl 100 nominal
Minimum price movement (tick size) and value:	Dfl 0.01 = Dfl 25
Trading hours:	09.00 - 17.00, Amsterdam time
Initial margin:	Margin short call/put: (options price + % (2 × the price of the underlying value - exercise price)) × the unit of trading. For daily margin percentages, consult the *Daily Official List*
Price limit:	If the price of FTO futures changes more than 1 point relative to the closing price on the previous business day, trading in all contracts, with the exception of contracts due to be settled in the current month, ceases for a period of 30 minutes. When trading has resumed, there is no further break in that day
Delivery:	Delivery is be made solely on the basis of positions which remain open at the end of the last day of trading. For each open contract, delivery is required of nominal Dfl 250,000 of Dutch government bonds. The seller specifies which bonds will be delivered. These must be Dutch government bonds, selected from public issues with an outstanding amount of at least Dfl 1bn, a single redemption date, and having on the first day of the delivery month a remaining life of at least 8 and not more than 10 years. The delivery obligation arising from a single contract must be satisfied by the delivery of a single issue. Bonds allowing early redemption are not acceptable for delivery
Settlement price:	The delivery price of the bonds is equal to the closing price on the last day of trading, multiplied by the conversion factor for the particular bonds delivered, as published by the FTA. Accrued interest on the delivered bonds starts on the last day of trading of the expiring guilder bond futures.

Figure 21.44 FTA Dutch government bond futures (FTO) - contract specifications

Note: The price of the FTO future depends on the price and conversion factor of the cheapest-to-deliver bond, the life of the contract and the difference between short-term interest and the coupon interest of the cheapest-to-deliver bond and is calculated as follows:

Futures price = (the price of the cheapest-to-deliver bond + the cost of financing - coupon receipts) / the conversion factor.

The conversion factor is the theoretical price of the bond on the last day of trading if yield-to-maturity is 7% divided by 100.

The FTA has published a brochure that contains all conversion factors, so that investors do not have to make these calculations themselves. The FTA has also developed a computer program that deals with this product.

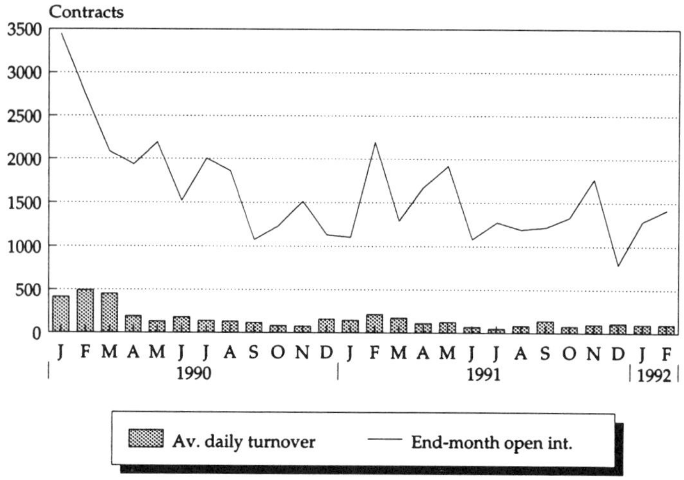

Figure 21.45 FTA bond futures - average daily volumes and end-month open interest.

21.15 Money markets

Overview

Dutch guilder money market instruments are both relatively small in number and underdeveloped. The bulk of short-term money goes into the active deposit market, although other products which fall into the broad definition of the Dutch money market (that is, financial instruments with maturities shorter than two years), are also available. There is a wide spectrum of market participants although, in practice, the principal players are the banks, local authorities and a limited number of large companies and institutional investors, while the Dutch government's participation is rather limited.

The most important instruments are short-term deposits (maturities of 1, 2, 3, 6 and 12 months), short-term cash loans (fixed-interest, maturities of 1, 2, 3, 6 and 12 months, minimum amount Dfl 1m), roll-overs (mid-term cash loan with interest based on AIBOR, the Amsterdam Interbank Offered Rate), commercial paper, certificates of deposit and forward-rate agreements. Since 1986, floating-rate notes (FRNs) have been permitted but, to date, only two issues have been recorded.

Commercial paper and certificates of deposit

Since January 1986 the issue of both guilder commercial paper (CP, issued by companies and municipalities) and guilder certificates of deposit (CDs, issued by financial institutions) has been permitted. At the end of 1991 the total value of announced CP programmes was Dfl 17.8bn, while CD programmes amounted to Dfl 17.2bn. The amount of CP and CDs actually outstanding on the market was Dfl 3.6bn and Dfl 4.5bn, respectively.

Coupon

The coupon is usually fixed and set as a spread over/under AIBOR.

Maturity

Not less than 14 days and no more than two years.

Interest payment

These are non-interest-bearing securities and are issued at a discount.

Prices

Prices are quoted on a yield-to-maturity basis.

Interest and yield calculation

Interest calculation is on an actual/360 day basis. The formula for calculating yield for maturity shorter than one year is:

$$\frac{B}{(1+\frac{P \times R}{360 \times 100})} = D$$

where,

B	face value
P	number of days from settlement to maturity
R	rate of discount %
D	discount amount (present value, price)

Where the maturity is longer than one year, a compound interest calculation is applied. First the calculation is made for the last part (a broken part of a year), then a present value calculation of this is made for the full years of maturity.

■ Example:

Amount: NLG 1,000,000
Maturity: 546 days
Interest: 9.00%

Step 1:
546 - 365 = 181 days

$$\frac{1{,}000{,}000}{(1+\frac{181 \times 9.00}{360 \times 100})} = \text{NLG}\,956{,}708.92$$

Step 2:

$$\frac{956{,}708.52}{(1+\frac{365 \times 9.00}{360 \times 100})} = \text{NLG}\,876{,}709.21$$

Issuers

The outstanding balance of domestic CP remains relatively small. Issuers include both Dutch and non-Dutch corporations. At the moment neither a rating nor a specific back-up credit line is necessary. Additionally, there are no restrictions governing either the geographical origin or any other classification of investors.

The Dutch central bank requires that organizations (i.e. companies and banks) report, on a monthly basis, the amount of CP/CDs they have outstanding, if such a figure exceeds Dfl 50m. The minimum size of an issue is Dfl 1m.

Investors

Banks, financial and investment institutions and institutional investors.

Settlement and clearing

Clearing is mainly handled through the Dutch central bank. In principle, the money is available to the client on the same day as transaction - thereby substantially adding to the negotiability of the paper. The notes are traded with the help of a giro system and, instead of expensive physical distribution, entitlement is denoted by a book-entry known as 'Global Note'.

21.16 Interest rate history

History seems to suggest that guilder rates follow German rates, full stop. However, there is actually more to it than that.

Looking at Figure 21.46, it cannot be denied that, for a long time, there has been a very strong relationship between both bond markets (it should also be noted that, recently, this has also been the case with regard to the correlation between the guilder and Ecu markets).

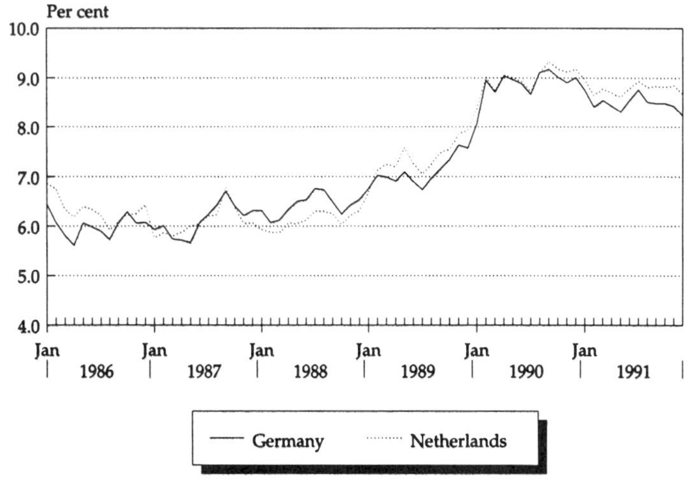

Figure 21.46 Interest rates in Holland and Germany, 1986-1991
Source: Datastream

This strong correlation means that guilder bonds could be, indeed have been, considered by international investors as *de facto* bunds, albeit with a certain risk associated with the guilder/bund spread. For the period 1987-1991, the correlation between the guilder and bund was approximately 0.81 while the standard deviation of total returns in local currency was 5.1 per cent for the guilder bond market and 5.5 per cent for the German bond market. The guilder/bund spread fluctuated between +20 (Dutch long-term interest rates below Germany) and -70 basis points.

The deep-seated cause of this traditionally strong relationship lies in the Dutch central bank's historical monetary policy, which has been fully dedicated to the task of stabilizing the guilder/Deutschemark exchange rate.

The Dutch central bank has been quite successful in optimizing its monetary policy in two ways. Firstly, it succeeded in establishing a very gentle day-to-day management of the money market, a policy which enabled creative fine-tuning of the market based, for the greater part, on a 'gentleman's agreement' with the banks. Controlling the money market in this way resulted in the very close tracking of German interest rates, thereby establishing a relative stable long-term guilder/Deutschemark relationship.

Secondly, in contrast with other industrial countries, the Dutch central bank does not have a target-oriented monetary policy. The bank's sole interest is in controlling M1 (the so-called 'little monetary policy'), it has no targets relating to either M2 or M3.

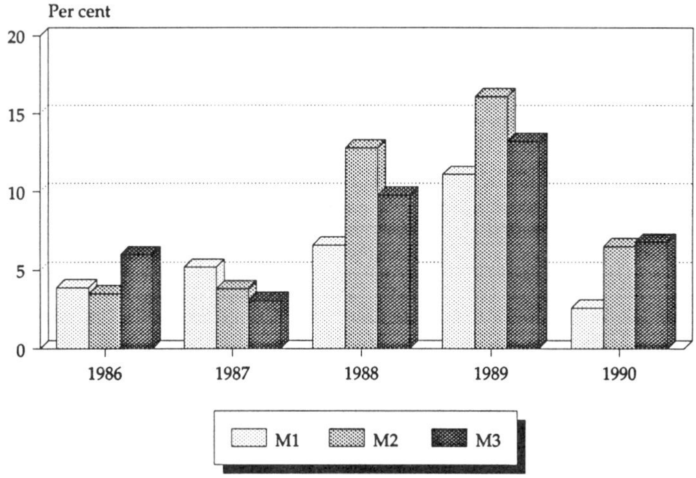

Figure 21.47 Dutch money supply growth 1986-1991
Source: 1990 Annual Report of De Nederlandsche Bank (Dutch Central Bank)

As Figure 21.47 shows, the growth rates in M2 and M3 have, at times, been very high. However, this has never led to any worries about inflation, largely due to the policy of Dutch unions which has been, and still is, to stay in line with the trend in German labour costs. The central bank's policy allowed freedom for both M2 and M3 and, at the same time, succeeded in isolating the position of the guilder, and the liquidity of the money market, from the broader capital market liquidity.

As the European money markets and capital markets are in a process of integration, it will be rather unlikely that the history of Dutch monetary policy can repeat itself and a re-orientation in money-supply growth is unavoidable. This means a break with the past and in the relative freedom gained by an undervaluation of the importance of M2 and M3. This change in stance probably accounts for the fact that, at year-end 1991, inflationary expectations for Holland are higher than for Germany. The occasionally very high growth rates in M2 and M3 were, in terms of liquidity, a blessing for the Dutch stock market and created a smooth pattern in long-term interest rates. However, it is clear that the trend of low standard deviations seen in the past in Dutch bond market returns, is unlikely to be repeated.

21.17 *Inter-market spreads*

Bond traders in the Netherlands often analyse yield differentials between several sectors of the fixed-income market. Primarily, the difference in yields on private placements relative to publicly-issued government bonds, is an item which is followed daily by professional fixed-income investors. The character of private placements makes it difficult to construct a long-term series of yields, because market participants (for instance the central government) are often either inactive in the market for protracted periods or interested in a varying maturity sectors.

Figure 21.48 shows the yield differential between 10-year government bonds and private placements, issued by the Dutch government, with an average life

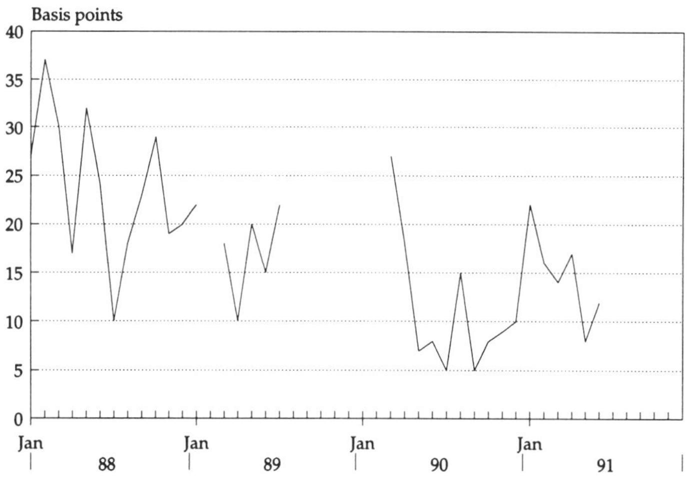

Figure 21.48 Yield differential: 10-yr government bonds minus government private placements

of 10.5 years. At times, there were no quotations for private placements in this particular maturity sector, for the reasons given above. During the second half of 1991, this lack of activity was caused by the government's demand for loans with longer maturities (30 to 40 years). Nevertheless, despite this lack of data, it can be seen that the yield gap between private placements and publicly-issued

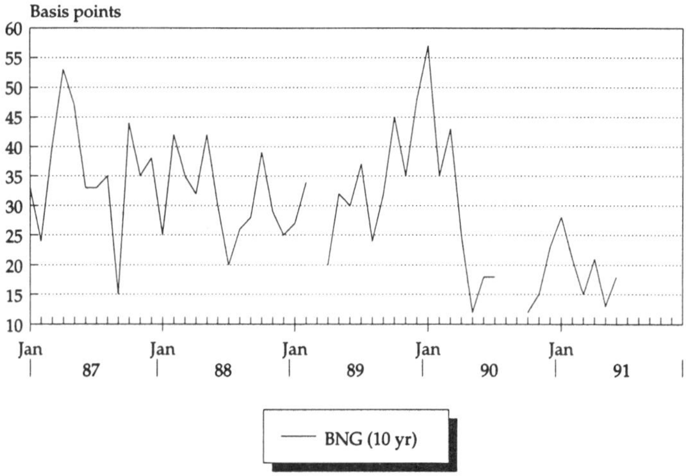

Figure 21.49 Yield differential: 10-yr government bonds minus BNG private placements

government bonds has recently tended to decrease to an average level of 15 basis points.

A market participant that is more active in the private placements market is the Bank for Dutch Municipalities (BNG). In the recent past, this institution only issued 2 or 3 public bonds a year, but was very active in the private placements market, especially in the medium-term note sector. Figure 21.49 shows the yield differential between 10-year government bonds and 10-year private loans to the BNG and, when Figures 21.48 & 21.49 are compared, it can be seen that a greater decline has been experienced. The yield gap of BNG loans relative to government bonds ranged from 20 to about 60 basis points in the period 1987 to 1990, while the yield gap in the government sector peaked at 36 basis points in early 1988.

Another category of yield spreads includes the differentials between several sectors within the public bond market. The most important issuer of new bonds in the Netherlands is the central government, which has to finance about Dfl 40bn to 45bn each year. To a lesser extent, other market participants operate on the demand side of the bond market. In a publication by the Dutch Central Bureau of Statistics (CBS), bond yields are calculated for government bonds, bonds issued by commercial banks (ordinary and subordinated capital bonds), bonds issued by supranational institutions (EIB, World Bank) and mortgage

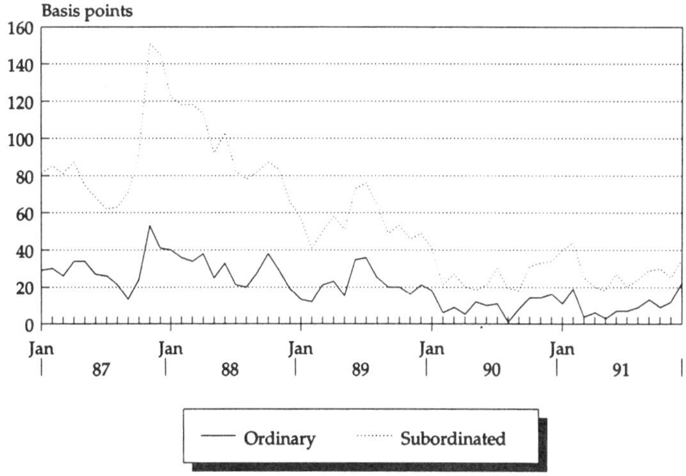

Figure 21.50 Yield differential: banking sector bonds minus Dutch government bonds

bonds. These figures are calculated as monthly averages, starting in January 1987. From these series it is possible to get a consistent view of the size of the yield spreads relative to government bond yields, because the source and the method of calculation are the same[1]. However, comparisons can be misleading because the CBS does not calculate duration figures for the published yield series.

During the past few years, the yield differential between bonds issued by the banking sector and government bonds has decreased dramatically. This holds true for both ordinary bonds and subordinated capital bonds. Recently, the average spread has amounted to about 10-20 basis points for both categories. Furthermore, it can be concluded from Figure 21.50 that fluctuations have diminished as well. This is further illustrated by Figure 21.51, in which the average yield spread and the standard deviation (as a measure of the fluctuations in the spread), are summarized.

1 *These CBS figures for government bonds differ from the bond yields used in the comparison with private loans, German bond yields and money market rates. While the CBS yields are calculated as monthly averages for bonds with an average life of 2 years or more, the other bond yields represent month-end figures for 10-year bonds.*

	Ordinary bonds	Subordinated bonds
1987/1991		
Average spread	20	59
Standard deviation	11	33
1989/1991		
Average spread	14	37
Standard deviation	8	16

Figure 21.51 Average yield spreads and standard deviations (in bp) between bonds issued by banks and central government

The spreads of yields on subordinated bonds (and the fluctuations in these spreads), have diminished particularly sharply relative to those on comparable government bonds.

The same conclusions can be drawn from Figure 21.52 where the yields on bonds issued by supranational institutions are shown relative to government bonds. The average yield differential for the whole period 1987 - 1991 amounts to 24bp and, from 1989 onwards, the average has decreased to 13 bp. In July 1991, there was no average yield difference at all. Spread fluctuations have fallen from 16 to 7bp.

Figure 21.53 shows that the fluctuations in the additional yield on mortgage bonds relative to state loans are consistently very high (the standard deviation stabilizes at around 7bp for both periods). On average, yields on this type of bonds exceed government bond yields by about 20bp.

There are two more spreads that are worth mentioning, as they are relevant to Dutch bond trading. The first is the difference between long-bond yields and money market rates, shown in Figure 21.54, which gives a clue to the shape of the yield curve shown in Figure 21.55. During the last 6 years, the yield curve began by showing a normal pattern, implying that long-bonds yielded more than money market instruments. However, since 1989, an inverted yield curve can frequently be observed, due partly to the close connection of the monetary policy of the Dutch central bank and the German Bundesbank. During 1991, Dutch money market rates exceeded long-bond yields by about 60 basis points. In December, the money market tightened further while the bond market showed a strong recovery, resulting in a spread of money rates over bond yields, of over 100bp.

The spread between Dutch and German bonds (see Figure 21.56) is also continuously analysed by traders. Because of the connection of the monetary policies in both countries, there is a high degree of correlation in bond yields.

Normally, Dutch bond yields exceed their German counterparts although, on one occasion in 1988, this position was reversed as rumours spread about the possible introduction of a withholding tax on German bonds.

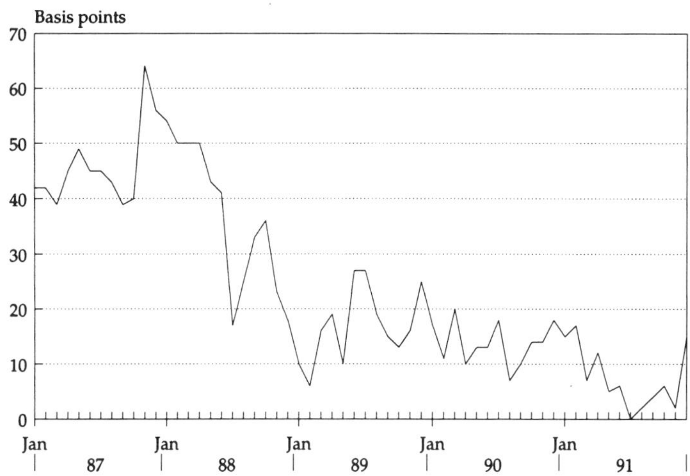

Figure 21.52 Yield differential: supranational bonds minus Dutch government bonds

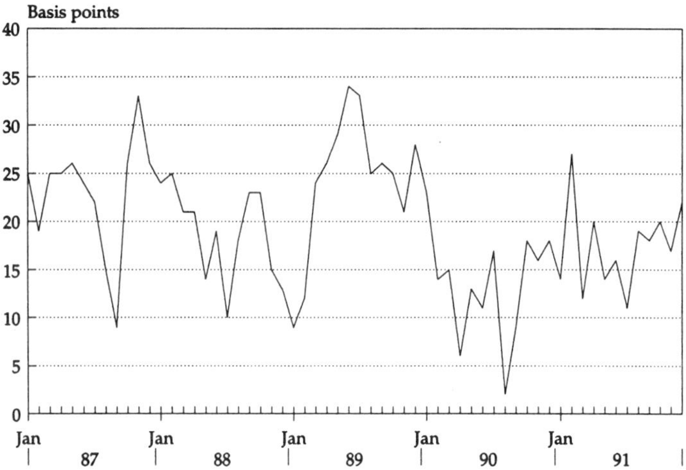

Figure 21.53 Yield differential: mortgage bonds minus Dutch government bonds

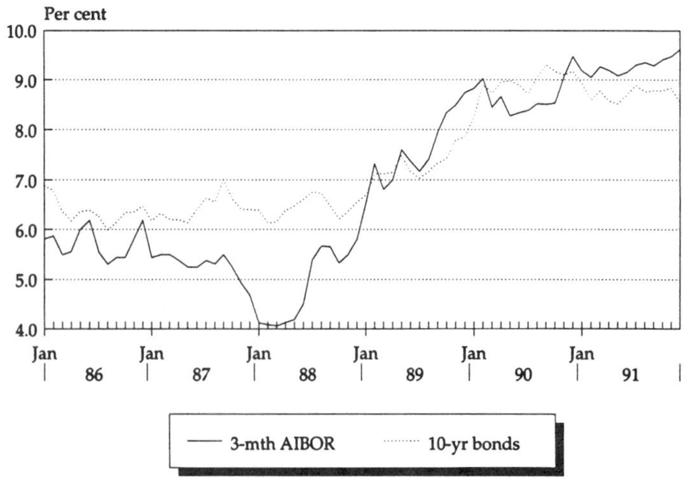

Figure 21.54 Money market rates and bond yields

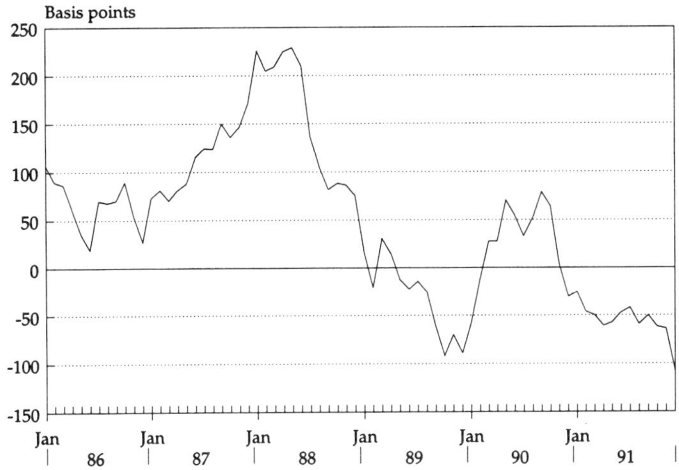

Figure 21.55 Yield differential: Dutch 10-yr bonds minus 3-month AIBOR

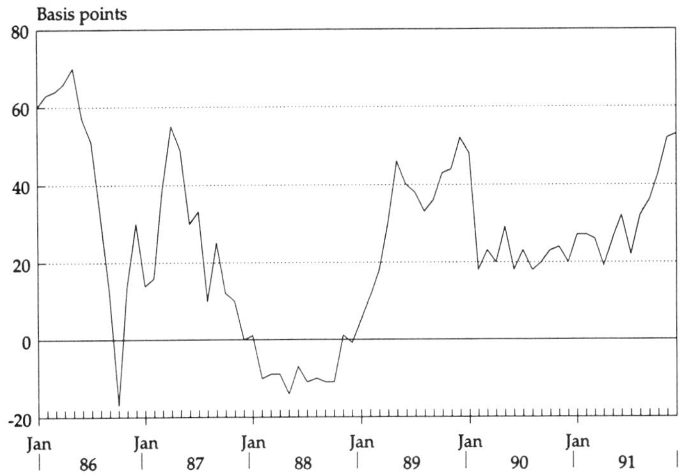

Figure 21.56 Yield differential: Dutch minus German 10-yr bonds

21.18 *Sources of reference*

Financial data

- Monthly bulletins of financial statistics of CBS, Centraal Bureau voor de Statistiek (the Netherlands Central Bureau of Statistics).
- *Quarterly and Annual Report* of De Nederlandsche Bank N.V. (Dutch Central Bank).
- *Beursplein 5* - a bulletin of the Vereniging voor de Effectenhandel (The Association for Trade in Securities).
- *Facts and Figures - Amsterdamse Effectenbeurs* (Amsterdam Stock Exchange).
- *Officiële Prijscourant* - official daily quotation record of the Amsterdam Stock Exchange , Europese Optiebeurs EOE (European Option Exchange) and Financiële Termijnmarkt Amsterdam FTA (Financial Futures Market Amsterdam).

Financial Press

- *Het Financiele Dagblad* - the Dutch financial newspaper.

Quote vendors and news agencies

- Reuters carry information on the Dutch market, as shown in Figure - 21.57

Page No.	Contributor	Subject
Prices		
DNBG/M	Central bank	Money market
AFGB (index)	Agent of the Ministry of Finance	Bonds/Private loans
HFLA	Multi-contributor	Money market
FWEB	Multi-contributor	Forward & deposit
QQIV	Multi-contributor	Forward & deposit
QQFN	Multi-contributor	Forward & deposit
QQHF/G	Multi-contributor	Forward & deposit
ADGF	Multi-contributor	Forward & deposit
AANB (index)	ABN AMRO	Money market
AANA (index)	ABN AMRO	Bonds
CBNB	Commerzbank	Forward & deposit
CLAT	Credit Lyonnais	Forward & deposit
OOLD	Oolders	Forward & deposit
OOLG/H	Oolders	Forward & deposit
THKB/C	OAT/Troost	Forward & deposit
WENN	Wallich Matthes	Forward & deposit
NLAA (index)	Stock Exchange	
EOEI (index)	EOE	Options
FTAA (index)	FTA	Futures

Figure 21.57 Reuters pages

Appendix 1

Public issues on the Netherlands capital market, 1990 & 1991

Coupon date	Details		Amount (NLG million)
Government			
15 February	Nederland 8.25%	90-00	5000
15 May	Nederland 9.00%	90-00	9600
01 May	Nederland 8.75%	90-00	3000
01 July	Nederland 9.00%	90-00	3250
01 August	Nederland 8.75%	90-00	1250
16 October	Nederland 9.00%	90-00	4300
30 November	Nederland 9.25%	90-00	5000
15 January	Nederland 9.00%	91-01	7700
15 March	Nederland 8.50%	91-01	10,000
01 June	Nederland 8.50%	91-06	10,000
15 September	Nederland 8.75%	91-01	13,250
Financial institutions			
15 February	Aegon 0.00% A$	90-00 (eur)	363
15 April	ABN Amro 9.50%	90-01/05 (a)	250
15 November	BNG 0.00%	90-02	1000
15 March	ING 10.00%	91-01 (a)	1000
27 June	Rabobank 9.00% Ecu	91-94 (eur)	519
01 August	BNG 0.00%	91-03	1000
15 September	Aegon 7.00% US$	91-01 (a/c/eur)	755
16 September	ABN Amro 9.25%	91-01 (a/eur)	750
Trade and industry			
02 July	Unilever 9.00%	90-00 (eur)	500
19 November	Ned. Gasunie 9.00%	90-95 (eur)	250
17 October	Energie Beh. Ned. 9.00% US$	90-95 (eur)	500
Foreign borrowers			
01 March	IBRAD 8.375%	90-97 (eur)	300
15 June	SHV Holdings 9.375%	90-00 (eur)	300

(cont.)

Coupon date	Details		Amount (NLG million)
Foreign borrowers (cont)			
05 July	IADB 9.25%	90-00 eur	250
19 December	EIB 9.25%	90-00 eur	300
27 December	IBRAD 9.25%	90-00 eur	300
05 August	IADB 8.875%	91-98 eur	250
03 December	EIB 8.875%	91-01 eur	300

Key:
a = subordinated
c = convertible
eur = eurobond

Note: Only loans with a nominal value equal to, or above, NLG 250m are included..

Appendix 2

Bank for Dutch Municipalities - medium-term note issues

Due date	Coupon	Amount outstanding (NLG million)
02 January 1992	7.2000	30
03 January 1992	5.7500	20
14 January 1992	5.7500	20
03 August 1992	5.7500	56
02 October 1992	5.6500	10
04 January 1993	6.1250	20
04 January 1993	7.2000	25
14 January 1993	6.1250	20
01 March 1993	7.2000	50
03 May 1993	5.7500	60
01 October 1993	6.0000	15
17 November 1993	6.1000	51
01 February 1994	6.2500	10
01 February 1994	6.6250	30
01 February 1994	9.3750	300
01 March 1994	8.2500	25
10 March 1994	7.3750	50
02 May 1994	7.2000	50
01 June 1994	6.2500	10
01 July 1994	7.3750	25
01 August 1994	9.0000	200
01 November 1994	6.0000	51
01 November 1994	7.2500	25
01 December 1994	8.2500	50
28 July 1995	7.3500	25
01 August 1995	7.3000	25
02 August 1995	9.0000	300
16 January 1996	6.1875	36
16 January 1996	9.5000	300

(cont.)

Due date	Coupon	Amount outstanding (NLG million)
16 April 1996	8.8750	300
01 July 1996	9.0000	300
15 April 1998	6.3750	75
29 April 1998	6.3750	25
18 May 1998	6.6250	50
01 December 1998	7.8750	25
01 February 1999	6.9000	50
01 March 1999	7.0000	50
01 March 1999	7.0000	50
01 April 1999	7.5000	210
03 May 1999	7.3750	100
01 June 1999	7.7000	150
28 July 1999	7.5000	100
02 August 1999	7.7500	300
29 September 1999	7.4000	200
29 November 1999	7.7500	300
03 January 2000	8.2500	500
01 February 2000	8.7500	750
01 March 2000	7.0000	25
01 March 2000	9.5000	300
16 May 2000	9.0000	750
03 July 2000	7.8000	100
03 July 2000	9.1700	153
10 July 2000	8.9000	300
29 September 2000	7.5000	500
16 November 2000	9.5000	800
02 January 2001	9.5000	750
04 January 2001	0.0000	150
16 February 2001	9.5000	750
30 August 2001	7.8750	500
17 September 2001	9.0000	1500
01 November 2001	8.8750	500
17 December 2001	9.0000	750
16 January 2002	8.7500	500
15 March 2002	8.8000	300

Appendix 3

Most-traded Dutch government bonds in 1991

No.		Bond		Turnover 1991 (NLG million)
1	8.5%	Netherlands 1991 I-III	2001	21,831
2	8.75%	Netherlands 1991 I-II	2001	21,017
3	9.0%	Netherlands 1991 I-II	2001	20,469
4	8.5%	Netherlands 1991 I-II	2006	14,458
5	9.0%	Netherlands 1990 I-II	2000	13,517
6	9.25%	Netherlands 1990	2000	7922
7	6.25%	Netherlands 1988	1994	6334
8	9.0&	Netherlands 1990 IV	2000	4641
9	7.5%	Netherlands 1989 II	1999	3576
10	8.5%	Netherlands 1987	1992/1995	3482
11	6.75%	Netherlands 1988	1998	2917
12	7.5%	Netherlands 1989 I	1999	2914
13	9.5%	Netherlands 1986	1990/93	2850
14	8.5%	Netherlands 1989	1995/1999	2814
15	8.25%	Netherlands 1990	2000	2673
16	6.0%	Netherlands 1988	1995	2673
17	6.25%	Netherlands 1987 I	1995	2475
18	7.0%	Netherlands 1989 III	1999	2348
19	6.75%	Netherlands 1989	1999	2301
20	6.25%	Netherlands 1986	1996	2243

Appendix 4

Redemption schemes on the Dutch government private loan market

Average life	Redemption scheme	Issue volumes (NLG million)				
		1987	1988	1989	1990	1991
30.0	30f	-	-	-	5.0	143.0
29.0	29f	-	-	-	38.9	-
25.5	20+10	-	-	-	30.0	78.0
25.0	25f	-	-	-	-	5.0
21.0	21f	-	-	-	17.5	-
20.0	20f	0.30	-	460.0	418.5	550.9
18.0	15+5	-	-	-	-	50.0
18.0	18f	-	-	-	-	7.7
18.0	10+15	-	-	-	57.0	-
16.0	16f	-	-	-	-	10.0
15.5	10+10	50.0	-	-	43.0	76.0
15.0	15f	-	65.0	-	10.0	210.5
14.0	14f	-	50.0	-	10.0	10.0
13.0	10+5	785.0	10.0	5.0	-	50.0
13.0	13f	50.0	50.0	40.0	65.0	85.0
12.5	10+4	50.0	-	-	-	10.0
12.5	9+6	-	-	-	-	5.0
12.0	12f	440.0	236.0	120.0	261.0	169.3
11.5	10+2	60.0	15.0	6.0	-	-
11.5	9+4	-	-	-	-	5.0
11.0	8+5	330.0	5.0	-	-	-
11.0	11f	347.5	429.0	490.0	184.0	1792.7
11.0	9+3	480.0	-	200.0	-	-
10.5	0+20	10.0	10.0	-	-	-
10.5	5+10	1301.5	412.0	20.0	-	-
10.5	4+12	-	7.5	-	-	-
10.5	7+6	-	35.0	6.0	-	-

(cont.)

Average life	Redemption scheme	Issue volumes (NLG million)				
		1987	1988	1989	1990	1991
10.5	8+4	-	416.0	-	-	-
10.5	9+2	1572.5	6343.5	7334.0	6715.5	3655.3
10.0	8+3	-	60.0	-	-	-
10.0	10f	309.0	405.0	1334.1	-	10.0
9.5	5+8	10.0	-	-	-	-
9.0	9f	-	50.0	-	-	-
8.0	8f	-	50.0	-	-	-
7.0	7f	-	50.0	-	-	-
	Total	5891.8	9628.0	8681.0	7855.4	6923.4
	Number	15	19	10	9	16
	Average life	11.1	10.5	11.1	11.4	12.3

Note:
xf = x years bullet
x+y = x years no redemption, redemption in y years

Interest(ed)

in

AMSTERDAM?

FTA

Chapter

22

The bond markets of

Norway

Baste Nepstad
Vital Forsikring

Bjarne Brynning
Vesta-group

Jan Pollestad
Carl Kirulf & Co.

Leif Ola Rød
Pre Invest

Odd Sigmund Røste
Oslo Stock Exchange

Morten Steinsland
Vestenfjeldske Bykreditt

Halvard Tretvoll
Central Securites Depository (VPS)

Alexandra Larsen
(Translator)

Note:: In general text, the abbreviation 'NKr' is used to denote the Norwegian kroner. Elsewhere, the international mnemonic 'NOK' is used.

22.1 Introduction

Right up until 1980, the Norwegian bond market was characterized by strict regulation by the authorities. A policy of low interest rates was an important instrument used by the government in rebuilding the economy in the post-war years. In the implementation of this policy, the supply of bonds was severely regulated through the Regulations for New Issues, through which the government controlled who should have access to the market, new issue volume and on what terms the funding could be made.

Banks and insurance companies were obliged to purchase these bonds, thereby ensuring demand. This market was of little interest to other groups of investors, owing to the low returns available.

During the first half of the 1980s, a liberalization process was initiated in the Norwegian bond market. The strict control over new issues was relaxed, and obligatory investment in bonds for banks and insurance companies was abolished. Interest rates were gradually adjusted to market levels. As a result, new groups came into the market, and the secondary market began to function. The market developed, and new instruments were introduced, based on models existing in the international markets.

- floating-rate notes
- convertible bonds
- bonds with warrants
- put and call issues
- certificates

The Regulations for New Issues, in their present form, still provide limitations. This applies in particular to choice of model. It is still impossible to issue long, straight bonds, unless dispensation has been granted in advance. Zero-coupon issues are forbidden.

The flourishing secondary market facilitated another important development: the transition to a paperless securities market through the establishment of the Norwegian Registry of Securities in 1986. All securities are now registered electronically. This revolutionized the secondary market, and can be said to be an important factor in the rapid growth in turnover volume.

Liberalization of the credit market allowed, amongst other things, mortgage institutions to increase market share. The bond market became an important factor in the supply and demand for credit. As a result, mortgage institutions took on an important role in the development of the secondary market.

The market for Kingdom of Norway issues has, in recent years, been coloured by the fact that the Norwegian government did not make any issues between 1986 and 1991. In fact, a large amount of the existing volume of outstanding issues was redeemed in that period. At the same time, demand has been maintained at a relatively high level, as banks have sought to increase holdings of government bonds in order to meet requirements imposed by the government. This has gradually lead to the creation of risk-free interest as the Norwegian markets have, to far too great an extent, been influenced by the banks need for Government issues. Liquidity in the market for these bonds has therefore been reduced.

In recent years, development seems to have been greatest in the market for mortgage institutions, even though not even this market has demonstrated that it functions sufficiently. The market for mortgage institution issues has given the impression that it is more liquid than the market for Kingdom of Norway issues, and has therefore attracted many investors who really ought to be in government issues.

Based on signals given in the Budget for 1992, there is reason to believe that a number of the problems mentioned above will straighten themselves out over the next few years. The government's borrowing requirement appears to be increasing which, to the extent this requirement is covered through the Norwegian Bond market, combined with suitable methods of issuance and necessary organization of the secondary market, will lead to a better functioning market. This applies in particular to its role as reference market for long-term funding.

The Oslo Stock Exchange has announced intentions to introduce trading in interest rate futures and options. Trading in standardized derivatives will undoubtedly have a positive effect on the market.

However, whilst the market has flourished, other factors have not been given the same degree of attention. This applies in particular to the documentation necessary for issuance, and the function of the agents, who are supposed to take care of the interests of the bondholders.

22.2 Economics

Introduction

Over the last ten years, the Norwegian economy has experienced considerable fluctuation. The mid-eighties were characterized by an upturn, fuelled by consumption and investment, with extremely strong growth in domestic demand in the period from 1984 to 1986. Private consumption was stimulated by high wage-growth. A negative rate of interest after tax and liberalization of the credit markets resulted in strong growth in credit, which amplified the upturn in the economy for mainland Norway, particularly in sheltered sectors. A relatively high oil price served to support this growth in activity.

The strong growth in demand and accumulation of debt, suggested a need for a tighter economic policy. Moreover, between 1985 and 1986, the balance of trade weakened by NKr 60m, equivalent to 11-12 per cent of GNP; half of the fall being attributable to the price of oil (which plummeted in 1986), with the remainder resulting from reduced exports and increased imports. The fall in the price of oil led to a marked weakening of the Norwegian kroner, which was devalued in May 1986.

To reduce pressure on the domestic economy, financial policy was tightened from 1986. Additionally, from 1987, the tax system saw a gradual reform which was aimed at dampening debt-financed consumption whilst, in 1988 and 1989, income regulation was introduced. The combination of all these factors resulted not only in a decline in domestic demand and GDP (see Figure 22.1), but also sharply increased unemployment.

The number of unemployed, including persons on various public employment schemes, has risen from some 40,000 in mid-1987, to approximately 160,000 (7.6 per cent of the work-force), by mid-1992.

An expansive financial policy has been pursued since 1989 which, in the three years from 1989 to 1992, has provided a stimulant to domestic demand equivalent to some 6.75 per cent of GDP.

Inflation

During the 1980s, a number of imbalances developed in the Norwegian economy, including a high growth in domestic costs which again led to a marked worsening of competitive ability. Wage costs in industry rose by an average of over ten per cent annually in the period 1980-1988. However, successive devaluations (amounting to a total of 11.75 per cent) during the first half of the eighties, countered the competitive weakness. Additionally, income regulation

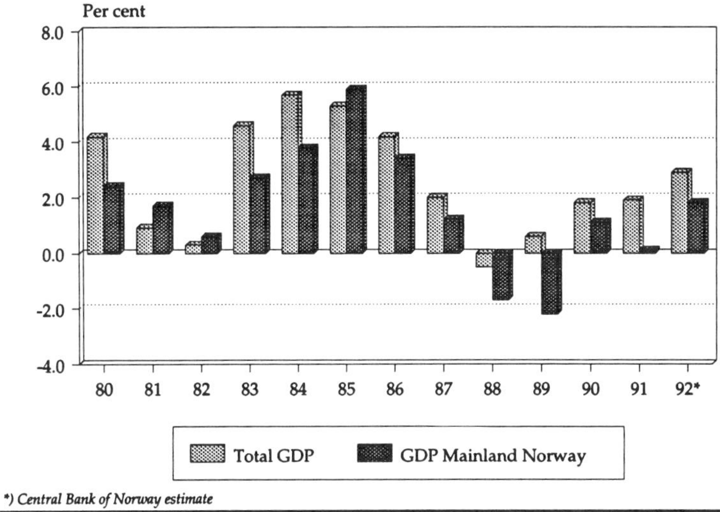

Figure 22.1 **Growth in total GDP and mainland Norway**
Source: Carl Kierulf & Co. A.S

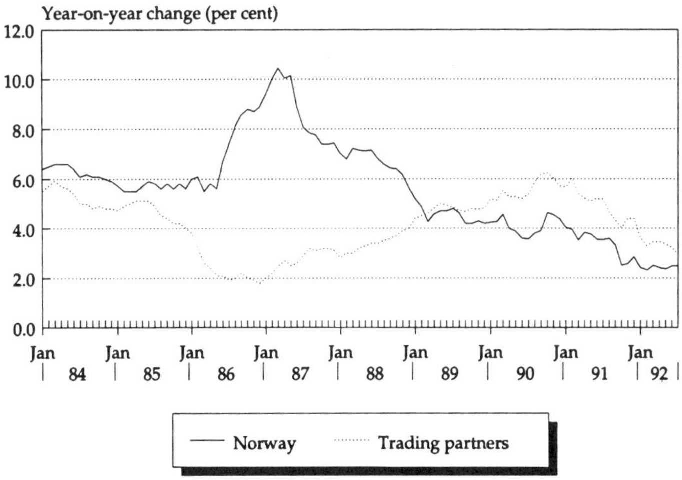

Figure 22.2 **Inflation in Norway and the average of its trading partners**
Source: Carl Kierulf & Co. A.S

imposed in 1988 and 1989, and a subsequent decline in wage-growth, has further enhanced industry's competitiveness but, nevertheless, the level of costs in Norway continues to lie some 20 per cent above the general level of its trading partners.

A strong growth in domestic consumption in the mid-eighties, and a devaluation implemented in 1986 resulted in very strong price-growth in a period when the rate of inflation was declining internationally. Over the last couple of years, the combination of weak domestic demand and a dampening of cost-growth has resulted in a substantial improvement, with the rate of inflation falling to below that of its trading partners, at around 2.5 per cent (see Figure 22.2).

Balance of trade

With the international economic upturn of 1987-90 contributing to a growth in the export of traditional goods, an opposite trend in domestic demand led to a decline in imports. As a result, a gradual reduction in trade deficit was experienced towards the end of the 1980s, culminating in the achievement of a balanced position in 1989. Increased oil production, and a sharp rise in the price of oil in the second half of 1990 (due to the Gulf War), helped the trade balance to move into a position of substantial surplus, a trend which was continued in 1991, when a further rise was seen (see Figures 22.3 & 22.4). This was in spite of the fact that the economies of Norway's most important export markets had begun to weaken from the second half of 1990.

A poor record of foreign trade in the years prior to 1989 meant that, by the end of that year, Norway's net foreign debt had reached a level equivalent to some 20 per cent of GDP. However, the considerable improvement subsequently achieved caused the net debt to be roughly halved by the end of 1991. Furthermore, assuming that the real price of crude oil remains unchanged from 1992 levels, the trade surplus is likely to be maintained at a high level and should lead to net foreign debt being eliminated within three or four years.

Interest and exchange rates

Because of widespread devaluations early in the eighties (most recently in 1986), foreign investors required a risk margin in order to invest in the kroner. Towards the end of the 1980s, though, there was broad political agreement that devaluation was not a solution to the problem of negative developments in prices and costs. It was announced that devaluation would no longer be used as an instrument of policy and that confidence in the kroner would be re-established, with consideration of a stable kroner exchange rate (see Figure 22.6) becoming a primary aim in monetary policies. The domestic level of interest rates was to be adapted to achieving this goal whilst, at the same time, Norges Bank

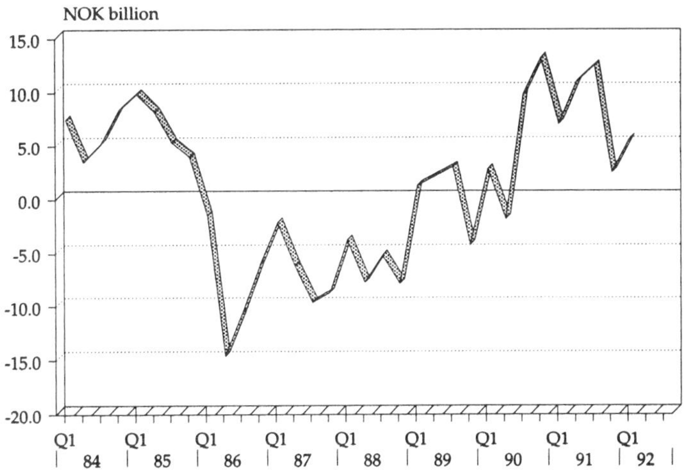

Figure 22.3 Norway's current account
Source: Carl Kierulf & Co. A.S

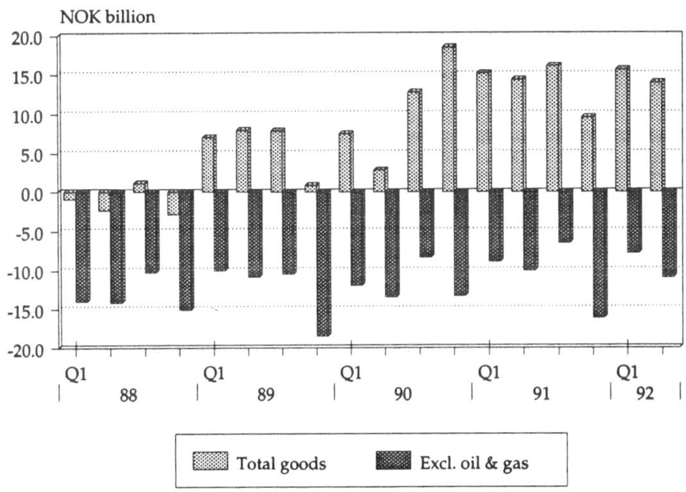

Figure 22.4 Norway's trade balance
Source: Carl Kierulf & Co. A.S

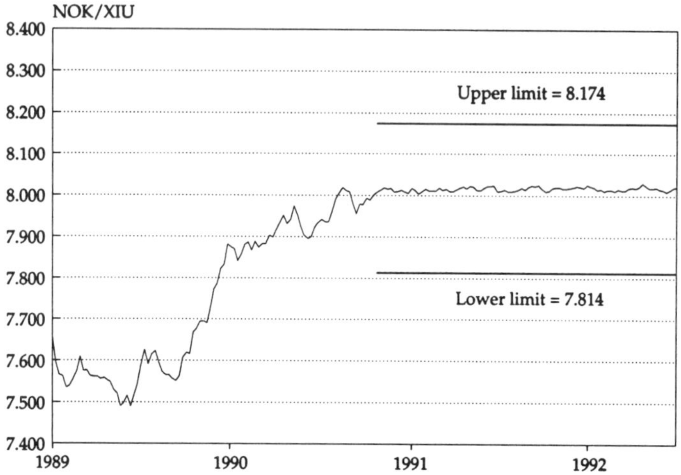

Figure 22.5 Exchange rate: NOK vs. XIU weekly average
Source: Carl Kierulf & Co. A.S

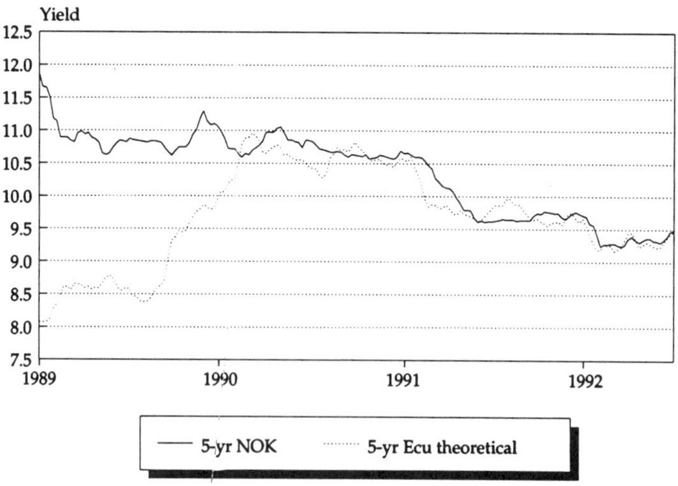

Figure 22.6 Long-term interest rates: 5-yr government bonds, weekly average
Source: Carl Kierulf & Co. A.S

(the Norwegian central bank) prepared for more active intervention in the currency market to maintain a stable kroner rate .

A restoration of the Norwegian economy, as well as increased confidence in foreign exchange policies has led to a reduction in domestic interest rates in recent years (see Figure 22.6). Levels of confidence were further enhanced when the government linked the international value of the kroner to the Ecu, in October 1990.

During periods of pressure on the kroner, Norges Bank has used interest rates to stabilize the kroner rate. This new system of exchange rates involves less variation in rates between the Norwegian kroner and the currencies which comprise the Ecu and, therefore, less need for a risk premium for NKr-denominated investment. For its part, the development of the domestic rate of interest is more dependent on the interest rates for Ecu-currencies.

Politics

In spite of shifting parliamentary alliances and various minority governments, the Norwegian political system is characterized by stability. In parliament (*Stortinget*), this stability has led to broad political accord over matters of economic policy.

Following the most recent general election in 1989, a conservative, three-party government came into power. However, the coalition collapsed after a year, as a result of internal disagreements over European conformity and the negotiation of an agreement between the EC and Efta. In the autumn of 1990, it was replaced by a new Labour government which, although strictly speaking a minority in parliament has, in practice, a broad parliamentary basis and achieves approval for its policies with alternating support from other parties.

22.3 *Market composition*

Composition by issuing sector

The market is dominated by two big groups of borrowers - the government and private mortgage institutions, which account for 25.49 per cent and 42.21 per cent respectively of total volume outstanding (see Figure 22.7). In recent years, new categories of borrowers (commercial and savings banks, and foreign borrowers) have been allowed access to the market.

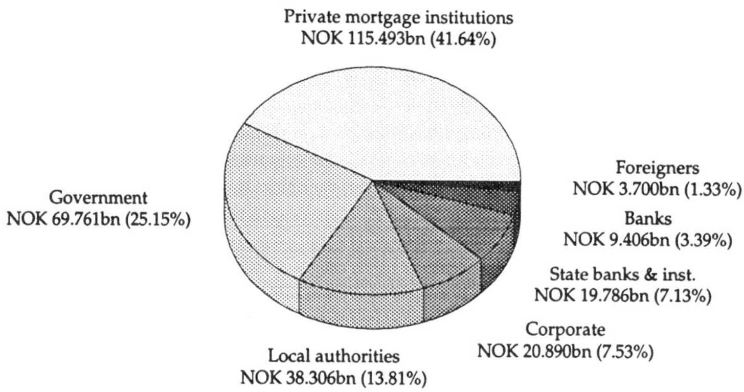

Figure 22.7 Norwegian market by issuer

Government bonds

The extent to which the government raises funds in the bond market is dependent, to a large degree, on whether the national budget shows a deficit. Until 1980, the government was the largest borrower in the bond market but, following the process of liberalizing the market which began in 1980, its relative pro-

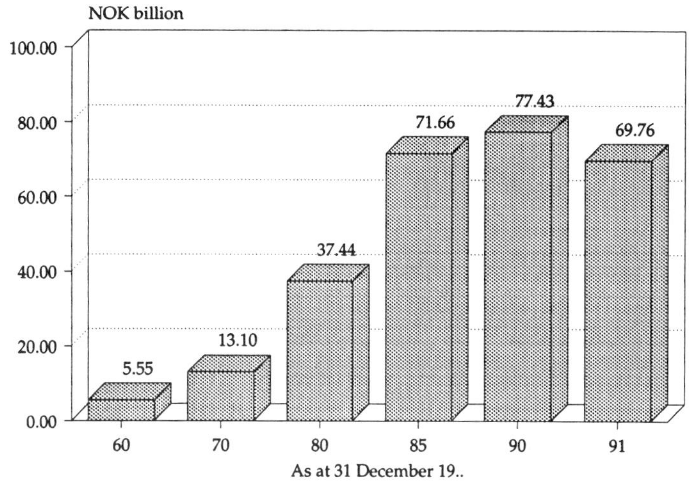

Figure 22.8 Outstanding volumes of Kingdom of Norway bonds

portion declined and, with the sharp increase in oil revenue in the period 1980-1985, net issuance of Kingdom of Norway bonds became even smaller.

Since 1987, the government has had no borrowing requirement although, in 1989, a placement was made with the National Insurance Fund.

In February 1991, however, the government issued NKr 12bn in a new five-year bullet and this bond (10 per cent 1991-96) is currently regarded as the best benchmark in the Norwegian market.

Some NKr 27bn of bonds matured in 1991. The substantial deficit in the national budget for the year was covered mostly through borrowing abroad and through calling in receivables with Norges Bank, although the government did issue US$ 1bn and Ecu 1bn, abroad.

The national budget is expected to show a deficit again in 1992, and the market therefore has strong expectations of an increasing volume of government issues in the years ahead. For 1992, the government has fixed a ceiling of NKr 50bn for new issuance in the domestic market. Loans will also be taken up in the international financial markets; indeed, two issues, one in yen and one in Deutschemarks, had been made by the end of January 1992. Total borrowing in international markets, in 1992, is limited to NKr 40bn.

Outstanding volumes of Kingdom of Norway bonds are shown in Figure 22.8.

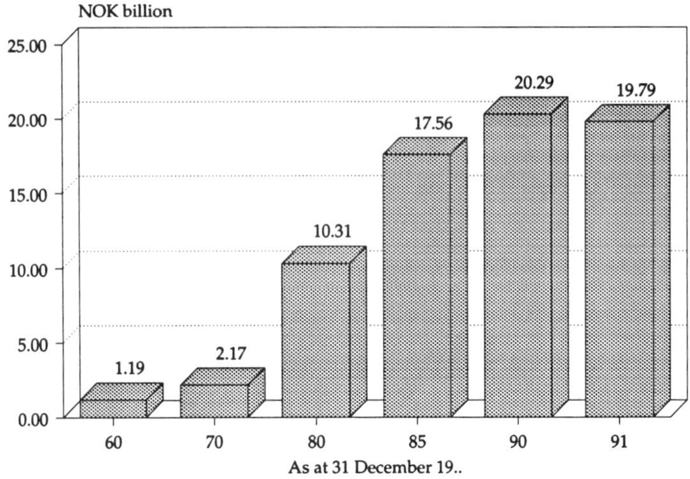

Figure 22.9 Outstanding volumes of government-guaranteed bonds

State banks and institutions with government guarantee

The state banks have an annual borrowing quota which is fixed by the national budget. Both Norges Kommunalbank and Den Norske Industribank AS raise funds by issuing bonds and certificates guaranteed by the Norwegian government. This quota will always be sensitive to changes in the economic and political environment. In the light of the problems experienced by commercial and savings banks in recent years, the quotas for state banks have been increased. Outstanding volumes in this sector are shown in Figure 22.9.

Local authorities and institutions with local authority guarantees

Local authorities have a large degree of autonomy over their funding activities in the bond market. Each issue, however, must be separately approved by public authorities at a high level. The vast majority of borrowing taken up by local authorities has been used to finance the municipal electricity supply.

Local authorities may either borrow directly in the bond market, or cover their financial needs through borrowings from Norges Kommunalbank or, to a certain degree, through commercial and savings banks, as well as through private mortgage institutions. The increasing focus on diversification by Norwe-

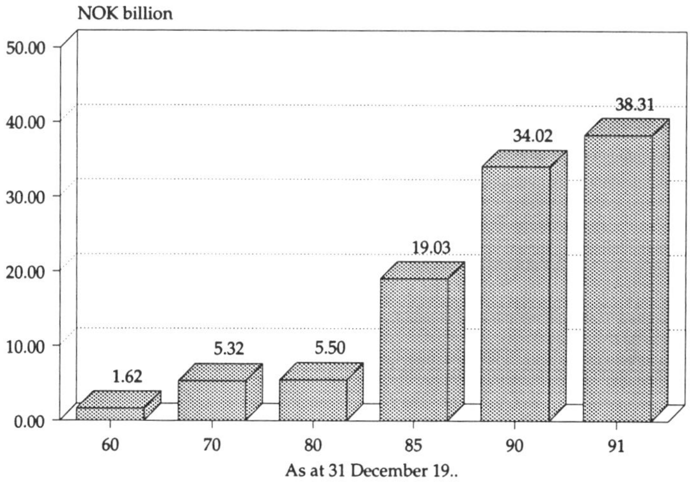

Figure 22.10 Outstanding volumes of bonds issued by local authorities and institutions with local authority guarantees.

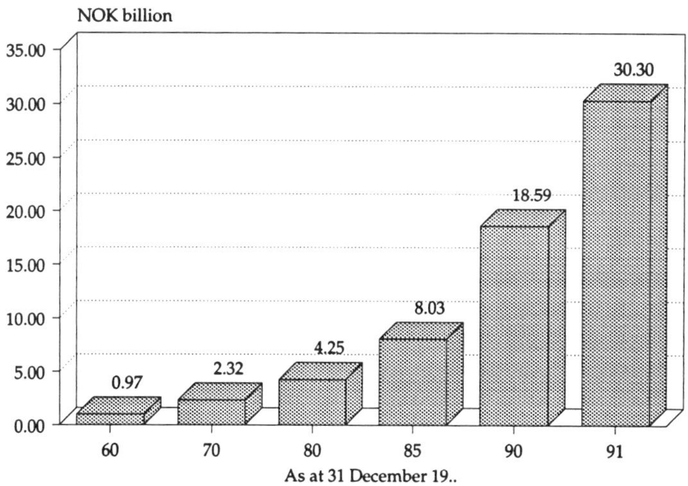

Figure 22.11 Outstanding volumes of corporate bonds

gian investors, combined with the desire for good-quality borrowers, has made it possible to make issues with principal amounts of NKr 25m, the lowest permitted. Outstanding volumes in this sector are shown in Figure 22.10.

Corporate borrowers

With the exception of shipping and offshore financing, this sector was completely deregulated in 1980. Many borrowers within this category have found it both more practical, and cheaper, to borrow from mortgage institutions, rather than issue bonds in their own name. The 'best' companies have often been able to achieve better terms by borrowing abroad. In 1990 and 1991, however, a number of the largest Norwegian companies issued bonds in the Norwegian market on very competitive terms. Examples are Norsk Hydro, Aker, Elkem, Norske Skog, Orkla, Hafslund and Saga. Outstanding volumes in this sector are shown in Figure 22.11.

Mortgage institutions

Most mortgage institutions make loans against collateral in the form of real estate, usually within a maximum limit of 70-80 per cent of the market value of the property. Funds are lent to the housing sector, industry and the public sector. Furthermore, there are companies which make loans against security to, amongst others, the shipping, fishing and agricultural industries.

Until the mid-1980s, the Norwegian credit market was characterized by regulation at a low level. For the bond market, the most important regulations were limitations on new issues, and the obligatory investment in bonds. Regulation of the supply of bonds, combined with the obligatory demand for these securities, enabled interest rates to be maintained at levels below normal market rates.

Following the abolition of the regulation of new issues and obligatory investment, interest rates on bonds began to rise. Simultaneously, the mortgage institutions' proportional share of total supply of credit started to increase. This was particularly evident after 1987, when regulations covering new issues by mortgage institutions for housing loans were scrapped. While mortgage institutions accounted for approximately 12 per cent of total credit supply in the period from 1982-85, their share increased to 27.4 per cent in the latter half of the decade and, by 1990, had this figure had increased to 44.7 per cent.

The sharp rise in market share towards the end of the 1980s occurred in a period in which the total credit supply increased dramatically, following the general liberalization of credit markets. Mortgage institutions experienced a formidable growth in lending to the general public in this period. In addition to the liberalization, this growth was fuelled by an expansive monetary policy, together with the fact that many groups had a negative real rate of after-tax interest.

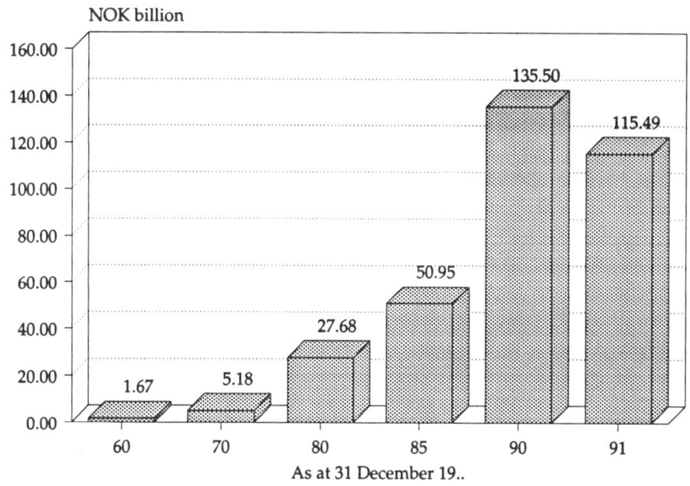

Figure 22.12 Outstanding volumes of mortgage institution bonds

As well as experiencing a liberalization in lending operations, mortgage institutions have also been given access to new sources of funding in recent years. In the middle of 1987, the certificate market was opened to this group and, in 1989, they were permitted to take up loans in foreign currencies. In May 1989, the Norwegian bond market was re-opened to foreign investors.

Demarcation lines within the credit market have faded in the course of the last few years. The move, in July 1989, to allow banks the right to issue bonds on the same terms as mortgage institutions, is of particular importance. Although the banks have so far made little use of this facility, it is expected that it will nevertheless become more common in the future - partly as a result of the banks' need for alternative sources of funding - and mortgage institutions may notice a resultant increase in competition.

An increase in losses and non-performing loans gives some cause for concern, even though the situation for mortgage institutions is far better than that for the banks. Losses have increased from 0.01 per cent of gross lending in 1987, to 0.87 per cent in 1990. This trend is due to the weak economy (and resultant fall in property markets), high unemployment and the sharply-rising real rate of interest after tax. The future development of losses and non-performing loans will depend on the development of the Norwegian economy in general, movements in property values, and the real rate of interest after tax.

Weakened confidence in Ncrwegian financial institutions, combined with a considerable imbalance between the supply and demand for mortgage institution bonds, contributed to an extremely turbulent market for this type of issue in 1991. Liquidity worsened and mortgage institutions had to pay a high-risk premium for new issuance. Outstanding volumes in this sector are shown in Figure 22.12.

In response to this situation, the latter half of 1991 saw a rapid movement towards major changes in the structure of the sector. The weakest institution, Den Norske Hypotekforening - DNH, began to be wound up while Realkreditt, the largest institution, commenced a merger with Den norske Bank. Other mortgage institutions are currently either considering mergers and co-operation agreements with other financial institutions, and/or are evaluating plans to apply for a bank concession. The main reason behind such moves is the institutions' desire to gain access to the same operational guidelines which apply to the banks and, thereby, increasing the potential for more flexibility on the liability side of the balance sheet.

Nevertheless, for both economic and structural reasons, there is little reason to believe that this group will increase market share further in the next few

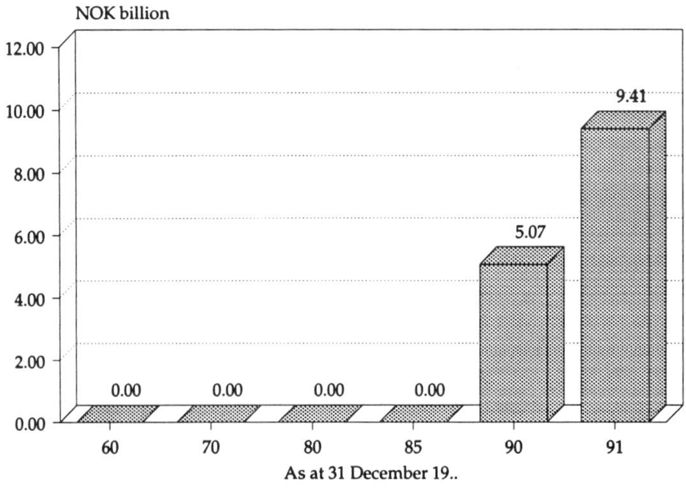

Figure 22.13 Outstanding volumes of bank bonds

years and, therefore, net bond issuance will be minimal. However, the large volume of redemptions will require large gross new issuance.

Banks

Prior to 1987, banks were not permitted to issue bonds. In 1987, however, banks were allowed to issue loans with a maximum two-year life. In 1989, this limitation on maturity was extended to three years, but it was not until 1990 that banks were able to issue bonds on the same terms as other groups of borrowers. Since 1990, a number of banks have used the bond market as a source of funding and this trend is expected to continue in the years to come. Outstanding volumes in this sector are shown in Figure 22.13.

Foreign borrowers

The domestic bond market was opened to foreign borrowers in 1989. Since then, four issues have been made, all from the Nordic countries. Outstanding volumes in this sector are shown in Figure 22.14.

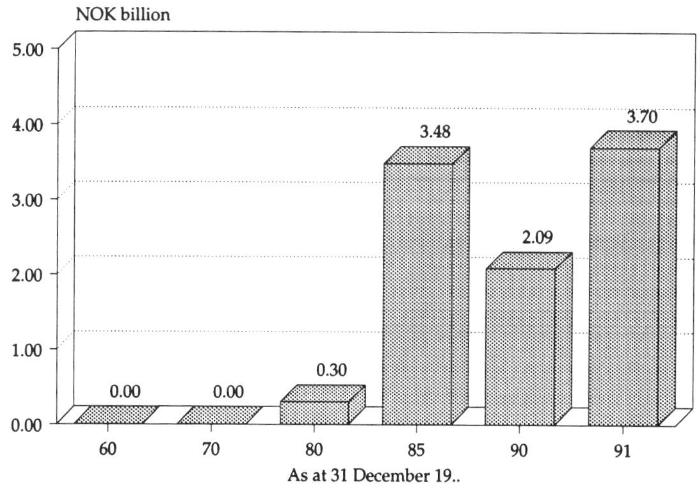

Figure 22.14 Outstanding volumes of bonds issued by foreign borrowers

22.4 Types of security

Until 1980, the Norwegian market was dominated by long-term, fixed-coupon loans, with or without a short period of grace before repayment started, and with either serial or annuity repayments. As the decade progressed, there was an increasing demand for, and supply of, issues carrying interest-regulation clauses. Initially, the clauses for adjustable interest rates were typically formu-

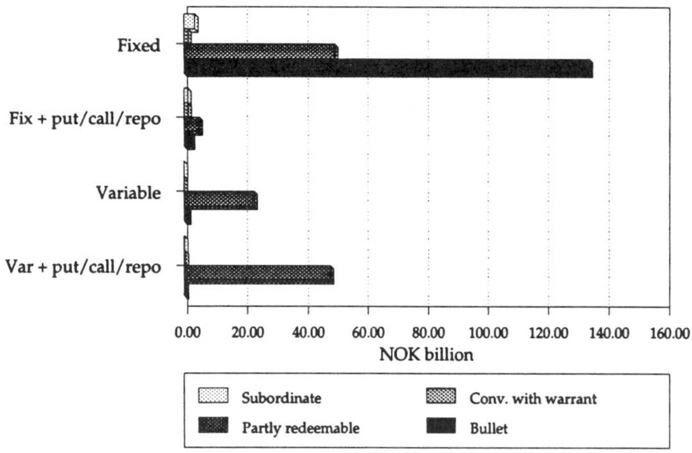

Figure 22.15 Composition of market by type of bond

lated in such a way that the interest rate would be adjusted to the same level as the market rate for new issues of the same quality, and the same redemption plan. This type of clause allowed for the considerable use of estimation, and led to major problems in the fixing of prices in the secondary market.

From the mid-eighties, these issues were replaced by issues with 20- to 30-year maturities, with an interest rate-regulation clause combined with a put option (the investor's right to redeem the bond), and an equivalent call option (the borrower's right to redemption).

In recent years, the trend has moved towards simpler bond types and this has led to an improvement in market liquidity, reflected in a strong rise in turnover volume on the secondary market.

Since 1988, most new issues have been bullet bonds with a life of up to five years. The mortgage institutions have paved the way for this development and bonds issued by this group have been among the most liquid in recent years. In 1991, a few bullet bonds with 10-year maturities have been issued by both the corporate sector and mortgage institutions. The maturity and coupon structures of the different types of security are shown in Figures 22.16 - 22.31, at the end of this section.

A number of bonds exist in the Norwegian market with clauses which diverge from the more typical examples described above. Such bonds, which are described below, are typified by small outstanding volumes and low turnover in the secondary market.

Callable bonds

Issues with a coupon fixed for the entire life of the bond, which may include a clause allowing for redemption at a price above par (which gradually decreases towards par over the life of the bond).

Bonds with repurchase clause

There are two variations on this kind of issue in the Norwegian market:

- Repurchase instead of instalment payment
- Repurchase to write-down debt outstanding

Other bonds

Other bond types in the Norwegian market include premium bonds and bonds with stepped-coupons.

Composition of market by type of guarantee

In the Norwegian market, issues fall into one of seven categories according to type of guarantee.

- 1. Kingdom of Norway bonds and bonds guaranteed by the government
- 2. Issues by local and county councils, and institutions guaranteed by same.

- 3. Issues by mortgage institutions and banks
- 4. Mortgage loans
- 5. Negative pledge
- 6. Unsecured loans
- 7. Subordinated loan capital

Guaranteed issues (1 and 2)

Loans in this category are most-commonly guaranteed by the Norwegian government, or local government/authorities

Issues by mortgage institutions and banks (3)

The security for issues made by mortgage companies is the institution's own funds (defined as equity, subordinated loan capital, *en bloc* reserves etc.), plus commitments made by the institution's borrowers/members.

Most mortgage institutions grant loans against collateral in the form of real estate. The maximum size of a loan is some 70 to 80 per cent of the assessed value of the mortgaged property. The Articles of Association of each individual mortgage institution (approved by the Norwegian Banking, Insurance and Securities Commission), provide the basis for the operations of the company.

Mortgage loans (4)

The borrower offers a first-priority mortgage in real estate, as security for the bond. These issues are usually regulated by the guidelines which apply for investments made by life insurance companies.

Negative pledge (5)

Negative pledge implies that the borrower commits himself not to offer specified collateral against later debt, without offering similar security to the earlier issue. However, it is important to note that some loan agreements allow the borrower to deviate from the definition of negative pledge.

Unsecured loans (6)

With an unsecured loan, the borrower does not provide any security for the bond. The lender makes the loan in good faith, assuming that the borrower will service the debt in the future.

Subordinated loan capital (7)

This type of debt is usually issued by finance institutions. It is unsecured and has lower priority than all other debt.

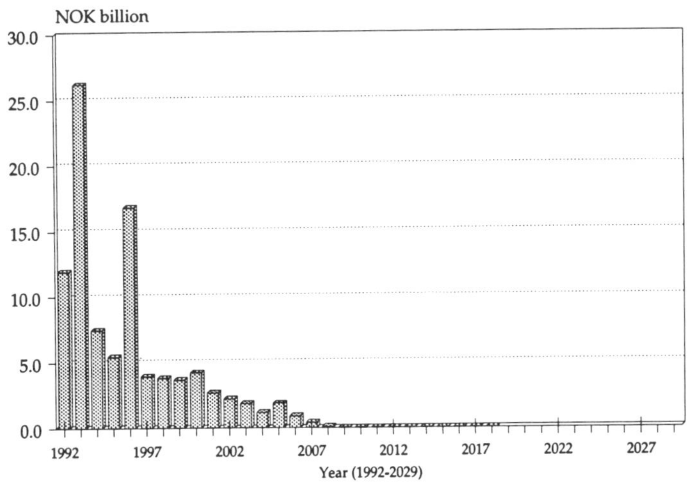

Figure 22.16 Maturity structure of the government bond market (incl. guaranteed issues)

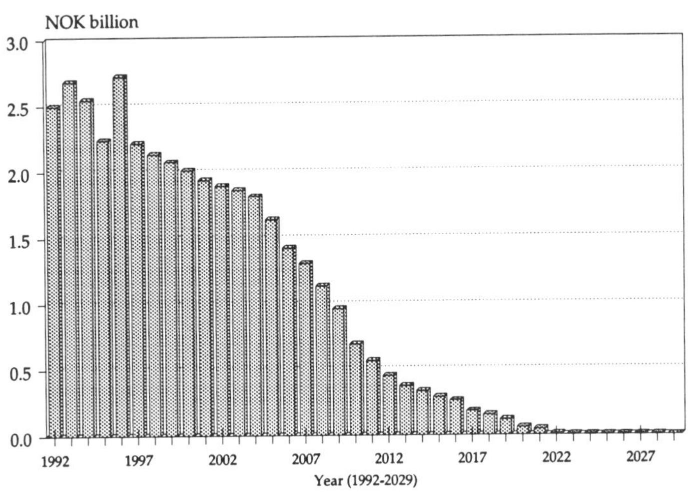

Figure 22.17 Maturity structure of the local authority bond market

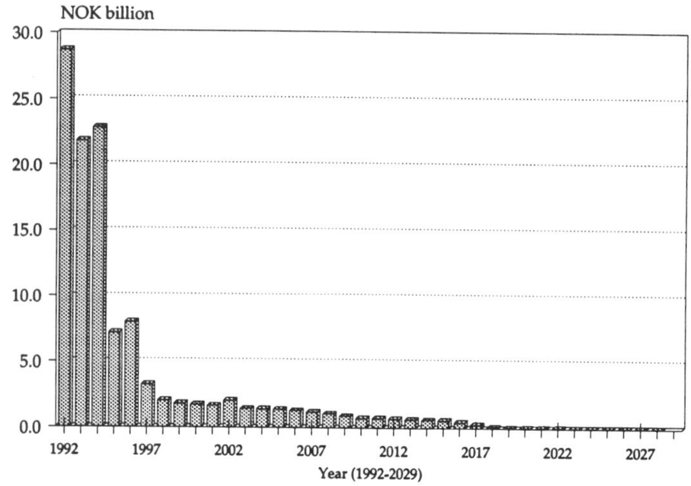

Figure 22.18 Maturity structure of the mortgage bond market

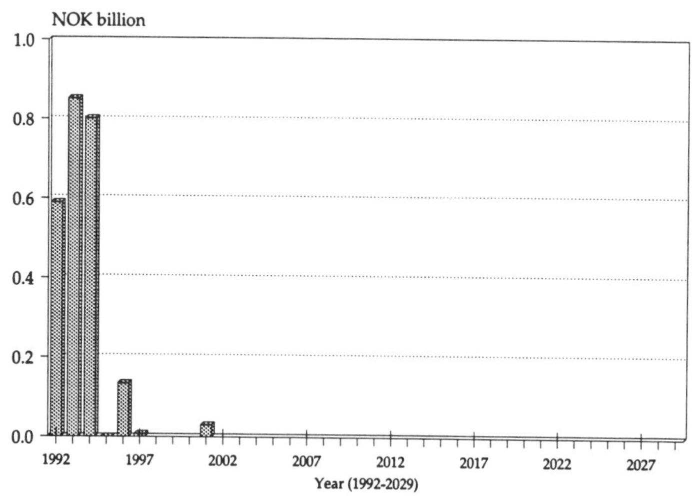

Figure 22.19 Maturity structure of the bank bond market

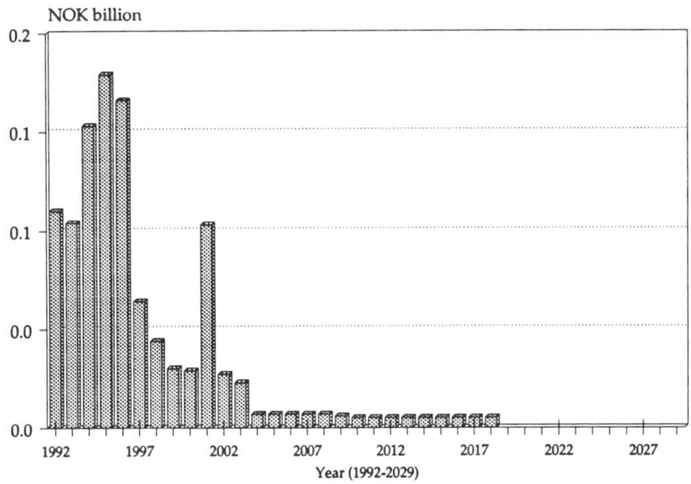

Figure 22.20 Maturity structure of the corporate bond market

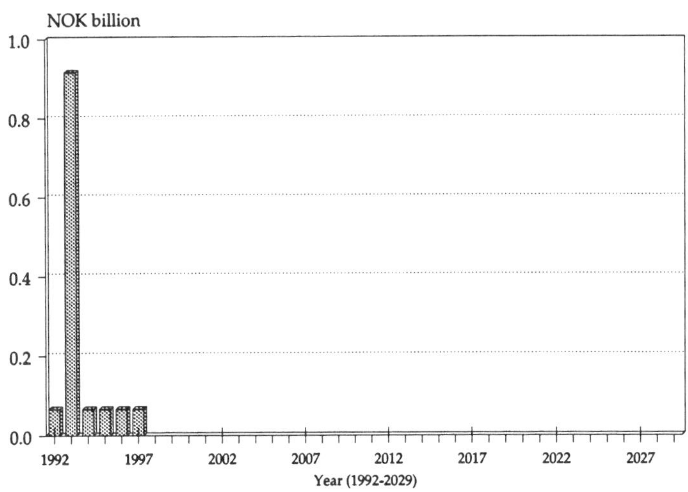

Figure 22.21 Maturity structure of the foreign bond market

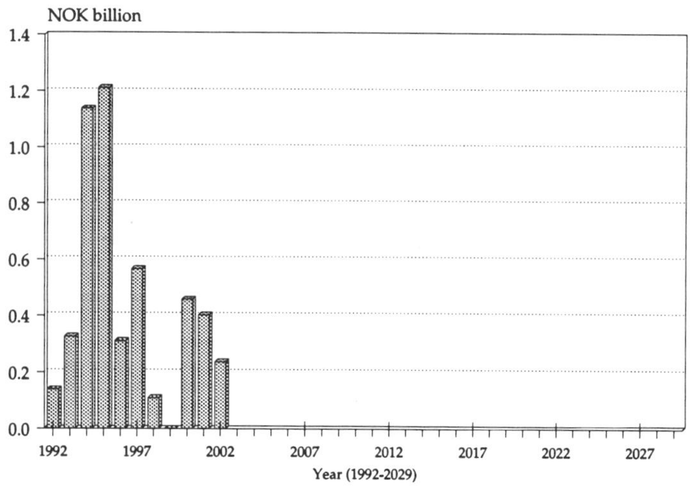

Figure 22.22 Maturity structure of the subordinated loan capital market

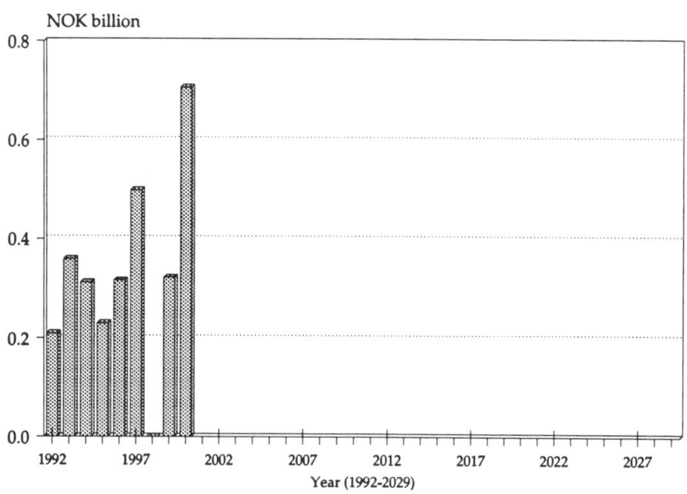

Figure 22.23 Maturity structure of the convertible bond market

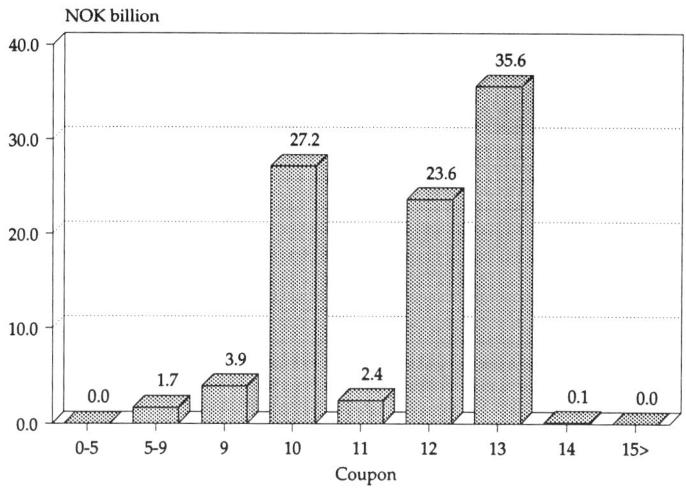

Figure 22.24 Coupon structure of the government bond market (incl. guaranteed bonds)

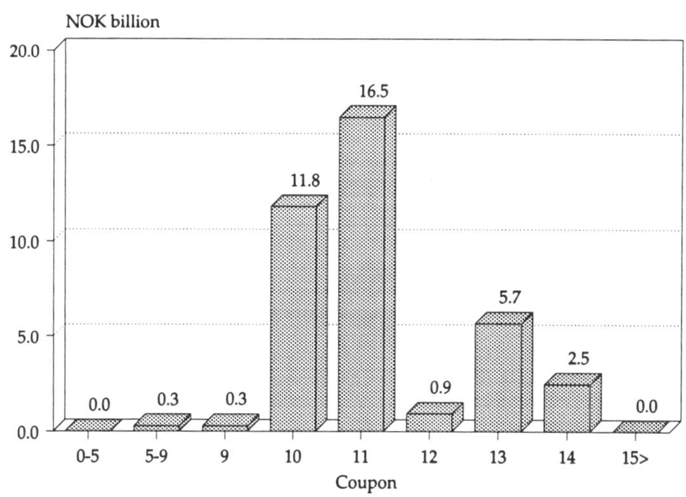

Figure 22.25 Coupon structure of the local authority bond market

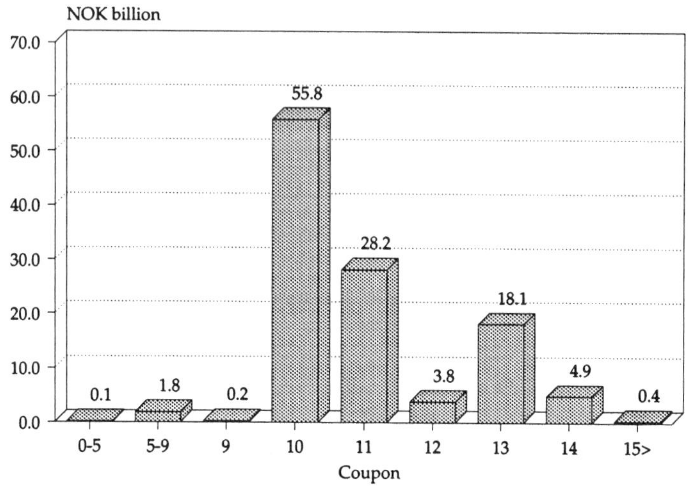

Figure 22.26 Coupon structure of the mortgage bond market

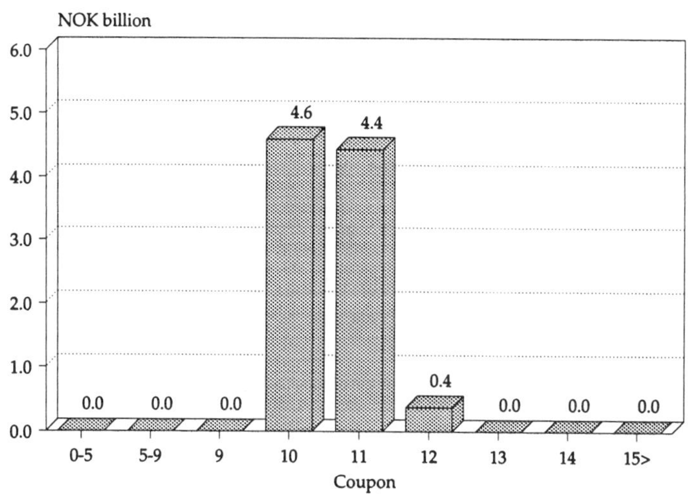

Figure 22.27 Coupon structure of the bank bond market

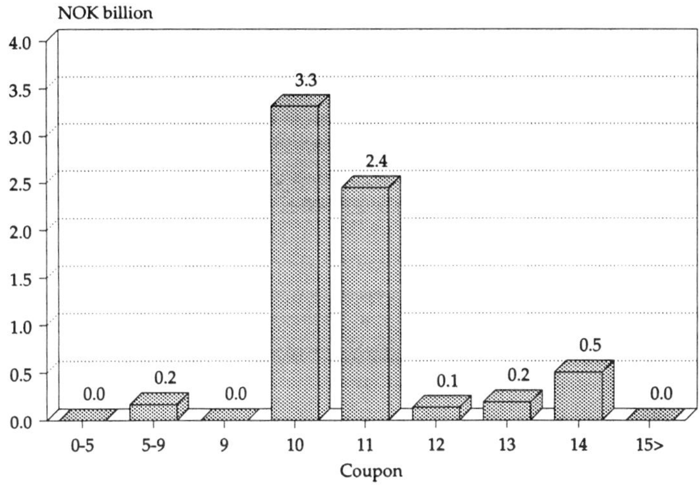

Figure 22.28 Coupon structure of the corporate bond market

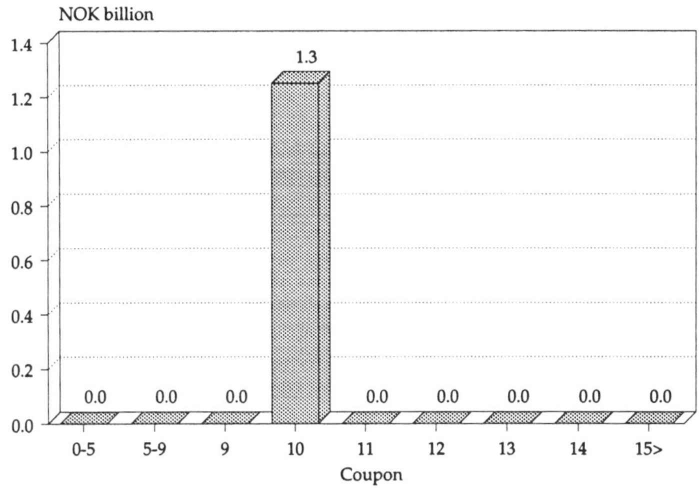

Figure 22.29 Coupon structure of the foreign bond market

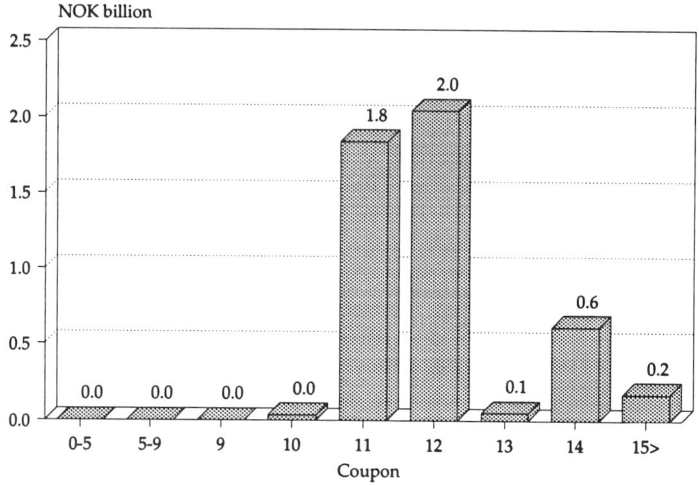

Figure 22.30 Coupon structure of the subordinated loan capital market

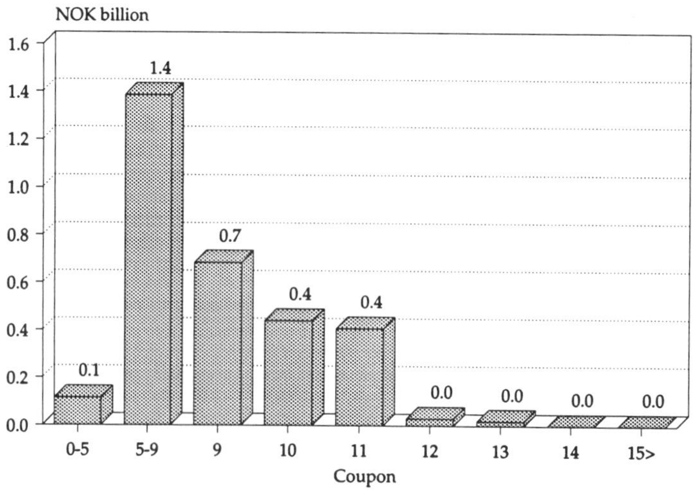

Figure 22.31 Coupon structure of the convertible bond market

22.5 *Issuers*

As illustrated in Figure 22.32, credit institutions represent the largest group of issuers in the Norwegian market for listed bonds, accounting for 41.2 per cent of the total volume of NKr 26,961.6m outstanding as at 31 December 1991. The government's share amounts to 26.2 per cent, local authorities account for 13.15 per cent, thereafter government guaranteed with 7.12 per cent, industry with 6.1 per cent, bank and insurance with 4.8 per cent and foreign issuers account for 1.4 per cent.

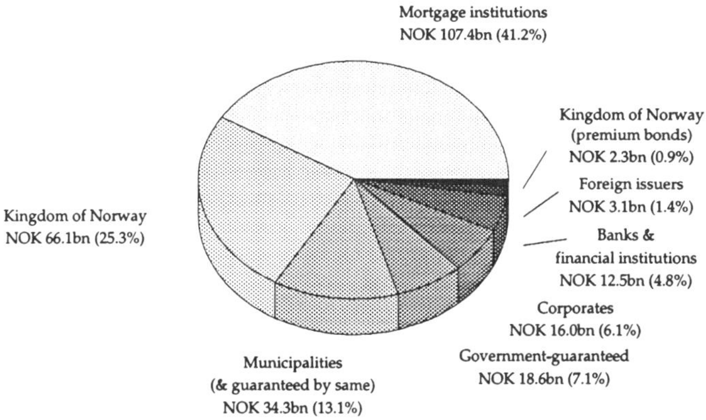

Figure 22.32 Issuers in the Norwegian bond market

The Norwegian Government

The Norwegian government's borrowing in the bond market must be seen in relation to the deficit in the National Budget, which basically defines the government's borrowing requirement. In the period from 1987 to 1990, no new government issues were made in Norway, but borrowing was carried out in international financial markets in JPY, USD and GBP. In 1991, the government made issues in USD and Ecu and in JPY in 1992. The Debt Office, a department in the Treasury, implements foreign borrowing for the Norwegian government. The government's foreign debt has developed as follows:

31 December 1985	NOK 52.5m
31 December 1986	NOK 6578.2m
31 December 1987	NOK 9324.1m
31 December 1988	NOK 15,050.8m
31 December 1989	NOK 17,289.4m
31 December 1990	NOK 16,862.9m
31 December 1991	NOK 25,953.3m

Source: The Treasury

Norges Bank has acted as lead-manager for issues in Norway. The government is not subject to regulations covering new issues but even so, has made use of stockbrokers and offered bonds for public subscription in previous issues. As lead-manager, Norges Bank has been responsible for publicizing the issue, preparation of the subscription offer document and so on, whilst subscriptions have taken place with brokers.

In February 1991, the government issued a bond (security no. 100459 - s459) for the first time since 1986. Norges Bank was the sole subscription place. The tradition of public offers for sale was broken with this issue, and NKr 6bn was sold by Dutch auction. The remaining NKr 6bn was reserved for Norges Bank (NKr 4bn) and other central instances (NKr 2bn). The right has been reserved to make subsequent increases in the issue. The notes carry a 10 per cent coupon, with a five year fixed maturity. A tender offer of 98.90 was accepted from all the offers made, which prices the notes at a yield of 10.29 per cent. The issue has one annual coupon payment, again diverging from the norm of two semi-annual payments.

In January 1992, the government issued a new Kingdom of Norway bond (security no. 100462 - S462). The same procedure as in the issue of S459 was followed: Norges Bank as the only subscription place, Dutch auction of NKr 4bn and NKr 4bn reserved for Norges Bank. Again, the government reserves the right to make subsequent extensions to the issue. The coupon is 9 per cent, seven year term with fixed maturity and one annual coupon payment. The lowest accepted tender was 99.3, equivalent to a yield of 9.14 per cent.

In order to support liquidity, Norges Bank operates in the market through stockbrokers. Every four months, Norges Bank invites offers from Norwegian stockbrokers for to undertake a "market-maker" function for government bonds. Through these brokers, Norges Bank currently makes two-way prices in 5 issues and bid prices, alone, in 6 bonds.

Issues with government guarantee

Borrowers with loans carrying a government guarantee are: Den norske Industribank, Norges Kommunalbank, Selskapet for Industrivekst, Låneinstituttet for Skip, A/S Sydvaranger, A/S Fastlandsfinans.
Låneinstituttet for Skip has merged with Norsk Skibs Hypothekbank, under the name Norsk Skibs Hypothekbank AS and new issues of the merged company are not eligible for government guarantee.

Issues by Norsk Skibs Hypothekbank are listed on the Oslo Stock Exchange under the section for mortgage institutions. Selskapet for Industrivekst A/S (SIVA) is a government organization which now has 3 issues listed on the Oslo Stock Exchange. The bonds have been issued through public subscriptions, and are bullet loans. For its most recent issue, 9.40 per cent 1991/1994, dispensation from the regulations covering new issues was granted, such that this is an open series and subsequent tranches may be issued without an underwriting syndicate, and at market price. So far, NKr 200m of the bond has been issued, by means of a public offer for sale.

October 1991 saw the entrance of a new borrower with a government guarantee - A/S Fastlandsfinans. This company is owned by five county councils/local authorities. Total liabilities are guaranteed by the government, Møre og Romsdal county council and private banks in the ratio 50 - 40 - 10. Each individual issue is guaranteed separately by one of the underwriters. In 1991, an issue of NKr 200m carrying a government guarantee was made through of a public offer for sale, at par. The nominal coupon is 9.80 per cent p.a. with interest adjustment and the option to exercise a put/call after one year. The issue has five years of grace, and is then repayable over fifteen years at the rate of one instalment annually. Earlier in 1991, the same borrower issued a bond through public subscription, this time with a local authority guarantee, with a 10.75 per cent coupon, again with an interest rate adjustment clause and a put/call option.

Den Norske Industribank A/S is 51 per cent owned by the Norwegian state and 49 per cent by private shareholders. The bank's primary role is to provide investment loans for the extension, modernization and adaptation of Norwegian industry. Since 1987, Industribanken has generally issued bullet bonds, that is, fixed-interest and fixed maturity. In 1990, Industribanken raised a total of NKr 1860m in the domestic bond market. This is split between NKr 1400m offered for sale at par in three new issues and NKr 460m through extending open series. In 1991, Industribanken issued 4 new bonds totalling NKr 1200m at par through public offers for sale. A further NKr 1075m has since been raised through direct placements in the market, at market prices.

Norges Kommunalbank is a state bank which lends to local authorities with a view to encouraging projects given priority by central government. Previously, Kommunalbanken covered its borrowing requirement in both the domestic and international capital markets. However, since 1988, the bank has held itself to the domestic market on instructions from the Treasury. Since 1987, Kommunalbanken has generally issued bonds with a fixed-coupon, fixed maturity and a call option for the borrower. In 1990, Kommunalbanken made six new issues. Five of these included a call option for the borrower, maturities of ten to fifteen years and were offered for sale at par. The sixth issue was a two year fixed bond, in which first two tranches were offered for public subscription, NKr 400m at par and NKr 300m at 100.15 per cent. Thereafter, NKr 200m was sold over the counter at market prices. In addition, a further NKr 1100m was issued through increasing open series from 1989. In 1991, Kommunalbanken has made one issue of NKr 350m through public offer for sale at par. It has 15 years to redemption, and includes a call option for the borrower. Both Industribanken and Kommunalbanken have older issues carrying a fixed-coupon and a period of grace followed by repayment in semi-annual instalments. Some of these issues also have a put/call option on the interest regulation dates. Industribanken now has six issues and Kommunalbanken 4 bonds quoted in the Section for Major Issues on the Oslo Stock Exchange. Bonds quoted in the Section for Major Issues have a minimum size of NKr 500m, and are bullet issues without any put/call clauses.

This group of borrowers has no market-maker arrangements linked to its issues.

Local authority, municipal bonds and issues guaranteed by same

At the end of December 1991, the nominal value of issues listed in this sector of the Oslo Stock Exchange was NKr 34,313.0m. This was divided between 340 issues. Borrowers with a county council or local authority guarantee are generally power stations, but also includes some road companies. New legislation covering power stations came into effect on 1 January 1991, with a view to ensuring free competition within the electricity market. Consumers should now be able to purchase electricity from the cheapest generator. Distributors of electricity remain in a monopoly situation.

Issues made by this group are offered for sale by public subscription as described above. Most are in series, with no period of grace, and are governed by the Regulation of New Issues, Section 7.

Issuers in this sector borrow partially in their own right and partially through Den norske Stats Husbank, Den norske Kommunalbank and mortgage institutions. Borrowers vary considerable in size. Oslo Kommune, with outstanding bond debt of NKr 10,157m at 31 December 1990 is one of the largest. Other major borrowers within this group are Trondheim Kommune, Bergen Kommune and a number of electricity utilities such as: Bergenshalvøens Kommunale Kraftselskap, Lyse Kraft, Tafjord Kraft and Øvre Otra. Issues vary in size from NKr 25m to NKr 500m. A number of borrowers within this group also operate in international markets. To mention a few examples, Oslo Kommune has an AA (long-term) rating from Standard & Poor's, and Oppland Energiverk was granted a licence for long-term borrowing in foreign currencies equivalent to NKr 1300m in 1987. It should be noted that some borrowers within this sector have also issued bonds secured by collateral and without a local authority guarantee, for example, Nordkraft.

In October 1991, Oslo Kommune was granted dispensation from Section 7 of the Regulations of New Issues, and issued a NKr 500m bullet with a nominal coupon of 10 per cent and redemption in 1996. The bond was offered for sale by public subscription, and will be quoted in the section for large issues on the Oslo Stock Exchange. In March 1992, Bergen Kommune also made an issue of NKr 500m, with fixed maturity, a five year term and 9.75% coupon. Dispensation from section 7 of Regulations for New Issues has been applied for, so that the issue may be made as an open series.

This group of borrowers has not taken advantage of any market-maker arrangements.

Banks, insurance and finance companies

Banks and finance companies used to cover their funding requirements in the international capital markets. From 1 July 1987, they were permitted to issue bonds of up to 2 years duration and later, on 12 April 1989, this was extended to three years. Finally, these limitations were entirely lifted on 6 July 1990 and they were then able to issue bonds according to the same guidelines which applied to mortgage institutions. Bonds in this sector may either be offered for public subscription, or be placed privately. Nowadays, banks often issue open series, whereby the first tranche is offered for public subscription at par, with later tranches being placed directly in the market, at market terms. As a rule, banks do not establish specific security for these issues.

A market-maker panel makes two-way prices in two issues by Den norske Bank and one each by Christiania Bank og Kreditkasse and Sparebanken NOR.

Insurance companies may not take up loans through the issuance of bonds. However, in order to meet the authorities' equity requirements, they are nevertheless permitted to take up subordinated loan capital in the form of bonds and convertible issues, subject to the approval of the Treasury. For banks and finance institutions, the requirement for separate approval from the Treasury to take up subordinated loan capital in the form of bonds, was abolished in July 1990.

There are now 36 issues of subordinated notes listed on the Oslo Stock Exchange, of which 20 are issued by banks, 7 by mortgage institutions and 9 by insurance companies.

Mortgage institutions

There were twelve active mortgage institutions in Norway at the end of 1991.

- Bolig- og Næringskreditt A/S

Bolig- og Næringskreditt A/S is a joint-stock company in which commercial banks hold some 45 per cent of the share capital. The company has applied for a concession to operate as a bank. Total assets and gross lending as at 31 December 1991 were NKr 20.7bn and NKr 18.8bn respectively.

- A/S Eksportfinans

A/S Eksportfinans is owned by Norwegian commercial and savings banks. The company is a central institution in Norway in financing exports of Norwegian produced capital goods. Lending in foreign currencies is financed through borrowing in international money and capital markets. The company is rated A1+ (short-term) and AAA (long-term) by Standard and Poor's, and P1 (short-term) and AAA (long-term) by Moody's. Total assets and gross lending as at 31 December 1991 were NKr 29.7bn and NKr 16.1bn respectively.

- Norgeskreditt

Norgeskreditt is organized as an association of borrowers. The company has adopted a resolution to convert to a joint-stock company. Norgeskreditt makes medium and long-term loans, primarily to industry. Total assets were NKr 21.3bn and gross lending was NKr 19.5bn as at 31 December 1991.

- Realkreditt

Realkreditt was converted from an association to a joint-stock company in 1991. The company has since been taken over by Den norske Bank, which intends to operate the company as a wholly owned subsidiary. Realkreditt's industrial portfolio will probably be transferred to Den norske Bank, whilst the portfolio of housing loans will remain in Realkreditt. Total assets and gross lending per 31 December 1991 were NKr 25.3bn and NKr 23.2bn respectively.

- Sparebankkreditt

Sparebankkreditt is 76.5 per cent owned by Sparebanken NOR, following the expiry of Sparebanken NOR's takeover bid on 13th March 1992. Sparebankkreditt provides loans to industry and the public sector. It also gives mortgages for housing purposes. Total assets and gross lending as at 31 December 1991 were NKr 17.5bn and NKr 15.8bn respectively.

- Vestenfjelske Bykreditt A/S

Vestenfjelske Bykreditt A/S was converted from an association to a joint stock company in 1991. In 1992, the company has applied for a concession to achieve bank status. The company provides medium and long-term loans to industry, public sector projects and in the form of mortgages to housebuyers. Total assets and gross lending as at 31 December 1991 were NKr 11.5bn and NKr 10.3bn respectively.

- Norges Hypotekinstitutt A/S
- Norsk Skibs Hypothekbank A/S
- Skipskredittforeningen

These institutions make loans primarily to the shipping industry.

- Eiendomslån AS

One new mortgage institution, Eiendomslån AS, has been established in 1990. The company's principal aims are to provide housing mortgages, and to finance renovations and improvements for existing housing. The company has borrowed in the certificate market but, in October 1991, it issued an open bond, in which an initial NKr 100m was offered for public subscription, at par.

With many small issues, mortgage institutions have, in the past, have been very active in the primary market. In the period 1980-1984, such a bond usually featured a fixed-coupon and a period of grace followed by repayment in equal semi-annual, or annual, instalments. From 1985-6, put/call options were introduced on a number of issues; some of the older issues also have a repurchase option. In more recent years, the trend has been towards fewer but larger issues, in open series with a fixed redemption date. Mortgage institutions issued 75 new bonds in 1989, 24 in 1990 and 12 in 1991.

In 1991, Norsk Skibs Hypothekbank issued an open series with a coupon of 6-months NIBOR + 0.20 percentage points. The coupon shall be fixed two days prior to IMM dates in September and March. Initially, NKr 300m was offered for public subscription, and this was later increased to NKr 550m. This is the very first issue in the Norwegian market in which the coupon is fixed in connection with IMM dates. Two mortgage institutions have since made two equivalent issues. In December, Norgeskreditt offered a three year bond, coupon 6-month NIBOR + 0.50 percentage points to be fixed two banking days prior to IMM dates in December and June. The principal amount for this issue was also NKr 300m, and so far has not been extended. In 1992, Vestenfjelske Bykreditt A/S has issued a two-year bond, coupon equal to 6-month NIBOR + 70 basis points. The coupon is to be set on IMM dates in March and September. The principal amount was NKr 80m, and was issued by private placement. This issue may not be extended.

There have been major changes in this sector in recent years. Partly as a result of the new capital adequacy requirements, mortgage institutions which were previously organized as associations, are now being reorganized into limited companies, a number of which intend to be, or already are, listed on the stock exchange. To varying degrees, mortgage institutions have been affected by the recent problems in the Norwegian financial sector.

Mortgage Institutions generally issue open series, offered directly in the market.

Almost all bonds issued by mortgage institutions are listed on the Oslo Stock Exchange, and some 40 issues are quoted in the section for Large Issues. The average size of these issues is NKr 1 to 2bn , the largest being NKr 4bn . Realkreditt, Bolig-og Næringskreditt A/S, SparebanKreditt A/S, Vestenfjeldske Bykreditt A.S and Norgeskreditt, additionally have issues listed on the Copenhagen Exchange.

Most mortgage institutions also have their own pages on Reuters, where a market-maker panel make prices via the Oslo Stock Exchange in a number of selected issues. Generally, these are two-way prices but, for some issues, solely bid prices are made. The liquidity of these issues has been good.

Industrial and trading companies

Bonds in this section are issued through public subscription. Borrowers are not only the larger Norwegian corporations (such as Norsk Hydro, Orkla, Hafslund, Saga and Statoil), but also smaller companies (such as power stations, and so on). Generally, loans in this sector are repayable in instalments, but larger borrowers who have taken up loans over the last couple of years have also issued bonds with a fixed maturity. Security is usually in the form of negative pledge or ordinary collateral.

As at March 1992, Norsk Hydro has eight issues quoted in the Large Issues section of the Oslo Stock Exchange and Orkla, two. In September 1990, Norske Skog was granted a dispensation from the Regulations for New Issues, and issued an open series, of which NKr 500m was offered for sale by public subscription, at par. This issue has later been extended by NKr 405m, placed directly in the market, at market terms.

In December 1991, Orkla was granted dispensation from the Regulations for New Issues and issued a five year bullet with a 10.5 per cent coupon. NKr 500m was offered for public subscription, at par. In February 1992, Saga Petroleum received a similar dispensation and issued a ten year bond, fixed maturity, 10.5 per cent coupon and NKr 1bn principal amount.

A number of listed companies within industry, shipping and oil have also issued convertible bonds, and 16 such issues are listed on the Oslo Stock Exchange.

Foreign borrowers

From December 1989, foreigners have been permitted to issue NKr-denominated bonds in Norway (subject to receiving a licence from Norges Bank), and four foreign borrowers, Den Nordiske Investeringsbank, Okobank, SAS and Swedish Export Credit issued such loans in 1990. All four were offered for sale by public subscription, with Norwegian lead-managers, as is stipulated for this kind of issue. The bonds are quoted in a separate section on the Oslo Stock Exchange.

Issuance of these bonds is governed by the Section, in the Regulation of New Issues, which deals with long-term loans taken up by those other than finance institutions.

22.6 *Investors*

Overview

The Norwegian bond market is, to all extents and purposes, dominated by institutional investors, of which the National Insurance Fund is the largest individual participant (see Figure 22.33).

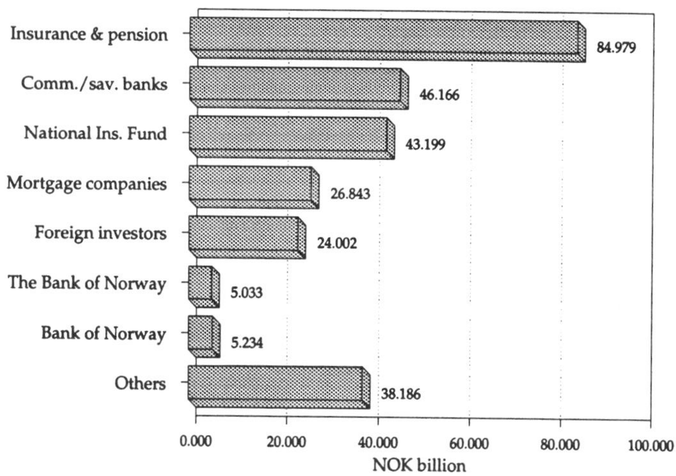

Figure 22.33 Composition of the market by investor

The National Insurance Fund

The National Insurance Fund was formed in 1967, as a step towards the establishment of a central state pension fund covering all adults in Norway.

A large proportion of the Fund's assets is invested in bearer-bonds (see Figure 22.34), and on deposit with commercial and savings banks. In the last few years, the public authorities have not made any transfers to the National Insurance Fund, so that any increase in assets is purely due to earned interest.

The Fund is obliged to hold a large proportion of its investment in the form of government and government-guaranteed bonds. The Fund purchases government bonds directly from Norges Bank. The National Insurance Fund's operational guidelines are currently under revision.

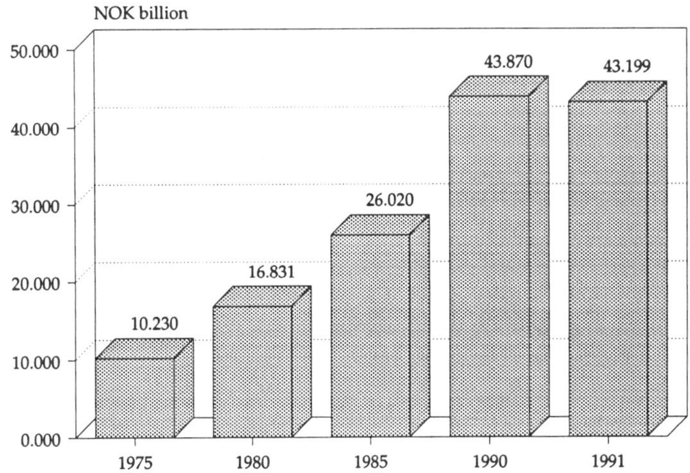

Figure 22.34 The development of the National Insurance Fund's bond portfolio:

Post Office Savings Bank and Postgiro

These two government-owned institutions are subject to quota regulations on lending and are obliged to place a large proportion of combined assets in government and government-guaranteed bonds. As at 31 December 1991, the Post Office Savings Bank and Postgiro held bond portfolios worth a total of NKr 5.033bn.

Norges Bank

Norges was founded in 1916. Its tasks with respect to the bond market are, amongst others:

- the arranging the issue of all new Kingdom of Norway bonds, either by public subscription or by direct sales.

- the carrying out of market operations. In the event that there is too much liquidity in the market, the central bank can withdraw funds through the sale of government bonds. Conversely, on occasions when liquidity is tight, government bonds can be purchased to ease the situation. For this system to function it is, of course, pre-requisite that the yield on government bonds is in line with the market at all times, so that institutional investors are willing to purchase/sell these securities.

Of the total outstanding volume in government bonds of NKr 67.761bn, Norges Bank holds NKr 5.214bn, equivalent to 7.7 per cent.

Commercial and savings banks

By tradition, commercial banks invest a proportion of their funds in bonds. The level of investment rose considerably in 1969, following the introduction of the obligatory bond investment requirement.

However, as a result of the abolition of this requirement in 1985 and, more recently, as a result of funding problems and adaptation to new, more rigorous, capital adequacy requirements, the banks have reduced their relative share of bondholding (see Figure 22.35).

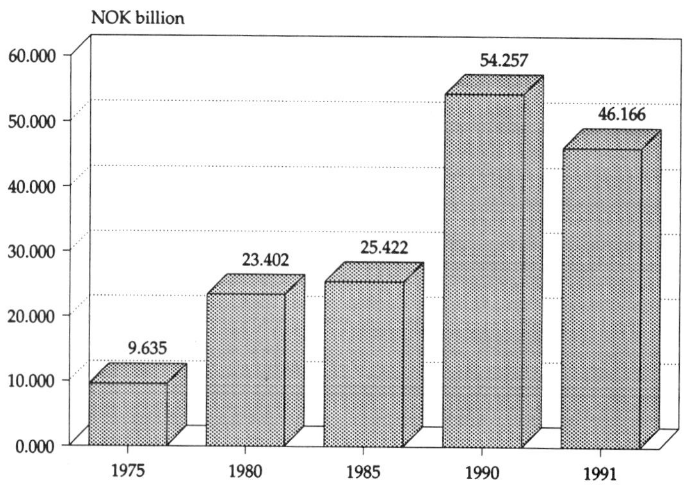

Figure 22.35 Development of bondholdings by commercial and savings banks

Banks are subject to a liquidity reserve requirement, which is met through the banks' holding of government bonds and government certificates. In 1991, the liquidity reserve requirement was slackened, and this has resulted in a reduction in the need to hold government and government-guaranteed bonds.

Insurance companies and pension funds

Life insurance companies receive their funds in the form of paid-up insurance premiums, and until 1985, were required to place up to 60 per cent of asset growth in bonds.

Following the abolition of the obligatory bond investment requirement in 1985, the relative share of bondholdings from this group has gradually been reduced. Over the last couple of years, life insurance companies have been more concerned about diversification, one consequence of which has been a reduction of this sector's holdings of mortgage institution bonds. Amendments made in 1990, to the law governing insurance companies, has resulted in a liberalization of their asset management.

Private pension funds have been subject to regulation which mirrors that of the life insurance companies, with the result that the development of both has been almost completely parallel (see Figure 22.36).

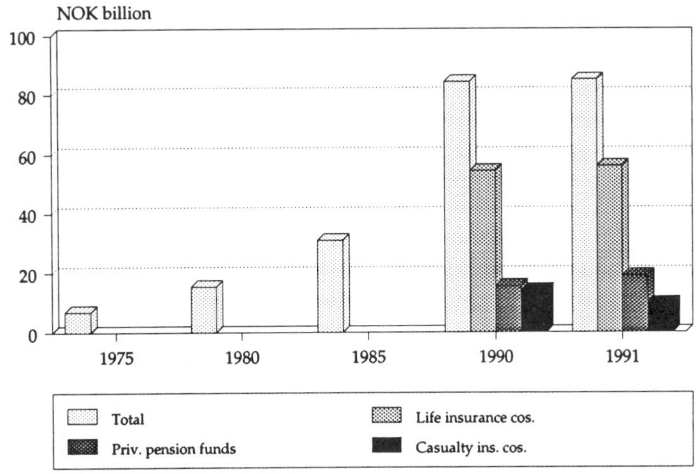

Note: 1975-85 figs. unclassified

Figure 22.36 Development of bondholdings of insurance companies and pension funds

Mortgage institutions

Over the last few years, mortgage institutions have increased their holding of bonds. This factor has more to do with their own re-financing activities, and support of their own bonds in the market, rather than their role as investor. Statistics also indicate that mortgage institutions are large holders of their own bonds.

Foreign investors

The domestic bond market was reopened to foreign investors in May 1989. Since then, foreign investors have increased holdings to NKr 24.002bn at the end of 1991. In particular, foreign holdings of private mortgage institution bonds increased sharply NKr 17.997bn It is assumed that this is due to the importance foreigners place on liquidity in the secondary market, together with the considerable yield gap between Kingdom of Norway bonds and mortgage institutions.

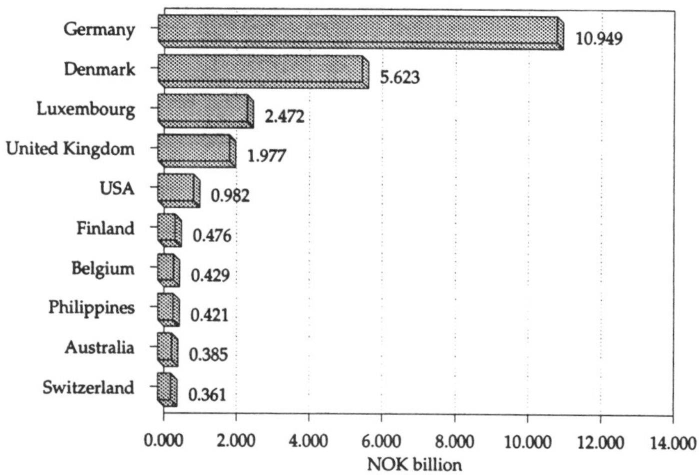

Figure 22.37 Origin of foreign investors

22.7 *Methods of issuance*

Public subscription

Most borrowers in the Norwegian market issue through public subscription. The borrower first approaches a number of brokers, who then tender for the issue. The broker offering the best terms is appointed lead-manager, responsible for placing the issue in the market. In this context, 'terms' refer to coupon, underwriting, commission and subscription fees. The next stage is for the lead-manager to establish an underwriting group, comprising contacts/investors.

The lead-manager prepares both the subscription offer document and prospectus for the bond, and makes an application to Norges Bank for approval of the issue. In accordance with Section 9 of the Securities Trading Act, the Oslo Stock Exchange shall "review the content of every offer to subscribe for, or similarly acquire, securities when the offer is made to more than fifty persons and the size of the issue is over NKr 5m". All subscription documents must be submitted to the Board of the Oslo Stock Exchange for review no later than one week prior to the offer. Stock Exchange Regulations lay down requirements concerning the content of both the subscription offer document and the prospectus. The issue cannot be made until a written confirmation has been received from Norges Bank, that the conditions for the issue have been fulfilled.(Regulations for New Issues S14).

Once approval has been received from the Oslo Stock Exchange, and prior to any subscription taking place, the lead-manager distributes the documents and prospectus to the subscription places. Immediately following the close of subscription, the Oslo Stock Exchange is informed of the result. The borrower usually has a clause in the subscription offer document reserving the right to reduce, or annul, any subscription if the issue is oversubscribed. If the loan is not fully subscribed, then the underwriters take up the issue, in accordance with the underwriting agreement. Should the lead-manager be left with the majority of the issue, as a result of its underwriting commitment, the bonds are usually sold later in the secondary market.

Issues offered for public subscription must apply for a stock exchange listing and the principal amount must be at least NKr 25m. The lead-manager makes an application for a listing, together with the announcement of the result of the subscription. As a rule, bonds are listed on the first Friday following the settlement date. Furthermore, the stock exchange listing implies that the borrower has a duty of information towards the exchange/market. Announcements of new coupon, puts/calls, results and so on, must always be sent to the Oslo Stock Exchange, which will then publicize the information.

The function of lead-manager can be assumed by private broking houses or banks' broking subsidiaries. Often, the banks are agents, while private brokers arrange the offering. In this connection, a contract is drawn up between borrower and agent/organizer. The agent enters into the contract on behalf of the lender and, in some areas, is also given the authority to act on behalf of same. The most important points in the contract of issue form part of the subscription offer document/prospectus.

The following brokers acted as lead-manager for a public issue in 1991:

- Bergen Fondsmeglerforretning
- Christiania Fonds
- DnB Fonds
- Elcon Securities
- Fearnley Finans
- Finanshuset
- Fokus Fonds
- Fondsfinans
- Invest Securities
- Oslo Securities
- Pre fonds
- SPN Fonds

The underwriting syndicate often comprises commercial and savings banks, insurance companies, stockbrokers, pension funds and larger industrial or trading corporations.

Private placement

Issuance in the form of a private placement may only be made by mortgage institutions, banks and insurance companies. This method is usually used for open series, either the introduction of a new series or the extension of an existing series.

In the case of the extension of an existing series, a new subscription offer document is not prepared. The issue is made either by the borrower approaching a number of brokers who then tender for the issue, as with a public subscription; or by a broker making contact with, say, a mortgage company, and bidding for a certain amount in a particular issue. With the nominal coupon having already been agreed, the broker which offers the lowest yield is awarded the issue. New bonds do not differ from the existing securities, and are registered in the NRS and traded on the Oslo Stock Exchange from the payment date.

Open issues must be closed one year prior to maturity at the latest (or one year prior to the first opportunity to make a put or call).

Regulatory legislation

New issues in the Norwegian bond market are regulated by

- Securities Trading Act of 14 June 1985
- Regulations for New Issues of 27 February 1989 (pursuant to Money and Credit Act)
- Regulations for the Stock Exchange of 21 December 1989 (pursuant to the Stock Exchange Act)
- Companies Act of 04 June 1976 (for convertible bonds)
- Act of 14 June 1985 governing the Norwegian Registry of Securities

Issues in the Norwegian market must be offered for public subscription, that is to say that the issue is made, and sold through, stockbroking companies (Regulations for New Issues S1.2) An underwriting group which guarantees full subscription of the issue must also be established. Bond issues smaller than NKr 25m may not be taken up without the approval of the Treasury. According to S13, issues may not be made at a price below par which is equivalent to more than 0.1 per cent of the yield calculated to the first interest-regulation date, or alternatively, the maturity date. Separate regulations apply to mortgage companies, state banks, commercial banks, savings banks and financing companies; these may take up loans without a public offering, and without a guarantee consortium. (Regulations for New Issues S3,4).

The guidelines covering new issues are expected to be liberalized in the near future, to become more in line with international practice.

22.8 *New issue volumes*

As illustrated in Figure 22.38 below, Kingdom of Norway issues and bonds carrying a government guarantee together with those issued by mortgage institutions, dominate the new issues market. In the period from 1980 to 1991, new issue volume in government and government guaranteed bonds accounted for an average of 42.7 per cent of total new issues volume for listed bonds. The figure for mortgage institutions is 32.7 per cent whilst the equivalent volume for local authorities, county councils and borrowers guaranteed by these was 12.7 per cent. Industrial companies accounted for 3.2 per cent of new issue volume.

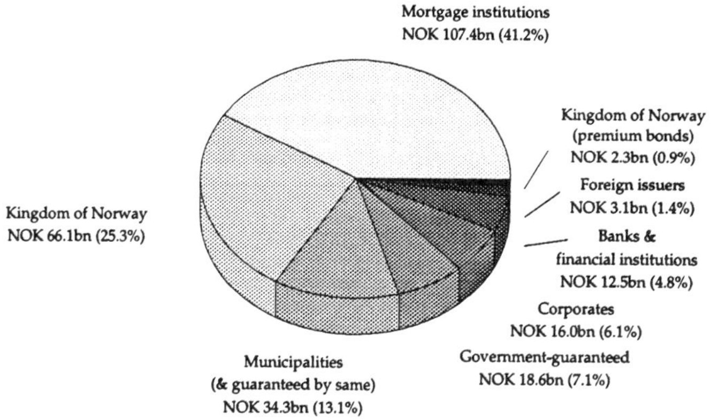

Figure 22.38 Composition of the Norwegian bond market

Government issues

As Figure 22.39 illustrates, new issue volume by the government was rising in the period from 1980 to 1986, with a sharp increase in 1983 and 1986. From 1980 to 1983, government issues accounted for some 20 to 25 per cent of total new issues volume. In 1983, the figure was 68.9 per cent and in 1986, 70.1 per cent. No new government issues were made in the years from 1987 to 1990. In February 1991, the government made a NKr 12bn issue, with a 10 per cent coupon and fixed redemption in 1996. A new domestic government bond was issued in January 1992. The principal amount was NKr 8bn, 9 per cent coupon and fixed maturity an 1999. From November 1991 to end 1992, the government has a limit of NKr 30bn on domestic borrowing, and NKr 40bn on borrowing in international markets.

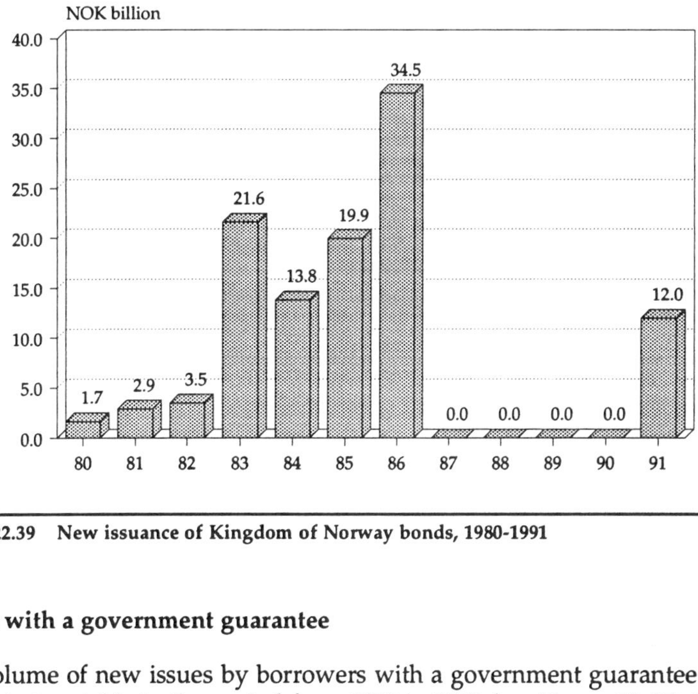

Figure 22.39 New issuance of Kingdom of Norway bonds, 1980-1991

Issues with a government guarantee

The volume of new issues by borrowers with a government guarantee has been somewhat variable in the period from 1980 to 1991 (see Figure 22.40). The share of total new issue volume was greatest in the years from 1980 to 1982, fluctuating between 20 and 27 per cent. In the period from 1983 to 1986, this group of borrowers accounted for between 4.7 per cent and 6.4 per cent of new issues volume, increasing somewhat thereafter. From 1987 to 1991, the share of total new issuance volume was between 8.8 per cent and 17.6 per cent.

Borrowers which currently have bonds with a government guarantee are: Den norske Industribank, Norges Kommunalbank, Selskapet for Industrivekst, Låneinstituttet for Skip, A/S Sydvaranger. In October 1991, A/S Fastlandsfinans obtained a government guarantee for its NKr 200m issue, 9.8 per cent 1991/2011.

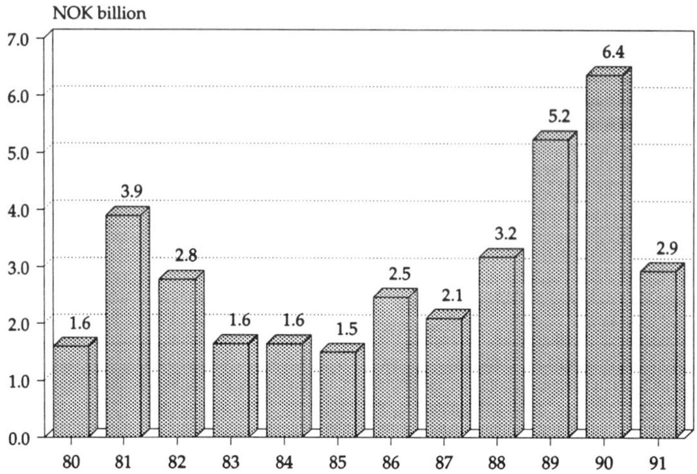

Figure 22.40 New issuance of government-guaranteed bonds, 1980-1991

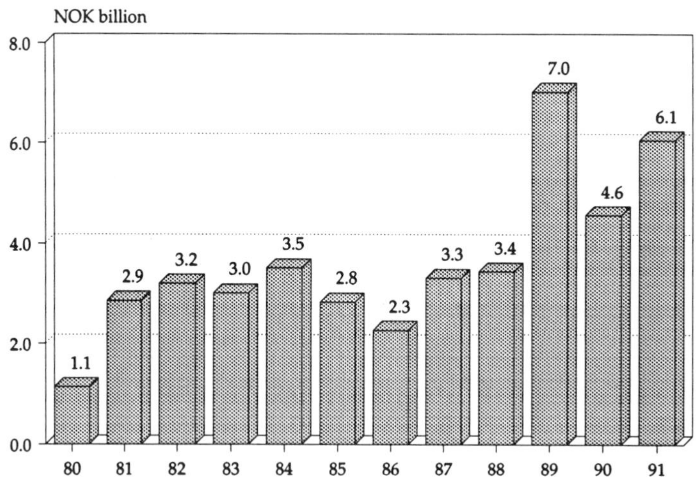

Figure 22.41 New issuance of municipal bonds and bonds guaranteed by same, 1980-1991

County council, local authority, municipal issues and issues guaranteed by same

The share of total new issues volume accounted for by this group varies from 4.6 per cent in 1986 to 23 per cent in 1982. In 1991, County councils, local authorities and power stations have been able to achieve better terms in the market than previously, which has resulted in increased new issuance volume. As at 31.12.1991, the volume of new issuance was NKr 6058m, against NKr 4553m in 1990 (see Figure 22.41). Compared with the total new issuance volume, this accounted for 18.3 per cent in 1991, up from 12.6 per cent in 1990.

Bank and finance companies

Bank and finance companies were permitted to issue bonds in the domestic market in July 1987. As illustrated in Figure 22.42, the first ordinary issues made by the banks were in 1989. Volume has increased steadily from 2.3 per cent of total new issuance volume in 1989 to 10 per cent in 1991.

Mortgage institutions

Mortgage institutions have been a dominant group in the Norwegian new issues market. The share of total new issues volume has varied between 9.8 per cent in 1981 and 65.9 per cent in 1989. In 1989, this sector issued 75 new bonds, in 1990 and 1991, the figure was 24 and 12 respectively (see Figure 22.43). The trend has been towards fewer, but larger issues. There are also continuous issues in open series.

In 1991 and 1992, three mortgage institutions have issued floating-rate bonds in which the coupon is fixed semi-annually at IMM dates:

- Security no. 153892 (KM92) Norgeskreditt 1991/1994
- Security no. 157772 (KQ72) Norsk Skibs Hypothekbank 1991/1994
- Security no. 156039 (KX39) Vestenfjelske Bykreditt A/S 1992/1994

Industrial issues

The volume of new issues within this sector has been extremely variable in the years from 1980 to 1991 (see Figure 22.44), accounting for 1.8 per cent of total new issues volume in 1985 and 20 per cent in 1981. In kroner terms, volume was greatest in 1990 at NKr 4.1bn. The biggest borrowers in this group also fund themselves in the international money markets.

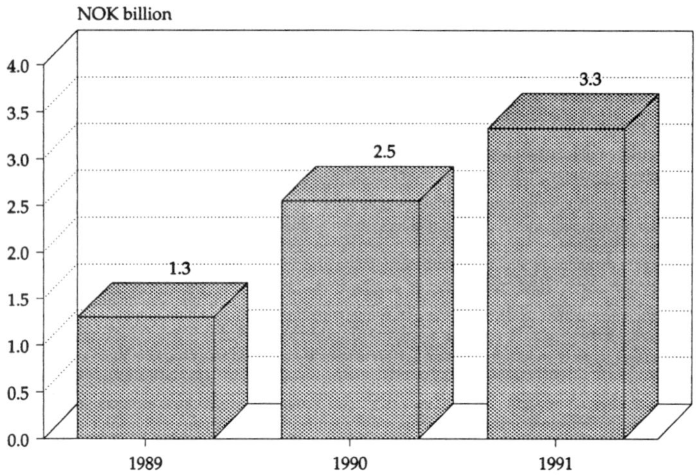

Figure 22.42 New issuance of bank & finance institution bonds, 1980-1991

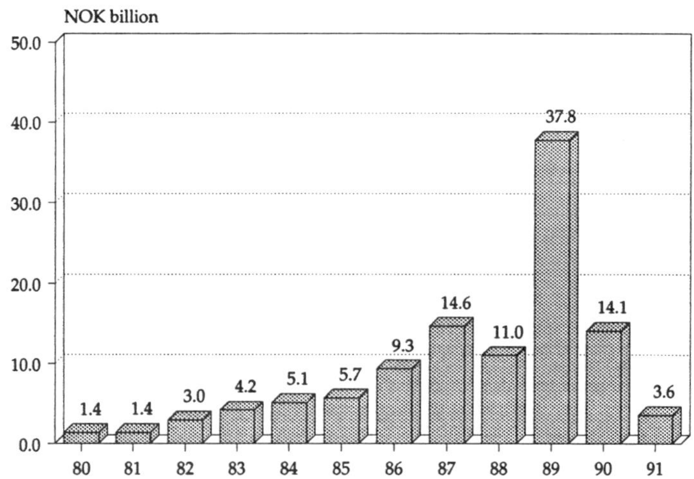

Figure 22.43 New issuance of mortgage institution bonds, 1980-1991

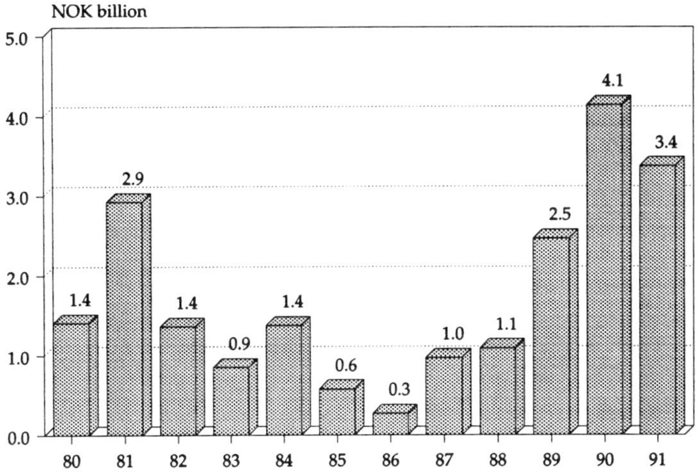

Figure 22.44 New issuance of industrial bonds, 1980-1991

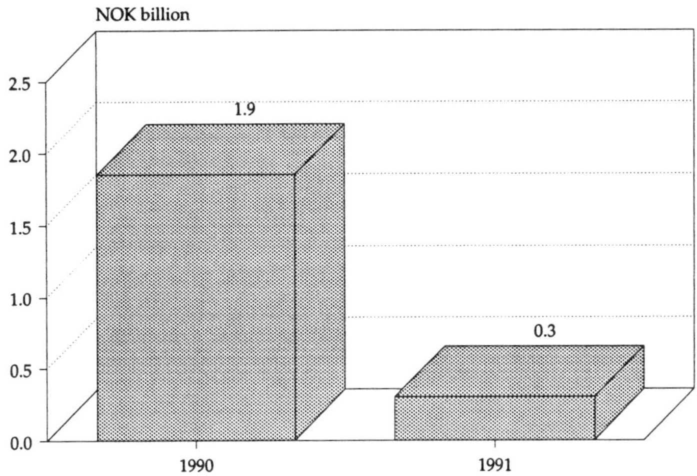

Figure 22.45 New issuance of NKr-denominated foreign bonds, 1980-1991

Foreign issues of NKr-denominated bonds

Four foreign borrowers only have issued NKr-denominated bonds in Norway. These issues were all made in 1990 (see Figure 22.45).

Foreign issues

There are six such issues listed in this sector of the Oslo Stock Exchange, four of which are eurokroner issues offered for public subscription in 1985. These are bullet bonds, maturing in 1992 and 1993.

In 1990, SAS issued a package comprising a bond in Danish kroner, one in Swedish kronor and one in Norwegian kroner. All three were listed simultaneously on the Oslo Stock Exchange, the Copenhagen Stock Exchange and the Stockholm Exchange. The issues in Danish kroner and Swedish kronor are both open issues, offered for sale by public subscription. In the terms of the NKr-denominated bond, the borrower reserves the right to extend the issue, in the event that legislation is amended to allow for this. The bond was offered for public subscription. As at 31 December 91, none of the issues had been increased.

Issuance volumes are shown in Figure 22.46.

Subordinated loan capital

Insurance companies may not take up loans through the issuance of bonds. However, in order to meet the authorities' equity requirements, they are permitted to take up subordinated loan capital in the form of bonds and convertible issues, subject to the approval of the Treasury. The requirement for separate approval from the Treasury in order to take up subordinated loan capital in the form of bonds, was abolished for banks and finance institutions in July 1990.

There are now 36 issues of subordinated notes listed on the Oslo Stock Exchange, of which 20 are issued by banks, 7 by mortgage institutions and 9 by insurance companies. All of these issues were offered for sale by public subscription, at par, in the period from 1987 to 1991. All are straight issues, some with a call option for the borrower. The volume of new issues was at its greatest in 1989 (see Figure 22.47), accounting for 3.9 per cent of the total new issues volume. This sank to 3.4 per cent in 1990 and to 2.6 per cent in 1991.

Subordinated notes are quoted in a separate section on the Oslo Stock Exchange, owing to their special status.

Convertible bonds

In volume terms, convertible issues account for only a small share of the Norwegian market (see Figure 22.48). The percentage of new issue volume was relatively even in the years from 1989 to 1991, at 2.1 per cent. As at 31.12.1991, there

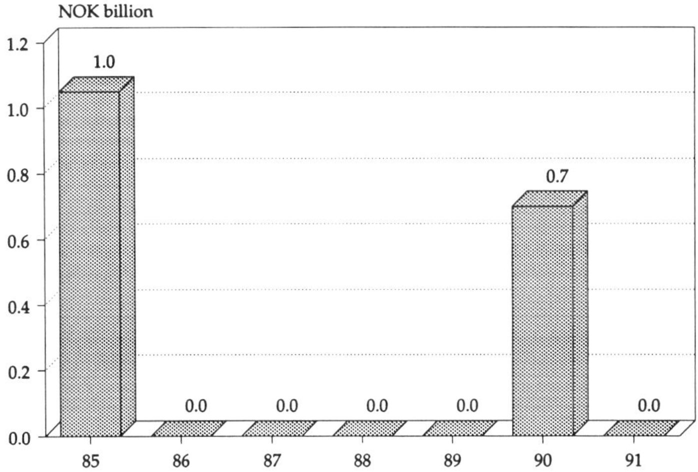

Figure 22.46 New issuance of foreign bonds, 1980-1991

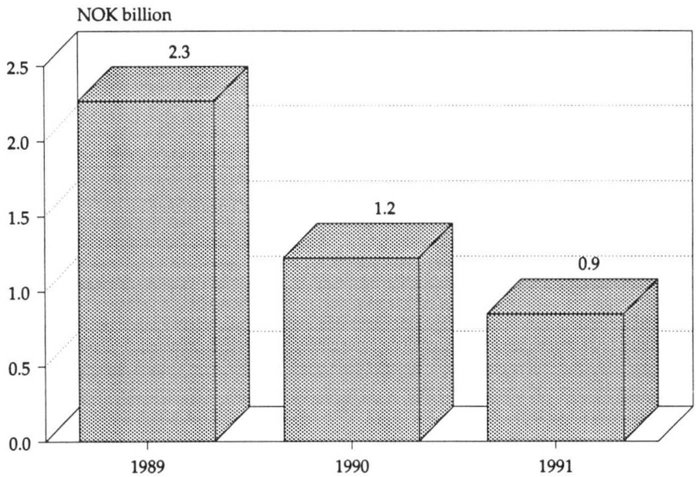

Figure 22.47 New issuance of subordinated loan capital;, 1980-1991

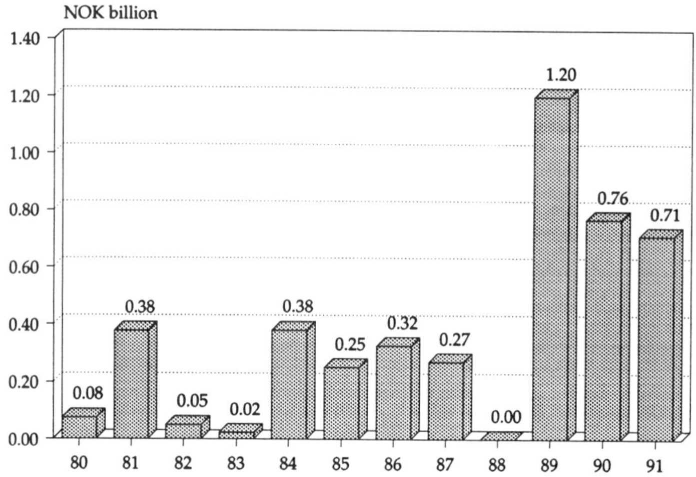

Figure 22.48 New issuance of convertible / warrant bonds, 1980-1991

are 16 such issues listed on the exchange. All borrowers are listed public limited companies in industry, shipping and oil. A total of 14 of the issues were offered for sale by public subscription, at par. Ross Offshore's loan from 1989 was a private placement made at market terms.

In 1991, only one new issue was made in this sector, namely Norske Skogindustriers bond, security no. 185108 (PV08) which was issued as an 'international offering'. The managers to the issue were Enskilda Securities, Christiania Fonds, Kleinwort Benson, Deutsche Bank, BnP, Credit Suisse First Boston, Paribas.

All the issues in this section have a fixed-coupon and maturity; a few also include a call option.

Section 5 of the Norwegian Companies Act includes regulations concerning taking up loans on 'special terms', hereunder convertible bonds, and bonds carrying warrants to purchase shares. A resolution to issue convertible bonds requires a two thirds majority at the company's Ordinary General Meeting. The size of the issue is limited to the amount which, when converted to equity, increases the share capital by maximum 50 per cent. The conversion price is therefore of vital importance when setting the upper limit of the size of the issue. For convertible issues, Treasury approval is not required even though the principal amount is under NKr 25m.

The conversion right may not be detached from the liability, and cannot therefore be traded separately. This means that the right to convert into shares can only be claimed by the holder of the convertible bond at that time.

The prospectus and subscription offer document are subject to the Stock Exchange Regulations for both bonds and shares.

22.9 *Methods of trading*

Most bonds in Norway are listed on the Oslo Stock Exchange. Brokers can access the Oslo Stock Exchange's trading system from their offices, and make prices in the listed issues. In some issues, these prices are passed on by Oslo Stock Exchange via information systems such as Reuters and Telerate.

This applies in particular to issues by banks and mortgage institutions, where the majority of borrowers have made agreements with groups of brokers with respect to two-way pricing of a number of issues. The prices are quoted on the Oslo Exchange which passes them on to specific pages on Reuters. Some issues are also listed on the Copenhagen Exchange, where Danish brokers operate as market-makers.

In the absence of a liquid market for government bonds, the market for mortgage institution bonds has been most active so far.

Primary dealers

Norges Bank acts as subscription place in new issues by the government. These issues are open to anyone. Normally, Norges Bank itself subscribes for a substantial amount, which is later used to support the market. Norges Bank selects a broker for a period of four months at a time, and this broker makes prices in agreed amounts on the Oslo Exchange, on behalf of Norges Bank. Norges Bank's prices may be found on Reuters pages CBOP and CBOQ.

Mortgage institutions and banks issue through their market-makers, who are obliged to make a price in a larger amount, on request by the the borrower. More recently, mortgage institutions have tended to use the Dutch auction principle. Market-makers receive a commission from the issuer in return for making prices. The size of this commission can vary.

Quotations

Prices are quoted on the Oslo Stock Exchange's trading system between 9 am and 3 pm on trading days. In this period, market-makers quote binding two-way prices in mortgage institution and bank issues, whilst Norges Bank's broker quotes similar prices in the issues Norges Bank wishes to support.

Quotes are made as prices, and as a rule, the spread is between 10 and 30 points. That is, if a price of 99.15 - 25 is quoted in sec. no. 158507 10.50 per cent Bolig-og Næringskreditt 1990/1995, which is the most actively traded issue in Norway, then the market-maker will purchase at a price of 99.15 and sell at 99.25.

As mentioned above, prices for Norges Bank are made by a broker on Norges Bank's behalf. This means that commission is payable in addition to these prices. The size of this commission is negotiable, between the instigator of the transaction, and the broker carrying it out.

Dealing

All transactions are effected by telephone. The trade can be confirmed by telex/fax should the client so require.

Benchmark bonds

Two Kingdom of Norway issues function as benchmark bonds in Norway, but owing to the small total outstanding volume of government issues, some mortgage institution bonds are traded just as actively as these government issues. The ten most traded issues so far this year (as at March 1992) are:

Security no.	Coupon (%)	Borrower	Maturity	Turnover (NOK bn)
100459	10.00	Kingdom of Norway	1991/1996	13.520
158500	10.85	Bolig-og Næringskreditt	1989/1994	8.488
158507	10.50	Bolig-og Næringskreditt	1990/1995	7.406
159509	10.90	Bolig-og Næringshreditt	1990/1993	7.124
100462	9.00	Kingdom of Norway	1992/1999	5.293
100438	12.50	Kingdom of Norway	1983/2000	5.377
159611	10.80	Sparebank Kreditt	1990/1996	4.786
153890	10.75	Norgeskreditt	1990/1996	4.659
153875	10.90	Norgeskreditt	1989/1994	4.310
159609	10.80	Sparebank Kreditt	1989/1994	3.827

The Oslo Stock Exchange

Most issues in Norway are listed on the Oslo Stock Exchange. Brokers enter their prices in the trading system from their offices and all transactions must be reported to the exchange, with details of the volume and price, within five minutes of the trade being completed. Turnover is then available to all systems which have access to the Oslo Stock Exchange's information system.

The following specifications must be fulfilled in order for a bond to be listed on the Exchange:

- the minimum principal amount is NKr 25m

- the issue must be of general public interest
- the minimum holding must not be larger than one trading lot (NKr 100,000.-)
- a subscription offer document and prospectus must be compiled

In order to separate the most interesting issues, the Oslo Stock Exchange introduced a Section for Major Issues. Bonds listed in this section must fulfill the following requirements:

- simple redemption plan
- no put/call clauses
- minimum issue of NKr 500m
- fixed coupon over the life of the bond

The Oslo Stock Exchange produces an official list daily. This includes all Kingdom of Norway issues together with all bonds listed in the Section for Major Issues which have been traded that week. Friday's official list includes all bonds.

22.10 *Market practices*

Denomination

The nominal value of Norwegian bonds is from NKr 1000.- and upwards.

Trading volumes

Prices quoted in market-maker issues are good for NKr 5m. It is not unusual to have prices quoted for larger amounts on request. Prices quoted by Norges Bank usually apply for between NKr 30m and NKr 50m.

Transaction cost

Brokers will claim a commission for trades in Kingdom of Norway issues against Norges Bank, whereas for transactions against market-makers in mortgage institution and bank bonds, their income is earned in the form of the spread.

Spread trading

Norges Bank normally quotes prices with a spread of 15 to 30 points. Prices made by market-makers in other issues usually have a spread of 10 to 20 points.

Ex-coupon trading

Quoted prices do not include accrued interest, whilst the purchase sum will normally include accrued interest. The following rules apply for calculation of interest:

- Accrued interest is calculated on the basis of actual no. of days/365 from last interest payment date to trade-date.
- If the trade-date is less than 14 days prior to an interest payment date, the seller receives the full coupon. In this situation, the purchaser pays minus days - that is, the interest is deducted.

The Stock Exchange Official List contains information about interest payment dates.

Withholding tax

Coupons are paid gross, in other words, no taxes are deducted at source.

22.11 Settlement

Primary market

Settlement dates within the primary market vary from two banking days, to several months. A security is issued by a company's account operator into the Norwegian Registry of Securities, showing the various subscription places; this ensures that the correct holding is transferred to each individual investor.

Secondary market

Settlement procedures in the secondary market changed radically following the establishment of the Norwegian Registry of Securities (NRS), as this involved the transition to a paperless system, at least in the case of listed companies. The Norwegian Registry of Securities was established in 1985 following the adoption of a specific law for the purpose. The legislation meant that, through the NRS, a Central Securities Depository (CSD), was established. However, the NRS is more than just a securities depository, it also carries legal protection. Unlike most other national CSDs (with the exception of Sweden and Denmark), registration in the NRS is made in the name of the final investor, and not just in the name of the broker, or custodian. However, in some particular cases involving foreign investors, registration in the name of the custodian has been accepted.

Through the establishment of the NRS, together with later modifications, Norway has to a large degree, satisfied the recommendations made by the Group of Thirty in 1989:

- A paperless system has been established.
- A matching system for inter-broker trading has been established.
- Settlement between brokers is made in the form of "Delivery against payment in same-day funds", whereby data is transferred from the NRS to Norges Bank, in which all brokers have settlement accounts. Settlements between broker and client are made by the broker directly and are not, as yet, connected to the settlement procedure of the NRS, although such a modification is under development and, during the first half of 1992, will be extended to include custodians.
- The settlement period has been standardized to a rolling T + 3 (trade-day + 3) system.
- Comprehensive ISIN (International Securities Identification Number) codes have been adopted to identify the individual securities. NRS has also been appointed National Numbering Agency for Norway.

At the moment, work is in progress to establish routines covering the borrowing and lending of securities, an extension of the existing matching system between brokers, and for Delivery against Payment settlement through Norges Bank to include a greater number of user groups. Efforts are also being made to link up to CSDs in other countries, to facilitate cross-border trading, including a system for Delivery against Payment in same-day funds.

Maturity

Redemption, instalment payments and interest payments, are also made through the NRS. Investors specify in their NRS accounts to which bank account both interest and capital repayments are to be credited. The NRS makes the actual calculations and is also responsible for drawings by lot, with advice to the investor, in the case of issues with instalment repayments. The NRS provides the necessary data which is transferred to the banks' clearing system for settlement. Funds are available to the investor on the due date, or the first following business day.

22.12 Yield calculation

Most issues in the Norwegian market pay interest semi-annually though, steadily, more issues are being made with an annual interest payment. Yield is calculated on the principle that one investor holds all the bonds in any one issue. The calculated yield can be interpreted as an expected yield for investors who hold only part of the issue.

Mathematically, yield is calculated according to the following formula:

$$P + I = v^{t/365} \sum_{j=1}^{n} A_j \, . \, v^{(n-1)/s}$$

where:

P	the price of the bond
I	accrued interest[1] (negative if applicable)
v	$1(1+i)$ annual yield discount factor
i	yield
t	number of calendar days to the next coupon-date (including leap days)[2]
n	number of instalments remaining
Aj	annuity amount due on coupon-date j, sum interest and capital repayment. Aj will vary according to the type of issue i.e. series, annuity, straight.
s	number of instalments per year

For issues with adjustable coupons, but without a put option for the borrower, it is usually assumed that the issue stands at a discount on the coupon-adjustment date (often 99 per cent). The reason for this is that issues without a put option are less liquid, and often stand at a discount on the adjustment date.

[1] *Accrued interest is calculated from the preceding coupon-date to settlement date based on no. days divided by 365. Negative interest occurs for settlement within 14 calendar days of the coupon-date. It is calculated as for accrued interest. Note that accrued interest is calculated on the basis of number of days divided by 365, whilst interest is paid, on the coupon-date, on the basis of 360/360 or 180/360*

[2] *An option does exist to use actual number of days in the life of the bond, although such a method is seldom used*

22.13 Taxation

Overview

These comments on the Norwegian tax system are limited to the taxation of interest-bearing instruments. Firstly, the regulations covering the taxation of securities in Norway will be described, after which, the consequences for foreign investors will be considered. Taxation of capital gains and interest income is based on the realization principle, that is, the income becomes taxable on the realization (sale) of the security. From the 1992 tax year, the FIFO principle is applicable.

Prior to spring 1990

Capital gains on bonds, except those held as trade investments, were not subject to tax until May 1990; the reason being, or so it was argued, that there was no capital gains over the entire life of a bond issued at par. The coupon interest was taxed as ordinary income; equally, interest expenses were deductible against ordinary income.

Prior to spring 1992

In 1990, it was decided that capital gains on bonds not held as a trade investment should be eligible for tax. Effective May 1990, capital gains on bond sales was taxed as ordinary income, as for coupon interest. This change in the tax regulations was based on the international development of bonds being issued way below par (for example, zero-coupon bonds), which made it appropriate in order to avoid tax distortions.

1992 Tax Reform

The entire tax system has been reformed, with effect from 1992. All capital income such as gains on sales of shares and bonds and interest income is now defined as ordinary income, and subject to 28 per cent tax; equally, losses on securities are now deductible against ordinary income.

Taxation by category of instrument

Bonds

According to the new tax system, all securities are now, in principle, subject to one flat rate of taxation: 28 per cent. This applies to all types of bonds.

Convertible bonds

Convertible bonds are treated as ordinary bonds for tax purposes, as long as they are not converted. On conversion, the shares will be taxed as ordinary shares, at a flat rate of 28 per cent. In order to avoid double taxation of profits on share sales, consideration is made of the company's taxed capital in the course of the shareholder's period of ownership. Profit or loss is defined as the difference between the sale value and the acquisition price. The acquisition price is regulated up or down, in line with the company's taxed capital in the course of the shareholder's period of ownership. The acquisition price is presented as the shareholder's purchase cost, plus a certain figure.

This figure is calculated on the basis of the company's taxable annual income, less taxes and dividends paid that year, divided between all shares, on a proportional basis according to the nominal value of the shares, as at 31 December in the tax year in question. This figure will first become available once the company's taxable income is fixed. In practice, this implies that the figure will normally be calculated in the autumn following the end of the tax year.

Derivative instruments

Derivative instruments, such as options, futures, FRAs, interest rate and currency swaps, and so on, will, until further notice, be taxed in accordance with the same principles, and at the same rate, as the underlying instrument. The realization principle applies as a general rule. In other words, a gain becomes taxable following the sale/redemption of the instrument and, equally, losses are deductible against ordinary income taxed at 28 per cent. The authorities intend to prepare a more detailed set of regulations covering the taxation of derivatives.

Bond funds

Dividends distributed by bond funds are eligible for tax in full, as for interest income, payable by the unit holder.

Taxation of foreigners

When considering the question of liability to pay taxes in Norway, it should be ascertained, first, whether the authority for taxation exists in Norwegian Law and, then, whether a taxation agreement exists with Norway and, if so, whether this limits the tax liability to Norway. In the event that a taxation agreement does not exist between the country in question and Norway, or a specific factor falls outside the conditions of the tax agreement, then taxation is to be applied according to Norwegian Law. This however does not apply to securities.

Taxation of bonds

The taxation of a foreign creditor for interest received from a Norwegian borrower has no precedent in Norwegian domestic laws. In a number of double taxation agreements, the right to tax interest income is split between the country of domicile and the source of the interest. The country of source is given the right to tax interest income by a certain per cent of the gross amount. This applies, for example, to: Japan, Belgium, Canada, Turkey, Israel and Brazil. There are also some agreements by which the source country has the complete right of taxation (such as Thailand). The opposite case is provided by agreements in which the right to tax the income is awarded to the country of domicile; this applies to the Nordic tax agreement. In the event that the receiver is domiciled outside Norway, Norwegian domestic law has no precedent allowing taxation, unless the interest is earned in connection with business operations in this country.

22.14 *Futures and options*

The market for futures and options on interest-bearing securities is limited - indeed, no such stock exchange-listed instruments exist. The best organized section of the OTC market is in eurokroner FRAs (future rate agreements). Additionally, there are *ad hoc* agreements covering bond deals with delayed settlement.

The Oslo Stock Exchange plans to launch a futures contract with one of the most recent NKr Kingdom of Norway issues as the underlying security (see Figure 22.49). This is expected to take place later in 1992, or in spring 1993.

Underlying security:	NKr Kingdom of Norway issue
Contract size:	Contract size: NOK 1,000,000 nominal
Delivery months:	March, June, September, December
Series:	Two parallel series. A future with six months maturity is introduced every quarter
Settlement days:	On IMM days (International Money Market Days), normally every third Wednesday
Quotation:	Based on rate/price
Contract standard:	Physical delivery of underlying security via the NRS at a pre-agreed settlement price on expiry
Restrictions:	A clearing customer may not issue or purchase more futures on the bond that exceeds 20 per cent of the total volume of underlying security

Figure 22.49 Oslo Stock Exchange bond futures - anticipated specification

Eurokroner FRA

Organization of the FRA market commenced in 1985/86. In 1987, participants in the market agreed to standardize maturity dates, contract sizes and terms in general, such that effective price quotation on the screens could be achieved.

Indications are now made for 3, 6 and 12-month contracts. The major banks act as market-makers. Reuters pages are FRRU/V/W.

22.15 Money markets

In recent years, the Norwegian money market has gained in importance following the deregulation of credit markets. The money market basically comprises a certificate market, a promissory note market and an interbank market. As participants in the money market become more professional, money market funds will become a good alternative for small and medium-sized investors.

The certificate market

The Norwegian certificate market is relatively young. It started after the government announced plans, in the 1985 national budget, to launch a new money market instrument. The main guidelines were published, in December 1984, in the Provisions for New Issues. Alterations to detail have since been made several times, but the main points are generally unchanged.

Certificates are negotiable securities registered in the NRS, with a maximum life of 12 months. They are usually unsecured, and are reserved for first-class borrowers. The principal amount and accrued interest are due for payment on maturity.

There were originally four categories of certificate:

- government certificates, issued by the Norwegian government (listed)
- bank certificates, issued by banks
- finance certificates, issued by financing companies
- loan certificates, issued by companies, institutions etc.

A fifth category was later introduced:

- mortgage certificates, issued by mortgage institutions

Although the certificate market was intended to be open to first-class borrowers only, several issues have been in default. As a result, the spread between the various categories, and between different issuers within the same group, has increased by comparison to the early years. The volume of various categories of certificate issued each year since 1986, is shown in Figure 22.50.

Norges Bank uses government certificates and bank certificates to regulate short-term liquidity. Norges Bank quotes binding prices for government certificates in the Oslo Stock Exchange's trading system. Prices are quoted in terms of yield (Reuters CBOO). A number of brokers quote indications in other types of certificates. Prices are made as interest for the period. An overview of the most recent new issues is available on Reuters pages NMNF/G. Interest rates are calculated on the basis of actual days/365. The various types of investor in the certificate market, are shown in Figure 22.51.

Promissory note market

The market for promissory notes has existed for a long time in Norway, and prior to the introduction of certificates, made up the core of the money market, together with special-term deposits and deposits with banks and financing companies. Following the establishment of the certificate market, the dimension of the promissory note market has been considerably reduced, particularly with respect to large issues from professional borrowers. The last time the market for promissory notes was used in any degree by major participants, was prior to the abolition of the quota regulation of mortgage institutions' lending for mortgages in months/years. A market for guaranteed promissory notes still exists, but it is dominated by smaller issuers and borrowers. This is partially due to a lack of interest in providing guarantees.

Promissory notes are not regulated in the same way as certificates. Maturity can be unlimited, and there are no particular requirements regarding the method in which interest payments are made. However, instalments are usually set at six-monthly intervals, or on maturity. The rate of interest may be either fixed or floating.

There are no binding, or good, price indications either on the Oslo Stock Exchange or on the screens, so promissory notes must be regarded as illiquid money market instruments. However, it can be said that financial institutions which have problems raising funds in the certificate or bond market, often make use of promissory notes. Interest is normally calculated on the basis of 30/360.

The interbank market / NIBOR

The interbank market is a limited market in which only the largest banks with foreign exchange traders participate. Usually, when the big banks lend each other money, swaps are made between kroner deposits and deposits in US dollars. Maturities can be as much as a year, but the market is dominated by the shortest maturities, especially demand deposits. NIBOR (Norwegian interbank offered rate) is, however, used as a reference in pricing certificates and coupon regulation for some bonds.

Money market funds

Money market funds are relatively new in Norway. They are not specifically defined in any legislation, so that the Norwegian money market funds are, officially, bond funds. The first fund to be called a money market fund saw the

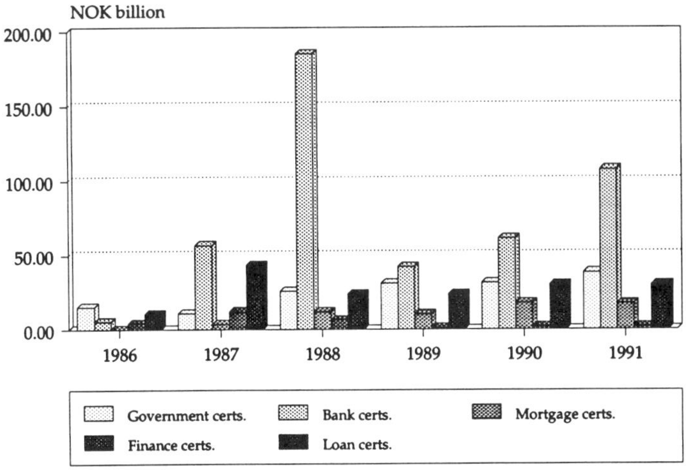

Figure 22.50 Volume of issues in the various certificate categories (per year, 1986-1991)
Source: Central Statistical Office (CSO)

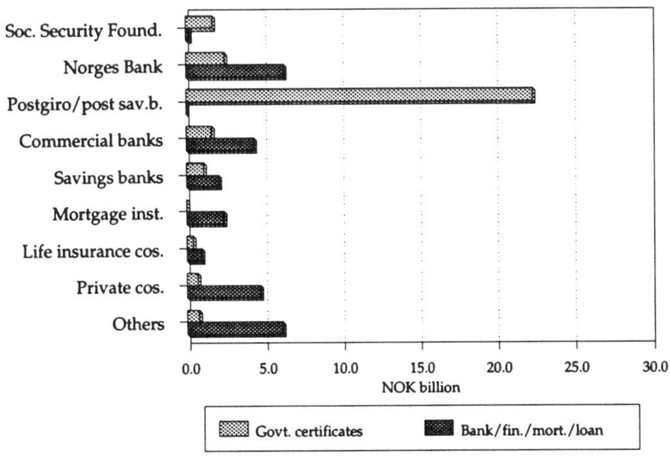

Figure 22.51 Investors in the certificate market, by type of cert. (as at 31 December 1991)
Source: NRS

light of day in 1987. Since then, more funds have been launched and volume was some NKr 4.5bn by 31 December 1991. It is difficult to give any exact figures showing the development, due to the lack of a precise definition and an obscure boundary between money market funds and bond funds.

22.16 *Interest rate history*

Overview

Looking at recent years as a whole, interest rate levels have generally been falling, despite a steep rise in 1986. There have, however, been sharp short-term fluctuations, which can be partly attributed to Norges Bank's use of interest rates to maintain stability of the kroner. Short-term rates of interest have always been higher than the long-term rates, that is to say, Norway has had an inverse yield curve.

1986

The year started with sharply-falling oil prices; the price of Brent oil fell from some US$30 per barrel (pb) to $12 pb in the course of three months. The fall in oil prices, together with rumours of a devaluation and an uncertain political situation, resulted in a sharp rise in interest rates. Norges Bank supported the kroner, and overnight rates shot up to 50 per cent for a few days. The change of government, combined with a 12 per cent devaluation, resulted in interest rates stabilizing, but at a higher level. Renewed rumours of a devaluation at the end of the year again led to an upturn in interest rates. At the end of the year, the bond market was experiencing an all-time high, as one-year notes issued by a first-class mortgage institution were priced at a yield of 17 per cent.

1987

During the spring and summer, oil prices maintained a level higher than that of the previous year. This resulted in a slight decline in interest rates, until the presentation of the national budget confirmed a reduction in exports of traditional goods, whilst a lower oil price had weakened the Norwegian economy. The resulting uneasiness in the currency again led to a marked increase in the short-term interest rates towards the end of the year. Interest rates for bonds also rose, though not by as much as the short rates.

1988

When Norges Bank resisted the pressure on the kroner at the end of the previous year, without making any changes to the D-loan rates (interest rate on the banks' marginal loans in the central bank), the kroner strengthened substantially at the start of the year, with a consequent fall in interest rates. The increased

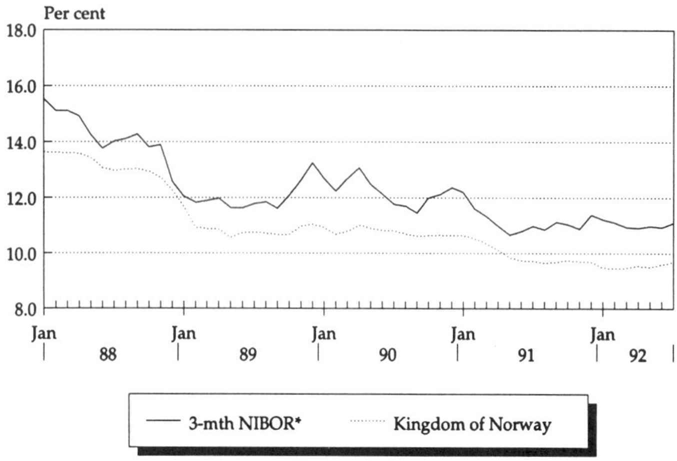

Note: NIBOR converted to actual/365 days and annualized

Figure 22.52 Development of 3-mth NIBOR and Kingdom of Norway, duration 3 years
Source: Carl Kierulf & Co. A.S

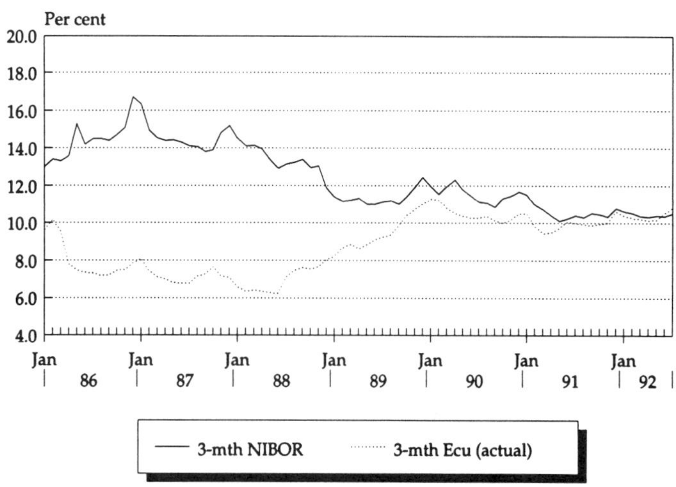

Figure 22.53 Development of 3-mth NIBOR and 3-mth Ecu (actual)
Source: Carl Kierulf & Co. A.S

confidence in the kroner allowed Norges Bank to reduce D-loan rates several times, in line with a general fall in interest rates. In November, rumours of a devaluation again began to flourish, and the kroner became unsettled, which led to a temporary rise in interest rates, particularly at the short end. Norges Bank again resisted substantial pressure on the kroner without raising D-loan rates - a move which was widely anticipated; interest rates fell again towards the end of the year. The interest rate gap with Norway's most-important trading partners was a mere 3 per cent at the end of the year.

1989

The downward trend in interest rates continued in 1989. D-loan rates were cut four times within the first six months, down to 10 per cent. At the half-year stage, interest rates were at their lowest for almost ten years. On 9 May, the domestic bond market was re-opened to foreign investors, thereby providing a stimulant to the market. The interest rate gap with Norway's most-important trading partners fell throughout the year and, by September, was only 0.5 per cent. Rising interest rates abroad, though, looked set to reverse the rapid fall in Norwegian rates; indeed, at the end of the year, rates were again on their way up. In November, Norges Bank raised D-loan rates by 1 per cent. The interest rate gap with Norway's trading partners had risen to 1.5 per cent by the year-end.

1990

The interest rate gap with Norway's trading partners is now so marginal, that the movement of interest rates abroad has an increased influence on the development of the domestic rate. In February, the interest rate gap was negative; rising levels abroad, however, led to a greater increase in Norway - and a larger gap. Interest rates declined again as the year progressed, and Norges Bank was able to reduce rates for D-loans, to 10.5 per cent. The Norwegian government decided that, effective 22 October, the Norwegian kroner should be pegged to the Ecu, as though Norway were a member of the EMS. The middle value against Ecu was fixed at NKr 7.9940, with a margin of +/- 2.25 per cent. Since then, the kroner has remained stable at around NKr 8.01 - 8.02 against the Ecu. The pegging resulted in an immediate reduction in interest rates but, towards the end of the year, interest rates started moving up again, following the pattern of the last few years.

1991

From the start of the year, until the end of May, both short- and long-term rates fell substantially. In this period, Norges Bank cut D-loan rates 4 times, down to 9.5 per cent (which is the lowest level for many years). The interest rate gap

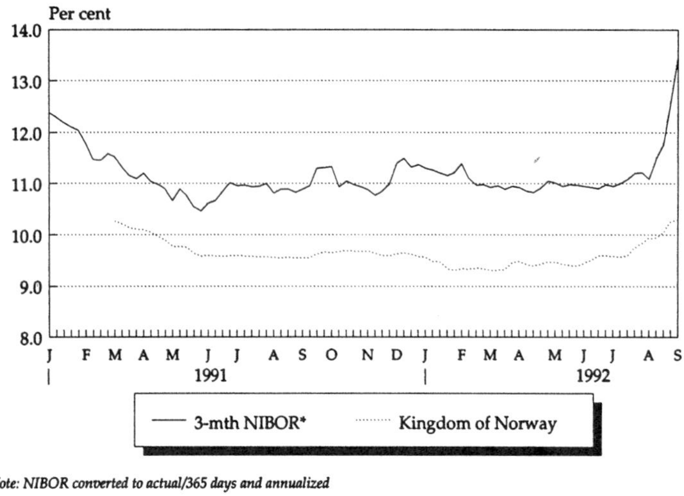

Figure 22.54 Development of 3-mth NIBOR and Kingdom of Norway 100459 (28.02.96)
Source: Carl Kierulf & Co. A.S

against the Ecu was also reduced following the fall in levels and, by May, was only 0.1 per cent against the theoretical Ecu rate for both short- and long-term rates. The picture in the second half of the year has been more varied, as pressure on the kroner pushed short rates up in September, and Norges Bank elected to raise D-loan rates to 10.5 per cent. Later that autumn, domestic unrest in the market for mortgage institutions lead to a sharp re-pricing of paper issued by this group. This coincided with a devaluation of the Finnish markka, which resulted in a jump in interest rates, initially by 1 per cent and then a further 6 per cent rise in the Swedish central bank's interbank rate. This spread to the Norwegian market and for a short period, interest rates were at the same level as at the start of the year. Norges Bank made substantial interventions in the market to support the kroner at the end of the year and succeeded in maintaining a stable currency. Short-term interest rates remained relatively high throughout the rest of the year. At the very end of 1991, some normalization in the market for mortgage institution bonds became evident. This lead to declining interest rates for these bonds. Anticipation of a new Kingdom of Norway issue in NKr resulted in renewed interest, and demand for, government bonds. At the start of 1992, the trend for both government and mortgage institution bonds was downwards. The interest rate gap between Norwegian levels and

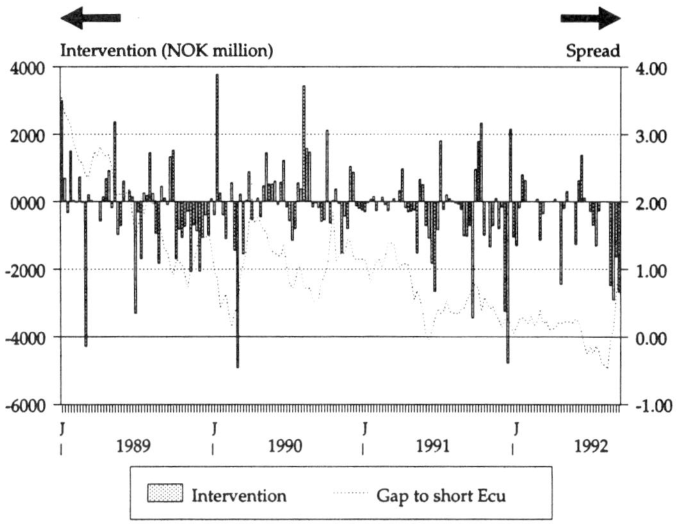

Figure 22.55 Norge Bank's intervention in NOK and the gap against short Ecu rates
Source: Carl Kierulf & Co. A.S

Ecu was extremely narrow at the end of 1991, such that Norwegian interest rates are extremely sensitive to changes in Ecu rates.

As illustrated in Figure 22.55, the policy, followed over recent years, of using interest rates to maintain a stable currency, has proved successful. Furthermore, pegging to the Ecu has had an even more stabilizing effect on the kroner.

22.17 Inter-market spreads

The most interesting and assertive inter-market spread which can be observed in the Norwegian market exists between mortgage institution bonds and government bonds.

As the market for government certificates is not particularly efficient, and there exist very few eurokroner bonds, continual monitoring of the spread against these markets is difficult.

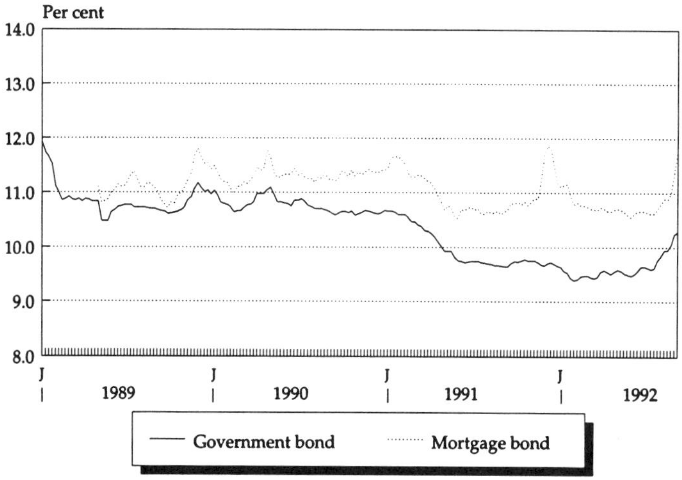

Figure 22.56 Yield on 3-yr government bond against yield on 3-yr benchmark mortgage bond
Source: Carl Kierulf & Co A/S

This spread has been followed closely, particularly over the last year, as mortgage institutions have shown a weak economic development. However, there have been considerable differences between the various mortgage institutions, as some can report relatively good results whilst one has actually opened negotiations with its creditors. As a result, the spread between the various institutions has also been significant, as much as 2 per cent at times. For the sake of simplicity, the figure illustrates the the spread between the best- priced mortgage institution, and government bonds with an equivalent maturity. The spread has been increasing for some time, with a noticeable jump at end-

November/early December 1991. This was most probably caused by psychological factors, although major groups of investors had been net sellers of mortgage institution bonds for some time. This in turn has temporarily reduced the investor base. The spread narrowed at the turn of the year, and into the new year. Several factors played a part in this development, one of the most important being Norges Bank's decision to provide liquidity loans for mortgage institutions experiencing refinancing problems. Another important development is that several mortgage institutions have applied for banking concessions. These will most probably be granted, and thus give access to Norges Bank's general lending facilities. Furthermore, two of the largest mortgage institutions have been either merged with, or taken over by major banks. The spread is anticipated to narrow towards 1 per cent.

Spread between short-term interest rates in the Scandinavian countries

The Scandinavian countries are often considered together, partly because all the currencies are denominated in kroner and the countries comprise a geographical unit, and because the language and cultures are similar.

As illustrated in Figure 22.57, the Norwegian and Danish interest rates have generally been more stable than the Swedish. For Norway, the policy followed in recent years to maintain a stable exchange rate, together with linking up with

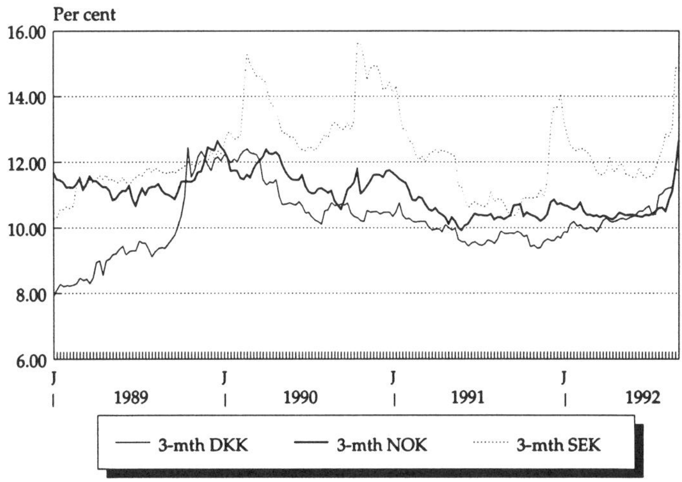

Figure 22.57 Development of short-term interest rates in Denmark, Norway and Sweden
Source: Carl Kierulf & Co A/S

Ecu, has been very significant. The figure also shows how movement in the Norwegian and Danish rates show considerable correlation although marked fluctuations in the Swedish interest rates will also affect the level in Norway.

22.18 *Sources of reference*

The main sources of reference for this chapter have been:

- The Norwegian Central Bureau of Statistics
- National Budgets
- The Oslo Stock Exchange
- Norges Bank (Bank of Norway)
- The Norwegian Registry of Securities (NRS)
- Carl Kierulf & Co. A.S.

The following persons, all member of the Norwegian Bond Commission, have contributed to this book by writing the Norwegian part:

Baste Nepstad, Vital Forsikring, Chairman
Bjarne Brynning, Vesta-group
Jan Pollestad, Carl Kierulf & Co
Leif Ola Rød, Pre Invest
Odd Sigmund Røste, Oslo Stock Exchange
Morten Steinsland, Vestenfjeldske Bykreditt
Halvard Tretvoll, Central Securities Depository (VPS)

Mailing Adress	Telephone	Telefax
P.O.Box 1276 Vika	+47 2 832444	+47 2 833953
N-0111 Oslo	(f.1993-01-29) +47 22832444	(f.1993-01-29) +47 22833953

Chapter

23

The bond markets of

Poland

Jacek Brzezinski
Creditanstalt-Bankverein, Vienna

Stanislaw Markowski
Bank Creditanstalt S.A., Warsaw

This chapter has been supplied by the Austrian Bond Commission

Note: In general text, the abbreviation 'Zl' is used to denote the Polish zloty. The corresponding international mnemonic, although not used here, is 'PLZ'.

23.1 General synopsis

Legal framework

The law that governs the issuance and trading of bonds was enacted on 27 September 1988. According to Polish law, bonds can be bearer bonds or registered bonds. They can be issued by the State Treasury, banks, legal entities carrying on business activities and foundations involved in economic activities.

The First Issue (1989)

On 16 June 1989, the minister of finance decided to issue Treasury bonds, for the first time since World War II, amounting to Zl 600bn. These bearer bonds could be bought by Polish citizens and had a fixed-interest rate of 60 per cent per annum. Bank Gospodarstwa Krajowego acted as lead-manager for the issue. Any bondholder could use the bonds to redeem debt to the State Treasury after four months from the date of purchase. Investors who held the bonds for more than 182 days were granted an additional 20 per cent premium. Expiry of bonds from this First Issue was 31 December 1990.

Convertible Treasury bonds (the Second Issue of 1989/1991)

Convertible Treasury bonds (CTBs), called 'Treasury Bonds of the Second Issue', were issued in November 1989. They were available between December 1989 and April 1991 in four denominations: Zl 5m, Zl 1m, Zl 400,000 and Zl 200,000. The total volume of the Second Issue amounted to Zl 500bn. The purpose of the issue was to support the budget of the first post-World War II non-communist government.

CTBs are floating-rate notes. The coupon is adjusted every month to equal the rate of inflation. Interest is paid from the month following the purchase (e.g. if the bond is bought in January, interest is calculated as of February). At the end of 1990, the total nominal value sold amounted to Zl 405.5bn. The bonds will expire on 31 December 2000.

During the period in which they were available on the primary market, the CTBs could only be sold to private investors. Those who purchased them were allowed to purchase shares of privatized companies at a 20 per cent discount. Some state-owned enterprises were also allowed to obtain CTBs, but only for the purpose of paying bonuses to their staff; thereby companies were able to increase their staff's salaries without having to pay taxes for wage increases.

The appearance of the CTBs strongly affected the secondary market of the Warsaw Stock Exchange. The effective issue price for stocks bought for CTBs was 20 per cent lower than the actual issue price. Employees of the privatized companies were granted additional discounts when they purchased shares from the tranche reserved for them.

CTBs were originally planned to be introduced on the secondary market of the Warsaw Stock Exchange at the end of September 1991, but their launch was postponed, and then suspended, due to both technical and legal difficulties. CTBs are currently traded through authorized brokerage offices only.

Inflation-linked bonds

In April 1991, the Ministry of Finance decided to cease the issuance of convertible bonds and, from 6 May 1991, it started offering Treasury bills. For the next year, these short-term instruments remained the only form of internal government finance (alternative to bank loans, that is). However, since they are targeted towards banks, rather than to the general public, they are therefore not really a suitable means of financing a structural budget deficit.

More appropriate instruments appeared in May 1992, as the Ministry of Finance unveiled two new types of bond, with maturities of one and three years, respectively. The one-year bond (the first auction of which was in May 1992) is targeted to the Polish general public, while the three-year issue (first issued in August 1992) is also open to foreign investors.

Both issues are inflation-linked; the one-year bond pays interest at maturity at a rate of inflation, plus 5 per cent, whilst interest on the three-year issue is calculated using the average of the yields of the four latest auctions of 13-week Treasury bills, which is then multiplied by a factor of 1.10.

Both bonds are in a non-material form. They are divided into four series each, and issued every quarter. The total volume for the three-year bond, which carries a denomination of Zl 1m per bond, is expected to reach Zl 7000bn in 1992/3. Proposed issue dates for the four series are 3 August and 2 November, 1992 (Zl 2000bn each), and 3 February and 4 May, 1993 (Zl 1500bn each).

Chapter

24

The bond markets of

Portugal

Miguel de Bragança & João Ermida
Citibank-Portugal S.A.

with thanks to:

Lisbon Stock Exchange

Portuguese Association of Mutual Funds Management Companies

Bank of Portugal

Note: In general text, the abbreviation 'Esc' is used to denote the Portuguese escudo. Elsewhere, the international mnemonic 'PTE' is used.

24.1 Introduction

At the beginning of the century, the Treasury began issuing bonds, denominated in pounds, with a maturity of 100 years. In the late 1940s, the government issued four series of perpetual bonds, named *Consolidados*, which reflected a policy of consolidation of the public deficit which existed in those times. These bonds had fixed coupons varying from 2.75 per cent to 4 per cent. The public debt issues during the 1950s and 60s were always denominated in escudos and had fixed coupons which varied from 3.5 per cent in 1959, to 5 per cent in 1969. In 1973, the year of the last fixed-rate issue, the nominal rate was also 5 per cent.

In terms of corporate names, the main issuers in the 1950s and 1960s were the electricity companies, the railway company, and the water distribution company. These issues had always fixed-rate coupons, which varied from 4.5 per cent to 6 per cent, and maturities ranging from 10 to 30 years.

The 1970s witnessed the Revolution, an event which caused the bond market effectively to disappear between 1974 and 1976 (the Lisbon Stock Exchange[1] also closed during this period). In 1976, however, the government began to issue public debt again, largely to rectify the acute problems in the public accounts which had arisen in the two years following the Revolution. The first issue of that year was a floating-rate note (FRN) with a first semi-annual coupon of 32.5 per cent. The indexation was the discount rate plus 5 per cent, and the amount was Esc 11bn (cf. the Esc 3bn, 5 per cent fixed-rate issue of 1973). In 1977, the state issued several billion escudos worth of fixed-rate bonds to indemnify the former owners of nationalized companies - with very unattractive conditions for the shareholders of those companies. The largest issue, of the twelve made, had a fixed-rate of 2.5 per cent and a final maturity of 28 years; inflation at the time was running near to 30 per cent per annum.

The beginning of the 80s saw state-owned companies returning to the market to join the Treasury issues. Along with EDP, some other state-owned companies, such as Petrogal, Portugal e Colonias, Quimigal, TLP, CTT, and Lisnave, started to issue FRNs in the domestic market. These had indexation against the discount rate and maturities ranging from 7 to 9 years. Government bond issues between 1980 and 1986 were particularly successful, mainly due to their attractive yields.

[1] *In this chapter, data concerning bond prices and turnover has been obtained from the Lisbon Stock Exchange and reflects only those transactions which occurred on the exchange up to 12 December 1991. Only bonds listed on the Lisbon Stock Exchange are analysed.*

Issuer	Rate	Amount (PTE million)	Maturity	Indexation	Int. payment
1960s:					
Cred. Prec	5.0	25	1985	Fixed	Qua.
Sid. Nac.	5.0	150	1985	Fixed	Sem.
Nitratos	5.0	20	1984	Fixed	Sem.
CD	4.5	120	1987	Fixed	Sem.
1970s:					
Metro	5.75	40	1984	Fixed	Sem.
Aguas	6.0	60	1985	Fixed	Sem.
CUF	6.0	150	1972-83	Fixed	Sem.
CP	6.75	130	1975-85	Fixed	Sem.
CTT	6.75	120	1975-84	Fixed	Sem.
Gas	7.0	100	1976-87	Fixed	Qua.
Electricity	7.0	250	1975-87	Fixed	Sem.
BFN	6.5	200	1976-83	Fixed	Sem.
1980s:					
Quimigal	17.5	1000	1983-87	Floating	Sem.
Petrogal	17.0	1000	1983-87	Floating	Sem.
Cimpor	17.5	500	1983-87	Floating	Sem.
Sid. Nac.	17.0	1200	1984-88	Floating	Sem.
EDP	18.0	1000	1983-87	Floating	Sem.
CTT	18.0	1000	1983-87	Floating	Sem.
Portucel	16.0	1200	1984-88	Floating	Sem.
EDP	17.0	1200	1984-88	Floating	Sem.
Colonias	16.5	800	1984-88	Floating	Sem.

Figure 24.1 Corporate issues prior to 1983

The main issues launched in the embryonic period prior to 1983, are shown in Figures 24.1 & 24.2.

In 1984/1985, the volume of issues increased, with the appearance of new issuers such as leasing and financial companies; examples include Locapor (a leasing company) and SPI (a financial company), which started to issue small amounts in 1984. In 1985, the government launched its first two big public issues, amounting to nearly Esc 100bn (cf. Esc 20bn issued in 1984). This issue, which was basically instigated by IMF requirements, was designed both to halt inflation and to avoid the increasing problem of external debt. In 1986, after years of FRN issuance, the government bond market introduced two innovative

Year	Rate	Maturity	Amount (PTE million)	Indexation
1959	3.5	1960-84	500	Fixed
1960	3.5	1966-85	500	Fixed
1963	3.5	1969-83	500	Fixed
1963	3.5	1970-84	500	Fixed
1965	3.5	1971-85	600	Fixed
1966	3.5	1972-86	500	Fixed
1969	5.0	1974-83	500	Fixed
1971	5.0	1976-85	1000	Fixed
1973	5.0	1978-87	3000	Fixed
1976	32.5	1979-84	11,000	Discount rate + 5%
1977	30.0	1980-84	12,000	Discount rate + 4%
1978	29.0	1981-85	15,000	Discount rate + 3%
1979	20.5	1982-86	10,000	Discount rate + 2%
1980	18.5	1983-87	15,000	Discount rate + 2%
1981	16.5	1985-89	7000	Discount rate + 2%
1982	16.5	1986-90	15,000	Discount rate + 2%

Figure 24.2 Treasury issues prior to 1983

fixed-rate issues. These were followed by zero-coupon issues, although the market reaction was not as enthusiastic as had been expected, with the largest investors being the state-owned banks.

Meanwhile, 1986/1987 was a boom period for life insurance companies, mutual funds, investment banks, financial houses and some pension funds. This development led to an increase in the number of both investors and issuers and, as a result, the foundation was laid for the start of liquid fixed-income market. Not only did the number of issuers increase dramatically in 1987, but they were favourably-influenced by fiscal changes which provided advantages for those issuing securities with lives of over 8 years. It was a time when investors were looking everywhere for paper, and investment bankers were looking for each company to make a bond issue. Until the October Crash, though, small investors were mainly buying only equities. The same year saw EDP come to the market with two issues, amounting to Esc 35bn - nearly half of the state's total 1987 volume. In 1988, as a result of the Crash, the corporate bond market showed important growth, with all issues being of the FRN variety. The government continued to issue FRNs - known as FIPs in Portugal - with a total amount, in that year, of Esc 38bn. The same year saw the first supranational escudo-denominated issue (by the European Investment Bank, EIB), which was mainly taken up by domestic investors. This deal was the first fixed-rate issue to have been seen since 1986, and the investor-reaction was very good, especially that of the insurance companies. 1989 was a year of change: A fiscal reform was initiated, introducing withholding tax for all bonds subsequently issued, and this affected the differential return, after tax, for the various segments of investors. As a consequence, there was a stronger development of the secondary market because some institutional investors swapped their bond portfolios. The primary market suffered from the tax uncertainly until the first semester. With a huge public deficit, the government issued Esc 516bn, with two types of instrument being used - an FIP and an OCA (see Section 24.3, Market composition). The secondary market revived this year with the swap of portfolios between banks, insurance and pension funds on one side, and mutual funds on the other.

In 1990, investment in bonds by non-residents grew, this being attributable both to the increased professionalism of the agents in the bond market and a strong growth in euro-issues (with placements coming from EIB, IFC, Council of Europe and CECA). In 1991, a new code defining the legal framework of the capital markets was introduced. Due to the uncertainty in terms of the regulatory environment, and also to the general expectation of a decrease in interest rates, the primary market saw low volumes. Meanwhile, the growth of capital flow into Portugal was very significant, due to:

- a high interest rate differential between escudo-denominated investments and those of other European currencies
- the favourable exchange rate behaviour of the escudo
- Portuguese banks using the offshore zone of Madeira to fund themselves in euroescudos, whilst investing in bonds
- the excellent reception given to fixed-rate government bond issues, mainly by non-residents who were keen to invest in high-yielding securities. Both the improved outlook and European integration, led to a much higher interest in these securities than had been seen in 1986.

This very high capital inflow led the central bank, in the third quarter of the year, to forbid non-residents from buying floating-rate notes, while even pressuring some of the banks with offshore branches to repatriate securities held abroad (as noted above, many of these securities had been acquired by offshore branches of Portuguese banks that were financing them in the euroescudo market). The prices of the fixed-rate government bonds showed a marked appreciation whilst escudo yields came down significantly, discounting the effect of the nominal convergence of the European currencies. As a consequence, later euro-issues that year met with far less enthusiasm from investors. Another important development in 1991 was the failure of some of the corporations that had issued in 1987, to pay any interest. Since this concerned not just a few, but rather several companies, it promoted the concept of credit risk awareness in the market, and the associated importance of rating procedures.

The period 1990-1991 was, therefore, a confirmation of the trend shown in previous years, with an increase in the primary market issuance as well as improved liquidity in the secondary market.

24.2 *Economics*

Gross domestic product

Over the last few years, Portugal has experienced strong growth, with the real GDP growth rate, from 1987 to 1990, consistently exceeding 4 per cent (see Figure 24.3). This favourable development can be attributed to a variety of factors, including political stability and the expectation of a convergence in the real economies in Europe.

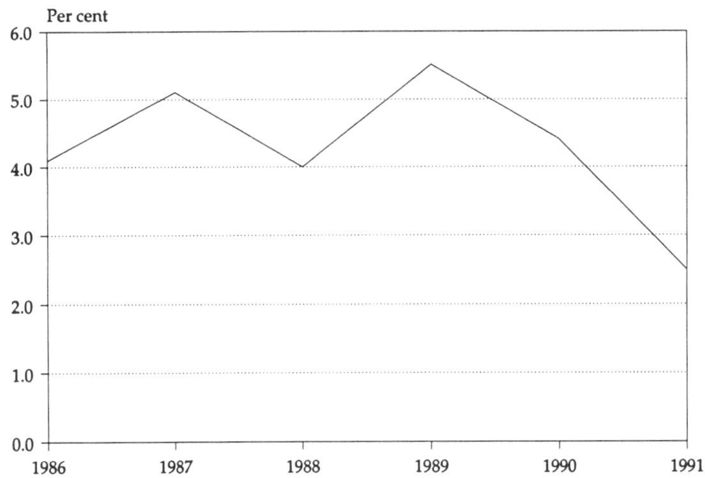

Figure 24.3 Growth in Portuguese GDP

It is estimated that, in 1991, this growth declined to a level of around 2 per cent, mainly due to the external recessionary environment, and to the behaviour of the exchange rate. The political stability mentioned above, together with a generally positive view of Portugal, both explain the growth of foreign direct investment over the last few years (see Figure 24.4). In 1987 and 1988, this investment was one of the main driving forces behind the growth in GDP. In 1989, too, external demand had an unusually positive effect on GDP but, more

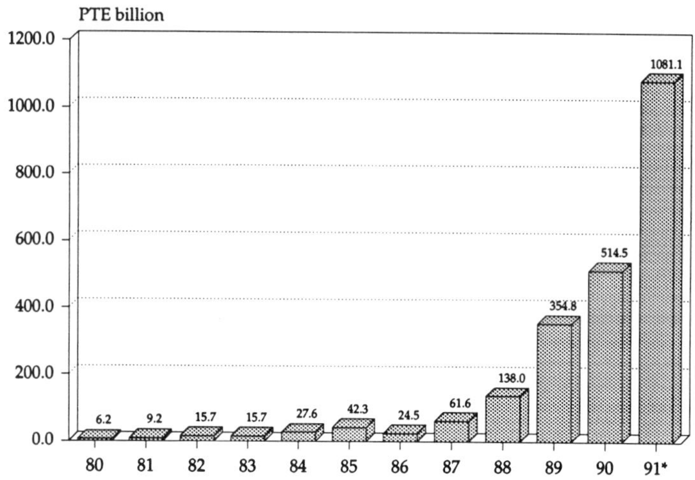

*) estimated

Figure 24.4 **Foreign direct investment**
Source: ICEP

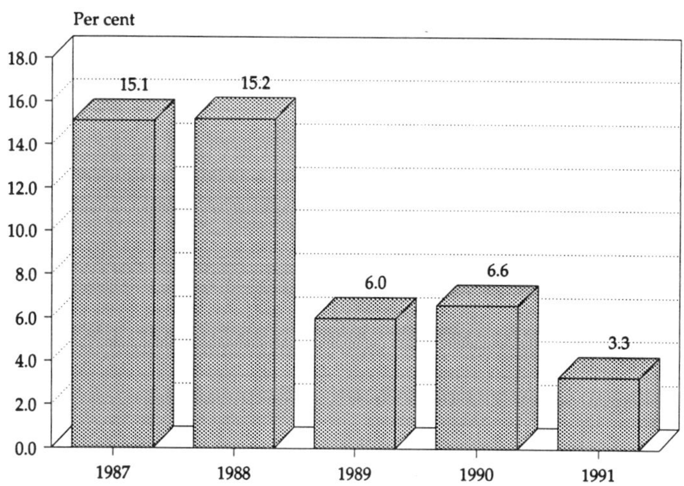

Figure 24.5 **Portuguese capital investment growth**

recently, however, domestic consumption (see Figure 24.6) has been the principal contributor to growth.

Unemployment

The growth in GDP tends to imply a low unemployment rate and, indeed, it has been consistently under 6 per cent (and with a decreasing trend), since 1988 (see Figure 24.7). However, this does not necessarily mean that there is a totally healthy situation in the labour market, because:

- there are some structural imbalances between the educational system and the needs of the economy, resulting in some long-term unemployment
- the last reductions in unemployment were largely caused by short-term contracts taken by unskilled labour, and an increase in self-employment.

Inflation

The high rate of growth and low unemployment mentioned above have occurred alongside a relatively high rate of inflation (see Figure 24.8).

One of the main macroeconomic objectives of the government has been the reduction of inflation, in order that Portugal may participate in the European monetary union. This objective has been pursued through a restrictive monetary policy and, consequently, high interest rates. These high interest rates have implied a slower pace of depreciation of the escudo than the inflation differential would justify.

Monetary policy

From 1978 to mid-1990, the escudo was smoothly depreciated *vis-à-vis* a basket of currencies by the Bank of Portugal according to a predefined objective, which called for a range of between 3 per cent and 4 per cent. The basket replicated the currencies of the economies with which Portugal had the most important economic relationships.

This predictability of the escudo depreciation stimulated capital inflow into Portugal and hindered efforts to reduce domestic inflation since it actually imported inflation. In mid-1990, this policy was stopped so that the escudo no longer had to follow a predefined depreciation pattern. In October 1990, the basket of currencies against which the depreciation is measured was changed to only five European currencies (Deutschemark, Spanish peseta, French franc, British pound and Italian lira), with all major currencies being actively and directly traded against the escudo. Furthermore, the Bank of Portugal started

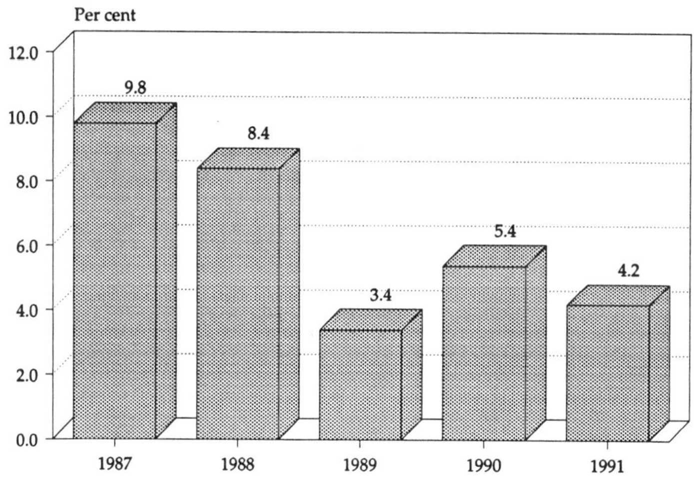

Figure 24.6 Growth in Portuguese domestic demand

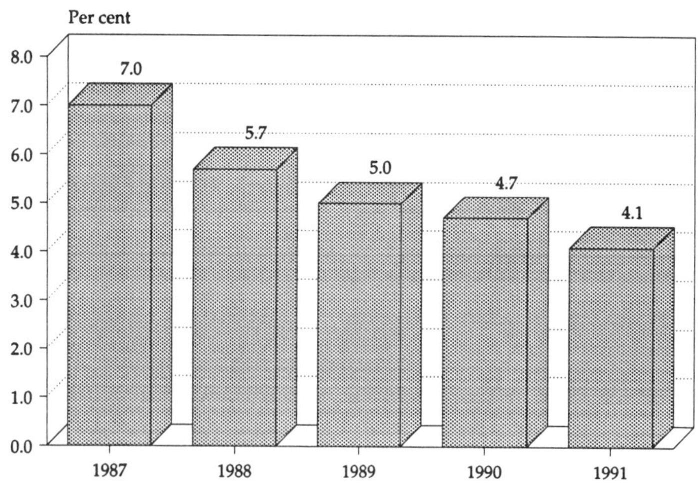

Figure 24.7 Portuguese unemployment

intervening in the market through open-market operations, without the former procedure involving the prior indication of firm price ranges. Since this policy was abandoned, the escudo has had a very stable exchange rate against the Ecu (see Figure 24.9), reflecting the discounting of the effect (or, at least, part of the effect) of the escudo joining the Ecu basket.

Trade balance

On the one hand, this currency behaviour has favoured the control of inflation, but on the other it has led to a deterioration in the trade deficit, with imports generally expanding more than exports (see Figure 24.10).

Alongside the exchange rate behaviour, other causes of this trade imbalance are the external recessionary environment and a crisis in the paper pulp industry, one of the main sources of export for Portugal. In spite of this deficit, however, the country is not dependent on foreign borrowing, due to the healthiness of the capital account. As noted earlier, growth opportunities on the one hand and high domestic interest rates on the other, have together attracted both foreign capital and emigrants' remittances. At the moment reserves even exceed foreign debt by a significant amount (see Figure 24.11).

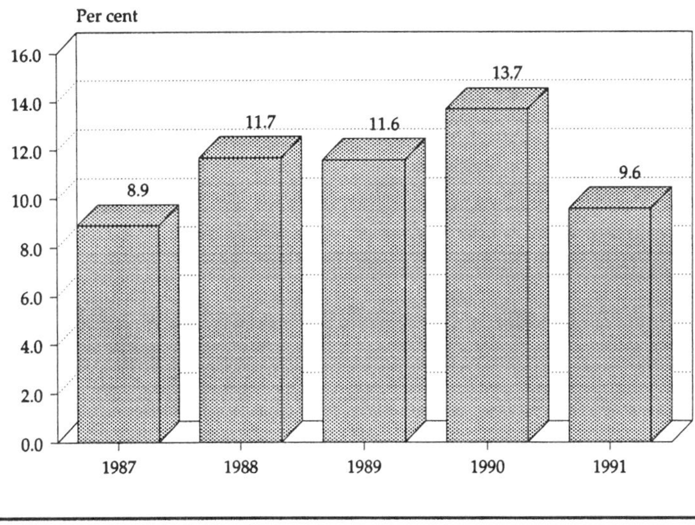

Figure 24.8 **Portuguese inflation (per cent, year-on-year)**

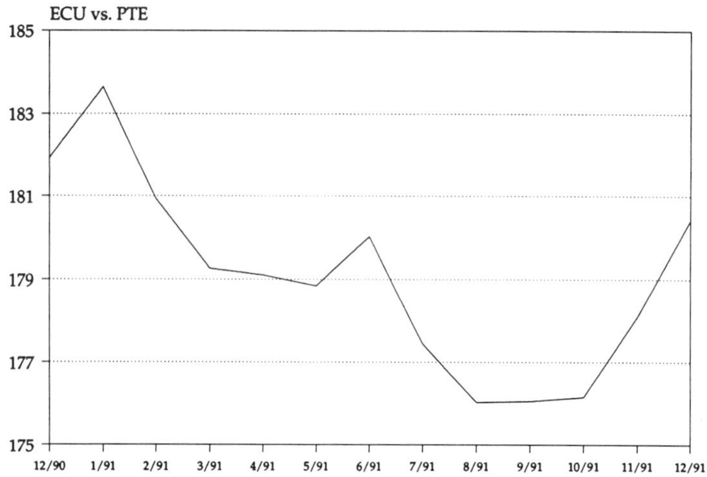

Figure 24.9 ECU/PTE exchange rate (average monthly value)

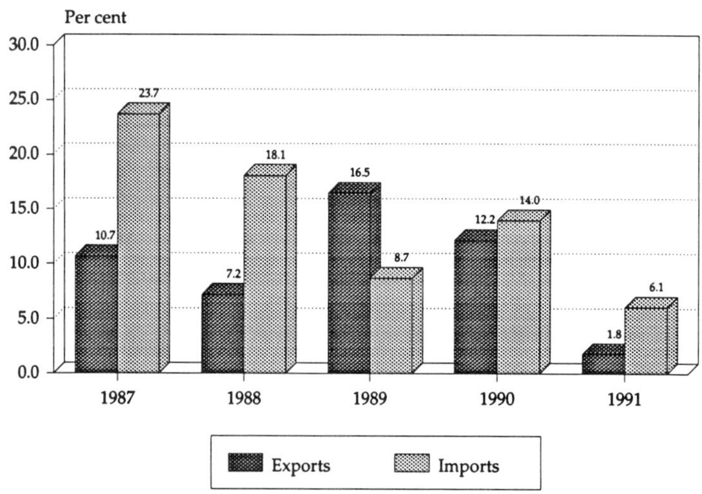

Figure 24.10 Portuguese import/export growth

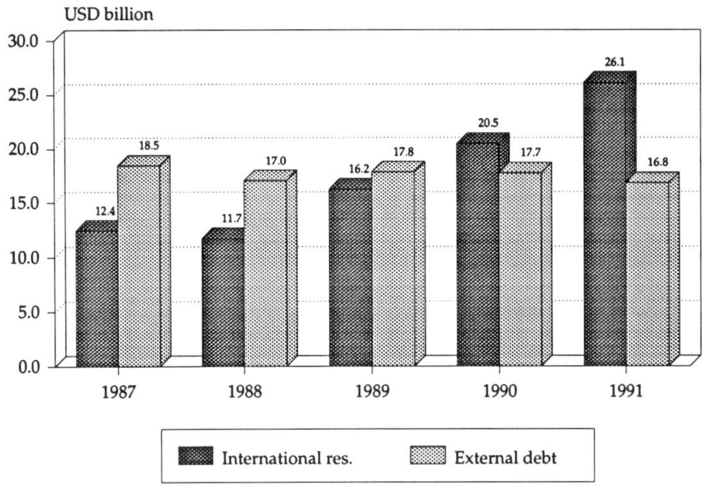

Figure 24.11 International reserves & external debt

24.3 *Market composition*

Note: All the data in this section refers to securities listed on the Lisbon Stock Exchange, as at 12 December 1991 (unless otherwise stated).

Composition by maturity structure

Government bonds

Most government bonds mature between 1996 and 1998. Those that mature in 1998, and those that mature in 1996, are the most liquid (see Figures 24.12 & 24.13).

Corporate bonds

The maturity of corporate bonds is quite uniform in the period from 1992 to 1996, followed by a peak in 1997. However, in terms of turnover, the bonds with maturities from 1995 to 1997 are more liquid (see Figures 24.14 & 24.15).

State agencies and supranationals

Most bonds issued by state agencies and supranationals in the Portuguese market mature in 1997, and they have the higher liquidity (see Figures 24.16 & - 24.17).

Composition by coupon structure

Government bonds

Most of the coupons of floating-rate government bonds are in the range from 17.5 per cent to 20 per cent. This is the case both in terms of amount outstanding, as well as in terms of turnover. The next most significant coupons are those between 15 per cent and 17 per cent, followed by those between 12.5 per cent and 15 per cent. It should be stressed that most of these bonds are floating-rate notes, so that their coupon values can be explained mainly by taxation differences (see Section 24.13). There are some bonds with very low coupons outstanding, although they have almost no liquidity (see Figures 24.18 & 24.19).

Corporate bonds

As far as corporate bonds are concerned, most of their coupons are quite evenly spread in the ranges from 12.5 per cent to 15 per cent, 15 per cent to 17.5 per cent, 17.5 per cent to 20 per cent and 20 per cent to 22.5 per cent. In terms of turnover, the most liquid bonds are those with coupons between 17.5 per cent and 20 per cent (see Figures 24.20 & 24.21).

State agencies and supranationals

The coupons of fixed-rate supranational bonds lie mainly in the 12.0 to 15.0 per cent range, while state agency FRNs are generally found in the 17.5 to 20.0 per cent range. In terms of turnover, bonds with coupons between 12.0-15.0 per cent and 17.5-20.0 per cent are more evenly spread (see Figures 24.22 & 24.23).

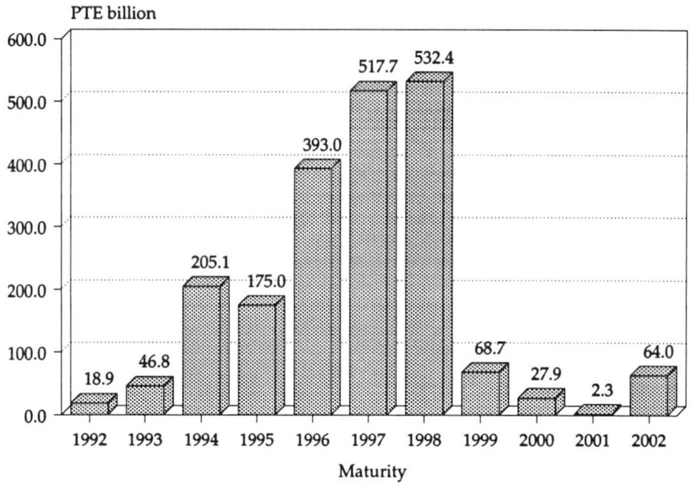

Figure 24.12 Maturity structure of the government bond market (by volume outstanding)
Source: Lisbon Stock Exchange

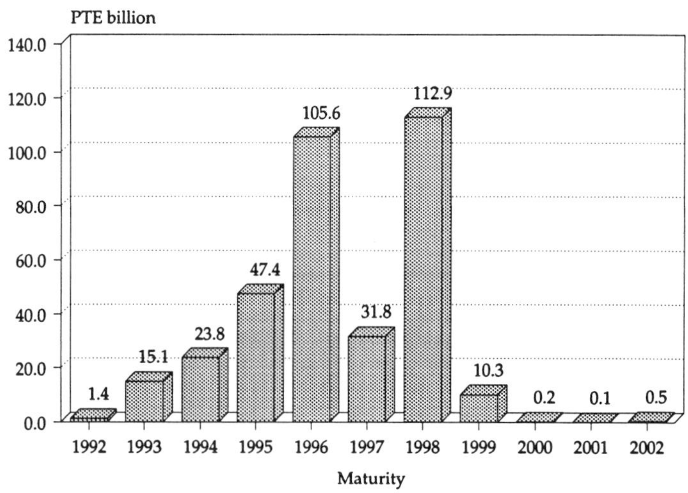

Figure 24.13 Maturity structure of the government bond market (by turnover)
Source: Lisbon Stock Exchange

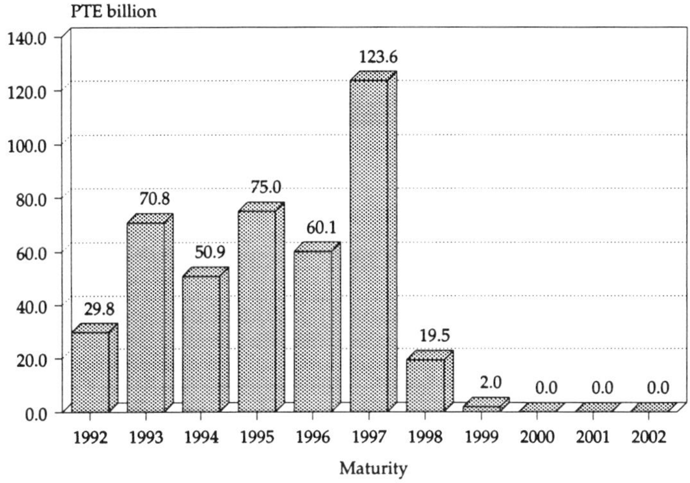

Figure 24.14 Maturity structure of the corporate bond market (by volume outstanding)
Source: Lisbon Stock Exchange

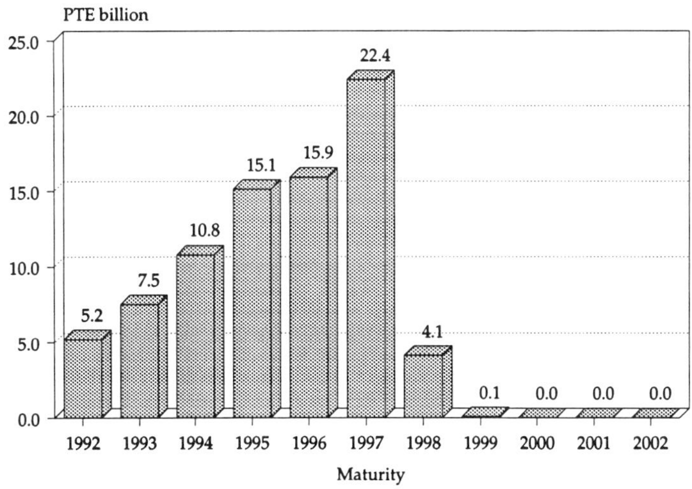

Figure 24.15 Maturity structure of the corporate bond market (by turnover)
Source: Lisbon Stock Exchange

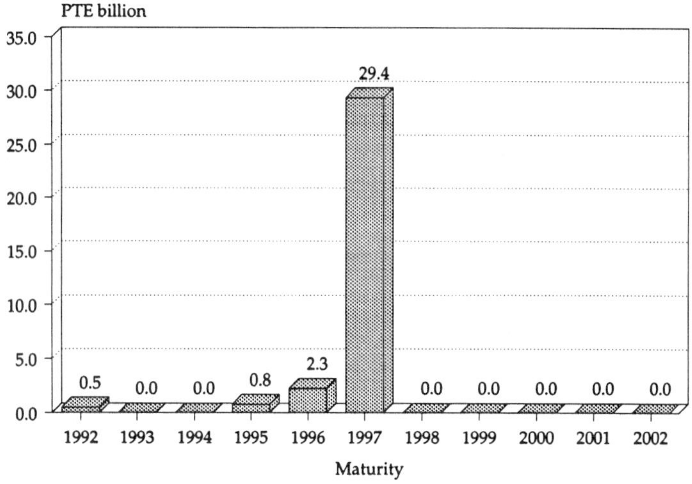

Figure 24.16 Maturity structure of the state agency & supranational mkt. (by vol. outstanding)
Source: Lisbon Stock Exchange

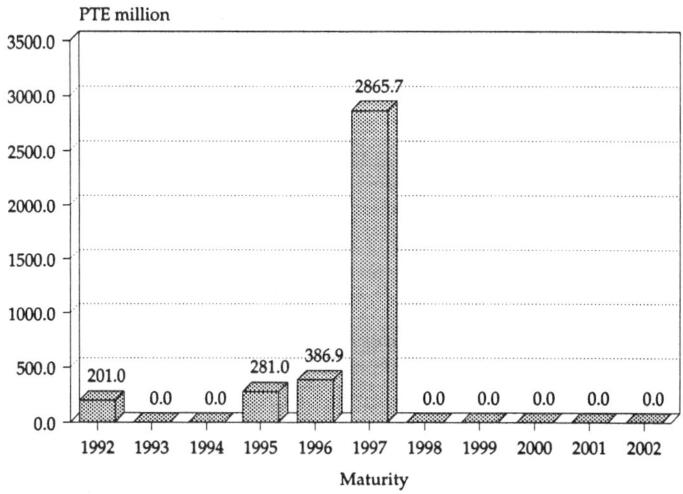

Figure 24.17 Maturity structure of the state agency & supranational bond market (by turnover)
Source: Lisbon Stock Exchange

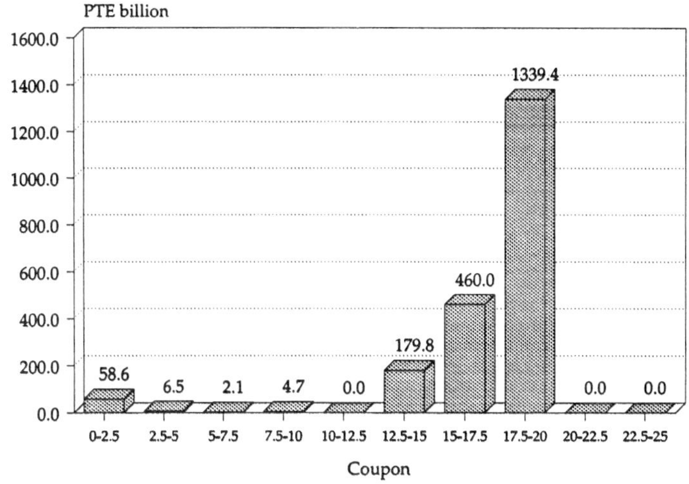

Figure 24.18 Coupon structure of the government bond market (by volume outstanding)
Source: Lisbon Stock Exchange

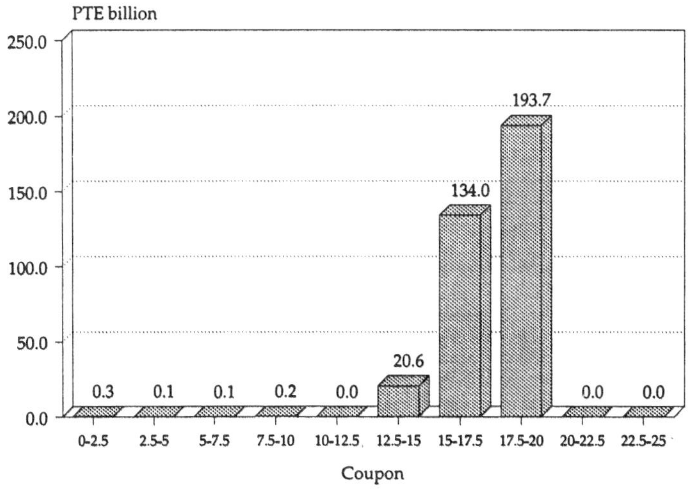

Figure 24.19 Coupon structure of the government bond market (by turnover)
Source: Lisbon Stock Exchange

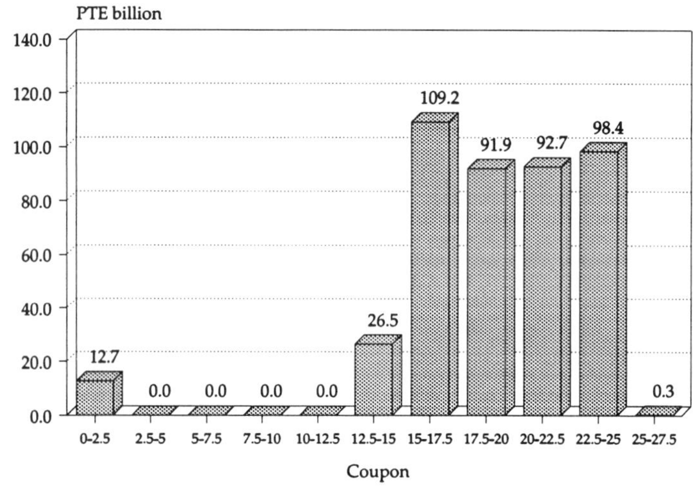

Figure 24.20 Coupon structure of the corporate bond market (by volume outstanding)
Source: Lisbon Stock Exchange

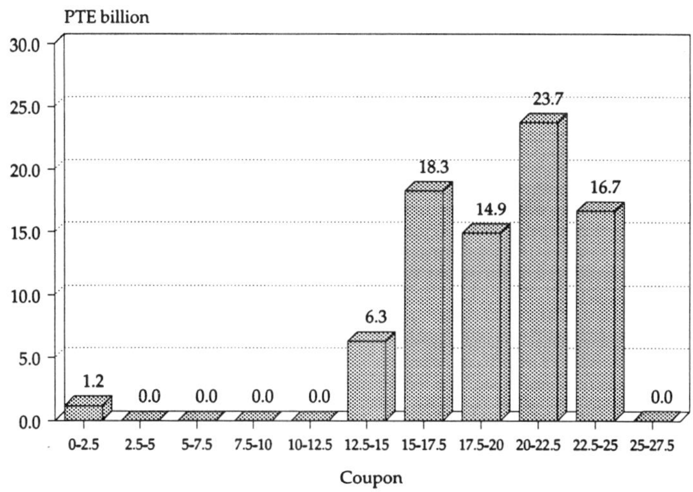

Figure 24.21 Coupon structure of the corporate bond market (by turnover)
Source: Lisbon Stock Exchange

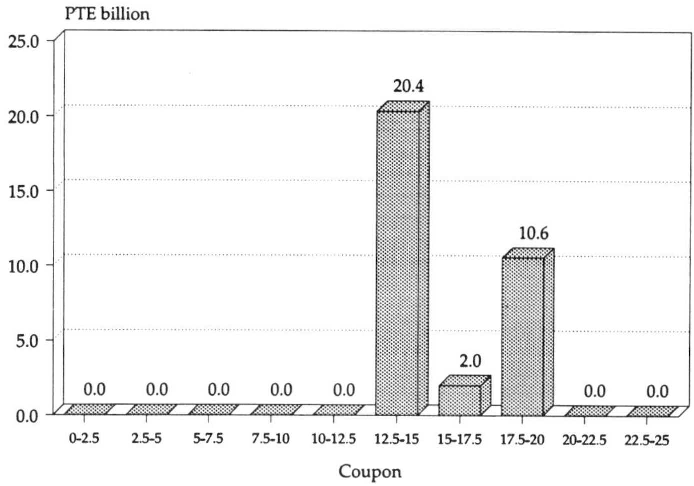

Figure 24.22 Coupon structure of the state agency & supranational mkt. (by vol. outstanding)
Source: Lisbon Stock Exchange

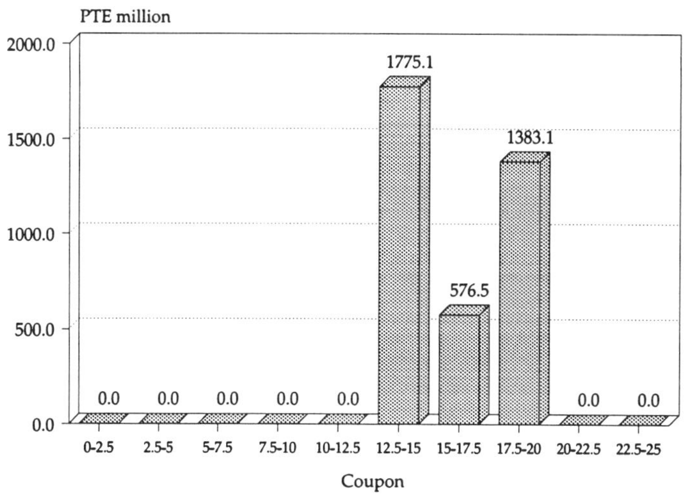

Figure 24.23 Coupon structure of the state agency & supranational bond market (by turnover)
Source: Lisbon Stock Exchange

24.4 Types of security

Overview

There are three ways to classify Portuguese bonds, namely by:

- redemption method
- coupon variation
- coupon payment

Redemption method

There are several different redemption methods:

Lottery method

In this method, each security has a number and at the date of the redemption, the decision on which bonds are redeemed and which are not, is made by lottery. This method may be implemented by identifying either individual bond numbers or large numbered series of bonds. The latter method was once used very frequently (indeed, until 1988, it was the most frequent method), but is now less common due to the administrative costs involved. In Figures 24.24 to 24.29, this method can be identified by the x-axis code (1) for annual redemptions, and (3) for semi-annual redemptions.

Reduction of nominal value

This method became more prevalent in 1989, as the government began to utilize it in its own issues. In Figures 24.24 to 24.29, this method can be identified by the x-axis code (2) for annual redemptions, and (4) for semi-annual redemptions.

Irredeemable

The government has been the sole issuer of irredeemable bonds. Three issues were placed between 1940 and 1943, but they have almost no liquidity. In Figures 24.24 to 24.29, this method can be identified by the x-axis code (5).

Bullet redemption

This redemption method was used most recently in the last FRN issues of the government. In Figures 24.24 to 24.29, this method can be identified by the x-axis code (6).

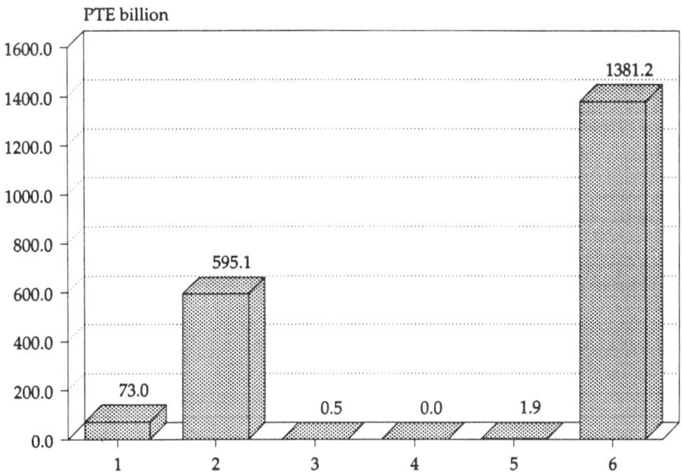

Figure 24.24 Government bond redemption methods (by volume outstanding)
Source: Lisbon Stock Exchange

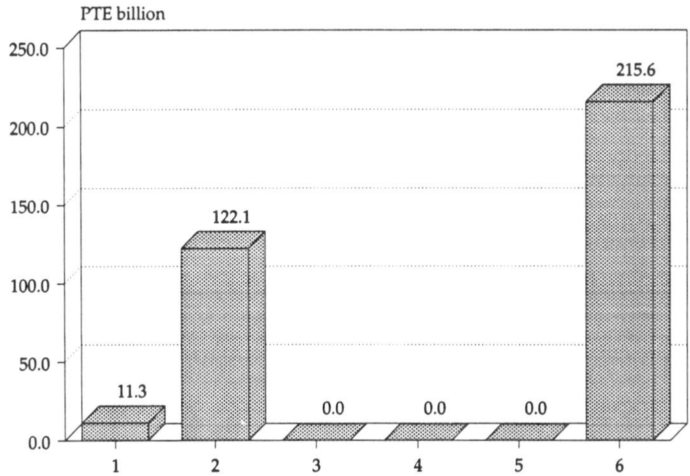

Figure 24.25 Government bond redemption methods (by turnover)
Source: Lisbon Stock Exchange

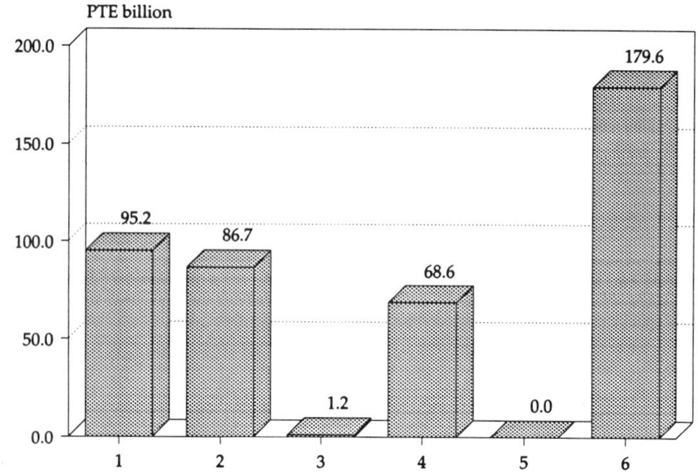

Figure 24.26 Corporate bond redemption methods (by volume outstanding)
Source: Lisbon Stock Exchange

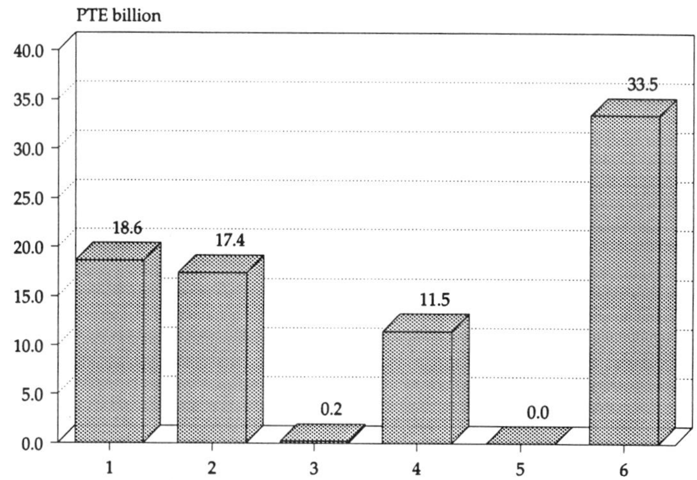

Figure 24.27 Corporate bond redemption methods (by turnover)
Source: Lisbon Stock Exchange

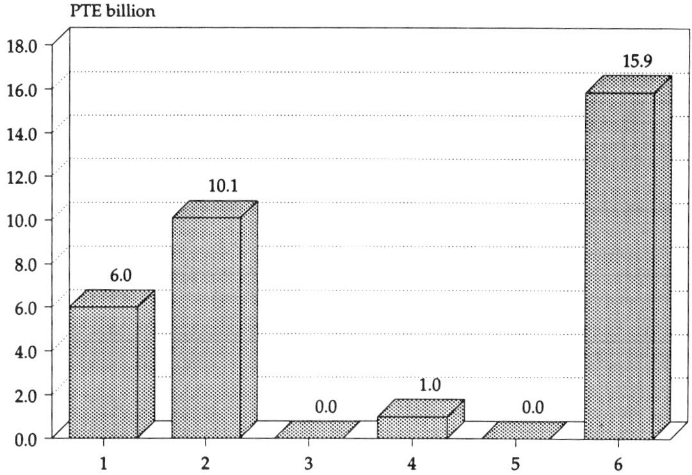

Figure 24.28 State agency & supranational bond redemption methods (by volume outstanding)
Source: Lisbon Stock Exchange

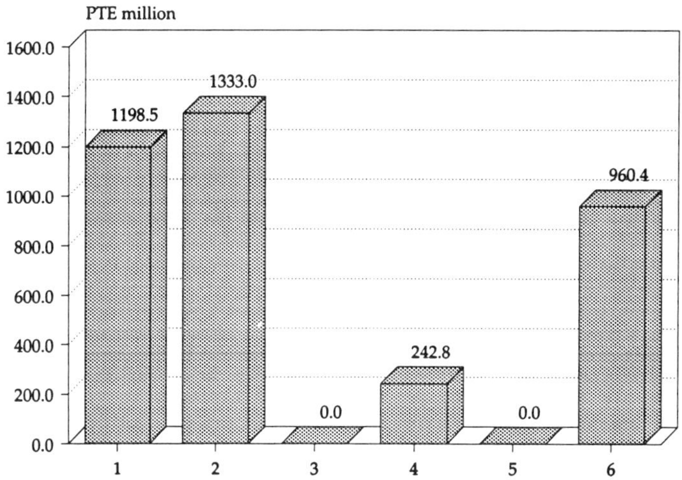

Figure 24.29 State agency & supranational bond redemption methods (by turnover)
Source: Lisbon Stock Exchange

■ Government bonds
Most government bonds have bullet redemptions (see Figures 24.24 & 24.25), although another very important redemption method is by annual decrease of nominal value. A small percentage of bonds are redeemed annual by a lottery method. Almost all redemptions are annual.

■ Corporate bonds
The majority of the corporate bonds have bullet redemptions (see Figures 24.26 & 24.27). However, there are also some bonds with annual redemptions either by lottery, or by decrease of nominal value. There are also some corporate bonds with semi-annual decrease of nominal value.

■ State agencies and supranationals
State agency and supranational issues normally have bullet redemption (see Figures 24.28 & 24.29), although annual redemption by decrease of nominal value and lottery method are also common, particularly for state agency bonds.

Coupon variation

In the Portuguese market, coupons may vary in several ways as described below:

Fixed-rate

Until the beginning of 1991, fixed-rate bonds were not very popular in the Portuguese bond market due to the high degree of uncertainty over inflation. They were first issued in 1986 and followed in 1990 by further issues, although they were not listed.

Due to a stronger international projection of Portugal in 1991 and also due to the fact that non-residents tend to prefer this type of security, fixed-rate issues enjoyed an enthusiastic market reception in 1991. These bonds enable investors to take a better view on the nominal convergence of the European economies. At the same time, they are more straightforward than the rather complex floating-rate issues, in which the investor has to monitor the behaviour of the underlying rate.

Puttable bonds with reset coupons

These bonds are a hybrid between fixed-rate and floating-rate. They were issued by the EIB in 1988 and 1989, albeit rather infrequently. However, with the strong development of fixed-rate bonds, it can be expected that the market for this type of security will develop further.

Floating-rate notes

In recent years, these securities have become much more common in the Portuguese bond market, because inflation has been one of the most uncertain variables of the economy. For FRNs, it is useful to distinguish between the reference rate of the bonds and the spread at which they vary relative to the underlying rate.

The reference rates that are currently used in the Portuguese bond market are mainly the TRO (the reference rate fixed by the Bank of Portugal), the average term deposit rate, APB (the lending rate of the Portuguese Association of Banks), and the TBA (the average rate of the last twelve Treasury bill auctions). Recently, use has also been made of the maximum of several indexations in order to determine the coupon. In Figures 24.30 - 24.35, the following x-axis codes are used:

1	Fixed-rate	7	APB 90 days
2	Discount rate of central bank	8	Treasury bill rate
3	TRO	9	APB 180 days
4	Term deposit rate	10	Mixed APB and BTS
5	Puttable bonds with reset coupons	11	Others
6	Ecu-LIBOR		

■ Government bonds

Government bonds indexed to the average Treasury bill rate form the largest group (see Figures 24.30 & 24.31), followed by those indexed to the term deposit rate of the three largest institutions, in terms of this instrument. The third largest group of bonds is composed of those with coupons indexed to the TRO. In terms of turnover, the ranking is similar, although here, fixed-rate bonds form the third-largest group. It should be noted that, recently, FRNs have been called 'FIPs' and fixed-rate bonds, 'OTs'.

■ Corporate bonds

Most corporate bonds are TRO-linked (see Figures 24.32 & 24.33), with only a very small amount being linked to the average Treasury bill rate, and this is the case both in terms of amount outstanding and turnover.

■ State agency and supranational bonds

Bonds of state agencies and supranationals have either coupons indexed to the TRO, or are puttable with reset coupons (see Figures 24.34 & 24.35). Puttable

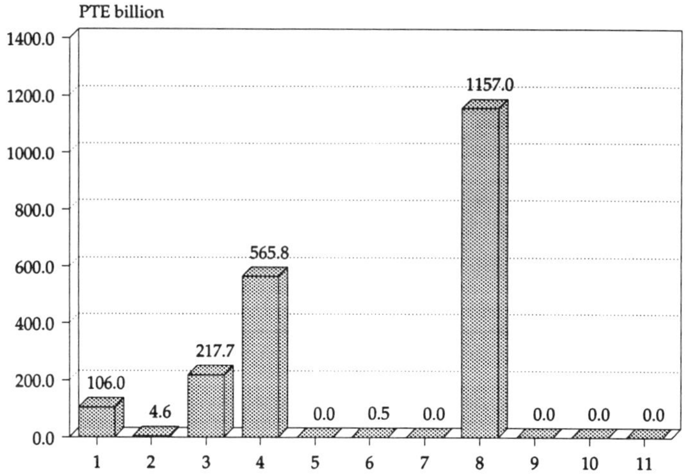

Figure 24.30 Indexation of government bonds (by volume outstanding)
Source: Lisbon Stock Exchange

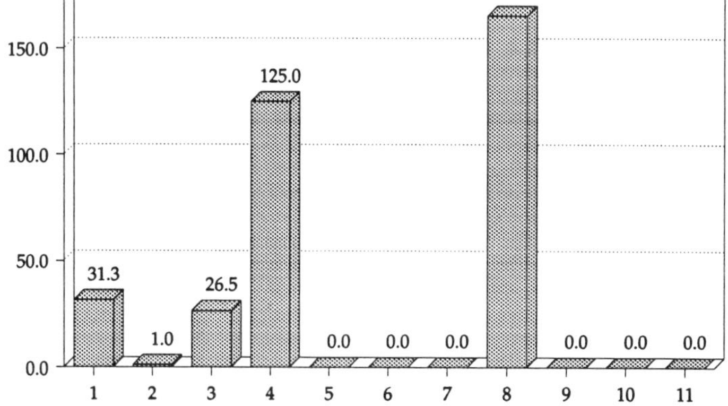

Figure 24.31 Indexation of government bonds (by turnover)
Source: Lisbon Stock Exchange

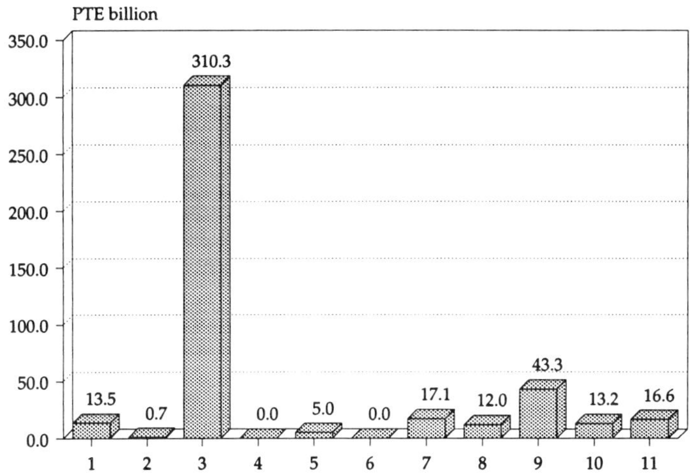

Figure 24.32 Indexation of corporate bonds (by volume outstanding)
Source: Lisbon Stock Exchange

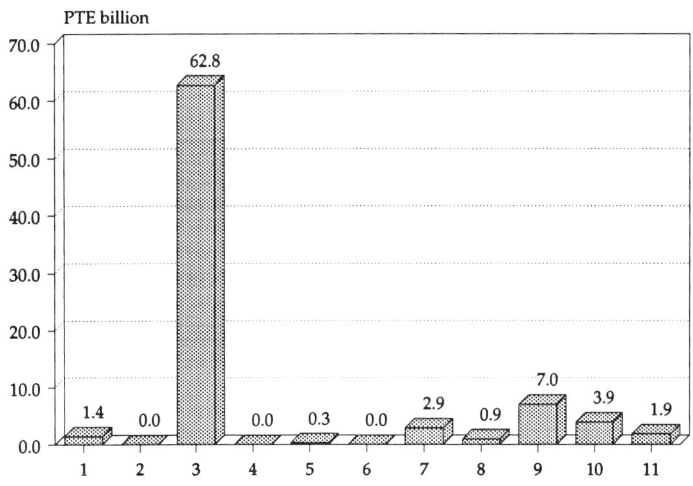

Figure 24.33 Indexation of corporate bonds (by turnover)
Source: Lisbon Stock Exchange

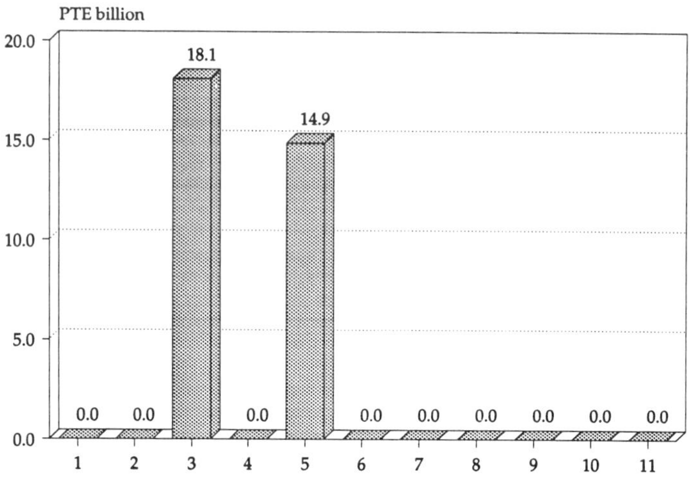

Figure 24.34 Indexation of state agency & supranational bonds (by volume outstanding)
Source: Lisbon Stock Exchange

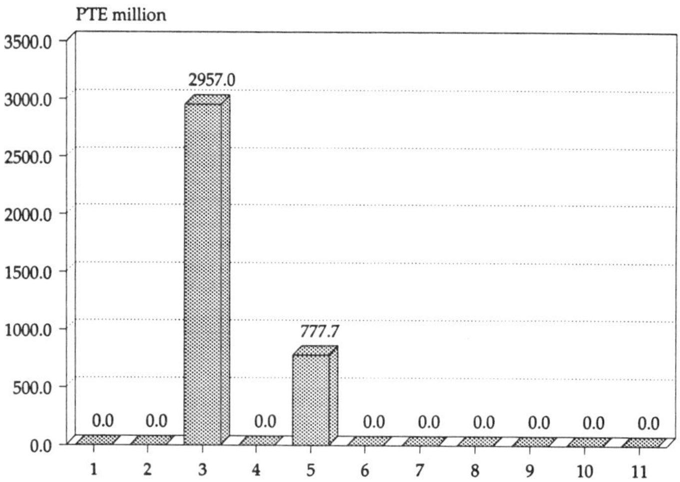

Figure 24.35 Indexation of state agency & supranational bonds (by turnover)
Source: Lisbon Stock Exchange

bonds with reset coupons do not have much liquidity in the Portuguese market because they have only been issued by EIB and have low transaction volumes.

Types of spread

■ Stepped variable
Some issues have variable spreads typically ascending with the number of the coupons. Most of the bonds with stepped spread are government bonds (see Figure 24.36). However, most of the turnover is in corporate bonds (see Figure 24.37).

■ Fixed
The most common type of spread is the fixed spread, and this may take different forms:

- Multiplicative
  This spread (see Figures 24.38 & 24.39) has recently been used more frequently, principally due to expectations of decreasing interest rates.

- Additive
  This is the most common form of spread above the reference rate, especially in relation to bonds indexed to the TRO and to APB. The spreads have varied significantly mainly because the changes in the reference rate have not reflected the changes in the market rates, but also because of taxation differences. Typically, the spread is positive above the TRO and Treasury bills and negative for coupons that vary with APB.

Coupon payment

Zero-coupon

There are very few securities with this characteristic. Recently there has been one issue - EDP 1990. In Figures 24.40 to 24.45, these bonds can be identified by the x-axis code (0).

Annual

Annual coupons are very rare in the Portuguese market, as may be seen in Figures 24.40 to 24.45, where these bonds can be identified by the x-axis code (1).

Semi-annual

This is the most usual coupon payment period. A special example of semi-annual coupons is the OCA. This is a floating-rate security that capitalizes interest

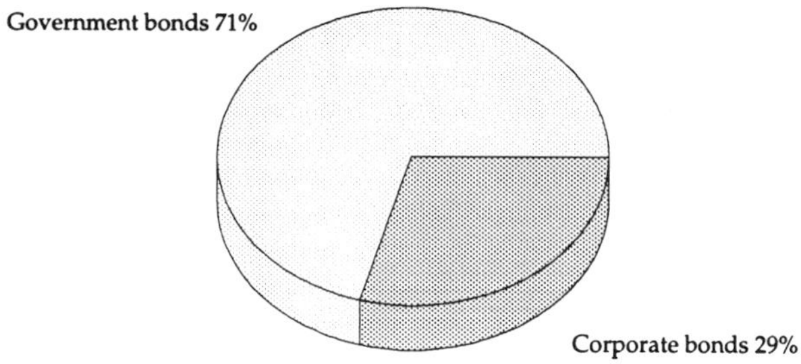

Figure 24.36 Stepped-spread bonds (by volume outstanding)

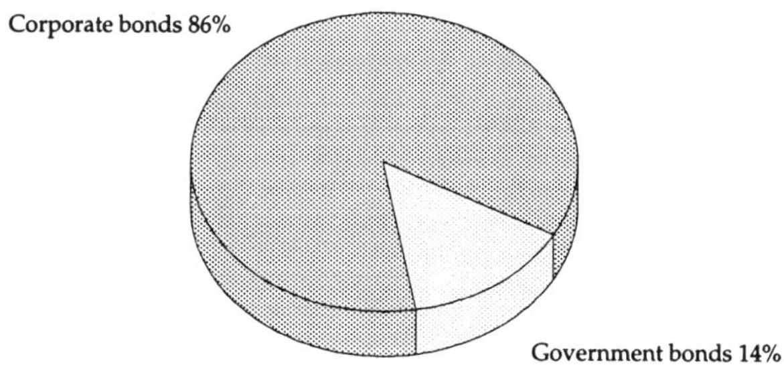

Figure 24.37 Stepped-spread bonds (by turnover)

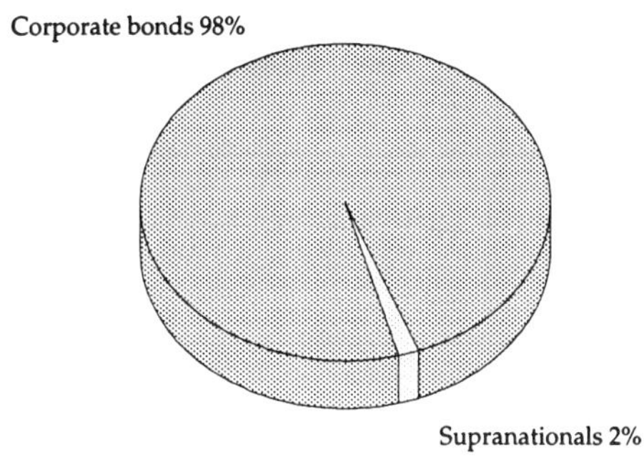

Figure 24.38 Bonds with multiplicative spread (by amount outstanding)

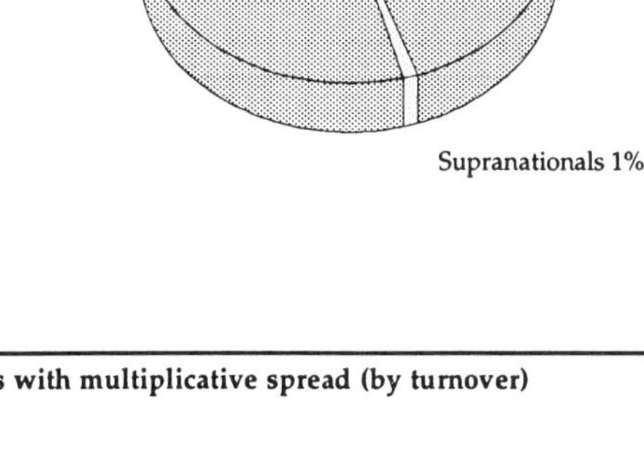

Figure 24.39 Bonds with multiplicative spread (by turnover)

semi-annually, only paying it at maturity. Consequently, each time the coupon matures, it accrues to the nominal value. These securities have been issued in 1986 and 1989/90. In 1991, a significant volume of OCAs were budgeted for but, as that year's fixed-rate bonds were so well received in the market, no OCAs were issued to the public. In Figures 24.40 to 24.45, OCAs can be identified by the x-axis code (2).

Quarterly

This type of coupon payment is very rare in the Portuguese market. A couple of examples, though, are BPI 87. In Figures 24.40 to 24.45, these bonds can be identified by the x-axis code (3).

Other bonds

Convertibles and bonds with warrants

There are very few convertible bonds listed. The equity market has shown very poor performance since 1987, and hence the volume of equity-linked issues has been very low. Two examples, though, are BPI 90 and BCM 90.

Cash bonds

Cash bonds are issued by financial institutions and usually have short maturities (which, nevertheless, have to exceed two years). They have simplified issuance procedures and may be issued either in series or continuously. Examples of issuers are Banco Fomento e Exterior, Banco Português de Investimento and Deutsche Bank de Investimento. Issuance since 1987 is shown in Figure 24.46

Mortgage bonds

Mortgage bonds, which provide the investor with a special indemnity relative to the real estate of the issuer, were only regulated in 1990. Their maturity must range between 3 and 30 years and, like cash bonds, they may be issued either in series or continuously. The volume outstanding is quite low, which is attributable on the one hand to the novelty of the instrument and, on the other, to the still rather early stage in the development of rating awareness by some investors. The only issuer in 1991 has been Caixa Geral de Depósitos, the biggest Portuguese financial institution, which has issued two bonds of Esc 2.5bn each (see Figure 24.47).

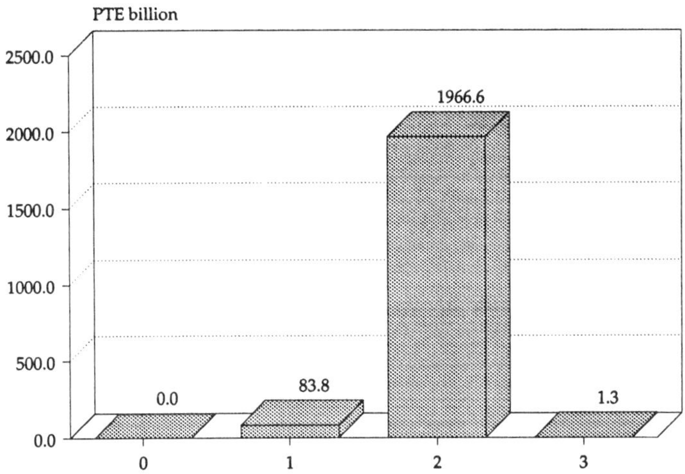

Figure 24.40 Types of coupon payment in the government bond market (by vol. outstanding)
Source: Lisbon Stock Exchange

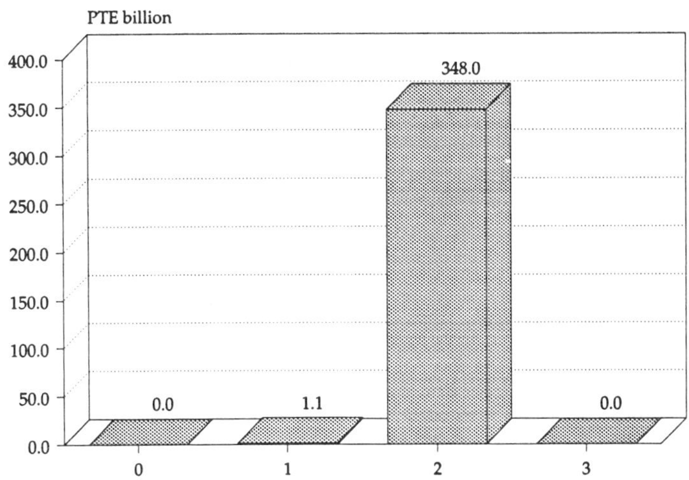

Figure 24.41 Types of coupon payment in the government bond market (by turnover)
Source: Lisbon Stock Exchange

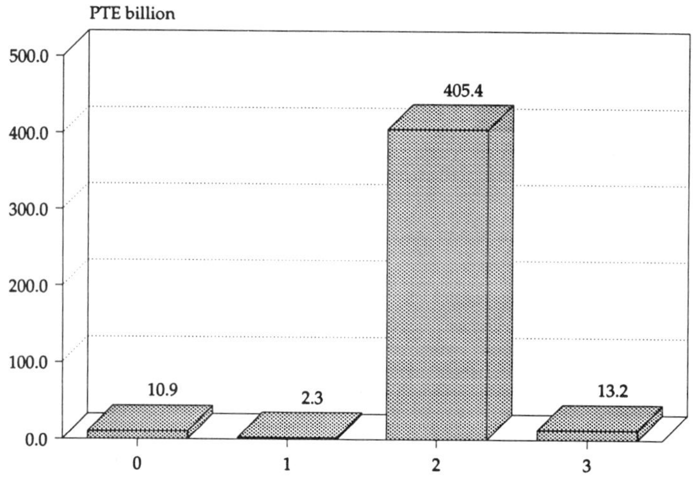

Figure 24.42 Types of coupon payment in the corporate bond market (by amount outstanding)
Source: Lisbon Stock Exchange

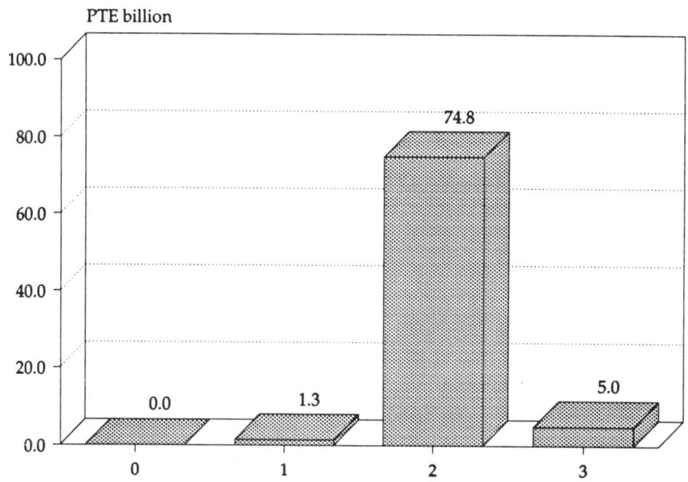

Figure 24.43 Types of coupon payment in the corporate bond market (by turnover)
Source: Lisbon Stock Exchange

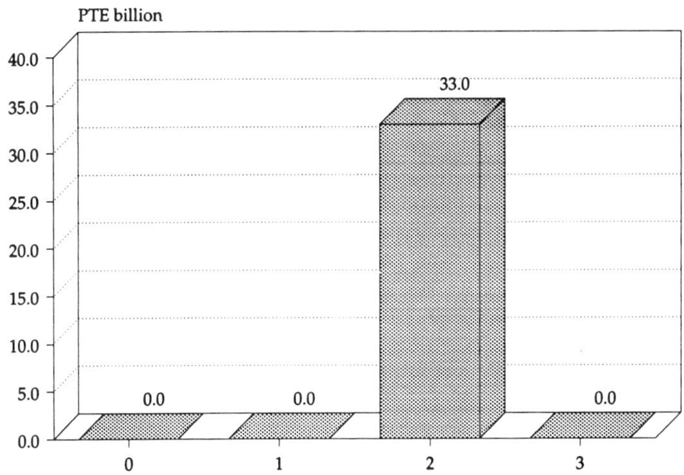

Figure 24.44 Types of coupon payment in the state ag. / supranat. mkt. (by vol. outstanding)
Source: Lisbon Stock Exchange

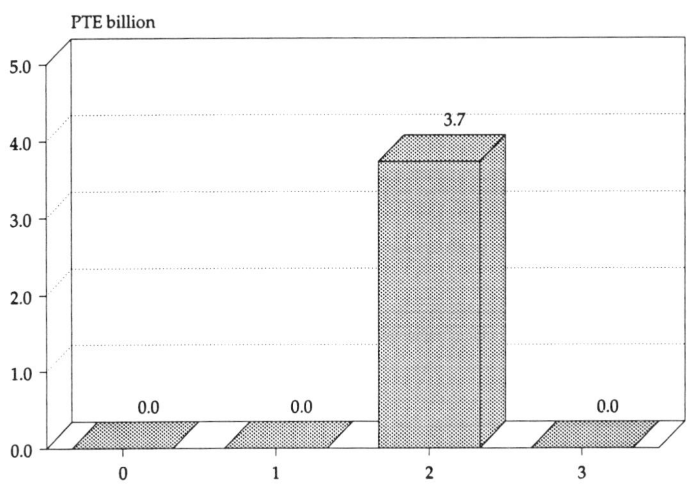

Figure 24.45 Types of coupon payment in the state ag. / supranat. market (by turnover)
Source: Lisbon Stock Exchange

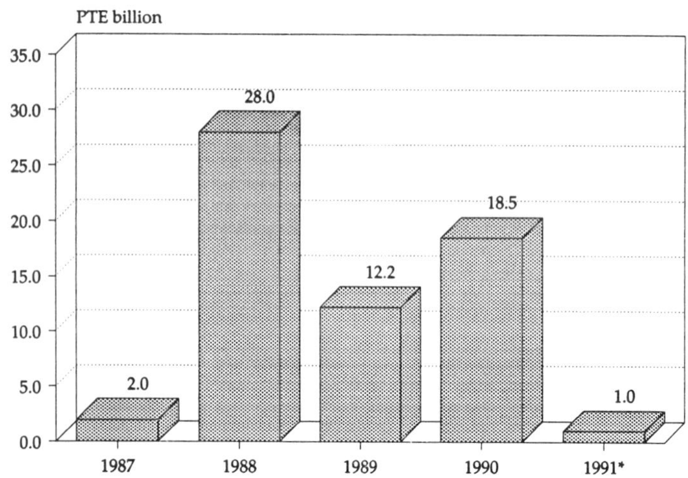

*) to September

Figure 24.46 New issuance of cash bonds
Source: Bank of Portugal

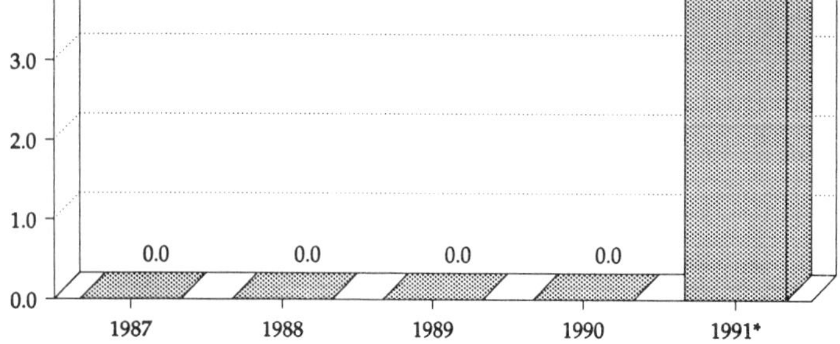

*) to September

Figure 24.47 New issuance of mortgage bonds
Source: Bank of Portugal

24.5 *Issuers*

Portuguese government

The most important issuer in the Portuguese bond market both in terms of volume outstanding and liquidity is the Portuguese government (see Figure 24.48). Its importance has increased, because:

- there is a relatively high level of public debt
- in order to ease monetary pressures, the government has increasingly utilized the bond market rather than other money-creating methods such as funding through the central bank, or through foreign debt.

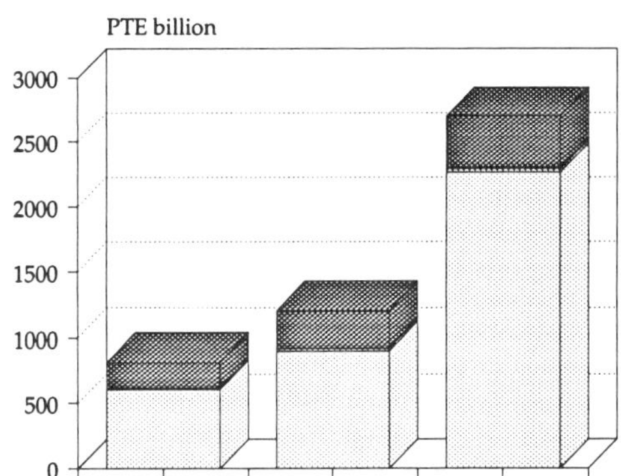

	1989	1990	1991
Corporates	198.72	279.891	409.048
Government agencies	12.438	22.686	32.734
Government	604.477	900.354	2260.116

Figure 24.48 Official market capitalization
Source: SIIB

Corporate issuers

As may be seen in the following graphs, the main corporate issuers are from the financial sector, the energy sector (mainly EDP), and the communication sector.

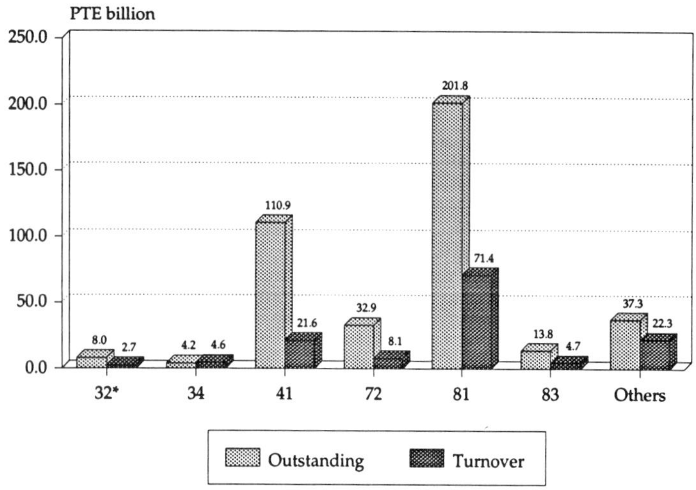

*) see below for key to codes

Figure 24.49 Corporate issuers in the Portuguese bond market
Source: SIBB

Note: x-axis codes for the different economic sectors are as follows:

32	*Textiles, clothing & leather*
34	*Paper, graphics, and publishing*
41	*Electricity, gas & steam*
72	*Communications*
81	*Banks & other financial institutions*
83	*Real estate transactions & services rendered to companies*

It should be stressed that, whilst in the energy sector EDP is almost the sole issuer, in the financial sector there are many issuers, principally leasing companies and investment societies. Bonds are one of the few instruments that these financial companies can use to fund themselves, since they cannot accept deposits. Investment banks have also used this market, as the bond market enables them to meet their specialized requirement for long-term funding.

Commercial banks have not been frequent issuers of bonds, mainly because they have access to sources of cheaper funding.

EDP is a state-owned company that produces almost all the electricity in Portugal. It is clearly the single-most important issuer, reflecting the high investment demands needed for its electricity-producing infrastructures, as well as the need to finance credit to some municipalities. In order to reduce its high leverage, it has recently followed a strategy of asset sales, namely its new power stations.

24.6 *Investors*

Overview

The main investors in the Portuguese bond market are, in decreasing order of importance:

- commercial banks
- insurance companies
- mutual funds
- pension funds
- investment banks
- foreign investors

This order reflects the recent situation but, until 1988 , investment banks were second in the ranking, a situation which reflected a special tax benefit. However, this position was merely temporary, as mutual and pension funds began to gain strength in the market. In 1991, foreign investors, especially foreign banks, started to invest in the domestic bond market, mainly due to the appearance of euroescudo issues and to the escudo being strong against major European currencies. This attractiveness led foreign investors, especially banks and investment houses based in Europe, to play a major role in the upward price movement seen in the fixed- and floating-rate note issues in 1991 .

Commercial banks

The historical influence of commercial banks as investors in the Portuguese bond market is very strong, particularly in the period prior to 1991, when all the major commercial banks were state-owned and were consequently the main investors in both public debt issues and corporate bonds. Until 1989, their interest as investors was always in long-term investments, which had seen little trading activity due to the low liquidity of the market.

From 1989, however, this situation changed, particularly after the creation of domestic banks' offshore branches in Madeira. As a result, commercial banks are today the major investors in the bond market (see Figure 24.50), and will probably remain in this position for some time.

As at the end of June 1991, the commercial banks holding the most bonds and Treasury bills were: Caixa Geral de Depósitos, Banco Totta & Açores, Banco Português do Atlântico, Banco Pinto Sotto Mayor, Banco Espirito Santo e Comercial Lisboa.

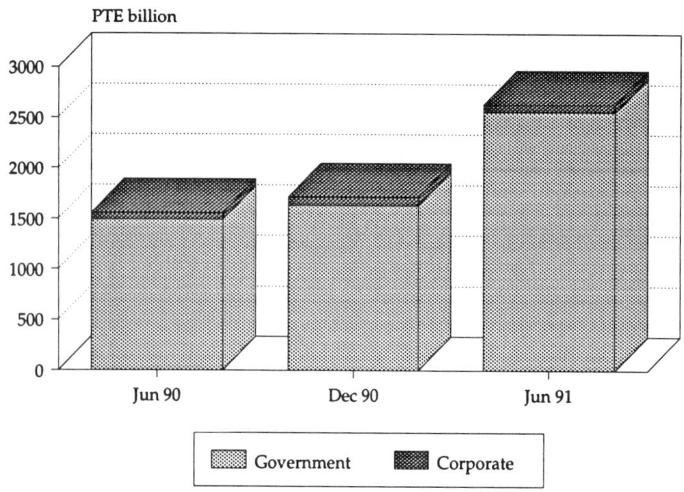

Figure 24.50 Fixed-income holdings of commercial banks
Source: APB

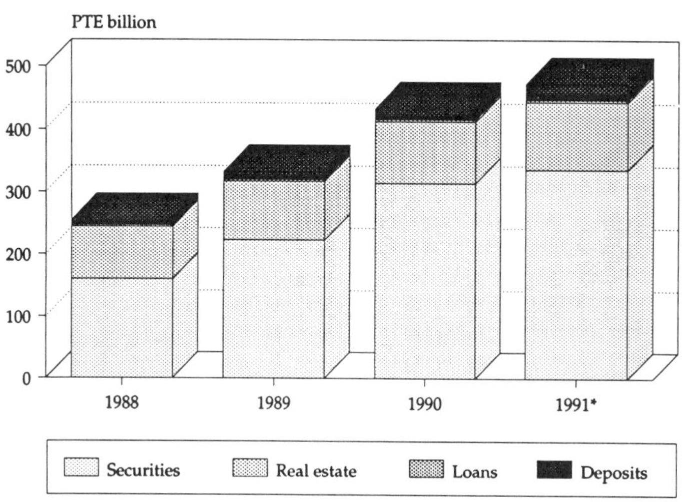

**) to June*

Figure 24.51 Portfolio structure of Portuguese insurance companies

Insurance companies

As is common in all the developed markets, insurance companies in Portugal are major investors in the bond market. Their rise to prominence as an investor group was due on the one hand to tax benefits and, on the other, to the rate of growth in the life segment following their creation in 1986/87. Their new investment in securities has been very important, increasing from 77 per cent in 1989 to 91.3 per cent in 1990 although, in the first semester of 1991, the figure has fallen to only 55.3 per cent, largely due to the attraction of real estate investments. Due to a legal requirement, insurance companies were obliged, until the end of 1991, to invest a minimum of 40 per cent (of their technical provision) in public debt issuance. This situation led many insurance companies to invest money only in Treasury issues and, consequently, their role as large investors in all types of bonds seen in 1988 and 1989, diminished in the following years.

Their investment in government bonds has consistently been the most important feature of this investment group. In 1989 such investment was particularly strong, mainly due to the tax reform that occurred that year. However, in 1990 and 1991, its relative importance has decreased. The fall in 1990 can be attributed to stronger investment in the equity market, whilst in 1991, it can be

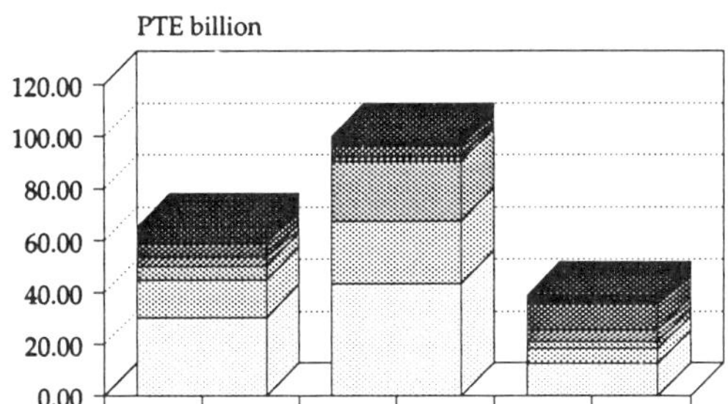

	1989	1990	1991*
Others	6.43	3.86	3.80
Real estate	5.46	4.37	9.59
Treasury bills	3.37	1.48	4.89
Shares/partic. bonds	5.27	22.80	2.51
Corporate bonds	14.36	24.03	5.83
Government bonds	30.52	43.56	12.48

*) *to June*

Figure 24.52 Net investments of Portuguese insurance companies

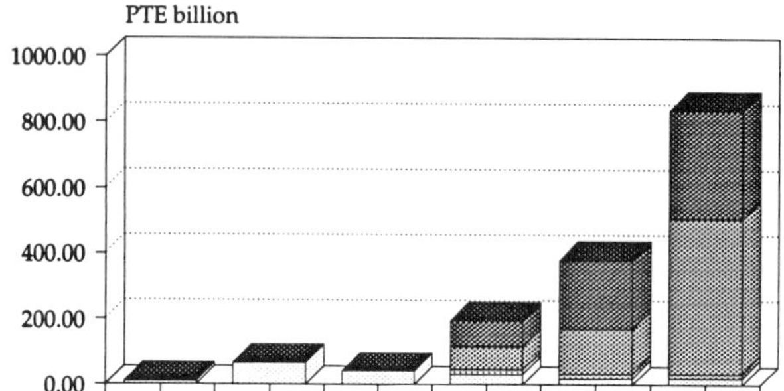

	1986	1987	1988	1989	1990	1991*
PPR funds	0.00	0.00	0.00	0.00	0.20	0.34
MM funds	0.00	0.00	0.13	81.12	210.33	330.24
Bond funds	0.00	0.00	0.00	69.21	135.55	471.52
Stock funds	0.00	0.00	0.00	14.61	14.49	15.10
Mixed funds	10.75	66.14	40.49	31.08	19.97	19.76

*) to October

Figure 24.53 Portuguese investment funds
Source: ASGFM

explained by an increased investment in real estate, as well as in Treasury bills, which was motivated by the high prices that the bonds attained in that year.

For 1992, the 40 per cent minimum investment ratio in public debt issuance has been reduced to 30 per cent. Investment in corporate bonds remained relatively stable in 1989 and 1990, but decreased sharply in 1991, mainly due to the lack of primary market activity.

Mutual funds

When mutual funds began their activities in 1986/87, they initially focused on the equity market. However, after the 1987 Crash, further growth in the mutual funds industry was seen, aided particularly by the creation of bond funds and the fact that Treasury funds changed their focus to bonds. These types of fund grew very fast as commercial banks wanted new and varied types of product to sell to their individual customer base. It should be stressed that, while bank deposits are subject to reserve requirements at the central bank, money market funds are free from such restrictions. Since 1989, mutual funds, and especially those that specialize in long-term and short-term income, have become the second largest investor group in Portugal. Since they are only obliged to invest 25 per cent of their assets in Treasuries, these funds are the main investors in corporate issues' private placements and, in the future, they are almost certain to

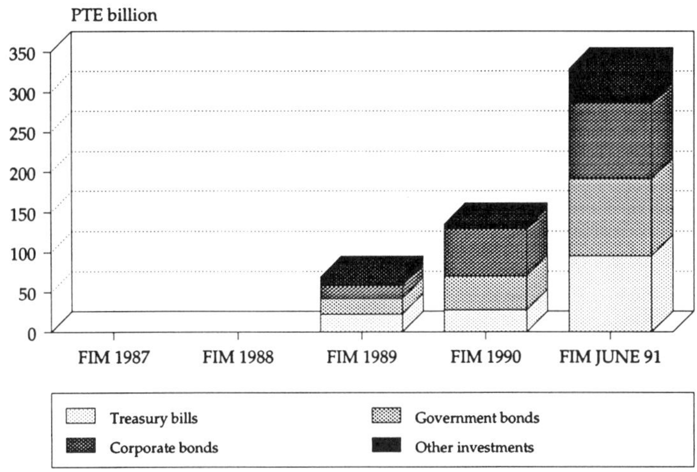

Figure 24.54 Portuguese bond funds
Source: ASGFM

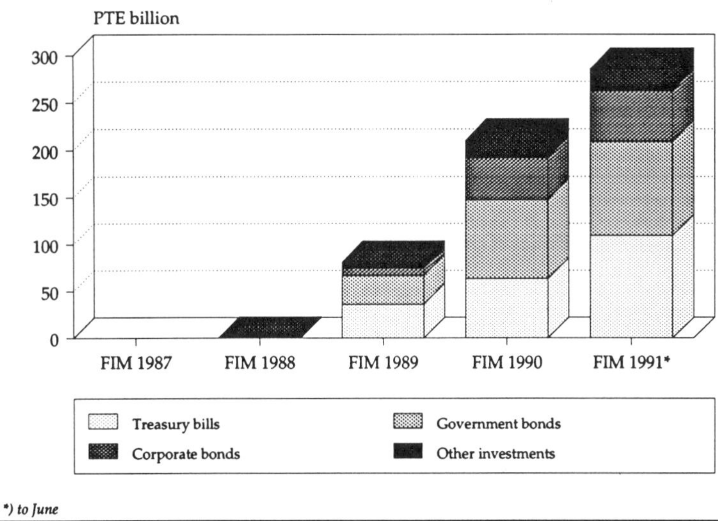

Figure 24.55 Treasury funds
Source: ASGFM

lead the market in terms of new product investment (such as derivatives, and so on). As at October 1991, the money market and bond funds together represented more than 90 per cent of the market; consequently, the importance of these funds in the bond market has become very substantial. From 1989 to 1990, in terms of asset allocation, there was very important growth in both the corporate and government bond segments. From January 1991 to October 1991, holdings of Treasury bills and government bonds have increased substantiality, while corporate bondholdings have seen reduced importance in percentage terms.

As noted above, the most important types of fund have been bond funds and money market funds. This has come about because, in the past, term deposits have been the single major application of the savings of the Portuguese people (in a manner similar to the French *sicavization*). This explains why Caixagest became the most important fund management company, since it is owned by Caixa Geral de Depositos which, in terms of deposits, is the largest Portuguese bank. The most important fund management companies, in terms of assets, are owned by Portuguese retail banks (as a result of the aforementioned *sicavization*):

- Caixagest - Caixa Geral de Depositos
- Interfundos - Banco Comercial Portugues
- Primogest - Banco Portugues do Atlantico
- Uniger - Uniao de Bancos Portugueses

Asset evolution

In the bond funds, there has recently been very important growth in Treasury bills (see Figure 24.54), coupled with a decrease in the importance of corporate bonds, this being mainly due to the lack of corporate primary market activity in 1991. As far as Treasury funds are concerned (see Figure 24.55), this movement has been even more pronounced due to the volatility of bond prices in 1991 and, consequently, the higher risk for short-term investors.

Pension funds

Since 1987, the pension fund industry has been a major investor in the corporate bond market, especially at the beginning of the period, since they had no obligation to invest a set amount in Treasury bonds. Since 1990, however, this situation has changed and, today, pension funds must have 30 per cent of their assets invested in Treasury bonds. The fiscal reform of 1989 re-introduced withholding tax on government issues and, as pension funds' income was tax-exempt, they swapped their portfolios, that year, from assets without withholding tax to others that had the tax, in which they had the highest comparative advantage. Nowadays, and with the weight of commercial banks, mutual funds and foreign investors in the market, the role of pension funds in the turnover of securities is rather small. In the future, their major involvement will probably be with private placements and derivatives.

Some insurance companies also play a major role in this market segment, particularly Tranquilidade, which ranks number one in the market and manages several funds with assets of Esc 32bn. The second-biggest name in the industry is Previsao, which manages two funds with assets of Esc 30bn.

In 1987, the assets managed by this industry were Esc 16bn. By 1989, this figure had grown to Esc 108bn and, by the end of 1990, it had reached Esc 170bn. Data for 1990 shows the total number of funds to be 185, with the average individual size being Esc 900m.

The biggest names in the pension fund management industry are:

- Tranquilidade Vida
- Previsão
- Praemium
- Vanguarda
- Futuro

Investment banks

As mentioned in the introduction, investment banks played a major role in the bond industry in the early eighties, being the first financial institutions to issue

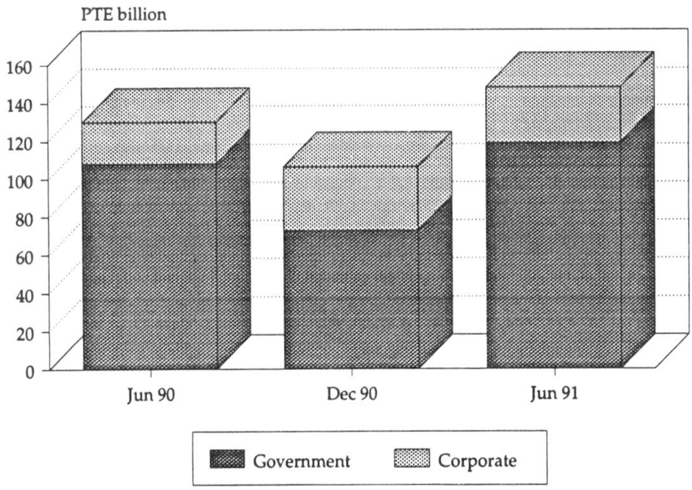

Figure 24.56 Fixed-income holdings of investment banks
Source: APB

bonds on a regular basis and, at the same time, being the main leading banks for new issues of corporate names. As investors, investment banks and investment houses played an particularly important role from 1985 to 1988, when their activities were mainly driven by a special tax benefit. With the loss of this benefit in 1988, and under funding pressure, both investment banks and investment houses have significantly reduced their security holdings - this being particularly so in the case of investment houses which do not have access to the money market. As a result, investment banks focused more on the origination of issues, which diminished the role of investment houses in the primary market. On the other hand, investment banks lost their position as big investors to commercial banks, mainly due to the cheaper funding obtained by the latter.

During 1990 and 1991, some Portuguese investment banks have increased their holdings in bonds, mainly due to the attraction of funding offshore in Madeira where such funding can be made at euroescudo rates, which are considerably cheaper than domestic rates. As at the end of June 1991, the major Portuguese investment banks, in terms of securities holdings, were:

- Banco Português de Investimento
- Banco Fomento e Exterior
- Sociedade Financeira Portuguesa

Foreign investment

Foreign investment in the Portuguese bond market increased substantially between 1989 and 1991 (see Figures 24.57 - 24.61), mainly due to the establishment of Madeira's offshore zone, where several Portuguese banks were able to finance Portuguese bonds at the lower euroescudo rates. Another major influence has been the growth in the importance of Macau, due mainly the presence of Portuguese banks there.

From 1990 to 1991 the importance of Madeira became particularly strong, but also of importance was the impact of purchasing by Spanish and Danish nationals. Great Britain, meanwhile, had substantially smaller net purchases of government bonds as at September 1991 (see Figure 24.63), this being mainly due to the decrease in market yields which motivated some British institutional investors to sell. As may be seen in Figure 24.64 - 24.69, the main investors in the Portuguese market are banks - mainly the offshore branches of Portuguese banks, but also some foreign banks, with those of Denmark and Spain being particularly important (see above).

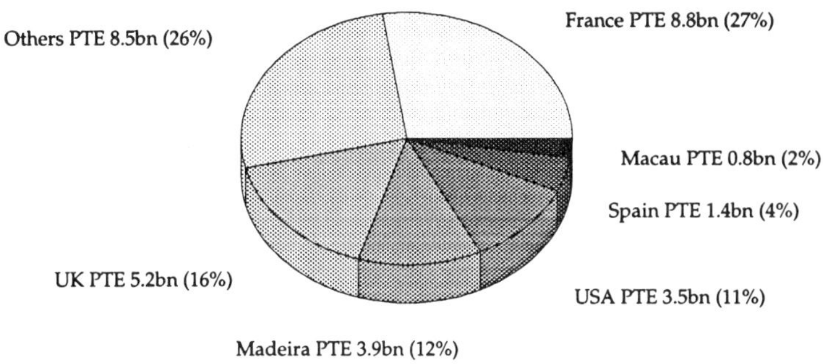

TOTAL: PTE 32.29bn

Figure 24.57 Foreign purchases of Portuguese government bonds by country of origin, 1989
Source: Bank of Portugal

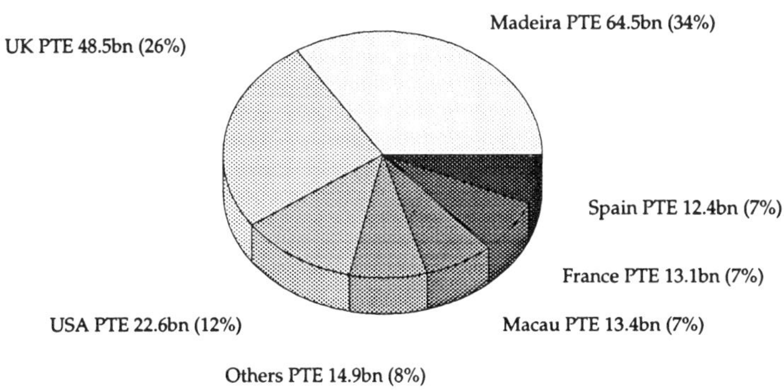

TOTAL: PTE 189.5bn

Figure 24.58 Foreign purchases of Portuguese government bonds by country of origin, 1990
Source: Bank of Portugal

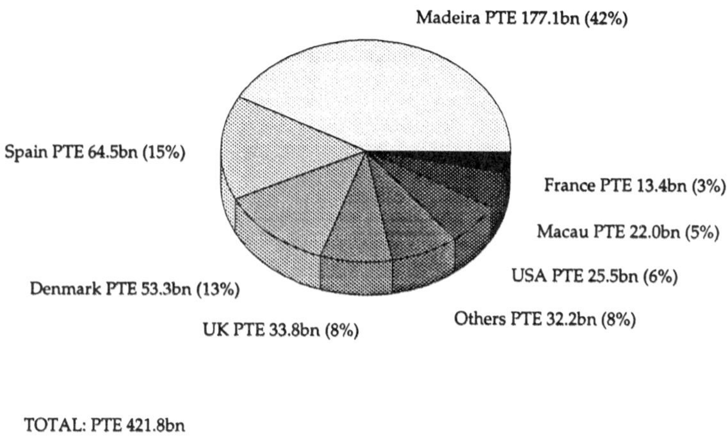

Figure 24.59 Foreign purchases of Portuguese government bonds, by country of origin, September 1991
Source: Bank of Portugal

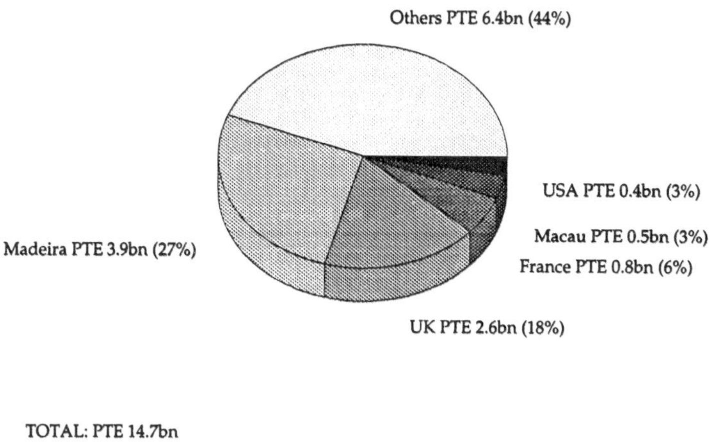

Figure 24.60 Foreign purchases of Portuguese corporate bonds by country of origin, 1990
Source: Bank of Portugal

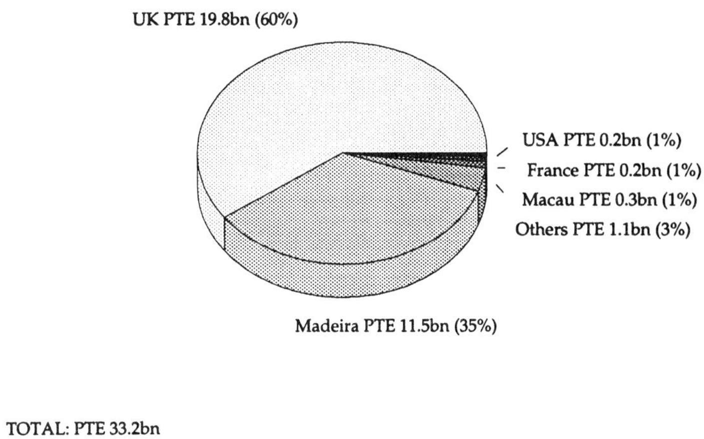

Figure 24.61 Foreign purchases of Portuguese corporate bonds by country of origin, September 1991

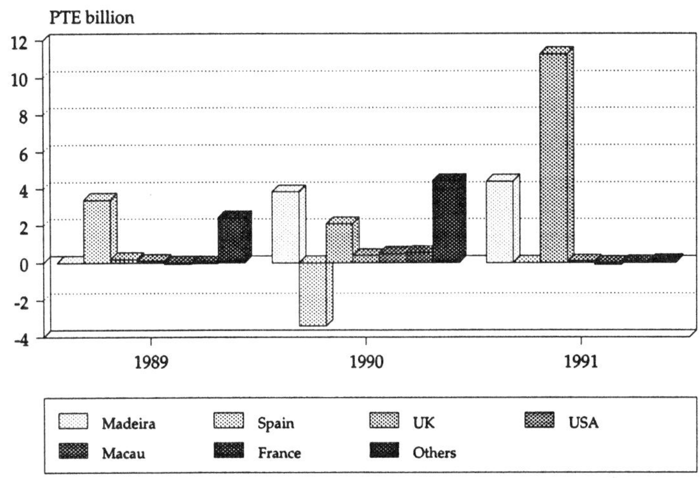

Figure 24.62 Net purchases of Portuguese corporate bonds, 1989 - September 1991
Source: Bank of Portugal

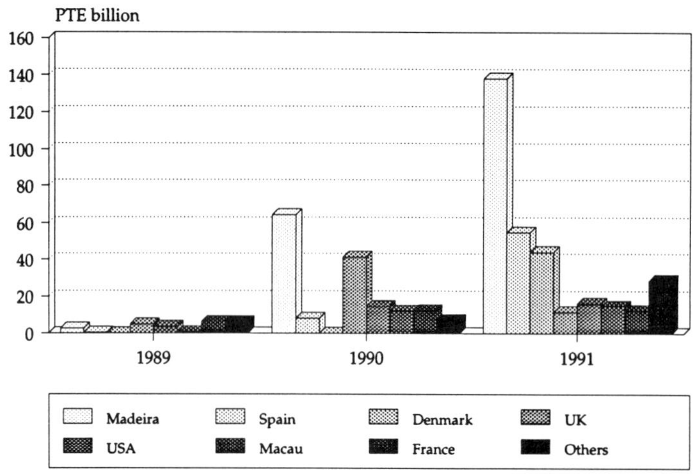

Figure 24.63 Net purchases of Portuguese government bonds, 1989 - September 1991
Source: Bank of Portugal

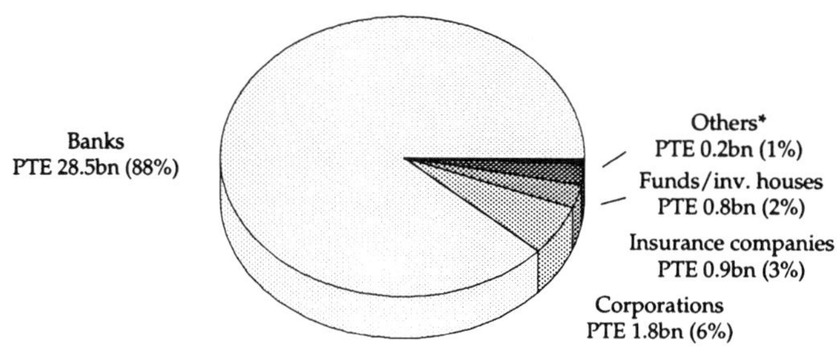

*) *others incl. private investors & international finance organizations*

Figure 24.64 Foreign purchases of Portuguese government bonds by investor group, 1989
Source: Bank of Portugal

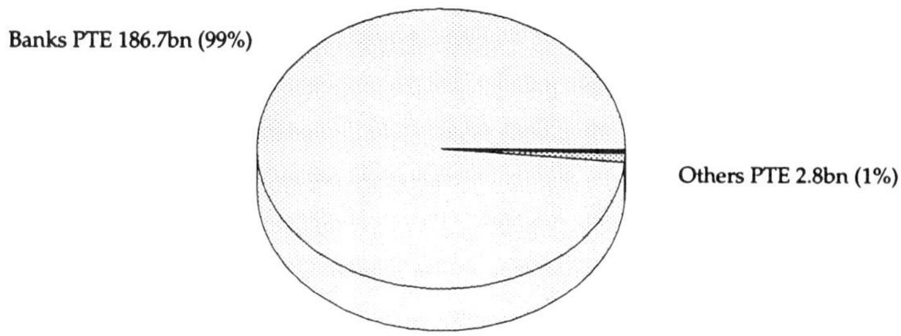

*) others incl. corporations, brokers, funds, insurance companies, & private

Figure 24.65 Foreign purchases of Portuguese government bonds by investor group, 1990
Source: Bank of Portugal

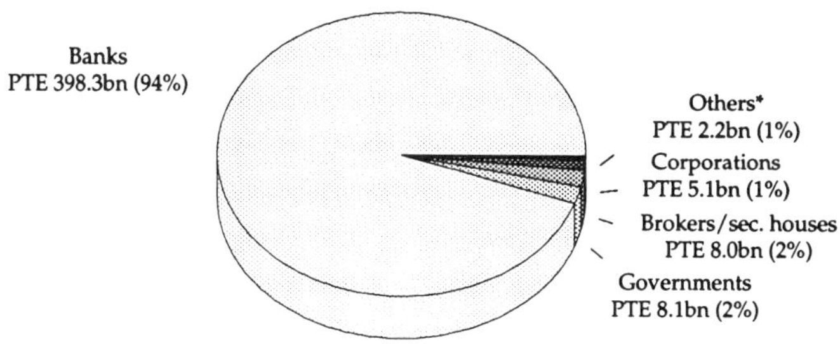

*) others incl. insurance companies, funds/inv. houses, & private

Figure 24.66 Foreign purchases of Portuguese government bonds by investor group, Sept. 1991
Source: Bank of Portugal

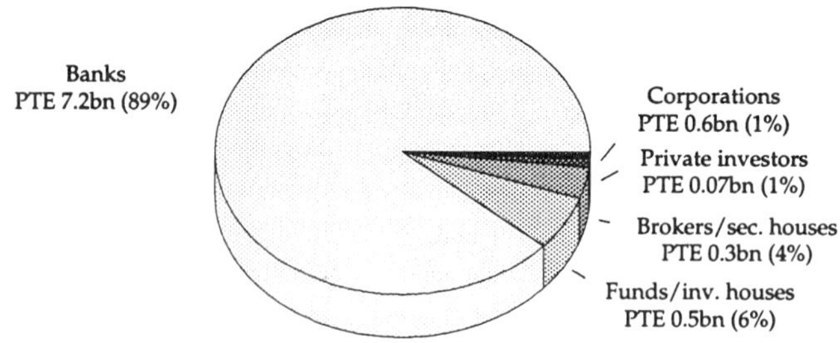

Figure 24.67 Foreign purchases of Portuguese corporate bonds by investor group, 1989
Source: Bank of Portugal

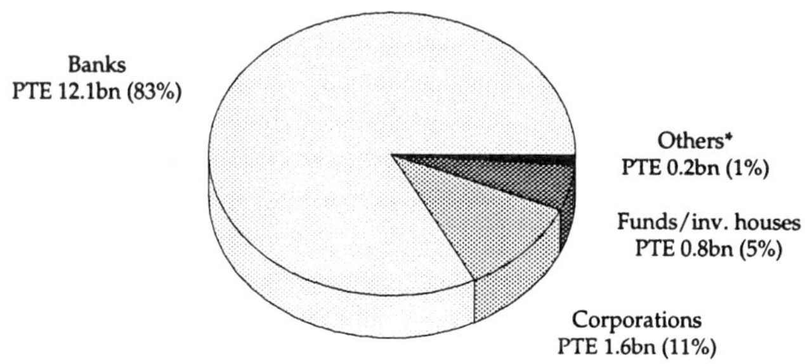

**) others incl. insurance companies, funds, insurance companies & private holdings*

Figure 24.68 Foreign purchases of Portuguese corporate bonds by investor group, 1990
Source: Bank of Portugal

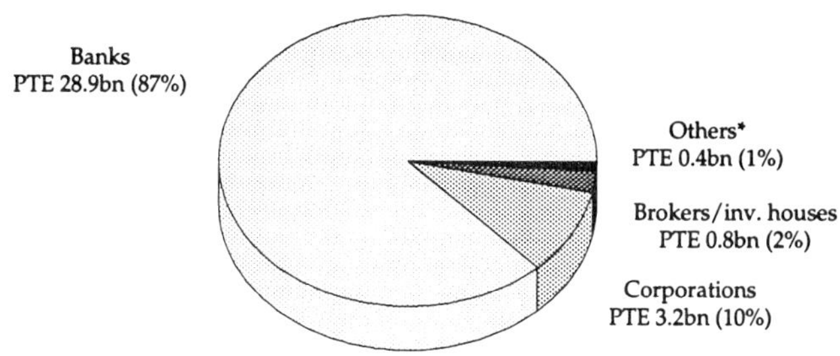

*) *others incl. funds/inv. houses, & private investors*

Figure 24.69 Foreign purchases of Portuguese corporate bonds by investor group, Sept. 1991
Source: Bank of Portugal

24.7 *Methods of issuance*

Before the reform of the financial system in 1991, almost all issues had to be authorized by the regulatory authorities. More recently, though, it is mainly just the issues of non-residents, issues in foreign currencies, index-linked bonds and those of some state-owned companies, that have had to be authorized. However, practically all bond issues above Esc 100m have to be registered at the CMVM (a commission that supervises the capital markets).

Government bonds

Floating-rate issues

Typically, the Treasury announces, at the beginning of each year, a calendar of those issues set to take place during that year. Normally, an auction by a government institution (JCP - Junta de Crédito Público) is arranged, in which the financial institutions that have access to the auction deliver a set of bids (with a maximum of five bids per institution) prior to 10.50 on, normally, the first Tuesday of each month. The bids are sorted by price, with volume allocated to the highest price first. Very often, new issues are fungible with former issues so that price is paid with accrued interest; the appointed market-makers then have a right to buy a certain amount of the security at the lowest price of the auction.

Fixed-rate issues

Fixed-rate securities are issued in a manner similar to floating-rate issues. However the auction is performed by the Bank of Portugal, with the dates of the auctions being provisionally defined at the beginning of each year. The auctions are confirmed by the Bank of Portugal at least two business days prior to the provisional date. Bids are subsequently made until 16.30 on the last business day before the auction. As in the case of the FIPs, the maximum number of bids is five. However, the auction is not conducted in terms of price, but rather in terms of yield, in multiples of 1/16 per cent. The bids with rates that are superior to the maximum rate that the state is willing to accept are disregarded. Starting with the lowest yields the bids are then fulfilled. The settlement of the auction lasts five business days. Typically, in the first auction of a certain type of security, the average yield of the auction then becomes the coupon rate. The price paid by each financial institutions is therefore found by the following formula:

$$P = \sum_{k=0}^{n-1} \frac{10{,}000 \times \frac{i}{2}}{(1+\frac{j}{2})^{(k+\frac{d}{182})}} + \frac{10{,}000}{(1+\frac{j}{2})^{(n-1+\frac{d}{182})}}$$

where,

n number of coupons
d actual days of the first coupon period
i coupon rate
j yield
10,000 face value

As a consequence, the auction price already includes accrued interest.

Other processes

As noted elsewhere, liquidity in Portugal used to be controlled through a 'credit ceiling' mechanism. When the Bank of Portugal changed the system to an indirect control of liquidity, there was too much liquidity in the banking system, mainly in the form of short-term deposits at the central bank. In order to absorb this excess liquidity the government, together with the Bank of Portugal, exchanged the short-term deposits of the banks held at the Bank of Portugal with government bonds, following a protocol signed with the banks. These securities are called *protocolo* and, in some cases, they are fungible with later issues.

Corporate bonds

Corporate bonds may be issued either to the public or through private placement. A very significant volume has been issued by private placement, because on the one hand private placements have a simplified approval process and, on the other, the law has allowed some discretion in the definition of an issue as a private placement. Presently, no authorization is needed to issue such bonds, although it is nevertheless necessary to register the issue at the CMVM. Private placements have, in some cases, simple registration processes; however the distinction between private and public subscription is now much sharper than before the new law was approved. A subscription is defined as public if, in all the following cases:

- the bonds are offered to an undetermined number of investors
- the bonds are offered to a determined number of investors not previously identified
- the bonds are offered to the public by any means of public marketing.

All public issues have to be indirect. An indirect subscription is an issue that is first underwritten by a financial institution, and only afterwards offered to investors. Direct subscriptions are, as their name implies, directly offered by the issuer to the investor with, or without, support from financial institutions. In all subscriptions in which financial institutions participate, the financial institutions and the issuers have to sign a contract specifying whether the financial institution is underwriting, committing to buy every unsold bond, or is only acting on a best-effort basis.

In larger issues a syndicate is very often created, in which the lead-manager has the function of structuring the syndicate and representing the syndicate in the relationship with the issuer and the CMVM.

24.8 *New issue volumes*

Government bonds

The amount of bonds issued by the government has increased significantly since 1987 (see Figure 24.70). Most of the volume is offered through public subscription.

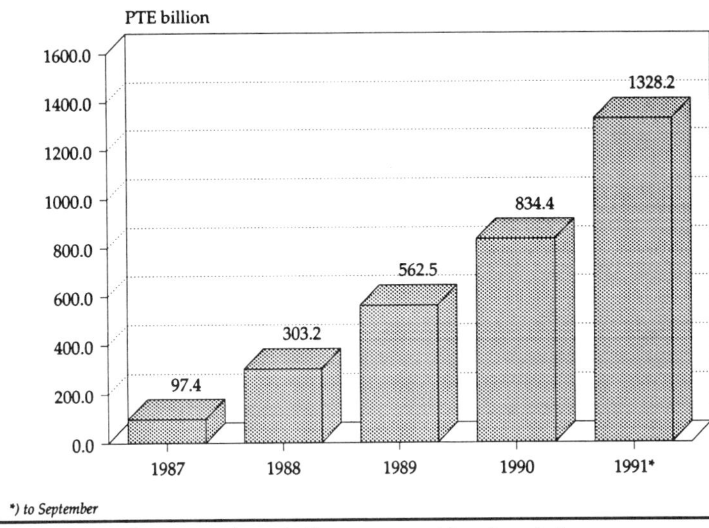

Figure 24.70 New issuance volume in the government bond market

Corporate bonds

Banks

Banks issued a number of bonds in 1987, largely as a result of the the tax incentives that existed at that time, and again in 1990 and 1991 (See Figure 24.71). Their activity in the market has been generally limited, though, because they have access to cheaper financing sources.

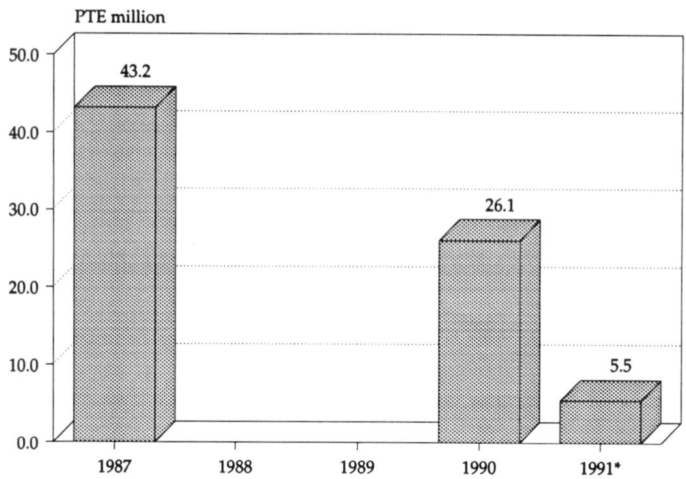

*) to September

Figure 24.71 New issuance volume in the bank bond market

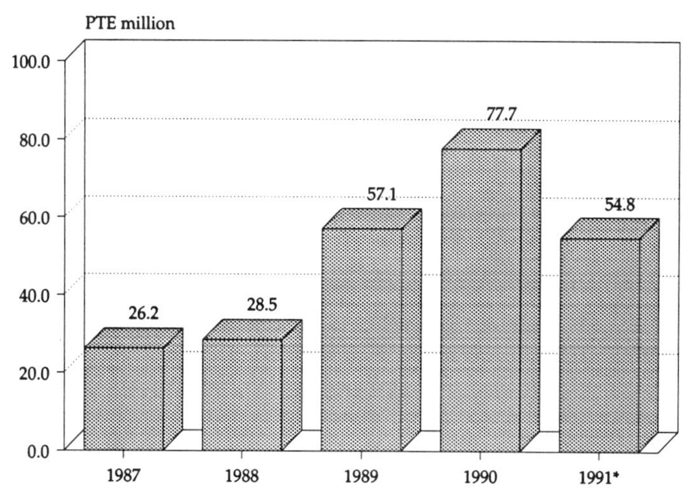

*) to September

Figure 24.72 New issuance volume in the market of other financial institutions

Other financial institutions

Other financial institutions, mainly investment societies and leasing companies, have regularly issued bonds (see Figure 24.72) since, as they cannot take deposits, bonds are one of the few funding sources they may use.

State-owned companies

As discussed earlier, state-owned capital-intensive companies (particularly the Electricity Company, the Telephone Company and the Post Company) use bonds as a source of funding. Figure 24.73 shows that there was a marked decrease in issuance in 1988, this reflecting the removal of the tax benefits which existed in 1987. After the state, issues from this sector are typically the most liquid and are subject to relatively low funding costs.

Private companies

Private companies have also entered the bond market but, by comparison to non-banking financial institutions and state-owned companies, their importance has decreased. Despite a large increase from 1987 to 1988 (See Figure 24.74), their growth in annual issuance volumes has failed to keep pace with that of other issuers. Some of the reasons for this are as follows:

- Portuguese private companies generally tend to prefer bank credit
- the size of Portuguese private companies generally precludes the issuance of large, 'interesting,' issues
- the difference between euro and domestic rates encourages the companies to euro-linked short-term trade finance as much as possible.

Euro-issues

As a result of the development of the market, and general interest from foreign investors in the Portuguese escudo, euro-issues have been a feature since 1988 (See Figure 24.75). The issues of supranationals have almost no liquidity in the Portuguese domestic market since they are mainly transacted abroad.

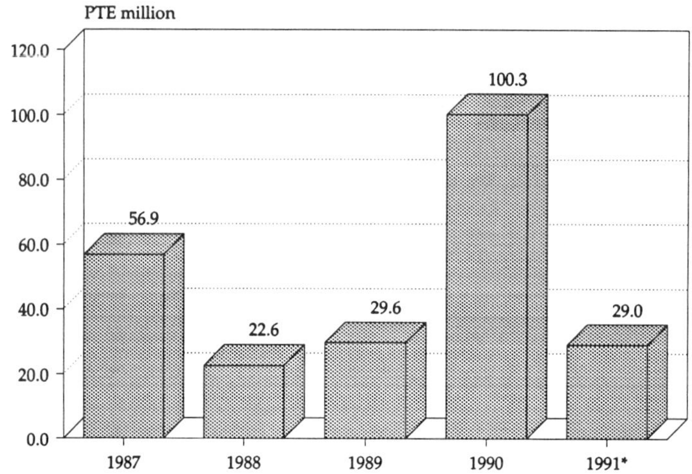

*) to September

Figure 24.73 New issuance volume in the non-financial public sector bond market

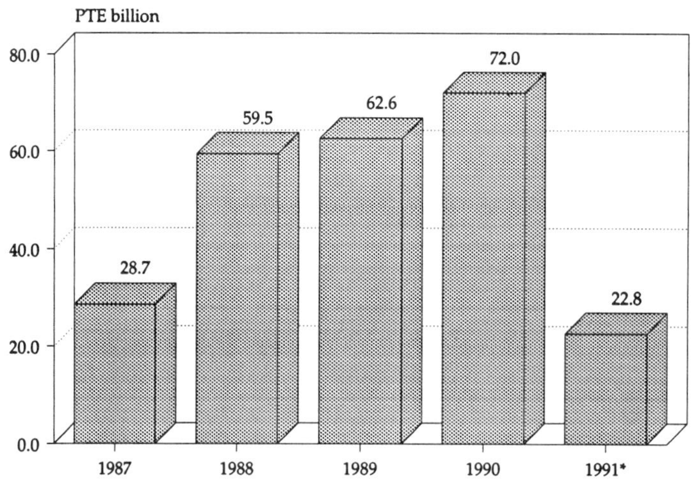

*) to September

Figure 24.74 New issuance volume in the corporate bond market

	Issuer	Amount (PTE billion)
1988	EIB	5
1989	EIB 1	10
	EIB 2	5
	Eurofima	7
1990	Council of Europe	5
	EIB 1	10
	EIB 2	12.5
	ECSC	5
	IFC	10
1991	EIB 1	15
	EIB 2	20
	EIB 3	10
	Eurofima	7
	Council of Europe	10
	IBRD	15
	IFC	11
	IADB	11.5

Figure 24.75 Euro-issues 1988-1991

24.9 Methods of trading

Markets

There are two stock exchanges in Portugal, to which only brokers and dealers have direct access. However, with the implementation of the Reform Act, a single country-wide stock exchange market will be established for most of the liquid securities. Nevertheless, some securities will remain traded in only one of the markets. In addition, there is a very active over-the-counter market mainly between banks and institutional investors.

Lisbon Stock Exchange

The prices of the bonds are established in the morning by an automatic system which receives orders and then derives their first price. At mid-morning, another price is formed by a call system.

Oporto Stock Exchange

In the Oporto Stock Exchange, one price is made per day through a call system. However, a subsequent price may be determined, if requested by a broker.

Over-the-counter

The over-the-counter market is not standardized, a fact which enables counterparties to define the features of their transactions on a case-by-case basis. Because prices are not subject to third-party influence, and also because some transactions are done as part of larger agreements, the prices reached on this market are sometimes not a truly representative market evaluation of the bonds.

Outlook

In 1992, it is expected that the pricing of most liquid securities will be on a continuous basis, this being particularly the case for government FRNs (FIPs) and government fixed-rate bonds (OTs). However, the least-liquid securities will continue to be traded by the call system, at least for the time being.

Agents in the market

The main agents in the secondary market are banks and mutual funds, these being followed by pension funds and insurance companies. Individuals are of no significance. Only brokers have direct access to the stock exchanges, and so they act as intermediaries in all transactions that are made on those exchanges. Banks are very active, mainly in the over-the-counter market which, until the end of 1989, was the market with the highest turnover.

Recently, market-makers for public debt have been chosen by the Treasury. To enjoy this privilege, each institution-designated market-maker must meet a set of conditions which typically include a commitment to quote government bonds with spreads not exceeding 0.5 per cent for volumes up to Esc 500m and a commitment to place a certain volume of orders in the primary market. These market-makers are:

- Banco Comercial de Macau
- Banco Comercial Português
- Banco Espírito Santo e Comercial de Lisboa
- Banco de Fomento e Exterior
- Banco Nacional Ultramarino
- Banco Pinto e Sotto Mayor
- Banco Português do Atlântico
- Banco Português de Investimentos
- Banco Totta e Açores
- Caixa Geral de Depósitos
- Citibank Portugal
- Crédito Predial Português
- Deutsche Bank de Investimento
- Manufacturers Hannover Bank

24.10 *Market practices*

Coupon payment

Most domestic bonds pay interest semi-annually. Very few, such as the issue of BPI, pay interest quarterly. Eurobonds in escudos pay interest annually.

First coupon

It is not uncommon to have odd first coupons for domestic bonds. Typically, the coupon is calculated on a 30/360 basis.

Ex-interest

Typically, bonds cease to be negotiable at the stock exchange three business days before the coupon. Until this date, they are traded with full interest.

Redemptions

Almost all recent issues redeem at par. The only notable exception is when a bond has either a call or a put option, or when it has a zero-coupon structure as in the case of one issue by Sofinloc.

Put and calls

Since 1991, issues with put and call options have become extremely frequent.

Form

Almost all bonds are in bearer form. Although the law allows for registered bonds and nominative bonds, such forms are almost solely used for equities.

Denomination

Most non-government bonds have a face value of Esc 1000, this usually being the smallest denomination. Government bonds issued after 1986 generally have a nominal value of 10,000. An exception is found in the case of the OCAs, the nominal value of which changes each time the coupon matures.

Withholding tax

Withholding tax is due when the coupon is paid. Some investors (like individuals and investment funds) are subject to withholding tax whilst others (like pension funds and insurance companies) are not. Some international investors may have their withholding tax reduced, depending upon whether their country has a double taxation treaty with Portugal.

Dealing quotations

Until 1991, there were no formal market-makers, so it was very uncommon to find bid/offer prices. In 1991, however, the Portuguese government created a market-maker structure for the Treasury bond market. As noted earlier, these are specially-appointed financial institutions which, in return for a commitment to provide liquidity to the market, enjoy the privilege of subscribing to a certain amount of government bonds in each auction, at the minimum price.

Accrued interest

Accrued interest is computed on a 30/360 basis from the last coupon-date until the trade-date. Prior to the reform of the Portuguese capital markets, it was computed up until the settlement date.

Commissions

A proposed new law foresees higher flexibility in the determination of the commissions. For the moment, however, they are legally fixed as follows:

Brokerage Fees

■ Stock exchange market

	Up to PTE 5m	5m to 20m	20m to 50m	Above 50m
Government bonds exc. OTMP	0.2%	0.15%	0.1%	Free
OTMP		0.16%		
Other bonds	0.3%	0.25%	0.15%	Free

■ Over-the-counter market

Listed securities:

Government bonds exc. OTMP	0.4%
OTMP	0.16%
Other bonds	0.5%

Unlisted securities:

	Up to PTE 5m	5m to 10m	Above 10m
Government bonds/OTMP	0.5%	0.45%	0.5%
Other bonds	0.6%	0.55%	0.5%

Transaction fees

In addition to brokerage, a special transaction fee is also charged:

Stock exchange transactions

FIP & OCA	0.02% (for market-makers)
	0.025% (for others)
OTMP	0.004%
Other bonds	0.025%

Over-the-counter transactions

All bonds	0.05%

Yield calculation

For most bonds, there is no formal convention in terms of yield, so that the market prefers to deal on a price basis. An exception is the primary market for OTs which has an auction based on yield according to the formula described. However, it is not uncommon in the Portuguese market for participants to use the concept of yield-to-maturity, even for floating-rate notes. As there is no market consensus on this matter, an investor is always advised to investigate which kind of formula is being used (i.e. is it with net coupons?, is it annualized?, how are the days counted?, etc.).

24.11 Settlement

Over-the-counter trades

Settlement of over-the-counter trades is performed by the physical delivery of the securities to the counterparty's custodian bank, with financial settlement made either by cheque payments or bank-to-bank transfers. Detailed settlement terms are freely determined by both parties, and may include 'delivery versus payment' instructions. It should, however, be stressed that when dealing with listed securities in the over-the-counter market, only spot transactions are allowed.

Stock exchange trades

In the event of non-performance of stock exchange transactions, a buy-in is made by the stock exchange, with the cost being borne by the defaulting party.

In terms of settlement it is useful to distinguish between fungible securities, non-fungible securities and dematerialized securities:

Fungible securities

Fungible securities are financially settled at the central bank on a T+4 basis. Physical settlement requires a provisional ledger credit on T+4, and a continuous net settlement with fixed settlement dates every two weeks (five business days after the last day of the month and five business days after Day 14 of the month). Most of the bonds that do not redeem through a lottery mechanism are considered fungible for this purpose.

Physical settlement is performed among custodian banks under supervision of the stock exchange, which indicates the net amounts to be received/delivered, and to which counterparties, every two weeks (five business days after the last day of the month and five business days after Day 14 of the month).

Non-fungible securities

Non-fungible securities (registered shares, and some bonds depending on the type of redemption), have a financial settlement done at the central bank on T+4, with physical settlement occurring in the following way:

- selling bank to broker: T+1
- or buying broker to buying bank: T+4

Dematerialized securities

Dematerialized securities are securities with no physical underlying, consequently there is no physical settlement, but rather a ledger credit on trade-date +4. Financial settlement occurs on trade-date +4. At the moment, these securities are being settled through a central depository system. All listed securities will eventually be settled through this system.

24.12 Yield calculation

It is not normal market practice to quote bonds in terms of yields, and transactions are usually made in terms of price. Consequently, there is no set market formula, in terms of the yields of bonds, which is used by all market agents. Some participants prefer to work with annualized yields, others with nominal semi-annual yields; some compute the yields using actual days, others use 30/360, whilst still others use actual days for the days until the first coupon and thereafter only use 30/360. However, the Bank of Portugal publishes the yield-to-maturity of corporate and government bonds according to the following formula:

$$P + AI = \sum_{j=1}^{m} \frac{v_j + i_j \times K'(1 - t) \times A_j + v_j \times B_j \times [1 + \frac{R_j}{v_j} \times (1 - t')]}{(1 + k \times r)^{(j-1)} \times (1 + k'_j \times r)}$$

where,

P	price
AI	accrued interest
V_j	Nominal value in period j
i_j	daily interest rate in period j. If the rate underlying the coupon has changed, then this new rate is considered for the next periods
t	tax rate of interest
t'	tax rate of redemption premium
K'	number of days in the first coupon period
R	redemption premium
B_j	probability of redemption
A_j	probability of interest being paid, mainly important in lottery redemptions
k	number of days in the period
r	daily rate to maturity

After the calculation of individual yields, the Bank of Portugal calculates average yields (see below) for both the government bond market and the corporate bond market. In order to avoid possible distortions, securities with less than six-month maturities are not considered. As weights, it uses the turnover of the securities.

$$TR = \frac{R_i \times V_i}{V_i}$$

24.13 Taxation

Taxation in the Portuguese bond market varies according to the issue dates of the bonds, and to the type of issuer.

Taxation of interest

Generally, the taxation of interest occurs only when the interest is paid. Some investors pay withholding tax, although this tax is not consistent for all types of bonds (see Figures 24.76 & 24.77). Most government bonds have a 20 per cent withholding tax. The most important corporate bonds, in terms of both amount outstanding and turnover, are the ones exempted from withholding tax, the ones with a 20 per cent tax rating and those with a 25 per cent rating. Bonds of state agencies and supranationals are either withholding tax-exempt, or have a 20 per cent rate.

Resident individuals

Resident individuals only pay withholding tax. However, the amount of withholding tax paid is dependent on the issue date of the bond and on whether the issuer is a corporate or the state.

	1987	1988	1989	1990	1991
Corporate bonds	0%[1]	6%	20%	25%	25%
Government bonds	0%	0%	20%	20%	20%

[1] *For more than eight years maturity*

Resident corporations

Resident corporations pay withholding tax as an advance tax payment. When they pay corporate taxes (the normal rate is 36 per cent with 3.6 per cent municipal taxes) they may deduct the withholding tax paid from their liability - the withholding tax therefore effectively being a payment in advance. Before 1989, bonds had a different tax treatment dependent upon the issue year. With the tax reform in 1989, it become necessary to compensate these bonds, so that they could maintain their relative advantages. Consequently, the legislator created tax benefits for each bond.

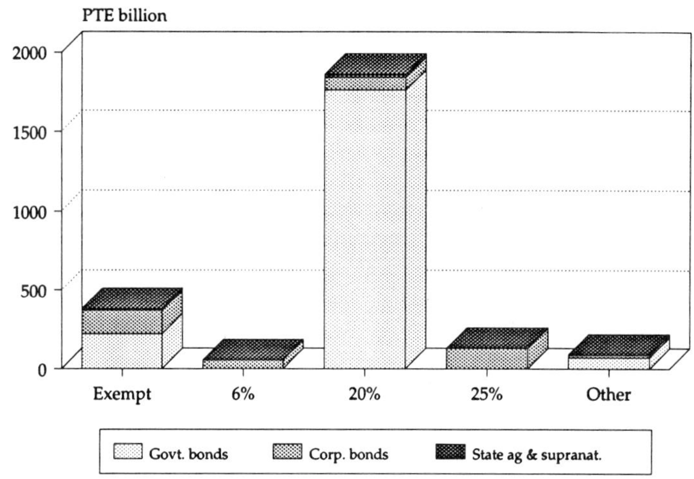

Figure 24.76 Taxation of different types of security (by volume outstanding)

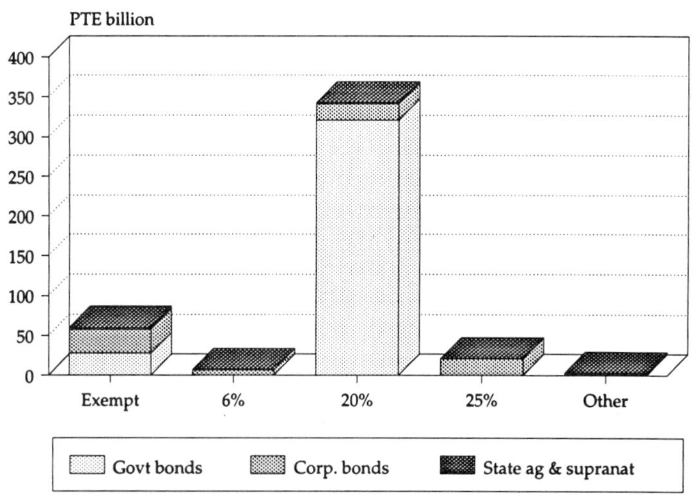

Figure 24.77 Taxation of different types of security (by turnover)

Tax benefit

The amount of tax resident corporations can deduct from their income taxes is shown below:

The values shown above were computed using a corporate tax rate of 36 per cent and a municipal tax rate of 10 per cent × 36 per cent = 3.6 per cent

		1987	1988	1989	1990	1991
Government	Tax benefit	45%	45%	20%	20%	0%
	Effective tax rate[1]	23%	23%	32%	32%	39%
Corporate	Tax benefit	45%	35%	20%	0%	0%
	Effective tax rate[1]	23%	27%	32%	39%	39%

[1] *Approximate effective tax rate: corporation tax rate × (1 - tax benefit) + municipal taxes*

Insurance companies

Insurance companies in the non-life sector are not subject to withholding tax; however, they have to include interest income when they pay global taxes. As a result, it is possible for them to profit from the company tax benefits shown above. Insurance companies in the life sector are also not subject to withholding tax. In contrast to those in the non-life sector, however, they pay global taxes on only 15 per cent of their revenue, which makes it very difficult for them to profit from the tax benefits described above, since their tax base is substantially reduced.

Investment funds

Investment funds are subject to withholding tax. When their certificates are held by an individual investor, however, the income distributed to the individual is not subject to tax. When the certificates are held by a corporation, the corporation pays taxes on the income received from the fund, but the withholding tax paid by the fund may be deducted from the global taxes paid by the corporation.

Pension funds

Pension funds do not pay taxes on income received.

Banks

Banks are taxed in a manner similar to the taxation of non-life insurance companies. They are exempt from withholding tax, although they must include the interest received in their global income for tax purposes.

Non-residents

Non-residents pay only withholding tax on the Portuguese market. However there are some double taxation treaties which reduce this withholding tax to reduced levels at source. Where a double taxation treaty exists, a non-resident investor may deduct the withholding tax paid in Portugal from any global tax liability, provided there are no excess foreign tax credits.

Current account with the state

It is normal practice in the Portuguese bond market to compute accrued interest on a net basis. However, there are investors (such as banks and insurance companies) who are not taxed when they receive the coupon. So, in order to avoid wash-sales of coupons, some investors who are exempt from withholding tax have a current account with the tax authorities to compensate for this effect.

Taxation of capital gains

Individuals

Individuals are exempt from taxes on capital gains from bonds.

Corporations

Corporations pay global taxes on capital gains except if they reinvest such gains, before the end of December of year N+2, in real assets, shares or government bonds.

Insurance companies

Insurance companies are not taxed on capital gains as long as the proceeds are reinvested.

Investment funds

Investment funds are exempt from capital gains taxes.

Pension funds

Pension funds are exempt from taxes.

Banks

Banks are not taxed on capital gains, as long as the proceeds are reinvested.

Non-residents

Non-residents are not subject to taxes on capital gains.

Other taxes

Gift and inheritance tax

Since 1986, there are have been no bonds subject to gift and inheritance tax. At the moment there is a tax exemption, in this respect, for bonds issued until 1992. After this date, if the exemption is not renewed for new issues, there will be a payment of this tax, together with withholding tax.

Taxes on bond issuance

No taxes are imposed on bond issuance. However, most corporate bond issues have to be registered at the notary, which charges a fee of 0.3 per cent. Additionally, the underwriting and distribution fees charged by the financial intermediaries are subject to a stamp tax of 9 per cent.

24.14 *Money markets*

In the domestic market, known locally as MMI (interbank money market), access is determined by the central bank and only financial institutions may participate. Basically, the market is used to balance the liquidity needs of the banking system, but it is also used for speculative positioning. Although there is an on-going process of deregulation, the local market is not yet accessible for non-residents, thus explaining the existence of two different yield curves for the domestic escudo and the euroescudo.

The domestic money market uses a 365-day base and standard operations are allowed for 1-day to 1-year contracts with same-day clearance by Banco de Portugal. Market depth decreases sharply for maturities over 1 month, and some 85 per cent of the average Esc 100bn daily turnover is dealt overnight. Following the liberalization of credit ceilings (i.e. the maximum amount of credit allowed by the central bank) in January 1991, the direct control of liquidity gave place to a form of indirect control by which interest rates are determined by demand and supply within a band set by central bank supply and mop-up intervention rates. The current reserve requirements are 17 per cent on resident liabilities

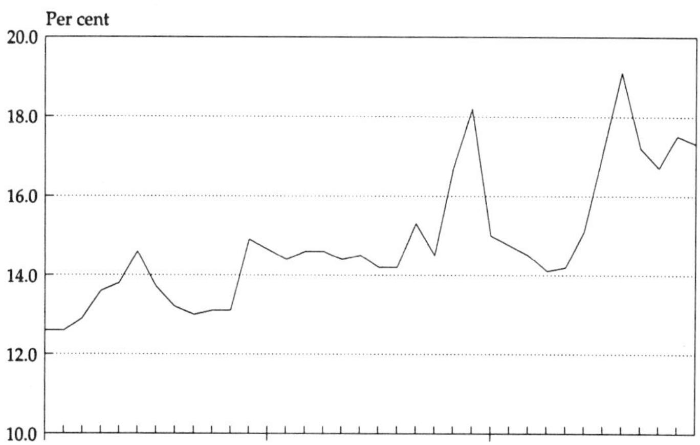

Figure 24.78 Average interest rate on the interbank money market, 24h - 5 days

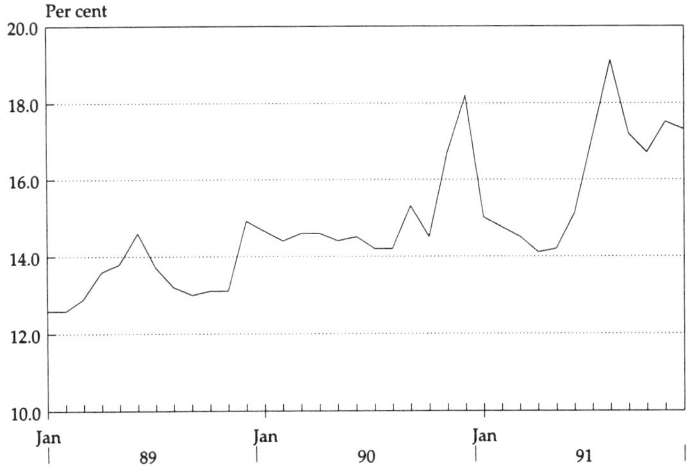

Figure 24.79 Average interest rate on the interbank money market, 6 - 30 days

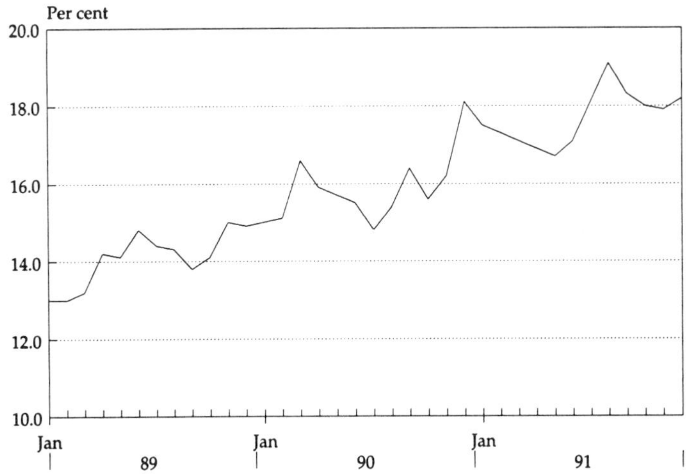

Figure 24.80 Average interest rate on the interbank money market, 31 - 90 days

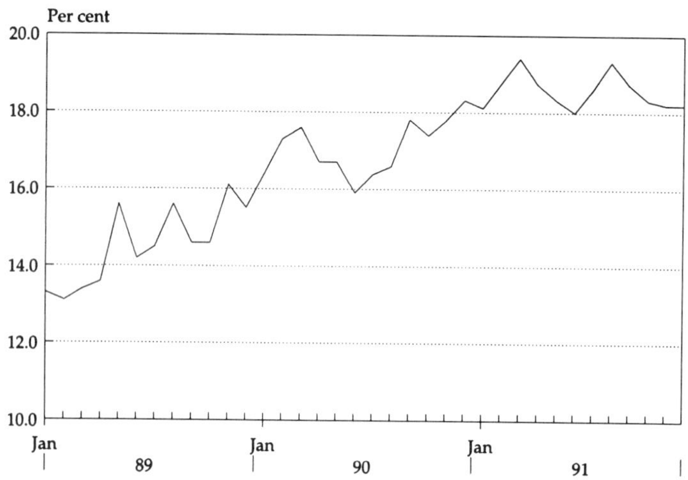

Figure 24.81 Average interest rate on the interbank money market, 91 - 180 days

and 90 per cent or 40 per cent on non-resident escudo-denominated liabilities, depending upon whether the depositor has an affiliation relationship with the bank, or not. The euroescudo market follows major currency standards, using a 360-day base, and without any restriction on length of term.

Treasury bills

This short-term public debt instrument was introduced in Portugal in 1985 and is issued in 3-, 6- and 12-month auctions, in which only those financial institutions permitted by the central bank may participate. It is a highly liquid instrument which is negotiable in the interbank secondary market (central bank included), or with the resident general public through repos or sales to maturity. Bids are received one day before the result is announced and three working days before the settlement date. Rates are determined by demand and supply, although there is an unknown intervention rate set by the Treasury for each auction. There is no fixed calendar and the amounts issued have proven quite flexible, respecting on the one hand the needs of the Treasury and, on the other, the monetary policy of the central bank. T-bills are discounted according to the following central bank formula:

$$PV = \frac{NV \bullet 36500}{36500 + D \bullet R}$$

where,

PV	present value
NV	nominal value
D	number of days
R	interest rate

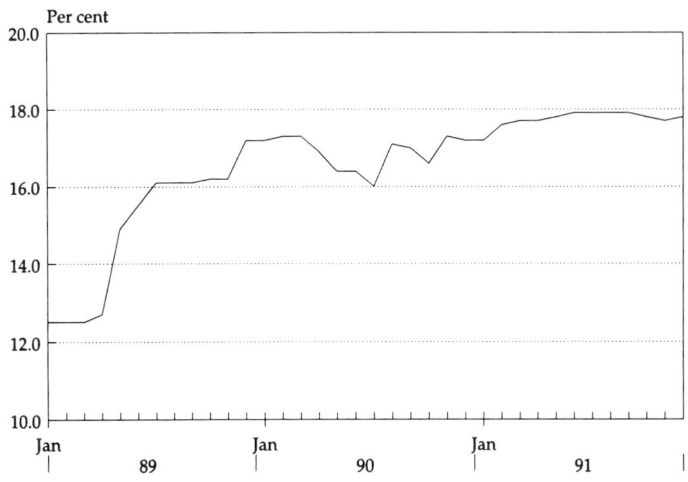

Figure 24.82 Average interest rates on Treasury bills, 91 days

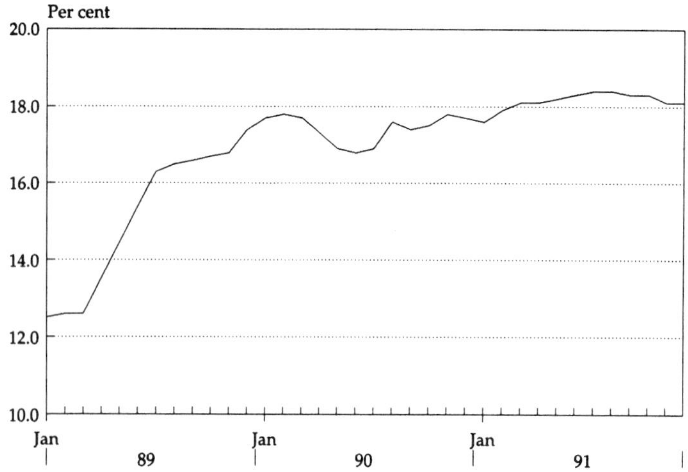

Figure 24.83 Average interest rates on Treasury bills, 182 days

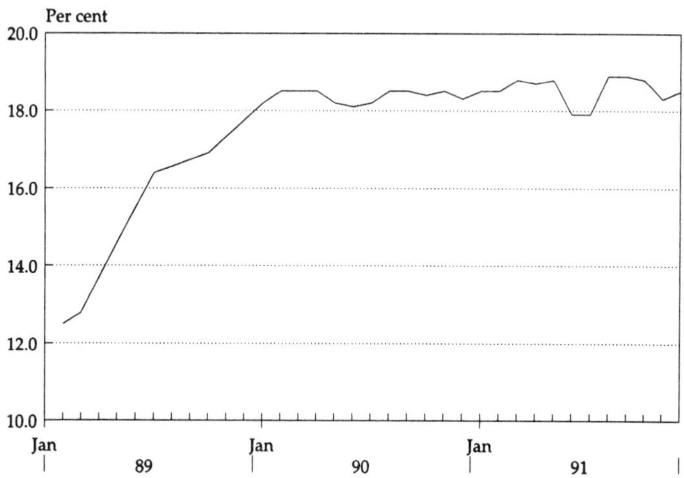

Figure 24.84 Average interest rates on Treasury bills, 364 days

Interbank securities market

First introduced in 1978, to absorb the large liquidity surpluses in the banking system due to the tight credit controls established by the central bank, interbank securities later became instruments of monetary control. They are issued by the central bank and can be either a long-term public debt or a repurchase mix of the central bank's own debt. They may range from 1 day to 26 weeks and rates can be either fixed or auctioned, depending on the instrument and the particular conditions announced for the issue. Amounts may, or may not, be pre-fixed; again, it depends upon the conditions of the announcement. For the past few months, the central bank has been issuing TRMs (*Titulos de Regularização Monetária* - see Figure 24.85) with fixed-rates and no volume limit for ranges of 1 to 9 days (thereby setting a floor for short-term rates) and TIMs (*Titulos de Intervenção Monetária* - see Figure 24.86) with rate determined by auction and amounts announced in advance, for 4, 13 and 26 weeks. These instruments are negotiable in the domestic market between banks (central bank included) with the mandatory requirement that all operations are cleared and reported to the central bank.

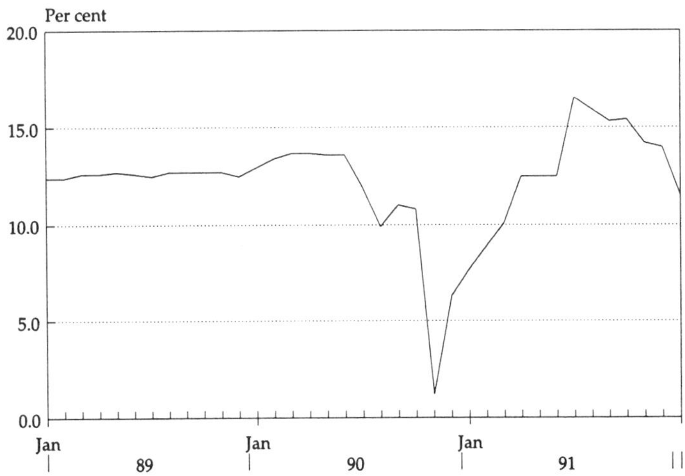

Figure 24.85 Average interest rates of central bank monetary certificates (TRM)

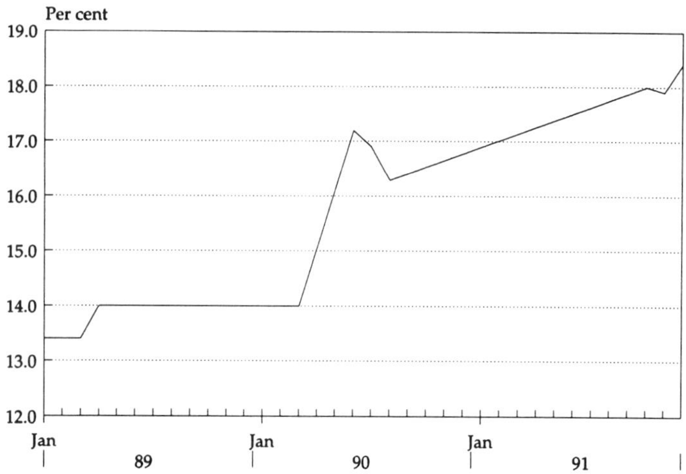

Figure 24.86 Average interest rates of central bank fixed-interest monetary certificates (TIM)

24.15 *Interest rate history*

Overview

The general interest rate behaviour since 1984 has been marked by a substantial decrease, reflecting the reduction in the inflation rate. More important than this quantitative decrease, however, is the qualitative meaning of interest rates. Until the end of the eighties, the money supply was controlled through credit ceilings and administratively-fixed rates. Thus, in practice, interest rates did not represent the result of supply and demand forces. With the development of the market and consequent deregulation, the Bank of Portugal abolished most of the interest rate limits and started the indirect control of the monetary base.

Bond yields

Until very recently, there were almost no fixed-rate bonds, thus it is very difficult to analyze the impact of bond yields. However, the Bank of Portugal calculates bond yields according to the formula described in Section 24.12.

As a result of the recent issuance of a significant volume of fixed-rate bonds, together with an expectation of a fall in long-term interest rates, this yield has decreased (see Figure 24.87). Furthermore, at the end of 1991 and at the beginning of 1992, the prices of floating-rate notes increased. This was due to a positioning movement, reflecting the expectations of most Portuguese banks that, with the liberalization of purchase restrictions on FIPs by non-residents, these securities will face a price appreciation. On the other hand, these bonds float imperfectly, because their coupons do not vary with the market rate directly, but rather with a moving average of the 12 last TB auctions. So, in a scenario of sharply decreasing interest rates, their coupon rate has lagged.

Interest rates underlying bonds

TRO

The TRO is a rate determined by the Bank of Portugal, which was originally designed to serve as a reference rate for floating-rate notes. In the first years following its creation it changed rather frequently, reflecting market movements. However, it has not changed since March 1989, due to smaller market interest rate oscillations than those which occurred in the eighties, and also to a greater emphasis on market-determined rates.

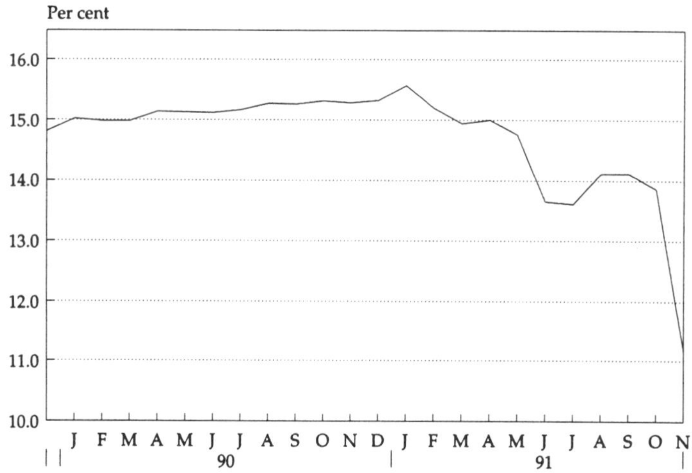

Figure 24.87 Government bond yields

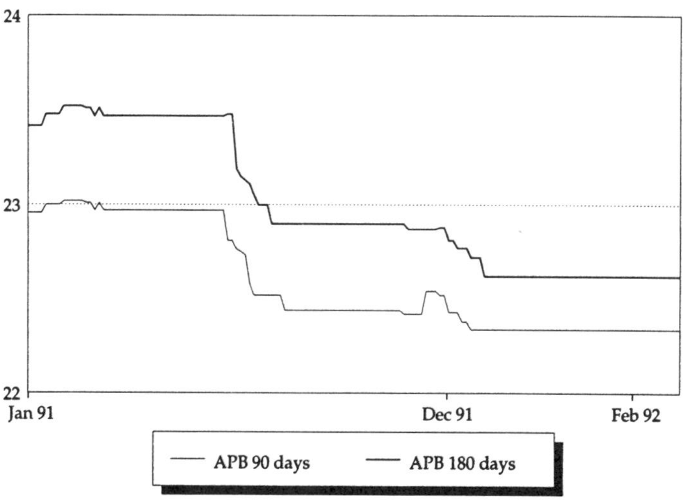

Figure 24.88 Reference rates for Portuguese floating-rate notes (i)
Source: APB, BVL

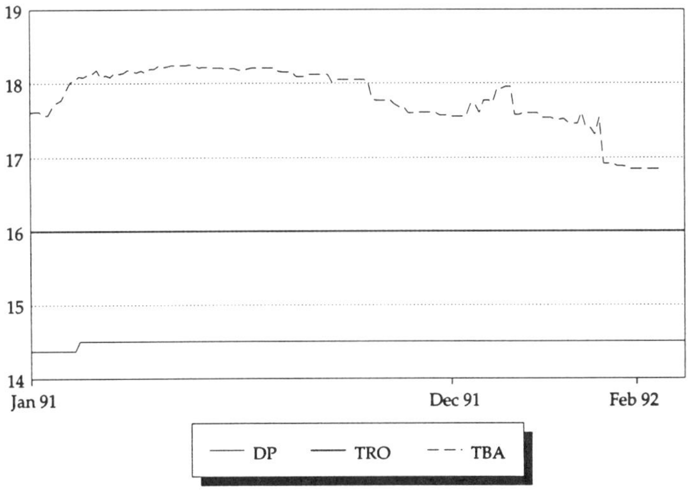

Figure 24.89 Reference rates for Portuguese floating-rate noes (ii)
Source: APB, BVL

APB

APB is an average lending rate of the commercial banks determined by the Portuguese Banks Association. It has been highly criticized for not accurately reflecting interest rate movements, and following further recent criticism, it has now dropped to more realistic levels.

TBA (Treasury bill average rate)

As described in Section 24.4, the TBA is a weighted average rate of the last twelve Treasury bill auctions.

Average-term deposit rate

As described in Section 24.4, the average-term deposit rates are the weighted average of the 180-360 nominal term deposit rate of the three largest institutions, in terms of these deposits.

24.16 *Inter-market spreads*

Treasury bills vs. government bonds

The difference between government bond yields and Treasury bills may be explained mainly by:

- totally different liquidities in each market
- different transaction costs
- difficulties in the evolution of the indexes.

However, as noted earlier, a significant volume of fixed-rate bonds has recently been issued. Since there is a general expectation of a decrease in interest rates, the yield curve between T-bills and bonds has become inverted (see Figure 24.90).

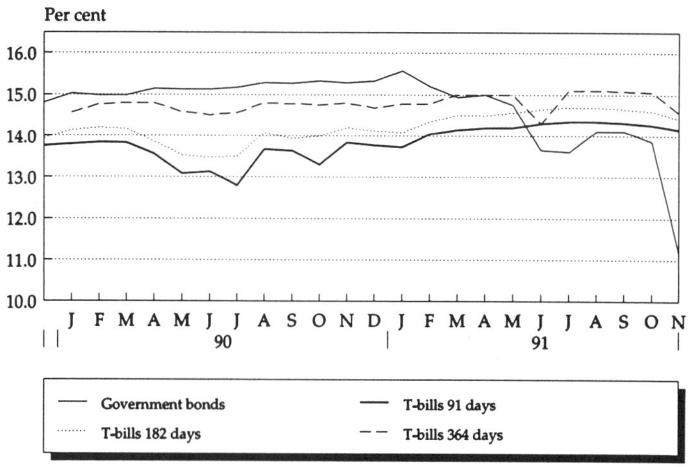

Figure 24.90 Yield spread: government bonds vs. Treasury bills

Term structure

The general interest rate structure is downward sloping, reflecting the general expectation of decrease in interest rates for maturities longer than 2/3 years. However, the shorter OT bond sector has revealed a somewhat irregular movement, attributable to its very low liquidity (see Figure 24.91).

Corporate bonds vs. government bonds

It is difficult to interpret the spread between corporate and government bonds, due to the absence of rating, to difficulties in applying the concept of yield-to-maturity to floating-rate notes (especially if they have different underlying rates), and to the existence of different taxation rates. However, typically, the 'yields' (as calculated by the Bank of Portugal) of these bonds issued by solid corporations, have been around 0.5 to 1 per cent over government issues. Recently, the difference has become larger (see Figure 24.92), mainly due to the distorting effect of the higher weight of the turnover of fixed-rate bonds by comparison to floating-rate bonds in the average of government issues. Furthermore, the floating-rate government bonds have seen an appreciation in price, reflecting the factors explained above.

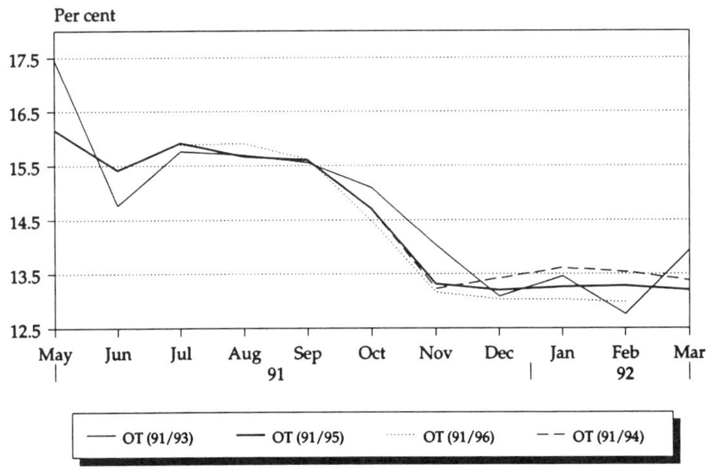

Figure 24.91 Yield curve of OTs

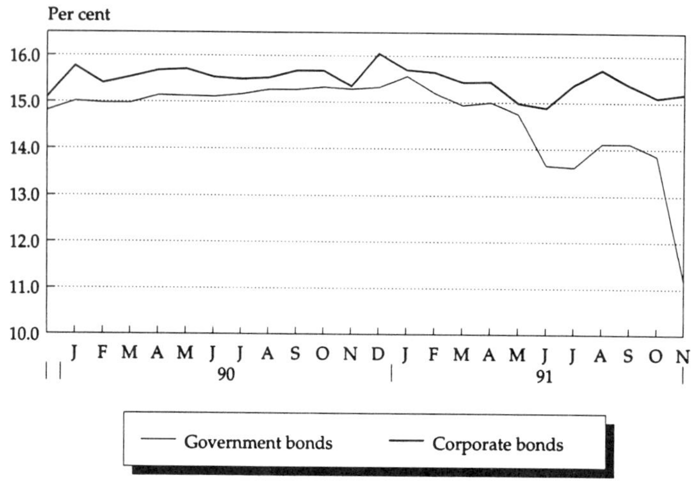

Figure 24.92 Yield spread: government bonds vs. corporate bonds

24.17 *Sources of reference*

Financial data

- APB *Information Report*
- Lisbon Stock Exchange *Financial Report* (yearly)
- APS *Market Report* (yearly)
- Bank of Portugal *Economic Statistics* (monthly)
- Bank of Portugal *Economic Statistics* (quarterly)
- Bank of Portugal financial data: investors
- ASGFIM investment funds' data
- SIIB - Stock Exchange Interactive Information Services

“If there were a contest in the banking business for the most 'global' bank, there is little doubt which would win: Citibank.”

FINANCIAL TIMES 24 July 1991

Chapter

25

The bond markets of

Spain

Rodrigo Sousa
Banco Hipotecario De España
(Editor)

Sonsoles Gallego
Ignacio Ezquiaga
José Ramón Jara
Analistas Financieros Internacionales

Enrique García
Ahorro Corporacion Financiera, Svb

Pilar Medina
Rodrigo Sousa
Banco Hipotecario De España

Note: In general text, the abbreviation 'Pta' is used to denote the Spanish peseta. Elsewhere, the international mnemonic 'ESP' is used.

25.1 Economics

The process of economic and financial liberalization which started with the entry of Spain into the European Economic Community (EEC) in 1986, can be interpreted as the origin of a structural change for the Spanish economy and society. This change allowed the start of a new phase of expansion in the real sector and the modernization of both the productive structures and the principal infrastructure. The development of this phase during the past few years can be seen to have occurred in two distinct periods.

1987-89

The first period, 1987-1989, saw three years of huge expansion as GDP growth achieved an annual average rate of 5.2 per cent, showing clear signs of an overheated economy. Over the same period, gross fixed-capital formation increased at an average annual rate of 15.4 per cent in real terms. However, while production was growing at an annual rate of 5.2 per cent, aggregate domestic demand was approaching 8 per cent, three percentage points over output growth and a direct impact of such growth, on both inflation and current deficit, was expected to result.

Exports of goods and services were growing at an average annual rate of 6.2 per cent in real terms, but imports expanded at an average annual rate of 18.4 per cent during the period. The current account deficit reached 3 per cent of the GDP in 1990 whilst inflation accelerated from a rate of 5.6 per cent in 1988, to 7.3 per cent in 1990. As a result of this overheating, the Spanish economy was consequently suffering a deterioration in its long-term goals.

This situation led to a tightening of economic policy which, since 1987, has mainly consisted of a very strict monetary policy based on three main instruments, implemented as a whole:

- 1. The Bank of Spain, which had practised a market-orientated monetary policy since the seventies, allowed a large appreciation of the peseta exchange rate against the Deutschemark in 1986 and 1987, seeking a level that could be stabilized for a prolonged period. However, market pressures in favour of the peseta necessitated the Bank of Spain to buy huge amounts of assets denominated in other currencies, in order to curb the market trend. The Bank of Spain was looking for an equilibrium between domestic competitiveness and the impact of the structural changes in the Spanish economy on its balance of payments (an inflow of new foreign capital larger than the current account deficit), and on the credibility of anti-inflationary policy. This task needed exchange controls for long periods. Most of these controls were imposed and maintained in an exceptional way (within a context of general liberalization), until the end of 1990. The entry of the peseta into the exchange rate mechanism of the European monetary system (EMS) institutionalized the Bank of Spain's exchange rate stability policy. The chosen central parity (65 pesetas per Deutschemark), and a 6 per cent band, were as a result of that equilibrium. Since the peseta's entry, Spain's currency has been negotiated at the upper limits of the exchange rate mechanism.

- 2. As the stability of the exchange rate against the Deutschemark has been shown to be the primary anchor of an anti-inflationary programme, interest rates have occupied a secondary role within monetary policy over the past few years. The behaviour of the monetary authorities was therefore influenced by the upward pressure exerted on the peseta, although they have carried out a policy of high interest rates, in real terms, in order both to maintain restrictions on domestic monetary conditions (not all the sectors of the economy show a high-grade sensitivity to the exchange rate) and to guarantee the credibility of the anti-inflationary policy. Exchange controls and fiscal barriers allowed very high interest rates in real terms during the 1987-1990 period and, in particular, during 1989 and 1990. As a result, the yield curve has been defined by the market with a very pronounced negative slope, overall, between six-month and one-year maturities.
- 3. For a very short period, and as a transitory measure, the monetary authorities imposed credit ceilings during the second half of 1989, and throughout 1990. The reason for this measure was the need to curb the intensity of the growth of domestic demand with instruments other than, for example, interest rates, which had a perverse effect on the peseta exchange rate. Additionally, credit ceilings could reinforce the impact of interest rates and exchange rates on the economy, thereby accelerating their restrictive effects.

As a result of the application of the strict monetary policy based on these instruments, the Spanish economy began to register an important slowdown from 1990, thus beginning its second phase - a phase which lasts until today.

1990 to present

In this second phase, the growth rate of domestic demand has slowed down, as in other industrialized nations. However, their respective cyclical patterns are not completely similar. The buoyancy of the Spanish economy was considerably greater during the economic upswing and, now, with the cyclical downturn behind it, it has continued to maintain a higher rate of growth. In recent months, all the components making up domestic demand have stabilized at about 2.5

per cent in the first half of 1991, continuing the process started in 1990 (that year showed a rate of growth of domestic demand of 4.6 per cent). The second half of showed more accelerated growth, thanks to consumption behaviour, and 1991 closed with a 3 per cent rate of growth in domestic demand.

In 1991, Spanish monetary policy adjusted to the new circumstances of domestic demand, and to the new interest rate cuts implemented by most of the industrialized countries. Evidence of this was seen in the lifting of credit restrictions and the reduction of domestic interest rates, enforcing the drive towards the full liberation of capital movements. However, the slowness with which the inflation rate is falling, the size of the external deficit, and the continuing presence of demand and output growth rates above the EMS average have necessitated caution in adapting monetary policy to the economy's new conditions. Therefore, the Bank of Spain's intervention rate, which had been cut by close to two points since the beginning of the year, did not fall significantly below 12.75 per cent (only 25 basis points), after 16 May.

In fact, today it can be said that the problem which causes Spain's persistently high inflation rate is no longer the excess of internal aggregate demand over production, but rather the excessive rise of prices in the service sector. The implementation of a tight monetary policy has generated a dual situation in the economy and process of inflation. On the one hand, the sector most sensitive to monetary policy (the manufacturing sector) now shows a very low rate of growth, while the sector impervious to monetary policy (services) still grows at a high rate in real terms. This level of dualism produces very negative conditions for investment and concentrates all the economy's growth on the demand for consumption. Additionally, consumption prices show a parallel process of dual inflation: industrial prices grow at a rate which is half the rate of growth of the prices of services.

Considering that Spanish fiscal policy, in the atmosphere of the greater flexibility introduced by Germany after unification, has dismissed the possibility of maintaining the public deficit level close to zero, and after the failure of the social pact proposed by the government in 1991, anti-inflationary policy should continue to lean heavily on monetary policy (which is, in fact, practically acting alone) and on government-announced structural microeconomic policies which are designed to impact on those sectors which are causing the most inflation.

The fight against inflation in Spain may not be easy in 1992. The concentration of important events such as the Olympic Games, the Universal Exhibition, the 500th Anniversary of the Discovery of the Americas - together with Madrid being designated the cultural capital of Europe - will all have an effect on the economy, stressing dualism whilst hindering deflation in the service sector; at the same time, these factors will not directly assist a resurgence in investment - such a resurgence will only be possible when productivity manages to compensate for the loss of competitiveness which the excessive growth of salary and service costs have caused in the industrial sector. Only then would a recupera-

	Dec 90	Sep 91	Oct 91	
			Forecast AFI	*Real*
CPI (A+B+C+D+E) (100%)	6.5	5.7	5.2	5.5
Underlying inflation (B+C+D) (77.54%)	6.1	6.1	6.0	6.2
A) Non-processed food (15.46%)	7.2	5.3	3.4	4.2
B) Processed food (17.56%)	3.6	3.3	3.3	3.5
C) Industrial non-energy goods (25.74%)	4.8	4.9	4.8	4.9
Non-energy goods (A+B+C) (58.76%)	5.1	4.5	4.0	4.3
D) Services (34.24%)	8.4	8.3	8.3	8.4
E) Energy (7.00%)	11.0	2.0	-1.2	-1.0

Figure 25.1 Year-on-year CPI growth rates

tion of expected benefits for investment be possible. Such an increase in productivity is, however, being achieved by way of a slowdown in the growth of employment. The expansive effects of the above-mentioned events may delay this slowdown in 1992, but they will not stop it. In 1993, a substantial fall in the rate of inflation may be expected as a result of the situation in the industrial sector, which has gone through a period of re-adjustment, of the spread of these effects to the construction sector, and of their impact on Spain's inflationary nucleus, namely the service sector.

Growth expectations for GDP in 1992 should be 2.7 per cent in real terms, the same as for 1991. This rate of growth may be possible as the result of an increase in the growth of the demand for consumption, offsetting a very low rate for investment in fixed capital. The current account deficit could increase its percentage of GDP to 3.7, from 3.5 in 1991. The inflation rate, meanwhile, could reach a 5.9 per cent rate at the end of 1992, in contrast to a projected 5.5 per cent level at the end of 1991 (because of the effect of increased taxes), but could go down below 5 per cent at the start of 1993.

25.2 *Market composition*

Government securities market

The Ministry of the Treasury is the main fixed-income issuer in Spain. During the last two years, Spanish authorities have placed great effort in developing the Treasury's debt management policy, which has been designed to achieve a two-fold objective: a more rational management of its liabilities, and the creation of a more transparent and liquid public debt market.

To achieve these objectives the Treasury has focused on three main areas:

- 1. A switch from partial financing by the Bank of Spain (BoS), to direct access to the market. By progressively substituting all former financial sources with the BoS, the Treasury has sought to introduce a more orthodox financing method, further enhanced by the gradual reduction of the compulsory investment ratio with which financial institutions had to cope.
  - Development of financial instruments designed to increase the range of products to be offered, and to create new issuance techniques (such as the implementation of a 'second round' in primary market auctions).
  - Achievement of a more liquid market by grouping issues of debt by maturity, and issuing them at a minimum of three fungible auctions. Currently, at least 5 bonds are traded every day with a total outstanding amount of more than Pta 2964bn. The latter figure does not include the 10-year 11.30 per cent coupon debenture, mainly held by non-residents, the outstanding amount of which is Pta 746.3bn.
  - Development of a settlement and clearing system - a computerized book-entry system - via the BoS. This system is available to account holders and also to third parties operating with management entities, the advantage being that trades and coupon payments are settled on the value-date on which funds are received. The Euroclear system for settlement and clearing is also available through security deposit accounts opened with Spanish management entities holding third-party accounts.
- 2. The marketing of bonds through specialized mutual funds called *Fontesoros*, consisting exclusively of government securities. This policy aims to improve mutual funds by enhancing the development of the public debt secondary market.

- 3. The lifting of withholding tax liability for the foreign investor. The Royal Decree 5/1990 of 20 December 1990 established that EC investors residing in Spain are exempt from Spanish taxation on interest payments and capital gains. Non-EC investors residing in Spain enjoy a tax exemption when holding public debt or Matador bonds.

The recent establishment of a futures and options market offering derivative instruments which allow hedging strategies, has further contributed to the strength experienced by the market. Presently futures and options are being traded on notional bonds (of 3-, 5- and, recently, 10-year maturities), as well as on the Madrid interbank offered rate (MIBOR). The volume traded throughout 1991 reached Pta 9932bn for futures and Pta 5538bn for options. Options on futures on notional bonds and MIBOR have been traded from 3 April 1992.

The amount of outstanding central government debt between 1980 and 1990 can be seen in Figure 25.2 It shows the development of public debt as a percentage of GDP over the last ten years. Figure 25.3 shows comparative gross public debt, including the debt of local authorities, as a percentage of GDP for EC countries. The net lending and borrowing position of those countries is shown in Figure 25.4, and reveals the effort made by the Spanish government to reduce its debt in relation to GDP. This effort has led to significant improvement in solvency risk compared to other EC countries.

Corporate bond market

The corporate bond market, unlike that for government bonds, is perhaps one of the segments of the Spanish bond market which is taking longer to reach the standards of other European and international financial markets.

The development of this market has been characterized by the following features:

- There has been generally poor liquidity. In addition to low issuance volumes, secondary markets have not been active because of an inability to speed up transactions. Also, most investors, especially institutions, continued to apply bond-accumulation policies, sometimes backed up by a tax and accounting ruling which promoted keeping bond portfolios while discouraging active strategies in bond portfolio management.
- Historically, the design of issues has been heterogeneous with a large number of different systems of repayment, calls and redemption, indexing formulas, different nominal values, etc. This made, for instance, the calculation of yields very difficult, even for expert dealers. In addition, each issuer used to launch many similar issues, but of low volume each. Therefore, even though the total volume issued could have promoted

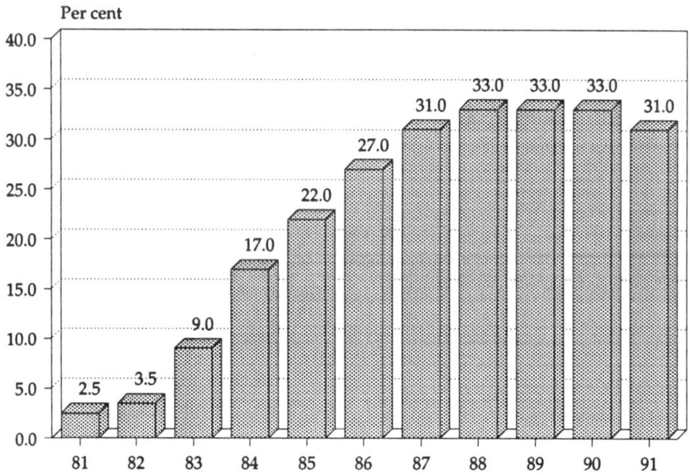

Figure 25.2 Outstanding central government debt as a percentage of GDP

	1980	1986	1989	1990	1991[1]
Belgium	76.9	123.7	129.9	129.4	129.4
Denmark	39.3	67.2	63.3	62.8	63.3
Germany	32.7	42.7	43.6	43.7	45.2
Greece	28.8	65.3	85.1	89.5	94.3
Spain	18.1	48.5	45.2	44.7	42.6
France	24.6	34.2	36.0	36.1	36.1
Ireland	76.8	115.7	104.7	101.4	99.4
Italy	59.0	88.5	98.9	100.9	102.9
Luxembourg	13.8	13.8	8.8	7.8	6.8
Netherlands	45.9	71.7	77.6	77.8	78.5
Portugal	37.1	68.4	71.5	67.8	64.7
United Kingdom	54.3	58.1	45.7	43.0	41.8
EUR 12	41.0	58.5	59.0	58.9	59.2

Figure 25.3 Gross public debt in EC countries (as percentage of GDP)

[1] *forecast*

Source: Commission of the European Community

	1983	1985	1987	1989	1990	1991[1]
EUR 12	-5.3	-5.2	-4.2	-3.0	-3.9	-4.1
High-deficit countries						
Greece	-8.3	-13.8	-12.0	-18.4	-18.6	-17.1
Italy	-11.8	-12.5	-11.2	-10.2	-10.0	-9.4
High-debt countries						
Belgium	-11.2	-8.5	-7.2	-6.6	-5.6	-5.9
Ireland	-11.8	-11.3	-9.1	-3.2	-3.3	-3.5
Netherlands	-6.4	-4.8	-6.5	-5.3	-5.4	-4.7
Portugal	-9.0	-10.1	-6.8	-3.8	-6.0	-5.6
Other countries						
Denmark	-7.2	-2.2	+2.2	-0.8	-1.4	-1.6
Germany	-2.5	-1.1	-1.9	+0.2	-3.2	-4.8
Spain	-4.8	-7.0	-3.2	-2.7	-3.0	-1.8
France	-3.2	-2.9	-2.0	-1.5	-1.2	-1.1
Luxembourg	+2.0	+5.3	+1.3	+3.4	+3.3	+1.1
United Kingdom	-3.3	-2.7	-1.3	+0.9	-0.2	-0.7

Figure 25.4 **Central government net lending (+) or borrowing (-)**
[1] *forecast*
Source: Commission of the European Community

	Treasury bills	Treasury notes[1]	T-bonds (3-5yr)	10-yr debentures
Dec 1987	2538.0	5332.0	2250.5	774.4
Dec 1988	3657.9	5051.4	3242.3	740.4
Dec 1889	5403.7	4570.9	3901.1	667.1
Dec 1990	7382.3	3707.8	4158.7	649.5
Dec 1991	7711.9	2775.7	5777.3	1090.0

Figure 25.5 **Recent evolution of central government debt outstanding (ESP billion)**
[1] *until 1992, Treasury notes had a specific tax treatment. Now, they are close to being defunct*

their secondary market, the lack of homogeneous issues, terms and conditions removed any chance of them gaining importance in the market.

- The lack of standard rating systems for issues and issuers has made it difficult to determine the minimum risks each manager should deal with. In general, the traditionally poor transparency regarding issuers' financial statements has given rise to a prevailing attitude of distrust, and has prevented this market's development in pace with the public debt market.
- Issue systems have been a further hindrance. Firstly, placement periods have been very long, and dealing availability, i.e., the acceptance for listing in the stock exchange, takes over three months. Many issuers have been used to appealing to captive markets, such as those derived from mandatory ratios of banks and, especially, savings banks.
- Finally, and very importantly, due to the current trend in the market, there has been a lack of portfolios really focused on fixed-income, as well as a lack of portfolio managers who know how to distinguish and choose between the different ways or strategies to invest in fixed-income. There are only a few fixed-income funds - at present, money market funds (FIAM, *Fondos de Inversión en Activos del Mercado Monetario*) and fixed-income funds (FIM, *Fondos de Inversión Mobiliaria*) together represent around Pta 4tr, and in the mid-90s this amount is expected to reach Pta 10tr. Furthermore, pension funds have only recently acquired the increasing significance they now display.

Private bond issuers

This market is controlled by the issuers of three specific sectors: banks, utilities and telecommunications. The remaining sectors have a very low share, with the vast majority of their issues being convertible bonds.

Financial institutions

In 1990 financial institutions represented 36.79 per cent of new issues volume listed on the stock exchange (see Figure 25.6). In fact, these issues are not offered to the open capital market, since they are placed through the banking office network and are part of the range of products offered by the banks and savings banks to their clients. The only exception is placement of convertible bonds and mortgage and secured bonds issued by state-owned banks. Also very common is the issue of subordinated debt in order to cover the guarantee ratio of banks, since this type of bond is computable as equity. For the reasons given above, there is no real secondary market for these issues, and in many cases, banks themselves regulate the secondary market among their own clients. The interest rate of these issues, as well as other conditions, are principally determined by the supply and demand levels of other typical bank products - current accounts, time deposits, etc. -, and not by other fixed-income issues of the market. During the first 10 months of 1991, this figure was as much as 50 per cent of the total issued by institutions other than public administrations. A similar percentage is shown by the outstanding balance of medium- and long-term bonds issued by finance companies, by comparison to total issuance (excluding government bonds).

Utilities (water, gas and electricity)

This is the main sector, in terms of both issue volume - 45.05 per cent of the total in 1990 - and turnover of its bonds. These issues financed the high investment needs of the electricity sector in the 1980s for new power stations, etc. In this respect, the electricity sector had two advantages,

- the acceptance of the sector's issues in the mandatory investment ratios of banks and savings banks
- the possibility of issuing with special discounts in respect of income tax and corporate tax - credit institutions excluded - and a specific withholding tax treatment on the paid coupons

The first advantage was removed in 1985. Since then, there has been an ongoing transfer of these bonds from financial institutions to individuals, who can benefit from tax advantages. Bond yields implied in their prices in secondary markets discount the above-mentioned tax advantages. The spread, versus other issues without that tax status, is usually between 50 and 100 basic points, depending on the time left until the coupon due date. At present, these debentures are still issued, but their volume is very small and they will tend to disappear due to the legal provisions under which they are governed. When withholding tax was applied to all fixed-income issues, placement to foreign investors was relatively significant - since, amongst other tax advantages, withholding tax was just 1.20 per cent of the paid coupon.

At present, most electricity companies launch issues of similar design to those of state bonds and debentures. The issuance of convertible bonds, although widely-used by this sector, was not possible at specific times during the eighties, due to the fact that bond prices were very close to the nominal value of the shares of their respective companies and, according to Spanish law, shares cannot be issued under par value. However, since the recovery of these companies' share prices from 1987, issues have started again and the financial strategy of all these companies includes the option of issuing convertible bonds.

Telecommunications

Almost all issues by this sector - 13.48 per cent in 1990 - are accounted for by Telefónica, which had to tap the market in order to meet the strong investment

	1989	% Total	1990	% Total
PUBLIC SECTOR				
Includes public debt, town councils, autonomous governments, international bodies etc.	5,142,850		3,253,239	
PRIVATE SECTOR				
Banks	773,260	30.88	786,994	36.79
Utilities	1,106,303	44.18	963,713	46.05
Telecommunications	297,047	11.86	298,946	13.98
Chemicals	52,666	2.10	16,164	0.76
Building sector	26,450	1.06	25,705	1.20
Remaining sectors	248,554	9.93	47,631	2.23
Total (private sector)	2,504,250	100.00	2,139,103	100.00
GRAND TOTAL	7,647,130		5,392,342	

Figure 25.6 Issued listed in the stock exchange (ESP million)

requirements needed both to increase service capacity and to cover a high growth in the demand for new lines, which started in the late eighties. Telefónica was the first issuer to implement an auction system for its bonds and debentures, which were open to financial institutions.

As far as the remaining issues are concerned, they account for less than 5 per cent of the market. In many cases, the lack of rating systems makes placement of these issues in the market very difficult.

Composition by coupon structure

The coupon structure of the Spanish government bond market (see Figure 25.7) shows a large concentration in high-coupon bonds, i.e. those between 11 per cent and 14 per cent. There are very few low-coupon bonds, and they belong to very old issues. Due to the recent development of the Spanish debt market and the existence of high interest rates in Spain during the last few years, (especially in 1989 and 1990), a remarkable effort was required in the Treasury's funding policy to promote the government's debt market. Given this situation, it was only logical that coupons would remain relatively high. However, the expectations of lower interest rates in 1991 allowed both larger issues and somewhat lower coupons (around 11-12 per cent). At the time of writing, the coupon rates for the most recent issues are 11.90 per cent for the three-year maturity bond (1995), 11.60 per cent for the five-year maturity bond (1997) and 11.30 per cent for the ten-year debenture (2002).

Composition by maturity structure

Until mid-1991, a high percentage of the outstanding amount issued in the Spanish medium- and long-term debt market was concentrated in the short-term (between 1 and 5 years). The reason for this was the particular kind of marketing technique employed by Spanish financial institutions - the main agents in this market until that time - which was directed to short-term repo operations. It was only the widespread expectations, seen from the beginning of 1991, of a downward trend in interest rates which impelled financial institutions to acquire long-term debt portfolios, which increased the average life of the debt outstanding.

Another factor determining the average increase in maturities that took place in 1991 was the significant volume of foreign investment received by the Spanish debt market as a result of new liberalization policies and the new tax exemption regulation, which went into effect on 1 January 1991. Given its larger investment horizon, this investment focused on long-term assets.

It is likely that once the government's debt market is sufficiently developed, more institutions (foreign investors, investment and pension funds) will be attracted to it. At the same time, as expectations of convergence (arising from European monetary union) become firmer, maturities are likely to extend and the market is likely to become more liquid.

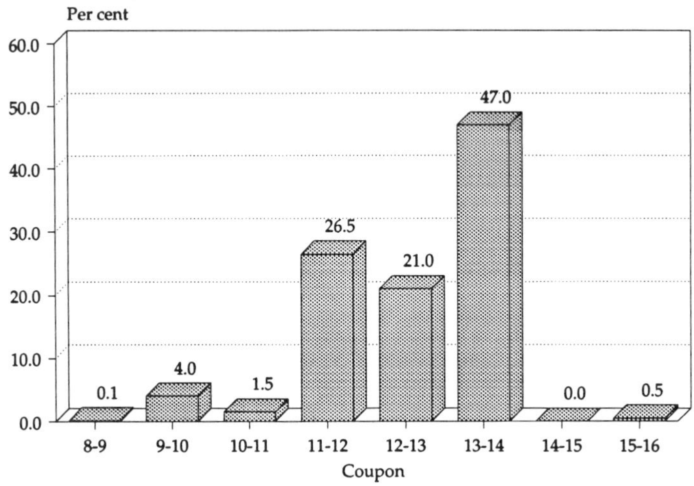

Figure 25.7 Coupon structure of the medium- and long-term government market

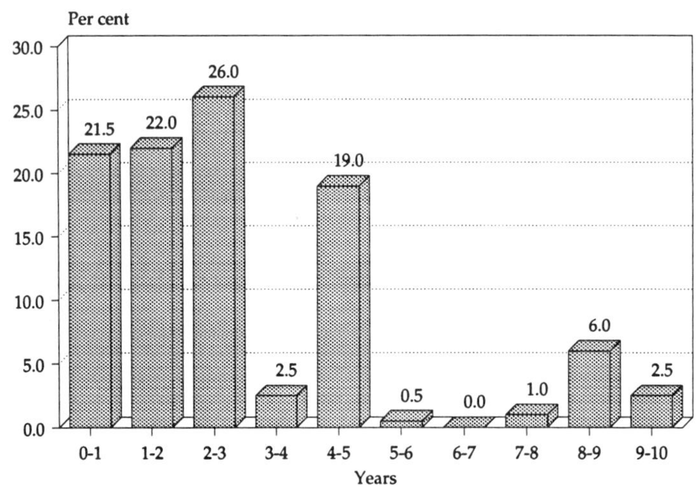

Figure 25.8 Maturity structure of the medium- and long-term government market

25.3 Types of security

Government market

The Spanish Treasury basically issues two types of security: T-bills (one-year maturity assets), called *Letras del Tesoro* and T-bonds (consisting of two longer maturity assets), called *Bonos del Estado* (3 and 5 years) and *Obligaciones del Estado* (10 years). A third type of asset, the *Pagaré del Tesoro*, has also been issued, in the past but, given its special tax characteristics and, more importantly, its imminent obsolescence, it does not warrant further consideration in this analysis.

Letras del Tesoro (T-bills) are the Treasury's newest instrument. They were created in June 1987 and, since then, they have become the main vehicle used to meeting the state's funding needs. They are issued as discount zero-coupon bonds with maturities which cannot exceed 18 months - in practice, only one-year and three-month T-bills have so far been issued. Their nominal value is Pta 1,000,000 and they can only be represented by settlement in book-entry form (i.e. not as material assets).

Their role as monetary policy instruments has also been outstanding, both in open-market operations and in three-month repo auctions developed by the Bank of Spain until late 1991. From 1987 until the beginning of 1991, the interest rate fixed by the Bank of Spain for three-month T-bill repo auctions was the basic reference for shorter-term interbank rates. Changes in this rate were seen as a clear sign that the direction of monetary policy had shifted. Since 1991, this auction has only been another way of funding and was just implemented temporarily by the Bank of Spain, while the Treasury acquired the legal status to issue assets shorter than one year to maturity.

On the other hand, *Bonos* and *Obligaciones del Estado* are coupon bullet bonds with a nominal value of Pta 10,000 which may be represented both as settlements and value assets. Redemption, as is usual in coupon bonds, is at par value.

Private sector

As noted earlier, issues of the private sector were characterized by their wide variety of terms and conditions. Nevertheless, the need to extend the market is forcing issuers to consider issuing with a standard set of conditions, similar to those of government bonds. Bearing in mind the wide diversity of issues, the main types of outstanding security may be listed as follows:

Bonds

These are bullet issues with a 3- to 5-year maturity term. They usually have fixed coupons, fixed to their maturity dates, and have neither puts nor calls. Their IRR is determined in the issue by a spread to public debt rates.

Debentures

These are bullet issues with, in general, maturity terms of 5 years. Companies in the electricity sector have been the major issuers of such bonds.

Convertible bonds

These bonds are usually issued with a 3-year term - at specified dates during which, they are convertible into shares of the company, with a discount expressed in a percentage of the price of shares during an earlier period of time - usually, one month. In some cases there is a call after the last conversion option. Traditionally, the yield of this type of bond has been 100-200 basis points below the rate of other types of gilt issued by same issuer. In general, their secondary market is small, since most investors buy the bonds in the primary market in order to exercise conversion.

Floating-rate notes

In Spain, there is no FRN market like that of other countries. The main reason for this is that very few bonds are directly MIBOR-indexed (Madrid interbank offered rate). Issues have an initial term of one or two years at a fixed-interest rate. After that, the indexation period is determined according to different parameters such as the nominal rates of public debt at similar terms, average prime rates of several banks, deposit rates, etc. The indexation of issues to the consumer price index was forbidden in 1989. Additionally, financial institutions are not allowed to index issues to their own interest rates, either those on credits or deposits. Floating-rate notes have virtually no secondary market, mainly due to their barely useful reference formulae, which are often at wide variance to short-term interest rates. The main issuers of this instrument have been the autonomous governments, and the utilities sector.

Callable bonds

As is the case for other types of bond, there are no standard terms and conditions for callable bonds. These bonds include, primarily, bonds with redemption options all along their term, at which redemption is exercised through previous notice by the issuer. Secondly, there is another type of callable bond that can only be redeemed on pre-determined dates, usually at prices over par value. Unlike government bonds, issuers have not always chosen the option to exercise calls when the apparent rate differential was positive for issuer, due to problems in the re-funding processes. There have been other types of advanced redemption, by drawing and by annual reduction of the nominal value. At present, callable bonds usually have one or two fixed dates for exercise, usually with a small premium. In situations such as currently exist, when there is a trend of falling interest rates, market yields always take into account the date of the first call.

Puttable bonds

Most puttable bonds are medium-term - between five and seven years - and usually include puts in the third and fifth years. The put exercise price is at par, and very often it coincides with call exercise at prices over par value. In general, bond coupon conditions do not change after the put or call exercise term.

Zero-coupon

Issues of this type have been increasing. The main issuers are state-owned banks and Telefónica, which implemented a new auction system for 3-, 5-and 10-year zero-coupon bonds. 10-year bonds are the ones preferred by investors, since they increase portfolio average life. Note that the average life of 10-year gilts is 6.3 years, and that these are the longest government bonds.

Warrant bonds

During the late eighties, when the stock exchange underwent a bullish period, bonds which included the right to purchase shares of the company (or other of its group) at a pre-determined price, were issued. Sometimes, that right could be negotiated in the stock exchange, but due to the relatively high liquidity of warrants, the low number of issues and their overall number, there is no warrant market as such. Some examples are those issued by Tubacex and Banco Hispano.

Financial institution market

Subordinated bonds

Subordinated bonds are bonds issued either on a fixed- or variable-interest rate basis, which as far as the investor who acquires them is concerned, are somewhat similar to shares, as interest on them is subordinated or subject to the profitability of the issuing companies, in the absence of which, payment thereof is cancelled. In addition, resulting accrued and unpaid interest may be accumulated in a debit, which is also subordinated, and which is paid only when the company achieves profitability again, and up to 1/3 thereof. Payment of late-payment interest on this debit is subject to previous authorization by Banco de España, and in no case can exceed the interest-rate of the issue.

As far as the issuing institutions - mainly savings banks and banks, but also co-operative savings banks - are concerned, subordinated debt serves as an instrument which can be used to increase their capital, making it highly-attractive. As a procedure used to increase equity, subordinated financing is relatively new to the Spanish financial system. It first appeared with Act 13/85, dated 25 May 1985, which dealt with investment ratios, equity and obligation of finance companies pass on information, and for most savings banks (which showed a deficit of such equity) was the only chance to attain the minimum legal levels, until the participation shares provided by Act 16/1988 on Procedure and Monitoring of Credit Companies were regulated.

Act 13/85, mentioned above, states the need "to determine criteria on companies' equity and to open up new options for those having insufficient capital", and introduces a significant new instrument among those included in minimum equity, namely, subordinated debentures. In particular, section 7.e of the Act states that "the financing received by the company which, on a credit-priority basis, is second to regular creditors, will be considered as capital, provided that the initial term of said financing is not less than 5 years, and that the remaining term up to its maturity date is not less than one year." Also, "this type of subordinated funding will be computable by the maximum amount authorized by Banco de España in each case."

Later on, the Banco de España Circular Letter 19/1989, dated 13 December, on determination and control of minimum equity establishes (in 2.c) that "subordinated funding exceeding 30 per cent of equity will not be computed as capital. Neither will be computable for capital the subordinated funding or part thereof which, added up to the remaining capital, exceeds by more than 20 per cent the equity required by the ratio. The latter restraint will not be applied to perpetual debt, provided that its eventual redemption clauses are subject to previous authorization by Banco de España and are not enforceable at least during 20 years from and after the issuing date."

The above provisions therefore serve to underline the following basic features:

- Initial term no shorter than five years
- No pre-payment; where clauses of this type exist, they must be authorized by Banco de España
- They cannot be acquired by the company itself, by companies of the consolidated group, or by other companies or individuals having been granted credits by the issuing company, or by a company of the consolidated group
- They can be denominated both in pesetas and in foreign currency
- They can be convertible in stock or shares of the issuing company, or consolidated group

With regard to issue types, there is a clear preference for a variable interest rate, to the extent that, in 1990-1991, almost all bonds were of this type.

On a tax basis, yields derived from investment in this type of bonds are subject to withholding tax, payable in the return of the income and corporate taxes.

Finally, they can be negotiated in organized official markets (stock exchanges), and in the AIAF OTC market (AIAF is the Asociación de Intermediarios Financieros, or Finance Brokers Association).

Matador bonds

Matador bonds are medium- and long-term debentures, denominated in pesetas and issued - in the Spanish market - by non-resident companies. They are bearer bonds, with annual coupons and 3-10 year maturities, although issues with a 5-year repayment term are prevalent - and guaranteed by financial companies operating in Spain. They are not exactly eurobonds, but rather part of a 'domestic market' with an 'international vocation', in which issuing parties are non-resident companies which issue peseta-denominated bonds in Spain. As a result, these bonds can be regarded as similar to yankee bonds (bonds denominated in dollars, issued in the USA by non-residents), samurai bonds (denominated in yen), Bulldog bonds (denominated in British pounds), and so on.

These issues have their legal basis in the Ministry Order dated 3 February 1987, which dealt with the issue, negotiation and listing in Spain of securities denominated in pesetas, and issued by international bodies of which Spain is a member. This provision determined the framework for these issues, which must be authorized by the *Dirección General del Tesoro y Política Financiera* (the Director General of the Treasury) - following a Report by the *Comisión Interministerial de Financiación Exterior* (Foreign Financing Inter-Ministry Commission) and which, for stock market listing purposes, are deemed to be government bonds. Also, it was determined that payment and settlement of transactions relating to these securities would take place in Spain until 1987. After that year, it was decided to let market forces act freely, so that the Spanish stock market could compete efficiently with overseas systems, most particularly, with those of the euromarket. At present, these bonds may be settled in any clearing centre - with Euroclear in Brussels and Cedel in Luxembourg being the most representative clearing houses in Europe.

From a tax point of view (see also Section 25.13), Matador bonds may be subscribed by private or public investors - either non-resident, in which case interest is exempt from taxation in Spain, or resident, and therefore subject to withholding tax, income tax or the tax. For Spaniards, these bonds are considered foreign investments and are thus subject to the exchange control information requirements.

Their exemption from taxes in Spain, their high yields (based on currency yields), the rating offered to issuers, and the settling through Euroclear and

Cedel, all explain the high degree of attraction of these bonds for foreign investors (who can transfer the capital and the interest overseas and convert them in other currencies by means of swaps).

The creation of the fixed-income OTC market of the AIAF in 1991, a secondary market with a non-official organization, has increased trading opportunities and has given higher liquidity to this market, which is characterized by the fact that investors tend to keep these bonds in their portfolios until maturity.

In 1991, there have been some notable changes in the new issuance of Matador bonds. On the one hand, the issues of the Republics of Austria and Mexico have been added to the traditional list of supranational entities. On the other, the coupon interest rate has changed, not only in terms of issuer, but also according to maturity. At the beginning of the year, some bonds were offered at an interest rate of 14.5 per cent - a level which fell throughout the year to stand at around 11.15 per cent at year-end. The only exception was the issue by the United States of Mexico, which offset the higher risk with an increase in the coupon to 14.25 per cent.

Another notable change was introduced by the Nordic Investment Bank, which launched the first issue of 3-year Matador bonds, with an indexed yield, based upon the development of the FIEX-35 index of the Madrid Stock Exchange (a selection of the 35 most-liquid stocks). Thus, on the bond maturity date, the investor will receive 90 per cent of the increase registered by the index during the 3-year term of the issue. If, for the sake of argument, the index dropped during this period of time, full repayment of the bonds is guaranteed by the issuer.

A full list of Matador bond issues may be found in the Appendix.

Bank zero-coupon bonds

Bank zeros are bonds which are similar to commercial paper, but with the particular difference that they are issued by banks or savings banks. These bonds, which are issued at a discount, include a payment promise for a fixed date, so that the issuing institution undertakes to return their nominal value. The usual term is 3 - 12 months and the bond's nominal value is usually Pta 1m.

From a tax point of view, the paid interest is subject to the relevant withholding on account of income tax and profit tax. Often, these bonds have been issued as withholding-at-source bonds (AFRO) (see Section 25.13, Taxation).

Banks' capital debentures (cash bonds & Treasury bonds)

These are debentures which are issued by banks and savings banks, with repayment terms from 3 to 5 years. Cash bonds were created in 1963 and Treasury bonds in 1980, usually with clauses that made them convertible into shares of the issuer. Like mortgage bonds, these bonds are considered as part of the money market, since, although they have a medium repayment term, they are highly-liquid assets.

The main difference between both types of bonds lies in the issuing entities. Cash bonds can only be issued by industrial banks, while Treasury bonds can be issued by savings banks and any other kind of bank, according to the Companies Act. Also, cash bonds imply some tax advantages, although both are subject to withholding on account of income tax and corporate tax. In this sense, they are exempt from inheritance tax, provided that they are kept by the holder for at least two years, and also from *Impuesto General sobre Transmisiones Patrimoniales y Actos Jurídicos Documentados*, capital transfer tax.

Capital debentures all have a very active secondary market (especially true in the case of cash bonds) in stock exchanges and in the AIAF market - provided that they are not convertible in shares. In 1990, dealings in the Madrid Stock Exchange amounted to Pta 97,670m, a figure which represented some 23 per cent of the total of bonds traded there.

Convertible issues and issues with warrants

Convertible issues, as their name implies, allow the possibility of converting bonds into shares of the issuing company, on selected dates. Since they can be converted into shares, these bonds have features typical both of debentures and shares. Conversion is voluntary, while failure to convert makes them become straight bonds.

Spanish convertible issues are characterized by the fact that the conversion price is not fixed in pesetas, but rather estimated by discounting a specific percentage - usually around 10-20 per cent - from the stock exchange average price of the company's shares during a given period of time. In addition, conversion is European-style in that there are some pre-determined dates to convert, unlike American-style which allows conversion at any time. Additionally, conversion is not always into new shares; sometimes, the issuing company gives old shares in exchange for debentures and, in such a case, they are termed 'exchangeable issues'. An exchangeable issue is always worth more than a convertible one, since conversion implies a non-dilution clause[1], whilst exchange does not. In addition, old shares are fully-liquid and can be sold immediately, while new shares usually imply illiquidity terms, ranging from three months (for the most active) to six months although, in some cases, this term is even longer. Sometimes, the issuing companies themselves are interested in the new securities being illiquid, since the offer of more shares may result in a fall in the share price.

From the issuer's point of view, convertible issues offer a way of reducing companies' self-portfolio excess.

As an additional feature to convertibility, warrants are included in some cases. These issues are characterized by the fact that each issued bond has an attached right - but not an obligation - to acquire a given number of shares of the issuer, who undertakes to deliver them at a pre-fixed date, in accordance with the issue's terms and conditions. Therefore, for subscribers, the warrant is like an issue premium and, as a result, its existence facilitates placement by the issuer. The main difference between these securities and convertible debentures lies in the fact that in debentures with warrants there is no conversion, but rather the subscription to a security at an agreed price - this allows a warrant to be used as a risk-coverage instrument. From a legal point of view, the warrant is deemed a security and can therefore be traded in stock markets.

The theoretical value of a warrant bond depends upon: its exercise price, share prices, interest rates, the period of time from appraisal to exercise, etc. Therefore, two elements have to be considered for its appraisal:

- The intrinsic value
- The temporary value

The intrinsic value is determined by the difference between the share price and its exercise price.

$$W = CN - PN = (C - P)\,N$$

where,

W	intrinsic value
C	share market price
N	number of shares that can be acquired with one warrant
P	share cost

The warrant is exercised when $C > P$, i.e., when the share price in the market is higher than its cost, since, otherwise, going directly to the market would be better. As a drop in share prices would make the warrant inoperative, the exercise price is fixed in terms of a discount on the share's stock exchange average price in a given period. This way, the warrant intrinsic value is always positive,

$$W = (C - T)\,N$$

[1] *In the case of a capital increase on account of capital (reserves), where the debenture holder has no preferential right of subscription, said clause is applied, which maintains the share proportion. The number of shares to be allotted per debenture, after the capital increase, is calculated according to the following formula,*

$$\frac{\textit{Number of shares allotted per debenture before the capital increase, according to the exchange equation}}{\textit{Total number of outstanding shares before the capital increase}} = \frac{\textit{Number of shares allotted per debenture after the capital increase}}{\textit{Total number of shares after the capital increase}}$$

where,

T pre-fixed discount

The temporary value includes the expected profit until the warrant coupon's exercise, resulting from the share price's development. The theoretical value of these coupons is estimated by applying the Black-Scholes option-appraisal model, which is expressed by the following formula,

$$Wt = C\,N(d1) - Ee^{-rt}\,N(d2)$$

where,

$$d1 \quad \left[\frac{In\left(\frac{C}{E\,e^{-rt}}\right)}{\sigma\sqrt{t}}\right] + 0.5\sigma\sqrt{t}$$

$$d2 \quad d1 - \sigma\sqrt{t}$$

Wt warrant's theoretical value
C daily share's price
E warrant's exercise price
r instant compound capitalization rate in the interbank market
t time to the warrant coupon's maturity date, expressed on an annual basis
σ share price volatility
$N(di)$ standard variable distribution on di, i=1,2.

During the past five years, financial companies have issued just one issue of this type. It was Banco Hispano Americano which, in 1988, issued the 'May 1988 Issue' of subordinated Treasury bonds - convertible into shares - which also included warrant coupons.

Mortgage bonds

In the early 1980s, Act 2/81, dated 25 May, extended by later Royal Decree 685/1982, dated 17 March, marked the beginning of the new Spanish mortgage market, by creating the following:

- The banking system's deregulation process: The Finance Ministry's Order, dated January 17, 1981, deregulated all interest rates and commissions of deposit banks, as well as bank dividends. It also promoted long-term financing and reduced the minimum investment ratio compulsory for banks, as well as the compulsory investment percentage for savings banks.

- The company funding deregulation process: The commercial paper market was officially created in October, 1982.
- New funding systems for the government: The *Pagarés del Tesoro* were created in 1980. These issues were the first signs of the beginning of a more orthodox Treasury approach to the market for short-term funding.

The mortgage market was created with the main aim of ensuring the existence of a certain volume of medium/long financial resources which would allow for the expansion of the real-estate market in general, and more specifically, the housing market. For this purpose, three types of bonds were created: *Cédulas Hipotecarias* (CH), *Bonos Hipotecarios* (BH), and *Participaciones Hipotecarias* (PH).

CH are bonds guaranteed by all the mortgage credits of the issuing company, and have the following features:

- In the beginning, CH issue was restricted to BHE and other official banks, savings banks and mortgage credit companies (MCC). Later, Act 26/1988, dated 19 July, which dealt with the Procedure and Monitoring of Credit Entities, opened up the facility for private banks and co-operative savings banks. Most recently, the Royal Decree 1289/1991, dated 2 August, which amends some sections of the Royal Decree 685/1982, authorized the Confederación Española de Cajas de Ahorro (Spanish Confederation of Savings Banks) also to issue them.
- There is a wide range of issue types: variable- or fixed- interest rates, zero-coupons, series issues, private issues, auction issues, etc.
- They are highly-liquid securities, like bonds, since they have a very active secondary market.
- There is no requirement for public deed or registration on Official Property Books.
- Like bonds, the issue volume is restricted to 90 per cent of the outstanding balance of mortgage credits suitable to serve as legal coverage.

BH are bonds guaranteed by specific mortgage credits. They are characterized by the following:

- They can be issued by official and private banks, savings banks, co-operative savings banks, MCCs and finance companies.
- Public deed and their inscription in the Mercantile Register is required.
- The creation of a bondholders' syndicate is required.
- Terms and interest rates are adapted to loans.
- Mortgage registration on the Official Property Books is required.

In the case of an issuer's default, mortgage/secured bondholders are considered, under the law, to be privileged creditors.

In addition, the issuing companies may have third parties participate - either fully or partially - in one or several mortgage credits of their portfolio, through issue of registered securities called PH, while PH of credits guaranteeing an issue of secured bonds cannot be issued.

The star securities of this market have been, since their creation, CH which, together with BH and PH, are included in the money market because, although in the beginning they were medium- and long-term bonds, the last amendment allows for the issue of short-term CH which have a very high potential liquidity and, therefore, are an investment alternative to other more 'strictly monetary' bonds.

The capacity and efficiency of the primary market for bonds in general, and specifically for mortgage bonds, depends on the attraction they have for the saver, i.e. their security, liquidity and profitability. These three features are largely fulfilled by mortgage securities, since security is a guarantee inherent to the securities themselves; their profitability depends on the conditions imposed by the market, and liquidity is ensured by the existence of secondary markets: the official market - the stock exchange, the market among the issuers themselves, and the non-official secondary markets (Mortgage Market Regulation Public Fund and AIAF).

As far as CH interest rates are concerned, an analysis per institution shows a high spread between issuers. The BHE's average nominal interest rate is the highest - 12 per cent in 1991 -, since it is determined by the interest rates applied in the market, mainly by government bonds. On the other hand, fund acquisition through bonds by savings banks was around 1.5 points below the BHE, this being due not only to their branch network, which makes direct placement to the public easier, but also to the fact that these resources are computable for cash ratio purposes. In order to acquire funds, mortgage credit companies (MCC) are forced to issue at more-competitive interest rates, lower than those of Banco Hipotecario, but higher than those of savings banks. In 1991, the interest rates applied by MCCs were, on average, around 11.9 per cent. Also that year, private banks launched their first issue of bonds as such - usually they operate through their subsidiaries mortgage credit companies -, at an 11 per cent-nominal interest rate.

With regard to issue types, Act 2/1981 (Section 11), empowers authorized companies to issue CH and BH of different types: "registered, order or bearer bonds, with regular or non-regular repayment terms, with fixed- or floating-interest rate, with or without premium, in series or singular."

In general, fixed-coupon issues are prevalent. Thus, in the case of CH, out of the Pta 270,400m face value issued in 1991, 5 per cent was accounted for by floating-rate coupon issues, with the remaining 50 per cent and 45 per cent accounted for by fixed and zero-coupons, respectively.

The increase in zero-coupon issues is mainly due to the BHE issues' auction procedure. In this new type of issue, which first appeared in March 1990, the cost and the funding volume is fixed in terms of demand and of the needs of BHE itself. Also, it meant the introduction of the discount issue system, never used until then for this type of bond.

Since July, 1987, BHE has also issued singular bonds. They are individual credit operations, implemented through a bond, with the issue terms and conditions being negotiated directly with the borrower. The special features of these issues, by comparison to traditional series issues, are that, besides having shorter maturity terms, they imply lower costs, both of issue and placement. The yields demanded by investors are higher than those of series bonds, and they have lower liquidity. Maturity can go from 3 to 12 years, and coupons can be either regular or zero.

The recent Royal Decree 1289/1991, dated 2 August which introduces changes in mortgage market regulation, is aimed at making the creation and issue of mortgage bonds easier, and is a step towards securitizing mortgages from PH.

The changes have the following basic effects:

- Measures aimed at promoting issue of CH are implemented.
- The obligation to reinvest a percentage of funds obtained through issues in CH is removed.
- The requirement for a minimum percentage of mortgage credits in order to issue CH is lowered and, in some cases, removed.
- The issue of bonds based upon PH acquired is feasible.
- PH are promoted. Section 62, point 3, states that: "where PH are fixed at term, i.e. without repurchase agreement nor issuer's commitment, PH shall not compute as risk assets for the issuing bank, since they are excluded from the issuer balance sheet".

Of particular note is the repeal of the provision that imposed a minimum term of three years for issues of CH, and so now their issue term can be shorter. As a result, in November, Banco Hipotecario issued the first issues of an auction programme of short-term CH for six, nine and twelve months. Being less-restrictive, CH have therefore become a common vehicle for deposit-acquisition for an increasing number of entities.

On a tax basis, the coupons of mortgage bonds are subject to withholding tax at payment dates, and to income or corporate taxes. In addition, issue, assignment, repayment and cancellation of mortgage bonds are exempt from the *Impuesto sobre Transmisiones Patrimoniales y Actos Jurídicos Documentados* (capital transfer tax).

25.4 Issuers

Financial institutions market

See Figures 25.9 & 25.10

Matador bonds

Until recently, issuers had to be international bodies of which Spain was a full member, such as Eurofima, the World Bank, the European Economic Community and the International Finance Corporation. More recently, however, foreign governments (Kingdom of Denmark, Republic of Ireland, Republic of Austria, etc.) have been included, as well as other institutions - all of them rated by Standard & Poor's and Moody's.

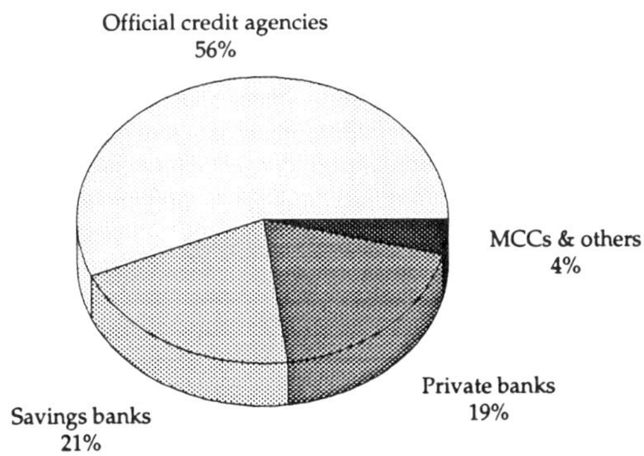

Figure 25.9 Financial institutions market - gross issuance by entity, 1990

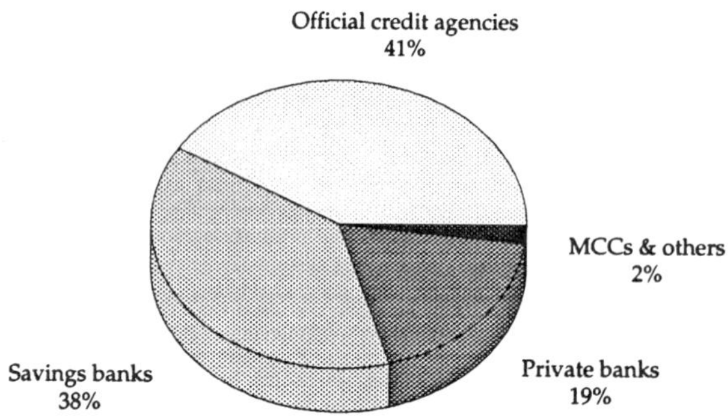

Figure 25.10 Financial institutions market - gross issuance by entity, 1991 (to October)

25.5 *Investors*

At the beginning of the period covered in this analysis (1987), the largest investors in public debt were mainly account holders (i.e. basically financial institutions), while foreign investment was practically non-existent (see Figure 25.11). Between 1987 and 1989, private investment by Spanish residents steadily increased, mainly due to the marketing strategies of the financial institutions concerned while the amount of debt owned by these institutions decreased significantly. Foreign investment, however, has followed a clear upward trend over the last few years, reaching its highest level to date, in 1991.

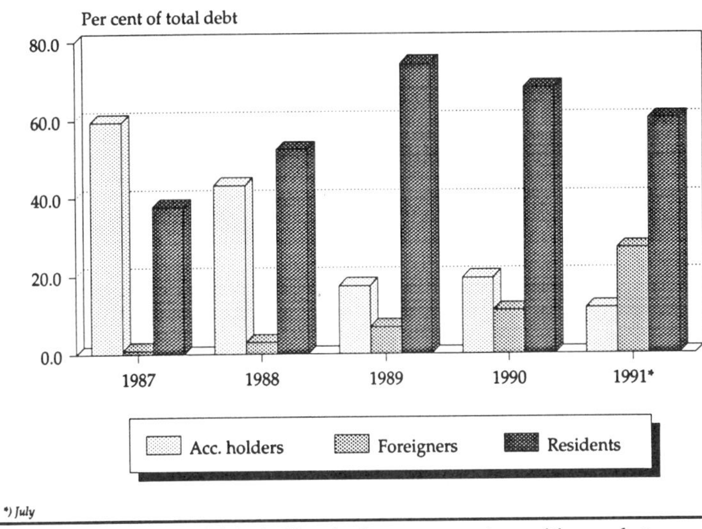

Figure 25.11 Distribution of debt holders in the government securities market

25.6 Methods of issuance

Government market

Three are three methods of issuance established by Spanish law:

- Competitive auction.
- Public offer at fixed conditions.
- Direct issue to the BoS, without auction. In this case, the amount of debt issued may be added on to the last auction held or become a new issue with the same characteristics. The price is determined to maintain yield (in the case of bonds) or the effective interest rate (in the case of T-bills).

During most of the 1980s, other methods of issuance were used by the Spanish Treasury. However, since 1989, the competitive auction method has been used for bonds and debentures, as well as for T-bills, while the now obsolete asset (the Treasury note) was issued through public offer at fixed conditions.

The minimum period between T-bill issues is two weeks (every other Friday). In the case of bonds, it is one month. Currently, bond auctions are held at the beginning of every month, although the value-date is around the 15th. Extraordinary auctions can be convened outside this timetable.

Auction system

In competitive auctions (see Figures 25.12 - 25.15) , bids can be placed for a minimum nominal value of Pta 1,000,000 for T-bills, and Pta 500,000 for bonds. (Under special conditions, a higher minimum value may be fixed in an auction, although such a figure cannot exceed Pta 1bn). Bids may be competitive (whereby pricing is established by the bidders, with an unlimited number of bids at different prices) or non-competitive (whereby the average price resulting from the auction is accepted to a general limit of Pta 25m). Non-competitive bids, at which only one price is acceptable, can only be presented in T-bill auctions.

The Bank of Spain handles the receipt of bids. The primary market should be considered a 'wholesale' market, since it is not directly open to the private investor. Where necessary, final investors must contact the Treasury via a financial institution.

Auctions are resolved in the following way. A committee formed by two members from the BoS, and two others from the Treasury, decide on the stop-out rate and the volume to be issued. For T-bill auctions, once the bidding is

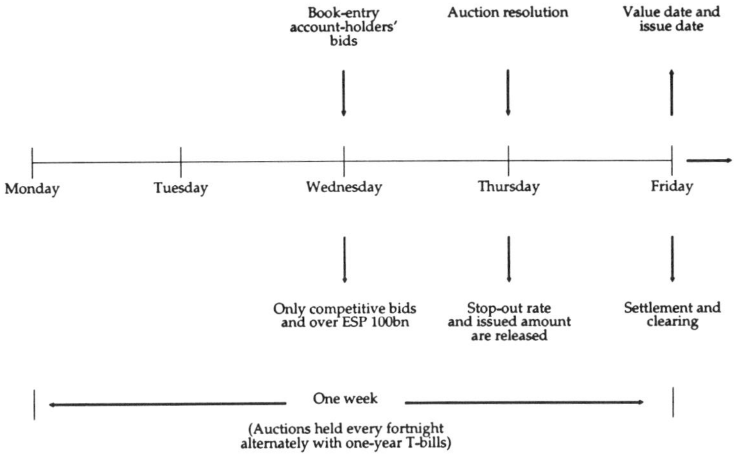

Figure 25.12 The three-month T-bill primary market

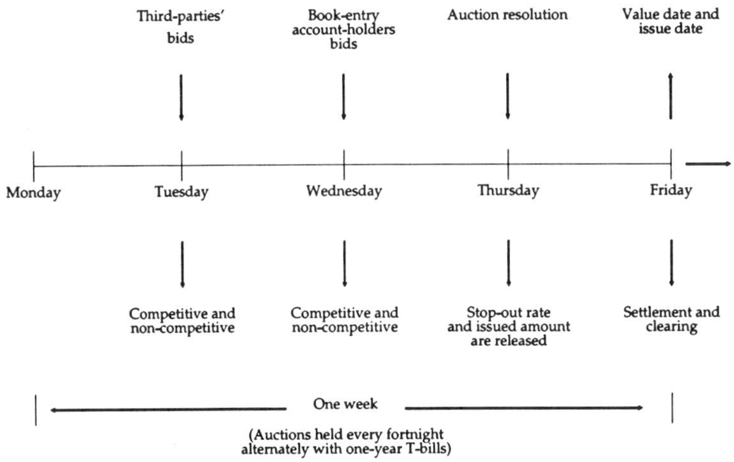

Figure 25.13 The one-year T-bill primary market

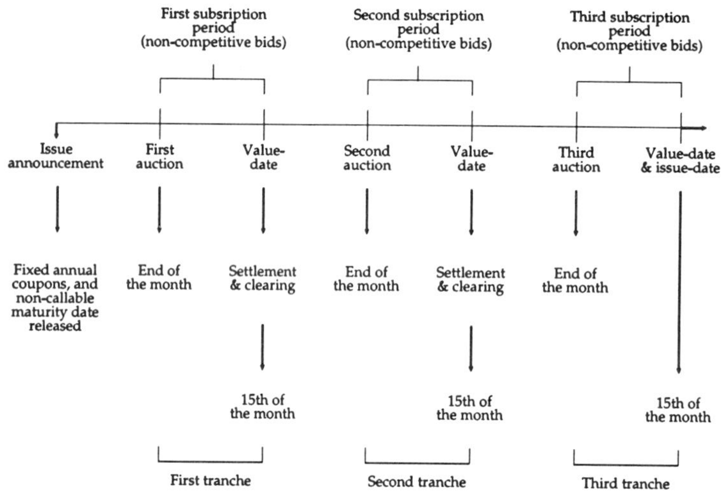

Figure 25.14 The primary market and the book-entry system - a general overview

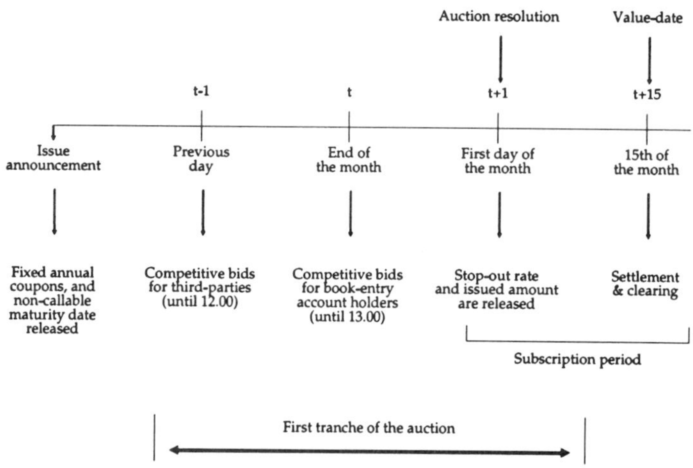

Figure 25.15 Primary market tranche issuance - a detailed view

finished, the committee then decides what amount they are willing to issue in nominal terms. The minimum accepted price among the competitive bids is then simultaneously set. Bids at, or above, the minimum price are automatically awarded, unless there is a great demand at this price, in which case only a percentage of these bids are allocated. All bids at the stop-out rate are awarded at the price offered. Bids at a higher price are awarded at this price when it is lower than the average auction, and are awarded at the average price when the bid price is higher. Finally, on the whole, non-competitive bids which are accepted, must pay the average price set in the auction.

The same procedure is applied to both bond and debenture auctions. As non-competitive bids were not allowed until 1992, this was compensated by the provision of a 'subscription period', a period that lasted from the auction resolution to the issue date. Bids made in this period were awarded at the average price set at the auction. At this stage any person or entity could mark a bid for a minimum nominal amount of Pta 10,000 and a maximum of Pta 3m.

Three tranches, two rounds

Since 27 July 1991 the Treasury has established a new 'second round' auction within the primary market auction arrangement (see Figure 25.16). It is important to distinguish between the two procedures:

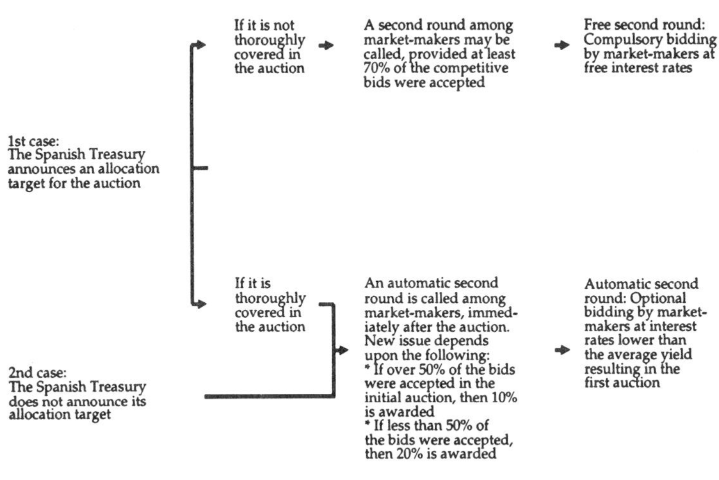

Figure 25.16 The 'second round' auction system

The first type takes place when the allocation target set is not reached in the first round by the Treasury. The Treasury may then announce an additional auction (second round) with the same roles as those of the first round, provided at least 70 per cent of the bids were accepted. Only market-makers can (indeed, are obliged to) place bids, although without requirements on the implied interest rates of their bids (all bids applied by any market-maker must be higher than the ratio of the amount of bonds to be placed in the second round and the number of applicants), unlike the second method where some restrictions exists. However the Treasury may, or may not, accept such bids.

The second procedure takes place when either the volume has been achieved or when no volume has been previously set. In either case, a second round is automatically convened with the Treasury being obliged to award at least 10 per cent of the bids accepted in the first round, if such an amount is greater than 50 per cent of the volume of bids previously placed, and 20 per cent if the amount accepted was less than 50 per cent Bids are also restricted to market-makers (and to a maximum of 3 bids). When using this second procedure in the second round, bids are not compulsory, but implied interest rates by the bids cannot be greater than the weighted average price set in the first round.

Corporate bond market

Underwriting

This is the most common issue system for corporate bonds. The issuer chooses a proposal from a lead-manager who, in turn, distributes the issue among co-managers and participants. For big companies, this system has turned into what could be called a private tender, wherein several banks or stock companies bid to lead the operation. Also, each issue must be registered and approved by the CNMV - Comisión Nacional del Mercado de Valores - which is similar to the Securities and Exchange Commission. However, they can be placed through private placement, provided that the final tender is not made to individual investors. This is how Renfe, BCI (Banco de Crédito Industrial) and the other state-owned banks usually offer.

The drawbacks of these issue systems were, firstly, the excessively long placement period, around one month, and secondly, the lack of liquidity, as issues were only listed after two or three additional months. Fortunately, the new market structures, and the implementation of the account-record system, are already helping to solve these problems.

Auctions

Until 1991, only government bonds and the commercial paper of big companies were issued through the tender-panel system. It was Telefónica which implemented the first corporate issue system of this type. A number of financial institutions now adhere to this system, bidding in each auction for bonds which are issued at 3- 5- and 10-year terms, with zero-coupons and with maturity dates which remain the same for all auctions in a yearly period. This means that the volume of each issue is sufficient to ensure the existence of a developed secondary market with high levels of liquidity.

Through the nineties, a large number of major issuers - private institutions, utilities, banks, etc. - are likely to implement similar systems to make issue processes more transparent, more competitive and less risky for underwriters.

Financial institutions market

Matador bonds

Issuance procedure starts with an application for authorization by the Dirección General del Tesoro y Política Financiera (Director General of the Treasury). Then, the issuer signs an issue letter - containing general terms and conditions - with the lead-manager, a resident bank. The former leads the underwriting group with other financial companies, which facilitates issue placement. Following this, a grey market for the security appears. Finally, the issue is offered to the public and, after its placement, clearing and settlement procedures start.

Since Matador bonds are deemed to be public debt, as far as their acceptance for listing on the stock exchange is concerned, they can be negotiated in the stock markets.

25.7 New issue volumes

Financial insitutions market

Figures 25.17 - 25.19 show the overall evolution of this sector in terms of both issuing entity and instrument. The issuance of individual security types is analysed in detail below.

Subordinated bonds

Figures 25.20 - 25.23 show the development of these bonds in the Spanish market. In 1988, Pta 187,600m was issued, a remarkable increase on the 1987 figure of Pta 36,200m. The increase in equity ratios, as stated in the Banco de España circular letter 25/1987, explains this (more than) five-fold increase. However, in 1989, issues dropped significantly - and this drop has continued to the present. The special features of subordinated bonds, second to regular bonds on a priority basis, require that they are issued with a risk premium on the interest rate of the latter. During high-interest rate periods, such as the one experienced during the past few years, this increases the issue cost significantly and is the prime cause of these recent lower volumes.

Matador bonds

The first issue of this type of bond was on 5 May 1987 by Eurofima, a European company which finances of railway material. In 1987, a total of 3 issues, with an overall amount of Pta 30,000m, were issued whilst, in 1988, issues increased to 7 with a total amount of Pta 85,800m. Since then, the growth of this market has been very high, to the point that, in just 5 years, 64 issues have been issued, with an overall amount of Pta 764,800m (see Figure 25.24). The European Investment Bank, the World Bank and Eurofima are the most active issuers (see Figure 25.25).

During 1991, around twenty Matador issues, with an overall amount of Pta 233bn, were issued. The positive peseta spread of the exchange rate, with nominal interest rates among the highest in the EC, favoured the subscription of these bonds abroad. As a result, the amount issued during 1991 exceeded that of the previous year by more than 36 per cent, and was very similar to the volume issued in 1989 - a boom year - when Pta 245bn was issued.

Bank zero-coupon bonds

After the 1983 alteration to the cash ratio, these assets became deemed as liabilities, and computable for that ratio. This, together with the publication of Act

	1987	1988	1989	1990	1991[1]
Private banks					
Cash bonds	35.2	60.1	13.0	0.6	0.2
Treasury bonds	127.9	120.6	90.5	40.0	14.9
Mortgage bonds	0.4	4.4	2.0	0.3	3.3
Subordinated debentures	32.6	46.4	95.7	44.0	56.5
Savings banks					
Mortgage bonds	36.9	64.5	88.3	65.8	98.2
Debentures[2]	12.3	3.4	1.1	9.9	5.0
Subordinated debentures	2.9	101.6	16.7	16.8	49.6
Co-operative Savings Bank					
Debentures	0.1	-	-	-	-
Subordinated debentures	-	0.2	0.1	-	-
Official credit agencies					
Debentures	80.4	140.3	77.9	159.6	86.3
Mortgage bonds	39.2	34.4	41.4	92.4	79.6
Mortgage credit companies					
Mortgage bonds	13.4	56.8	24.4	18.3	7.9
TOTALS					
Cash bonds	35.2	60.1	13.0	0.6	0.2
Treasury bonds	127.9	120.6	90.5	40.0	14.9
Mortgage bonds	89.9	160.1	156.1	176.8	189.0
Debentures	92.8	143.7	79.0	169.5	91.3
Subordinated debentures	35.5	148.2	112.5	60.8	106.1

Figure 25.17 Gross issuance of medium- & long-term bonds by financial institutions (ESP billion)

[1] *as at October*

[2] *includes non-mortgage bonds, except subordinated debentures whatever currency in which they are denominated*

Source: Banco de España and BHE

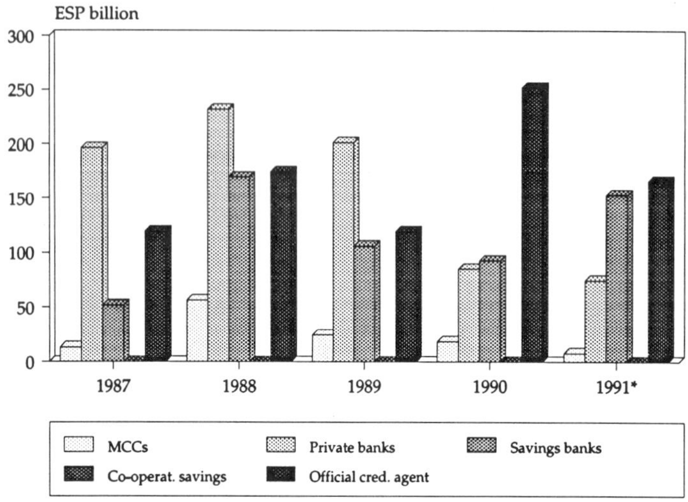

*) as at October

Figure 25.18 **Financial institutions market - gross issuance of medium- and long-term bonds by entity**

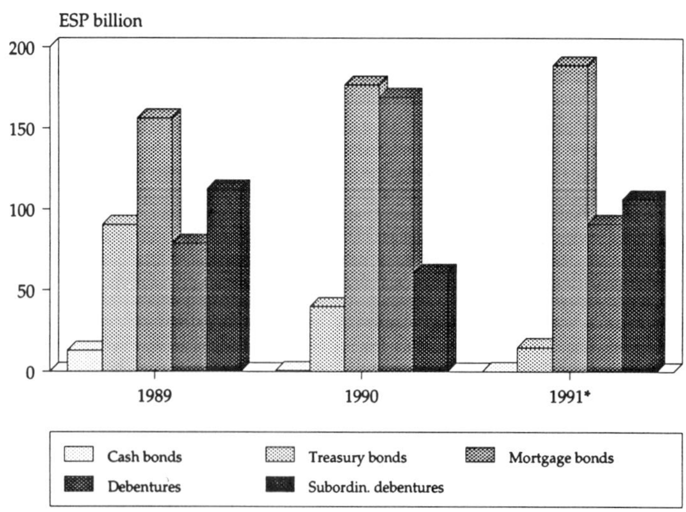

*) as at October

Figure 25.19 **Financial institutions market - gross issuance of medium- and long-term bonds by instrument**

14/1985 (dated 29 May and dealing with the tax system of selected bonds), which granted tax privileges to Treasury zero-coupon bonds and established mandatory withholding tax, for income tax and corporate tax liability, are some of the reasons for the removal of bank zeros from the market. From mid-1985, bank zeros were no longer issued and, as a result, the outstanding balance started to fall, from Pta 3360.2bn in December 1984, to Pta 2838.1bn in 1985 and Pta 601.8bn in 1986.

In 1987, however, official credit agencies started to issue bank zeros since, at that time, these agencies were not liable to any cash requirement ratio, and zeros were a useful means of expanding liabilities without branch networks. Since then, these institutions have been playing a very significant role as issuers in this market. The growth of issues has been encouraged by the dynamics of finance markets which, characterized by great uncertainty regarding the trend in interest rates, have created an increasing interest in bank zeros, both in terms of supply and demand. This has, in turn, created a continuing increase in the outstanding balance during the past few years (see Figure 25.26).

Banks' capital debentures

Figure 25.27 shows the development of these bonds during the last five years and illustrates the higher relative weight of cash bonds and the continuing fall in outstanding balances in both markets.

Convertible issues & issues with warrants

Figure 25.28 shows 1988 as an outstanding year for convertible issues - exchangeable issues are also included. Later, investors' lack of confidence in the development of stock markets caused issues to be mostly of convertible bonds, and made holders of these bonds exercise conversion options only very seldom. During the past few years there has been a significant fall in the issuance of these bonds, largely due to uncertainty in the share market, as well as to the high interest rates experienced during the period.

Mortgage bonds

Activity on the mortgage market was very strong in the beginning, being mainly carried out by savings banks - which used mortgage bonds as an instrument to obtain funds other than longer term deposits - and Banco Hipotecario de España (see Figures 25.29 - 25.31). Savings banks were the first to issue bonds, in July 1982. That same year, total issuance by all market participants amounted to Pta 85,600m of nominal value.

The tax advantages that were created with these bonds helped to increase market activity during 1983-1986. Even though the Bond Act of 1986 removed

	Fixed-rate	Floating-rate	Total	% of total convertible
1987	16.6	83.4	100.0	91.3
1988	33.7	66.3	100.0	25.3
1989	60.6	39.4	100.0	76.5
1990	26.0	74.0	100.0	25.2
1991	-	100.0	100.0	-

Figure 25.20 Subordinated bonds, types of issue (per cent)
Source: Official State Bulletin

	1987	1988	1989	1990	1991
Private banks	33.0	55.5	101.5	40.0	40.0
Savings banks	3.2	132.1	14.9	59.1	3.6
Total	36.2	187.6	116.4	99.1	43.6

Figure 25.21 Subordinated bonds - authorized issues (ESP billion)
Source: Official State Bulletin

	Total		Banks		Savings banks		Co-operative savings	
	Gross	*Net*	*Gross*	*Net*	*Gross*	*Net*	*Gross*	*Net*
1987	35.5	33.1	32.6	30.2	2.9	2.9	-	-
1988	148.2	133.1	46.4	31.5	101.6	101.6	0.2	-
1989	112.5	52.2	95.7	35.5	16.7	16.7	0.1	-
1990	60.8	-6.9	44.0	-23.7	16.8	16.8	-	-
1991[1]	102.1	96.9	56.5	47.3	45.6	49.6	-	-

Figure 25.22 Subordinated bond issuance (ESP billion)
Source: Banco de España

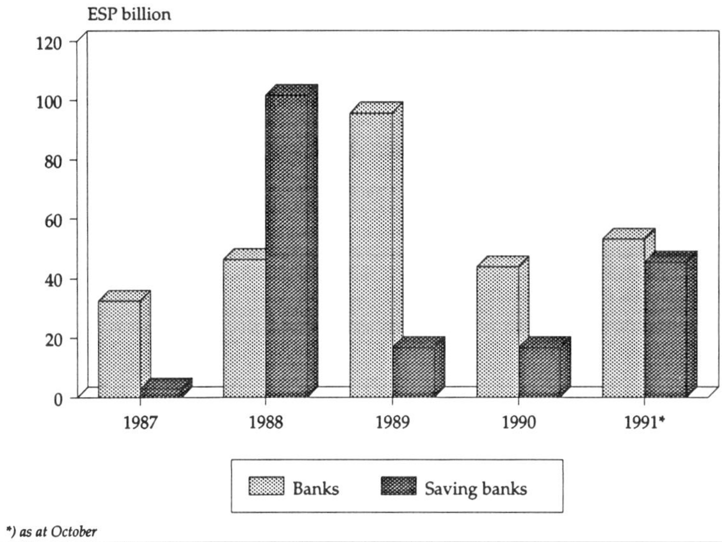

Figure 25.23 Financial institutions market - gross issuance of subordinated bonds

the tax advantage of CH, the announcement of the imminent removal, in 1987, of tax deductions for investors, caused an unprecedented increase of these medium- and long-term bond issues. In 1987, placements dropped significantly, and whilst in the period 1983-1986, the gross issue average total of CH amounted to Pta 193,700m, gross funding dropped to Pta 90,000m in 1987. Therefore, the removal of tax deductions for investments - 15 per cent deduction from income and profit tax -, the eventual increase in interest rates during 1987, the creation of Treasury bills (Ministry Order of 11 June 1987) with very high initial interest rates, and the deregulation of interest rates on current accounts and other short-term deposits (Order of 3 March 1987), all together created an increase in these instruments over medium- and long-term bonds.

In 1988, the primary market of CH overcame the 1987 slump, although gross issues were not as high as those of earlier years. The profitability of these bonds was affected by the maintenance of high interest rates, by the high appeal of government bonds and Treasury bills, and by the prevalence of issues of subordinated debt and debentures by official credit agencies and international bodies.

With regard to 1989, that year was marked by difficulties experienced by issuers in obtaining medium- and long-term funding at a reasonable cost. Investors, meanwhile, could choose from a wide range of financial products characterized by short-terms, high yields and, in some cases, low risk. Among these financial products were public debt bonds, Treasury bills, commercial paper, 'financial accounts' (usually backed up by government securities), and 'super-accounts' (very high-yielding current-accounts). These were the realization of the 'deposit war' process, which caused a major increase in liability costs for a large number of banking institutions.

During 1990, interest rates were kept at high levels, largely due to the restrictive policy applied by the monetary authorities and the strong issue needs of the Treasury, which was more and more committed to an orthodox deficit-financing policy.

The proliferation of issues of commercial paper at highly-competitive interest rates, determined by the restriction on bank credit growth and by the general use of 'super accounts' among deposit banks, caused a significant reduction in the issuance of debenture loans.

In spite of the above, CH continued to be an important fixed-interest rate medium- and long-term instrument, as shown by the Pta 334,000m of bonds issued in 1990, the highest-ever volume to date, which amounted to 61 per cent of all medium- and long-term bonds issued by financial companies. Again, in 1991, a significant volume of CH was issued in the market, amounting to Pta 303,700m of nominal value, although slightly lower than that of the previous year.

However, the above figures are not truly representative since, besides not including non-publicized extensions nor partnership bonds, they do not match the actual volume subscribed. Gross issues, which do include the above-mentioned items, amounted to Pta 176,800m in 1990 (see Figure 25.31), representing 40 per cent of medium- and long-term bonds issued by finance companies.

The positive development of CH continued during 1991 and, in the January-October period (the latest data available at the time of writing), bonds amounting to Pta 189,000m were subscribed which, in relative terms, represented a 39 per cent increase over the first ten months of 1990.

Considering a classification per item of issues by finance companies for January-October 1990 (see Figures 25.32), mortgage bonds accounted for over 39 per cent of the total issued; in the same period of 1991 (see Figures 25.33), this percentage was over 42 per cent. Also, bank bonds and debentures showed a slight drop, while subordinated debt attracted higher interest.

The Pta 189,000m of CH actually subscribed up to October 1991 exceeded, by some 39 per cent, the amount subscribed in 1990 (Pta 135,800m). This is a significant percentage, especially considering that, besides the competition of public debt, the existence of credit restrictions increased the company securitization process of turning directly to the market through the issue of commercial paper and short-term bonds with high yields. An analysis per institution shows that there is a significant increase in bonds subscribed by private banks and savings banks, with the latter having the highest market share, of 52 per cent. The Banco Hipotecario de España's issues increased to a lesser extent and this caused a fall in its market share when measured against the period January-October 1990. Mortgage credit companies, as a result of a reduction in issuance of over 45 per cent, saw their market share drop from around 11 per cent in 1990, to 2 per cent in 1991.

Figure 25.34 shows the overall funds obtained in the stock market during the past few years. The behaviour patterns of the capital and money markets for the January-October period of 1991 were quite different. Whilst in the capital market around Pta 3134bn was obtained, net issuance in the money market was negative to the tune of Pta 425,500m, largely as a result of the high degree of public debt repayment during the period. The increase registered by the placement of bonds in the capital market was basically due to the great success of bonds issued by the government. Public administrations as a whole obtained an overall amount of Pta 1895bn, i.e. over 60 per cent of the total amount of funds obtained in the market.

In the context of the money markets, the share of CH was very significant; Pta 79,000m was obtained in 1991, compared to Pta 8800m drawn in the January-October period of 1990. Nevertheless, despite this and the large amount of funds obtained through commercial paper, the high volume of repayments of Treasury bills and *Pagarés del Tesoro* caused a draw in the money markets, which was offset by the funds obtained in the capital market.

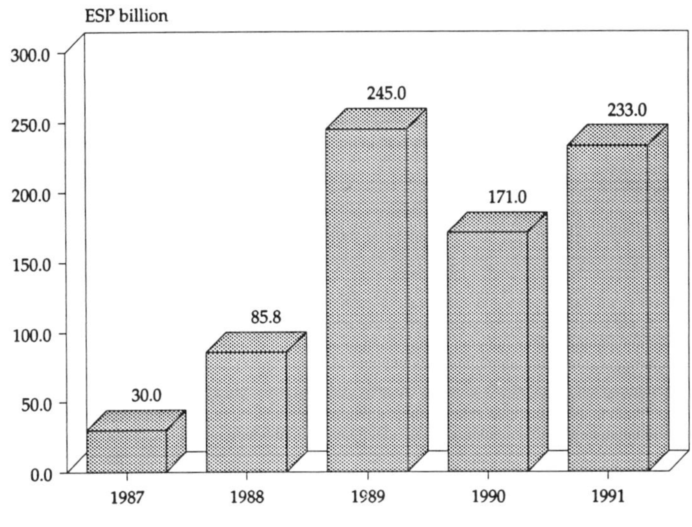

Figure 25.24 New issuance of matador bonds

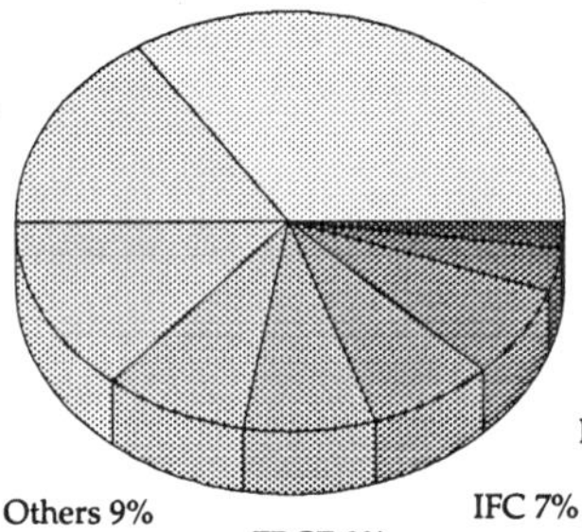

Figure 25.25 Issuance of matador bonds by entity

	Private banks	Savings banks	Official credit agencies	Total
1987	854.9	70.8	20.0	945.7
1988	410.3	115.2	75.5	601.0
1989	771.9	197.7	387.1	1356.7
1990	705.8	140.3	586.5	1432.6
1991[1]	474.1	222.3	705.6	1402.0

Figure 25.26 Bank zero-coupons - amount outstanding (ESP billion)
[1] *as at October*
Source: Banco de España

	Private banks		Savings banks[1]	Total
	Cash bonds	*Treasury bonds*	*Treasury bonds*	
1987	509.9	199.1	150.5	859.5
1988	405.4	165.1	109.7	680.2
1989	249.8	143.8	58.0	451.6
1990	164.5	89.3	17.7	271.5
1991[1]	137.3	78.7	17.0	233.0

Figure 25.27 Cash and Treasury bonds - outstanding amounts (ESP billion)
[1] *non-convertible bonds issued by savings banks, Treaury bonds*
[2] *as at October*
Source: Banco de España

	Total	Treasury bonds	Cash bonds	Straight bonds	Subordinated bonds	Pro-memory: warrant
1987	132.5	89.5	10.0	-	33.0	-
1988	189.8	98.3	6.0	38.0	47.5	10.0
1989	167.8	52.8	1.0	25.0	89.0	-
1990	33.4	8.4	-	-	25.0	-
1991	13.5	-	-	13.5	-	-

Figure 25.28 Deposit banks - issuance of convertible bonds (ESP billion)
Note: non-publicized extensions are not included
Source: Official State Bulletin

	1987		1988		1989		1990		1991[1]	
	Gross	*Net*	*Gross*	*Net*	*Gross*	*Net*	*Gross*	*Net*	*Gross*	*Net*
Private banks	0.4	-3.4	4.4	-1.0	2.0	1.8	0.3	-1.4	3.3	2.6
Savings banks	36.9	-78.5	64.5	-71.2	88.3	88.3	65.8	-70.1	98.2	42.0
BHE	39.2	13.0	34.4	30.7	41.4	41.4	92.4	87.8	79.6	57.6
MCCs	13.4	-3.8	56.8	34.6	24.4	24.4	18.3	-2.2	7.9	-23.1
Total	89.9	-72.7	160.1	-6.9	156.1	156.1	176.8	14.1	189.0	79.1

Figure 25.29 Issuance of mortage bonds, effective value (ESP billion)
[1] *as at October*
Source: Banco de España and BHE

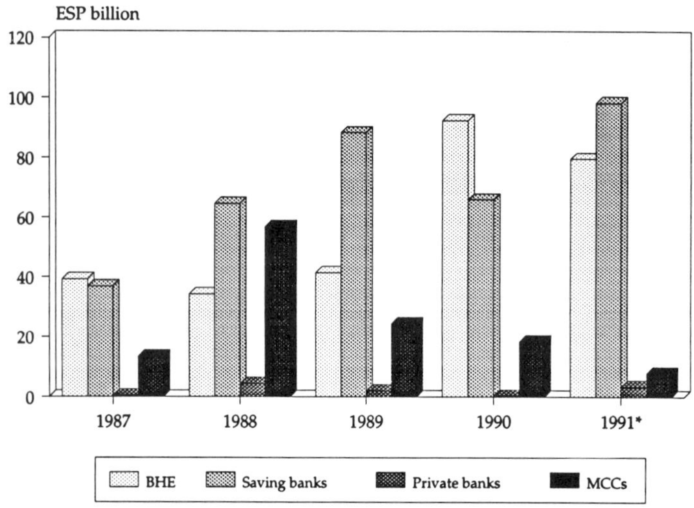

*) as at October

Figure 25.30 Gross issuance of mortage bonds

	Issuing entity	Total amount (ESP bn)	No. of issues	Av. issue amount (ESP bn)	% issued in terms of yield: Fixed-rate		Floating rate	Average interest rate	Av.erage repayment term[1]
					Regular	*Zero*			
1986	Several	242,900	71	3421.1	74.0	11.5	14.5	9.16	4.0
1987	Several	100,000	24	4166.7	76.0	9.5	14.5	9.55	4.5
1988	Several	102,400	35	2925.7	83.4	6.1	10.5	10.20	3.8
1989	Several	128,750	29	4439.7	84.9	3.9	11.2	10.87	3.8
1990	Several	275,750	34	8810.3	67.0	34.0	1.9	11.99	4.9
1991	Several	270,400	40	6760.0	50.0	45.2	4.8	11.13	3.4

Figure 25.31 Mortgage bond series issues

[1] *in years. BHE's at-a discount issues, placed by auction, are not included*

Source: BHE (using data from the Official State Bulletin)

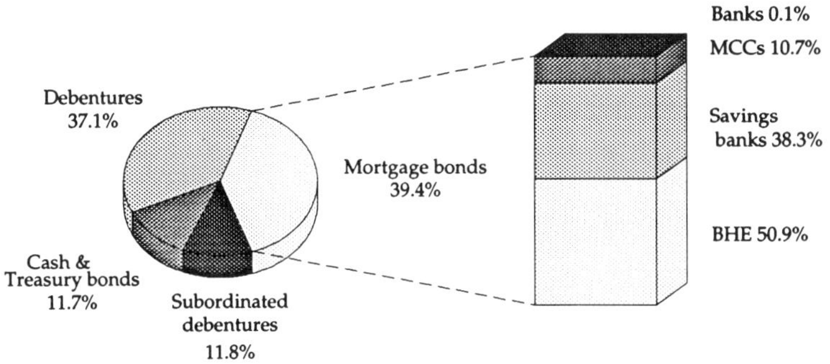

Figure 25.32 **Gross issuance by finance companies, January - October 1990**

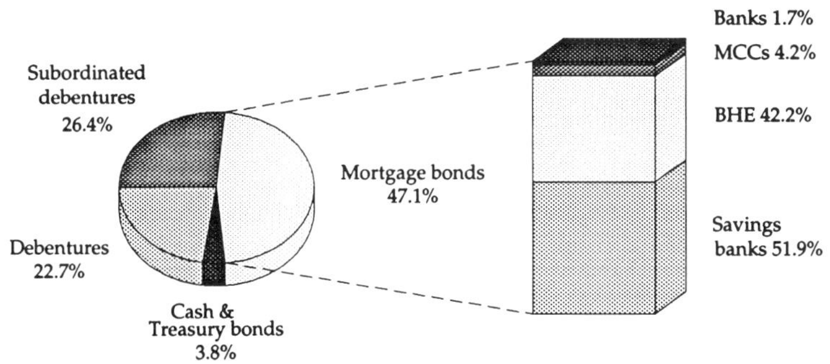

Figure 25.33 **Gross issuance by finance companies, January - October 1991**

	1987	1988	1989	1990	1991[1]	91/90[2]
Capital market	888.4	1809.0	877.8	1393.2	3133.8	159.7
Shares[3]	572.5	544.0	403.0	614.3	682.3	43.0
Bonds:	315.9	1265.0	474.8	778.9	2451.5	236.0
Public administrations	306.9	959.4	275.1	602.6	1894.5	237.6
Finace companies[4]	74.1	256.2	88.2	5.5	124.5	186.2
Non-finance & non-resident companies	-65.1	49.4	111.5	170.8	432.5	245.7
Money market	1310.1	905.1	1119.5	2575.9	-425.5	-120.9
Fixed-interest money bonds:	-235.1	-183.1	-337.0	-158.6	34.1	125.2
Bank bonds[5]	-162.4	-176.2	-230.3	-172.7	-44.9	64.6
Mortgage bonds	-72.7	-6.9	-106.7	14.1	79.0	997.7
Short-term money market instruments:	1545.2	1088.2	1456.5	2734.5	-459.6	-121.1
Promissory notes & T-bills	1907.2	839.3	1265.3	1115.5	-697.9	-193.5
Company promissory notes[6]	-362.0	248.9	191.2	1619.0	238.3	-83.3
Stock market total	2198.5	2714.1	1997.3	3969.1	2708.3	-16.5

Figure 25.34 Net issuance on the stock market (ESP billion)
[1]*as at October*
[2]*Oct 91/Oct 90 difference, in per cent*
[3]*issues placed by finance and non-finance comapnies with fund contribution*
[4]*official credit agencies and subordinated debentures*
[5]*cash and Treasury bonds*
[6]*negotiated through banks, savings banks and money brokers (SMMD)*
Source: Banco de España and BHE

25.8 Methods of trading

Stock exchange

Traditionally, all bonds issued by private institutions have been listed in the stock exchange. Until 1989, the date of the stock exchange reform, market participants were individual stockbrokers, who always acted on behalf of their clients and who never focused - save for rare exceptions - on bond markets. The non-existence of market-making, together with other factors noted earlier, made the market very narrow and, more importantly, kept major institutional investors well away as they restricted their operations to the primary markets.

Since 1989, following the creation of stock companies, market behaviour has been very different. With a focus on investment banking, bond-dealing departments have been created and they have become very active, engaged in both government bonds and corporate bonds and in both primary and secondary markets. Some of the major bond dealers are those of:

- A.B. Asesores Bursátiles
- A.C.F. Ahorro Corporación Financiera
- F.G. Inversiones Bursátiles

A new system of stock exchange dealing for corporate bonds was implemented in 1992, through an electronic network inter-linked with all the four stock exchanges which exist in Spain. This is similar to the Computer-Aided Trading System, CATS, used for stocks and is solving the inefficiency and poor transparency of stock exchanges although, given its infancy, adequate liquidity levels have yet to be reached.

Despite this recent innovation, most operations by bond dealers are still executed by telephone (as in an OTC market), after which they are publicized through stock exchange systems.

AIAF (Asociación de Intermediarios de Activos Financieros - Finance Brokers Association)

In 1991, the Ministry of Finance granted the AIAF (a domestic association similar to ISMA) the status of Regulated Market - which was a pre-requisite for investment funds to invest in securities negotiated in that market. This is similar to the eurobond market, where dealer members and market-makers get in contact by telephone and inform one another of all operations. There are Reuters pages where executed operations can be viewed (AIAI-AIAP). In turn, clearing

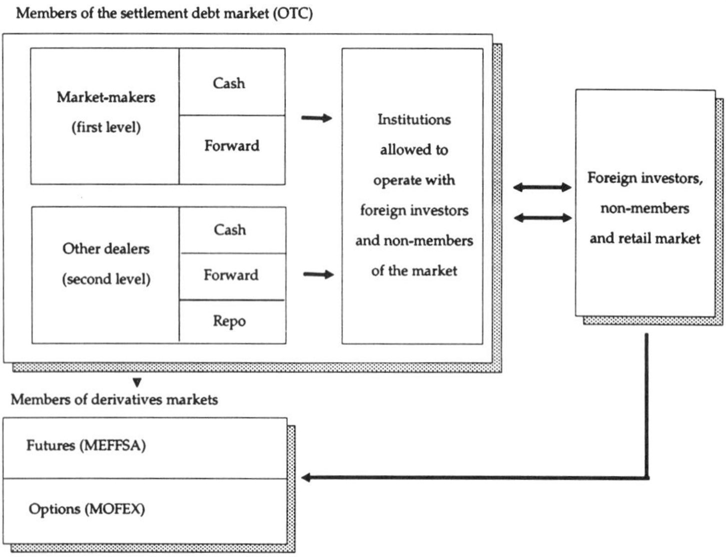

Figure 25.35 Spanish government debt secondary market

is done through Espaclear, by means of account records. This company allows cross operations with Cedel and Euroclear, so operating procedures for foreign investors are much easier.

Market participants are big banks and some stock companies. Therefore, the range of participants and their capacity is higher than that of the stock exchanges. Also, the main issuers - Instituto Nacional de Industria (National Institute of Industry, I.N.I.), Telefónica and the utilities, are offering their new issues in this market, where costs for the issuers are lower. Instead of fixed commissions, as found in the stock exchange, participants fix bid and ask prices. In the future, strong growth and consolidation of the market's current liquidity levels can be expected.

The secondary market

The basic structure of the BoS's book-entry system, which is the most liquid government securities secondary market, is made up of two different segments:

- The first segment is the members' market, dealing with operations among those financial institutions which specialize in government bond trading (primary dealers).

- The second segment, outside the members' market, deals with operations amongst, on the one hand, resident companies or families (the public) and all non-residents, and, on the other, those members (financial institutions) which are allowed to manage investors' bonds.

In quality terms, the principal market is the first one, where price and reference interest rates are formed. The second segment only constitutes, in practice, the spreads that market conditions allow against the first segment. These spreads depend mainly on the competitiveness among institutions to increase their share of the clients' market. The basic activity of the clients' market is in 'repo' operations. However, this is not a retail market, since it is denominated by insitutions of which domestic corporate treasuries and international investors are significant (in 1991, 70 per cent of the (gross) issuance of bonds and debentures was bought by non-residents).

	Treasury bills	Bonds	
		'Blind'	*Second level*
1989	235.5	23.8	123.8
1990	193.9	30.6	127.0
1991	440.8	217.8	444.2

Figure 25.36 Liquidity of members' secondary market: spot market (monthly average turnover in ESP billion)

Source: Analistas Financieros Internacionales, S.A.

The members' market includes a 'blind' segment which is considered the 'core' of the market: trading partners do not know their respective counterparts, and trade is conducted by specialized interdealers (termed 'blind' brokers) in an electronic network system. This is called the first level of the members' market. The conditions of this market allow, theoretically at least, a large volume of cash and forward trading. The participants (around 30 institutions) must ensure market liquidity by quoting bids and offers at the lowest price spreads. This first level can only trade bonds in cash and forward operations.

The second level is supported by the Bank of Spain's money market telephone service; trading partners are known to each other and a repo market is conducted together with other operations. In a quantitative sense, the second level is larger than the first. In 1991, the members' market turnover stood at around US $6bn monthly, a much higher figure than that of 1990, which was under US $2bn. It could be said that foreign investment indirectly boosted the liquidity of the members' market.

However, much trading also takes place outside the borders of the book-entry system. Trading between non-resident counterparts is developing in the Cedel and Euroclear systems which, in any case, are integrated in the price formation process of the domestic book-entry system, as a result of the market-makers' arbitrage.

A non-resident can purchase or sell bonds through any of the authorized member management entities (called *gestoras*), which can open sub-accounts (securities deposit accounts) in the book-entry system by order of their clients. All non-member resident investors operate in this way. The member issues a contract for each of its clients, as well as an official Treasury receipt for each operation carried out and deposited in its sub-account.

The book-entry system

The composition of the Spanish money bond market is dominated by the Treasury's issues which cover government funding needs. As in many other countries, the development of the bond market has been led by Treasury issuance which, in Spain, constitutes the only bond market with sufficient breadth and liquidity. Other markets, although growing in importance in line with the government bond market, are not as liquid. Nevertheless, it may be expected that the official 'organized market,' which was established in September 1991 by the fixed-income market (AIAF) and is highly significant for the investments of mutual funds and non-residents alike, will provide for significant development in 1992.

By the end of 1990 the nominal value outstanding of the Spanish bond market had reached US$ 90.4bn. This figure represented 0.8 per cent of the world bond market outstanding (based on estimates made by Salomon Brothers). The largest component of the market (58 per cent) was that of the government bond sector, which was estimated at US$ 49.6bn. By comparison, the corporate bond sector only amounted to US$ 20.8bn for the same period - the relatively low figure being basically attributable to the (still) low degree of securitization in the area of corporate liability. The development of market infrastructures in this sector of the bond market can be seen as a significant, and proper, approach in the quest for future growth. The AIAF non-government bond market has recently implemented a very important clearing and settlement system in order to attract the confidence of investors and improve the liquidity of the market. The AIAF market now concentrates on the wholesale segments of the bond market, which includes both corporate bonds and Matador bonds. The appearance of rating agencies can also be expected in 1992, although certain important issuers have already been been rated.

The government debt market, which is basically an over-the-counter market supported by a book-entry system, enjoyed a structural change in 1991, thanks to the implementation of universal tax-exemption for foreign investors involved in the sector. The two major consequences of this change have been a more integrated performance in European bond markets, and an increased amount of medium- and long-term maturities in the very short-term maturity profile of the Spanish Treasury's outstanding debt (the average maturity for outstanding debt is no more than one year). At the time of writing, the nominal value outstanding for Treasury bonds was US $66bn, while for T-bills it was US $76bn.

It should be noted that, although tax exemption on government bonds was implemented for foreign investors, from 1 January 1991, matching the tax status of Matadors, the market for the latter did not fall during the year, contrary to what might have been predicted. In fact, many supranational issuers chose to issue Matadors that year, among them Eurofima, BEI, and BID. Today, the amount of total Matadors outstanding approaches US $8bn, in contrast to US $5.6bn, at the end of 1990.

Financing of long positions in pesetas

There are two basic alternatives methods to finance a long position in Spanish government debt. The first one is a repo short position in the Spanish domestic market (the repo market is a very large and liquid market in Spain). However, this procedure does require an investor's bonds to be registered in the BoS's book-entry system through the third parties' account of any Spanish financial institution (a member).

The alternative is europeseta financing (via a swap). In this case it does not matter whether the debt is registered in Euroclear (via the Banco de Santander), Cedel (via the banco Bilbao Vizcaya) or the Bos's book-entry system (which links the investor directly to a very liquid domestic market, without administrative red tape). However, the opportunity cost of not using the repo market is evident, as may be observed in the charts (long periods of unfavourable below, spreads against eurodeposit financing)

25.9 Settlement

Overview

Government securities are registered through a computerized public debt book-entry office run by the Bank of Spain. It works through a telephone service from the money market and avoids the need to issue physical securities. The Bank of Spain establishes several categories of account holders in the system, with most Spanish financial institutions being classed as holder entities (members), (i.e. they can only hold their own accounts). Management entities (*entidades gestoras*) also hold their own accounts but they are also allowed to manage accounts for third parties. The third kind of account holder is that of market-makers, who have the obligation to quote prices on a continuous basis through the system of blind interdealer brokers ('MEDAS'), in order to guarantee the liquidity of the market.

There are three ways to implement settlement and clearing:

- Through BoS's book-entry system, by means of a management entity
- Through the Euroclear system
- Through the Cedel system

BoS's book-entry system

A final investor can trade public debt through management entities. These entities, which are permitted to hold accounts for third parties in the central book-entry office, register the deal in an account for third parties by opening a securities' deposit account in its third parties' account, or by transferring the deal to another entity chosen by the investor, with the advantage that the latter can trade through any of the management entities while centralizing all positions in one self-designed single account. After trading, an investor will ask for an official Treasury receipt certifying the details and ownership of the investment. The advantage of this system is that trades and coupon payments are settled when the funds are received on the value-date.

Euroclear system

The final investor can also settle and clear Spanish Treasury debt through this system. Banco de Santander has opened a securities' deposit account in Euroclear, where all the capital movements of Euroclear customers are registered in the third parties' account held by the above-mentioned bank at the Bank of Spain.

Cedel system

This system is similar to Euroclear but, in this case, it is Banco Bilbao Vizcaya (BBV) which manages Cedel's securities deposit account; capital movements are registered in the third parties' account held by BBV in the BoS's book-entry office.

The Euroclear/Cedel systems are subject to some communication and administrative problems. Because of this, normally when settling through Euroclear, it is common practice for non-resident investors to carry out cash trades with value-dates set seven days forward, in order to avoid the impact of potential errors in communication procedures on prices.

25.10 *Yield calculation*

Government bonds

■ Zero-coupon Treasuries with maturities below 378 days:

$$P = \frac{1000000}{(1 + i\,(t/360))}$$

■ Zero-coupon Treasuries with maturities exceeding 378 days:

$$P = \frac{1000000}{(1 + i)^{(t/360)}}$$

where,

P	effective price paid for each Pta 1 m nominal
i	effective yield-to-maturity
t	number of days to maturity

■ Regular coupon bonds' internal rate of return (IRR) computation is done as follows:

Obligaciones del Estado and *Bonos del Estado*:

$$P = (1 + I)^{-(t/365)} \left\{ \frac{1}{2} C \frac{[1-(1+I)^{(-N/2)}]}{[1-(1+I)^{(-N/2)}]} + A\,(1+I)^{(-N/2)} \right\} t$$

where,

P	price
C	year coupon value
I	bond yield
N	number of coupons to redemption
A	asset redemption value

■ Repo rates are computed on the base of 360 days a year.

■ Accrued interest:

$$\frac{(\text{coupon value} \times \text{number of days last payment date})}{\text{number of days between last payment and next one}}$$

In official statistics, dates used in computations are theoretical; the eventual coupon payment on Saturday, Sunday or Holiday is not considered in formulae.

■ Withholding tax
Withholding taxes are never considered in computation for zero-coupon Treasuries. In yield-to-maturity calculations for regular coupon securities, it is usual to compute the yield net of withholding tax. There is no official method, but the most common way is to consider withholding tax at payment dates, and its refund every 30 June.

■ When the life to maturity for one regular coupon bond is below one year, the appropriate computation is:

$$P = \sum_{i=1}^{H} \frac{Ci}{(1 + \frac{y}{100}\frac{ti}{365})} + \frac{A}{(1 + \frac{y}{100}\frac{tH}{365})}$$

where,

Ci	coupon amount at moment i
H	max. {*i*}
ti	number of days until payment *i* (*ti* < 365)

Non-government securities

Yield calculation largely follows the same formulae as for government securities. There are, however, two important differences on short-term paper yields.

When dealing, it is necessary to specify whether one is talking in compound terms (see the formula for zeros with lives longer than 378 days) or in non-compound terms, and if one is considering a 360-day base or a 365-day base.

It is necessary to compute the withholding tax effect on the yield, which can be very important, mainly in the first half of every year, as *Letras del Tesoro* do not carry this tax.

$$P = \frac{P + (N-P)(1-wt)}{(1 + \frac{y}{100})^{(t/365)}} + \frac{(N-P)\,wt}{(1 + \frac{4}{100})^{(T/365)}}$$

where,

wt withholding tax (25 per cent)
T number of days till the 30 June of the *following* year.

Matador bonds

ISMA formulae are used for these securities.

25.11 Taxation

Overview

During the past two years, bond taxation for non-resident investors has been significantly changed although, for residents in Spain, fiscal structures have remained largely unchanged. In the case of non-residents, the offsetting of withholding tax for Matador coupons and the removal of any kind of taxation on government bonds (and all other bonds under certain conditions) has led to sharp improvements in both liquidity and potential outstanding within the peseta bond markets.

Withholding tax

Withholding tax on gross coupon value is 25 per cent for every resident investor. This amount is directly settled upon coupon payment. There is the same level of withholding tax on zero-coupon bonds at the redemption date, and after every trade based on the difference between the purchase and sale values. On the other hand, *Letras del Tesoro* and *Pagarés del Tesoro* are not subject to any withholding tax (see Law 14/1985, 24/5/1985, which deals with taxation on specific assets).

Zero-coupon bonds called AFROS (*Activos Financieros con Retención unica en el Origen*) bear a very high withholding tax (55 per cent). However withholding tax is only executed at issuance, so later trades are exempted. Yields on these coupons must be higher than 15 per cent.

Deep-discount bonds and premium bonds, where the coupon rate is less than official base rate (9 per cent), are liable to withholding tax on the gross coupon value and on capital gains. Where the coupon rate is above official base rate (according to the 3rd additional statement, no. 3 of the Law 37/1988, 28/12/88), withholding tax is computed only on the gross coupon value. Withholding tax is computed on the conversion premiums of every convertible bond with a gross coupon rate below the official base rate.

Certain issues, mostly electric power corporations and highway bonds, bear only 1.2 per cent withholding tax. Subscribers who are subject to income or corporate taxes (with the exception of insurance corporations and credit or savings institutions) are entitled to deduct 24 per cent of the gross coupon from their liability to such taxes. The *Cédulas de Inversión* bear no withholding tax but corporations (subscribers were, until recently, financial institutions meeting a compulsory investment requirement) can deduct a withholding tax amounting to 20 per cent of the gross coupon value.

Special taxation frame for non-residents

The coupon values of Matador bonds belonging to non-residents are not subject to withholding taxes.

Non-resident investors must pay 35 per cent of their capital gains (if they reside in countries with no double-taxation agreement) and 20 per cent of their other proceeds. However, in cases where double-taxation agreements exist, lower rates are applicable.

The Real Decreto-Law 5/1990, 20/12/90, stated that coupons from government bonds would be tax-free for every non-resident investor, except those based in off-shore financial markets (the Real Decreto 1080/1991, 5/7/91, stated the list of the 48 places in the world considered to be off-shore financial markets). Furthermore, the coupons of all other bonds were to be be tax-free for residents based in EC countries.

Finally, the Real Decreto 1285/1991, 2/8/91, explained the methodology for settle coupon payments, avoiding withholding tax in a first step and the final settlement some weeks before. Non-residency may be stated directly to some *entidad gestora* by the institutional investors which keep Spanish bonds in their portfolios, or through the dealers or clearing systems (Cedel and Euroclear) when trading.

Income taxes and corporate taxes

For the purposes of income and corporate taxes, gross coupon values are deemed to be capital earnings[1]. With the exception of AFROS, an investor's total withholding tax amount can be deducted from both income and corporate tax liabilities.

The effective proceeds from deep-discount bonds, premium bonds and convertible bonds are considered as capital earnings and taxed accordingly when the nominal rate is below the official base rate. Individuals and non-financial corporations cannot present capital losses (the minimum being zero earnings) in their tax sheets.

When the nominal rate is over the official base rate, proceeds are considered as capital gains. For corporate taxes (with the exception of unit trusts) the capital gain of an asset is computed as the selling price (or redemption price, or conversion price of the share, in the case of convertibles) minus the net accounted value (or market price of a share for convertibles). Taxes amount to 35 per cent of this value, only 1 per cent over mutual fund profits. For income tax (and corporate tax, in the case of unit trusts) capital gains are calculated as the

[1] *Income taxes are progressive in Spain. Corporate tax is 35 per cent of taxable profits.*

selling price (or redemption price, or conversion price of the share in the case of convertibles) minus the purchase price (or market price of a share for convertibles), weighted by a coefficient dependent on time. Capital gains are divided by the number of years of holding. This quotient is added (or subtracted in case of capital losses) to other taxable income to compute the total amount to pay.

AFRO yields increase the average tax rate in income taxes. However, AFRO yields are not used to calculate the tax amount among the whole taxable income applying the average tax.

Some bonds bear another special taxation feature which involves the deduction of 95 per cent of the taxed coupon value from the corporate tax amount (35 per cent).

Property taxes

Resident bondholders are subject to property taxes. Amounts below Pta 9 m. per individual are tax-free. The bands for property taxes are quite low (highest being 2 per cent for tranches of more than Pta 2.5bn and lowest being 0.02 per cent for tranches of less than Pta 25 m).

The whole of non-resident bondholders' properties are taxable.

Other taxes

Bond portfolios are subject to inheritance and gift tax. Stamp taxes on trading activities are no longer in force.

25.12 *Futures & options*

Overview

Futures and options have only recently been introduced in Spain since it was only in March 1989 that the Spanish Treasury permitted the establishment of organized markets for derivatives. As a result of the Treasury's resolution two companies, MEFFSA (for futures) and MOFEX (for options) were formed, and the first option contract was launched in November 1889, shortly followed, in March 1990, by the first futures contract.

	18 March 1991		17 June 1992		16 September 1992	
Settlement	*Yield*	*Open interest*[4]	*Yield*	*Open interest*[4]	*Yield*	*Open interest*[4]
Futures[1]	96.69	79.47	97.00	3.09	-	-
Futures[2]	64.55	1.53	-	-	-	-
Option[3]	-	nd	-	-	-	-

Figure 25.37 Options and futures contracts (settlement price December 16)
[1] *yield for the notional 3-yr bond price, converted to the cheapest deliverable bond: 12% coupon*
[2] *yield for the notional 5-yr bond price, converted to the cheapest deliverable bond: 11.90% coupon*
[3] *calls & puts*
[4] *open interest in ESP billion*

Despite the short period of time since the inception of futures and options trading, both markets have achieved acceptable levels of liquidity and are already seen as important and useful tools in the portfolio management of Spanish public debt, both by resident institutions and those that are non-resident.

The origin of derivative markets in Spain can be traced back to December 1988, when forward transactions for government debt trading between book-entry system members registered with the BoS's system, was authorized. It was then that the two market segments started their trading:

Forward markets

Blind forward markets

'Blind' forward markets are a part of the market-makers' first level in the global system of secondary markets. At this level, primary dealers, 'blind' brokers and

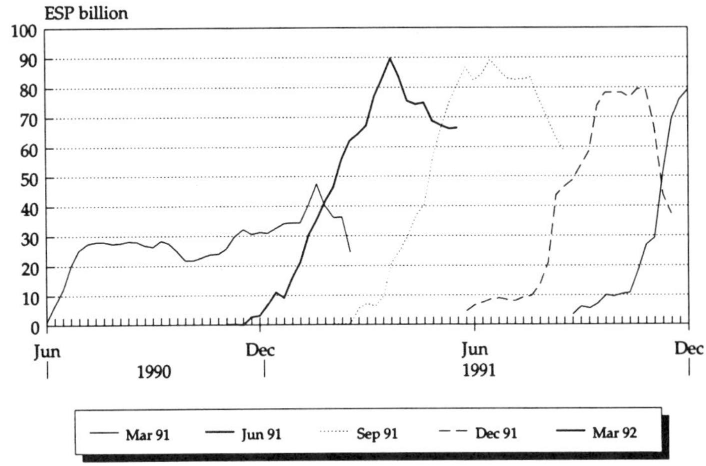

Figure 25.38 Futures market open interest (ESP billion)

the Bank of Spain have organized standardized trading, with daily marking-to-market, thus minimizing counterparty risks (which is particularly important in this market as buyers and sellers do not know the identity of their counterparties). Theoretically, the role of this segment is to guarantee the liquidity of forward contracts at the four delivery dates, two of which are the third Wednesday in the months closest to the March/June/September/December cycle. This market, which is designed for electronic trading, are quite similar in character to futures markets.

Other members' forward market

The other members' forward market is a traditional forward market in which contracts are not standardized, and there is no daily mark-to-market system. Following notification, the BoS administers, records, settles and clears the trades. However, it should be noted that the BoS does not act as clearing house in the usual futures market sense.

Futures market - MEFFSA

As noted earlier, besides the BoS's book-entry system market, there are two organized markets: one for futures and one for options. Both of them have a dual

	Forward (Bonds and debentures)		Notional bond	
	'Blind'	Second level	Futures	Options
1989	97.5	134.1	-	-
1990	147.9	302.5	138.4	70.5
Ene	192.5	734.0	424.0	366.0

Figure 25.39 Liquidity of derivative markets in public debt instruments (monthly average turnover in ESP billion)
Source: Analistas Financieros Internacionales, S.A.

exchange and clearing capacity. The MEFFSA futures market includes four types of membership:

- Full clearing members, who can trade and clear for their own accounts, and for other members and for their clients
- Ordinary clearing members, who can trade and clear for their own accounts and for their clients
- Self-clearing members, who can only trade for their own accounts
- Non-clearing members, who can only act as brokers between clients and full clearing members

The trading system implemented by MEFFSA is a fully-integrated electronic network. Members issue their orders from their trading desks to a central processing unit which then stores, matches and executes them as necessary. It also sends confirmation messages to the issuing members.

Options market - MOFEX

MOFEX also features integrated clearing and accounting for its members, who are Spain's most important financial institutions. The exchange regulations allow the following types of membership:

- Intermediaries, who can trade and clear for their own accounts, for other members and for their clients
- Self-clearing members, who can only trade for their own accounts (they are not allowed to manage clients' accounts)
- Specialized brokers, who can only act as brokers between clients and other members (they have access to the trading system but they are not clearing members)

The trading system implemented by MOFEX is a effective combination of electronic and telephone-based trading. As a result, costs for members can be very low, since while the level of information-flow normally found in pit-trading is maintained, the associated costs are avoided.

Underlying assets

The underlying assets of futures and option contracts are two notional bonds:

- A three-year notional bond, theoretically issued at par on the expiration date, and with an annual 10 per cent coupon (paid semi-annually
- A five-year notional bond, theoretically issued at par, with a 10 per cent coupon on the same date

Contracts are traded with four expiration dates following the March/June/September/December cycle. A margin deposit (which is updated daily) is required for each contract. When the futures contract falls due, settlement must be effected by the delivery of one of the bonds previously deemed as acceptable for delivery by MEFFSA. If the buyer of a call option decides to exercise it on the expiration date, settlement must be effected by means of the delivery of one of the bonds designated by MEFFSA (the seller of the bond chooses the security). The relatively low-coupon rate of the notional bonds (10 per cent), against the 11.5+ per cent seen in recent government bond issues, has an important consequence in the delivery process. Since the conversion factors disclosed by MEFFSA are calculated as an exchange rate (hedge rate) between the price of each government bond from the set of deliverables at a yield of 10.25 per cent, and the notional bond's price at par (10.25 per cent yield), only one of the bonds listed in each contract can be the cheapest to deliver - the others being too expensive. Thus, the specific list of bonds accepted for delivery is of fundamental importance and, for this reason, MEFFSA cannot change the list once a contract has been set.

25.13 Money markets

Commercial paper market

The company promissory notes market has increased since the passing of the first Act regulating this type of notes, in 1986. Later, the creation of Espaclear, S.A., a company specialized in commercial-paper clearing, and the negotiation through AIAF members, increased market's liquidity and its absolute volume. Also, major issuers had no short-term financing system other than bank short-term credits. Therefore, the removal of brokerage costs caused significant reductions in their financial expenses, besides increasing their diversification regarding borrowers.

Also, the high increase in the assets of money market funds, caused a rise in the offer of this type of securities, which was followed by a relevant demand rise. The biggest problem still unsolved is that many issuers do not have their short-term debt rated. Some of them have already been rated as Prime-1, and the recent introduction of two rating firms in Spain: Standard & Poor's in Madrid and IBCA in Barcelona, will solve this problem in the medium-term.

Issue of these instruments must be previously authorized by the CNMV. In many cases, annual issue programmes are authorized, so issuers' operation in the market is not hindered.

The most common issue system is through competitive auction. A number of financial institutions offer purchase prices in auctions which are usually held monthly. The main issuers are electrical companies, Telefónica, Autonomous governments, industrial companies, State-owned banks and some Town Councils:

The main issuers are:

- INI (National Institute of Industry)
- Sevillana
- Iberdrola I
- ENHER
- Endesa
- Hidrocantábrico
- REDESA
- NISSAN
- INESPAL
- TELEFONICA
- RENFE
- Andalusia's Regional Government

- Madrid Autonomous Government
- Valencia Autonomous Government
- Barcelona Town Council

Commercial paper is negotiated at a discount - zero-coupon - and issue terms are usually 3, 6, 12 and 18 months. Yields are fixed by the market in terms of the MIBOR rates and, according to the issuer rating, a specific spread is usually negotiated. For the best issues, the spread is up to -30 bp and, for the worst, the same as, or higher than, the MIBOR.

Agents are banks, stockbrokers and investment banks; there are also inter-dealer brokers. There are no commissions, since bid and ask prices are fixed for clients. Clients are mostly institutions: funds, banks, insurance companies and other companies that use these instruments to make their cash profitable.

25.14 *Inter-market spreads*

In analysing the inter-market spreads of the Spanish government market, it is important to take into account the very negative slope of the Spanish yield curve. High short-term interest rates, together with the recent development of the debt market have brought about high yields in three- and five-year bonds, whilst expectations associated with European monetary union (Emu) have had greater repercussions on the ten-year debenture yield.

In 1991, a significant narrowing of the spread between the ten-year debenture yield and the five-year bond yield took place (see Figure 25.40), as levels ended the year close to 10 bp, down from the 60 bp level seen at the beginning. The reason for this is once again related to the developments which took place in the government debt market during the year as the market acquired enough liquidity in all maturities to improve price formation throughout. Previously, ten-year debenture prices were somewhat unconnected with those of shorter maturities, due mainly to the fact that demand longer maturities had been traditionally scarce in the Spanish market. Now, though, the yield structure has acquired a more 'normal' profile. Ten-year debenture yields went down from 12.30 per

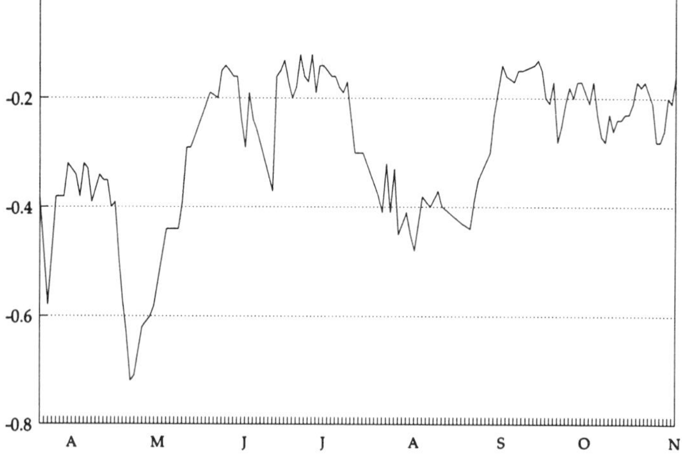

Figure 25.40 Yield spread between 5- and 10-yr Spanish government debt

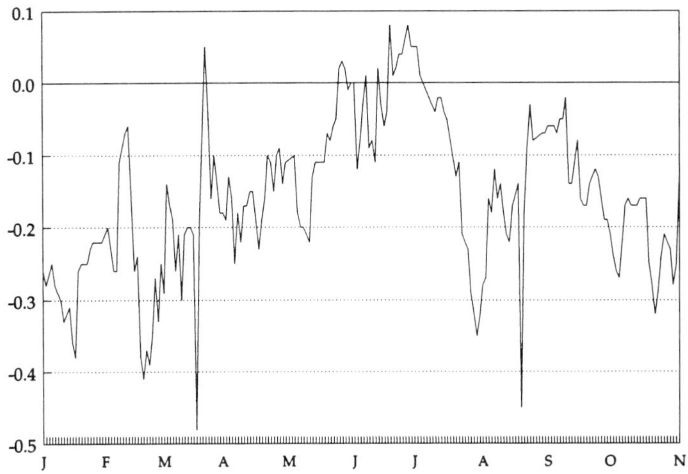

Figure 25.41 Yield spread between 3- and 5-yr Spanish government bonds

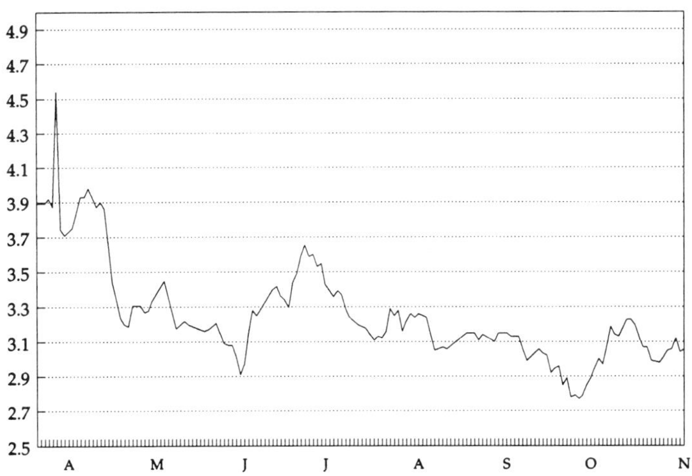

Figure 25.42 Yield spread between Spanish and German government debt (10-year)

cent in March to 11.40 per cent in October, while five-year bond yields decreased from 13.45 per cent to 11.50 per cent, in the same period.

The yield spread between three- and five-year bonds (see Figure 25.41), however, has not revealed such a definite trend, although it has been subject to a much higher degree of volatility. During the first six months of 1991, it became increasingly narrow as it moved from over 20 bp to levels close to 0 bp, reflecting the pressure of increased demand for the five-year bond - a demand which was partly encouraged by the interest of foreign investors. After a period of instability during the months of June and July (when the spread even turned positive for the five-year bond), it began to widen again until it returned to the levels previously seen at the beginning of the year.

At first glance, it may seem surprising that the three- to five-year yield spread (now 20 bp) is the same as the five- to ten-year yield spread, but a suitable explanation may be found in the traditional liquidity problem of longer maturities in the Spanish debt market. Given the level of development already attained by the bond markets, a further lowering in the yield of ten-year debentures seems rather probable in the near future.

Yield curve expectations

Since the recent implementation of new tax-exemption measures, price formation in the Spanish bond market has been determined by 'convergence-based' investment strategies. Many investors have been borrowing, on a short-term basis, from low interest rate ERM currencies and then investing, on a longer-term basis, in the Spanish bond market, as well as in other high-yield European markets. This strategy has been the cause of the narrowing effect experienced by the Spanish bond's long-term spread against the German bond (see Figure 25.42). In the second half of 1991, the market seemed to be groping for a trend to continue the yield convergence process. The ten-year spread experienced a cut to 2.70 basis points from around 3.40 during the June to September period but afterwards went up again, to the 3.00 basis point level.

While yield spreads were very high at the beginning of 1991, things were easier for convergence-based strategies. The only problem was the uncertainty regarding the moment of returning withholding tax on bond coupons to non-residents. The Spanish authorities stated that tax returns should be made automatically, but no additional regulation appeared until September 1991 (as from 25 September, non-residents no longer had to pay withholding tax). Although the uncertainty over taxation policy was lifted, tax yield spreads have not reduced their level.

If the ten-year Spanish/German yield spread stands at the 3.00 basis points level, it implies that the forward exchange rate stands at 83 pesetas for each Deutschemark, in contrast with the 63 peseta spot rate. If one believes that future market expectations regarding the peseta exchange rate could be close to

Figure 25.43 Yield spread between Spanish and French government debt (10-year)

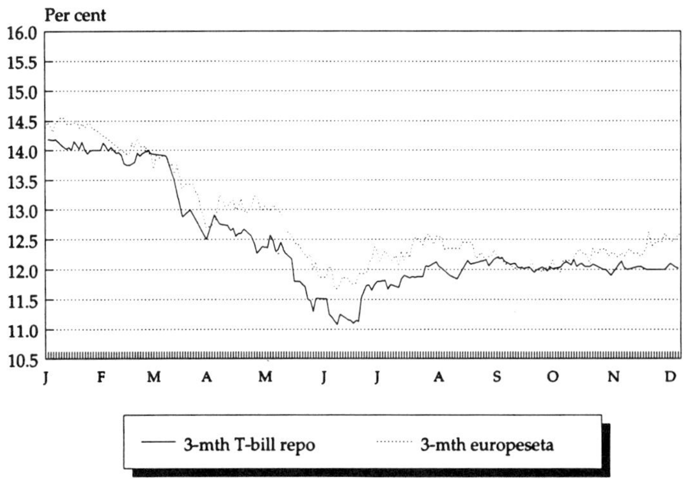

Figure 25.44 T-bill repo rate & peseta eurodeposit rate (3-month maturity)

the long-term equilibrium of purchasing power parity (PPP), that is around 70 pesetas for each Deutschemark, then the three points include a 1.7 per cent risk premium.

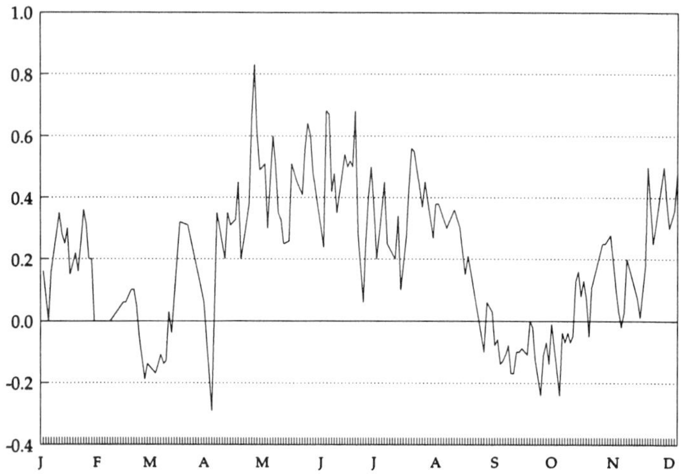

Figure 25.45 Spread between T-bill repo rate & peseta eurodeposit rate (3-month maturity)

	1 Inflation rate 1986-1990 average	2 Long-term yields 1986-1990 average	3 Current yield[1]	4 Long-term expected inflation rate[2]	5 Expected real yield (3-4)
Germany	1.4	6.90	8.26	3.2	5.06
France	3.1	8.57	8.75	3.0	5.76
UK	5.9	9.93	9.80	3.8	6.00
Italy	5.7	10.93	12.69	4.5	8.19
Spain	6.5	13.27	11.30	4.3	7.05

Figure 25.46 Government bond yields and inflation rates in selected EMS countries
[1] *as at 18 October 1991*
[2] *convergence at 3% in 2002*
Source: Analistas Financieros Internacionales, S.A.

	Yield spread	Inplied forward exchange rate vs. DEM	EMS exchange rates	
			Central parity	*Upper limit*
France	-0.49	3.5652	3.3539	3.4302
UK	-1.54	0.3952	0.3390	0.3599
Italy	-2.79	963.71[1]	748.22	765.25
Spain	-3.04	83.065	65.000	69.017

Figure 25.47 10-year Bund yields vs. other 10-yr bonds in selected EMS countries
[1] *calculated with yields after taxes*
Source: Analistas Financieros Internacionales, S.A.

	Yield spread[1]	Implied forward exchange rate	Parity of purchasing power (PPP) (estimate)	Annual risk premium implied in yield spread
France	0.49	3.5652	3.40	0.5
Spain	3.04	83.0650	70.00	1.7

Figure 25.48 Yield spread determinants of French/Spanish 10-year yields
[1] *as at 18 October 1991*
Source: Analistas Financieros Internacionales, S.A.

Appendix

Matador bonds

(annual coupon unless stated)

	Iss. date	Term (years)	Amount (ESP bn)	Coupon (per cent)	Yield-to-maturity	Iss. price
1987						
Eurofima	05 May 87	10.0	10,000	12.500	12.500	100.000
World Bank	09 Aug 87	10.0	10,000	12.250	12.250	100.000
European Community	16 Nov 87	8.0	10,000	12.375	12.375	100.000
1988						
Int'l Finance Corp (IFC)	21 Jan 88	5.0	8300	12.500	12.500	100.000
Eurofima	17 Mar 88	7.0	10,000	12.000	12.000	100.00
World Bank	09 Sep 88	10.0	10,000	10.625	10.625	100.000
Eurofima	15 Sep 88	10.0	10,000	10.500	10.500	100.000
European Invest. Bank (EIB)	10 Oct 88	10.0	10,000	10.350	10.350	100.000
World Bank	27 Oct 88	10.0	15,000	10.375	10.375	100.000
EIB	19 Dec 88	7.0	12,500	11.400	11.400	100.000
1989						
IFC	18 Jan 89	5.0	10,000	11.250	11.250	100.000
Euro. Council's Reinstall. Fund	15 Feb 89	4.9	15,000	11.375	11.375	100.000
Eurofima	16 Feb 89	10.0	10,000	11.375	11.375	100.000
EIB	22 Feb 89	7.0	20,000	11.400	11.400	100.000
World Bank	09 Mar 89	5.0	10,000	11.750	11.750	100.000
Euro. Council's Reinstall. Fund	21 Mar 89	5.0	10,000	12.000	12.000	100.000
EIB	03 May 89	10.0	10,000	12.100	12.100	100.000

(cont.)

	Iss. date	Term (years)	Amount (ESP bn)	Coupon (per cent)	Yield-to-maturity	Iss. price
Euro. Council's Reinstall. Fund	05 May 89	5.0	10,000	12.625	12.625	100.000
IFC	31 May 89	5.0	10,000	12.500	12.049	101.625
Eurofima	14 Jun 89	5.0	15,000	12.375	11.994	101.375
World Bank	21 Jun 89	5.0	10,000	12.375	11.994	101.375
EIB	28 Jun 89	5.0	10,000	12.200	12.200	100.000
EEC	24 Jul 89	4.0	15,000	12.375	11.669	101.625
African Development Bank	05 Aug 89	7.0	10,000	12.500	12.197	101.375
EIB	21 Aug 89	5.0	10,000	11.850	11.474	101.375
Eurofima	30 Aug 89	4.0	10,000	11.750	11.304	101.375
Euro. Council's Reinstall. Fund	18 Sep 89	7.0	15,000	11.750	11.454	101.375
World Bank	21 Oct 89	5.0	10,000	11.375	11.003	101.375
EIB	14 Nov 89	8.0	15,000	11.400	11.132	101.375
IFC	25 Nov 89	5.0	10,000	11.600	11.159	101.625
Eurofima	30 Dec 89	5.0	10,000	12.625	12.311	101.125
1990						
World Bank	20 Feb 90	5.0	10,000	13.450	13.165	101.000
IEB	22 Feb 90	5.0	15,000	13.500	13.500	100.000
IEB	22 Mar 90	10.0	15,000	13.900	13.900	100.000
World Bank	25 Apr 90	4.5	6000	11.375	13.836	91.972
Euro. Council's Reinstall. Fund	27 Apr 90	5.0	10,000	14.000	13.711	101.000
EIB	29 May 90	9.8	20,000	13.900	13.970	99.500
IFC	22 Jun 90	5.0	10,000	13.750	13.391	101.250
Eurofima	28 Jun 90	5.0	10,000	13.750	13.498	100.875
World Bank	14 Jul 90	5.0	10,000	13.750	13.349	101.400
Kingdom of Denmark	20 Jul 90	5.0	10,000	13.750	13.249	101.750
EIB	03 Oct 90	5.0	10,000	14.350	14.058	101.000
Nordic Investment Bank	20 Nov 90	5.0	10,000	13.925	13.925	100.000
ECSC	01 Dec 90	5.0	15,000	13.500	13.016	101.700
EIB	08 Dec 90	7.0	20,000	13.350	13.011	101.500

(cont.)

	Iss. date	Term (years)	Amount (ESP bn)	Coupon (per cent)	Yield-to-maturity	Iss. price
1991						
Republic of Austria	15 Jan 91	6.0	15,000	13.550	13.098	101.800
Inter-Am. Development Bank	08 Feb 91	5.0	10,000	14.150	13.680	101.625
World Bank	16 Feb 91	5.0	15,000	13.625	13.161	101.625
IFC	11 Mar 91	5.0	8000	13.375	12.914	101.625
EIB	27 Apr 91	5.0	20,000	12.250	11.945	101.100
Republic of Ireland	23 May 91	7.0	10,000	11.800	11.434	101.700
Eurofima	05 Jun 91	5.0	10,000	11.600	11.179	101.550
EIB	26 Jun 91	3.0	15,000	11.300	10.770	101.300
United States of Mexico	08 Aug 91	5.0	10,000	14.250	14.397	99.500
EIB	13 Sep 91	5.0	20,000	11.150	10.773	101.550
World Bank	05 Oct 91	5.0	15,000	11.000	10.665	101.250
Nordic Investment Bank	05 Oct 91	3.0	5000	Coupon 0 (indexed)		100.000
Reconst. Credit Institute	16 Oct 91	5.0	10,000	11.250	10.846	101.500
EIB	23 Oct 91	5.0	20,000	11.150	10.564	102.190
Eurofima	31 Oct 91	5.0	10,000	11.200	10.763	101.625
Electricite France	07 Nov 91	4.0	10,000	11.150	10.670	101.500
KFW Int. Fin. Delaware, USA	13 Nov 91	5.0	10,000	11.250	10.846	101.500
Inter-Am. Development Bank	13 Nov 91	7.0	10,000	11.250	10.880	101.750
EIB	17 Dec 91	5.0	10,000	11.150	10.365	102.950

Source: BHE (using data from the Official State Bulletin)

Chapter

26

The bond markets of

Sweden

Stefan Clevhammar
Kommunernas Pensionsanstalt

Andrejs Landsmanis
Läns Kapital AB

Jan Gurander
Patricia Treasury AB

Arne Lidén
Arcona Fastighetsutveckling AB

Malin Hedman Björkmo
Stockholm School of Economics & Öhman Fondkommission AB

Bernt Nilsson

Sven Jarlöv
Skandinaviska Enskilda Banken

Erik Sjöberg
Enskilda Kapitalförvaltning

Pehr Wissén
Svenska Handelsbanken

Note: In general text, the abbreviation 'SKr' is used to denote the Swedish krona. Elsewhere, the international mnemonic 'SEK' is used.

26.1 *Introduction*

Recent development

The Swedish bond market has undergone major changes over the last decade. It has developed from a very domestic and strongly-regulated market (the main purposes of which were to provide low-cost financing of government debt and to be a source of subsidy for the regulated real estate market) into a market which is deregulated, market-orientated and of a good international standard.

The changed market is the result of:

- phased deregulation
- a strong growth of market liquidity
- the currency devaluation in 1982
- continuing securitization
- more, and better-educated, market players
- the introduction of new loan instruments

In addition to the above, many technical improvements, in the form of new information systems and computerized business tools and routines, have been introduced.

The Swedish bond market has always been focused on government and mortgage bonds. This has been emphasized during recent years when relatively small volumes have been issued for municipalities and corporate borrowers. An important reason for this has been the strong growth of the commercial paper market, which has been one of the main sources of funds for these categories.

Swedish household savings have been at a low level for many years. Individuals have never been important investors in interest-bearing bonds - and for good reasons; both inflation and marginal taxes have been high, resulting in a negative yield after tax. This situation changed completely in 1991 with the introduction of a fiscal reform which set tax on capital income at a low, flat 30 per cent. In addition, inflation in 1992 is expected to drop to 3 per cent which is, in turn, expected to result in a substantial real interest yield after tax.

Hopefully, Swedish private investors will therefore become a major source of funding, especially for the mortgage institutes which face very large refinancing needs in the coming years.

It is therefore only natural that much effort has been made to widen the market and to facilitate investment in bonds by individuals. To that end, the market has seen the recent introduction of a book-entry system (the new paperless VP-system), as well as custom-designed bonds for private investors. In 1991, the introduction of zero-coupon bonds was permitted and this has been particularly appreciated by private investors who now have the possibility of deferring tax payments. Since November 1991, a selected number of bonds targeted at private investors are traded daily on the Stockholm Stock Exchange 'SOX' market.

The linking of the krona to the Ecu in the spring of 1991, as well as the application to join the EC, have both increased faith in the krona and the interest markets, thereby making bond investments more attractive. The tax on interest will be further reduced in 1993 (from 30 per cent to 25 per cent), thereby additionally stimulating demand.

Composition of Swedish bond market

The Swedish bond market consists of 1100 loans with a total debt of SKr 1080bn. 300 of the loans are government and mortgage bullet bond loans with a total debt of SKr 650bn. They are considered the most liquid bonds on the market and are quoted on the **daily** *Stockholm Stock Exchange Bond List.*

The remaining 800 loans, with a total debt of SKr 400bn, are the less liquid bonds issued by mortgage institutions, municipalities, credit institutions, corporates and banks. Their illiquidity can be attributed to bond structure; the loans usually have amortization features and interest adjustment clauses. The loans in this group are all quoted on the **monthly** *Stockholm Stock Exchange Bond List.*

Additionally, there are 40 eurokronor bond loans, with a total debt of SKr 18bn, which are not quoted on the Stockholm Stock Exchange.

The reported turnover in bonds quoted on the daily list for 1991 was SKr 1870bn. The turnover in bonds quoted on the monthly list, for the same period, is not reported but is estimated to be less than SKr 10bn.

The deregulation of the market has been implemented gradually during the last decade. Many of the internationally-recognized varieties of bonds, such as FRNs, perpetuals, zero-coupon bonds and index-linked have therefore been unable to be issued in Sweden until very recently and, accordingly, there are relatively few such loans to be found on the market.

Government bonds and mortgage bonds have always dominated the Swedish bond market (see Figures 26.1 & 26.2).

As shown, government and mortgage bonds made up 85 per cent of the market in 1980 versus 87 per cent in 1991. However, more noticeable is the relative growth of the mortgage bond market against the relative decline of the volume of government bonds.

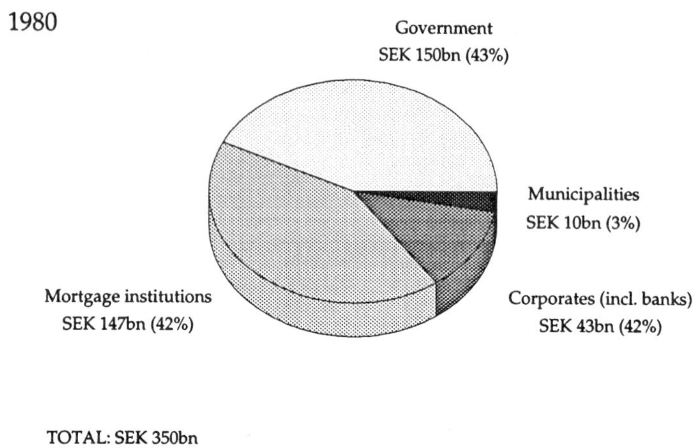

Figure 26.1 Composition of the Swedish bond market - 1980

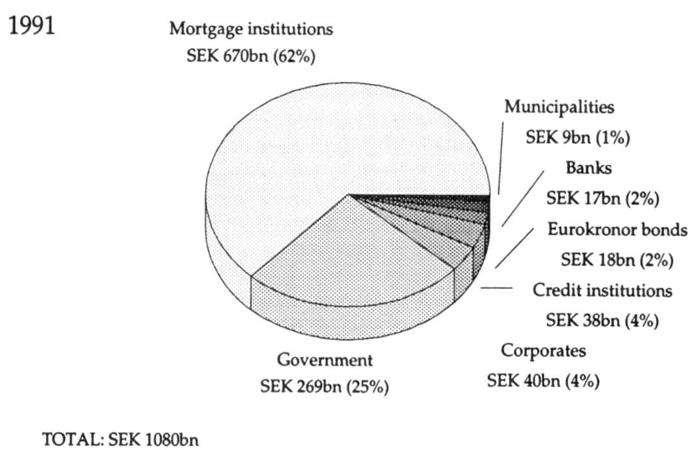

Figure 26.2 Composition of the Swedish bond market - 1991

History of Swedish bond market deregulation

1983	Liberalization of bond issue controls. Interest rates and other loan conditions for corporate and municipal bonds able to be set according to market conditions
1986	Abolition of investment requirements for financial institutions. Market rates for all government and mortgage bonds
1989	Most currency regulations abolished
	Krona-denominated eurobonds introduced
1991	Remaining regulations abolished
	Zero-coupon bonds allowed
	Index-linked bonds allowed
	The only remaining requirement from the central bank is to be informed about bond issues having been launched on the market

Figure 26.3 History of Swedish bond market deregulation

During the 1980s, credit controls have been abolished gradually and most regulations have now been dropped. In June 1983, bond issuance controls were liberalized (and totally abolished in October 1991). At the end of 1986, investment requirements compelling financial institutions, mainly the National Pension Fund, and the insurance companies, to invest a certain ratio of their funds in government bonds and mortgage bonds were abolished. In July 1989, foreign investors were allowed to invest in SKr-denominated securities.

The general tax reform in 1991 made it possible for the central bank to allow zero-coupon bonds on the Swedish market and, from October 1991, it is also possible to issue index-linked bond loans.

26.2 Economics

Introduction

The years from 1988 to 1991 saw dramatic changes in Swedish economic policy. At the beginning of the period the economy was overheated with rates of wage growth and price inflation which not only exceeded that of Sweden's major trading partners, but were also unsustainable in the long run. Sweden had - and still has - a fixed exchange rate policy, but in the late 80's and early 90's doubts about the ability of the Swedish government to maintain the policy in the long-term, became widespread.

The background to the situation in 1990-1991 can be found in the series of devaluations which the Swedish government made in the late 1970s and which culminated in the major devaluation of October 1982, when the Swedish krona was marked down by 16 per cent against its major trading partners. During the period 1977-1982, the overall devaluation of the krona, against its major trading partners, amounted to some 40 per cent. These devaluations created an undervalued krona, but then, that was the purpose of the policy.

Back in the 1970s, the competitiveness of Swedish industry had gradually declined and this had led to a contraction in the trade and manufacturing sector whilst, in contrast, the public sector expanded, thereby ensuring - amongst other things - full employment. The increase in the size of the public sector led to higher taxes and a tendency towards a structural deficit in the balance of payments. In the early 1980s it became obvious that the decline in the trade and manufacturing sector had to be stopped.

The chosen remedy was a major depreciation of the currency, which was expected to increase profits and investment in the trade and manufacturing sector. At the same time, a restrictive fiscal policy was intended not only to restrict growth in the public sector to leave room for the expansion in the private sector, but also to halt the inflationary tendencies which so often follow devaluations. This strategy, developed by the Social Democratic Party which formed a minority government, was called the 'Third Way', indicating that its purpose was to find a way of growing which avoided both inflation and unemployment.

The first years of the 1980s seemed to bring success for the Third Way. The economy grew without excessive inflation and, above all, without the high rate of unemployment which was a major problem in the rest of Europe.

Sweden had a fixed exchange rate against a trade-weighted basket of fifteen major trading partners. During the period the rigorous controls and regulations of Swedish capital markets were abolished, leading to the creation of securities markets of a good international standard. The growth of the securities markets led to an important internationalization of the Swedish financial sector and, over time, currency flows grew more sensitive to changes in the Swedish economy. This tendency was further strengthened when capital controls were abolished in July 1989.

In the autumn of 1990 it became obvious that the policy of the Swedish government, which produced an extremely low rate of unemployment but a high rate of inflation, was not compatible, in the long run, with a fixed exchange rate. The Third Way had come to an end. The Swedish authorities had to choose between sticking to the fixed exchange rate, whilst accepting that any anti-inflationary policy would inevitably lead to higher rates of unemployment, or devaluing the currency yet again. The consensus among Swedish politicians was that a new round of devaluations would only lead to higher inflation. The lesson of the 1980s was clear: There was no 'third way' - Sweden had to undergo a period of deflation in very much the same way as other European countries.

Politics

The Swedish economy was in a state of acute crisis in October 1990, when a consistently high rate of inflation led to doubts in the financial markets about the ability of the Swedish government to maintain the policy of a fixed exchange rate. There were expectations of a forthcoming Swedish devaluation and, to prevent a massive outflow of currency, the Swedish central bank drastically increased the spread between Swedish and international interest rates. The high spread also meant very high nominal interest rates in Sweden.

Amongst other things, the 1980s had seen a period of high financial leverage, above all in the real estate sector which had become particularly highly leveraged. High nominal interest rates naturally lead to financial distress for leveraged firms and there were real fears that a long period of such rates would lead to serious problems in the financial sector. As a result, pressure grew for a change in the direction of economic policy to bring the rates down.

With some simplification, it can be claimed that October 1990 saw a watershed in Swedish economic policy. The currency crisis of that month led to an important political decision - Sweden declared its intention to apply for membership of the European Community. It also declared that economic policy would be changed to give higher priority to the fight against inflation, effectively terminating the Third Way, in favour of a period of deflation. The decision to apply for membership of the Community was put into effect by an application which was completed in June 1991 and underlined by a change in the exchange rate regime. In May 1991, the Swedish central bank declared that it intended to keep an exchange rate fixed against the Ecu.

These decisions had far reaching consequences. Inflation in Sweden had to be brought down to European standards and this, in turn, had implications for the degree of expansion in fiscal policy. The decision to apply for membership of the EC also meant that the level of taxation in Sweden had to be harmonized with the rest of Europe. For political life in Sweden this had even wider consequences, because it necessarily pointed to a reduction in the size of the public sector.

These changes basically meant making the Swedish economy more market-oriented. Since the Swedish Social Democratic Party has been associated with a large public sector and a high level of taxation, it came as no big surprise that they lost the election in the autumn of 1991, to be replaced by a new government led by the Conservative Party.

The changes in Swedish political life which have been sketched here have taken place very recently and it is therefore too early to say exactly where they will lead. In the 1980s, Sweden had tried to go its own way - the Third Way. By the autumn of 1991, it had become obvious that the Third Way had failed - the persistently high rate of inflation had proved the impossibility of trying to pursue an economic policy which, at the same time, both kept inflation down and provided for full employment.

As noted above, the policy choice made in 1990-1991 resulted in an application for membership of the EC and a fixed exchange rate against the Ecu, leading to a period of deflation, similar to that experienced elsewhere in Europe. It is likely that the choice will also result in a change in the relative composition of the economy, with less emphasis on the public sector and more on the private sector leading, in the end, to a lower level of taxation. The net result will be that Sweden will become more like the existing EC economies to which it has declared closer co-operation.

Gross domestic product

During the 1980s, Sweden has had consistently lower rates of growth in GDP than the average of the G7 countries. The difference has increased over time, as can be seen in Figure 26.4. In 1991, GDP actually fell by 1.1 per cent, and a further decline is expected in 1992.

The Swedish economy obviously has a structural growth problem, reflected particularly by the low rate of productivity increase both in industry and the rest of the economy. The major factor behind this is probably the fact that, in not embarking on policy of deflation until 1991-92, Sweden has lagged behind the rest of Europe.

The devaluation policy pursued in the 1980s led to high profits in Swedish industry and, hence, not much pressure to increase productivity. With expectations of further devaluations, Swedish industry came to depend on the benefits of cost-competitiveness resulting from such devaluations, despite the inflationary nature of the policy. However, that road has now been closed and Swedish industry has no choice but to undergo a period of rationalization to increase productivity and thereby improve competitiveness. The slow growth of Swedish

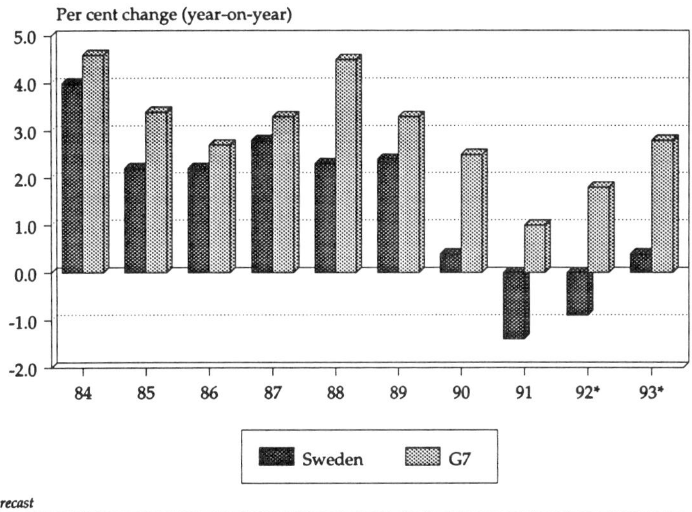

Figure 26.4 **GDP in Sweden and the G7 countries 1984-1991 - percentage change**
Source: Svenska Handelsbanken Economic Research

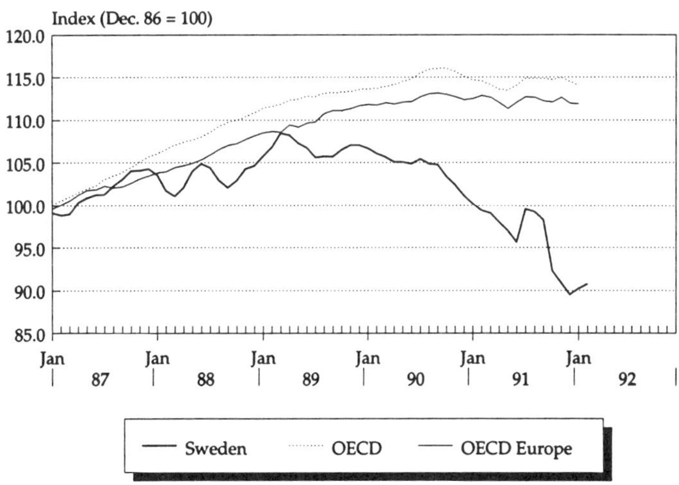

Figure 26.5 **Industrial production in Sweden and OECD - seasonally-adjusted annual rate of change, 3-month moving average** *Source: Svenska Handelsbanken Economic Research*

industry during the 1980s can be seen illustrated in Figure 26.5, where it is compared to the OECD average.

Trade balance

The Swedish trade balance has shown surpluses since 1983 while, in contrast, the current account has shown deficits every year (with the exceptions of 1984 and 1986), as can be seen in Figure 26.6.

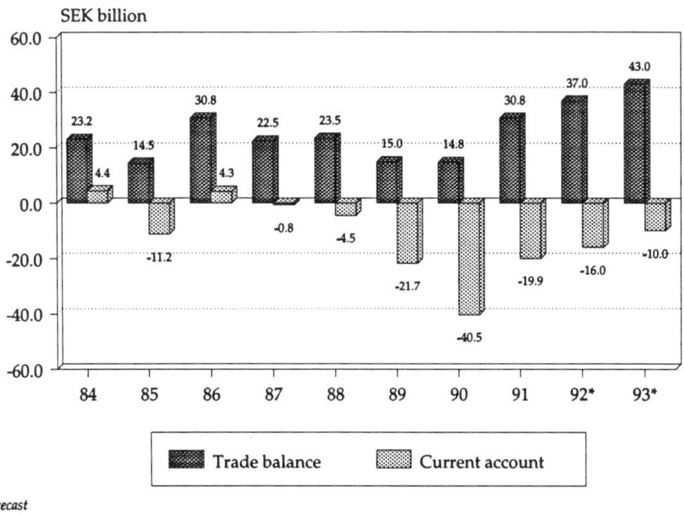

Figure 26.6 Trade balance and current account 1983-1991
Source: Svenska Handelsbanken Economic Research

The trade balance - the difference between the export and import of goods - has been positive, but not sufficiently so as to give balanced currency flows. The reason for this is that Sweden has had a negative balance of services as well as net transfers, such as foreign aid. Sweden also has had a net debt in foreign currencies, which means that interest payments on the debt adds to the need for currency inflow. The sum of these factors - trade balance, service balance and net transfers - has been negative during most of the 1980s and this has created a need for a compensating inflow of foreign currencies to maintain the fixed exchange rate.

During the latter part of the 1980s there have been substantial Swedish net investments in the rest of the world and this has meant a capital outflow in addition to the outflow created by the deficit in the current account. These investments have been both industrial and financial, one example being the real estate sector. The sum of the current account deficit and the capital outflows have increased the need for an inflow of capital, as can be seen in Figure 26.7.

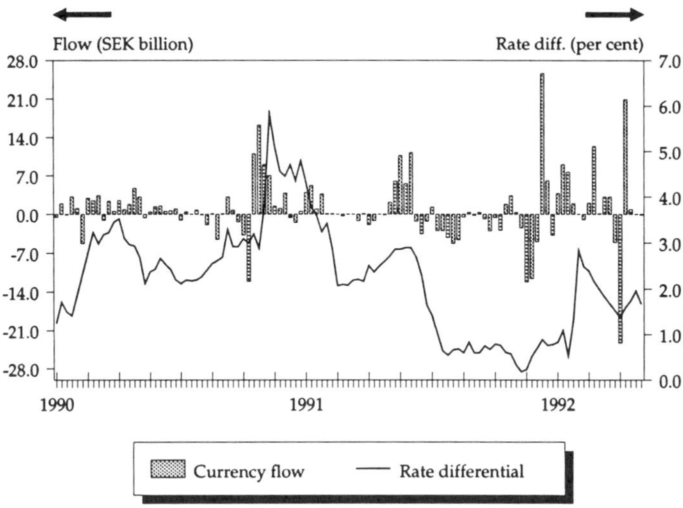

Figure 26.7 Currency flows and interest rate spread 1983-1991
Source: Svenska Handelsbanken Economic Research

The central bank has had to pursue a monetary policy which provides interest rates which are high enough to attract financial flows to compensate for the underlying outflow of currency.

Unemployment

One consequence of the Third Way was that the rate of unemployment, by international comparison, was very low in Sweden during the 1980s, indeed, this was one of the aims of the policy. Figure 26.8 shows the unemployment trend during the period 1986-1991.

From the figure, it can be seen that the rate of unemployment was generally as low as 1.5 per cent, and even slightly lower on occasions, in the late 1980s. Although it is true that international comparisons of unemployment figures may be misleading, these are nevertheless very low numbers and, perhaps, not unexpectedly so given the high rates of inflation (as shown in Figure 26.6).

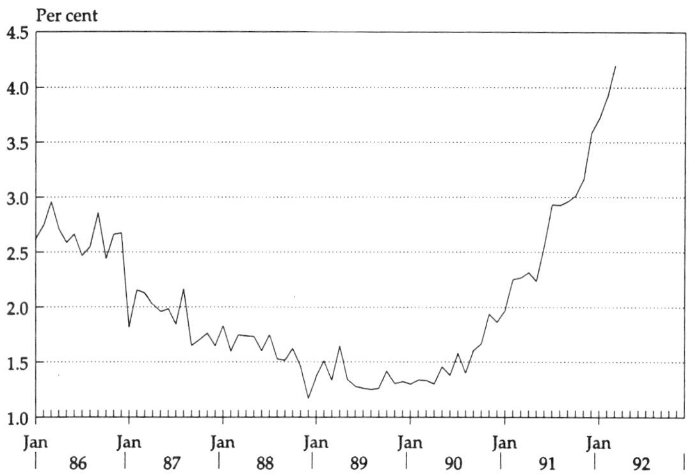

Figure 26.8 Unemployment in Sweden 1986-1991
Source: Svenska Handelsbanken Economic Research

During 1990 and 1991 unemployment has increased dramatically in Sweden. This can be explained both as a business cycle phenomenon, and as a part of the structural change the Swedish economy is undergoing in the deflationary process. However, despite this increase, the 1992 rate of unemployment, of 4 per cent, still compares favourably with other countries.

Inflation

The high level of growth in both wages and prices has been one of the major problems for the Swedish economy during the period 1987-1991. The driving force behind this growth has been the overheated situation in the labour market. Figure 26.9 depicts the development of consumer prices in Sweden in comparison with its eight major trading partners.

The figure shows that, by comparison to the others, the Swedish CPI rate has been consistently higher. The rate jumped considerably in 1990, but this increase is distorted because of a change in fiscal policy. With effect from early 1990, Sweden implemented a major tax reform which essentially shifted the burden from direct (income) tax to indirect (value added) tax. Total tax revenue remained unchanged but the shift had the effect of boosting the consumer price index. Attempts to measure the underlying rate of inflation have indicated,

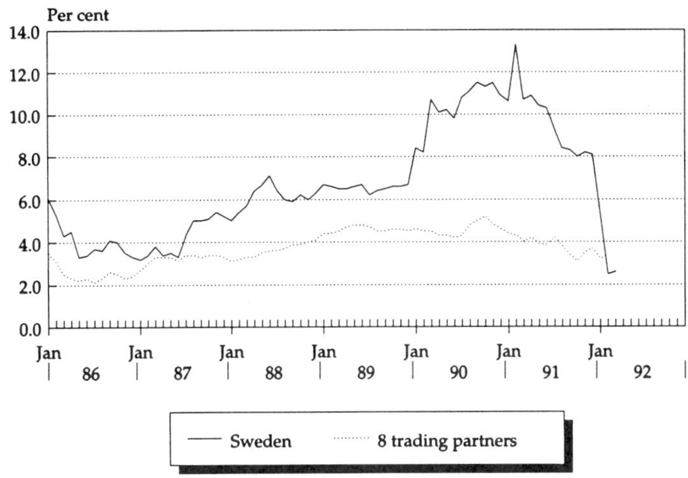

Figure 26.9 **Inflation - rate of change in consumer prices on a 12-month basis.**
Source: Svenska Handelsbanken Economic Research

though, that it is still higher in Sweden than in most other countries in Western Europe. The underlying rate of inflation in Sweden during the whole period is approximately five to six per cent.

In 1992, the rate of inflation is decreasing rapidly, and is soon expected to be below 3 per cent.

Monetary policy

The central bank has pursued two different goals in its monetary policy during the period. In the late 1980s, when the economy was overheated, the central bank followed a tight monetary policy (meaning high nominal interest rates) with the aim of reducing domestic demand - the goal was therefore internal. Later, the central bank activated its open market operations with the ambition of maintaining a fixed exchange rate - the goal therefore being external. The net result of these divergent activities meant that Sweden has tended towards a fixed exchange rate and high nominal interest rates.

In rather simple terms, the Swedish economy was overheated during 1985-1989 and fiscal policy was not restrictive enough to dampen domestic demand. The lack of a tight fiscal policy was partly substituted by a tight monetary policy, which meant that the central bank kept nominal interest rates as high as possible, given the fixed exchange rate against the basket. This led to an upward pressure on the currency and a tendency for the currency reserve to increase.

After 1989, this pressure led to speculation that the krona might be devalued. The central bank then had to shift emphasis and devote its monetary policy to defending the fixed exchange rate - and this again meant high nominal interest rates.

During the 1980s the Swedish capital markets were deregulated. A tightly-imposed and very restrictive system of quantitative controls was abolished and replaced by a market-orientated monetary policy. The last step in the process of deregulation was taken in 1989, when capital controls were abolished, after which the central bank began to conduct monetary policy primarily by open-market operations, adding or withdrawing liquidity as necessary from the banking system by either buying or selling government paper in the open market or by repos with the commercial banks.

Public sector deficit

In the early 1980s there was a substantial public sector deficit. In 1982, one of the aims of the new Social Democratic government was to reduce the size of the deficit and, as can be seen in Figure 26.10, they were successful in achieving this.

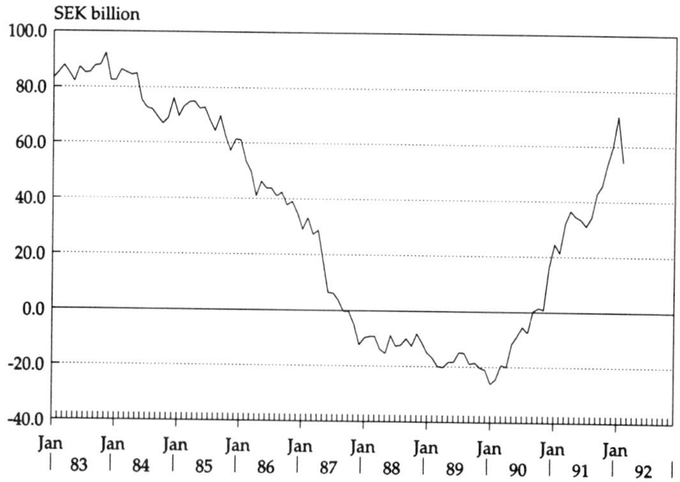

Figure 26.10 The Swedish public sector deficit
Source: Svenska Handelsbanken Economic Research

The deficit in the public sector was gradually decreased during the 1980s. This was partly due to the effect of deliberate attempts to hold back the increase in public spending, and partly due to the effect of an economy which was working close to full-capacity with high tax revenue and a low demand for unemployment benefit payments.

As a result of the cyclical downturn of the economy in 1990 and 1991, the deficit started growing again . However, during this period it did not reach a level where it was considered to be a major political problem - as had been the case in the late 1970s.

Exchange rate history

The exchange rate history of the Swedish krona is relatively straightforward. Following the devaluations in the late 1970s and early 1980s, the krona has had a fixed exchange rate. In the period between 1982 and 1991 the value was fixed against a basket of currencies of the 15 most important trading partners, the weights given to the various currencies being determined by a five year moving

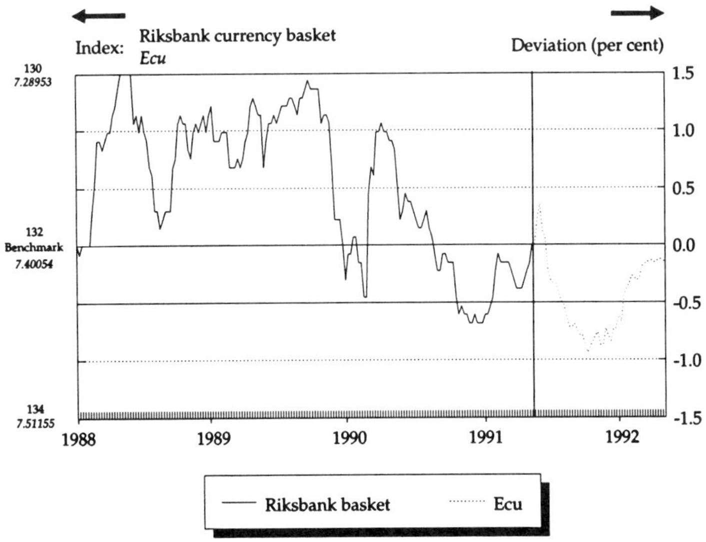

Figure 26.11 The performance of the Swedish krona - Riksbank currency basket/Ecu
Note: The Riksbank's currency basket index is allowed to vary +/- 1.5 per cent, i.e. from 130 to 134. The Ecu rate is allowed to vary +/- 1.5 per cent, i.e. from 7.28953 to 7.51155

Source: Svenska Handelsbanken Economic Research

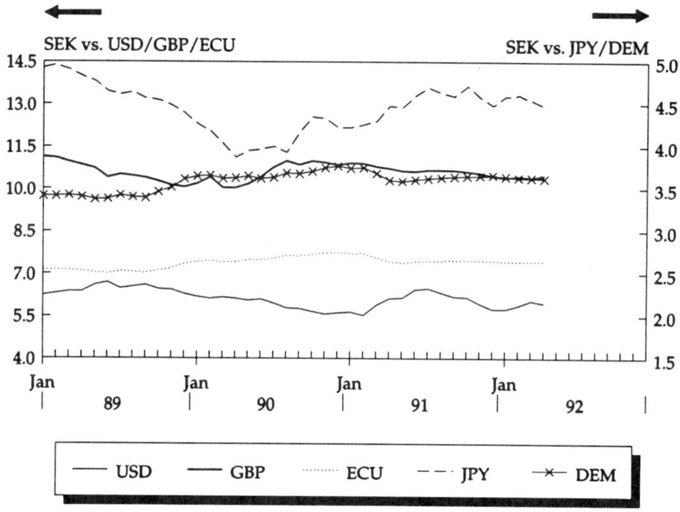

Figure 26.12 The performance of the Swedish krona - SEK vs. USD, GBP, ECU, JPY, DEM
Source: Svenska Handelsbanken Economic Research

average of the shares in foreign trade. The only exception was the US dollar which, in view of its role as an invoicing currency in Sweden's foreign trade, was given double its trade-weight. In 1991, the exchange rate arrangement was changed and the krona became pegged against the Ecu at the central Ecu/SKr rate of 7.40054. The past performance of the krona is shown in Figures 26.11 - 26.18.

The krona has had a fluctuation band of +/- 1.5 per cent against both of the baskets shown in Figure 26.11. It has tended to be on the stronger side of the band as a result of a tight monetary policy which has kept interest rates high with a resulting inflow of currency and upward pressure on the exchange rate.

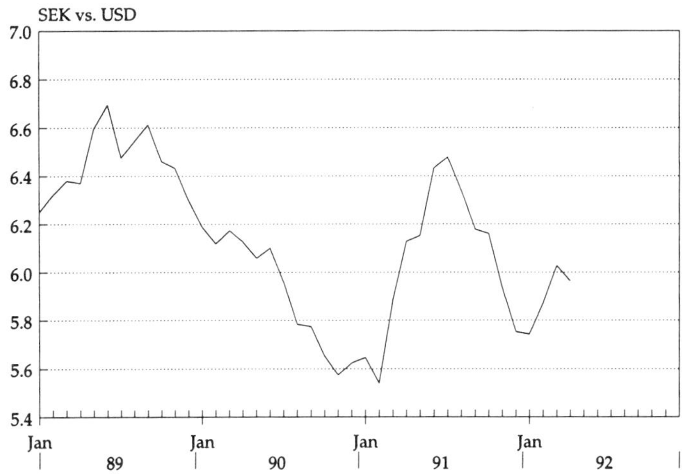

Figure 26.13 The performance of the Swedish krona - SEK vs. USD
Source: Svenska Handelsbanken Economic Research

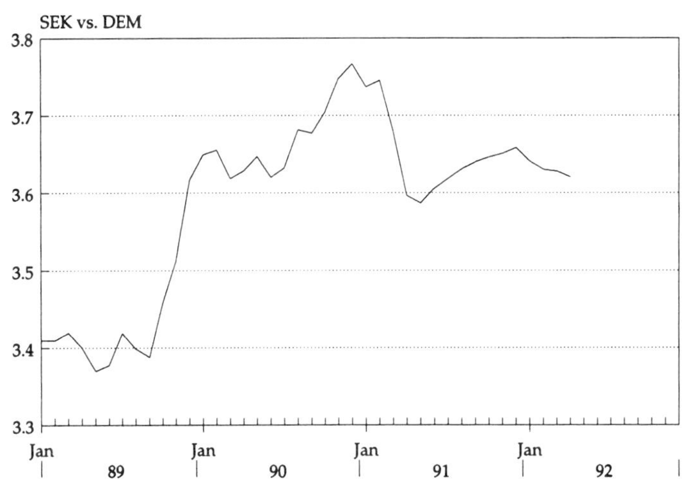

Figure 26.14 The performance of the Swedish krona - SEK vs. DEM
Source: Svenska Handelsbanken Economic Research

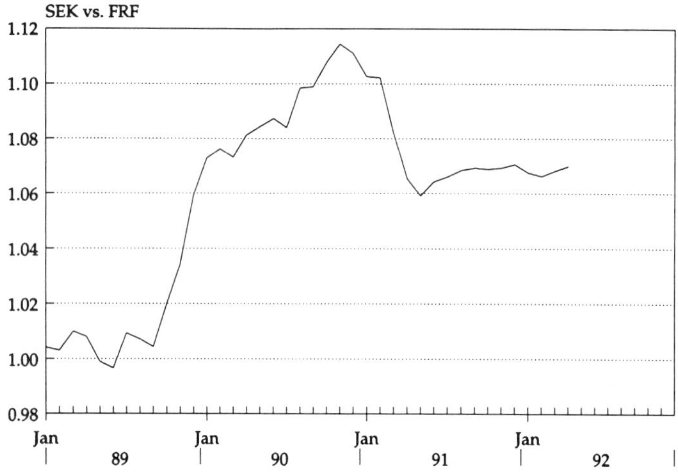

Figure 26.15 The performance of the Swedish krona - SEK vs. FRF
Source: Svenska Handelsbanken Economic Research

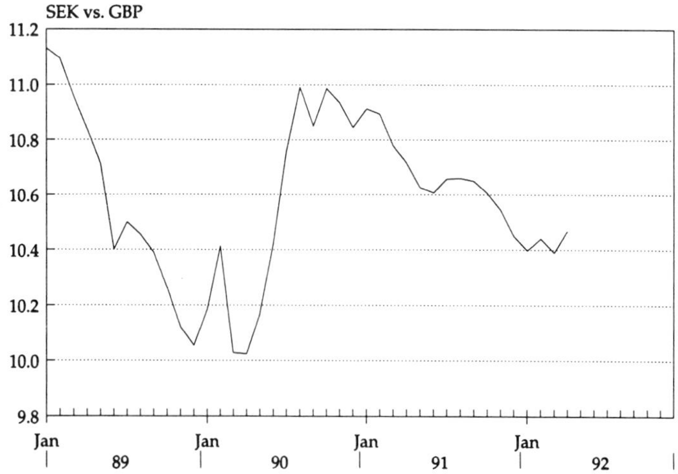

Figure 26.16 The performance of the Swedish krona - SEK vs. GBP
Source: Svenska Handelsbanken Economic Research

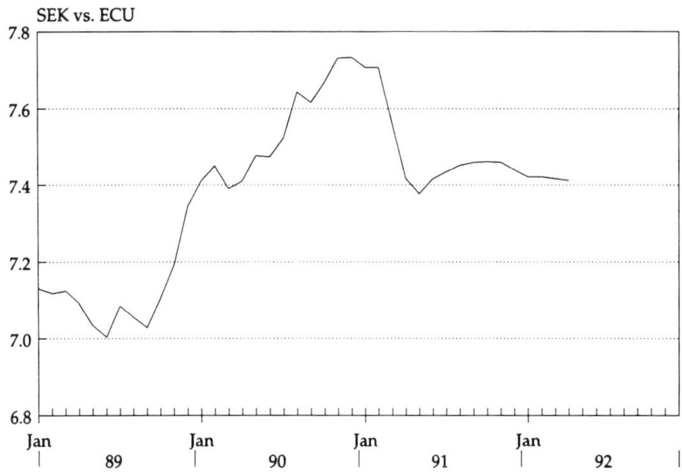

Figure 26.17 The performance of the Swedish krona - SEK vs. ECU
Source: Svenska Handelsbanken Economic Research

Figure 26.18 The performance of the Swedish krona - SEK vs. JPY
Source: Svenska Handelsbanken Economic Research

26.3 *Market composition*

The Swedish bond market consists of approximately 1100 loans with a total debt of SKr 1080bn. Some 300 of the loans are bullet loans issued by the Kingdom of Sweden and mortgage institutions with a total debt of SKr 650bn. They are considered the most liquid bonds in the market and are therefore quoted on the daily *Stockholm Stock Exchange Bond List*. In this context, the bonds comprise what is referred to as the 'bullet bond market'.

Bullet bond market

This section of the market has been growing rapidly, as nearly all new borrowing is in the form of bullet loans. Moreover, the amount of new borrowing increased considerably in 1991 as a result of larger government budget deficits, as well as the higher lending and larger refinancing needs of the mortgage institutions. The composition of the bullet bond market with respect to size, growth and turnover is shown in Figure 26.19 below.

	Debt as of 31 Dec 1991	Bonds issued in 1991	Reported market turnover in 1991
Kingdom of Sweden	267	76	1387
Stadshypotekskassen (Caisse)	113	49	} 483
Other mortgage institutions	275	75	
Total	655	200	1870

Figure 26.19 Size, growth and turnover in the Swedish bullet bond market (SEK billion)

The performance of the Swedish bond market was excellent in 1991 and the return to investors was among the best in the world. Average yield of the bullet bond market decreased over 1991 from 13.4 to 11.1 per cent (see Figure 26.21), resulting in an increase in the price index of 18.4 per cent (see Figure 26.22).

The development of yields and price indices for bonds of different issuers and maturities as given by the Stockholm Stock Exchange is shown in Figure 26.20.

	Average yield-to-maturity			Indices		
	Year-end 1991	Year-end 1990	+/-	Year-end 1991	Year-end 1990	+/-
Kingdom of Sweden						
1-3 years	11.33	13.60	-2.27	138.96	121.14	+14.71
3-5 years	10.47	12.79	-2.32	142.14	120.15	+18.30
5- years	10.10	12.36	-2.26	143.97	116.96	+23.09
Weighted average	10.34	12.71	-2.37	142.25	119.34	+19.20
Stadshypotekskassan (Caisse)						
1-3 years	12.22	14.58	-2.36	140.73	121.07	+16.24
3-5 years	11.66	13.98	-2.32	139.05	116.98	+18.87
5- years	-	13.63	-	138.48	114.01	+21.46
Weighted average	11.88	14.11	-2.23	139.38	118.48	+17.64
Other mortgage institutions						
1-3 years	12.08	14.59	-2.51	141.04	120.78	+16.77
3-5 years	11.86	14.07	-2.21	139.12	117.18	+18.72
5- years	11.82	13.65	-1.83	140.86	117.57	+19.81
Weighted average	11.94	14.18	-2.24	140.07	118.68	+18.02
All bonds						
1-3 years	11.88	14.24	-2.36	140.20	120.92	+15.94
3-5 years	11.39	13.55	-2.16	140.10	118.19	+18.54
5- years	10.36	12.68	-2.32	142.94	116.84	+22.34
Weighted average	11.07	13.41	-2.34	140.87	118.96	+18.42

Figure 26.20 **Yield and indices of bonds traded on the daily *Stockholm Stock Exchange Bond List***

The National Debt Office has been able to create a rather well-balanced maturity structure (see Figure 26.23), through the use of Treasury bonds with maturities from 2 to 12 years.

The maturity structure of mortgage bonds (see Figure 26.24), reveals that the mortgage institutions face a heavy burden of refinancing the large amount of bonds which are due for redemption over the next few years. This reflects heavy borrowing, over several years, in the form of 5-year loans.

The coupon structure of the market (see Figures 26.25 & 26.26) reveals that interest rates in Sweden have long been in the range of 10-12 per cent.

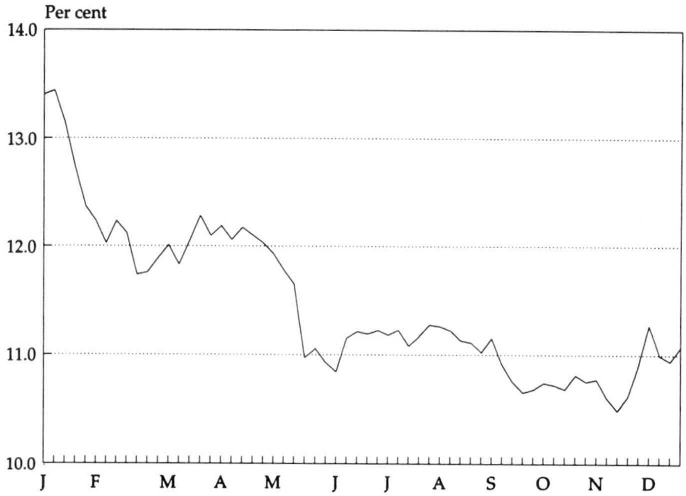

Figure 26.21 Average yield-to-maturity for all bonds on the bullet market in 1991 (Stockholm Stock Exchange)

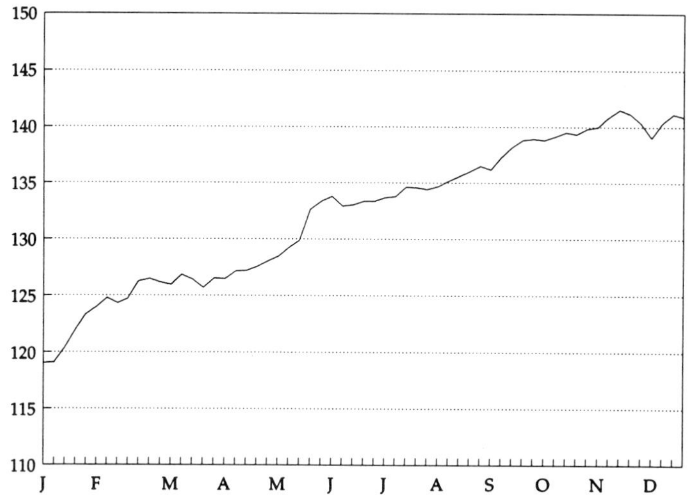

Figure 26.22 Index for all bonds on the bullet market, in 1991 (Stockholm Stock Exchange)

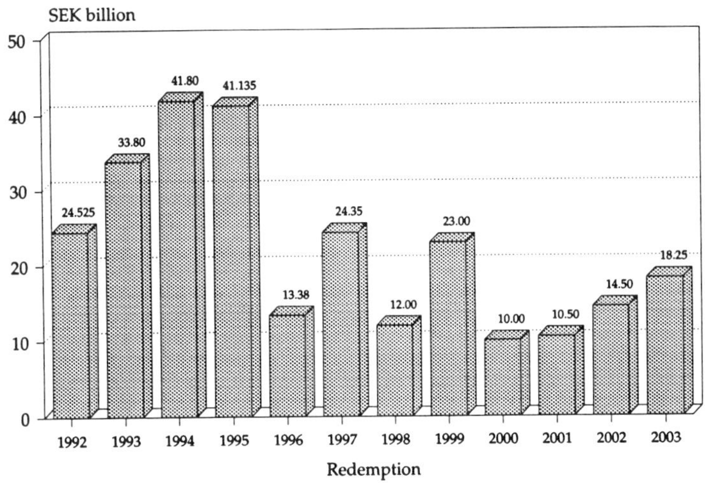

Figure 26.23 Composition of bullet market by maturity - Kingdom of Sweden issues

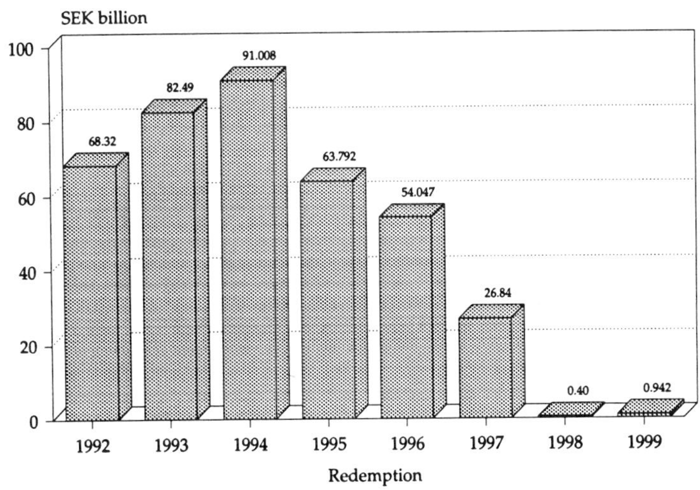

Figure 26.24 Composition of bullet market by maturity - mortgage institutions issues

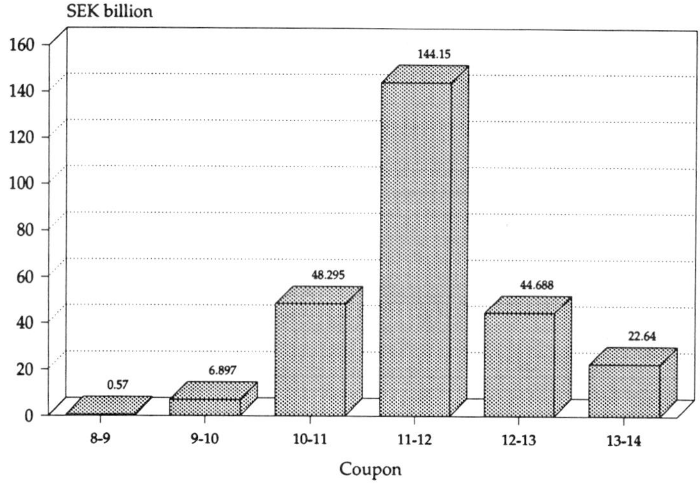

Figure 26.25 Composition of bullet market by coupon structure - Kingdom of Sweden issues

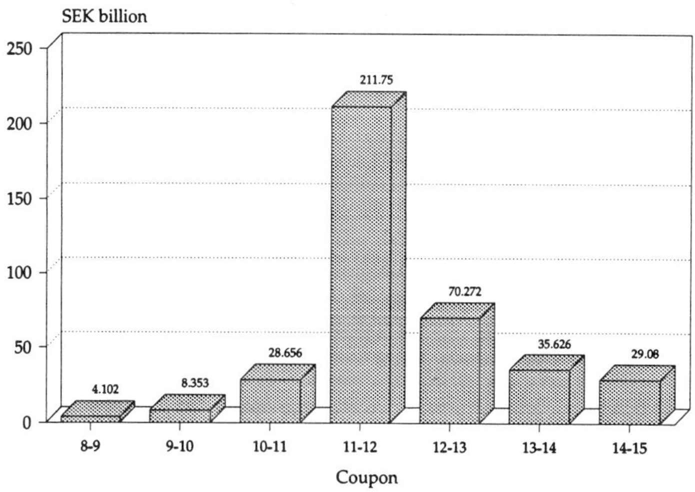

Figure 26.26 Composition of bullet market by maturity - mortgage institution issues

The SOX market

In November 1991, a new bond market-place for private investors, 'SOX', was opened by the Stockholm Stock Exchange.

The SOX market consists of 25 bond loans and has the following composition:

	Debt as of 31 December 1991 (SEK billion)
Bullet bonds	
Mortgage institutions	4.8
Zero-coupon bonds	
Mortgage institutions	0.3
Banks	1.2
Total	6.3

Maturities range from 2 to 10 years and coupons from 10.5 to 15 per cent, with 11 per cent being the most common.

Eurokronor bond market

The eurokronor bond market consists of 40 loans with a total debt of SKr 18bn. Issuers are first-rated Swedish, and internationally well-known, banks and corporates. The loans are not quoted on the Stockholm Stock Exchange. Coupons are all in the range of 10 to 11 per cent and maturities, with few exceptions, are 1994 - 97.

The market for less-liquid bonds

The remaining 900 loans, with a total debt of SKr 400bn, are the less liquid bonds issued by mortgage institutions, municipalities, credit institutions, corporates and banks. Their illiquidity can be attributed to bond structure. The loans usually have amortization features and interest-adjustment clauses. The loans in this group are all quoted on the monthly *Stockholm Stock Exchange Bond List*.

This group also includes the relatively limited number of floating-rate notes, variable-rate notes, perpetuals and zero-coupon loans.

Information about the composition of this segment of the market is rather scarce.

Government bonds

There are only 7 loans in this group, with a total debt of SKr 1.5bn. The loans were issued in the 1930s and 1940s, and therefore have coupons of 3 - 3.5 per cent. Maturities are 1992 - 1997.

Mortgage bonds

With a total debt of SKr 300bn, this category consists of approximately 300 loans, most of them being of the older type, with amortization and interest-adjustment clauses. The coupon structure is very wide - from 2.5 per cent (Caisse 1938/2008) to 14.375 per cent (Caisse 1985/90/95/00/2005), while maturities are 1992 - 2009.

In addition, there are three FRN loans with a total debt of SKr 3bn. Interest is 3-month STIBOR and maturities are 1992, and 2000 (two loans). Two perpetuals, for SBAB and Spintab, were issued in 1991 with interest-adjustment every 5 years.

Credit institution bonds

There are approximately 90 such loans, with a total debt of SKr 17bn, issued by Industrikredit, Svensk Exportkredit, Svenska Skeppshypotekskassan and Sveriges Allmänna Hypoteksbank.

Some of the loans are very old and, accordingly, their coupons are very low (Sveriges Allmänna Hypoteksbank 3% 1935/2005). Others have had their coupon adjusted in the early 1990s and will therefore have a relatively high-coupon for another couple of years (Sveriges Allmänna Hypoteksbank 14.50% 1980/90/95/00). Maturities are 1992 - 2014.

Municipal bonds

There are approximately 150 municipal loans, with a total debt of SKr 9bn, including those of the intermediary bond issuers, Kommunkredit and Nordbanken Kredit. Coupons range from 5.25 per cent (Stockholm 5.25% 1962/92), to 15 per cent (Stockholms läns landsting 15% 1987/90/00). Maturities are 1992 - 2005.

Corporate bonds

There are more than 300 corporate bond loans, with a total debt of SKr 40bn. Most of the bonds were issued before 1980 with a 15-year life at issue and, accordingly, they will soon reach final redemption. Maturities are 1992 - 2005, with a majority being in the range 1992 - 1995. The coupon structure is 6 to 15 per cent, with a majority being around 11 per cent.

In addition, there are a few FRN and VRN loans, with a total debt of SKr 4bn, which have interest related to STIBOR.

Bank bonds

There are 40 bank bond loans, all of them subordinated debt. 19 of the loans are either bullet loans or loans with amortization. The remaining loans are FRNs, zero-coupon bonds, or perpetuals.

Maturities are relatively short, with the majority being redeemed 1992 - 1995. The coupon structure is from 7.5 to 14.3 per cent, with the majority of bonds being found in the 10-12 per cent range.

26.4 Types of security

Overview

The majority of Swedish bond loans are straight bullet bonds[1], issued in the last decade. In addition, there are still a large number of small loans which were issued before 1985 and feature long maturities, amortization plans and, in many cases, interest-adjustment clauses.

The market owes its structure to the following historical factors. Until to the mid-1980s, the Swedish bond market was regulated to reflect the permanent lack of long-term capital. Government bond loans were meant to be rolled over and could therefore be structured as bullet loans, whereas other issuers' bond loans were designed according to the financial needs of the borrower. Mortgage bonds had a 20-year life and an amortization plan based on a 50-year life, corporate bonds had a 15- to 25-year life with amortization and municipal bonds were similarly designed. The market was clearly not investor-orientated.

As a result of the rising inflation throughout the 1970s, investors nevertheless succeeded in getting interest adjustment clauses which allowed the interest on loans to be adjusted, at certain intervals, to the prevailing market rate. Many such bonds are still outstanding on the market but are, for obvious reasons, very illiquid.

In 1983 the National Debt Office introduced a new type of government bond, namely, Treasury notes (*Riksobligationer*). Treasury notes were simple bullet bonds designed to attract good liquidity. The marketing of such bonds was successful and other groups of issuers followed suit to achieve the same liquidity and, thereby, a better price structure. The mortgage institutes started to issue bullet loans in 1985 and thereafter converted all their maturing bond debt into bullet loans. In March 1992, the National Debt Office declared that all government bonds and notes should be referred to as 'Treasury bonds'.

This has had a major impact on the liquidity and trading feasibility of Swedish bonds. Approximately SKr 500bn, or 50 per cent of the outstanding bond debt, can be regarded as liquid and therefore actively traded.

The deregulation of the market has been implemented gradually during the last decade. Many internationally well-known types of bonds such as FRNs, perpetuals, zero-coupon bonds and index-linked bonds have therefore not been issued in Sweden until very recently. Accordingly there are relatively few such loans on the Swedish market.

[1] *Bullet bonds are bonds with a fixed-coupon paid annually, with no amortization and with a single fixed maturity date.*

Government bond market

The principal features of the government bond market are as follows:

Issuer:	Kingdom of Sweden
Size of the market:	SKr 269bn (31 December 1991)
Types of security:	Treasury bonds • Most Treasury bonds are modern government bonds issued in bearer form. They are bullet loans with a maturity of 2-12 years at issue, a fixed annual coupon and a denomination of SKr 1m (some issues SKr 100,000) • Moreover, there are some bonds of an older type which are now straight bullet loans. Denomination is as low as SKr 1000 and coupons are as low as 3 per cent.
Interest calculation:	30/360 days
Typical issue size and maturity:	Sizes typically range from SKr 5 to 10 bn with maturities from 2 to 12 years
Rating:	AAA (Standard & Poor's), Aa1 (Moody's)
Listing:	Stockholm Stock Exchange

Bullet bonds

The total SKr-denominated bond debt amounts to 269bn (see Figure 26.27), which comprises 51 loans of which 49 are bullet loans, i.e. loans with a fixed-coupon and a single, fixed, maturity date. The following six bullet bonds, which are registered as government benchmark bonds, are the most liquid bonds on the Swedish bond market:

No.	Coupon (%)	Redemption	Debt amount (SEK billion)
199	11.20	01 September 1994	25.3
202	11.50	01 September 1995	33.9
1020	10.75	23 January 1997	24.3
1028	11.00	21 January 1999	20.0
1030	13.00	15 June 2001	14.0
1033	10.25	05 May 2003	25.3

see also Appendix 1

Amortization bonds

There are only two government bond loans with amortization still outstanding on the market. They were issued in 1937, with a final redemption date of 1997 and a coupon of 3 per cent.

Low-coupon bonds

Until the 1950s, interest rates were very low in Sweden, while the lives of bonds were very long. There are still eight loans with a 3 or 3.5 per cent coupon outstanding on the market, of which two are the amortization bonds mentioned above.

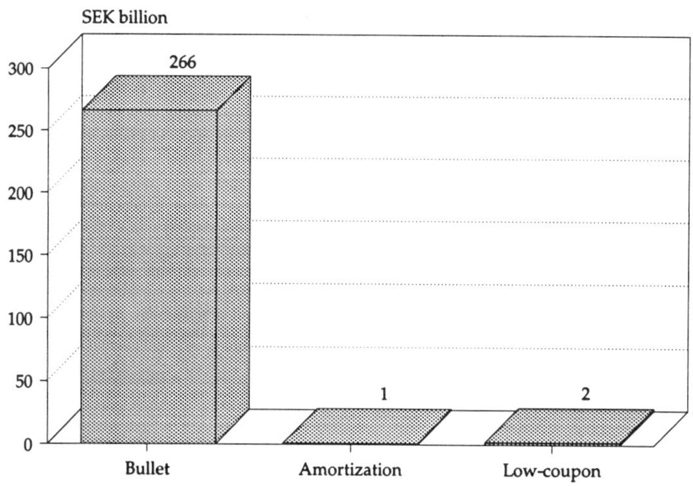

Figure 26.27 Types of issue in the government bond market

Zero-coupon bonds

The Swedish central bank did not allow the issuance of zero-coupon bonds until 1991. As yet, however, the National Debt Office has not issued any zeros.

In the autumn of 1991, the Finance Inspection Board accepted - in a legal sense - the stripping of Treasury bonds. Although no stripping has yet taken place, it is nevertheless likely to occur in the near future.

Mortgage bond market

The principal features of the mortgage bond market are as follows:

Issuers:	Several mortgage institutions (see below)
Size of the market:	SKr 670bn
Types of security:	See below
Interest calculation:	30/360 days
Typical issue size and maturity:	Sizes typically range from SKr 5 to 10 bn, although there are benchmark loans in the size range SKr 10 to 15bn. A standard maturity is 5 years at issue, but maturities range from 3 to 10 years
Rating:	See below
Listing:	Stockholm Stock Exchange

Until 1986, the Swedish bond market was regulated and loans could therefore be structured to fit the needs of the issuers. Bonds had amortization plans, call options and interest adjustment clauses; accordingly they were rather illiquid. The abolition, in 1986, of the requirement for financial institutions to invest in mortgage bonds changed the issuer-investor relationship altogether. Mortgage institutions started to issue simple bullet loans, in large volumes, in order to achieve the best possible liquidity. The larger part of today's mortgage bond market consists of bullet loans.

Bullet bonds

As noted above, the majority of the mortgage bond market comprises bullet bonds. There are 200 such loans, with a total volume of SKr 356bn (see Figure 26.28). All new mortgage bonds are bullet loans with 3- to 5-year lives. *See also Appendix 2.*

Amortization bonds

There are still several hundred loans on the market which were issued before 1986 with amortization plans; many of them carry interest adjustment clauses. When issued, most of them had a 20-year life and an amortization plan based on 50 years. Such bonds are very illiquid today and will be gradually exchanged for new bullet loans when redeemed.

FRN and VRN bonds

Floating-rate note (FRN) loans were introduced on the Swedish market in 1986 and have been mostly used by banks. Two FRN loans have been issued by

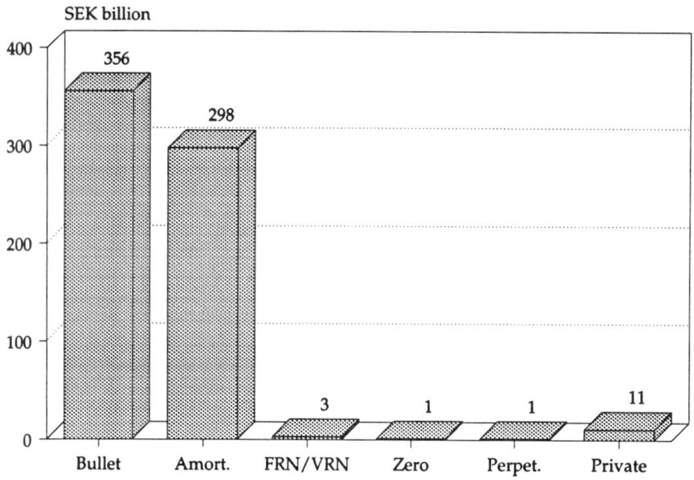

Figure 26.28 Types of issue in the mortgage bond market

Caisse in the form of subordinated debt with a 10-year life and one by Handelsbanken Hypotek. Both have interest related to STIBOR

Two variable-rate note (VRN) loans have also been issued; one by Handelsbanken Hypotek and the other by Svensk Fastighetskredit.

Zero-coupon bonds

The Swedish central bank did not allow zero-coupon bonds to be issued on the Swedish market until 1991, following the tax reform. During 1991, about 10 loans have been issued for different mortgage institutions. As these bonds are aimed at private investors, their yield has therefore been able to be set at approximately 60 basis points below that of mortgage benchmark bonds.

In March 1992, the first stripping of mortgage bonds occurred in the Swedish market. The strips, called 'Principal strips' and 'Coupon strips', are aimed at institutional investors. The latest strip was SKr 712m of the Spintab 5-year loan 155, due 1997.

Perpetual bonds

There are only six perpetual bond loans on the Swedish market, one of which is the 1991 issue by SPINTAB.

Bonds for private investors

With the exception of savings bonds and premium bonds, private investors have historically had very little incentive to invest in bonds generally. However, the tax reform of 1991 has provided an incentive by considerably improving the net return on bond investments. As a result, mortgage companies are now trying to tap this potential market by issuing specially-designed bonds with small denominations in non-physical form, which can easily be bought by a simple telephone call. Caisse, Svensk Fastighetskredit and SPINTAB have shown the strongest interest in this growing market.

To improve liquidity, the Stockholm Stock Exchange opened (in November 1991) the SOX market which provides for the daily trading of 25 bond loans for private investors.

Credit institution bond market

The principal features of the credit institution bond market are as follows:

Issuers:	5-6 companies and institutions (Industrikredit, Sveriges Allmänna Hypoteksbank, Svenska Skeppshypotekskassan, Svensk Exportkredit, Teleinvest) set up as intermediaries to finance small and medium-sized companies in industry, shipping and agriculture (excluded are two credit companies financing municipalities. Their bonds are included in the section on the municipal bond market, below)
Size of the market:	SKr 38bn
Types of security:	See below
Interest calculation:	30/360 days
Typical issue size and maturity:	Sizes typically range from SKr 200 to 500m with maturities from 2 to 5 years
Listing:	Stockholm Stock Exchange

Credit institutions perform an intermediary function in the Swedish capital market. They all have good credit-standing and are able to issue bond loans to raise capital which is then transformed into loans to medium- and small-sized companies in industry, shipping and agriculture.

Bullet bonds

Practically all bond loans issued after 1986 are of the bullet type. There are 30 such loans, totalling SKr 20bn (see Figure 26.29), and carrying lives of 2-5 years. Issuers of such loans are Industrikredit, Sveriges Allmänna Hypoteksbank and Teleinvest.

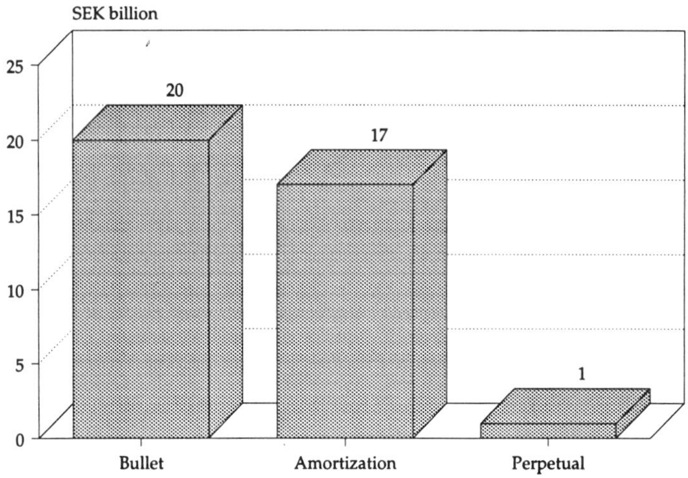

Figure 26.29 Types of issue in the credit institution bond market

Amortization bonds

There are still approximately 90 loans on the market of the older type of bonds, issued before 1986, with amortization plans and interest-adjustment clauses. All of the bonds issued by Svenska Skeppshypotekskassan are of this type as, too, are most of the issues of Sveriges Allmänna Hypoteksbank.

Perpetual bonds

There are six loans of this type on the market, three of them being issued in 1991 by Industrikredit.

Municipal bond market

The principal features of the municipal bond market are as follows:

Issuers:	The cities of Stockholm, Göteborg and Malmö plus the local municipality of the Greater Stockholm Area. There are in addition a few loans issued by smaller municipalities. Included are also loans issued by Kommunkredit and Nordbanken Kredit, two credit companies that fund themselves partly on the bond market and lend their funds to smaller municipalities

Size of the market:	SKr 9bn
Type of bonds:	See below
Interest calculation:	30/360 (actual days for FRN)
Typical issue size and maturity:	Sizes typically range from SKr 300m to 1000m with maturities from 3 to 5 years for new loans
Listing:	Stockholm Stock Exchange

Only four Swedish municipal borrowers have had regular direct access to the Swedish bond market, namely, the cities of Stockholm, Göteborg and Malmö and the local municipality of the Greater Stockholm Area. Smaller municipalities have had indirect access to the bond market via the intermediary bond issuers Kommunkredit and Nordbanken Kredit, which provide lending to smaller municipalities.

There are nearly 150 municipal bond loans on the market, most of them issued before 1986 and therefore carrying amortization plans and, in many cases, interest-adjustment clauses.

Municipalities have borrowed very little on the bond market in recent years and there are therefore few loans of the modern type in existence. Municipal bonds are generally very illiquid.

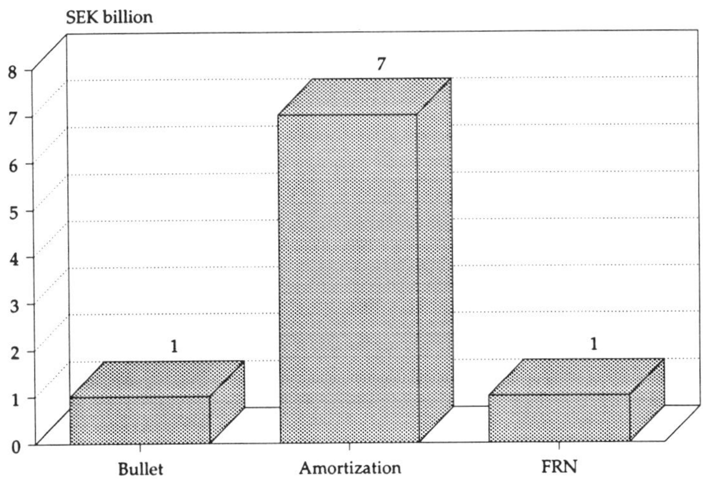

Figure 26.30 Types of issue in the municipal bond market

Bullet bonds

There are only a few bullet bond loans on the market, totalling less than SKr 1bn.

Amortization bonds

Nearly all of the 140 municipal bond loans were issued before 1986. Such loans have amortization plans and, in most cases, interest-adjustment clauses. To a large extent, the loans will be amortized within the next few years.

FRN bonds

The local municipality of the Greater Stockholm Area has issued two FRN bond loans with 1996 and 2005 maturities, respectively.

Corporate bond market

As many as 330 of the 1200 loans listed on the Stockholm Stock Exchange are corporate bonds. However, they represent only 4 per cent of the total bond debt. Most of the loans are relatively small, issued between 1975-1985 and with original lives of 15-20 years. Most of them are of the older type of bond (see Figure 26.31), that is to say, structured more to suit the borrower rather than the investor.

Bullet bonds

Most of the corporate bond loans that have been issued after 1985 are bullet loans. A special category of bullet loans consists of 35 subordinated loans issued around 1984 originally with detachable stock warrants and therefore featuring low coupons, usually around 7 per cent. Such loans were issued to company stockholders and, as a result, they are well distributed throughout the market. Many of the loans are rather large. They are listed without warrants on the Stockholm Stock Exchange monthly bond list.

Amortization bonds

As mentioned earlier, most of the outstanding corporate bond loans are of the older type with amortization plans and interest-adjustment clauses. The loans are relatively small and market liquidity is poor.

FRN and VRN bonds

There are 4 FRN and 4 VRN corporate bond loans on the market. Two of the FRN loans have their interest adjusted on the IMM days. The VRN loans have

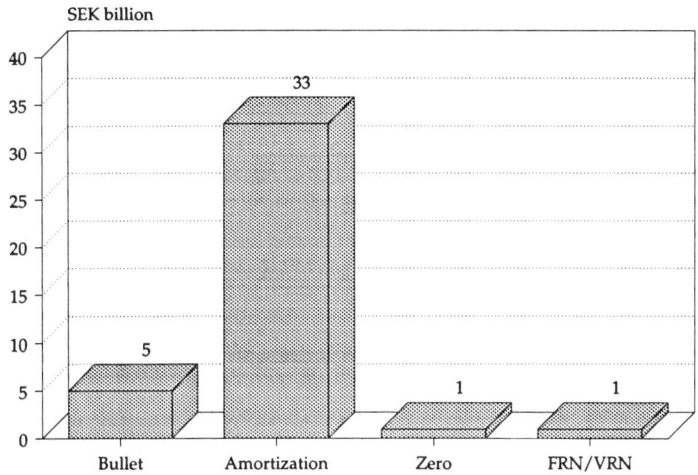

Figure 26.31 Types of issue in the corporate bond market

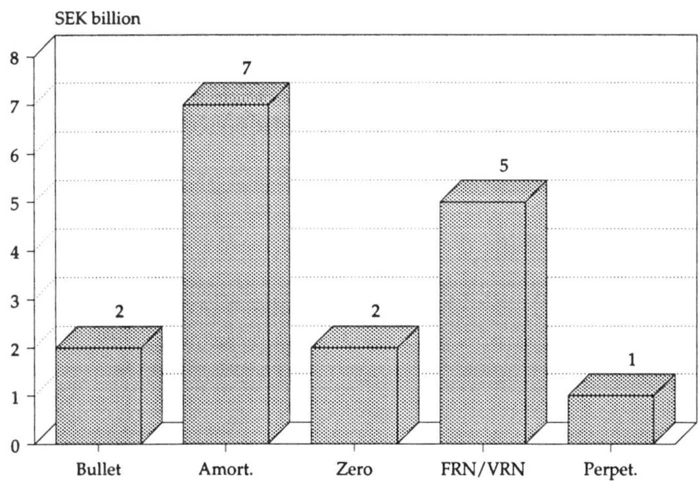

Figure 26.32 Types of issue in the bank bond market

no formula for interest adjustment, interest instead being set by the issuer before each new interest period - the bondholders have an option to call their bonds if they do not wish to accept the new rate.

Zero-coupon bonds

There are three corporate zero-coupon loans. Two of them were issued by the energy company, OKG, and carried 4-year lives. The third, with a 5-year life, was issued by Electrolux and, as it is aimed at private investors, it features a yield somewhat below that of mortgage bonds.

Bank bond market

There are about 40 bank bond loans on the market - all of them subordinated debt (see Figure 26.32). Nineteen of the loans are either bullet loans, or loans with amortization plans.

Bullet bonds

There are relatively few bullet bank bonds as, lately, banks have chosen to issue loans with floating interest.

Amortization bonds

There are still a number of older-type bank bond loans on the market, but the total outstanding debt is rather small due to the final redemption dates being very close.

FRN and VRN bonds

The FRN market in Sweden started in 1986 when the first loan was issued by Skandinaviska Enskilda Banken. There are now 14 FRN and 4 VRN bank bond loans on the market - all of them with interest adjustments every 3 months, usually on the IMM days. Interest is mostly linked to STIBOR.

Zero-coupon bonds

The zero-coupon market started relatively late, in 1991, following the major tax reform. The market is orientated towards the private investor. All the major banks have each issued one or more loans on the market. The loans have maturities from 3 to 10 years.

Perpetual bonds

The perpetual bond market also opened in 1991. Only 2 bank perpetuals have been issued so far, one for Svenska Handelsbanken and one for Skandinaviska Enskilda Banken.

Eurokronor bond market

The eurokronor bond market opened in 1988, with an issue for the World Bank. At the end of 1991, the total outstanding debt of such bonds was SKr 18bn and the total number of issues was 40. During January and February 1992, another 10 loans were issued, with a total debt of SKr 4.9bn.

Most of the issues have relatively short maturities, the longest being 1999. The issuers are well-known Swedish and international institutions and corporates. All of these loans are bullet loans.

Also, there are many mortgage bonds, issued in Sweden, but aimed additionally at the Danish market. Such bonds are quoted both in Stockholm and Copenhagen.

MTN and FTN bond market

In 1991, the market for MTNs (medium-term notes) and FTNs (flexible-term notes) was opened. The first issuer of an MTN bond programme was Teleinvest, a borrowing vehicle for Swedish Telecom. The programme allows Teleinvest to issue bonds with maturities of between 2 and 10 years, within a programme size of SKr 14bn (including Teleinvest's CP programme and general bond programme). The notes are zero-coupon bonds.

The first FTN programme was issued by AB Svensk Exportkredit (SEK), an internationally-recognized borrower. The size of the programme is SKr 4bn and it allows SEK to issue notes with any maturity. They can either be zero-coupon instruments, or they can carry a specified coupon.

26.5 *Issuers*

In terms of nominal value of bonds outstanding, the Swedish bond market is the tenth largest in the world. The market is dominated on the issuers' side by the Kingdom of Sweden and the mortgage institutions, together accounting for more than 85 per cent of total outstanding bond debt (see Figure 26.33). The outstanding volume as of 31 December 1991 was SKr 970bn (US$170bn).

Government

All government borrowing is the responsibility of the National Debt Office which has been a government agency since 1989 (subordinate to the Ministry of Finance).

The Swedish government has managed to keep a balanced state budget over the last five years. Long-term kronor debt actually decreased, both in terms of nominal value (SKr 257bn in 1986 versus SKr 245bn in 1990), and in relative terms (54 per cent of total SKr debt in 1986, versus 47 per cent in 1990). Bond loans due for payment have been replaced by straight bullet loans with better liquidity. New issues amounted to SKr 18bn in 1990 and increased to SKr 76bn in 1991, owing to the much weaker development of the Swedish economy and, hence, an increasing government budget deficit.

	1987	1988	1989	1990	1991	Outstanding debt
		(Percentage share)				(SEK bn, as at 31.12.91)
Interest-bearing loans[1]	38.5	34.9	30.6	27.4	18.6	118.1
Treasury notes[1]	16.3	18.1	18.8	19.6	23.7	150.6
Treasury bills	17.0	14.5	15.6	17.2	48.1	304.8
Total capital market	71.8	67.5	65.1	64.2	90.4	573.5
Lottery bonds	11.1	10.8	12.0	9.8	7.1	45.6
Savings certificates	7.4	6.9	6.0	4.6	1.5	9.9
General public savings scheme	7.6	9.9	12.6	11.1	10.4	66.0
Total household market	26.1	27.6	30.6	25.5	19.0	121.5
Other	2.1	4.9	4.3	10.2	-9.4	-61.0
Total per cent	100.0	100.0	100.0	100.0	100.0	
State debt (SEK billion)	481.0	487.5	486.1	498.9	634.0	634.0

[1] *now called 'Treasury bonds'*

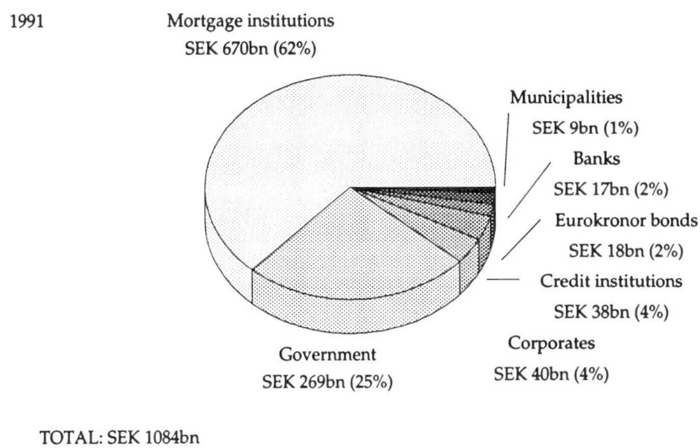

Figure 26.33 Issuers in the Swedish bond market (31 December 1991)

Mortgage institutions (Housing credit institutions)

The Swedish real estate market consists of approximately 85 per cent non-commercial properties and 15 per cent commercial properties, with a total value of approximately SKr 4500bn.

Most of the non-commercial housing - apartment buildings and private homes - is financed by government loans and by mortgage institutions under a politically-arranged framework of interest subsidies and individual subsidies.

Commercial properties are financed by mortgage institutions, insurance companies and other long-term lenders.

From 1992, a new system of financing has been in introduced, under which government loans for new buildings will be abolished, and all housing finance will be provided by mortgage institutions or other lenders. In order to offset risk in new second-mortgage lending, mortgage institutions can buy a credit guarantee from a government agency at an annual cost of 0.5 per cent.

Financing of newly-constructed multi-family buildings or single-family houses is typically arranged as follows:

First mortgage from mortgage institute	⇒	65-75 per cent of property value
Second mortgage offset against a government credit guarantee	⇒	5-25 per cent of property value
Cash payment	⇒	5-20 per cent of property value

The total amount of subsidies to the housing sector, in 1991, came to SKr 54bn.

The mortgage institutions participate in two areas of the property market; one being the financing of both new construction and the rebuilding of properties, while the other being the financing of properties in connection with changes of ownership. Each sector accounts for 50 per cent of the total market.

Property values decreased considerably during 1990-1991, causing financial distress for many property companies. The market is therefore concerned that mortgage institutions may be badly affected by loan defaults and other credit losses.

A recent study on the financial strength of the mortgage institutions, however, indicates that credit losses have been rather low in 1991, at around 0.15 per cent of total lending. When evaluating risks in mortgage institutions' portfolios, it is essential to look at lending from 1987 onwards as, during this period, property prices at first increased, but thereafter fell considerably. The risk is mainly in newly-financed properties that do not give owners a positive cash-flow. The study concludes that the mortgage institutions, as a group, are well-cushioned against credit losses. Even if loan losses were to increase in 1992, say, to SKr 2.5bn, they would not equate to more than 0.3 per cent of total outstanding debt.

The mortgage institutions are either bank-owned or co-operative mortgage associations. SBAB, which until 1991, provided secondary mortgages within the subsidy system, is government-owned.

The mortgage institutions active on the Swedish bond market are briefly described below:

Caisse, Konungariket Sveriges Stadshypotekskassa (The Urban Mortgage Bank Group of Sweden)

Caisse is a co-operative mortgage institution backed by a government guarantee fund of SKr 27bn. Total bond volume is SKr 250bn, of which 150bn is in the form of straight bullet bond loans. Caisse, which is rated AA+ by S & P, will most likely be transformed into a limited company by January 1993.

SPINTAB, Sparbankernas Intecknings AB (SPINTAB Swede Mortgage)

SPINTAB is the largest of the bank-owned mortgage institutions. It is a subsidiary of the central savings bank, Swedbank. Total bond volume is SKr 175bn, of which 123bn is in the form of straight bullet bond loans. SPINTAB is rated Aa2 by Moody's.

Svensk Fastighetskredit AB (SEB Mortgage)

SFK is a wholly-owned subsidiary of Skandinaviska Enskilda Banken. Total bond volume is SKr 65bn, of which 50bn is in the form of straight bullet bond loans. SFK is not rated, but Skandinaviska Enskilda Banken is rated AA- by S & P and Aa2 by Moody's.

Handelsbanken Hypotek AB

Handelsbanken Hypotek is a wholly-owned subsidiary of Svenska Handelsbanken. Total bond volume is SKr 30bn, of which 25bn is in the form of straight bullet bond loans. Handelsbanken Hypotek is not rated, but Svenska Handelsbanken is rated AA- by S & P and Aa3 by Moody's.

Nordbanken Kredit AB and Nordbanken Hypotek AB

Nordbanken Kredit and Nordbanken Hypotek are wholly-owned by Nordbanken, of which the government owns 71 per cent. Total bond volume is SKr 40bn, all of which is in the form of straight bullet bond loans. Nordbanken Kredit and Nordbanken Hypotek have no rating of their own, but Nordbanken (the parent company) has been rated Aa3 by Moody's.

Föreningsbanken Kredit AB

Föreningsbanken Kredit AB is wholly-owned by Sveriges Föreningsbank, the central bank of the co-operative FB bank group. Total bond volume is SKr 18bn of which most is in the form of straight bullet bond loans. Sveriges Föreningsbank has not been rated.

SBAB, Statens Bostadsfinansierings AB (The Swedish National Housing Finance Corporation)

SBAB is a government-owned company which hitherto has provided secondary mortgages within the government subsidy system. Total bond volume is SKr

75bn of which SKr 50bn is in the form of straight bullet bond loans. SBAB has an AAA rating by S & P and Aa1 by Moody's.

Credit institutions

Credit institutions' bond borrowing amounts to SKr 38bn. A short description of the largest credit institutions is given below.

Sveriges Allmänna Hypoteksbank (Hypoteksbanken)

This is a co-operative credit institution set up to provide long-term credits to the agricultural sector. The government has provided a guarantee fund of SKr 2.3bn. Total outstanding bond debt is SKr 24bn. Hypoteksbanken is rated AA+ by S & P.

Industrikredit AB (Finance for Swedish Industry)

This institution issues medium-term bond loans in the Swedish market for the purpose of lending to small and medium-sized companies in the industrial sector. Industrikredit is owned half by the government and half by the commercial banks. Total outstanding bond debt amounts to approximately SKr 10bn, all in the form of straight bullet bonds. Industrikredit has an AA rating by S & P.

Teleinvest AB

This institution is the borrowing vehicle for Swedish Telecom, a government agency which guarantees its borrowing. Total outstanding bond debt is approximately SKr 4bn, all in the form of straight bullet loans. Teleinvest is not rated.

Municipalities

Since they have the right to levy local taxes, Swedish municipalities have always been considered first-class borrowers. However, over the past few years, many Swedish municipalities have come under financial pressure; moreover, the government has introduced, in connection with its tax reform, a temporary ban on municipal tax increases. Sweden's largest cities - Stockholm, Göteborg and Malmö - as well as the local municipality of the Greater Stockholm Area, all have many bond loans on the Swedish market. Smaller municipalities have had indirect access to the bond market via the intermediary bond issuers Kommunkredit and Nordbanken Kredit.

Over the last few years Swedish municipalities have borrowed very little on the Swedish bond market and therefore, there are only a few loans of the straight bullet type. Total debt of Swedish municipalities at the end of 1991 was

SKr 74bn of which only 6.5bn was bond debt while 2.5bn was from credit institutions funding themselves on the Swedish bond market.

The City of Stockholm has an AAA rating by S & P and Göteborg has an Aa1 rating by Moody's. Malmö and the local municipality of the Greater Stockholm Area have no rating.

Corporations

As the level of Swedish long-term interest rates has been relatively high for a number of years, Swedish corporates have chosen either to borrow abroad, or to use the commercial paper market.

Therefore, in recent years, corporate bond loans have rarely been issued in the Swedish bond market. There are still a large number of corporate bond loans outstanding, but most of them are illiquid since they are relatively small. They are subject to amortization, and usually have interest-adjustment clauses.

Internationally-recognized Swedish industrial companies such as Volvo, Ericsson and ASEA, have not been borrowers in the domestic Swedish bond market for a long time. However, they have issued loans in the eurokronor market.

The energy sector, which includes several first-class borrowers, has always used the Swedish bond market as a major source of long-term funds. Sydkraft, OKG, Forsmarks Kraftgrupp and Stockholm Energi all have a considerable bond debt in the Swedish market, but most of their bond loans are rather illiquid and the turnover in the secondary market is very limited.

In summary, the Swedish corporate bond market is rather inactive.

Banks

Borrowing by Swedish banks in the Swedish bond market is limited to subordinated debt. Most issues are in the form of floating-rate notes (FRNs) or variable-rate notes (VRNs).

All major Swedish banks have such loans outstanding in the market. The liquidity of these bonds, however, is rather limited.

26.6 *Investors*

The Swedish capital market has traditionally been dominated by large investors. A breakdown of investors in terms of bond holding is shown in Figure 26.34.

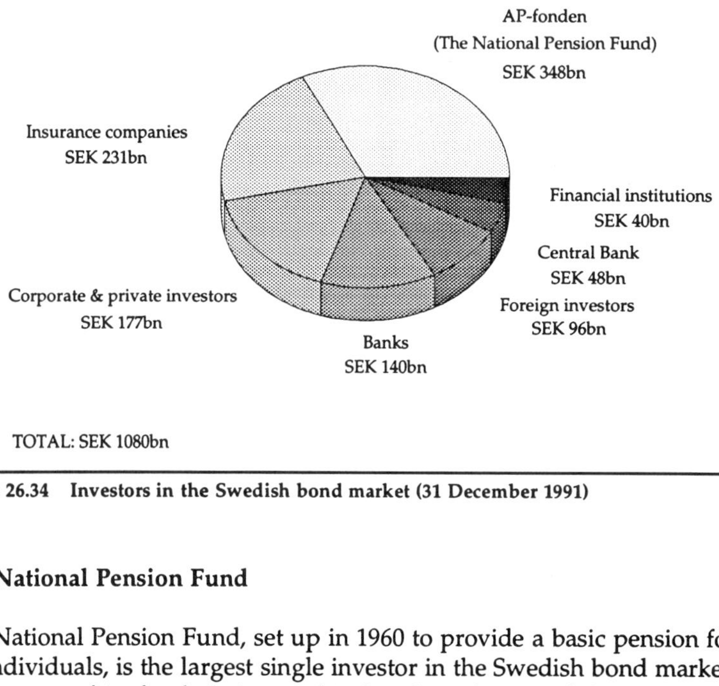

Figure 26.34 Investors in the Swedish bond market (31 December 1991)

The National Pension Fund

The National Pension Fund, set up in 1960 to provide a basic pension for Swedish individuals, is the largest single investor in the Swedish bond market. About 83 per cent of its funds is invested in bonds and most of the remaining 20 per cent in loans to municipalities and mortgage institutions. After a long period of growth, the National Pension Fund today has a relative balance between premiums received and pension paid; it is therefore not the major source of long-term funds that it once was. However, the size of capital income and the bond portfolio, about SKr 350bn, plus the large cashflows related to it, still make the National Pension Fund a very important factor on the Swedish bond market.

The National Pension Fund is restricted by law as to the type of investments it can make. The restrictions have been somewhat modified lately but, as yet, most of its assets have to be in Swedish bonds.

Total fund growth over the period 1986-91 is shown in Figure 26.35.

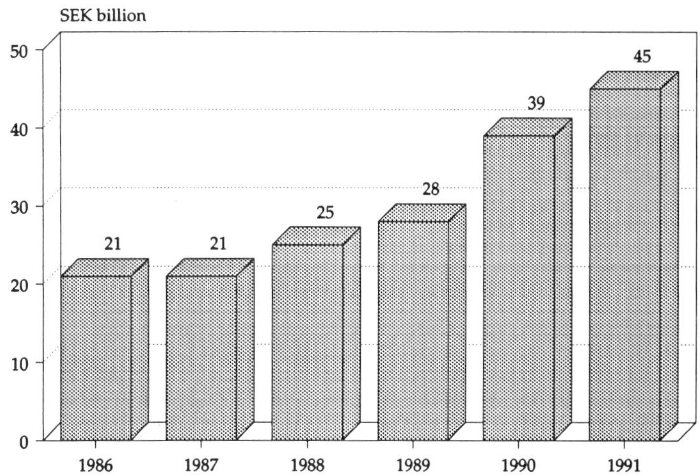

Figure 26.35 National Pension Fund - growth of funds 1986-1991

Insurance companies

The Swedish life and property insurance companies, which have assets of SKr 600bn, must invest their funds in low-risk investments, i.e. primarily in bonds and property loans. Additionally, they may invest in stocks and properties. The five largest life insurance companies account for 80 per cent of the total investment of all insurance companies.

The Swedish insurance companies were, until 1986, obliged to invest a major part of their new funds in government and mortgage bonds with yields below market level.

About 60 per cent of the assets of the insurance companies once consisted of bonds. However, since the abolition of the mandatory investment regulations, they have tended to put new funds in investments other than bonds - mainly shares and properties. However, this trend changed in 1991, due to the beginning of the recession and falling property values. Real interest rates of 6 to 7 per cent induced the insurance companies to increase their investment in bonds.

Due to the favourable tax treatment of private pension schemes, insurance companies have received, during recent years, a large amount of new funds to invest. Despite the tendency to diversify investment portfolios into investments other than bonds, the insurance companies have, nevertheless, increased their share of outstanding bonds over the last few years.

The largest life and property insurance company groups on the Swedish market are:

	Assets (SEK bn, 31.12. 1991)	Premium income (1991, SEK bn)	Net investments (1991, SEK bn)
Trygg Hansa SPP	194	17	15
Skandia	120	32	10
Folksam	38	11	4
AMF-Pension	55	5	6
Wasa	40	7	2
Länsförsäkringar	22	6	3
AMF-sjuk	38	4	6

Total fund growth over the period 1986-91 is shown in Figure 26.36, below.

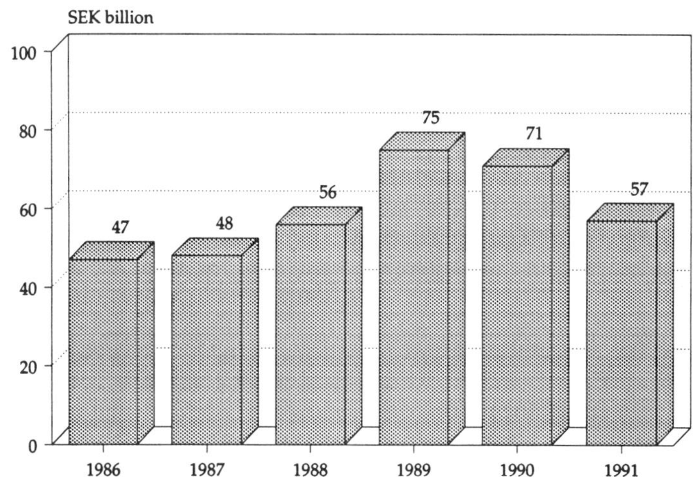

Figure 26.36 Insurance companies - growth of funds 1986-1991

Banks

Until 1986, banks were also obliged to invest in low-yielding government and mortgage bonds. When this requirement was abolished most banks decreased the size of their bond portfolios relative to total assets. Swedish banks are, nevertheless, substantial bondholders and important participants on the market not only as investors, but also as dealers and market-makers.

After a period of mergers and re-structuring, the Swedish banking sector is now limited to just nine groups: Skandinaviska Enskilda Banken, Svenska Handelsbanken, Nordbanken, Sparbankernas Bank (Swedbank), Gota Bank, Föreningsbankerna, Östgöta Enskilda Bank, JP Bank and Bohusbanken.

Corporate and private investors

The 1982 devaluation of the Swedish krona by 16 per cent was a major factor in the development of the Swedish money and capital markets. Profitability and liquidity in the corporate sector increased considerably (although this was also due, in part, to large government budget deficits and favourable business conditions) and, as a result, many companies established sophisticated financial units to handle the investment of excess funds.

Initially, investment from the corporate sector was primarily concerned with money market instruments, but the higher yield on longer-term investments prompted companies to invest considerable amounts in bonds. Of particular importance is the investment role played by corporates in the introduction of the FRN instrument on the Swedish market in 1986. Today, corporates are crucial players on the Swedish bond market.

By international comparison, the Swedish private investor has never been of any importance as a market for interest-bearing bonds. However, this situation has recently changed. A significantly lower inflation rate, together with the recent tax reform (which provided a flat rate of taxation of only 30 per cent on interest and capital gains) have both considerably improved the attraction of interest-bearing bonds.

At first, the growth came mainly from specially-designed mutual funds set up for tax-planning purposes and a total of SKr 70bn was invested in such bond funds at the end of 1989. While changes in the tax system have, on one hand, led to a decrease in the size of the market (to a present level of approximately SKr 20bn) they have also led, on the other, to a strong growth in direct private ownership of bonds.

With the government budget deficit expected to increase and with mortgage institutions needing to undertake very large refinancing of their bond stocks, it will be important to try to switch the savings of the private sector into bond investment.

Foreign investors

Until July 1989, foreign investors were not allowed to invest on the domestic Swedish bond market. However, since the removal of this restriction, foreign trading in liquid Swedish government and mortgage bonds has grown steadily.

In order to keep currency flows in balance, the central bank has encouraged Swedish corporates to borrow abroad by keeping Swedish short-term interest rather high. This has had a secondary effect on long-term rates.

The Swedish application to the EC and the associated linkage of the krona to the Ecu, together with the recent election of a new non-socialist government, have all induced confidence in krona investments.

Additionally, in an environment of converging interest rates, investors in Europe, the USA and increasingly, the Far East, have realized the advantage of investment in high-yielding Swedish bonds. The high volatility has provided many opportunities for big international investors to take trading positions in the Swedish market. By the end of 1991, foreign investors held approximately SKr 90bn worth of Swedish bonds, of which SKr 40bn was held in government bonds.

26.7 *Methods of issuance*

In the Swedish market there are several issuance techniques; auctions, tap issuing and underwriting are most commonly used.

The method employed varies according to the issuer, but there is a common denominator in that issuers do not have direct contact with investors but rely, instead, on the marketing knowledge of dealers and underwriters.

Government bonds

Swedish government securities are issued by auction. The National Debt Office, which is responsible for all government borrowing, has signed an agreement with 12 banks and brokerage firms authorizing them to act as dealers and sole distributors ('primary dealers') for government bonds. The dealers have undertaken to put in tenders at all issues, these tenders including both the dealers' own bids, as well as the bids received from investors.

The Debt Office issues information about ensuing half-yearly issues, each June and December. Normally there are ten issues each year, all of them being straight bullet loans. Terms for each separate issue are given at the time of the issue. A tranche amount is announced - usually several billion kronor - and dealers ask investors for bids, including price and volume. Bids are then reported to the Debt Office which ranks them by price. Bids which match, or are better than, the price at which the issue volume is covered are accepted and result in the receipt of bonds at the bid price.

Bids of SKr 5m may be given without stating any price, in which case such bids are accepted and priced at a level which is equal to that of the highest accepted bid. The result of an issue, giving details of the number of bids tendered/accepted, highest/lowest accepted price and the weighted average price, is published by Reuters, Telerate and PmI.

Loans will frequently be re-opened in the form of new tranches in order to obtain higher volumes and better liquidity.

The agreement between the Debt Office and the dealers includes the undertaking not only to participate in each issue, but also to deal actively in the secondary market, as market-makers, by always quoting bid and offer prices with a specified narrow spread, for a number of government benchmark loans.

Dealers receive fees geared to their results in both the primary and secondary markets.

Mortgage bonds

There is keen competition in the financial markets between the different mortgage institutions and borrowing costs are, therefore, of vital importance. Mortgage institutions normally have a continuing need for funds and so their bonds, issued in the form of straight bullet loans, are primarily sold on a tap basis via established dealer groups.

All the mortgage institutions have reached agreements with different dealers who have undertaken to both sell bonds and act as market-makers to ensure satisfactory liquidity in the secondary market. An agreement may include an undertaking from the participating dealers always to consent to buy, say, SKr 20m at their bid price. This method normally means that a mortgage institution will need to ask several dealers for bids to obtain the lowest price on the market. The technique is flexible and allows dealers who have a demand for bonds with a particular maturity to take the initiative in the issue and sale of new bonds.

Since loan terms and issuer-quality are similar for all the issues, the liquidity of a bond issue is of vital importance . A good price level is the result of large issue volumes, a good network of market-makers, timing of issuance according to market-maker demand and a generally flexible approach to market innovations.

Stadshypotekskassan (Caisse) has been able to meet these requirements and is therefore a market leader. Caisse normally issues four new loans each year. Moreover, they have both two-year and five-year synthetic futures contracts of very high liquidity (see Section 26.14, Futures & options). The bank-owned mortgage houses of SPINTAB, SFK, Handelsbanken Hypotek and Nordbanken Kredit are all smaller than Caisse and have therefore been unable to match Caisse's volumes. As a result, they have made an agreement with their parent banks in an attempt to overcome this size disadvantage.

Under the name of MBB (Mortgage Benchmark Bonds) the institutions have undertaken to issue a number of identical bond loans in large volumes, while the banks have undertaken to accept delivery of any one institution's bonds of a particular issue which is sold in the name of MBB. The liquidity of the bonds has thereby been considerably improved. At present, there are three MBBs in the market: MBB-95, -96 and -97, due in 1995, 1996 and 1997, respectively.

Credit institution bonds

In the Swedish capital markets there are some credit institutions which offer medium- and long-term loans to primarily small and medium-sized companies in industry, agriculture and shipping. They obtain funds partly by issuing bonds. The issuance methods used have been auctions and tap issuing via selling groups with which they have long-term dealer agreements.

Municipal bonds

There have been very few bond issues from the municipal sector over the last few years. The loans issued have been sold either by underwriting, or by selling through commission on a best-effort basis.

Corporate bonds

The corporate sector has borrowed relatively little on the Swedish bond market during the last decade. Borrowing needs have been met either from abroad or in the form of commercial paper.

Apart from straight bullet issues, corporates have chosen to tap the rather new FRN and VRN market. The issuing techniques used have either been underwriting, or selling through commission on a best-effort basis.

Bank bonds

Swedish banks have had a continuing need to strengthen their capital base by issuing subordinated debt in the form of bonds. For obvious reasons, they have preferred to issue floating-rate debt.

Skandinaviska Enskilda Banken introduced FRNs into the Swedish market in 1986 and, since then, about 20 such bank loans have been issued.

The issuing techniques have been either underwriting by a small selling group, or selling through commission on a best-effort basis.

26.8 New issuance volume

As shown in Figure 26.37, mortgage and government bonds dominate the new issue market. Mortgage institutions have, in addition, obtained substantial funds from international bond issuance and from the Swedish CP market.

	1986	1987	1988	1989	1990	1991	Total	%
Government	33	20	21	19	19	76	188	23
Mortgage	75	50	81	108	94	123	531	66
Municipal	3	1	1	-	1	-	6	1
Credit institutions	5	2	4	4	3	11	29	4
Corporates	5	2	1	-	7	1	16	2
Banks	2	1	5	3	4	3	18	2
Euro-SEK	-	-	1	8	2	7	18	2
Total	123	78	114	142	140	222	807	100

Figure 26.37 New issue volume 1986-1991 (SEK billion)

Government bonds

The government's net borrowing needs correspond mainly to budget figures, which include interest payments on government debt. In 1991, interest payments amounted to SKr 62bn (on a government debt of SKr 693bn).

The budget position improved from a deficit of SKr 35bn in 1986, to a surplus of SKr 20bn in 1989. However, in 1990 and 1991, there were once again budget deficits, amounting to SKr 16bn and SKr 50bn, respectively. Of the total debt of SKr 693bn at the end of 1991, SKr 634bn was borrowed on the Swedish market and SKr 59bn abroad. New issuance volume is shown in Figure 26.38.

Mortgage bonds

Mortgage institutions' bond issuance (see Figure 26.39), corresponds directly with same institutions' lending. Lending over the same period has developed as shown in Figure 26.40.

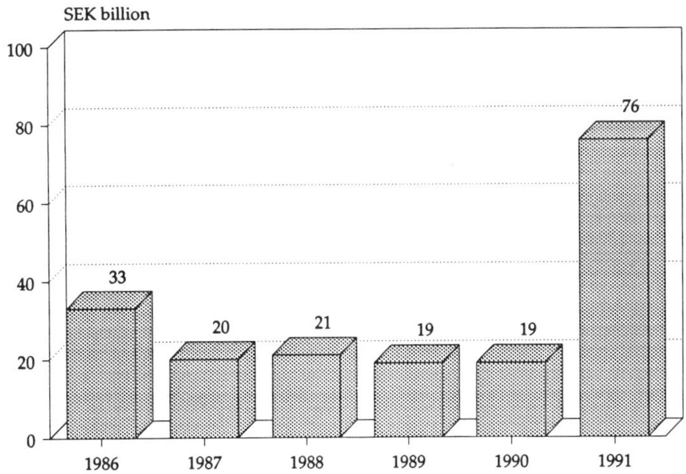

Figure 26.38 **New issuance volume of government bonds (1986-1991)**

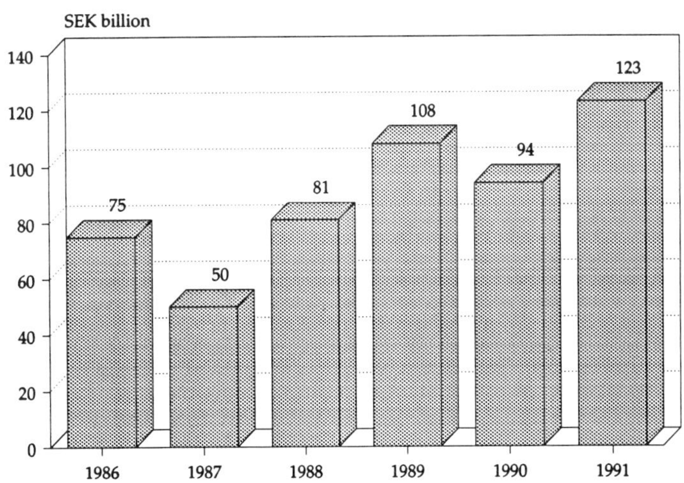

Figure 26.39 **New issuance volume of mortgage bonds (1986-1991)**

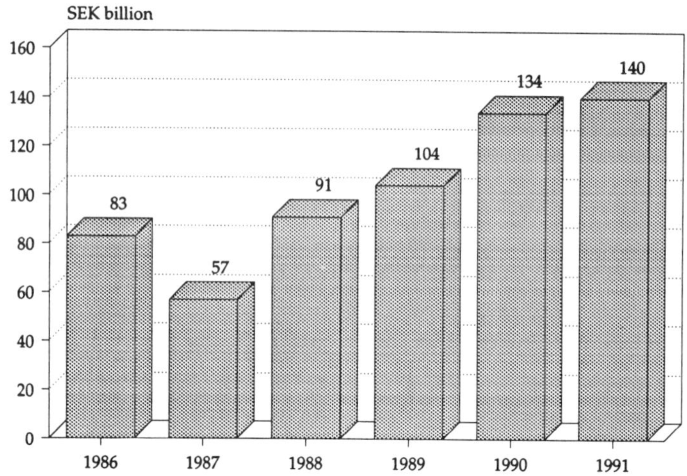

Figure 26.40 Lending by mortgage institutions (1986-1991)

The considerable increase in lending and bond issuance over the period can be attributed mainly to the new opportunities for mortgage institutions to issue large volumes of modern bonds with good liquidity and, thereby, the ability to offer loans at competitive prices. Considerable stocks of loans have been transferred to mortgage institutions from banks and finance companies.

Most of the new debt is in the form of 5-year bullet bonds. The mortgage institutions will therefore have to refinance the large amount of bonds due in the coming years.

Municipal bonds

Municipalities, and the credit institutions financing municipalities, have issued only a rather small amount of bonds over the period (see Figure 26.41). This is mainly due to the opportunity to borrow directly from the National Pension Fund. It should be noted, though, that municipalities have been very active in the domestic commercial paper market.

Credit institution bonds

Small and medium-sized companies have been able to tap the Swedish bond market using credit institutions as intermediaries. Owing to the general business

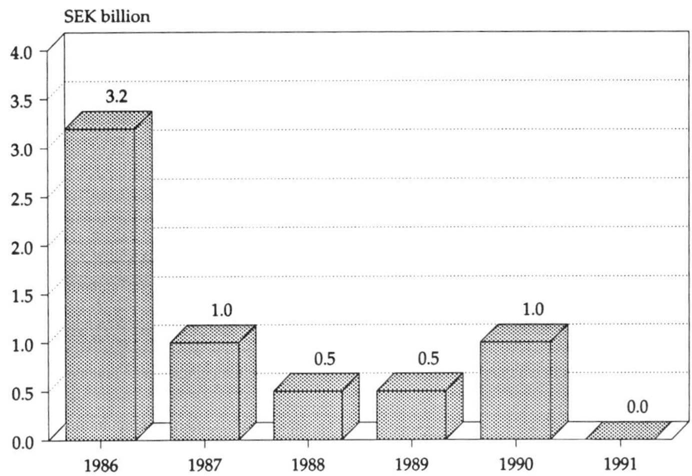

Figure 26.41 **New issuance volume of municipal bonds (1986-1991)**

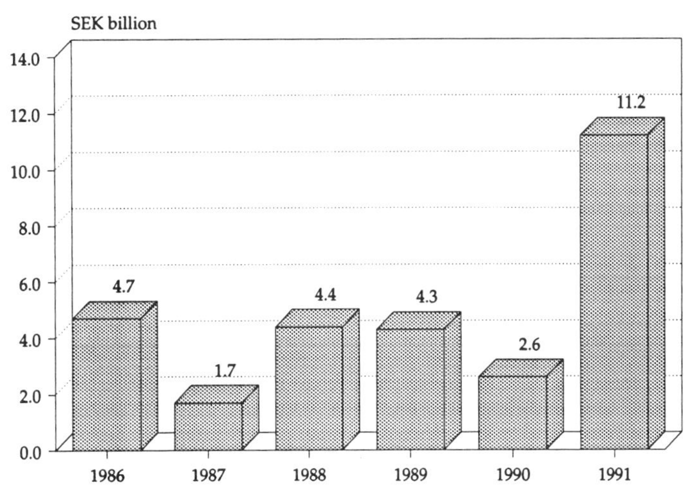

Figure 26.42 **New issuance volume of credit institution bonds (1986-1991)**

conditions, demand for credit has levelled out in 1991, but volumes have nevertheless increased owing to larger refinancing needs (see Figure 26.42).

Corporate bonds

Relatively few corporate bonds have been issued during the period (see Figure 26.43). Corporates have mainly financed themselves on the domestic CP market, as well as abroad where interest rates have been more favourable. The difference between Swedish long-term corporate interest rates and Ecu rates has generally been around 300 basis points.

Bank bonds

Banks have been able to tap the market (see Figure 26.44), in the form of subordinated bonds, to improve their capital structure. Most of the borrowing has been in the form of FRN loans.

Eurokronor bonds

The eurokronor bond market opened in 1988 with an issue for the World Bank. In 1989 the market was flooded with eurokronor loans, making it necessary to decrease volumes considerably in 1990 (see Figure 26.45).

During 1991, the eurokronor market has been tapped regularly, not only by Swedish issuers, but also by well-known international borrowers. The total number of issues is 40, with a overall volume of SKr 18bn.

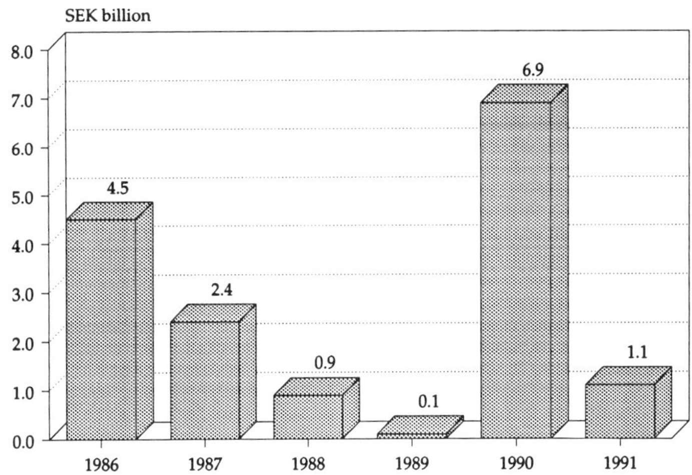

Figure 26.43 New issuance volume of corporate bonds (1986-1991)

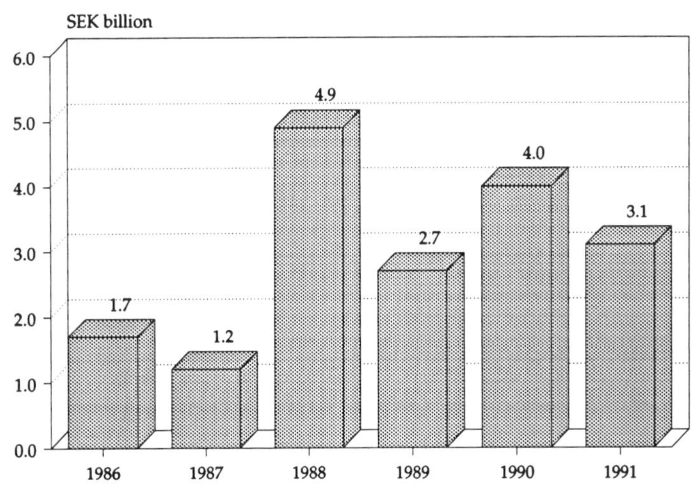

Figure 26.44 New issuance volume of bank bonds (1986-1991)

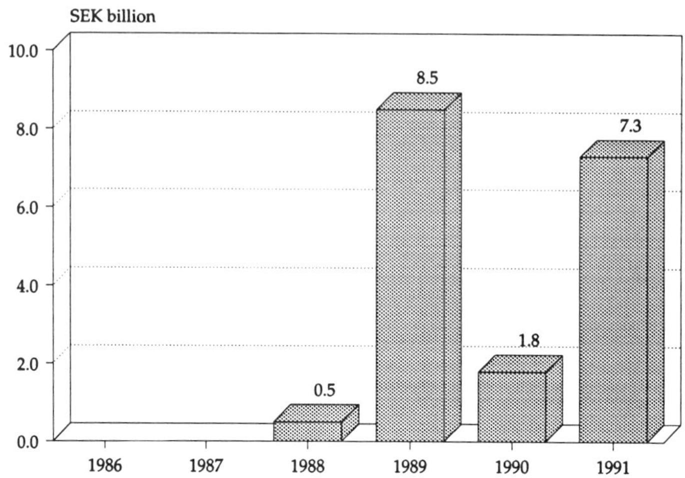

Figure 26.45 New issuance volume of eurokronor bonds (1986-1991)

26.9 *Methods of trading*

The Swedish bond market is an over-the-counter market built around a market-maker system by which market-makers quote two-way prices for a limited number of benchmark bonds. All trading - except the recently opened SOX bond market for bonds aimed at private investors - takes place outside the Stockholm Stock Exchange.

The Swedish market-maker trading system is a function of the central role that Swedish banks have always played in the bond market - as both intermediaries and investors.

Primary dealers

The National Debt Office has appointed twelve banks and stockbrokers to act as primary dealers and market-makers in government bonds.

They are:

- Carnegie Fondkommission
- Consensus Fondkommission
- Gota Bank
- JP Bank
- Nordbanken
- Skandinaviska Enskilda Banken
- Sparbankernas Bank
- Svenska Handelsbanken
- Sveriges Föreningsbank
- Transferator Fondkommission
- United Securities
- Öhman Fondkommission

Two Danish banks, Den Danske Bank and Unibörs, act as market-makers although they have not been formally appointed. Additionally, there are some brokers (Fulton, Harlow Butler and Interviking) who act on the interbank bond market.

The primary market-makers have undertaken (and are therefore obliged) to submit bids to the National Debt Office at auctions of government bonds and, furthermore, to act as market-makers in the secondary market for government bonds by always quoting two-way prices for benchmark issues. They receive commissions from the Debt Office related to their results in both the primary and secondary markets.

Quotations

Trading takes place every bank business day from 09.00 to 15.30 (from 1 September 1992, trading will be extended to 16.00). Market-makers give two-way price quotations on the Reuters, Telerate and PmI (Penningmarknadsinformation) systems, for government and mortgage benchmark bonds. Indicative prices are also given for other loans issued by the government, certain mortgage institutions and credit companies.

Prices are stated in the form of yield for all available maturities; for example, Caisse 96 11.25-30, means that the market-maker is indicating that he is willing to buy/sell bonds issued by Konungariket Sveriges Stadshypotekskassa (Caisse) with a 1996 maturity, at a price giving a yield of 11.25 per cent and 11.30 per cent respectively.

The quoted yield spread is normally three basis points for benchmark bonds, and five basis points for other daily-traded bonds. Benchmark quotations in the form of price are also available (see Reuters page SEBK)

Dealing

Business deals are closed over the telephone. Non-Swedish customers receive a fax confirmation of the deal.

Benchmark bonds

There are at present six government benchmark loans and twelve mortgage benchmark loans on the market (see Figures 26.46 & 26.47).

New benchmark loans will be added to the lists, whilst existing ones may, over time, be substituted.

Loan No.	Coupon (%)	Maturity/Coupon day	Debt amount (SEK bn)
199	11.20	01 September 1994	25.3
202	11.50	01 September 1995	33.9
1020	10.75	23 January 1997	24.3
1028	11.00	21 January 1999	20.0
1030	13.00	15 June 2001	14.0
1033	10.25	05 May 2003	25.3

Figure 26.46 Government benchmark bonds

Loan No.	Coupon (%)	Maturity/Coupon day	Debt amount (SEK bn)
MBB-95[1]	11.00	21 June 1995	24.7
MBB-96[2]	12.00	18 September 1996	25.9
MBB-97[3]	12.00	17 December 1997	13.3
SBAB 111	13.00	20 September 1995	17.9
SBAB 112	12.50	23 January 1997	12.3
Caisse 1539	10.75	02 June 1997	5.0

Figure 26.47 Mortgage benchmark bonds
[1] *SFK 526, Handelsbanken Hypotek 933, Nordbanken 5503, Spintab 154*
[2] *SFK 529, Handelsbanken Hypotek 935, Nordbanken 5505, Spintab 156*
[3] *SFK 530, Handelsbanken Hypotek 936, Nordbanken 5701, Spintab 157*

Stockholm Stock Exchange

Swedish bonds are, with few exceptions, listed on the Stockholm Stock Exchange although, as mentioned previously, no bond trading takes place on the Exchange itself. The published quotations and the turnover reported in the **daily** *Stockholm Stock Exchange Bond List* therefore only constitute the deals made in the market by the market-makers, and reported to the Stock Exchange, and their price quotations at the close of each business day.

The **daily** *Stock Exchange List* contains all bonds that meet certain criteria. For listing, bonds should:

- be loans issued by the government, mortgage institutions or some other credit institutions
- carry a coupon over 8 per cent
- not be subject to amortization
- not have any future adjustment of the coupon

The daily bond list contains information concerning not only the price, but also the yield, price risk and duration, of each loan. The daily list also includes a series of bond indices. Six maturities and three segments of the market are covered. The segments are bonds issued by 1) the government, 2) Caisse and 3) other mortgage institutions. Yields, yield-index and durations are presented daily in three matrices.

All other bonds can be found in the **monthly** *Stock Exchange List*.

26.10 *Market practices*

Denomination

For bond loans aimed at the institutional capital market, the smallest bond denomination is normally SKr 1m. For bond loans aimed at private investors, the smallest denomination is SKr 1000 or SKr 10,000.

Trading volumes

Prices quoted by market-makers apply to the standard trading volume of SKr 20m, although SKr 50m to 100m is often transacted at the same price.

Transaction costs

There are no transaction costs involved in a normal bond deal. Market-makers make their profit from trading spreads.

Spread trading

The bid/offer spread for benchmark bonds is 3 basis points (in yield). Spreads for other government and mortgage loans are normally 3 to 5 basis points. Bonds of a more illiquid character rarely have a two-way quotation.

Ex-coupon trading

Price quotations do not include accrued interest. A purchase will therefore normally include payment of accrued interest. A purchase after a specific day (i.e. the registration day) will, however, be made ex-coupon, and with a negative interest. The registration day occurs,

- for Treasury bonds nos. 1-300 : 10 days before the next coupon day
- for Treasury bonds nos. 1001- : 15 days before the next coupon day
- for mortgage bonds: 5-30 days before the next coupon day
- for VPC bonds: 5 days before the next coupon day

The daily Stockholm Stock Exchange List contains information on the registration day for each bond loan listed.

Withholding tax

Resident individuals are subject to a withholding tax which is 30 per cent, on interest paid in 1992, and 25 per cent from 1993. Non-resident investors are not subject to this withholding tax (see also Section 1.13, Taxation).

First coupon

It is common practice in the Swedish market that the loan date, coupon dates and maturity date of a loan have the same yearly day. Bonds carry coupons paying a yearly interest and this also applies to the first coupon. Swedish bond loans therefore do not have a 'short' or 'long' first coupon.

As it is common that bonds are issued well in advance of the loan date - this is a rule for mortgage bonds sold on tap - the settlement then includes a negative interest, calculated from the settlement day to the loan date, to be deducted upon settlement.

26.11 *Settlement*

Settlement day is normally two business days after the transaction day for money market instruments and five business days after the transaction day for bonds. Value day is the settlement day.

Physical delivery may take place on the settlement day. If, however, the transaction takes place between a bank and an investor who has a trust account with the bank, or between two investors with trust accounts with the same bank, a book-entry transaction substitutes the delivery.

Physical delivery takes place within the MVPC - *Manuella Värdepappers Centralen* - a clearing place where banks, stockbrokers and the largest institutional investors exchange securities for payment at 09.00 each business day. In order to facilitate bond holding, Swedish issuers normally also have a book-entry system in which all bonds are registered. Interest is paid to holders on the registration day occurring a specific number of days before each coupon day. It is therefore of importance that bonds are properly registered on that particular day.

Bond loans can also be registered with the VPC - clearing house for all stocks on the Stockholm Stock Exchange. VPC keeps a special book-entry system for bonds. The VPC system is normally used for loans intended for private investors.

Non-Swedish bond investors are obliged to deposit their bonds in a Swedish bank, or brokerage house, as Swedish bonds may not be removed from Sweden.

26.12 Yield calculation

Coupon bonds

Prices are calculated in accordance with the ISMA method, albeit with a minor adjustment.

The quoted yield, which is a simple interest rate if the maturity is one year or shorter (or a compounded yield in other cases), is used to discount all cash flows of the bond. This gives the clean price, plus accrued interest:

$$P + a = \sum_{i=1}^{n} \frac{\frac{c}{f}}{(1+\frac{r}{100})^{\frac{d_i}{360}}} + \frac{100}{(1+\frac{r}{100})^{\frac{d_n}{360}}}$$

where,

P clean price
a accrued interest
c coupon in per cent
n number of coupons to maturity
f number of coupons per year
r interest rate in per cent
d_i days from settlement to coupon i, 30/360 days basis

When there is only one coupon payment per year, which is the case for all Treasury bonds, the expression above is slightly simplified:

$$P + a = \sum_{i=1}^{n} \frac{c}{(1+\frac{r}{100})^{\frac{d_i}{360}}} + \frac{100}{(1+\frac{r}{100})^{\frac{d_n}{360}}}$$

It is important to note that the settlement price (dirty price) on the Swedish bond market will **not** be equal to (face value/100) × (P+a). Instead, let P^1 equal P rounded to three decimals, then:

Settlement price = (face value/100)*(P^1 + a)

Treasury bills and other zero-coupon bonds

For Treasury bills, the interest rate quoted is always a simple interest rate, regardless of time to maturity, and the pricing formula is therefore:

$$P = \frac{F}{1 + \frac{r}{100}\frac{d}{360}}$$

where,

P price
F face value
r interest rate (per cent)
d days to maturity, 30/360 days basis

Floating-rate notes

For pricing FRNs, the following formula should be used:

$$P + a = \sum_{i=1}^{n} \frac{k_i}{disc_i} + \frac{100}{disc_n}$$

where,

$$k_1 = c\,\frac{d_1}{360}$$

$$K_i = \frac{(r_s + m_f)}{100}\frac{d_i}{360},\; i = 2,..,n$$

$$disc_i = (1 + \frac{(r_{s+m_q})}{100}\frac{d_1}{360})\;(1 + \frac{(r_{s+m_q})}{100}\frac{d_2}{360})\cdots(1 + \frac{(r_{s+m_q})}{100}\frac{d_i}{360})$$

and,

P clean price
a accrued interest rate
n number of coupon payments
c coupon (per cent)
r_s quoted STIBOR (per cent)
m_f fixed margin (per cent)

m_q	quoted margin (per cent)
d_1	number of actual days from settlement to first coupon
d_i	number of actual days from coupon i-1 to coupon i,
i	$= 2,...,n$

26.13 *Taxation*

Taxation of resident individuals

Resident individuals are subject to national and municipal income tax on their world-wide income, and to net wealth tax on their world-wide capital. Individuals are liable to pay national and municipal income tax on the sum of employment income and un-incorporated business income (earned income). Municipal income tax is imposed at an aggregate rate of about 31 per cent. National income tax is imposed at a flat rate of 20 per cent on earned income exceeding the amount of SKr 170,000 (income year 1991). The last mentioned amount is index-adjusted every income year. The highest marginal tax rate on earned income is thus about 51 per cent.

Income from capital is taxed separately from earned income and subject to a flat 30 per cent national tax rate only. It is proposed that the tax rate on capital income be reduced to 25 per cent from the 1993 income year. However, due to a proposed transitional rule, shares disposed during the 1992 income year will be taxed at an effective rate of 25 per cent.

Income of capital includes interest, dividends and all other income derived from capital investment. Capital gains on the disposal of debt instruments are taxed in their entirety, regardless of the period of possession. In general, the taxable gain equals the difference between the selling price and the acquisition costs. In a case where a bondholder owns bonds of the same class that are acquired at different prices, the acquisition costs are defined as the average acquisition costs. If part of the purchase-sum for an acquired coupon-bearing debt instrument constitutes a payment for accrued interest, the interest amount is treated as part of the acquisition cost. As a consequence, the accrued-interest amount will only be subject to deduction at the date of the disposal of the acquired instrument. Furthermore, capital gains and losses on listed debt instruments will be treated as interest income and interest expense. This rule does not, however, apply to convertible bonds which, from a tax point of view, are treated as shares.

Interest expenses are fully deductible from taxable capital revenues. Capital losses on listed debt instruments are, as mentioned above, always treated as interest expense. Capital losses on unlisted debt instruments are only 70 per cent deductible. Capital losses on listed shares are fully deductible from gains made on similar shares. Any excess loss on listed shares, and losses on unlisted shares, are only 70 per cent deductible.

The calculation of taxable capital income is made separately from the earned income category. Tax deductible costs are thus deducted from the taxable revenues.

A net surplus is taxed at the normal rate. If a deficit, of an amount up to SKr 100,000, arises, 30 per cent of the deficit may be used as a tax credit against income taxes on earned income whilst, on any amount exceeding SKr 100,000, only 21 per cent may be used as a tax credit. As an effect of the reduced tax rate that will be applied in the 1993 income year, the above-mentioned tax credit percentages will consequently be reduced to 25 and 18 per cent, respectively.

On dividends and interest payments to resident individuals a preliminary income tax of 30 per cent is withheld at source. In the 1993 income tax year, the rate will be reduced to 25 per cent. The withheld amount is credited against the final tax that is levied on the taxpayer's total income.

A net wealth tax of 1.5 per cent is levied on net wealth exceeding SKr 800,000. This tax will be abolished as from the 1994 income year.

Taxation of resident companies

The taxable base for resident companies is their world-wide profit less allowable deductions. The only category of income is business income. National income tax is levied at a flat rate of 30 per cent. Taxable income is generally calculated in accordance with the accruals concept. Interest income and capital gains are treated as normal business income. Interest expenses and capital losses are generally deductible as business expenses. However, certain specific rules apply when shares held for capital investment purposes are sold at a loss.

Taxation of non-resident individuals

Non-resident individuals are subject to Swedish income taxes only if they receive income which is derived through a permanent establishment, or from immovable property which they have in Sweden, or from personal services performed there. Thus non-resident individuals are not normally liable to pay Swedish income tax on interest and capital gains received from Sweden. There is no form of withholding tax on interest payments to non-residents. However, information containing the name of the recipient, and the amount paid out, has to be submitted to the national tax board.

Taxation of non-resident companies

Non-resident companies are subject to Swedish income tax only if they receive business income effectively connected with immovable property or a permanent establishment in Sweden. Thus non-resident companies are not normally liable to pay income tax on interest income or capital gains. There is no form of withholding tax on interest payments and no information need be submitted to the tax authorities.

26.14 *Futures & options*

Introduction

Interest rate futures and options in the Swedish market were introduced in 1986, through the establishment of the Stockholm Options Market (OM), a corporation acting as both market-place and clearing house.

The first contract was based on a specified five-year Swedish government bond. The turnover was quite substantial throughout 1988 but, due to the government introduction of a turnover tax in 1989, the contract was withdrawn. The contract was re-introduced in April 1989, but volume was limited due to the effect of the turnover tax. In April 1990, turnover tax was abolished on bonds and other instruments related to interest rates. By then, with trade in Swedish fixed-interest instruments opened to foreigners, new contracts based on a notional seven-year 11% government bond, were introduced.

Further instruments have been introduced since then, including contracts with underlying securities of other maturities, mortgage bonds and currencies. In response to market demand, two new bond contracts were added, in September 1990, to replace the seven-year contracts, one being based on a five-year notional government bond and the other on a similar ten-year bond.

Along with the market for listed derivative products, there is an active market in over-the-counter, interest and currency-related, forward and option contracts. One of the most actively traded is the IMM three-month forward interbank interest rate. There is also an active market in interest rate swaps for maturities up to seven years. In currencies, the Swedish banks actively act as market-makers in currency forwards and options.

Bond contracts

For contract specifications, see Figures 26.48 - 26.54.

Money market contracts

For contract specifications, see Figure 26.55.

Contract size:	SEK 1,000,000 notional bond with 11% coupon
Delivery months:	March, June, September, December
Delivery day:	IMM standards, normally the third Wednesday in expiry month
Last trading day:	12.00 noon, six banking days before settlement
Quotation:	Yield-to-maturity with two decimals, e.g. 10.34%
Minimum price movement (tick size) and value:	0.01% of the yield
Trading hours:	09.30 - 15.30 Stockholm time.
Initial margin:	Related to OM's margin system
Price limit:	None
Contract standard:	Physical delivery of government bonds with a duration not differing more than approximately half a year from the fixing using a conversion factor
Reuters pages:	TERL, TERM
Telerate pages:	9298

Figure 26.48 Long-term 11.00% 5-year notional government bond (OMR5) futures - contract specification.

Contract size:	SEK 1,000,000 notional bond with 11% coupon
Delivery months:	March, June, September, December
Delivery day:	IMM standards, normally the third Wednesday in expiry month
Last trading day:	12.00 noon, six banking days before settlement
Quotation:	Yield-to-maturity with two decimals, e.g. 10.34%
Minimum price movement (tick size) and value:	0.01% of the yield
Trading hours:	09.30 - 15.30 Stockholm time
Initial margin:	Related to OM's margin system
Price limit:	None
Contract standard:	Physical delivery of government bonds with a duration not differing more than approximately half a year from the fixing using a conversion factor
Reuters pages:	OMKN
Telerate pages:	-

Figure 26.49 Long-term 11.00% 5-year notional government bond (OMR5) options - contract specification.

Contract size:	SEK 1,000,000 notional bond with 11% coupon
Delivery months:	March, June, September, December
Delivery day:	IMM standards, normally the 3rd Wednesday in expiry month
Last trading day:	12.00 noon, six banking days before settlement
Quotation:	Yield-to-maturity with two decimals, e.g. 10.34%
Minimum price movement (tick size) and value:	0.01% of the yield
Trading hours:	09.30 - 15.30 Stockholm time
Initial margin:	Related to OM's margin system
Price limit:	None
Contract standard:	Physical delivery of government bonds with a duration not differing more than approximately half a year from the fixing using a conversion factor
Reuters pages:	TERL, TERM
Telerate pages:	9298

Figure 26.50 Long-term 11.00% 10-year notional government bond (OMR10) futures - contract specification.

Contract size:	SEK 1,000,000 notional bond with 11% coupon
Delivery months:	March, June, September, December
Delivery day:	IMM standards, normally the 3rd Wednesday in expiry month
Last trading day:	12.00 noon, six banking days before settlement
Quotation:	
Minimum price movement (tick size) and value:	
Trading hours:	09.30 - 16.00 Stockholm time
Initial margin:	OM margin system
Price limit:	None
Contract standard:	Cash settlement of all futures contracts against settlement yield. For net positions delivery of deliverable mortgage bonds at settlement yield. Deliverable bonds are 1/4 of each MBB (Handelsbanken Hypotek, SFK and Nordbanken Kredit, Spintab) and SBAB
Reuters pages:	TERJ
Telerate pages:	9298

Figure 26.51 Long-term 11.00% 5-year notional mortgage bond (OMBO5) futures - contract specification.

Contract size:	SEK 1,000,000 notional bond with 11% coupon
Delivery months:	March, June, September, December
Delivery day:	IMM standards, normally the 3rd Wednesday in expiry month
Last trading day:	12.00 noon, six banking days before settlement
Quotation:	
Minimum price movement (tick size) and value:	
Trading hours:	09.30 - 16.00 Stockholm time
Initial margin:	OM margin system
Price limit:	None
Contract standard:	Cash settlement of all futures contracts against settlement yield. For net positions delivery of deliverable mortgage bonds at settlement yield. Deliverable bonds are 1/4 of each MBB (Handelsbanken Hypotek, SFK and Nordbanken Kredit, Spintab) and SBAB
Reuters pages:	-
Telerate pages:	-

Figure 26.52 Long-term 11.00% 2-year notional mortgage bond (OMBO2) futures contract spec.

Contract size:	SEK 1,000,000 notional bond with 11% coupon
Delivery months:	March, June, September, December
Delivery day:	IMM standards, normally the 3rd Wednesday in expiry month
Last trading day:	12.00 noon, six banking days before settlement
Quotation:	
Minimum price movement (tick size) and value:	
Trading hours:	09.30 - 16.00 Stockholm time
Initial margin:	OM margin system
Price limit:	None
Contract standard:	Cash settlement of all futures contracts against settlement yield. For net positions delivery of deliverable mortgage bonds at settlement yield. Deliverable bonds are Stadshypotekskassan (Caisse)
Reuters pages:	TEMH
Telerate pages:	9298

Figure 26.53 Long-term 11.00% 5-year Caisse bond (C5) futures - contract specification.

Contract size:	SEK 1,000,000 notional bond with 11% coupon
Delivery months:	March, June, September, December
Delivery day:	IMM standards, normally the 3rd Wednesday in expiry month
Last trading day:	12.00 noon, six banking days before settlement
Quotation:	
Minimum price movement (tick size) and value:	
Trading hours:	09.30 - 16.00 Stockholm time
Initial margin:	OM margin system
Price limit:	None
Contract standard:	Cash settlement of all futures contracts against settlement yield. For net positions delivery of deliverable mortgage bonds at settlement yield. Deliverable bonds are Stadshypotek (Caisse)
Reuters pages:	TEVZ
Telerate pages:	9298

Figure 26.54 Short-term 11.00% 2-year Caisse bond (C2) futures - contract specification.

Contract size:	SEK 1,000,000
Delivery months:	March, June, September, December
Delivery day:	IMM standards, normally the 3rd Wednesday in expiry month
Last trading day:	11.00 a.m, three bank days prior to expiration settlement day
Quotation:	Six-month rate
Minimum price movement (tick size) and value:	
Trading hours:	08.30 - 16.15 Stockholm time (08.30 - 13.00 on expiry day)
Initial margin:	OMS system
Price limit:	None
Contract standard:	Cash settlement of all futures contracts against yield. Thereafter delivery of treasury bills at fixing of net position of all futures contracts. Treasury bills with maturity during the fifth, sixth or seventh months after the future's expiry day are deliverable
Delivery settlement price:	The fixing yield determined in Statsfix at 11.00 (Stockholm time) on the expiry day of the futures contract which is derived from Treasury bills with six months to maturity
Reuters pages:	TERK
Telerate pages:	9298

Figure 26.55 Treasury bill futures (OMSVX180) - contract specification.

26.15 *Money markets*

Sweden has a well developed domestic money market, with a complete array of instruments available to investors. The following is a brief description of some of the short-term instruments available.

Treasury bills (SSV)

Treasury bills are promissory bearer notes issued by the National Debt Office. The Swedish Treasury bill market started in 1982 and has, at times, been the largest and most efficient segment of the money market with high volumes and good liquidity. The volume outstanding by year-end 1991, was SKr 305bn.

Coupon

Treasury bills are issued at a discount and have no interest payments.

Maturities

3, 6 and 12 months at issue.

Interest payment

Discount securities.

Denomination

SKr 1, 5, 10, 20, 50, 100m.

Issuing intervals

Usually every second week.

Issue volumes

SKr 1 - 7bn.

Price information

Reuters, Telerate, PmI.

Prices

Prices are quoted on a discount yield basis.

Interest calculation

30/360 days.

Issue technique

Auction. Tenders through dealers approved by the Debt Office.

Investors

All sectors are investors in this paper and it is of course to a large extent used by the central bank in its open market operations.

Commercial paper

Commercial paper (CP) is a short-term, negotiable, unsecured promissory note in bearer form and issued within the framework of a CP programme, with which a borrower can raise short-term funds to the limit of the programme with a minimum borrowing amount of SKr 1m (although 20-50m is a normal borrowing amount).

The Swedish CP market started in 1983 and has developed very rapidly to become the fourth-largest domestic CP market in the world. There are nearly 200 programmes with a total programme size of about SKr 300bn. Approximately 30 per cent of the total programme volume is estimated to be outstanding debt.

The market was severely hurt in October 1990, when several finance companies were unable to roll-over their commercial paper. The incident triggered a general loss of market confidence towards second-rated borrowers. The market has since recovered, but investors are still generally reluctant to buy unrated CPs.

Yield

Usually set at a spread over STIBOR (Stockholm Interbank Offered Rate).

Maturity

From 7 days to two years.

Prices

Prices are quoted on a yield-to-maturity basis.

Interest and yield calculation

Interest is on a 30/360 days basis.

Issuers

Corporations, mortgage institutions, credit companies, municipalities and finance companies.

Investors

Corporations, municipalities, money market funds, capital market institutions and others with surplus liquidity.

Certificates of deposit

Certificates of deposit, evidence of a time deposits made with issuing banks, are negotiable instruments . In contrast to FRNs, CDs are treated as bank deposits and rank *pari passu* with all other deposits, while FRNs are subordinated to deposits.

Coupon

Fixed-rate.

Maturity

From 1 day to two years.

Interest payment

Interest is paid at maturity.

Prices

Prices are quoted on a yield-to-maturity basis.

Interest calculation

Interest is on a 30/360 days basis. CDs are discount papers.

Issuers

Banks.

Investors

Banks, financial institutions, large co-operations and municipalities.

Floating-rate notes (FRN)

FRNs are medium- or long-term bonds in which the coupon, linked to money market rates, is adjusted at regular intervals.

Coupon

Normally spread over/under 3-month STIBOR (Stockholm Interbank Offered Rate).

Interest adjustment

Normally per IMM-days (third Wednesday in March, June, September and December).

Maturity

Normally 5-10 years when issued.

Interest payment

Normally at the same time as interest adjustment.

Prices

Prices are quoted as yield-to-maturity. In addition, information is given about margin between yield and 3-month Treasury bills.

Interest and yield calculation

Interest is on a 365/360 days basis.

Issuers

Mainly banks and mortgage institutions. FRNs have also been issued by municipalities and corporates.

Investors

Banks, insurance companies, pension funds, corporates etc.

Calls

No loans have call options outstanding at present.

Other structures

There are still a few issues on the market in which the coupon is fixed to 3-month Treasury bills. However, no loans have recently been issued with this type of interest fixing.

26.16 Interest rate history

1989

During 1989, and particularly during the latter part of the year, the participants in the Swedish market started to acknowledge the growing problems of imbalance in the Swedish economy. Great concern was focused on the current account deficit which re-appeared after a few years of balance or surplus. The

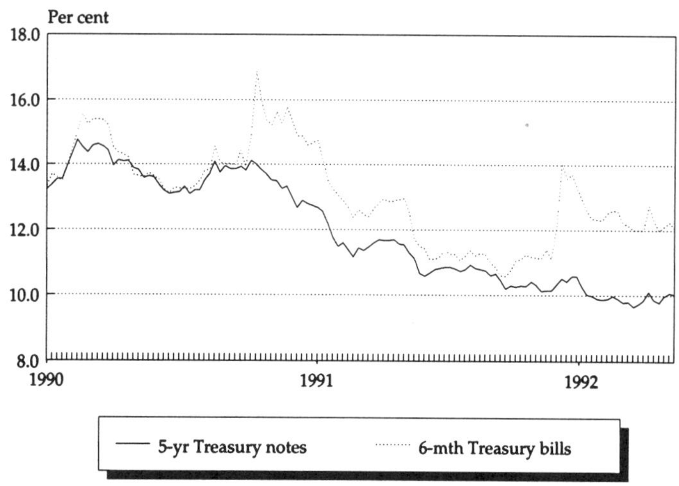

Figure 26.56 Swedish interest rates, 1987-1992
Source: S-E-Bank Economic Research Group

deficit caused money market rates to increase and, at the same time, the krona weakened - resulting in an outflow of currency. The central bank had to concentrate on the defence of the krona and it was the maintenance of a stable exchange rate which came to be the policy-target of 1990. The money market, therefore, had little choice but to adjust to this policy.

1990

As a consequence of the higher spreads between Swedish interest rates and international interest rates, the outflow of currency stopped at the beginning of

1990. At the same time, the krona weakened within its index span, with the result that krona investments therefore became more attractive. However, in spite of this, no inflow of currency was registered. In the beginning of 1990, a labour conflict in the banking sector occurred, causing most major operations in the financial markets to halt; only minor trades in the currency market could be maintained.

During the strike, the government proposed a package of economic and political measures in an attempt to halt cost-inflation and the weakening of external balances. This led to a government crisis to which the financial markets responded immediately - a new outflow of currency was registered (despite the continuing strike). Emphasizing its goal of a stable krona, the central bank responded forcefully to the situation by tightening monetary policy and forcing up the banks' borrowing rate at the central bank, from 12 per cent to 15 per cent.

When the conflict in the banking sector was over and the markets re-opened, money market interest rates were up by 200 basis points and Swedish interest rate spreads against major currencies, measured on a 6-month basis, were up from 2.2 per cent to 4 per cent. The 5-year bond yield went up by only 100 basis points, causing the yield curve to become negative. An inflow of currency was registered and the krona strengthened. As the governmental crisis settled at the end of February and the political situation returned to normal, the central bank was able to ease interest rates and, by the end of May, they were almost back to where they were before the turmoil.

In April 1990, the notorious turnover tax on interest-bearing instruments was removed, leading to an immediate and substantial rise in turnover and thus improving the function of the markets.

The calmness that prevailed during the spring, and most of the summer, was abruptly ended by the Iraqi invasion of Kuwait. Short-term interest rates rose by 100 basis points while the krona weakened once again. Even long-term interest rates rose by 100 basis points, which was somewhat more than elsewhere in the world.

One reason for Swedish interest rates rising more than those abroad was the fear that, with an uncertain global outlook, the Swedish economy would be hit harder than others because of its perceived financial weakness. At the end of September 1990, the market learned that some of the largest financial companies had run into severe problems, suffering major defaults in their credit portfolios. The event made big headlines internationally and caused foreign investors and other market participants to take a more cautious attitude towards krona investments.

At the beginning of October 1990, rumours spread that Sweden was going to change its currency policy. Such rumours were strengthened by the entry of sterling into the ERM - the market speculating that, after a depreciation, the krona would be linked to the Ecu. The rumours spread internationally, which was not surprising given the uncertainty surrounding both Swedish economic development and policy. Substantial outflows of currency were registered. To defend its firm monetary policies, the central bank was forced, once again, to raise interest rates by market operations. In spite of a rise of 200 basis points for loans from the central bank, no signs of currency inflows were registered. The central bank raised marginal lending rates to 17 per cent and, at the same time, it intervened heavily on the market by selling large amounts of Treasury bills. This policy resulted in an immediate response and currency flows turned. An announcement by the government that public spending would be curbed contributed to this effect, as did the decision to speed-up the process of gaining full membership of the European Community. Slowly, money market rates came down, as did long-term interest rates, although this was perhaps more due to the evidence of a true recessionary environment.

It is important to recall that, as of 1 July 1989, foreign investors were allowed to invest directly in the Swedish markets. The turbulent situation during 1990 and the ensuing high yields, caused a net inflow from foreign investors, of around SKr 120bn.

1991

Swedish interest rates fell comparatively steeply for most of 1991. The main factors were lower international interest rates, weaker inflationary expectations and the pegging of the krona to the Ecu.

The pegging of the krona to the Ecu in May, was followed in June by the application for full membership of the EC. This resulted in strengthened confidence in the central bank's exchange policy and accordingly, in May and June, interest rates fell by one to two percentage points. Foreign investors became highly interested in krona investments in the early summer, resulting in an inflow of currencies of nearly SKr 30bn in May and June. Investors became convinced that Sweden was going to adjust its economy to the requirements inherent in EC membership, including a lowering of the relatively high inflation rate to that of the existing EC-member countries.

During the summer, interest rates continued to fall, even though a net outflow of currencies (of SKr 23bn) was registered from July through to September. At the beginning of September, the Swedish interest rate was just above 10 per cent. As there had been no corresponding fall in international interest rates the difference between Swedish interest rates and Ecu interest rates narrowed to approximately 50 basis points. The summer of 1991 therefore saw a weakening of the krona. The reduced interest differential discouraged Swedish corporates from borrowing abroad and investing in krona interest-bearing papers, with the result that an outflow of currency was registered in late summer.

The central bank reacted by raising short-term interest rates to stem the outflow and, in October and November, it was stabilized. With persistent expectations of a further reduction in the rate of inflation, bond rates continued to fall; in October, the rate for five year government bonds was less than 10 per cent, a level not seen since 1986.

In the middle of November the Finnish markka was devalued. This raised doubts as to whether Sweden was going to be able to pursue its exchange rate policy, which had led to substantial currency outflows. In the last weeks of November and the first week of December, the registered outflow was SKr 31bn. There were several other reasons for the outflow. There was an uncertainty over whether the budget plan (to be presented in January 1992) would be sufficiently tight and also over whether Swedish corporates would renew their foreign-currency borrowing as and when the interest rate differential returned to less than 100 basis points.

In late November and early December, the central bank tightened its monetary policy by raising the overnight rates, initially from 10.5 to 11 per cent and subsequently (since the first rise had not stemmed the outflow), by an additional 6 percentage points, to 17.5 per cent. As a result, the differential *vis-à-vis* the Ecu widened to 4.5 percentage points. The currency flow showed an immediate response, with an inflow of SKr 26bn reported for the second week in December. Confidence in Swedish exchange policy returned and interest rates continued to fall. By comparison to the levels seen at the beginning of the year, five-year government bonds showed a fall of about two percentage points while six-month Treasury bills fell one percentage point.

The drop in interest rates has continued further in 1992.

26.17 Inter-market spreads

The most interesting inter-market spreads are as follows:

- mortgage bond yield vs. government bond yield (see Figure 26.57)
- eurokronor bond yield vs. government bond yield
- STIBOR vs. Treasury bills (see Figure 26.59)
- domestic commercial paper vs. Treasury bills (see Figure 26.60)

The mortgage bond - government bond spread

This spread has been closely watched by Swedish investors since 1986, when the central bank deregulated interest rates for government and mortgage bonds. Through 1986 and in the beginning of 1987, the spread was as high as 125 basis points (bp), but it narrowed down to 20bp during 1987 and 1988. This can be attributed to an improved liquidity in mortgage bonds - the credit rating of the mortgage institutes being regarded as high. From that narrow spread of 20 bp, a

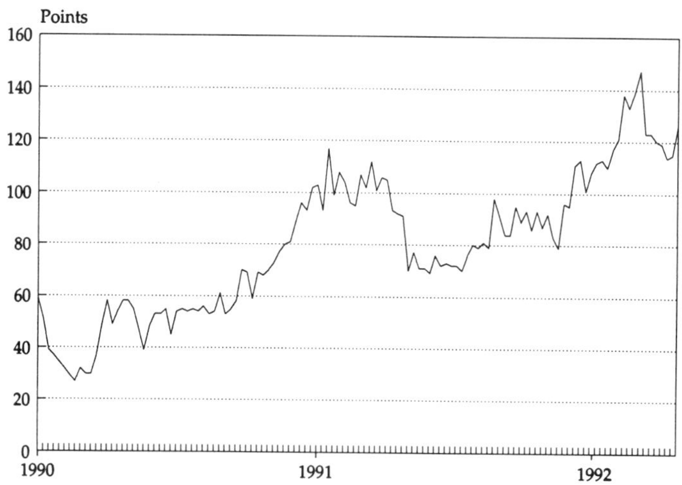

Figure 26.57 Mortgage bond (Caisse) yield vs. government bond yield
Source: Svenska Handelsbanken Economic Research

slow widening was seen during 1989 and 1990, to approximately 50 bp. In autumn of 1990, the crises within the real estate and finance company sectors occurred, leading to a widening of the spread from 50 bp to 110 bp. After that, the spread narrowed to 70 bp in mid-1991, only to rebound to 130 bp at the end of 1991, the rebound being due to falling prices in the property market and worries that mortgage institutions might suffer credit losses as a result.

Since the autumn of 1991, there has also been a widening yield differential between mortgage bonds issued by different mortgage institutions; for example, the spread between bonds issued by Caisse and bonds issued by Spintab and Nordbanken Kredit was 35 bp at the end of 1991.

The eurokronor bond - government bond spread

When eurokronor bonds were issued in late-1988, the yield on the euros were lower than those of Swedish government bonds. This negative spread continued in 1989, but narrowed when Swedish currency regulations were abolished in mid-1989. Most of the eurokronor bonds were issued for arbitrage opportunities. The proceeds from a eurokronor issue could be invested in Swedish government or mortgage bonds that had a much higher yield than the yield of the issue. The yield on eurokronor bonds were higher than the government bond yield in December 1991, but issues with a high-rating still trade at a lower yield than mortgage bonds.

The STIBOR - Treasury bill spread

The spread between Treasury bills and STIBOR, which has normally been in the range of 30-40 basis points, is due to a difference in credit-standing and liquidity. There is an obvious correlation between the size of the spread and the level of the market interest rate. At times, when the central bank has taken measures to increase the short-term market rates, the spread has widened.

The commercial paper - Treasury bill spread

Until autumn 1990, the best Swedish corporate CP borrowers (rated K1 by Nordisk Rating) had a borrowing cost that was approximately 25 bp higher than the T-bill yield. The spread increased to 35 bp during 1990 and 1991 for the same reasons that caused the higher spread between mortgage bonds and government bonds. The biggest shift in spreads has occurred for the non-K1 papers. Until autumn 1990, very little difference (5-10 bp) existed between the top-rated and other issuers of commercial paper. A year later, in October 1991, only a few issuers with a K2 rating were able to issue commercial paper and the spread over T-bills could be as high as 100 bp. The investors had a very different view of credit risk in 1991 than earlier.

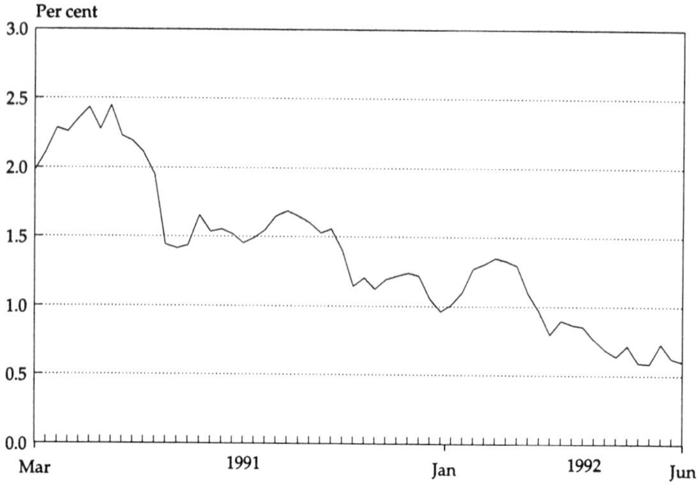

Figure 26.58 10-yr Treasury bond 2001 vs. Ecu 2001
Source: Svenska Handelsbanken Economic Research

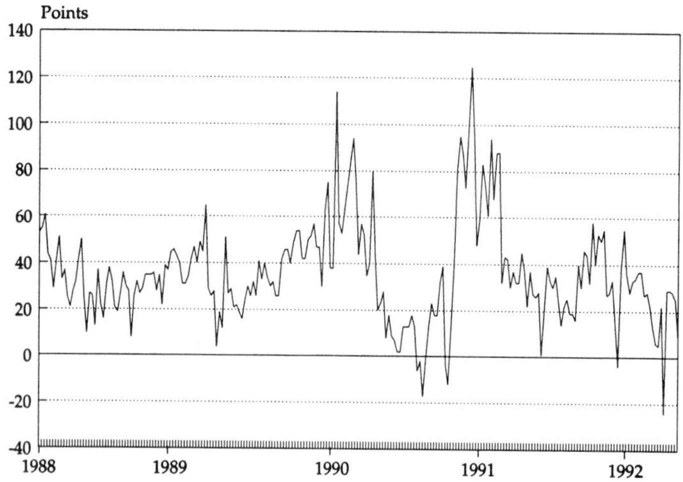

Figure 26.59 STIBOR vs. Treasury bills
Source: Svenska Handelsbanken Economic Research

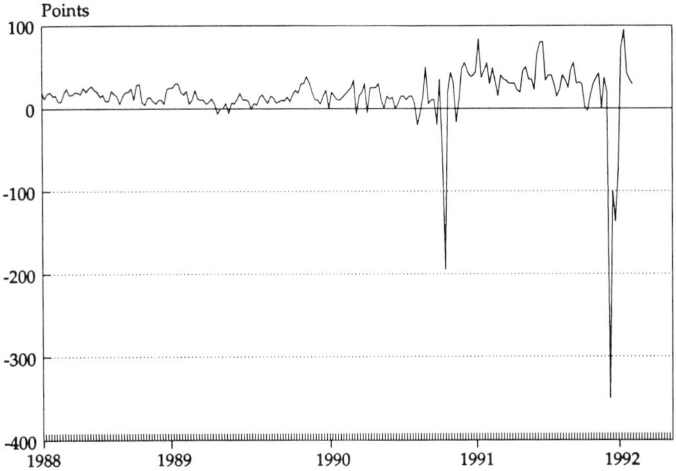

Figure 26.60 Domestic commercial paper vs. Treasury bills
Source: Svenska Handelsbanken Economic Research

26.18 *Sources of reference*

Financial data

Swedish Central Bureau of Statistics (Statistiska Centralbyrån)

- *Official Statistics of Sweden* (yearly)
- *Monthly Digest of Swedish Statistics* (monthly)
- Statistical reports with summaries in English on:
  - Credit market (about 14/year)
  - National accounts (about 11/year)
  - Public finance (about 20/year)
  - Prices and consumption (about 50/year)

These publications are chargeable and can be obtained on application to SCB Förlag (+46 019 17 6800).

Ministry of Finance (Finansdepartementet)

- *The Swedish Budget,* in summary (once a year in January)
- *The Revised Budget Statement* (yearly)
- *The Revised Finance Bill* (yearly)

These publications are chargeable and can be obtained on application to Allmänna Förlaget (+46 8 739 96 30).

Bank of Sweden (Sveriges Riksbank)

- *Annual Report* (yearly)
- *Quarterly Review* (Money and Foreign Exchange policy)
- *Statistical Yearbook*
- *Assets and Liabilities* (weekly and monthly)
- *Credit and Foreign Exchange* (yearly)
- Occasional papers

These publications are chargeable and can be obtained on application to the Library, Sveriges Riksbank (Bank of Sweden) (+46 8 787 00 00).

The Swedish National Debt Office (Riksgäldskontoret)

- *Annual Report* (yearly)
- *Statistical Yearbook*

- *Monthly Statement of the National Debt of Sweden*

These publications are obtainable free of charge on application to the Information Department. The Swedish National Debt Office (+46 8 613 45 00).

Financial press (in Swedish)

Daily:

- *Dagens Industri* (with a short summary in English)
- *Finanstidningen*
- *Svenska Dagbladet*
- *Dagens Nyheter*

Weekly:

- *Affärsvärlden*
- *Veckans Affärer*

Quote vendors and news agencies

Reuters and Telerate both provide information on the Swedish market (see Figures 26.61 & 26.62).

Page No.	Contributor	Subject
Central Bank		
RIKA	Bank of Sweden	Recent prices of T-bills and bonds
RIKD-J	Bank of Sweden	Turnover, repo information
RIKN-O	Bank of Sweden	Economics
RIKR-Z	Bank of Sweden	Lending, statistics
Swedish National Debt Office		
PMRH-O	National Debt Off.	Auction results, interest rates
Economics		
SCUB	Statistics Sweden	Index page
Prices		
General		
PMJP	Multi-contributor	Index page
Bond and money markets		
PMJP	JP Bank	
PMHD	Svenska Handelsbanken	
PMSE	Skandinaviska Enskilda Banken	
PMGO	Gota Bank	
PMBF	Swedbank	
PMFD	Föreningsbanken	
PMUS	United Securities	
PMNH	Nordbanken	
PMCF	Carnegie Fondkommission	
PMTR	Transferator Fondkommission	
PMCO	Consensus Fondkommission	
PMOR	Öhman Fondkommission	
PMMU	Midland Montagu Bank	

Figure 26.61 Reuters pages

Page No.	Contributor	Subject
Central Bank		
3342-43	Bank of Sweden	
Swedish National Debt Office		
3344-46	National Debt Off.	
Economics		
6266	Statistics Sweden	
Prices		
9298	Multi-contributor	
6293	Multi-contributor	
6263	Multi-contributor	

Figure 26.62 Telerate pages

Appendix 1: Government bonds

No.	Coupon (%)	Redemption date	Amount outstanding (SEK million)	Denomination
Treasury bonds				
181	11.875	12 August 1992	500	a
183	12.125	10 November 1992	1200	a
186	11.500	15 January 1993	3600	a
188	11.700	12 February 1993	7700	a
190	12.500	18 March 1993	1700	a
191	11.400	08 April 1993	1600	a
192	12.000	10 September 1993	700	a
193	11.300	10 September 1993	6000	a
194	12.000	11 October 1993	100	a
195	11.500	11 October 1993	1900	a
196	11.550	08 December 1993	100	b
197	11.100	02 February 1994	5000	b
198	10.800	01 May 1994	2500	b
199	11.200	01 September 1994	25,300	b
200	13.050	05 April 1995	700	b
201	13.750	01 June 1995	2000	b
202	11.500	01 September 1995	33,900	b
203	11.000	02 September 1996	6000	b
204	10.000	04 October 1996	1300	b
205	8.500	20 November 1996	600	b

For key to denominations, see end of table

No.	Coupon (%)	Redemption date	Amount outstanding (SEK million)	Denomination
Treasury bonds				
1010	13.000	28 August 1992	1800	b
1012	13.00	21 May 1992	4000	b
1013	11.850	15 January 1993	3000	b
1015	10.650	03 may 1993	2000	b
1016	9.750	23 January 1992	2200	b
1017	9.250	21 January 1994	3000	b
1019	9.250	23 August 1993	3000	b
1020	10.750	23 January 1997	24,300	b
1022	11.650	23 February 1995	8000	b
1023	10.750	21 April 1994	6000	b
1025	11.750	23 January 1998	12,000	b
1026	11.600	10 February 1999	3000	b
1027	11.400	24 August 1997	3600	b
1028	11.000	21 January 1999	20,000	b
1029	11.000	05 May 2000	10,000	c
1030	13.000	15 June 2001	14,000	c
1031	13.000	10 December 1996	5500	c
1032	11.000	23 April 2002	14,500	c
1033	10.250	05 May 2003	25,300	c

Key to denominations:

a: Minimum denomination of SEK 1000

b: Minimum denomination of SEK 1,000,000

c: Minimum denomination of SEK 100,000

Appendix 2: Mortgage bonds

Selected straight issues, no call.

No.	Coupon (%)	Redemption date	Amount outstanding (SEK million)	Denomination
Stadshypotekskassan (Caisse)				
*1515	12.25	01 August 1992	4140	b
*1516	11.75	01 November 1992	2795	b
*1517	11.50	01 December 1992	4589	b
*1518	11.00	01 December 1992	1389	b
*1519	11.50	01 March 1993	3589	b
*1520	11.00	01 April 1993	2751	b
*1521	10.50	02 May 1993	1771	b
*1522	11.00	01 June 1993	6063	b
*1523	11.00	01 August 1993	1959	b
*1524	10.75	01 September 1993	3546	b
*1525	11.25	01 November 1993	8039	b
*1526	11.50	01 December 1993	4652	b
*1527	11.25	01 February 1994	5388	b
*1528	10.25	01 March 1994	2108	b
*1529	10.50	02 May 1994	2366	b
*1530	11.00	01 June 1994	6479	b
*1531	11.25	01 September 1994	5318	b
*1532	11.25	01 March 1995	5831	b
*1533	14.50	03 July 1995	11,434	b
*1534	14.00	01 March 1996	12,788	b
*1535	12.25	03 June 1996	7378	b
*1536	11.25	02 September 1996	7700	b
*1537	11.50	02 December 1996	12,647	b
*1538	10.75	03 March 1997	10,158	b
*1539	10.75	02 June 1997	5000	b

For key to denominations, see end of table

No.	Coupon (%)	Redemption date	Amount outstanding (SEK million)	Denomination
Spintab				
104	12.25	15 September 1992	4520	b
105	11.75	15 December 1992	3501	b
106	11.75	15 March 1993	11034	b
107	10.50	15 June 1993	2330	b
108	11.00	15 September 1993	12363	b
109	11.50	15 December 1993	4695	b
110	11.00	01 February 1994	10,202	b
150	11.00	10 April 1994	4594	b
151	11.25	15 June 1994	3470	b
152	11.50	15 December 1994	1540	a
153	11.50	15 December 1994	8654	a
154	11.00	21 June 1995	9284	a
155	13.00	19 September 1997	16,959	b
156	12.00	18 September 1996	9487	a
157	12.00	17 December 1997	7003	c
158	11.00	19 March 1997	5960	c
Statens Bostadsfinansieringsaktiebolag (SBAB)				
104	12.50	10 December 1992	3055	b
105	11.50	10 March 1993	3025	b
106	12.00	10 June 1993	95	b
107	11.50	10 November 1993	3310	b
108	10.50	15 April 1994	1720	b
109	11.25	15 June 1994	3971	b
110	11.50	15 September 1994	3431	b
111	13.00	20 September 1995	17,930	b
112	12.50	23 January 1997	12,286	b

For key to denominations, see end of table

No.	Coupon (%)	Redemption date	Amount outstanding (SEK million)	Denomination
Svensk Fastighetskredit (SEB Mortgage)				
513	13.00	01 October 1992	979	b
514	12.25	01 October 1992	710	b
515	11.875	15 December 1992	1208	b
516	11.75	01 April 1993	540	b
517	11.00	01 April 1993	1544	b
518	11.75	01 July 1993	1861	b
519	11.75	01 October 1993	1455	b
*520	11.20	15 January 1994	2793	b
521	12.00	15 January 1994	1303	b
523	10.50	10 April 1994	1670	b
524	11.25	30 September 1994	2529	b
*525	11.00	10 July 1994	1650	b
*526	11.00	21 June 1995	8340	b
*529	12.00	18 September 1996	5833	c
*530	12.00	17 December 1997	1616	c
534	11.00	19 March 1997	420	c

Key to denominations:

*: SEK 10,000 denominations via Euroclear

a: Minimum denomination of SEK 1000

b: Minimum denomination of SEK 1,000,000

c: Minimum denomination of SEK 100,000

Chapter

27

The bond markets of

Switzerland

Ernst Zbinden
Bank Leu

Dr. Werner Stricker

Note: In general text, the abbreviation 'SFr' is used to denote the Swiss franc. Elsewhere, the international mnemonic 'CHF' is used.

27.1 Introduction

Within the Swiss economy, the financial sector plays an important role whilst, in an international context, its attraction as a financial centre ranks far above average. Traditionally the primary factors contributing to its position have been:

- a stable political system and neutrality
- a high GNP per capita, low inflation, a high savings rate and, predominant budget surpluses
- a stable currency and low interest rates
- a well-developed banking system, with an emphasis on international asset management

However, in almost all of the above, Switzerland has recently lost some of its comparative advantage. Domestically, the fundamentals of the Swiss economy, as measured by the relative inflation rate and anticipated budget deficits, have worsened considerably. As far as Switzerland's international role is concerned, discussions on whether or not to join the European Economic Area (EEA), and eventually the EC, have only just begun, but it is clear that any move in this direction will have a major impact on the political, economical and social structure of the country. A referendum to ratify the EEA treaty is to be taken in 1992.

The fixed-interest securities sector, an important part of the financial marketplace, has also assumed an above-average importance in an international context. However, it differs markedly in structure from other markets as indicated by:

- the relatively small significance of the Swiss franc government bond market
- the above-average importance of the Swiss franc foreign bond market
- an absence of a Swiss franc eurobond market
- a high proportion of private placements
- the virtual absence of a money market
- the importance of the warrants market
- the importance of Japanese issuers

The Swiss bond market's development over the last few years has been marked by:

- the removal of fixed trading commissions
- a significance increase in institutional investment
- the introduction of securities lending and borrowing

- the introduction of screen-based trading of interest rate futures contracts
- changes in the syndication structures
- the increasing significance of the swap-driven market

The prime factors determining the exchange rate and interest rates in Switzerland will continue to be: relative inflation trends, budget deficits at all levels of government and the yield differential *vis-à-vis* Germany.

As far as the capital markets are concerned, the following developments are likely:

- the introduction of an electronic trading system for bonds (EBS), planned for 1994
- the complete or partial abolition of the turnover tax
- the introduction of options on futures
- the issuance of more benchmark bonds
- increasing liquidity in the government bond market

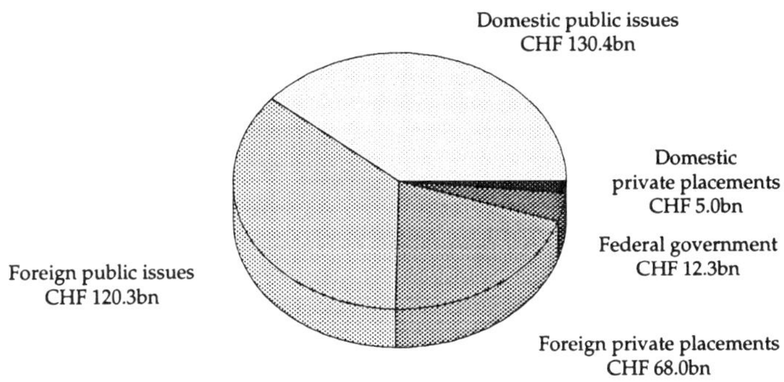

Figure 27.1 The structure of the Swiss bond market

The Swiss bond market comprises five primary sectors (see Figure 27.1):

- federal government issues
- public issues of Swiss borrowers
- private placements of Swiss borrowers
- public issues of foreign borrowers
- private placements of foreign borrowers

Note: Official statistics in Switzerland are restricted primarily to new issues and outstanding volumes on listed bonds. There are few statistics available for private placements. For these reasons, certain figures produced in this chapter are based on estimates provided by Bank Leu.

27.2 Economics

Introduction

Switzerland has no natural resources to speak of and there is very little large-scale production of basic industrial goods yet, paradoxically, the Swiss enjoy the highest income per capita in Europe.

Traditionally, the Swiss population enjoy a high standard of education and this, together with a strong work-ethic, has favoured the manufacture of value-added products such as specialized chemicals, pharmaceuticals and precision machines. The same qualities have helped to build up the strong service sector in areas such as banking, insurance and engineering. Since the domestic market is comparatively small, those corporations wishing to expand are dependent upon exports and the establishment of interests abroad and, for this reason, the interdependence of the Swiss economy and the world economy has steadily increased. Swiss production facilities were left unscathed by the Second World War and therefore enjoyed a favourable post-war economic position by comparison to other European countries. Additionally, political neutrality and stability (as well as strong banking secrecy), attracted a great deal of foreign capital which contributed to the rapid growth of Switzerland as a financial centre. The relatively high savings rate also was conducive to the growth of the economy.

As noted earlier, however, the comparative advantages of Switzerland have seen erosion in recent years and there are both internal and external reasons for this. Internally, Switzerland has had a generally higher inflation rate than its major trading partners; additionally, the economy has recently suffered unprecedented rates of interest as well as gradually rising taxes. Externally, other countries have caught up with Switzerland in certain areas due, in no small part, to the creation of the EC's 12-nation single market and the subsequent goal of economic and monetary union. The population of Switzerland will soon decide, by referendum, whether or not to join the EEA (and later, the EC), a move which the majority of the federal government and business community seems to favour.

Politics

Switzerland's political system is based upon direct democracy. Within the confederation, there are 20 cantons and 6 half-cantons. The cantons enjoy a relatively strong autonomy. The legislature on the federal level consists of two bodies: On one side are the 200 representatives making up the National Council (lower house) whilst on the other are the 46 members of the Council of States (upper house). Together, they form the parliament and are subject to election every four years (the last elections were held in the autumn of 1991). Due to the multi-party system, and the inclination of the Swiss population to avoid extreme changes, elections have never resulted in major political shifts. Thus, for the last few decades, Switzerland has enjoyed a long period of relative political stability. An additional contribution to this stability is the fact that the government, elected by the Parliament, cannot be removed from power by a vote of no confidence. The political attitude of the population is predominantly conservative/liberal, favouring a market-driven economy. Radicals and communists have never played a major role in Swiss political life. In the legislative process, representatives of the business community have traditionally held a strong position and, for this reason, politics has had no major influence on the Swiss capital markets or the determination of interest and exchange rate developments.

Political aspects will however take centre stage in the near future. The successful conclusion of the draft treaty for joining the European Economic Area (EEA) and the decision of the government to press for membership of the 18-nation EEA, have already increased the pressure for Swiss interest rates to converge, upward, to general European interest rates. As noted earlier, whether or not Switzerland will eventually become a member of the EEA is subject to a national referendum to be held in 1992. Beyond the EEA, the government intends to apply for membership of the EC but, again, whether this will come to fruition is open to question.

Gross domestic product

Between 1983 and 1990, Switzerland experienced the most prolonged expansion of business since the Second World War. Real gross domestic product (GDP), the most comprehensive measure of domestic output of goods and services, showed quarterly growth rates of between 2.5 per cent and 3.5 per cent (year-on-year rate, seasonally-adjusted). The Swiss economy therefore expanded beyond its long-term growth path (set at 2 per cent to 2.5 per cent). Since the first half of 1990, however, the business cycle has clearly turned downward. While industrial production and services were still producing at full capacity until the third quarter of 1990, construction activity had already slowed down, due to high interest rates. In the fourth quarter of 1990, economic growth declined considerably, although a major recession was avoided by consumer demand, which held up well; Switzerland incurred the first negative quarterly real growth rate since 1982 (see Figure 27.2). This fall in growth was due to the slowdown in international business activity, the high level of domestic interest rates and uncertainties created by the war in the Gulf. In the first quarter of 1991, economic activity fell further, although the majority of researchers felt that the economy bottomed out in the first half of the year. For the whole year, real GDP is projected to have fallen by between 0.5 per cent and 0.75 per cent. For 1992, little

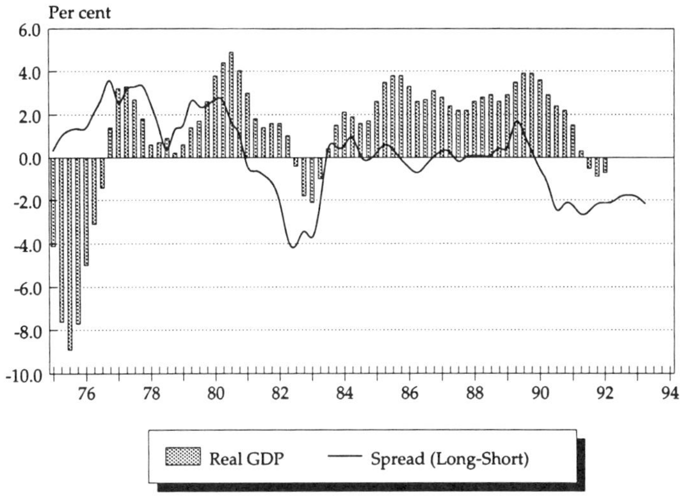

Figure 27.2 Swiss GDP (y-o-y) & interest structure (interest spread advanced by one year)
Source: Bank Leu

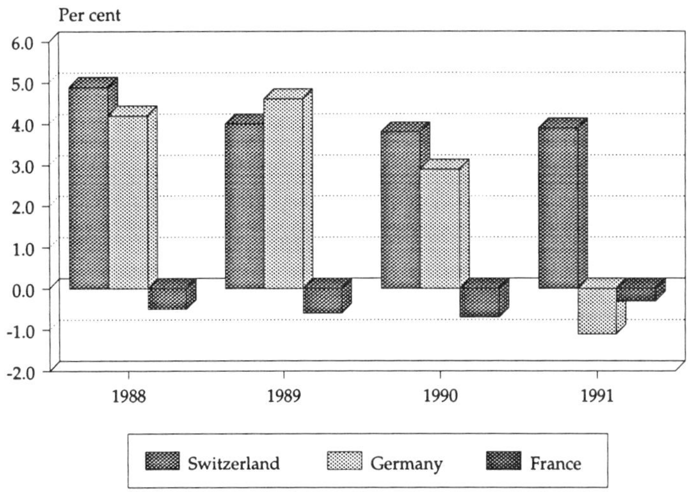

Figure 27.3 Current accounts of Switzerland and selected countries (as percentage of GDP)
Source: Bank Leu

growth in activity is forecast; indeed, a relapse is possible. However, although investment in plant and equipment will probably continue to decline, real GDP may grow by 0.5 per cent to 1 per cent and both consumer expenditure and exports are likely to grow by slightly more, thereby stimulating modest growth and preventing the economy from sliding into a serious recession.

Trade balance

Foreign trade plays a vital role in the growth and well-being of the Swiss economy. Germany is, by far, the biggest trading partner (accounting for 25 per cent of exports and 33 per cent of imports), followed by France, Italy and the USA. Switzerland's most important export items are precision machines and chemicals.

Switzerland's traditional quarterly trade deficit increased between 1987 and 1989 (see Figure 27.3), but showed a considerable decrease in 1990 - due to increasing export volumes and an improvement in the terms of trade following the revaluation of the Swiss franc. This trend continued during the first half of 1991, as the Swiss export sector continued to be stimulated by demand from its trading partners, notably Germany.

While the Swiss trade balance has, by tradition, remained in deficit, the current account has continually shown large surpluses. Due to the positive net income derived from tourism, other services (e.g. insurance) and, above all, from foreign interest and dividend income, the current account comfortably compensates for any trade deficit. The improvement in foreign trade during 1990, contributed to the growing surplus in the current account, whilst an increase in net interest income and a greater surplus in the service sector produced an even better current account position in 1991.

Unemployment

Since the Second World War, Switzerland has had few problems of high unemployment. In the oil-induced recession of 1974-76, employment declined by 8 per cent; however, two-thirds of the unemployed were foreigners who subsequently left Switzerland. Unemployment increased gradually between 1982 and 1984, although the extent of the increase was quite modest. Thereafter, a declining trend began which continued until it reached a figure of just 0.5 per cent in mid-1990 (see Figure 27.4).

From around July 1990, as employment growth started to decrease, the unemployment rate began to rise and, from October 1990, this upward trend began to accelerate. Since then, unemployment has continued to rise and, October 1991, it reached a figure of 1.5 per cent, or 45,692 people. In a period of difficulty, the first reaction of industry is often to put workers on short-time, consequently the number of short-time workers doubled between the first and second

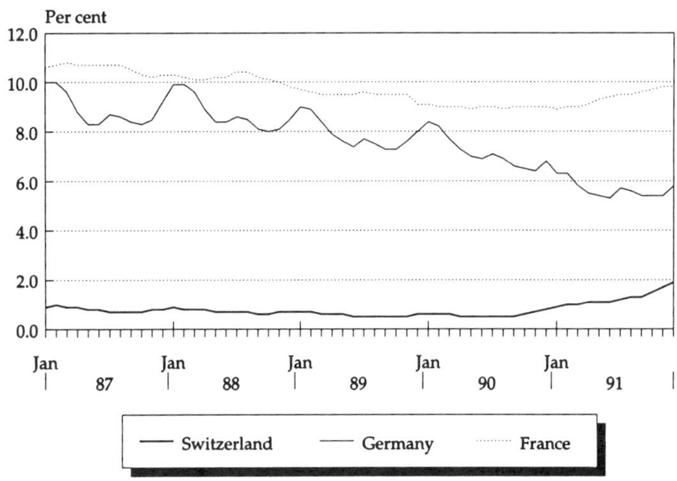

Figure 27.4 **Unemployment in Switzerland and selected countries (as percentage of workforce)**
Source: OECD

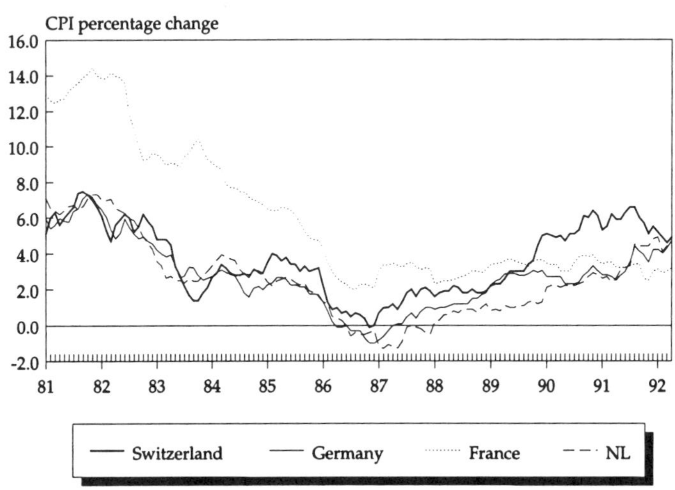

Figure 27.5 **Inflation in Switzerland and selected countries, 1981-1992**
Source: OECD

quarters of 1991 (to a figure of 22,000). Given the economic situation, unemployment will probably continue to worsen, although some respite may be gained from a mild recovery in 1992; however, structural problems and intensified international competition are likely to inhibit a speedy return to the formerly low rates of unemployment.

Inflation

Until the late eighties, Switzerland was consistently among the world's lowest inflation countries. Since then, however, its position has worsened considerably and it now has one of the highest rates to be found among the most important industrialized countries. The origin of this increasing trend dates back to 1987. Before that, declining crude oil prices and the strength of the Swiss franc had masked the underlying problem, namely home-made inflationary pressures. Subsequently, though, the prices of domestic goods and services started to increase rapidly. During the last two months of 1989, the rate of inflation showed particular acceleration - due mainly to both increased mortgage rates (which fed through as hefty rent hikes) and the rising crude oil price. The same factors had an impact once again in 1990. In 1991, the high degree of administrated prices, the passing on of rising wage costs, as well as weather-related factors for foods, all combined to push the inflation rate up further (see Figure 27.5).

However, the basis effect, a weaker US dollar, somewhat lower oil prices and the likely end of the high interest-rate cycle, should contribute to a gradual lowering of the inflation rate. In the course of 1992, Switzerland should converge down to the German inflation rate which, since 1989, has trended substantially below the Swiss level.

Monetary policy

Since the flotation of the Swiss franc, in January 1973, the Swiss National Bank (SNB) has operated a fully autonomous monetary policy, the backbone of which is to manage and influence the money supply (see Figure 27.6). After initially concentrating on the M1 definition of money, the SNB changed (in 1980) to central bank money (M0) as an indicator. It comprises coins and notes as well as commercial banks' reserves at the central bank and, until 1987, M0 seemed to serve the purpose well. However, as new liquidity requirements for commercial banks and a new payment system were introduced (1988-89), the SNB found that it could no longer rely on M0 as a reliable aggregate. The underestimated, and rapid, decline in the balances of commercial banks at the central bank surprised the SNB - suddenly its monetary policy had become too expansive (and it was to remain so, for some time). This phase contributed a great deal to the problems of high inflation which ensued in 1990 and 1991. But, as from 1990, the SNB once again conducted monetary policy according to M0, because it was

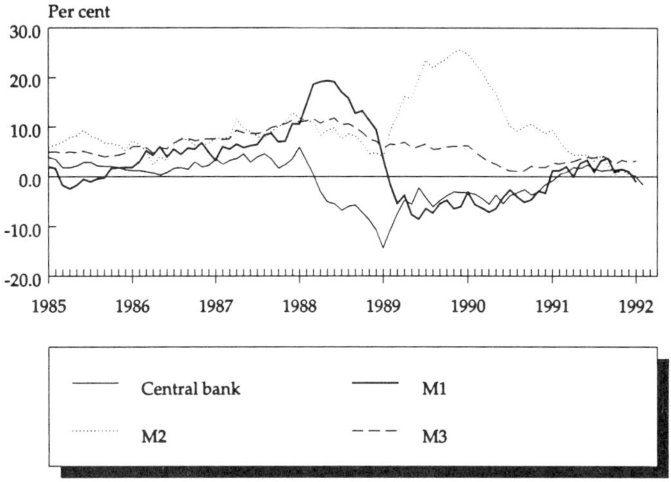

Figure 27.6 **Swiss money supply (percentage change, year-on-year)**
Source: SNB

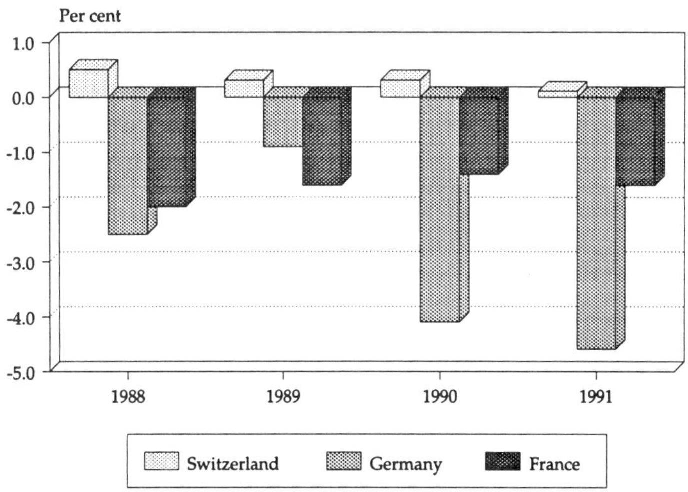

Figure 27.7 **Budget deficits of Switzerland and selected countries (as percentage of GDP/GNP)**
Source: Bank Leu

believed that the technical aberrations were now corrected and no longer distorting the figures.

The most important task of the SNB is to stabilize the internal price level in Switzerland. Inflationary cycles cannot, however, be avoided because monetary policy in Switzerland takes 2 to 3 years to have an effect on real economic variables, particularly inflation. Besides the business cycle, the SNB also looks very closely at the exchange rate, considerations of which can severely restrict the flexibility to operate an independent monetary policy. The National Bank had, for instance, to abandon the attempts to counter the cyclical strength of the franc in 1978, and again in 1987. Nowadays, the Deutschemark/franc exchange rate plays a major role in preventing, for the time being, an expansionary monetary policy while, at the same time, leading to gradually lower interest rates.

During 1989 and particularly during the first half of 1990, the SNB followed a very restrictive monetary policy. In the second half of 1990 however, it decided on a slight expansion of central bank money whilst, in 1991, the growth in M0 was slightly above the National Bank's target of 1 per cent. For 1992, the SNB also envisages an expansion rate of marginally above 1 per cent.

Public sector deficit

Since Switzerland, as a confederation, has a decentralized political structure, an analysis of the public sector deficit includes all levels of governments - federal, cantonal and communal. Naturally, the federal government attracts the most attention.

After several years of public sector deficits, the favourable economic trend in the second half of the eighties led to budget surpluses (see Figure 27.7), particularly at federal government level. As is common in such situations, there followed a expenditure boom, particularly in the luxury goods sector of the market. In 1989, a much higher inflation rate and a declining growth in tax monies led to an overall public sector deficit although, at that point in time, the federal government was still in a surplus position. However, in the 1991 fiscal year, the federal government incurred a deficit, too. For 1992, the three levels of governments are going to have an estimated combined deficit of SFr 5bn. This accelerating deterioration of the economy is likely to lead to deficits for the next few years and can only to be corrected by savings or new sources of revenues. It is certain that the federal government, which in the period of 1986-1988 even paid back bonds on a net basis, will come to the market more frequently.

With the prospect of continuing deficits, the public sector is unlikely to provide any incentive for a short-term decline in interest rates. Indeed, at times, the market may well be unable to absorb its demands, thereby actually putting upward pressure on rates.

Exchange rate history

Although the French franc, Italian lire, British pound and Japanese yen are all important to the Swiss economy, the Deutschemark and the US dollar carry the most significance. Their prominence is due on one hand to the fact that Germany is the biggest trading partner whilst, on the other, many prices are denominated in dollars. Additionally, both exchange rates play a major role both as investment and transaction currencies. The US dollar exchange rate showed a steady decline from 1985 to 1987, with only a few minor recoveries. The beginning of 1988, however, saw the start of a strong uptrend (see Figure 27.8). Initially, the Swiss National Bank intervened in favour of the dollar, causing a substantial revaluation. However, before long, it had to switch sides and, along with other central banks, intervene in favour of the franc. Against the Deutschemark, meanwhile, the franc's trend had been slightly weaker. However, during 1989, the franc lost ground against all currencies. The following recovery was due to the introduction of a flexible Lombard rate in Switzerland as well as interventions by the central bank. In the course of the fourth quarter of 1989, the Deutschemark climbed to SFr 0.91. Around the end of 1989 and the beginning of 1990, the central bank again intervened to support the franc which promptly showed a recovery, largely due to rising interest rates in the money market.

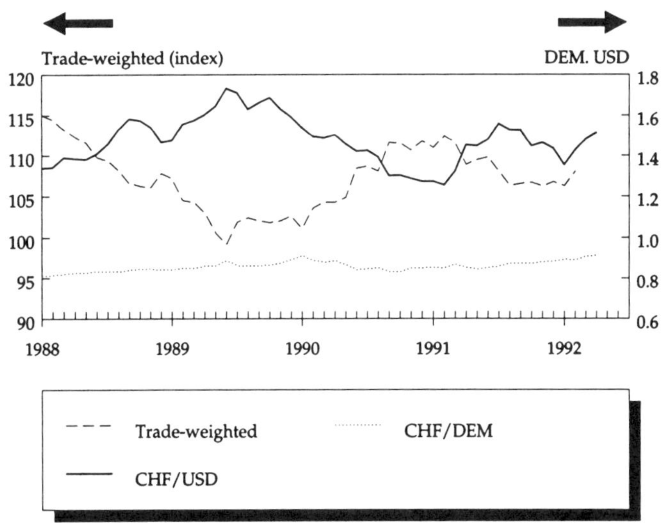

Figure 27.8 **Swiss franc exchange rate, 1988-1992**
Source: SNB

Meanwhile, the dollar had started a renewed slide in the middle of 1989 and this bearish trend was set to continue throughout 1990.

The first half of 1991 saw the franc once again weakening against all currencies and, together with other central banks, the SNB sold the dollar against the franc. While the weakness of the franc against most currencies - mainly those in the European exchange rate mechanism - continued, the dollar came under pressure due to declining interest rates and weak economic growth in the United States, ending 1991 at the depressed level of SFr 1.36.

27.3 *Market composition*

Overview

Government bond market

In terms of outstanding volume, the government bond sector is very small in relation to the whole market (see Figures 27.9 & 27.10). Indeed, due to the budget surpluses of the federal government during the last few years, its relative size has shown a steady decrease. However, given the downturn in the

		31 Dec 1990	% Total	31 Dec 1991	% Total
LISTED					
	Government	11.4	3.6	12.3	3.7
	Domestic	116.3	36.7	125.6	37.4
	Foreign	112.3	35.5	116.2	34.6
	Total	240.0	75.8	254.1	75.7
OTC					
	Domestic	4.6	1.5	4.8	1.4
	Foreign	5.2	1.6	4.1	1.2
	Total	9.8	3.1	8.9	2.6
PRIVATE PLACEMENTS					
	Domestic	5.0	1.6	5.0	1.5
	Foreign	62.0	19.6	68.0	20.2
	Total	67.0	21.2	73.0	21.7
	Total domestic	137.3	43.3	147.7	44.0
	Total foreign	179.5	56.7	188.3	56.0
	GRAND TOTAL	316.8	100.0	336.0	100.0

Figure 27.9 Nominal value of outstanding bonds (CHF billion)
Sources: Zurich Stock Exchange Annual Report (listed bonds), estimates of Bank Leu (OTC and private placement), Swiss Bank Corporation

	31 Mar 1990	% Total	31 Dec 1991	% Total
DOMESTIC MARKET				
Federal government				
Straight	12.3	5.9	12.3	4.7
Cantons & municipalities				
Straight	18.6	8.9	17.0	6.4
Banks & financial institutions				
Straight	41.1		84.2	
Convertible	0.5		1.0	
Warrant	4.1		4.4	
Floating-rate	0.3		-	
Total	46.0	22.1	89.7	34.1
Industry & others				
Straight	24.3		18.2	
Convertible	1.0		2.1	
Warrant	4.6		2.9	
Floating-rate	0.3		-	
Zero-coupon	0.3		0.3	
Total	30.5	14.6	23.7	9.0
Total domestic	107.4	51.5	142.3	54.2
FOREIGN MARKET				
Straight	81.6		104.9	
Convertible	3.9		4.5	
Warrant	5.1		3.4	
Floating-rate	1.3		1.0	
FIPS	2.1		1.8	
Dual-currency	4.8		2.4	
Zero-coupon	2.2		2.2	
Total foreign	101.0	48.5	120.2	45.8
GRAND TOTAL	208.4	100.0	262.5	100.0

Figure 27.10 Structure of the market by sector (CHF billion nominal, listed and OTC bonds only)

Swiss economy from late 1990 and the expected demands from some rather large projects coming up in the next few years, the financial position of the government will deteriorate. As a result, there is likely to be an increasing number of government issues in the future, which should bring about a considerable improvement in liquidity.

Domestic bonds

The majority of domestic bonds are made up of:

- local government bonds (cantons & municipalities)
- bank bonds
- corporate bonds

Most of these bonds are placed through public subscription, with just a few being placed privately.

Foreign bonds

The foreign sector's relative share of the Swiss bond market has been on the increase over the last few years and is now very significant, with public issues and private placements making up 56 per cent of the outstanding market. As far as the privately-placed bond sector is concerned, this features equity-linked instruments and a preponderance of Japanese borrowing.

Composition of market by maturity

Federal government bonds

The average maturity of government bonds has shortened (see Figure 27.11), owing to the fact that very few new issues have been brought to the market. However, average maturity should begin to lengthen considerably, as the federal government is scheduled to issue at an increasing rate from 1992 onwards.

Domestic mortgage bonds

Mortgage bonds placed through a central-issuing agency generally have a life of 8 to 12 years (see Figure 27.12). As issuing activity will likely decline over the next few years (due to the economic downturn), the average maturity of the outstanding volume will become shorter.

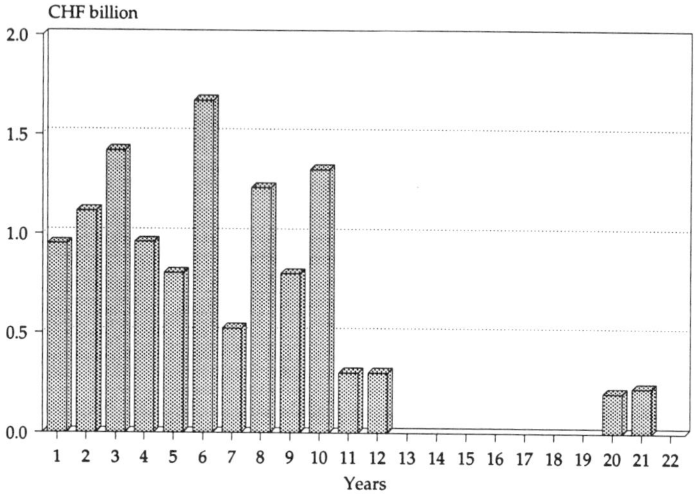

Figure 27.11 Maturity structure of the federal government bond market
Source: Bank Leu - Bond Research

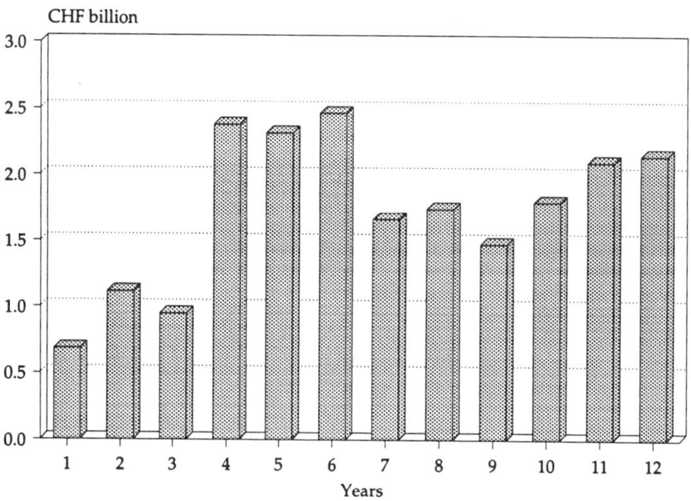

Figure 27.12 Maturity structure of the domestic mortgage bond market
Source: Bank Leu - Bond Research

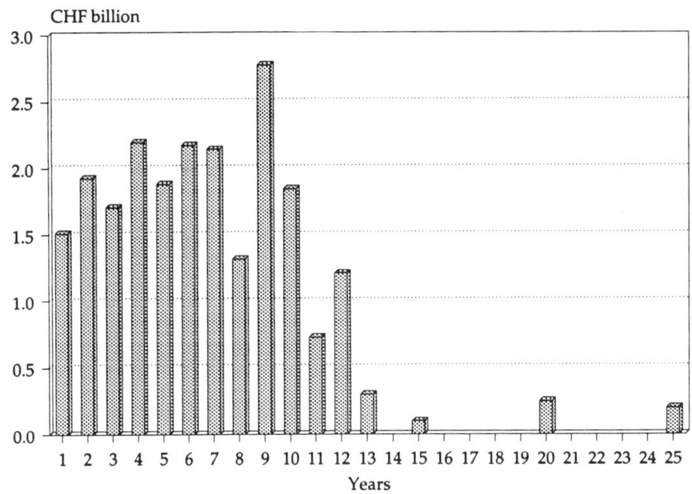

Figure 27.13 Maturity structure of the bank bond market
Source: Bank Leu - Bond Research

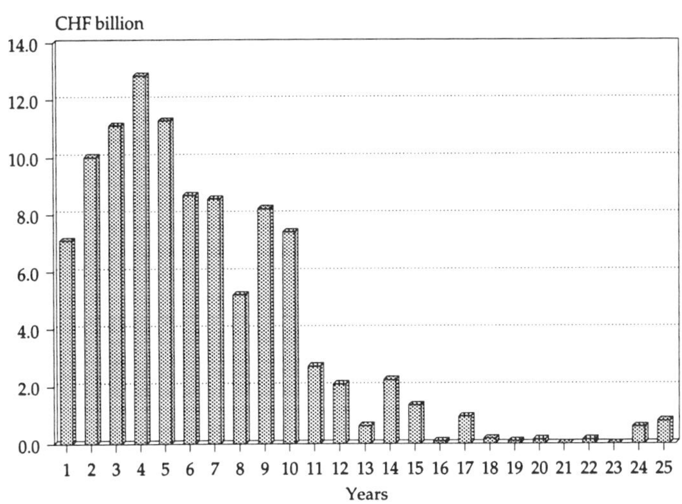

Figure 27.14 Maturity structure of the foreign bond market
Source: Bank Leu - Bond Research

Domestic bank bonds

Newly-issued bonds carry maturities of 8 to 12 years, and there is a steady supply of these securities (see Figure 27.13). In the domestic market, bank bonds will remain the most important sector and the average maturity is likely to remain stable.

Foreign bonds

As yields have peaked, the maturities of newly-placed bonds have recently become longer - the average life in 1991 was around 10 years (see Figure 27.14). As a result, the average life of outstanding bonds will also lengthen.

Composition of market by coupon structure

Federal government bonds

Although traditionally low, government bond coupons have recently become generally higher, with the highest levels in this yield cycle reaching 6.75 per cent (see Figure 27.15). The coupons of new issues in 1992 are likely to be marginally lower, but a return to the low levels seen in the eighties can be ruled out for a long time.

Domestic mortgage bonds

Given the twin factors of the cyclical high in yields in 1991, and the difficulties of some regional banks with exposure to real estate, coupons have recently exceeded 7 per cent (see Figure 27.16). A gradual decrease in coupon levels may be expected during 1992.

Domestic bank bonds

Traditionally, bank bonds have the highest coupons in the domestic market (see Figure 27.17). This is so because they command a sizeable share of the market and have to be priced more cheaply in order to attract new investment. Coupon levels are likely to decline marginally in 1992.

Foreign bonds

Coupons of foreign bonds are somewhat higher than for domestic bonds (see Figure 27.18). Because lower-quality bonds can no longer be placed, the spread of the current coupons has diminished. The forecast trend for 1992 is for slightly lower coupons.

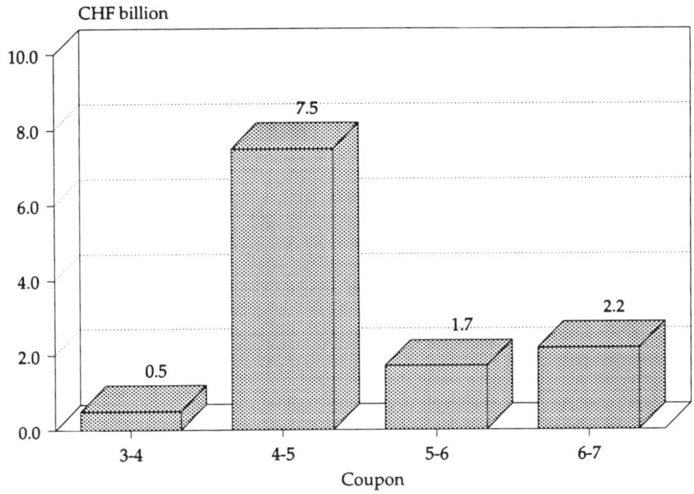

Figure 27.15 Coupon structure of the federal government bond market
Source: Bank Leu - Bond Research

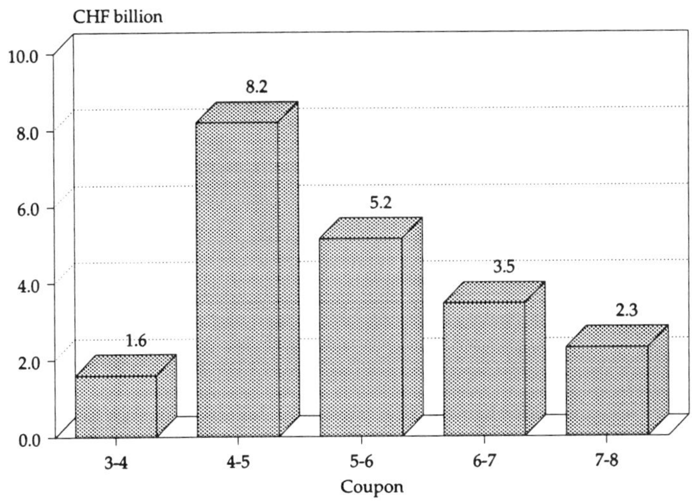

Figure 27.16 Coupon structure of the domestic mortgage bond market
Source: Bank Leu - Bond Research

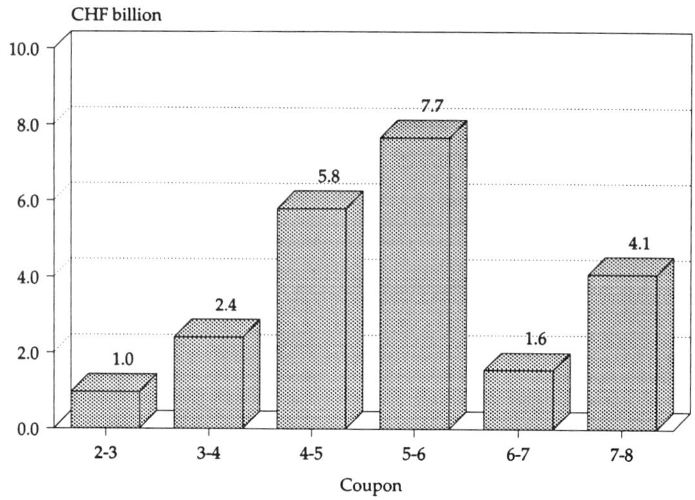

Figure 27.17 Coupon structure of the domestic bank bond market
Source: Bank Leu - Bond Research

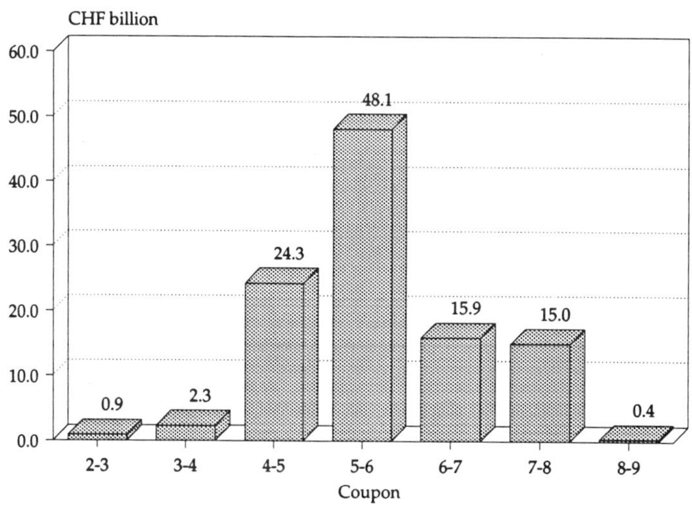

Figure 27.18 Coupon structure of the foreign bond market
Source: Bank Leu - Bond Research

27.4 Types of security

Domestic bonds

Federal government bonds

The majority of federal government bonds (80 per cent) are callable, while the remainder are in bullet form. There are no instruments outstanding other than straight bonds with fixed-coupons. The total number of listed issues amounts to only 45. The longest bond matures in 2012, and the highest coupon is 6.75 per cent.

Cantonal and municipal government bonds

The 26 cantons and half-cantons, as well as more than 3000 municipalities, function as autonomous financial entities. They have their own budgets and their capital requirements are met in the markets. The new issues of the cantons, certain cities and larger communities are floated directly in the capital market, whereas smaller communities go through the Central Issuing Organization of Swiss Municipalities (in order to save costs and obtain acceptable conditions).

Bond type	**1990**		**1991**	
	CHF bn	Per cent	CHF bn	Per cent
Straight	216.1	86.6	236.6	90.1
Convertible	7.7	3.1	7.2	2.7
Warrant	16.7	6.7	10.9	4.2
Floating-rate	1.3	0.5	1.1	0.4
FIPS	1.8	0.7	1.8	0.7
Dual-currency	3.5	1.4	2.4	0.9
Zero-coupon	2.5	1.0	2.5	1.0
Total	249.5	100.0	262.5	100.0

Figure 27.19 Issuance by type of security, 1990-91

The most important cantons, in terms of outstanding issues are Basel, Bern, Geneva and Zurich.

The majority of these bonds (90 per cent) are callable, with the remainder appearing in bullet form.

Bank and corporate bonds

By volume, bank and corporate bonds constitute the largest portion of the domestic market. The straight bonds are unsecured and mostly callable. Within the equity-related sector, warrant bonds prevail. Floating-rate and zero-coupon bonds are insignificant.

The big three banks, SBC, UBS and Credit Suisse, along with the cantonal banks, are the most important issuers in this sector.

Mortgage bonds

These are long-term mortgage-collateralized bonds which, under Swiss law, may only be issued to finance mortgages or real estate loans. The Mortgage Bond Act has empowered two central institutions to issue these bonds: The Central Mortgage Bond Institution of the Swiss Cantonal Banks and The Mortgage Bond Bank of the Swiss Mortgage Institutions. The bonds are secured by mortgage deeds whose coverage is monitored by law. All of them are callable.

Foreign bonds

This sector once showed an innovative drive with respect to new instruments, but this ceased in the late eighties.

Warrant bonds

Bonds with warrant certificates attached entitle the holder to purchase, within a predetermined period and at a pre-set price:

- equities
- bonds
- raw materials
- precious metals
- foreign currencies
- indexes

The warrant is detachable from the bond and may be traded separately (a bond without the warrant is known as 'ex-warrant'). Warrant bonds are popular with both issuers and investors. There are currently no outstanding warrant bonds of the type which actually have bonds as the underlying instrument.

Convertible bonds

These are issued with inseparable conversion rights attached and may be converted into specific securities, or some other assets, within a predetermined period and at a pre-set price. The instrument is very popular with Japanese issuers who prefer issuance by private placement. While domestic convertibles are callable, Japanese issuers have floated a large number of puttable bonds.

Dual-currency bonds

With this type of bond, the issue price and coupon amount are payable in Swiss francs, whereas the principal is repayable in a pre-set amount of US or Canadian dollars. The coupon is stated as a percentage of the Swiss franc issue price and is always somewhat higher than the usual rate on Swiss franc bonds. The amount repayable is sometimes significantly higher than the issue price, which makes these bonds discounted. Generally, they appear with both put and call option, allowing the investor and the borrower to opt out before the bond's maturity. In the secondary market, their trading prices are quoted as percentages of the repayment amount in US or Canadian dollars, with accrued interest already included, i.e. the quotation is flat. The dual-currency nature of these bonds makes it considerably more difficult for the investors to assess their desirability. The most common approach involves analysing the two currency components separately, in order to be able to compare them on either the bond's present value, or its yield.

FIPS

Foreign-interest payment securities or FIPS are perpetual Swiss franc bonds with dollar coupons. Their coupons are adjusted every ten years and are equivalent to the, then, current yield on ten-year US Treasury bonds. The coupon, the bond's nominal value and a fixed-exchange rate, are used to calculate the amount paid out in dollars. Borrowers have the right to exercise their call option and repay the issue every ten years when the interest rate is adjusted. Investors may also exercise their early redemption right at this time and, in such a case, the redemption price in Swiss francs will depend upon the exchange rate of the dollar at the time; if it is at, or above, the predetermined dollar price, the bonds will be redeemed at their nominal value; if it is below this present rate, the redemption price will be adjusted downwards accordingly.

There are only seven issues of this type, one example being the 7 1/2% Pepsi Co., callable and puttable in 1996.

Perpetual bonds

Because Swiss law requires a maturity date to be stipulated for bonds, perpetual bonds constitute securities which are repayable at the date of a company's liquidation. Since their introduction in 1985, a good number of perpetual bonds have appeared in the foreign sector. All have been issued with a call provision, allowing the borrower to repay them at a predetermined time.

Floating-rate notes

Floaters are usually medium- and long-term bonds whose coupons are periodically adjusted to market conditions. In the Swiss market the coupons are adjusted with reference to:

- LIBOR (London interbank offered rate)
- LIMEAN (London interbank mean rate)
- average yield on federal bonds
- rates on six- or twelve-month time deposits (at major banks)
- mortgage rates of Zurich Cantonal Bank
- average yield on Swiss franc foreign bonds

There are approximately 40 floaters outstanding and no new issues have come to the market in the last few years, having failed to gain popularity with investors.

27.5 *Issuers*

Domestic market

The structure of the domestic market is dominated by the issues of commercial and mortgage banks, followed by the provinces and municipalities (see Figure 27.20).

Foreign market

In the Swiss franc foreign bond market, bank and corporate borrowers prevail. Also of some significance are supranational institutions, which have a market share of 10 per cent.

	1990		1991	
	Domestic	Foreign	Domestic	Foreign
Sovereigns	1.1	0.8	1.4	1.1
Prov. & municipalities	2.5	1.3	3.9	1.6
Banks & financial institutions	11.2	11.0	9.4	8.0
Corporates	2.3	16.3	2.0	17.1
Supranationals	0.7	4.0	0.6	3.0
Total	18.2	33.4	17.2	30.7

Figure 27.20 Volume by issuer, 1990-1991 (CHF billion nominal)

27.6 *Investors*

The lack of data on the subject makes it difficult to analyse the final investors in the Swiss capital market by type. Of course, viewed from the other perspective, it is an example of the protection of the investor's identity offered by Swiss banks. Naturally, Swiss institutional investors have grown in importance and privately-organized pension funds have had an above-average growth (see Figure 27.21). From a market point of view, they tend to be conservative investors - investing principally in Swiss franc rather than foreign-currency bonds and also showing a preference for domestic borrowers. In a way, this conservatism is helping to preserve the interest rate differential against foreign interest rates, thereby hindering rapid convergence of Swiss rates to the general European level.

It is only in the area of domestic bonds that the involvement of foreign investors is publicly-known - at the end of 1990, it was approximately 13 per cent. As far as foreign bonds are concerned, the share of the foreign investor is much higher - probably as high as 30 to 40 per cent - although the trend has been downward over the last few years, due to relatively low interest rates and the

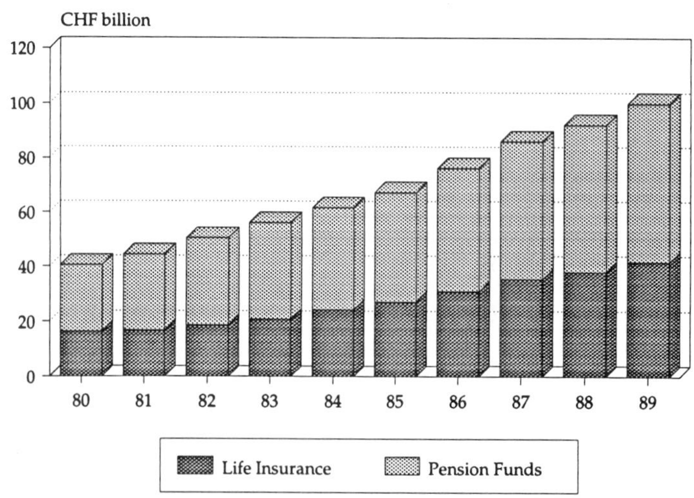

Figure 27.21 Growth of bond investment by pension funds and life insurers
Source: Federal Office of Private Insurance

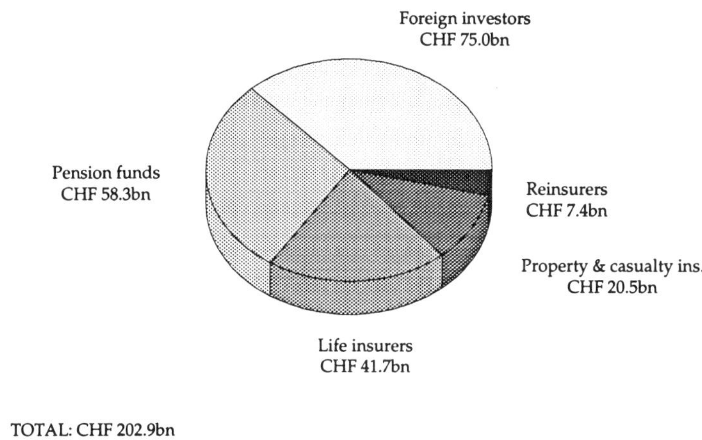

Figure 27.22 Investors in the Swiss market, 1989

weakening Swiss franc. In the absence of statistics, it is probably fair to assume that their involvement in private placements is much higher than in public bonds. Figure 27.22, which shows investor categories, is quite imprecise as far as the foreign investors are concerned, but should nevertheless illustrate the major breakdown of invested amounts.

27.7 *Methods of issuance*

Overview

There are a number of different issuing methods, the application of each depending upon the borrower's category and the mode of placement (public or private). The Swiss National Bank stipulates that only banks and financial institutions domiciled in Switzerland may issue SFr-bonds. This regulation has not only ensured that SFr-issues remain within Switzerland (despite the adverse impact of the stamp tax), but has also prevented the development of a Swiss franc-eurobond market.

Federal government

The Swiss federal government has been marketing its bonds by tender since 1980. The Cantons of Zurich and Geneva, as well as the City of Zurich and some other issuers, all use this procedure from time to time. The issuer sets the coupon rate, maturity and approximate amount to be floated, while determination of the issue price is left to the market. Investors may participate in a tender through a Swiss bank on a net basis, without any taxes or commissions being added to the price.

Other borrowers

All other categories of borrowers, with the exception of banks, use firm underwriting through banks, bank syndicates, or groups of syndicates to float their issues. For public bonds, subscription with a prospectus takes place. Private placements, on the other hand, are sold through syndicate members and only require a short information memorandum; they also have a denomination of SFr 50,000.

Commission structure

Commission costs incurred by the borrower vary according to the type of placement (public or private), and time to maturity. Fees for private placements are much lower than for public issues.

Syndicate structure

Following a ruling by the Swiss cartel commission, formal syndicates were prohibited as of January 1991. This has led to the closer co-operation among the big three universal banks which commanded a market share of 60.5 per cent of the

Swiss franc foreign bond sector in 1991 (somewhat down on the 1987 figure of 70 per cent). For domestic bond issues, the cantonal banks were the market leaders with 38.4 per cent in 1991.

Lead-managers

In 1991, the following banks were the main lead-managers for foreign bonds:

- Credit Suisse
- Swiss Bank Corporation
- Union Bank of Switzerland
- Banque Paribas (Suisse)

Swap transactions

In the last few years, swap arrangements have rapidly gained importance in the area of foreign SFr-denominated issuance. It is estimated that 80 per cent of non-Japanese issues are linked to swaps.

27.8 *New issue volumes*

The annual issuing potential in the Swiss market seems unable to break the SFr 50bn mark (see Figure 27.23). As a result, in relation to the growing eurobond market, the Swiss franc bond market has lost some market share during the last few years.

Figure 27.24 shows that, in 1991, total issuance (both public and private placement) decreased by 7.3 per cent to a figure of SFr 47.9bn. (587 issues), compared with SFr 51.7bn (561 issues) in 1990. The slight contraction in volume may be the result of the reduced interest rate differential between Switzerland and other countries, as well as the developing world-wide recession.

The domestic sector absorbed SFr 17.2bn (36 per cent of issuance), down 6 per cent on 1990. Average maturities were 10 years in the public sector and 7 years for private placements. Bank bonds had a market share of 51 per cent.

Foreign issues, meanwhile, were down by 8 per cent on 1990 levels, to SFr 30.7bn (a market share of 64 per cent). The average maturities were 8 years for

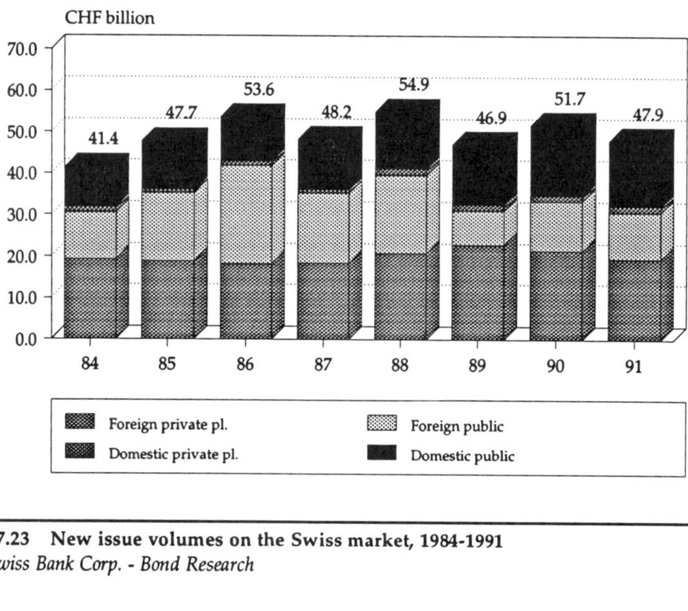

Figure 27.23 New issue volumes on the Swiss market, 1984-1991
Source: Swiss Bank Corp. - Bond Research

	1990		1991	
	CHF bn	Per cent	CHF bn	Per cent
Domestic - public	17.1	33.1	15.7	32.8
Domestic - private placement	1.2	2.3	1.5	3.1
Total	18.3	35.4	17.2	35.9
Foreign - public	11.9	23.0	11.3	23.6
Foreign - private placement	21.4	41.4	19.4	40.5
Total	33.3	64.4	30.7	64.1
GRAND TOTAL	51.7	100.0	47.9	100.0

Figure 27.24 Breakdown of issuing volumes by sector

public issues and 4.5 years for private placements. Among the issuers, Japanese borrowers had by far the biggest market share, at 42.5 per cent.

27.9 Methods of trading

The secondary market can be divided into four basic sectors:

- the stock exchange
- the pre-market
- the over-the-counter market (OTC)
- the grey market

Only the first two of these operate under governmental supervision, with all their trading occurring on one of Switzerland's three stock exchanges of Zurich, Geneva and Basel.

Transactions on the official stock exchanges are restricted to those securities that have been admitted to listing and are, hence, essentially limited to public issues. Currently, however, only 20 to 30 per cent of all public issues are traded on a stock exchange, with the rest of the volume being handled on the OTC market.

Pre-market trading, which is primarily composed of public issues which are not listed on the exchanges, generally occurs in such instances wherein:

- listing-approval for newly-issued bonds is awaiting the printing and delivery of finalized documents
- an application for listing is still under consideration by the authorities
- the borrower wants the issue to continue being traded in the pre-market

Off-floor trading by telephone (OTC) usually accounts for the sizeable remainder of public offerings, as well as the entire private placement business.

The major market-makers are the big banks, as well as a few smaller specialized banks. In recent years a number of Geneva-based foreign bank subsidiaries have led in the development of the so-called 'grey market', which functions alongside the traditional market areas. Grey market trading occurs within the narrow time-span between the fixing of terms for a new issue and their pre-market trading.

Transaction costs in the secondary market are no longer regulated. Other costs, such as stamp tax, cantonal fees and stock exchange fees, are fiscal in nature and covered in Section 27.12, Taxation.

27.10 Market practices

Coupon payment

Interest on bonds is paid annually. The following bonds are exceptions to this rule:

- floating-rate notes, which often carry semi-annual coupons
- many of foreign convertible bonds, which carry semi-annual coupons

First coupon

Normally, payment on the first coupon occurs one year after the issue payment date. The so-called 'irregular' coupons diverge from this pattern, in that payment on their first coupon typically coincides with the later redemption date and involves only the broken-period interest accrued up to then. However, all subsequent coupons attached to the bond follow the normal yearly payment pattern.

Redemption

All issues redeem at par except those bonds with calls, which are often redeemed at a premium determined by the terms of the individual issue.

Put options

Put options, with the associated right of the creditor to demand early redemption, are only rarely attached either to Swiss domestic bonds or to public SFr-denominated foreign issues. In contrast, they are commonly found on the convertibles of Japanese borrowers in the private placement sector.

Partial repayment

Partial repayment can be made by either a sinking fund, or purchase fund, method. Under the sinking fund arrangement, the repayment schedule has to be implemented regardless of the market situation. If the market price is above par, bonds are drawn for repayment by lottery. Under the purchase procedure, the buy-back is simply made in the open market when the price is below par.

Calls

Convertible bonds are also sometimes issued with a call provision which is based on a relationship between market price and conversion price, or exchange rate factors.

Denomination

In Switzerland, public issues are typically offered in denominations of SFr 5000 and SFr 100,000. Private placements have denominations of SFr 50,000.

Form

Bonds are issued in the form of bearer certificates.

Dealing quotations

Bond trading is done on the basis of a price quoted in per cent exclusive of accrued interest. The spread between bid and offered prices varies from issue to issue. Lower-grade bonds trade at substantial spreads, while good-quality bonds trade at spreads of around 50 basis points.

Settlement

Settlement of a transaction occurs on value day, which is three working days after the trade-date.

27.11 *Yield calculation*

Current yield method

This method is only used with convertible bonds that are trading above par and allows their market value to be compared with the underlying stock.

current yield = (interest rate/bond's market price) × 100 per cent

Yield to (average) life and to call

Since Swiss franc bonds are similar in form to eurobonds, i.e. generally issued with annual coupons attached, the ISMA's definition can be applied to them. In addition to current income, this method also takes into account any capital gain or loss, as well as the current value of all payments due at different dates, and then calculates the reinvestment of all coupons at the same yield. This method allows the comparison of bonds having the same maturities and credit quality.

The current price of a bond plus accrued interest equals the sum of all future payments (coupons and redemption), discounted to present values. The discount rate used to calculate the current value is the yield-to-maturity or yield-to-call, the value of which is found by solving the equation below:

$$p + a = \frac{c_1}{\left(1+\frac{y}{100}\right)^{L_1}} + \ldots + \frac{c_x}{\left(1+\frac{y}{100}\right)^{L_x}} + \ldots + \frac{c_n}{\left(1+\frac{y}{100}\right)^{L_n}}$$

where:

p the bond's current price as a percentage of its nominal value
a accrued interest on the bond expressed in currency units (0 if bond is traded flat)
y yield in per cent
n number of anticipated payments (coupons and repayment(s))
cx xth payment in currency per units per bond
Lx remaining life to the xth payment in years.

In Switzerland, the following conditions generally hold:

- The discount period is on a yearly basis.

- Interest accrual is calculated on the basis of a year equalling 360 days and a month equalling 30 days. Interest is calculated from the last coupon payment date to the settlement date, which generally falls three days after the trade-date. Should the next coupon payment date fall between the trade-date and the settlement date, accrued interest is calculated for more than 360 days.

Yields on floating-rate notes

Since the coupons on these bonds are adjusted periodically with reference to some key rate, the only interest rate known is the current coupon. As a rule, therefore, this rate is used to calculate the yield in the manner described above.

27.12 Taxation

The federal, cantonal and communal governments, all levy taxes independently on income, capital gains, and turnover. They vary according to whether a domestic or foreign issue is involved, and where the investor is domiciled.

Domestic investors

Withholding tax

A withholding tax of 35 per cent is deducted directly from the coupon income of all domestic bonds. For foreign issues there is no tax withheld at the source.

Income tax

Income tax is levied on all interest income. In the case of zero-coupon bonds, the tax authorities of the federal and cantonal levels differ greatly in their approach. In view of this, and the possibility of a change in the practice, it is recommended that potential investors inquire about the current regulations prior to purchase.

Capital gains tax

Capital gains tax (which is calculated on the difference between the purchase and sales price of the principal) is only levied by some cantons, if the investor is naturalized Swiss. The tax rate varies from canton to canton.

Foreign investors

Foreign investors also pay withholding tax on domestic issues, but not on foreign issues. However, those domiciled in countries which have a double taxation agreement with Switzerland can request reimbursement of all or part of this tax.

Investors domiciled abroad do not have to pay Swiss capital gains tax.

Transaction taxes

These taxes must be paid regardless of the investor's nationality or domicile. The so-called stamp tax is levied by the federal government on all capital transactions in which one of the parties is a securities dealer resident in either Switzerland or Liechtenstein. The charge is 0.3 per cent for foreign securities and

0.15 per cent on domestic issues. Each of the two parties to the contract is liable for half of the tax.

Cantonal fees, which are charged at 0.01 per cent (Canton Zurich), may also be regarded as a type of tax. The same is also true of the stock exchange fee of 0.005 per cent (Zurich Stock Exchange) levied on issues listed on the exchange. Both of these taxes are charged at the stated rates equally to both parties.

Effects of taxation

Foreign investors are very reluctant to purchase domestic bonds since some tax must be paid, even if they are resident in a country that has a double tax agreement with Switzerland (also, they often resent the fact that their identity must be revealed in order to request reimbursement of the tax). Additionally, the withholding tax has prevented the issue of domestic puttable bonds, while the turnover tax has hampered the development of a money market.

27.13 *Futures & options*

Early in 1991, the Swiss Option and Financial Futures Exchange (SOFFEX) launched a 3-month LIBOR futures contract (see Figure 27.25). This was soon followed by a 5-year swap rate futures contract (see Figure 27.26).

Contract size:	CHF 1,000,000
Delivery months:	Nearest 5 months of C-cycle: March, June, September, December.
Last trading day:	2 days prior to the 3rd Wednesday of the respective contract month at 11.00 London time.
Quotation:	100 minus interest rate p.a.
Minimum price movement (tick size) and value:	0.01 = CHF 25
Trading hours:	08.30 -16.30 Swiss time (no break).
Initial margin:	CHF 750 (spread margin: CHF 300).
Price limit:	None
Contract standard:	Cash settlement based on the LIBOR for 3-month euro-Swiss francs. The final settlement price is 100 minus LIBOR
Position limits:	None

Figure 27.25 3-mth euro-Swiss franc futures - contract specification

Contract size:	CHF 100,000. nominal 5-year synthetic bond with 6% coupon.
Delivery months:	Nearest 4 months of C-cycle: March, June, September, December.
Last trading day:	2 days prior to the 3rd Wednesday of the respective contract month at 11.00 GMT.
Quotation:	In per cent of the nominal value
Minimum price movement (tick size) and value:	0.01% = CHF 10
Trading hours:	09.00-16.30 Swiss time (no break).
Initial margin:	CHF 1000 (spread margin: CHF 250).
Price limit:	None
Contract standard:	Cash settlement based on the discounted value of the synthetic bond. Discount rates are: for 1 year: LIMEAN; for 2 to 5 years: SWIMEAN.
Position limits:	None

Figure 27.26 5-yr Swiss franc interest rate futures - contract specification

27.14 *Money markets*

The Swiss money market is not well-developed, a fact which is largely due to the federal turnover tax which is applied to issues and transactions of short-term instruments. In view of the lack of short-term instruments, investors tend to place funds predominantly in the euromarket in the form of short-term deposits. The Swiss National Bank has, however, launched money market claims for the federal government (*Geldmarktbuchforderungen*) with maturities of 1 to 6 months, and which are not liable for turnover tax. The disadvantage, though, is that there is no secondary market for them. The three major banks have also started to develop instruments, with the same characteristics, for foreign issuers and in different currencies.

27.15 History of interest rates

A strong Swiss franc, and the crash of the stock market in the autumn of 1987, provided the signals for the Swiss National Bank to pursue an expansive monetary policy in 1987 and the first quarter of 1988. In the first few months of 1988, interest rates therefore sank to levels not seen during the preceding few years (see Figure 27.27). From December 1987 to February 1988, three-month rates declined from 3.64 per cent to 1.63 per cent. The SNB adjusted the money supply too slowly. As a result of the introduction of new liquidity requirements for commercial banks, as well as a new interbank clearing system, the demand for money declined more than the SNB had anticipated and the differential in short-term interest rates between Switzerland and other countries thus increased quite considerably. Meanwhile, the average yield of federal government bonds decreased, reaching a low of 3.75 per cent by the end of April 1988. In the second quarter of 1988, money market rates increased (along with firming interest rates abroad and the strengthening of the US dollar), as a consequence of which, capital market sentiment took a turn for the worse. In both July and August of 1988, the SNB augmented the Lombard rate, whilst in August, it also raised the discount rate. Initially, yield movements in the bond market were negligible, since newly-issued bonds, which were predominantly of good quality, were easily absorbed by the considerable demand of institutional investors. However, due to the restrictive monetary policy which had prevailed since the beginning of November 1988, money market rates crossed long-term rates and, from early 1989, pressures for higher yields in the capital market began to develop. The rising trend then continued until spring of 1990.

Against a background of full employment and rising inflation, short-term rates kept rising even faster than long-term rates, thereby creating a steeper inversion of the yield curve. Additionally, short-term Swiss franc rates were higher than the corresponding Deutschemark rates from May to September 1989 and, again, at the end of the year. Because eurodollar rates declined, the differential to them also narrowed - and reversed altogether at the end of 1989. The beginning of the revaluation of the Swiss franc at the beginning of 1990, along with the temporary stability of the Deutschemark rates, created expectations that the peak of the interest cycle had been reached. Indeed, money market rates turned down, as did long-term rates (from May), having peaked at 6.7 per cent (government bonds). However, with the beginning of the Gulf crisis in August of 1990, domestic yields reversed their trend and started rising again. Meanwhile, investors began increasingly to differentiate between different qualities of issue. Rising short-term Deutschemark rates and high domestic inflation prevented Swiss money market rates from declining further. Since September 1990, Swiss short-term interest rates were again below the German rates, but still above US dollar rates. From the beginning of 1991 onwards, the level of interest rates in Switzerland tended gradually lower. In June of that year, however, the SNB decided (in view of the sustained high inflation level and the weakness of the franc) to become even more restrictive. In the middle of August, together with other central banks, it increased the discount rate by one percentage point. In the fourth quarter of 1991, inflationary expectations and the conclusion of the EEA negotiations once again created pressure for higher long-term interest rates, which were about to test the previous high (reached in 1990). At the beginning of 1992, two opposite forces are influencing the level of interest rates in Switzerland: A weakening economy points to lower interest rates, but the continuing restrictive monetary policy of the German Bundesbank, as well as persistently high domestic inflation, both tend to counter any downward tendency.

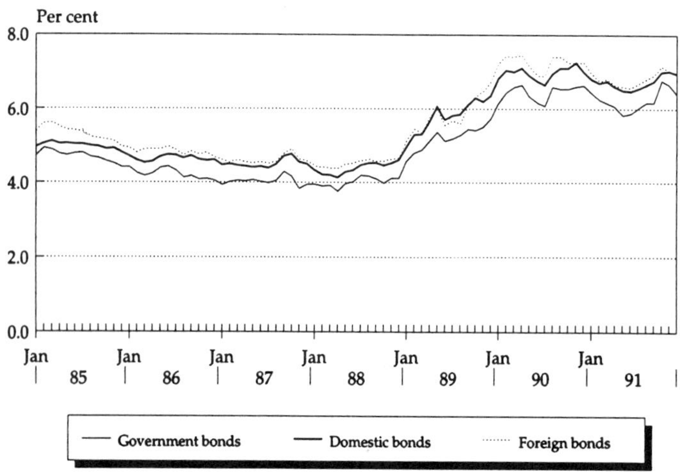

Figure 27.27 History of Swiss interest rates, 1985-1991
Source: Bank Leu

27.16 *Inter-market spreads*

Federal government bonds/domestic bonds

The yield differential between domestic issues and federal government bonds (see Figure 27.28) varies over time according to the interest rate movements and quality concerns of the investors. It always widens when interest rates increase, as was the case in 1987 and 1989. In both instances, there also were quality concerns, which triggered a flight to those issues which were deemed to be of a higher investment standard. The average spread, over time, was around 40 basis points.

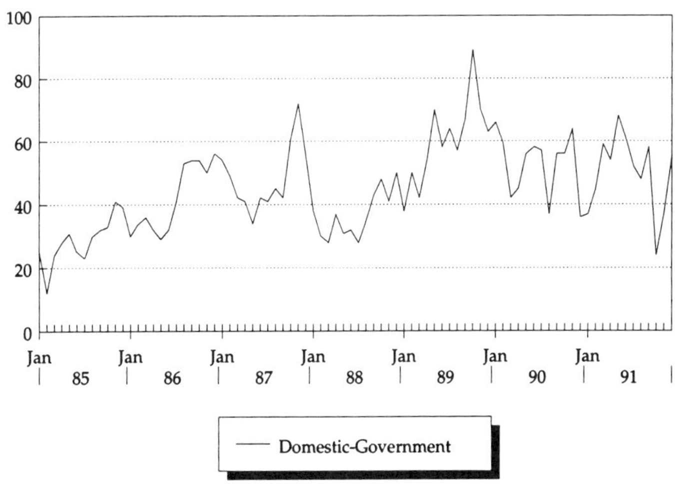

Figure 27.28 Yield spread: federal government bonds / domestic bonds
Source: Bank Leu

Domestic/foreign bonds

The yield differential between foreign and domestic issues tends to be quite volatile over a period (see Figure 27.29). It is driven by the demand of domestic institutions for domestic issues and the relative attraction of the Swiss market

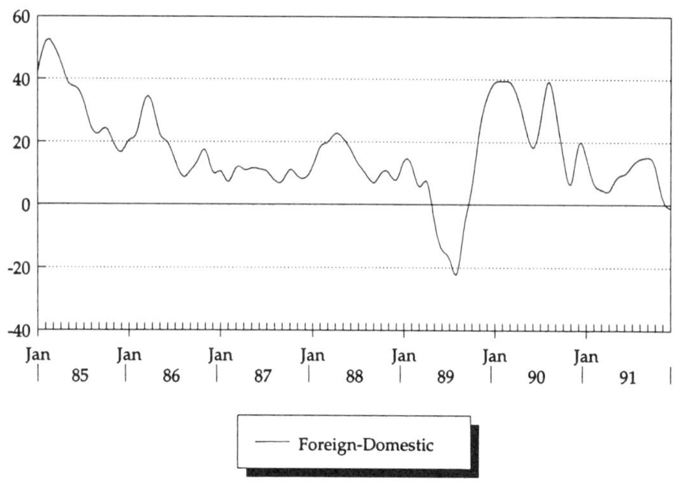

Figure 27.29 Yield spread: domestic bonds / foreign bonds
Source: Bank Leu

for those foreign investors who concentrate on foreign securities. Over time, the spread has substantially narrowed because the (withholding) tax-free foreign issues appeal more to the private investor. As the Swiss franc is likely to become more attractive as an investment currency in the course of 1992, the differential will remain narrow, or even reverse.

Yield spread between foreign bond qualities

During the early- and mid-eighties, investors made little of differences of quality, despite the fact that the Swiss market was afloat with many lesser-quality issues. From 1989 onwards, though, quality became a major factor as a number of predominantly British and American borrowers got into trouble. In 1991, the crisis peaked and although an improvement is expected, it is likely to be rather slow, since other European and Japanese issuers are likely to experience difficulties as well. The yield spread between qualities is shown in Figure 27.30.

German / Swiss government bonds

The yield differential between Swiss government bonds and German *Bundesanleihen* has been very volatile (see Figure 27.31), reflecting relative developments

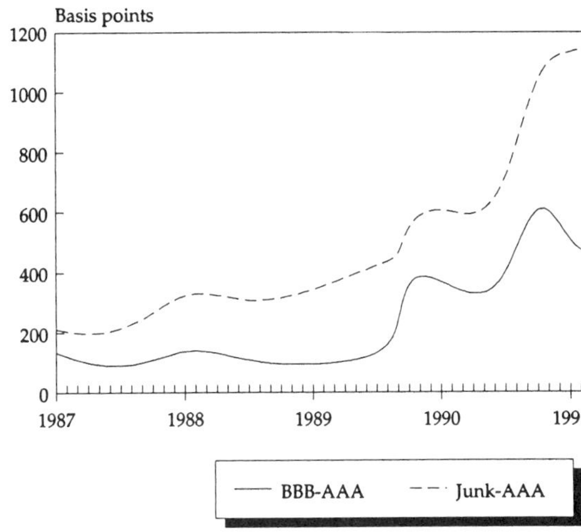

Figure 27.30 Yield spread among different qualities of foreign bonds
Source: Bank Leu

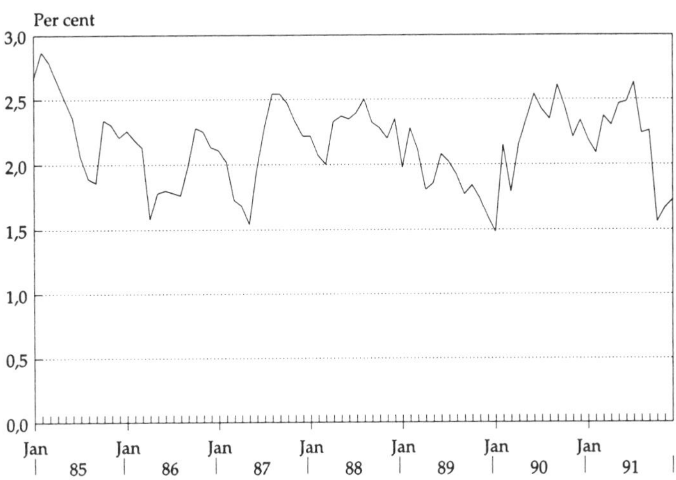

Figure 27.31 Yield spread: German / Swiss government bonds
Source: Bank Leu

with respect to economic growth, monetary policy, inflation and budget deficit. Reunification and currency union had an adverse effect in Germany, widening the differential in 1989/90. However, in 1991, the differential narrowed as higher inflation and the conclusion of the EEA treaty both had adverse impacts in Switzerland. The yield spread is expected to decline even further in 1992, as the general convergence of European interest rates continues.

27.17 Sources of reference

Financial data

The following publications are available to those interested in obtaining further information about investing in Switzerland. (Those marked with an asterisk are not available in English, but a translation of the title in English is provided in parenthesis).

- *International Financial Review,* with comments on events in the capital market, appears weekly.
- *Die Volkswirtschaft** (The National Economy) is published by the Ministry of Economic Affairs, and appears monthly. It focuses on macroeconomic conditions.
- *Statistisches Jahrbuch der Schweiz** (Statistical Almanac of Switzerland) appears annually. It gives an overview of the Swiss economy.
- *Schweizerische Nationalbankberichte** (Swiss National Bank reports) appear on a monthly, quarterly and annual basis. They present a statistical summary of economic events.
- *Annual Report* of the Zurich Stock Exchange.

Financial press

Daily newspapers with comprehensive financial sections are:

- *Neue Zuercher Zeitung**
- *Tages Anzeiger**
- *Basler Zeitung**
- *Journal de Geneve**

There are also specialist financial papers:

- *L'Agefi** (daily)
- *Finanz und Wirtschaft** (twice a week)
- *Schweizerische Handelszeitung** (weekly)
- *Cash** (weekly)
- *Bilanz** (monthly)
- *Schweizer Bank** (monthly)
- *Finanzmarkt und Portfolio management** (monthly)

Quote vendors and news agencies

- Telekurs provide information on system pages: 401,NZ; 401,NS; 40,5; 85,EK; 340,Valor,1; 85,MDY
- Reuters provide information on system pages: SNBS; FWDV; SFR3-9; SWAA-H
- Bloomberg provide information on system pages: IYC; MDY

Further reading

Books

- Haemmerli, H: *Aspekte des Schweizerischen Emissionsgeschaeftes** (Aspects of Swiss Underwriting Business), 1986.
- Loeffler, A: *Anleihen** (Bonds), 1987.
- Hoffmann, P: *Bonitätsbeurteilung durch Credit Rating** (Creditworthiness), 1991.

Other Publications

A number of Swiss banks and financial institutions have their own publications:

- *The Swiss Capital Market*, Credit Swiss, 1986
- *The Swiss Capital Market*, Swiss Bank Corp., 1986
- *The Swiss Capital Market by International Comparison*, Union Bank of Switzerland, 1986
- *Capital Market Trends*, Bank Leu, appears on a monthly and quarterly basis

Chapter

28

The bond markets of the

United Kingdom

Stuart McLean
UNI Storebrand Investment Managers

Christopher Anthony
UBS Phillips & Drew

Steven Bell
Morgan Grenfell

with help from

Richard Williams
Credit Suisse First Boston

Grant Mackie
County Natwest Securities

Note: In general text, the £-sign is used to denote the British pound (sterling). Elsewhere, the international mnemonic 'GBP' is used.

28.1 Introduction

The United Kingdom bond markets have been undergoing a period of major change. The now famed 'Big Bang' in October 1986 saw a total revision of the structure of the securities markets. This included the abolition of single capacity (the old brokers and jobbers), the introduction of dual capacity, the expansion of security houses to include the admission of foreign security houses, the change to screen-based trading (from a physical trading floor) and the removal of fixed commissions. The stock exchange had two years to adapt and a very high investment in technology. In the gilt-edged market, for example, the number of companies choosing to make markets (GEMMs) expanded to 27. However, although turnover increased, revenues fell sharply, competition increased and many houses lost money. The introduction of the BIS rules for banks and the collapse in bond turnover in London in the euro-markets, put pressure on the London trading houses and resulted in several closing either or both their gilts and/or eurobond departments. The result was a dramatic reduction in staffing levels and a reduction to only 17 GEMMs. The structural changes are still continuing and one must wait for the situation to settle before assessing how the markets will evolve to their final form.

The Thatcher government also embarked on a process of major tax reform which resulted in large scale reduction of income tax rates and the removal of many of the tax anomalies that were exploited by market participants to reduce their tax liabilities. The highest rate of income tax was reduced over a number of years from 98.0 per cent, on unearned income, to 40.0 per cent; corporate taxation was also reduced, to 35 per cent, while capital gains tax (CGT) was equated to income tax thereby removing any anomaly between interest and capital gain (note that gilt-edged bonds, their derivatives and the majority of non-government fixed-interest bonds are free of CGT). At the same time, various institutional tax rates were harmonized and differentials removed. Government expenditure was brought under control and the budget brought into surplus enabling a fall in government borrowing. The dramatic turnaround was such that government bonds were bought back and retired, the result being that the proportion of gilts, both as a percentage of GNP and in UK portfolios, fell dramatically.

At a meeting of the European Bond Commission in 1991, a comment was made by one of the continental European members that the UK government bond market was now probably one of the most 'primitive' in Europe. With the lack of issuance since 1987 there had been no need to maintain or evolve the UK market. In contrast, however, many continental European markets had been deregulating and making major advances in the form and structure of their markets with actions such as the removal of withholding tax, the development of futures/options markets, etc. Indeed, several emerging markets such as Belgium, Spain and Italy had features that were thought pre-requisite for a major market yet were not to be found in the UK gilt-edged market, which currently lacks all the following features:

- automatic payment of interest without withholding tax
- a repo market
- securities held in Euroclear/Cedel
- a futures/options market on a 10-year bond

These deficiencies are surprising when one considers that London has become the major trading centre for many European government bond markets, often with volumes that exceed those with in that country. With bonds being a very low proportion of domestic UK funds, the government may, with the return to a budget deficit, undertake a major restructuring of the market in order to appeal to international investors who need to be persuaded that the UK Gilt Edged market is again one of the major bond markets in the world.

Market composition

Throughout the 1970s, and early 1980s, the size of the total bond market was almost entirely determined by the UK government's funding needs. Such was

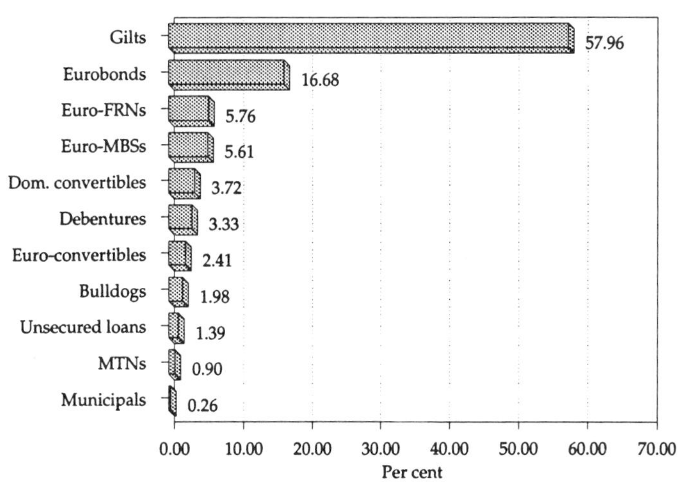

Figure 28.1 Composition of UK bond market

demand for funds by the government that rates rose to a level high enough to cause issuance in all other sectors of the sterling bond market to virtually dry up completely in the 1970s. The first market to show any sign of revival was the Bulldog market in 1980; this being shortly followed by a few local authority (and a number of corporate) issues. More recently, though, there has been a relative paucity of issues in the domestic markets. Overall, therefore, the growth of the domestic bond markets, with the exception of straight corporate issues and the convertible market, has been slow but this has been more than compensated by the dramatic growth of the eurosterling market (including MTNs): from just over £4bn outstanding in 1984, to over £30.3bn in 1988 and to £65.4bn in 1991.

While the government public sector debt repayment (PSDR) enabled the government to buy back considerable debt, it also led to a lack of new issues, thereby reducing the proportion of the gilt-edged market of the total sterling market, from 74.88 per cent in 1988 to 57.92 per cent in 1991 (see Figure 28.2). In contrast, eurosterling 'straight' bonds rose from 8.88 per cent to 16.71 per cent while other areas of growth included: mortgage-backed securities 'MBSs' from 0.77 per cent to 5.61 per cent, euro-convertibles from 1.81 per cent to 2.40 per cent and domestic convertibles from 2.21 per cent to 3.72 per cent. Due to the sharp fall in gilts, modest rises were seen in floating-rate notes (FRNs), Bulldogs

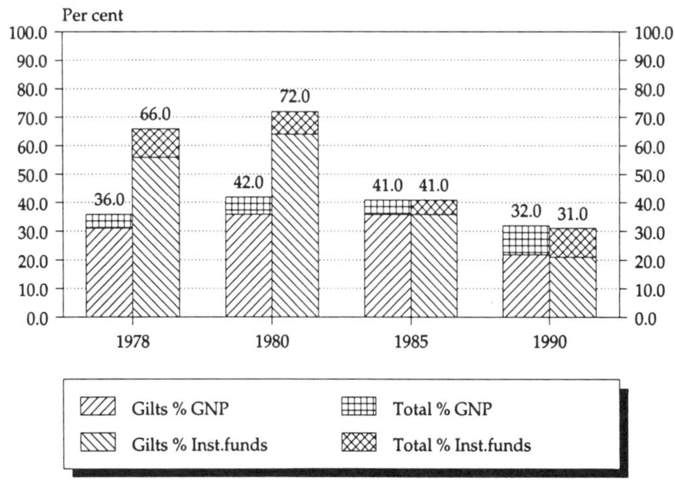

Figure 28.2 Relative size of the market

and corporate bonds, although municipal bonds have fallen. A new sector, for medium-term notes (MTNs), opened during this period and has already grown to exceed the municipal or local authority market, although is still relatively small, at £1.88bn outstanding, 0.90 per cent of the total sterling market and 6th largest euro-MTN currency market after US dollars, Australian dollars, Ecu, Italian lira and Yen.

The gilt-edged market grew, as a proportion of GNP, to 36.0 per cent in the mid-1980s. However, following the Thatcher government's decision to tighten control on government spending and to reduce the public sector deficit, it has since shrunk to 22.0 per cent. Until the mid-1980s, non-gilt-edged bonds represented about 5.0 per cent of GNP, but with the growth of the other sterling markets (led mainly by the expansion of the eurosterling market and the liberalization of mortgage finance techniques that enabled the creation of MBSs), it has grown to 10.0 per cent.

Bond market deregulation

The government has enacted a programme of reform to deregulate the UK financial markets. This started with the removal of exchange controls in 1979. This fundamental move, made it then appropriate to eliminate the many anomalies that existed both between the UK and other countries and also internally between the domestic markets and the eurosterling markets. Changes to the legislation allowed UK corporates to borrow in the eurosterling market and

1979	Exchange controls suspended (later abolished)
1984	Non-gilt sterling bonds exempted from capital gains tax (subject to qualifications)
1986	Stamp duty on non-government bonds removed following unpopular re-imposition
	First euro-commercial paper issue
	First long-dated eurosterling issue
	First eurosterling convertible issue
1987	First mortgage-backed security issue
1988	Size restriction on eurosterling issues lifted
1989	Control of Borrowing Order abolished - bond issues of shorter than 5 years and as small as £100 000 permitted, opening up the possibility of issuing medium-term notes etc.
1990	First medium-term note

Figure 28.3 History of UK bond market deregulation

pay interest gross; later, UK building societies were allowed to access the wholesale money markets and issue bonds. The result was a dramatic growth in eurosterling issues for both UK and international borrowers. An article in the *Bank of England Quarterly* (February 1988) entitled 'Recent Developments in the Corporate and Bulldog sectors of the Sterling Bond Market', discussed many of the attractions of eurosterling in comparison with domestic bond markets.

Mortgage-backed securities

Another major change was in the deregulation of the banking and mortgage institutions - the building societies who provide house financing, usually on a variable-rate basis, and raise funds by offering savers a variety of deposit schemes. There had been a number of fiscal and structural advantages to these institutions over the banks that supported them in maintaining their dominant position in both these areas. The government removed many of the constraints and, at the same time, allowed other companies to enter the area of providing home finance. An early leader, The Mortgage Corporation (TMC) (a Salomon Brothers company) was shortly joined by a wide variety of insurance companies and banks, often UK branches of overseas institutions. Other special-purpose or centralized lending companies, similar to TMC, were formed. They included: National Home Loans, Household Mortgage Corporation and Mortgage Funding Corporation. All these institutions, including the building societies were able to tap the wholesale money markets to raise the necessary finance. Building societies became issuers of both fixed- and floating-rate notes. On the other hand, the centralized mortgage borrowers issued AAA-rated mortgage-backed securities (MBSs), a *pass-through* security. These instruments, similar to pay-through mortgage-backed securities from the United States, exposing the bondholder not only to the interest rate risk but also pre-payment risk of the underlying mortgage loan portfolio. This is because, as mortgages are repaid, capital flow passes through to the bondholder as an early partial redemption. In the US, this market has grown to be second only to US government at US$ 3 trillion, ahead of corporate bonds. As banks, e.g. Bank of Ireland and CIBC, came under pressure from the BIS rules, many of them repackaged their home lending books and either sold portfolios privately or they issued into the MBS market. The first issue was in March 1987 and this sector now has £11.78bn outstanding. There has only been one genuine, fully fixed-rate MBS: the Bear Stearns Mortgage Securities No.1 11.75 per cent 2017 (£124m). This is probably because the vast majority of mortgages in the UK are floating-rate. Following the violent rises in mortgage interest rates during 1989-91 (peaking at 15.75 per cent), there may be a temptation amongst UK households to take out fixed-rate mortgages when, and if, the rates fall below 9.00 per cent; more fixed-rate issues could then be seen. Other, short maturity, synthetic fixed-rate securities have been manufactured from variable-rate mortgage pools. More recently, there have been a number of fixed-rate issues which have been created by swapping a tranche of a FRN issue. The one CMS 101 issue and three HMC 101-103 issues total £425m.

Because this market is growing rapidly and there is considerable interest in developing similar markets in other European countries, a more detailed description is given in Section 28.4

Convertibles and preference shares

In recent years there has been a massive increase in convertible issuance, mainly through the eurosterling market. This market is attractive to issuers in that they can often achieve higher premiums and target a wide distribution, especially amongst overseas investors and hence a surge in issuance was witnessed before the October Crash, almost exclusively by lower multiple companies. These issues offered investors a put after five years often at a premium as high as 30 per cent over the redemption value. The aim was that, if the bond was converted to equity then the issuer would achieve equity at a higher level than at the time of issuance and if the bond was put, it would be a cheaper form of debt than borrowing in the open market.

So widespread was the positive view of a future rise in equity prices that little thought was given, by the borrowers, to these puts being operated. Indeed, such was the size of issues that, as the put-dates approached and the conversions became worthless, there was a serious fall in the equity prices reflecting investors' growing concerns that companies would be unable to finance the puts. Major refinancing operations had to be undertaken by a number of these companies, Saatchi & Saatchi being the most prominent. Nevertheless, the euro-convertible market has still been a major source of finance, with some issuers offering conversion into shares of other companies they hold (covered convertibles).

The convertible market has not been without further controversy. In the UK, when a company raises money by the issue of equity (or future equity as in the case of convertibles) for cash, the company has first to offer it to existing shareholders who then have three weeks to either accept or reject it (the *pre-emptive right*). A number of borrowers felt that this did not apply to euro-issues, especially as one of the reasons for issuing in this markets was to widen the investor group and place equity in the hands of overseas investors, especially at high premiums (rights issues in the UK are usually undertaken at a discount to existing share values.)

Following intense pressure from UK investors it was agreed that these securities would not have to be first offered to existing shareholders if the offer for new cash did not exceeded 7.5 per cent of existing shares. Additionally, convertibles issued to finance take-overs were excluded. The net result is that most large issues take place in the international market rather than the domestic convertible market. Nevertheless, a few have been issued domestically, either because exemptive rights applied or that the name was not well recognized internationally (or the company had not been credit-rated).

Medium-term notes (MTNs)

In February 1990, the rules concerning euro-commercial paper were changed to allow issues up to five years to be known as medium-term notes, or MTNs. These issues are part of a programme which has an upper limit on total issuance and usually covers several currencies. Issues are made by agreement between the issuers and the investor and full flexibility as to maturity date, coupon and form are allowed. These securities are, therefore, very attractive to certain types of investors and are usually issued close to market levels. Any premium that would be exacted due to the need to meet investors' specific requirements are offset by a lack of liquidity.

Municipal (or local authority & public bodies) bonds

This sector has continued to decline with no public issuance for some considerable time. This is because these bodies have been able to raise finance at very attractive rates and for very long periods, directly from central government via the Public Works Loan Board (PWLB). Local authorities have been borrowing an estimated steady £4-6bn a year from the PWLB, well in excess of their own borrowing requirement of £0.5bn. This excess was initially used to repay bank and longer term debt (the retirement of existing bonds) as well as to release privatization monies - previously lent internally - for investment in so-called 'external investment funds'. As at the end of March 1989, the total amount of local authority debt was £50.8bn of which £44.1bn was owed to the PWLB with short term assets at £9.6bn. Evidence exists that PWLB rates are too low and there is considerable discussion about the future of local authority funding. Already, the arrangements with regard to quotas and lending rules have been altered and further reviews can be expected, with expectations that PWLB rates will rise sharply and/or that quotas will be put in place. This means that local authorities will have to return to banking finance and, when rates are low enough, to the issuance of long-term debt.

There has also been some concern by investors about the credit-quality of some local authorities (although there are many whose credit-quality cannot be questioned), especially those which are Labour-controlled, e.g. the London Boroughs of Haringey, Southwark, Islington and Lambeth, also some major cities such as Liverpool (which experienced problems in 1985) as well as the interest rate swaps debacle of 1988-90. Therefore, not all authorities will have access to this market.

It should be noted that these bonds do not have an implicit government guarantee and, indeed, the government has allowed one public body, the Mersey Docks & Harbour Board, to default.

It has often been said that the government would not allow any local authority to default. While this has not happened yet, the tension between many Labour controlled local authorities and the Conservative government is such that it is more likely than previously assumed.

Types of issue

Due to a lack of new issuance in the domestic bond market, most of the more innovative structures in the UK are to be found in the gilt-edged and eurosterling markets. In the gilt-edged, two notable sectors are convertibles (i.e. bonds with short-dated maturities which may be converted into longer-dated bonds) and index-linked bonds (the coupon and maturity value of which are linked to the Retail Price Index (RPI).

The eurosterling market has a considerable volume of floating-rate notes (FRNs) outstanding and while other structures such as bonds with warrants, puts and conversions into other securities are available, most are in the form of bullets. The growth of eurosterling convertible markets at the expense of the domestic convertible market, as previously discussed, is of particular note.

In the UK domestic market, corporate bonds are available in two forms: debentures and unsecured loans. The debenture market consists of securities which are secured, in most cases, on the assets of the company - commonly property. However, a few securities have been issued which have a prior call on the general revenue of the issuer. It is often thought that UK institutions have an exclusive demand for secured loans; however, the growth of the eurosterling market shows how this situation has changed. The re-emergence of domestic corporate bonds in the 1980s (after being effectively closed in the 1970s by the high levels of interest and the massive demands by central government), has attracted those borrowers who are able to offer security, such as property companies and breweries, but has also enabled large corporates, such as ICI, BAT and banks to raise funds in considerable size, in unsecured form.

Funding of corporate sector

Although it has been government policy to promote the issuance of corporate debt this has, however, been only been partially successful. The domestic corporate sector's reliance upon the banking system for finance has remained strongly in evidence in the past five years and, given the highly developed state of the banking system in the UK, there is little reason to believe that the capital markets will be in a position where they can supply a dominant proportion of the corporate sector's funding needs in the years ahead. It can be seen in Figure 28.4

that capital issues are relatively small, with surges in equity issuance in the run up to the October Crash in 1987 and in 1991, followed by heavy reliance on banks in the intervening three years.

Year	Total external borrowings	Bank borrowings	Debs & pref.	Other capital issues	Equities
1986	20.2	9.1	2.5	1.1	5.5
1987	35.3	12.1	3.6	2.2	13.4
1988	49.5	31.0	3.6	2.5	4.4
1989	62.2	33.3	5.6	7.7	1.9
1990	40.0	18.8	3.5	5.9	2.6

Figure 28.4 Funding of the corporate sector (GBP billion)

The economic policies of the Conservative administrations during the 1980s had a profound effect on the markets. The lowering of inflation, restoration of competitiveness by industry, strong economic growth and a dramatic increase in productivity all resulted in a stable currency and a falling government borrowing requirement. This, in turn, resulted in strong inflows from overseas investors which allowed the growth of the eurosterling market to be maintained. However, the heady days of 1987 were about to come to a dramatic and disastrous end. The Conservative Chancellor, Lawson, who is a firm believer in the European exchange rate mechanism, decided to shadow the Deutschemark at a Dm 3.00 level. With the marked differential in interest rates between the two countries, overseas investors decided that the UK was a one-way bet and moved considerable volumes of money into the UK, not only into bonds but also uncovered deposits. Interest rates began to fall from 11.00 per cent to nearly 7.50 per cent (London interbank offered rate, LIBOR, in 1988) and to 9.00 per cent in long-bond yields. These reductions fuelled a major expansion in the economy which, coupled with the deregulation of the financial community, saw borrowing levels explode. Property prices escalated. Fears of overheating in the economy led the government to initiate an interest rate rise of 0.50 per cent.

The surge in consumption in early 1988, triggered by the relaxed credit conditions and the series of tax cuts introduced in the spring budget, exacerbated the deterioration in the balance of payments and along with an already tight labour market, these created conditions in the economy which fuelled the rise in retail price inflation, a variable which peaked some 18 months later at 10.90 per cent - a rise of 8.50 per cent from the floor. Short-term interest rates were forced to unsustainable low levels, a view supported by the bond market, where yields failed to follow base rates lower.

The trend in UK interest rates was reversed, not so much by evidence of the deterioration in economic performance (which, due to statistical shortcomings appeared to be some way off), but by concerted tightening moves by the bulk of industrialized countries. Short-term interest rates were moved progressively higher, a reaction to a deterioration in sterling's fortunes on the foreign exchanges, further tightening in international credit conditions and mounting problems on the domestic economic front. By the end of the year, base rates had risen 5.50 percentage points from their late-May floor of 7.50 per cent.

International interest in UK bonds is reflected in the sales of gilt-edged bonds to overseas investors. These sales had been growing gradually from £211m in 19801/82 to £3549m in 1987/88; however, they fell to a resale of just £26 million. In 1989/90, overseas investors, particularly Japanese, decided to sell and UK resales saw £3110m. The trend continued in 1990/91, albeit at a lower level of £1730m.

28.2 Economics

Political background

The UK has a two-party system of parliamentary democracy in the sense that every government in modern times has been formed by either the Conservative or Labour parties. There have been thirteen general elections since the war, not counting the one due in 1992; the Conservatives have won a majority in seven, Labour in six. The UK's first-past-the-post system means that minority parties tend to be under-represented in parliament relative to their share of the vote, particularly if their support is spread nationally. The Liberal Party, in its various guises and alliances, has suffered most from this. In the 1987 election it attracted 23 per cent of the vote but gained just 3 per cent of the seats in parliament. In 1983, its share of the vote was 25 per cent, just 2 percentage points below Labour, yet the Liberal/SDP Alliance won only 23 seats compared with 209 for Labour.

Mrs Thatcher won the 1979 election and continued as prime minister until she was toppled from power in November 1990. John Major replaced her without the need for a general election - the British prime minister is not elected directly but is normally the leader of the party with an overall majority of seats in parliament.

The Conservative Party has traditionally been more popular among the middle classes and in the prosperous south of the country. By contrast, the Labour Party, with its roots in the union movement, has more of its support in inner city areas and the north. The Labour Party's vote is becoming increasingly concentrated so that, in the constituencies where it already holds control, its majority is tending to increase in relative terms. Given the UK's electoral system, this works to Labour's disadvantage in that, on an even share of the vote, the Conservatives would normally win more seats in Parliament. When the boundary commission re-designates constituencies in 1993, this electoral penalty on Labour will increase - some estimates put its potential loss as high as 20 seats.

The Labour Party has enjoyed a revival under the leadership of Neil Kinnock, as a result both of its shift towards the centre and the unpopularity of the government. The Labour Party are now highly pro-Europe, reversing the position relative to the Conservatives that prevailed in the past. Nationalization is no longer a key part of their policy and, in line with the general strategy of distancing themselves from the union movement, they have played-down earlier commitments to reverse much of the labour market legislation passed under Mrs Thatcher.

Following Mrs Thatcher's demise, John Major has promoted a much more centrist strategy, distinguished by being more pro-European (though still showing scepticism in key areas), generally right-wing on economic issues, but more centrist on social issues. The differences between the two major parties at the beginning of the 1990s are arguably less than they have been at any time since the late sixties.

Neither of the two main parties, nor the smaller parties, take an avowedly anti-European stance. Indeed, the bulk of the debate *vis-à-vis* Europe has been within the Conservative Party. There is a split in public opinion over the need for closer political and economic integration within Europe, although a majority would seem to disapprove of any move to leave the EC or the ERM. As the prospect of European political integration has grown, a number of nationalist groups within the UK, notably the Scottish National Party, have seen this as a way of securing devolution of power from Westminster, if not full independence. The running sore of Northern Ireland, however, remains as intractable as ever.

National income

The UK has traditionally been a relatively low-growth economy compared with other western European, or OECD, nations. As a result, its relative position in world national-income league tables has tended to slip. The UK has been overtaken by France and pushed to the bottom of the Group of Five league, with the Italian government suggesting that their economy is actually now bigger if account is taken of the 'hidden economy'. Although the OECD have been persuaded of this argument and placed Italy at number five, just ahead of the UK, alternative indicators of living standards, such as numbers of specific consumer goods per capita, tend to suggest that the UK remains ahead. The UK is unusual in having few passenger cars on a per capita basis but, along with North America and Japan, shows a heavy demand for television sets with an average of over one for every two inhabitants.

Figure 28.5 shows that the relative growth rates of the UK and other major countries converged, and even reversed, in the late 1980s. This now seems to have been a cyclical phenomenon with the UK economic boom occurring earlier, and being stronger, than in other major countries. Figure 28.6 shows the recent pattern of growth rates as the UK has moved into heavy recession. The peak trough-to-trough loss of GDP in the 1990-91 recession is estimated to be 3-4 per cent. This is similar to the 1974-75, recession but much less than in 1980-81, when non-oil GDP fell by 6 per cent. Many of the old uncertainties about the UK's ability to sustain a growth rate at, or close to, the international average have now returned. One improvement that does appear to have been sustained is the rise in manufacturing productivity growth. However, there has been no benefit from this in terms of either an increased share of manufacturing output

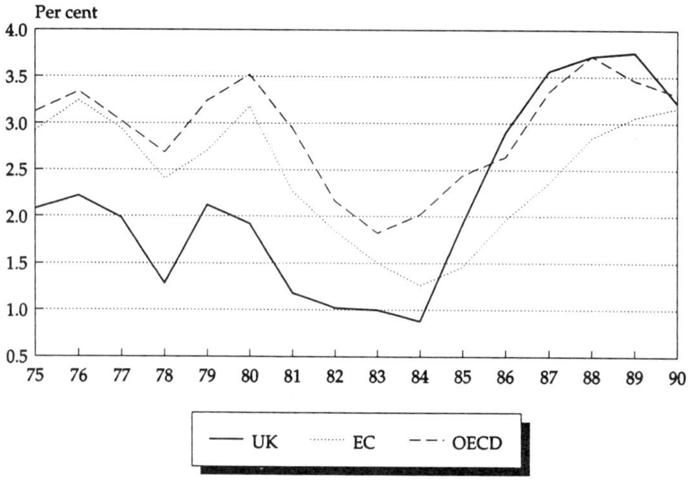

Figure 28.5 **Long-term UK growth trend - percentage change in real GDP (5-yr. moving av.)**
Source: OECD

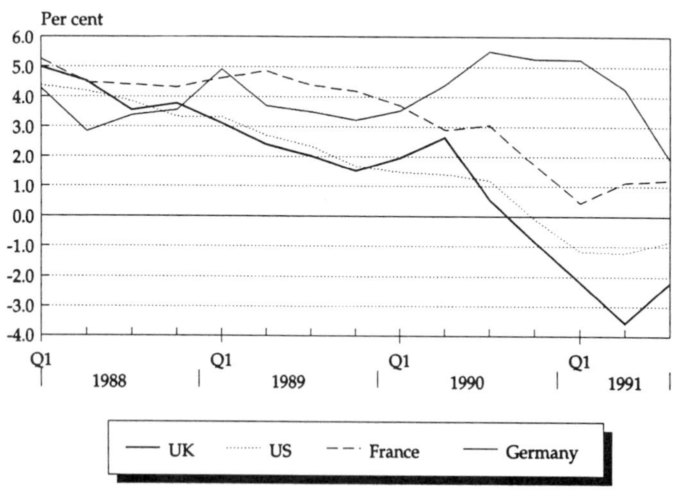

Figure 28.6 **UK GDP/GNP**
Source: Datastream

in national income, or a faster absolute rate of growth; the impact has been seen in lower manufacturing employment. Morgan Grenfell estimate that the UK's trend growth-rate is now some 2 1/4 per cent per annum, very close to the average in the 1970s and 1980s.

Trade balance

The UK has traditionally had a surplus on the invisible account but a deficit on trade, as a result of which, the current account has moved between surplus and deficit. Due to the strength of the economic boom in the late 1980s (a much stronger cyclical position than in the UK's main export markets), the current account deficit reached very high levels, peaking at over £20bn, or 4 per cent of GDP, in 1989 (see Figure 28.7).

The UK's foreign assets are dominated by holdings of direct investments and equities, whereas the liabilities are more heavily weighted towards interest-bearing securities and deposits. Capital gains on the UK's net asset position do not feature in the balance of payments figures and, therefore, a continuing current account deficit can be consistent with a stable net foreign asset position. In fact, year-to-year movements in net assets are dominated by the effect of currency conversion. The dominant currency denomination of assets is the US dollar

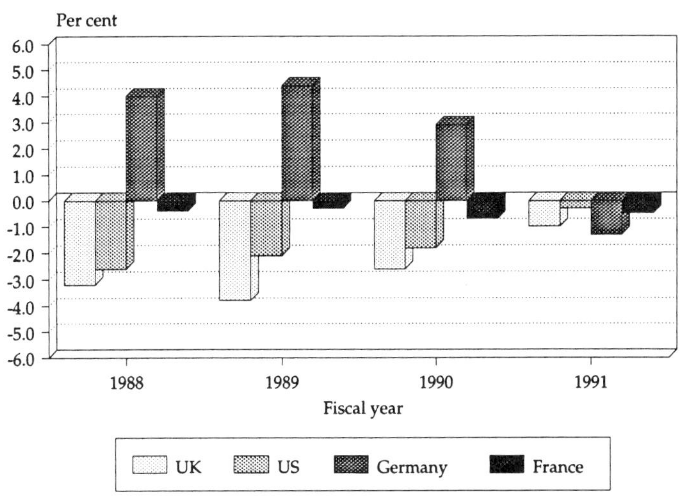

Figure 28.7 UK current account (as percentage of GDP/GNP)
Source: Morgan Grenfell

while most liabilities are set in sterling. This was the reason behind the very large fall in UK net assets in 1990, the latest year for which full figures are available. The UK remains one of the largest international creditors.

Although the current account deficit shrank to 1 per cent of GNP in 1991, it has failed to move into surplus despite the very beneficial effects of the cyclical position in the UK *vis-à-vis* the rest of the world, particularly Germany, which is now the UK's largest trade partner (the US held this position a decade ago). When more robust growth is evident in the UK, the current account may once again return as a constraint on economic policy. Indeed, if the current account deficit were to return to 2 or 3 per cent of GDP, it may call into question the ability to sustain sterling's exchange rate parity within the ERM. However, Morgan Grenfell take a relatively sanguine view of this. The substantial increase in direct investment into the UK, particularly by the car industry, suggests that the output of internationally-tradeable goods will be sustained in the UK, whilst a decision to opt for European monetary union (Emu) would reduce, and ultimately eliminate, the importance of balance of payments flows.

Unemployment

After a substantial and extended decline in unemployment in the late 1980s, the trend has been rapidly reversed by the 1990-91 recession (see Figure 28.8). Once thought to be a lagging indicator of the economy, both the rise and the deceleration in unemployment have occurred more swiftly than in past recessions. Business was much more sensitive to economic conditions and began to shed labour quickly in the 1990-91 recession. Also, the downturn was concentrated on those sectors with high labour-turnover, notably construction and retailing. One particular feature is that outflows from the unemployment register started to rise in the spring of 1991, less than a year after the economy moved into recession. This reflects the fact that layoffs have been greatest in the south where the level of unemployment is relatively low. This (and the fact that many of those made redundant are highly-skilled) suggests that unemployment is unlikely to increase to the same degree as in the recession a decade ago. Nonetheless, the UK, like many other European countries, sustains a level of unemployment that is much higher in relation to the figures for the 1960s and 1970s or, indeed, those experienced by Japan and the US in the 1990s.

Monetary policy

The decision by the UK government to join the ERM in October 1990 was part of a long-term trend towards greater integration within Europe. It also reflected disappointment with past experiments at conducting an independent monetary policy. Monetary targets have been adopted, revised, redefined and abandoned, and augmented on some occasions by quantitative restrictions. Almost every

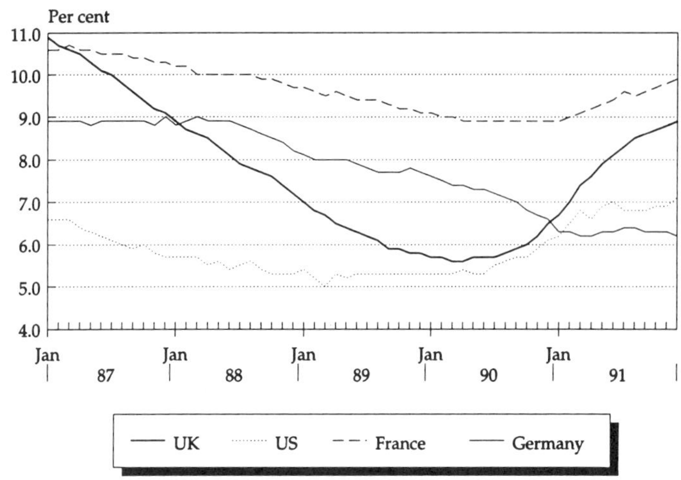

Figure 28.8 UK unemployment (percentage of work-force)
Source: OECD

combination of interest rate and funding strategy has been tried in attempts by the monetary authorities to achieve sustainable low inflation. In the early 1980s, the Conservative government published their *Medium-Term Financial Strategy* which sought to reduce the growth of M3, then the main monetary aggregate, without excessive reliance on interest rates - thus implying firm control of the budget deficit. Short-term control of the monetary aggregate was to be via short-term interest rates.

In the event, increasing short-term interest rates appeared, if anything, to boost the growth of M3, which persistently overshot targets. The main influence of monetary policy was seen to be through the exchange rate, which rose very strongly in response to interest rate increases which were taken on purely domestic grounds. The associated recession was seen by many as the sole root by which inflation was reduced, with monetary policy itself having a limited direct influence. The disenchantment with the instability of broad money-growth, combined with the difficulty of controlling it with short-term interest rates, led the government through its Chancellor, Nigel Lawson, to abandon monetary targeting and cease issuing greater quantities of debt than were needed to finance the public sector deficit (a technique known as over-funding), in the mid-1980s. Many commentators believe that this represented a monetary relaxation which led to the subsequent boom and inflation in the economy. What is undoubtedly true is that the progressive deregulation of credit, and the financial system more generally, provided the background in which a surge in consumer spending could be financed to a much greater degree than in past upswings.

As the government moved away from monetary targets, the exchange rate began to have an increasing role in monetary policy decision-making and Lawson attempted to shadow the Deutschemark, a policy which was opposed by the then prime minister, Margaret Thatcher. Before she resigned, Mrs Thatcher had accepted the principle of ERM membership although she did set tough conditions. The chancellor of the Exchequer at the time of entry to the ERM, in October 1990, was John Major and he can therefore be closely identified with both the principle and the level of the parity. By adopting for the wider 6 per cent band within the system, the authorities accepted that the UK economy was far from fully-converged towards the sustained low inflation rates of the core members, such as France. There is a clear intention under the present government to move to narrow bands around the existing parity of Dm 2.95.

In line with increasing integration into Europe, day-to-day movements in money market rates and, to an increasing degree, longer-term interest rates, are influenced by developments in Germany. In contrast to the position in the 1970s when movements in US rates were almost fully transmitted to London, UK money market interest rates now trade as a spread over those in Germany. This spread, in turn, reflects the range of economic and political factors, notably relative inflation rates, balance of payments and probability of a realignment of the parity.

In terms of day-to-day management of the money markets, the Bank of England attempts to achieve a surplus on its transactions with the banking system. This leaves the market with a shortage on most days in the money market, which must then be relieved by transactions with the Bank of England. Normally this is achieved by the Bank of England buying bills (i.e. accepted commercial bills and Treasury bills) from the market. The discount houses offer bills to the Bank, which may accept or decline. Transactions are separated into four bands, according to maturity, from one-day to three-month. Since May 1989, the Bank of England has normally transacted in bands one and two, i.e. maturities up to one month. When market shortages are particularly large over several days, the Bank may enter into a repurchase agreement, or 'repo'. The maturity is typically for three weeks and may be with the discount houses against bills, or with banks generally against gilt-edged securities. Although not an official rate, banks' base rates, which underpin the lending and, to some extent, the deposit-rate system in the UK, are the most widely-used measure of officially-influenced short-term rates in the UK. The Bank of England is always strained by having, on the one hand, a desire to avoid creating arbitrage opportunities by its activities whilst, on the other, having a role (as agent for the Treasury) in setting the overall level of interest rates. Another problem for the monetary authorities is that, in conducting its operations largely via the discount market, they are operating on a very thin pivot for the UK monetary system. There have been moves to extend the range of intermediaries with whom they deal, but the concern of the authorities is that their wish to retain control over the structure may be diminished if they were to deal directly with the major clearing banks. Unlike many other countries, the UK has neither a pre-announced discount rate nor a specific emergency-funding rate, while the rates at which the money market operations are conducted tend to be constant on a day-to-day basis, with discrete movements when the authorities wish to change banks' base rates. Nor does the government have a required-reserve system, except for a tiny non-interest-bearing requirement, known as the cash ratio, which is recognized as a mechanism by which the Bank of England itself is financed. The cash ratio currently stands at 0.35 per cent of banks' eligible liabilities, which broadly equates to their deposits. Traditionally, increases in interest rates have typically been one or two (and on rare occasions three) percentage points. In the recent cycle of interest rate reductions, apart from the first move from the 15 per cent peak down to 14 per cent, all the changes have been by 1/2 per cent. At some stage, a move to 1/4 per cent changes is likely.

Under the terms of the Maastricht treaty, the UK must establish an independent central bank as part of the process of moving to Stage Three, if it wishes to participate in Emu.

Budget deficit

Traditionally, the UK has had a wide budget deficit but, in the latter part of the 1980s, the combination of economic boom, firm control of public spending and privatization receipts generated a substantial surplus. In the 1987 fiscal year, for example, the surplus amounted to 3 per cent of GDP (see Figure 28.9). No other major country was running a budget surplus in this period and the UK's position was one of the most remarkable turnarounds in the history of fiscal policy. However, together with a relaxation of public spending controls and the cost of ameliorating the introduction of poll tax, the recession has pushed the budget back into deficit. A further big deterioration in the size of the deficit is projected for the 1992 fiscal year and, whichever government is in power, an early reversal of the trend is unlikely. Nonetheless, as the economy recovers, the fiscal deficit will tend to narrow and, in this indicator at least, the UK out-performs many other major countries, notably Germany and the US.

The convergence criteria for Emu include detailed conditions on the fiscal side relating to the outstanding stock of public sector debt, expressed as a percentage of GDP, and the budget deficit itself. At present the UK meets the debt/GDP requirement of 60 per cent with a considerable margin. It is also within the 3 per cent fiscal deficit/GDP ratio, although this is likely to be breached temporarily over the next 2-3 years.

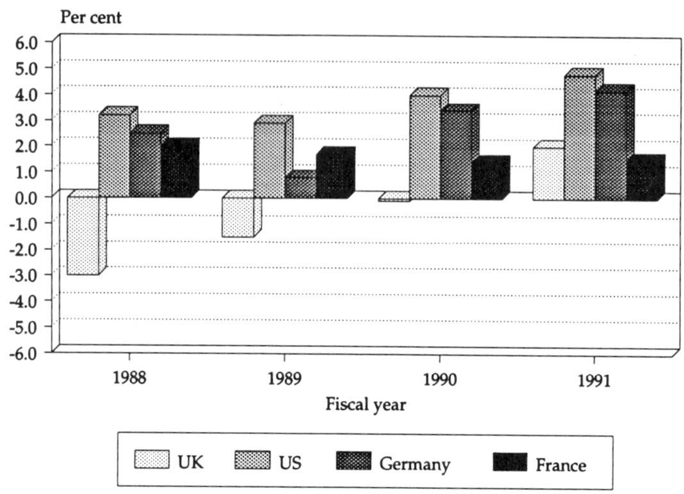

Figure 28.9 **Fiscal balance (by national definition, percentage of GNP/GDP)**
Source: Morgan Grenfell

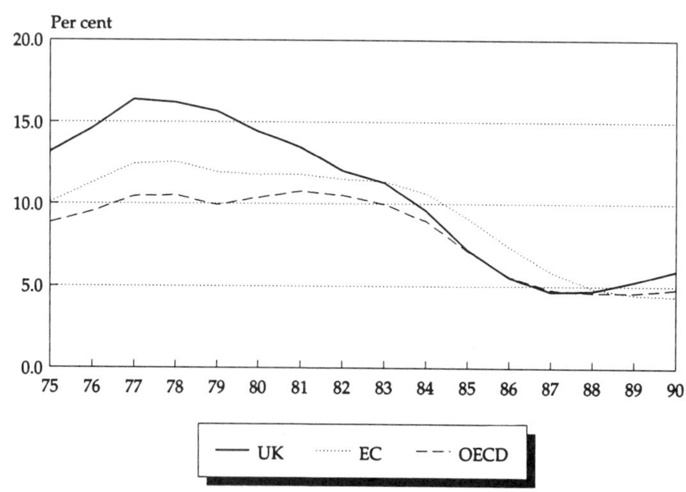

Figure 28.10 **Long-term inflation rates (CPI percentage change, year-on-year 5-yr. moving av.)**
Source: OECD

Figure 28.10 shows that UK inflation in the 1970s and early-1980s, was above the average both of the EC and OECD. There was a considerable absolute and relative improvement in the mid- and late-1980s but the boom at the end of the decade reversed much of this improvement. UK inflation is now declining rapidly towards the European average (see Figure 28.11), although Morgan Grenfell believe that the underlying trend remains a little above that in the US, France and Germany. Measurement of inflation is distorted in the UK by the heavy weight given to mortgage rates in the widely-observed retail price index (RPI). A one per cent increase in mortgage rates adds approximately 1/2 per cent to the RPI. In 1988-1990, the steep rise in mortgage rates added to the RPI both directly and, via its effect on wage settlements, also had a more sustained indirect impact. From October 1990 onwards, this process was reversed and substantial cuts in mortgage rates pushed the headline RPI rate well below the underlying level. The depth of the recession has guaranteed a full follow-through into lower wage settlements and Morgan Grenfell judge that the UK has moved to being a 4 per cent trend-inflation economy. This is rather above the best performance within the core of the ERM and it remains to be seen whether there is any slippage as the economy recovers.

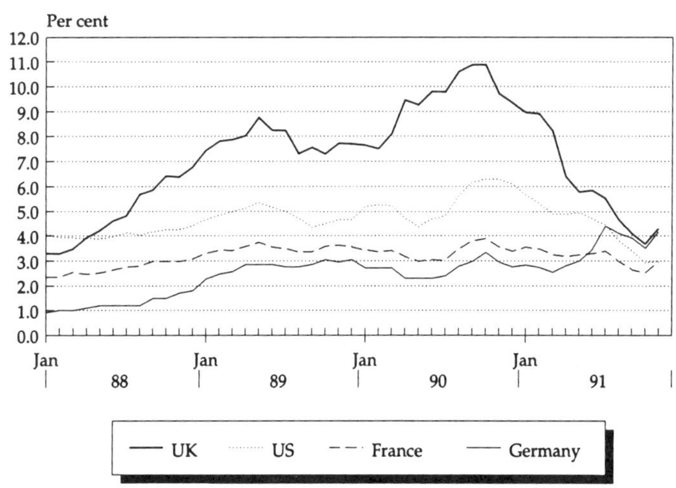

Figure 28.11 Inflation - consumer prices
Source: Datastream

Exchange rate history

There has been a significant shift in the structure of the UK exchange rate, away from direct or indirect linkage with the US dollar towards membership of the ERM and the associated greater ability vis-à-vis the Deutschemark (see Figures 28.11 & 28.12).

The future movements in sterling against those currencies outside the ERM, will be dominated by the performance of the Deutschemark versus these currencies. The greater part of sterling's volatility against the dollar, therefore, is determined by the Deutschemark's movement against the US currency.

There is a debate over whether there will be a devaluation of sterling within the ERM. This will continue to be an issue until the UK joins full-blown Emu at the end of this decade, assuming it decides not to opt out. There are considerable pressures which make devaluation an unpleasant option for governments. Increasing intra-EC trade means that the direct effect of increased import prices on inflation is trending higher. A 10 per cent devaluation would tend to add 2 per cent to RPI inflation within a year. The benefits, in terms of improved competitiveness, therefore tend to get eroded more quickly. Devaluations have never, at least within Europe, been regarded as political successes after the event. Moreover, as Europe moves towards Emu, any country which devalues will effectively be reducing the real value of benefits received in long-term

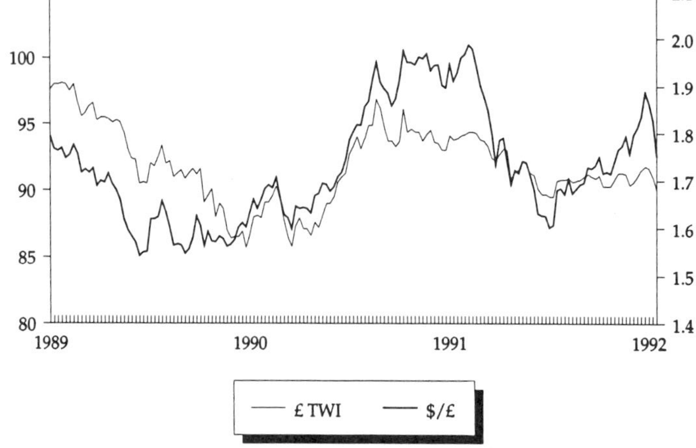

Figure 28.12 Sterling exchange rates
Source: Morgan Grenfell

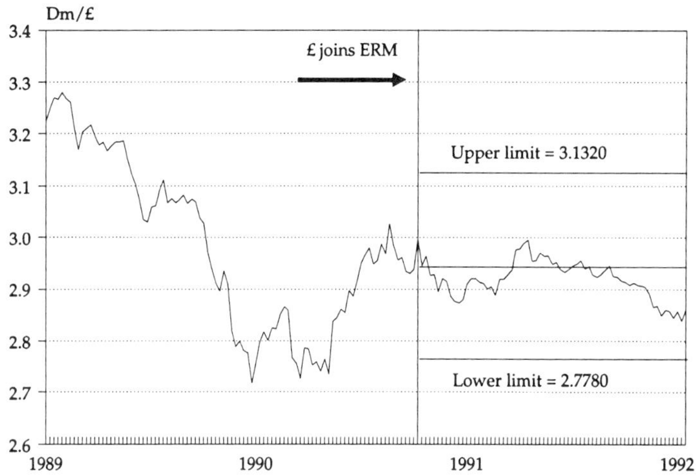

Figure 28.13 Sterling vs. Deutschemark in the ERM
Source: Morgan Grenfell

contracts in their domestic currency, which will ultimately be paid in Ecu. Thus, for example, a 5 per cent devaluation in sterling would reduce the real value of all pension commitments after Emu. Of course, the government could decide to offset this by raising pension payments themselves, but this would not apply to other forms of long-term contracts and the comparison with other European countries which had not devalued (or had, perhaps, revalued), would make the political cost of devaluation even greater. Also, with possibly one exception, devaluations within the ERM have been forced on those governments which have been either unable to accept the level of interest rates needed to defend their currencies, or have exhausted their foreign-exchange reserves. The UK has considerable, but not unlimited, resources in both of these areas.

28.3 *Market composition*

Overview

Gilt-edged market

One major aim of the Thatcher administration was to reduce the public sector deficit and consequently we saw the gilt-edged market decline by 20.0 per cent by the end of 1990, in nominal terms, since 1988. During 1991, the government began to raise finance and this fall reduced to 12.1 per cent. While irredeemable bond volumes have declined only slightly, bullet bonds have fallen by 5.7 per cent, convertible bonds by 79.4 per cent (although the outstanding issue is not convertible and is effectively a bullet bond) and callable bonds by 30.0 per cent. Index-linked volumes have risen, although by only 2.4 per cent.

The UK government not only stopped issuing bonds and let the outstandings fall due to redemptions but also began to buy back bonds in the market for retirement. This was especially true of bullet bonds. However, nearly all new issuance has been in the form of bullet bonds with a small amount of index-linked. The reduction in convertibles occurred as many were converted into longer-dated bonds, leaving those unconverted to retire as bullets, the conversion options having expired worthless. There have been no callable bonds issued for sometime and really the reduction represents only the run off in redemptions.

Eurosterling market

The eurosterling market had, in the past, been primarily utilized by foreign borrowers of sterling, with issues being structured to attract foreign investors. However, since 1984, tax and regulatory changes have allowed UK borrowers, such as building societies and corporates, to access the market directly, increasing the proportion of this sector from 3.4 per cent in 1984, to almost 16.6 per cent in 1988 and 48.8 per cent in 1991.

This sector has undergone a considerable change in composition: from primarily only bullet bonds with lives of five years, to a wide range of instruments such as FRNs, convertibles and MBSs (see below). Maturity ranges have extended to over 30 years, and even include a perpetual FRN.

■ Eurosterling fixed-rate bonds

The fixed-rate market has grown from £0.34bn issuance in 1980, to £9.71bn in 1991. This growth has occurred for a number of reasons. In the main, it has been

	March 1988	% Total	January 1992	% Total
GOVERNMENT				
Gilt-edged bonds				
Bullet	93.36	50.43	88.08	41.94
Callable	23.00	12.42	16.10	7.67
Index-linked	12.75	6.89	13.05	6.21
Irredeemables	3.24	1.75	3.21	1.53
Convertible	6.27	3.39	1.29	0.61
Total	138.62	74.88	121.72	57.96
EURO				
Eurosterling				
Bullet	13.92	7.52	29.87	14.22
Bullet with features	2.52	1.36	5.17	2.46
Total	16.44	8.88	35.04	16.68
Floating-rate notes (FRN)				
FRN fixed			0.05	0.02
FRN asset-backed			0.78	0.37
FRN bullet			4.15	1.98
FRN callable			3.83	1.82
FRN call/sub			0.08	0.04
FRN increasing margin	10.17	5.49	0.20	0.10
FRN puttable			0.28	0.13
FRN sinking fund			0.30	0.14
FRN subordinated			0.71	0.34
FRN tap			0.30	0.14
FRN unsubordinated			1.28	0.61
FRN & warrants			0.15	0.07
Total	10.17	5.49	12.10	5.76
Mortgage-backed securities (MBS)				
Mortgage-backed FRN	1.43	0.77	11.23	5.35
Mortgage-backed fixed	0.00	0.00	0.12	0.06
Mortgage-backed swapped	0.00	0.00	0.43	0.20
Total	1.43	0.77	11.78	5.61

(cont.)

	(March 1988)	*(% Total)*	*(January 1992)*	*(% Total)*
Convertibles				
Bullet	3.36	1.81	2.81	1.34
Convertible capital bonds	-	-	1.61	0.76
Preference share	-	-	0.63	0.30
Total	3.36	1.81	5.05	2.41
Medium-term notes				
Bullet	0.00	0.00	0.75	0.36
Floating-rate notes	0.00	0.00	0.33	0.16
Zero-coupon	0.00	0.00	0.26	0.12
Discount coupon	0.00	0.00	0.37	0.17
Premium	0.00	0.00	0.01	0.00
Total	0.00	0.00	1.88	0.90
DOMESTICS				
Debentures				
Bullet	2.63	1.42	6.22	2.96
Callable	3.50	1.89	0.32	0.15
Call/drop lock	-	-	0.02	0.01
Callable/SF	-	-	0.09	0.04
Index-linked	0.00	0.00	0.08	0.04
Stepped-up	0.60	0.32	0.16	0.07
Zero	0.10	0.05	0.12	0.06
Total	6.83	3.69	7.00	3.33
Unsecured loans				
Bullet	-	-	1.16	0.55
Bullet/warrants	-	-	0.02	0.01
Callable	-	-	1.23	0.59
Callable SF	-	-	0.01	0.01
Callable/warr	-	-	0.01	0.00
Deep-discount	-	-	0.13	0.06
Index-linked	-	-	0.16	0.08
No interest	-	-	0.03	0.01
Zero-coupon	-	-	0.19	0.09
Total	-	-	2.93	1.39

(cont.)

	(March 1988)	(% Total)	(January 1992)	(%Ttotal)
Convertibles				
NCCRP - callable			2.84	1.35
NCCRP - bullet			2.27	1.08
CULS - bullet			0.82	0.39
CCB			0.78	0.37
NCCRP - irredeemable	4.10	2.21	0.57	0.27
CULS - callable			0.32	0.15
CULS - irredeemable			0.11	0.05
GCCRP - bullet			0.04	0.02
GCCRP - callable			0.03	0.01
CULS - zero			0.01	0.01
Bulldog bonds				
Bullet	3.31	1.79	2.34	1.11
Puttable	0.05	0.03	0.08	0.04
Purchase fund			1.58	0.75
Tender			0.10	0.05
Currency-indexed			0.03	0.01
Serial			0.03	0.01
Total	3.36	1.81	4.15	1.98
Municipal bonds				
Bullet	0.39	0.21	0.29	0.14
Callable	0.30	0.16	0.13	0.06
Irredeemables	0.08	0.04	0.08	0.04
L.A. bonds	0.05	0.03	0.05	0.02
Total	0.82	0.44	0.55	0.26
GRAND TOTAL	185.13	100.00	210.00	100.00

Figure 28.14 Composition of the UK market (GBP billion nominal)

due to UK companies now regularly using this market in preference to the domestic markets. In addition, UK institutions are regular investors in the international markets - this means that they are familiar with the credits and regularly using the international clearing houses. Previously, they had been particularly parochial in their investments. Finally, international investors had grown more confident of sterling, the UK political and economic performance therefore increasing demand for sterling bonds.

The size of issues has grown. Initially, there were restrictions on issues of £100m and below. 1991 saw issues of £400m for GEFCO, £350m for British Gas and £250m for Deutsche Bank (a zero-coupon bond) and GEFCO.

■ Mortgage-backed securities (MBS)

The first MBS issue was for The Mortgage Corporation, a specialist company set up by Salomon Brothers to provide mortgage finance to the UK public, which was brought to market in March 1987. Since then the sector has grown to almost £12bn (which is 5.61 per cent of the total sterling bond market). With the rapid rise in property values and a rush to purchase property in 1988, many special-purpose mortgage companies were created which re-packaged existing mortgage portfolios and issued MBSs. However, since then, interest rates have risen and a severe recession has set in; the resultant fall in house prices leading to a much lower volumes of mortgage activity in 1990 and 1991.

The BIS capital adequacy rules have had a significant impact on banks. As part of an organized attempt to manage their BIS ratios, several have securitized their mortgage portfolios. A variety of bank originated issues have been brought to market by banks such as Chemical (Domus), Barclays (Gracechurch) and Bank of Ireland (Residential). With growing acceptance of MBS issues further refinement has taken place. The CMS A1, A2 and A3 issues were the first three tranche collateralized mortgage obligations (CMOs). At the start of 1991, concerns about the Bank of England weightings for mortgage-backed securities (to be increased to 100 per cent in January 1993, in line with European practice), and the insurance credits that backed these issues, resulted in spreads widening. Nevertheless, the market stabilized and proved resilient, even in the light of potential problems reflected by the liquidity difficulties at National Home Loans (NHL). Indeed, spreads from January to July 1991 narrowed from 70 bp to 45 bp over LIBOR.

■ Floating-rate note market

The FRN market has continued to grow: from 3.1 per cent in 1986, to 5.6 per cent in 1988 and stayed at that level in 1991. Most of the issuance is by UK building societies which are funding their floating-rate mortgage portfolios. However, also included are: a number of UK and international banks, corporates such as All Nippon Airways, a sovereign borrower (New Zealand) and a number of special-purpose company issues which are the result of repackaged securities such as CARPS and STRIPES and asset-backed issues, being auto loans, such as Auto Finance, CARS and Drive Securities (see Section 28.5).

■ Eurosterling convertible bond market

As with the MBS market, the euro-convertible market has also shown growth: from its first issue in 1987, to 1.81 per cent of the total market in 1988 and to 2.40 per cent in 1991. All the issuers are UK companies which are using the facilities of the eurosterling market to make their issues attractive to international investors, thereby hoping to widen investor base. However, as discussed in Section 28.1, it has not been a market without controversy.

Companies with low P/E ratios often issued eurosterling convertibles with a high conversion premium before the October Crash. These issues offered investors a put option normally after 5 years - often at a premium of as much as 30.00 per cent to the redemption value. If the bond was converted, then the issuer would have succeeded in issuing equity at a higher level than would have been achievable in the equity market whilst also having had the benefit of borrowing at a lower rate. However, a number of companies assumed that the equity markets would continue to rise and rise, and that conversion would occur. Accordingly, a number of companies did not make provisions for the possibility of the bonds being put. After the Crash, and the severe recession in the UK, concern began to mount that some would be unable to pay the option. So far, only one company - Saatchi & Saatchi - has had to restructure its debt because of the put. Rules have now been introduced by the Accounting Standards Authority forcing companies to account for the put from the outset, regardless of the likelihood of the conversion.

Corporate market (debentures & unsecured loans)

The domestic corporate market, had languished for a number of years as a result of the very high long-term interest rates which have deterred corporates from issuing and has, therefore, not been a major source of funds for the corporate sector. Investment trusts are amongst the most active and innovative issuers in this market, having issued preference stock, debentures with stepped-coupons, index-linked issues and zero-coupon bonds; such innovations, though, remain a very small part of the market. During the 1980s, issues have been dominated by secured debt for property companies and breweries and unsecured debt for banks.

Several companies have chosen to issue in the domestic, rather than the eurosterling market. At first glance, this may appear strange, since one would think that the ability to issue to overseas investors would be attractive. However, despite being well-known to UK investors, many of these companies are small and relatively unknown overseas. Domestic issues do not necessarily require a credit rating, an important consideration to international investors. Furthermore, in order to issue on the best terms in the UK, these companies have issued secured debt which, while being highly prized by UK investors, is afforded little, if any, value by overseas investors.

Domestic convertible bond market

The popularity of the convertible capital bond has led to a downturn in issuance of convertible preference and convertible unsecured loan stocks. As many trade in both bearer and registered form, they appeal to both domestic and international investors as well as attracting favourable accounting treatment for the issuers. However, it grew from 2.21 per cent of the total market in 1988 to 3.72 per cent in 1991 and remains larger than the euro market. Most of the issuance has been for small UK borrowers which are not well-known internationally. Nevertheless, a number of larger issues such as British Airways (£320.2m), Williams Holdings (£318.5m), Cable & Wireless (£313.2m), British Aerospace (£270.1m), Rank Organisation (£228.3m), Tate & Lyle (£214.7m) and Reckitt & Colman (£200.8m) have been brought in this market due to the pre-emptive rights problem (see Section 28.1).

Bulldog market

The Bulldog market was created in July 1980 by the issuance of Denmark 13.00 per cent 2005 and can be considered as a domestic market for foreign borrowers - being structured generally to attract UK domestic investors. However, many of the issues carry the facility of bearer bonds and allow international investors to receive interest without deduction of withholding tax.

Prior to 1980, supranational borrowers (such as the World Bank) raised finance in the UK domestic market. These borrowers pay interest free of tax. Commonwealth borrowers (ranging from Australia to the Kenya Railways and Nigerian Port Authorities) also raised finance in the UK. These borrowers paid interest subject to tax and were not considered Bulldog issues, but Commonwealth issues. In reality, there is no difference between these issues and current Bulldog issues, but it became popular to give such markets descriptive names as with 'Yankee' and 'Samurai', in the US and Japan respectively.

In the early years of its revival, the market showed significant growth, although, recently, borrowers have begun to turn increasingly to the eurosterling market for their financing needs. Since 1985, the main borrower has been the European Investment Bank (EIB). However, Portugal in 1986 (£140m) and 1988 (£10m), the World Bank in 1989 (£35m), Barbados in 1990 (£30m) and Gibraltar in 1991 (£50m), have all tapped the market. The two pioneer issues for Guaranteed Export Credit Finance (a UK government guaranteed agency) in 1989 (£250m) and 1990 (£250m), may be considered anomalies since they were probably brought to this market because of overseas investors' unfamiliarity with the credit and the long maturities (2010 and 2002 respectively). GEFCO has recently begun to tap the eurosterling market directly.

This market contains two of the largest non-government bond issues: the £426m EIB 9.5 per cent 2009 and £376m EIB 10.375 per cent 2004, as well as the two £250m GEFCO issues.

Medium-term note market

The medium-term note market opened in January 1990 and has grown steadily, if unspectacularly, to be larger than the local authority market at over £1.1 billion. This market allows a continuous issuance of bonds, with maturities between one and five years, within the total size limit of the programme. Investors can customize an issue in all facets to meet both their own, and the borrower's requirements.

Municipal market

As discussed in Section 28.1, the local authority market has declined to virtual insignificance in the last seven years as a result of the government's debt management policies. These institutions have been able to finance from central government via the Public Works Loan Board on more favourable terms than would otherwise be possible in the market. Indeed, a great number of authorities borrowed monies from this source to retire public quoted debt. There has also been some concern by investors about the credit quality of some authorities, especially those which have been rate-capped and would have encountered considerable difficulty in raising finance in the market-place . It is expected that there may be a return to the public market in the years ahead, as the Public Works Loan Board (PWLB) becomes both less generous in its terms and subject to quotas. Currently, the authorities would expect to raise finance from the PWLB at least 1.00 per cent over gilts, with different rates being applied to different authorities. Nevertheless, the problem of credit rating will act as considerable drag upon the ability of such borrowers to raise funds on the finest terms.

Composition of market by maturity

Gilt-edged market

The gilt-edged market has seen a gradual shortening in the life of its bonds. This had been due to a number of factors including the lack of issuance. It has been the belief of the UK government that interest rates would converge on those of continental Europe, especially Germany, and therefore, it did not wish to issue high-coupon (then current coupon) bonds with long maturities in a falling yield environment. One way it was able to issue long-term debt more cheaply was by the issuance of convertible bonds. These short-dated bonds had maturities up to 5 years with options to convert into fixed nominal amounts of a

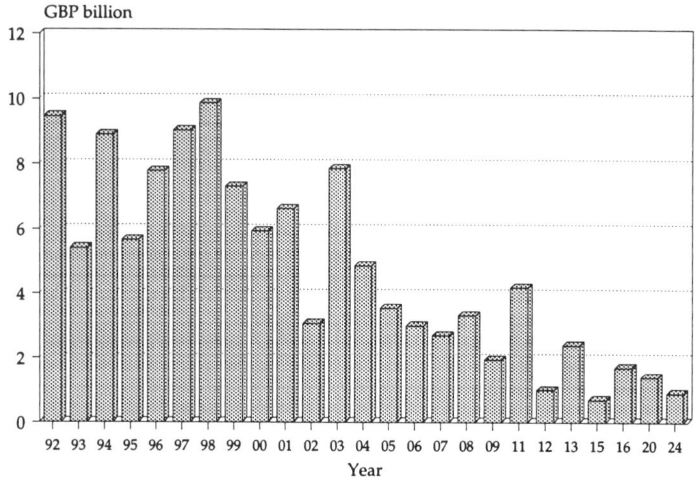

Figure 28.15 Maturity structure of the gilt-edged market

long-dated bond at yields below the, then current, long-bond rate. As yields fell, many investors were able to have long-dated exposure, while holding short-dated bonds. The terms declined as time past and the two bonds left are now short-dated bullets.

As can be seen, there is a considerable volume of bonds to be redeemed in 1992 and 1993. These will have to be refinanced and one can expect maturities to be extended. During 1991/92, the Bank of England has begun to issue a number of benchmark issues with maturities of 5, 10 ,15 and 20 year maturities, as well as adding to existing issues including some long-dated bonds through its tap method. The UK's commitment to ERM has resulted in a lower interest rate environment and narrower spreads to other European countries. This has encouraged the Bank to extend its maturity structure.

The very long-dated bonds are nearly all index-linked bonds, with maturities at the 22, 25, 29 and 33 year. The other long-dated bonds are relatively old issues with call features.

Eurosterling market

The majority of eurosterling straight bonds (56.1 per cent) have lives of less than 5 years. This is because much of the issuance has been targeted at overseas investors by issuing securities with lives of 5 or less years. However, with the

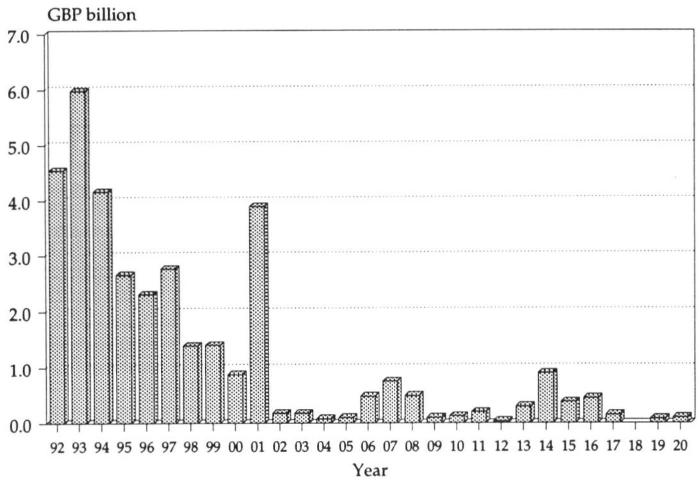

Figure 28.16 Maturity structure of the eurosterling market

opening of the market to UK borrowers, there has been a notable growth in bonds with lives of over 15 years targeted at the UK insurance companies and pension funds. Indeed, almost 15 per cent of issues have a life in excess of 10 years. The longest bond in this sector is the Lucas 10.875 per cent 2020 issues with the £400m Italy 10.5 per cent 2014 being one of the largest and longest. Most of the long-dated issues are for UK corporates with only issues by the World Bank (£350m 2007), Finland (£100m 2008), EDF (£100m 2009), Italy, Hydro-Quebec (£150m 2015) and AMP (£150m 2015) from overseas borrowers who would have traditionally issued in the Bulldog market.

Eurosterling FRN market

Most eurosterling FRNs again reflect the initial issue maturity range of 5 years. However, there have been a number of longer-dated issues particularly by UK building societies and banks with maturities in excess of 2000, e.g. TSB 2003 (£100m), Abbey National 2004 (£50m) and Royal Bank of Scotland 2005 (£100m). The Standard Chartered Perpetual (£150m) is of particular note; at the time of issuance, many investors felt that there was little risk involved in this type of security and thought they were just maintaining the spread of this issue for perpetuity - but because it is effectively a dividend-capped equity with equity risk it has collapsed in price as part of the 'Perpetual Fiasco'.

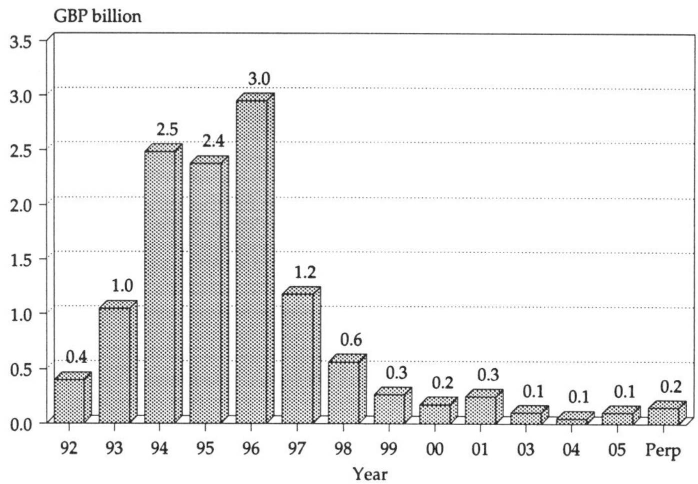

Figure 28.17 Maturity structure of the eurosterling FRN market

Eurosterling MBS market

Home mortgages are usually issued with lives of 25 years, although shorter mortgages are also granted. The exact life of the mortgage is usually determined by the borrower with standard terms of 20, 25, 30 and 35 years being the most common. The final maturity is often linked to the borrower's period to retirement at age 60 or 65. It is a requirement of the rating agencies that MBSs have a maturity at least 2 years beyond that of the longest mortgage in the underlying pool. This allows sufficient time for foreclosure in the event that the mortgage defaults at maturity. As a consequence, most MBSs are issued with final maturities in excess of 20 years. However, the average life of the security will be considerably less, being dependent on the mortgage borrower's pre-payments, usually at the time of moving or windfall cash receipts such as inheritances, bonuses and insurance policy maturities, but more recently refinancing in the light of intense competition between banks, building societies and special mortgage finance companies.

It is impossible to calculate the exact average life of MBS since they are effectively partial callable bonds with the mortgage holder determining when, and how much of, the mortgage is repaid. Therefore, at issuance, models of the possible course of pre-payment are used to determine the effective average life of the bond assuming a certain level of pre-payment. This is shown in Figure

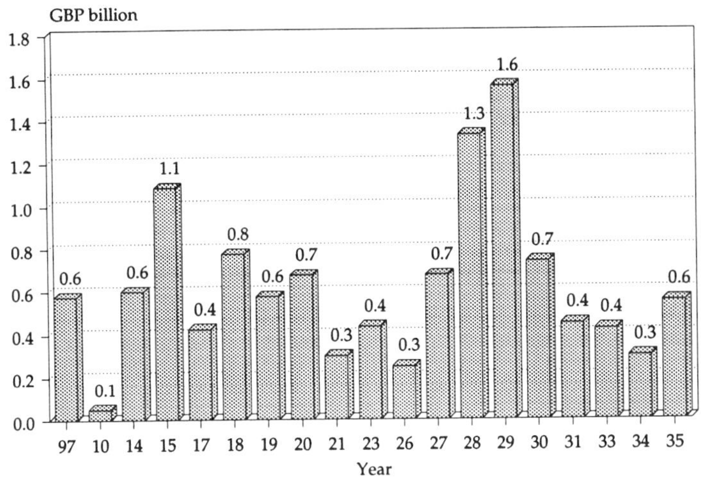

Figure 28.18 Final maturity structure of the eurosterling MBS market

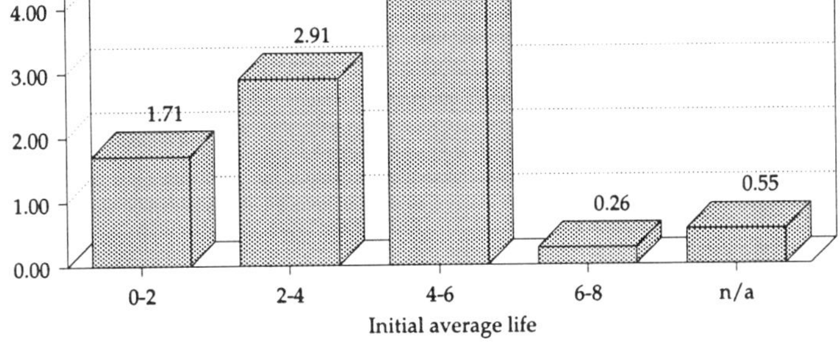

Figure 28.19 Maturity structure of the average life of the eurosterling MBS market

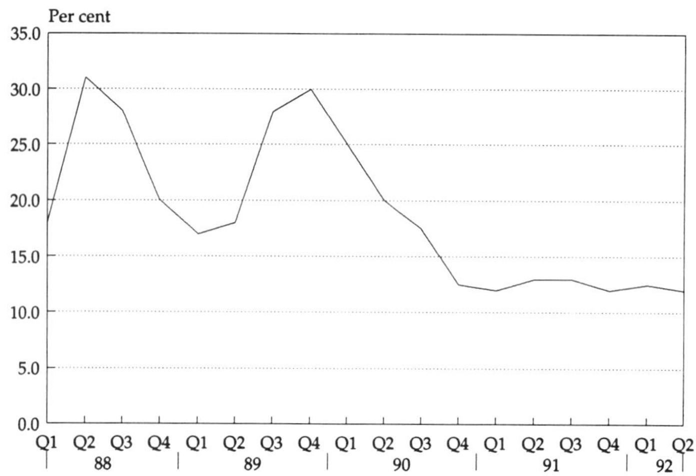

Figure 28.20 Secondary market pre-payment index for eurosterling MBSs
Source: CSFB

28.19. It should be noted that, if pre-payment rates fall, the effective average life increases, and vice versa if pre-payment rates rise.

As can be seen in Figure 28.20, based on Credit Suisse First Boston analysis, the actual pre-payment rates have greatly exceeded the 10 to 15 per cent rates expected at the market's inception. This is linked to a number of factors. For example, higher pre-payment rates in 1988 can be associated with the end of double tax relief for joint home-buyers and the fact the special-purpose mortgage companies were very competitive in lending relative to the building societies. This led to a considerable switching away from building societies to these companies. However, since 1989-90, the building societies have been more competitive and, with a lower cost base from personal savings, compared with the wholesale cost of funds. In this environment, there has been a switch back of borrowers to the building societies.

Eurosterling convertible bond market

The dearth of short-dated euro-convertible issues reflects the fact that this market did not open until 1987. There are no irredeemables in contrast to the domestic convertible market - a fact which reflects international investors' preferences. Euro-convertibles are nearly all callable, usually at a premium and after five years, whilst the domestic convertibles are usually non-callable, except for the convertible capital bonds which trade in both bearer and registered form. However, maturities are very long usually with most issues having lives of 15 years. Amongst the largest are Hanson 9.50 per cent 2006 (£500m), Elf (Enterprise) 8.75 per cent 2006 (£437.8m), Sainsbury 8.50 per cent 2005 (£200m) and Tesco 9.00 per cent 2005 (£200m).

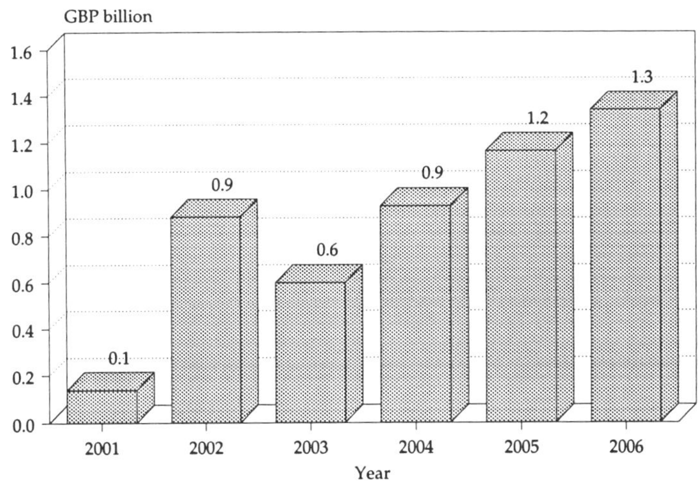

Figure 28.21 Maturity structure of the eurosterling convertible bond market

It should be noted that most investors are particularly concerned about the period of conversion into equity and this varies considerably from issue to issue, but is usually between two and five years, depending on the expected rate of ordinary dividend growth.

Corporate market

There is a dramatic difference in the maturity patterns of debenture and unsecured loans. There are few short-dated debentures; on the other hand there is a major increase from almost nil in the 12-14 year range to £355m in the 16-18 year range, rising to a peak of £1,455m in the 24-26 year range. This declines gradually to the 38-40 year area with another peak of £679m in the 32-34 year range and lows of £15m (30-32 years) and £nil (36-38 years). The main reason

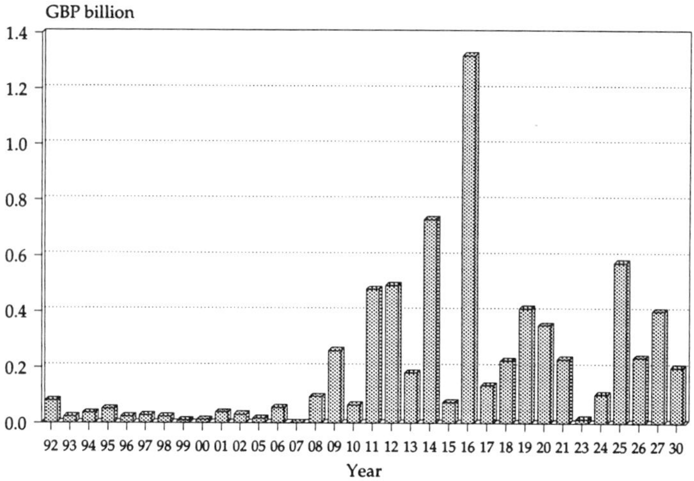

Figure 28.22 Maturity structure of the debenture bond market

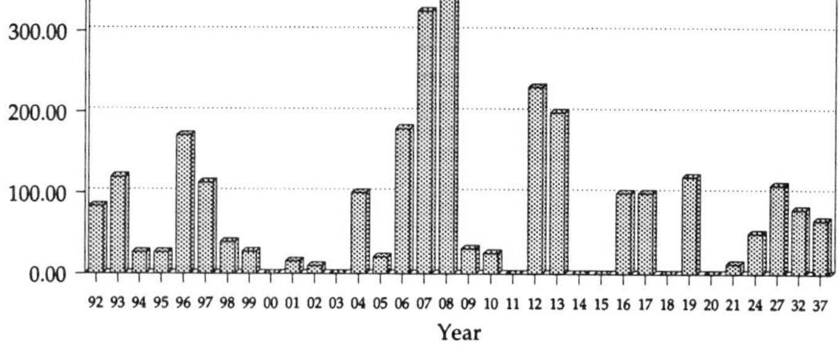

Figure 28.23 Maturity structure of the unsecured loans market

for these long maturities is that the bonds both finance, and are secured on, property (especially offices). The borrowers and maturities would be unattractive to overseas investors and are therefore more suited to the domestic markets.

Unsecured loans are mainly to be found in the shorter-dated maturity ranges and reflect the run-off of older bonds. The major unsecured issues such as those for BAT and the banks is to be seen with the volumes in the 14-16, 16-18 and 20-22 year ranges. However, it should be noted that there are few issues beyond this. Yet, the longest issue in the corporate sector is an unsecured loan for the North Housing Association with a maturity of 2037!!

Domestic convertible bond market

The maturity range of domestic convertibles is very marked when compared to that of euro-convertibles. Firstly, there is a full range of maturities reflecting continuing issuance and failed conversion (see Figure 28.24). Although there has been little issuance of this type of security recently, there were five issues in 1988 and three in 1989. The life at issuance varies dramatically and reflects the type and size of borrower. Many smaller borrowers issue bonds with lives of 10 years while larger borrowers have much longer lives. Of note are the British

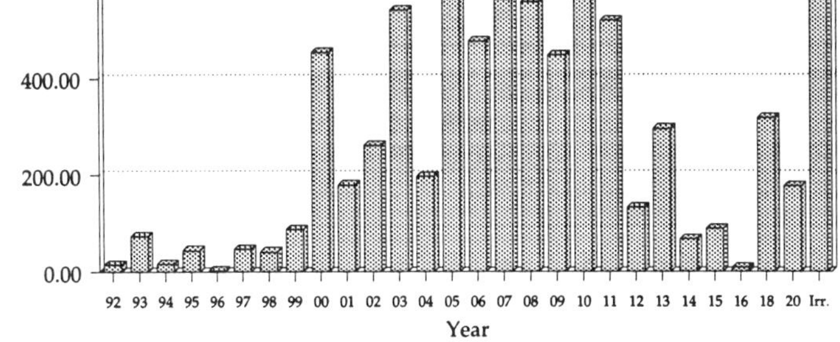

Figure 28.24 Maturity structure of the domestic convertible bond market

Land 8.625 per cent 2011 (£78.80m), Queens Moat 7.50 per cent 2011 (£188.9m), Tate & Lyle 7.25 per cent 2013 (£214.7m), Williams Holdings 8.000 per cent 2018 (£318.5m) and BICC 6.75 per cent 2020 (£177.1m) issues which are amongst the longest, being issued with initial lives of 20 years, 25 years and 30 years. It should also be remembered that the conversion period may only be a relatively short period of, say, 5 years, although there are some bonds with very long conversion periods.

Bulldog market

There is only one short-dated Bulldog issue (see Figure 28.25), and this will shortly redeem. In the beginning issues would be brought with either short lives of 5 or 10 years or else very long lives (such as the Quebec 2020 issue, which had a life of 36 years). With the decline in the Bulldog market and the upsurge of the eurosterling market, all shorter-dated issues have been brought in the eurosterling market and there has therefore been no issuance in this area. All other issues have been brought with long lives of just over 10 years from the Guaranteed Export Finance Corporation and the European Investment Bank (EIB). However, the old Commonwealth borrowers of Barbados were able to issue a bond with a life of 24 years and Gibraltar with a life of 15 years.

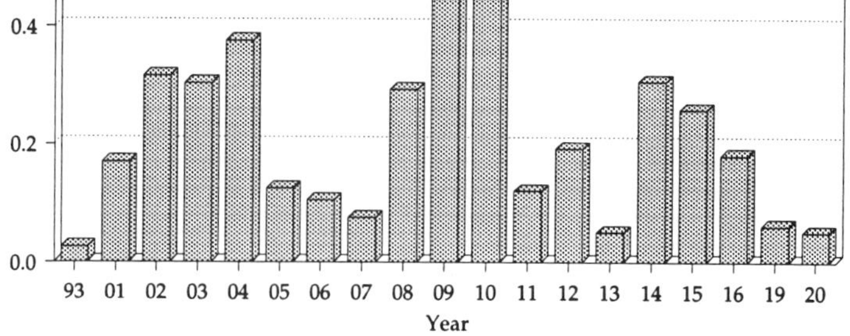

Figure 28.25 Maturity structure of the Bulldog market

Medium-term notes

The main purpose of the MTN market is to allow borrowers and lenders to tap particular maturity dates for particular amounts. Therefore, it is not surprising to find that the majority are small issues. However, there are some large issues which dominate a particular maturity. Most of the issues are between one and five years, as per the terms of the definition of a sterling MTN. There is a large Abbey National issue in 1994 (£80m).

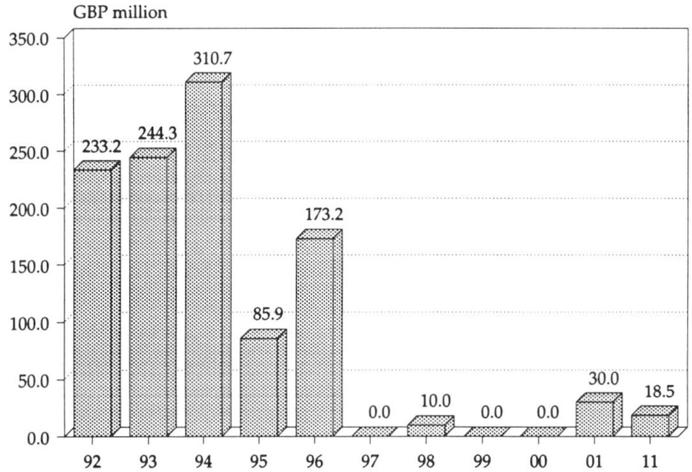

Figure 28.26 Maturity structure of the medium-term note market

Local authority market

With only a short period of issuance of long-dated bonds in the mid-1980s, the maturity structure (see Figure 28.27) reflects those very old issues now running off, the very old irredeemables, and the 1980s with maturities ranging from 2006 to the Kirklees 11.60 per cent 2031. Many of the very old issues have nominal values of less £100,000, some less than £10,000. Although the full nominal of the 1980s issues has been recorded many have, in fact, been bought in and virtually retired.

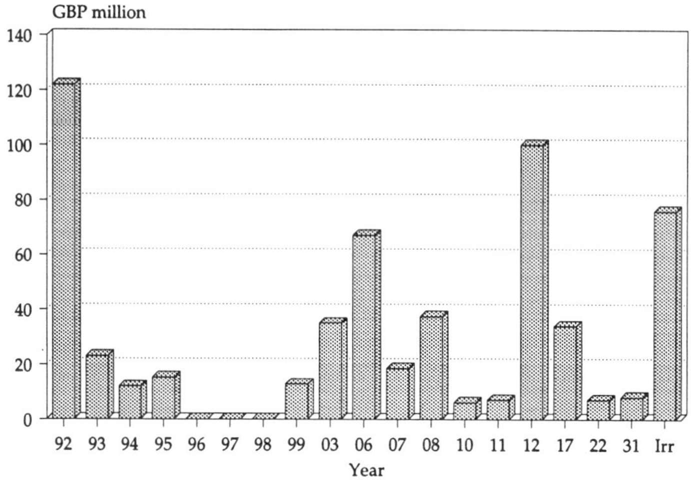

Figure 28.27 Maturity structure of the local authority market

Composition of market by coupon structure

Gilt-edged market

At look at the coupon structure of the gilt-edged market shown in Figure 28.28 may, at first sight, appear puzzling. There are, however, special factors at play. For example, the low-coupon bonds, i.e. 2-4 per cent, are mainly made up of 2.0 and 2.5 per cent index-linked bonds (£13.05bn), irredeemables (£2.852bn), two very old callable issues (Gas 3 per cent 90/95 and Funding 3 1/2 per cent 99/04) and a single 3.0 per cent issue. Historically, the UK government issued discount short-dated bonds designed for private individuals but, with the reduction in income tax levels and a concerted move to reduce 'tax-breaks', there has not been any new issuance of this type of bond for some time.

Most issues carry coupons of 9 to 10.5 per cent and 12 to 13 per cent reflecting the periods when interest rates traded in these ranges. There are a number of high-coupon bonds ranging up to 15.5 per cent but these are less liquid. The market is stratified in yield terms, reflecting the coupon structure.

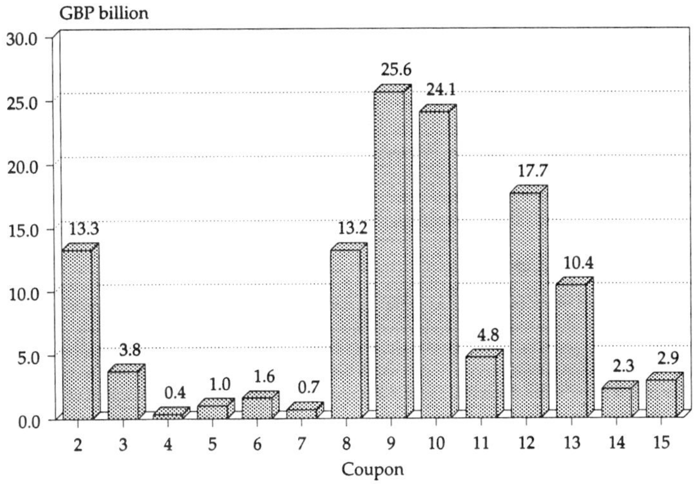

Figure 28.28 Coupon structure of the gilt-edged market

Eurosterling market

The coupon structure of the eurosterling market is shown in Figure 28.29. After a number of zero-coupon bonds in the mid-80s, there have been three £200.00m issues in late 1989 and early 1990: Alliance & Leicester 1995, British Telecom 2000 and Guaranteed Export Finance 2000. 1991 saw further issues of £250m Deutsche Bank, £200m SBC Finance and £100m Nationwide Anglia BS. The mid-coupon issues are the result of issues with warrants and the vast majority of issues are within the 9.00 per cent to 12.00 per cent range. The high-coupon issues are all due for redemption in 1992/3, and include the £515.7m British Telecom 13.75 per cent 1993, the result of four tranche issues.

Eurosterling FRN market

Surprisingly, the lowest quoted margin in the eurosterling FRN market (see Figure 28.30) is not offered by a sovereign, but a bank! The £250m Compagnie Bancaire 1995 issue offers a margin of LIBOR flat, but provides a put option (even if it is not a generous one), as does the STRIPES 1996 issue. Most of the older building society issues carry a spread of 1/16th over LIBOR. Other UK building societies, and many bank issues, carry a spread of 1/8th over LIBOR.

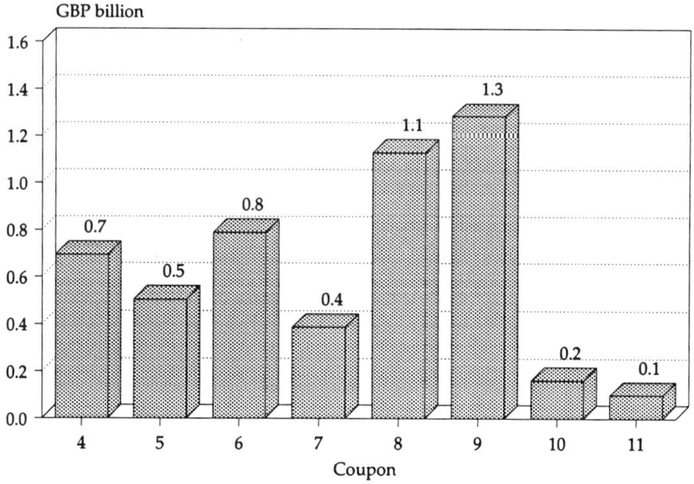

Figure 28.29 Coupon structure of the eurosterling market

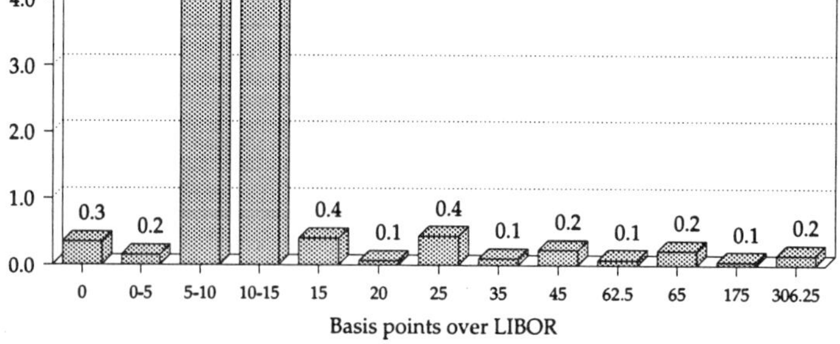

Figure 28.30 Coupon structure of the eurosterling FRN market

The wider spreads of 35 bp or more can be found on the subordinated building society issues and asset backed loans. Higher spreads are available on the £200m subordinated Halifax 1998 issue with a margin of 62.5 bp over LIBOR (but it has a 20 per cent sinking fund per annum from 1994), and the £112m Alliance & Leicester 1998, a 65 bp margin. The highest margins are 175 bp, found on the £50m Halifax 1992 issue, which resulted from conversion from a fixed-rate issue and the Standard Chartered 1996 issue with 306.25 bp.

Eurosterling MBS market

The coupon structure of the eurosterling market is shown in Figure 28.31. The lower margin issues are usually the first (shortest) tranche of a multi-tranche CMO deal. Most issues carry a margin of between 25 bp to around 45bp. The higher margin has resulted after clarification of the BIS rules and the Bank of England's application of them to MBSs.

Of the lower margin issues are the CMO first tranche of £110.0m CMS 1 A1 2016 (10.0 bp), £250.0m CMS 2A 2026 (18.0 bp) and £200.0m Maes Funding 1 2018. The large £500.0m TMC No.11 2020 carries a margin of 27.5 bp. Recent issues such as £200.0m CMS 8 2028 have a coupon of 52.5 bp, while £210.0m TMC Pimbs No7 2029 carries 50.0 bp and £75.0m Temple Court 2A 2031, 55.0 bp.

The first issues in 1987 such as TMC1, NHL1 and HMC1 were mis-priced at between 20 bp to 25 bp in a misunderstood market. In 1988, following investor education spreads were between 35bp (HMC2 and 42.5 bp (MFC1 A1). Later NHL, TMC and HMC deals saw spreads fall from 35 bp to 20 bp from 1988 to 1989, as demand for sterling securities, sterling and floating-rate securities grew. This trend was reversed from mid-1989 through to 1990 as credit fears began to grow. Following the Bank of England announcements, in January 1991, on the BIS rules spreads widened to 50 bp, later to fall to around 45 bp.

Eurosterling convertible bond market

The coupon range for euro-convertibles (see Figure 28.32) is obviously lower than that for straight eurosterling issues and domestic convertibles, reflecting the conversion option and the longer period of issuance in the domestic convertible market. The lower coupon issues were brought to market before the October Crash and reflect the extremely positive sentiment at the time. Following the Crash, a more realistic valuation was adopted and enhanced by the put feature. Most recent issues have been at rates about 50 to 100 basis points below gilt-edged securities. It should be remembered that in setting the coupon, a lot will depend on the yield on the underlying equity.

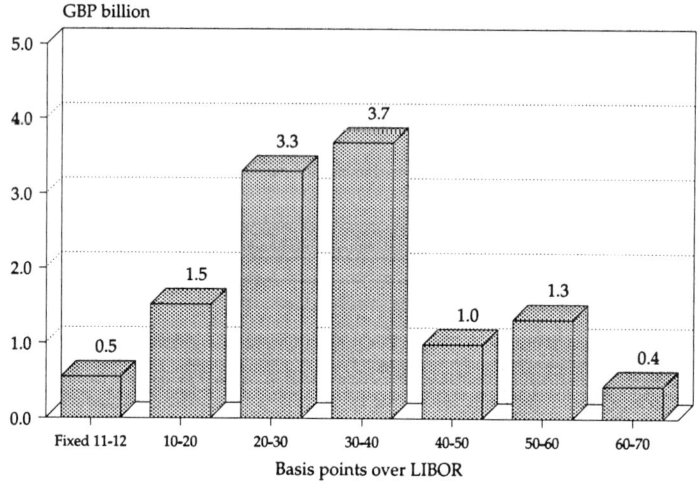

Figure 28.31 Margin structure of the eurosterling MBS market

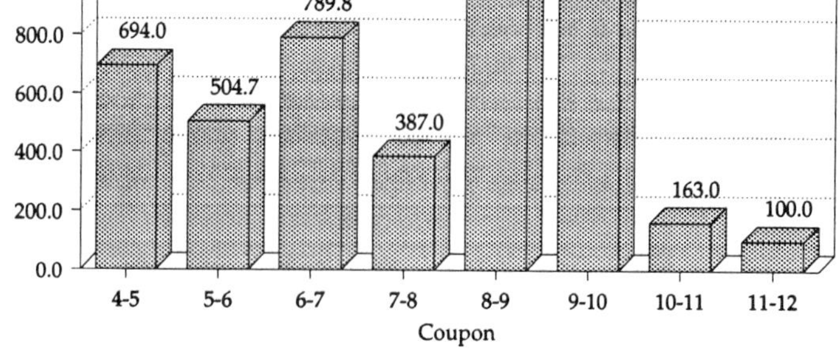

Figure 28.32 Coupon structure of the eurosterling convertible bond market

Corporate market

■ Debentures

There are two zero-coupon debentures: a £93.5m Housing Finance 2012 and a £22.5m New Throgmorton Trust issue (an Investment Trust). The £60.0m THFC 5.625 per cent 2020, Dartmoor 6.25 per cent 2005 issues (both actually index-linked to the UK Retail Price Index, RPI) and £50.95m Housing Finance 5.00 per cent 2027 issues are the most recent issues with this level of coupon. All others are the result of old issues which are due to shortly be redeemed. A few short-dated issues which were brought to market in 1987/88 (the bottom of that UK rate cycle) also carry coupons in this range.

During this period, many property companies and investment trusts also raised long-term debt with coupons between 9.50 per cent and 10.00 per cent. The largest of these issues are the £350m Allied Lyons 9.75 per cent 2019 (which is secured on pubs) and the £400m Land Securities 10.00 per cent 2025 (secured on property). The vast majority of the remaining issues (see Figure 28.33) carry coupons between 10.00 per cent and 12.00 per cent, reflecting the interest rate levels of the 1986-1989 period. It should be remembered that debentures carry coupons up to 100 basis points below unsecured loans. The highest coupons are

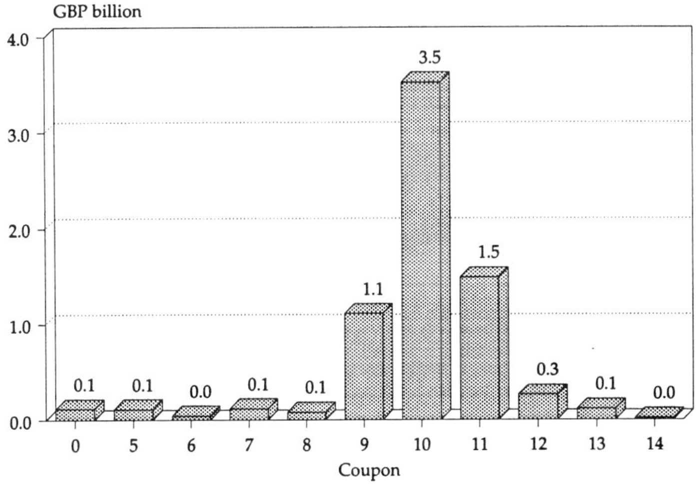

Figure 28.33 Coupon structure of the debenture bond market

those issued in the early 1980s, but these are small issues of between £10m and £30m.

■ Unsecured loans

There are two zero-coupon issues in the unsecured loan market (see Figure 28.34), both for North Housing Association: £80.0m 2019 and £110.0m 2027. There are three index-linked issues: £13.0m Nationwide Building Society 3.875 per cent 2021, £50.0m Nationwide BS 4.25 per cent 2024 and £100.0m Anglian Water 5.125 per cent 2008. In addition there is a £27.0m International Business Communications 4.00 per cent 1996 issue, which pays no interest until 1994 when it starts to pay 4.00 per cent but, being an subordinated debenture, it reverts to an unsecured loan. Tesco, a supermarket chain, raised finance by issuing an unsecured deep-discount £125.0m 4.00 per cent 2006 issue.

Most issues with coupons from 6.00 per cent to 10 per cent are the result of issues from the mid 1960s. There are two large issues that dominate the 10.00 per cent - 12.00 per cent range: the £231.4m British & Commonwealth 10.50 per cent 2012, which is in administration, and the £200.0m Enterprise Oil 10.75 per cent 2013.

The 12.00 per cent - 14.00 per cent range is also dominated by a large issue - the £337.89m BAT Industries 12.25 per cent 2008, which was issued to finance the purchase of Eagle Star Insurance. There were a number of £100.0m bank unsecured loans issued in 1982. The highest coupon is carried by the Barclays 16.00 per cent 2007 issue, most of which has been bought back and retired.

Domestic convertible bond market

The coupon structure of the domestic convertible market (see Figure 28.35) not only reflects on its obvious extensive history of issuance and failure of some issues to convert, but also on its wide range of issue sizes and credit quality. With a number of small UK companies using the market as an alternative means of raising finance, coupons in excess of 13.00 per cent can be found, but they are very small issues. However, the vast majority of coupons are to be found in the 6.00 per cent to 8.00 per cent range.

Another feature of the domestic convertible market is that there are issues with coupons net of tax and others that pay gross.

Bulldog market

The coupon structure of the Bulldog market (see Figure 28.36) reflects the two main periods of issuance. The lower coupons of 9-10 per cent (mid-86, and late 1988 to mid-89) and 10-12 per cent (the early years from 1981 to 1985). There are some very high coupons in this market reflecting the interest rate levels for very

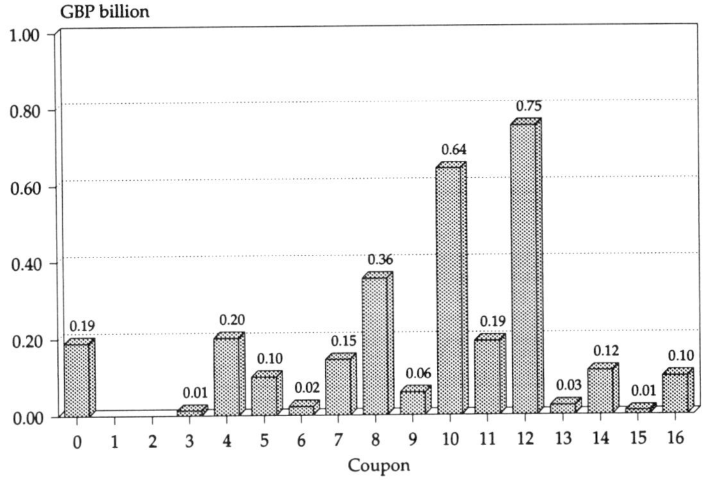

Figure 28.34 Coupon structure of the unsecured loan market

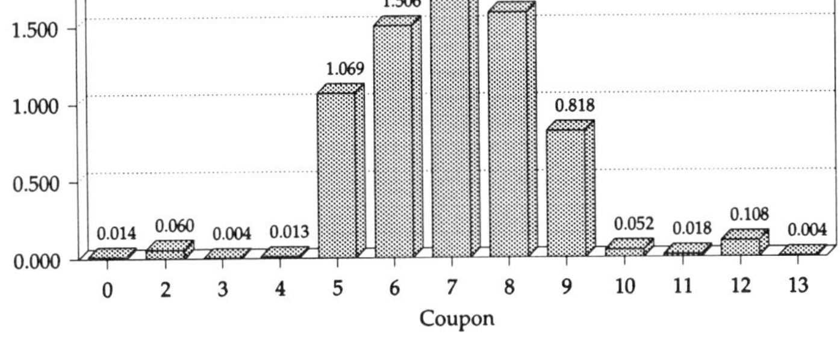

Figure 28.35 Coupon structure of the domestic convertible bond market

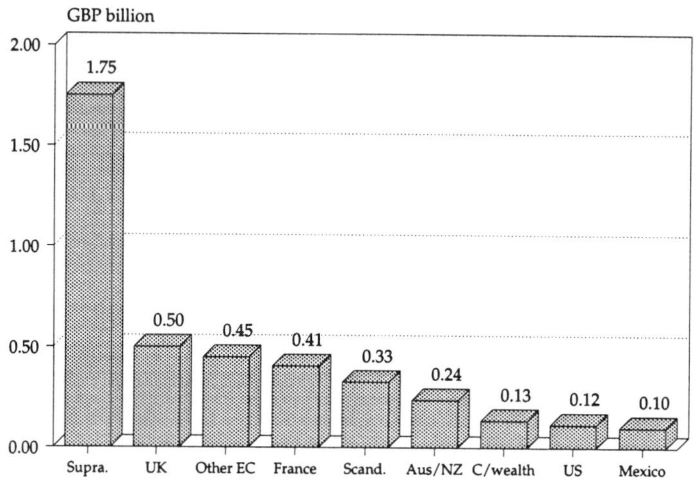

Figure 28.36 Coupon structure of the Bulldog market

long bonds in 1981/82. Of these coupons, the Mexico issue has a put option and the Inco issue's coupon can be paid in US$ at a rate of £1= US$1.98.

The largest issues in the 9.00 per cent - 10.00 per cent range are the £170.0m EIB 9.00 per cent 2001 and £426.3m EIB 9.75 per cent 2009. These, together with the £300.0m EIB 10.375 per cent 2004 and £235.0m World Bank 11.50 per cent 2003 are the largest issues in this market and dominate their coupon ranges. The highest coupon issues are the £50.0m United Mexican States 16.5 per cent 1988/2008 and £25.0m Transcanada Pipelines 16.5 per cent 1st Mortgage Pipe Line Bonds 2007, both of which are held mainly by private clients.

Medium-term note market

A large proportion of MTNs are issued as zero-coupon bonds or, in fact, as discount instruments (see Figure 28.37). This, therefore, inflates the nominal value of the low-coupon bonds. Surprisingly, there are two discount issues with low coupons: Abbey National 0.75 per cent 1995 (£7.375m) and 1996 (£11.9m). These have obviously been issued to meet a particular need. In addition there have a few discount and premium issues, e.g.. 15.0 per cent issues for National & Provincial Building Society (£10m), ANZ Bank (£10m) and Coles Meyer (£10m), 15.5 per cent Compagnie Bancaire (10m), 15.98 per cent Abbey National

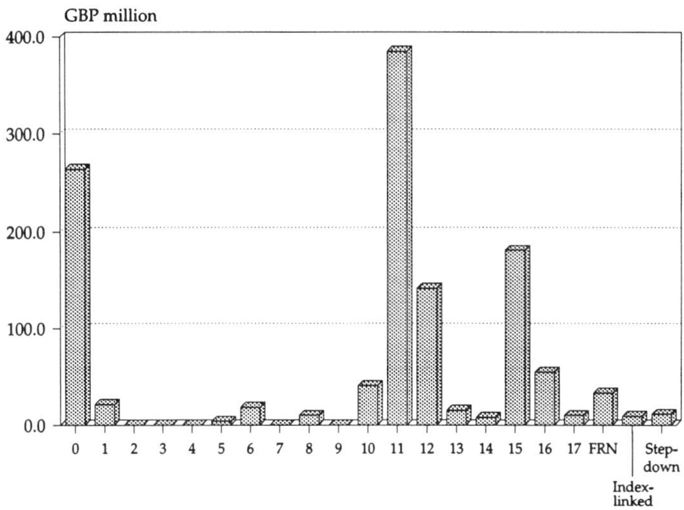

Figure 28.37 Coupon structure of the medium-term note market

(£10m),16.25 per cent Toronto-Dominion (£10m), as well as a 5.0 per cent issue for Compagnie Bancaire (£4m) and a 5.375 per cent issue for Nationwide Building Society (£18.5m). The rest were issued at current levels.

All the Kingfisher issues are zero-coupon bonds, some of which are only for £1.0m. There are £20.0m zero-coupon issues for Nationwide BS 1992 and SBC 1993. The two £15.0m issues for National Westminster and Deutsche Bank have 1996 redemption dates.

Local authority market

The coupon structure (Figure 28.38) again reflects the history of issuance. The lower coupon bonds from 1.00 per cent to 5.00 per cent are commonly the very old issues which are usually irredeemable and very small, e.g. Glasgow Water 1.00 per cent Irr. (£70,000). Those issues with coupons between 5.00 per cent and 10.50 per cent are very old issues, too, but are usually callable, with redemptions due in the 1990s (the largest issue being £40m GLC. 6.75 per cent 1990/92).

The higher coupons are the 1980s issues. There was a short period of local authority issuance which saw 15 issues with coupons from 10.80 per cent to 13.75 per cent, with most around 11.50 per cent. The largest issues are Birmingham 11.50 per cent 2012 (£100m) and Leeds 13.50 per cent 2006 (£50m). The size

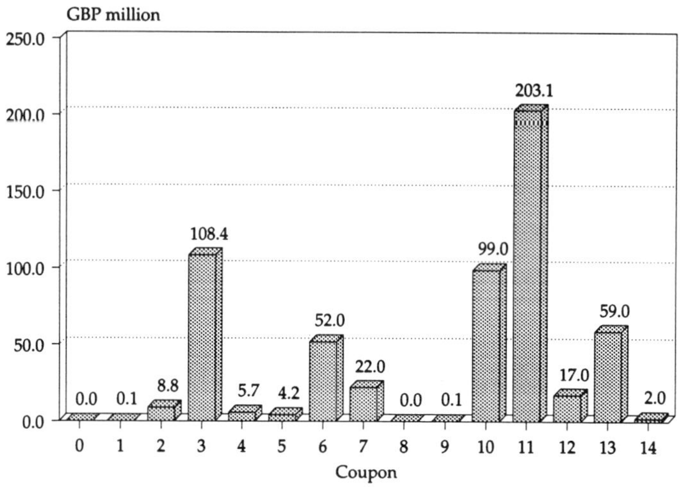

Figure 28.38 Coupon structure of the local authority bond market

of these issues are greatly inflated over actual outstandings as many of these issues have been bought back by the local authority and retired. Exact outstandings are hard to establish but it is estimated that less than £10m exists in the Birmingham issue. The two Scottish Agricultural Mortgage issues (13.00 per cent 1999 and 14.00 per cent 1993) are very small at only £2m.

28.4 Types of security

Gilt-edged market

Bullet bonds

The majority of gilt-edged securities (see Figure 28.39) are bullet bonds, i.e. with a single fixed maturity date. However,the proportion of these has continued to decline in recent years.

Callable bonds

Nearly 13 per cent of the gilt-edged market comprises callable bonds. These are securities which are redeemable at a date prior to final maturity on three months' notice by the UK government. Most of these issues in the past were low-coupon stocks and many have been redeemed. As a result, few can be found in the shorter medium-dated area. Most of the callable bonds have call-dates between 1998 and 2004 and were issued at a time when interest rates were

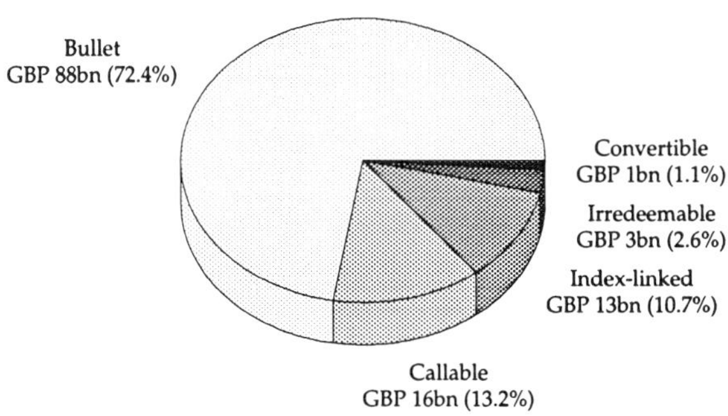

Figure 28.39 Types of issues in the gilt-edged market

very high and the government wished to avoid contracting itself into paying high coupons for the full term. Consequently, coupons on these securities are nearly all over 11.25 per cent. At current yield levels the market expects these securities to be redeemed early. However, there are a number of bonds, most particularly Treasury 9 per cent 1992/96 which, should interest rates fall, will trade to their earliest maturity date.

Convertible bonds

The UK government has issued a number of short-dated securities which offer the holder the option to convert for every £100 nominal into a predetermined nominal value of a longer-dated bond, usually with a lower coupon. These securities are actually convertible for a number of years, for example up to three, every half year. The terms of the conversion, however, usually deteriorate with time. Convertible bonds have been issued which give the holder the option to convert into an existing medium- or long-dated stock. For example, at issue, Treasury Convertible 10 per cent 1991 had the following conversion options:

- Either into:

Conversion 9.50% 2001:

Conversion date	Conversion terms[1]
12/7/87	£102
12/1/88	£101
12/7/88	£100
12/1/89	£99
12/7/89	£98

[1]*The conversion terms are set on a nominal basis. For example, on 12 July 1987, £100 nominal of Treasury Convertible 10% 1991 may be converted into £102 nominal of Conversion 9.50% 2001*

- Or into:

Conversion 9.00% 2011:

Conversion date	Conversion terms
12/7/87	£105
12/1/88	£103
12/7/88	£101
12/1/89	£99
12/7/89	£97

The majority of gilt-edged securities are bullet bonds (i.e. with a single, fixed, maturity date), but the proportion of these has declined in recent years.

Index-linked bonds

In response to growing inflation and investors' concern about real rates of return on their investments, the UK government issued securities with interest payments and final redemption value linked to the RPI. These securities, which initially offered real rates of return of just over 2.5 per cent, now offer returns in excess of 4.25 per cent. This sector of the market has grown from £6.9bn, in 1984, to around £13bn and has been stable at this level for the last four years. It is part of the government's intention to expand this sector of the market. It should be noted that these securities were initially only offered to (and designed for) UK pension funds, but this restriction was later removed. Two issues are available to overseas investors who, on application, may receive the interest payments free of tax.

Irredeemable bonds

The UK government has nearly £3.25bn nominal outstanding of what are known as irredeemable bonds. Although they carry no final maturity, these securities are redeemable after a certain date on three months' notice. In all cases the earliest date has passed. The most important of these securities is War Loan 3 1/2 per cent 1952 or After of which there is £1.9bn nominal outstanding and pays interest gross to ALL holders and is available in bearer form. It should be noted that when interest rates were much lower after the Second World War some of those securities traded above par, but it is unlikely that interest rates in the near future will fall to such a level that these securities will be redeemed.

Eurosterling market

Bullet bonds

Nearly £30bn nominal of eurosterling issues (see Figure 28.40) are in the form of bullet bonds. These securities offer the international investor fixed maturity dates. There are very few callable bonds.

Callable bonds

With the international aversion to callable securities, there have only been seven callable issues most issued in the mid-1980s. The exception is the £100.0m Lucas 10.875 per cent 2020 which is callable from January 1994 at the higher of par and the price which yields the same as Exchequer 12.0 per cent 2013/17.

Convertible into FRN

There is one issue which entitled the holder to convert into a FRN. The £35.0m CEPME 11.25 per cent 1995 was convertible until 1988 into 6-month LIBOR or

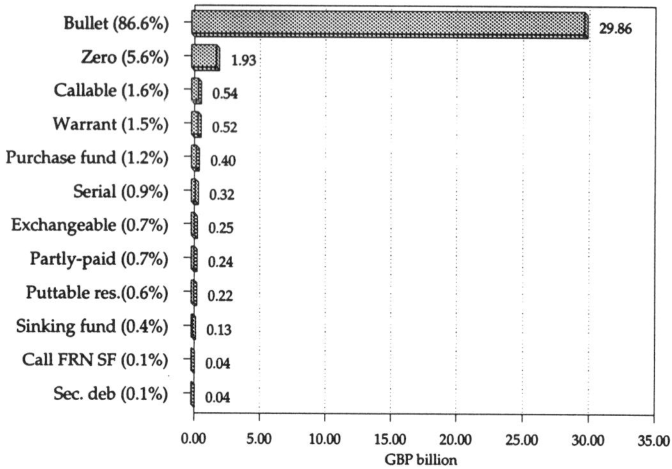

Figure 28.40 Types of issue in the eurosterling market

minimum of 5.25 per cent where one bond = $1,550 Face with a Sinking Fund from 1993 which retires 40.0 per cent each year until 20.0 per cent in the last year.

Exchangeable issues

The £500m British Telecom 13.75 per cent 1993 was initially issued in exchange for £150m 9.50 per cent 1993 and £100m 9.25 per cent 1993 issues.

Ex-warrant securities

A number of warrant issues have been made, the largest of which is the £100.0m Unilever 12.25 per cent 1994. However, most of these issues are redeemed in 1992.

Partly-paid securities

The Finland 10.125 per cent 2008 and Pearson 10.50 per cent 2008 were issued in partly-paid form.

Purchase fund securities

The European Investment Bank appears unique in that has purchase funds. To stabilize the price, the EIB applies a purchase fund in its first few years if the bond's price falls below par. The amount of money applied is not very much, usually about £3.0m per annum for the first three years.

Puttable bonds with reset coupons

There are two types of this security, which are puttable at a specific date. If the bond is not put, then either the bond becomes a floating-rate note or a fixed-rate bond with a different coupon. The former issues are £75.0m Banco di Roma 9.625 per cent 1993 (puttable 1991 if not reset as FRN with LIBOR plus 10 bp) and the latter are £100.0m Abbey National 11.625 per cent 1995 (puttable 1993 if not reset at two swap rate plus 10 bp).

Semi-annual payment

In 1991, a number of bonds were issued in the eurosterling market which paid interest semi-annually as is the UK normal practice. However, there is some confusion as to the correct method to adopt. The £150m British Land 12.5 per cent 2016 pays interest on a 360-day (euro) basis while the £100m Associated British Ports 11.875 per cent 2011, £100m BAA 11.75 per cent 2016 and £150m British Aerospace 11.875 per cent 2008 pay on a 365 day (UK) basis.

Serial redemption bonds

There are three serial bonds:

- £100.0m EDF 10.50 per cent 2006/09 with equal serial redemptions in the years 2006 to 2009.
- £125.0m ICI 11.25 per cent 1994/95 with equal serial redemptions in the years 1994 to 1995.
- £100.0m Lloyds Bank 11.375 per cent 1994/98 with equal serial redemptions in the years 1994 to 1998.

Zero-coupon securities

A number of zero-coupon issues can be found in the eurosterling market. The largest is the £300.0m Dow Chemical 1997 issue. £250m Deutsche bank 2001 was issued in 1991 and £200.0m issues can be found for Alliance & Leicester 1995, SBC Finance 2001, British Telecom 2000 and Guaranteed Export Finance 2000.

Eurosterling FRN bonds

Before discussing the variations in types of FRNs (see Figure 28.41), it would be appropriate to point out that, while the vast majority of issues have a quarterly coupon payment period, there are a number of issues with:

a) Monthly coupon payment:

- Halifax 1996 'A'
- Nationwide 1996

b) Semi-annual coupon payment:

- Alliance & Leicester 1993 Mismatch
- Bristol & West 1993 Mismatch
- Halifax 1996 'B'
- Halifax 1997

Asset-backed securities (ABS)

There is currently three ABS one of which the largest is the £328m CARS (UK) (Cardiff Automobile Receivables Securitization) 1995 issue. This is a special-purpose

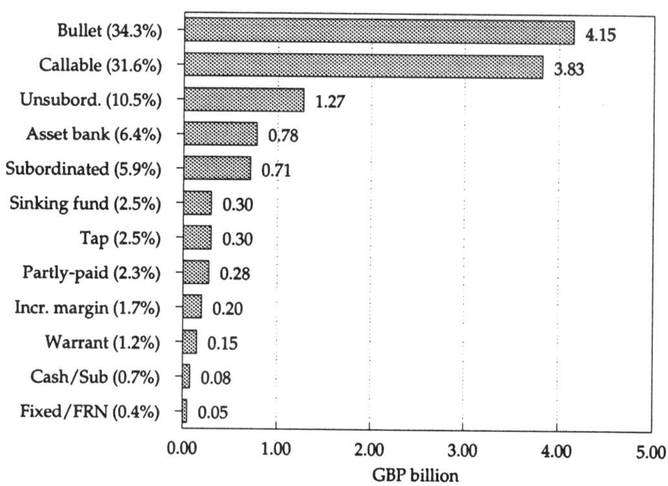

Figure 28.41 Types of issues in the eurosterling FRN market

company created solely for the issue of the security which is secured on a portfolio of motor vehicle hire purchase contracts with an initial value of not less than £328m and an assignment of the issuer's rights under a Swap Agreement.

CARS (UK) plc has entered into an agreement with Chartered Trust as counterparty and UBS as swap guarantor, whereby CARS will make fixed monthly payments, equivalent to 13.7 per cent of the principal amount outstanding, to Chartered Trust who then make payments to CARS equivalent to the interest on the FRNs.

The others are £220m Auto Funding 1996 (LIBOR + 65 bp) and £230m Drive Securities 1996 (LIBOR + 45 bp).

Bullet bonds

The largest group of FRNs are the bullet bonds with a fixed final maturity date.

Callable notes

There are a large number of callable issues. Many of these issues are by building societies, but the terms of the call are only operable if the issuer were to cease to be a building society. The reason for this is that there was considerable concern that the credit quality of the borrower might fall if the society de-mutualized, therefore the call is actual an event-risk protection feature. These issues were mainly brought to market between 1986-88, when this fear was at its highest. So far only one building society, the Abbey National, has become a public bank.

Conversions from fixed-rate bonds

There are two issues which arose from initially fixed-rate issues:

- Halifax BS 1992. Converted from 8.75 per cent 1992 in June 1990
- Woolwich BS 1995. Converted from 9.75 per cent 1995 in June 1991

Mismatches

A mismatch issue has different coupon periods and index-rate periods. The issues with mismatched coupon payments are:

- Alliance & Leicester 1993 Mismatch. Pays the higher of 6.25bp over 6-month LIBOR or 1-month LIBOR flat with a semi-annual coupon payment period.
- Bristol & West 1993 Mismatch. Pays the higher of 6.25bp over 6-month LIBOR or 1-month LIBOR flat with a semi-annual coupon payment period.

Perpetual

There is only one perpetual issue: the Standard & Chartered issue, which ranks as junior subordinated unsecured debt with a margin 18.75bp over 3-month LIBOR.

Puttable notes

A number of issues allow the lenders to put the notes to the borrower, the most important being:

- Compagnie Bancaire 1995, puttable from 1991 at 99.80 rising 0.05 per annum to 1994

Sinking funds

A number of issues with sinking funds can be found:

- Halifax 1998 with a 20 per cent S/F from 1994
- Lloyds Euro 1996 with a S/F operating between 1992 and 1996
- Royal Bank of Scotland 2005 with a 20 per cent S/F operating between 2001 and 2005

Tap issues

A number of issues have taps, i.e. the issue can be increased by supply notes to the market:

- National & Provincial BS 1999
- Yorkshire BS 1997

Stepped margins

These issues have margins which are increased during the life of the issue:

- Alliance & Leicester BS 1995. Initial margin 10bp stepped up to 17bp from May 1992.
- Leeds BS 1994. Initial margin 12.5bp stepped up to 15bp in October 1990.

Senior and subordinate notes

Several FRN issues by banks and building societies have either senior or subordinated status. The former has a higher claim on assets should a bank be wound up and therefore has the higher credit rating. Senior notes are:

- Birmingham Midshires BS 1995
- Halifax BS 1992
- Leeds BS 1997
- Nationwide Anglia BS 1993
- Nationwide Anglia BS 1995
- Yorkshire Bank International 1994
- Woolwich BS 1994
- Woolwich BS 1995

Warrants

The Standard & Chartered Irredeemable was issued with warrants to apply for fixed-rate US$ bonds.

Eurosterling MBS bonds

Mortgage-backed securities are *pass-through* instruments in that principal and interest is collected by the administrator and passed to the investor, according to the bonds specifications (see Figure 28.42).

The administrator bundles together a pool of mortgages. The interest payments are collected from the borrower and the interest on the bond (usually the mortgage interest less the costs of servicing) is paid to the bondholder. As borrowers either wholly or partially pre-pay their loans, these principal payments are repaid to the bondholders on a pro-rata basis. A number of variations are discussed below.

In order to ensure, to some degree, the average life of some notes, a collateralized mortgage obligation (CMO) structure is employed (see Figure 28.42). This means that interest is still paid to all bondholders but, as principal is prepaid, the first tranche will receive all principal payments until it is redeemed, the second likewise and then, the final tranche. An example of such an issue would be CMS 1 A1, A2 and A3 which were marketed in January 1990 with average lives of 1.5 years, 4.8 years and 6.5 years respectively.

Floating-rate notes

The vast majority of MBS public issues are floating-rate notes (see Figure 28.43). Sterling mortgage-backed floating-rate notes combine characteristics of traditional sterling floating-rate notes with those mortgage securities in the US dollar bond markets. However, the predominantly floating-rate nature of UK mortgage market endows the sterling security with features which are absent in its US dollar relative. The most important advantage is the absence of an interest rate cap made possible by the use of floating-rate collateral which in most cases pays interest at a level that floats well above LIBOR. Where temporary fixed-

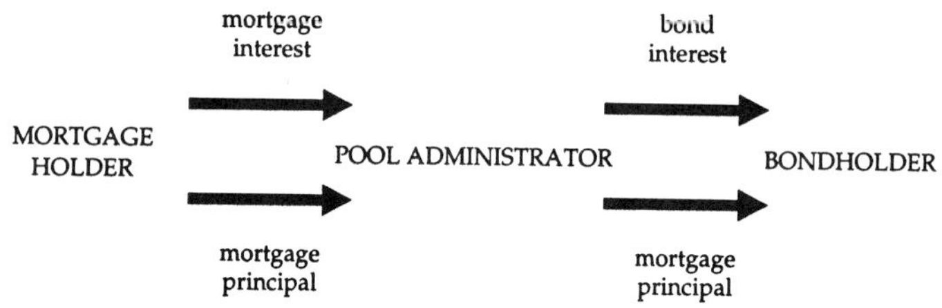

Figure 28.42 Pass-through structure of the eurosterling MBS market

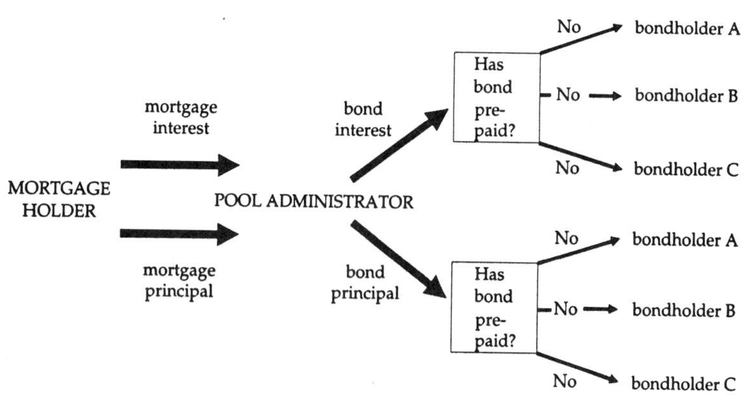

Figure 28.43 CMO structure of eurosterling MBS market

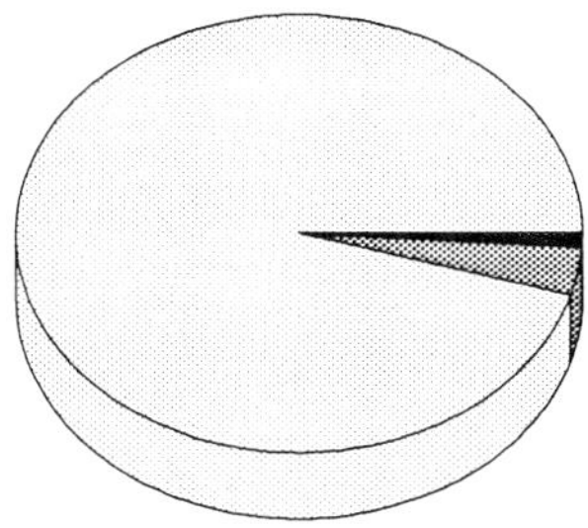

Figure 28.44 Types of issue in the MBS markets

rate mortgage collateral is used, the securitization structure will incorporate an interest rate swap during the fixed-rate period to ensure a floating-rate coupon payment can be guaranteed.

To date, all sterling mortgage-backed FRNs carry a coupon that is reset quarterly at a spread over three-month LIBOR. On the highest quality tranches of deals launched, spreads have ranged from LIBOR plus 10 basis points, to LIBOR plus 70 basis points. Subordinated or longer-life tranches have carried quoted margins as high as 1.50 per cent. Typically, quoted margins step up from their initial level after a number of years. The majority of deals carry a step up after ten years, although an earlier step up is possible. More recently, step up levels have been set at 60 to 70 basis points, substantially higher than the more traditional 50 bp over LIBOR on earlier deals.

Average life and principal redemption

Different features can act to shorten, or extend, the average life of an MBS. To reduce the rate at which pre-payments are transferred to bondholders, many security structures permit limited substitution of new mortgages to replace mortgages that have prepaid. Substitutions have been limited to a fixed amount over a fixed period or simply limited to the first three to five years, without restrictions on amount.

Another device that enables an issuer to re-deploy principal in a mortgage pool is the use of further advances. In the event that borrowers wish to increase the size of their individual mortgage, lenders can extend additional funds subject to stringent credit criteria. The majority of sterling mortgage-backed FRNs permit the limited use of principal redemptions from the mortgage pool in making further advances. Such advances extend the average life of the FRN. Occasionally, security issues explicitly forbid further advances, in which case, the issuer usually has the option of either making an entirely separate loan or repurchasing the existing mortgage from the pool an action that would effectively shortening the average life of the MBS.

The earliest redemption technique was to distribute principal redemptions pro rata amongst investors. A pool factor is published to allow investors to track the current principal balance of their investment. Redemption techniques were refined towards the end of 1987 with the use of a purchase fund (plus optional sinking fund) to make principal repayments. Mortgage interest repayments are accumulated during each three month coupon period. Using the purchase fund facility, the issuer may use any principal funds remaining at the next coupon-date to bid for notes in the open market. When notes are trading below par, the issuer may buy them back at a discount, thereby making a profit. The issuer may purchase notes and cancel them. The advantage of a purchase fund is that it ensures only complete notes are redeemed at any time, removing the need for a pool factor.

A sinking fund option allows the issuer to retire notes at par on each date if there are sufficient principal funds available. In general, this option will act as a depressant in times of market strength, since sinking fund redemptions are made at par and by drawing lots. This is a less desirable alternative for the investor, as principal repayment cashflow is most uncertain. Conversely, the sinking fund option protects the issuer against too high a market price and ensures the integrity of the deal's credit quality.

Credit quality

The credit quality of UK MBSs is very high. All but about seven of the securities issued to date have carried AAA ratings at launch. Credit quality depends upon the high quality of mortgage collateral, the amount and form of any credit enhancement and the legal structure that ensures cashflows reach investors in a complete and timely manner. The credit quality of mortgage collateral can be demonstrated by examining the geographical diversity, the range of insurance schemes and specific financial information such as loan-to-value (LTV) ratios.

The lending criteria employed in granting mortgages generally require either:

- a) income multiples of 3 times the primary wage earner plus the income of one additional party to the mortgage, or
- b) approximately 2.5 to 2.75 times the joint income of similar income joint-applicants.

The ratio of mortgage loan amount to the value of the underlying property (LTV ratio) typically falls in a range from 20 per cent to 95 per cent although, in some cases, 100 per cent loans have been made. Where larger LTV levels occur, however, the excess amount must be insured by a mortgage indemnity policy if it is to be eligible for inclusion in a high quality securities pool.

A life assurance policy is used as part of the security for each endowment mortgage. Most borrowers opting for repayment mortgages will also take out a life assurance policy to ensure mortgage repayment in the event of their death. The life policies and the insurance companies providing them are an important aspect of collateral credit quality. In a securitized mortgage pool, a broader diversity of life assurance providers improves the quality of the pool. In the past, rating agencies have either limited the proportion of a pool that can be covered by any one insurer, or have demanded additional capital as the proportion covering a single insurer is increased.

Pool insurance policies provide for any losses resulting from mortgage default by a borrower after all steps have been taken to enforce repayment of the mortgage. The proportion of losses covered for a pool as a whole by the pool policy and the rating of the insurer determines the rating granted to the issue by Standard and Poor's Corporation. Recently, downgrading of life assurance companies has affected the rating of individual bonds, although in most cases steps have been taken to correct this.

An alternative form of protection against mortgage default losses is the establishment of a subordinate (or 'B') tranche for the issue. This form of credit enhancement has the advantage of removing a third party insurance company dependence from the security structure. The size of the underlying mortgage pool matches the size of the senior 'A' tranche plus the subordinated 'B' tranche. The 'B' tranche is subordinated to the extent that it is used to absorb any losses resulting from the default of any mortgages in the pool. In some cases, principal is not repaid to the 'B' tranche until all 'A' tranche principal has been returned. Clearly, as principal is repaid, the cover afforded by a static 'B' tranche increases enormously. To restore the balance of insurance cover, some issues permit limited repayment of 'B' notes after an earlier period of, say, seven years. 'B' tranche investors receive higher margin payments in return for the additional risk of capital loss. 'B' tranche notes are usually issued as unlisted securities and/or in the form of a private placement.

Collateralized mortgage obligations (CMOs)

As shown above, it is possible, by splitting an issue into various parts or tranches, to direct all principal pre-payments to one tranche until that tranche is paid off, before then directing them to the next tranche. Thus, the average life of the first tranche is the shortest and that of the others extends accordingly. Naturally, the exact life is dependent on the rate of pre-payment.

Examples of such issues are the CMS 1 2016 issues, with £110.0m A1, £65.0m A2 and £35.0m A3 tranches, CMS 7 2028 with £135.0m A1 and £120.0m A2 tranches, MFC 4 2035 with two £100.0m A1 and A2 tranches and the TMC Pimbs No.4 2029 with two £100.0m A and B tranches.

Fixed-rate bonds

To date, four fixed-rate sterling mortgage-backed securities have been launched in the public market. The first two, HMC 101 and HMC 102, carried five-year maturities and were collateralized by a pool of primarily floating-rate mortgages. The fixed-rate coupon payments were generated by swapping the floating-rate cashflows from the mortgage pool for fixed-rate payments. The short life was generated by employing a take-out process, whereby a large institutional investor agreed to purchase, at par, the remaining floating-rate mortgage pool at the end of five years.

The only outstanding truly fixed-rate MBSs are the £124.0m Bear Stearns No.1 11.75 per cent 2017 issue which had an expected average life of ten years at issue in 1990 and the £100.0m Household Mortgage Corp (HMC) 11.125 per cent 1993.

Swapped fixed-rate bonds

In November 1988, HMC created a five year fixed-rate MBS by swapping the underlying collateral of HMC 101 Mortgage Assets, swap provided by Morgan Guaranty Trust and the maturity take out provided by AIG Financial Products. This structure was repeated in 1989 with HMC 102. In 1991, two issues were created, one for CMS and another for HMC.

Eurosterling convertible bonds

Convertible capital bonds (CCBs)

The main attraction of these bonds to issuers lies in the beneficial accounting treatment which these instruments attract:

- Interest on CCBs is deductible from corporation tax which is more advantageous than raising capital by a convertible preference issue.

- CCBs are treated as equity in the balance sheet, as share capital. The reason for this treatment lies in the mechanics of the conversion process. Unlike convertible preference shares and convertible unsecured loan stock which convert straight into equity, CCBs convert into preference shares before they convert into equity. Since, in many cases, the issuer can force conversion into the preference shares it is argued that the CCBs should be treated in the same way as convertible preference shares.
- For issuers wishing to target European investors, these bonds have the advantage of paying interest gross unlike preference shares whose dividends are subject to advance corporation tax. For this reason, an increasing number have been issued in eurosterling form, with holders have the option to hold the bond in bearer or registered form and dealable in either the domestic or euro-convertible markets.

The first issue in 1989 was the £200m Boots 6.00 per cent 2005 issue. While many of these issues are very large, over £100.0m, there have been a number of

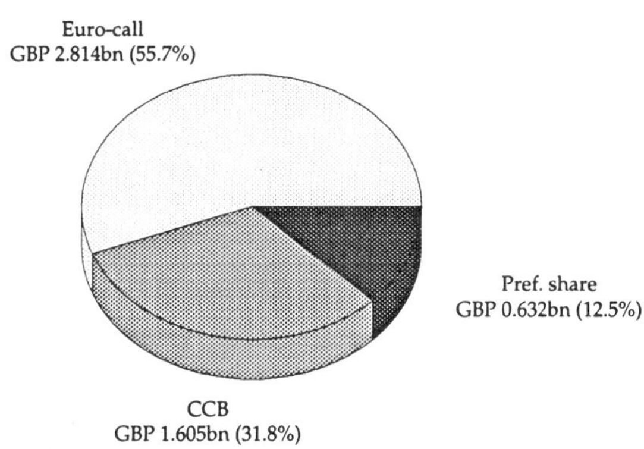

Figure 28.45 Types of issue in the eurosterling convertible bond market

small issues including the £28.0m Premier Consolidated Oilfields 8.00 per cent 2005.

Callable loans and preference shares

Many of the euro-convertibles (see Figure 28.45) are callable with the £500m Hanson 9.50 per cent 2006 and £437.8m Elf/Enterprise 8.75 per cent 2006 being the largest. The latter issue by Elf Aquitaine offers conversion into Enterprise shares, which were bought by Elf from ICI, and is a means of placing a large stake without the need to place at a discount, especially when the price of the equity is being held low as investors fear both how and when the stake will be placed.

The difference between loans and preference shares lies in the treatment of interest and in bankruptcy. Interest on loans is paid by the company before deduction of corporation tax while preference share dividends are paid after such taxes. For holders of preference shares who themselves pay corporation tax, no further tax is payable. Since a dividend is only payable after all loan interest has been paid, it is possible that a dividend may not be paid. However, nearly all preference shares have cumulative terms of conditions, i.e. if a dividend is not paid, or only partly paid, the balance should be paid at the next dividend date. If this is again missed, the outstanding balance is rolled forward until paid. Therefore, the yield on such a share is not guaranteed. Furthermore, while the preference share ranks before ordinary equity for dividend payment, it still ranks as equity in the case of bankruptcy. Therefore, all loans rank before equity or convertible holders.

All the eurosterling issues are callable, usually with hard call protection of 5 years and are then subject to the 130 per cent rule that requires the equity to trading at 130 per cent of issuing price.

Puttable convertible bonds

These issues have been infamous in the UK. Undeservedly so! The issues were often for low multiple UK companies seeking to place equity with a wider investor base than the UK presented and at a level that the company believed to be reasonable, i.e. at premiums of 20.0 per cent above the initial prevailing level. In order to overcome investors' fears, a put option was given which allowed the investor to put the bonds after five years at a premium price to issue, sometimes at over 120 per cent, to give a yield equivalent to gilt-edged securities.

Thus, the puttable convertibles meant that the company would be raising equity at a higher rate than current levels or, if the bonds were out, then the cost of borrowing would be considerably lower than normally available. Unfortunately, many of these companies assumed that the rise in the equity market would continue and did not make provisions against the put option being operated. Therefore, when the equity market fell and the UK economy went into severe recession, several of these companies could not repay the bonds which were being put. Saatchi & Saatchi had to enter into negotiations with the bondholders to come up with a refinancing package. At one time, some issues such as Next were trading at yields close to 100 per cent as investors were concerned that the effect of exercising the put could result in the company going into bankruptcy.

These issues have all been redeemed.

Puttable preference shares

See above for discussion on preference shares and put options. One of the largest issues is the £89.0m Thorn EMI 5.75 per cent 2004.

Preference bullet shares

See discussion above. Among the larger issues is the £100.0m United News (Reuters) 8.00 per cent 2004, which offers the holder conversion into Reuters shares.

Puttable convertible capital bonds

There is only one such issue, the £155.0m Boots 6.00 per cent 2005 issue.

Corporate market

Debentures

■ Bullet bonds
The vast majority of debentures (see Figure 28.46) are bullet bonds.

■ Callable bonds
There are a few callable bonds. However, most of these were issued in the mid-60s and early 70s and usually had issue sizes of just £10.0m to £20.0m. The only recent issues are the £15.0m Tops Estates 10.25 per cent 2016 and £10.0m Peel South-East 12.50 per cent 2020 issues, brought to market in 1986 and 1982 respectively. They are not, however, significant issues. Many of the earlier callable bonds also have sinking funds.

■ Index-linked bonds
The £60.0m THFC 5.625 per cent 2020, Dartmoor 6.25 per cent 2005 (both index-linked to the UK RPI) and £50.95m Housing Finance 5.00 per cent 2027 are the most recent issues with this level of coupon.

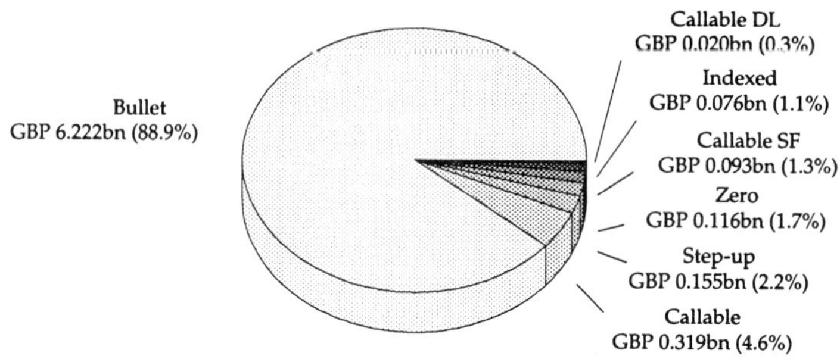

Figure 28.46 Types of issue in the debenture corporate bond market

■ Stepped-coupon bonds

The Scottish Mortgage Trust has issued two stepped-coupon issues: 1982 £20.0m 2020 (which stepped from 8.00 per cent in 1983 to 14.00 per cent in 1989, in 1.00 per cent steps) and the 1986 £50.0m 2026 (which stepped from 6.00 per cent in 1987 to 12.00 per cent in 1993, in 1.00 per cent steps). Whitbread Investment also issued a £15.0m 2010 (which stepped from 7.00 per cent in 1986 to 12.00 per cent in 1991, in 1.00 per cent steps) in 1985. These issues are little understood and therefore little traded. It was surprising, therefore, to see a £70.0m Letinvest 2012 (which stepped from 10.25 per cent in 1990 to 11.25 per cent in 1992, in 0.50 per cent steps) issued in March 1989.

■ Zero-coupon bonds

There are two zero-coupon debentures: a £93.5m Housing Finance 2012 and a £22.5m New Throgmorton Trust issue (an Investment Trust).

Unsecured corporate loans market

It should be noted that there is far less unsecured loan stock outstanding, compared with debenture issues(see Figure 28.47). The main reason for this is that any unsecured issues of size have been issued in the eurosterling market. With

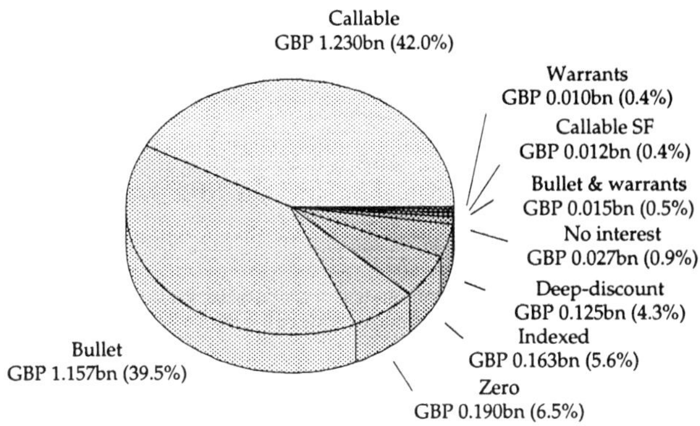

Figure 28.47 Types of issue in the unsecured corporate loans market

the UK institutions preference for security, issuance of unsecured loans has been limited. The main issues have been those by the banks and finance houses.

■ Bullet loans

These are the second largest type of loans available, representing 39.5 per cent of all unsecured loans.

■ Callable loans

This is the largest sector with 42.0 per cent. There are a number of callable loans, mainly the result of issues brought to market in the 60s and 70s. Of the more recent issues, the largest are the bank bonds of Barclays (£100m 1985), Midland (£100m 1982) and Standard Chartered (£100m 1982). Other large callable issues are BAT (£338m 1984) and BOC (£100m 1982).

■ Delayed interest loan

The £27.0m International Business Communications 4.00 per cent 1996 issue, which was brought to market in December 1990, pays no interest until 1994 when it starts to pay 4.00 per cent but, being an subordinated debenture, it reverts to an unsecured loan.

■ Index-linked loans

There are three index-linked issues: the £13.0m Nationwide Building Society 3.875 per cent 2021, £50.0m Nationwide BS 4.25 per cent 2024 and £100.0m Anglian Water 5.125 per cent 2008. These securities are similar to the index-linked gilt-edged bonds.

■ Unsecured deep-discount loans

Tesco, a supermarket chain, raised finance by issuing an unsecured deep discount £125.0m 4.00 per cent 2006 issue. The annualized gain from issue price is taxed as income in the UK.

■ Zero-coupon loans

There are two zero-coupon North Housing Association issues: the £80.0m 2019 and £110.0m 2027.

Domestic convertible bonds

This market has grown in recent years and there is just over £7.8bn UK domestic convertibles available (see Figure 28.48), compared with £5.05bn of euroster-

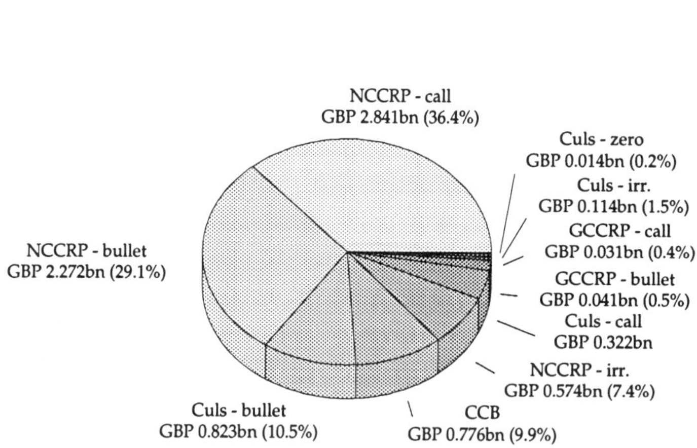

Figure 28.48 Types of issue in the domestic convertible bond market

ling convertibles, most of which have been brought to the market in the last three years.

Convertible capital bond (CCB)

See the section on eurosterling convertibles for more details of this structure. In the domestic sector, the largest issues are £320.2m British Airways 9.75 per cent 2005, £200.8m Reckitt & Colman 9.50 per cent 2005 and £177.1m BICC 6.75 per cent 2020.

Convertible unsecured loans (CULS)

These securities are unsecured loan stocks and therefore they pay interest, in contrast to preference shares which pay dividends. The two largest issues are the £313.2m Cable & Wireless 7.00 per cent 2008 and £146.3m Kingfisher 8.50 per cent 2000. The £114.3m Jefferson Smurfitt 9.75 per cent issue is irredeemable.

Convertible unsecured loans (callable) (CULS)

The same as CULS but each carries a call option. There have been no issues for some time although in December 1990, Grovewood issued a £23m bond.

Gross cumulative convertible redeemable preference share (GCCRP)

These securities are able to pay dividends gross, similar to euro-securities, yet they are domestic issues. There are only two of this type at present: the £31.0m Merlin International 9.00 per cent 2002/07 (which is callable) and the £40.5m Attwoods 8.50 per cent 2008.

Net cumulative convertible bullet preference share (NCCP)

This class of securities have the same features as NCCRPs (see below), but are irredeemable securities. The largest issues are the £100.1m National Home Loans 7.50 per cent and £92.8m Capital & Counties 5.75 per cent bonds.

Net cumulative convertible redeemable bullet preference share (NCCRP)

These preference shares, which pay their dividends net of basic rate tax, are the largest and most common security in this group. In the event of the dividend being passed for some reason, any cumulative short-fall will be added to the next dividend payment. These preference shares are redeemable, in contrast to several that are irredeemable (see above).

The largest issue in the whole sector is of the NCCRP type: the £318.5m Williams Holdings 8.00 per cent 2018. Another large issue is the £162.2m MB Caradon.

Net cumulative convertible redeemable callable preference share (NCCRP)

The calls terms for each issue vary, some being event-driven. However, most just shorten the final life by up to 5 years. redemption at the earlier date is usually if 75.0 per cent or more of the bond has been converted. This is beneficial to holders because if the majority of the bond had been converted, the bonds would trade at a discount and be illiquid. All the large issues are of this kind, the most important being the £188.9m Queens Moat 7.50 per cent 2006/11, £214.7m Tate & Lyle 7.25 per cent 29908/13, £228.3m Rank Organisation 8.25 per cent 2003/07 and £270.1m British Aerospace 7.75 per cent 2007/10.

Bulldog market

Bullet bonds

Nearly all Bulldogs have been issued in the form of bullet bonds (see Figure 28.49).

Serial bonds

There are two serial redemption bonds. These are: Credit Foncier de France 10.25 per cent Guaranteed serial Loan 2011/14 which will be redeemed at par by equal instalment in August 2011/12/13 and (finally) 2014, and the Electricite de France 11.75 per cent Guaranteed Serial Loan 2009/2012 which will be redeemed at par by equal instalment in Aug 2009/10/11 and (finally) 2012.

Puttable bonds

There are two issues with puttable options: the Mexico 16.5 per cent 2008 issue, which is puttable at par annually from 1988, and the Trinidad & Tobago 12.25 per cent 2009 issue, which is puttable at par every 5th year, i.e. 1994, 1999 and 2004.

Callable bonds

There are no callable bonds in the Bulldog market.

Currency repayment option bonds

The Inco 15.75 per cent 2006 U/L has a US dollar repayment option. On redemption, the holder can elect to receive either £100 sterling or US$ 198.

Purchase fund

For several of the first issues in this market, it was considered important to stabilize new issues through the first three years by have a purchase fund. In

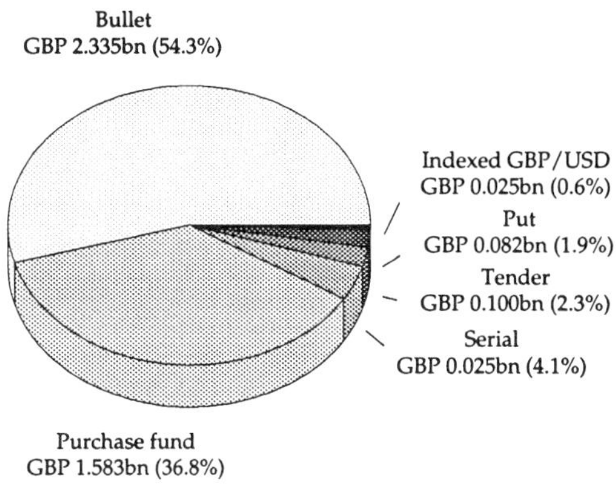

Figure 28.49 Types of issue in the Bulldog market

most cases, this amounts to 3.00 per cent of initial nominal and operates below par. In reality, they had little real value and have for the most part been dropped from later issues. The main borrower who offers this facility is the EIB.. Others were African Development Bank, Australia, Inter-American Development Bank, Ireland and New Zealand. The most recent borrower has been Bank of Greece.

Tender issue

During a time of volatile markets, the UK government used the tender system to price new issues. This method was copied by Sweden with its 9.75 per cent 2014 issue.

Medium-term note market

Bullet notes

Most issues are bullets (see Figure 28.50), as one would expect if the main driver of an issue is the lender.

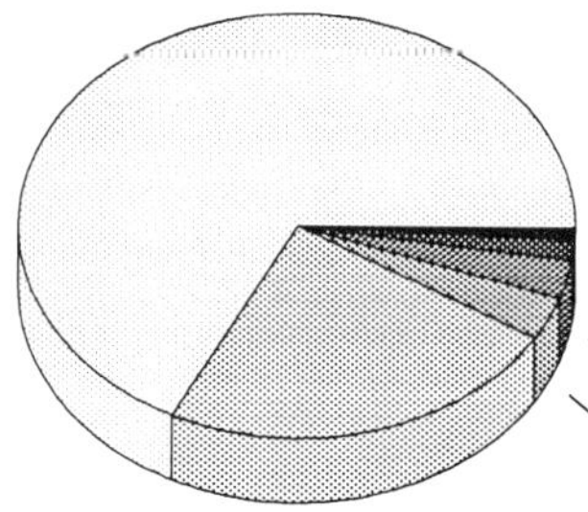

Figure 28.50 Types of issue in the medium-term note market

Discount coupon bonds

There are two such issues: an Abbey National 0.75 per cent 1995 issue and a Compagnie Bancaire 5.00 per cent 1995 issue. These have obviously been issued to meet a particular investor's requirements.

Floating-rate notes

There is a £15m three-year FRN for Halifax Building Society, and a £18m five-year issue for Nationwide Building Society.

Indexed notes

There are two indexed issues for Abbey National, both of which carry coupons and are indexed to the FT-SE 100 equity index.

Zero-coupon bonds

These issues are effectively Treasury bill equivalents, with all the Kingfisher issues being of this type.

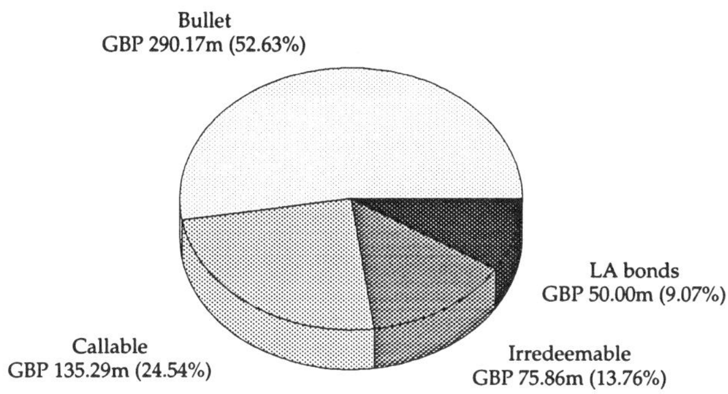

Figure 28.51 Types of issue in the municipal market

Municipal market

Bullet bonds

Most of the 1980s issues were in the form of bullet bonds (see Figure 28.51), while very few of the earlier issues were so structured.

Callable bonds

Nearly all of the earlier issues from the 1950s and 1960s were in the form of callable bonds. However, since the coupons of most of these securities are considerably below current levels, it is unlikely that any of these bonds will be called at present.

Irredeemable bonds

With little issuance, the proportion of irredeemables continues to grow as dated bonds are redeemed. There is about £80m nominal outstanding of irredeemable bonds in domestic corporates.

28.5 Issuers

Eurosterling market

The initial growth of the eurosterling market (see Figures 28.52 & 28.53) in 1984 and 1985 was fuelled by the UK building societies' and banks' need for funds. As a consequence, banks (17.0 per cent) are the largest sector, with sovereign (13.35 per cent) and supranational (12.33 per cent) issuers next. UK building societies (9.13 per cent) and Utilities are strong issuers.

Banks

A wide range of banks have raised finance in the eurosterling market. Some have done so to finance their London branches and sterling loans. Other have used the opportunities in the swaps market to create other synthetic loans such as a floating-rate yen loan. Most major international banks can be found. The largest issues are the £250m Deutsche Bank 0.00 per cent 2001, £200m SBC Finance 0.00 per cent 2001, £150.0m OKB 12.00 per cent 1992 (Austrian Bank), £150.0m Lloyds Bank 10.25 per cent 1998, and three £250.0m Barclays Bank issues of 9.50 per cent 1993, 10.25 per cent 1997 and 12.75 per cent 1997. This last issue has been partially bought in.

Corporates

This sector encompasses a wide range of corporations, both by type and country of origin. The largest issues are: £300.0m Dow Chemical Zero 1997, £300.0m Elders IXL 10.25 per cent 1992, £215.7m British Telecom 13.75 per cent 1993 and £200.0m issues for Land Securities 9.50 per cent 2007 and British Telecom Zero 2000.

Financial

A number of finance companies have accessed this market. They are mainly UK companies although there are issues for American Express and General Finance. As in the case of banks, these loans are probably financing UK operations.

Sovereign

Several governments have tapped this market. Many have moved from the Bulldog market to access the wider investor base (which still includes UK institutions).

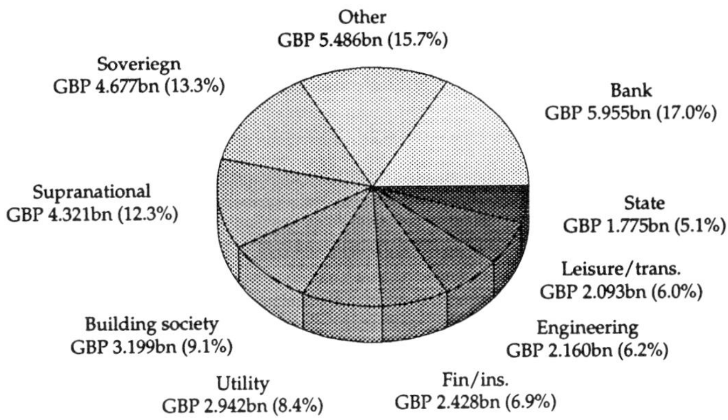

Figure 28.52 Types of issuer in the eurosterling bond market (per cent)

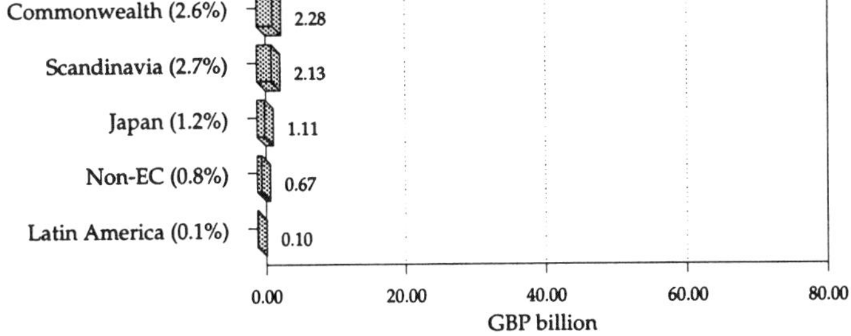

Figure 28.53 Country of origin of issuers in the eurosterling bond market

The largest issue in the eurosterling market is the £400.0m Italy 10.50 per cent 2014 and GEFCO 10.625 per cent 2001 issues. There are also £200.0m Finland 10.375 per cent 1998, GEFCO 0.00 per cent 2000 and Norway 10.50 per cent 1994 issue. Other government issues of about £100.0m can be found for Australia, Austria, Denmark, Export-Import Bank of Japan, Finland, French government agencies, Ireland, Mexico, New Zealand, Oesterreichische Postsparkasse and Sweden with maturities between 1993 and 2009.

State

A wide range of state borrowers can be seen covering both export and other state agencies. The US Sallie Mae has a £100.0m 11.00 per cent 1994 issue. Other borrowers come from Australia, Canada, Finland, France, Japan and Sweden. The UK agencies include '3i', the £120.0m Agricultural Mortgage Corporation and £200.0m Guaranteed Export Finance Corporation.

Supranationals

All the major supranationals have eurosterling issues, of which the £350.0m World Bank 9.25 per cent 2007 is the largest.

UK building societies

There is a large number of issues for UK building societies, most having been issued with 5 year terms. The largest issues are the £200.0m issues of Alliance & Leicester Zero 1995 and 14.25 per cent 1995.

Foreign borrowers

The supranationals (4.9 per cent) are the third largest borrower after the UK (79.9 per cent). European borrowers come next, both EC (5.7 per cent) and non-EC (3.5 per cent of which 2.7 per cent is from Scandinavian borrowers). The US represents 2.6 per cent, while the Commonwealth also makes up 2.6 per cent (the smaller Commonwealth countries still use the Bulldog market). Japan only makes 1.2 per cent, a far smaller figure than can be found in US dollars and Swiss francs.

UK borrowers

As can be seen, the UK borrowers make up 79.9 per cent. This is because the issuance methods of the market are easier, the investor base is much wider and many UK borrowers believe that UK institutions require too high a rate of interest for similar loans in the domestic market.

Floating-rate note market

The FRN market is dominated by UK building societies and banks (see Figures 28.54 & 28.55), the former in order to finance their floating-rate mortgages and the latter to provide floating-rate funds with the Standard & Chartered raising junior subordinated capital in this form. There is one sovereign issue and one corporate.

Asset-backed issues

There are three asset backed issues supported by auto loans. They are Auto Finance (£220m), CARS (£328m) and Drive Securities (£230m).

Building societies

The largest issues are Nationwide 199 (£300m), Halifax 1995 (£350m) and the Alliance & Leicester 1994 (£300m) with five further issues of £250m and thirteen issues of £200m. These issues are in several forms including unsubordinated and subordinated debt as well as stepped margin and mismatches. Investors should refer to Section 28.4, which deals with types of securities.

Banks

The largest issue for a bank is the £250m Midland Bank Subordinated 2001 issue with £200m issues for Lloyds Euro 1996 (the first eurosterling FRN) and Compagnie Bancaire which has put options. Standard & Chartered has a £150m Perpetual issue which ranks as junior subordinated debt.

Finance

The broad title 'Finance' includes a number of special-purpose company issues:

- £100m STRIPES (Securities Transferred & Repackaged into Pound Equivalent Securities) 1996

This is a special-purpose company created solely for the issue of the security which is secured by a fixed charge on US$154m Kingdom of Denmark FRN 1996. In the event of early redemption of the Denmark issue, the FRN's money will be placed on deposit with Dresdner Bank AG which has undertaken to pay an equal rate of interest. STRIPES will enter into agreement with Morgan Guaranty Trust Company of New York, London branch, whereby STRIPES will make payment to them equal to the interest on the Denmark's FRNs in return for

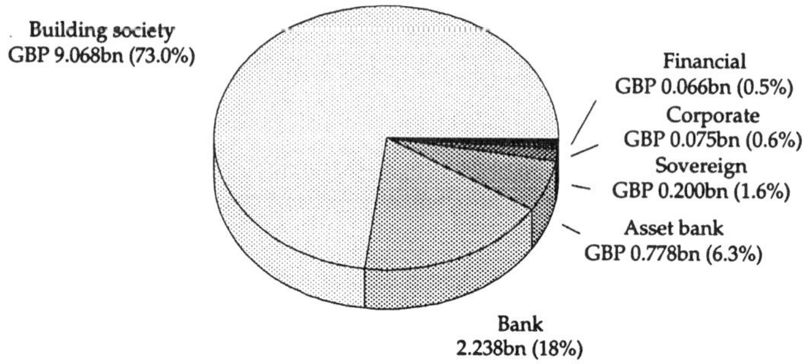

Figure 28.54 Types of issuer in the eurosterling FRN market (per cent)

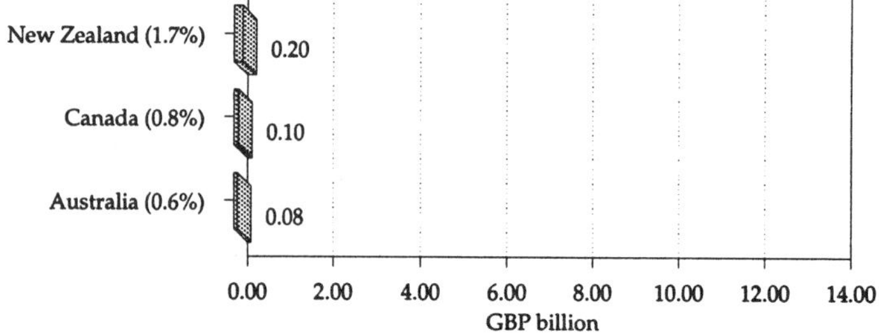

Figure 28.55 Country of origin of issuers in the eurosterling FRN market

payments by Morgan Guaranty Trust Company of New York equal to the interest on the STRIPES FRNs.

- £66m CARPS 3 1999

This is a special-purpose company created solely for the issue of the security which is secured by a first charge on US$ 104,089,050 of Devonshire Finance Ltd. Secured Amortising Bonds, due 1995, and an assignment of the issuers rights under a swap agreement. CARPS 3 Ltd has entered into agreements with Prudential Global Funding Inc. whereby CARPS undertakes to make payments to Prudential equal to the principal and interest on the bonds forming the security against payments by Prudential equal to the principal and interest on the CARPS FRNs. This bond has a semi-annual sinking fund which retires 92.06 per cent prior to maturity.

Mortgage-backed securities market

The MBS market resulted from the deregulation of the financial markets and liberalization of home lending. The first company to be created to finance home lending was the Salomon Brothers International's subsidiary, The Mortgage Corporation (TMC). This was later joined most notably by National Home

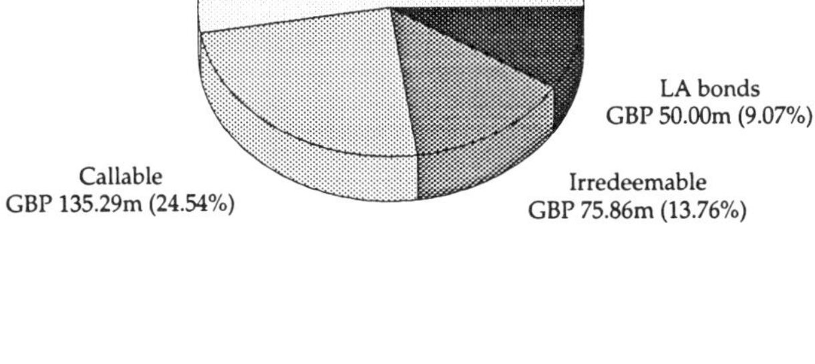

Figure 28.56 Types of issuer in the eurosterling MBS market (per cent)

Loans (NHL), Household Mortgage Corporation (HMC). Other MBS issuers are special-purpose companies which were created to repackage the home mortgages of institutions such as banks and insurance companies (see Figure 28.56).

The Mortgage Corporation (TMC)

This Salomon Brothers International subsidiary was the first in the market-place and issued the first MBS. It has a high public profile and often advertises on television and in the press thereby generating a large proportion of the mortgage market and providing 30.0 per cent of the MBS securities. It was considered necessary to create a separate company in order to save issuing expenses: Program for Issuance of Mortgage-backed Securities (PIMBS).

National Home Loans (NHL)

This is the second largest company in this area. It issues both in its own name and that of Collateralized Mortgage Securities (CMS), together responsible for 21.5 per cent of the market.

Household Mortgage Corporation (HMC)

This is the third largest company and, together with its other issuing vehicle SRF accounts for 13.7 per cent of issues.

Other special-purpose companies

Other mortgage providers are the Mortgage Funding Corporation (MFC, accounting for 7.2 per cent of issues), Mortgage Intermediary Nominees International (MINI - £50m) and Mortgage Securities - the issuing vehicle for First Mortgage Securities (4.0 per cent)

Re-packaged mortgage companies

These companies re-package the mortgages of banks and insurance companies. Those currently to be found are:

- Domus - Chemical Bank (0.85 per cent)
- Exclusive Finance - Trustee Savings Bank (1.15 per cent)
- Gracechurch - Barclays Bank (1.49 per cent)
- Maes Funding - Canadian Imperial Banking Corporation (4.2 per cent)
- Residential - Bank of Ireland (3.4 per cent)
- Temple Court - Legal & General Insurance Company (2.8 per cent)

Eurosterling convertible bond market

Surprisingly, most issuers are UK companies (see Figures 28.57). Whilst one would expect the domestic authorities of any company to demand that a company issue equity and equity related securities in their own market to allow domestic investors to participate, it is surprising that companies wishing to attract UK investors have not explored this market. The currency risk should not be a deterrent, as the use of currency swap techniques can cover any perceived risk. The largest issuers are stores, followed by chemical and oil companies. The overseas issuers all have issued covered convertibles into UK equities, being Elf (French) into Enterprise Oil, News Corp (Australian) into Pearson and ADT (Bermuda) into BAA.

Building companies

The biggest issues are for £107.5m Tarmac 9.50 per cent 2006, £100.0m Hepworth 11.25 per cent 2005, £90.0m Blue Circle 10.50 per cent 2005 and the £78.0m RMC Group 8.75 per cent 1996/2006. Of these, all but the Blue Circle issue were issued in 1991 as convertible capital bonds (CCBs), during a period of severe recession and very low stock price in the construction industry.

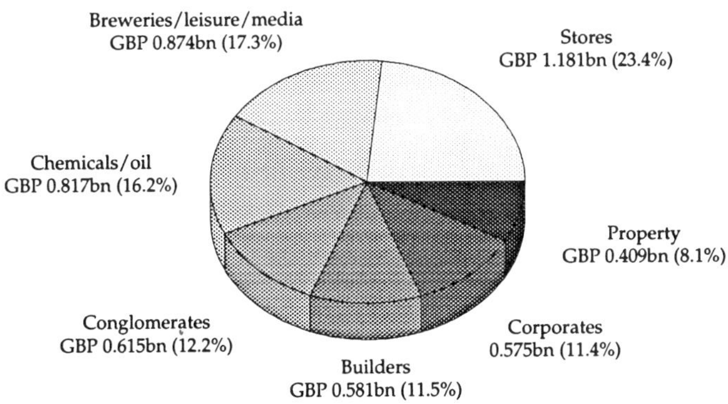

Figure 28.57 Types of issuer in the eurosterling convertible bond market (per cent)

Chemical & oil companies

The dominate issue in this sector is that of £437.8m Elf/Enterprise 8.75 per cent 2006. This issue by Elf Aquitaine (UK) is for conversion into its major stake in the UK oil company, Enterprise Oil. It is second only to the Hanson Convertible and one of the largest in the sterling market. The £200.8m Reckitt & Colman 9.50 per cent 2005, £90.0m LASMO and £90.0m Smith & Nephew 4.00 per cent 2002 (issued in 1987) are the other major companies. The structure of the Elf/Enterprise issue is copied from eurobond issues which have carried warrants to buy equities held by the issuer. While warrants are well understood in the international markets, they are considered a private investor instrument and, by UK investors, a highly speculative one. The euro-convertible structure has, therefore, greater appeal to UK institutions.

Conglomerates

The £500.0m Hanson 9.50 per cent 2006 dominates not only this sector, but also the sterling bond market. The other issues are £75.0m Harrisons & Crosfield 7.50 per cent 2003 and £40.0m ECC. Group 6.50 per cent 2003.

Corporates

This general category embraces the third largest issue for £320.2m British Airways 9.75 per cent 2005, £150.0m Hillsdown Holdings 4.50 per cent 2002 (a food manufacturer), £98.0m Coats Viyella 7.25 per cent 2004 (a textile company) and £98.0m United Biscuits 5.75 per cent 2003 (a food manufacturer).

Electrical & engineering companies

The longest issue in this sector is for £177.1m BICC 6.75 per cent 2020 (which also rates as one of the longest euro-convertible issues).

Leisure companies

This sector embraces brewers, hotels and media. The largest issue is for £150.0m Ladbroke 5.25 per cent 2004 (a hotel/betting company which owns the Hilton International chain). Others are: £100.0m issues for Independent Newspapers 6.00 per cent 2006, United News (Reuters) 8.00 per cent 2004 (the bond is convertible into Reuters shares) and Grand Metropolitan (which owns restaurant chains and hotels).

Property companies

The two big issues in this sector are £175.0m Land Securities 9.375 per cent 2004 and £150.0m Slough Estates. It should be remembered that these issues are unsecured, while all straight bond issues are debentures.

Stores

This sector is the largest and dominated by the £200.0m issues for supermarket chains Sainsbury (8.50 per cent 2005) and Tesco (9.00 per cent 2005). Further large issues are: £155.0m Boots 6.00 per cent 2005 (a pharmaceutical retailer), £110.0m Burton 4.75 per cent 2005 (a clothes retailer) and £108.0m ASDA 4.75 per cent 2002 (a supermarket chain).

Corporate bond markets

There is a marked difference between the issues of debentures (secured loans) and unsecured loans. The main issues of debentures (see Figure 28.58), are associated with property companies, breweries (secured on their pubs) and investment trusts (secured on the assets of the trust). On the other hand, banks and

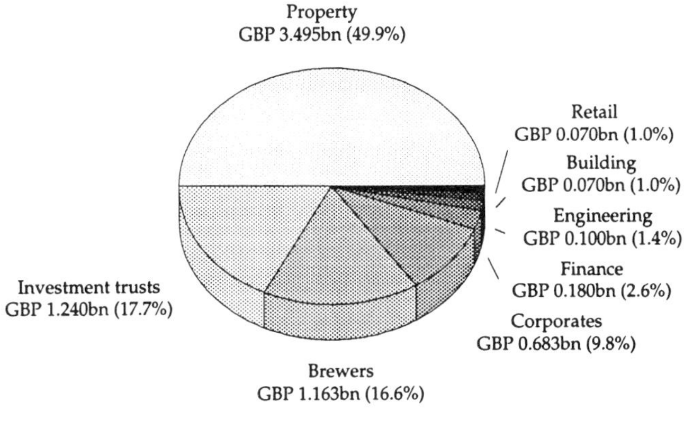

Figure 28.58 Types of issuer in the debenture market (per cent)

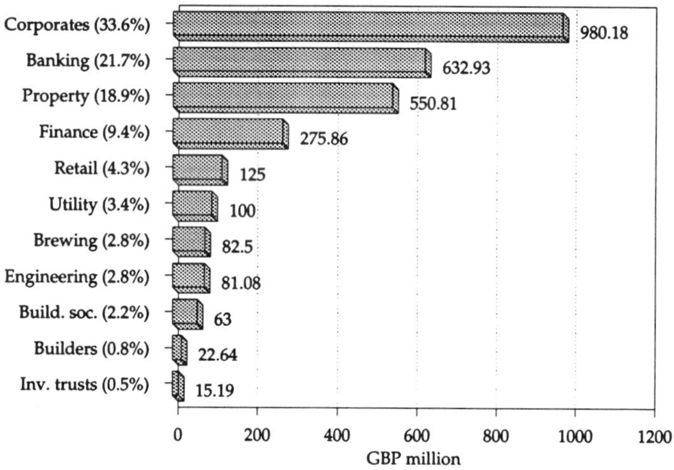

Figure 28.59 Types of issuer in the unsecured loans market (per cent)

building societies have only issued unsecured loans (see Figure 28.59). The corporate sector has both types of issues, the type used by the issuer being dependent on the credit quality of the borrower. Large borrowers such as BAT (£337.9m - 12.25 per cent 2008) and Enterprise Oil (£200m - 10.75 per cent 2013) can borrow unsecured, as was possible for the leading banks (Midland, National Westminster, Barclays and Standard & Chartered, all raised finance in 1982 in this form, the issue size being limited to £100m at the time. Barclays and the Trustee Savings Bank were able to raise similar amounts in 1988).

The largest issues in the debenture market are two £200m issues for Land Securities (10.00 per cent 2025 and 10.00 per cent 2030), £200m Mount Charlotte 10.75 per cent 2014 and £200m Allied Lyons 9.75 per cent 2019. Also, £150m issues for Lasmo (10.375 per cent 2009), Allied Lyons 9,75 per cent 2019 and Bass 10.375 per cent 2016 can be found. All debenture issuers come to the domestic market rather than the euro-market because security is highly valued by UK investors and the companies are well-known domestically. Real estate companies have always been considered safe investments, whilst in many countries this is certainly not the case and therefore, these companies could have raised funds more cheaply here than in the euro-market.

A recent innovation has been the creation of a special-purpose company to raise funds for a number of small borrowers. The special-purpose bond is of a size that will be liquid and therefore very attractive to investors. The first debenture issue for five small investment trusts (Trustco) was for £55m and the second, for four small breweries (Pubco), was also for £55m. However, both are open-ended and further issuance is allowed. By using this format, these small companies were able to access the domestic corporate bond market and refinance their bank borrowings.

Banks

There were a number of very old and small debenture issues for UK banks, but the majority of them have been redeemed. The large issuance of long-dated bonds seen in 1988 and 1990 were all in the form of unsecured loans. The largest issues are each for £100.0m: Barclays Bank (16.00 per cent 2007), Midland Bank (14.00 per cent 2007), National Westminster (12.50 per cent 2004), Standard & Chartered 12.875 per cent 2007 and Trustee Savings Bank (10.625 per cent 2008 - most which has been bought back and retired).

Building societies

There are no debentures issued by building societies as these would contravene the status of other lenders. All the issues are unsecured loans, although these borrowers prefer to borrow in the FRN market as their mortgages are nearly all in floating-rate form. The two building societies issues are index-linked and both by Nationwide: £13.0m 3.875 per cent IL 2021 and £50m 4.25 per cent IL 2024.

Breweries

The reverse of the banks' issuing pattern is seen in this sector. Nearly all the old issues were in unsecured loan form, whilst all the recent issues were debentures. The largest issues are: £400.0m Allied Lyons 9.75 per cent 2019, £350.0m Bass 10.375 per cent 2016 and £135.0m Whitbread 11.625 per cent 2011.

Corporates

This is an all-embracing sector and covers many industries. In the unsecured loans market the largest issues are for £337.89m BAT 12.25 per cent 2008 (issued to finance the take-over of Eagle Star), £200.0m Enterprise Oil 10.75 per cent 2013, £125.0m Tesco 4.00 per cent 2006 (a deep discount issue) and £100.0m BOC 12.25 per cent 2017 (an industrial gases company). The largest debenture issues are £150.0m British Sugar 10.75 per cent 2013 and £150.0m LASMO 10.375 per cent 2009

Financial companies

These companies have issued both debentures and unsecured loans. The former are all small issues, while the latter is dominated by the £231.4m British & Commonwealth 10.50 per cent 2012, which is held in administration after the company went into receivership.

Investment trusts

These companies invest in securities, often overseas and differ from unit trusts in that they are closed end. They are also able to raise loans to create further gearing; however, this is always in the form of debentures. It should be remembered that the security of these companies is the assets of the fund, i.e. equities. Should equity prices fall sharply then the cover will be severely eroded and, if the assets fall far enough, then the value of the security may be worthless. Nearly all issues are small, often under £25.0m, with the largest, by far, being the £100.0m Foreign & Colonial IT 11.25 per cent 2014.

Oil companies

The UK oil companies have very little domestic issuance, most of their finance being raised in the form of equity or in the international bond markets in a variety of currencies, including eurosterling.

Property companies

In the past, both unsecured bonds and debentures were seen for this type of company. However, following the property crisis, investors became concerned about their creditworthiness and, as a result, all the most recent issues have been debentures. The unsecured loans market has seen the zero-coupon issues for North Housing Association £80.0m 2019 and £110.0m 2027. In the debenture market, the largest issues are: £400.0m and £200.0m Land Securities 10.00 per cent issues, of 2025 and 2030 respectively, £200.0m Mount Charlotte 10.75 per cent 2014 and the £200.0m Peel Holding 9.875 per cent 2011. However, recently this sector has been under severe pressure as companies extended themselves building major office developments just as the UK economy went into severe recession (Peel Holdings is currently undergoing a refinancing programme). Whilst, in the past, property values and rentals have risen sharply, there is concern that the currently glut of offices will constrain the market and, because cover is usually based on rental escalation, thereby lead to pressure on property companies.

Retail companies

Most retail company non-equity finance has been raised in the form of convertibles. However, with increased demands for security by investors, most recent issues have been in the form of small debentures issues.

Domestic convertible bond market

As noted earlier, many of these issues (see Figure 28.60), are issued to finance take-overs and acquisitions.

Building companies

The largest issues are: £86.7m AMEC 6.50 per cent 2009, £82.9m W. Lawrence 8.50 per cent 2003/06 and £75.0m Blue Circle 7.625 per cent 2010/12.

Chemical & oil companies

This is a very small sector made up of several issues below £40.0m.

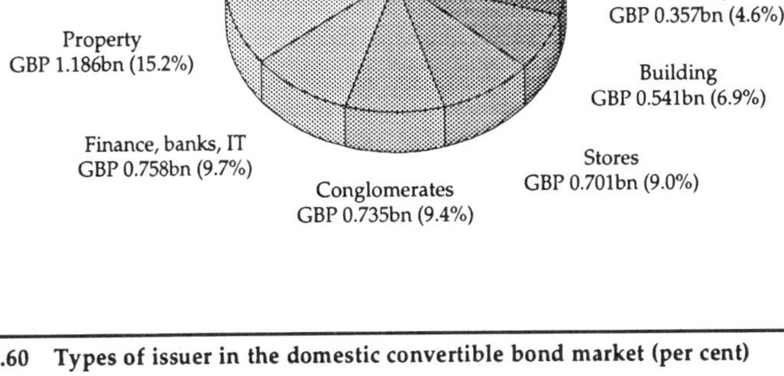

Figure 28.60 Types of issuer in the domestic convertible bond market (per cent)

Conglomerates

The largest issue is the £318.5m Williams Holdings 8.00 per cent 2018.

Corporations

This is the widest group and contains food manufacturers, car parts/repairs, paper, etc. The largest issues are: £214.7m Tate & Lyle 7.25 per cent 2008/13 and £114.3m Jefferson Smurfitt 9.75 per cent Irredeemable.

Electrical & engineering companies

The largest issues are: £270.1m British Aerospace 7.75 per cent 2007/10 and £313.2m Cable & Wireless 7.00 per cent 2008.

Finance

The largest issues are: £120.0m Hambros Bank 7.50 per cent 2004/09 and £100.1m National Home Loans 7.50 per cent Irredeemable.

Leisure

This sector includes breweries, hotels and media companies. The largest issue is the £228.3m Rank Organisation (Xerox, hotels, bingo and cinemas) 8.25 per cent 2003/07, £188.9m Queens Moat (hotels) 7.50 per cent 2006/11, £173.7m Granada (television, restaurants and TV rentals) 7.50 per cent 2003/09 and £162.2m Carlton Communications (television) 6.500 per cent 2005/10.

Property companies

The largest issue is the £141.0m Slough Estates 8.25 per cent 2006/11.

Stores

The largest issues are: £186.2m Dixons 5.00 per cent 2003/07, £146.3m Kingfisher 8.50 per cent 2000 and £75.5m Iceland Frozen Foods 5.50 per cent 2003/08.

Bulldog market

The major borrowers in this market have been sovereign nations and supranationals (see Figures 28.61 & 28.62). The corporate and state borrowers were drawn from the old Commonwealth country of Canada as well as a few corpo-

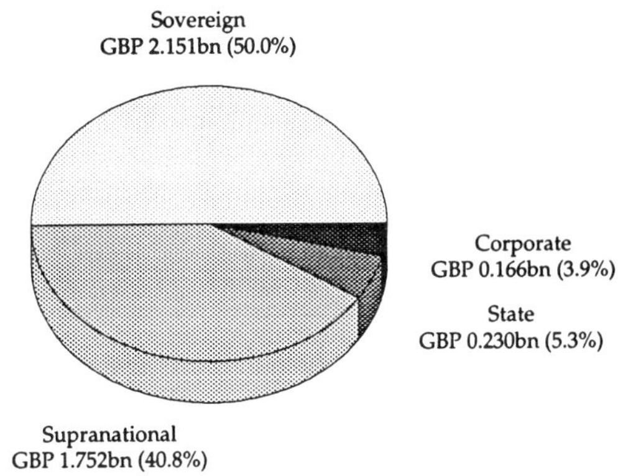

Figure 28.61 Types of issuer in the Bulldog market (per cent)

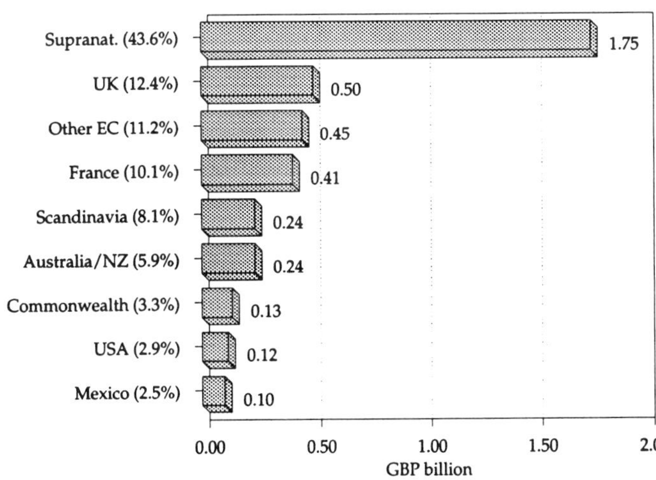

Figure 28.62 Country of origin of issuers in the Bulldog market

rations from the United States. The main reason for this was that the UK investors had not seen issuance in the domestic markets for almost ten years and therefore were unable to assess credit risk. By issuing bonds for sovereign and supranational borrowers, the UK merchant banks were able to overcome this problem.

Supranationals

The EIB is a major borrower in this market and continues to use it today by issuing further tranches of existing issues. This has resulted in the £500m issue of 9.5 per cent 2009 and £400m issue of 10.375 per cent 2004. The World Bank has two long-dated issues: £100m 9.5 per cent 2010 and £235m 11.5 per cent 2003.

Other supranationals, namely, the African Development Bank, Asian Development Bank and Inter-American Development Bank have also issued into the market.

Sovereign

The main borrowers in the Bulldog market have been European borrowers, both major countries such as France, Sweden and Denmark as well as a number of smaller ones such as Finland, Greece, Iceland, Portugal and Spain. The old Commonwealth countries of Australia, Barbados, New Zealand, Trinidad & Tobago and Gibraltar have also been able to take advantage of their historical connections with the UK. Australia has been buying back its debt and retiring it. Mexico tapped this market in 1981 with issues in its own name and via PEMEX during a period when it was raise finance in many currencies.

State

The main state borrowers have been those of Canada: Hydro-Quebec, Nova Scotia and Quebec. Again they have been able to take advantage of their historical connections with the UK.

Corporates

In addition to the Canadian borrowers of Inco and Trans-Canada Pipelines, the corporates that have tapped this market have been mainly from the US: American Brands, American Medical, CIGNA and Eaton. The latter has been buying back its issue and retiring bonds.

Medium-term note market

The blanket criterion for a company to qualify to issue sterling MTNs, is a minimum net asset amount of £25 million. Specific criteria are:

- A UK company must also have either debt or equity listed on the International Stock Exchange or shares traded on the Unlisted Securities Market (USM).
- An overseas company must be listed on an authorized stock exchange.
- Public sector bodies need only to have debt securities trading on an authorized stock exchange.

Note that *UK local authorities can issue MTNs.*

The main borrowers are the UK building societies and the banks (see Figures 28.63 & 28.64). Corporates are, as yet, not major players - neither are supranationals. However, there is the Council of Europe with £42m, and small programmes for Finnish Export Credit and Nordic Investment Bank are available. GECC became very active in 1991.

The most successful programmes appear to be those for Compagnie Bancaire, GECC and Kingfisher who issue regularly with issues of between £3m-£10m for the first, £2m-23m for GECC, and £1m-£3m for the latter.

Auto finance

There is one issue for Ford Motor company.

Banks

This sector is led by Compagnie Bancaire and includes Deutsche Bank, National Westminster, SBC Finance and Toronto-Dominion

Building societies

The Abbey National, Cheltenham, Halifax, Nationwide and National & Provincial all issue in this market.

Corporates

The only corporate borrowers are Coles Meyer and Kingfisher. However, the latter has a very large programme and is very active.

Finance companies

GECC is the only borrower in this sector.

State agency

The only borrower is Finnish Export Credit

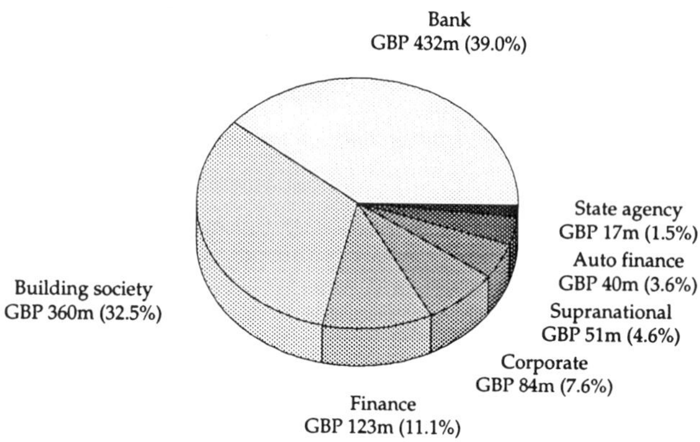

Figure 28.63 Types of issuer in the medium-term note market (per cent)

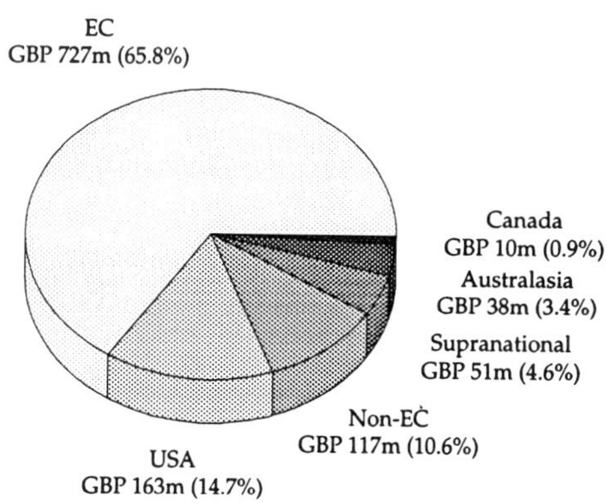

Figure 28.64 Country of origin of issuers in the medium-term note market

Supranationals

Both Council of Europe and Nordic Investment Bank have issued sterling MTNs.

Municipals

While most of large issues outstanding are by local authorities or cities such as Birmingham, Leeds and the London Boroughs of Islington, Kensington & Chelsea, these issues have been bought in. Of the irredeemables, a few are for cities such as Manchester, Hull, Swansea, etc. while the rest are for the old utilities which were later nationalized such as water companies, gas companies and port authorities.

The remaining borrowers are the two Agricultural Mortgage Corporations (AMC and Scottish AMC), which are public bodies that lend to farmers. Most recently, the AMC borrowed in the eurosterling bond market with £100m 11.375 per cent 1996 (April 1991) and £150m 11.5 per cent 1994 (August 1989) issues.

As previously noted, all these borrowers have been able to raise funds by borrowing from the PWLB (see Section 28.1), but there is some expectation that they may return in their own right to the market-place.

28.6 Investors

In the 1960s, most investment portfolios in the UK were heavily biased towards bonds with over 50.0 per cent in such securities (see Figures 28.65 - 28.68 inc.). However, this proportion was being eroded until the 1970s when the level of government borrowing grew dramatically and levels were maintained at 30.0 per cent. Note that the private sector held approximately 30.0 per cent while the local authority funds held 35.0 per cent and other public sector interests held only 22.0 per cent. During the 1980s, with the rapid expansion of equity values (particularly overseas equity), the level of bonds has been eroded until, in 1990, only 8.0 per cent is held in the form of UK fixed-interest. However, the level of index-linked, since their introduction has been held at around 3.0 per cent with overseas bonds held at 2.0 per cent.

Gilt-edged market

An important feature of the gilt market has been that different categories of investors dominate different sectors of the market and consequently, localized

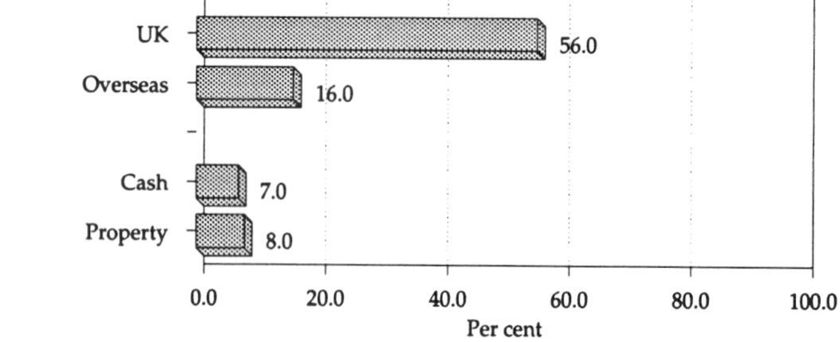

Figure 28.65 Distribution of assets held by UK private sector, 1990

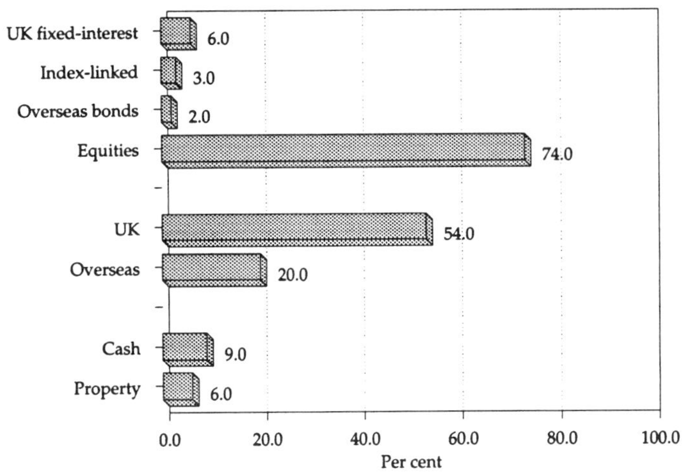

Figure 28.66 Distribution of assets held by UK local authority sector, 1990

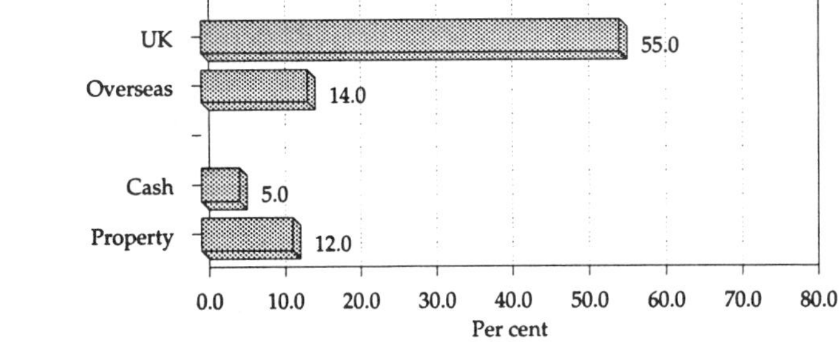

Figure 28.67 Distribution of assets held by UK other public sector, 1990

areas of the market have fluctuated along with the investment requirements of these separate groups. In the past, these groups of investors have limited themselves to a single activity, such as mortgages, or life insurance, or pension funds. However, there is now a trend towards diversification and this signals a change in approach by the fund managers within the market.

Building societies

The prime role of building societies has been to take short-term deposits from private investors and to provide mortgages for domestic housing, against the surety of property. In 1984, major changes in the taxation of these institutions, together with a greater liberalization of their activities, have resulted in them borrowing wholesale funds in the markets, in addition to widening their activities into other various forms of loans, with the result that these institutions are becoming increasingly similar to banks. Most of their bond market assets are in the form of short-dated securities (i.e. up to five years) and it is very rare to find these institutions investing longer.

	1991					1990				
	Total	%	0-5 yrs	5-15 yrs	15+ yrs	Total	%	0-5 yrs	5-15 yrs	15+ yrs
Monetary sector[1]	6.5	5.3	3.4	2.0	1.1	7.9	6.3	3.8	2.8	1.3
Insurance companies	67.2	54.9	n/a	n/a	n/a	34.9	27.9	2.3	18.2	14.4
Pension funds						22.4	17.9	1.1	10.5	10.8
Other ofis[2]	0.8	0.6	0.3	0.3	0.2	0.5	0.4	0.1	0.3	0.1
Overseas	14.4	11.8	6.2	6.0	2.2	15.3	12.2	6.2	8.0	1.0
Other holders[3]	18.1	14.8	n/a	n/a	n/a	27.0	21.6	17.7	6.6	2.7
Official holders	15.4	12.6	5.0	7.2	3.2	17.0	13.6	5.3	6.9	4.8
Total	122.4	100.0	34.9	56.3	31.2	125.0	99.9	36.5	53.4	35.1

Figure 28.68 Distribution of gilt-edged holding (£bn) as at 31 March 1991

[1] *includes banks, building societies and discount houses*

[2] *other financial institutions*

[3] *includes personal sector, industrial and commercial companies, and other public sector*

Insurance companies

UK insurance companies can be divided into two types:

- i) Life insurance companies

These companies take on long-term liabilities in the form of death benefits or 'with profits' endowment policies. Due to the long-term nature of these liabilities, most of their funds are invested in securities with lives over 15 years, but it is the nature of the gilt-edged market for yields to decline after 15 years, so some of these companies invest in maturities slightly shorter than 15 years to take advantage of the higher yields. There is a strong history of these institutions matching their liabilities against their assets, so, in any event, it is unlikely that they will hold short-dated maturities.

- ii) Property/casualty companies

These companies are involved in insuring homes, cars, etc. and also offer short, fixed term policies. Due to the short-term nature of their liabilities, most of their investments can be found in the maturity range of up to ten years.

Pension funds

Pension funds have, for the most part, very long-term liabilities and provide pensions on retirement for fund members. As a consequence, most of their funds are invested in maturities of over 15 years. Again, as with the life offices, some proportion of those funds is invested in the under 15-year area to take advantage of the higher yields. However, due to a belief that equities offer better long-term real rates of return than bonds, many of these institutions have been reducing their exposure to bonds.

Banks

Most bank investments are held in the one- to ten-year area, and it is only in extreme cases that these institutions hold longer bonds. In recent years, the number of banks holding gilt-edged securities as a proportion of their assets has declined greatly due mainly to the application of the BIS rules which has made government securities more attractive than corporate bonds. This relationship is dependent on the rate of return on capital as computed using the BIS rules which apply different weightings to different asset classes.

Individual and private trusts

The UK government once targeted high net-worth individuals and attracted this group of investors to the gilt-edged market by the issue of deep discount, low-coupon bonds. However, with the borrowing surplus and a reduction in the highest marginal rate, this practice has now stopped, leaving only one bond in this range.

Overseas investors

The sterling bond market, being one of the major liquid government bond markets in the world with its greatly expanded eurosterling sector, attracts considerable interest from overseas, as well as domestic, investors.

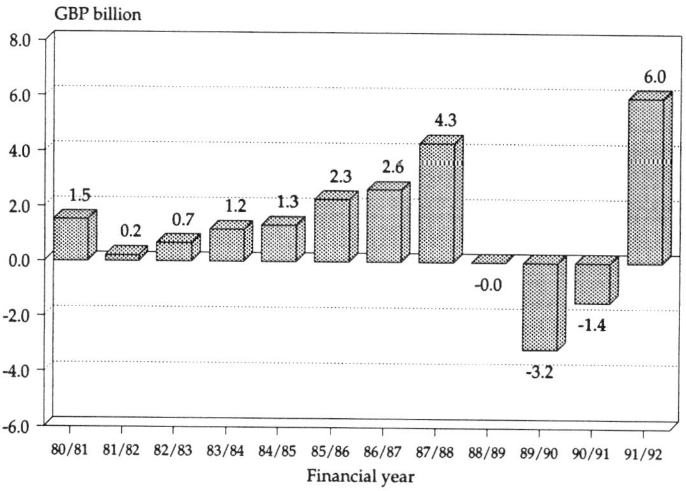

Figure 28.69 Net purchases of gilt-edged bonds by overseas investors

International investors in the sterling bond markets have historically been scarce and short-term in nature; generally being attracted to the market only by the possibility of speculative gains in the bond market and currency considerations. Since 1985, though, international investors have increased their purchases of sterling as may be seen in Figure 28.69 and it is widely expected that every major internationally-diversified portfolio will contain a reasonable proportion of sterling (up to ten per cent of total value). However, following the sterling crisis and the rise in interest rates, the majority of bonds have been sold back.

In the past, when UK interest rates have risen and the pound has been weak, international participation in the market has been very limited. It is hoped that the 1990 entry in to the European exchange rate mechanism (ERM) will have the long-term effects of strengthening the economy and stabilize the pound. Many international investors have been attracted by high nominal and real yields and, being familiar with shorter-term securities, have their major influence in the one- to ten-year area. Some overseas investors have maturities out to the very longest dates, but these are the exception, as the majority are used to the shorter maturity spectrum of their own markets and feel uncomfortable about buying bonds with lives in excess of 15 years.

Corporates

UK and multinational corporations who are cash-rich invest in the gilt-edged maturities of up to five years; very rarely does this type of institution invest longer. Most of this money is held in the up-to-two-year area, as an alternative to other money market instruments.

Eurosterling market

The eurosterling market attracts a wide range of investors. Foreign investors dominate the shorter- and medium-term areas (up to ten years), with the central banks being particularly attracted to sovereign and supranational names. The longer-term area of this market (over 15 years), which has only recently been opened, is the main domain of UK institutions such as life offices and pension funds.

Eurosterling FRN and MBS markets

The major investors in these sectors are banks, building societies and money managers.

Eurosterling convertible bond market

Despite the original intention to widen the international investor base, much of the issuance overseas has gradually seeped back to the UK market, with main investors being UK pension and insurance funds.

Corporate bond market

The major investors in these markets are insurance companies and pension funds. Few foreigners are attracted to these markets because the bonds are in registered form and subject to withholding tax. Building societies are restricted in the type of securities they may hold and, as a consequence, rarely invest in this area.

Domestic convertible bond market

See corporate bond markets.

Bulldog market

The Bulldog profile of investors is very similar to that of gilt-edged bonds. Those Bulldogs that are available in bearer-form and can pay gross (i.e. without withholding tax), have attracted international investment.

Medium-term note market

Most holders are money managers. Due to the flexibility of the instrument, at present, the number of participants is quite low.

Local authority bond market

See corporate bond market.

28.7 *Methods of issuance*

Within the UK bond markets there is a vast array of different methods of issuance and most of these are to be found in the gilt-edged market. They have evolved to allow the Bank of England greater flexibility both in issuing and meeting investor demand.

Gilt-edged market

Offer for sale by tender

The traditional method of issuing gilt-edged securities is the offer for sale. This involves the announcement of an issue, most frequently on a Friday, with the date on which the offer is closed, typically 10 a.m. the following Wednesday, with first dealings the next day. Applications are made direct to the Bank of England using the form published in leading UK newspapers such as the *Financial Times*, *The Times* and the *Daily Telegraph*. In the past, a fixed-issue price was used but, more recently the Bank has solicited tenders with a minimum price which is set in line with market prices at the time the issue is announced (note that tenders for index-linked gilts normally have no minimum price). It should be noted that these offers for sale are not always fully subscribed and when this occurs, any outstandings are then offered to the market through the tap system, which involves the Bank of England taking up those securities not subscribed for and gradually selling them to the market direct. While the Bank is a steady seller, it will alter the price at which it is prepared to sell the bonds, thus giving it both flexibility and a measure of control over long-term interest rates. Frequently, these issues are offered in partly-paid form.

If a further issue of an existing bond is made, it will usually have a separate tranche identifier such as 'A', 'B', 'C', etc. and will trade separately until fungible with the existing issue on the first coupon-date of that tranche. It will carry a different accrued-interest value reflecting the interest since issue and any partly-paid element.

Taplets or tranchettes

The Bank of England also uses, for existing bonds, another method of funding commonly referred to as *taplets* or *tranchettes*. This is a series of relatively small-sized releases of further bonds which are indistinguishable from an existing issue; they are instantly fungible and made directly available to primary market-makers. This method allows the Bank of England to meet demand by issuing small amounts of bonds when market conditions are not sufficiently strong enough to absorb a large new issue. The securities are therefore acquired through the market, in the usual manner.

Auctions

In 1987, as part of the continuing deregulation following Big Bang, the Bank of England introduced auctions. These were experimental in nature, and were used to test the feasibility of putting part of the funding programme more permanently on an auction system. This process has continued although auction dates are irregular and maturities vary, unlike many European markets which use a benchmark maturity. There is no official commitment on the part of primary dealers to underwrite issues and both investors and primary market-makers can bid the Bank of England directly, with bids being made on either a competitive or non-competitive basis. Although there is a maximum size of £100,000 for any non-competitive bid, only one can be submitted for the benefit of an investor. During the period of public sector surplus, the Bank of England held reverse auctions with investors offering stock to the Bank at various prices.

Official operations in the secondary market

The Bank of England will, on occasion, operate in the secondary market, either buying or selling bonds. This is done by the primary market-maker approaching the Bank of England and offering, or bidding, for a particular stock. The Bank of England, whenever possible, responds to bids for tap and tranchette issues, but other securities may be bought or sold dependent upon the Bank of England's overall position (although this activity is relatively modest, normally amounting to no more than £50m in any one gilt bond).

Rules for lead-management of sterling issues

The rules governing who may lead issues in the UK are laid out in the following Bank of England statement:

"In order to promote the orderly development of the sterling capital markets, the Bank will continue to require all capital market issues denominated in sterling (whether in the form of debt or equity, including securities carrying a sterling option or a sterling-related element, except issues of commercial paper or medium-term notes) to be managed in the UK, under the lead-management of a UK-based firm which has satisfied the Bank that it has the capacity in the UK to act as an issuing house. Foreign-owned firms with such a capacity will be eligible to lead manage sterling issues only if in the Bank's view there are reciprocal opportunities in their domestic capital markets for UK owned firms to lead manage issues. Firms which do not meet the guidelines for lead-management are able to participate in sterling issues in a co-management position (but not as a co-lead-manager).

'The International Stock Exchange and the British Merchant Banking and Securities Houses Association have established procedures, operated by the Bank of England, for an exchange of information about the timing proposed for new sterling capital market issues of £20 million or more. Advisers to a new issue should give prior notification to the Bank of the proposed timing and main features of the issue. The Bank will indicate whether there is likely to be a clash with a competing issue. The advisers will then be able to consider whether to proceed on the specified date, or to change the timing, notifying the Bank accordingly. If a clash is likely to remain, the Bank will inform the sponsors of the competing issues. The Bank also requires to be notified for the record of main details of any new capital market issue in sterling for an amount of £20 million or more at the time it is made. These notifications should be made to the Bank of England's Gilt-Edged and Money Markets Division."

Eurosterling markets (including euro-convertibles, FRNs & MBSs)

Bought deal

Eurosterling issues are brought to the market using traditional eurobond methods. Most commonly, the issue is underwritten by the lead-manager as a bought deal, with the terms both fixed and agreed. The lead-manager then selects a number of co-managers who, together with the lead-manager, underwrite and agree to distribute the issue. The proportions that are allocated to the co-managers are determined by the lead-manager and vary according to the lead-manager's placing power. The managers normally offer these securities to their investor base, but investors can approach the managers directly. The amount available depends on the success of the issue and the relationship with the manager.

Fixed price re-offer

Recently, the leading houses have introduced the fixed-price re-offer system. This involves the managers of the deal agreeing not to offer bonds below an agreed price until the syndicate is broken and was instituted in order to stop the practice by which some managers in a deal, with no placing capacity, would dump the bonds in the market-place, thereby requiring the lead-manager to absorb them. The period of syndication can be as little as a day or up to three weeks dependent upon the success in placing the deal. Often the syndicate would be very small with, sometimes, as few as four managers.

Lead-managers

The following security houses are the main lead-managers of eurosterling markets:

- Barclays de Zoete Wedd
- Baring Brothers

- County NatWest Securities
- Credit Suisse First Boston
- Deutsche Bank
- Goldman Sachs
- Hambros
- JP Morgan Securities
- Kleinwort Benson
- Lehman Brothers International
- Merrill Lynch International
- Morgan Grenfell (now part of Deutsche Bank)
- Paribas
- SG Warburgs
- Salomon Brothers International
- Samuel Montagu
- UBS Phillips & Drew

Corporate and domestic convertible bond markets

Historically, two methods of issuance have been employed in the domestic bond markets - offer for sale and private placement.

Offer for sale

Securities are offered for sale, in a manner similar to that found in the gilt-edged market. However, the exact terms of the issue are usually determined on the Wednesday evening prior to first trading and are derived by the calculation of a spread over a designated gilt-edged security, for example 100 basis points over Treasury 9 per cent 2008 at 3.30 p.m. on Wednesday.

Private placement

The most common form of issuance is for the lead-manager to approach investors with a potential issue, on the Monday through to the Wednesday, to find firm underwriting. As before, the terms of issuance are set at the close of business on the Wednesday. In the past, issuers have been offered underwriting fees, with the underwriting group often being much larger than those institutions subscribing. For example, a particular institution may subscribe to £10m securities but only be offered underwriting for £5m. Issues are usually placed, predominantly with UK institutions, by this means. However, there is a requirement that some proportion (up to ten per cent) is placed with market-makers to allow them to meet the demands of other investors.

When there were advantages of liquidity and lower commission rates for sovereign and supranational issues prior to Big Bang,these were made available via offerings. However, all other issuers (for example, corporate borrowers), issued using the placement method. With the removal of fixed commissions, there is no reason for issues (both domestic and Bulldog) to be brought to the market in any other form. Indeed, those few issues that have been brought since Big Bang have all employed this method.

In the case of offers for sale, investors can apply direct to the issuing house using the form available in the UK newspapers. Otherwise an investor can, as in the case of private placements, approach the lead-manager directly.

Lead-managers

The following security houses are the main lead-managers of domestic issues:

- Barclays de Zoete Wedd
- Baring Brothers
- County NatWest Securities
- Goldman Sachs
- Hambros
- Kleinwort Benson
- SG Warburgs
- UBS Phillips & Drew

Bulldog market

See above for domestic bonds.

Medium-term note market

MTNs are on constant offer by the dealers of the issue. When a borrower wishes to use the facilities of the programme, the dealers approach lenders to try to place the securities with them. However, often, an investor will approach the dealer and ask which issuers would be interested in issuing a security with the features that the lender requires. The dealer then approaches the appropriate borrowers on his programme list to see who would like to issue, along with their terms. Should both parties agree the security is then issued, subject to total limit. The size of issue and all other features of the security can be varied to meet the requirements of the parties.

Each programme will have its own dealer list which can vary from just one dealer to over eight. Obviously, the more dealers there are, the more likely the programme will be activated (and the higher the liquidity level).

Dealers in medium-term note programmes

Regular dealers for sterling issues:

- Bankers Trust International
- Barclays de Zoete Wedd Limited
- Baring Brothers & Co Limited
- BNP Capital Markets Limited
- Citicorp Investment Bank
- Credit Suisse First Boston
- Daiwa Europe Limited
- Deutsche Bank Capital Markets Limited
- Goldman Sachs International Limited
- J.P. Morgan Securities Limited
- Kidder Peabody International
- Lehman Brothers International
- Merrill Lynch International Limited
- Midland Montagu Commercial Paper
- Morgan Grenfell & Co Limited
- Morgan Stanley International Limited
- NatWest Capital Markets Limited
- Nomura International
- SG Warburg Securities
- Salomon Brothers International
- Swiss Bank Corporation
- UBS Phillips & Drew Securities Limited
- Yamaichi International (Europe) Limited

It should be noted that many of the above are only dealers for one sterling MTN programme.

Local authority Market

Local authority issues used the 'offer for sale' method, but there has been no issuance since 1984. However, should issuance begin one would expect it to follow the method used for domestic corporate bonds.

28.8 *New issue volumes*

Gilt-edged market

The UK government was able to achieve a remarkable feat in buying back and retiring debt in the period 1988/89 to 1990/91. However, such has been the depth of the recession that, in 1991/92, this trend has been completely reversed, with the government needing to raising over £15.0bn. The government issues gilt-edged securities both to take advantage of funding levels that it finds attractive and as part of its overall funding strategy.

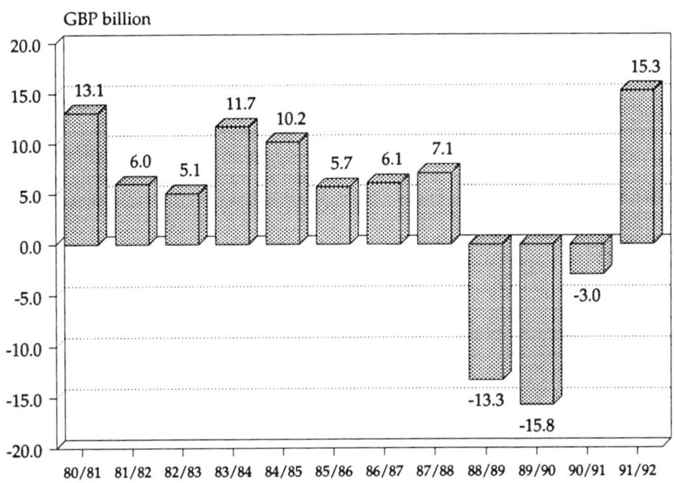

Figure 28.70 New issuance volumes in the gilt-edged bond market

Eurosterling market

Eurosterling market new issue volumes have been growing rapidly as a result of international demand for sterling (see Figure 28.71). However, the growth has been erratic, with large issuance in the early part of each year recently, when demand for sterling assets has been particularly high prior to the spring budgets.

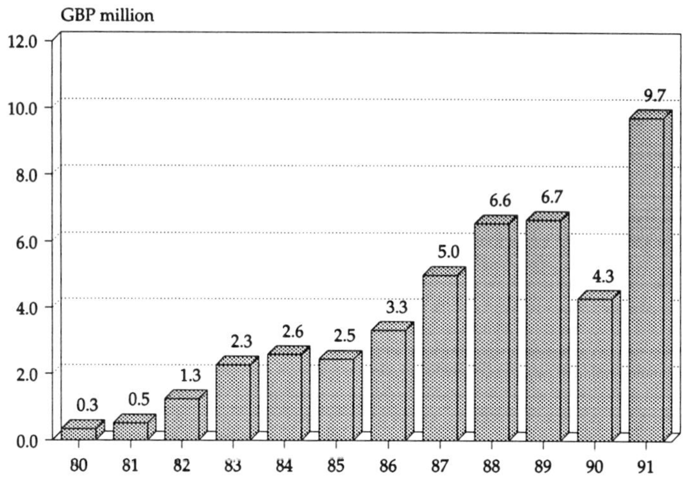

Figure 28.71 **New issuance volumes in the eurosterling bond market**

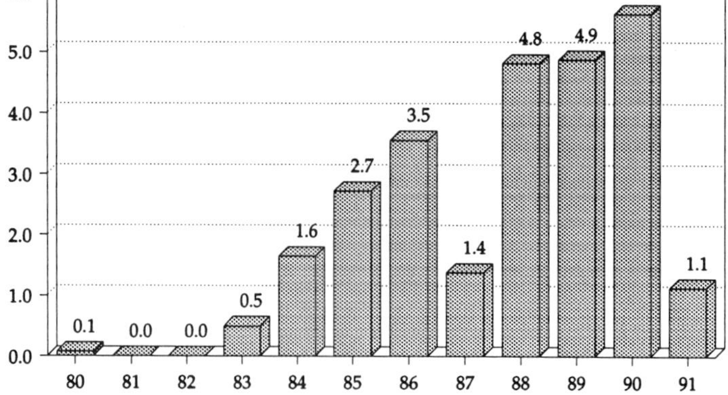

Figure 28.72 **New issuance volumes in the eurosterling FRN market**

Since many of the borrowers are UK companies, they have been able to access continuously.

Eurosterling FRN market

While most FRN markets under went a period of contraction following the Perpetual Crisis and LDC debt crisis that has plagued the bank sector, the UK sterling FRN market has continued to expand (see Figure 28.72). Since much of the issuance is for UK building societies, the growth reflected both the demand for home loans and the societies' expansion into consumer lending.

Eurosterling MBS market

After its opening in 1987, the UK home-financing market saw a major swing towards the new lenders such as TMC, NHL and HMC (the highest quality servicer in the market), who were very competitive. However, as the economy came under pressure and house prices, particularly in the London and South-east area fell over 20.0 per cent, demand for new loans fell. Alongside growing pressure to meet home loan payments, many existing borrowers decided to stay with their traditional lenders and, as a result, securitization fell (see Figure - 28.73).

Eurosterling convertible bond market

After the Crash, new issue volumes fell (see Figure 28.74). However, the 1987 level was exceeded in 1990 and 1991. The 1990 is made up a number of large issues being £200m Sainsbury 8.5 per cent 2005, £155m Boots 6.0 per cent 2005, £100m Independent Newspapers 6.0 per cent 2006, £100m Hepworth 11.25 per cent 2005 and £200m Tesco 9.0 per cent 2005. The 1991 figures similarly reflect a few very large issues being the £107.5m Tarmac 9.5 per cent 2006, £437.8m Elf/Enterprise issue and £500m Hanson.

Corporate bond market

As illustrated in Figures 28.75 & 28.76, issuance in the domestic corporate markets has been very low and sporadic, often only one or two issues per month. Some of these issues in the debenture market have been small issues for water authorities who regularly tap the UK market. The large issuance in May 1987 actually consisted of three issues for Northern Housing (two of which were zero-coupon bonds), all with lives in excess of 30 years, the actual cash raised being relatively small. Since then, there has been very little issuance. Issuance of unsecured loans has also been greatly reduced. With only one issue in June 1990 of £100m Anglian Water 5.125 per cent 2008, one of £27.0 4.0 per cent Delayed

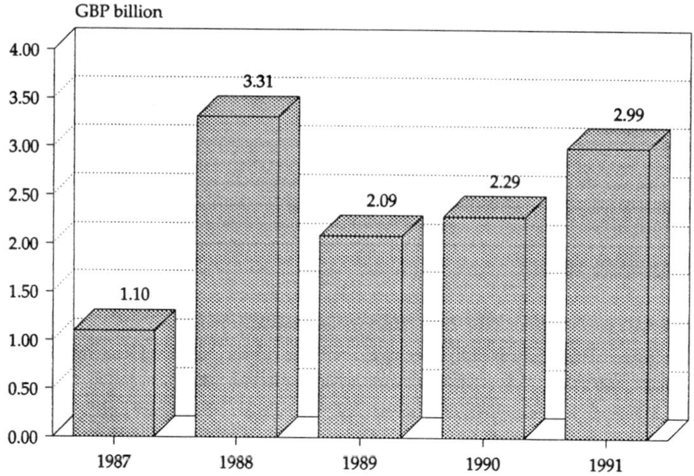

Figure 28.73 New issuance volumes in the eurosterling MBS market

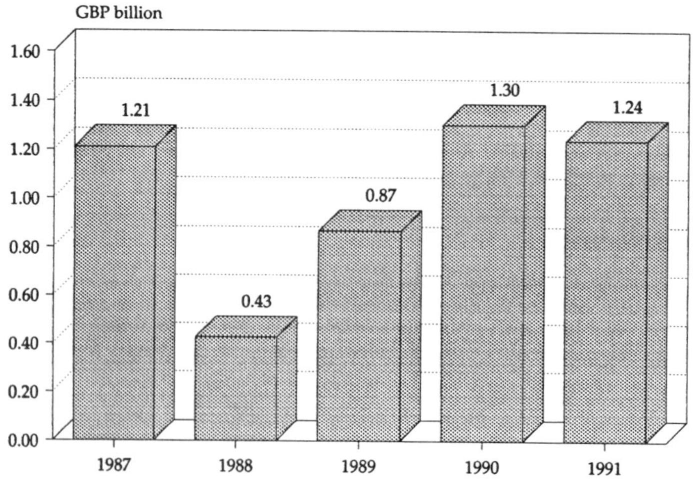

Figure 28.74 New issuance volumes in the euro-convertible bond market

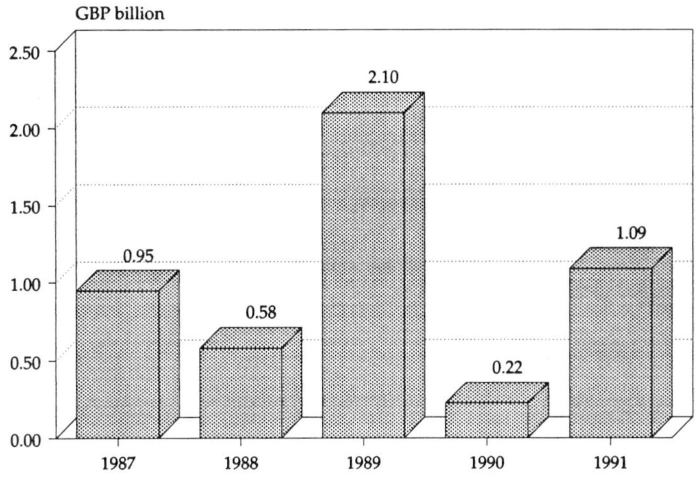

Figure 28.75 New issuance volumes in the debenture market

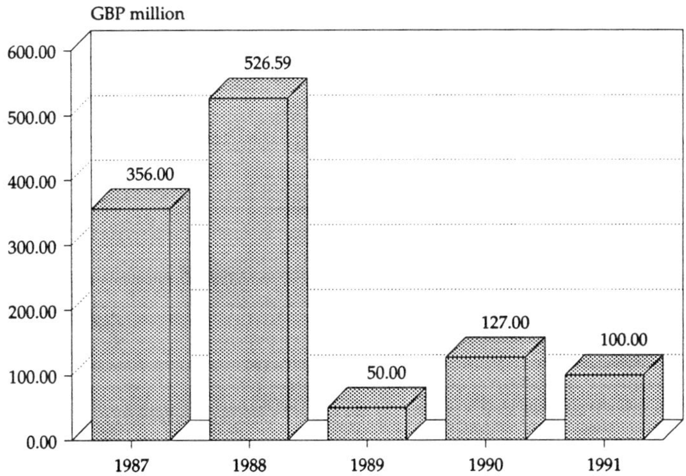

Figure 28.76 New issuance volumes in the unsecured loans market

Interest 1996 for International Business Communications in December 1990 and finally a £100m Enterprise Oil 11.625 per cent issue in April 1991. Issuance of debentures was sporadic in 1990 but picked up significantly in 1991 to over £1.0bn. The major issues were £150m for British Steel (11.5 per cent 2016 in July), £100m Great Portland Estates (10.75 per cent 2021 in October), £100m Housing Finance (11.5 per cent 2016 in November) and £200m Land Securities (10.0 per cent 2027 in September) all of whom achieved significantly finer terms in the domestic market than would have been available in the eurosterling market.

In June 1987 there was an increase when UK corporates were able to issue discount securities which were specially structured to take advantage of UK tax regulations and thus were attractive to UK investors. This opportunity is, however, no longer available.

Domestic convertible bond market

In contrast to the eurosterling convertible issues, 1988 and 1989 were the highest level, with sharp falls in 1990 and 1991 (see Figure 28.77). The 1990 figures reflect three major issues, £200.8m Reckitt & Colman 2005, £177.1m BICC 2020 and £228.3m Rank 2007. In 1991, there were only 5 issues with two very large issues

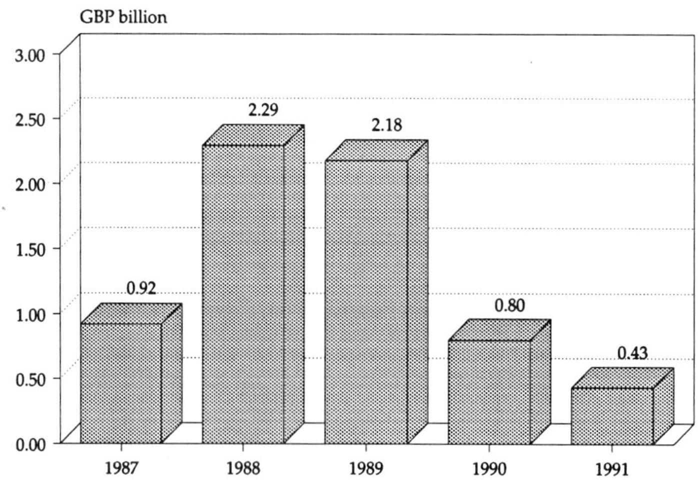

Figure 28.77 New issuance volumes in the domestic convertible market

being the £188.9m Queens Moat 7.5 per cent 2011 and £141m Slough Estates 8.25 per cent 2011.

Bulldog market

Bulldog issuance has declined quite sharply (see Figure 28.78). Indeed, were it not for the EIB continuing to issue further tranches of existing issues there would hardly be any issuance at all. Note that the £50.0m Gibraltar issue, in April 1991, could only have been achieved in this market.

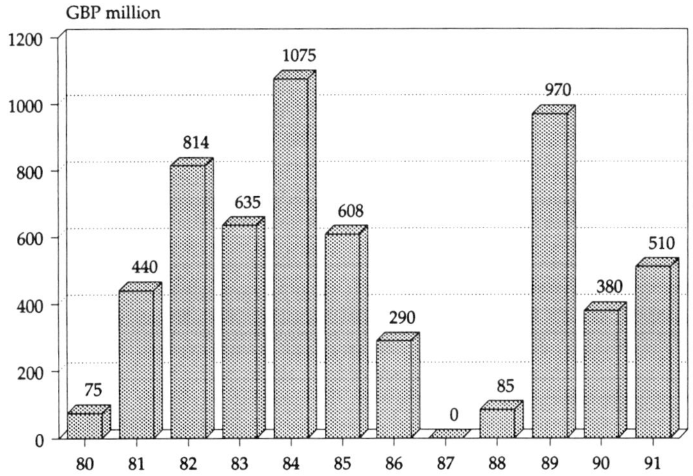

Figure 28.78 New issuance volumes in the Bulldog market

Medium-term note market

The market was slow to start with the £40.0m Ford 1992 issue being the only large issue until December 1990, when there was a flurry of activity (see Figure 28.79). January 1991 saw several large issues: £80.0m Abbey National 1994, £30.0m Council of Europe 1993 and £30.0m SBC Finance 1993. Thereafter, volumes were low until May 1991, when seven borrowers raised finance with three programmes, issuing more than twice, and the Compagnie Bancaire programme,

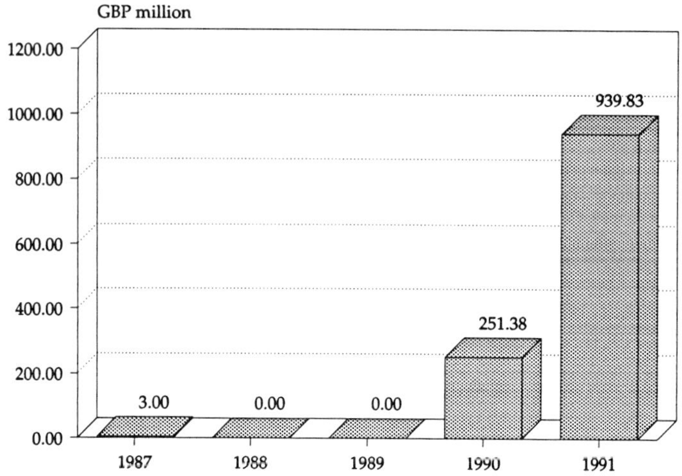

Figure 28.79 New issuance volumes in the medium-term note market

four times. Deutsche Bank raised £50m in one issue in June, as did SBC Finance. There was a £30m issue for CCF in November.

Municipal bonds

Each week, local authorities issue approximately £2-£3m local authority bonds (LABs). These all carry the same coupon and are issued in the names of various local authorities. There has been no major issuance of municipal bonds since 1986 because the UK local authorities and municipalities have been able to access funds from the PWLB (see Section 28.1).

28.9 Methods of trading

Prior to October 1986, securities other than eurosterling bonds were traded on the stock market using a single-capacity method with brokers, who acted as agents for investors, approaching jobbers who were wholesale market-makers. As a consequence of Big Bang, this single-capacity role was replaced with the dual-capacity primary market-maker. Initially there were 27 of these GEMMS, but this figure has since decreased to 17 (see Section 28.1).

Gilt-edged market

Primary market-makers

The 17 gilt-edged market-makers (GEMMs) now include a large number of international investment banks. This has increased price competitiveness, as well as the total overall capitalization of market-makers. As a result, bid/offer spreads have narrowed dramatically from between 1/2 per cent to 2 -4/32nds. The primary market-makers, using their own sales teams, interact with investors and trade with each other, mainly through the use of inter-dealer brokers (see below). The Bank of England supervises the activities of the primary dealers and offers certain facilities to those who demonstrate capacity and are prepared to accept the Bank of England's prudential oversight. These facilities are:

- direct dealing with the Bank of England in gilts
- the facility to borrow bonds
- favourable tax treatment
- borrowing facilities at the Bank of England
- access to inter-dealer brokers

In return, the market-makers agree to provide continuous effective two-way prices, on demand, under any trading conditions of an appropriate size for those issues which have been agreed in advance with the Bank, thereby providing continuous liquidity with the investing public. The Bank of England also applies limits on both the total and net positions of the market-makers, relative to their capital base.

Current GEMMs are:

- Aitken Campbell & Co.
- Barclays de Zoete Wedd
- Baring Brothers
- Bankers Trust

- County NatWest
- Credit Suisse First Boston
- Daiwa Securities
- Deutsche Bank International
- Gerrard & National
- Goldman Sachs
- Greenwell Montagu
- Kleinwort Benson
- JP Morgan
- James Capel
- Nikko Securities
- Nomura International
- UBS Phillips & Drew
- Salomon Brothers International
- Shearson Lehman
- SG Warburgs

Agency brokers

At the time of Big Bang, a number of former stockbrokers decided that they did not wish to become primary dealers and retained their roles as brokers, i.e. acting as intermediaries on behalf of the investor. These brokers are paid a small commission for their services.

	Short-dated			**Medium/long-dated**		
	Value	Bargains	Av. size (GBP mill.)	Value	Bargains	Av. size (GBP mill.)
UK Individuals	8.3	80.0	42.1	3.8	60.2	49.0
Fund Managers	14.8	4.4	1377.6	17.0	12.8	1043.3
Major Institutions	24.3	3.8	2558.7	42.8	13.1	2560.2
Overseas Sector	26.4	4.9	2213.0	18.4	6.2	2337.2
Total	100.0	100.0	405.2	100.0	100.0	782.9

Figure 28.80 Gilt-edged turnover - percentage of totals (1990)

Year	Shorts	Mediums	Longs	Index-linked	Av. per day
1970	12.9	-	14.4	-	0.1
1980	75.2	-	76.5	-	0.6
1986	186.4	-	238.0	-	1.7
1988	525.9	276.0	290.2	37.0	4.5
1990	367.5	335.0	242.0	28.6	3.8
1991	411.8	434.7	237.6	28.6	4.4

Figure 28.81 Gilt-edged turnover -totals (£bn)
Note:
i) Prior to 1987, gilt turnover was categorized in two groups only: 5 years and under, and over 5 years.
ii) Figures after 1987 include customer and intra-market business following the end of single capacity

Eurosterling markets including FRNs & MBSs

Although many eurosterling issues are listed on London's International Stock Exchange, the vast majority of trading occurs in over-the-counter form. In this way, market-makers deal directly with each other although, for new issues and occasionally for liquid issues, inter-dealer brokers may be used.

Major UK and international houses are all active in the eurosterling bond markets, but fewer are active in the FRN and MBS markets.

Major market-makers in eurosterling FRN & MBS markets:

- Barclays de Zoete Wedd
- Baring Brothers
- Credit Suisse First Boston
- Goldman Sachs
- JP Morgan
- Kidder Peabody International
- Salomon Brothers International
- UBS Phillips & Drew
- SG Warburg

Corporate bond market

Prior to Big Bang, domestic bonds were traded on the stock exchange in a manner similar to gilt-edged securities, i.e. by the means of brokers and jobbers. Since October 1987, a number of primary dealers have expanded their market trading capacity to include domestic bonds. There are no inter-dealer brokers in this sector of the market, and consequently the traders deal directly with each other.

Main houses:

- Barclays de Zoete & Bevan
- Baring Brothers
- UBS Phillips & Drew
- SG Warburg

Domestic convertible bond market

These are traded by the specialized convertible desks which can be found in many security houses. Since these securities are more closely related to equity during their conversion period, they usually are traded by the large UK equity houses but, once the conversion period has passed unexercised, they tend to become illiquid and are traded only by the major UK bond houses as discount bonds.

Bulldog market

See 'Corporate bond market'

Medium-term note market

These securities are traded on a yield basis. Since a variety of maturities and both coupon and discount instruments are available, it is advisable to agree the yield method being used.

Note: These securities are effectively highly illiquid private placements and therefore rarely traded. A seller would have some difficulty in getting competitive market prices. Buyers would actually just access the relevant programme as a new issue.

Local authority bonds

These bonds are effectively illiquid. The larger issues with coupons in excess of 10.00 per cent have been bought back and retired. Should any remaining stock in these issues become available, they would be sold back to the relevant local authority. Only small amounts of these bonds are held, however - usually by individuals.

28.10 *Market practices*

Coupon payment

All gilt-edged markets pay semi-annually in arrears, the one exception being Consuls 2.50 per cent, which pays quarterly. Most eurosterling fixed-rate bonds are paid annually. Sterling FRNs generally pay quarterly. Most domestic bonds pay semi-annually.

First coupon

It is common to find, in both gilt-edged securities and domestic bonds, that the first coupon is not one full coupon period after the date of issuance. As a consequence, this payment is usually pro-rated in relation to the number of days between the date of issue and date of payment. Note that this may be greater, or less, than 182 days. The coupon payment may be adjusted further to reflect whether the bond was partly-paid.

Partly-paid

It is a common for both gilt-edged securities and domestic bonds to be issued in the partly-paid form, i.e. an initial down-payment together with up to three further future part-payments or calls.

Ex-dividend

As a general rule, UK gilt-edged securities go ex-dividend (or ex-interest), 37 days before the next interest payment, after which date they trade with the negative accrued-interest until the coupon-date. If this date falls on a non-business day, such as a weekend, the first day that the security is deemed ex-dividend is the next business date. For domestic bonds and Bulldogs, a similar method of determining the first ex-dividend date is used, but the period is usually one calendar month, but this varies from bond to bond and an exact formula cannot be provided. It is essential that all investors consult the International Stock Exchange's Daily Official List for exact data on bonds that are trading ex-dividend. Eurosterling issues do not trade ex-dividend.

Special ex-dividend

Before reaching the ex-dividend period there is a period of three weeks when those UK domestic securities with lives of over five years, can be traded either cum (i.e. with) dividend or special ex-dividend, the next coupon payment. The exception to this is War Loan 3.5 per cent 1952 or After, which does not trade special issue.

Redemption

All domestic issues redeem at par except those eurosterling bonds with calls which are redeemed at a premium determined by the terms of the individual issue.

Puts

No gilt-edged securities give the holder the right to put bonds; neither do any domestic bonds. However, two Bulldog issues: Mexico 16.5 per cent 1988/2008 and Trinidad & Tobago 12.25 per cent 2009, give the holder this option. A few eurosterling issues have a put option.

Sinking funds

Two gilt-edged securities have sinking funds, the most powerful being Conversion 3.5 per cent which requires that one per cent of the value outstanding be applied each half-year while the price is below 90. Most of the domestic bonds issued in the 1950s and 1960s have sinking funds, varying in intensity. Some Bulldogs and eurosterling issues can be found with purchase funds, although these usually have little effect.

Denomination

All domestic issues can be bought and sold in units of one pence. Eurosterling issues can be found in denominations of £1000, £5000, £10,000 and so on, varying from issue to issue.

Form

All gilt-edged securities are available in registered form, the register being held by the Bank of England. Some are available in bearer form, the most important of which is War Loan 3.50 per cent 1952 or After. Those bonds which are called Treasury may be converted to bearer form. However, it should be noted that a very small proportion of the total gilt market is in the form of bearer bonds (approximately £72 million). All eurosterling is in bearer form, although a very few issues can be held in registered form. All domestic bonds are in registered form with the registrar usually being a bank. All Bulldogs are available in registered form, although some may be available in bearer form (this varies from issue to issue). Again, the registrar is usually a bank.

Dealing quotations

Most gilt-edged securities are quoted with bid/offer spreads between 2/32nds and 4/32nds. The spread is narrower in the shorter maturity range than that at the longer end. Eurosterling fixed-rate bonds are quoted with between 8 and 16/32nds spreads. Naturally, spreads will narrow during periods of activity in highly liquid securities. However, if the market experiences extreme instability, or if a particular issue is considered highly illiquid, spreads will widen. Most eurosterling FRNs are quoted on 5-10 basis point spreads, while domestic bonds (and Bulldog issues) are quoted between 12 and 20/32nds, dependent on maturity and liquidity. Since MTN issues are highly illiquid, prices will be wide and dependent upon market conditions, structure and borrower.

The following quotes are good in the specified markets:

- Gilts: £5 million
- Eurosterling: £500,000
- Bulldog: £250,000
- Domestic: £100,000

Withholding tax

All gilt-edged securities are paid subject to withholding tax at the basic rate, currently 25 per cent, with the exception of War Loan 3 1/2 1952 or After, which pays gross in all cases. International investors may have their interest payments paid without deduction of withholding tax (see Section 28.13). Eurosterling issues are not subject to withholding tax unless a UK paying agent is used, whilst all domestic bonds are subject to withholding tax. All supranational Bulldog issues, whether registered or in bearer form, are paid gross. All other Bulldog issues in registered form are subject to withholding tax, except to overseas investors (see Section 28.13). Bulldog issues in bearer form, but using a UK paying agent, are subject to withholding tax; if an overseas paying agent is used, however, payments will be gross.

Commissions

There are no commissions charged in the UK by primary dealers. However, should an agent be employed, then a small charge may be levied (and should be agreed beforehand). The level will depend upon the liquidity of the asset.

28.11 Settlement

Gilt-edged market

Gilt-edged securities are normally settled on the next business day after the date of trade. However, it is possible to sell a security before 11 a.m. for cash settlement on the same day. By special arrangement, it is also possible to trade in securities for future settlement, but this period cannot be greater than three weeks.

Eurosterling market

These securities use seven-day settlement and are usually held in a clearing system such as Euroclear or Cedel.

Corporate bond market

These securities once settled using the equity market account date method, but now they use seven-day settlement.

It is possible in all cases to arrange forward settlement with the agreement of the market-maker, but this is usually restricted to no more than three weeks and naturally involves appropriate changes to reflect both price and accrued interest.

Bulldog market

Those bonds (usually sovereign and supranational issues) which were dealt in the gilt-edged market, settled the next business day. For all other Bulldogs, settlement was two days after the date of trade. However, nowadays they use seven-day settlement.

Medium-term notes

See 'Eurosterling market'.

Municipal bonds

See 'Corporate bonds'.

28.12 *Yield calculation*

Gilt-edged market

Conventional gilts

The redemption yield is expressed as a rate of return per chosen time period. The convention in the gilt market is to use a time period equal to the standard coupon period - half a year - but to quote the yield in annual terms.

In order to clarify the definition of what constitutes a yield, the terminology 'effective' is used, which applies to the period to which the interest rate relates. For example, if a sum of £100 is invested for one year at an interest rate of 9 per cent effective annually, it will amount to a sum of £109 a year later. If a sum of £100 is invested for one year at an interest rate of 4.5 per cent effective semi-annually, it will amount to a sum of £104.5 half a year later, and to a sum of £104.5 × 1.045 = £109.2025 a year later.

The convention in the gilt market is to quote a redemption yield as twice the effective semi-annual interest rate. Appropriate adjustments should be made to this yield before it can be compared with yields on the securities, which are often based on an annual yield.

In order to calculate the redemption yield, all cashflows are discounted at a single interest rate. The interest rate at which the sum of all the discounted cashflows equals the price, is the redemption yield.

There are a number of variations in the details of the calculation of redemption yield:

■ Standard approach
The standard approach to the method of calculating gross redemption yield is to assume that, after the first coupon-date, the following coupons are paid at equal six-monthly periods.

For the investor free of tax on both income and capital gains, the effective semi-annual interest rate is found by solving the following equation:

$$P{+}a = v^{d/182.5}\,[C_1 + \frac{C}{2} \times (v + v^2 \ldots\ldots v^n) + R \times v^n\,]$$

or,

$$P{+}a = v^{d/182.5}\,[\,C_1 + \frac{C}{2} \times \frac{v\,(1 - v^n)}{(1 - v)} + R\,v^n\,]$$

where:

i effective semi-annual interest rate, derived from v by the formula:

$$i = \frac{1}{v} - 1.$$

giving the redemption yield of 200 × i per cent, and where:

P clean price
a accrued interest at purchase
d days to next coupon-date
C_1 first coupon payment
C annual rate of coupon
$n + 1$ number of coupons
R redemption proceeds (normally 100)

■ Actual days denominator
The number of days between coupon dates can vary between 181 and 184, depending on whether the coupon period straddles February. One approach is to base the calculation on this basis, rather than on exact half periods.

■ Exact payment periods
The calculation can be based on the actual dates of payment of each cashflow. This method makes allowance for both uneven dividend periods and delays in payment due to Bank Holidays. This has the advantage of most accurately determining the internal rate of return from the available information.

The redemption yield is then calculated by solving the following equation for v:

$$P + a = v^{2t_1} C_1 + \frac{C}{2} (v^{2t_2} + v^{2t_3} + v^{2t_4} \ldots\ldots . v^{2t_n}) + R\, v^{2t_n}$$

where:

i = effective semi-annual interest rate, derived from v by the formula:

$$i = \frac{1}{v} - 1$$

giving the redemption yield of 200 × i per cent, and where:

P	clean price
a	accrued interest at purchase
t_k	time in years to kth coupon-date
C_1	first coupon payment
C	annual rate of coupon
$n+1$	number of coupons
R	redemption proceeds (normally 100)

The range of methods currently in use sometimes gives rise to discrepancies in the quoted yield, by as much as around 10 basis points on bonds with up to two years to maturity, declining to around 2 basis points for bonds with over five years to maturity. Although this may seem insignificant to many investors, such discrepancies can lead to significant opportunities.

Index-linked

There are two types of redemption yield used to evaluate index-linked bonds: money yield, which is sometimes called nominal yield, and real yield.

The money yield is calculated by projecting inflation, at some assumed rate, from the most recently published RPI figure in order to estimate, in money terms, all future interest and capital payments. The money yield is calculated from these interest and capital payments in a manner similar to the redemption yield on a fixed-income gilt.

The real yield is calculated by converting the money interest and capital payments into real payments in terms of the change in the RPI between settlement day and the day in which the payments are received. In other words, the interest and capital payments are divided by an inflation adjustment factor, which represents the change in RPI level between the two days:

$$\frac{\text{RPI } \textit{on paymentdate}}{\text{RPI } \textit{on settlement date}}$$

The real yield is then calculated form these inflation adjusted payments in a manner similar to the calculation of redemption yield on fixed income bonds.

■ Money yield

In order to calculate the money yield, all future cashflows must be estimated. These cashflows are derived from both published and forecast values of the RPI. The standard approach used to establish forecast values of the RPI is to project inflation at a constant rate, from the most recently published RPI, to the date to which the forecast value relates.

The forecast value is therefore calculated as:

$$RPI_k = RPI_m \times (1 + I_k)^{T_k}$$

where:

RPI_k RPI for month k

RPI_m RPI for month m, the most recent month for which the RPI has been published

T_k the time period, in years, between the days in months k and m to which the RPI values relate

I_k the estimated rate of inflation between the days in months k and m to which the RPI value relates. This is usually assumed to be constant over all future periods

For example, the RPI for March 1987 was calculated using prices collected on 20 March 1987 and was 100.6. The RPI for June 1988, based on prices collected on 14 June, can be derived from this value assuming an inflation rate of 4.50 per cent per annum, as follows:

$$100.6 \times \left\{1 + (\frac{4.5}{100})\right\}^{\frac{464}{365}} = 106.389$$

The future cashflows are then given in money terms by their known value or, if unknown, as in the case of payments fixed by an RPI value not yet published, by:

$$D_k = \frac{C}{2} \times \frac{RPI_{k-8}}{RPI_b},\ R = 100 \times \frac{RPI_{n-8}}{RPI_b}$$

where:

D_k the coupon payment in month k

C the nominal annual coupon

R the redemption proceeds

RPI_b the base RPI

The money yield is then calculated by solving the following equation for v:

$$P + a = D_1 v^{2t_1} + D_2 v^{2t_2} + D_3 v^{2t_3} + \ldots\ldots + D_n v^{2t_n} + R v^{2t_n}$$

where:

P the clean price
a the accrued interest
t_k the time in years to the kth coupon payment

The money yield is then derived from v as follows:

$$\text{Money yield} = \left\{\frac{1}{v} - 1\right\} \times 200 \text{ per cent}$$

The equation above is subject to the same qualifications as the equation for the redemption yield for fixed income bonds.

Real yield equation

In the case where inflation is projected at a constant assumed rate, the real yield is related to the money yield simply by deflating the money yield by the rate of inflation as described by the following equation:

$$\left\{1 + \frac{\text{money yield}}{200}\right\} = \left\{1 + \frac{\text{inflation rate}}{100}\right\} \times \left\{1 + \frac{\text{real yield}}{200}\right\}$$

For example, if a bond has a redemption money yield of 10 per cent then, by rearranging the formula, the real yield can be derived using the same inflation assumption as used to calculate the money yield.

If inflation is assumed to be 5 per cent, the real yield can, therefore, be calculated as follows:

$$\left\{\frac{(1 + \frac{10}{200})}{(1 + \frac{5}{100})^{\frac{1}{2}}} - 1\right\} \times 200 = 4.94 \text{ per cent}$$

Alternatively, the real yield can be calculated directly. The equation of real yield is essentially the same equation as above, but with the money payments converted into real payments. The equation below illustrates this alternative approach, which is to divide each money amount by the retail price index on the date the amount is paid or received. In this way, each payment is converted into equivalent real terms.

The equation for the real yield then becomes:

$$\frac{P_c + a}{RPI_0} = \frac{D_1 w^{2t_1}}{RPI_1} + \frac{D_2 w^{2t_2}}{RPI_2} + \frac{D_3 w^{2t_3}}{RPI_3} + \ldots\ldots + \frac{D_n w^{2t_n} + R w^{2t_n}}{RPI_n}$$

where:

RPI_t	the RPI on the date of the cashflow
P_c	the clean price
a	the accrued interest
D_k	the kth coupon payment
t_k	the time in years to the kth coupon payment
R	the redemption proceeds.

The real yield is calculated by solving the equation above, for w. Then the real yield is derived from w as follows:

$$\text{Real yield} = \left\{\frac{1}{w} - 1\right\} \times 200 \text{ per cent}$$

Eurosterling market

Eurosterling fixed-rate bonds

It is the market convention to use the ISMA formula in determining yields. Note that this is not directly comparable to other yields used in the sterling market.

For a fully paid fixed-coupon bond, paying h times per year with an assumed single redemption date, the redemption yield formula may be written as:

$$P + A = v^{f_1} \times \left\{k + \sum_{i=1}^{n-1} \frac{g}{h} \times v^i\right\} + \left\{RV + \frac{g}{h} \times f_2\right\} \times v^{n + f_1 + F_2 - 1}$$

where:

P	clean price
A	accrued interest
g	annual coupon rate per cent
k	first/next coupon payment per cent
h	number of coupon payments per year. Therefore, each normal coupon payment is g/h.
n	number of coupon payments to assumed redemption, excluding any fractional payment on redemption
f_1	fraction of a period from value-date to the first/next interest payment. A period is defined as the normal time between two consecutive coupon payments

f_2 fraction of a period from the last normal coupon-date to the assumed redemption
RV redemption value
v discounting factor, i.e. where:

$$v = \frac{1}{\left\{1 + \frac{y}{h}\right\}}$$

y required redemption yield compounded h times per annum ($y = 0.08$ for a yield of 8.00 per cent).

It should be noted that solving this equation produces an annualized redemption yield for bonds with annual coupon payments, a semi-annualized yield for bonds with semi-annual coupon payments, and so on. The above formula calculates the same redemption yield for a semi-annual bond as for an annual bond with half the annual coupon rate, and twice the life. However, the yield for the former has a compounding frequency of six months and, for the latter, of one year.

This formula can be rewritten as:

$$P = v^{F_1} \times \left\{k + \frac{g}{h} \times \frac{v(1 - v^{n-1})}{(1 - v)} + \left\{C + \frac{g}{h} \times f_2\right\} \times v^{(n + f_2 - 1)}\right\}$$

For full details on eurobond yields, see the ISMA publication, *Formulae for Yield and Other Calculations* and the CSFB publication, *Yield Calculations.*
Accrued interest is calculated as follows:

Fixed-rate eurobonds

Based on a 360-day year, with the 31st of the month always being treated as the 30th, divided by 360. 'Since bonds days elapsed' are used to calculate the number of days between date 1 (d1,m1.y1) and date 2 (d2,m2,y2), this can be derived by:

$$\text{Bond days elapsed} = (y_2 - y_1) \times 360 + (m_2 - m_1) \times 30 + (d_2 - d_1)$$

Floating-rate eurobonds

Based on actual days accrued divided by:
a) non-sterling: 360.
b) sterling: 365, or normally 366 if the next coupon-date is in a leap year.

Eurosterling floating-rate notes

The following are the recommended formulae to be used for evaluating margins on FRNs and were developed by Credit Suisse First Boston and J P Morgan. While the two formulae given are both often used, the discounted margin is the recommended form.

■ i) Simple margin

The recommended simple margin formulae is:

$$\text{simple margin} = \frac{RV - (P + A) - (I + QM) \times (\frac{d}{360}) + \text{coupon}}{\text{Life}} + QM$$

where:

$P + A$ price plus accrued interest
I index rate from settlement to next coupon-date
d number of days to next coupon
QM quoted margin.
RV redemption value.
Life life from settlement to maturity

■ ii) Discounted margin

The recommended iterative solution formulae is:

$$(P + A) \times \left\{1 + \frac{(I + Dm)}{100} \times h\right\} - C_1 = \sum_{i=1}^{n} \frac{(I_a + QM) \times h}{\left\{1 + \frac{(I_a + Dm)}{100} \times h\right\}^i} + \frac{RV}{\left\{1 + \frac{(I_a + Dm)}{100} \times h\right\}^n}$$

where:

$P + A$ price plus accrued interest
I index rate from settlement to next coupon-date
I_a index rate
n number of whole coupon periods
f number of coupon periods per year

h $\frac{365.25}{360} \times \frac{1}{f}$

DM discounted margin
QM quoted margin
RV redemption value

Mortgage-backed securities

■ Discounted margin

The recommended iterative solution formula for MBSs is as above, except that the last term is:

$$+\sum_{i=1}^{n} \frac{RV_i}{\left\{1 + \frac{(I_a + Dm)}{100} \times h\right\}^n}$$

where:

RV_i redemption values at time i (i.e. principal pre-paid)

Since future exact redemptions values are not known in advance, it is the market convention to assume some constant annual rate of mortgage pre-payments. However, note that, should a higher or lower rate than that actually experienced be used, then the discount margin will be distorted accordingly.

Corporate bond market

This market uses the formulae applied in the gilt-edged market.

Bulldog market

This market uses the formulae applied in the gilt-edged market.

Medium-term notes

It is the market convention to use the ISMA formula in determine yields. Note that this is not directly comparable to other yields in the sterling market. For zero-coupon bonds, see Treasury bill yield calculations.

Local authority bonds

This market uses the formulae applied in the gilt-edged market.

28.13 Taxation

Domestic investors

Income and withholding tax

UK paying agents are required to withhold tax on coupons, whether in registered or bearer form, at the lowest basic rate of income tax, at present 25 per cent. The only securities exempt from this are: War Loan 3 1/2 per cent 1952 or After, Ireland 12.5 per cent 2008 and supranational issues for borrowers such as the World Bank and European Investment Bank. Overseas investors may, however, receive coupon payments free of tax (see later in this section).

In the past, UK institutions were taxed at a wide variety of rates. As a consequence these institutions could take advantage of lower-coupon bonds and the disparity between income tax and capital gains tax. The Thatcher government carried out major reforms of corporate taxation which has resulted in a more equitable system. All institutions are charged a tax rate of 35 per cent of income, with pension funds charged at zero, but individual investors and Lloyds funds are charged at their highest marginal rate - the top rate of which has been reduced to 40 per cent.

In February 1985, the Inland Revenue announced that, from 28 February 1986, income on gilts and other fixed-interest securities would be taxed on an accrual basis rather than on an income-received basis.

Capital gains tax

In the past, CGT was charged at 30 per cent with all gains indexed against inflation. In the 1988 Budget this rate was changed to the highest marginal rate of income tax and, as a result, the tax differential between income and CGT has been reduced to zero. Gilt-edged securities and 'qualified bonds', as well as gains on futures and options warrants, are not subject to CGT.

Overseas investors

Withholding tax

■ Gilt-edged market

Unless special arrangement had been made, all interest payments on gilt-edged securities, with the exception of War Loan 3 1/2 per cent 1952 or After, is paid after the deduction of the basic rate of tax, at present 25 per cent. Non-UK residents can take a number of measures in order to receive these payments gross, or at a reduced withholding tax rate.

■ Double taxation relief agreements
The UK has a wide range of double taxation agreements. Full exemption exists with:

Austria, Denmark, Faro Island, Finland, Germany, Greece, Hungary, Eire, Luxembourg, Mauritius, Netherlands Antilles, Norway, Poland, Sweden, Switzerland, USA.

Investors from many countries can gain partial exemption from these agreements which range between 15 per cent and 7.5 per cent, or even nil in certain restricted cases. For those overseas investors not wishing to utilize double taxation agreement, other methods are available.

■ FOTRA bonds
A number of gilt-edged securities are designated as 'free of tax to residents abroad' (FOTRA bonds - see Figure 28.82). Non-residents may apply independently to the Inspector of Foreign Dividends in order to have interest paid on these securities gross. Separate applications must be made for each bond held and, if a holding is sold, a new application will have to be made if it is repurchased. It should be noted that non-UK mutual funds may not be able to utilize this facility if they are unable to prove that all members are non-UK residents.

■ 'E arrangement'
It is also possible for non-residents to obtain a concession through what is known as the 'E arrangement'. This is a concession, by the Board of the Inland Revenue, enabling banks and corporate members of the stock exchange in the UK to obtain exemptions from the UK income tax on behalf of clients who are not resident in the UK. These concessions are subject to a number of restrictions and are not applicable to:

- i) Japanese investors
- ii) Investments under one year
- iii) Securities which form part of a trust or settlement
- iv) Holdings that are sold specially ex-dividend
- Eurosterling market

All eurosterling issues are paid gross, with the exception of instances in which investors choose to use a UK paying agent (should one exist for these securities); in such cases the basic rate of tax is applied.

Nominal £m	Name	Coupon (%)	Maturity date
775	Treasury	12.75	22 Jan 1992
1550	Treasury	8.00	13 Apr 1992
1288	Treasury Convertible	10.50	07 May 1992
1850	Treasury	10.00	15 Apr 1993
1100	Treasury	12.50	14 Jul 1993
600	Funding	6.00	15 Sep 1993
1065	Treasury	13.75	23 Nov 1993
550	Treasury	14.50	01 Mar 1994
1900	Treasury	10.00	09 Jun 1994
1600	Treasury	9.00	17 Nov 1994
840	Treasury	12.75	15 Nov 1995
750	Treasury	9.00	15 Mar 1992/96
1150	Treasury	15.25	03 May 1996
800	Exchequer	13.25	15 May 1996
1290	Treasury	13.25	22 Jan 1997
3600	Treasury	8.75	01 Sep 1997
1000	Treasury	6.75	01 May 1995/98
935	Treasury	15.50	30 Sep 1998
1250	Treasury	9.50	15 Jan 1999
2759	Conversion	9.00	03 Mar 2000
1800	Treasury	8.00	05 Oct 2002/06
1547	Treasury	8.50	16 Jul 2007
3321	Treasury	9.00	13 Oct 2008
233	Conversion	9.00	12 Jul 2011
1000	Treasury	5.50	10 Sep 2008/12
700	Treasury	7.75	26 Jan 2012/15
1909	War Loan	3.50	1952 or after
650	Index-linked	2.00	23 Mar 1992
900	Index-linked	2.50	17 Jul 2024

Figure 28.82 List of FOTRA gilts. *Note: Not all bonds called 'Treasury' are FOTRA bonds.*

Bulldog market

Those issues for supranational borrowers and Ireland 12.50 per cent 2008, are free from withholding tax. Several issues are available in both registered and bearer form. Should these securities be held in bearer form and paying agents outside the UK used, payments are not be subject to UK withholding tax.

Corporate bond market

UK domestic bonds are subject to the same income tax and CGT rules as gilt-edged securities. However, the capital gains tax exemption only applies to 'qualified bonds'. The rules to determine what qualifies as a qualified bond are quite complex. However, most recent issues from the 1980s are qualified bonds. For the very old outstanding bonds, it is recommended to seek advice from your dealer.

Domestic convertible bond market

UK domestic convertible bonds are subject to the same income tax as domestic corporate securities. However, the taxation of domestic preference shares is different, in that the share is equity. Interest is effectively a dividend and is taxed as such. If a company which pays UK corporation tax holds the preference share, then the dividend received is not taxed again, the interest being termed 'franked income'. For some types of investors, such as Investment Trust, this is very attractive. For borrowers, loan interest is paid from gross profits while dividends are paid from net (after tax) profits - hence the difference. There is a difference in the taxation of capital gains: while capital gains on loans are free of tax, capital gains on convertibles are subject to CGT, which indexes gains. The gains on deep-discount issues are especially of note: there was considerable controversy over the application of CGT when applied to puttable securities, since many were puttable at large premiums to the issue price.

Medium-term notes

The normal rules concerning medium-term securities apply including deep-discount or deep-gain legislation, if relevant. Interest paid ranks as annual interest. If a UK paying agent is used withholding tax is deducted, unless the bond qualifies as a 'quoted eurobond'.

Local authority bonds

See 'Corporate bond market'.

28.14 *Futures & options*

The London International Financial Futures Exchange 'Liffe' was the first Exchange to trade financial futures in Europe. The Exchange was established in 1981, independent from the existing International Stock Exchange and commodity futures Exchanges, and began trading on 30th September 1982 in the Royal Exchange building opposite the Bank of England. The first contracts to be traded on Liffe were currency futures, 3-month eurodollar and sterling interest rate futures and long-term UK government bond (long gilt) futures. In 1984, Liffe introduced US Treasury bond and Financial Times - Stock Exchange (FT-SE) 100 stock index futures. Options were introduced in 1985.

In 1987, Liffe expanded its range of interest rate contracts to include contracts denominated in currencies other than sterling or US dollars. A Japanese government bond (JGB) future was introduced in 1987, followed by a German government bond (Bund) future in 1988, the latter having subsequently grown to be Liffe's second most active contract in 1989.

In 1989, Liffe launched three-month euromark interest rate futures which was followed by three-month Ecu futures later in the year -the first Ecu interest rate contract to be traded in the world. More recently, the Exchange has added Ecu bond futures in 1990 and Italian government bond futures in 1991.

The bulk of volume on Liffe is concentrated in interest rate contracts; Liffe now has the widest and most international range of such contracts of any Exchange in the world, with short-term interest rate contracts in four major currencies - sterling, US dollar, Deutschemark and Ecu - and long-term interest rate contracts on six of the largest government bond markets - US Treasuries, Japanese government bonds, UK gilts, German bonds, Italian government bonds and Ecu bonds. Since its inception, volumes on Liffe have grown steadily.

Business on Liffe is cleared by an independent clearing house - the London Clearing House or LCH. The LCH is owned by six UK clearing banks: Barclays, Lloyds, Midland, National Westminster, Royal Bank of Scotland and Standard Chartered. Like the Chicago Exchanges, Liffe is principally a floor-based 'open outcry' market with continuous trading between 08.00 and 16.15. However, in November 1989, Liffe successfully introduced an Automated Pit Trading System (APT), for evening trading sessions (16.30 - 18.00) in euromark and Bund futures contracts.

UK government long bond (long gilt) futures

Long gilt futures (see Figure 28.83) were the first government bond futures to be launched on Liffe and, by 1987, became the most active contract on the Exchange. The early success of the contract stemmed mainly from the size of the

Contract size:	£50,000 nominal value notional gilt with 9 per cent coupon.
Delivery months:	March, June, September, December
Delivery day:	Any business day in the delivery month (at seller's choice).
Last trading day:	11.00, two business days prior to last business day in the delivery month.
Quotation:	Per £100 nominal.
Minimum price movement (tick size) and value:	1/32 per cent= £15.625.
Trading hours:	08.30-16.15
Initial margin:	1.5 per cent = £750.
Price limit:	None
Contract standard:	Physical delivery may be made of any gilt with maturities of between 1 January 2003 and 31 December 2009, as listed by Liffe. Stocks with optional dates will be deliverable only if both earliest and latest dates meet this criterion. No variable rate index-linked convertible or partly-paid may be delivered. Stocks are not deliverable within the period of three weeks and one day, or on, the ex-dividend day
Exchange Delivery Settlement Price (EDSP):	The Liffe market price at 11.00 on the second business day prior to delivery. The invoicing amount in respect of each deliverable stock is calculated by the price factor system. Price factors are calculated by the Exchange and announced before trading for the relevant contract month has commenced
Reuters pages:	LIEP
Telerate pages:	1994

Figure 28.83 Long gilt futures - contract specification

gilt market (the world's third largest, after US Treasuries and Japanese government bonds), and from the spectacular increase in turnover following London's Big Bang in 1986, when the number of market-makers was increased, from a handful of small British firms to 27 large international houses.

Since 1988, the UK government has began to buy back gilt from the market, reducing both turnover and volatility. As a result, volume in 1989 declined by some 27 per cent to 4.1m contracts, making it the third most active contract on the Exchange in 1989. However, market conditions improved in 1990 when volumes in the first half reached 3.1 million contracts against 2.2m during the same period in 1989.

The contract itself was initially designed along conventional lines: as a deliverable contract allowing the seller to choose which gilt to deliver, with an adjustment being made to the invoice amount by means of a price factor. Originally, delivery could be made of any gilt, as listed by Liffe, with a maturity

Stock	Price factor[1]	Daily accrued[2]	Initial accrued[3]
Treasury 11.75% 22 Jan 2003/07	1.1809062	16.0959	-853.08
Treasury 10.00% 08 Sep 2003	1.0681802	13.6986	1136.99
Treasury 12.50% 21 Nov 2003/05	1.2412503	17.1233	154.11
Treasury 13.50% 26 May 2004/08	1.3155523	18.4932	1202.05
Conversion 9.50% 25 Oct 2004	1.0360234	13.0137	468.49
Conversion 9.50% 18 Apr 2005	1.0368092	13.0137	559.59
Treasury 8.50% 16 Jul 2007	0.9600662	11.6438	-547.26
Treasury 9.00% 13 Oct 2008	0.9999282	12.3288	591.78
Treasury 8.00% 25 Sep 2009	0.9143034	10.9589	723.29

Figure 28.84 Long gilt futures (9% coupon) - price factors & accrued interest [contract month June 1990]

[1] *expressed as a fraction of par*
[2] *accrued interest per day on £50,000 face value*
[3] *accrued interest on £50,000 face value as of the last day of the month prior to the delivery month*
Invoicing amount = (500 x EDSP x price factor) + initial accrued + (daily accrued x delivery day in month)
Issue date: 19 March 1992

of between 15 and 25 years. However, because of the lack of new issues in this area, the contract was re-designed in 1989 to allow delivery of gilts with redemption dates between 01 January 2003 and 31 December 2009. Thus, from 01 January 1990, for example, gilt with maturities of between 12 and 19 years can be delivered.

Liffe also introduced short gilt futures in 1985 and medium gilt futures in 1988, but these contracts were de-listed in January 1990.

UK government long bond (long gilt) options

Long gilt options (see Figure 28.85) were launched on Liffe in March 1986 and grew quickly to become Liffe's most active options contract in 1988. However, for the same reasons that caused the decline in long gilt futures, contract turnover fell in 1989, by 36 per cent to 727,000 contracts, and it became the third most active options contract on the Exchange. As is common for Exchange traded interest rate options, the long gilt option is an option on the futures contract with the same face value and expiry cycle as the futures contract. However, the long gilt option expires before trading ceases in the futures contract and has a minimum price movement of 1/64, i.e. half the minimum price movement of the futures contract. Long gilt options may be exercised on any business

Options type:	American
Unit of trading:	One long gilt futures contract.
Delivery months:	March, June, September, December
Assignment of futures:	On the first business day after the exercise day
Last trading day:	16.15, six business days prior to the first delivery day of the long gilt futures contract
Quotation:	Multiples of 1/64
Minimum price movement (tick size) and value:	1/64 per cent = £7.8125
Trading hours:	08.32-16.15
Initial margin:	Initial margin for long and short options positions is calculated with reference to daily published risk factors
Reuters pages:	LIGU
Telerate pages:	15990-15993

Figure 28.85 Long gilt options - contract specification

day prior to expiry (American style), with exercise resulting in the assignment of a futures position.

Three-month sterling interest rate ('short sterling') futures

Three-month sterling interest rate, or 'short sterling', futures (see Figure 28.86) were launched in 1982, and have grown to be Liffe's most active contract in 1989, when volumes rose by 102 per cent to 7.1m contracts. This increase has been due mainly to the sharp increase in short-term sterling interest rate volatility since mid-1988. In the first half of 1990, volumes increased to 4.2m contracts against 3.3m contracts in the same period in 1989. The short sterling contract is 'cash-settled' i.e. there is no exchange of the underlying unit of trading on the delivery day. Instead, all positions are closed out against the exchange delivery settlement price, or EDSP. This price is set by Liffe in the following way: quotes for 3-month London interbank offered rate (LIBOR) are taken from sixteen banks between 9.30 and 11.00 on the last trading day. The three highest and three lowest quotes are excluded, and an average is taken of the remaining ten. The EDSP is then 100.00 less this average, e.g. a price of 90.00 reflects a rate of interest of 10.00 per cent.

Three-month sterling interest rate ('short sterling') options

Three-month sterling interest rate, or 'short sterling', options (see Figure 28.87) were launched on Liffe in November 1987 and have grown to become Liffe's

Contract size:	£500,000
Delivery months:	March, June, September, December
Delivery day:	First business day after the last trading day
Last trading day:	11.00 on the third Wednesday of the delivery month
Quotation:	100.00 minus rate of interest
Minimum price movement (tick size) and value:	0.01 per cent = £12.50
Trading hours:	08.20-16.02
Initial margin:	0.75 per cent = £3750
Price limit:	None
Contract standard:	Cash settlement
Settlement price:	Based on LIBOR sampled between 09.30 and 11.00 on the last trading day from a random sample of 16 banks from a list of designated banks. Having disregarded the three highest and three lowest quotes, the settlement price is 100.00 minus the average of the remaining 10 rates
Reuters pages:	LIIA
Telerate pages:	995

Figure 28.86 Short sterling futures - contract specification

Option type:	American
Unit of trading:	One 3-month sterling futures contract
Delivery months:	March June September December
Assignment of futures:	First business day after the exercise day
Last trading day:	11.00 on the last trading day of the 3-month sterling futures contract
Quotation:	Multiples of 0.01
Minimum price movement (tick size) and value:	0.01 per cent = £12.50
Trading hours:	08.22-16.02
Initial margin:	Initial margin for long and short option positions is calculated with reference to daily published risk factors
Price limit:	None
Exercise (strike) prices:	Intervals of 25 basis points
Reuters pages:	LIIB, LFXP - LFXU
Telerate pages:	15742-15745

Figure 28.87 Short sterling options - contract specification

most active options contract with a volume of 824,000 contracts in 1989, up 85 per cent on 1988. In the first half of 1990, volume increased again to 542,000 contracts against 366,000 in the same period in 1989.

Like other Liffe interest rate options, the three-month sterling option is an option on the futures contract with the same contract features, e.g. face value, expiry cycle months, minimum price movements and last trading day. Like all Liffe options, three-month sterling options may be exercised on any business day prior in a futures position.

28.15 Money markets

The UK has very well developed money markets, not only in sterling, but in nearly all major currencies. The following is a brief description of some of the very short-term sterling instruments available for investors:

Floating-rate notes (see also eurosterling FRNs)

These are instruments where the coupon, linked to money market rates, is adjusted at regular intervals. A large number of issues are mortgage-backed. (For more details, see the sections on eurosterling FRNs and MBSs).

Coupon

Normally spread over/under set-term LIBOR, e.g. 3-month LIBOR.

Maturity

1993 to 2030, with one perpetual issued by Standard Chartered Bank.

Interest payment

Normally at the same time as coupon refix. Paid net or gross depending on type of issue and where paying agent resides. There are a number of variations available, such a bond that pays the higher of 0.0625 over 6-month LIBOR or 1-month LIBOR flat and a stepped-margin rate over a period of years.

Prices

Prices are quoted as a price per par value to two decimal places.

Interest and yield calculation

Interest is on an actual days over 365-day basis. For details on the formulae for calculating simple and discounted margins see the section on yield calculations.

Issuers

Mainly banks, building societies and housing finance companies. There is one sovereign issue (by the New Zealand government), one corporate (the Milk

Marketing Board), and one asset-backed security (CARS (UK)). There is a very large mortgage-backed securities market (discussed separately).

Investors

Banks, insurance companies and pension funds.

Calls

Most issues callable at par before maturity.

Other structures

Rolling-rate interest payment and setting-date mismatch, e.g. interest paid every 3 months, with coupon set monthly. There are also mortgage-backed and asset-backed FRNs.

Sterling commercial paper (SCP)

Sterling commercial paper is a short-term, negotiable, unsecured promissory note issued on a programme basis whereby borrowers can raise additional finance subject to the limit of the overall programme size, which often covers several currencies with a minimum issue size of £100,000.

The SCP market started in 1986 and has only grown slowly since its inception, to reach a level of £4.7bn outstanding at the end of 1990, with a total programme volume of £19.5bn. There has been a continuing divergence of opinion on the prospects for the market with the bulls pointing out that commercial paper in the US grew from nil to US$300bn (in its first 10 years), while the bears point out the lack of depth and diversity. There is no doubt that the default by Polly Peck has cast a cloud over the market. With many dealers having withdrawn, citing an inability to participate profitably in a market that is both too small and beset with a less than desirable general credit quality, the future of the market has yet to be determined.

Coupon

Either fixed or floating and usually set as a spread over/under LIBOR.

Maturity

Not less than 7 days, and not more than one year.

Interest payment

These are non-interest-bearing securities and are issued at a discount. Normally paid gross.

Prices

Prices are quoted on a yield-to-maturity basis.

Interest and yield calculation

Interest is on an actual days over 365-day basis. The formula for calculating yield is:

$$P = F \times \left\{1 - \frac{R}{100} \times \frac{D_{sm}}{365}\right\}$$

where:

P price
F face value
R rate of discount per cent
D_{sm} number of days from settlement to maturity

The rate of discount can be converted to a yield, for comparison with money market instruments traded on a yield basis, using the formula:

$$Y = \frac{100 \times R \times 365}{(100 \times 365 - R \times D_{sm})}$$

where:

Y yield per cent
R rate of discount per cent
D_{sm} number of days from settlement to maturity.

Issuers

Typically banks and corporates. Changes in the regulations have been made to allow non-UK borrowers to use this market. The blanket criterion for a company to qualify to issue sterling SCP, is a minimum net asset amount of £25 million. Specific criteria are:

- A UK company must also have either debt or equity listed on the International Stock Exchange or shares traded on the Unlisted Securities Market (USM).
- An overseas company must be listed on an authorized stock exchange.
- Public sector bodies need only to have debt securities trading on an authorized stock exchange.

Note that UK local authorities can issue SCP.

Investors

Banks, financial and investment institutions. (*Note*: building societies are not permitted to buy paper issued by corporates.)

Sterling certificates of deposits (SCDs)

SCDs are negotiable instruments evidencing a time deposit made with an issuing bank or building society at a fixed, or variable, rate for a fixed period. A few UK corporates are authorized to issue SCDs. In contrast to FRNs, SCDs are treated as bank deposits and rank *pari passu* with all other deposits, while most FRNs are subordinated to deposits.

Coupon

Generally fixed-rate, a few variable-rate certificates have been issued.

Maturity

One month to 5 years, although the majority are issued with original maturities of less than 6 months.

Interest payment

These are interest-bearing securities and therefore the coupon is paid on maturity on SCDs with one year or less original maturity, otherwise these securities pay semi-annually. Interest is paid either gross or net depending on the issuer and where the certificates are lodged.

Prices

Prices are quoted on a yield-to-maturity basis for fixed-rate SCDs and price basis for floating-rate issues.

Interest calculation

Interest is on actual days over 365-day basis. For SCDs paying one coupon, the formula for calculating yield can be derived as shown below. At issue, SCDs are priced at par. At maturity, the investor receives par, plus a coupon payment. The coupon of an SCD is expressed as an annual rate based on 365-day year. The value at maturity of a SCD is given by the formula:

$$\text{value at maturity} = F \times \left\{1 + \frac{G}{100} \times \frac{D_{im}}{365}\right\}$$

where:

F face value of SCD
G coupon rate per cent
D_{im} number of days from issue date to maturity

At issue the yield of an SCD is equal to its coupon. After issue the yield will change in response to movements in interest rates. To calculate the price of an SCD for a given yield the formula is:

$$P = F \times \frac{\left\{1 + \frac{G}{100} \times \frac{D_{im}}{365}\right\}}{\left\{1 + \frac{Y}{100} \times \frac{D_{sm}}{365}\right\}}$$

where:

P price
F face value
G coupon rate per cent
Y yield per cent
D_{im} number of days from issue to maturity
D_{sm} number of days from settlement to maturity

Issuers

Primarily banks and corporations.

Investors

Banks, financial and investment institutions.

Treasury bills ('T-bills')

Treasury bills are promissory notes issued by the government in anticipation of future revenues. The Treasury bill market in the UK had been historically a very small market with weekly issuance of around £200m of 91-day Treasury bills. The bills were sold primarily to discount houses and banks and were rarely bought by other investors who preferred to purchase certificates of deposits (CDs), floating-rate notes (FRNs), or make bank deposits.

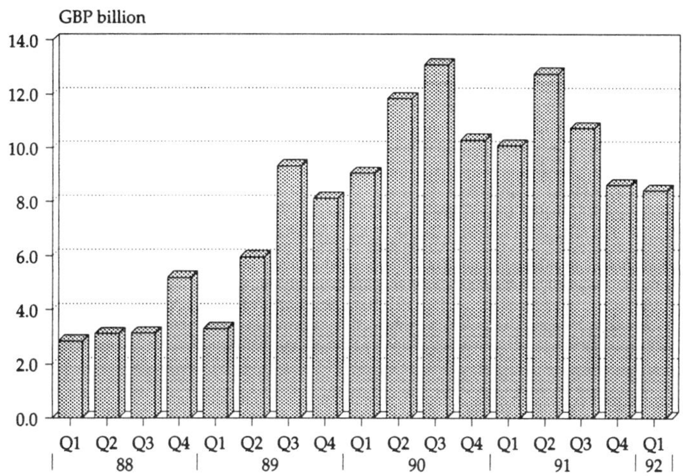

Figure 28.88 Treasury bill outstandings

When the Bank of England started to buy back gilt-edged securities in 1989, it began to issue Treasury bills in order to absorb the surplus cash thus generated. Therefore, an increase in outstandings in the 3rd quarter 1989 can be seen (see Figure 28.88). [It should be noted that there is seasonal effect in outstandings because the government receives much of its corporate taxes in the 1st quarter and, therefore, the budget is usually in surplus which then turns into deficit in the 3rd & 4th quarter.]

The government's intention in 1989 was also to sell extra volumes to non-banks, as sales to banks and building societies (see Figure 28.89), do not count towards funding the public sector borrowing requirement (PSBR). However, it was appreciated that a more liquid and larger market was needed.

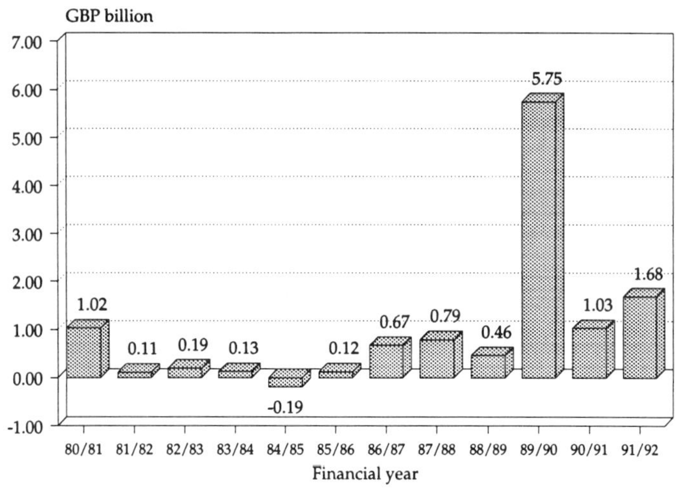

Figure 28.89 Treasury bill net issuance

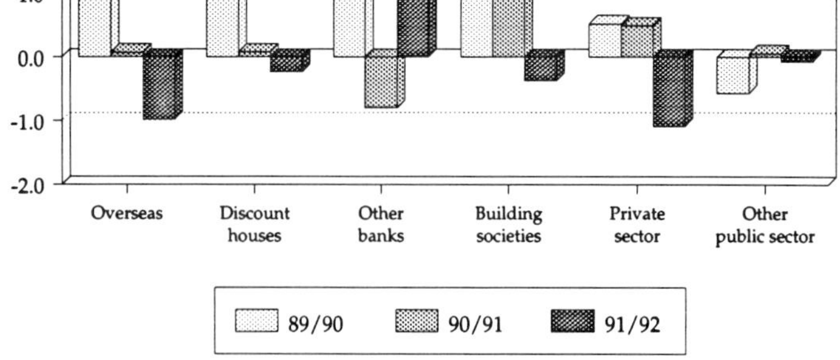

Figure 28.90 Treasury bill net sales by type of institution

Coupon

These securities are issued at a discount and have no interest payments.

Maturities

While there are issues out to one year, the vast majority of issues are for three months/91 days.

Interest payment

On maturity.

Prices

Quoted on a discount yield basis.

Interest calculation

Interest is on actual days over 365-day basis. The formula for calculating yield is the same as SCPs (see above).

Issuers

The UK government.

Investors

Primarily financial institutions and central banks, but all sectors are investors in this paper.

Other promissory bills

Other issuers of bills are trading companies and local authorities. Company bills can be divided into two types, 'eligible' and 'non-eligible'. The former can be discounted at the Bank of England, while the latter cannot.

28.16 *Interest rate history*

Overview

UK interest rates have experienced a chequered history in the past six years. This is nothing unusual for a country which has had more than its fair share of currency crises, major shifts in economic policies and notable changes in the style of political management. But, for an economy which appeared to be showing signs of responding to the government's anti-inflation drive - and hence giving rise to hopes of a more stable path of development, the second half of the last decade must have been viewed with some disappointment. With hindsight, a volatile profile would hardly have been surprising given some of the events

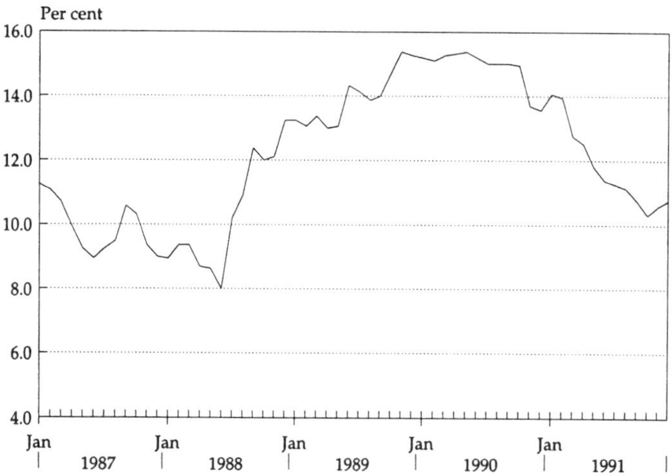

Figure 28.91 UK interest rates 1987 - 1991

which have taken place - ranging, to name but a few, from the stock market's October 1987 Crash, major policy disagreements within the Conservative Party leading to the loss of a chancellor as well as prime minister, the Gulf War and sterling's entry to the European exchange rate mechanism. However, the fact that much of the period was characterized by the need to maintain relatively high short-term interest rates, suggested the UK's post-war problems had not been conquered entirely.

1986

The year commenced on an uncertain note, principally in response to the weakness of sterling on the foreign exchanges. The currency had suffered from a significant decline in international crude oil prices, a development regarded as having far-reaching consequences for the trade balance - which was already showing signs of a gradual deterioration from the strong position in evidence earlier in the decade. The problems of the pound were compounded by mounting political uncertainty surrounding the gradual diminution of the Conservative Party's popularity in the opinion polls and the tensions associated with the Westland Affair, which featured the resignations of two key members of Prime Minister Thatcher's government.

Nevertheless, the impact of these problems on domestic interest rates was diluted by the generally favourable trend in international rates. The easing in global credit conditions, facilitated by the fall in oil prices and the resulting steep fall in inflation in the majority of leading industrialized countries, provided a background against which short- and long-term interest rates in the UK were able to decline, albeit only temporarily. By the late spring, further evidence of the deterioration in the performance of the balance of payments and, more importantly, the revival of political uncertainty, served to place renewed downward pressure upon the currency, a development which obliged the authorities to embark upon support operations via money rates. Interest rates moved higher during the summer months, with bank base rates peaking in early-October at 11 per cent.

In the final stages of the year, the fortunes of the markets had again begun to improve. Short-term interest rates held steady in spite of the continued weakness of the currency, which saw sterling fall below $1.40 at one stage (late October). The pressure on rates was, in large part, relieved by evidence that the government's problems with respect to dwindling popularity were at an end. This factor meant the bond markets could benefit more fully from the favourable performance of key economic indicators such as retail price inflation, which fell below 2 1/2 per cent in mid-year. In addition, the advent of the new market structure, heralded in by Big Bang (27 October), served to improve the attractions of the government bond market, initially via a substantial improvement in liquidity.

1987

The rally in the market did not commence in earnest until the initial stages of 1987, however. Then, a dramatic swing in the political fortunes of the government eliminated much of the risk investors had attached to investing in fixed-interest markets. Domestic and international demand for sterling securities increased substantially, giving rise to a fall in long-dated yields of more than 200 basis points, and provided the background against which base rates could be cut by 2 percentage points. The performance of rates in the period to mid-year, compared with the shift in government popularity is illustrated in Figure 28.92.

End month	MORI poll ratings				Base rates	Gilt yields 03/07	STWI[1]
	Con	Lab	Lib	Other			
Nov 1986	41	39	18	2	11.00	10.92	68.1
Dec 1986	39	38	21	2	11.00	10.44	69.2
Jan 1987	39	38	21	2	11.00	10.12	68.5
Feb 1987	41	35	21	3	11.00	9.66	69.9
Mar 1987	41	29	29	1	10.00	9.18	71.4
Apr 1987	44	31	23	2	9.50	8.87	73.2
May 1987	44	31	24	1	9.00	8.82	72.7
Jun 1987	44	32	32	2	9.00	8.83	73.4

Figure 28.92 Poll ratings and the market
[1] *Sterling trade-weighted index*

The bulk of the favourable movement had been seen by April, the decline in yields being reinforced, not just by optimism over the longer term prospects for the economy, but also by the view that a further Conservative victory at the election would trigger a surge of international funds into the UK, including the gilt-edged market.

In the event, the well-discounted election result failed to produce the anticipated influx of overseas funds and long-term interest rates edged higher. Bonds failed to perform in line with the equity market, which still reflected undue optimism over the prospects for corporate growth and profitability in the years ahead. Indeed, by mid-summer, the authorities delivered the first of a series of shocks to the financial markets. Official interest rates were raised on the grounds - correctly as it eventually turned out - that the economy was showing signs of overheating, especially on the balance of payments front.

The financial markets continued to be carried forward on a wave of euphoria into the autumn. Then, signs of competitive interest hikes by leading industrialized nations, in particular Germany and the USA, triggered a major sell-off in the world equity markets - the 1987 stock market Crash. Fears of depression, on the grounds that the history of the 1930s would be repeated, sparked an influx of funds to government bonds and forced long-term interest rates lower. Short-term interest rates were reduced as part of an international drive to stem the flight from long-term securities, a development which helped to underpin the favourable gilt-edged market performance into the new year.

1988

The post-Crash year commenced on a nervous, though favourable, note for UK interest rates. Nevertheless, the authorities were aware of the dangers of excessive growth both for the balance of payments and inflation. By early-February it appeared the Bank of England had managed to overcome the worries associated with the Crash and return to the policy course first embarked upon in August 1987. Official interest rates were raised an unexpected 1/2 per cent in response to fears that the economy was in danger of overheating. Nevertheless, this policy course was apparently abandoned at an early stage. Poor official statistics on the health of the economy, residual fears over the effects of the recession upon consumer and industrial confidence and the misguided informal pegging of the sterling/Deutschemark exchange rate at Dm 3.00 conspired to push interest rates to excessively low levels and to fuel economic growth to what eventually turned out to be unsustainably high levels.

The surge in consumption in early 1988, triggered by the relaxed credit conditions and the series of tax cuts introduced in the spring budget, exacerbated the deterioration in the balance of payments and created conditions in the economy - including the already tight labour market - which fuelled the rise in retail price inflation, a variable which peaked some 18 months later at 10.9 per cent - a rise of 8 1/2 per cent from the floor. Short-term interest rates were forced to unsustainably low levels, a conclusion supported by the bond market, where yields failed to follow base rates lower.

The trend in UK interest rates was reversed, not so much by evidence of the deterioration in economic performance - which, in view of the poorness of statistic, was still some time in materializing - but by concerted tightening moves by the bulk of industrialized countries. Short-term interest rates were moved progressively higher in reaction to a deterioration in sterling's fortunes on the foreign exchanges, further tightening in international credit conditions and mounting problems on the domestic economic front. By the end of the year, base rates had risen 5 1/2 percentage points from their late-May floor of 7 1/2 per cent.

It was in 1988, however, that the UK market saw the decoupling of the relationship between short and long-term interest rates. The movement of the public sector's finances to a substantial surplus position, itself a consequence of the very strong growth in the economy and the heavy privatization programme, saw the adoption of a new variation of monetary policy - the so-called 'full funding' policy. This required the authorities to counter the contractionary effects of their surplus position upon the monetary aggregates by injecting funds back into the economy. Rather than embark upon arguably inflationary expansions to public spending programmes, this was achieved by the purchase of public sector debt from the non-monetary sector of the economy, in the main gilt-edged securities. The effect of this tactic, embarked upon a high-profile basis between mid-1988 and mid-1990, was to hold long-term interest rates below where they would otherwise have been, given the performance of the economy and mounting political uncertainty.

1989

The firmer trend in short-term interest rates continued through 1989. The problems of the domestic economy, labelled as a mere blip by Chancellor Lawson, were proving more resilient than had been assumed officially. The continued deterioration in the economic background virtually ruled out any hope of an early relaxation in monetary policy, although the words chosen by the chancellor continued to suggest that an improvement would soon be in evidence.

Tensions on the foreign exchanges, present during much of 1988, remained in evidence with heavy official intervention by central banks to halt the advance of the US dollar, proving largely ineffective. In addition to this, the rise in key international interest rates, especially Japan and Germany created an environment in which a further hike in the UK would be deemed appropriate for international as well as domestic considerations. Base rates were raised again in mid-May. During much of the early part of the year simmering political tensions remained an unsettling background influence. Disagreements in government about the UK's relationship with Europe and, in particular, the timing of any linkage with the ERM, appeared from time to time and this tended to compound the difficulties of the currency and money market through much of the first half of the year.

The currency and bond market experienced a modest rally following the May hike in base rates (up 1 per cent, to 14 per cent), but the euphoria failed to persist in the face of continuing signs of a deteriorating economy, further rises in international interest rates (which triggered another 1 per cent increase in base rates to 15 per cent in the early days of October) and the ever-present uncertainty over the political background. Indeed, this influence came well and truly to the fore in late October and tended to mask the benefits which might otherwise have been gained from the successful central bank assault upon the US dollar's position on the foreign exchanges earlier than month. Then, disagreements over sterling and the ERM finally forced the resignation of Chancellor Lawson from the Thatcher government, an event which itself led to an unsuccessful bid to oust the prime minister from office.

During the entire year, long-term interest rates remained virtually immune from all the adverse developments. While the trend was generally higher, in sympathy with the deteriorating economic and political background, the government's active pursuit of its full funding policy ensured there was a very effective ceiling above which yields would not rise. The authorities' policy was aimed not just at avoiding the problems a large public sector surplus might create for the availability of credit but also to provide conditions which would ensure the active issuance of non-government sterling fixed-interest securities, a policy which proved successful. It was only in the closing stages of the year, when speculation about the demise of the public sector surplus and a resulting return of the government to the gilt market as a borrower strengthened, that long-term interest rates began to edge gradually higher.

1990

1990 was the first year since 1969 when there was only a single alteration in official interest rates. However, this lack of movement masks over a period in which there was no shortage of market volatility. Political uncertainty and disappointing economic performance dominated sentiment and, this year, the realization that it was only a matter of time before the deterioration in public sector finances forced the government to issue gilts meant long-term interest rates were more susceptible to adverse shifts in sentiment. The year started on a very poor note, worries over the path of official funding tending to undermine the attractions of the sterling sector. This gave way to the even stronger influence of

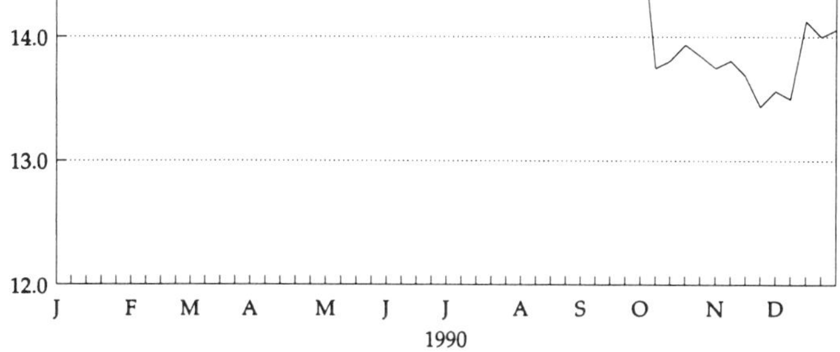

Figure 28.93 UK interest rates in 1990

political uncertainty, exacerbated by the obvious unpopularity of the new poll tax. Short- and long-term interest rates moved higher in the first quarter in reaction to this unfavourable consideration, the money market at one stage discounting a potential rise in base rates to 16 per cent, (an event which never materialized).

Political tensions subsided in the late spring when slightly better than expected local government election results heralded a modest improvement in the government's fortunes in the opinion polls. The relief of the market was evident in the recovery of gilt prices and the small subsidence of short-term money rates, a recovery which turned into a full blown rally on the back of strong rumours that sterling would enter the ERM in the 'near future'. However, the rally proved relatively short-lived, the poise of all markets being undermined by the Iraqi invasion of Kuwait (in August), a development which threatened to spark a significant rise in oil prices and hence to damage the prospects for long run growth and inflation.

The influence of the Gulf tended to subside in the autumn and although the outlook for the economy remained unclear, sterling's entry to the ERM (8 October) provided the authorities with the opportunity to cut official interest rates by a full percentage point. Long-term interest rates also moved lower, although the favourable trend was cut short by the question over Mrs Thatcher's ability to remain leader of the Conservative Party. In the event, a challenge to the prime minister was successfully launched in November.

The recovery in the government's popularity upon the elevation of John Major to the position of PM, and unmistakable evidence that the UK was in the midst of a severe recession, provided the background against which a rally in the market could carry through into the new year.

1991

The strengthening in sterling in the early stages of 1991, mounting evidence of recession in the domestic economy, and the wave of euphoria in the international financial markets which arose at the start of the military operations in the Gulf, combined to create conditions in which a fall in interest rates was possible. In addition to these considerations, the relaxation in credit conditions in the USA and some key ERM countries, notably Spain and France, enabled the authorities to pursue a cautious policy of ease, in spite of deteriorating political background and mounting worries over the size of the official gilt funding requirement in the years ahead. Indeed, the significant rally in the US dollar which commenced around mid-March helped to boost the pound relative to the Deutschemark, a development which was clearly beneficial towards a cut in official interest rates.

By mid-year base lending rates had been cut 2 1/2 percentage points from their post-ERM level while, at their best, long-dated gilt yields had declined 80

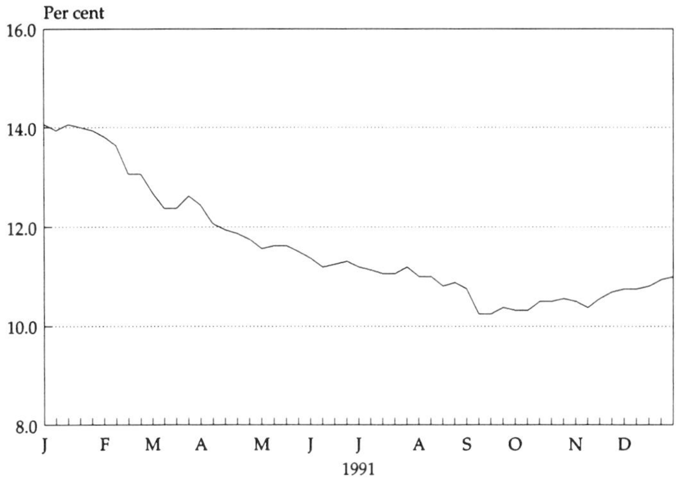

Figure 28.94 UK interest rates in 1991

basis points. However, the strength of the bond market did not continue unabated. Political and funding uncertainties, followed at a later stage by some weakening in sterling within the ERM, cut short the rally in bond prices and triggered the start of a long process of consolidation. The threatened return of the government to the gilt-edged market finally occurred in late January with the issue of a £500m tranche of the Conversion 10% 1996 short-dated benchmark bond, an event which heralded the steady flow of new paper. Political uncertainty, on the other hand, followed the course of the government's popularity in the opinion polls which, in spite of the promised demise of the emotive poll tax, charted a steadily deteriorating trend to mid-year.

The consolidation continued through to late summer, but was reversed when the US authorities reacted to evidence that the recovery in economic activity was faltering. The steep fall in short-term interest rates triggered a strong rally in US Treasury bonds and created the environment for a recovery in the sterling market. Sentiment received an additional boost from a notable improvement in the political background. Prime Minister Major's successes in the international political field, associated with, for example, the failed coup in the Soviet Union, helped to lift the government's popularity in the opinion polls. The consequent improvement in sterling's fortunes in the ERM enabled the authorities to cut short-term interest rates to a level of 10.5 per cent. This position failed to be bettered in subsequent months. A decline in government popularity, as the attention of the electorate shifted back towards the ills of the domestic economy, coupled with rising German rates and a weaker currency, ruled out scope for further easing and created a background against which the bond market ended the year on a disappointing note.

28.17 *Inter-market spreads*

Overview

The behaviour of yield spreads within the UK has been very diverse in the last five years, a factor which has helped to create a significant number of investment opportunities both between, and within, specific securities markets. The analysis of spread relationships is not a new concept, but it is probably fair to say that the number of areas compared now is very much greater than it was, say, ten or even five years ago. The globalization of investment management since the mid-1980s and the greater awareness of the opportunities available to fund managers in markets outside the sterling sector, has served to concentrate attention upon the yield spreads between different currency blocks and markets with widely different inflation performances. Indeed, the move towards economic and monetary union in Europe is set to intensify the debate on spread relationships in the years ahead, specifically between the two schools of thought on European yield convergence.

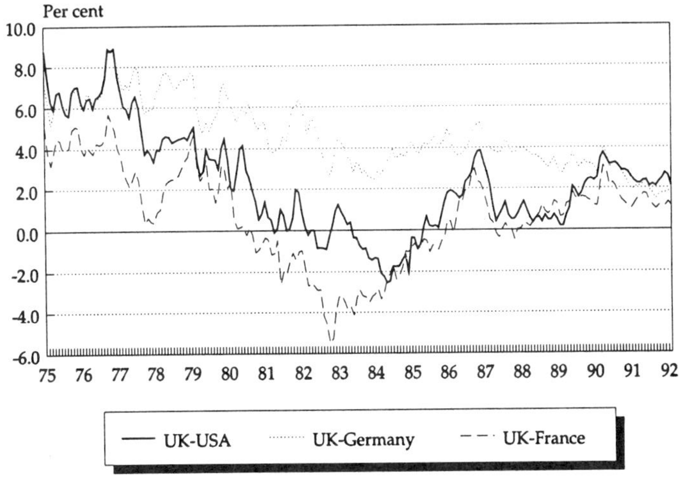

Figure 28.95 Yield spreads: UK vs. USA, Germany & France

Within the UK, a vast array of spreads are examined frequently by investors, a few of the more interesting of these can be listed as follows:

- the gilt/non-gilt fixed-coupon yield differential
- the equity/gilt yield ratio
- the equity/index-linked gilt yield difference

The relationship between government and eurosterling bonds underwent a significant transformation during the second half of the 1980s. Then, two events in particular had a major effect upon the yield spreads:

> 1) Primary activity in the eurosterling market mushroomed as issuers took advantage of the steep increase in international demand for sterling-denominated instruments. The growth in this market was also aided by the adoption of a much more positive attitude to the corporate bond markets by the UK authorities, via the lifting of numerous restrictions which had limited its attractions to potential users.
>
> 2) Official assistance did not stop at the lifting of technical restrictions. The government's adoption of a policy of buying-in public sector debt to offset the effects of the large public sector surplus upon the overall availability of credit - an aspect of the so-called 'full funding' rule - was designed in such a way to promote growth in corporate issuance. Buying-in was concentrated in areas of the maturity range which would depress yields to levels where issuance was attractive.

The policies were a success. New issuance increased dramatically and this, together with the artificial depression of gilt-edged yields, caused yield spreads to widen sharply.

Since early 1990, however, the cessation of the government's aggressive gilt buying-in policy and their eventual return to the gilt market as a high profile borrower in January 1991 contributed to a reversal of the trend, a development also encouraged by a decline in the volume of non-government bond issuance, (itself a consequence of the relatively high level of yields).

While the relationship is set to remain erratic, it seems unlikely that spreads will trade out towards their 1989/90 levels. Issuance by non-government borrowers will remain strongly in evidence, but the predominance of the government as a borrower will almost certainly be the most significant feature of the primary markets, in the next two to three years at the very least.

Spreads between gilts and equities have been studied by market practitioners for decades, although it is probably true to say that with the increased institutionalization of the equity and bond markets, and the greater segregation between different security types, these relationships are not watched as closely as

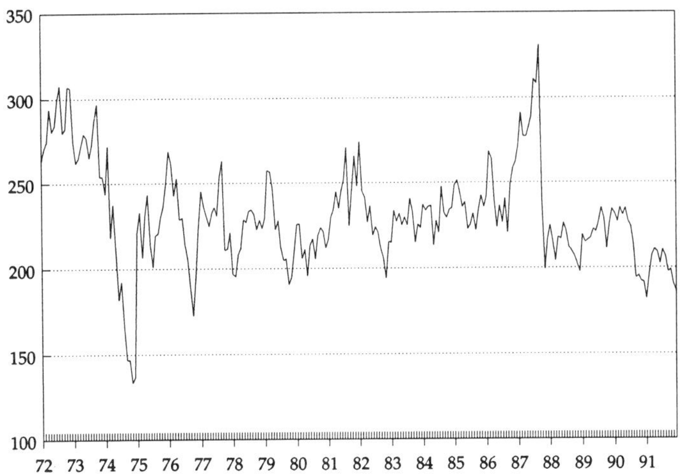

Figure 28.96 Long gilt yield / All-Share dividend yield

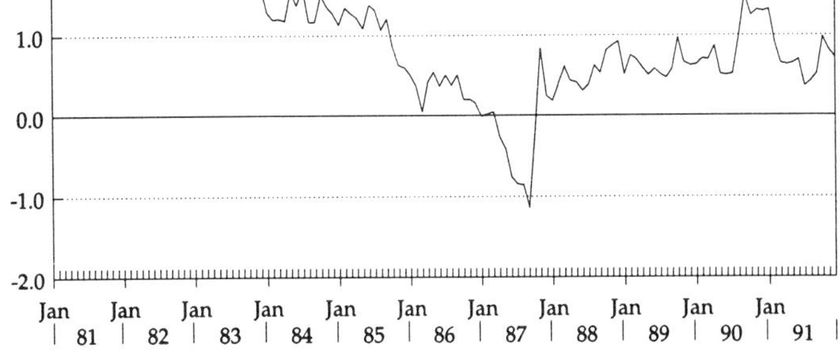

Figure 28.97 All-Share yield minus long-dated index-linked yield

they used - or, arguably, ought - to be. The yield ratio depicted in Figure 28.96 shows a distinct trading range in the ratio over the years, as does the equity/index-linked yield gap (see Figure 28.97).

The relationship moved well outside its limits in 1987 and underlines the unmistakable shift in the equity market to an excessively expensive position relative to gilts ahead of the October Crash. Now the relationship tends to trade at the lower end of the range. A debate has begun as to whether there has been a fundamental change in the ratio as a consequence of sterling's membership of the ERM. The prospect of a shift towards a low inflation/low growth economy subject to a fixed exchange rate regime, with implications for profits growth, is advanced as good reason to believe that there should be a step-down in the so-called trading range seen during the past decade. Only time will tell whether a change has indeed taken place and, in the mean time, the debate will continue.

Sterling bond markets

Bulldog bonds

1991 saw a gradual narrowing in the yield differential between gilt-edged securities and Bulldog bonds. It will become apparent from the analysis of different

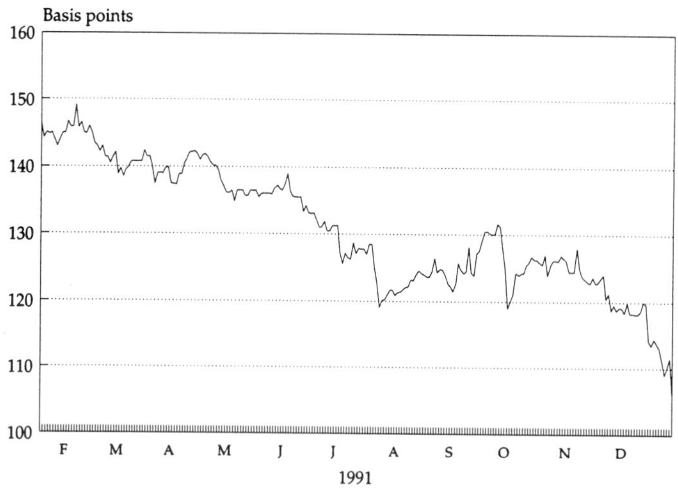

Figure 28.98 Yield spread: Denmark 13% 2005 minus Treasury 9% 2008

spreads which follows, that the decline in this sector has been among the most pronounced. While part of the movement can be attributed to lack of supply, the market's perception of the high credit quality offered by the bulk of issues has clearly been of importance at a time when the depth of the UK recession has underlined the significance of credit quality. With a few notable exceptions, the bulk of Bulldog issues carry triple-A status, a consideration which contrasts with the much wider quality distribution in, for example, eurosterling issues.

With the exception of 1989, supply to the Bulldog market remained modest during the past six years owing, in large part, to the relative cost attractions of borrowing in the eurosterling market, as well as the advantages the latter sector offers to issuers in terms of the wider level of investor participation. In addition to this, sterling's entry to the ERM has had a profound effect upon the willingness of sovereign and supranational issuers, major users of the Bulldog market in the past, to tap the sterling sector while interest rates remain high. For, in an environment of fixed exchange rates, borrowers can no longer rely upon the effects of probable currency depreciation to reduce non-sterling denominated redemption costs and thereby counter the relatively high-coupon at which paper is offered. Issuing in alternative lower-coupon currencies will appear more attractive under these circumstances. Lack of issuance, combined with the perceived quality of the paper currently in issue, support the argument that yield spreads will remain narrow for the foreseeable future.

Eurosterling

Yield spreads in the eurosterling sector have also followed a declining trend. There are some reasons behind the general narrowing in differentials, specifically:

1) The reduction in the volume of issue activity, borrowers being deterred by a reduction in the number and frequency of attractive swap opportunities and the desire, against a background of falling international bond yields, to wait for cheaper funding opportunities.

2) The effect upon spreads of a combination of reduced supply of eurosterling paper and the return of the UK government to the gilt-edged market as a major borrower of funds. During calendar 1991, gilt issuance, net of redemptions, amounted to £6.4bn, compared with official gilt purchases of £8.8bn in 1990 and an even higher £14.1bn in 1989.

The trends in different sectors of the eurosterling market have been varied, however. This is illustrated in Figures 28.99 - 28.101. As in the case of Bulldog issues, the two most important determinants have been the frequency and size of supply during the past twelve months and the concern about credit quality, not just in reaction to the recession in the UK economy, but also the financial

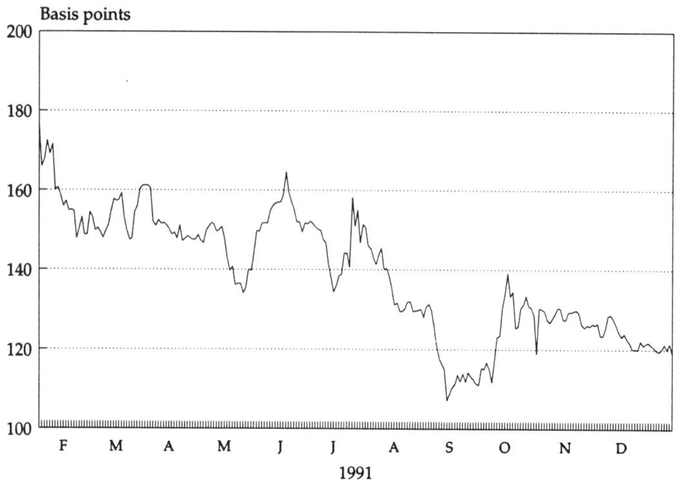

Figure 28.99 Yield spread: ICI 9 3/4% 2005 minus Treasury 9% 2008

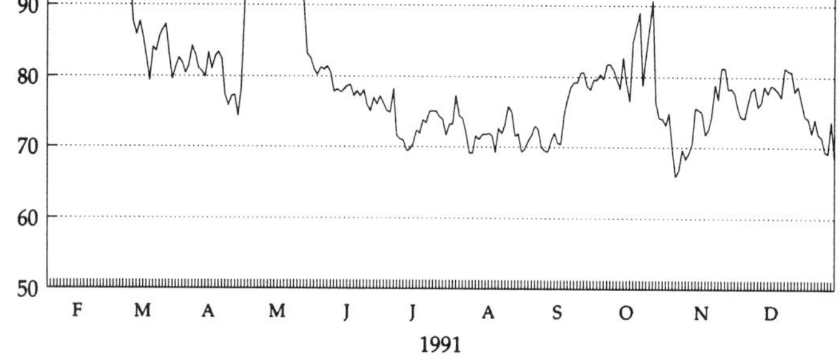

Figure 28.100 Yield spread: Treasury 10 1/2% minus Barclays 12 3/4% 1997

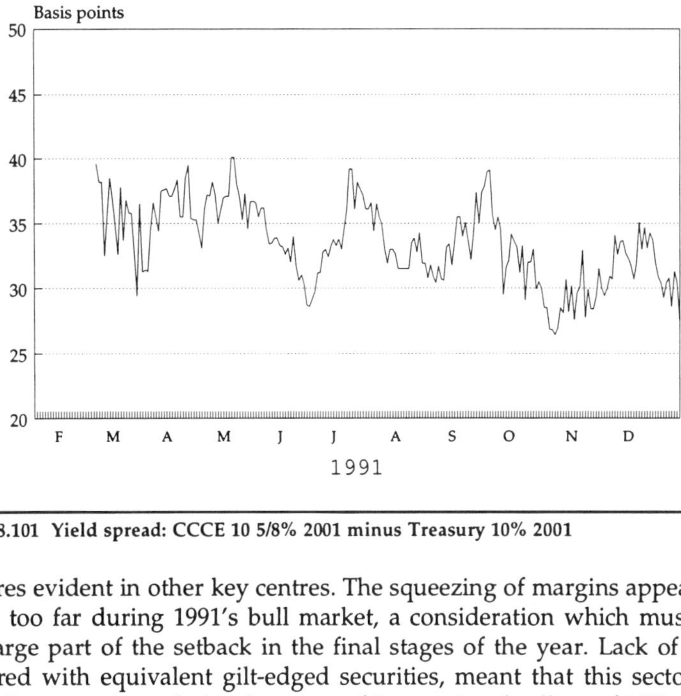

Figure 28.101 Yield spread: CCCE 10 5/8% 2001 minus Treasury 10% 2001

pressures evident in other key centres. The squeezing of margins appeared to be carried too far during 1991's bull market, a consideration which must account for a large part of the setback in the final stages of the year. Lack of liquidity, compared with equivalent gilt-edged securities, meant that this sector was affected disproportionately by the wave of international selling of UK markets at the time of currency and bond market uncertainty, associated with the run up to the EC's Maastricht Treaty negotiations and the unexpectedly sharp hike in German interest rates around the same time.

Domestic fixed-income

Quality considerations have had an even greater impact upon the relative performance of spreads in the domestic sterling market. The effect of the recession in the UK had a profound effect upon investor preferences, concerned with the quality of balance sheets and, in more extreme cases, the long run viability of the borrower. Clearly, this had a major bearing upon the strength of demand for secured and unsecured paper during the past year, a background influence of great significance in the movement of yield differentials.

Economic considerations were also of significance in determining the relative performance of different securities. It is clear that considerations of quality of issuer bore great weight, but so did the market's assessment of the attractions of

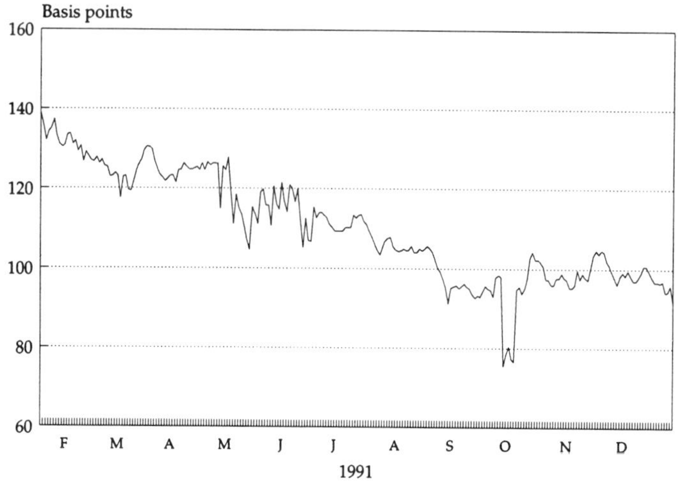

Figure 28.102 Yield spread: Allied Lyons 9 3/4% 2019 minus Treasury 9% 2008

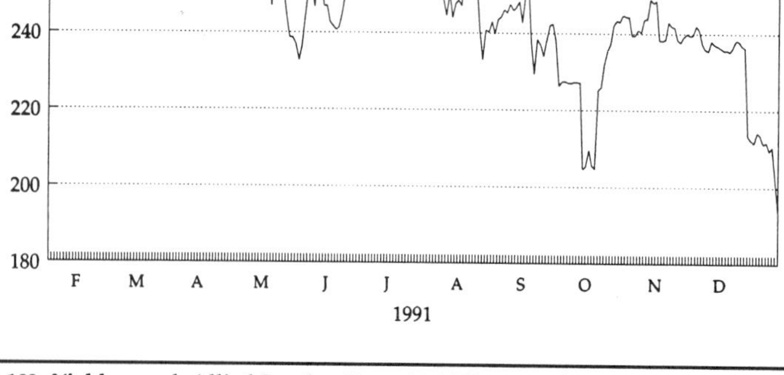

Figure 28.103 Yield spread: Allied London Prop. 10 3/4% 2025 minus Treasury 9% 2008

different sectors of the economy. Property-related debt was a particular example of a market affected adversely by:

- economic downturn
- worries about the health of balance sheets
- the value of assets against which issues were secured

The effect of these considerations upon the relative performance of yields can be seen in Figure 28.103. Worries about the health of the corporate sector, together with the ongoing threat of event risk, hindered a narrowing of yield spreads, especially in the area of lower quality and subordinated issues.

28.18 *Sources of reference*

Financial data

• *CSO. Financial Statistics* (monthly):
Detailed data on money supply, bank lending, debt issuance, debt outstanding, government borrowing, flow of funds, etc.

• *CSO. Monthly Digest and Economic Trends* (monthly):
General economic data on the UK, GDP, consumer spending, prices, etc.

• *Bank of England Quarterly Bulletin*:
Detailed banking data. Articles on banking, monetary control and monetary policy, etc.

- *Financial Statement and Budget Report* (published at time of Budget in March or April) and *Autumn Statement*

- General government forecasts, statements of monetary policy, government financial plans.

Note: All of the above can be obtained via Her Majesty's Stationery Office

Financial Press

Daily:
- *Daily Telegraph*
- *Financial Times*
- *The Guardian*
- *The Independent*
- *The Times*

Sundays:
- *The Independent on Sunday*
- *The Sunday Times*

Quote vendors and news agencies

- Reuters, Telerate, Bloomberg & Datastream International all provide extensive coverage on the UK bond markets.

Other sources

Brokers publishing information on the UK bond markets on a regular basis:

- Barclays de Zoete Wedd
- Credit Suisse First Boston
- County NatWest Securities
- Goldman Sachs
- Greenwell Montagu
- Lehman Brothers International
- Kleinwort Benson
- Merrill Lynch
- J.P. Morgan
- Salomon Brothers International
- UBS Phillips & Drew
- S.G. Warburg

Further reading

- *UBS Phillips & Drew's Sterling Bond Statistical Data* by UBS Phillips & Drew, July 1991
- *The UK Government Bond Markets* by Christopher Bellchamber (published by CSFB Research, pp.416)
- *Inside the Gilt-Edged Market* by Patrick Phillips, Barclays de Zoete Wedd
- *Index-Linked Gilts* by Roger Bootle (published by Woodland Faulkner)
- *The Gilt-Edged Market* by J.Wormell (published by Allen & Unwin
- A section on Liffe is contained in *The European Options & Futures Markets.* by the European Bond Commission (published by Probus, pp. 1100).

Year after Year the
Union Bank of Switzerland
Group...

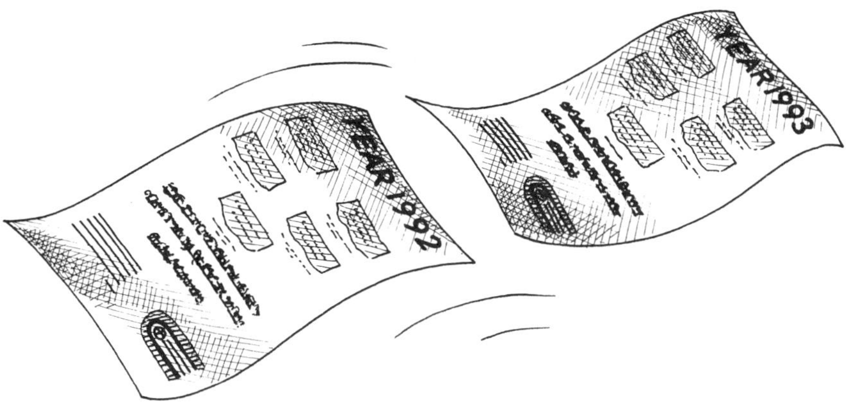

Index

Sponsors

(cont.)

■ Associate sponsors *(cont.)*